THE SEAGULL READER

Literature

W. W. Norton & Company, Inc., also publishes

THE SEAGULL READER: POEMS

THE SEAGULL READER: STORIES

THE SEAGULL READER: PLAYS

THE SEAGULL READER: ESSAYS

THE SEAGULL READER

Literature

edited by Joseph Kelly

College of Charleston

W. W. Norton & Company, Inc. • New York • London

W. W. Norton & Company has been independent since its founding in 1923, when William Warder Norton and Mary D. Herter Norton first published lectures delivered at the People's Institute, the adult education division of New York City's Cooper Union. The Nortons soon expanded their program beyond the Institute, publishing books by celebrated academics from America and abroad. By mid-century, the two major pillars of Norton's publishing program—trade books and college texts—were firmly established. In the 1950s, the Norton family transferred control of the company to its employees, and today—with a staff of four hundred and a comparable number of trade, college, and professional titles published each year—W. W. Norton & Company stands as the largest and oldest publishing house owned wholly by its employees.

Since this page cannot legibly accommodate all the copyright notices, pages 1225–1231 constitute an extension of the copyright page.

The text of this book is composed in Adobe Garamond with the display set in Bernhard Modern.
Book design by Chris Welch.
Composition by PennSet, Inc.
Manufacturing by R. R. Donnelley & Sons—Haddon, Bloomsburg Division.
Production Manager: Ben Reynolds.

Library of Congress Cataloging-in-Publication Data
The seagull reader. Literature / edited by Joseph Kelly.
p. cm.
Includes bibliographical references and index.

ISBN 0-393-92677-X (pbk.)

1. Literature—Collections. I. Kelly, Joseph, 1962–

PN6014.S334 2004
808.8—dc22

2004061708

W. W. Norton & Company, Inc., 500 Fifth Avenue, New York, N.Y. 10110
www.wwnorton.com
W. W. Norton & Company Ltd., Castle House, 75/76 Wells Street,
London W1T 3QT

2 3 4 5 6 7 8 9 0

Contents

Poems * 363

*

Acknowledgments

I want to thank Susan Farrell for her help and kindness and, for inspiration, Spencer, Owen, and Hannah. Peter Simon, Marian Johnson, Kurt Wildermuth, and Rob Bellinger, all at W. W. Norton, deserve much of the credit for putting together this volume. Every book is a collaboration; the Seagull Readers, more than most.

Along with the publisher, I thank the following for their assistance during various stages of this project:

John Aber (College of Mount Saint Joseph); Timothy Adams (West Virginia University); Jay Adler (Los Angeles Southwest College); Elizabeth Ann Altruda (Middlesex County College); Leslie Antonette (East Stroudsburg University); Thomas Austenfeld (Drury College); Paul Aviles (Onondaga Community College); Leslie G. Bailey (Saint Martin's College); Raymond L. Baubles, Jr. (Western Connecticut State University); Terrell Beck (University of Wisconsin at La Crosse); G. R. Benzinger (Duquesne University); David Bergman (Towson University); Michael Berndt (University of Minnesota); Stephen Bernstein (University of Michigan at Flint); Martin Bickman (University of Colorado); Eric Birdsall (University of Akron); George Bishop (D'Youville College); Jonathan Blake (Worcester State College); Elvena Boliek (Georgia Southern University); Stuart C. Brown (New Mexico State University); Anthony Boyle (State University of New York at Potsdam); Jenny Brantley (University of Wisconsin at River Falls); Edward H. Brodie, Jr. (University of South Carolina); Donna Burney (Howard Payne University); Rex Burns (University of Colorado at Denver); John Carlson (Waldorf College); William Carpenter (College of the Atlantic); Tom Chandler (Bryant College); Lisa Chen; Kevin Clark (California Polytechnic State University at San Luis Obispo); Patricia Clark (Grand Valley State University); Bruce Clarke (Texas Tech University); Joseph Rocky Colavito (Northwestern State University); Gina Claywell (Murray State University); Gerald Concannon (Massachuseetts Maritime Academy); Thomas F. Connolly (Suffolk University); Seamus Cooney (Western Michigan University); Ruth L. Copp (Saginaw Valley State University and Northwood University); Denise Coulter (Atlantic Community College); Karen Cox (Bronx Community College); Carolyn M. Craft (Longwood College); Virginia Crank (Rock Valley College); A. T. Crosland (University of South Carolina, Spartanburg); Koos Daley (Adams State College); Debbie Danowski (Sacred Heart University); Robert Darling (Keuka College); Charles L. Darr (University of Pittsburgh at Johnstown); Adam Brooke Davis (Truman State University); Cathy Day (Minnesota State University); Louise Dibble; John Dick (University of Texas at El Paso); Paul B. Diehl (University of Iowa); Marylynne Diggs (Clark College); William Doreski (Keene University), Gregory Eiselein (Kansas State University); S. K. Eisiminger (Clemson University); B. L. Farley (Ocean County Community College); Shir Filler (North County Community College); Sharon S. Fong (University of Nevada at Las Vegas); Marilyn Fontane (St. Louis College of Pharmacy); Chris Forhan (Trident Technical College); Kyle Friedow (Kent State University); Robert Fuhrel (Community College of Southern Nevada); David Galef (University of Mississippi); Victoria Gaydosik (Southwestern Oklahoma State University); Amy Getty (Augustana College); Robert L. Giron (Montgomery College); Len Gougeon (University of Scranton); George Greenlee (Missouri Southern State College); Charles Grogg (Santa Barbara City College); Amanda Gulla (New York University); Carol Harding (Western Oregon University); Pamela S. Hardman; Clarinda Harris (Towson University); Muriel Harris (Purdue University); Lois Head (St. Cloud State University); John Healy (Baker University); Michael Hennessy (Southwest Texas State University); Walter J. Hickey; John Hildebidle (Massachusetts Institute of Technology); Mark Hochberg (Juniata College); Charles Hood (Antelope Valley College); Shari Horner (Shippensburg University); George Hudson (Colgate University); Jefferson Hunter (Smith College); James D. Johnson (Humboldt State University); Kathleen Jacquette (State University of New York at Farmingdale); Linda

Karlen (Oakton Community College); Deborah A. Kearney (California State University, Sacramento); Robert Johnson (Midwestern State University); Bruce W. Jorgensen (Brigham Young University); Richard Kelly; Christopher B. Kennedy (Duke University); Brian Gordon Kennelly (Webster University); De'Lara Khalili; David Kidd (Norfolk Academy); Millie M. Kidd (Mount Saint Mary's College, Los Angeles); Herbert W. Kitson (University of Pittsburgh at Titusville); Linda Kittell (Washington State University); Steve Klepetar (St. Cloud State University); Diane Koenig (Columbia-Greene Community College); Leonard Kress (Owens Community College); Stanley Krohmer (Grand Valley State University); Brigitte LaPresto (Pikeville College); Emily Law; Joy Leasure (New York University); Dennis Leavens (Truman State University); Michael Leddy (Eastern Illinois University); Dennis Lynch (Elgin Community College); James L. Machor (Kansas State University); Chris Mackowski (University of Pittsburgh at Bradford); Michael Mattison (University of Massachusetts at Amherst); David Mazel (Adams State College); J. L. McClure (Kirkwood Community College); David McCordick (University of Wisconsin); Douglas J. McMillan (East Carolina University); David Melzer (Florida State University); G. Douglas Meyers (University of Texas at El Paso); Patricia Meyers (Grand Canyon University); Charles W. Mignon (University of Nebraska at Lincoln); Ruth Misheloff (Borough of Manhattan Community College, City University of New York); James J. Mooney (Immaculata College); Debroah Murray (Kansas State University); Mike Mutschelknaus (Saint Mary's University of Minnesota); Lisa Nakamura (Sonoma State University); Ruth Newberry (Duquesne University); Rolf Norgaard (University of Colorado at Boulder); Barry H. Novick (College of New Jersey); Stephen O'Neill (Bucks County Community College); Angela M. Pellettiere (New York University); Diane Penrod (Rowan University); Barry Phillips (College of Public and Community Service); Brian R. Plant (Mary Baldwin College); Donna Potts (Kansas State University); Gordon M. Pradl (New York University); Diane Putnam (Cabrillo College); Mark Putnam (Northwestern College); David Rachels (Virginia Military Institute); Stacey A. Rannik (Paradise Valley Community College); Steven L. Reagles (Bethany Lutheran College); Jason Rosenblatt (Georgetown University); Robert E. Rubin (Wright

State University); Marsha Rutter (Southwestern College); Carol de Saint Victor (University of Iowa); David Schelhaas (Dordt College); Ana Schnellman (Lindenwood University); Barbara Goldstein Scott (New York University); Craig L. Shurtleff (Illinois Central College); Shirley Simpson (Nicholls State University); Elliott L. Smith; Adam Sorkin (Penn State Delaware County); Jamieson Spencer (St. Louis Community College at Florissant Valley); Karen Stewart (Beloit College); Kip Strasma (Illinois Central College); Anthony Stubbs (Iowa Lakes Community College); Carolyn P. Sturm (Valley College); Debra Sutton (Jefferson College); Timothy Stump; Dan K. Thorpe (College of DuPage); Maurice Tome (New York University); Mary Troy (University of Missouri—St. Louis); Sandra Varone (Brookdale Community College); Mark Vinz (Moorhead State University); Suzanne Waldenberger (Pima County Community College); Ronald G. Walker (Western Illinois University); Heidemarie Z. Weidner (Tennessee Technological University); David Winn (Hunter College, City University of New York); Alan Zhang (Darton College).

What Is Literature?

I've asked my students this question at the start of each semester for nearly twenty years. Some students (often the kind who are headed toward the humanities) answer with a sort of reverence for the "greats" like Shakespeare and Hemingway. But they are few. More answer with a sort of bored indifference, but because I'm an English teacher and they don't want to hurt my feelings, they bow to the enthusiasm of the few. They accept the notion that "Literature"—with a capital *L*—is good for you in much the same way that they accept that spinach is good for you, but it's not something they'd read except for school. A third group faces "Literature" almost angrily, the way someone who's been dragged to an art museum against his will might regard a sixteenth-century portrait of the Spanish royal family.

This book is going to try to prove to you that none of those answers is right. Literature is not the kind of thing we need to reverence. It doesn't do us much good to think of the "greats" as geniuses who were different from you and me, and it doesn't help to put literature on a pedestal, as if it were some rare, untouchable object. And even those students most hostile to English probably take some of their greatest pleasures from literature—whether they realize it or not. Of all things, literature should not be regarded as a chore or a duty or an obligation. It should be fun.

The problem is that our society tends to spell *literature* with a capital *L*. You might be surprised to learn that the belief that "Literature" is a special, high-brow, hard-to-understand or fancy type of writing is not that old. In fact, it's a belief that's not much older than English departments, which have been in universities for little more than a century. Certainly these two phenomena are related: the rise of English departments in colleges and the growing belief that "Literature" is some special kind of writing that doesn't have much to do with our everyday reading habits.

It's well beyond the scope of this introduction to figure out exactly who's to blame for this state of affairs, although I ought to admit that English teachers and the editors of literature anthologies are near the top of the list. The Romantic poets, like Lord Byron and William Wordsworth, must take some responsibility also. Wordsworth's Romantic manifesto elevated poets to an almost superhuman status, and Lord Byron, cashing in on this new notion of the writer, was poetry's first superstar. Some professors have tried to define "Literature" as a type of writing that is fundamentally different from normal, everyday discourse because it uses more figures of speech, like metaphors and symbols. But others (including me) would argue that there's nothing special about literary language— that the figures of speech we find even in the most poetic writing are the same we use in our everday conversations. Suffice it to say that whoever's to blame, our culture has mystified "Literature" so that today it seems to be something you deal with only in English classes.

I want to persuade you that *literature* should be spelled with a little *l*. You swim in literature every day. You consume it every time you turn on the television. Every time you go to a movie and whenever you listen to a song on the radio, you're "reading" literature. You couldn't escape literary culture if you wanted to. It's as much a part of our nature as eating and dreaming.

But what exactly *is* "literature"? Just about the only consensus is that the term refers to imaginative writing. Admittedly, that's a broad definition. But any attempt to narrow it will exclude pieces of writing that most of us would consider literary, and we'd start spelling the word with a capital *L* again. So we're stuck with a broad category.

Such an undiscriminating definition raises a tough question: if literature is all around us, if we consume it all the time in our ordinary lives, how can a book like this one that you're reading right now claim it is more important to read a poem by William Wordsworth than the lyrics to a song by Eminem? I'm presenting you with another anthology of literature, and while it includes the usual sonnets by Shakespeare, there's not a single song by Nirvana. How come? I must have used some standard that separates the early American poet Anne Bradstreet from the contemporary American singer Alanis Morrissette. Even if I think *literature* should be spelled with a lowercase *l*, I must have some idea about value, or I wouldn't think that certain works ought to be read in an English class year after year while others needn't be. You should legitimately demand to know how I decided which pieces of literature should go in this anthology.

The best criterion I've ever come across is one of the simplest: *good* literature is writing that you like to read more than once. That distinguishes it from everything you read just to get the information it contains. News articles, for example, become stale after you've read them once. You use up whatever pleasure or utility they give you the first time you read them. The words of a news article are like the shell of nut. Once you've eaten the kernel—the information contained in the article—there's nothing left to do with the words but throw them away. The same is true of many (though certainly not all) "dime novels," the kind of reading you might take to the beach. We often call these books page-turners because their plots are so exciting we can hardly put them down: we want to see what happens next. But once you've read such a book, there's hardly any incentive to reread it. You already know what's going to happen. The words are used up. You give the book away; you leave it at the beach house; you toss it in the garbage.

Good literature is not like that. Literary writing is more than a vehicle that transports information to a reader. Whether it's for the emotion it stirs in you, or for that powerful sensation that makes you think you're experiencing the events yourself, or for the fresh perspective it gives you on your own world, or merely for the delight in the sounds of the words, we return to good literature and take pleasure in it a second time. Good literature is the kind of writing that gets better with every reading. Even the fifth time through, you see something you didn't see when you read it the fourth time, and you delight in it just as much the tenth time round as you did the first time. Maybe you delight in it more. For example, think about how you come back again and again to the lyrics of a good song. They never grow stale. They get better and better the more you think about them. That's good literature.

In my junior year of high school, my English class read *Moby-Dick*. It was a tough slog. There was a popular clownish guy in the class, a defensive lineman on the football team, and even though our football team was terrible, he still commanded a lot of attention—not only from other students but also from Mrs. Baker, the teacher. He mocked Nathaniel Hawthorne. He scorned Stephen Crane. Even Mark Twain—funny, irreverent Twain—he trashed.

One gray day in October not long before Homecoming, Mrs. Baker was reciting her dreary list of things that Captain Ahab's white whale represents—purity, God, the Tree of Knowledge of Good and Evil, male sexuality—when this lineman exploded with a single comment: "Boring!"

"Why's it boring?" Mrs. Baker asked.

"If he was trying to talk about that stuff," the football player said, "why didn't he just say it? What's the deal with all this symbolism? Isn't the whale just a whale?" (I'm not sure if these were his exact words, but they're close.)

The class laughed.

Mrs. Baker, a tiny woman in her forties, was a mouse facing a falcon. She asked mildly, "If he didn't want us to interpret his symbols, why do you think Melville wrote the book?"

"To make money?"

The class laughed again. Mrs. Baker smiled indulgently.

I, the future English teacher who had that reverent feeling for the "greats," got a sick feeling in my heart. But it wasn't because I disagreed with the football player. It was because I agreed with him. I secretly thought *Moby-Dick* was boring. The lineman voiced my own fainthearted suspicion: *Moby-Dick* wasn't nearly as interesting as a book by a writer like Tom Clancy.

I was forced to read *Moby-Dick* again in college, and I liked it better the second time around. I reread it in graduate school, and it improved again. I haven't read it from cover to cover a fourth time, but I dip into it now and again, and it never bores me. Not too long ago I took a second look at *The Hunt for Red October*, Tom Clancy's first best seller. I couldn't get past the fifth page. I've read Mary Shelley's *Frankenstein* a dozen times, and it delights me more each year. But I got so bored in my second reading of Stephen King's *The Shining* that I couldn't finish it: I knew everything that was going to happen, and that ruined the pleasure. If the pleasure of a text *diminishes* with each fresh reading, then I think it should be left out of an anthology.

Good literature, then, is not a different *kind* of writing. It uses the same techniques that we find in the most ephemeral writing. Even the anecdote I told about the football player uses the techniques of literature: metaphor, symbolism, personification, alliteration, conflict, and so on. Good literature is just writing that is *better written* than most of what we encounter in the marketplace. I know that criteria is mighty vague. People will disagree on what is better and worse writing. But it's a definition that's elastic enough to cover popular genres—for example, I've included song lyrics by Bruce Springsteen in this volume. I'm sure there are dozens of popular song writers today who are writing good literature. Even many English teachers recognize that hip-hop can be good free verse. (Maybe Eminem does belong in an English class; maybe I've excluded him because of my own prejudice.) There's no reason to exclude even something as undervalued in our society as the script of a television sitcom episode. I wasn't so bold as to include a script of *The Simpsons*, but I've seen many an episode that I think would be worthy. I've seen some episodes of *The Simpsons* half a dozen times, and they still delight me even though I know all of the jokes ahead of time. No matter our personal tastes, if we agree that good literature is writing we like to reread, I think the definition will serve.

How Do You Read Literature?

That definition serves particularly well because it means that everyone already knows how to read good literature. In reading any poem or play or story in this book, you use exactly the same skills and techniques that you use already in your everyday life. The introduction to each section of this book will discuss the vocabulary of literary analysis that is appropriate to the genre. But you'll find nothing new here, nothing that you don't know in your bones. If you've ever puzzled over the lyrics of a favorite song or argued with friends as you left a movie theater, you're already a well-practiced interpreter of literature. Interpreting literature is a skill you picked up as naturally as you learned to speak English.

In fact, literature is like a language, and you might think of the **genres** represented here—poems, stories, and plays—as three dialects of that language. Just like the English language, literature has a grammar. You can understand English even if you don't consciously know grammatical conventions, because you've internalized them. And certainly one can speak and write well without consciously thinking about grammar. You can function perfectly well in English without ever learning the difference between a noun and a verb. You can internalize the conventions without ever studying them. In short, you do not need to know grammar to be competent in a language. But your understanding deepens when you know the conventions—what we often refer to as the rules of grammar—and can see them at work. And if you've studied the conventions of English, if you know a noun from a verb and an object from a subject, you'll have an easier time understanding complicated sentences and intricate paragraphs.

Likewise, you can read and understand a work of literature without consciously knowing literary conventions. The moment you click on a television program, you'll know whether or not it's a sitcom. You might not be conscious of the conventions you're "reading" (maybe the style of music, maybe the laugh track, maybe the set), but you do a fine job of interpreting them anyway. Similarly, you can already "read" the conventions that pertain to the genres in this book. They might be less practiced than your highly honed skill of interpreting television programs, but just growing up in our culture has taught you how to read poems and stories and plays. The introductions to the sections of this book try to make you more *conscious* of those conventions you've already internalized. They'll remind you of the vocabulary and techniques of literary analysis appropriate to each genre—what are often called the skills of **close reading**. But remember: **close reading** is nothing different from what you do already when you read; you'll just get better at it as you master the skills.

It might be useful to think of the three genre introductions as supplying you with tools. Certainly everyone knows what a saw does, but if you're taught how to handle one—how to use the grain of the wood to your advantage, when to ease up on the pressure and when to apply it—you'll saw better than the novice. The master carpenter will build a better cabinet than the weekend amateur. By learning the tools of analysis, you'll interpret with more skill and greater precision.

And **interpretation** is the final purpose of reading literature. That term is a little more complex than we typically think. We tend to equate our interpretation of a text with a summary of its meaning. That's a fine equation—so long as we remember that "meaning" is itself a complex thing. We cannot reduce meaning to a simple formula the way we reduce a fable to a "moral," like "Slow and steady wins the race" or "Beware the flatterer." True, the meaning of a work might include unequivocal aphorisms ("War is bad" or "Love is more important than money"), but invariably literary meaning is more expansive. It's more difficult to pin down. It includes your emotional experience while reading the text, and rarely does it lay itself out like a pithy, brief truism. When we talk of *meaning* in literature, we use that term the way we do when we talk about the *meaning* of a friendship, or the *meaning* of some historical event, or the *meaning* of life itself. Interpreting meaning, then, is not like decoding a cipher. It is much more an art than a science. A rich and expansive imagination is as important as the tools I'll lay out in this book. Be a *creative* reader.

I'll end with a caution: Your interpretation, though it's founded on your own imagination and constructed by your own handling of the tools of analysis, can be wrong. Don't fall into the mistaken belief that because interpretations are personal, everyone's is equally valid. It is true that interpretations are matters of opinion, but there are two types of opinion. There are opinions such as "I like rainy days." No one can dispute my authority on an opinion like that. But an interpretation of literature is not that manner of opinion. It is like the other type, which includes statements like these: "We need a Republican in the White House" and "Only a Democrat can salvage our foreign policy."

Those opinions deal in what rhetoricians call probable truths, as opposed to the kind of "absolute" truths mathematicians deal in. You can prove absolutely that the sum of the squares of the legs of a right triangle equals the square of the hypotenuse. But no one can prove absolutely that we need a Republican in the White House. It is the responsibility of someone who voices such an opinion (which is an *interpretation* of the current political situation) to persuade others that she is *probably* right. Some opinions are good, some are bad. Generally, we think poorly defended opinions are probably wrong. This book should help you to better defend your own interpretations.

Once you've voiced your interpretation of a text, it is your responsibility to show others how you came to that opinion. You need to be able to persuade them that you're probably right. And to accomplish that task, you'll find that the skills of close reading are particularly useful.

Stories

*

What Are Stories?

We can't escape stories. We read them in the newspaper; we see them on television; and over lunch or coffee or on the phone, we tell each other stories about ourselves, our friends, our enemies, our heroes. Stories keep us afloat. We need to both hear and tell stories to make sense of the world and our place in it.

There's that story your roommate told you last week about his old girlfriend: she was a fine person, but he left her for selfish reasons and feels guilty about it now. Or the one you told your parents about why you got a D in your first semester at school: it had something to do with a crooked-faced teacher. We tell stories to define and judge character, and there's hardly a more interesting topic in the world. Our own characters have fascinated us since before the first scribe thought to write down the heroic tales he heard told round the fire, and we're no less spellbound today. **Short stories** are nothing more than these tales told by men and women who have studied the art of telling, refined it through long practice, and adapted it to the demands of a sophisticated reading—as opposed to a listening—audience. As a result, short stories tend to be more complex and sophisticated than the anecdotes we tell one another.

Even so, short stories are fundamentally no different from the anecdote you heard this morning while walking to class.

You have probably already mastered every element of the short story simply by growing up in society. *Point of view, character, plot, setting, symbols, motifs, theme*—these are some of the terms critics use to break stories down, and each of these terms refers to something or things with which you already are familiar. You might not realize that you're an expert, but you are. Already, you probably interpret each of these elements intuitively whenever you hear or read a story. The purpose of this introduction is to bring what you do intuitively into the light of your consciousness so that you can interpret stories more confidently and accurately, so that your interpretations will gain sophistication, and so that you can understand sophisticated stories.

How Do You Read Stories?

In each section below, I discuss an element of short stories. These discussions are in no particular order. You do not necessarily need to analyze point of view before character or character before symbols. Analyzing a short story is a more organic, sloppy affair. You will consider these elements as your needs demand. You might puzzle over a strange ending and then think about who was telling the story. You might get bored in a long description of place and wonder why the writer put it there. If you are reading a story for pleasure—that is, outside the context of school—you might never bother to define in your own mind who the protagonist is, but you would sense it intuitively. Or you might interpret a symbol without consciously recognizing it as a symbol. In the context of school, however, you should at some time consider each of these elements formally.

Point of view

Every story has its teller. For example, when you listen to one friend bad-mouth another, you tend to take into account the source of the gossip: Does the teller have an ax to grind? Is he capable of lying? Will she distort the truth? Is he too dull to take into account the full picture? Every person has his or her own **point of view,** and the same event will sound different when reported by different people. Sometimes these differences will be dramatic—each driver in a car crash might hold the other at fault, for example. More often, the differences will be more subtle. Ask two people long married about their first date, and though the facts might remain the same, each will color the event with his or her own perceptions, which derive from his or her own prejudices. This is natural. Everyone has a particular version of events.

We call the person who "tells" a story the **narrator.** When the narrator is a character in the story, whether he or she is involved in the events or merely reporting them from the sidelines, we are usually pretty aware of the point of view. We know that the narrator has witnessed the events from his or her own perspective. This type of narrator is called a **first-person narrator** because he or she uses the first-person pronoun: *I* or *we.* If the story is told from the periphery of the action, the narrator is a **first-person observer:** "I saw the thief run off with the queen's jewels." If the narrator is in the midst of the action, he or she is a **first-person participant:** "Just as I ran off with the queen's jewels, I realized that I'd been seen." If we have reason to doubt the information we're getting, if the narrator is naïve or dim-witted or mentally handicapped or dishonest or extremely prejudiced, we call the narrator **unreliable.** Clearly, all first-person narrators are unreliable to some degree, since they all have their own perspectives and therefore cannot present a purely objective reality, but we reserve the term *unreliable* for those few narrators who severely distort the tales they're telling. When reading a story by such a narrator, part of the reader's pleasure comes from piecing together a more reliable account of the events.

The point of view of a story is less obvious when the narrator is not a character at all. Such narrators are called **third-person narrators** because they do not refer to themselves as *I:* "Completely unobserved, the thief made off with the queen's jewels." No one was in the room to see the thief, yet his action is reported to us, almost as if the narrator were a fly on the wall. Often the perspective of a third-person narrator does not seem to belong to a real person. The narrator gives us information no human could. He might tell us about events that occur in different places at the same time or about the biographical histories of unrelated characters, or he might enter into the thoughts of different characters. If there is no limit to what the third-person narrator knows, if he can eavesdrop on the minds of characters and reveal their unspoken thoughts, we call him **omniscient.** If there are limits—for example, if the narrator tells us the thoughts of only one character but not the thoughts of others—he has what we call **limited omniscience.**

With all third-person narrators, you can be pretty certain that the information you get is trustworthy. To put it more precisely, the author does not intend for you to question the narrator's perspective. The author expects you to regard the narrator's information, even the narrator's value judgments, as objective, undistorted truth. If the narrator tells you the day was dreary, the day was dreary. If the narrator says this character is evil and that one is good, then it is so. For example, if the narrator says, "The good-hearted thief stole the queen's jewels out of devotion to his own wife," we can be sure that the author wants us to believe the thief is a good man. Sometimes third-person narrators get heavy-handed in their value judgments. For example, the narrator might address readers directly: "Now we mustn't judge our thief too harshly. His disrespect for private property is more than amply compensated for by his love of humanity. He is the type of person whom any of us would cherish as a friend." This is called **editorializing.** Of course, we do not have to accept the third-person narrator's point of view. We might decide the narration is distorted by the author's prejudices or by the prejudices of the time or place in which the author wrote. But within the fictional world of the short story itself, a third-person narrator is generally reliable. (The use of a central consciousness, which is discussed below, is one significant exception to this rule.)

(I should comment on my use of the pronoun *he* in this discussion of the third-person narrator. Normally, I would substitute *she* now and then, but I haven't here because I do not want to imply that third-person narrators are sometimes male and sometimes female. They are neither, typically. *It* would be a neutral pronoun, but *it* denies personhood, and it is best to think of a third-person narrator as a person. So here I stick with the unsatisfactory old use of *he* to mean "anyone.")

About a hundred years ago, writers began experimenting with a narrator who combined aspects of the first and third person. This narrator never uses the personal pronoun *I;* he is not a character in the story; and if you don't read closely, he might seem to be a third-person narrator with limited omniscience, for his knowledge is limited to the thoughts and perceptions of a single character. But more careful attention reveals that everything this type of narrator says comes to us as if filtered through the consciousness of that one single character. The perceptions of the events given voice by the narrator are the perceptions of the character. This type of narrator is called the **central consciousness.** Though the narrator seems to be third person, we must take into account the distorting prejudices of the central consciousness just as we would take into account the prejudices of a first-person narrator.

Use of the central consciousness was the first step toward the development of a radical method of narration perfected by James Joyce and Virginia Woolf: **stream of consciousness.** The American psychologist William James coined the term *stream of consciousness* to describe the flux of thoughts—many of them preverbal—that run through our minds when we are awake. If you have ever tried to capture even a couple of moments of your own consciousness, you know how idiosyncratic and various and layered our thought patterns are. A writer using stream of consciousness approximates the thoughts of a character in a technique called **interior monologue.** The narrator is not precisely third person because it is as if we were witnessing the thought process of one character—so we will see the word *I.* Even so, the character is not telling a story. Instead, we are witnessing the story through the character's mind. All the events, then, are conveyed to us through a lens even more distorting than the lens of an unreliable first-person narrator. In stream-of-consciousness style, the story of the thief that I've been using as an example might read like this: "Dark. Darker than I thought it would be. Wait a minute. There. Shapes emerge. A bureau. Right where they're supposed to be, the whole lot of them. These pearls on Jenny. How she looks in that dress. The sunlight on her, that day at the seashore, how she said she would. I could still turn back. Pocket them and I'm a thief forever after. No—already if someone turns on the light and me standing here in the room where I'm not supposed to be, in these clothes, the necklace hanging in my fingers, I'm a thief already. Explain I decided not to? Just putting them back. On my way out. Don't you believe me?" As you can see, with stream of consciousness, it is difficult to make out what is literally happening.

Both central-consciousness and stream-of-consciousness narratives reflect the shift toward psychological drama in literature that took place around World War I. Few writers today use either type.

Character

The purpose of stories is to reveal **character.** The focus might be human character in general or the character of particular individuals, but either way, everything in a story serves this end. The main character of a story, the person you would say the story is about, is called the **protagonist.** Protagonists do not need to be good people; generally they are a complex mix of good and bad. But typically, a story will make us sympathize with its protagonist and perhaps also identify with him. In most short stories, the protagonist will face some physical or psychological challenge, usually a moral choice, and grappling with that challenge will change her. Protagonists, then, are usually **dynamic characters:** they change.

Most other characters in a story do not change: they are **static.** Folklorists have developed catalogs of the different types of static characters—what we might call stock characters—that are defined by the roles they play in stories. But the most important character besides the protagonist is the **antagonist.** This is a character who opposes or impedes the protagonist. Not all stories have an antagonist. In many of the psychological stories written in the twentieth century, protagonists struggle against themselves instead of against another person.

In stories, character is revealed in the same way it is revealed in real life. What a character says, what others say about him, physical descriptions, items (such as clothes) associated with the character, and what a character does all contribute to our understanding of that character. Some narrators provide even more information: what is going on in a character's head, for example. You judge characters, then, the same way you judge people. Though some English teachers tend to discourage simple questions such as, Do you *like* this guy? and Would you like to *be* this woman? they are actually extremely useful: they activate the very skills of interpretation you will need to use. Characters who appeal to us and have our good wishes are called **sympathetic characters,** and perhaps the most fundamental question to ask yourself about any character, especially a protagonist, is Is she *sympathetic*? Then you should figure out what in the story made you react the way you did: why is the character sympathetic or unsympathetic?

One warning about this last bit of advice: sometimes our reactions to stories can be idiosyncratic. I might like a character despite his faults, while my wife thinks he is a jerk. Our reactions might be affected by our background—class, race, education, and so on. Therefore, a more sophisticated way to think about character is to ask, Does the author *want* me to find this character sympathetic? You might find that Hemingway wants the reader to sympathize with a character whom you detest or that Hawthorne wants you to disapprove of someone you admire. When you analyze a story, you are not so much seeking to determine what you think as what the author wants you to think.

If you don't react to a character the way you think the author meant for you to react, it could be because the writer is not very good at his craft. Or it might be because you are not the audience the writer had in mind when she wrote the story. If you find your own judgments differing from those you think the writer wanted you to make, you should try to figure out whom the writer expected to read the story. Generally, writers tend to write for people like themselves, so a little biographical information—the kind provided in the headnotes and in the biographical sketches in this volume—can tell you a great deal.

Your consideration of character should go well beyond this initial question of whether a character is sympathetic or not. You should define the protagonist's character as thoroughly as you can. What motivates him to do what he does? Why does she hesitate when she ought to act? How does he change? These and similar questions—

the kind you might ask yourself about someone in real life—will help you understand each character. The discussion in the next section will also help you to analyze and understand characters.

Plot

Critics have developed a wide array of terms to help them analyze **plots.** Most of them were first used to describe the plots of plays (in fact, you'll find a similar discussion of plot elements in the introduction to plays, on pp. 608–11). But they can be adapted to analyze the plots of short stories also. As you learn to apply these terms, don't lose sight of why you're analyzing plot: to help you understand the characters. The various elements of stories described below, then, are not ends in themselves; they are crucial to understanding character.

There is a difference between a plot and a mere recitation of incidents. Consider this example, made famous by the English novelist E. M. Forster: The queen died; then the king died. No connection is made between these events; they are coincidental. So this is not a plot. A plot is a series of incidents that are unified: The queen died; then the king died of grief. In this case, the incidents are not coincidental. They are united by the king's love for his wife. The second event *results* from the first event.

A plot, then, is a linked chain of events. Sometimes—perhaps most often—these events are not presented to readers in chronological order. The story might begin **in medias res**—that is, in the middle of the plot. Or the narrator might begin at the end and relate the story through **flashbacks.** But if you rearranged the incidents in chronological order, you would find that every story begins in a situation of **equilibrium:** the protagonist might not be satisfied with the status quo, but her life is in a state of relative order and calm. Something then happens to disrupt that order. Consider, for example, the biblical story of the Prodigal Son:

> There was a man who had two sons; and the younger of them said to his father, "Father, give me the share of property that falls to me." And he divided his living between them. Not many days later, the younger son gathered all he had and took his journey into a far country, and there he squandered his property in loose living.

And when he had spent everything, a great famine arose in that country, and he began to be in want. So he went and joined himself to one of the citizens of that country, who sent him into his fields to feed swine. And he would gladly have fed on the pods that the swine ate; and no one gave him anything. But when he came to himself he said, "How many of my father's hired servants have bread enough to spare, but I perish here with hunger! I will arise and go to my father, and I will say to him, 'Father, I have sinned against heaven and before you; I am no longer worthy to be called your son; treat me as one of your hired servants.' " And he arose and came to his father. But while he was yet at a distance, his father saw him and had compassion and ran and embraced him and kissed him. And the son said to him, "Father, I have sinned against heaven and before you; I am no longer worthy to be called your son." But the father said to his servants, "Bring quickly the best robe, and put it on him; and put a ring on his hand, and shoes on his feet; and bring the fatted calf and kill it, and let us eat and make merry; for this my son was dead, and is alive again; he was lost, and is found." And they began to make merry.

Now his elder son was in the field; and as he came and drew to the house, he heard music and dancing. And he called one of the servants and asked what this meant. And he said to him, "Your brother has come, and your father has killed the fatted calf, because he has received him safe and sound." But he was angry and refused to go in. His father came out and entreated him, but he answered his father, "Lo, these many years I have served you, and I never disobeyed your command; yet you never gave me a kid, that I might make merry with my friends. But when this son of yours came, who has devoured your living with harlots, you killed for him the fatted calf!" And he said to him, "Son, you are always with me, and all that is mine is yours. It was fitting to make merry and be glad, for this your brother was dead, and is alive; he was lost, and is found."

The state of equilibrium in this story is a time we must infer because it exists before the story actually begins. There is a rich man who has two sons grown to young adulthood living under his roof. They are prosperous, and everything is fine.

This status quo is disrupted when the younger son demands his inheritance. Such a disruption is called a **complication.** A complication introduces the story's **conflict,** which is a struggle between the protagonist and some other person (the antagonist) or force. You may have seen a list of possible conflicts before: human versus human, human versus nature, human versus society, the individual versus him- or herself. This list suggests just how wide is the range of things that the protagonist might struggle against. It could be nature, even human nature; it could be an unjust society; it could be a part of herself. It is crucial that you be able to define this conflict. Make sure you can answer the question, What does the protagonist struggle against?

In the Prodigal Son, the conflict is between the younger son and his father: the son wants to live a life that he cannot live while he's under his father's roof and authority. The subsequent events in the story—the squandering of the inheritance, the famine, the job feeding pigs—are parts of the **rising action.** They raise the tension in the conflict to a breaking point. The father is not present in the foreign country, so the son is not struggling against him *literally*. But we know that his dissolute life is a rebellion against his father, especially when we reach the **climax** of the story, which is the point in a story where the conflict is decided. In other words, the climax decides who wins. Sometimes, you will sense when the tension has reached its peak. But be aware that though the climax is sometimes the emotional high point of a story, sometimes it is not. Rather than looking for your own heightened emotion, look for the point when the conflict disappears. Often the climax requires the protagonist to make a decisive choice. In the Prodigal Son, the climax is the moment the son decides to return to his father and beg his forgiveness. At this moment, the conflict ends. The father has "won," so to speak, and the son has lost.

But the end of the conflict is not the end of the story. Following the climax is a **resolution,** or **denouement.** A new situation of equilibrium is established, often quite different from the state that existed before the initial complication. Sometimes the resolution is a **reversal** of fortunes. In a tragedy, the plot resolves itself with the protagonist's fall from prosperity to poverty. This situation is the opposite in a comedy: the protagonist begins in a state of figurative or literal poverty and ends up in prosperity. But these *terms—*

tragedy and *comedy*—apply to plays more readily than to stories. In stories, the change revealed in the resolution is often more subtle than these obvious reversals.

In the Prodigal Son, the son expected a reversal. Instead, he was surprised to find his original status restored by his forgiving father. This is a good example of why you cannot automatically equate the emotional high point of a story with its climax. I feel a flush of emotion not when the son has made his decisive choice to live under his father's authority again but when the father rushes to welcome his returning son. My own emotion at this point comes from the father's unexpected generosity: the prodigal son's final status is equivalent to the initial state of equilibrium.

Or it is nearly so. The last episode in the story, which reveals the jealousy of the older brother, indicates that despite his father's forgiveness, the prodigal son's brief life of debauchery does have permanent consequences. It has altered his relationship with his brother, and it has altered the older son's relationship with the father. But as strained as the relations within this house are, the conflict is resolved: we have returned to a state of relative order and stability.

Not all stories have plots that can be mapped out so neatly. For example, many writers in the early twentieth century, influenced by the rise of psychology, devised plots that took place entirely inside the main character's psyche, and these can be harder to analyze. These usually are the individual-versus-herself (or human-versus-human nature) plots in which two aspects of the protagonist's psyche struggle against each other. Because there is no antagonist, you might find it hard to identify the complication and rising action, and the climax in these stories is often nothing more dramatic than a personal insight that comes upon the protagonist suddenly. The insight might be about human nature in general, though usually it is about the protagonist's own self. These types of climaxes are called **epiphanies,** and a good example is the conclusion to James Joyce's "Araby," in which the protagonist suddenly recognizes that he is "a creature driven and derided by vanity."

But even in modern stories, you will probably find it useful to summarize the plot. A plot summary should identify each of these elements: initial equilibrium, complication, conflict, rising action, climax, and resolution. If you can identify these, you have gone a long way toward understanding the protagonist.

Setting

The **setting** is the locale in which you find the characters. If the story were performed on stage, the setting would be the scenery and the stage props, the landscapes or cityscapes, or the rooms in which the characters move. You might think initially that setting is neutral so far as a story's meaning goes. After all, there has to be ground on which the characters walk; the ground doesn't *mean* anything. Sometimes this might be true. The setting is so spare in the story of the Prodigal Son that we probably cannot glean any meaning from it. But if the setting is described in a story, you can be pretty well assured that it has some meaning. Short stories are such an economical art form that they leave little room for neutral details. If the ground is mentioned, you can mine it for meaning. For example, a description of the setting can establish the **atmosphere,** or **mood,** of the story, the emotional state the writer wants you to be in while you read. This technique is most obvious in ghost stories, in which the setting—for example, a giant ramshackle house on a rainy night—makes you feel apprehensive and vulnerable. Though it might not be so obvious elsewhere as it is in horror fiction, setting is a feature of nearly all short stories. Usually in the opening pages of a story, you will find some description of the setting, and that description will establish the story's atmosphere.

Setting might also serve as a window onto the emotional state of a character. This technique is called **projection,** because the writer projects onto the setting the emotions of the character. If we were to slip some projection into the Prodigal Son, we might use the setting to communicate the father's joy at seeing his son return. The time of day would be morning; the sun would have just burst from the horizon, banishing the last darkness of night; birds would be singing in the trees; and the air would be fresh and bracing. Kate Chopin uses this technique in her "The Story of an Hour": the description of the world outside the window reflects the protagonist's mental state.

In some stories, the setting alludes to events in the world beyond the little circle of the characters. The drama of the protagonist's story might be surrounded by a larger drama involving all society. There might be a war going on or some other social unrest. Just as the protagonist's state of equilibrium has been disturbed by a complication, so the wider world may be convulsed in some conflict. Such a conflict is called an **enveloping action.** The dominance in literature of internal, psychological drama during the last hundred years means that few modern stories contain an enveloping action, but those stories that do tend to use that action to comment on the smaller plight of the protagonist. The larger social events will probably parallel or contrast with the protagonist's difficulties, either trivializing them or making them seem more profound. For example, the civil rights movement envelops the action of Alice Walker's "Everyday Use," and this wider context might influence our judgment of Dee's character.

Symbolism

A **symbol** is an object that represents something else, sometimes another object but more often an abstraction. For example, consider Robert E. Lee's surrender to Ulysses S. Grant at Appomattox. One object represented another: General Lee stood for the defeated Army of Northern Virginia, and by surrendering himself to General Grant he surrendered his entire command. So he dressed in his last clean uniform and belted on his sword in order to present his ragtag army in the best possible light. Grant might have taken Lee prisoner, but he didn't. He refused, even, to confiscate Lee's sword. In this context, the sword represented a number of abstractions, not the least of which was Lee's honor. Grant's refusal to take the sword communicated his esteem for Lee and for the soldiers who had until that minute been his enemies.

Some things, usually things in the natural world, carry the same symbolic meaning in just about any culture. The sunrise will probably call to mind birth or new beginnings no matter where you go, just as the sunset seems to naturally represent death or an ending. These symbols are perceived in Bali just as they are in Belgium. Similarly, all ferocious predators might represent evil in many different cultures, and a dense forest might symbolize the unknown.

These are **universal symbols.** For example, the journey into the catacombs in Edgar Allan Poe's "The Cask of Amontillado" might represent a journey into death, for the underground is a universal symbol of the realm of the dead, probably because most cultures bury their dead.

Other objects carry meaning only in the context of a particular culture. You're driving across the United States, and in St. Louis you see a giant, soaring arch towering over buildings and trees and silhouetted against the blue sky. It's the gateway to the West, and it calls to your mind the American conquest of the Great Plains in the nineteenth century. You might feel a mix a respect for the accomplishment, regret for the people displaced by the migration, and all the ambivalence that usually accompanies thoughts of progress. Citizens of St. Louis probably take the arch as a symbol of their city and enjoy some degree of civic pride whenever they see it. Other travelers, those unfamiliar with American monuments, would puzzle over its significance. The arch might have no meaning for an Australian touring the States by Greyhound bus. The symbol is not universal: it is a convention contrived by a particular population of people. Such symbols are called **conventional symbols.**

Sometimes it is obvious that the symbolic meanings of conventional symbols are contrived. The regalia of clubs and political organizations are good examples. The mascot of a sports team is chosen by the team's owner or by a committee of professional marketers, and thereafter the Major League Baseball team in Arizona is symbolized by a rattlesnake. A flag is sewn by Betsy Ross and adopted by a committee, and instantly it symbolizes a nation.

But most conventional symbols have an anonymous genealogy; it is impossible to say who created them. It is as if they arose out of the culture itself. Who can say when apple pie came to symbolize the values of Middle America? Did any one person decide that the Midwest would represent wholesomeness and naïveté? or that the American West would symbolize rugged individualism? Show almost anyone who grew up in American culture a picture of John Wayne on a horse in a western landscape, and he or she will understand the symbolism. In fact, many people around the globe would recognize it too, for the icon of the American cowboy, and the notions of self-reliance and freedom and violence that he represents, is one of our cultural exports, courtesy of Hollywood. But show the picture of John Wayne to a farmer in rural China, and he would see just a man on a horse. No one person or committee decided that these objects would convey symbolic meaning in our culture; nevertheless, they do. And outside our culture, they are meaningless. Raymond Carver's "Cathedral" uses a conventional symbol. Outside Western culture, a medieval cathedral would carry no meaning. It is just a big building. You couldn't say whether it was a government building or a library or a temple. But for us, it carries all sorts of symbolic meanings.

A **literary symbol** is an object with symbolic meaning limited to the very narrow context of a particular work of literature. Outside the short story, the object does not mean what it does inside the short story. A literary symbol is authored neither by nature nor by a culture, but by a writer. As with a conventional symbol, when you take a literary symbol out of its original context, it stops being a symbol. In John Steinbeck's "The Chrysanthemums," for example, the chrysanthemums represent a number of things, including the love and care and kindness of the protagonist. But outside the story, they carry no such meanings.

So far I've discussed only the different types of symbols. It takes a good deal of interpretive skill to recognize that an object in a story is not just its literal self but also representative of something else. Identifying literary symbols is an art, but there are a few tricks you can count on to help you. If the title of a story is an object, you can be pretty sure it symbolizes something—thus the symbolic meaning of the chrysanthemums in John Steinbeck's story. By calling attention to the chrysanthemums in the title, Steinbeck alerts us to their importance. On even your first reading of the story, you should be asking yourself, What could the chrysanthemums represent? But for the most part, it is impossible to teach someone a foolproof way to recognize which objects are symbolic and which are not. You have to trust your own gut feelings. If you find your attention drawn to an object, if you suspect that something might have more than literal significance, you're probably right. The text itself will call attention to its literary symbols. Even if Steinbeck had called his story "A Day in California," we could still have figured out that the chrysanthemums were symbolic because the story itself draws our attention to them.

After you've identified which objects might be symbols, you still have a tougher task: figuring out what the objects represent. Again, this is a skill impossible to teach. You have to trust your instincts. Read the story a few times and an idea will more than likely come to you: the object represents love; it represents death; it represents the American dream; it represents hope. Usually, a symbol represents abstractions: love, death, dreams, hopes. Trust your gut. Even so, be prepared to revise your gut feelings. If you try to interpret an object symbolically and it just does not seem to work, maybe you were wrong. Maybe the object is not a symbol. Or maybe you were wrong about what the object represents. Keep revising and refining your ideas until you think you get it right.

After you have done all this, there is one thing left to do. To interpret the symbol fully, you must follow what happens to the literal object in the story and then apply that to whatever the object represents. I don't want to ruin Steinbeck's story for you by telling you how it ends, but when you read it, be sure to note what happens to the chrysanthemums. What happens to them also happens to love and care and kindness.

Allegory is a special use of symbolism. In an allegory, characters or objects have a one-to-one correspondence to whatever they represent. Often in allegory, all the characters participate in a web of symbolism: one character might represent Sin, another Virtue, and yet a third Mercy. In allegory, the literal level is much less important than the symbolic level. The literal objects or characters are merely devices by which the writer explores the abstractions they represent. Allegory was popular in the Middle Ages, but current tastes, which tend to demand a high degree of realism, make it rare today. A few stories in this volume include some elements of allegory: Nathaniel Hawthorne's "Young Goodman Brown," for example, and Gabriel García Márquez's "A Very Old Man with Enormous Wings."

Motifs

A **motif** is an image, object, character, situation, theme, even a word, that the writer uses repeatedly throughout a work. For example, there is a motif of decay in William Faulkner's "A Rose for Emily." Emily decays; her house decays; her entire way of life decays; and something else decays too, though I won't ruin the story by telling you ahead of time. This motif helps give you, the reader, a sense of the story's unity. More important, it tips you off to an important theme—maybe the most important theme—in the story.

Recognizing motifs draws your attention to something important to a story, and that attention will help you understand the story. For example, if an object keeps popping up again and again, you will know that the writer is calling your attention to it. To use a famous example, if you see a gun in the opening scene of a story, safely holstered and out of the way, you might think it is just part of the setting, but if it turns up a second time, you should begin to suspect it is a motif. Probably, you will begin to suspect that someone will shoot it by the end of the story, and the motif will thus contribute to the rising sense of tension as you approach the climax of the story.

If the motif is an object, more than likely that object will, by the end of the story, carry symbolic meaning. Dirt and dust crop up again and again in Katherine Ann Porter's "The Jilting of Granny Weatherall," so we suspect that they might represent something. In fact, dust is a conventional symbol: it represents our mortality, as when a priest on Ash Wednesday says, "for dust thou art, and unto dust shalt thou return." If dust were not a motif in the story, we might hesitate to equate it with mortality and with a host of other meanings Porter might have given it. But because it is a motif, we read great meaning into Granny's persistent attempts to get rid of the dirt.

Sometimes a particular motif might be characteristic of stories in a subgenre or a particular period. Detective stories, for example, often end with the variety of suspects gathered in one room to hear the sleuth unravel the mystery and identify the guilty party. That scene is a motif of mysteries. Similarly, the isolated, intelligent, lonely protagonist trying to overcome feelings of alienation is a motif common to stories written in the modern period, in the years just before and after World War I. To recognize these motifs, you will have to become familiar with a lot of stories—far more than are represented in this volume. Your instructor can help you.

Theme

A story's **theme** is what that story is about, though not in a literal sense. Literally, the story of the Prodigal Son is about one man who chooses a wayward life and ends up begging forgiveness from his father. Themes are more universal: prodigality, remorse of conscience, mercy. In a larger sense, the Prodigal Son is about these abstractions. It has something to say about prodigality, remorse, and mercy—and jealousy, too; it teaches us something about these themes.

Theme is one thing that distinguishes fictional stories from most of the stories you read in newspapers. A newspaper will tell a story merely because it happened: a plane crashed, and everyone on board died; the president gave a speech in a nearby city; a famous actor got married. These stories generally do not have any larger thematic significance. Sometimes they do. When the "unsinkable" *Titanic* sank on its maiden voyage, many saw the event as an enormous reminder of the puniness of humans as compared to nature or God and as a rebuke of our pride. But most stories you read in the papers do not explore abstract themes. They are written simply to tell us what happened yesterday, and we read them because they are "news." Just think how stale yesterday's paper is, or last week's. Fictional stories last longer because their themes broaden their scope.

At the same time, we do not read short stories to extract a moral, as we would when we read a fable. Short stories do not offer some universally applicable lesson that can be easily paraphrased, such as "Slow and steady wins the race," which is the lesson of Aesop's fable of the tortoise and the hare.

But short stories, like fables, are about more than just the particular characters who enliven them. Frank O'Connor's "Guests of the Nation," for example, is not just about a couple of IRA members during the Anglo-Irish War; it is also about war in general and its effects on soldiers. To interpret the story, to comprehend its meaning, you have to draw some conclusion about the story's theme. You have to ask—and answer—questions such as, What does Frank O'Connor have to say about war?

Conclusion

Ultimately, this is why we analyze stories. We examine point of view and consider symbols and root out motifs so we can better understand what a story tells us about its themes. You might instinctively shy away from analysis because you're afraid that it ruins the story. After all, any reader who feels a visceral emotion at the end of "Guests of the Nation" *gets* the story. You don't need to analyze the story to feel the emotion swelling in your throat. That instinct against analysis is a good precaution. It *is* irreverent to ignore your visceral response in order to pursue questions about, say, narrative point of view with the clinical attitude of a scientist dissecting a cadaver.

But rather than letting that precautionary instinct turn you away from analysis altogether, you should let it lead you back to the story, back to the coherent whole story, *after* you've taken it apart in analysis. You will find that detailed analysis doesn't ruin a story. It increases the intensity of your unreflecting response. And added to the impossible-to-articulate meaning that a good story injects into your blood will be the intellectual pleasure of understanding. You will be able to articulate what Frank O'Connor has to say about war, about friendship, about duty, guilt, and death.

Chinua Achebe

1930—

> *Achebe is a Nigerian writer who grew up listening to the old Igbo
> stories told by his mother and reading the literature of Britain,
> which ruled Nigeria as a colony until 1960. Like the cultures of
> many colonized peoples, Achebe says, the Igbo culture "had been
> branded as inferior and bad by British oppressors, when they did
> not say it was non-existent. It appeared to be a vital cultural neces-
> sity to fight and rebel against that view." "Uncle Ben's Choice" ex-
> plores this conflict between native beliefs and customs imposed by
> colonialism, but Uncle Ben himself is unusual because he peaceably
> combines Igbo and Christian beliefs. Achebe regrets that modern
> Nigeria has lost the magic of tales told and retold orally, and here
> he tries to approximate that tradition. Reading a story cannot re-
> place listening to a storyteller, according to Achebe, but the writer
> can try to minimize what is lost.*

Uncle Ben's Choice

In the year nineteen hundred and nineteen I was a young clerk
in the Niger Company at Umuru. To be a clerk in those days is
like to be a minister today. My salary was two pounds ten. You
may laugh but two pounds ten in those days is like fifty pounds today. You could buy a big goat with four shillings. I could remember
the most senior African in the company was one Saro[1] man on ten-
thirteen-four. He was like Governor-General in our eyes.

Like all progressive young men I joined the African Club. We
played tennis and billiards. Every year we played a tournament with
the European Club. But I was less concerned with that. What I
liked was the Saturday night dances. Women were surplus. Not all

---

1. Yoruba (Nigerian language and people) term for freed British and American slaves reset-
tled in Africa via Sierra Leone who eventually made their way back to their ancestral home-
lands in southern Nigeria.

the waw-waw women you see in townships today but beautiful things like this.

I had a Raleigh bicycle, brand new, and everybody called me Jolly Ben. I was selling like hot bread. But there is one thing about me—we can laugh and joke and drink and do otherwise but I must always keep my sense with me. My father told me that a true son of our land must know how to sleep and keep one eye open. I never forget it. So I played and laughed with everyone and they shouted "Jolly Ben! Jolly Ben!" but I knew what I was doing. The women of Umuru are very sharp; before you count A they count B. So I had to be very careful. I never showed any of them the road to my house and I never ate the food they cooked for fear of love medicines. I had seen many young men kill themselves with women in those days, so I remembered my father's word: Never let a handshake pass the elbow.

I can say that the only exception was one tall, yellow, salt-water girl like this called Margaret. One Sunday morning I was playing my gramophone, a brand-new HMV Senior. (I never believe in second-hand things. If I have no money for a new one I just keep myself quiet; that is my motto.) I was playing this record and standing at the window with my chewing-stick in my mouth. People were passing in their fine-fine dresses to one church nearby. This Margaret was going with them when she saw me. As luck would have it I did not see her in time to hide. So that very day—she did not wait till tomorrow or next tomorrow—but as soon as church closed she returned back. According to her she wanted to convert me to Roman Catholic. Wonders will ever end! Margaret Jumbo! Beautiful thing like this. But it is not Margaret I want to tell you about now. I want to tell you how I stopped all that foolishness.

It was one New Year's Eve like this. You know how New Year can pass Christmas for jollity, for we end-of-month people. By Christmas Day the month has reached twenty-hungry but on New Year your pocket is heavy. So that day I went to the Club.

When I see you young men of nowadays say you drink, I just laugh. You don't know what drink is. You drink one bottle of beer or one shot of whisky and you begin to holler like crazeman. That night I was taking it easy on White Horse. *All that are desirous to pass from Edinburgh to London or any other place on their road, let them repair to the White Horse cellar. . . .* God Almighty!

One thing with me is I never mix my drinks. The day I want to drink whisky I know that that is whisky-day; if I want to drink beer tomorrow then I know it is beer-day; I don't touch any other thing. That night I was on White Horse. I had one roasted chicken and a tin of Guinea Gold. Yes, I used to smoke in those days. I only stopped when one German doctor told me my heart was as black as a cooking-pot. Those German doctors were spirits. You know they used to give injections in the head or belly or anywhere. You just point where the thing is paining you and they give it to you right there—they don't waste time.

What was I saying? . . . Yes, I drank a bottle of White Horse and put one roasted chicken on top of it . . . Drunk? It is not in my dictionary. I have never been drunk in my life. My father used to say that the cure for drink is to say no. When I want to drink I drink, when I want to stop I stop. So about three o'clock that night I said to myself, you have had enough. So I jumped on my new Raleigh bicycle and went home quietly to sleep.

At that time our senior clerk was jailed for stealing bales of calico and I was acting in that capacity. So I lived in a small company house. You know where G.B. Olivant is today? . . . Yes, overlooking the River Niger. That is where my house was. I had two rooms on one side of it and the store-keeper had two rooms on the other side. But as luck would have it this man was on leave, so his side was vacant.

I opened the front door and went inside. Then I locked it again. I left my bicycle in the first room and went into the bedroom. I was too tired to begin to look for my lamp. So I pulled my dress and packed them on the back of the chair, and fell like a log into my big iron bed. And to God who made me, there was a woman in my bed. My mind told me at once it was Margaret. So I began to laugh and touch her here and there. She was hundred per cent naked. I continued laughing and asked her when did she come. She did not say anything and I suspected she was annoyed because she asked me to take her to the Club that day and I said no. I said to her: if you come there we will meet, I don't take anybody to the Club as such. So I suspected that is what is making her vex.

I told her not to vex but still she did not say anything. I asked her if she was asleep—just for asking sake. She said nothing. Although I told you that I did not like women to come to my house, but for every rule there must be an exception. So if I say that I was very angry to find Margaret that night I will be telling a white lie. I was still laughing when I noticed that her breasts were straight like the breasts of a girl of sixteen—or seventeen, at most. I thought that perhaps it was because of the way she was lying on her back. But when I touched the hair and it was soft like the hair of a European my laughter was quenched by force. I touched the hair on her head and it was the same. I jumped out of the bed and shouted: "Who are you?" My head swelled up like a barrel and I was shaking. The woman sat up and stretched her hands to call me back; as she did so her fingers touched me. I jumped back at the same time and shouted again to her to call her name. Then I said to myself: How can you be afraid of a woman? Whether a white woman or a black woman, it is the same ten and tenpence. So I said: "All right, I will soon open your mouth," at the same time I began to look for matches on the table. The woman suspected what I was looking for. She said, "Biko akpakwana oku."

I said: "So you are not a white woman. Who are you? I will strike the matches now if you don't tell me." I shook the matches to show her that I meant business. My boldness had come back and I was trying to remember the voice because it was very familiar.

"Come back to the bed and I will tell you," was what I heard next. Whoever told me it was a familiar voice told me a lie. It was sweet like sugar but not familiar at all. So I struck the matches.

"I beg you," was the last thing she said.

If I tell you what I did next or how I managed to come out of that room it is pure guesswork. The next thing I remember is that I was running like a crazeman to Matthew's house. Then I was banging on his door with both my hands.

"Who is that?" he said from inside.

"Open," I shouted. "In the name of God above, open."

I called my name but my voice was not like my voice. The door opened very small and I saw my kinsman holding a matchete in his right hand.

I fell down on the floor, and he said, "God will not agree."

It was God Himself who directed me to Matthew Obi's house that night because I did not see where I was going. I could not say whether I was still in this world or whether I was dead. Matthew poured cold water on me and after some time I was able to tell him what happened. I think I told it upside down otherwise he would not keep asking me what was she like, what was she like.

"I told you before I did not see her," I said.

"I see, but you heard her voice?"

"I heard her voice quite all right. And I touched her and she touched me."

"I don't know whether you did well or not to scare her away," was what Matthew said.

I don't know how to explain it but those words from Matthew opened my eyes. I knew at once that I had been visited by Mami Wota,[2] the Lady of the River Niger.

Matthew said again: "It depends what you want in life. If it is wealth you want then you made a great mistake today, but if you are a true son of your father then take my hand."

We shook hands and he said: "Our fathers never told us that a man should prefer wealth instead of wives and children."

Today whenever my wives make me vex I tell them: "I don't blame you. If I had been wise I would have taken Mami Wota." They laugh and ask me why did I not take her. The youngest one says: "Don't worry, Papa, she will come again; she will come tomorrow." And they laugh again.

But we all know it is a joke. For where is the man who will choose wealth instead of children? Except a crazy white man like Dr. J.M. Stuart-Young. Oh, I didn't tell you. The same night that I drove Mami Wota out she went to Dr. J.M. Stuart-Young, a white merchant and became his lover. You have heard of him? . . . Oh yes, he became the richest man in the whole country. But she did not allow him to marry. When he died, what happened? All his wealth went to outsiders. Is that good wealth? I ask you. God forbid.

1966

---

2. A legendary seductress in West African mythology who brings wealth to her lover but prevents his fathering children.

Raymond Carver
1938–1988

Carver is famous for his minimalist style of prose, which he often described as stripped down to not just the bone but the marrow. His characters are also typically pessimistic and unhappy. But in the context of Carver's life's work, "Cathedral" marks a turn toward a fuller prose style and more congenial (if not entirely happy) characters. Carver himself recognized that "Cathedral" is "more generous and maybe more affirmative" than the "smallness of vision and execution" of his previous work. In one interview he commented on the building of cathedrals to emphasize the collaborative and anonymous character of art. How does this give you some sense of what he's trying to achieve in the final scene of this story?

Cathedral

This blind man, an old friend of my wife's, he was on his way to spend the night. His wife had died. So he was visiting the dead wife's relatives in Connecticut. He called my wife from his in-laws'. Arrangements were made. He would come by train, a five-hour trip, and my wife would meet him at the station. She hadn't seen him since she worked for him one summer in Seattle ten years ago. But she and the blind man had kept in touch. They made tapes and mailed them back and forth. I wasn't enthusiastic about his visit. He was no one I knew. And his being blind bothered me. My idea of blindness came from the movies. In the movies, the blind moved slowly and never laughed. Sometimes they were led by seeing-eye dogs. A blind man in my house was not something I looked forward to.

That summer in Seattle she had needed a job. She didn't have any money. The man she was going to marry at the end of the summer was in officers' training school. He didn't have any money, either. But she was in love with the guy, and he was in love with her, etc. She'd seen something in the paper: HELP WANTED—*Reading to Blind Man,* and a telephone number. She phoned and went over, was hired on the spot. She'd worked with this blind man all summer. She read stuff to him, case studies, reports, that sort of thing. She helped him organize his little office in the county social-service department. They'd become good friends, my wife and the blind man. How do I know these things? She told me. And she told me something else. On her last day in the office, the blind man asked if he could touch her face. She agreed to this. She told me he touched his fingers to every part of her face, her nose—even her neck! She never forgot it. She even tried to write a poem about it. She was always trying to write a poem. She wrote a poem or two every year, usually after something really important had happened to her.

When we first started going out together, she showed me the poem. In the poem, she recalled his fingers and the way they had moved around over her face. In the poem, she talked about what she had felt at the time, about what went through her mind when the blind man touched her nose and lips. I can remember I didn't think much of the poem. Of course, I didn't tell her that. Maybe I just don't understand poetry. I admit it's not the first thing I reach for when I pick up something to read.

Anyway, this man who'd first enjoyed her favors, the officer-to-be, he'd been her childhood sweetheart. So okay. I'm saying that at the end of the summer she let the blind man run his hands over her face, said goodbye to him, married her childhood etc., who was now a commissioned officer, and she moved away from Seattle. But they'd kept in touch, she and the blind man. She made the first contact after a year or so. She called him up one night from an Air Force base in Alabama. She wanted to talk. They talked. He asked her to send him a tape and tell him about her life. She did this. She sent the tape. On the tape, she told the blind man about her husband and about their life together in the military. She told the blind man she loved her husband but she didn't like it where they lived and she didn't like it that he was a part of the military-industrial thing. She told the blind man she'd written a poem about what it was like to be an Air Force officer's wife. The poem wasn't finished yet. She was still writing it. The blind man made a tape. He sent her the tape. She made a tape. This went on for years. My wife's officer was posted to one base and then another. She sent tapes from Moody AFB, McGuire, McConnell, and finally Travis, near Sacramento, where one night she got to feeling lonely and cut off from people she kept losing in that moving-around life. She got to feeling she couldn't go it another step. She went in and swallowed all the pills and capsules in the medicine chest and washed them down with a bottle of gin. Then she got into a hot bath and passed out.

But instead of dying, she got sick. She threw up. Her officer—why should he have a name? he was the childhood sweetheart, and what more does he want?—came home from somewhere, found her, and called the ambulance. In time, she put it all on a tape and sent the tape to the blind man. Over the years, she put all kinds of stuff on tapes and sent the tapes off lickety-split. Next to writing a poem every year, I think it was her chief means of recreation. On one tape, she told the blind man she'd decided to live away from her officer for a time. On another tape, she told him about her divorce. She and I began going out, and of course she told her blind man about it. She told him everything, or so it seemed to me. Once she asked me if I'd like to hear the latest tape from the blind man. This was a year ago. I was on the tape, she said. So I said okay, I'd listen to it. I got us drinks and we settled down in the living room. We made ready to listen. First she inserted the tape into the player and adjusted a couple of dials. Then she pushed a lever. The tape squeaked and someone began to talk in this loud voice. She lowered the volume. After a few minutes of harmless chitchat, I heard my own name in the mouth of this stranger, this blind man I didn't even know! And then this: "From all you've said about him, I can only conclude—" But we were interrupted, a knock at the door, something, and we didn't ever get back to the tape. Maybe it was just as well. I'd heard all I wanted to.

Now this same blind man was coming to sleep in my house.

"Maybe I could take him bowling," I said to my wife. She was at the draining board doing scalloped potatoes. She put down the knife she was using and turned around.

"If you love me," she said, "you can do this for me. If you don't love me, okay. But if you had a friend, any friend, and the friend came to visit, I'd make him feel comfortable." She wiped her hands with the dish towel.

"I don't have any blind friends," I said.

"You don't have *any* friends," she said. "Period. Besides," she said, "goddamn it, his wife's just died! Don't you understand that? The man's lost his wife!"

I didn't answer. She'd told me a little about the blind man's wife. Her name was Beulah. Beulah! That's a name for a colored woman.

"Was his wife a Negro?" I asked.

"Are you crazy?" my wife said. "Have you just flipped or something?" She picked up a potato. I saw it hit the floor, then roll under the stove. "What's wrong with you?" she said. "Are you drunk?"

"I'm just asking," I said.

Right then my wife filled me in with more detail than I cared to know. I made a drink and sat at the kitchen table to listen. Pieces of the story began to fall into place.

Beulah had gone to work for the blind man the summer after my wife had stopped working for him. Pretty soon Beulah and the blind man had themselves a church wedding. It was a little wedding—who'd want to go to such a wedding in the first place?—just the two of them, plus the minister and the minister's wife. But it was a church wedding just the same. It was what Beulah had wanted, he'd said. But even then Beulah must have been carrying the cancer in her glands. After they had been inseparable for eight years—my wife's word, *inseparable*—Beulah's health went into a rapid decline. She died in a Seattle hospital room, the blind man sitting beside the bed and holding on to her hand. They'd married, lived and worked together, slept together—had sex, sure—and then the blind man had to bury her. All this without his having ever seen what the goddamned woman looked like. It was beyond my understanding. Hearing this, I felt sorry for the blind man for a little bit. And then I found myself thinking what a pitiful life this woman must have led. Imagine a woman who could never see herself as she was seen in the eyes of her loved one. A woman who could go on day after day and never receive the smallest compliment from her beloved. A woman whose husband could never read the expression on her face, be it misery or something better. Someone who could wear makeup or not—what difference to him? She could, if she wanted, wear green eye-shadow around one eye, a straight pin in her nostril, yellow slacks and purple shoes, no matter. And then to slip off into death, the blind man's hand on her hand, his blind eyes streaming tears—I'm imagining now—her last thought maybe this: that he never even knew what she looked like, and she on an express to the grave. Robert was left with a small insurance policy and half of a twenty-peso Mexican coin. The other half of the coin went into the box with her. Pathetic.

So when the time rolled around, my wife went to the depot to pick him up. With nothing to do but wait—sure, I blamed him for that—I was having a drink and watching the TV when I heard the car pull into the drive. I got up from the sofa with my drink and went to the window to have a look.

I saw my wife laughing as she parked the car. I saw her get out of the car and shut the door. She was still wearing a smile. Just amazing. She went around to the other side of the car to where the blind man was already starting to get out. This blind man, feature this, he was wearing a full beard! A beard on a blind man! Too much, I say. The blind man reached into the back seat and dragged out a suitcase. My wife took his arm, shut the car door, and, talking all the way, moved him down the drive and then up the steps to the front porch. I turned off the TV. I finished my drink, rinsed the glass, dried my hands. Then I went to the door.

My wife said, "I want you to meet Robert. Robert, this is my husband. I've told you all about him." She was beaming. She had this blind man by his coat sleeve.

The blind man let go of his suitcase and up came his hand.

I took it. He squeezed hard, held my hand, and then he let it go. "I feel like we've already met," he boomed.

"Likewise," I said. I didn't know what else to say. Then I said, "Welcome. I've heard a lot about you." We began to move then, a little group, from the porch into the living room, my wife guiding him by the arm. The blind man was carrying his suitcase in his other hand. My wife said things like, "To your left here, Robert. That's right. Now watch it, there's a chair. That's it. Sit down right here. This is the sofa. We just bought this sofa two weeks ago."

I started to say something about the old sofa. I'd liked that old sofa. But I didn't say anything. Then I wanted to say something else, small-talk, about the scenic ride along the Hudson. How going *to* New York, you should sit on the right-hand side of the train, and coming *from* New York, the left-hand side.

"Did you have a good train ride?" I said. "Which side of the train did you sit on, by the way?"

"What a question, which side!" my wife said. "What's it matter which side?" she said.

"I just asked," I said.

"Right side," the blind man said. "I hadn't been on a train in nearly forty years. Not since I was a kid. With my folks. That's been a long time. I'd nearly forgotten the sensation. I have winter in my beard now," he said. "So I've been told, anyway. Do I look distinguished, my dear?" the blind man said to my wife.

"You look distinguished, Robert," she said. "Robert," she said. "Robert, it's just so good to see you."

My wife finally took her eyes off the blind man and looked at me. I had the feeling she didn't like what she saw. I shrugged.

I've never met, or personally known, anyone who was blind. This blind man was late forties, a heavy-set, balding man with stooped shoulders, as if he carried a great weight there. He wore brown slacks, brown shoes, a light-brown shirt, a tie, a sports coat. Spiffy. He also had this full beard. But he didn't use a cane and he didn't wear dark glasses. I'd always thought dark glasses were a must for the blind. Fact was, I wished he had a pair. At first glance, his eyes looked like anyone else's eyes. But if you looked close, there was something different about them. Too much white in the iris, for one thing, and the pupils seemed to move around in the sockets without his knowing it or being able to stop it. Creepy. As I stared at his face, I saw the left pupil turn in toward his nose while the other made an effort to keep in one place. But it was only an effort, for that eye was on the roam without his knowing it or wanting it to be.

I said, "Let me get you a drink. What's your pleasure? We have a little of everything. It's one of our pastimes."

"Bub, I'm a Scotch man myself," he said fast enough in this big voice.

"Right," I said. Bub! "Sure you are. I knew it."

He let his fingers touch his suitcase, which was sitting alongside the sofa. He was taking his bearings. I didn't blame him for that.

"I'll move that up to your room," my wife said.

"No, that's fine," the blind man said loudly. "It can go up when I go up."

"A little water with the Scotch?" I said.

"Very little," he said.

"I knew it," I said.

He said, "Just a tad. The Irish actor, Barry Fitzgerald? I'm like that fellow. When I drink water, Fitzgerald said, I drink water. When I drink whiskey, I drink whiskey." My wife laughed. The blind man brought his hand up under his beard. He lifted his beard slowly and let it drop.

I did the drinks, three big glasses of Scotch with a splash of water in each. Then we made ourselves comfortable and talked about Robert's travels. First the long flight from the West Coast to Connecticut, we covered that. Then from Connecticut up here by train. We had another drink concerning that leg of the trip.

I remembered having read somewhere that the blind didn't smoke because, as speculation had it, they couldn't see the smoke they exhaled. I thought I knew that much and that much only about blind people. But this blind man smoked his cigarette down to the nubbin and then lit another one. This blind man filled his ashtray and my wife emptied it.

When we sat down at the table for dinner, we had another drink. My wife heaped Robert's plate with cube steak, scalloped potatoes, green beans. I buttered him up two slices of bread. I said, "Here's bread and butter for you." I swallowed some of my drink. "Now let us pray," I said, and the blind man lowered his head. My wife looked at me, her mouth agape. "Pray the phone won't ring and the food doesn't get cold," I said.

We dug in. We ate everything there was to eat on the table. We ate like there was no tomorrow. We didn't talk. We ate. We scarfed. We grazed that table. We were into serious eating. The blind man had right away located his foods, he knew just where everything was on his plate. I watched with admiration as he used his knife and fork on the meat. He'd cut two pieces of meat, fork the meat into his mouth, and then go all out for the scalloped potatoes, the beans next, and then he'd tear off a hunk of buttered bread and eat that. He'd follow this up with a big drink of milk. It didn't seem to bother him to use his fingers once in a while, either.

We finished everything, including half a strawberry pie. For a few moments, we sat as if stunned. Sweat beaded on our faces. Finally, we got up from the table and left the dirty plates. We didn't look back. We took ourselves into the living room and sank into our places again. Robert and my wife sat on the sofa. I took the big chair. We had us two or three more drinks while they talked about the major things that had come to pass for them in the past ten years. For the most part, I just listened. Now and then I joined in. I didn't want him to think I'd left the room, and I didn't want her to think I was feeling left out. They talked of things that had happened to them—to them!—these past ten years. I waited in vain to hear my name on my wife's sweet lips: "And then my dear husband came into my life"—something like that. But I heard nothing of the sort. More talk of Robert. Robert had done a little of everything, it seemed, a regular blind jack-of-all-trades. But most recently he and his wife had had an Amway distributorship, from which, I gathered, they'd earned their living, such as it was. The blind man was also a ham radio operator. He talked in his loud voice about conversations he'd had with fellow operators in Guam, in the Philippines, in Alaska, and even in Tahiti. He said he'd have a lot of friends there if he ever wanted to go visit those places. From time to time, he'd turn his blind face toward me, put his hand under his beard, ask me something. How long had I been in my present position? (Three years.) Did I like my work? (I didn't.) Was I going to stay with it? (What were the options?) Finally, when I thought he was beginning to run down, I got up and turned on the TV.

My wife looked at me with irritation. She was heading toward a boil. Then she looked at the blind man and said, "Robert, do you have a TV?"

The blind man said, "My dear, I have two TVs. I have a color set and a black-and-white thing, an old relic. It's funny, but if I turn the TV on, and I'm always turning it on, I turn on the color set. It's funny, don't you think?"

I didn't know what to say to that. I had absolutely nothing to say to that. No opinion. So I watched the news program and tried to listen to what the announcer was saying.

"This is a color TV," the blind man said. "Don't ask me how, but I can tell."

"We traded up a while ago," I said.

The blind man had another taste of his drink. He lifted his

beard, sniffed it, and let it fall. He leaned forward on the sofa. He positioned his ashtray on the coffee table, then put the lighter to his cigarette. He leaned back on the sofa and crossed his legs at the ankles.

My wife covered her mouth, and then she yawned. She stretched. She said, "I think I'll go upstairs and put on my robe. I think I'll change into something else. Robert, you make yourself comfortable," she said.

"I'm comfortable," the blind man said.

"I want you to feel comfortable in this house," she said.

"I am comfortable," the blind man said.

After she'd left the room, he and I listened to the weather report and then to the sports roundup. By that time, she'd been gone so long I didn't know if she was going to come back. I thought she might have gone to bed. I wished she'd come back downstairs. I didn't want to be left alone with a blind man. I asked him if he wanted to smoke some dope with me. I said I'd just rolled a number. I hadn't, but I planned to do so in about two shakes.

"I'll try some with you," he said.

"Damn right," I said. "That's the stuff."

I got our drinks and sat down on the sofa with him. Then I rolled us two fat numbers. I lit one and passed it. I brought it to his fingers. He took it and inhaled.

"Hold it as long as you can," I said. I could tell he didn't know the first thing.

My wife came back downstairs wearing her pink robe and her pink slippers.

"What do I smell?" she said.

"We thought we'd have us some cannabis," I said.

My wife gave me a savage look. Then she looked at the blind man and said, "Robert, I didn't know you smoked."

He said, "I do now, my dear. There's a first time for everything. But I don't feel anything yet."

"This stuff is pretty mellow," I said. "This stuff is mild. It's dope you can reason with," I said. "It doesn't mess you up."

"Not much it doesn't, bub," he said, and laughed.

My wife sat on the sofa between the blind man and me. I passed her the number. She took it and toked and then passed it back to me. "Which way is this going?" she said. Then she said, "I shouldn't be smoking this. I can hardly keep my eyes open as it is. That dinner did me in. I shouldn't have eaten so much."

"It was the strawberry pie," the blind man said. "That's what did it," he said, and he laughed his big laugh. Then he shook his head.

"There's more strawberry pie," I said.

"Do you want some more, Robert?" my wife said.

"Maybe in a little while," he said.

We gave our attention to the TV. My wife yawned again. She said, "Your bed is made up when you feel like going to bed, Robert. I know you must have had a long day. When you're ready to go to bed, say so." She pulled his arm. "Robert?"

He came to and said, "I've had a real nice time. This beats tapes, doesn't it?"

I said, "Coming at you," and I put the number between his fingers. He inhaled, held the smoke, and then let it go. It was like he'd been doing it since he was nine years old.

"Thanks, bub," he said. "But I think this is all for me. I think I'm beginning to feel it," he said. He held the burning roach out for my wife.

"Same here," she said. "Ditto. Me, too." She took the roach and passed it to me. "I may just sit here for a while between you two guys with my eyes closed. But don't let me bother you, okay? Either one of you. If it bothers you, say so. Otherwise, I may just sit here with my eyes closed until you're ready to go to bed," she said. "Your bed's made up, Robert, when you're ready. It's right next to our room at the top of the stairs. We'll show you up when you're ready. You wake me up now, you guys, if I fall asleep." She said that and then she closed her eyes and went to sleep.

The news program ended. I got up and changed the channel. I sat back down on the sofa. I wished my wife hadn't pooped out. Her head lay across the back of the sofa, her mouth open. She'd turned so that her robe had slipped away from her legs, exposing a juicy thigh. I reached to draw her robe back over her, and it was then that I glanced at the blind man. What the hell! I flipped the robe open again.

"You say when you want some strawberry pie," I said.

"I will," he said.

I said, "Are you tired? Do you want me to take you up to your bed? Are you ready to hit the hay?"

"Not yet," he said. "No, I'll stay up with you, bub. If that's all right. I'll stay up until you're ready to turn in. We haven't had a chance to talk. Know what I mean? I feel like me and her monopolized the evening." He lifted his beard and he let it fall. He picked up his cigarettes and lighter.

"That's all right," I said. Then I said, "I'm glad for the company."

And I guess I was. Every night I smoked dope and stayed up as long as I could before I fell asleep. My wife and I hardly ever went to bed at the same time. When I did go to sleep, I had these dreams. Sometimes I'd wake up from one of them, my heart going crazy.

Something about the church and the Middle Ages was on the TV. Not your run-of-the-mill TV fare. I wanted to watch something else. I turned to the other channels. But there was nothing on them, either. So I turned back to the first channel and apologized.

"Bub, it's all right," the blind man said. "It's fine with me. Whatever you want to watch is okay. I'm always learning something. Learning never ends. It won't hurt me to learn something tonight. I got ears," he said.

We didn't say anything for a time. He was leaning forward with his head turned at me, his right ear aimed in the direction of the set. Very disconcerting. Now and then his eyelids dropped and then they snapped open again. Now and then he put his fingers into his beard and tugged, like he was thinking about something he was hearing on the television.

On the screen, a group of men wearing cowls was being set upon and tormented by men dressed in skeleton costumes and men dressed as devils. The men dressed as devils wore devil masks, horns, and long tails. This pageant was part of a procession. The Englishman who was narrating the thing said it took place in Spain once a year. I tried to explain to the blind man what was happening.

"Skeletons," he said. "I know about skeletons," he said, and he nodded.

The TV showed this one cathedral. Then there was a long, slow look at another one. Finally, the picture switched to the famous one in Paris,[1] with its flying buttresses and its spires reaching up to the clouds. The camera pulled away to show the whole of the cathedral rising above the skyline.

There were times when the Englishman who was telling the thing would shut up, would simply let the camera move around over the cathedrals. Or else the camera would tour the countryside, men in fields walking behind oxen. I waited as long as I could. Then I felt I had to say something. I said, "They're showing the outside of this cathedral now. Gargoyles. Little statues carved to look like monsters. Now I guess they're in Italy. Yeah, they're in Italy. There's paintings on the walls of this one church."

"Are those fresco paintings, bub?" he asked, and he sipped from his drink.

I reached for my glass. But it was empty. I tried to remember what I could remember. "You're asking me are those frescoes?" I said. "That's a good question. I don't know."

The camera moved to a cathedral outside Lisbon. The differences in the Portuguese cathedral compared with the French and Italian were not that great. But they were there. Mostly the interior stuff. Then something occurred to me, and I said, "Something has occurred to me. Do you have any idea what a cathedral is? What they look like, that is? Do you follow me? If somebody says cathedral to you, do you have any notion what they're talking about? Do you know the difference between that and a Baptist church, say?"

He let the smoke dribble from his mouth. "I know they took hundreds of workers fifty or a hundred years to build," he said. "I just heard the man say that, of course. I know generations of the same families worked on a cathedral. I heard him say that, too. The men who began their life's work on them, they never lived to see the completion of their work. In that wise, bub, they're no different from the rest of us, right?" He laughed. Then his eyelids drooped again. His head nodded. He seemed to be snoozing. Maybe he was imagining himself in Portugal. The TV was showing another cathedral now. This one was in Germany. The Englishman's voice droned on. "Cathedrals," the blind man said. He sat up and rolled his head back and forth. "If you want the truth, bub, that's about all I know.

---

1. Notre Dame.

What I just said. What I heard him say. But maybe you could describe one to me? I wish you'd do it. I'd like that. If you want to know, I really don't have a good idea."

I stared hard at the shot of the cathedral on the TV. How could I even begin to describe it? But say my life depended on it. Say my life was being threatened by an insane guy who said I had to do it or else.

I stared some more at the cathedral before the picture flipped off into the countryside. There was no use. I turned to the blind man and said, "To begin with, they're very tall." I was looking around the room for clues. "They reach way up. Up and up. Toward the sky. They're so big, some of them, they have to have these supports. To help hold them up, so to speak. These supports are called buttresses. They remind me of viaducts, for some reason. But maybe you don't know viaducts, either? Sometimes the cathedrals have devils and such carved into the front. Sometimes lords and ladies. Don't ask me why this is," I said.

He was nodding. The whole upper part of his body seemed to be moving back and forth.

"I'm not doing so good, am I?" I said.

He stopped nodding and leaned forward on the edge of the sofa. As he listened to me, he was running his fingers through his beard. I wasn't getting through to him, I could see that. But he waited for me to go on just the same. He nodded, like he was trying to encourage me. I tried to think what else to say. "They're really big," I said. "They're massive. They're built of stone. Marble, too, sometimes. In those olden days, when they built cathedrals, men wanted to be close to God. In those olden days, God was an important part of everyone's life. You could tell this from their cathedral-building. I'm sorry," I said, "but it looks like that's the best I can do for you. I'm just no good at it."

"That's all right, bub," the blind man said. "Hey, listen. I hope you don't mind my asking you. Can I ask you something? Let me ask you a simple question, yes or no. I'm just curious and there's no offense. You're my host. But let me ask if you are in any way religious? You don't mind my asking?"

I shook my head. He couldn't see that, though. A wink is the same as a nod to a blind man. "I guess I don't believe in it. In anything. Sometimes it's hard. You know what I'm saying?"

"Sure, I do," he said.

"Right," I said.

The Englishman was still holding forth. My wife sighed in her sleep. She drew a long breath and went on with her sleeping.

"You'll have to forgive me," I said. "But I can't tell you what a cathedral looks like. It just isn't in me to do it. I can't do any more than I've done."

The blind man sat very still, his head down as he listened to me.

I said, "The truth is, cathedrals don't mean anything special to me. Nothing. Cathedrals. They're something to look at on late-night TV. That's all they are."

It was then that the blind man cleared his throat. He brought something up. He took a handkerchief from his back pocket. Then he said, "I get it, bub. It's okay. It happens. Don't worry about it," he said. "Hey, listen to me. Will you do me a favor? I got an idea. Why don't you find us some heavy paper? And a pen. We'll do something. We'll draw one together. Get us a pen and some heavy paper. Go on, bub, get the stuff," he said.

So I went upstairs. My legs felt like they didn't have any strength in them. They felt like they did after I'd done some running. In my wife's room, I looked around. I found some ballpoints in a little basket on her table. And then I tried to think where to look for the kind of paper he was talking about.

Downstairs, in the kitchen, I found a shopping bag with onion skins at the bottom of the bag. I emptied the bag and shook it. I brought it into the living room and sat down with it near his legs. I moved some things, smoothed the wrinkles from the bag, spread it out on the coffee table.

The blind man got down from the sofa and sat next to me on the carpet.

He ran his fingers over the paper. He went up and down the sides of the paper. The edges, even the edges. He fingered the corners.

"All right," he said. "All right, let's do her."

He found my hand, the hand with the pen. He closed his hand over my hand. "Go ahead, bub, draw," he said. "Draw. You'll see. I'll follow along with you. It'll be okay. Just begin now like I'm telling you. You'll see. Draw," the blind man said.

So I began. First I drew a box that looked like a house. It could have been the house I lived in. Then I put a roof on it. At either end of the roof, I drew spires. Crazy.

"Swell," he said. "Terrific. You're doing fine," he said. "Never thought anything like this could happen in your lifetime, did you, bub? Well, it's a strange life, we all know that. Go on now. Keep it up."

I put in windows with arches. I drew flying buttresses. I hung great doors. I couldn't stop. The TV station went off the air. I put down the pen and closed and opened my fingers. The blind man felt around over the paper. He moved the tips of his fingers over the paper, all over what I had drawn, and he nodded.

"Doing fine," the blind man said.

I took up the pen again, and he found my hand. I kept at it. I'm no artist. But I kept drawing just the same.

My wife opened up her eyes and gazed at us. She sat up on the sofa, her robe hanging open. She said, "What are you doing? Tell me, I want to know."

I didn't answer her.

The blind man said, "We're drawing a cathedral. Me and him are working on it. Press hard," he said to me. "That's right. That's good," he said. "Sure. You got it, bub. I can tell. You didn't think you could. But you can, can't you? You're cooking with gas now. You know what I'm saying? We're going to really have us something here in a minute. How's the old arm?" he said. "Put some people in there now. What's a cathedral without people?"

My wife said, "What's going on? Robert, what are you doing? What's going on?"

"It's all right," he said to her. "Close your eyes now," the blind man said to me.

I did it. I closed them just like he said.

"Are they closed?" he said. "Don't fudge."

"They're closed," I said.

"Keep them that way," he said. He said, "Don't stop now. Draw."

So we kept on with it. His fingers rode my fingers as my hand went over the paper. It was like nothing else in my life up to now.

Then he said, "I think that's it. I think you got it," he said. "Take a look. What do you think?"

But I had my eyes closed. I thought I'd keep them that way for a little longer. I thought it was something I ought to do.

"Well?" he said. "Are you looking?"

My eyes were still closed. I was in my house. I knew that. But I didn't feel like I was inside anything.

"It's really something," I said.

1981

John Cheever
1912–1982

> *Many of Cheever's stories deal with American suburbia's promise of heaven on earth, and quite a few use the strange mix of realism and fantasy that we find in "The Swimmer." Cheever wrote this story for the* New Yorker, *so we might think of his primary audience as that magazine's upper-middle-class clientele, in New York but also throughout the country. Many readers have struggled to figure out exactly what* happens *in this story. Cheever himself was a bit disdainful whenever he was asked about "The Swimmer." Tongue in cheek, he suggested that Neddy was a latter-day Narcissus pursuing the reflection of his own face and pursuing death. Cheever also pointed out how the story was popular in communist Russia, presumably for its portrayal of capitalists. The incongruous details, Cheever insisted, "ought to be taken at face value." In other words, when Neddy sees autumn leaves and smells wood smoke, it is* autumn.

The Swimmer

It was one of those midsummer Sundays when everyone sits around saying, "I *drank* too much last night." You might have heard it whispered by the parishioners leaving church, heard it from the lips of the priest himself, struggling with his cassock in the *vestiarium*,[1] heard it from the golf links and the tennis courts, heard it from the wildlife preserve where the leader of the Audubon group was suffering from a terrible hangover. "I *drank* too much," said

---

1. Vestry, a room attached to the church where the clergy put on their vestments.

Donald Westerhazy. "We all *drank* too much," said Lucinda Merrill. "It must have been the wine," said Helen Westerhazy. "I *drank* too much of that claret."

This was at the edge of the Westerhazys' pool. The pool, fed by an artesian well with a high iron content, was a pale shade of green. It was a fine day. In the west there was a massive stand of cumulus cloud so like a city seen from a distance—from the bow of an approaching ship—that it might have had a name. Lisbon. Hackensack. The sun was hot. Neddy Merrill sat by the green water, one hand in it, one around a glass of gin. He was a slender man—he seemed to have the especial slenderness of youth—and while he was far from young he had slid down his banister that morning and given the bronze backside of Aphrodite on the hall table a smack, as he jogged toward the smell of coffee in his dining room. He might have been compared to a summer's day, particularly the last hours of one, and while he lacked a tennis racket or a sail bag the impression was definitely one of youth, sport, and clement weather. He had been swimming and now he was breathing deeply, stertorously as if he could gulp into his lungs the components of that moment, the heat of the sun, the intenseness of his pleasure. It all seemed to flow into his chest. His own house stood in Bullet Park, eight miles to the south, where his four beautiful daughters would have had their lunch and might be playing tennis. Then it occurred to him that by taking a dogleg to the southwest he could reach his home by water.

His life was not confining and the delight he took in this observation could not be explained by its suggestion of escape. He seemed to see, with a cartographer's eye, that string of swimming pools, that quasi-subterranean stream that curved across the county. He had made a discovery, a contribution to modern geography; he would name the stream Lucinda after his wife. He was not a practical joker nor was he a fool but he was determinedly original and had a vague and modest idea of himself as a legendary figure. The day was beautiful and it seemed to him that a long swim might enlarge and celebrate its beauty.

He took off a sweater that was hung over his shoulders and dove in. He had an inexplicable contempt for men who did not hurl themselves into pools. He swam a choppy crawl, breathing either with every stroke or every fourth stroke and counting somewhere well in the back of his mind the one-two one-two of a flutter kick. It was not a serviceable stroke for long distances but the domestication of swimming had saddled the sport with some customs and in his part of the world a crawl was customary. To be embraced and sustained by the light green water was less a pleasure, it seemed, than the resumption of a natural condition, and he would have liked to swim without trunks, but this was not possible, considering his project. He hoisted himself up on the far curb—he never used the ladder—and started across the lawn. When Lucinda asked where he was going he said he was going to swim home.

The only maps and charts he had to go by were remembered or imaginary but these were clear enough. First there were the Grahams, the Hammers, the Lears, the Howlands, and the Crosscups. He would cross Ditmar Street to the Bunkers and come, after a short portage, to the Levys, the Welchers, and the public pool in Lancaster. Then there were the Hallorans, the Sachses, the Biswangers, Shirley Adams, the Gilmartins, and the Clydes. The day was lovely, and that he lived in a world so generously supplied with water seemed like a clemency, a beneficence. His heart was high and he ran across the grass. Making his way home by an uncommon route gave him the feeling that he was a pilgrim, an explorer, a man with a destiny, and he knew that he would find friends all along the way; friends would line the banks of the Lucinda River.

He went through a hedge that separated the Westerhazys' land from the Grahams', walked under some flowering apple trees, passed the shed that housed their pump and filter, and came out at the Grahams' pool. "Why, Neddy," Mrs. Graham said, "what a marvelous surprise. I've been trying to get you on the phone all morning. Here, let me get you a drink." He saw then, like any explorer, that the hospitable customs and traditions of the natives would have to be handled with diplomacy if he was ever going to reach his destination. He did not want to mystify or seem rude to the Grahams nor did he have the time to linger there. He swam the length of their pool and joined them in the sun and was rescued, a few minutes later, by the arrival of two carloads of friends from Connecticut. During the uproarious reunions he was able to slip away. He went down by the front of the Grahams' house, stepped over a thorny hedge, and crossed a vacant lot to the Hammers'. Mrs.

Hammer, looking up from her roses, saw him swim by although she wasn't quite sure who it was. The Lears heard him splashing past the open windows of their living room. The Howlands and the Cross-cups were away. After leaving the Howlands' he crossed Ditmar Street and started for the Bunkers', where he could hear, even at that distance, the noise of a party.

The water refracted the sound of voices and laughter and seemed to suspend it in midair. The Bunkers' pool was on a rise and he climbed some stairs to a terrace where twenty-five or thirty men and women were drinking. The only person in the water was Rusty Towers, who floated there on a rubber raft. Oh, how bonny and lush were the banks of the Lucinda River! Prosperous men and women gathered by the sapphire-colored waters while caterer's men in white coats passed them cold gin. Overhead a red de Haviland trainer was circling around and around and around in the sky with something like the glee of a child in a swing. Ned felt a passing affection for the scene, a tenderness for the gathering, as if it was something he might touch. In the distance he heard thunder. As soon as Enid Bunker saw him she began to scream: "Oh, look who's here! What a marvelous surprise! When Lucinda said that you couldn't come I thought I'd *die*." She made her way to him through the crowd, and when they had finished kissing she led him to the bar, a progress that was slowed by the fact that he stopped to kiss eight or ten other women and shake the hands of as many men. A smiling bartender he had seen at a hundred parties gave him a gin and tonic and he stood by the bar for a moment, anxious not to get stuck in any conversation that would delay his voyage. When he seemed about to be surrounded he dove in and swam close to the side to avoid colliding with Rusty's raft. At the far end of the pool he bypassed the Tomlinsons with a broad smile and jogged up the garden path. The gravel cut his feet but this was the only unpleasantness. The party was confined to the pool, and as he went toward the house he heard the brilliant, watery sound of voices fade, heard the noise of a radio from the Bunkers' kitchen, where someone was listening to a ball game. Sunday afternoon. He made his way through the parked cars and down the grassy border of their drive-way to Alewives Lane. He did not want to be seen on the road in his bathing trunks but there was no traffic and he made the short distance to the Levys' driveway, marked with a PRIVATE PROPERTY sign and a green tube for *The New York Times*. All the doors and windows of the big house were open but there were no signs of life; not even a dog barked. He went around the side of the house to the pool and saw that the Levys had only recently left. Glasses and bottles and dishes of nuts were on a table at the deep end, where there was a bathhouse or gazebo, hung with Japanese lanterns. After swimming the pool he got himself a glass and poured a drink. It was his fourth or fifth drink and he had swum nearly half the length of the Lucinda River. He felt tired, clean, and pleased at that moment to be alone; pleased with everything.

It would storm. The stand of cumulus cloud—that city—had risen and darkened, and while he sat there he heard the percussiveness of thunder again. The de Haviland trainer was still circling overhead and it seemed to Ned that he could almost hear the pilot laugh with pleasure in the afternoon; but when there was another peal of thunder he took off for home. A train whistle blew and he wondered what time it had gotten to be. Four? Five? He thought of the provincial station at that hour, where a waiter, his tuxedo concealed by a raincoat, a dwarf with some flowers wrapped in newspaper, and a woman who had been crying would be waiting for the local. It was suddenly growing dark; it was that moment when the pinheaded birds seemed to organize their song into some acute and knowledgeable recognition of the storm's approach. Then there was a fine noise of rushing water from the crown of an oak at his back, as if a spigot there had been turned. Then the noise of fountains came from the crowns of all the tall trees. Why did he love storms, what was the meaning of his excitement when the door sprang open and the rain wind fled rudely up the stairs, why had the simple task of shutting the windows of an old house seemed fitting and urgent, why did the first watery notes of a storm wind have for him the unmistakable sound of good news, cheer, glad tidings? Then there was an explosion, a smell of cordite, and rain lashed the Japanese lanterns that Mrs. Levy had bought in Kyoto the year before last, or was it the year before that?

He stayed in the Levys' gazebo until the storm had passed. The rain had cooled the air and he shivered. The force of the wind had stripped a maple of its red and yellow leaves and scattered them over the grass and the water. Since it was midsummer the tree must be blighted, and yet he felt a peculiar sadness at this sign of autumn. He braced his shoulders, emptied his glass, and started for the Welchers' pool. This meant crossing the Lindleys' riding ring and he was surprised to find it overgrown with grass and all the jumps dismantled. He wondered if the Lindleys had sold their horses or gone away for the summer and put them out to board. He seemed to remember having heard something about the Lindleys and their horses but the memory was unclear. On he went, barefoot through the wet grass, to the Welchers', where he found their pool was dry.

This breach in his chain of water disappointed him absurdly, and he felt like some explorer who seeks a torrential headwater and finds a dead stream. He was disappointed and mystified. It was common enough to go away for the summer but no one ever drained his pool. The Welchers had definitely gone away. The pool furniture was folded, stacked, and covered with a tarpaulin. The bathhouse was locked. All the windows of the house were shut, and when he went around to the driveway, in front he saw a FOR SALE sign nailed to a tree. When had he last heard from the Welchers—when, that is, had he and Lucinda last regretted an invitation to dine with them? It seemed only a week or so ago. Was his memory failing or had he so disciplined it in the repression of unpleasant facts that he had damaged his sense of the truth? Then in the distance he heard the sound of a tennis game. This cheered him, cleared away all his apprehensions and let him regard the overcast sky and the cold air with indifference. This was the day that Neddy Merrill swam across the county. That was the day! He started off then for his most difficult portage.

Had you gone for a Sunday afternoon ride that day you might have seen him, close to naked, standing on the shoulders of Route 424, waiting for a chance to cross. You might have wondered if he was the victim of foul play, had his car broken down, or was he merely a fool. Standing barefoot in the deposits of the highway—beer cans, rags, and blowout patches—exposed to all kinds of ridicule, he seemed pitiful. He had known when he started that this was a part of his journey—it had been on his maps—but confronted with the lines of traffic, worming through the summery light, he found himself unprepared. He was laughed at, jeered at, a beer can was thrown at him, and he had no dignity or humor to bring to the situation. He could have gone back, back to the Westerhazys', where Lucinda would still be sitting in the sun. He had signed nothing, vowed nothing, pledged nothing, not even to himself. Why, believing as he did, that all human obduracy was susceptible to common sense, was he unable to turn back? Why was he determined to complete his journey even if it meant putting his life in danger? At what point had this prank, this joke, this piece of horseplay become serious? He could not go back, he could not even recall with any clearness the green water at the Westerhazys', the sense of inhaling the day's components, the friendly and relaxed voices saying that they had *drunk* too much. In the space of an hour, more or less, he had covered a distance that made his return impossible.

An old man, tooling down the highway at fifteen miles an hour, let him get to the middle of the road, where there was a grass divider. Here he was exposed to the ridicule of the northbound traffic, but after ten or fifteen minutes he was able to cross. From here he had only a short walk to the Recreation Center at the edge of the village of Lancaster, where there were some handball courts and a public pool.

The effect of the water on voices, the illusion of brilliance and suspense, was the same here as it had been at the Bunkers' but the sounds here were louder, harsher, and more shrill, and as soon as he entered the crowded enclosure he was confronted with regimentation. "ALL SWIMMERS MUST TAKE A SHOWER BEFORE USING THE POOL. ALL SWIMMERS MUST USE THE FOOTBATH. ALL SWIMMERS MUST WEAR THEIR IDENTIFICATION DISKS." He took a shower, washed his feet in a cloudy and bitter solution, and made his way to the edge of the water. It stank of chlorine and looked to him like a sink. A pair of lifeguards in a pair of towers blew police whistles at what seemed to be regular intervals and abused the swimmers through a public address system. Neddy remembered the sapphire water at the Bunkers' with longing and thought that he might contaminate himself—damage his own prosperousness and charm—by swimming in this murk, but he reminded himself that he was an explorer, a pilgrim, and that this was merely a stagnant bend in the Lucinda River. He dove, scowling with distaste, into the chlorine and had to swim with his head above water to avoid collisions, but even so he was bumped into, splashed, and jostled. When he got to the shallow end both lifeguards were shouting at him: "Hey, you, you without the identification disk, get outa the water." He did, but they had no way of pursuing him and he went through the reek of suntan oil and chlorine out through the hurricane fence and passed the handball courts. By crossing the road he entered the wooded part of the Halloran estate. The woods were not cleared and the footing was treacherous and difficult until he reached the lawn and the clipped beech hedge that encircled their pool.

The Hallorans were friends, an elderly couple of enormous wealth who seemed to bask in the suspicion that they might be Communists. They were zealous reformers but they were not Communists, and yet when they were accused, as they sometimes were, of subversion, it seemed to gratify and excite them. Their beech hedge was yellow and he guessed this had been blighted like the Levys' maple. He called hullo, hullo, to warn the Hallorans of his approach, to palliate his invasion of their privacy. The Hallorans, for reasons that had never been explained to him, did not wear bathing suits. No explanations were in order, really. Their nakedness was a detail in their uncompromising zeal for reform and he stepped politely out of his trunks before he went through the opening in the hedge.

Mrs. Halloran, a stout woman with white hair and a serene face, was reading the *Times*. Mr. Halloran was taking beech leaves out of the water with a scoop. They seemed not surprised or displeased to see him. Their pool was perhaps the oldest in the country, a fieldstone rectangle, fed by a brook. It had no filter or pump and its waters were the opaque gold of the stream.

"I'm swimming across the county," Ned said.

"Why, I didn't know one could," exclaimed Mrs. Halloran.

"Well, I've made it from the Westerhazys'," Ned said. "That must be about four miles."

He left his trunks at the deep end, walked to the shallow end, and swam this stretch. As he was pulling himself out of the water he heard Mrs. Halloran say, "We've been *terribly* sorry to hear about all your misfortunes, Neddy."

"My misfortunes?" Ned asked. "I don't know what you mean."

"Why, we heard that you'd sold the house and that your poor children . . ."

"I don't recall having sold the house," Ned said, "and the girls are at home."

"Yes," Mrs. Halloran sighed. "Yes . . ." Her voice filled the air with an unseasonable melancholy and Ned spoke briskly. "Thank you for the swim."

"Well, have a nice trip," said Mrs. Halloran.

Beyond the hedge he pulled on his trunks and fastened them. They were loose and he wondered if, during the space of an afternoon, he could have lost some weight. He was cold and he was tired and the naked Hallorans and their dark water had depressed him. The swim was too much for his strength but how could he have guessed this, sliding down the banister that morning and sitting in the Westerhazys' sun? His arms were lame. His legs felt rubbery and ached at the joints. The worst of it was the cold in his bones and the feeling that he might never be warm again. Leaves were falling down around him and he smelled wood smoke on the wind. Who would be burning wood at this time of year?

He needed a drink. Whiskey would warm him, pick him up, carry him through the last of his journey, refresh his feeling that it was original and valorous to swim across the county. Channel swimmers took brandy. He needed a stimulant. He crossed the lawn in front of the Hallorans' house and went down a little path to where they had built a house for their only daughter, Helen, and her husband, Eric Sachs. The Sachses' pool was small and he found Helen and her husband there.

"Oh, *Neddy*," Helen said. "Did you lunch at Mother's?"

"Not *really*," Ned said. "I *did* stop to see your parents." This seemed to be explanation enough. "I'm terribly sorry to break in on you like this but I've taken a chill and I wonder if you'd give me a drink."

"Why, I'd *love* to," Helen said, "but there hasn't been anything in this house to drink since Eric's operation. That was three years ago."

Was he losing his memory, had his gift for concealing painful facts let him forget that he had sold his house, that his children were in trouble, and that his friend had been ill? His eyes slipped from Eric's face to his abdomen, where he saw three pale, sutured scars, two of them at least a foot long. Gone was his navel, and what, Neddy thought, would the roving hand, bed-checking one's gifts at 3 A.M., make of a belly with no navel, no link to birth, this breach in the succession?

"I'm sure you can get a drink at the Biswangers'," Helen said. "They're having an enormous do. You can hear it from here. Listen!"

She raised her head and from across the road, the lawns, the gardens, the woods, the fields, he heard again the brilliant noise of voices over water. "Well, I'll get wet," he said, still feeling that he had no freedom of choice about his means of travel. He dove into the Sachses' cold water and, gasping, close to drowning, made his way from one end of the pool to the other. "Lucinda and I want *terribly* to see you," he said over his shoulder, his face set toward the Biswangers'. "We're sorry it's been so long and we'll call you *very* soon."

He crossed some fields to the Biswangers' and the sounds of revelry there. They would be honored to give him a drink, they would be happy to give him a drink. The Biswangers invited him and Lucinda for dinner four times a year, six weeks in advance. They were always rebuffed and yet they continued to send out their invitations, unwilling to comprehend the rigid and undemocratic realities of their society. They were the sort of people who discussed the price of things at cocktails, exchanged market tips during dinner, and after dinner told dirty stories to mixed company. They did not belong to Neddy's set—they were not even on Lucinda's Christmas card list. He went toward their pool with feelings of indifference, charity, and some unease, since it seemed to be getting dark and these were the longest days of the year. The party when he joined it was noisy and large. Grace Biswanger was the kind of hostess who asked the optometrist, the veterinarian, the real-estate dealer, and the dentist. No one was swimming and the twilight, reflected on the water of the pool, had a wintry gleam. There was a bar and he started for this. When Grace Biswanger saw him she came toward him, not affectionately as he had every right to expect, but bellicosely.

"Why, this party has everything," she said loudly, "including a gate crasher."

She could not deal him a social blow—there was no question about this and he did not flinch. "As a gate crasher," he asked politely, "do I rate a drink?"

"Suit yourself," she said. "You don't seem to pay much attention to invitations."

She turned her back on him and joined some guests, and he went to the bar and ordered a whiskey. The bartender served him but he served him rudely. His was a world in which the caterer's men kept the social score, and to be rebuffed by a part-time barkeep meant that he had suffered some loss of social esteem. Or perhaps the man was new and uninformed. Then he heard Grace at his back say: "They went for broke overnight—nothing but income—and he showed up drunk one Sunday and asked us to loan him five thousand dollars. . . ." She was always talking about money. It was worse than eating your peas off a knife. He dove into the pool, swam its length and went away.

The next pool on his list, the last but two, belonged to his old mistress, Shirley Adams. If he had suffered any injuries at the Biswangers' they would be cured here. Love—sexual roughhouse in fact—was the supreme elixir, the pain killer, the brightly colored pill that would put the spring back into his step, the joy of life in his heart. They had had an affair last week, last month, last year. He couldn't remember. It was he who had broken it off, his was the upper hand, and he stepped through the gate of the wall that surrounded her pool with nothing so considered as self-confidence. It seemed in a way to be his pool, as the lover, particularly the illicit lover, enjoys the possessions of his mistress with an authority unknown to holy matrimony. She was there, her hair the color of brass, but her figure, at the edge of the lighted, cerulean water, excited in him no profound memories. It had been, he thought, a lighthearted affair, although she had wept when he broke it off. She seemed confused to see him and he wondered if she was still wounded. Would she, God forbid, weep again?

"What do you want?" she asked.

"I'm swimming across the county."

"Good Christ. Will you ever grow up?"

"What's the matter?"

"If you've come here for money," she said, "I won't give you another cent."

"You could give me a drink."

"I could but I won't. I'm not alone."

"Well, I'm on my way."

He dove in and swam the pool, but when he tried to haul himself up onto the curb he found that the strength in his arms and shoulders had gone, and he paddled to the ladder and climbed out. Looking over his shoulder he saw, in the lighted bathhouse, a young man. Going out onto the dark lawn he smelled chrysanthemums or marigolds—some stubborn autumnal fragrance—on the night air, strong as gas. Looking overhead he saw that the stars had come out, but why should he seem to see Andromeda, Cepheus, and Cassiopeia? What had become of the constellations of midsummer? He began to cry.

It was probably the first time in his adult life that he had ever cried, certainly the first time in his life that he had ever felt so miserable, cold, tired, and bewildered. He could not understand the rudeness of the caterer's barkeep or the rudeness of a mistress who had come to him on her knees and showered his trousers with tears. He had swum too long, he had been immersed too long, and his nose and his throat were sore from the water. What he needed then was a drink, some company, and some clean, dry clothes, and while he could have cut directly across the road to his home he went on to the Gilmartins' pool. Here, for the first time in his life, he did not dive but went down the steps into the icy water and swam a hobbled sidestroke that he might have learned as a youth. He staggered with fatigue on his way to the Clydes' and paddled the length of their pool, stopping again and again with his hand on the curb to rest. He climbed up the ladder and wondered if he had the strength to get home. He had done what he wanted, he had swum the county, but he was so stupefied with exhaustion that his triumph seemed vague. Stooped, holding on to the gateposts for support, he turned up the driveway of his own house.

The place was dark. Was it so late that they had all gone to bed? Had Lucinda stayed at the Westerhazys' for supper? Had the girls joined her there or gone someplace else? Hadn't they agreed, as they usually did on Sunday, to regret all their invitations and stay at home? He tried the garage doors to see what cars were in but the doors were locked and rust came off the handles onto his hands. Going toward the house, he saw that the force of the thunderstorm had knocked one of the rain gutters loose. It hung down over the front door like an umbrella rib, but it could be fixed in the morning. The house was locked, and he thought that the stupid cook or the stupid maid must have locked the place up until he remembered that it had been some time since they had employed a maid or a cook. He shouted, pounded on the door, tried to force it with his shoulder, and then, looking in at the windows, saw that the place was empty.

1964

Anton Chekhov
1860–1904

> *At the age of thirty, already the most famous writer in Russia with the exception of Tolstoy and suffering from tuberculosis, Chekhov decided to attempt the arduous three-month journey across Siberia to visit the penal colony on Sakhalin Island in the North Pacific. Chekhov was a doctor as well as a writer, and he went to inspect the conditions of the convicts and to report the information back to Moscow. "In Exile" is one of two stories inspired by the experience. The story came out in 1892, just after Chekhov, who was known for his political quietude, started publishing in liberal, reformist newspapers. Though the choice facing the Tartar in the story might symbolize Chekhov's view of the human condition, it is also disturbingly realistic. Families were permitted to accompany an exiled convict, since to be forced to live on Sakhalin was considered punishment enough. "In Exile," as Chekhov surely hoped it would, helped spark reforms on Sakhalin.*

In Exile[1]

Old Semyon, whose nickname was Preacher, and a young Tartar, whose name no one knew, were sitting by a campfire on the bank of the river; the other three ferrymen were inside the hut. Semyon, a gaunt, toothless old man of sixty, broadshouldered and still healthy-looking, was drunk; he would have

---

1. Translated by Ann Dunnigan.

gone to bed long ago, but he had a bottle in his pocket and was afraid his comrades in the hut would ask him for a drink of vodka. The Tartar was worn out and ill, and, wrapping himself in his rags, he talked about how good it was in the province of Simbirsk,[2] and what a beautiful and clever wife he had left at home. He was not more than twenty-five, and in the firelight his pale, sickly face and woebegone expression made him seem like a boy.

"Well, this is no paradise, of course," said Preacher. "You can see for yourself: water, bare banks, nothing but clay wherever you look. . . . It's long past Easter and there's still ice on the river . . . and this morning there was snow."

"Bad! Bad!" said the Tartar, surveying the landscape with dismay.

A few yards away the dark, cold river flowed, growling and sluicing against the pitted clay banks as it sped on to the distant sea. At the edge of the bank loomed a capacious barge, which ferrymen call a *karbas*. Far away on the opposite bank crawling snakes of fire were dying down then reappearing—last year's grass being burned. Beyond the snakes there was darkness again. Little blocks of ice could be heard knocking against the barge. It was cold and damp. . . .

The Tartar glanced at the sky. There were as many stars as there were at home, the same blackness, but something was lacking. At home, in the province of Simbirsk, the stars and the sky seemed altogether different.

"Bad! Bad!" he repeated.

"You'll get used to it!" said Preacher with a laugh. "You're still young and foolish—the milk's hardly dry on your lips—and in your foolishness you think there's no one more unfortunate than you, but the time will come when you'll say to yourself: may God give everyone such a life. Just look at me. In a week's time the floods will be over and we'll launch the ferry; you'll all go gadding about Siberia, while I stay here, going back and forth, from one bank to the other. For twenty-two years now that's what I've been doing. Day and night. The pike and the salmon under the water and me on it. That's all I want. God give everyone such a life."

The Tartar threw some brushwood onto the fire, lay down closer

2. In southeast central Russia, along the Volga River.

to it, and said, "My father is sick man. When he dies, my mother, my wife, will come here. Have promised."

"And what do you want a mother and a wife for?" asked Preacher. "Just foolishness, brother. It's the devil stirring you up, blast his soul! Don't listen to him, the Evil One! Don't give in to him. When he goes on about women, spite him: I don't want them! When he talks to you about freedom, you stand up to him: I don't want it! I want nothing! No father, no mother, no wife, no freedom, no house nor home! I want nothing, damn their souls!"

Preacher took a swig at the bottle and went on, "I'm no simple peasant, brother; I don't come from the servile class; I'm a deacon's son, and when I was free I lived in Kursk,[3] and used to go around in a frock coat; but now I've brought myself to such a point that I can sleep naked on the ground and eat grass. And God give everyone such a life. I don't want anything, I'm not afraid of anyone, and the way I see it, there's no man richer or freer than I am. When they sent me here from Russia, from the very first day I jibbed: I want nothing! The devil was at me about my wife, about my kin, about freedom, but I told him: I want nothing! And I stuck to it; and here, you see, I live well, I don't complain. But if anyone humors the devil and listens to him even once, he's lost, no salvation for him. He'll be stuck fast in the bog, up to his ears, and he'll never get out.

"It's not only the likes of you, foolish peasants, that are lost, but even the well-born and educated. Fifteen years ago they sent a gentleman here from Russia. He forged a will or something—wouldn't share with his brothers. It was said he was a prince or a baron, but maybe he was only an official, who knows? Well, the gentleman came here, and the first thing, he bought himself a house and land in Mukhortinskoe.[4] 'I want to live by my own labor,' says he, 'in the sweat of my brow, because I'm no longer a gentleman, but an exile.' . . . 'Well,' says I, 'may God help you, that's the right thing.' He was a young man then, a hustler, always on the move; he used to do the mowing himself, catch fish, ride sixty versts on horseback. But here

3. City in Russia, south of Moscow.
4. A town in the Krasnodo region of Siberia.

was the trouble: from the very first year he began riding to Gyrino to the post office. He used to stand on my ferry and sigh, 'Ah, Semyon, for a long time now they haven't sent me any money from home.' . . . 'You don't need money, Vasily Sergeich. What good is it? Throw off the past, forget it as if it had never happened, as if it was only a dream, and start life afresh. Don't listen to the devil,' I tell him, 'he'll bring you to no good; he'll tighten the noose. Now you want money,' says I, 'and in a little while, before you know it, you'll want something else, and then more and more. But,' says I, 'if you want to be happy, the very first thing is not to want anything.' Yes. . . . 'And if fate has cruelly wronged you and me,' says I, 'it's no good going down on your knees to her and asking her favor; you have to spurn her and laugh at her, otherwise she'll laugh at you.' That's what I said to him. . . .

"Two years later I ferried him over to this side, and he was rubbing his hands together and laughing. 'I'm going to Gyrino,' says he, 'to meet my wife. She has taken pity on me and come here. She's so kind and good!' He was panting with joy. Next day he comes with his wife. A young, beautiful lady in a hat, carrying a baby girl in her arms. And plenty of baggage of all sorts. My Vasily Sergeich was spinning around her; couldn't take his eyes off her; couldn't praise her enough. 'Yes, brother Semyon, even in Siberia people can live!' . . . 'Well,' thinks I, 'just you wait; better not rejoice too soon.' . . . And from that time on, almost every week he went to Gyrino to find out if money had been sent from Russia. As for money—it took plenty! 'It's for my sake that her youth and beauty are going to ruin here in Siberia,' he says, 'sharing with me my bitter fate, and for this,' he says, 'I ought to provide her with every diversion.' To make it more cheerful for his lady he took up with the officials and with all sorts of riffraff. And there had to be food and drink for this crowd, of course, and they must have a piano, and a fuzzy little lap dog on the sofa—may it croak! . . . Luxury, in short, indulgence. The lady did not stay with him long. How could she? Clay, water, cold, no vegetables for you, no fruit; uneducated and drunken people all around, no manners at all, and she a pampered lady from the capital. . . . Naturally, she grew tired of it. Besides, her husband, say what you like, was no longer a gentleman, but an exile—not exactly an honor.

"Three years later, I remember, on the eve of the Assumption,[5] someone shouted from the other side. I went over in the ferry, and what do I see but the lady—all muffled up, and with her a young gentleman, an official. There was a troika. . . . And after I ferried them across, they got in it and vanished into thin air! That was the last that was seen of them. Toward morning Vasily Sergeich galloped up to the ferry. 'Didn't my wife pass this way, Semyon, with a gentleman in spectacles?' . . . 'She did,' says I. 'Seek the wind in the fields!' He galloped off in pursuit of them, and didn't stop for five days and five nights. Afterwards, when I took him over to the other side, he threw himself down on the ferry, beat his head against the planks, and howled. 'So that's how it is,' says I. . . . I laughed and recalled to him: 'Even in Siberia people can live!' And he beat his head all the more.

"After that he began to long for freedom. His wife had slipped away to Russia, so, naturally, he was drawn there, both to see her and to rescue her from her lover. And, my friend, he took to galloping off every day, either to the post office or the authorities; he kept sending in petitions, and presenting them personally, asking to be pardoned so he could go back home; and he used to tell how he had spent some two hundred rubles on telegrams alone. He sold his land, and mortgaged his house to the Jews. He grew gray, stooped, and yellow in the face, as if he was consumptive. He'd talk to you and go: khe-khe-khe . . . and there would be tears in his eyes. He struggled with those petitions for eight years, but now he has recovered his spirits and is more cheerful: he's thought up a new indulgence. His daughter, you see, has grown up. He keeps an eye on her, dotes on her. And, to tell the truth, she's all right, a pretty little thing, black-browed, and with a lively disposition. Every Sunday he goes to church with her in Gyrino. Side by side they stand on the ferry, she laughing and he not taking his eyes off her. 'Yes, Semyon,' says he, 'even in Siberia people can live. Even in Siberia there is happiness. Look,' says he, 'see what a daughter I've got! I suppose you wouldn't find another like her if you went a thousand versts.' . . . 'Your daughter,' says I, 'is a fine young lady, that's true, certainly. . . .'

5. August 15, observed in commemoration of the Assumption of the Virgin Mary (that is, the taking of Mary up to heaven).

But I think to myself: Wait a while. . . . The girl is young, her blood is dancing, she wants to live, and what life is there here? And, my friend, she did begin to fret. . . . She withered and withered, wasted away, fell ill; and now she's completely worn out. Consumption.

"That's your Siberian happiness for you, the pestilence take it! That's how people can live in Siberia! . . . He's taken to running after doctors and taking them home with him. As soon as he hears that there's a doctor or quack two or three hundred versts away, he goes to fetch him. A terrible lot of money has been spent on doctors; to my way of thinking, it would have been better to spend it on drink. . . . She'll die anyway. She's certain to die, and then he'll be completely lost. He'll hang himself from grief, or run away to Russia—that's sure. He'll run away, they'll catch him, there'll be a trial, and then hard labor; they'll give him a taste of the lash. . . ."

"Good, good," muttered the Tartar, shivering with cold.

"What's good?" asked Preacher.

"Wife and daughter. . . . Let hard labor, let suffer; he saw his wife and daughter. . . . You say: want nothing. But nothing is bad! Wife was with him three years—God gave him that. Nothing is bad; three years is good. How you not understand?"

Shivering and stuttering, straining to pick out the Russian words, of which he knew so few, the Tartar said God forbid one should fall sick and die in a strange land, and be buried in the cold, sodden earth; that if his wife came to him even for one day, even for one hour, he would be willing to accept any torture whatsoever, and thank God for it. Better one day of happiness than nothing.

After that he again described the beautiful and clever wife he had left at home; then, clutching his head with both hands, he began crying and assuring Semyon that he was innocent and had been falsely accused. His two brothers and his uncle stole some horses from a peasant, and beat the old man till he was half dead, and the commune had not judged fairly, but had contrived a sentence by which all three brothers were sent to Siberia, while the uncle, a rich man, remained at home.

"You'll get u-u-used to it!" said Semyon.

The Tartar relapsed into silence and fixed his tearful eyes on the fire; his face expressed bewilderment and fright, as though he still did not understand why he was here in the dark, in the damp, among strangers, instead of in the province of Simbirsk. Preacher lay down near the fire, chuckled at something, and began singing in an undertone.

"What joy has she with her father?" he said a little later. "He loves her, she's a consolation to him, it's true; but you have to mind your p's and q's with him, brother: he's a strict old man, a severe old man. And strictness is not what young girls want. . . . They want petting and ha-ha-ha and ho-ho-ho, scents and pomades! Yes. . . . Ekh, life, life!" sighed Semyon, getting up with difficulty. "The vodka's all gone, so it's time to sleep. Eh? I'm going, my boy."

Left alone, the Tartar put more brushwood onto the fire, lay down, and, looking into the blaze, began thinking of his native village, and of his wife: if she would come only for a month, even for a day, then, if she liked, she might go back again. Better a month or even a day than nothing. But if she kept her promise and came, how could he provide for her? Where could she live?

"If not something to eat, how you live?" the Tartar asked aloud.

He was paid only ten kopecks for working at the oars a day and a night; the passengers gave him tips, it was true, but the ferrymen shared everything among themselves, giving nothing to the Tartar, but only making fun of him. And he was hungry, cold, and frightened from want. . . . Now, when his whole body was shivering and aching, he ought to go into the hut and lie down to sleep, but he had nothing there to cover himself with, and it was colder there than on the river bank; here, too, he had nothing to put over him, but at least he could make a fire. . . .

In another week, when the floods had subsided and the ferry could sail, none of the ferrymen except Semyon would be needed, and the Tartar would begin going from village to village, looking for work and begging alms. His wife was only seventeen years old; beautiful, pampered, shy—could she possibly go from village to village, her face unveiled, begging? No, even to think of it was dreadful. . . .

It was already growing light; the barge, the bushes of rose-willow, and the ripples on the water were clearly distinguishable, and looking back there was the steep clay precipice, below it the little hut thatched with brown straw, and above clung the huts of the villagers. The cocks were already crowing in the village.

The red clay precipice, the barge, the river, the strange, unkind people, hunger, cold, illness—perhaps all this did not exist in reality. Probably it was all a dream, thought the Tartar. He felt that he was asleep, and hearing his own snoring. . . . Of course, he was at home in the province of Simbirsk, and he had only to call his wife by name for her to answer, and in the next room his mother. . . . However, what awful dreams there are! Why? The Tartar smiled and opened his eyes. What river was this? The Volga?

"Bo-o-at!" someone shouted from the other side. "Karba-a-s!"

The Tartar woke up and went to wake his comrades, to row over to the other side. Putting on their torn sheepskins as they came, the ferrymen appeared on the bank, swearing in hoarse, sleepy voices, and shivering from the cold. After their sleep, the river, from which there came a piercing gust of cold air, evidently struck them as revolting and sinister. They were not quick to jump into the barge. The Tartar and the three ferrymen took up the long, broad-bladed oars, which looked like crabs' claws in the darkness. Semyon leaned his belly against the long tiller. The shouting from the other side continued, and two shots were fired from a revolver; the man probably thought that the ferrymen were asleep or had gone off to the village tavern.

"All right, plenty of time!" said Preacher in the tone of a man who is convinced that there is no need to hurry in this world—that it makes no difference, really, and nothing will come of it.

The heavy, clumsy barge drew away from the bank and floated between the rose-willows; and only because the willows slowly receded was it possible to see that the barge was not standing still but moving. The ferrymen plied the oars evenly, in unison; Preacher hung over the tiller on his belly, and, describing an arc in the air, flew from one side of the boat to the other. In the darkness it looked as if the men were sitting on some antideluvian animal with long paws, and sailing to a cold, bleak land, the very one of which we sometimes dream in nightmares.

They passed beyond the willows and floated out into the open. The rhythmic thump and splash of the oars were now audible on the further shore, and someone shouted, "Hurry! Hurry!" Another ten minutes passed and the barge bumped heavily against the landing stage.

"And it keeps coming down, and coming down!" muttered Semyon, wiping the snow from his face. "Where it comes from, God only knows!"

On the other side stood a thin old man of medium height wearing a jacket lined with fox fur and a white lambskin cap. He was standing at a little distance from his horses and not moving; he had a concentrated, morose expression, as if, trying to remember something, he had grown angry with his unyielding memory. When Semyon went up to him with a smile and took off his cap, he said, "I'm hastening to Anastasyevka. My daughter is worse again, and they say there's a new doctor at Anastasyevka."

They dragged the tarantass[6] onto the barge and rowed back. The man, whom Semyon called Vasily Sergeich, stood motionless all the way back, his thick lips tightly compressed, his eyes fixed on one spot; when the coachman asked permission to smoke in his presence, he made no reply, as if he had not heard. And Semyon, hanging over the tiller on his belly, glanced mockingly at him and said, "Even in Siberia people can live. Li-i-ve!"

There was a triumphant expression on Preacher's face, as if he had proved something and was rejoicing that it had turned out exactly as he had surmised. The helpless, unhappy look of the man in the fox-lined jacket evidently afforded him great satisfaction.

"It's muddy driving now, Vasily Sergeich," he said when the horses were harnessed on the bank. "You'd better have waited a week or two till it gets drier. . . . Or else not have gone at all. . . . If there were any sense in going, but, as you yourself know, people have been driving about for ever and ever, by day and by night, and there's never any sense in it. That's the truth!"

Vasily Sergeich tipped him without a word, got into the tarantass, and drove off.

"See there, he's gone galloping off for a doctor!" said Semyon, shrinking with cold. "Yes, looking for a real doctor is like chasing the wind in the fields, or catching the devil by the tail, damn your soul! What freaks! Lord forgive me, a sinner!"

The Tartar went up to Preacher and, looking at him with hatred and abhorrence, trembling, mixing Tartar words with his broken

6. A type of carriage used in Russia in the 1800s.

Russian, said, "He is good—good. You bad! You bad! Gentleman is good soul, excellent, and you beast, you bad! Gentleman alive and you dead. . . . God created man to be live, be joyful, be sad and sorrow, but you want nothing. . . . You not live, you stone, clay! Stone want nothing and you want nothing. . . . You stone—and God not love you, love gentleman!"

Everyone laughed; the Tartar frowned scornfully and, with a gesture of despair, wrapped himself in his rags and went to the fire. Semyon and the ferrymen trailed off to the hut.

"It's cold," said one of the ferrymen hoarsely as he stretched out on the straw that covered the damp floor.

"Well, it's not warm!" one of the others agreed. "It's a hard life!"

They all lay down. The door was blown open by the wind, and snow drifted into the hut. No one felt like getting up and closing the door; it was cold and they were lazy.

"I'm all right!" said Semyon, falling asleep. "God give everyone such a life."

"You're a hard case, we know that. Even the devils won't take you!"

From outside there came sounds like the howling of a dog.

"What's that? Who's there?"

"It's the Tartar crying."

"He'll get u-u-used to it!" said Semyon, and instantly fell asleep. Soon the others fell asleep too. And the door remained unclosed.

1892

Kate Chopin

1851–1904

> *Chopin wrote "The Story of an Hour" in the spring of 1894, but it was rejected by many magazine editors, at least once for being unethical. Finally,* Vogue *published it in December, paying Chopin ten dollars and also the compliment of presenting her to the public as a daring writer. Like the writing of Charlotte Perkins Gilman, Chopin's work helped energize feminists in her own day and continues to do so today. The theme of this story is autobiographical, though the details are not. Chopin, the mother of six, was widowed*

at the age of thirty-two. A month after finishing this story, she wrote in her diary that if her husband had lived, she "would have to forget the past ten years of my growth—my real growth." Nevertheless, she does not dismiss marriage as merely a prison for women. A sentence later she admits that she would have given up her ten years of growth in "the spirit of perfect acquiescence."

The Story of an Hour

Knowing that Mrs. Mallard was afflicted with a heart trouble, great care was taken to break to her as gently as possible the news of her husband's death.

It was her sister Josephine who told her, in broken sentences; veiled hints that revealed in half concealing. Her husband's friend Richards was there, too, near her. It was he who had been in the newspaper office when intelligence of the railroad disaster was received, with Brently Mallard's name leading the list of "killed." He had only taken the time to assure himself of its truth by a second telegram, and had hastened to forestall any less careful, less tender friend in bearing the sad message.

She did not hear the story as many women have heard the same, with a paralyzed inability to accept its significance. She wept at once, with sudden, wild abandonment, in her sister's arms. When the storm of grief had spent itself she went away to her room alone. She would have no one follow her.

There stood, facing the open window, a comfortable, roomy armchair. Into this she sank, pressed down by a physical exhaustion that haunted her body and seemed to reach into her soul.

She could see in the open square before her house the tops of trees that were all aquiver with the new spring life. The delicious breath of rain was in the air. In the street below a peddler was crying his wares. The notes of a distant song which some one was singing reached her faintly, and countless sparrows were twittering in the eaves.

There were patches of blue sky showing here and there through the clouds that had met and piled one above the other in the west facing her window.

She sat with her head thrown back upon the cushion of the chair, quite motionless, except when a sob came up into her throat and shook her, as a child who has cried itself to sleep continues to sob in its dreams.

She was young, with a fair, calm face, whose lines bespoke repression and even a certain strength. But now there was a dull stare in her eyes, whose gaze was fixed away off yonder on one of those patches of blue sky. It was not a glance of reflection, but rather indicated a suspension of intelligent thought.

There was something coming to her and she was waiting for it, fearfully. What was it? She did not know; it was too subtle and elusive to name. But she felt it, creeping out of the sky, reaching toward her through the sounds, the scents, the color that filled the air.

Now her bosom rose and fell tumultuously. She was beginning to recognize this thing that was approaching to possess her, and she was striving to beat it back with her will—as powerless as her two white slender hands would have been.

When she abandoned herself a little whispered word escaped her slightly parted lips. She said it over and over under her breath: "free, free, free!" The vacant stare and the look of terror that had followed it went from her eyes. They stayed keen and bright. Her pulses beat fast, and the coursing blood warmed and relaxed every inch of her body.

She did not stop to ask if it were or were not a monstrous joy that held her. A clear and exalted perception enabled her to dismiss the suggestion as trivial.

She knew that she would weep again when she saw the kind, tender hands folded in death; the face that had never looked save with love upon her, fixed and gray and dead. But she saw beyond that bitter moment a long procession of years to come that would belong to her absolutely. And she opened and spread her arms out to them in welcome.

There would be no one to live for her during those coming years; she would live for herself. There would be no powerful will bending hers in that blind persistence with which men and women believe they have a right to impose a private will upon a fellow-creature. A kind intention or a cruel intention made the act seem no less a crime as she looked upon it in that brief moment of illumination.

And yet she had loved him—sometimes. Often she had not. What did it matter! What could love, the unsolved mystery, count for in face of this possession of self-assertion which she suddenly recognized as the strongest impulse of her being!

"Free! Body and soul free!" she kept whispering.

Josephine was kneeling before the closed door with her lips to the keyhole, imploring for admission. "Louise, open the door! I beg; open the door—you will make yourself ill. What are you doing, Louise? For heaven's sake open the door."

"Go away. I am not making myself ill." No; she was drinking in a very elixir of life through that open window.

Her fancy was running riot along those days ahead of her. Spring days, and summer days, and all sorts of days that would be her own. She breathed a quick prayer that life might be long. It was only yesterday she had thought with a shudder that life might be long.

She arose at length and opened the door to her sister's importunities. There was a feverish triumph in her eyes, and she carried herself unwittingly like a goddess of Victory. She clasped her sister's waist, and together they descended the stairs. Richards stood waiting for them at the bottom.

Some one was opening the front door with a latchkey. It was Brently Mallard who entered, a little travel-stained, composedly carrying his grip-sack and umbrella. He had been far from the scene of accident, and did not even know there had been one. He stood amazed at Josephine's piercing cry; at Richards' quick motion to screen him from the view of his wife.

But Richards was too late.

When the doctors came they said she had died of heart disease— of joy that kills.

1894

Stephen Crane

1871–1900

> *In 1897, Crane was working as a reporter when he boarded the* Commodore, *a gunrunning freighter supplying Cuban rebels out of Jacksonville, Florida. After running aground twice, the ship finally made it out to sea, where it began to slowly sink. Most of the crew and the Cuban fighters were evacuated on three big lifeboats, but Crane waited to the very end and escaped in a ten-foot dinghy with the ship's captain, an oiler named William Higgins, and the cook. One of the lifeboats foundered, and the men in the dinghy watched seven others drown. After thirty hours at sea, the four finally came ashore at Daytona. Crane wrote a newspaper dispatch right away. Six months later he wrote "The Open Boat," which covered the ordeal on the sea. Contemporary readers did not think of it as fiction, and neither did Crane (consider the story's subtitle). "The Open Boat" is considered one of the finest examples of American naturalism: an irreligious philosophy that views the universe as indifferent to the existence and struggles of humans.*

The Open Boat

A Tale Intended to Be after the Fact: Being the Experience of Four Men from the Sunk Steamer COMMODORE

I

None of them knew the color of the sky. Their eyes glanced level and were fastened upon the waves that swept toward them. These waves were of the hue of slate, save for the tops, which were of foaming white, and all of the men knew the colors of the sea. The horizon narrowed and widened, and dipped and rose, and at all times its edge was jagged with waves that seemed thrust up in points like rocks.

Many a man ought to have a bathtub larger than the boat which here rode upon the sea. These waves were most wrongfully and barbarously abrupt and tall, and each froth-top was a problem in small-boat navigation.

The cook squatted in the bottom, and looked with both eyes at the six inches of gunwale which separated him from the ocean. His sleeves were rolled over his fat forearms, and the two flaps of his unbuttoned vest dangled as he bent to bail out the boat. Often he said, "Gawd! that was a narrow clip." As he remarked it he invariably gazed eastward over the broken sea.

The oiler, steering with one of the two oars in the boat, sometimes raised himself suddenly to keep clear of water that swirled in over the stern. It was a thin little oar, and it seemed often ready to snap.

The correspondent, pulling at the other oar, watched the waves and wondered why he was there.

The injured captain, lying in the bow, was at this time buried in that profound dejection and indifference which comes, temporarily at least, to even the bravest and most enduring when, willy-nilly, the firm fails, the army loses, the ship goes down. The mind of the master of a vessel is rooted deep in the timbers of her, though he command for a day or a decade; and this captain had on him the stern impression of a scene in the grays of dawn of seven turned faces, and later a stump of a topmast with a white ball on it that slashed to and fro at the waves, went low and lower, and down. Thereafter there was something strange in his voice. Although steady, it was deep with mourning, and of a quality beyond oration or tears.

"Keep'er a little more south, Billie," said he.

"A little more south, sir," said the oiler in the stern.

A seat in his boat was not unlike a seat upon a bucking broncho, and by the same token a broncho is not much smaller. The craft pranced and reared and plunged like an animal. As each wave came, and she rose for it, she seemed like a horse making at a fence outrageously high. The manner of her scramble over these walls of water is a mystic thing, and, moreover, at the top of them were ordinarily these problems in white water, the foam racing down from the summit of each wave requiring a new leap, and a leap from the air. Then, after scornfully bumping a crest, she would slide and race and splash down a long incline, and arrive bobbing and nodding in front of the next menace.

A singular disadvantage of the sea lies in the fact that after successfully surmounting one wave you discover that there is another behind it just as important and just as nervously anxious to do something effective in the way of swamping boats. In a ten-foot dinghy one can get an idea of the resources of the sea in the line of waves that is not probable to the average experience, which is never at sea in a dinghy. As each slaty wall of water approached, it shut all else from the view of the men in the boat, and it was not difficult to imagine that this particular wave was the final outburst of the ocean, the last effort of the grim water. There was a terrible grace in the move of the waves, and they came in silence, save for the snarling of the crests.

In the wan light the faces of the men must have been gray. Their eyes must have glinted in strange ways as they gazed steadily astern. Viewed from a balcony, the whole thing would, doubtless, have been weirdly picturesque. But the men in the boat had not time to see it, and if they had had leisure, there were other things to occupy their minds. The sun swung steadily up the sky, and they knew it was broad day because the color of the sea changed from slate to emerald green streaked with amber lights, and the foam was like tumbling snow. The process of the breaking day was unknown to them. They were aware only of this effect upon the color of the waves that rolled toward them.

In disjointed sentences the cook and the correspondent argued as to the difference between a life-saving station and a house of refuge. The cook had said: "There's a house of refuge just north of the Mosquito Inlet Light, and as soon as they see us they'll come off in their boat and pick us up."

"As soon as who see us?" said the correspondent.

"The crew," said the cook.

"Houses of refuge don't have crews," said the correspondent. "As I understand them, they are only places where clothes and grub are stored for the benefit of shipwrecked people. They don't carry crews."

"Oh, yes, they do," said the cook.

"No, they don't," said the correspondent.

"Well, we're not there yet, anyhow," said the oiler in the stern.

"Well," said the cook, "perhaps it's not a house of refuge that I'm thinking of as being near Mosquito Inlet Light; perhaps it's a life-saving station."

"We're not there yet," said the oiler in the stern.

II

As the boat bounced from the top of each wave the wind tore through the hair of the hatless men, and as the craft plopped her stern down again the spray slashed past them. The crest of each of these waves was a hill, from the top of which the men surveyed for a moment a broad tumultuous expanse, shining and wind-riven. It was probably splendid, it was probably glorious, this play of the free sea, wild with lights of emerald and white and amber.

"Bully good thing it's an on-shore wind, said the cook. "If not, where would we be? Wouldn't have a show."

"That's right," said the correspondent.

The busy oiler nodded his assent.

Then the captain, in the bow, chuckled in a way that expressed humor, contempt, tragedy, all in one. "Do you think we've got much of a show now, boys?" said he.

Whereupon the three were silent, save for a trifle of hemming and hawing. To express any particular optimism at this time they felt to be childish and stupid, but they all doubtless possessed this sense of the situation in their minds. A young man thinks doggedly at such times. On the other hand, the ethics of their condition was decidedly against any open suggestion of hopelessness. So they were silent.

"Oh, well," said the captain, soothing his children, "we'll get ashore all right."

But there was that in his tone which made them think; so the oiler quoth, "Yes! if this wind holds."

The cook was bailing. "Yes! if we don't catch hell in the surf."

Canton-flannel gulls flew near and far. Sometimes they sat down on the sea, near patches of brown seaweed that rolled over the waves with a movement like carpets on a line in a gale. The birds sat comfortably in groups, and they were envied by some in the dinghy, for the wrath of the sea was no more to them than it was to a covey of prairie chickens a thousand miles inland. Often they came very close and stared at the men with black bead-like eyes. At these times they were uncanny and sinister in their unblinking scrutiny, and the men hooted angrily at them, telling them to be gone. One came, and evidently decided to alight on the top of the captain's head. The bird flew parallel to the boat and did not circle, but made short sidelong jumps in the air in chicken fashion. His black eyes were wistfully fixed upon the captain's head. "Ugly brute," said the oiler to the bird. "You look as if you were made with a jackknife." The cook and the correspondent swore darkly at the creature. The captain naturally wished to knock it away with the end of the heavy painter, but he did not dare do it, because anything resembling an emphatic gesture would have capsized this freighted boat; and so, with his open hand, the captain gently and carefully waved the gull away. After it had been discouraged from the pursuit the captain breathed easier on account of his hair, and others breathed easier because the bird struck their minds at this time as being somehow gruesome and ominous.

In the meantime the oiler and the correspondent rowed; and also they rowed. They sat together in the same seat, and each rowed an oar. Then the oiler took both oars; then the correspondent took both oars, then the oiler; then the correspondent. They rowed and they rowed. The very ticklish part of the business was when the time came for the reclining one in the stern to take his turn at the oars. By the very last star of truth, it is easier to steal eggs from under a hen than it was to change seats in the dinghy. First the man in the stern slid his hand along the thwart and moved with care, as if he were of Sèvres.[1] Then the man in the rowing-seat slid his hand along the other thwart. It was all done with the most extraordinary care. As the two sidled past each other, the whole party kept watchful eyes on the coming wave, and the captain cried: "Look out, now! Steady, there!"

The brown mats of seaweed that appeared from time to time were like islands, bits of earth. They were travelling, apparently, neither one way nor the other. They were, to all intents, stationary. They informed the men in the boat that it was making progress slowly toward the land.

The captain, rearing cautiously in the bow after the dinghy soared on a great swell, said that he had seen the lighthouse at Mosquito Inlet. Presently the cook remarked that he had seen it. The correspondent was at the oars then, and for some reason he too

1. I.e., as if he were made of china.

wished to look at the lighthouse; but his back was toward the far shore, and the waves were important, and for some time he could not seize an opportunity to turn his head. But at last there came a wave more gentle than the others, and when at the crest of it he swiftly scoured the western horizon.

"See it?" said the captain.

"No," said the correspondent, slowly; "I didn't see anything."

"Look again," said the captain. He pointed. "It's exactly in that direction."

At the top of another wave the correspondent did as he was bid, and this time his eyes chanced on a small, still thing on the edge of the swaying horizon. It was precisely like the point of a pin. It took an anxious eye to find a lighthouse so tiny.

"Think we'll make it, Captain?"

"If this wind holds and the boat don't swamp, we can't do much else," said the captain.

The little boat, lifted by each towering sea and splashed viciously by the crests, made progress that in the absence of seaweed was not apparent to those in her. She seemed just a wee thing wallowing, miraculously top up, at the mercy of five oceans. Occasionally a great spread of water, like white flames, swarmed into her.

"Bail her, cook," said the captain, serenely.

"All right, Captain," said the cheerful cook.

III

It would be difficult to describe the subtle brotherhood of men that was here established on the seas. No one said that it was so. No one mentioned it. But it dwelt in the boat, and each man felt it warm him. They were a captain, an oiler, a cook, and a correspondent, and they were friends—friends in a more curiously iron-bound degree than may be common. The hurt captain, lying against the water jar in the bow, spoke always in a low voice and calmly; but he could never command a more ready and swiftly obedient crew than the motley three of the dinghy. It was more than a mere recognition of what was best for the common safety. There was surely in it a quality that was personal and heart-felt. And after this devotion to the commander of the boat, there was this comradeship, that the correspondent, for instance, who had been taught to be cynical of men, knew even at the time was the best experience of his life. But no one said that it was so. No one mentioned it.

"I wish we had a sail," remarked the captain. "We might try my overcoat on the end of an oar, and give you two boys a chance to rest." So the cook and the correspondent held the mast and spread wide the overcoat; the oiler steered; and the little boat made good way with her new rig. Sometimes the oiler had to scull sharply to keep a sea from breaking into the boat, but otherwise sailing was a success.

Meanwhile the lighthouse had been growing slowly larger. It had now almost assumed color, and appeared like a little gray shadow on the sky. The man at the oars could not be prevented from turning his head rather often to try for a glimpse of this little gray shadow.

At last, from the top of each wave, the men in the tossing boat could see land. Even as the lighthouse was an upright shadow on the sky, this land seemed but a long black shadow on the sea. It certainly was thinner than paper. "We must be about opposite New Smyrna,"[2] said the cook, who had coasted this shore often in schooners. "Captain, by the way, I believe they abandoned that life-saving station there about a year ago."

"Did they?" said the captain.

The wind slowly died away. The cook and the correspondent were not now obliged to slave in order to hold high the oar. But the waves continued their old impetuous swooping at the dinghy, and the little craft, no longer underway, struggled woundily over them. The oiler or the correspondent took the oars again.

Shipwrecks are *apropos* of nothing. If men could only train for them and have them occur when the men had reached pink condition, there would be less drowning at sea. Of the four in the dinghy none had slept any time worth mentioning for two days and two nights previous to embarking in the dinghy, and in the excitement of clambering about the deck of a foundering ship they had also forgotten to eat heartily.

For these reasons, and for others, neither the oiler nor the corre-

2. A town about eighty miles south of Jacksonville, Florida.

spondent was fond of rowing at this time. The correspondent wondered ingenuously how in the name of all that was sane could there
be people who thought it amusing to row a boat. It was not an
amusement; it was a diabolical punishment, and even a genius of
mental aberrations could never conclude that it was anything but a
horror to the muscles and a crime against the back. He mentioned
to the boat in general how the amusement of rowing struck him,
and the weary-faced oiler smiled in full sympathy. Previously to the
foundering, by the way, the oiler had worked a double watch in the
engine-room of the ship.

"Take her easy, now, boys," said the captain. "Don't spend yourselves. If we have to run a surf you'll need all your strength, because
we'll sure have to swim for it. Take your time."

Slowly the land arose from the sea. From a black line it became a
line of black and a line of white—trees and sand. Finally the captain
said that he could make out a house on the shore. "That's the house
of refuge, sure," said the cook. "They'll see us before long, and come
out after us."

The distant lighthouse reared high. "The keeper ought to be able
to make us out now, if he's looking through a glass," said the captain. "He'll notify the life-saving people."

"None of those other boats could have got ashore to give word of
the wreck," said the oiler, in a low voice, "else the life-boat would be
out hunting us."

Slowly and beautifully the land loomed out of the sea. The wind
came again. It had veered from the northeast to the southeast. Finally a new sound struck the ears of the men in the boat. It was the
low thunder of the surf on the shore. "We'll never be able to make
the lighthouse now," said the captain. "Swing her head a little more
north, Billie."

"A little more north, sir," said the oiler.

Whereupon the little boat turned her nose once more down the
wind, and all but the oarsman watched the shore grow. Under the
influence of this expansion doubt and direful apprehension were
leaving the minds of the men. The management of the boat was still
most absorbing, but it could not prevent a quiet cheerfulness. In an
hour, perhaps, they would be ashore.

Their backbones had become thoroughly used to balancing in

the boat, and they now rode this wild colt of a dinghy like circus men. The correspondent thought that he had been drenched to the skin, but happening to feel in the top pocket of his coat, he found therein eight cigars. Four of them were soaked with sea-water, four were perfectly scatheless. After a search, somebody produced three dry matches; and thereupon the four waifs rode impudently in their little boat and, with an assurance of an impending rescue shining in their eyes, puffed at the big cigars, and judged well and ill of all men. Everybody took a drink of water.

IV

"Cook," remarked the captain, "there don't seem to be any signs of life about your house of refuge."

"No," replied the cook. "Funny they don't see us!"

A broad stretch of lowly coast lay before the eyes of the men. It was of low dunes topped with dark vegetation. The roar of the surf was plain, and sometimes they could see the white lip of a wave as it spun up the beach. A tiny house was blocked out black upon the sky. Southward, the slim lighthouse lifted its little gray length.

Tide, wind, and waves were swinging the dinghy northward. "Funny they don't see us," said the men.

The surf's roar was here dulled, but its tone was nevertheless thunderous and mighty. As the boat swam over the great rollers the men sat listening to this roar. "We'll swamp sure," said everybody.

It is fair to say here that there was not a life saving station within twenty miles in either direction; but the men did not know this fact, and in consequence they made dark and opprobrious remarks concerning the eyesight of the nation's life-savers. Four scowling men sat in the dinghy and surpassed records in the invention of epithets.

"Funny they don't see us."

The light-heartedness of a former time had completely faded. To their sharpened minds it was easy to conjure pictures of all kinds of incompetency and blindness and, indeed, cowardice. There was the shore of the populous land, and it was bitter and bitter to them that from it came no sign.

"Well," said the captain, ultimately, "I suppose we'll have to make a try for ourselves. If we stay out here too long, we'll none of us have strength left to swim after the boat swamps."

And so the oiler, who was at the oars, turned the boat straight for the shore. There was a sudden tightening of muscles. There was some thinking.

"If we don't all get ashore," said the captain—"if we don't all get ashore, I suppose you fellows know where to send news of my finish?"

They then briefly exchanged some addresses and admonitions. As for the reflections of the men, there was a great deal of rage in them. Perchance they might be formulated thus: "If I am going to be drowned—if I am going to be drowned—if I am going to be drowned, why in the name of the seven mad gods who rule the sea, was I allowed to come thus far and contemplate sand and trees? Was I brought here merely to have my nose dragged away as I was about to nibble the sacred cheese of life? It is preposterous. If this old ninny-woman, Fate, cannot do better than this, she should be deprived of the management of men's fortunes. She is an old hen who knows not her intention. If she has decided to drown me, why did she not do it in the beginning and save me all this trouble? The whole affair is absurd. . . . But no; she cannot mean to drown me. She dare not drown me. She cannot drown me. Not after all this work." Afterward the man might have had an impulse to shake his fist at the clouds. "Just you drown me, now, and then hear what I call you!"

The billows that came at this time were more formidable. They seemed always just about to break and roll over the little boat in a turmoil of foam. There was a preparatory and long growl in the speech of them. No mind unused to the sea would have concluded that the dinghy could ascend these sheer heights in time. The shore was still afar. The oiler was a wily surfman. "Boys," he said, swiftly, "she won't live three minutes more, and we're too far out to swim. Shall I take her to sea again, Captain?"

"Yes; go ahead!" said the captain.

This oiler, by a series of quick miracles and fast and steady oarsmanship, turned the boat in the middle of the surf and took her safely to sea again.

There was a considerable silence as the boat bumped over the furrowed sea to deeper water. Then somebody in gloom spoke: "Well, anyhow, they must have seen us from the shore by now."

The gulls went in slanting flight up the wind toward the gray, desolate east. A squall, marked by dingy clouds and clouds brick-red, like smoke from a burning building, appeared from the southeast.

"What do you think of those life-saving people? Ain't they peaches?"

"Funny they haven't seen us."

"Maybe they think we're out here for sport! Maybe they think we're fishin'. Maybe they think we're damned fools."

It was a long afternoon. A changed tide tried to force them southward, but wind and wave said northward. Far ahead, where coast-line, sea, and sky formed their mighty angle, there were little dots which seemed to indicate a city on the shore.

"St. Augustine?"

The captain shook his head. "Too near Mosquito Inlet."

And the oiler rowed, and then the correspondent rowed; then the oiler rowed. It was a weary business. The human back can become the seat of more aches and pains than are registered in books for the composite anatomy of a regiment. It is a limited area, but it can become the theatre of innumerable muscular conflicts, tangles, wrenches, knots, and other comforts.

"Did you ever like to row, Billie?" asked the correspondent.

"No," said the oiler, "hang it!"

When one exchanged the rowing-seat for a place in the bottom of the boat, he suffered a bodily depression that caused him to be careless of everything save an obligation to wiggle one finger. There was cold sea-water swashing to and from in the boat, and he lay in it. His head, pillowed on a thwart, was within an inch of the swirl of a wave-crest, and sometimes a particularly obstreperous sea came inboard and drenched him once more. But these matters did not annoy him. It is almost certain that if the boat had capsized he would have tumbled comfortably out upon the ocean as if he felt sure that it was a great soft mattress.

"Look! There's a man on the shore!"

"Where?"

"There? See 'im? See 'im?"

"Yes, sure! He's walking along."

"Now he's stopped. Look! He's facing us!"

"He's waving at us!"

"So he is! By thunder!"

"Ah, now we're all right! Now we're all right! There'll be a boat out here for us in half an hour."

"He's going on. He's running. He's going up to that house, there."

The remote beach seemed lower than the sea, and it required a searching glance to discern the little black figure. The captain saw a floating stick, and they rowed to it. A bath towel was by some weird chance in the boat, and, tying this on the stick, the captain waved it. The oarsman did not dare turn his head, so he was obliged to ask questions.

"What's he doing now?"

"He's standing still again. He's looking, I think. . . . There he goes again—toward the house. . . . Now he's stopped again."

"Is he waving at us?"

"No, not now; he was, though."

"Look! There comes another man!"

"He's running."

"Look at him go, would you!"

"Why, he's on a bicycle. Now he's met the other man. They're both waving at us. Look!"

"There comes something up the beach."

"What the devil is that thing?"

"Why, it looks like a boat."

"Why, certainly, it's a boat."

"No; it's on wheels."

"Yes, so it is. Well, that must be the life-boat. They drag them along shore on a wagon."

"That's the life-boat, sure."

"No, by God, it's—it's an omnibus."

"I tell you it's a life-boat."

"It is not! It's an omnibus. I can see it plain. See? One of these big hotel omnibuses."

"By thunder, you're right. It's an omnibus, sure as fate. What do you suppose they are doing with an omnibus? Maybe they are going around collecting the life-crew, hey?"

"That's it, likely. Look! There's a fellow waving a little black flag. He's standing on the steps of the omnibus. There come those other two fellows. Now they're all talking together. Look at the fellow with the flag. Maybe he ain't waving it!"

"That ain't a flag, is it? That's his coat. Why, certainly, that's his coat."

"So it is; it's his coat. He's taken it off and is waving it around his head. But would you look at him swing it!"

"Oh, say, there isn't any life-saving station there. That's just a winter-resort hotel omnibus that has brought over some of the boarders to see us drown."

"What's that idiot with the coat mean? What's he signaling, any-how?"

"It looks as if he were trying to tell us to go north. There must be a life-saving station up there."

"No; he thinks we're fishing. Just giving us a merry hand. See? Ah, there, Willie!"

"Well, I wish I could make something out of those signals. What do you suppose he means?"

"He don't mean anything; he's just playing."

"Well, if he'd just signal us to try the surf again, or to go to sea and wait, or go north, or go south, or go to hell, there would be some reason in it. But look at him! He just stands there and keeps his coat revolving like a wheel. The ass!"

"There come more people."

"Now there's quiet a mob. Look! Isn't that a boat?"

"Where? Oh, I see where you mean. No, that's no boat."

"That fellow is still waving his coat."

"He must think we like to see him do that. Why don't he quit it? It don't mean anything."

"I don't know. I think he is trying to make us go north. It must be that there's a life-saving station there somewhere."

"Say, he ain't tired yet. Look at 'im wave!"

"Wonder how long he can keep that up. He's been revolving his coat ever since he caught sight of us. He's an idiot. Why aren't they getting men to bring a boat out? A fishing boat—one of those big yawls—could come out here all right. Why don't he do something?"

"Oh, it's all right now."

"They'll have a boat out here for us in less than no time, now that they've seen us."

A faint yellow tone came into the sky over the low land. The shadows on the sea slowly deepened. The wind bore coldness with it, and the men began to shiver.

"Holy smoke!" said one, allowing his voice to express his impious mood, "if we keep on monkeying out here! If we've got to flounder out here all night!"

"Oh, we'll never have to stay here all night! Don't you worry. They've seen us now, and it won't be long before they'll come chasing out after us."

The shore grew dusky. The man waving a coat blended gradually into this gloom, and it swallowed in the same manner the omnibus and the group of people. The spray, when it dashed uproariously over the side, made the voyagers shrink and swear like men who were being branded.

"I'd like to catch the chump who waved the coat. I feel like socking him one, just for luck."

"Why? What did he do?"

"Oh, nothing, but then he seemed so damned cheerful."

In the meantime the oiler rowed, and then the correspondent rowed, and then the oiler rowed. Gray-faced and bowed forward, they mechanically, turn by turn, plied the leaden oars. The form of the lighthouse had vanished from the southern horizon, but finally a pale star appeared, just lifting from the sea. The streaked saffron in the west passed before the all-merging darkness, and the sea to the east was black. The land had vanished, and was expressed only by the low and drear thunder of the surf.

"If I am going to be drowned—if I am going to be drowned—if I am going to be drowned, why, in the name of the seven mad gods who rule the sea, was I allowed to come thus far and contemplate sand and trees? Was I brought here merely to have my nose dragged away as I was about to nibble the sacred cheese of life?"

The patient captain, drooped over the water-jar, was sometimes obliged to speak to the oarsman.

"Keep her head up! Keep her head up!"

"Keep her head up, sir." The voices were weary and low.

This was surely a quiet evening. All save the oarsman lay heavily and listlessly in the boat's bottom. As for him, his eyes were just capable of noting the tall black waves that swept forward in a most sinister silence, save for an occasional subdued growl of a crest.

The cook's head was on a thwart, and he looked without interest at the water under his nose. He was deep in other scenes. Finally he spoke. "Billie," he murmured, dreamfully, "what kind of pie do you like best?"

V

"Pie!" said the oiler and the correspondent, agitatedly. "Don't talk about those things, blast you!"

"Well," said the cook, "I was just thinking about ham sandwiches, and——"

A night on the sea in an open boat is a long night. As darkness settled finally, the shine of the light, lifting from the sea in the south, changed to full gold. On the northern horizon a new light appeared, a small bluish gleam on the edge of the waters. These two lights were the furniture of the world. Otherwise there was nothing but waves.

Two men huddled in the stern, and distances were so magnificent in the dinghy that the rower was enabled to keep his feet partly warm by thrusting them under his companions. Their legs indeed extended far under the rowing-seat until they touched the feet of the captain forward. Sometimes, despite the efforts of the tired oarsman, a wave came piling into the boat, an icy wave of the night, and the chilling water soaked them anew. They would twist their bodies for a moment and groan, and sleep the dead sleep once more, while the water in the boat gurgled about them as the craft rocked.

The plan of the oiler and the correspondent was for one to row until he lost the ability, and then arouse the other from his sea-water couch in the bottom of the boat.

The oiler plied the oars until his head drooped forward and the overpowering sleep blinded him; and he rowed yet afterward. Then he touched a man in the bottom of the boat, and called his name. "Will you spell me for a little while?" he said meekly.

"Sure, Billie," said the correspondent, awaking and dragging himself to a sitting position. They exchanged places carefully, and the oiler, cuddling down in the sea-water at the cook's side, seemed to go to sleep instantly.

The particular violence of the sea had ceased. The waves came without snarling. The obligation of the man at the oars was to keep the boat headed so that the tilt of the rollers would not capsize her, and to preserve her from filling when the crests rushed past. The black waves were silent and hard to be seen in the darkness. Often one was almost upon the boat before the oarsman was aware.

In a low voice the correspondent addressed the captain. He was not sure that the captain was awake, although this iron man seemed to be always awake. "Captain, shall I keep her making for that light north, sir?"

The same steady voice answered him. "Yes. Keep it about two points off the port bow."

The cook had tied a life-belt around himself in order to get even the warmth which this clumsy cork contrivance could donate, and he seemed almost stove-like when a rower, whose teeth invariably chattered wildly as soon as he ceased his labor, dropped down to sleep.

The correspondent, as he rowed, looked down at the two men sleeping underfoot. The cook's arm was around the oiler's shoulders and, with their fragmentary clothing and haggard faces, they were the babes of the sea—a grotesque rendering of the old babes in the wood.[3]

Later he must have grown stupid at his work, for suddenly there was a growling of water, and a crest came with a roar and a swash into the boat, and it was a wonder that it did not set the cook afloat in his life-belt. The cook continued to sleep, but the oiler sat up, blinking his eyes and shaking with the new cold.

3. "Babes in the Wood" is the name of an old nursery rhyme about two orphans who are abandoned in the woods. Crane might be referring to the image evoked by the lines: "In one another's armes they dyed, / As babes wanting relief."

"Oh, I'm awful sorry, Billie," said the correspondent, contritely.

"That's all right, old boy," said the oiler, and lay down again and was asleep.

Presently it seemed that even the captain dozed, and the correspondent thought that he was the one man afloat on all the ocean. The wind had a voice as it came over the waves, and it was sadder than the end.

There was a long, loud swishing astern of the boat, and a gleaming trail of phosphorescence, like blue flame, was furrowed on the black waters. It might have been made by a monstrous knife.

Then there came a stillness, while the correspondent breathed with open mouth and looked at the sea.

Suddenly there was another swish and another long flash of bluish light, and this time it was alongside the boat, and might almost have been reached with an oar. The correspondent saw an enormous fin speed like a shadow through the water, hurling the crystalline spray and leaving the long glowing trail.

The correspondent looked over his shoulder at the captain. His face was hidden, and he seemed to be asleep. He looked at the babes of the sea. They certainly were asleep. So, being bereft of sympathy, he leaned a little way to one side and swore softly into the sea.

But the thing did not then leave the vicinity of the boat. Ahead or astern, on one side or the other, at intervals long or short, fled the long sparkling streak, and there was to be heard the *whirroo* of the dark fin. The speed and power of the thing was greatly to be admired. It cut the water like a gigantic and keen projectile.

The presence of this biding thing did not affect the man with the same horror that it would if he had been a picnicker. He simply looked at the sea dully and swore in an undertone.

Nevertheless, it is true that he did not wish to be alone with the thing. He wished one of his companions to awake by chance and keep him company with it. But the captain hung motionless over the water-jar and the oiler and the cook in the bottom of the boat were plunged in slumber.

VI

"If I am going to be drowned—if I am going to be drowned—if I am going to be drowned, why in the name of the seven mad gods who rule the sea, was I allowed to come thus far and contemplate sand and trees?"

During this dismal night, it may be remarked that a man would conclude that it was really the intention of the seven mad gods to drown him, despite the abominable injustice of it. For it was certainly an abominable injustice to drown a man who had worked so hard, so hard. The man felt it would be a crime most unnatural. Other people had drowned at sea since galleys swarmed with painted sails, but still——

When it occurs to a man that nature does not regard him as important and that she feels she would not maim the universe by disposing of him, he at first wishes to throw bricks at the temple, and he hates deeply the fact that there are no bricks and no temples. Any visible expression of nature would surely be pelleted with his jeers.

Then, if there be no tangible thing to hoot, he feels, perhaps, the desire to confront a personification and indulge in pleas, bowed to one knee, and with hands supplicant, saying, "Yes, but I love myself."

A high cold star on a winter's night is the word he feels that she says to him. Thereafter he knows the pathos of his situation.

The men in the dinghy had not discussed these matters, but each had, no doubt, reflected upon them in silence and according to his mind. There was seldom any expression upon their faces save the general one of complete weariness. Speech was devoted to the business of the boat.

To chime the notes of his emotions, a verse mysteriously entered the correspondent's head. He had even forgotten that he had forgotten this verse, but it suddenly was in his mind.

A soldier of the Legion lay dying in Algiers;
There was lack of woman's nursing,
  there was dearth of woman's tears;

But a comrade stood beside him,
and he took the comrade's hand,
And he said, "I never more shall see
my own, my native land."[4]

In his childhood the correspondent had been made acquainted with the fact that a soldier of the Legion lay dying in Algiers, but he had never regarded it as important. Myriads of his schoolfellows had informed him of the soldier's plight, but the dinning had naturally ended by making him perfectly indifferent. He had never considered it his affair that a soldier of the Legion lay dying in Algiers, nor had it appeared to him as a matter for sorrow. It was less to him than the breaking of a pencil's point.

Now, however, it quaintly came to him as a human, living thing. It was no longer merely a picture of a few throes in the breast of a poet, meanwhile drinking tea and warming his feet at the grate; it was an actuality—stern, mournful, and fine.

The correspondent plainly saw the soldier. He lay on the sand with his feet out straight and still. While his pale left hand was upon his chest in an attempt to thwart the going of his life, the blood came between his fingers. In the far Algerian distance, a city of low square forms was set against a sky that was faint with the last sunset hues. The correspondent, plying the oars and dreaming of the slow and slower movements of the lips of the soldier, was moved by a profound and perfectly impersonal comprehension. He was sorry for the soldier of the Legion who lay dying in Algiers.

The thing which had followed the boat and waited had evidently grown bored at the delay. There was no longer to be heard the slash of the cutwater, and there was no longer the flame of the long trail. The light in the north still glimmered, but it was apparently no nearer to the boat. Sometimes the boom of the surf rang in the correspondent's ears, and he turned the craft seaward then and rowed harder. Southward, some one had evidently built a watchfire on the beach. It was too low and too far to be seen, but it made a shimmering, roseate reflection upon the bluff in back

---

4. From "Bingen on the Rhine," a popular poem by the English poet and feminist Caroline Norton (1808–1877).

of it, and this could be discerned from the boat. The wind came stronger, and sometimes a wave suddenly raged out like a mountain-cat, and there was to be seen the sheen and sparkle of a broken crest.

The captain, in the bow, moved on his water-jar and sat erect. "Pretty long night," he observed to the correspondent. He looked at the shore. "Those life-saving people take their time."

"Did you see that shark playing around?"

"Yes, I saw him. He was a big fellow, all right."

"Wish I had known you were awake."

Later the correspondent spoke into the bottom of the boat. "Billie!" There was a slow and gradual disentanglement. "Billie, will you spell me?"

"Sure," said the oiler.

As soon as the correspondent touched the cold, comfortable sea-water in the bottom of the boat and had huddled close to the cook's life-belt he was deep in sleep, despite the fact that his teeth played all the popular airs. This sleep was so good to him that it was but a moment before he heard a voice call his name in a tone that demonstrated the last stages of exhaustion. "Will you spell me?"

"Sure, Billie."

The light in the north had mysteriously vanished, but the correspondent took his course from the wide-awake captain.

Later in the night they took the boat farther out to sea, and the captain directed the cook to take one oar at the stern and keep the boat facing the seas. He was to call out if he should hear the thunder of the surf. This plan enabled the oiler and the correspondent to get respite together. "We'll give those boys a chance to get into shape again," said the captain. They curled down and, after a few preliminary chatterings and trembles, slept once more the dead sleep. Neither knew they had bequeathed to the cook the company of another shark, or perhaps the same shark.

As the boat caroused on the waves, spray occasionally bumped over the side and gave them a fresh soaking, but this had no power to break their repose. The ominous slash of the wind and the water affected them as it would have affected mummies.

"Boys," said the cook, with the notes of every reluctance in his voice, "she's drifted in pretty close. I guess one of you had better take her to sea again." The correspondent, aroused, heard the crash of the toppled crests.

As he was rowing, the captain gave him some whiskey-and-water, and this steadied the chills out of him. "If I ever get ashore and anybody shows me even a photograph of an oar——"

At last there was an short conversation.

"Billie! . . . Billie, will you spell me?"

"Sure," said the oiler.

VII

When the correspondent again opened his eyes, the sea and the sky were each of the gray hue of the dawning. Later, carmine and gold was painted upon the waters. The morning appeared finally, in its splendor, with a sky of pure blue, and the sunlight flamed on the tips of the waves.

On the distant dunes were set many little black cottages, and a tall white windmill reared above them. No man, nor dog, nor bicycle appeared on the beach. The cottages might have formed a deserted village.

The voyagers scanned the shore. A conference was held in the boat. "Well," said the captain, "if no help is coming, we might better try a run through the surf right away. If we stay out here much longer we will be too weak to do anything for ourselves at all." The others silently acquiesced in this reasoning. The boat was headed for the beach. The correspondent wondered if none ever ascended the tall wind-tower, and if then they never looked seaward. This tower was a giant, standing with its back to the plight of the ants. It represented in a degree, to the correspondent, the serenity of nature amid the struggles of the individual—nature in the wind, and nature in the vision of men. She did not seem cruel to him then, nor beneficent, nor treacherous, nor wise. But she was indifferent, flatly indifferent. It is, perhaps, plausible that a man in this situation, impressed with the unconcern of the universe, should see the innumerable flaws of his life, and have them taste wickedly in his mind, and wish for another chance. A distinction between right and wrong seems absurdly clear to him, then, in this new ignorance of the grave-edge, and he understands that if he were given another opportunity he would mend his conduct and his words, and be better and brighter during an introduction or at a tea.

"Now, boys," said the captain, "she is going to swamp sure. All we can do is to work her in as far as possible, and then when she swamps, pile out and scramble for the beach. Keep cool now, and don't jump until she swamps sure."

The oiler took the oars. Over his shoulders he scanned the surf. "Captain," he said, "I think I'd better bring her about and keep her head-on to the seas and back her in."

"All right, Billie," said the captain. "Back her in." The oiler swung the boat then, and, seated in the stern, the cook and the correspondent were obliged to look over their shoulders to contemplate the lonely and indifferent shore.

The monstrous inshore rollers heaved the boat high until the men were again enabled to see the white sheets of water scudding up the slanted beach. "We won't get in very close," said the captain. Each time a man could wrest his attention from the rollers, he turned his glance toward the shore, and in the expression of the eyes during this contemplation there was a singular quality. The correspondent, observing the others, knew that they were not afraid, but the full meaning of their glances was shrouded.

As for himself, he was too tired to grapple fundamentally with the fact. He tried to coerce his mind into thinking of it, but the mind was dominated at this time by the muscles, and the muscles said they did not care. It merely occurred to him that if he should drown it would be a shame.

There were no hurried words, no pallor, no plain agitation. The men simply looked at the shore. "Now, remember to get well clear of the boat when you jump," said the captain.

Seaward the crest of a roller suddenly fell with a thunderous crash, and the long white comber came roaring down upon the boat.

"Steady now," said the captain. The men were silent. They turned their eyes from the shore to the comber and waited. The boat slid up the incline, leaped at the furious top, bounced over it, and swung down the long back of the wave. Some water had been shipped, and the cook bailed it out.

But the next crest crashed also. The tumbling, boiling flood of white water caught the boat and whirled it almost perpendicular. Water swarmed in from all sides. The correspondent had his hands on the gunwale at this time, and when the water entered at that place he swiftly withdrew his fingers, as if he objected to wetting them.

The little boat, drunken with this weight of water, reeled and snuggled deeper into the sea.

"Bail her out, cook! Bail her out!" said the captain.

"All right, Captain," said the cook.

"Now, boys, the next one will do for us sure," said the oiler. "Mind to jump clear of the boat."

The third wave moved forward, huge, furious, implacable. It fairly swallowed the dinghy, and almost simultaneously the men tumbled into the sea. A piece of life-belt had lain in the bottom of the boat, and as the correspondent went overboard he held this to his chest with his left hand.

The January water was icy, and he reflected immediately that it was colder than he had expected to find it off the coast of Florida. This appeared to his dazed mind as a fact important enough to be noted at the time. The coldness of the water was sad; it was tragic. This fact was somehow mixed and confused with his opinion of his own situation, so that it seemed almost a proper reason for tears. The water was cold.

When he came to the surface he was conscious of little but the noisy water. Afterward he saw his companions in the sea. The oiler was ahead in the race. He was swimming strongly and rapidly. Off to the correspondent's left, the cook's great white and corked back bulged out of the water, and in the rear the captain was hanging with his one good hand to the keel of the overturned dinghy.

There is a certain immovable quality to a shore, and the correspondent wondered at it amid the confusion of the sea.

It seemed also very attractive; but the correspondent knew that it was a long journey, and he paddled leisurely. The piece of life-preserver lay under him, and sometimes he whirled down the incline of a wave as if he were on a hand-sled.

But finally he arrived at a place in the sea where travel was beset with difficulty. He did not pause swimming to inquire what manner of current had caught him, but there his progress ceased. The shore was set before him like a bit of scenery on a stage, and he looked at it and understood with his eyes each detail of it.

As the cook passed, much farther to the left, the captain was calling to him, "Turn over on your back, cook! Turn over on your back and use the oar."

"All right, sir." The cook turned on his back, and, paddling with an oar, went ahead as if he were a canoe.

Presently the boat also passed to the left of the correspondent, with the captain clinging with one hand to the keel. He would have appeared like a man raising himself to look over a board fence if it were not for the extraordinary gymnastics of the boat. The correspondent marvelled that the captain could still hold to it.

They passed on nearer to shore—the oiler, the cook, the captain—and following them went the water-jar, bouncing gaily over the seas.

The correspondent remained in the grip of this strange new enemy, a current. The shore, with its white slope of sand and its green bluff topped with little silent cottages, was spread like a picture before him. It was very near to him then, but he was impressed as one who, in a gallery, looks at a scene from Brittany or Algiers.

He thought: "I am going to drown? Can it be possible? Can it be possible? Can it be possible?" Perhaps an individual must consider his own death to be the final phenomenon of nature.

But later a wave perhaps whirled him out of this small deadly current, for he found suddenly that he could again make progress toward the shore. Later still he was aware that the captain, clinging with one hand to the keel of the dinghy, had his face turned away from the shore and toward him, and was calling his name. "Come to the boat! Come to the boat!"

In his struggle to reach the captain and the boat, he reflected that when one gets properly wearied drowning must really be a comfortable arrangement—a cessation of hostilities accompanied by a large degree of relief; and he was glad of it, for the main thing in his mind for some moments had been horror of the temporary agony; he did not wish to be hurt.

Presently he saw a man running along the shore. He was undressing with most remarkable speed. Coat, trousers, shirt, everything flew magically off him.

"Come to the boat!" called the captain.

"All right, Captain." As the correspondent paddled, he saw the captain let himself down to bottom and leave the boat. Then the correspondent performed his one little marvel of the voyage. A large wave caught him and flung him with ease and supreme speed completely over the boat and far beyond it. It struck him even then as an event in gymnastics, and a true miracle of the sea. An overturned boat in the surf is not a plaything to a swimming man.

The correspondent arrived in water that reached only to his waist, but his condition did not enable him to stand for more than a moment. Each wave knocked him into a heap, and the undertow pulled at him.

Then he saw the man who had been running and undressing and undressing and running, come bounding into the water. He dragged ashore the cook, and then waded toward the captain; but the captain waved him away and sent him to the correspondent. He was naked—naked as a tree in winter; but a halo was about his head, and he shone like a saint. He gave a strong pull, and a long drag, and a bully heave at the correspondent's hand. The correspondent, schooled in the minor formulae, said, "Thanks, old man." But suddenly the man cried, "What's that?" He pointed a swift finger. The correspondent said, "Go."

In the shallows, face downward, lay the oiler. His forehead touched sand that was periodically, between each wave, clear of the sea.

The correspondent did not know all that transpired afterward. When he achieved safe ground he fell, striking the sand with each particular part of his body. It was as if he had dropped from a roof, but the thud was grateful to him.

It seems that instantly the beach was populated with men with blankets, clothes, and flasks, and women with coffee-pots and all the remedies sacred to their minds. The welcome of the land to the men from the sea was warm and generous; but a still and dripping shape was carried slowly up the beach, and the land's welcome for it could only be the different and sinister hospitality of the grave.

When it came night, the white waves paced to and fro in the moonlight, and the wind brought the sound of the great sea's voice to the men on the shore, and they felt that they could then be interpreters.

1897

William Faulkner
1897–1962

> "A Rose for Emily" was Faulkner's first published story. It combines
> two real-life events from Faulkner's home in Mississippi. One story
> was of a local woman who refused to release her dead son's body to
> the undertaker, and the other was of a romance between a Southern
> belle and a Northerner who came South to pave streets. When asked
> if the romance symbolized the persistent conflict between the North
> and South, Faulkner allowed that it "could have been a part of my
> background, my experience, without knowing it." Nearly all critics
> think Emily symbolizes the decay of the old order, the dissolution of
> the Southern aristocracy. Faulkner himself disowned symbolic read-
> ings and described the story as the tragedy of "a young girl that just
> wanted to be loved and to love and to have a husband and a fam-
> ily" but was "kept down by her father, a selfish man, who didn't
> want her to leave home because he wanted a housekeeper." Accord-
> ing to Faulkner, her impulses drove her to do things that she knew
> were wrong. If you're a bit confused by the course of Emily's life,
> that's to be expected. When you reread the story, try to straighten out
> in your own mind the chronology of events. Note that the narrator
> in this story is first person plural, which is uncommon.

A Rose for Emily

I

When Miss Emily Grierson died, our whole town went to
her funeral: the men through a sort of respectful affection
for a fallen monument, the women mostly out of curiosity
to see the inside of her house, which no one save an old manservant—a combined gardener and cook—had seen in at least ten years.

It was a big, squarish frame house that had once been white, decorated with cupolas and spires and scrolled balconies in the heavily
lightsome style of the seventies, set on what had once been our most
select street. But garages and cotton gins had encroached and oblit-
erated even the august names of that neighborhood; only Miss

Emily's house was left, lifting its stubborn and coquettish decay above the cotton wagons and the gasoline pumps—an eyesore among eyesores. And now Miss Emily had gone to join the representatives of those august names where they lay in the cedar-bemused cemetery among the ranked and anonymous graves of Union and Confederate soldiers who fell at the battle of Jefferson.

Alive, Miss Emily had been a tradition, a duty, and a care; a sort of hereditary obligation upon the town, dating from that day in 1894 when Colonel Sartoris, the mayor—he who fathered the edict that no Negro woman should appear on the streets without an apron—remitted her taxes, the dispensation dating from the death of her father on into perpetuity. Not that Miss Emily would have accepted charity. Colonel Sartoris invented an involved tale to the effect that Miss Emily's father had loaned money to the town, which the town, as a matter of business, preferred this way of repaying. Only a man of Colonel Sartoris' generation and thought could have invented it, and only a woman could have believed it.

When the next generation, with its more modern ideas, became mayors and aldermen, this arrangement created some little dissatisfaction. On the first of the year they mailed her a tax notice. February came, and there was no reply. They wrote her a formal letter, asking her to call at the sheriff's office at her convenience. A week later the mayor wrote her himself, offering to call or to send his car for her, and received in reply a note on paper of an archaic shape, in a thin, flowing calligraphy in faded ink, to the effect that she no longer went out at all. The tax notice was also enclosed, without comment.

They called a special meeting of the Board of Aldermen. A deputation waited upon her, knocked at the door through which no visitor had passed since she ceased giving china-painting lessons eight or ten years earlier. They were admitted by the old Negro into a dim hall from which a stairway mounted into still more shadow. It smelled of dust and disuse—a close, dank smell. The Negro led them into the parlor. It was furnished in heavy, leather-covered furniture. When the Negro opened the blinds of one window, they could see that the leather was cracked; and when they sat down, a faint dust rose sluggishly about their thighs, spinning with slow motes in the single sun-ray. On a tarnished gilt easel before the fireplace stood a crayon portrait of Miss Emily's father.

They rose when she entered—a small, fat woman in black, with a thin gold chain descending to her waist and vanishing into her belt, leaning on an ebony cane with a tarnished gold head. Her skeleton was small and spare; perhaps that was why what would have been merely plumpness in another was obesity in her. She looked bloated, like a body long submerged in motionless water, and of that pallid hue. Her eyes, lost in the fatty ridges of her face, looked like two small pieces of coal pressed into a lump of dough as they moved from one face to another while the visitors stated their errand.

She did not ask them to sit. She just stood in the door and listened quietly until the spokesman came to a stumbling halt. Then they could hear the invisible watch ticking at the end of the gold chain.

Her voice was dry and cold. "I have no taxes in Jefferson. Colonel Sartoris explained it to me. Perhaps one of you can gain access to the city records and satisfy yourselves."

"But we have. We are the city authorities, Miss Emily. Didn't you get a notice from the sheriff, signed by him?"

"I received a paper, yes," Miss Emily said. "Perhaps he considers himself the sheriff. . . . I have no taxes in Jefferson."

"But there is nothing on the books to show that, you see. We must go by the—"

"See Colonel Sartoris. I have no taxes in Jefferson."

"But, Miss Emily—"

"See Colonel Sartoris." (Colonel Sartoris had been dead almost ten years.) "I have no taxes in Jefferson. Tobe!" The Negro appeared. "Show these gentlemen out."

II

So she vanquished them, horse and foot,[1] just as she had vanquished their fathers thirty years before about the smell. That was

---

1. I.e., she vanquished them thoroughly. "Horse and foot" is a nineteenth-century phrase meaning, roughly, "the whole army, both cavalry and infantry."

two years after her father's death and a short time after her sweet-heart—the one we believed would marry her—had deserted her. Af-ter her father's death she went out very little; after her sweetheart went away, people hardly saw her at all. A few of the ladies had the temerity to call, but were not received, and the only sign of life about the place was the Negro man—a young man then—going in and out with a market basket.

"Just as if a man—any man—could keep a kitchen properly," the ladies said; so they were not surprised when the smell developed. It was another link between the gross, teeming world and the high and mighty Griersons.

A neighbor, a woman, complained to the mayor, Judge Stevens, eighty years old.

"But what will you have me do about it, madam?" he said.

"Why, send her word to stop it," the woman said. "Isn't there a law?"

"I'm sure that won't be necessary," Judge Stevens said. "It's prob-ably just a snake or a rat that nigger of hers killed in the yard. I'll speak to him about it."

The next day he received two more complaints, one from a man who came in diffident deprecation. "We really must do something about it, Judge. I'd be the last one in the world to bother Miss Emily, but we've got to do something." That night the Board of Al-dermen met—three graybeards and one younger man, a member of the rising generation.

"It's simple enough," he said. "Send her word to have her place cleaned up. Give her a certain time to do it in, and if she don't . . ."

"Dammit, sir," Judge Stevens said, "will you accuse a lady to her face of smelling bad?"

So the next night, after midnight, four men crossed Miss Emily's lawn and slunk about the house like burglars, sniffing along the base of the brickwork and at the cellar openings while one of them performed a regular sowing motion with his hand out of a sack slung from his shoulder. They broke open the cellar door and sprin-kled lime there, and in all the outbuildings. As they recrossed the lawn, a window that had been dark was lighted and Miss Emily sat in it, the light behind her, and her upright torso motionless as that of an idol. They crept quietly across the lawn and into the shadow of the locusts that lined the street. After a week or two the smell went away.

That was when people had begun to feel really sorry for her. People in our town, remembering how old lady Wyatt, her great-aunt, had gone completely crazy at last, believed that the Griersons held themselves a little too high for what they really were. None of the young men were quite good enough for Miss Emily and such. We had long thought of them as a tableau, Miss Emily a slender figure in white in the background, her father a spraddled silhouette in the foreground, his back to her and clutching a horsewhip, the two of them framed by the back-flung front door. So when she got to be thirty and was still single, we were not pleased exactly, but vindicated; even with insanity in the family she wouldn't have turned down all of her chances if they had really materialized.

When her father died, it got about that the house was all that was left to her; and in a way, people were glad. At last they could pity Miss Emily. Being left alone, and a pauper, she had become humanized. Now she too would know the old thrill and the old despair of a penny more or less.

The day after his death all the ladies prepared to call at the house and offer condolence and aid, as is our custom. Miss Emily met them at the door, dressed as usual and with no trace of grief on her face. She told them that her father was not dead. She did that for three days, with the ministers calling on her, and the doctors, trying to persuade her to let them dispose of the body. Just as they were about to resort to law and force, she broke down, and they buried her father quickly.

We did not say she was crazy then. We believed she had to do that. We remembered all the young men her father had driven away, and we knew that with nothing left, she would have to cling to that which had robbed her, as people will.

III

She was sick for a long time. When we saw her again, her hair was cut short, making her look like a girl, with a vague resemblance to those angels in colored church windows—sort of tragic and serene.

The town had just let the contracts for paving the sidewalks, and in the summer after her father's death they began the work. The construction company came with niggers and mules and machinery, and a foreman named Homer Barron, a Yankee—a big, dark, ready man, with a big voice and eyes lighter than his face. The little boys would follow in groups to hear him cuss the niggers, and the niggers singing in time to the rise and fall of picks. Pretty soon he knew everybody in town. Whenever you heard a lot of laughing anywhere about the square, Homer Barron would be in the center of the group. Presently we began to see him and Miss Emily on Sunday afternoons driving in the yellow-wheeled buggy and the matched team of bays from the livery stable.

At first we were glad that Miss Emily would have an interest, because the ladies all said, "Of course a Grierson would not think seriously of a Northerner, a day laborer." But there were still others, older people, who said that even grief could not cause a real lady to forget *noblesse oblige*—without calling it *noblesse oblige*.[2] They just said, "Poor Emily. Her kinsfolk should come to her." She had some kin in Alabama; but years ago her father had fallen out with them over the estate of old lady Wyatt, the crazy woman, and there was no communication between the two families. They had not even been represented at the funeral.

And as soon as the old people said, "Poor Emily," the whispering began. "Do you suppose it's really so?" they said to one another. "Of course it is. What else could . . ." This behind their hands; rustling of craned silk and satin behind jalousies closed upon the sun of Sunday afternoon as the thin, swift clop-clop-clop of the matched team passed: "Poor Emily."

She carried her head high enough—even when we believed that she was fallen. It was as if she demanded more than ever the recognition of her dignity as the last Grierson; as if it had wanted that touch of earthiness to reaffirm her imperviousness. Like when she bought the rat poison, the arsenic. That was over a year after they had begun to say "Poor Emily," and while the two female cousins were visiting her.

2. The responsibility to behave honorably associated with people of higher birth; literally, nobility obligates (French).

"I want some poison," she said to the druggist. She was over thirty then, still a slight woman, though thinner than usual, with cold, haughty black eyes in a face the flesh of which was strained across the temples and about the eye-sockets as you imagine a lighthouse-keeper's face ought to look. "I want some poison," she said.

"Yes, Miss Emily. What kind? For rats and such? I'd recom—"

"I want the best you have. I don't care what kind."

The druggist named several. "They'll kill anything up to an elephant. But what you want is—"

"Arsenic," Miss Emily said. "Is that a good one?"

"Is . . . arsenic? Yes, ma'am. But what you want—"

"I want arsenic."

The druggist looked down at her. She looked back at him, erect, her face like a strained flag. "Why, of course," the druggist said. "If that's what you want. But the law requires you to tell what you are going to use it for."

Miss Emily just stared at him, her head tilted back in order to look him eye for eye, until he looked away and went and got the arsenic and wrapped it up. The Negro delivery boy brought her the package; the druggist didn't come back. When she opened the package at home there was written on the box, under the skull and bones: "For rats."

IV

So the next day we all said, "She will kill herself"; and we said it would be the best thing. When she had first begun to be seen with Homer Barron, we had said, "She will marry him." Then we said, "She will persuade him yet," because Homer himself had re-marked—he liked men, and it was known that he drank with the younger men in the Elks' Club—that he was not a marrying man. Later we said, "Poor Emily" behind the jalousies as they passed on Sunday afternoon in the glittering buggy, Miss Emily with her head high and Homer Barron with his hat cocked and a cigar in his teeth, reins and whip in a yellow glove.

Then some of the ladies began to say that it was a disgrace to the town and a bad example to the young people. The men did not

want to interfere, but at last the ladies forced the Baptist minister—
Miss Emily's people were Episcopal—to call upon her. He would
never divulge what happened during that interview, but he refused
to go back again. The next Sunday they again drove about the
streets, and the following day the minister's wife wrote to Miss
Emily's relations in Alabama.

So she had blood-kin under her roof again and we sat back to
watch developments. At first nothing happened. Then we were sure
that they were to be married. We learned that Miss Emily had been
to the jeweler's and ordered a man's toilet set in silver, with the letters H. B. on each piece. Two days later we learned that she had
bought a complete outfit of men's clothing, including a nightshirt,
and we said, "They are married." We were really glad. We were glad
because the two female cousins were even more Grierson than Miss
Emily had ever been.

So we were not surprised when Homer Barron—the streets had
been finished some time since—was gone. We were a little disappointed that there was not a public blowing-off, but we believed
that he had gone on to prepare for Miss Emily's coming, or to give
her a chance to get rid of the cousins. (By that time it was a cabal,
and we were all Miss Emily's allies to help circumvent the cousins.)
Sure enough, after another week they departed. And, as we had expected all along, within three days Homer Barron was back in town.
A neighbor saw the Negro man admit him at the kitchen door at
dusk one evening.

And that was the last we saw of Homer Barron. And of Miss
Emily for some time. The Negro man went in and out with the
market basket, but the front door remained closed. Now and then
we would see her at a window for a moment, as the men did that
night when they sprinkled the lime, but for almost six months she
did not appear on the streets. Then we knew that this was to be expected too; as if that quality of her father which had thwarted her
woman's life so many times had been too virulent and too furious to
die.

When we next saw Miss Emily, she had grown fat and her hair
was turning gray. During the next few years it grew grayer and
grayer until it attained an even pepper-and-salt iron-gray, when it

ceased turning. Up to the day of her death at seventy-four it was still that vigorous iron-gray, like the hair of an active man.

From that time on her front door remained closed, save for a period of six or seven years, when she was about forty, during which she gave lessons in china-painting. She fitted up a studio in one of the downstairs rooms, where the daughters and granddaughters of Colonel Sartoris' contemporaries were sent to her with the same regularity and in the same spirit that they were sent to church on Sundays with a twenty-five-cent piece for the collection plate. Meanwhile her taxes had been remitted.

Then the newer generation became the backbone and the spirit of the town, and the painting pupils grew up and fell away and did not send their children to her with boxes of color and tedious brushes and pictures cut from the ladies' magazines. The front door closed upon the last one and remained closed for good. When the town got free postal delivery, Miss Emily alone refused to let them fasten the metal numbers above her door and attach a mailbox to it. She would not listen to them.

Daily, monthly, yearly we watched the Negro grow grayer and more stooped, going in and out with the market basket. Each December we sent her a tax notice, which would be returned by the post office a week later, unclaimed. Now and then we would see her in one of the downstairs windows—she had evidently shut up the top floor of the house—like the carven torso of an idol in a niche, looking or not looking at us, we could never tell which. Thus she passed from generation to generation—dear, inescapable, impervious, tranquil, and perverse.

And so she died. Fell ill in the house filled with dust and shadows, with only a doddering Negro man to wait on her. We did not even know she was sick; we had long since given up trying to get any information from the Negro. He talked to no one, probably not even to her, for his voice had grown harsh and rusty, as if from disuse.

She died in one of the downstairs rooms, in a heavy walnut bed with a curtain, her gray head propped on a pillow yellow and moldy with age and lack of sunlight.

V

The Negro met the first of the ladies at the front door and let them in, with their hushed, sibilant voices and their quick, curious glances, and then he disappeared. He walked right through the house and out the back and was not seen again.

The two female cousins came at once. They held the funeral on the second day, with the town coming to look at Miss Emily beneath a mass of bought flowers, with the crayon face of her father musing profoundly above the bier and the ladies sibilant and macabre; and the very old men—some in their brushed Confederate uniforms—on the porch and the lawn, talking of Miss Emily as if she had been a contemporary of theirs, believing that they had danced with her and courted her perhaps, confusing time with its mathematical progression, as the old do, to whom all the past is not a diminishing road but, instead, a huge meadow which no winter ever quite touches, divided from them now by the narrow bottleneck of the most recent decade of years.

Already we knew that there was one room in that region above stairs which no one had seen in forty years, and which would have to be forced. They waited until Miss Emily was decently in the ground before they opened it.

The violence of breaking down the door seemed to fill this room with pervading dust. A thin, acrid pall as of the tomb seemed to lie everywhere upon this room decked and furnished as for a bridal: upon the valance curtains of faded rose color, upon the rose-shaded lights, upon the dressing table, upon the delicate array of crystal and the man's toilet things backed with tarnished silver, silver so tarnished that the monogram was obscured. Among them lay a collar and tie, as if they had just been removed, which, lifted, left upon the surface a pale crescent in the dust. Upon a chair hung the suit, carefully folded; beneath it the two mute shoes and the discarded socks.

The man himself lay in the bed.

For a long while we just stood there, looking down at the profound and fleshless grin. The body had apparently once lain in the attitude of an embrace, but now the long sleep that outlasts love, that conquers even the grimace of love, had cuckolded him. What was left of him, rotted beneath what was left of the nightshirt, had become inextricable from the bed in which he lay; and upon him and upon the pillow beside him lay that even coating of the patient and biding dust.

Then we noticed that in the second pillow was the indentation of a head. One of us lifted something from it, and leaning forward, that faint and invisible dust dry and acrid in the nostrils, we saw a long strand of iron-gray hair.

1930

Gabriel García Márquez
1928–

> *Garciá Márquez was a central figure in the 1960s Latin American literary movement called "The Boom." The writers of this movement were cosmopolitan and wrote for an international Spanish-speaking audience. A few, like García Márquez, were also conscious of writing for audiences who would only read their work in translation. Even so, García Márquez typically grounds his stories in fairly isolated rural villages, as here, where myth and fantasy mix on equal terms with "reality." His technique has been dubbed magical realism, and you can devise a pretty good definition of that term by analyzing "A Very Old Man with Enormous Wings." We could regard the story as an allegory and, perhaps, compare its central character and theme to those of Kafka's "A Hunger Artist." But magical realism extends its effect beyond allegory. Of equal importance to the story line—who the protagonist is, what the conflict and resolution are—is the effect of García Márquez's style. Though the characters in the story regard the arrival of the angel as remarkable, still they accept the miraculous and supernatural as easily as they accept the crabs that have come up from the sea's floor. As you read this story, you live briefly in this world. What is the effect on you?*

A Very Old Man with Enormous Wings[1]

A Tale for Children

On the third day of rain they had killed so many crabs inside the house that Pelayo had to cross his drenched courtyard and throw them into the sea, because the newborn child had a temperature all night and they thought it was due to the stench. The world had been sad since Tuesday. Sea and sky were a single ash-gray thing and the sands of the beach, which on March nights glimmered like powdered light, had become a stew of mud and rotten shellfish. The light was so weak at noon that when Pelayo was coming back to the house after throwing away the crabs, it was hard for him to see what it was that was moving and groaning in the rear of the courtyard. He had to go very close to see that it was an old man, a very old man, lying face down in the mud, who, in spite of his tremendous efforts, couldn't get up, impeded by his enormous wings.

Frightened by that nightmare, Pelayo ran to get Elisenda, his wife, who was putting compresses on the sick child, and he took her to the rear of the courtyard. They both looked at the fallen body with mute stupor. He was dressed like a ragpicker. There were only a few faded hairs left on his bald skull and very few teeth in his mouth, and his pitiful condition of a drenched great-grandfather had taken away any sense of grandeur he might have had. His huge buzzard wings, dirty and half-plucked, were forever entangled in the mud. They looked at him so long and so closely that Pelayo and Elisenda very soon overcame their surprise and in the end found him familiar. Then they dared speak to him, and he answered in an incomprehensible dialect with a strong sailor's voice. That was how they skipped over the inconvenience of the wings and quite intelligently concluded that he was a lonely castaway from some foreign ship wrecked by the storm. And yet, they called in a neighbor woman who knew everything about life and death to see him, and all she needed was one look to show them their mistake.

1. Translated by Gregory Rabassa.

"He's an angel," she told them. "He must have been coming for the child, but the poor fellow is so old that the rain knocked him down."

On the following day everyone knew that a flesh-and-blood angel was held captive in Pelayo's house. Against the judgment of the wise neighbor woman, for whom angels in those times were the fugitive survivors of a celestial conspiracy, they did not have the heart to club him to death. Pelayo watched over him all afternoon from the kitchen, armed with his bailiff's club, and before going to bed he dragged him out of the mud and locked him up with the hens in the wire chicken coop. In the middle of the night, when the rain stopped, Pelayo and Elisenda were still killing crabs. A short time afterward the child woke up without a fever and with a desire to eat. Then they felt magnanimous and decided to put the angel on a raft with fresh water and provisions for three days and leave him to his fate on the high seas. But when they went out into the courtyard with the first light of dawn, they found the whole neighborhood in front of the chicken coop having fun with the angel, without the slightest reverence, tossing him things to eat through the openings in the wire as if he weren't a supernatural creature but a circus animal.

Father Gonzaga arrived before seven o'clock, alarmed at the strange news. By that time onlookers less frivolous than those at dawn had already arrived and they were making all kinds of conjectures concerning the captive's future. The simplest among them thought that he should be named mayor of the world. Others of sterner mind felt that he should be promoted to the rank of five-star general in order to win all wars. Some visionaries hoped that he could be put to stud in order to implant on earth a race of winged wise men who could take charge of the universe. But Father Gonzaga, before becoming a priest, had been a robust woodcutter. Standing by the wire, he reviewed his catechism in an instant and asked them to open the door so that he could take a close look at that pitiful man who looked more like a huge decrepit hen among the fascinated chickens. He was lying in a corner drying his open wings in the sunlight among the fruit peels and breakfast leftovers that the early risers had thrown him. Alien to the impertinences of the world, he only lifted his antiquarian eyes and murmured something in his dialect when Father Gonzaga went into the chicken coop and said good morning to him in Latin. The parish priest had his first suspicion of an imposter when he saw that he did not understand the language of God or know how to greet His ministers. Then he noticed that seen close up he was much too human: he had an unbearable smell of the outdoors, the back side of his wings was strewn with parasites and his main feathers had been mistreated by terrestial winds, and nothing about him measured up to the proud dignity of angels. Then he came out of the chicken coop and in a brief sermon warned the curious against the risks of being ingenuous. He reminded them that the devil had the bad habit of making use of carnival tricks in order to confuse the unwary. He argued that if wings were not the essential element in determining the difference between a hawk and an airplane, they were even less so in the recognition of angels. Nevertheless, he promised to write a letter to his bishop so that the latter would write to his primate so that the latter would write to the Supreme Pontiff in order to get the final verdict from the highest courts.

His prudence fell on sterile hearts. The news of the captive angel spread with such rapidity that after a few hours the courtyard had the bustle of a marketplace and they had to call in troops with fixed bayonets to disperse the mob that was about to knock the house down. Elisenda, her spine all twisted from sweeping up so much marketplace trash, then got the idea of fencing in the yard and charging five cents admission to see the angel.

The curious came from far away. A traveling carnival arrived with a flying acrobat who buzzed over the crowd several times, but no one paid any attention to him because his wings were not those of an angel but, rather, those of a sidereal bat. The most unfortunate invalids on earth came in search of health: a poor woman who since childhood had been counting her heartbeats and had run out of numbers; a Portuguese man who couldn't sleep because the noise of the stars disturbed him; a sleepwalker who got up at night to undo the things he had done while awake; and many others with less serious ailments. In the midst of that shipwreck disorder that made the earth tremble, Pelayo and Elisenda were happy with fatigue, for in less than a week they had crammed their rooms with money and the line of pilgrims waiting their turn to enter still reached beyond the horizon.

The angel was the only one who took no part in his own act. He spent his time trying to get comfortable in his borrowed nest, befuddled by the hellish heat of the oil lamps and sacramental candles that had been placed along the wire. At first they tried to make him eat some mothballs, which, according to the wisdom of the wise neighbor woman, were the food prescribed for angels. But he turned them down, just as he turned down the papal lunches[2] that the penitents brought him, and they never found out whether it was because he was an angel or because he was an old man that in the end he ate nothing but eggplant mush. His only supernatural virtue seemed to be patience. Especially during the first days, when the hens pecked at him, searching for the stellar parasites that proliferated in his wings, and the cripples pulled out feathers to touch their defective parts with, and even the most merciful threw stones at him, trying to get him to rise so they could see him standing. The only time they succeeded in arousing him was when they burned his side with an iron for branding steers, for he had been motionless for so many hours that they thought he was dead. He awoke with a start, ranting in his hermetic language and with tears in his eyes, and he flapped his wings a couple of times, which brought on a whirlwind of chicken dung and lunar dust and a gale of panic that did not seem to be of this world. Although many thought that his reaction had been one not of rage but of pain, from then on they were careful not to annoy him, because the majority understood that his passivity was not that of a hero taking his ease but that of a cataclysm in repose.

Father Gonzaga held back the crowd's frivolity with formulas of maidservant inspiration while awaiting the arrival of a final judgment on the nature of the captive. But the mail from Rome showed no sense of urgency. They spent their time finding out if the prisoner had a navel, if his dialect had any connection with Aramaic, how many times he could fit on the head of a pin, or whether he wasn't just a Norwegian with wings. Those meager letters might

2. Expensive meals.

have come and gone until the end of time if a providential event had not put an end to the priest's tribulations.

It so happened that during those days, among so many other carnival attractions, there arrived in town the traveling show of the woman who had been changed into a spider for having disobeyed her parents. The admission to see her was not only less than the admission to see the angel, but people were permitted to ask her all manner of questions about her absurd state and to examine her up and down so that no one would ever doubt the truth of her horror. She was a frightful tarantula the size of a ram and with the head of a sad maiden. What was most heartrending, however, was not her outlandish shape but the sincere affliction with which she recounted the details of her misfortune. While still practically a child she had sneaked out of her parents' house to go to a dance, and while she was coming back through the woods after having danced all night without permission, a fearful thunderclap rent the sky in two and through the crack came the lightning bolt of brimstone that changed her into a spider. Her only nourishment came from the meatballs that charitable souls chose to toss into her mouth. A spectacle like that, full of so much human truth and with such a fearful lesson, was bound to defeat without even trying that of a haughty angel who scarcely deigned to look at mortals. Besides, the few miracles attributed to the angel showed a certain mental disorder, like the blind man who didn't recover his sight but grew three new teeth, or the paralytic who didn't get to walk but almost won the lottery, and the leper whose sores sprouted sunflowers. Those consolation miracles, which were more like mocking fun, had already ruined the angel's reputation when the woman who had been changed into a spider finally crushed him completely. That was how Father Gonzaga was cured forever of his insomnia and Pelayo's courtyard went back to being as empty as during the time it had rained for three days and crabs walked through the bedrooms.

The owners of the house had no reason to lament. With the money they saved they built a two-story mansion with balconies and gardens and high netting so that crabs wouldn't get in during the winter, and with iron bars on the windows so that angels wouldn't get in. Pelayo also set up a rabbit warren close to town and gave up his job as bailiff for good, and Elisenda bought some satin pumps with high heels and many dresses of iridescent silk, the kind worn on Sunday by the most desirable women in those times. The chicken coop was the only thing that didn't receive any attention. If they washed it down with creolin[3] and burned tears of myrrh inside it every so often, it was not in homage to the angel but to drive away the dungheap stench that still hung everywhere like a ghost and was turning the new house into an old one. At first, when the child learned to walk, they were careful that he not get too close to the chicken coop. But then they began to lose their fears and got used to the smell, and before the child got his second teeth he'd gone inside the chicken coop to play, where the wires were falling apart. The angel was no less standoffish with him than with other mortals, but he tolerated the most ingenious infamies with the patience of a dog who had no illusions. They both came down with chicken pox at the same time. The doctor who took care of the child couldn't resist the temptation to listen to the angel's heart, and he found so much whistling in the heart and so many sounds in his kidneys that it seemed impossible for him to be alive. What surprised him most, however, was the logic of his wings. They seemed so natural on that completely human organism that he couldn't understand why other men didn't have them too.

When the child began school it had been some time since the sun and rain had caused the collapse of the chicken coop. The angel went dragging himself about here and there like a stray dying man. They would drive him out of the bedroom with a broom and a moment later find him in the kitchen. He seemed to be in so many places at the same time that they grew to think that he'd been duplicated, that he was reproducing himself all through the house, and the exasperated and unhinged Elisenda shouted that it was awful living in that hell full of angels. He could scarcely eat and his antiquarian eyes had also become so foggy that he went about bumping into posts. All he had left were the bare cannulae[4] of his last feathers. Pelayo threw a blanket over him and extended him the charity of letting him sleep in the shed, and only then did they notice that he had a temperature at night, and was delirious with the tongue twisters of an old Nor-

---

3. A disinfectant.
4. The tubes that attach feathers to the body.

wegian. That was one of the few times they became alarmed, for they thought he was going to die and not even the wise neighbor woman had been able to tell them what to do with dead angels.

And yet he not only survived his worst winter, but seemed improved with the first sunny days. He remained motionless for several days in the farthest corner of the courtyard, where no one would see him, and at the beginning of December some large, stiff feathers began to grow on his wings, the feathers of a scarecrow, which looked more like another misfortune of decrepitude. But he must have known the reason for those changes, for he was quite careful that no one should notice them, that no one should hear the sea chanteys[5] that he sometimes sang under the stars. One morning Elisenda was cutting some bunches of onions for lunch when a wind that seemed to come from the high seas blew into the kitchen. Then she went to the window and caught the angel in his first attempts at flight. They were so clumsy that his fingernails opened a furrow in the vegetable patch and he was on the point of knocking the shed down with the ungainly flapping that slipped on the light and couldn't get a grip on the air. But he did manage to gain altitude. Elisenda let out a sigh of relief, for herself and for him, when she saw him pass over the last houses, holding himself up in some way with the risky flapping of a senile vulture. She kept watching him even when she was through cutting the onions and she kept on watching until it was no longer possible for her to see him, because then he was no longer an annoyance in her life but an imaginary dot on the horizon of the sea.

1968

Charlotte Perkins Gilman

1860–1935

Gilman's "The Yellow Wallpaper" was closely based on her own experience. She married at the age of twenty-four and immediately got pregnant, had a child, and fell into depression. An eminent doc-

---

5. Songs sung by sailors to the rhythm of their work.

tor, S. Weir Mitchell, treated her with his now notorious "rest cure," which was identical to Jane's treatment in the story. The "inevitable result," as Gilman wrote in her autobiography, was "progressive insanity." She said that her own treatment drove her "as far as one could go [toward insanity] and get back." After leaving her husband and moving to California, she regained her mental and physical health. When she published the story in 1892, doctors praised the accuracy of its psychological depiction, and apparently, Mitchell subsequently abandoned the rest cure. This was Gilman's avowed purpose: to "convince [Mitchell] of the error of his ways." Though Gilman had this narrow intention, the story has much to say about the general condition of women in late-nineteenth-century American society. Gilman's fiction and her studies of economics helped convince America of the consequences of denying women the range of personal development allowed men—especially in the workplace.

The Yellow Wallpaper

It is very seldom that mere ordinary people like John and myself secure ancestral halls for the summer.

A colonial mansion, a hereditary estate, I would say a haunted house and reach the height of romantic felicity—but that would be asking too much of fate!

Still I will proudly declare that there is something queer about it.

Else, why should it be let so cheaply? And why have stood so long untenanted?

John laughs at me, of course, but one expects that.

John is practical in the extreme. He has no patience with faith, an intense horror of superstition, and he scoffs openly at any talk of things not to be felt and seen and put down in figures.

John is a physician, and *perhaps*—(I would not say it to a living soul, of course, but this is dead paper and a great relief to my mind)—*perhaps* that is one reason I do not get well faster.

You see, he does not believe I am sick! And what can one do?

If a physician of high standing, and one's own husband, assures friends and relatives that there is really nothing the matter with one but temporary nervous depression—a slight hysterical tendency[1]—what is one to do?

My brother is also a physician, and also of high standing, and he says the same thing.

So I take phosphates or phosphites—whichever it is, and tonics, and journeys, and air, and exercise, and am absolutely forbidden to "work" until I am well again.

Personally, I disagree with their ideas.

Personally, I believe that congenial work, with excitement and change, would do me good.

But what is one to do?

I did write for a while in spite of them; but it *does* exhaust me a good deal—having to be so sly about it, or else meet with heavy opposition.

I sometimes fancy that in my condition if I had less opposition and more society and stimulus—but John says the very worst thing I can do is to think about my condition, and I confess it always makes me feel bad.

So I will let it alone and talk about the house.

The most beautiful place! It is quite alone, standing well back from the road, quite three miles from the village. It makes me think of English places that you read about, for there are hedges and walls and gates that lock, and lots of separate little houses for the gardeners and people.

There is a *delicious* garden! I never saw such a garden—large and shady, full of box-bordered paths, and lined with long grape-covered arbors with seats under them.

There were greenhouses, too, but they are all broken now.

There was some legal trouble, I believe, something about the heirs and co-heirs; anyhow, the place has been empty for years.

That spoils my ghostliness, I am afraid, but I don't care—there is something strange about the house—I can feel it.

I even said so to John one moonlight evening, but he said what I felt was a *draught,* and shut the window.

---

1. In the nineteenth century, the term *hysteria* was used to describe a host of symptoms indicating emotional disturbance or dysfunction thought to be especially prevalent among women and often considered to be either a manifestation of repressed sexual urges or an attempt by affected women to avoid their duties as wives and mothers.

I get unreasonably angry with John sometimes. I'm sure I never used to be so sensitive. I think it is due to this nervous condition.

But John says if I feel so, I shall neglect proper self-control; so I take pains to control myself—before him, at least, and that makes me very tired.

I don't like our room a bit. I wanted one downstairs that opened on the piazza and had roses all over the window, and such pretty old-fashioned chintz hangings! but John would not hear of it.

He said there was only one window and not room for two beds, and no near room for him if he took another.

He is very careful and loving, and hardly lets me stir without special direction.

I have a schedule prescription for each hour in the day; he takes all care from me, and so I feel basely ungrateful not to value it more.

He said we came here solely on my account, that I was to have perfect rest and all the air I could get. "Your exercise depends on your strength, my dear," said he, "and your food somewhat on your appetite; but air you can absorb all the time." So we took the nursery at the top of the house.

It is a big, airy room, the whole floor nearly, with windows that look all ways, and air and sunshine galore. It was nursery first and then playroom and gymnasium, I should judge; for the windows are barred for little children, and there are rings and things in the walls.

The paint and paper look as if a boys' school had used it. It is stripped off—the paper—in great patches all around the head of my bed, about as far as I can reach, and in a great place on the other side of the room low down. I never saw a worse paper in my life. One of those sprawling flamboyant patterns committing every artistic sin.

It is dull enough to confuse the eye in following, pronounced enough to constantly irritate and provoke study, and when you follow the lame uncertain curves for a little distance they suddenly commit suicide—plunge off at outrageous angles, destroy themselves in unheard-of contradictions.

The color is repellant, almost revolting; a smouldering unclean yellow, strangely faded by the slow-turning sunlight. It is a dull yet lurid orange in some places, a sickly sulphur tint in others.

No wonder the children hated it! I should hate it myself if I had to live in this room long.

There comes John, and I must put this away—he hates to have me write a word.

We have been here two weeks, and I haven't felt like writing before, since that first day.

I am sitting by the window now, up in this atrocious nursery, and there is nothing to hinder my writing as much as I please, save lack of strength.

John is away all day, and even some nights when his cases are serious.

I am glad my case is not serious!

But these nervous troubles are dreadfully depressing.

John does not know how much I really suffer. He knows there is no reason to suffer, and that satisfies him.

Of course it is only nervousness. It does weigh on me so not to do my duty in any way!

I mean to be such a help to John, such a real rest and comfort, and here I am a comparative burden already!

Nobody would believe what an effort it is to do what little I am able—to dress and entertain, and order things.

It is fortunate Mary is so good with the baby. Such a dear baby!

And yet I *cannot* be with him, it makes me so nervous.

I suppose John never was nervous in his life. He laughs at me so about this wallpaper!

At first he meant to repaper the room, but afterwards he said that I was letting it get the better of me, and that nothing was worse for a nervous patient than to give way to such fancies.

He said that after the wallpaper was changed it would be the heavy bedstead, and then the barred windows, and then that gate at the head of the stairs, and so on.

"You know the place is doing you good," he said, "and really, dear, I don't care to renovate the house just for a three months' rental."

"Then do let us go downstairs," I said. "There are such pretty rooms there."

Then he took me in his arms and called me a blessed little goose, and said he would go down cellar, if I wished, and have it white-washed into the bargain.

But he is right enough about the beds and windows and things.

It is as airy and comfortable a room as anyone need wish, and, of course, I would not be so silly as to make him uncomfortable just for a whim.

I'm really getting quite fond of the big room, all but that horrid paper.

Out of one window I can see the garden—those mysterious deep-shaded arbors, the riotous old-fashioned flowers, and bushes and gnarly trees.

Out of another I get a lovely view of the bay and a little private wharf belonging to the estate. There is a beautiful shaded lane that runs down there from the house. I always fancy I see people walking in these numerous paths and arbors, but John has cautioned me not to give way to fancy in the least. He says that with my imaginative power and habit of story-making, a nervous weakness like mine is sure to lead to all manner of excited fancies, and that I ought to use my will and good sense to check the tendency. So I try.

I think sometimes that if I were only well enough to write a little it would relieve the press of ideas and rest me.

But I find I get pretty tired when I try.

It is so discouraging not to have any advice and companionship about my work. When I get really well, John says we will ask Cousin Henry and Julia down for a long visit; but he says he would as soon put fireworks in my pillowcase as to let me have those stimulating people about now.

I wish I could get well faster.

But I must not think about that. This paper looks to me as if it *knew* what a vicious influence it had!

There is a recurrent spot where the pattern lolls like a broken neck and two bulbous eyes stare at you upside down.

I get positively angry with the impertinence of it and the ever-lastingness. Up and down and sideways they crawl, and those absurd unblinking eyes are everywhere. There is one place where two breadths didn't match, and the eyes go all up and down the line, one a little higher than the other.

I never saw so much expression in an inanimate thing before, and we all know how much expression they have! I used to lie awake as a child and get more entertainment and terror out of blank walls and plain furniture than most children could find in a toy-store.

I remember what a kindly wink the knobs of our big old bureau used to have, and there was one chair that always seemed like a strong friend.

I used to feel that if any of the other things looked too fierce I could always hop into that chair and be safe.

The furniture in this room is no worse than inharmonious, however, for we had to bring it all from downstairs. I suppose when this was used as a playroom they had to take the nursery things out, and no wonder! I never saw such ravages as the children have made here.

The wallpaper, as I said before, is torn off in spots, and it sticketh closer than a brother—they must have had perseverance as well as hatred.

Then the floor is scratched and gouged and splintered, the plaster itself is dug out here and there, and this great heavy bed which is all we found in the room, looks as if it had been through the wars.

But I don't mind it a bit—only the paper.

There comes John's sister. Such a dear girl as she is, and so careful of me! I must not let her find me writing.

She is a perfect and enthusiastic housekeeper, and hopes for no better profession. I verily believe she thinks it is the writing which made me sick!

But I can write when she is out, and see her a long way off from these windows.

There is one that commands the road, a lovely shaded winding road, and one that just looks off over the country. A lovely country too, full of great elms and velvet meadows.

This wallpaper has a kind of sub-pattern in a different shade, a particularly irritating one, for you can only see it in certain lights, and not clearly then.

But in the places where it isn't faded and where the sun is just so—I can see a strange, provoking, formless sort of figure that seems to skulk about behind that silly and conspicuous front design.

There's sister on the stairs!

Well, the Fourth of July is over! The people are all gone, and I am tired out. John thought it might do me good to see a little company, so we just had Mother and Nellie and the children down for a week.

Of course I didn't do a thing. Jennie sees to everything now.

But it tired me all the same.

John says if I don't pick up faster he shall send me to Weir Mitchell in the fall.

But I don't want to go there at all. I had a friend who was in his hands once, and she says he is just like John and my brother, only more so!

Besides, it is such an undertaking to go so far.

I don't feel as if it was worthwhile to turn my hand over for anything, and I'm getting dreadfully fretful and querulous.

I cry at nothing, and cry most of the time.

Of course I don't when John is here, or anybody else, but when I am alone.

And I am alone a good deal just now. John is kept in town very often by serious cases, and Jennie is good and lets me alone when I want her to.

So I walk a little in the garden or down that lovely lane, sit on the porch under the roses, and lie down up here a good deal.

I'm getting really fond of the room in spite of the wallpaper. Perhaps *because* of the wallpaper.

It dwells in my mind so!

I lie here on this great immovable bed—it is nailed down, I believe—and follow that pattern about by the hour. It is as good as gymnastics, I assure you. I start, we'll say, at the bottom, down in the corner over there where it has not been touched, and I determine for the thousandth time that I *will* follow that pointless pattern to some sort of conclusion.

I know a little of the principle of design, and I know this thing was not arranged on any laws of radiation, or alternation, or repetition, or symmetry, or anything else that I ever heard of.

It is repeated, of course, by the breadths, but not otherwise.

Looked at in one way, each breadth stands alone; the bloated curves and flourishes—a kind of "debased Romanesque" with delirium tremens[2]—go waddling up and down in isolated columns of fatuity.

But, on the other hand, they connect diagonally, and the sprawling outlines run off in great slanting waves of optic horror, like a lot of wallowing sea-weeds in full chase.

The whole thing goes horizontally, too, at least it seems so, and I exhaust myself trying to distinguish the order of its going in that direction.

They have used a horizontal breadth for a frieze,[3] and that adds wonderfully to the confusion.

There is one end of the room where it is almost intact, and there, when the crosslights fade and the low sun shines directly upon it, I can almost fancy radiation after all—the interminable grotesque seems to form around a common center and rush off in headlong plunges of equal distraction.

It makes me tired to follow it. I will take a nap, I guess.

I don't know why I should write this.

I don't want to.

I don't feel able.

And I know John would think it absurd. But I *must* say what I feel and think in some way—it is such a relief!

But the effort is getting to be greater than the relief.

Half the time now I am awfully lazy, and lie down ever so much.

John says I mustn't lose my strength, and has me take cod liver oil and lots of tonics and things, to say nothing of ale and wine and rare meat.

Dear John! He loves me very dearly, and hates to have me sick. I tried to have a real earnest reasonable talk with him the other day, and tell him how I wish he would let me go and make a visit to Cousin Henry and Julia.

2. A mental and nervous disorder, often associated with alcoholism, accompanied by violent trembling and hallucinations. Romanesque refers to a profuse ornamental style.

3. An ornamental band running along the top of a wall.

But he said I wasn't able to go, nor able to stand it after I got there; and I did not make out a very good case for myself, for I was crying before I had finished.

It is getting to be a great effort for me to think straight. Just this nervous weakness, I suppose.

And dear John gathered me up in his arms, and just carried me upstairs and laid me on the bed, and sat by me and read to me till it tired my head.

He said I was his darling and his comfort and all he had, and that I must take care of myself for his sake, and keep well.

He says no one but myself can help me out of it, that I must use my will and self-control and not let any silly fancies run away with me.

There's one comfort—the baby is well and happy, and does not have to occupy this nursery with the horrid wallpaper.

If we had not used it, that blessed child would have! What a fortunate escape! Why, I wouldn't have a child of mine, an impressionable little thing, live in such a room for worlds.

I never thought of it before, but it is lucky that John kept me here after all, I can stand it so much easier than a baby, you see.

Of course I never mention it to them any more—I am too wise—but I keep watch for it all the same.

There are things in that paper that nobody knows about but me, or ever will.

Behind that outside pattern the dim shapes get clearer every day.

It is always the same shape, only very numerous.

And it is like a woman stooping down and creeping about behind that pattern. I don't like it a bit. I wonder—I begin to think—I wish John would take me away from here!

It is so hard to talk with John about my case, because he is so wise, and because he loves me so.

But I tried it last night.

It was moonlight. The moon shines in all around just as the sun does.

I hate to see it sometimes, it creeps so slowly, and always comes in by one window or another.

John was asleep and I hated to waken him, so I kept still

and watched the moonlight on that undulating wallpaper till I felt creepy.

The faint figure behind seemed to shake the pattern, just as if she wanted to get out.

I got up softly and went to feel and see if the paper *did* move, and when I came back John was awake.

"What is it, little girl?" he said. "Don't go walking about like that—you'll get cold."

I thought it was a good time to talk, so I told him that I really was not gaining here, and that I wished he would take me away.

"Why darling!" said he. "Our lease will be up in three weeks, and I can't see how to leave before.

"The repairs are not done at home, and I cannot possibly leave town just now. Of course if you were in any danger, I could and would, but you really are better, dear, whether you can see it or not. I am a doctor, dear, and I know. You are gaining flesh and color, your appetite is better, I feel really much easier about you."

"I don't weigh a bit more," said I, "nor as much; and my appetite may be better in the evening when you are here but it is worse in the morning when you are away!"

"Bless her little heart!" said he with a big hug. "She shall be as sick as she pleases! But now let's improve the shining hours by going to sleep, and talk about it in the morning!"

"And you won't go away?" I asked gloomily.

"Why, how can I, dear? It is only three weeks more and then we will take a nice little trip of a few days while Jennie is getting the house ready. Really, dear, you are better!"

"Better in body perhaps—" I began, and stopped short, for he sat up straight and looked at me with such a stern, reproachful look that I could not say another word.

"My darling," said he, "I beg of you, for my sake and for our child's sake, as well as for your own, that you will never for one instant let that idea enter your mind! There is nothing so dangerous, so fascinating, to a temperament like yours. It is a false and foolish fancy. Can you not trust me as a physician when I tell you so?"

So of course I said no more on that score, and we went to sleep before long. He thought I was asleep first; but I wasn't, and lay there for hours trying to decide whether that front pattern and the back pattern really did move together or separately.

On a pattern like this, by daylight, there is a lack of sequence, a defiance of law, that is a constant irritant to a normal mind.

The color is hideous enough, and unreliable enough, and infuriating enough, but the pattern is torturing.

You think you have mastered it, but just as you get well under way in following, it turns a back-somersault and there you are. It slaps you in the face, knocks you down, and tramples upon you. It is like a bad dream.

The outside pattern is a florid arabesque, reminding one of a fungus. If you can imagine a toadstool in joints; an interminable string of toadstools, budding and sprouting in endless convolutions—why, that is something like it.

That is, sometimes!

There is one marked peculiarity about this paper, a thing nobody seems to notice but myself, and that is that it changes as the light changes.

When the sun shoots in through the east window—I always watch for that first long, straight ray—it changes so quickly that I never can quite believe it.

That is why I watch it always.

By moonlight—the moon shines in all night when there is a moon—I wouldn't know it was the same paper.

At night in any kind of light, in twilight, candlelight, lamplight, and worst of all by moonlight, it becomes bars! The outside pattern, I mean, and the woman behind it is as plain as can be.

I didn't realize for a long time what the thing was that showed behind that dim sub-pattern, but now I am quite sure it is a woman.

By daylight she is subdued, quiet. I fancy it is the pattern that keeps her so still. It is so puzzling. It keeps me quiet by the hour.

I lie down ever so much now. John says it is good for me, and to sleep all I can.

Indeed he started the habit by making me lie down for an hour after each meal.

It is a very bad habit I am convinced, for you see, I don't sleep.

And that cultivates deceit, for I don't tell them I'm awake—O no!

The fact is I am getting a little afraid of John.

He seems very queer sometimes, and even Jennie has an inexplicable look.

It strikes me occasionally, just as a scientific hypothesis, that perhaps it is the paper!

I have watched John when he did not know I was looking, and come into the room suddenly on the most innocent excuses, and I've caught him several times *looking at the paper!* And Jennie too. I caught Jennie with her hand on it once.

She didn't know I was in the room, and when I asked her in a quiet, a very quiet voice, with the most restrained manner possible, what she was doing with the paper—she turned around as if she had been caught stealing, and looked quite angry—asked me why I should frighten her so!

Then she said that the paper stained everything it touched, that she had found yellow smooches⁴ on all my clothes and John's, and she wished we would be more careful!

Did not that sound innocent? But I know she was studying that pattern, and I am determined that nobody shall find it out but myself!

Life is very much more exciting now than it used to be. You see I have something more to expect, to look forward to, to watch. I really do eat better, and am more quiet than I was.

John is so pleased to see me improve! He laughed a little the other day, and said I seemed to be flourishing in spite of my wallpaper.

I turned it off with a laugh. I had no intention of telling him it was *because* of the wallpaper—he would make fun of me. He might even want to take me away.

I don't want to leave now until I have found it out. There is a week more, and I think that will be enough.

————

4. Smudges, smears.

I'm feeling so much better!

I don't sleep much at night, for it is so interesting to watch developments; but I sleep a good deal during the daytime.

In the daytime it is tiresome and perplexing.

There are always new shoots on the fungus, and new shades of yellow all over it. I cannot keep count of them, though I have tried conscientiously.

It is the strangest yellow, that wallpaper! It makes me think of all the yellow things I ever saw—not beautiful ones like buttercups, but old, foul, bad yellow things.

But there is something else about that paper—the smell! I noticed it the moment we came into the room, but with so much air and sun it was not bad. Now we have had a week of fog and rain, and whether the windows are open or not, the smell is here.

It creeps all over the house.

I find it hovering in the dining-room, skulking in the parlor, hiding in the hall, lying in wait for me on the stairs.

It gets into my hair.

Even when I go to ride, if I turn my head suddenly and surprise it—there is that smell!

Such a peculiar odor, too! I have spent hours in trying to analyze it, to find what it smelled like.

It is not bad—at first—and very gentle, but quite the subtlest, most enduring odor I ever met.

In this damp weather it is awful, I wake up in the night and find it hanging over me.

It used to disturb me at first. I thought seriously of burning the house—to reach the smell.

But now I am used to it. The only thing I can think of that it is like is the *color* of the paper! A yellow smell.

There is a very funny mark on this wall, low, down, near the mopboard.[5] A streak that runs round the room. It goes behind every piece of furniture, except the bed, a long straight, even *smooch*, as if it had been rubbed over and over.

I wonder how it was done and who did it, and what they did it

5. Baseboard.

for. Round and round and round—round and round and round—
it makes me dizzy!

I really have discovered something at last.

Through watching so much at night, when it changes so, I have
finally found out.

The front pattern *does* move—and no wonder! The woman behind shakes it!

Sometimes I think there are a great many women behind, and
sometimes only one, and she crawls around fast, and her crawling
shakes it all over.

Then in the very bright spots she keeps still, and in the very
shady spots she just takes hold of the bars and shakes them hard.

And she is all the time trying to climb through. But nobody
could climb through that pattern—it strangles so; I think that is
why it has so many heads.

They get through, and then the pattern strangles them off and
turns them upside down, and makes their eyes white!

If those heads were covered or taken off it would not be half so
bad.

I think that woman gets out in the daytime!

And I'll tell you why—privately—I've seen her!

I can see her out of every one of my windows!

It is the same woman, I know, for she is always creeping, and
most women do not creep by daylight.

I see her in that long shaded lane, creeping up and down. I see
her in those dark grape arbors, creeping all around the garden.

I see her on that long road under the trees, creeping along, and
when a carriage comes she hides under the blackberry vines.

I don't blame her a bit. It must be very humiliating to be caught
creeping by daylight!

I always lock the door when I creep by daylight. I can't do it at
night, for I know John would suspect something at once.

And John is so queer now that I don't want to irritate him. I wish
he would take another room! Besides, I don't want anybody to get
that woman out at night but myself.

I often wonder if I could see her out of all the windows at once.

But, turn as fast as I can, I can only see out of one at one time.

And though I always see her, she *may* be able to creep faster than I can turn! I have watched her sometimes away off in the open country, creeping as fast as a cloud shadow in a wind.

If only that top pattern could be gotten off from the under one! I mean to try it, little by little.

I have found out another funny thing, but I shan't tell it this time! It does not do to trust people too much.

There are only two more days to get this paper off, and I believe John is beginning to notice. I don't like the look in his eyes.

And I heard him ask Jennie a lot of professional questions about me. She had a very good report to give.

She said I slept a good deal in the daytime.

John knows I don't sleep very well at night, for all I'm so quiet!

He asked me all sorts of questions, too, and pretended to be very loving and kind.

As if I couldn't see through him!

Still, I don't wonder he acts so, sleeping under this paper for three months.

It only interests me, but I feel sure John and Jennie are affected by it.

Hurrah! This is the last day, but it is enough. John is to stay in town over night, and won't be out until this evening.

Jennie wanted to sleep with me—the sly thing, but I told her I should undoubtedly rest better for a night all alone.

That was clever, for really I wasn't alone a bit! As soon as it was moonlight and that poor thing began to crawl and shake the pattern, I got up and ran to help her.

I pulled and she shook, I shook and she pulled, and before morning we had peeled off yards of that paper.

A strip about as high as my head and half around the room.

And then when the sun came and that awful pattern began to laugh at me, I declared I would finish it today!

We go away tomorrow, and they are moving all my furniture down again to leave things as they were before.

Jennie looked at the wall in amazement, but I told her merrily that I did it out of pure spite at the vicious thing.

She laughed and said she wouldn't mind doing it herself, but I must not get tired.

How she betrayed herself that time!

But I am here, and no person touches this paper but Me—not *alive!*

She tried to get me out of the room—it was too patent! But I said it was so quiet and empty and clean now that I believed I would lie down again and sleep all I could; and not to wake me even for dinner—I would call when I woke.

So now she is gone, and the servants are gone, and the things are gone, and there is nothing left but that great bedstead nailed down, with the canvas mattress we found on it.

We shall sleep downstairs tonight, and take the boat home tomorrow.

I quite enjoy the room, now it is bare again.

How those children did tear about here!

This bedstead is fairly gnawed!

But I must get to work.

I have locked the door and thrown the key down into the front path.

I don't want to go out, and I don't want to have anybody come in, till John comes.

I want to astonish him.

I've got a rope up here that even Jennie did not find. If that woman does get out, and tries to get away, I can tie her!

But I forgot I could not reach far without anything to stand on!

This bed will *not* move!

I tried to lift and push it until I was lame, and then I got so angry I bit off a little piece at one corner—but it hurt my teeth.

Then I peeled off all the paper I could reach standing on the floor. It sticks horribly and the pattern just enjoys it! All those strangled heads and bulbous eyes and waddling fungus growths just shriek with derision!

I am getting angry enough to do something desperate. To jump out of the window would be admirable exercise, but the bars are too strong even to try.

Besides I wouldn't do it. Of course not. I know well enough that a step like that is improper and might be misconstrued.

I don't like to *look* out of the windows even—there are so many of those creeping women, and they creep so fast.

I wonder if they all come out of that wallpaper as I did?

But I am securely fastened now by my well-hidden rope—you don't get *me* out in the road there!

I suppose I shall have to get back behind the pattern when it comes night, and that is hard!

It is so pleasant to be out in this great room and creep around as I please!

I don't want to go outside. I won't, even if Jennie asks me to.

For outside you have to creep on the ground, and everything is green instead of yellow.

But here I can creep smoothly on the floor, and my shoulder just fits in that long smooch around the wall, so I cannot lose my way.

Why there's John at the door!

It is no use, young man, you can't open it!

How he does call and pound!

Now he's crying to Jennie for an axe.

It would be a shame to break down that beautiful door!

"John dear!" said I in the gentlest voice. "The key is down by the front steps, under a plantain leaf!"

That silenced him for a few moments.

Then he said—very quietly indeed, "Open the door, my darling!"

"I can't," said I. "The key is down by the front door under a plantain leaf!"

And then I said it again, several times, very gently and slowly, and said it so often that he had to go and see, and he got it of course, and came in. He stopped short by the door.

"What is the matter?" he cried. "For God's sake, what are you doing!"

I kept on creeping just the same, but I looked at him over my shoulder.

"I've got out at last," said I, "in spite of you and Jane! And I've pulled off most of the paper, so you can't put me back!"

Now why should that man have fainted? But he did, and right across my path by the wall, so that I had to creep over him every time!

1892

Nathaniel Hawthorne
1804–1864

"Young Goodman Brown" was not especially admired until the twentieth century, when it came to be recognized as one of America's best short stories. Its allegorical treatment of innocence and sin seems to anticipate Freud's descriptions of the psyche's repressed sexual impulses. In allegory, various figures stand for virtues and vices we each might possess: for example, Faith, Brown's wife, represents Brown's faith in God. The devil's proclamation, "This night it shall be granted you to know their secret deeds," perhaps also has a political dimension: its reference to the unacknowledged truths of our own history. Three of the women in the story were modeled after women actually accused of witchcraft in Salem, two of whom were executed in 1692. Goodman Brown's father and grandfather are based on Hawthorne's own ancestors: his great-great-grandfather had a Quaker woman stripped half-naked and roped to a cart that pulled her through the streets while a constable followed behind whipping her; another kinsmen burned an Indian village and, as magistrate, actually presided over some witch trials. In this sense, the allegory is not of our personal struggles between innocence and sin, but of our nation's struggle between justice and corruption.

Young Goodman Brown

Young Goodman Brown came forth at sunset into the street of Salem village,[1] but put his head back, after crossing the threshold, to exchange a parting kiss with his young wife. And Faith, as the wife was aptly named, thrust her own pretty head

---

1. Salem, Massachusetts, where the famous witch trials of 1692 took place. Goodman: title of respect for a man below the rank of gentleman.

into the street, letting the wind play with the pink ribbons of her cap while she called to Goodman Brown.

"Dearest heart," whispered she, softly and rather sadly, when her lips were close to his ear, "prithee put off your journey until sunrise and sleep in your own bed to-night. A lone woman is troubled with such dreams and such thoughts that she's afeard of herself sometimes. Pray tarry with me this night, dear husband, of all nights in the year!"

"My love and my Faith," replied young Goodman Brown, "of all nights in the year, this one night must I tarry away from thee. My journey, as thou callest it, forth and back again, must needs be done 'twixt now and sunrise. What, my sweet, pretty wife, dost thou doubt me already, and we but three months married?"

"Then God bless you!" said Faith, with the pink ribbons; "and may you find all well when you come back."

"Amen!" cried Goodman Brown. "Say thy prayers, dear Faith, and go to bed at dusk, and no harm will come to thee."

So they parted; and the young man pursued his way until, being about to turn the corner by the meeting-house, he looked back and saw the head of Faith still peeping after him with a melancholy air, in spite of her pink ribbons.

"Poor little Faith!" thought he, for his heart smote him. "What a wretch am I to leave her on such an errand! She talks of dreams, too. Methought as she spoke there was trouble in her face, as if a dream had warned her what work is to be done to-night. But no, no; 't would kill her to think it. Well, she's a blessed angel on earth; and after this one night I'll cling to her skirts and follow her to heaven."

With this excellent resolve for the future, Goodman Brown felt himself justified in making more haste on his present evil purpose. He had taken a dreary road, darkened by all the gloomiest trees of the forest, which barely stood aside to let the narrow path creep through, and closed immediately behind. It was all as lonely as could be; and there is this peculiarity in such a solitude, that the traveller knows not who may be concealed by the innumerable trunks and the thick boughs overhead; so that with lonely footsteps he may yet be passing through an unseen multitude.

"There may be a devilish Indian behind every tree," said Goodman Brown to himself; and he glanced fearfully behind him as he added, "What if the devil himself should be at my very elbow!"

His head being turned back, he passed a crook of the road, and, looking forward again, beheld the figure of a man, in grave and decent attire, seated at the foot of an old tree. He arose at Goodman Brown's approach and walked onward side by side with him.

"You are late, Goodman Brown," said he. "The clock of the Old South was striking as I came through Boston; and that is full fifteen minutes agone."[2]

"Faith kept me back a while," replied the young man, with a tremor in his voice, caused by the sudden appearance of his companion, though not wholly unexpected.

It was now deep dusk in the forest, and deepest in that part of it where these two were journeying. As nearly as could be discerned, the second traveller was about fifty years old, apparently in the same rank of life as Goodman Brown, and bearing a considerable resemblance to him, though perhaps more in expression than features. Still they might have been taken for father and son. And yet, though the elder person was as simply clad as the younger, and as simple in manner too, he had an indescribable air of one who knew the world, and would not have felt abashed at the governor's dinner table or in King William's[3] court, were it possible that his affairs should call him thither. But the only thing about him that could be fixed upon as remarkable was his staff, which bore the likeness of a great black snake, so curiously wrought that it might almost be seen to twist and wriggle itself like a living serpent. This, of course, must have been an ocular deception, assisted by the uncertain light.

"Come, Goodman Brown!" cried his fellow-traveller, "this is a dull pace for the beginning of a journey. Take my staff, if you are so soon weary."

"Friend," said the other, exchanging his slow pace for a full stop, "having kept covenant by meeting thee here it is my purpose now to return whence I came. I have scruples touching the matter thou wot'st[4] of."

---

2. Boston is some fifteen miles from Salem. This might indicate the supernatural speed of the speaker's travel.

3. King William III of England (ruled 1689–1702).

4. Know.

"Sayest thou so?" replied he of the serpent, smiling apart. "Let us walk on, nevertheless, reasoning as we go; and if I convince thee not thou shalt turn back. We are but a little way in the forest yet."

"Too far, too far!" exclaimed the goodman, unconsciously resuming his walk. "My father never went into the woods on such an errand, nor his father before him. We have been a race of honest men and good Christians since the days of the martyrs; and shall I be the first of the name of Brown that ever took this path and kept—"

"Such company, thou wouldst say," observed the elder person, interpreting his pause. "Well said, Goodman Brown! I have been as well acquainted with your family as with ever a one among the Puritans; and that's no trifle to say. I helped your grandfather, the constable, when he lashed the Quaker woman so smartly through the streets of Salem; and it was I that brought your father a pitch-pine knot, kindled at my own hearth, to set fire to an Indian village, in King Philip's war.[5] They were my good friends, both, and many a pleasant walk have we had along this path, and returned merrily after midnight. I would fain be friends with you for their sake."

"If it be as thou sayest," replied Goodman Brown, "I marvel they never spoke of these matters; or, verily, I marvel not, seeing that the least rumor of the sort would have driven them from New England. We are a people of prayer, and good works to boot, and abide no such wickedness."

"Wickedness or not," said the traveller with the twisted staff, "I have a very general acquaintance here in New England. The deacons of many a church have drunk the communion wine with me; the selectmen of divers towns make me their chairman; and a majority of the Great and General Court are firm supporters of my interest. The governor and I, too—But these are state secrets."

"Can this be so?" cried Goodman Brown, with a stare of amazement at his undisturbed companion. "Howbeit, I have nothing to do with the governor and council; they have their own ways, and are no rule for a simple husbandman like me. But, were I to go on with thee, how should I meet the eye of that good old man, our minister, at Salem village? Oh, his voice would make me tremble both Sabbath day and lecture day."

5. War between Native Americans and white settlers (1675–76).

Thus far the elder traveller had listened with due gravity; but now burst into a fit of irrepressible mirth, shaking himself so violently that his snake-like staff actually seemed to wriggle in sympathy.

"Ha! ha! ha!" shouted he again and again; then composing himself, "Well, go on, Goodman Brown, go on; but, prithee, don't kill me with laughing."

"Well, then, to end the matter at once," said Goodman Brown, considerably nettled, "there is my wife, Faith. It would break her dear little heart; and I'd rather break my own."

"Nay, if that be the case," answered the other, "e'en go thy ways, Goodman Brown. I would not for twenty old women like the one hobbling before us that Faith should come to any harm."

As he spoke he pointed his staff at a female figure on the path, in whom Goodman Brown recognized a very pious and exemplary dame, who had taught him his catechism in youth, and was still his moral and spiritual adviser, jointly with the minister and Deacon Gookin.

"A marvel, truly, that Goody[6] Cloyse should be so far in the wilderness at nightfall," said he. "But with your leave, friend, I shall take a cut through the woods until we have left this Christian woman behind. Being a stranger to you, she might ask whom I was consorting with and whither I was going."

"Be it so," said his fellow-traveller. "Betake you to the woods, and let me keep the path."

Accordingly the young man turned aside, but took care to watch his companion, who advanced softly along the road until he had come within a staff's length of the old dame. She, meanwhile was making the best of her way, with singular speed for so aged a woman, and mumbling some indistinct words—a prayer, doubt-less—as she went. The traveller put forth his staff and touched her withered neck with what seemed the serpent's tail.

"The devil!" screamed the pious old lady.

"Then Goody Cloyse knows her old friend?" observed the trav-eller, confronting her and leaning on his writhing stick.

"Ah, forsooth, and is it your worship indeed?" cried the good

6. Short for "goodwife," a title of respect for a married woman below the rank of lady.

dame. "Yea, truly is it, and in the very image of my old gossip,[7] Goodman Brown, the grandfather of the silly fellow that now is. But—would your worship believe it?—my broomstick hath strangely disappeared, stolen, as I suspect, by that unhanged witch, Goody Cory, and that, too when I was all anointed with the juice of smallage, and cinquefoil, and wolf's-bane—"[8]

"Mingled with fine wheat and the fat of a new-born babe," said the shape of old Goodman Brown.

"Ah, your worship knows the recipe," cried the old lady, cackling aloud. "So, as I was saying, being all ready for the meeting, and no horse to ride on, I made up my mind to foot it; for they tell me there is a nice young man to be taken into communion to-night. But now your good worship will lend me your arm, and we shall be there in a twinkling."

"That can hardly be," answered her friend. "I may not spare you my arm, Goody Cloyse; but here is my staff, if you will."

So saying, he threw it down at her feet, where, perhaps, it assumed life, being one of the rods which its owner had formerly lent to the Egyptian magi.[9] Of this fact, however, Goodman Brown could not take cognizance. He had cast up his eyes in astonishment, and, looking down again, beheld neither Goody Cloyse nor the serpentine staff, but this fellow-traveller alone, who waited for him as calmly as if nothing had happened.

"That old woman taught me my catechism," said the young man; and there was a world of meaning in this simple comment.

They continued to walk onward, while the elder traveller exhorted his companion to make good speed and persevere in the path, discoursing so aptly that his arguments seemed rather to spring up in the bosom of his auditor than to be suggested by himself. As they went he plucked a branch of maple, to serve for a walking stick, and began to strip it of the twigs and little boughs, which were wet with evening dew. The moment his fingers touched them

---

7. Friend.

8. Plants sometimes associated with witchcraft.

9. Reference to Exodus 7.8–12, in which God instructs Aaron to show Pharaoh a miracle by casting a rod before him, whereupon it will become a serpent. Pharaoh, in order to show that this is sorcery and not a miracle, has his magicians replicate the transformation. Hawthorne's line suggests that the rods used by the Egyptian magicians (magi) were lent to them by the devil.

they became strangely withered and dried up as with a week's sunshine. Thus the pair proceeded, at a good free pace, until suddenly, in a gloomy hollow of the road, Goodman Brown sat himself down on the stump of a tree and refused to go any farther.

"Friend," said he, stubbornly, "my mind is made up. Not another step will I budge on this errand. What if a wretched old woman do choose to go to the devil when I thought she was going to heaven: is that any reason why I should quit my dear Faith and go after her?"

"You will think better of this by and by," said his acquaintance, composedly. "Sit here and rest yourself a while; and when you feel like moving again, there is my staff to help you along."

Without more words, he threw his companion the maple stick, and was as speedily out of sight as if he had vanished into the deepening gloom. The young man sat a few moments by the roadside, applauding himself greatly, and thinking with how clear a conscience he should meet the minister in his morning walk, nor shrink from the eye of good old Deacon Gookin. And what calm sleep would be his that very night, which was to have been spent so wickedly, but so purely and sweetly now, in the arms of Faith! Amidst these pleasant and praiseworthy meditations, Goodman Brown heard the tramp of horses along the road, and deemed it advisable to conceal himself within the verge of the forest, conscious of the guilty purpose that had brought him thither, though now so happily turned from it.

On came the hoof tramps and the voices of the riders, two grave old voices, conversing soberly as they drew near. These mingled sounds appeared to pass along the road, within a few yards of the young man's hiding-place; but, owing doubtless to the depth of the gloom at that particular spot, neither the travellers nor their steeds were visible. Though their figures brushed the small boughs by the wayside, it could not be seen that they intercepted, even for a moment, the faint gleam from the strip of bright sky athwart which they must have passed. Goodman Brown alternately crouched and stood on tiptoe, pulling aside the branches and thrusting forth his head as far as he durst without discerning so much as a shadow. It vexed him the more, because he could have sworn, were such a thing possible, that he recognized the voices of the minister and Deacon Gookin, jogging along quietly, as they were wont to do, when bound to some ordination or ecclesiastical council. While yet within hearing, one of the riders stopped to pluck a switch.

"Of the two, reverend sir," said the voice like the deacon's, "I had rather miss an ordination dinner than to-night's meeting. They tell me that some of our community are to be here from Falmouth and beyond, and others from Connecticut and Rhode Island, besides several of the Indian powwows, who, after their fashion, know almost as much deviltry as the best of us. Moreover, there is a goodly young woman to be taken into communion."

"Mighty well, Deacon Gookin!" replied the solemn old tones of the minister. "Spur up, or we shall be late. Nothing can be done, you know, until I get on the ground."

The hoofs clattered again; and the voices, talking so strangely in the empty air, passed on through the forest, where no church had ever been gathered or solitary Christian prayed. Whither, then, could these holy men be journeying so deep into the heathen wilderness? Young Goodman Brown caught hold of a tree for support, being ready to sink down on the ground, faint and overburdened with the heavy sickness of his heart. He looked up to the sky, doubting whether there really was a heaven above him. Yet there was the blue arch, and the stars brightening in it.

"With heaven above and Faith below, I will yet stand firm against the devil!" cried Goodman Brown.

While he still gazed upward into the deep arch of the firmament and had lifted his hands to pray, a cloud, though no wind was stirring, hurried across the zenith and hid the brightening stars. The blue sky was still visible, except directly overhead, where this black mass of cloud was sweeping swiftly northward. Aloft in the air, as if from the depths of the cloud, came a confused and doubtful sound of voices. Once the listener fancied that he could distinguish the accents of towns-people of his own, men and women, both pious and ungodly, many of whom he had met at the communion table, and had seen others rioting at the tavern. The next moment, so indistinct were the sounds, he doubted whether he had heard aught but the murmur of the old forest, whispering without a wind. Then came a stronger swell of those familiar tones, heard daily in the sunshine at Salem village, but never until now from a cloud of night. There was one voice, of a young woman, uttering lamentations, yet with an uncertain sorrow, and entreating for some favor, which, perhaps, it would grieve her to obtain; and all the unseen multitude, both saints and sinners, seemed to encourage her onward.

"Faith!" shouted Goodman Brown, in a voice of agony and desperation; and the echoes of the forest mocked him, crying, "Faith! Faith!" as if bewildered wretches were seeking her all through the wilderness.

The cry of grief, rage, and terror was yet piercing the night, when the unhappy husband held his breath for a response. There was a scream, drowned immediately in a louder murmur of voices, fading into far-off laughter, as the dark cloud swept away, leaving the clear and silent sky above Goodman Brown. But something fluttered lightly down through the air and caught on the branch of a tree. The young man seized it, and beheld a pink ribbon.

"My Faith is gone!" cried he, after one stupefied moment. "There is no good on earth; and sin is but a name. Come, devil; for to thee is this world given."

And, maddened with despair, so that he laughed loud and long, did Goodman Brown grasp his staff and set forth again, at such a rate that he seemed to fly along the forest path rather than to walk or run. The road grew wilder and drearier and more faintly traced, and vanished at length, leaving him in the heart of the dark wilderness, still rushing onward with the instinct that guides mortal man to evil. The whole forest was peopled with frightful sounds—the creaking of the trees, the howling of wild beasts, and the yell of Indians; while sometimes the wind tolled like a distant church bell, and sometimes gave a broad roar around the traveller, as if all Nature were laughing him to scorn. But he was himself the chief horror of the scene, and shrank not from its other horrors.

"Ha! ha! ha!" roared Goodman Brown when the wind laughed at him. "Let us hear which will laugh loudest. Think not to frighten me with your deviltry. Come witch, come wizard, come Indian powwow, come devil himself, and here comes Goodman Brown. You may as well fear him as he fear you."

In truth, all through the haunted forest, there could be nothing more frightful than the figure of Goodman Brown. On he flew among the black pines, brandishing his staff with frenzied gestures, now giving vent to an inspiration of horrid blasphemy, and now shouting forth such laughter as set all the echoes of the forest laughing like demons around him. The fiend in his own shape is less hideous than when he rages in the breast of man. Thus sped the demoniac on his course, until, quivering among the trees, he saw a red light before him, as when the felled trunks and branches of a clearing have been set on fire, and throw up their lurid blaze against the sky, at the hour of midnight. He paused, in a lull of the tempest that had driven him onward, and heard the swell of what seemed a hymn, rolling solemnly from a distance with the weight of many voices. He knew the tune; it was a familiar one in the choir of the village meeting-house. The verse died heavily away, and was lengthened by a chorus, not of human voices, but of all the sounds of the benighted wilderness pealing in awful harmony together. Goodman Brown cried out, and his cry was lost to his own ear, by its unison with the cry of the desert.

In the interval of silence he stole forward until the light glared full upon his eyes. At one extremity of an open space, hemmed in by the dark wall of the forest, arose a rock, bearing some rude, natural resemblance either to an altar or a pulpit, and surrounded by four blazing pines, their tops aflame, their stems untouched, like candles at an evening meeting. The mass of foliage that had overgrown the summit of the rock was all on fire, blazing high into the night and fitfully illuminating the whole field. Each pendent twig and leafy festoon was in a blaze. As the red light arose and fell, a numerous congregation alternately shone forth, then disappeared in shadow, and again grew, as it were, out of the darkness, peopling the heart of the solitary woods at once.

"A grave and dark-clad company," quoth Goodman Brown.

In truth they were such. Among them, quivering to and fro between gloom and splendor, appeared faces that would be seen next day at the council board of the province, and others which, Sabbath after Sabbath, looked devoutly heavenward, and benignantly over the crowded pews, from the holiest pulpits in the land. Some affirm that the lady of the governor was there. At least there were high dames well known to her, and wives of honored husbands, and widows, a great multitude, and ancient maidens, all of excellent repute, and fair young girls, who trembled lest their mothers should espy them. Either the sudden gleams of light flashing over the obscure field bedazzled Goodman Brown, or he recognized a score of the church members of Salem village famous for their especial sanctity. Good old Deacon Gookin had arrived, and waited at the skirts of that venerable saint, his revered pastor. But, irreverently consorting with these grave, reputable, and pious people, these elders of the church, these chaste dames and dewy virgins, there were men of dissolute lives and women of spotted fame, wretches given over to all mean and filthy vice, and suspected even of horrid crimes. It was strange to see that the good shrank not from the wicked, nor were the sinners abashed by the saints. Scattered also among their pale-faced enemies were the Indian priests, or powwows, who had often scared their native forest with more hideous incantations than any known to English witchcraft.

"But where is Faith?" thought Goodman Brown; and, as hope came into his heart, he trembled.

Another verse of the hymn arose, a slow and mournful strain, such as the pious love, but joined to words which expressed all that our nature can conceive of sin, and darkly hinted at far more. Unfathomable to mere mortals is the lore of fiends. Verse after verse was sung, and still the chorus of the desert swelled between like the deepest tone of a mighty organ; and with the final peal of that dreadful anthem there came a sound, as if the roaring wind, the rushing streams, the howling beasts, and every other voice of the unconverted wilderness were mingling and according with the voice of guilty man in homage to the prince of all. The four blazing pines threw up a loftier flame, and obscurely discovered shapes and visages of horror on the smoke wreaths above the impious assembly. At the same moment the fire on the rock shot redly forth and formed a glowing arch above its base, where now appeared a figure. With reverence be it spoken, the apparition bore no slight similitude, both in garb and manner, to some grave divine of the New England churches.

"Bring forth the converts!" cried a voice that echoed through the field and rolled into the forest.

At the word, Goodman Brown stepped forth from the shadow of the trees and approached the congregation, with whom he felt a loathful brotherhood by the sympathy of all that was wicked in his heart. He could have well-nigh sworn that the shape of his own dead father beckoned him to advance, looking downward from a smoke wreath, while a woman, with dim features of despair, threw out her hand to warn him back. Was it his mother? But he had no power to retreat one step, nor to resist, even in thought, when the minister and good old Deacon Gookin seized his arms and led him to the blazing rock. Thither came also the slender form of a veiled female, led between Goody Cloyse, that pious teacher of the catechism, and Martha Carrier, who had received the devil's promise to be queen of hell. A rampant hag was she. And there stood the proselytes beneath the canopy of fire.

"Welcome, my children," said the dark figure, "to the communion of your race. Ye have found thus young your nature and your destiny. My children, look behind you!"

They turned; and flashing forth, as it were, in a sheet of flame, the fiend worshippers were seen; the smile of welcome gleamed darkly on every visage.

"There," resumed the sable form, "are all whom ye have reverenced from youth. Ye deemed them holier than yourselves, and shrank from your own sin, contrasting it with their lives of righteousness and prayerful aspirations heavenward. Yet here are they all in my worshipping assembly. This night it shall be granted you to know their secret deeds: how hoary-beared elders of the church have whispered wanton words to the young maids of their households; how many a woman, eager for widows' weeds, has given her husband a drink at bedtime and let him sleep his last sleep in her bosom; how beardless youths have made haste to inherit their fathers' wealth; and how fair damsels—blush not, sweet ones—have dug little graves in the garden, and bidden me, the sole guest, to an infant's funeral. By the sympathy of your human hearts for sin ye shall scent out all the places—whether in church, bed-chamber, street, field, or forest—where crime has been committed, and shall exult to behold the whole earth one stain of guilt, one mighty blood spot. Far more than this. It shall be yours to penetrate, in every bosom, the deep mystery of sin, the fountain of all wicked arts, and which inexhaustibly supplies more evil impulses than human power—than my power at its utmost—can make manifest in deeds. And now, my children, look upon each other."

They did so; and, by the blaze of the hell-kindled torches, the wretched man beheld his Faith, and the wife her husband, trembling before that unhallowed altar.

"Lo, there ye stand, my children," said the figure, in a deep and solemn tone, almost sad with its despairing awfulness, as if his once angelic nature could yet mourn for our miserable race. "Depending upon one another's hearts, ye had still hoped that virtue were not all a dream. Now are ye undeceived. Evil is the nature of mankind. Evil must be your only happiness. Welcome again, my children, to the communion of your race."

"Welcome," repeated the fiend worshippers, in one cry of despair and triumph.

And there they stood, the only poor, as it seemed, who were yet hesitating on the verge of wickedness in this dark world. A basin was hollowed, naturally, in the rock. Did it contain water, reddened by the lurid light? or was it blood? or, perchance, a liquid flame? Herein did the shape of evil dip his hand and prepare to lay the mark of baptism upon their foreheads, that they might be partakers of the mystery of sin, more conscious of the secret guilt of others, both in deed and thought, than they could now be of their own. The husband cast one look at his pale wife, and Faith at him. What polluted wretches would the next glance show them to each other, shuddering alike at what they disclosed and what they saw!

"Faith! Faith!" cried the husband, "look up to Heaven, and resist the wicked one."

Whether Faith obeyed he knew not. Hardly had he spoken when he found himself amid calm night and solitude, listening to a roar of the wind which died heavily away through the forest. He staggered against the rock and felt it chill and damp, while a hanging twig, that had been all on fire, besprinkled his cheek with the coldest dew.

The next morning young Goodman Brown came slowly into the street of Salem village, staring around him like a bewildered man. The good old minister was taking a walk along the graveyard, to get an appetite for breakfast and meditate his sermon, and bestowed a blessing, as he passed, on Goodman Brown. He shrank from the venerable saint as if to avoid an anathema. Old Deacon Gookin was at domestic worship, and the holy words of his prayer were heard through the open window. "What God doth the wizard pray to?"

quoth Goodman Brown. Goody Cloyse, that excellent old Christian, stood in the early sunshine, at her own lattice, catechizing a little girl who had brought her a pint of morning's milk. Goodman Brown snatched away the child as from the grasp of the fiend himself. Turning the corner by the meeting-house, he spied the head of Faith, with the pink ribbons, gazing anxiously forth, and bursting into such joy at sight of him that she skipped along the street and almost kissed her husband before the whole village. But Goodman Brown looked sternly and sadly into her face, and passed on without a greeting.

Had Goodman Brown fallen asleep in the forest, and only dreamed a wild dream of a witch-meeting?

Be it so if you will; but, alas! it was a dream of evil omen for young Goodman Brown. A stern, a sad, a darkly meditative, a distrustful, if not a desperate man did he become from the night of that fearful dream. On the Sabbath day, when the congregation were singing a holy psalm, he could not listen because an anthem of sin rushed loudly upon his ear and drowned all the blessed strain. When the minister spoke from the pulpit with power and fervid eloquence, and, with his hand on the open Bible, of the sacred truths of our religion, and of saint-like lives and triumphant deaths, and of future bliss or misery unutterable, then did Goodman Brown turn pale, dreading lest the roof should thunder down upon the gray blasphemer and his hearers. Often, awaking suddenly at midnight, he shrank from the bosom of Faith; and at morning or eventide, when the family knelt down at prayer, he scowled and muttered to himself, and gazed sternly at his wife, and turned away. And when he had lived long, and was borne to his grave a hoary corpse, followed by Faith, an aged woman, and children and grandchildren, a goodly procession, besides neighbors not a few, they carved no hopeful verse upon his tombstone, for his dying hour was gloom.

1835

Ernest Hemingway
1899–1961

> *Hemingway finished writing "Hills Like White Elephants" while on his honeymoon in France in May 1927. His second wife was Catholic, and Hemingway also considered himself to be Catholic at the time, which could be significant, given the subject matter of this story. Perhaps that's why he set the story in Spain, one of the most traditional and Catholic countries in Europe in the 1920s. Hemingway explained, "I met a girl in Prunier where I'd gone to eat oysters before lunch. I knew she'd had an abortion. I went over and we talked, not about that, but on the way home I thought of the story, skipped lunch, and spent that afternoon writing it." This anecdote exemplifies Hemingway's writing technique: what is said merely hints at and suggests the wealth of what is not said.*

Hills Like White Elephants

The hills across the valley of the Ebro[1] were long and white. On this side there was no shade and no trees and the station was between two lines of rails in the sun. Close against the side of the station there was the warm shadow of the building and a curtain, made of strings of bamboo beads, hung across the open door into the bar, to keep out flies. The American and the girl with him sat at a table in the shade, outside the building. It was very hot and the express from Barcelona would come in forty minutes. It stopped at this junction for two minutes and went on to Madrid.

"What should we drink?" the girl asked. She had taken off her hat and put it on the table.

"It's pretty hot," the man said.

"Let's drink beer."

"Dos cervezas," the man said into the curtain.

"Big ones?" a woman asked from the doorway.

"Yes. Two big ones."

The woman brought two glasses of beer and two felt pads. She

---

1. River in northern Spain.

put the felt pads and the beer glasses on the table and looked at the man and the girl. The girl was looking off at the line of hills. They were white in the sun and the country was brown and dry.

"They look like white elephants," she said.

"I've never seen one," the man drank his beer.

"No, you wouldn't have."

"I might have," the man said. "Just because you say I wouldn't have doesn't prove anything."

The girl looked at the bead curtain. "They've painted something on it," she said. "What does it say?"

"Anis del Toro. It's a drink."

"Could we try it?"

The man called "Listen" through the curtain. The woman came out from the bar.

"Four reales."[2]

"We want two Anis del Toro."

"With water?"

"Do you want it with water?"

"I don't know," the girl said. "Is it good with water?"

"It's all right."

"You want them with water?" asked the woman.

"Yes, with water."

"It tastes like licorice," the girl said and put the glass down.

"That's the way with everything."

"Yes," said the girl. "Everything tastes of licorice. Especially all the things you've waited so long for, like absinthe."

"Oh, cut it out."

"You started it," the girl said. "I was being amused. I was having a fine time."

"Well, let's try and have a fine time."

"All right. I was trying. I said the mountains looked like white elephants. Wasn't that bright?"

"That was bright."

"I wanted to try this new drink. That's all we do, isn't it—look at things and try new drinks?"

"I guess so."

2. Spanish coins.

The girl looked across at the hills.

"They're lovely hills," she said. "They don't really look like white elephants. I just meant the coloring of their skin through the trees."

"Should we have another drink?"

"All right."

The warm wind blew the bead curtain against the table.

"The beer's nice and cool," the man said.

"It's lovely," the girl said.

"It's really an awfully simple operation, Jig," the man said. "It's not really an operation at all."

The girl looked at the ground the table legs rested on.

"I know you wouldn't mind it, Jig. It's really not anything. It's just to let the air in."

The girl did not say anything.

"I'll go with you and I'll stay with you all the time. They just let the air in and then it's all perfectly natural."

"Then what will we do afterward?"

"We'll be fine afterward. Just like we were before."

"What makes you think so?"

"That's the only thing that bothers us. It's the only thing that's made us unhappy."

The girl looked at the bead curtain, put her hand out and took hold of two of the strings of beads.

"And you think then we'll be all right and be happy."

"I know we will. You don't have to be afraid. I've known lots of people that have done it."

"So have I," said the girl. "And afterward they were all so happy."

"Well," the man said, "if you don't want to you don't have to. I wouldn't have you do it if you didn't want to. But I know it's perfectly simple."

"And you really want to?"

"I think it's the best thing to do. But I don't want you to do it if you don't really want to."

"And if I do it you'll be happy and things will be like they were and you'll love me?"

"I love you now. You know I love you."

"I know. But if I do it, then it will be nice again if I say things are like white elephants, and you'll like it?"

"I'll love it. I love it now but I just can't think about it. You know how I get when I worry."

"If I do it you won't ever worry?"

"I won't worry about that because it's perfectly simple."

"Then I'll do it. Because I don't care about me."

"What do you mean?"

"I don't care about me."

"Well, I care about you."

"Oh, yes. But I don't care about me. And I'll do it and then everything will be fine."

"I don't want you to do it if you feel that way."

The girl stood up and walked to the end of the station. Across, on the other side, were fields of grain and trees along the banks of the Ebro. Far away, beyond the river, were mountains. The shadow of a cloud moved across the field of grain and she saw the river through the trees.

"And we could have all this," she said. "And we could have everything and every day we make it more impossible."

"What did you say?"

"I said we could have everything."

"We can have everything."

"No, we can't."

"We can have the whole world."

"No, we can't."

"We can go everywhere."

"No, we can't. It isn't ours any more."

"It's ours."

"No, it isn't. And once they take it away, you never get it back."

"But they haven't taken it away."

"We'll wait and see."

"Come on back in the shade," he said. "You mustn't feel that way."

"I don't feel any way," the girl said. "I just know things."

"I don't want you to do anything that you don't want to do—"

"Nor that isn't good for me," she said. "I know. Could we have another beer?"

"All right. But you've got to realize—"

"I realize," the girl said. "Can't we maybe stop talking?"

They sat down at the table and the girl looked across at the hills on the dry side of the valley and the man looked at her and at the table.

"You've got to realize," he said, "that I don't want you to do it if you don't want to. I'm perfectly willing to go through with it if it means anything to you."

"Doesn't it mean anything to you? We could get along."

"Of course it does. But I don't want anybody but you. I don't want any one else. And I know it's perfectly simple."

"Yes, you know it's perfectly simple."

"It's all right for you to say that, but I do know it."

"Would you do something for me now?"

"I'd do anything for you."

"Would you please please please please please please please stop talking?"

He did not say anything but looked at the bags against the wall of the station. There were labels on them from all the hotels where they had spent nights.

"But I don't want you to," he said, "I don't care anything about it."

"I'll scream," the girl said.

The woman came out through the curtains with two glasses of beer and put them down on the damp felt pads. "The train comes in five minutes," she said.

"What did she say?" asked the girl.

"That the train is coming in five minutes."

The girl smiled brightly at the woman, to thank her.

"I'd better take the bags over to the other side of the station," the man said. She smiled at him.

"All right. Then come back and we'll finish the beer."

He picked up the two heavy bags and carried them around the station to the other tracks. He looked up the tracks but could not see the train. Coming back, he walked through the barroom, where people waiting for the train were drinking. He drank an Anis at the bar and looked at the people. They were all waiting reasonably for the train. He went out through the bead curtain. She was sitting at the table and smiled at him.

"Do you feel better?" he asked.

"I feel fine," she said. "There's nothing wrong with me. I feel fine."

1927

O. Henry
1862–1910

> *O. Henry (born William Sidney Porter) wrote most of his stories for newspapers. Because his stories were so popular with common readers, newspapers competed to get his work, and so he always wrote under the pressure of deadlines. Sometimes he even paid friends for plots that he could then flesh out. He wrote "The Furnished Room" for a newspaper, the* World, *and he republished it in his 1906 collection,* Four Million. *A short preface explained the title: a socialite had remarked "that there were only 'Four Hundred' people in New York City who were really worth noticing." But O. Henry used "the census taker" to come up with a "larger estimate of human interest." Four million people lived in New York in 1900; each lived a story worthy of notice. As the preface advertised, O. Henry relished his reputation for ennobling the life of the unheralded and lowly. Critics in Soviet Russia valued his record of the effects of capitalism on the masses, and his fiction is still a touchstone of high versus low culture.*

The Furnished Room

Restless, shifting, fugacious as time itself is a certain vast bulk of the population of the red brick district of the lower West Side. Homeless, they have a hundred homes. They flit from furnished room to furnished room, transients forever—transients in abode, transients in heart and mind. They sing "Home, Sweet Home" in ragtime; they carry their *lares et penates*[1] in a bandbox; their vine is entwined about a picture hat; a rubber plant is their fig tree.

---

1. Cherished possessions of a family or household. Lares and Penates were household gods in ancient Rome.

Hence the houses of this district, having had a thousand dwellers, should have a thousand tales to tell, mostly dull ones, no doubt; but it would be strange if there could not be found a ghost or two in the wake of all these vagrant guests.

One evening after dark a young man prowled among these crumbling red mansions, ringing their bells. At the twelfth he rested his lean hand-baggage upon the step and wiped the dust from his hatband and forehead. The bell sounded faint and far away in some remote, hollow depths.

To the door of this, the twelfth house whose bell he had rung, came a housekeeper who made him think of an unwholesome, surfeited worm that had eaten its nut to a hollow shell and now sought to fill the vacancy with edible lodgers.

He asked if there was a room to let.

"Come in," said the housekeeper. Her voice came from her throat; her throat seemed lined with fur. "I have the third-floor back, vacant since a week back. Should you wish to look at it?"

The young man followed her up the stairs. A faint light from no particular source mitigated the shadows of the halls. They trod noiselessly upon a stair carpet that its own loom would have forsworn. It seemed to have become vegetable; to have degenerated in that rank, sunless air to lush lichen or spreading moss that grew in patches to the stair-case and was viscid under the foot like organic matter. At each turn of the stairs were vacant niches in the wall. Perhaps plants had once been set within them. If so they had died in that foul and tainted air. It may be that statues of the saints had stood there, but it was not difficult to conceive that imps and devils had dragged them forth in the darkness and down to the unholy depths of some furnished pit below.

"This is the room," said the housekeeper, from her furry throat. "It's a nice room. It ain't often vacant. I had some most elegant people in it last summer—no trouble at all, and paid in advance to the minute. The water's at the end of the hall. Sprowls and Mooney kept it three months. They done a vaudeville sketch. Miss B'retta Sprowls—you may have heard of her—Oh, that was just the stage names—right there over the dresser is where the marriage certificate hung, framed. The gas is here, and you see there is plenty of closet room. It's a room everybody likes. It never stays idle long."

"Do you have many theatrical people rooming here?" asked the young man.

"They comes and goes. A good proportion of my lodgers is connected with the theatres. Yes, sir, this is the theatrical district. Actor people never stays long anywhere. I get my share. Yes, they comes and they goes."

He engaged the room, paying for a week in advance. He was tired, he said, and would take possession at once. He counted out the money. The room had been made ready, she said, even to towels and water. As the housekeeper moved away he put, for the thousandth time, the question that he carried at the end of his tongue.

"A young girl—Miss Vashner—Miss Eloise Vashner—do you remember such a one among your lodgers? She would be singing on the stage, most likely. A fair girl, of medium height and slender, with reddish, gold hair and dark mole near her left eyebrow."

"No, I don't remember the name. Them stage people has names they change as often as their rooms. They comes and they goes. No, I don't call that one to mind."

No. Always no. Five months of ceaseless interrogation and the inevitable negative. So much time spent by day in questioning managers, agents, schools and choruses; by night among the audiences of theatres from all-star casts down to music halls so low that he dreaded to find what he most hoped for. He who had loved her best had tried to find her. He was sure that since her disappearance from home this great, water-girt city held her somewhere, but it was like a monstrous quicksand, shifting its particles constantly, with no foundation, its upper granules of to-day buried to-morrow in ooze and slime.

The furnished room received its latest guest with a first glow of pseudo-hospitality, a hectic, haggard, perfunctory welcome like the specious smile of a demirep.[2] The sophistical comfort came in reflected gleams from the decayed furniture, the ragged brocade upholstery of a couch and two chairs, a foot-wide cheap pier-glass between the two windows, from one or two gilt picture frames and a brass bedstead in a corner.

The guest reclined, inert, upon a chair, while the room, confused

---

2. A woman of doubtful or compromised reputation, often a prostitute.

in speech as though it were an apartment in Babel,[3] tried to discourse to him of its divers tenantry.

A polychromatic rug like some brilliant-flowered, rectangular, tropical islet lay surrounded by a billowy sea of soiled matting. Upon the gay-papered wall were those pictures that pursue the homeless one from house to house—The Huguenot Lovers, The First Quarrel, The Wedding Breakfast, Psyche at the Fountain. The mantel's chastely severe outline was ingloriously veiled behind some pert drapery drawn rakishly askew like the sashes of the Amazonian ballet. Upon it was some desolate flotsam cast aside by the room's marooned when a lucky sail had borne them to a fresh port—a trifling vase or two, pictures of actresses, a medicine bottle, some stray cards out of a deck.

One by one, as the characters of a cryptograph became explicit, the little signs left by the furnished room's procession of guests developed a significance. The threadbare space in the rug in front of the dresser told that lovely women had marched in the throng. The tiny fingerprints on the wall spoke of little prisoners trying to feel their way to sun and air. A splattered stain, raying like the shadow of a bursting bomb, witnessed where a hurled glass or bottle had splintered with its contents against the wall. Across the pier-glass had been scrawled with a diamond in staggering letters the name "Marie." It seemed that the succession of dwellers in the furnished room had turned in fury—perhaps tempted beyond forbearance by its garish coldness—and wreaked upon it their passions. The furniture was chipped and bruised; the couch, distorted by bursting springs, seemed a horrible monster that had been slain during the stress of some grotesque convulsion. Some more potent upheaval had cloven a great slice from the marble mantel. Each plank in the floor owned its particular cant and shriek as from a separate and individual agony. It seemed incredible that all this malice and injury had been wrought upon the room by those who had called it for a time their home; and yet it may have been the cheated home instinct surviving blindly, the resentful rage at false household gods

---

3. The biblical Tower of Babel was built to reach heaven. God punished its builders by changing the one language of the world into several different languages so people would not understand one another (Genesis 11.1–9).

that had kindled their wrath. A hut that is our own we can sweep and adorn and cherish.

The young tenant in the chair allowed these thoughts to file, soft-shod, through his mind, while there drifted into the room furnished sounds and furnished scents. He heard in one room a tittering and incontinent, slack laughter; in others the monologue of a scold, the rattling of dice, a lullaby, and one crying dully; above him a banjo tinkled with spirit. Doors banged somewhere; the elevated trains roared intermittently; a cat yowled miserably upon a back fence. And he breathed the breath of the house—a dank savor rather than a smell—a cold, musty effluvium as from underground vaults mingled with the reeking exhalations of linoleum and mildewed and rotten woodwork.

Then suddenly, as he rested there, the room was filled with the strong, sweet odor of mignonette.[4] It came as upon a single buffet of wind with such sureness and fragrance and emphasis that it almost seemed a living visitant. And the man cried aloud: "What, dear?" as if he had been called, and sprang up and faced about. The rich odor clung to him and wrapped him around. He reached out his arms for it, all his senses for the time confused and commingled. How could one be peremptorily called by an odor? Surely it must have been a sound. But, was it not the sound that had touched, that had caressed him?

"She has been in this room," he cried, and he sprang to wrest from it a token, for he knew he would recognize the smallest thing that had belonged to her or that she had touched. This enveloping scent of mignonette, the odor that she had loved and made her own—whence came it?

The room had been but carelessly set in order. Scattered upon the flimsy dresser scarf were half a dozen hairpins—those discreet, indistinguishable friends of womankind, feminine of gender, infinite of mood and uncommunicative of tense. These he ignored, conscious of their triumphant lack of identity. Ransacking the drawers of the dresser he came upon a discarded, tiny, ragged handkerchief. He pressed it to his face. It was racy and insolent with

4. A perfume sold by Sears Roebuck at the turn of the twentieth century; the fragrance was meant to resemble that of the greenish flower of the same name.

heliotrope;[5] he hurled it to the floor. In another drawer he found odd buttons, a theatre programme, a pawnbroker's card, two lost marshmallows, a book on the divination of dreams. In the last was a woman's black satin hair bow, which halted him, poised between ice and fire. But the black satin hair bow also is feminity's demure, impersonal common ornament and tells no tales.

And then he traversed the room like a hound on the scent, skimming the walls, considering the corners of the bulging matting on his hands and knees, rummaging mantel and tables, the curtains and hangings, the drunken cabinet in the corner, for a visible sign, unable to perceive that she was there beside, around, against, within, above him, clinging to him, wooing him, calling him so poignantly through the finer senses that even his grosser ones became cognizant of the call. Once again he answered loudly: "Yes, dear!" and turned, wild-eyed, to gaze on vacancy, for he could not yet discern form and color and love and outstretched arms in the odor of mignonette. Oh, God! whence that odor, and since when have odors had a voice to call? Thus he groped.

He burrowed in crevices and corners, and found corks and cigarettes. These he passed in passive contempt. But once he found in a fold of the matting a half-smoked cigar, and this he ground beneath his heel with a green and trenchant oath. He sifted the room from end to end. He found dreary and ignoble small records of many a peripatetic tenant; but of her whom he sought, and who may have lodged there, and whose spirit seemed to hover there, he found no trace.

And then he thought of the housekeeper.

He ran from the haunted room downstairs and to a door that showed a crack of light. She came out to his knock. He smothered his excitement as best he could.

"Will you tell me, madam," he besought her, "who occupied the room I have before I came?"

"Yes, sir. I can tell you again. 'Twas Sprowls and Mooney, as I said. Miss B'retta Sprowls it was in the theatres, but Missis Mooney she was. My house is well known for respectability. The marriage certificate hung, framed, on a nail over——"

---

5. A fragrance meant to imitate the scent of the purplish flowers of the same name.

"What kind of a lady was Miss Sprowls—in looks, I mean?"

"Why, black-haired, sir, short, and stout, with a comical face. They left a week ago Tuesday."

"And before they occupied it?"

"Why, there was a single gentleman connected with the draying[6] business. He left owing me a week. Before him was Missis Crowder and her two children, that stayed four months; and back of them was old Mr. Doyle, whose sons paid for him. He kept the room six months. That goes back a year, sir, and further I do not remember."

He thanked her and crept back to his room. The room was dead. The essence that had vivified it was gone. The perfume of mignonette had departed. In its place was the old, stale odor of mouldy house furniture, of atmosphere in storage.

The ebbing of his hope drained his faith. He sat staring at the yellow, singing gaslight. Soon he walked to the bed and began to tear the sheets into strips. With the blade of his knife he drove them tightly into every crevice around windows and door. When all was snug and taut he turned out the light, turned the gas full on again and laid himself gratefully upon the bed.

It was Mrs. McCool's night to go with the can for beer. So she fetched it and sat with Mrs. Purdy in one of those subterranean retreats where housekeepers foregather and the worm dieth seldom.

"I rented out my third-floor-back this evening," said Mrs. Purdy, across a fine circle of foam. "A young man took it. He went up to bed two hours ago."

"Now, did ye, Mrs. Purdy, ma'am?" said Mrs. McCool, with intense admiration. "You do be a wonder for rentin' rooms of that kind. And did ye tell him, then?" she concluded in a husky whisper laden with mystery.

"Rooms," said Mrs. Purdy, in her furriest tones, "are furnished for to rent. I did not tell him, Mrs. McCool."

" 'Tis right ye are, ma'am; 'tis by renting rooms we kape alive. Ye have the rale sense for business, ma'am. There be many people will rayjict the rentin' of a room if they be tould a suicide has been after dyin' in the bed of it."

6. Hauling.

"As you say, we has our living to be making," remarked Mrs.
Purdy.

"Yis, ma'am; 'tis true. 'Tis just one wake ago this day I helped ye
lay out the third-floor-back. A pretty slip of a colleen she was to be
killin' herself wid the gas—a swate little face she had, Mrs. Purdy,
ma'am."

"She'd a-been called handsome, as you say," said Mrs. Purdy, as-
senting but critical, "but for that mole she had a-growin' by her left
eyebrow. Do fill up your glass again, Mrs. McCool."

1904

James Joyce
1882–1941

*Joyce wrote "Araby" in September 1905 while living in Trieste. That
year he had left Ireland to find a less restrictive atmosphere on the
Continent. Ireland, he felt, was paralyzed by a combination of
Catholic ideology and British imperial capitalism, and he wrote
this story and the fourteen others that make up* Dubliners *in order
to give his Irish readers "one good look at themselves in my nicely
polished looking-glass." By comparing his stories to a mirror, Joyce
put them in the category of realism—literature that tries to faith-
fully mirror reality, often to expose to readers some defect in themselves or society. But critics often point to the highly literary
character of "Araby," which compares the narrator's trip to the
bazaar to a romantic quest. The narrator's experience at the conclusion is a fine example of an* epiphany, *a literary term Joyce
invented. An epiphany, according to Joyce, is "a sudden spiritual
manifestation" revealed usually in some mundane or seemingly
trivial gesture or phrase.*

Araby

Northworth Richmond Street, being blind,[1] was a quiet street except at the hour when the Christian Brothers'[2] School set the boys free. An uninhabited house of two storeys stood at the blind end, detached from its neighbours in a square ground. The other houses of the street, conscious of decent lives within them, gazed at one another with brown imperturbable faces.

The former tenant of our house, a priest, had died in the back drawing-room. Air, musty from having been long enclosed, hung in all the rooms, and the waste room behind the kitchen was littered with old useless papers. Among these I found a few paper-covered books, the pages of which were curled and damp: *The Abbot*, by Walter Scott, *The Devout Communicant* and *The Memoirs of Vidocq*. I liked the last best because its leaves were yellow. The wild garden behind the house contained a central apple-tree and a few straggling bushes under one of which I found the late tenant's rusty bicycle-pump. He had been a very charitable priest; in his will he had left all his money to institutions and the furniture of his house to his sister.

When the short days of winter came dusk fell before we had well eaten our dinners. When we met in the street the houses had grown sombre. The space of sky above us was the colour of ever-changing violet and towards it the lamps of the street lifted their feeble lanterns. The cold air stung us and we played till our bodies glowed. Our shouts echoed in the silent street. The career of our play brought us through the dark muddy lanes behind the houses where we ran the gantlet of the rough tribes from the cottages, to the back doors of the dark dripping gardens where odours arose from the ashpits, to the dark odorous stables where a coachman smoothed and combed the horse or shook music from the buckled harness. When we returned to the street light from the kitchen windows had filled the areas. If my uncle was seen turning the corner we hid in the shadow until we had seen him safely housed. Or if Mangan's sister came out on the doorstep to call her brother in to his tea we

1. A dead end.

2. A Roman Catholic order that catered to the poor.

watched her from our shadow peer up and down the street. We waited to see whether she would remain or go in and, if she remained, we left our shadow and walked up to Mangan's steps resignedly. She was waiting for us, her figure defined by the light from the half-opened door. Her brother always teased her before he obeyed and I stood by the railings looking at her. Her dress swung as she moved her body and the soft rope of her hair tossed from side to side.

Every morning I lay on the floor in the front parlour watching her door. The blind was pulled down to within an inch of the sash so that I could not be seen. When she came out on the doorstep my heart leaped, I ran to the hall, seized my books and followed her. I kept her brown figure always in my eye and, when we came near the point at which our ways diverged, I quickened my pace and passed her. This happened morning after morning. I had never spoken to her, except for a few casual words, and yet her name was like a summons to all my foolish blood.

Her image accompanied me even in places the most hostile to romance. On Saturday evenings when my aunt went marketing I had to go to carry some of the parcels. We walked through the flaring streets, jostled by drunken men and bargaining women, amid the curses of labourers, the shrill litanies of shop-boys who stood on guard by the barrels of pigs' cheeks, the nasal chanting of street-singers, who sang a *come-all-you* about O'Donovan Rossa,[3] or a ballad about the troubles in our native land. These noises converged in a single sensation of life for me: I imagined that I bore my chalice safely through a throng of foes. Her name sprang to my lips at moments in strange prayers and praises which I myself did not understand. My eyes were often full of tears (I could not tell why) and at times a flood from my heart seemed to pour itself out into my bosom. I thought little of the future. I did not know whether I would ever speak to her or not or, if I spoke to her, how I could tell her of my confused adoration. But my body was like a harp and her words and gestures were like fingers running upon the wires.

3. Jeremiah O'Donovan ("Dynamite Rossa") (1831–1915) was a member of the Fenians, who were precursors to the present-day Irish Republican Army. O'Donovan Rossa was banished from Ireland, but a number of nationalist ballads (which often began with the words "Come all you . . .") kept his anti-English exploits in the popular imagination.

One evening I went into the back drawing-room in which the priest had died. It was a dark rainy evening and there was no sound in the house. Through one of the broken panes I heard the rain impinge upon the earth, the fine incessant needles of water playing in the sodden beds. Some distant lamp or lighted window gleamed below me. I was thankful that I could see so little. All my senses seemed to desire to veil themselves and, feeling that I was about to slip from them, I pressed the palms of my hands together until they trembled, murmuring: *O love! O love!* many times.

At last she spoke to me. When she addressed the first words to me I was so confused that I did not know what to answer. She asked me was I going to *Araby*.[4] I forget whether I answered yes or no. It would be a splendid bazaar, she said; she would love to go.

—And why can't you? I asked.

While she spoke she turned a silver bracelet round and round her wrist. She could not go, she said, because there would be a retreat[5] that week in her convent. Her brother and two other boys were fighting for their caps and I was alone at the railings. She held one of the spikes, bowing her head towards me. The light from the lamp opposite our door caught the white curve of her neck, lit up her hair that rested there and, falling, lit up the hand upon the railing. It fell over one side of her dress and caught the white border of a petticoat, just visible as she stood at ease.

—It's well for you, she said.

—If I go, I said, I will bring you something.

What innumerable follies laid waste my waking and sleeping thoughts after that evening! I wished to annihilate the tedious intervening days. I chafed against the work of school. At night in my bedroom and by day in the classroom her image came between me and the page I strove to read. The syllables of the word *Araby* were called to me through the silence in which my sould luxuriated and cast an Eastern enchantment over me. I asked for leave to go to the bazaar on Saturday night. My aunt was surprised and hoped it

4. When Joyce was a boy, a charity bazaar called "Araby" did visit Dublin. Admission was one shilling.

5. A special gathering for prayer and moral instruction. The "convent" is a Catholic school.

was not some Freemason affair.[6] I answered few questions in class. I watched my master's face pass from amiability to sternness; he hoped I was not beginning to idle. I could not call my wandering thoughts together. I had hardly any patience with the serious work of life which, now that it stood between me and my desire, seemed to me child's play, ugly monotonous child's play.

On Saturday morning I reminded my uncle that I wished to go to the bazaar in the evening. He was fussing at the hallstand, looking for the hat-brush, and answered me curtly:

—Yes, boy, I know.

As he was in the hall I could not go into the front parlour and lie at the window. I left the house in bad humour and walked slowly towards the school. The air was pitilessly raw and already my heart misgave me.

When I came home to dinner my uncle had not yet been home. Still it was early. I sat staring at the clock for some time and, when its ticking began to irritate me, I left the room. I mounted the staircase and gained the upper part of the house. The high cold empty gloomy rooms liberated me and I went from room to room singing. From the front window I saw my companions playing below in the street. Their cries reached me weakened and indistinct and, leaning my forehead against the cool glass, I looked over at the dark house where she lived. I may have stood there for an hour, seeing nothing but the brown-clad figure cast by my imagination, touched discreetly by the lamplight at the curved neck, at the hand upon the railings and at the border below the dress.

When I came downstairs again I found Mrs. Mercer sitting at the fire. She was an old garrulous woman, a pawnbroker's widow, who collected used stamps for some pious purpose. I had to endure the gossip of the tea-table. The meal was prolonged beyond an hour and still my uncle did not come. Mrs. Mercer stood up to go: she was sorry she couldn't wait any longer, but it was after eight o'clock and she did not like to be out late, as the night air was bad for her. When she had gone I began to walk up and down the room, clenching my fists. My aunt said:

---

6. The Masons were a quasi-religious, semi-secret society devoted to, among other things, the demise of Roman Catholicism.

—I'm afraid you may put off your bazaar for this night of Our Lord.

At nine o'clock I heard my uncle's latchkey in the halldoor. I heard him talking to himself and heard the hallstand rocking when it had received the weight of his overcoat. I could interpret these signs. When he was midway through his dinner I asked him to give me the money to go to the bazaar. He had forgotten.

—The people are in bed and after their first sleep now, he said.

I did not smile. My aunt said to him energetically:

—Can't you give him the money and let him go? You've kept him late enough as it is.

My uncle said he was very sorry he had forgotten. He said he believed in the old saying: *All work and no play makes Jack a dull boy.* He asked me where I was going and, when I had told him a second time he asked me did I know *The Arab's Farewell to his Steed.*[7] When I left the kitchen he was about to recite the opening lines of the piece to my aunt.

I held a florin[8] tightly in my hand as I strode down Buckingham Street towards the station. The sight of the streets thronged with buyers and glaring with gas recalled to me the purpose of my journey. I took my seat in a third-class carriage of a deserted train. After an intolerable delay the train moved out of the station slowly. It crept onward among ruinous houses and over the twinkling river. At Westland Row Station a crowd of people pressed to the carriage doors; but the porters moved them back, saying that it was a special train for the bazaar. I remained alone in the bare carriage. In a few minutes the train drew up beside an improvised wooden platform. I passed out on to the road and saw by the lighted dial of a clock that it was ten minutes to ten. In front of me was a large building which displayed the magical name.

I could not find any sixpenny entrance and, fearing that the bazaar would be closed, I passed in quickly through a turnstile, handing a shilling to a weary-looking man. I found myself in a big hall girdled at half its height by a gallery. Nearly all the stalls were

7. Sentimental poem by Caroline Norton (1808–1877), in which an Arab boy sells his horse, but as the horse is being led away, changes his mind and runs after the man he sold it to in order to return the money and reclaim his love.

8. British coin worth two shillings.

closed and the greater part of the hall was in darkness. I recognised a silence like that which pervades a church after a service. I walked into the centre of the bazaar timidly. A few people were gathered about the stalls which were still open. Before a curtain, over which the words *Café Chantant*[9] were written in coloured lamps, two men were counting money on a salver. I listened to the fall of the coins.

Remembering with difficulty why I had come I went over to one of the stalls and examined porcelain vases and flowered tea-sets. At the door of the stall a young lady was talking and laughing with two young gentlemen. I remarked their English accents and listened vaguely to their conversation.

—O, I never said such a thing!

—O, but you did!

—O, but I didn't!

—Didn't she say that?

—Yes. I heard her.

—O, there's a . . . fib!

Observing me the young lady came over and asked me did I wish to buy anything. The tone of her voice was not encouraging; she seemed to have spoken to me out of a sense of duty. I looked humbly at the great jars that stood like eastern guards at either side of the dark entrance to the stall and murmured:

—No, thank you.

The young lady changed the position of one of the vases and went back to the two young men. They began to talk of the same subject. Once or twice the young lady glanced at me over her shoulder.

I lingered before her stall, though I knew my stay was useless, to make my interest in her wares seem the more real. Then I turned away slowly and walked down the middle of the bazaar. I allowed the two pennies to fall against the sixpence in my pocket. I heard a voice call from one end of the gallery that the light was out. The upper part of the hall was now completely dark.

Gazing up into the darkness I saw myself as a creature driven and derided by vanity; and my eyes burned with anguish and anger.

1904

---

9. Singing Café (French), a café offering musical entertainment.

Franz Kafka
1883–1924

> *Kafka wrote this story in February 1922, when he was suffering
> from tuberculosis and a depression that manifested itself in insom-
> nia and extreme fatigue. But the physical deterioration of the cen-
> tral figure in this story goes well beyond Kafka's own physical
> condition. In fact, you have to suspend disbelief to enjoy Kafka's sto-
> ries, which tend toward allegory. Many critics believe that the
> hunger artist stands for artists in general and that the story depicts
> Kafka's relation to his own audiences. Kafka was what we would
> today call a "modernist." Modernism produced a refined and intel-
> lectual style that often alienated the artist from general readers by
> pursuing as its goal art for art's sake, rather than art that edifies so-
> ciety. At the same time, modernists criticized the banality of Euro-
> pean life after World War I—especially the life of the middle
> class—and made artists the heroes of their fiction, at least in so
> much as their alienated, self-sacrificing, doomed protagonists can
> be called "heroes."*

A Hunger Artist[1]

During these last decades the interest in professional fasting
has markedly diminished. It used to pay very well to stage
such great performances under one's own management, but
today that is quite impossible. We live in a different world now. At
one time the whole town took a lively interest in the hunger artist;
from day to day of his fast the excitement mounted; everybody
wanted to see him at least once a day; there were people who
bought season tickets for the last few days and sat from morning till
night in front of his small barred cage; even in the nighttime there
were visiting hours, when the whole effect was heightened by torch
flares; on fine days the cage was set out in the open air, and then it
was the children's special treat to see the hunger artist; for their elders he was often just a joke that happened to be in fashion, but the

---

1. Translated by Edwin and Willa Muir.

children stood open-mouthed, holding each other's hands for greater security, marveling at him as he sat there pallid in black tights, with his ribs sticking out so prominently, not even on a seat but down among straw on the ground, sometimes giving a courteous nod, answering questions with a constrained smile, or perhaps stretching an arm through the bars so that one might feel how thin it was, and then again withdrawing deep into himself, paying no attention to anyone or anything, not even to the all-important striking of the clock that was the only piece of furniture in his cage, but merely staring into vacancy with half shut eyes, now and then taking a sip from a tiny glass of water to moisten his lips.

Besides casual onlookers there were also relays of permanent watchers selected by the public, usually butchers, strangely enough, and it was their task to watch the hunger artist day and night, three of them at a time, in case he should have some secret recourse to nourishment. This was nothing but a formality, instituted to reassure the masses, for the initiates knew well enough that during his fast the artist would never in any circumstances, not even under forcible compulsion, swallow the smallest morsel of food: the honor of his profession forbade it. Not every watcher, of course, was capable of understanding this, there were often groups of night watchers who were very lax in carrying out their duties and deliberately huddled together in a retired corner to play cards with great absorption, obviously intending to give the hunger artist the chance of a little refreshment, which they supposed he could draw from some private hoard. Nothing annoyed the artist more than such watchers; they made him miserable; they made his fast seem unendurable; sometimes he mastered his feebleness sufficiently to sing during their watch for as long as he could keep going, to show them how unjust their suspicions were. But that was of little use; they only wondered at his cleverness in being able to fill his mouth even while singing. Much more to his taste were the watchers who sat close up to the bars, who were not content with the dim night lighting of the hall but focused him in the full glare of the electric pocket torch given them by the impresario.[2] The harsh light did not trouble him at all, in any case he could never sleep properly, and he could always

2. Promoter and manager of an entertainment.

drowse a little, whatever the light, at any hour, even when the hall was thronged with noisy onlookers. He was quite happy at the prospect of spending a sleepless night with such watchers; he was ready to exchange jokes with them, to tell them stories out of his nomadic life, anything at all to keep them awake and demonstrate to them again that he had no eatables in his cage and that he was fasting as not one of them could fast. But his happiest moment was when the morning came and an enormous breakfast was brought them, at his expense, on which they flung themselves with the keen appetite of healthy men after a weary night of wakefulness. Of course there were people who argued that this breakfast was an unfair attempt to bribe the watchers, but that was going rather too far, and when they were invited to take on a night's vigil without a breakfast, merely for the sake of the cause, they made themselves scarce, although they stuck stubbornly to their suspicions.

Such suspicions, anyhow, were a necessary accompaniment to the profession of fasting. No one could possibly watch the hunger artist continuously, day and night, and so no one could produce first-hand evidence that the fast had really been rigorous and continuous; only the artist himself could know that, he was therefore bound to be the sole completely satisfied spectator of his own fast. Yet for other reasons he was never satisfied; it was not perhaps mere fasting that had brought him to such skeleton thinness that many people had regretfully to keep away from his exhibitions, because the sight of him was too much for them, perhaps it was dissatisfaction with himself that had worn him down. For he alone knew, what no other initiate knew, how easy it was to fast. It was the easiest thing in the world. He made no secret of this, yet people did not believe him, at the best they set him down as modest, most of them, however, thought he was out for publicity or else was some kind of cheat who found it easy to fast because he had discovered a way of making it easy, and then had the impudence to admit the fact, more or less. He had to put up with all that, and in the course of time had got used to it, but his inner dissatisfaction always rankled, and never yet, after any term of fasting—this must be granted to his credit— had he left the cage of his own free will. The longest period of fasting was fixed by his impresario at forty days, beyond that term he was not allowed to go, not even in great cities, and there was good reason for it, too. Experience had proved that for about forty days the interest of the public could be stimulated by a steadily increasing pressure of advertisement, but after that the town began to lose interest, sympathetic support began notably to fall off; there were of course local variations as between one town and another or one country and another, but as a general rule forty days marked the limit. So on the fortieth day the flower-bedecked cage was opened, enthusiastic spectators filled the hall, a military band played, two doctors entered the cage to measure the results of the fast, which were announced through a megaphone, and finally two young ladies appeared, blissful at having been selected for the honor, to help the hunger artist down the few steps leading to a small table on which was spread a carefully chosen invalid repast. And at this very moment the artist always turned stubborn. True, he would entrust his bony arms to the outstretched helping hands of the ladies bending over him, but stand up he would not. Why stop fasting at this particular moment, after forty days of it? He had held out for a long time, an illimitably long time; why stop now, when he was in his best fasting form, or rather, not yet quite in his best fasting form? Why should he be cheated of the fame he would get for fasting longer, for being not only the record hunger artist of all time, which presumably he was already, but for beating his own record by a performance beyond human imagination, since he felt that there were no limits to his capacity for fasting? His public pretended to admire him so much, why should it have so little patience with him; if he could endure fasting longer, why shouldn't the public endure it? Besides, he was tired, he was comfortable sitting in the straw, and now he was supposed to lift himself to his full height and go down to a meal the very thought of which gave him a nausea that only the presence of the ladies kept him from betraying, and even that with an effort. And he looked up into the eyes of the ladies who were apparently so friendly and in reality so cruel, and shook his head, which felt too heavy on its strengthless neck. But then there happened yet again what always happened. The impresario came forward, without a word—for the band made speech impossible—lifted his arms in the air above the artist, as if inviting Heaven to look down upon its creature here in the straw, this suffering martyr, which indeed he was, although in quite another sense; grasped him round the emaciated waist, with exaggerated caution, so that the frail condition he was in might be appreciated; and committed him to the care of the blenching[3] ladies, not without secretly giving him a shaking so that his legs and body tottered and swayed. The artist now submitted completely; his head lolled on his breast as if it had landed there by chance; his body was hollowed out; his legs in a spasm of self-preservation clung close to each other at the knees, yet scraped on the ground as if it were not really solid ground, as if they were only trying to find solid ground; and the whole weight of his body, a feather-weight after all, relapsed onto one of the ladies, who, looking round for help and panting a little—this post of honor was not at all what she had expected it to be—first stretched her neck as far as she could to keep her face at least free from contact with the artist, when finding this impossible, and her more fortunate companion not coming to her aid but merely holding extended on her own trembling hand the little bunch of knucklebones that was the artist's, to the great delight of the spectators burst into tears and had to be replaced by an attendant who had long been stationed in readiness. Then came the food, a little of which the impresario managed to get between the artist's lips, while he sat in a kind of half-fainting trance, to the accompaniment of cheerful patter designed to distract the public's attention from the artist's condition; after that, a toast was drunk to the public, supposedly prompted by a whisper from the artist in the impresario's ear; the band confirmed it with a mighty flourish, the spectators melted away, and no one had any cause to be dissatisfied with the proceedings, no one except the hunger artist himself, he only, as always.

So he lived for many years, with small regular intervals of recuperation, in visible glory, honored by the world, yet in spite of that troubled in spirit, and all the more troubled because no one would take his trouble seriously. What comfort could he possibly need? What more could he possibly wish for? And if some good-natured person, feeling sorry for him, tried to console him by pointing out that his melancholy was probably caused by fasting, it could happen, especially when he had been fasting for some time, that he reacted with an outburst of fury and to the general alarm began to

3. Flinching, shrinking back.

shake the bars of his cage like a wild animal. Yet the impresario had a way of punishing these outbreaks which he rather enjoyed putting into operation. He would apologize publicly for the artist's behavior, which was only to be excused, he admitted, because of the irritability caused by fasting; a condition hardly to be understood by well-fed people; then by natural transition he went on to mention the artist's equally incomprehensible boast that he could fast for much longer than he was doing; he praised the high ambition, the good will, the great self-denial undoubtedly implicit in such a statement; and then quite simply countered it by bringing out photographs, which were also on sale to the public, showing the artist on the fortieth day of a fast lying in bed almost dead from exhaustion. This perversion of the truth, familiar to the artist though it was, always unnerved him afresh and proved too much for him. What was a consequence of the premature ending of his fast was here presented as the cause of it! To fight against this lack of understanding, against a whole world of non-understanding, was impossible. Time and again in good faith he stood by the bars listening to the impresario, but as soon as the photographs appeared he always let go and sank with a groan back on to his straw, and the reassured public could once more come close and gaze at him.

A few years later when the witnesses of such scenes called them to mind, they often failed to understand themselves at all. For meanwhile the aforementioned change in public interest had set in; it seemed to happen almost overnight; there may have been profound causes for it, but who was going to bother about that; at any rate the pampered hunger artist suddenly found himself deserted one fine day by the amusement seekers, who went streaming past him to other more favored attractions. For the last time the impresario hurried him over half Europe to discover whether the old interest might still survive here and there; all in vain; everywhere, as if by secret agreement, a positive revulsion from professional fasting was in evidence. Of course it could not really have sprung up so suddenly as all that, and many premonitory symptoms which had not been sufficiently remarked or suppressed during the rush and glitter of success now came retrospectively to mind, but it was now too late to take any countermeasures. Fasting would surely come into fashion again at some future date, yet that was no comfort for those living in the present. What, then, was the hunger artist to do? He had been applauded by thousands in his time and could hardly come down to showing himself in a street booth at village fairs, and as for adopting another profession, he was not only too old for that but too fanatically devoted to fasting. So he took leave of the impresario, his partner in an unparalleled career, and hired himself to a large circus; in order to spare his own feelings he avoided reading the conditions of his contract.

A large circus with its enormous traffic in replacing and recruiting men, animals and apparatus can always find a use for people at any time, even for a hunger artist, provided of course that he does not ask too much, and in this particular case anyhow it was not only the artist who was taken on but his famous and long-known name as well, indeed considering the peculiar nature of his performance, which was not impaired by advancing age, it could not be objected that here was an artist past his prime, no longer at the height of his professional skill, seeking a refuge in some quiet corner of a circus; on the contrary, the hunger artist averred that he could fast as well as ever, which was entirely credible, he even alleged that if he were allowed to fast as he liked, and this was at once promised him without more ado, he could astound the world by establishing a record never yet achieved, a statement which certainly provoked a smile among the other professionals, since it left out of account the change in public opinion, which the hunger artist in his zeal conveniently forgot.

He had not, however, actually lost his sense of the real situation and took it as a matter of course that he and his cage should be stationed, not in the middle of the ring as a main attraction, but outside, near the animal cages, on a site that was after all easily accessible. Large and gaily painted placards made a frame for the cage and announced what was to be seen inside it. When the public came thronging out in the intervals to see the animals, they could hardly avoid passing the hunger artist's cage and stopping there for a moment, perhaps they might even have stayed longer had not those pressing behind them in the narrow gangway, who did not understand why they should be held up on their way toward the excitements of the menagerie, made it impossible for anyone to stand gazing quietly for any length of time. And that was the reason why

the hunger artist, who had of course been looking forward to these
visiting hours as the main achievement of his life, began instead to
shrink from them. At first he could hardly wait for the intervals; it
was exhilarating to watch the crowds come streaming his way, until
only too soon—not even the most obstinate self-deception, clung to
almost consciously, could hold out against the fact—the conviction
was borne in upon him that these people, most of them, to judge
from their actions, again and again, without exception, were all on
their way to the menagerie. And the first sight of them from the distance remained the best. For when they reached his cage he was at
once deafened by the storm of shouting and abuse that arose from
the two contending factions, which renewed themselves continuously, of those who wanted to stop and stare at him—he soon began
to dislike them more than the others—not out of real interest but
only out of obstinate self-assertiveness, and those who wanted to go
straight on to the animals. When the first great rush was past, the
stragglers came along, and these, whom nothing could have prevented from stopping to look at him as long as they had breath,
raced past with long strides, hardly even glancing at him, in their
haste to get to the menagerie in time. And all too rarely did it happen that he had a stroke of luck, when some father of a family
fetched up before him with his children, pointed a finger at the
hunger artist and explained at length what the phenomenon meant,
telling stories of earlier years when he himself had watched similar
but much more thrilling performances, and the children, still rather
uncomprehending, since neither inside nor outside school had they
been sufficiently prepared for this lesson—what did they care about
fasting?—yet showed by the brightness of their intent eyes that new
and better times might be coming. Perhaps, said the hunger artist to
himself many a time, things would be a little better if his cage were
set not quite so near the menagerie. That made it too easy for people to make their choice, to say nothing of what he suffered from
the stench of the menagerie, the animals' restlessness by night, the
carrying past of raw lumps of flesh for the beasts of prey, the roaring
at feeding times, which depressed him continually. But he did not
dare to lodge a complaint with the management; after all, he had
the animals to thank for the troops of people who passed his cage,
among whom there might always be one here and there to take an

interest in him, and who could tell where they might seclude him if
he called attention to his existence and thereby to the fact that,
strictly speaking, he was only an impediment on the way to the
menagerie.

A small impediment, to be sure, one that grew steadily less. People grew familiar with the strange idea that they could be expected,
in times like these, to take an interest in a hunger artist, and with
this familiarity the verdict went out against him. He might fast as
much as he could, and he did so; but nothing could save him now,
people passed him by. Just try to explain to anyone the art of fasting! Anyone who has no feeling for it cannot be made to understand it. The fine placards grew dirty and illegible, they were torn
down; the little notice board telling the number of fast days
achieved, which at first was changed carefully every day, had long
stayed at the same figure, for after the first few weeks even this small
task seemed pointless to the staff; and so the artist simply fasted on
and on, as he had once dreamed of doing, and it was no trouble to
him, just as he had always foretold, but no one counted the days, no
one, not even the artist himself, knew what records he was already
breaking, and his heart grew heavy. And when once in a time some
leisurely passer-by stopped, made merry over the old figure on the
board and spoke of swindling, that was in its way the stupidest lie
ever invented by indifference and inborn malice, since it was not
the hunger artist who was cheating; he was working honestly, but
the world was cheating him of his reward.

Many more days went by, however, and that too came to an end. An
overseer's eye fell on the cage one day and he asked the attendants
why this perfectly good cage should be left standing there unused
with dirty straw inside it; nobody knew, until one man, helped out
by the notice board, remembered about the hunger artist. They
poked into the straw with sticks and found him in it. "Are you still
fasting?" asked the overseer. "When on earth do you mean to stop?"
"Forgive me, everybody," whispered the hunger artist; only the
overseer, who had his ear to the bars, understood him. "Of course,"
said the overseer, and tapped his forehead with a finger to let the attendants know what state the man was in, "we forgive you." "I always wanted you to admire my fasting," said the hunger artist. "We

do admire it," said the overseer, affably. "But you shouldn't admire it," said the hunger artist. "Well, then we don't admire it," said the overseer, "but why shouldn't we admire it?" "Because I have to fast, I can't help it," said the hunger artist. "What a fellow you are," said the overseer, "and why can't you help it?" "Because," said the hunger artist, lifting his head a little and speaking, with his lips pursed, as if for a kiss, right into the overseer's ear, so that no syllable might be lost, "because I couldn't find the food I liked. If I had found it, believe me, I should have made no fuss and stuffed myself like you or anyone else." These were his last words, but in his dimming eyes remained the firm though no longer proud persuasion that he was still continuing to fast.

"Well, clear this out now!" said the overseer, and they buried the hunger artist, straw and all. Into the cage they put a young panther. Even the most insensitive felt it refreshing to see this wild creature leaping around the cage that had so long been dreary. The panther was all right. The food he liked was brought him without hesitation by the attendants; he seemed not even to miss his freedom; his noble body, furnished almost to the bursting point with all that it needed, seemed to carry freedom around with it too; somewhere in his jaws it seemed to lurk; and the joy of life streamed with such ardent passion from his throat that for the onlookers it was not easy to stand the shock of it. But they braced themselves, crowded round the cage, and did not want ever to move away.

1924

D. H. Lawrence
1885–1930

> *Lawrence wrote the first draft of "The Horse Dealer's Daughter" in 1915 while living in what he considered the wild, Celtic, pre-Christian environment of Cornwall, on the extreme coast of south-west England. His novel* The Rainbow *had just been suppressed because of its sexual explicitness, and its sequel,* Women in Love, *would be rejected by publishers for the same reason. After World War I, he wandered from Italy to Australia to the American South-west to Mexico, finding these places more congenial to his beliefs*

and reworking this story until its publication in 1922. The setting is based on his hometown, a coal town in central England, and he prided himself on capturing the language and manners of the poor. Peasants and other poor country folk, like the native peoples of the places to which he traveled, represented to Lawrence and to many intellectuals of the 1920s an antidote to the stupefying and corrupting influences of European civilization. According to Lawrence, our carnal, passionate impulse to sex has an unmatched power to free us and orient us to a moral life, as it does for Jack Ferguson in this story.

The Horse Dealer's Daughter

Well, Mabel, and what are you going to do with yourself?" asked Joe, with foolish flippancy. He felt quite safe himself. Without listening for an answer, he turned aside, worked a grain of tobacco to the tip of his tongue, and spat it out. He did not care about anything, since he felt safe himself.

The three brothers and the sister sat round the desolate breakfast-table, attempting some sort of desultory consultation. The morning's post had given the final tap to the family fortunes, and all was over. The dreary dining-room itself, with its heavy mahogany furniture, looked as if it were waiting to be done away with.

But the consultation amounted to nothing. There was a strange air of ineffectuality about the three men, as they sprawled at table, smoking and reflecting vaguely on their own condition. The girl was alone, a rather short, sullen-looking young woman of twenty-seven. She did not share the same life as her brothers. She would have been good-looking, save for the impressive fixity of her face, "bull-dog," as her brothers called it.

There was a confused tramping of horses' feet outside. The three men all sprawled round in their chairs to watch. Beyond the dark holly bushes that separated the strip of lawn from the high-road, they could see a cavalcade of shire horses[1] swinging out of their own yard, being taken for exercise. This was the last time. These were the

---

1. Breed of draft horse.

last horses that would go through their hands. The young men watched with critical, callous look. They were all frightened at the collapse of their lives, and the sense of disaster in which they were involved left them no inner freedom.

Yet they were three fine, well-set fellows enough. Joe, the eldest, was a man of thirty-three, broad and handsome in a hot, flushed way. His face was red, he twisted his black moustache over a thick finger, his eyes were shallow and restless. He had a sensual way of uncovering his teeth when he laughed, and his bearing was stupid. Now he watched the horses with a glazed look of helplessness in his eyes, a certain stupor of downfall.

The great draught-horses swung past. They were tied head to tail, four of them, and they heaved along to where a lane branched off from the high-road, planting their great hoofs floutingly in the fine black mud, swinging their great rounded haunches sumptuously, and trotting a few sudden steps as they were led into the lane, round the corner. Every movement showed a massive, slumbrous strength, and a stupidity which held them in subjection. The groom at the head looked back, jerking the leading rope. And the cavalcade moved out of sight up the lane, the tail of the last horse, bobbed up tight and stiff, held out taut from the swinging great haunches as they rocked behind the hedges in a motion-like sleep.

Joe watched with glazed hopeless eyes. The horses were almost like his own body to him. He felt he was done for now. Luckily he was engaged to a woman as old as himself, and therefore her father, who was steward of a neighbouring estate, would provide him with a job. He would marry and go into harness. His life was over, he would be a subject animal now.

He turned uneasily aside, the retreating steps of the horses echoing in his ears. Then, with foolish restlessness, he reached for the scraps of bacon-rind from the plates, and making a faint whistling sound, flung them to the terrier that lay against the fender.[2] He watched the dog swallow them, and waited till the creature looked into his eyes. Then a faint grin came on his face, and in a high, foolish voice he said:

"You won't get much more bacon, shall you, you little b——?"

---

2. Low metal screen before a fireplace.

The dog faintly and dismally wagged its tail, then lowered its haunches, circled round, and lay down again.

There was another helpless silence at the table. Joe sprawled uneasily in his seat, not willing to go till the family conclave was dissolved. Fred Henry, the second brother, was erect, clean-limbed, alert. He had watched the passing of the horses with more *sang-froid*.[3] If he was an animal, like Joe, he was an animal which controls, not one which is controlled. He was master of any horse, and he carried himself with a well-tempered air of mastery. But he was not master of the situations of life. He pushed his coarse brown moustache upwards, off his lip, and glanced irritably at his sister, who sat impassive and inscrutable.

"You'll go and stop with Lucy for a bit, shan't you?" he asked. The girl did not answer.

"I don't see what else you can do," persisted Fred Henry.

"Go as a skivvy,"[4] Joe interpolated laconically.

The girl did not move a muscle.

"If I was her, I should go in for training for a nurse," said Malcolm, the youngest of them all. He was the baby of the family, a young man of twenty-two with a fresh, jaunty *museau*.[5]

But Mabel did not take any notice of him. They had talked at her and round her for so many years, that she hardly heard them at all.

The marble clock on the mantelpiece softly chimed the half-hour, the dog rose uneasily from the hearth-rug and looked at the party at the breakfast-table. But still they sat in an ineffectual conclave.

"Oh, all right," said Joe suddenly, apropos of nothing. "I'll get a move on."

He pushed back his chair, straddled his knees with a downward jerk, to get them free, in horsey fashion, and went to the fire. Still he did not go out of the room; he was curious to know what the others would do or say. He began to charge his pipe, looking down at the dog and saying in a high, affected voice:

"Going wi' me? Going wi' me are ter? Tha't goin' further than tha counts on just now, dost hear?"

---

3. Coolness (French).
4. Female domestic servant.

5. Face; literally, "muzzle" (French).

The dog faintly wagged his tail, the man stuck out his jaw and covered his pipe with his hands, and puffed intently, losing himself in the tobacco, looking down all the while at the dog with an absent brown eye. The dog looked up at him in mournful distrust. Joe stood with his knees stuck out, in real horsey fashion.

"Have you had a letter from Lucy?" Fred Henry asked of his sister.

"Last week," came the neutral reply.

"And what does she say?"

There was no answer.

"Does she *ask* you to go and stop there?" persisted Fred Henry.

"She says I can if I like."

"Well, then, you'd better. Tell her you'll come on Monday."

This was received in silence.

"That's what you'll do then, is it?" said Fred Henry, in some exasperation.

But she made no answer. There was a silence of futility and irritation in the room. Malcolm grinned fatuously.

"You'll have to make up your mind between now and next Wednesday," said Joe loudly, "or else find yourself lodgings on the kerbstone."

The face of the young woman darkened, but she sat on immutable.

"Here's Jack Ferguson!" exclaimed Malcolm, who was looking aimlessly out of the window.

"Where?" exclaimed Joe loudly.

"Just gone past."

"Coming in?"

Malcolm craned his neck to see the gate.

"Yes," he said.

There was a silence. Mabel sat on like one condemned, at the head of the table. Then a whistle was heard from the kitchen. The dog got up and barked sharply. Joe opened the door and shouted:

"Come on."

After a moment a young man entered. He was muffled up in overcoat and a purple woollen scarf, and his tweed cap, which he did not remove, was pulled down on his head. He was of medium height, his face was rather long and pale, his eyes looked tired.

"Hello, Jack! Well, Jack!" exclaimed Malcolm and Joe. Fred Henry merely said: "Jack."

"What's doing?" asked the newcomer, evidently addressing Fred Henry.

"Same. We've got to be out by Wednesday. Got a cold?"

"I have—got it bad, too."

"Why don't you stop in?"

"*Me* stop in? When I can't stand on my legs, perhaps I shall have a chance." The young man spoke huskily. He had a slight Scotch accent.

"It's a knock-out, isn't it," said Joe, boisterously, "if a doctor goes round croaking with a cold. Looks bad for the patients, doesn't it?"

The young doctor looked at him slowly.

"Anything the matter with *you*, then?" he asked sarcastically.

"Not as I know of. Damn your eyes, I hope not. Why?"

"I thought you were very concerned about the patients, wondered if you might be one yourself."

"Damn it, no, I've never been patient to no flaming doctor, and hope I never shall be," returned Joe.

At this point Mabel rose from the table, and they all seemed to become aware of her existence. She began putting the dishes together. The young doctor looked at her, but did not address her. He had not greeted her. She went out of the room with the tray, her face impassive and unchanged.

"When are you off then, all of you?" asked the doctor.

"I'm catching the eleven-forty," replied Malcolm. "Are you goin' down wi' th' trap, Joe?"

"Yes, I've told you I'm going down wi' th' trap, haven't I?"

"We'd better be getting her in then. So long Jack, if I don't see you before I go," said Malcolm, shaking hands.

He went out, followed by Joe, who seemed to have his tail between his legs.

"Well, this is the devil's own," exclaimed the doctor, when he was left alone with Fred Henry. "Going before Wednesday, are you?"

"That's the orders," replied the other.

"Where, to Northampton?"

"That's it."

"The devil!" exclaimed Ferguson, with quiet chagrin.

And there was silence between the two.

"All settled up, are you?" asked Ferguson.

"About."

There was another pause.

"Well, I shall miss yer, Freddy, boy," said the young doctor.

"And I shall miss thee, Jack," returned the other.

"Miss you like hell," mused the doctor.

Fred Henry turned aside. There was nothing to say. Mabel came in again, to finish clearing the table.

"What are *you* going to do, then, Miss Pervin?" asked Ferguson. "Going to your sister's, are you?"

Mabel looked at him with her steady, dangerous eyes, that always made him uncomfortable, unsettling his superficial ease.

"No," she said.

"Well, what in the name of fortune *are* you going to do? Say what you mean to do," cried Fred Henry, with futile intensity.

But she only averted her head, and continued her work. She folded the white table-cloth, and put on the chenille cloth.

"The sulkiest bitch that ever trod!" muttered her brother.

But she finished her task with perfectly impassive face, the young doctor watching her interestedly all the while. Then she went out.

Fred Henry stared after her, clenching his lips, his blue eyes fixing in sharp antagonism, as he made a grimace of sour exasperation.

"You could bray[6] her into bits, and that's all you'd get out of her," he said, in a small, narrowed tone.

The doctor smiled faintly.

"What's she *going* to do, then?" he asked.

"Strike me if *I* know!" returned the other.

There was a pause. Then the doctor stirred.

"I'll be seeing you tonight, shall I?" he said to his friend.

"Ay—where's it to be? Are we going over to Jessdale?"

"I don't know. I've got such a cold on me. I'll come round to the 'Moon and Stars', anyway."

"Let Lizzie and May miss their night for once, eh?"

"That's it—if I feel as I do now."

"All's one——"

6. Crush or grind.

The two young men went through the passage and down to the back door together. The house was large, but it was servantless now, and desolate. At the back was a small brick house-yard and beyond that a big square, graveled fine and red, and having stables on two sides. Sloping, dank, winter-dark fields stretched away on the open sides.

But the stables were empty. Joseph Pervin, the father of the family, had been a man of no education, who had become a fairly large horse dealer. The stables had been full of horses, there was a great turmoil and come-and-go of horses and of dealers and grooms. Then the kitchen was full of servants. But of late things had declined. The old man had married a second time, to retrieve his fortunes. Now he was dead and everything was gone to the dogs, there was nothing but debt and threatening.

For months, Mabel had been servantless in the big house, keeping the home together in penury for her ineffectual brothers. She had kept house for ten years. But previously it was with unstinted means. Then, however brutal and coarse everything was, the sense of money had kept her proud, confident. The men might be foul-mouthed, the women in the kitchen might have bad reputations, her brothers might have illegitimate children. But so long as there was money, the girl felt herself established, and brutally proud, reserved.

No company came to the house, save dealers and coarse men. Mabel had no associates of her own sex, after her sister went away. But she did not mind. She went regularly to church, she attended to her father. And she lived in the memory of her mother, who had died when she was fourteen, and whom she had loved. She had loved her father, too, in a different way, depending upon him, and feeling secure in him, until at the age of fifty-four he married again. And then she had set hard against him. Now he had died and left them all hopelessly in debt.

She had suffered badly during the period of poverty. Nothing, however, could shake the curious, sullen, animal pride that dominated each member of the family. Now, for Mabel, the end had come. Still she would not cast about her. She would follow her own way just the same. She would always hold the keys of her own situation. Mindless and persistent, she endured from day to day. Why should she think? Why should she answer anybody? It was enough that this was the end, and there was no way out. She need not pass any more darkly along the main street of the small town, avoiding every eye. She need not demean herself any more, going into the shops and buying the cheapest food. This was at an end. She thought of nobody, not even of herself. Mindless and persistent, she seemed in a sort of ecstasy to be coming nearer to her fulfillment, her own glorification, approaching her dead mother, who was glorified.

In the afternoon, she took a little bag, with shears and sponge and a small scrubbing-brush, and went out. It was a grey, wintry day, with saddened, dark green fields and an atmosphere blackened by the smoke of foundries not far off. She went quickly, darkly along the causeway, heeding nobody, through the town to the churchyard.

There she always felt secure, as if no one could see her, although as a matter of fact she was exposed to the stare of everyone who passed along under the churchyard wall. Nevertheless, once under the shadow of the great looming church, among the graves, she felt immune from the world, reserved within the thick churchyard wall as in another country.

Carefully she clipped the grass from the grave, and arranged the pinky white, small chrysanthemums in the tin cross. When this was done, she took an empty jar from a neighbouring grave, brought water, and carefully, most scrupulously sponged the marble head-stone and the coping-stone.

It gave her sincere satisfaction to do this. She felt in immediate contact with the world of her mother. She took minute pains, went through the park in a state bordering on pure happiness, as if in performing this task she came into a subtle, intimate connection with her mother. For the life she followed here in the world was far less real than the world of death she inherited from her mother.

The doctor's house was just by the church. Ferguson, being a mere hired assistant, was slave to the country-side. As he hurried now to attend to the out-patients in the surgery, glancing across the graveyard with his quick eye, he saw the girl at her task at the grave. She seemed so intent and remote, it was like looking into another world. Some mystical element was touched in him. He slowed down as he walked, watching her as if spellbound.

She lifted her eyes, feeling him looking. Their eyes met. And each looked away again at once, each feeling, in some way, found out by the other. He lifted his cap and passed on down the road. There remained distinct in his consciousness, like a vision, the memory of her face, lifted from the tombstone in the churchyard, and looking at him with slow, large, portentous eyes. It *was* portentous, her face. It seemed to mesmerize him. There was a heavy power in her eyes which laid hold of his whole being, as if he had drunk some powerful drug. He had been feeling weak and done before. Now the life came back into him, he felt delivered from his own fretted, daily self.

He finished his duties at the surgery as quickly as might be, hastily filling up the bottles of the waiting people with cheap drugs. Then, in perpetual haste, he set off again to visit several cases in another part of his round, before tea-time. At all times he preferred to walk if he could, but particularly when he was not well. He fancied the motion restored him.

The afternoon was falling. It was grey, deadened, and wintry, with a slow, moist, heavy coldness sinking in and deadening all the faculties. But why should he think or notice? He hastily climbed the hill and turned across the dark green fields, following the black cinder-track. In the distance, across a shallow dip in the country, the small town was clustered like smouldering ash, a tower, a spire, a heap of low, raw, extinct houses. And on the nearest fringe of the town, sloping into the dip, was Oldmeadow, the Pervins' house. He could see the stables and the outbuildings distinctly, as they lay towards him on the slope. Well, he would not go there many more times! Another resource would be lost to him, another place gone: the only company he cared for in the alien, ugly little town he was losing. Nothing but work, drudgery, constant hastening from dwelling to dwelling among the colliers and the iron-workers. It wore him out, but at the same time he had a craving for it. It was a stimulant to him to be in the homes of the working people, moving, as it were, through the innermost body of their life. His nerves were excited and gratified. He could come so near, into the very lives of the rough, inarticulate, powerfully emotional men and women. He grumbled, he said he hated the hellish hole. But as a matter of fact it excited him, the contact with the rough, strongly-feeling people was a stimulant applied direct to his nerves.

Below Oldmeadow, in the green, shallow, soddened hollow of fields, lay a square, deep pond. Roving across the landscape, the doctor's quick eye detected a figure in black passing through the gate of the field, down towards the pond. He looked again. It would be Mabel Pervin. His mind suddenly became alive and attentive.

Why was she going down there? He pulled up on the path on the slope above, and stood staring. He could just make sure of the small black figure moving in the hollow of the failing day. He seemed to see her in the midst of such obscurity, that he was like a clairvoyant, seeing rather with the mind's eye than with ordinary sight. Yet he could see her positively enough, whilst he kept his eye attentive. He felt, if he looked away from her, in the thick, ugly falling dusk, he would lose her altogether.

He followed her minutely as she moved, direct and intent, like something transmitted rather than stirring in voluntary activity, straight down the field towards the pond. There she stood on the bank for a moment. She never raised her head. Then she waded slowly into the water.

He stood motionless as the small black figure walked slowly and deliberately towards the center of the pond, very slowly, gradually moving deeper into the motionless water, and still moving forward as the water got up to her breast. Then he could see her no more in the dusk of the dead afternoon.

"There!" he exclaimed. "Would you believe it?"

And he hastened straight down, running over the wet, soddened fields, pushing through the hedges, down into the depression of callous wintry obscurity. It took him several minutes to come to the pond. He stood on the bank, breathing heavily. He could see nothing. His eyes seemed to penetrate the dead water. Yes, perhaps that was the dark shadow of her black clothing beneath the surface of the water.

He slowly ventured into the pond. The bottom was deep, soft clay, he sank in, and the water clasped dead cold round his legs. As he stirred he could smell the cold, rotten clay that fouled up into the water. It was objectionable in his lungs. Still, repelled and yet not heeding, he moved deeper into the pond. The cold water rose over his thighs, over his loins, upon his abdomen. The lower part of his body was all sunk in the hideous cold element. And the bottom was so deeply soft and uncertain, he was afraid of pitching with his mouth underneath. He could not swim, and was afraid.

He crouched a little, spreading his hands under the water and moving them round trying to feel for her. The dead cold pond swayed upon his chest. He moved again, a little deeper, and again, with his hands underneath, he felt all around under the water. And he touched her clothing. But it evaded his fingers. He made a desperate effort to grasp it.

And so doing he lost his balance and went under, horribly, suffocating in the foul earthy water, struggling madly for a few moments. At last, after what seemed an eternity, he got his footing, rose again into the air and looked around. He gasped, and knew he was in the world. Then he looked at the water. She had risen near him. He grasped her clothing, and drawing her nearer, turned to take his way to land again.

He went very slowly, carefully, absorbed in the slow progress. He rose higher, climbing out of the pond. The water was now only about his legs; he was thankful, full of relief to be out of the clutches of the pond. He lifted her and staggered onto the bank, out of the horror of wet, grey clay.

He laid her down on the bank. She was quite unconscious and running with water. He made the water come from her mouth, he worked to restore her. He did not have to work very long before he could feel the breathing begin again in her; she was breathing naturally. He worked a little longer. He could feel her live beneath his hands; she was coming back. He wiped her face, wrapped her in his overcoat, looked round into the dim, dark grey world, then lifted her and staggered down the bank and across the fields.

It seemed an unthinkably long way, and his burden so heavy he felt he would never get to the house. But at last he was in the stable-yard, and then in the house-yard. He opened the door and went into the house. In the kitchen he laid her down on the hearth-rug and called. The house was empty. But the fire was burning in the grate.

Then again he kneeled to attend to her. She was breathing regularly, her eyes were wide open and as if conscious, but there seemed something missing in her look. She was conscious in herself, but unconscious of her surroundings.

He ran upstairs, took blankets from a bed, and put them before the fire to warm. Then he removed her saturated, earthy-smelling clothing, rubbed her dry with a towel, and wrapped her naked in the blankets. Then he went into the dining-room, to look for spirits. There was a little whisky. He drank a gulp himself, and put some into her mouth.

The effect was instantaneous. She looked full into his face, as if she had been seeing him for some time, and yet had only just become conscious of him.

"Dr. Ferguson?" she said.

"What?" he answered.

He was divesting himself of his coat, intending to find some dry clothing upstairs. He could not bear the smell of the dead, clayey water, and he was mortally afraid for his own health.

"What did I do?" she asked.

"Walked into the pond," he replied. He had begun to shudder like one sick, and could hardly attend to her. Her eyes remained full on him, he seemed to be going dark in his mind, looking back at her helplessly. The shuddering became quieter in him, his life came back to him, dark and unknowing, but strong again.

"Was I out of my mind?" she asked, while her eyes were fixed on him all the time.

"Maybe, for the moment," he replied. He felt quiet, because his strength had come back. The strange fretful strain had left him.

"Am I out of my mind now?" she asked.

"Are you?" he reflected a moment. "No," he answered truthfully. "I don't see that you are." He turned his face aside. He was afraid now, because he felt dazed, and felt dimly that her power was stronger than his, in this issue. And she continued to look at him fixedly all the time. "Can you tell me where I shall find some dry things to put on?" he asked.

"Did you dive into the pond for me?" she asked.

"No," he answered. "I walked in. But I went in over head as well."

There was silence for a moment. He hesitated. He very much wanted to go upstairs to get into dry clothing. But there was another desire in him. And she seemed to hold him. His will seemed to have gone to sleep, and left him, standing there slack before her. But he felt warm inside himself. He did not shudder at all, though his clothes were sodden on him.

"Why did you?" she asked.

"Because I didn't want you to do such a foolish thing," he said.

"It wasn't foolish," she said, still gazing at him as she lay on the floor, with a sofa cushion under her head. "It was the right thing to do. *I* knew best, then."

"I'll go and shift these wet things," he said. But still he had not the power to move out of her presence, until she sent him. It was as if she had the life of his body in her hands, and he could not extricate himself. Or perhaps he did not want to.

Suddenly she sat up. Then she became aware of her own immediate condition. She felt the blankets about her, she knew her own limbs. For a moment it seemed as if her reason were going. She looked round, with wild eye, as if seeking something. He stood still with fear. She saw her clothing lying scattered.

"Who undressed me?" she asked, her eyes resting full and inevitable on his face.

"I did," he replied, "to bring you round."

For some moments she sat and gazed at him awfully, her lips parted.

"Do you love me, then?" she asked.

He only stood and stared at her, fascinated. His soul seemed to melt.

She shuffled forward on her knees, and put her arms round him, round his legs, as he stood there, pressing her breasts against his knees and thighs, clutching him with strange, convulsive certainty, pressing his thighs against her, drawing him to her face, her throat, as she looked up at him with flaring, humble eyes of transfiguration, triumphant in first possession.

"You love me," she murmured, in strange transport, yearning and triumphant and confident. "You love me. I know you love me, I know."

And she was passionately kissing his knees, through the wet clothing, passionately and indiscriminately kissing his knees, his legs, as if unaware of everything.

He looked down at the tangled wet hair, the wild, bare, animal shoulders. He was amazed, bewildered, and afraid. He had never thought of loving her. He had never wanted to love her. When he rescued her and restored her, he was a doctor, and she was a patient. He had had no single personal thought of her. Nay, this introduction of the personal element was very distasteful to him, a violation of his professional honour. It was horrible to have her there embracing his knees. It was horrible. He revolted from it, violently. And yet—and yet—he had not the power to break away.

She looked at him again, with the same supplication of powerful love, and that same transcendent, frightening light of triumph. In view of the delicate flame which seemed to come from her face like a light, he was powerless. And yet he had never intended to love her. He had never intended. And something stubborn in him could not give way.

"You love me," she repeated, in a murmur of deep, rhapsodic assurance. "You love me."

Her hands were drawing him, drawing him down to her. He was afraid, even a little horrified. For he had, really, no intention of loving her. Yet her hands were drawing him towards her. He put out his hand quickly to steady himself, and grasped her bare shoulder. A flame seemed to burn the hand that grasped her soft shoulder. He had no intention of loving her: his whole will was against his yielding. It was horrible. And yet wonderful was the touch of her shoulders, beautiful the shining of her face. Was she perhaps mad? He had a horror of yielding to her. Yet something in him ached also.

He had been staring away at the door, away from her. But his hand remained on her shoulder. She had gone suddenly very still. He looked down at her. Her eyes were now wide with fear, with doubt, the light was dying from her face, a shadow of terrible greyness was returning. He could not bear the touch of her eyes' question upon him, and the look of death behind the question.

With an inward groan he gave way, and let his heart yield towards her. A sudden gentle smile came on his face. And her eyes, which never left his face, slowly, slowly filled with tears. He watched the strange water rise in her eyes, like some slow fountain coming up. And his heart seemed to burn and melt away in his breast.

He could not bear to look at her any more. He dropped on his knees and caught her head with his arms and pressed her face against his throat. She was very still. His heart, which seemed to have broken, was burning with a kind of agony in his breast. And he felt her slow, hot tears wetting his throat. But he could not move.

He felt the hot tears wet his neck and the hollows of his neck, and he remained motionless, suspended through one of man's eternities. Only now it had become indispensable to him to have her face pressed close to him; he could never let her go again. He could never let her head go away from the close clutch of his arm. He wanted to remain like that for ever, with his heart hurting him in a pain that was also life to him. Without knowing, he was looking down on her damp, soft brown hair.

Then, as it were suddenly, he smelt the horrid stagnant smell of that water. And at the same moment she drew away from him and looked at him. Her eyes were wistful and unfathomable. He was afraid of them, and he fell to kissing her, not knowing what he was doing. He wanted her eyes not to have that terrible, wistful, unfathomable look.

When she turned her face to him again, a faint delicate flush was glowing, and there was again dawning that terrible shining of joy in her eyes, which really terrified him, and yet which he now wanted to see, because he feared the look of doubt still more.

"You love me?" she said, rather faltering.

"Yes." The word cost him a painful effort. Not because it wasn't true. But because it was too newly true, the *saying* seemed to tear open again his newly-torn heart. And he hardly wanted it to be true, even now.

She lifted her face to him, and he bent forward and kissed her on the mouth, gently, with the one kiss that is an eternal pledge. And as he kissed her his heart strained again in his breast. He never intended to love her. But now it was over. He had crossed over the gulf to her, and all that he had left behind had shrivelled and become void.

After the kiss, her eyes again slowly filled with tears. She sat still, away from him, with her face drooped aside, and her hands folded in her lap. The tears fell very slowly. There was complete silence. He too sat there motionless and silent on the hearth-rug. The strange pain of his heart that was broken seemed to consume him. That he should love her? That this was love! That he should be ripped open in this way! Him, a doctor! How they would all jeer if they knew! It was agony to him to think they might know.

In the curious naked pain of the thought he looked again to her. She was sitting there drooped into a muse. He saw a tear fall, and his heart flared hot. He saw for the first time that one of her shoulders was quite uncovered, one arm bare, he could see one of her small breasts; dimly, because it had become almost dark in the room.

"Why are you crying?" he asked, in an altered voice.

She looked up at him, and behind her tears the consciousness of her situation for the first time brought a dark look of shame to her eyes.

"I'm not crying, really," she said, watching him, half frightened.

He reached his hand, and softly closed it on her bare arm.

"I love you! I love you!" he said in a soft, low vibrating voice, unlike himself.

She shrank, and dropped her head. The soft, penetrating grip of his hand on her arm distressed her. She looked up at him.

"I want to go," she said. "I want to go and get you some dry things."

"Why?" he said. "I'm all right."

"But I want to go," she said. "And I want you to change your things."

He released her arm, and she wrapped herself in the blanket, looking at him rather frightened. And still she did not rise.

"Kiss me," she said wistfully.

He kissed her, but briefly, half in anger.

Then, after a second, she rose nervously, all mixed up in the blanket. He watched her in her confusion as she tried to extricate herself and wrap herself up so that she could walk. He watched her relentlessly, as she knew. And as she went, the blanket trailing, and as he saw a glimpse of her feet and her white leg, he tried to remember her as she was when he had wrapped her in the blanket. But then he didn't want to remember, because she had been nothing to him then, and his nature revolted from remembering her as she was when she was nothing to him.

A tumbling, muffled noise from within the dark house startled him. Then he heard her voice: "There are clothes." He rose and went to the foot of the stairs, and gathered up the garments she had thrown down. Then he came back to the fire, to rub himself down and dress. He grinned at his own appearance when he had finished.

The fire was sinking, so he put on coal. The house was now quite dark, save for the light of a street-lamp that shone in faintly from beyond the holly trees. He lit the gas with matches he found on the mantelpiece. Then he emptied the pockets of his own clothes, and threw all his wet things in a heap into the scullery. After which he gathered up her sodden clothes, gently, and put them in a separate heap on the copper-top in the scullery.

It was six o'clock on the clock. His own watch had stopped. He ought to go back to the surgery. He waited, and still she did not come down. So he went to the foot of the stairs and called:

"I shall have to go."

Almost immediately he heard her coming down. She had on her best dress of black voile, and her hair was tidy, but still damp. She looked at him—and in spite of herself, smiled.

"I don't like you in those clothes," she said.

"Do I look a sight?" he answered:

They were shy of one another.

"I'll make you some tea," she said.

"No, I must go."

"Must you?" And she looked at him again with the wide, strained, doubtful eyes. And again, from the pain of his breast, he knew how he loved her. He went and bent to kiss her, gently, passionately, with his heart's painful kiss.

"And my hair smells so horrible," she murmured in distraction. "And I'm so awful, I'm so awful! Oh no, I'm too awful." And she broke into bitter, heartbroken sobbing. "You can't want to love me, I'm horrible."

"Don't be silly, don't be silly," he said, trying to comfort her, kissing her, holding her in his arms. "I want you, I want to marry you, we're going to be married, quickly, quickly—to-morrow if I can."

But she only sobbed terribly, and cried:

"I feel awful. I feel awful. I feel I'm horrible to you."

"No, I want you, I want you," was all he answered, blindly, with that terrible intonation which frightened her almost more than her horror lest he should *not* want her.

1922

James Alan McPherson
1943–

"A Loaf of Bread" is as ambiguous as any story in this collection. The meaning of Mr. Reed's gesture at the end, though apparently perfectly understood by Mr. Green, is a matter of interpretation. He might be making amends; he might be reversing an indignity. McPherson's story is unusual among twentieth-century fiction for its direct exploration of social issues. We would do the writer a disservice if, in addition to undertaking the usual literary analysis, we did not also let the story challenge our view of the human institutions with which we live. For example, does Thomas, Mr. Green's brother-in-law, accurately describe the marketplace in a capitalist society? What do you think McPherson concludes about the ethics of the situation? What should Mr. Green have done? And what should Mr. Reed have done?

A Loaf of Bread

It was one of those obscene situations, pedestrian to most people, but invested with meaning for a few poor folk whose lives are usually spent outside the imaginations of their fellow citizens. A grocer named Harold Green was caught red-handed selling to one group of people the very same goods he sold at lower prices at similar outlets in better neighborhoods. He had been doing this for many years, and at first he could not understand the outrage heaped upon him. He acted only from habit, he insisted, and had nothing personal against the people whom he served. They were his neighbors. Many of them he had carried on the cuff during hard times.

Yet, through some mysterious access to a television station, the poor folk were now empowered to make grand denunciations of the grocer. Green's children now saw their father's business being picketed on the Monday evening news.

No one could question the fact that the grocer had been overcharging the people. On the news even the reporter grimaced distastefully while reading the statistics. His expression said, "It is my job to report the news, but sometimes even I must disassociate myself from it to protect my honor." This, at least, was the impression the grocer's children seemed to bring away from the television. Their father's name had not been mentioned, but there was a close-up of his store with angry black people, and a few outraged whites, marching in groups of three in front of it. There was also a close-up of his name. After seeing this, they were in no mood to watch cartoons. At the dinner table, disturbed by his children's silence, Harold Green felt compelled to say, "I am not a dishonest man." Then he felt ashamed. The children, a boy and his older sister, immediately left the table, leaving Green alone with his wife. "Ruth, I am not dishonest," he repeated to her.

Ruth Green did not say anything. She knew, and her husband did not, that the outraged people had also picketed the school attended by their children. They had threatened to return each day until Green lowered his prices. When they called her at home to report this, she had promised she would talk with him. Since she could not tell him this, she waited for an opening. She looked at her husband across the table.

"I did not make the world," Green began, recognizing at once the seriousness in her stare. "My father came to this country with nothing but his shirt. He was exploited for as long as he couldn't help himself. He did not protest or picket. He put himself in a position to play by the rules he had learned." He waited for his wife to answer, and when she did not, he tried again. "I did not make this world," he repeated. "I only make my way in it. Such people as these, they do not know enough to not be exploited. If not me, there would be a Greek, a Chinaman, maybe an Arab or a smart one of their own kind. Believe me, I deal with them. There is something in their style that lacks the patience to run a concern such as mine.

If I closed down, take my word on it, someone else would do what has to be done."

But Ruth Green was not thinking of his leaving. Her mind was on other matters. Her children had cried when they came home early from school. She had no special feeling for the people who picketed, but she did not like to see her children cry. She had kissed them generously, then sworn them to silence. "One day this week," she told her husband, "you will give free, for eight hours, anything your customers come in to buy. There will be no publicity, except what they spread by word of mouth. No matter what they say to you, no matter what they take, you will remain silent." She stared deeply into him for what she knew was there. "If you refuse, you have seen the last of your children and myself."

Her husband grunted. Then he leaned toward her. "I will not knuckle under," he said. "I will *not* give!"

"We shall see," his wife told him.

The black pickets, for the most part, had at first been frightened by the audacity of their undertaking. They were peasants whose minds had long before become resigned to their fate as victims. None of them, before now, had thought to challenge this. But now, when they watched themselves on television, they hardly recognized the faces they saw beneath the hoisted banners and placards. Instead of reflecting the meekness they all felt, the faces looked angry. The close-ups looked especially intimidating. Several of the first pickets, maids who worked in the suburbs, reported that their employers, seeing the activity on the afternoon news, had begun treating them with new respect. One woman, midway through the weather report, called around the neighborhood to disclose that her employer had that very day given her a new china plate for her meals. The paper plates, on which all previous meals had been served, had been thrown into the wastebasket. One recipient of this call, a middle-aged woman known for her bashfulness and humility, rejoined that her husband, a sheet-metal worker, had only a few hours before been called "Mister" by his supervisor, a white man with a passionate hatred of color. She added the tale of a neighbor down the street, a widow-woman named Murphy, who had at first been reluctant to join the picket; this woman now was insisting it should be made a

daily event. Such talk as this circulated among the people who had
been instrumental in raising the issue. As news of their victory
leaked into the ears of others who had not participated, they received all through the night calls from strangers requesting verifica-
tion, offering advice, and vowing support. Such strangers listened,
and then volunteered stories about indignities inflicted on them by
city officials, policemen, other grocers. In this way, over a period of
hours, the community became even more incensed and restless than
it had been at the time of the initial picket.

Soon, the man who had set events in motion found himself a
hero. His name was Nelson Reed, and all his adult life he had been
employed as an assembly-line worker. He was a steady husband, the
father of three children, and a deacon in the Baptist church. All his
life he had trusted in God and gotten along. But now something in
him capitulated to the reality that came suddenly into focus. "I was
wrong," he told people who called him. "The onliest thing that
matters in this world is *money*. And when was the last time you seen
a picture of Jesus on a dollar bill?" This line, which he repeated over
and over, caused a few callers to laugh nervously, but not without
some affirmation that this was indeed the way things were. Many
said they had known it all along. Others argued that although it was
certainly true, it was one thing to live without money and quite another to live without faith. But still most callers laughed and said,
"You right. You *know* I know you right. Ain't it the truth, though?"
Only a few people, among them Nelson Reed's wife, said nothing
and looked very sad.

Why they looked sad, however, they would not communicate.
And anyone observing their troubled faces would have to trust his
own intuition. It is known that Reed's wife, Betty, measured all
events against the fullness of her own experience. She was skeptical
of everything. Brought to the church after a number of years of living openly with a jazz musician, she had embraced religion when
she married Nelson Reed. But though she no longer believed completely in the world, she nonetheless had not fully embraced God.
There was something in the nature of Christ's swift rise that had always bothered her, and something in the blood and vengeance of
the Old Testament that was mellowing and refreshing. But she had
never communicated these thoughts to anyone, especially her hus-

band. Instead, she smiled vacantly while others professed leaps of faith, remained silent when friends spoke fiercely of their convictions. The presence of this vacuum in her contributed to her personal mystery; people said she was beautiful, although she was not outwardly so. Perhaps it was because she wished to protect this inner beauty that she did not smile now, and looked extremely sad, listening to her husband on the telephone.

Nelson Reed had no reason to be sad. He seemed to grow more energized and talkative as the days passed. He was invited by an alderman, on the Tuesday after the initial picket, to tell his story on a local television talk show. He sweated heavily under the hot white lights and attempted to be philosophical. "I notice," the host said to him, "that you are not angry at this exploitative treatment. What, Mr. Reed, is the source of your calm?" The assembly-line worker looked unabashedly into the camera and said, "I have always believed in *Justice* with a capital *J*. I was raised up from a baby believin' that God ain't gonna let nobody go *too* far. See, in *my* mind God is in charge of *all* the capital letters in the alphabet of this world. It say in the Scripture He is Alpha and Omega, the first and the last. He is just about the *onliest* capitalizer they is." Both Reed and the alderman laughed. "Now, when *men* start to capitalize, they gets *greedy*. They put a little *j* in *joy* and a littler one in *justice*. They raise up a big *G* in *Greed* and a big *E* in *Evil*. Well, soon as they commence to put a little *g* in *god*, you can expect some kind of reaction. The Savior will just raise up the *H* in *Hell* and go on from there. And that's just what I'm doin', giving these sharpies *HELL* with a big *H*." The talk show host laughed along with Nelson Reed and the alderman. After the taping they drank coffee in the back room of the studio and talked about the sad shape of the world.

Three days before he was to comply with his wife's request, Green, the grocer, saw this talk show on television while at home. The words of Nelson Reed sent a chill through him. Though Reed had attempted to be philosophical, Green did not perceive the statement in this light. Instead, he saw a vindictive-looking black man seated between an ambitious alderman and a smug talk-show host. He saw them chatting comfortably about the nature of evil. The cameraman had shot mostly close-ups, and Green could see the set in Nelson Reed's jaw. The color of Reed's face was maddening. When his children came into the den, the grocer was in a sweat. Before he could think, he had shouted at them and struck the button turning off the set. The two children rushed from the room screaming. Ruth Green ran in from the kitchen. She knew why he was upset because she had received a call about the show; but she said nothing and pretended ignorance. Her children's school had been picketed that day, as it had the day before. But both children were still forbidden to speak of this to their father.

"Where do they get so much power?" Green said to his wife. "Two days ago, nobody would have cared. Now, everywhere, even in my home, I am condemned as a rascal. And what do I own? An airline? A multinational? Half of South America? *No!* I own three stores, one of which happens to be in a certain neighborhood inhabited by people who cost me money to run it." He sighed and sat upright on the sofa, his chubby legs spread wide. "A cab driver has a meter that clicks as he goes along. I pay extra for insurance, iron bars, pilfering by customers and employees. Nothing clicks. But when I add a little overhead to my prices, suddenly everything clicks. But for someone else. When was there last such a world?" He pressed the palms of both hands to his temples, suggesting a bombardment of brain-stinging sounds.

This gesture evoked no response from Ruth Green. She remained standing by the door, looking steadily at him. She said, "To protect yourself, I would not stock any more fresh cuts of meat in the store until after the giveaway on Saturday. Also, I would not tell it to the employees until after the first customer of the day has begun to check out. But I would urge you to hire several security guards to close the door promptly at seven-thirty, as is usual." She wanted to say much more than this, but did not. Instead she watched him. He was looking at the blank gray television screen, his palms still pressed against his ears. "In case you need to hear again," she continued in a weighty tone of voice, "I said two days ago, and I say again now, that if you fail to do this you will not see your children again for many years."

He twisted his head and looked up at her. "What is the color of these people?" he asked.

"Black," his wife said.

"And what is the name of my children?"

"Green."

The grocer smiled. "There is your answer," he told his wife. "Green is the only color I am interested in."

His wife did not smile. "Insufficient," she said.

"The world is mad!" he moaned. "But it is a point of sanity with me to not bend. I will not bend." He crossed his legs and pressed one hand firmly atop his knee. "*I will not bend*," he said.

"We will see," his wife said.

Nelson Reed, after the television interview, became the acknowledged leader of the disgruntled neighbors. At first a number of them met in the kitchen at his house; then, as space was lacking for curious newcomers, a mass meeting was held on Thursday in an abandoned theater. His wife and three children sat in the front row. Behind them sat the widow Murphy, Lloyd Dukes, Tyrone Brown, Les Jones—those who had joined him on the first picket line. Behind these sat people who bought occasionally at the store, people who lived on the fringes of the neighborhood, people from other neighborhoods come to investigate the problem, and the merely curious. The middle rows were occupied by a few people from the suburbs, those who had seen the talk show and whose outrage at the grocer proved much more powerful than their fear of black people. In the rear of the theater crowded aging, old-style leftists, somber students, cynical young black men with angry grudges to explain with inarticulate gestures. Leaning against the walls, huddled near the doors at the rear, tape-recorder-bearing social scientists looked as detached and serene as bookies at the track. Here and there, in this diverse crowd, a politician stationed himself, pumping hands vigorously and pressing his palms gently against the shoulders of elderly people. Other visitors passed out leaflets, buttons, glossy color prints of men who promoted causes, the familiar and obscure. There was a hubbub of voices, a blend of the strident and the playful, the outraged and the reverent, lending an undercurrent of ominous energy to the assembly.

Nelson Reed spoke from a platform on the stage, standing before a yellowed, shredded screen that had once reflected the images of matinee idols. "I don't mind sayin' that I have always been a sucker," he told the crowd. "All my life I have been a sucker for the words of Jesus. Being a natural-born fool, I just ain't never had the *sense* to learn no better. Even right today, while the whole world is sayin' wrong is right and up is down, I'm so dumb I'm *still* steady believin' what is wrote in the Good Book . . ."

From the audience, especially the front rows, came a chorus singing, "Preach!"

"I have no doubt," he continued in a low baritone, "that it's true what is writ in the Good Book: 'The last shall be first and the first shall be last.' I don't know about y'all, but I have *always* been the last. I never wanted to be the first, but sometimes it look like the world get so bad that them that's holdin' onto the tree of life is the onliest ones left when God commence to blowin' dead leafs off the branches."

"Now you preaching," someone called.

In the rear of the theater a white student shouted an awkward "Amen."

Nelson Reed began walking across the stage to occupy the major part of his nervous energy. But to those in the audience, who now hung on his every word, it looked as though he strutted. "All my life," he said, "I have claimed to be a man without earnin' the right to call myself that. You know, the *average* man ain't really a man. The average man is a *boot-licker*. In fact, the *average* man would *run away* if he found hisself standing alone facin' down a adversary. I have done that *too many a time* in my life! But *not no more*. Better to be *once* was than *never* was a man. I will tell you tonight, there is somethin' *wrong* in being average. *I intend to stand up!* Now, if your average man that ain't really a man stand up, two things gonna happen: *One*, he g'on bust through all the weights that been place on his head, and, *two*, he g'on feel a lot of pain. But that same hurt is what make things fall in place. That, and gettin' your hands on one of these slick four-flushers tight enough so's you can squeeze him and say, 'No more!' You do that, you g'on hurt some, but *you won't be average no more . . .*"

"No *more!*" a few people in the front rows repeated.

"I say *no more!*" Nelson Reed shouted.

"*No more! No more! No more!*" The chant rustled through the crowd like the rhythm of an autumn wind against a shedding tree.

Then people laughed and chattered in celebration.

As for the grocer, from the evening of the television interview he had begun to make plans. Unknown to his wife, he cloistered himself several times with his brother-in-law, an insurance salesman, and plotted a course. He had no intention of tossing steaks to the crowd. "And why should I, Tommy?" he asked his wife's brother, a lean, bald-headed man named Thomas. "I don't cheat anyone. I have never cheated anyone. The businesses I run are always on the up-and-up. So why should I pay?"

"Quite so," the brother-in-law said, chewing an unlit cigarillo. "The world has gone crazy. Next they will say that people in my business are responsible for prolonging life. I have found that people who refuse to believe in death refuse also to believe in the harshness of life. I sell well by saying that death is a long happiness. I show people the realities of life and compare this to a funeral with dignity, *and* the promise of a bundle for every loved one salted away. When they look around hard at life, they usually buy."

"So?" asked Green. Thomas was a college graduate with a penchant for philosophy.

"So," Thomas answered. "You must fight to show these people the reality of both your situation and theirs. How would it be if you visited one of their meetings and chalked out, on a blackboard, the dollars and cents of your operation? Explain your overhead, your security fees, all the additional expenses. If you treat them with respect, they might understand."

Green frowned. "That I would never do," he said. "It would be admission of a certain guilt."

The brother-in-law smiled, but only with one corner of his mouth. "Then you have something to feel guilty about?" he asked.

The grocer frowned at him. "*Nothing!*" he said with great emphasis.

"So?" Thomas said.

This first meeting between the grocer and his brother-in-law took place on Thursday, in a crowded barroom.

At the second meeting, in a luncheonette, it was agreed that the grocer should speak privately with the leader of the group, Nelson Reed. The meeting at which this was agreed took place on Friday afternoon. After accepting this advice from Thomas, the grocer resigned himself to explain to Reed, in as finite detail as possible, the economic structure of his operation. He vowed to suppress no information. He would explain everything: inventories, markups, sale items, inflation, balance sheets, specialty items, overhead, and that mysterious item called profit. This last item, promising to be the most difficult to explain, Green and his brother-in-law debated over for several hours. They agreed first of all that a man should not work for free, then they agreed that it was unethical to ruthlessly exploit. From these parameters, they staked out an area between fifteen and forty percent, and agreed that someplace between these two borders lay an amount of return that could be called fair. This was easy, but then Thomas introduced the factor of circumstance. He questioned whether the fact that one serviced a risky area justified the earning of profits, closer to the forty-percent edge of the scale. Green was unsure. Thomas smiled. "Here is a case that will point out an analogy," he said, licking a cigarillo. "I read in the papers that a family wants to sell an electric stove. I call the home and the man says fifty dollars. I ask to come out and inspect the merchandise. When I arrive I see they are poor, have already bought a new stove that is connected, and are selling the old one for fifty dollars because they want it out of the place. The electric stove is in good condition, worth much more than fifty. But because I see what I see I offer forty-five."

Green, for some reason, wrote down this figure on the back of the sales slip for the coffee they were drinking.

The brother-in-law smiled. He chewed his cigarillo. "The man agrees to take forty-five dollars, saying he has had no other calls. I look at the stove again and see a spot of rust. I say I will give him forty dollars. He agrees to this, on condition that I myself haul it away. I say I will haul it away if he comes down to thirty. You, of course, see where I am going."

The grocer nodded. "The circumstances of his situation, his need to get rid of the stove quickly, placed him in a position where he has little room to bargain?"

"Yes," Thomas answered. "So? Is it ethical, Harry?"

Harold Green frowned. He had never liked his brother-in-law, and now he thought the insurance agent was being crafty. "But," he answered, "this man does not *have* to sell! It is his choice whether to wait for other calls. It is not the fault of the buyer that the seller is in a hurry. It is the right of the buyer to get what he wants at the lowest price possible. That is the rule. That has *always* been the rule. And the reverse of it applies to the seller as well."

"Yes," Thomas said, sipping coffee from the Styrofoam cup. "But suppose that in addition to his hurry to sell, the owner was also of a weak soul. There are, after all, many such people." He smiled. "Suppose he placed no value on the money?"

"Then," Green answered, "your example is academic. Here we are not talking about real life. One man lives by the code, one man does not. Who is there free enough to make a judgment?" He laughed. "Now you see," he told his brother-in-law. "Much more than a few dollars are at stake. If this one buyer is to be condemned, then so are most people in the history of the world. An examination of history provides the only answer to your question. This code will be here tomorrow, long after the ones who do not honor it are not."

They argued fiercely late into the afternoon, the brother-in-law leaning heavily on his readings. When they parted, a little before 5:00 P.M., nothing had been resolved.

Neither was much resolved during the meeting between Green and Nelson Reed. Reached at home by the grocer in the early evening, the leader of the group spoke coldly at first, but consented finally to meet his adversary at a nearby drugstore for coffee and a talk. They met at the lunch counter, shook hands awkwardly, and sat for a few minutes discussing the weather. Then the grocer pulled two gray ledgers from his briefcase. "You have for years come into my place," he told the man. "In my memory I have always treated you well. Now our relationship has come to this." He slid the books along the counter until they touched Nelson Reed's arm.

Reed opened the top book and flipped the thick green pages with his thumb. He did not examine the figures. "All I know," he said, "is over at your place a can of soup cost me fifty-five cents, and two miles away at your other store for white folks you chargin' thirty-nine cents." He said this with the calm authority of an outraged soul. A quality of condescension tinged with pity crept into his gaze.

The grocer drummed his fingers on the counter top. He twisted his head and looked away, toward shelves containing cosmetics, laxatives, toothpaste. His eyes lingered on a poster of a woman's apple red lips and milk white teeth. The rest of the face was missing.

"Ain't no use to hide," Nelson Reed said, as to a child. "*I know you wrong, you* know you wrong, and before I finish, *everybody in this city* g'on know you wrong. God don't *like* ugly." He closed his eyes and gripped the cup of coffee. Then he swung his head suddenly and faced the grocer again. "Man, why you want to *do* people that way?" he asked. "We human, same as you."

"Before *God!*" Green exclaimed, looking squarely into the face of Nelson Reed. "Before God!" he said again. "*I am not an evil man!*" These last words sounded more like a moan as he tightened the muscles in his throat to lower the sound of his voice. He tossed his left shoulder as if adjusting the sleeve of his coat, or as if throwing off some unwanted weight. Then he peered along the counter top. No one was watching. At the end of the counter the waitress was scrubbing the coffee urn. "Look at these figures, please," he said to Reed.

The man did not drop his gaze. His eyes remained fixed on the grocer's face.

"All right," Green said. "Don't look. I'll tell you what is in these books, believe me if you want. I work twelve hours a day, one day off per week, running my business in three stores. I am not a wealthy person. In one place, in the area you call white, I get by barely by smiling lustily at old ladies, stocking gourmet stuff on the chance I will build a reputation as a quality store. The two clerks there cheat me; there is nothing I can do. In this business you must be friendly with everybody. The second place is on the other side of town, in a neighborhood as poor as this one. I get out there seldom. The profits are not worth the gas. I use the loss there as a write-off against some other properties." He paused. "Do you understand write-off?" he asked Nelson Reed.

"Naw," the man said.

Harold Green laughed. "What does it matter?" he said in a tone of voice intended for himself alone. "In this area I will admit I make a profit, but it is not so much as you think. But I do not make a profit here because the people are black. I make a profit because a profit is here to be made. I invest more here in window bars, theft losses, insurance, spoilage; I deserve to make more here than at the other places." He looked, almost imploringly, at the man seated next to him. "You don't accept this as the right of a man in business?"

Reed grunted. "Did the bear shit in the woods?" he said.

Again Green laughed. He gulped his coffee awkwardly, as if eager to go. Yet his motions slowed once he had set his coffee cup down on the blue plastic saucer. "Place yourself in *my* situation," he said, his voice high and tentative. "If *you* were running my store in this neighborhood, what would be *your* position? Say on a profit scale of fifteen to forty percent, at what point in between would you draw the line?"

Nelson Reed thought. He sipped his coffee and seemed to chew the liquid. "Fifteen to forty?" he repeated.

"Yes."

"I'm a churchgoin' man," he said. "Closer to fifteen than to forty."

"How close?"

Nelson Reed thought. "In church you tithe ten percent."

"In restaurants you tip fifteen," the grocer said quickly.

"All right," Reed said. "Over fifteen."

"How much over?"

Nelson Reed thought.

"Twenty, thirty, thirty-five?" Green chanted, leaning closer to Reed.

Still the man thought.

"Forty? Maybe even forty-five or fifty?" the grocer breathed in Reed's ear. "In the supermarkets, you know, they have more subtle ways of accomplishing such feats."

Reed slapped his coffee cup with the back of his right hand. The brown liquid swirled across the counter top, wetting the books. "*Damn this!*" he shouted.

Startled, Green rose from his stool.

Nelson Reed was trembling. "I ain't *you*," he said in a deep baritone. "I ain't the *supermarket* neither. All I is is a poor man that works *too* hard to see his pay slip through his fingers like rainwater. All I know is you done *cheat* me, you done *cheat* everybody in the neighborhood, and we organized now to get some of it *back!*" Then he stood and faced the grocer. "My daddy sharecropped down in Mississippi and bought in the company store. He owed them twenty-three years when he died. I paid off five of them years and then run away to up here. Now, I'm a deacon in the Baptist church. I raised my kids the way my daddy raise me and don't bother no-body. Now come to find out, after all my runnin', they done lift that *same company store* up out of Mississippi and slip it down on us here! Well, my daddy was a *fighter*, and if he hadn't owed all them years he would of raise him some hell. Me, I'm steady my daddy's child, plus I got seniority in my union. I'm a free man. Buddy, don't you know *I'm gonna raise me some hell!*"

Harold Green reached for a paper napkin to sop the coffee soaking into his books.

Nelson Reed threw a dollar on top of the books and walked away.

"I *will not* do it!" Harold Green said to his wife that same evening. They were in the bathroom of their home. Bending over the face bowl, she was washing her hair with a towel draped around her neck. The grocer stood by the door, looking in at her. "I will not bankrupt myself tomorrow," he said.

"I've been thinking about it, too," Ruth Green said, shaking her wet hair. "You'll do it, Harry."

"Why should I?" he asked. "You won't leave. You know it was a bluff. I've waited this long for you to calm down. Tomorrow is Saturday. This week has been a hard one. Tonight let's be realistic."

"Of course you'll do it," Ruth Green said. She said it the way she would say "Have some toast." She said, "You'll do it because you want to see your children grow up."

"And for what other reason?" he asked.

She pulled the towel tighter around her neck. "Because you are at heart a moral man."

He grinned painfully. "If I am, why should I have to prove it to *them?*"

"Not them," Ruth Green said, freezing her movements and looking in the mirror. "Certainly not them. By no means them. They have absolutely nothing to do with this."

"Who, then?" he asked, moving from the door into the room. "Who else should I prove something to?"

His wife was crying. But her entire face was wet. The tears moved secretly down her face.

"Who else?" Harold Green asked.

It was almost 11:00 P.M. and the children were in bed. They had also cried when they came home from school. Ruth Green said, "For yourself, Harry. For the love that lives inside your heart."

All night the grocer thought about this.

Nelson Reed also slept little that Friday night. When he returned home from the drugstore, he reported to his wife as much of the conversation as he could remember. At first he had joked about the exchange between himself and the grocer, but as more details returned to his conscious mind he grew solemn and then bitter. "He ask me to put myself in *his* place," Reed told his wife. "Can you imagine that kind of gumption? I never cheated nobody in my life. All my life I have lived on Bible principles. I am a deacon in the church. I have work all my life for other folks and I don't even own the house I live in." He paced up and down the kitchen, his big arms flapping loosely at his sides. Betty Reed sat at the table, watching. "This here's a low-down, ass-kicking world," he said. "I swear to God it is! All my life I have lived on principle and I ain't got a dime in the bank. Betty," he turned suddenly toward her, "don't you think I'm a fool?"

"Mr. Reed," she said. "Let's go on to bed."

But he would not go to bed. Instead, he took the fifth of bourbon from the cabinet under the sink and poured himself a shot. His wife refused to join him. Reed drained the glass of whiskey, and then another, while he resumed pacing the kitchen floor. He slapped his hands against his sides. "*I* think I'm a fool," he said. "Ain't got a dime in the bank, ain't got a pot to *pee* in or a wall to pitch it over, and that there *cheat* ask me to put myself inside *his* shoes. Hell, I can't even *afford* the kind of shoes he wears." He stopped pacing and looked at his wife.

"Mr. Reed," she whispered, "tomorrow ain't a work day. Let's go to bed."

Nelson Reed laughed, the bitterness in his voice rattling his wife. "The *hell* I will!" he said.

He strode to the yellow telephone on the wall beside the sink and began to dial. The first call was to Lloyd Dukes, a neighbor two blocks away and a lieutenant in the organization. Dukes was not at home. The second call was to McElroy's Bar on the corner of 65th and Carroll, where Stanley Harper, another of the lieutenants, worked as a bartender. It was Harper who spread the word, among those men at the bar, that the organization would picket the grocer's store the following morning. And all through the night, in the bedroom of their house, Betty Reed was awakened by telephone calls coming from Lester Jones, Nat Lucas, Mrs. Tyrone Brown, the widow-woman named Murphy, all coordinating the time when they would march in a group against the store owned by Harold Green. Betty Reed's heart beat loudly beneath the covers as she listened to the bitterness and rage in her husband's voice. On several occasions, hearing him declare himself a fool, she pressed the pillow against her eyes and cried.

The grocer opened later than usual this Saturday morning, but still it was early enough to make him one of the first walkers in the neighborhood. He parked his car one block from the store and strolled to work. There were no birds singing. The sky in this area was not blue. It was smog-smutted and gray, seeming on the verge of a light rain. The street, as always, was littered with cans, papers, bits of broken glass. As always the garbage cans overflowed. The morning breeze plastered a sheet of newspaper playfully around the sides of a rusted garbage can. For some reason, using his right foot, he loosened the paper and stood watching it slide into the street and down the block. The movement made him feel good. He whistled while unlocking the bars shielding the windows and door of his store. When he had unlocked the main door he stepped in quickly and threw a switch to the right of the jamb, before the shrill sound of the alarm could shatter his mood. Then he switched on the lights. Everything was as it had been the night before. He had already telephoned his two employees and given them the day off. He busied himself doing the usual things—hauling milk and vegetables from the cooler, putting cash in the till—not thinking about the silence of his wife, or the look in her eyes, only an hour before when he left home. He had determined, at some point while driving through the city, that today it would be business as usual. But he expected very few customers.

The first customer of the day was Mrs. Nelson Reed. She came in around 9:30 A.M. and wandered about the store. He watched her from the checkout counter. She seemed uncertain of what she wanted to buy. She kept glancing at him down the center aisle. His suspicions aroused, he said finally, "Yes, may I help you, Mrs. Reed?" His words caused her to jerk, as if some devious thought had been perceived going through her mind. She reached over quickly and lifted a loaf of whole wheat bread from the rack and walked with it to the counter. She looked at him and smiled. The smile was a broad, shy one, that rare kind of smile one sees on virgin girls when they first confess love to themselves. Betty Reed was a woman of about forty-five. For some reason he could not comprehend, this gesture touched him. When she pulled a dollar from her purse and laid it on the counter, an impulse, from no place he could locate with his mind, seized control of his tongue. "Free," he told Betty Reed. She paused, then pushed the dollar toward him with a firm and determined thrust of her arm. "Free," he heard himself saying strongly, his right palm spread and meeting her thrust with absolute force. She clutched the loaf of bread and walked out of his store.

The next customer, a little girl, arriving well after 10:30 A.M., selected a candy bar from the rack beside the counter. "Free," Green said cheerfully. The little girl left the candy on the counter and ran out of the store.

At 11:15 A.M. a wino came in looking desperate enough to sell his soul. The grocer watched him only for an instant. Then he went to the wine counter and selected a half-gallon of medium-grade red wine. He shoved the jug into the belly of the wino, the man's sour breath bathing his face. "Free," the grocer said. "But you must not drink it in here."

He felt good about the entire world, watching the wino through the window gulping the wine and looking guiltily around.

At 11:25 A.M. the pickets arrived.

Two dozen people, men and women, young and old, crowded the pavement in front of his store. Their signs, placards, and voices denounced him as a parasite. The grocer laughed inside himself. He felt lighthearted and wild, like a man drugged. He rushed to the meat counter and pulled a long roll of brown wrapping paper from the rack, tearing it neatly with a quick shift of his body resembling a dance step practiced fervently in his youth. He laid the paper on the chopping block and with the black-inked, felt-tipped marker scrawled, in giant letters, the word FREE. This he took to the window and pasted in place with many strands of Scotch tape. He was laughing wildly. "Free!" he shouted from behind the brown paper. "Free! Free! Free! Free! Free! Free!" He rushed to the door, pushed his head out, and screamed to the confused crowd, "*Free!*" Then he ran back to the counter and stood behind it, like a soldier at attention.

They came in slowly.

Nelson Reed entered first, working his right foot across the dirty tile as if tracking a squiggling worm. The others followed: Lloyd Dukes dragging a placard, Mr. and Mrs. Tyrone Brown, Stanley Harper walking with his fists clenched, Lester Jones with three of his children, Nat Lucas looking sheepish and detached, a clutch of winos, several bashful nuns, ironic-smiling teenagers and a few students. Bringing up the rear was a bearded social scientist holding a tape recorder to his chest. "Free!" the grocer screamed. He threw up his arms in a gesture that embraced, or dismissed, the entire store. "*All free!*" he shouted. He was grinning with the grace of a madman.

The winos began grabbing first. They stripped the shelf of wine in a matter of seconds. Then they fled, dropping bottles on the tile in their wake. The others, stepping quickly through this liquid, soon congealed it into a sticky, bloodlike consistency. The young men went for the cigarettes and luncheon meats and beer. One of them had the prescience to grab a sack from the counter, while the others loaded their arms swiftly, hugging cartons and packages of cold cuts like long-lost friends. The students joined them, less for greed than for the thrill of the experience. The two nuns backed toward the door. As for the older people, men and women, they stood at first as if stuck to the wine-smeared floor. Then Stanley Harper, the bartender, shouted, "The man said *free*, y'all heard him." He paused. "Didn't you say *free* now?" he called to the grocer.

"I said free," Harold Green answered, his temples pounding.

A cheer went up. The older people began grabbing, as if the secret lusts of a lifetime had suddenly seized command of their arms and eyes. They grabbed toilet tissue, cold cuts, pickles, sardines, boxes of raisins, boxes of starch, cans of soup, tins of tuna fish and salmon, bottles of spices, cans of boned chicken, slippery cans of olive oil. Here a man, Lester Jones, burdened himself with several heads of lettuce, while his wife, in another aisle, shouted for him to drop those small items and concentrate on the gourmet section. She herself took imported sardines, wheat crackers, bottles of candied pickles, herring, anchovies, imported olives, French wafers, an ancient, half-rusted can of pâté, stocked, by mistake, from the inventory of another store. Others packed their arms with detergents, hams, chocolate-coated cereal, whole chickens with hanging asses, wedges of bologna and salami like squashed footballs, chunks of cheeses, yellow and white, shriveled onions, and green peppers. Mrs. Tyrone Brown hung a curve of pepperoni around her neck and seemed to take on instant dignity, much like a person of noble birth in possession now of a long sought-after gem. Another woman, the widow Murphy, stuffed tomatoes into her bosom, holding a half-chewed lemon in her mouth. The more enterprising fought desperately over the three rusted shopping carts, and the victors wheeled these along the narrow aisles, sweeping into them bulk items—beer in six-packs, sacks of sugar, flour, glass bottles of syrup, toilet cleanser, sugar cookies, prune, apple and tomato juices—while others endeavored to snatch the carts from them. There were several fistfights and much cursing. The grocer, standing behind the counter, hummed and rang his cash register like a madman.

Nelson Reed, the first into the store, followed the nuns out, empty-handed.

In less than half an hour the others had stripped the store and vanished in many directions up and down the block. But still more people came, those late in hearing the news. And when they saw the shelves were bare, they cursed soberly and chased those few stragglers still bearing away goods. Soon only the grocer and the social scientist remained, the latter stationed at the door with his tape recorder sucking in leftover sounds. Then he too slipped away up the block.

By 12:10 P.M. the grocer was leaning against the counter, trying to make his mind slow down. Not a man given to drink during work hours, he nonetheless took a swallow from a bottle of wine, a dusty bottle from beneath the wine shelf, somehow overlooked by the winos. Somewhat recovered, he was preparing to remember what he should do next when he glanced toward a figure at the door. Nelson Reed was standing there, watching him.

"All gone," Harold Green said. "My friend, Mr. Reed, there is no more." Still the man stood in the doorway, peering into the store.

The grocer waved his arms about the empty room. Not a display case had a single item standing. "All gone," he said again, as if addressing a stupid child. "There is nothing left to get. You, my friend, have come back too late for a second load. I am cleaned out."

Nelson Reed stepped into the store and strode toward the counter. He moved through wine-stained flour, lettuce leaves, red, green, and blue labels, bits and pieces of broken glass. He walked toward the counter.

"All day," the grocer laughed, not quite hysterically now, "all day long I have not made a single cent of profit. The entire day was a loss. This store, like the others, is *bleeding* me." He waved his arms about the room in a magnificent gesture of uncaring loss. "Now do you understand?" he said. "Now will you put yourself in my shoes? I have nothing here. Come, now, Mr. Reed, would it not be so bad a thing to walk in my shoes?"

"Mr. Green," Nelson Reed said coldly. "My wife bought a loaf of bread in here this mornin'. She forgot to pay you. I, myself, have come here to pay you your money."

"Oh," the grocer said.

"I think it was brown bread. Don't that cost more than white?"

The two men looked away from each other, but not at anything in the store.

"In my store, yes," Harold Green said. He rang the register with the most casual movement of his finger. The register read fifty-five cents.

Nelson Reed held out a dollar.

"And two cents tax," the grocer said.

The man held out the dollar.

"After all," Harold Green said. "We are all, after all, Mr. Reed, in debt to the government."

He rang the register again. It read fifty-seven cents.

Nelson Reed held out a dollar.

1977

Joyce Carol Oates
1938–

One of Oates's inspirations for this story was a Life *magazine feature on the "Pied Piper of Tuscon," a serial killer who seduced and murdered teenaged girls. What attracted Oates to the story was that a group of teenagers knew about the man, but the killer's inexplicable charm prevented them from telling anyone. She described her first draft of the story as "realistic allegory," which she defined as "Hawthornean, romantic, shading into parable." The name of the story was "Death and the Maiden." The final draft may still combine these elements: many readers see Arnold Friend and Connie, despite their realistic portrayal, as mythic types. But in revision, Oates eliminated any "suggestion that 'Arnold Friend' has seduced and murdered other young girls, or even that he necessarily intends to murder Connie." Oates wonders herself if Friend's interest in Connie is " 'merely' sexual." Also gone was her original attraction to the story: a group of teenagers who knew what Friend was up to. What is left is a "shallow, vain, silly, hopeful, doomed" young girl who is capable, nonetheless, "of an unexpected gesture of heroism at the story's end. . . . We don't know the nature of her sacrifice," Oates says, "only that she is generous enough to make it."*

Where Are You Going, Where Have You Been?

for Bob Dylan[1]

Her name was Connie. She was fifteen and she had a quick, nervous giggling habit of craning her neck to glance into mirrors or checking other people's faces to make sure her own was all right. Her mother, who noticed everything and knew everything and who hadn't much reason any longer to look at her own face, always scolded Connie about it. "Stop gawking at yourself. Who are you? You think you're so pretty?" she would say. Connie would raise her eyebrows at these familiar old complaints and look right through her mother, into a shadowy vision of herself as she was right at that moment: she knew she was pretty and that was everything. Her mother had been pretty once too, if you could believe those old snapshots in the album, but now her looks were gone and that was why she was always after Connie.

"Why don't you keep your room clean like your sister? How've you got your hair fixed—what the hell stinks? Hair spray? You don't see your sister using that junk."

Her sister June was twenty-four and still lived at home. She was a secretary in the high school Connie attended, and if that wasn't bad enough—with her in the same building—she was so plain and chunky and steady that Connie had to hear her praised all the time by her mother and her mother's sisters. June did this, June did that, she saved money and helped clean the house and cooked and Connie couldn't do a thing, her mind was all filled with trashy daydreams. Their father was away at work most of the time and when he came home he wanted supper and he read the newspaper at supper and after supper he went to bed. He didn't bother talking much to them, but around his bent head Connie's mother kept picking at her until Connie wished her mother was dead and she herself was dead and it was all over. "She makes me want to throw up sometimes," she complained to her friends. She had a high, breathless,

---

1. Folk and rock singer and songwriter (1941–). Oates has said that the idea for this story came to her after listening to his song "It's All Over Now, Baby Blue."

amused voice that made everything she said sound a little forced, whether it was sincere or not.

There was one good thing: June went places with girl friends of hers, girls who were just as plain and steady as she, and so when Connie wanted to do that her mother had no objections. The father of Connie's best girl friend drove the girls the three miles to town and left them at a shopping plaza so they could walk through the stores or go to a movie, and when he came to pick them up again at eleven he never bothered to ask what they had done.

They must have been familiar sights, walking around the shopping plaza in their shorts and flat ballerina slippers that always scuffed the sidewalk, with charm bracelets jingling on their thin wrists; they would lean together to whisper and laugh secretly if someone passed who amused or interested them. Connie had long dark blond hair that drew anyone's eye to it, and she wore part of it pulled up on her head and puffed out and the rest of it she let fall down her back. She wore a pull-over jersey blouse that looked one way when she was at home and another way when she was away from home. Everything about her had two sides to it, one for home and one for anywhere that was not home: her walk, which could be childlike and bobbing, or languid enough to make anyone think she was hearing music in her head; her mouth, which was pale and smirking most of the time, but bright and pink on these evenings out; her laugh, which was cynical and drawling at home—"Ha, ha, very funny,"—but high-pitched and nervous anywhere else, like the jingling of the charms on her bracelet.

Sometimes they did go shopping or to a movie, but sometimes they went across the highway, ducking fast across the busy road, to a drive-in restaurant where older kids hung out. The restaurant was shaped like a big bottle, though squatter than a real bottle, and on its cap was a revolving figure of a grinning boy holding a hamburger aloft. One night in midsummer they ran across, breathless with daring, and right away someone leaned out a car window and invited them over, but it was just a boy from high school they didn't like. It made them feel good to be able to ignore him. They went up through the maze of parked and cruising cars to the bright-lit, fly-infested restaurant, their faces pleased and expectant as if they were entering a sacred building that loomed up out of the night to give

them what haven and blessing they yearned for. They sat at the
counter and crossed their legs at the ankles, their thin shoulders
rigid with excitement, and listened to the music that made everything so good: the music was always in the background, like music
at a church service; it was something to depend upon.

A boy named Eddie came in to talk with them. He sat backwards
on his stool, turning himself jerkily around in semicircles and then
stopping and turning back again, and after a while he asked Connie
if she would like something to eat. She said she would and so she
tapped her friend's arm on her way out—her friend pulled her face
up into a brave, droll look—and Connie said she would meet her at
eleven, across the way. "I just hate to leave her like that," Connie
said earnestly, but the boy said that she wouldn't be alone for long.
So they went out to his car, and on the way Connie couldn't help
but let her eyes wander over the windshields and faces all around
her, her face gleaming with a joy that had nothing to do with Eddie
or even this place; it might have been the music. She drew her
shoulders up and sucked in her breath with the pure pleasure of being alive, and just at that moment she happened to glance at a face
just a few feet from hers. It was a boy with shaggy black hair, in a
convertible jalopy painted gold. He stared at her and then his lips
widened into a grin. Connie slit her eyes at him and turned away,
but she couldn't help glancing back and there he was, still watching her. He wagged a finger and laughed and said, "Gonna get
you, baby," and Connie turned away again without Eddie noticing
anything.

She spent three hours with him, at the restaurant where they ate
hamburgers and drank Cokes in wax cups that were always sweating, and then down an alley a mile or so away, and when he left her
off at five to eleven only the movie house was still open at the plaza.
Her girl friend was there, talking with a boy. When Connie came
up, the two girls smiled at each other and Connie said, "How was
the movie?" and the girl said, "*You* should know." They rode off
with the girl's father, sleepy and pleased, and Connie couldn't help
but look back at the darkened shopping plaza with its big empty
parking lot and its signs that were faded and ghostly now, and over
at the drive-in restaurant where cars were still circling tirelessly. She
couldn't hear the music at this distance.

Next morning June asked her how the movie was and Connie said, "So-so."

She and that girl and occasionally another girl went out several times a week, and the rest of the time Connie spent around the house—it was summer vacation—getting in her mother's way and thinking, dreaming about the boys she met. But all the boys fell back and dissolved into a single face that was not even a face but an idea, a feeling, mixed up with the urgent insistent pounding of the music and the humid night air of July. Connie's mother kept dragging her back to the daylight by finding things for her to do or saying suddenly, "What's this about the Pettinger girl?"

And Connie would say nervously, "Oh, her. That dope." She always drew thick clear lines between herself and such girls, and her mother was simple and kind enough to believe it. Her mother was so simple, Connie thought, that it was maybe cruel to fool her so much. Her mother went scuffling around the house in old bedroom slippers and complained over the telephone to one sister about the other, then the other called up and the two of them complained about the third one. If June's name was mentioned her mother's tone was approving, and if Connie's name was mentioned it was disapproving. This did not really mean she disliked Connie, and actually Connie thought that her mother preferred her to June just because she was prettier, but the two of them kept up a pretense of exasperation, a sense that they were tugging and struggling over something of little value to either of them. Sometimes, over coffee, they were almost friends, but something would come up—some vexation that was like a fly buzzing suddenly around their heads—and their faces went hard with contempt.

One Sunday Connie got up at eleven—none of them bothered with church—and washed her hair so that it could dry all day long in the sun. Her parents and sister were going to a barbecue at an aunt's house and Connie said no, she wasn't interested, rolling her eyes to let her mother know just what she thought of it. "Stay home alone then," her mother said sharply. Connie sat out back in a lawn chair and watched them drive away, her father quiet and bald, hunched around so that he could back the car out, her mother with a look that was still angry and not at all softened through the windshield, and in the back seat poor old June, all dressed up as if she didn't know what a barbecue was, with all the running yelling kids and the flies. Connie sat with her eyes closed in the sun, dreaming and dazed with the warmth about her as if this were a kind of love, the caresses of love, and her mind slipped over onto thoughts of the boy she had been with the night before and how nice he had been, how sweet it always was, not the way someone like June would suppose but sweet, gentle, the way it was in movies and promised in songs; and when she opened her eyes she hardly knew where she was, the back yard ran off into weeds and a fence-like line of trees and behind it the sky was perfectly blue and still. The asbestos "ranch house" that was now three years old startled her—it looked small. She shook her head as if to get awake.

It was too hot. She went inside the house and turned on the radio to drown out the quiet. She sat on the edge of her bed, barefoot, and listened for an hour and a half to a program called XYZ Sunday Jamboree, record after record of hard, fast, shrieking songs she sang along with, interspersed by exclamations from "Bobby King": "An' look here, you girls at Napoleon's—Son and Charley want you to pay real close attention to this song coming up!"

And Connie paid close attention herself, bathed in a glow of slow-pulsed joy that seemed to rise mysteriously out of the music itself and lay languidly about the airless little room, breathed in and breathed out with each gentle rise and fall of her chest.

After a while she heard a car coming up the drive. She sat up at once, startled, because it couldn't be her father so soon. The gravel kept crunching all the way in from the road—the driveway was long—and Connie ran to the window. It was a car she didn't know. It was an open jalopy, painted a bright gold that caught the sunlight opaquely. Her heart began to pound and her fingers snatched at her hair, checking it, and she whispered, "Christ. Christ," wondering how bad she looked. The car came to a stop at the side door and the horn sounded four short taps, as if this were a signal Connie knew.

She went into the kitchen and approached the door slowly, then hung out the screen door, her bare toes curling down off the step. There were two boys in the car and now she recognized the driver: he had shaggy, shabby black hair that looked crazy as a wig and he was grinning at her.

"I ain't late, am I?" he said.

"Who the hell do you think you are?" Connie said.

"Toldja I'd be out, didn't I?"

"I don't even know who you are."

She spoke sullenly, careful to show no interest or pleasure, and he spoke in a fast, bright monotone. Connie looked past him to the other boy, taking her time. He had fair brown hair, with a lock that fell onto his forehead. His sideburns gave him a fierce, embarrassed look, but so far he hadn't even bothered to glance at her. Both boys wore sunglasses. The driver's glasses were metallic and mirrored everything in miniature.

"You wanta come for a ride?" he said.

Connie smirked and let her hair fall loose over one shoulder.

"Don'tcha like my car? New paint job," he said. "Hey."

"What?"

"You're cute."

She pretended to fidget, chasing flies away from the door.

"Don'tcha believe me, or what?" he said.

"Look, I don't even know who you are," Connie said in disgust.

"Hey, Ellie's got a radio, see. Mine broke down." He lifted his friend's arm and showed her the little transistor radio the boy was holding, and now Connie began to hear the music. It was the same program that was playing inside the house.

"Bobby King?" she said.

"I listen to him all the time. I think he's great."

"He's kind of great," Connie said reluctantly.

"Listen, that guy's *great*. He knows where the action is."

Connie blushed a little, because the glasses made it impossible for her to see just what this boy was looking at. She couldn't decide if she liked him or if he was just a jerk, and so she dawdled in the doorway and wouldn't come down or go back inside. She said, "What's all that stuff painted on your car?"

"Can'tcha read it?" He opened the door very carefully, as if he were afraid it might fall off. He slid out just as carefully, planting his feet firmly on the ground, the tiny metallic world in his glasses slowing down like gelatine hardening, and in the midst of it Connie's bright green blouse. "This here is my name, to begin with," he said. ARNOLD FRIEND was written in tarlike black letters on the side, with a drawing of a round, grinning face that reminded Connie of a pumpkin, except it wore sunglasses. "I wanta introduce myself, I'm Arnold Friend and that's my real name and I'm gonna be your friend, honey, and inside the car's Ellie Oscar, he's kinda shy." Ellie brought his transistor radio up to his shoulder and balanced it there. "Now, these numbers are a secret code, honey," Arnold Friend explained. He read off the numbers 33, 19, 17 and raised his eyebrows at her to see what she thought of that, but she didn't think much of it. The left rear fender had been smashed and around it was written, on the gleaming gold background: DONE BY CRAZY WOMAN DRIVER. Connie had to laugh at that. Arnold Friend was pleased at her laughter and looked up at her. "Around the other side's a lot more— you wanta come and see them?"

"No."

"Why not?"

"Why should I?"

"Don'tcha wanta see what's on the car? Don'tcha wanta go for a ride?"

"I don't know."

"Why not?"

"I got things to do."

"Like what?"

"Things."

He laughed as if she had said something funny. He slapped his thighs. He was standing in a strange way, leaning back against the car as if he were balancing himself. He wasn't tall, only an inch or so taller than she would be if she came down to him. Connie liked the way he was dressed, which was the way all of them dressed: tight faded jeans stuffed into black, scuffed boots, a belt that pulled his waist in and showed how lean he was, and a white pull-over shirt that was a little soiled and showed the hard small muscles of his arms and shoulders. He looked as if he probably did hard work, lifting and carrying things. Even his neck looked muscular. And his face was a familiar face, somehow: the jaw and chin and cheeks slightly darkened because he hadn't shaved for a day or two, and the nose long and hawklike, sniffing as if she were a treat he was going to gobble up and it was all a joke.

"Connie, you ain't telling the truth. This is your day set aside for a ride with me and you know it," he said, still laughing. The way he straightened and recovered from his fit of laughing showed that it had been all fake.

"How do you know what my name is?" she said suspiciously.

"It's Connie."

"Maybe and maybe not."

"I know my Connie," he said, wagging his finger. Now she remembered him even better, back at the restaurant, and her cheeks warmed at the thought of how she had sucked in her breath just at the moment she passed him—how she must have looked to him. And he had remembered her. "Ellie and I come out here especially for you," he said. "Ellie can sit in back. How about it?"

"Where?"

"Where what?"

"Where're we going?"

He looked at her. He took off the sunglasses and she saw how pale the skin around his eyes was, like holes that were not in shadow but instead in light. His eyes were like chips of broken glass that catch the light in an amiable way. He smiled. It was as if the idea of going for a ride somewhere, to someplace, was a new idea to him.

"Just for a ride, Connie sweetheart."

"I never said my name was Connie," she said.

"But I know what it is. I know your name and all about you, lots of things," Arnold Friend said. He had not moved yet but stood still leaning back against the side of his jalopy. "I took a special interest in you, such a pretty girl, and found out all about you—like I know your parents and sister are gone somewheres and I know where and how long they're going to be gone, and I know who you were with last night, and your best girl friend's name is Betty. Right?"

He spoke in a simple lilting voice, exactly as if he were reciting the words to a song. His smile assured her that everything was fine. In the car Ellie turned up the volume on his radio and did not bother to look around at them.

"Ellie can sit in the back seat," Arnold Friend said. He indicated his friend with a casual jerk of his chin, as if Ellie did not count and she should not bother with him.

"How'd you find out all that stuff?" Connie said.

"Listen: Betty Schultz and Tony Fitch and Jimmy Pettinger and

Nancy Pettinger," he said in a chant. "Raymond Stanley and Bob Hutter—"

"Do you know all those kids?"

"I know everybody."

"Look, you're kidding. You're not from around here."

"Sure."

"But—how come we never saw you before?"

"Sure you saw me before," he said. He looked down at his boots, as if he were a little offended. "You just don't remember."

"I guess I'd remember you," Connie said.

"Yeah?" He looked up at this, beaming. He was pleased. He began to mark time with the music from Ellie's radio, tapping his fists lightly together. Connie looked away from his smile to the car, which was painted so bright it almost hurt her eyes to look at it. She looked at that name, ARNOLD FRIEND. And up at the front fender was an expression that was familiar—MAN THE FLYING SAUCERS. It was an expression kids had used the year before but didn't use this year. She looked at it for a while as if the words meant something to her that she did not yet know.

"What're you thinking about? Huh?" Arnold Friend demanded. "Not worried about your hair blowing around in the car, are you?"

"No."

"Think I maybe can't drive good?"

"How do I know?"

"You're a hard girl to handle. How come?" he said. "Don't you know I'm your friend? Didn't you see me put my sign in the air when you walked by?"

"What sign?"

"My sign." And he drew an X in the air, leaning out toward her. They were maybe ten feet apart. After his hand fell back to his side the X was still in the air, almost visible. Connie let the screen door close and stood perfectly still inside it, listening to the music from her radio and the boy's blend together. She stared at Arnold Friend. He stood there so stiffly relaxed, pretending to be relaxed, with one hand idly on the door handle as if he were keeping himself up that way and had no intention of ever moving again. She recognized most things about him, the tight jeans that showed his thighs and buttocks and the greasy leather boots and the tight shirt, and even that slippery friendly smile of his, that sleepy dreamy smile that all the boys used to get across ideas they didn't want to put into words. She recognized all this and also the singsong way he talked, slightly mocking, kidding, but serious and a little melancholy, and she recognized the way he tapped one fist against the other in homage to the perpetual music behind him. But all these things did not come together.

She said suddenly, "Hey, how old are you?"

His smiled faded. She could see then that he wasn't a kid, he was much older—thirty, maybe more. At this knowledge her heart began to pound faster.

"That's a crazy thing to ask. Can'tcha see I'm your own age?"

"Like hell you are."

"Or maybe a coupla years older. I'm eighteen."

"Eighteen?" she said doubtfully.

He grinned to reassure her and lines appeared at the corners of his mouth. His teeth were big and white. He grinned so broadly his eyes became slits and she saw how thick the lashes were, thick and black as if painted with a black tarlike material. Then, abruptly, he seemed to become embarrassed and looked over his shoulder at Ellie. "*Him*, he's crazy," he said. "Ain't he a riot? He's a nut, a real character." Ellie was still listening to the music. His sunglasses told nothing about what he was thinking. He wore a bright orange shirt unbuttoned halfway to show his chest, which was a pale, bluish chest and not muscular like Arnold Friend's. His shirt collar was turned up all around and the very tips of the collar pointed out past his chin as if they were protecting him. He was pressing the transistor radio up against his ear and sat there in a kind of daze, right in the sun.

"He's kinda strange," Connie said.

"Hey, she says you're kinda strange! Kinda strange!" Arnold Friend cried. He pounded on the car to get Ellie's attention. Ellie turned for the first time and Connie saw with shock that he wasn't a kid either—he had a fair, hairless face, cheeks reddened slightly as if the veins grew too close to the surface of his skin, the face of a forty-year-old baby. Connie felt a wave of dizziness rise in her at this sight and she stared at him as if waiting for something to change the shock of the moment, make it all right again. Ellie's lips kept shaping words, mumbling along with the words blasting in his ear.

"Maybe you two better go away," Connie said faintly.

"What? How come?" Arnold Friend cried. "We come out here to take you for a ride. It's Sunday." He had the voice of the man on the radio now. It was the same voice, Connie thought. "Don'tcha know it's Sunday all day? And honey, no matter who you were with last night, today you're with Arnold Friend and don't you forget it! Maybe you better step out here," he said, and this last was in a different voice. It was a little flatter, as if the heat was finally getting to him.

"No. I got things to do."

"Hey."

"You two better leave."

"We ain't leaving until you come with us."

"Like hell I am—"

"Connie, don't fool around with me. I mean—I mean, don't fool *around*," he said, shaking his head. He laughed incredulously. He placed his sunglasses on top of his head, carefully, as if he were indeed wearing a wig, and brought the stems down behind his ears. Connie stared at him, another wave of dizziness and fear rising in her so that for a moment he wasn't even in focus but was just a blur standing there against his gold car, and she had the idea that he had driven up the driveway all right but had come from nowhere before that and belonged nowhere and that everything about him and even about the music that was so familiar to her was only half real.

"If my father comes and sees you—"

"He ain't coming. He's at a barbecue."

"How do you know that?"

"Aunt Tillie's. Right now they're—uh—they're drinking. Sitting around," he said vaguely, squinting as if he were staring all the way to town and over to Aunt Tillie's back yard. Then the vision seemed to get clear and he nodded energetically. "Yeah. Sitting around. There's your sister in a blue dress, huh? And high heels, the poor sad bitch—nothing like you, sweetheart! And your mother's helping some fat woman with the corn, they're cleaning the corn—husking the corn—"

"What fat woman?" Connie cried.

"How do I know what fat woman, I don't know every goddamn fat woman in the world!" Arnold Friend laughed.

"Oh, that's Mrs. Hornsby. . . . Who invited her?" Connie said. She felt a little lightheaded. Her breath was coming quickly.

"She's too fat. I don't like them fat. I like them the way you are, honey," he said, smiling sleepily at her. They stared at each other for a while through the screen door. He said softly, "Now, what you're going to do is this: you're going to come out that door. You're going to sit up front with me and Ellie's going to sit in the back, the hell with Ellie, right? This isn't Ellie's date. You're my date. I'm your lover, honey."

"What? You're crazy—"

"Yes, I'm your lover. You don't know what that is but you will," he said. "I know that too. I know all about you. But look: it's real nice and you couldn't ask for nobody better than me, or more polite. I always keep my word. I'll tell you how it is, I'm always nice at first, the first time. I'll hold you so tight you won't think you have to try to get away or pretend anything because you'll know you can't. And I'll come inside you where it's all secret and you'll give in to me and you'll love me—"

"Shut up! You're crazy!" Connie said. She backed away from the door. She put her hands up against her ears as if she'd heard something terrible, something not meant for her. "People don't talk like that, you're crazy," she muttered. Her heart was almost too big now for her chest and its pumping made sweat break out all over her. She looked out to see Arnold Friend pause and then take a step toward the porch, lurching. He almost fell. But, like a clever drunken man, he managed to catch his balance. He wobbled in his high boots and grabbed hold of one of the porch posts.

"Honey?" he said. "You still listening?"

"Get the hell out of here!"

"Be nice, honey. Listen."

"I'm going to call the police—"

He wobbled again and out of the side of his mouth came a fast spat curse, an aside not meant for her to hear. But even this "Christ!" sounded forced. Then he began to smile again. She watched this smile come, awkward as if he were smiling from inside a mask. His whole face was a mask, she thought wildly, tanned down to his throat but then running out as if he had plastered make-up on his face but had forgotten about his throat.

"Honey——? Listen, here's how it is. I always tell the truth and I promise you this: I ain't coming in that house after you."

"You better not! I'm going to call the police if you—if you don't—"

"Honey," he said, talking right through her voice, "honey, I'm not coming in there but you are coming out here. You know why?"

She was panting. The kitchen looked like a place she had never seen before, some room she had run inside but that wasn't good enough, wasn't going to help her. The kitchen window had never had a curtain, after three years, and there were dishes in the sink for her to do—probably—and if you ran your hand across the table you'd probably feel something sticky there.

"You listening, honey? Hey?"

"—going to call the police—"

"Soon as you touch the phone I don't need to keep my promise and can come inside. You won't want that."

She rushed forward and tried to lock the door. Her fingers were shaking. "But why lock it," Arnold Friend said gently, talking right into her face. "It's just a screen door. It's just nothing." One of his boots was at a strange angle, as if his foot wasn't in it. It pointed out to the left, bent at the ankle. "I mean, anybody can break through a screen door and glass and wood and iron or anything else if he needs to, anybody at all, and specially Arnold Friend. If the place got lit up with a fire, honey, you'd come runnin' out into my arms, right into my arms an' safe at home—like you knew I was your lover and'd stopped fooling around. I don't mind a nice shy girl but I don't like no fooling around." Part of those words were spoken with a slight rhythmic lilt, and Connie somehow recognized them—the echo of a song from last year, about a girl rushing into her boy friend's arms and coming home again—

Connie stood barefoot on the linoleum floor, staring at him. "What do you want?" she whispered.

"I want you," he said.

"What?"

"Seen you that night and thought, that's the one, yes sir. I never needed to look anymore."

"But my father's coming back. He's coming to get me. I had to wash my hair first—" She spoke in a dry, rapid voice, hardly raising it for him to hear.

"No, your daddy is not coming and yes, you had to wash your hair and you washed it for me. It's nice and shining and all for me. I thank you sweetheart," he said with a mock bow, but again he almost lost his balance. He had to bend and adjust his boots. Evidently his feet did not go all the way down; the boots must have been stuffed with something so that he would seem taller. Connie stared out at him and behind him at Ellie in the car, who seemed to be looking off toward Connie's right, into nothing. This Ellie said, pulling the words out of the air one after another as if he were just discovering them, "You want me to pull out the phone?"

"Shut your mouth and keep it shut," Arnold Friend said, his face red from bending over or maybe from embarrassment because Connie had seen his boots. "This ain't none of your business."

"What—what are you doing? What do you want?" Connie said. "If I call the police they'll get you, they'll arrest you—"

"Promise was not to come in unless you touch that phone, and I'll keep that promise," he said. He resumed his erect position and tried to force his shoulders back. He sounded like a hero in a movie, declaring something important. But he spoke too loudly and it was as if he were speaking to someone behind Connie. "I ain't made plans for coming in that house where I don't belong but just for you to come out to me, the way you should. Don't you know who I am?"

"You're crazy," she whispered. She backed away from the door but did not want to go into another part of the house, as if this would give him permission to come through the door. "What do you . . . you're crazy, you. . . ."

"Huh? What're you saying, honey?"

Her eyes darted everywhere in the kitchen. She could not remember what it was, this room.

"This is how it is, honey: you come out and we'll drive away, have a nice ride. But if you don't come out we're gonna wait till your people come home and then they're all going to get it."

"You want that telephone pulled out?" Ellie said. He held the radio away from his ear and grimaced, as if without the radio the air was too much for him.

"I toldja shut up, Ellie," Arnold Friend said, "you're deaf, get a hearing aid, right? Fix yourself up. This little girl's no trouble and's gonna be nice to me, so Ellie keep to yourself, this ain't your date— right? Don't hem in on me, don't hog, don't crush, don't bird dog, don't trail me," he said in a rapid, meaningless voice, as if he were running through all the expressions he'd learned but was no longer sure which of them was in style, then rushing on to new ones, making them up with his eyes closed. "Don't crawl under my fence, don't squeeze in my chipmunk hole, don't sniff my glue, suck my popsicle, keep your own greasy fingers on yourself!" He shaded his eyes and peered in at Connie, who was backed against the kitchen table. "Don't mind him, honey, he's just a creep. He's a dope. Right? I'm the boy for you and like I said, you come out here nice like a lady and give me your hand, and nobody else gets hurt, I mean, your nice old bald-headed daddy and your mummy and your sister in her high heels. Because listen: why bring them in this?"

"Leave me alone," Connie whispered.

"Hey, you know that old woman down the road, the one with the chickens and stuff—you know her?"

"She's dead!"

"Dead? What? You know her?" Arnold Friend said.

"She's dead—"

"Don't you like her?"

"She's dead—she's—she isn't here any more—"

"But don't you like her, I mean, you got something against her? Some grudge or something?" Then his voice dipped as if he were conscious of a rudeness. He touched the sunglasses perched up on top of his head as if to make sure they were still there. "Now, you be a good girl."

"What are you going to do?"

"Just two things, or maybe three," Arnold Friend said. "But I promise it won't last long and you'll like me the way you get to like people you're close to. You will. It's all over for you here, so come on out. You don't want your people in any trouble, do you?"

She turned and bumped against a chair or something, hurting

her leg, but she ran into the back room and picked up the telephone. Something roared in her ear, a tiny roaring, and she was so
sick with fear that she could do nothing but listen to it—the telephone was clammy and very heavy and her fingers groped down to
the dial but were too weak to touch it. She began to scream into the
phone, into the roaring. She cried out, she cried for her mother, she
felt her breath start jerking back and forth in her lungs as if it were
something Arnold Friend was stabbing her with again and again
with no tenderness. A noisy sorrowful wailing rose all about her and
she was locked inside it the way she was locked inside this house.

After a while she could hear again. She was sitting on the floor
with her wet back against the wall.

Arnold Friend was saying from the door, "That's a good girl. Put
the phone back."

She kicked the phone away from her.

"No, honey. Pick it up. Put it back right."

She picked it up and put it back. The dial tone stopped.

"That's a good girl. Now, you come outside."

She was hollow with what had been fear but what was now just
an emptiness. All that screaming had blasted it out of her. She sat,
one leg cramped under her, and deep inside her brain was something like a pinpoint of light that kept going and would not let her
relax. She thought, I'm not going to see my mother again. She
thought, I'm not going to sleep in my bed again. Her bright green
blouse was all wet.

Arnold Friend said, in a gentle-loud voice that was like a stage
voice, "The place where you came from ain't there any more, and
where you had in mind to go is cancelled out. This place you are
now—inside your daddy's house—is nothing but a cardboard box I
can knock down any time. You know that and always did know it.
You hear me?"

She thought, I have got to think. I have got to know what to do.

"We'll go out to a nice field, out in the country here where it
smells so nice and it's sunny," Arnold Friend said. "I'll have my arms
tight around you so you won't need to try to get away and I'll show
you what love is like, what it does. The hell with this house! It looks
solid all right," he said. He ran a fingernail down the screen and the
noise did not make Connie shiver, as it would have the day before.

"Now, put your hand on your heart, honey. Feel that? That feels solid too but we know better. Be nice to me, be sweet like you can because what else is there for a girl like you but to be sweet and pretty and give in?—and get away before her people come back?"

She felt her pounding heart. Her hand seemed to enclose it. She thought for the first time in her life that it was nothing that was hers, that belonged to her, but just a pounding, living thing inside this body that wasn't really hers either.

"You don't want them to get hurt," Arnold Friend went on. "Now, get up, honey. Get up all by yourself."

She stood.

"Now, turn this way. That's right. Come over here to me.—Ellie, put that away, didn't I tell you? You dope. You miserable creepy dope," Arnold Friend said. His words were not angry but only part of an incantation. The incantation was kindly. "Now, come out through the kitchen to me, honey, and let's see a smile, try it, you're a brave, sweet little girl and now they're eating corn and hot dogs cooked to bursting over an outdoor fire, and they don't know one thing about you and never did and honey, you're better than them because not a one of them would have done this for you."

Connie felt the linoleum under her feet; it was cool. She brushed her hair back out of her eyes. Arnold Friend let go of the post tentatively and opened his arms for her, his elbows pointing in toward each other and his wrists limp, to show that this was an embarrassed embrace and a little mocking, he didn't want to make her self-conscious.

She put out her hand against the screen. She watched herself push the door slowly open as if she were back safe somewhere in the other doorway, watching this body and this head of long hair moving out into the sunlight where Arnold Friend waited.

"My sweet little blue-eyed girl," he said in a half-sung sigh that had nothing to do with her brown eyes but was taken up just the same by the vast sunlit reaches of the land behind him and on all sides of him—so much land that Connie had never seen before and did not recognize except to know that she was going to it.

1966

Tim O'Brien
1946–

> *O'Brien fought in Vietnam as part of a unit like the one depicted in this story. Though O'Brien first published "The Things They Carried" as a short story in* Esquire *magazine, he eventually made it the first chapter in his 1990 novel bearing the same title, in which the lives of the characters in this story continue in the subsequent chapters. For example, Martha and Jimmy Cross meet again, long after the war, at a school reunion, but they do not rekindle their relationship; Martha has become a celibate missionary. Also, Jimmy Cross's conclusion at the story's end—that imagination is a killer, that he will stick to reality—is challenged in later chapters. Perhaps its style is the most striking feature of "The Things They Carried." Jimmy Cross's story is embedded within emotionless recitations of the weights of each item the soldiers carried into the field. Many readers might not consider this information important, but O'Brien's including it was surely purposeful. To figure out his meaning, pay particular attention to how these lists and their effects on you change from the beginning to the end of the story.*

The Things They Carried

First Lieutenant Jimmy Cross carried letters from a girl named Martha, a junior at Mount Sebastian College in New Jersey. They were not love letters, but Lieutenant Cross was hoping, so he kept them folded in plastic at the bottom of his rucksack. In the late afternoon, after a day's march, he would dig his foxhole, wash his hands under a canteen, unwrap the letters, hold them with the tips of his fingers, and spend the last hour of light pretending. He would imagine romantic camping trips into the White Mountains in New Hampshire. He would sometimes taste the envelope flaps, knowing her tongue had been there. More than anything, he wanted Martha to love him as he loved her, but the letters were mostly chatty, elusive on the matter of love. She was a virgin, he was almost sure. She was an English major at Mount Sebastian, and she wrote beautifully about her professors and roommates and midterm exams, about her respect for Chaucer and her great affection for Virginia Woolf. She often quoted lines of poetry; she never mentioned the war, except to say, Jimmy, take care of yourself. The letters weighed ten ounces. They were signed "Love, Martha," but Lieutenant Cross understood that "Love" was only a way of signing and did not mean what he sometimes pretended it meant. At dusk, he would carefully return the letters to his rucksack. Slowly, a bit distracted, he would get up and move among his men, checking the perimeter, then at full dark he would return to his hole and watch the night and wonder if Martha was a virgin.

The things they carried were largely determined by necessity. Among the necessities or near necessities were P-38 can openers, pocket knives, heat tabs, wrist watches, dog tags, mosquito repellent, chewing gum, candy, cigarettes, salt tablets, packets of Kool-Aid, lighters, matches, sewing kits, Military Payment Certificates, C rations, and two or three canteens of water. Together, these items weighed between fifteen and twenty pounds, depending upon a man's habits or rate of metabolism. Henry Dobbins, who was a big man, carried extra rations; he was especially fond of canned peaches in heavy syrup over pound cake. Dave Jensen, who practiced field hygiene, carried a toothbrush, dental floss, and several hotel-size bars of soap he'd stolen on R&R[1] in Sydney, Australia. Ted Lavender, who was scared, carried tranquilizers until he was shot in the head outside the village of Than Khe in mid-April. By necessity, and because it was SOP,[2] they all carried steel helmets that weighed five pounds including the liner and camouflage cover. They carried the standard fatigue jackets and trousers. Very few carried underwear. On their feet they carried jungle boots—2.1 pounds—and Dave Jensen carried three pairs of socks and a can of Dr. Scholl's foot powder as a precaution against trench foot. Until he was shot, Ted Lavender carried six or seven ounces of premium dope, which for him was a necessity. Mitchell Sanders, the RTO,[3] carried condoms. Norman Bowker carried a diary. Rat Kiley carried comic books. Kiowa, a devout Baptist, carried an illustrated New Testament that had been presented to him by his father, who taught Sunday school

---

1. Rest and recreation leave.
2. Standard operating procedure.

3. Radio and telephone operator.

in Oklahoma City, Oklahoma. As a hedge against bad times, however, Kiowa also carried his grandmother's distrust of the white
man, his grandfather's old hunting hatchet. Necessity dictated. Because the land was mined and booby-trapped, it was SOP for each
man to carry a steel-centered, nylon-covered flak jacket, which
weighed 6.7 pounds, but which on hot days seemed much heavier.
Because you could die so quickly, each man carried at least one large
compress bandage, usually in the helmet band for easy access. Because the nights were cold, and because the monsoons were wet,
each carried a green plastic poncho that could be used as a raincoat
or ground sheet or makeshift tent. With its quilted liner, the poncho weighed almost two pounds, but it was worth every ounce. In
April, for instance, when Ted Lavender was shot, they used his poncho to wrap him up then to carry him across the paddy, then to lift
him into the chopper that took him away.

They were called legs or grunts.
    To carry something was to "hump" it, as when Lieutenant Jimmy
Cross humped his love for Martha up the hills and through the
swamps. In its intransitive form, "to hump" meant "to walk," or "to
march," but it implied burdens far beyond the intransitive.
    Almost everyone humped photographs. In his wallet, Lieutenant
Cross carried two photographs of Martha. The first was a Koda-
chrome snapshot signed "Love," though he knew better. She stood
against a brick wall. Her eyes were gray and neutral, her lips slightly
open as she stared straight-on at the camera. At night, sometimes,
Lieutenant Cross wondered who had taken the picture, because he
knew she had boyfriends, because he loved her so much, and because
he could see the shadow of the picture taker spreading out against the
brick wall. The second photograph had been clipped from the 1968
Mount Sebastian yearbook. It was an action shot—women's volleyball—and Martha was bent horizontal to the floor, reaching, the
palms of her hands in sharp focus, the tongue taut, the expression
frank and competitive. There was no visible sweat. She wore white
gym shorts. Her legs, he thought, were almost certainly the legs of a
virgin, dry and without hair, the left knee cocked and carrying her entire weight, which was just over one hundred pounds. Lieutenant
Cross remembered touching that left knee. A dark theater, he remem-

bered, and the movie was *Bonnie and Clyde*, and Martha wore a tweed skirt, and during the final scene, when he touched her knee, she turned and looked at him in a sad, sober way that made him pull his hand back, but he would always remember the feel of the tweed skirt and the knee beneath it and the sound of the gunfire that killed Bonnie and Clyde, how embarrassing it was, how slow and oppressive. He remembered kissing her good night at the dorm door. Right then, he thought, he should've done something brave. He should've carried her up the stairs to her room and tied her to the bed and touched that left knee all night long. He should've risked it. Whenever he looked at the photographs, he thought of new things he should've done.

What they carried was partly a function of rank, partly of field specialty.

As a first lieutenant and platoon leader, Jimmy Cross carried a compass, maps, code books, binoculars, and a .45-caliber pistol that weighed 2.9 pounds fully loaded. He carried a strobe light and the responsibility for the lives of his men.

As an RTO, Mitchell Sanders carried the PRC-25 radio, a killer, twenty-six pounds with its battery.

As a medic, Rat Kiley carried a canvas satchel filled with morphine and plasma and malaria tablets and surgical tape and comic books and all the things a medic must carry, including M&M's for especially bad wounds, for a total weight of nearly twenty pounds.

As a big man, therefore a machine gunner, Henry Dobbins carried the M-60, which weighed twenty-three pounds unloaded, but which was almost always loaded. In addition, Dobbins carried between ten and fifteen pounds of ammunition draped in belts across his chest and shoulders.

As PFCs or Spec 4s,[4] most of them were common grunts and carried the standard M-16 gas-operated assault rifle. The weapon weighed 7.5 pounds unloaded, 8.2 pounds with its full twenty-round magazine. Depending on numerous factors, such as topography and psychology, the riflemen carried anywhere from twelve to twenty magazines, usually in cloth bandoliers, adding on another 8.4 pounds

---

4. PFC: Private First Class. Spec 4: Specialist Fourth Class, an army rank immediately above Private First Class.

at minimum, fourteen pounds at maximum. When it was available, they also carried M-16 maintenance gear—rods and steel brushes and swabs and tubes of LSA oil[5]—all of which weighed about a pound. Among the grunts, some carried the M-79 grenade launcher, 5.9 pounds unloaded, a reasonably light weapon except for the ammunition, which was heavy. A single round weighed ten ounces. The typical load was twenty-five rounds. But Ted Lavender, who was scared, carried thirty-four rounds when he was shot and killed outside Than Khe, and he went down under an exceptional burden, more than twenty pounds of ammunition, plus the flak jacket and helmet and rations and water and toilet paper and tranquilizers and all the rest, plus the unweighed fear. He was dead weight. There was no twitching or flopping. Kiowa, who saw it happen, said it was like watching a rock fall, or a big sandbag or something—just boom, then down—not like the movies where the dead guy rolls around and does fancy spins and goes ass over teakettle—not like that, Kiowa said, the poor bastard just flat-fuck fell. Boom. Down. Nothing else. It was a bright morning in mid-April. Lieutenant Cross felt the pain. He blamed himself. They stripped off Lavender's canteens and ammo, all the heavy things, and Rat Kiley said the obvious, the guy's dead, and Mitchell Sanders used his radio to report one U.S. KIA[6] and to request a chopper. Then they wrapped Lavender in his poncho. They carried him out to a dry paddy, established security, and sat smoking the dead man's dope until the chopper came. Lieutenant Cross kept to himself. He pictured Martha's smooth young face, thinking he loved her more than anything, more than his men, and now Ted Lavender was dead because he loved her so much and could not stop thinking about her. When the dust-off[7] arrived, they carried Lavender aboard. Afterward they burned Than Khe. They marched until dusk, then dug their holes, and that night Kiowa kept explaining how you had to be there, how fast it was, how the poor guy just dropped like so much concrete. Boom-down, he said. Like cement.

In addition to the three standard weapons—the M-60, M-16, and M-79—they carried whatever presented itself, or whatever seemed

5. Small arms lubricant.   7. Helicopter.
6. Killed in action.

appropriate as a means of killing or staying alive. They carried catch-as-catch-can. At various times, in various situations, they carried M-14s and CAR-15s and Swedish Ks and grease guns and captured AK-47s and Chi-Coms and RPGs and Simonov carbines and black-market Uzis and .38-caliber Smith & Wesson handguns and 66 mm LAWs and shotguns and silencers and blackjacks and bayonets and C-4 plastic explosives. Lee Strunk carried a slingshot; a weapon of last resort, he called it. Mitchell Sanders carried brass knuckles. Kiowa carried his grandfather's feathered hatchet. Every third or fourth man carried a Claymore antipersonnel mine—3.5 pounds with its firing device. They all carried fragmentation grenades—fourteen ounces each. They all carried at least one M-18 colored smoke grenade—twenty-four ounces. Some carried CS or tear-gas grenades. Some carried white-phosphorus grenades. They carried all they could bear, and then some, including a silent awe for the terrible power of the things they carried.

In the first week of April, before Lavender died, Lieutenant Jimmy Cross received a good-luck charm from Martha. It was a simple pebble, an ounce at most. Smooth to the touch, it was a milky-white color with flecks of orange and violet, oval-shaped, like a miniature egg. In the accompanying letter, Martha wrote that she had found the pebble on the Jersey shoreline, precisely where the land touched water at high tide, where things came together but also separated. It was this separate-but-together quality, she wrote, that had inspired her to pick up the pebble and to carry it in her breast pocket for several days, where it seemed weightless, and then to send it through the mail, by air, as a token of her truest feelings for him. Lieutenant Cross found this romantic. But he wondered what her truest feelings were, exactly, and what she meant by separate-but-together. He wondered how the tides and waves had come into play on that afternoon along the Jersey shoreline when Martha saw the pebble and bent down to rescue it from geology. He imagined bare feet. Martha was a poet, with the poet's sensibilities, and her feet would be brown and bare, the toenails unpainted, the eyes chilly and somber like the ocean in March, and though it was painful, he wondered who had been with her that afternoon. He imagined a pair of shadows moving along the strip of sand where things came together but also separated. It was phantom jealousy, he knew, but he couldn't help himself. He loved her so much. On the march, through the hot days of early April, he carried the pebble in his mouth, turning it with his tongue, tasting sea salts and moisture. His mind wandered. He had difficulty keeping his attention on the war. On occasion he would yell at his men to spread out the column, to keep their eyes open, but then he would slip away into daydreams, just pretending, walking barefoot along the Jersey shore, with Martha, carrying nothing. He would feel himself rising. Sun and waves and gentle winds, all love and lightness.

What they carried varied by mission.

When a mission took them to the mountains, they carried mosquito netting, machetes, canvas tarps, and extra bug juice.

If a mission seemed especially hazardous, or if it involved a place they knew to be bad, they carried everything they could. In certain heavily mined AOs,[8] where the land was dense with Toe Poppers and Bouncing Betties, they took turns humping a twenty-eight-pound mine detector. With its headphones and big sensing plate, the equipment was a stress on the lower back and shoulders, awkward to handle, often useless because of the shrapnel in the earth, but they carried it anyway, partly for safety, partly for the illusion of safety.

On ambush, or other night missions, they carried peculiar little odds and ends. Kiowa always took along his New Testament and a pair of moccasins for silence. Dave Jensen carried night-sight vitamins high in carotin. Lee Strunk carried his slingshot; ammo, he claimed, would never be a problem. Rat Kiley carried brandy and M&M's. Until he was shot, Ted Lavender carried the starlight scope, which weighed 6.3 pounds with its aluminum carrying case. Henry Dobbins carried his girlfriend's pantyhose wrapped around his neck as a comforter. They all carried ghosts. When dark came, they would move out single file across the meadows and paddies to their ambush coordinates, where they would quietly set up the Claymores and lie down and spend the night waiting.

Other missions were more complicated and required special equipment. In mid-April it was their mission to search out and de-

---

8. Areas of operations.

stroy the elaborate tunnel complexes in the Than Khe area south of Chu Lai. To blow the tunnels, they carried one-pound blocks of pentrite high explosives, four blocks to a man, sixty-eight pounds in all. They carried wiring, detonators, and battery-powered clackers. Dave Jensen carried earplugs. Most often, before blowing the tunnels, they were ordered by higher command to search them, which was considered bad news, but by and large they just shrugged and carried out orders. Because he was a big man, Henry Dobbins was excused from tunnel duty. The others would draw numbers. Before Lavender died there were seventeen men in the platoon, and whoever drew the number seventeen would strip off his gear and crawl in head first with a flashlight and Lieutenant Cross's .45-caliber pistol. The rest of them would fan out as security. They would sit down or kneel, not facing the hole, listening to the ground beneath them, imagining cobwebs and ghosts, whatever was down there—the tunnel walls squeezing in—how the flashlight seemed impossibly heavy in the hand and how it was tunnel vision in the very strictest sense, compression in all ways, even time, and how you had to wiggle in—ass and elbows—a swallowed-up feeling—and how you found yourself worrying about odd things—will your flashlight go dead? Do rats carry rabies? If you screamed, how far would the sound carry? Would your buddies hear it? Would they have the courage to drag you out? In some respects, though not many, the waiting was worse than the tunnel itself. Imagination was a killer.

On April 16, when Lee Strunk drew the number seventeen, he laughed and muttered something and went down quickly. The morning was hot and very still. Not good, Kiowa said. He looked at the tunnel opening, then out across a dry paddy toward the village of Than Khe. Nothing moved. No clouds or birds or people. As they waited, the men smoked and drank Kool-Aid, not talking much, feeling sympathy for Lee Strunk but also feeling the luck of the draw. You win some, you lose some, said Mitchell Sanders, and sometimes you settle for a rain check. It was a tired line and no one laughed.

Henry Dobbins ate a tropical chocolate bar. Ted Lavender popped a tranquilizer and went off to pee.

After five minutes, Lieutenant Jimmy Cross moved to the tunnel, leaned down, and examined the darkness. Trouble, he thought—a cave-in maybe. And then suddenly, without willing it, he was think-ing about Martha. The stresses and fractures, the quick collapse, the two of them buried alive under all that weight. Dense, crushing love. Kneeling, watching the hole, he tried to concentrate on Lee Strunk and the war, all the dangers, but his love was too much for him, he felt paralyzed, he wanted to sleep inside her lungs and breathe her blood and be smothered. He wanted her to be a virgin and not a vir-gin, all at once. He wanted to know her. Intimate secrets—why po-etry? Why so sad? Why that grayness in her eyes? Why so alone? Not lonely just alone—riding her bike across campus or sitting off by her-self in the cafeteria. Even dancing, she danced alone—and it was the aloneness that filled him with love. He remembered telling her that one evening. How she nodded and looked away. And how, later, when he kissed her, she received the kiss without returning it, her eyes wide open, not afraid, not a virgin's eyes, just flat and uninvolved.

Lieutenant Cross gazed at the tunnel. But he was not there. He was buried with Martha under the white sand at the Jersey shore. They were pressed together, and the pebble in his mouth was her tongue. He was smiling. Vaguely, he was aware of how quiet the day was, the sullen paddies, yet he could not bring himself to worry about matters of security. He was beyond that. He was just a kid at war, in love. He was twenty-two years old. He couldn't help it.

A few moments later Lee Strunk crawled out of the tunnel. He came up grinning, filthy but alive. Lieutenant Cross nodded and closed his eyes while the others clapped Strunk on the back and made jokes about rising from the dead.

Worms, Rat Kiley said. Right out of the grave. Fuckin' zombie.

The men laughed. They all felt great relief.

Spook City, said Mitchell Sanders.

Lee Strunk made a funny ghost sound, a kind of moaning, yet very happy, and right then, when Strunk made that high happy moaning sound, when he went *Ahhooooo*, right then Ted Lavender was shot in the head on his way back from peeing. He lay with his mouth open. The teeth were broken. There was a swollen black bruise under his left eye. The cheekbone was gone. Oh shit, Rat Kiley said, the guy's dead. The guy's dead, he kept saying, which seemed profound—the guy's dead. I mean really.

———

The things they carried were determined to some extent by super-stition. Lieutenant Cross carried his good-luck pebble. Dave Jensen carried a rabbit's foot. Norman Bowker, otherwise a very gentle per-son, carried a thumb that had been presented to him as a gift by Mitchell Sanders. The thumb was dark brown, rubbery to the touch, and weighed four ounces at most. It had been cut from a VC[9] corpse, a boy of fifteen or sixteen. They'd found him at the bottom of an irrigation ditch, badly burned, flies in his mouth and eyes. The boy wore black shorts and sandals. At the time of his death he had been carrying a pouch of rice, rifle, and three maga-zines of ammunition.

You want my opinion, Mitchell Sanders said, there's a definite moral here.

He put his hand on the dead boy's wrist. He was quiet for a time, as if counting a pulse, then he patted the stomach, almost affection-ately, and used Kiowa's hunting hatchet to remove the thumb.

Henry Dobbins asked what the moral was.

Moral?

You know. *Moral.*

Sanders wrapped the thumb in toilet paper and handed it across to Norman Bowker. There was no blood. Smiling, he kicked the boy's head, watched the flies scatter, and said, It's like with that old TV show—Paladin. Have gun, will travel.

Henry Dobbins thought about it.

Yeah, well, he finally said. I don't see no moral.

There it *is*, man.

Fuck off.

They carried USO[10] stationery and pencils and pens. They carried Sterno,[11] safety pins, trip flares, signal flares, spools of wire, razor blades, chewing tobacco, liberated joss sticks and statuettes of the smiling Buddha, candles, grease pencils, *The Stars and Stripes*, fin-gernail clippers, Psy Ops[12] leaflets, bush hats, bolos, and much more. Twice a week, when the resupply choppers came in, they car-

9. Vietcong.
10. United Service Organization, which provided entertainment to the troops.

11. Canned fuel for a portable stove.
12. Psychological Operations.

ried hot chow in green Mermite cans and large canvas bags filled
with iced beer and soda pop. They carried plastic water containers,
each with a two-gallon capacity. Mitchell Sanders carried a set of
starched tiger fatigues for special occasions. Henry Dobbins carried
Black Flag insecticide. Dave Jensen carried empty sandbags that
could be filled at night for added protection. Lee Strunk carried tan-
ning lotion. Some things they carried in common. Taking turns,
they carried the big PRC-77 scrambler radio, which weighed thirty
pounds with its battery. They shared the weight of memory. They
took up what others could no longer bear. Often, they carried each
other, the wounded or weak. They carried infections. They carried
chess sets, basketballs, Vietnamese-English dictionaries, insignia of
rank, Bronze Stars and Purple Hearts, plastic cards imprinted with
the Code of Conduct. They carried diseases, among them malaria
and dysentery. They carried lice and ringworm and leeches and
paddy algae and various rots and molds. They carried the land itself—Vietnam, the place, the soil—a powdery orange-red dust that
covered their boots and fatigues and faces. They carried the sky. The
whole atmosphere, they carried it, the humidity, the monsoons, the
stink of fungus and decay, all of it, they carried gravity. They moved
like mules. By daylight they took sniper fire, at night they were
mortared, but it was not battle, it was just the endless march, village
to village, without purpose, nothing won or lost. They marched for
the sake of the march. They plodded along slowly, dumbly, leaning
forward against the heat, unthinking, all blood and bone, simple
grunts, soldiering with their legs, toiling up the hills and down into
the paddies and across the rivers and up again and down just humping, one step and then the next and then another, but no volition,
no will, because it was automatic, it was anatomy, and the war was
entirely a matter of posture and carriage, the hump was everything,
a kind of inertia, a kind of emptiness, a dullness of desire and intellect and conscience and hope and human sensibility. Their principles were in their feet. Their calculations were biological. They had
no sense of strategy or mission. They searched the villages without
knowing what to look for, not caring, kicking over jars of rice, frisk-
ing children and old men, blowing tunnels, sometimes setting fires
and sometimes not, then forming up and moving on to the next village, then other villages, where it would always be the same. They

carried their own lives. The pressures were enormous. In the heat of early afternoon, they would remove their helmets and flak jackets, walking bare, which was dangerous but which helped ease the strain. They would often discard things along the route of march. Purely for comfort, they would throw away rations, blow their Claymores and grenades, no matter, because by nightfall the resupply choppers would arrive with more of the same, then a day or two later still more, fresh watermelons and crates of ammunition and sunglasses and woolen sweaters—the resources were stunning—sparklers for the Fourth of July, colored eggs for Easter. It was the great American war chest—the fruits of science, the smokestacks, the canneries, the arsenals at Hartford, the Minnesota forests, the machine shops, the vast fields of corn and wheat—they carried like freight trains; they carried it on their backs and shoulders—and for all the ambiguities of Vietnam, all the mysteries and unknowns, there was at least the single abiding certainty that they would never be at a loss for things to carry.

After the chopper took Lavender away, Lieutenant Jimmy Cross led his men into the village of Than Khe. They burned everything. They shot chickens and dogs, they trashed the village well, they called in artillery and watched the wreckage, then they marched for several hours through the hot afternoon, and then at dusk, while Kiowa explained how Lavender died, Lieutenant Cross found himself trembling.

He tried not to cry. With his entrenching tool, which weighed five pounds, he began digging a hole in the earth.

He felt shame. He hated himself. He had loved Martha more than his men, and as a consequence Lavender was now dead, and this was something he would have to carry like a stone in his stomach for the rest of the war.

All he could do was dig. He used his entrenching tool like an ax, slashing, feeling both love and hate, and then later, when it was full dark, he sat at the bottom of his foxhole and wept. It went on for a long while. In part, he was grieving for Ted Lavender, but mostly it was for Martha, and for himself, because she belonged to another world, which was not quite real, and because she was a junior at Mount Sebastian College in New Jersey, a poet and a virgin and uninvolved, and because he realized she did not love him and never would.

Like cement, Kiowa whispered in the dark. I swear to God—boom-down. Not a word.

I've heard this, said Norman Bowker.

A pisser, you know? Still zipping himself up. Zapped while zipping.

All right, fine. That's enough.

Yeah, but you had to see it, the guy just—

I *heard*, man. Cement. So why not shut the fuck *up*?

Kiowa shook his head sadly and glanced over at the hole where Lieutenant Jimmy Cross sat watching the night. The air was thick and wet. A warm, dense fog had settled over the paddies and there was the stillness that precedes rain.

After a time Kiowa sighed.

One thing for sure, he said. The Lieutenant's in some deep hurt. I mean that crying jag—the way he was carrying on—it wasn't fake or anything, it was real heavy-duty hurt. The man cares.

Sure, Norman Bowker said.

Say what you want, the man does care.

We all got problems.

Not Lavender.

No, I guess not. Bowker said. Do me a favor, though.

Shut up?

That's a smart Indian. Shut up.

Shrugging, Kiowa pulled off his boots. He wanted to say more, just to lighten up his sleep, but instead he opened his New Testament and arranged it beneath his head as a pillow. The fog made things seem hollow and unattached. He tried not to think about Ted Lavender, but then he was thinking how fast it was, no drama, down and dead, and how it was hard to feel anything except surprise. It seemed un-Christian. He wished he could find some great sadness, or even anger, but the emotion wasn't there and he couldn't make it happen. Mostly he felt pleased to be alive. He liked the smell of the New Testament under his cheek, the leather and ink and paper and glue, whatever the chemicals were. He liked hearing the sounds of night. Even his fatigue, it felt fine, the stiff muscles and the prickly awareness of his own body, a floating feeling. He enjoyed not being dead. Lying there, Kiowa admired Lieutenant Jimmy Cross's capacity for grief. He wanted to share the man's pain, he wanted to care as Jimmy Cross cared. And yet when he closed his eyes, all he could think was Boom-down, and all he could feel was the pleasure of having his boots off and the fog curling in around him and the damp soil and the Bible smells and the plush comfort of night.

After a moment Norman Bowker sat up in the dark.

What the hell, he said. You want to talk, *talk*. Tell it to me.

Forget it.

No, man, go on. One thing I hate, it's a silent Indian.

For the most part they carried themselves with poise, a kind of dignity. Now and then, however, there were times of panic, when they squealed or wanted to squeal but couldn't, when they twitched and made moaning sounds and covered their heads and said Dear Jesus and flopped around on the earth and fired their weapons blindly and cringed and sobbed and begged for the noise to stop and went wild and made stupid promises to themselves and to God and to their mothers and fathers, hoping not to die. In different ways, it happened to all of them. Afterward, when the firing ended, they would blink and peek up. They would touch their bodies, feeling shame, then quickly hiding it. They would force themselves to stand. As if in slow motion, frame by frame, the world would take on the old logic—absolute silence, then the wind, then sunlight, then voices. It was the burden of being alive. Awkwardly, the men would reassemble themselves, first in private, then in groups, becoming soldiers again. They would repair the leaks in their eyes. They would check for casualties, call in dust-offs, light cigarettes, try to smile, clear their throats and spit and begin cleaning their weapons. After a time someone would shake his head and say, No lie, I almost shit my pants, and someone else would laugh, which meant it was bad, yes, but the guy had obviously not shit his pants, it wasn't that bad, and in any case nobody would ever do such a thing and then go ahead and talk about it. They would squint into the dense, oppressive sunlight. For a few moments, perhaps, they would fall silent, lighting a joint and tracking its passage from man to man, inhaling, holding in the humiliation. Scary stuff, one of them might say. But then someone else would grin or flick his eyebrows and say, Roger-dodger, almost cut me a new asshole, *almost*.

There were numerous such poses. Some carried themselves with a sort of wistful resignation, others with pride or stiff soldierly discipline or good humor or macho zeal. They were afraid of dying but they were even more afraid to show it.

They found jokes to tell.

They used a hard vocabulary to contain the terrible softness. *Greased*, they'd say. *Offed, lit up, zapped while zipping.* It wasn't cruelty, just stage presence. They were actors and the war came at them in 3-D. When someone died, it wasn't quite dying, because in a curious way it seemed scripted, and because they had their lines mostly memorized, irony mixed with tragedy, and because they called it by other names, as if to encyst and destroy the reality of death itself. They kicked corpses. They cut off thumbs. They talked grunt lingo. They told stories about Ted Lavender's supply of tranquilizers, how the poor guy didn't feel a thing, how incredibly tranquil he was.

There's a moral here, said Mitchell Sanders.

They were waiting for Lavender's chopper, smoking the dead man's dope.

The moral's pretty obvious, Sanders said, and winked. Stay away from drugs. No joke, they'll ruin your day every time.

Cute, said Henry Dobbins.

Mind-blower, get it? Talk about wiggy—nothing left, just blood and brains.

They made themselves laugh.

There it is, they'd say, over and over, as if the repetition itself were an act of poise, a balance between crazy and almost crazy, knowing without going. There it is, which meant be cool, let it ride, because oh yeah man, you can't change what can't be changed, there it is, there it absolutely and positively and fucking well *is*.

They were tough.

They carried all the emotional baggage of men who might die. Grief, terror, love, longing—these were intangibles, but the intangibles had their own mass and specific gravity, they had tangible weight. They carried shameful memories. They carried the common secret of cowardice barely restrained, the instinct to run or freeze or hide, and in many respects this was the heaviest burden of all, for it could never be put down, it required perfect balance and perfect posture. They carried their reputations. They carried the soldier's greatest fear, which was the fear of blushing. Men killed, and died, because they were embarrassed not to. It was what had brought them to the war in the first place, nothing positive, no dreams of glory or honor, just to avoid the blush of dishonor. They died so as not to die of embarrassment. They crawled into tunnels and walked point and advanced under fire. Each morning, despite the unknowns, they made their legs move. They endured. They kept humping. They did not submit to the obvious alternative, which was simply to close the eyes and fall. So easy, really. Go limp and tumble to the ground and let the muscles unwind and not speak and not budge until your buddies picked you up and lifted you into the chopper that would roar and dip its nose and carry you off to the world. A mere matter of falling, yet no one ever fell. It was not courage, exactly; the object was not valor. Rather, they were too frightened to be cowards.

By and large they carried these things inside, maintaining the masks of composure. They sneered at sick call. They spoke bitterly about guys who had found release by shooting off their own toes or fingers. Pussies, they'd say. Candyasses. It was fierce, mocking talk, with only a trace of envy or awe, but even so, the image played itself out behind their eyes.

They imagined the muzzle against flesh. They imagined the quick, sweet pain, then the evacuation to Japan, then a hospital with warm beds and cute geisha[13] nurses.

They dreamed of freedom birds.

At night, on guard, staring into the dark, they were carried away by jumbo jets. They felt the rush of takeoff. *Gone!* they yelled. And then velocity, wings and engines, a smiling stewardess—but it was more than a plane, it was a real bird, a big sleek silver bird with feathers and talons and high screeching. They were flying. The weights fell off, there was nothing to bear. They laughed and held

---

13. Japanese girls and women trained to be professional entertainers and companions for men.

on tight, feeling the cold slap of wind and altitude, soaring, think-ing *It's over, I'm gone!*—they were naked, they were light and free—it was all lightness, bright and fast and buoyant, light as light, a helium buzz in the brain, a giddy bubbling in the lungs as they were taken up over the clouds and the war, beyond duty, beyond gravity and mortification and global entanglements—*Sin loi!*[14] they yelled, *I'm sorry, motherfuckers, but I'm out of it, I'm goofed, I'm on a space cruise, I'm gone!*—and it was a restful, disencumbered sensation, just riding the light waves, sailing that big silver freedom bird over the mountains and oceans, over America, over the farms and great sleeping cities and cemeteries and highways and the golden arches of McDonald's. It was flight, a kind of fleeing, a kind of falling, falling higher and higher, spinning off the edge of the earth and be-yond the sun and through the vast, silent vacuum where there were no burdens and where everything weighed exactly nothing. *Gone!* they screamed, *I'm sorry but I'm gone!* And so at night, not quite dreaming, they gave themselves over to lightness, they were carried, they were purely borne.

On the morning after Ted Lavender died, First Lieutenant Jimmy Cross crouched at the bottom of his foxhole and burned Martha's letters. Then he burned the two photographs. There was a steady rain falling, which made it difficult, but he used heat tabs and Sterno to build a small fire, screening it with his body, holding the photographs over the tight blue flame with the tips of his fingers.

He realized it was only a gesture. Stupid, he thought. Sentimen-tal, too, but mostly just stupid.

Lavender was dead. You couldn't burn the blame.

Besides, the letters were in his head. And even now, without pho-tographs, Lieutenant Cross could see Martha playing volleyball in her white gym shorts and yellow T-shirt. He could see her moving in the rain.

When the fire died out, Lieutenant Cross pulled his poncho over his shoulders and ate breakfast from a can.

There was no great mystery, he decided.

In those burned letters Martha had never mentioned the war, ex-

14. Sorry about that (Vietnamese).

cept to say, Jimmy, take care of yourself. She wasn't involved. She signed the letters "Love," but it wasn't love, and all the fine lines and technicalities did not matter.

The morning came up wet and blurry. Everything seemed part of everything else, the fog and Martha and the deepening rain.

It was a war, after all.

Half smiling, Lieutenant Jimmy Cross took out his maps. He shook his head hard, as if to clear it, then bent forward and began planning the day's march. In ten minutes, or maybe twenty, he would rouse the men and they would pack up and head west, where the maps showed the country to be green and inviting. They would do what they had always done. The rain might add some weight, but otherwise it would be one more day layered upon all the other days.

He was realistic about it. There was that new hardness in his stomach.

No more fantasies, he told himself.

Henceforth, when he thought about Martha, it would be only to think that she belonged elsewhere. He would shut down the daydreams. This was not Mount Sebastian, it was another world, where there were no pretty poems or midterm exams, a place where men died because of carelessness and gross stupidity. Kiowa was right. Boom-down, and you were dead, never partly dead.

Briefly, in the rain, Lieutenant Cross saw Martha's gray eyes gazing back at him.

He understood.

It was very sad, he thought. The things men carried inside. The things men did or felt they had to do.

He almost nodded at her, but didn't.

Instead he went back to his maps. He was now determined to perform his duties firmly and without negligence. It wouldn't help Lavender, he knew that, but from this point on he would comport himself as a soldier. He would dispose of his good-luck pebble. Swallow it, maybe, or use Lee Strunk's slingshot, or just drop it along the trail. On the march he would impose strict field discipline. He would be careful to send out flank security, to prevent straggling or bunching up, to keep his troops moving at the proper pace and at the proper interval. He would insist on clean weapons.

He would confiscate the remainder of Lavender's dope. Later in the day, perhaps, he would call the men together and speak to them plainly. He would accept the blame for what had happened to Ted Lavender. He would be a man about it. He would look them in the eyes, keeping his chin level, and he would issue the new SOPs in a calm, impersonal tone of voice, an officer's voice, leaving no room for argument or discussion. Commencing immediately, he'd tell them, they would no longer abandon equipment along the route of march. They would police up their acts. They would get their shit together, and keep it together, and maintain it neatly and in good working order.

He would not tolerate laxity. He would show strength, distancing himself.

Among the men there would be grumbling, of course, and maybe worse, because their days would seem longer and their loads heavier, but Lieutenant Cross reminded himself that his obligation was not to be loved but to lead. He would dispense with love; it was not now a factor. And if anyone quarreled or complained, he would simply tighten his lips and arrange his shoulders in the correct command posture. He might give a curt little nod. Or he might not. He might just shrug and say Carry on, then they would saddle up and form into a column and move out toward the villages of Than Khe.

1986

Flannery O'Connor
1925–1964

O'Connor, a Catholic from Georgia, always insisted that her faith informed her fiction, despite her stories' being filled with grotesques and violence. "A Good Man Is Hard to Find," she explained, is grotesque the way a child's drawing is. The child "doesn't intend to distort but to set down exactly what he sees." O'Connor advised readers to be on the lookout not for dead bodies but for "the action of grace." We should not be surprised to find the unpleasant grandmother the vehicle of grace, because, as O'Connor explained, grace "can and does use as its medium the imperfect, purely human, and even hypocritical." The choice facing the grandmother and the Mis-

fit in this story, as for the characters in most of O'Connor's stories, is to accept or cut oneself off from grace. The violence in the story forces this choice on the grandmother, just as her decision forces the choice on the Misfit.

A Good Man Is Hard to Find

The grandmother didn't want to go to Florida. She wanted to visit some of her connections in east Tennessee and she was seizing every chance to change Bailey's mind. Bailey was the son she lived with, her only boy. He was sitting on the edge of his chair at the table, bent over the orange sports section of the *Journal.* "Now look here, Bailey," she said, "see here, read this," and she stood with one hand on her thin hip and the other rattling the newspaper at his bald head. "Here this fellow that calls himself The Misfit is aloose from the Federal Pen and headed toward Florida and you read here what it says he did to these people. Just you read it. I wouldn't take my children in any direction with a criminal like that aloose in it. I couldn't answer to my conscience if I did."

Bailey didn't look up from his reading so she wheeled around then and faced the children's mother; a young woman in slacks, whose face was as broad and innocent as a cabbage and was tied around with a green headkerchief that had two points on the top like rabbit's ears. She was sitting on the sofa, feeding the baby his apricots out of a jar. "The children have been to Florida before," the old lady said. "You all ought to take them somewhere else for a change so they would see different parts of the world and be broad. They never have been to east Tennessee."

The children's mother didn't seem to hear her, but the eight-year-old boy, John Wesley, a stocky child with glasses, said, "If you don't want to go to Florida, why dontcha stay at home?" He and the little girl, June Star, were reading the funny papers on the floor.

"She wouldn't stay at home to be queen for a day," June Star said without raising her yellow head.

"Yes, and what would you do if this fellow, The Misfit, caught you?" the grandmother asked.

"I'd smack his face," John Wesley said.

"She wouldn't stay at home for a million bucks," June Star said. "Afraid she'd miss something. She has to go everywhere we go."

"All right, Miss," the grandmother said. "Just remember that the next time you want me to curl your hair."

June Star said her hair was naturally curly.

The next morning the grandmother was the first one in the car, ready to go. She had her big black valise that looked like the head of a hippopotamus in one corner, and underneath it she was hiding a basket with Pitty Sing,[1] the cat, in it. She didn't intend for the cat to be left alone in the house for three days because he would miss her too much and she was afraid he might brush against one of the gas burners and accidentally asphyxiate himself. Her son, Bailey, didn't like to arrive at a motel with a cat.

She sat in the middle of the back seat with John Wesley and June Star on either side of her. Bailey and the children's mother and the baby sat in the front and they left Atlanta at eight forty-five with the mileage on the car at 55890. The grandmother wrote this down because she thought it would be interesting to say how many miles they had been when they got back. It took them twenty minutes to reach the outskirts of the city.

The old lady settled herself comfortably, removing her white cotton gloves and putting them up with her purse on the shelf in front of the back window. The children's mother still had on slacks and still had her head tied up in a green kerchief, but the grandmother had on a navy blue straw sailor hat with a bunch of white violets on the brim and a navy blue dress with a small white dot in the print. Her collar and cuffs were white organdy trimmed with lace and at her neckline she had pinned a purple spray of cloth violets containing a sachet. In case of an accident, anyone seeing her dead on the highway would know at once that she was a lady.

She said she thought it was going to be a good day for driving, neither too hot nor too cold, and she cautioned Bailey that the speed limit was fifty-five miles an hour and that the patrolmen hid themselves behind billboards and small clumps of trees and sped out after you before you had a chance to slow down. She pointed

1. Pitti-Sing is a character in Gilbert and Sullivan's operetta *The Mikado* (1885).

out interesting details of the scenery: Stone Mountain; the blue granite that in some places came up to both sides of the highway; the brilliant red clay banks slightly streaked with purple; and the various crops that made rows of green lace-work on the ground. The trees were full of silver-white sunlights and the meanest of them sparkled. The children were reading comic magazines and their mother had gone back to sleep.

"Let's go through Georgia fast so we won't have to look at it much," John Wesley said.

"If I were a little boy," said the grandmother, "I wouldn't talk about my native state that way. Tennessee has the mountains and Georgia has the hills."

"Tennessee is just a hillbilly dumping ground," John Wesley said, "and Georgia is a lousy state too."

"You said it," June Star said.

"In my time," said the grandmother, folding her thin veined fingers, "children were more respectful of their native states and their parents and everything else. People did right then. Oh look at the cute little pickaninny!" she said and pointed to a Negro child standing in the door of a shack. "Wouldn't that make a picture, now?" she asked and they all turned and looked at the little Negro out of the back window. He waved.

"He didn't have any britches on," June Star said.

"He probably didn't have any," the grandmother explained. "Little niggers in the country don't have things like we do. If I could paint, I'd paint that picture," she said.

The children exchanged comic books.

The grandmother offered to hold the baby and the children's mother passed him over the front seat to her. She set him on her knee and bounced him and told him about the things they were passing. She rolled her eyes and screwed up her mouth and stuck her leathery thin face into his smooth bland one. Occasionally he gave her a faraway smile. They passed a large cotton field with five or six graves fenced in the middle of it, like a small island. "Look at the graveyard!" the grandmother said, pointing it out. "That was the old family burying ground. That belonged to the plantation."

"Where's the plantation?" John Wesley asked.

"Gone With the Wind,"[2] said the grandmother. "Ha. Ha."

When the children finished all the comic books they had brought, they opened the lunch and ate it. The grandmother ate a peanut butter sandwich and an olive and would not let the children throw the box and the paper napkins out the window. When there was nothing else to do they played a game by choosing a cloud and making the other two guess what shape it suggested. John Wesley took one the shape of a cow and June Star guessed a cow and John Wesley said, no, an automobile, and June Star said he didn't play fair, and they began to slap each other over the grandmother.

The grandmother said she would tell them a story if they would keep quiet. When she told a story, she rolled her eyes and waved her head and was very dramatic. She said once when she was a maiden lady she had been courted by a Mr. Edgar Atkins Teagarden from Jasper, Georgia. She said he was a very good-looking man and a gentleman and that he brought her a watermelon every Saturday afternoon with his initials cut in it, E.A.T. Well, one Saturday, she said, Mr. Teagarden brought the watermelon and there was nobody at home and he left it on the front porch and returned in his buggy to Jasper, but she never got the watermelon, she said, because a nigger boy ate it when he saw the initials, E.A.T.! This story tickled John Wesley's funny bone and he giggled and giggled but June Star didn't think it was any good. She said she wouldn't marry a man that just brought her a watermelon on Saturday. The grandmother said she would have done well to marry Mr. Teagarden because he was a gentleman and had bought Coca-Cola stock when it first came out and that he had died only a few years ago, a very wealthy man.

They stopped at The Tower for barbecued sandwiches. The Tower was a part-stucco and part-wood filling station and dance hall set in a clearing outside of Timothy. A fat man named Red Sammy Butts ran it and there were signs stuck here and there on the building and for miles up and down the highway saying, TRY RED SAMMY'S FAMOUS BARBECUE. NONE LIKE FAMOUS RED SAMMY'S! RED SAM! THE FAT BOY WITH THE HAPPY LAUGH. A VETERAN! RED SAMMY'S YOUR MAN!

2. Title of the best-selling novel (1936) by Margaret Mitchell about the passing of the old South.

Red Sammy was lying on the bare ground outside The Tower with his head under a truck while a gray monkey about a foot high, chained to a small chinaberry tree, chattered nearby. The monkey sprang back into the tree and got on the highest limb as soon as he saw the children jump out of the car and run toward him.

Inside, The Tower was a long dark room with a counter at one end and tables at the other and dancing space in the middle. They all sat down at a broad table next to the nickelodeon[3] and Red Sam's wife, a tall burnt-brown woman with hair and eyes lighter than her skin, came and took their order. The children's mother put a dime in the machine and played "The Tennessee Waltz," and the grandmother said that tune always made her want to dance. She asked Bailey if he would like to dance but he only glared at her. He didn't have a naturally sunny disposition like she did and trips made him nervous. The grandmother's brown eyes were very bright. She swayed her head from side to side and pretended she was dancing in her chair. June Star said play something she could tap to so the children's mother put in another dime and played a fast number and June Star stepped out onto the dance floor and did her tap routine.

"Ain't she cute?" Red Sam's wife said, leaning over the counter. "Would you like to come be my little girl?"

"No, I certainly wouldn't," June Star said. "I wouldn't live in a broken-down place like this for a million bucks!" and she ran back to the table.

"Ain't she cute?" the woman repeated, stretching her mouth politely.

"Aren't you ashamed?" hissed the grandmother.

Red Sam came in and told his wife to quit lounging on the counter and hurry up with these people's order. His khaki trousers reached just to his hip bones and his stomach hung over them like a sack of meal swaying under his shirt. He came over and sat down at a table nearby and let out a combination sigh and yodel. "You can't win," he said. "You can't win," and he wiped his sweating red face off with a gray handkerchief. "These days you don't know who to trust," he said. "Ain't that the truth?"

3. Jukebox.

"People are certainly not nice like they used to be," said the grandmother.

"Two fellers come in here last week," Red Sammy said, "driving a Chrysler. It was an old beat-up car but it was a good one and these boys looked all right to me. Said they worked at the mill and you know I let them fellers charge the gas they bought? Now why did I do that?"

"Because you're a good man!" the grandmother said at once.

"Yes'm, I suppose so," Red Sam said as if he were struck with this answer.

His wife brought the orders, carrying the five plates all at once without a tray, two in each hand and one balanced on her arm. "It isn't a soul in this green world of God's that you can trust," she said. "And I don't count nobody out of that, not nobody," she repeated, looking at Red Sammy.

"Did you read about that criminal, The Misfit, that's escaped?" asked the grandmother.

"I wouldn't be a bit surprised if he didn't attack this place right here," said the woman. "If he hears about it being here, I wouldn't be none surprised to see him. If he hears it's two cent in the cash register, I wouldn't be a tall surprised if he . . ."

"That'll do," Red Sam said. "Go bring these people their Co'-Colas," and the woman went off to get the rest of the order.

"A good man is hard to find," Red Sammy said. "Everything is getting terrible. I remember the day you could go off and leave your screen door unlatched. Not no more."

He and the grandmother discussed better times. The old lady said that in her opinion Europe was entirely to blame for the way things were now. She said the way Europe acted you would think we were made of money and Red Sam said it was no use talking about it, she was exactly right. The children ran outside into the white sunlight and looked at the monkey in the lacy chinaberry tree. He was busy catching fleas on himself and biting each one carefully between his teeth as if it were a delicacy.

They drove off again into the hot afternoon. The grandmother took cat naps and woke up every few minutes with her own snoring. Outside of Toombsboro she woke up and recalled an old plantation that she had visited in this neighborhood once when she was a young lady. She said the house had six white columns across the front and that there was an avenue of oaks leading up to it and two little wooden trellis arbors on either side in front where you sat down with your suitor after a stroll in the garden. She recalled exactly which road to turn off to get to it. She knew that Bailey would not be willing to lose any time looking at an old house, but the more she talked about it, the more she wanted to see it once again and find out if the little twin arbors were still standing. "There was a secret panel in this house," she said craftily, not telling the truth but wishing that she were, "and the story went that all the family silver was hidden in it when Sherman[4] came through but it was never found . . ."

"Hey!" John Wesley said. "Let's go see it! We'll find it! We'll poke all the woodwork and find it! Who lives there? Where do you turn off at? Hey Pop, can't we turn off there?"

"We never have seen a house with a secret panel!" June Star shrieked. "Let's go to the house with the secret panel! Hey, Pop, can't we go see the house with the secret panel!"

"It's not far from here, I know," the grandmother said. "It wouldn't take over twenty minutes."

Bailey was looking straight ahead. His jaw was as rigid as a horseshoe. "No," he said.

The children began to yell and scream that they wanted to see the house with the secret panel. John Wesley kicked the back of the front seat and June Star hung over her mother's shoulder and whined desperately into her ear that they never had any fun even on their vacation, that they could never do what THEY wanted to do. The baby began to scream and John Wesley kicked the back of the seat so hard that his father could feel the blows in his kidney.

"All right!" he shouted and drew the car to a stop at the side of the road. "Will you all shut up? Will you all just shut up for one second? If you don't shut up, we won't go anywhere."

"It would be very educational for them," the grandmother murmured.

"All right," Bailey said, "but get this. This is the only time we're

4. In 1864 the Union general William Tecumseh Sherman and his army marched from Atlanta to Savannah, burning many civilian farms and houses along the way.

going to stop for anything like this. This is the one and only time."

"The dirt road that you have to turn down is about a mile back," the grandmother directed. "I marked it when we passed."

"A dirt road," Bailey groaned.

After they had turned around and were headed toward the dirt road, the grandmother recalled other points about the house, the beautiful glass over the front doorway and the candle lamp in the hall. John Wesley said that the secret panel was probably in the fireplace.

"You can't go inside this house," Bailey said. "You don't know who lives there."

"While you all talk to the people in front, I'll run around behind and get in a window," John Wesley suggested.

"We'll all stay in the car," his mother said.

They turned onto the dirt road and the car raced roughly along in a swirl of pink dust. The grandmother recalled the times when there were no paved roads and thirty miles was a day's journey. The dirt road was hilly and there were sudden washes in it and sharp curves on dangerous embankments. All at once they would be on a hill, looking down over the blue tops of trees for miles around, then the next minute, they would be in a red depression with the dust-coated trees looking down on them.

"This place had better turn up in a minute," Bailey said, "or I'm going to turn around."

The road looked as if no one had traveled on it in months.

"It's not much farther," the grandmother said and just as she said it, a horrible thought came to her. The thought was so embarrassing that she turned red in the face and her eyes dilated and her feet jumped up, upsetting her valise in the corner. The instant the valise moved, the newspaper top she had over the basket under it rose with a snarl and Pitty Sing, the cat, sprang onto Bailey's shoulder.

The children were thrown to the floor and their mother, clutching the baby, was thrown out the door onto the ground; the old lady was thrown into the front seat. The car turned over once and landed right-side-up in a gulch on the side of the road. Bailey remained in the driver's seat with the cat—gray-striped with a broad white face and an orange nose—clinging to his neck like a caterpillar.

As soon as the children saw they could move their arms and legs, they scrambled out of the car, shouting, "We've had an ACCIDENT!" The grandmother was curled up under the dashboard, hoping she was injured so that Bailey's wrath would not come down on her all at once. The horrible thought she had had before the accident was that the house she had remembered so vividly was not in Georgia but in Tennessee.

Bailey removed the cat from his neck with both hands and flung it out the window against the side of a pine tree. Then he got out of the car and started looking for the children's mother. She was sitting against the side of the red gutted ditch, holding the screaming baby, but she only had a cut down her face and a broken shoulder. "We've had an ACCIDENT!" the children screamed in a frenzy of delight.

"But nobody's killed," June Star said with disappointment as the grandmother limped out of the car, her hat still pinned to her head but the broken front brim standing up at a jaunty angle and the violet spray hanging off the side. They all sat down in the ditch, except the children, to recover from the shock. They were all shaking.

"Maybe a car will come along," said the children's mother hoarsely.

"I believe I have injured an organ," said the grandmother, pressing her side, but no one answered her. Bailey's teeth were clattering. He had on a yellow sport shirt with bright blue parrots designed in it and his face was as yellow as the shirt. The grandmother decided that she would not mention that the house was in Tennessee.

The road was about ten feet above and they could see only the tops of the trees on the other side of it. Behind the ditch they were sitting in there were more woods, tall and dark and deep. In a few minutes they saw a car some distance away on top of a hill, coming slowly as if the occupants were watching them. The grandmother stood up and waved both arms dramatically to attract their attention. The car continued to come on slowly, disappeared around a bend and appeared again, moving even slower, on top of the hill they had gone over. It was a big black battered hearselike automobile. There were three men in it.

It came to a stop over them and for some minutes, the driver looked down with a steady expressionless gaze to where they were sitting, and didn't speak. Then he turned his head and muttered something to the other two and they got out. One was a fat boy in black trousers and a red sweat shirt with a silver stallion embossed on the front of it. He moved around on the right side of them and stood staring, his mouth partly open in a kind of loose grin. The other had on khaki pants and a blue striped coat and a gray hat pulled down very low, hiding most of his face. He came around slowly on the left side. Neither spoke.

The driver got out of the car and stood by the side of it, looking down at them. He was an older man than the other two. His hair was just beginning to gray and he wore silver-rimmed spectacles that gave him a scholarly look. He had a long creased face and didn't have on any shirt or undershirt. He had on blue jeans that were too tight for him and was holding a black hat and a gun. The two boys also had guns.

"We've had an ACCIDENT!" the children screamed.

The grandmother had the peculiar feeling that the bespectacled man was someone she knew. His face was as familiar to her as if she had known him all her life but she could not recall who he was. He moved away from the car and began to come down the embankment, placing his feet carefully so that he wouldn't slip. He had on tan and white shoes and no socks, and his ankles were red and thin. "Good afternoon," he said. "I see you all had you a little spill."

"We turned over twice!" said the grandmother.

"Oncet," he corrected. "We seen it happen. Try their car and see will it run, Hiram," he said quietly to the boy with the gray hat.

"What you got that gun for?" John Wesley asked. "Whatcha gonna do with that gun?"

"Lady," the man said to the children's mother, "would you mind calling them children to sit down by you? Children make me nervous. I want all you all to sit down right together there where you're at."

"What are you telling us what to do for?" June Star asked.

Behind them the line of woods gaped like a dark open mouth. "Come here," said their mother.

"Look here now," Bailey began suddenly, "we're in a predicament! We're in . . ."

The grandmother shrieked. She scrambled to her feet and stood staring.

"You're The Misfit!" she said. "I recognized you at once!"

"Yes'm," the man said, smiling slightly as if he were pleased in spite of himself to be known, "but it would have been better for all of you, lady, if you hadn't of reckernized me."

Bailey turned his head sharply and said something to his mother that shocked even the children. The old lady began to cry and The Misfit reddened.

"Lady," he said, "don't you get upset. Sometimes a man says things he don't mean. I don't reckon he meant to talk to you that-away."

"You wouldn't shoot a lady, would you?" the grandmother said and removed a clean handkerchief from her cuff and began to slap at her eyes with it.

The Misfit pointed the toe of his shoe into the ground and made a little hole and then covered it up again. "I would hate to have to," he said.

"Listen," the grandmother almost screamed, "I know you're a good man. You don't look a bit like you have common blood. I know you must come from nice people!"

"Yes mam," he said, "finest people in the world." When he smiled he showed a row of strong white teeth. "God never made a finer woman than my mother and my daddy's heart was pure gold," he said. The boy with the red sweat shirt had come around behind them and was standing with his gun at his hip. The Misfit squatted down on the ground. "Watch them children, Bobby Lee," he said. "You know they make me nervous." He looked at the six of them huddled together in front of him and he seemed to be embarrassed as if he couldn't think of anything to say. "Ain't a cloud in the sky," he remarked, looking up at it. "Don't see no sun but don't see no cloud neither."

"Yes, it's a beautiful day," said the grandmother. "Listen," she said, "you shouldn't call yourself The Misfit because I know you're a good man at heart. I can just look at you and tell."

"Hush!" Bailey yelled. "Hush! Everybody shut up and let me handle this!" He was squatting in the position of a runner about to spring forward but he didn't move.

"I pre-chate that, lady," The Misfit said and drew a little circle in the ground with the butt of his gun.

"It'll take a half a hour to fix this here car," Hiram called, looking over the raised hood of it.

"Well, first you and Bobby Lee get him and that little boy to step over yonder with you," The Misfit said, pointing to Bailey and John Wesley. "The boys want to ask you something," he said to Bailey. "Would you mind stepping back in them woods there with them?"

"Listen," Bailey began, "we're in a terrible predicament! Nobody realizes what this is," and his voice cracked. His eyes were as blue and intense as the parrots in his shirt and he remained perfectly still.

The grandmother reached up to adjust her hat brim as if she were going to the woods with him but it came off in her hand. She stood staring at it and after a second she let it fall on the ground. Hiram pulled Bailey up by the arm as if he were assisting an old man. John Wesley caught hold of his father's hand and Bobby Lee followed. They went off toward the woods and just as they reached the dark edge, Bailey turned and supporting himself against a gray naked pine trunk, he shouted, "I'll be back in a minute, Mamma, wait on me!"

"Come back this instant!" his mother shrilled but they all disappeared into the woods.

"Bailey Boy!" the grandmother called in a tragic voice but she found she was looking at The Misfit squatting on the ground in front of her. "I just know you're a good man," she said desperately. "You're not a bit common!"

"Nome, I ain't a good man," The Misfit said after a second as if he had considered her statement carefully, "but I ain't the worst in the world neither. My daddy said I was a different breed of dog from my brothers and sisters. 'You know,' Daddy said, 'it's some that can live their whole life out without asking about it and it's others has to know why it is, and this boy is one of the latters. He's going to be into everything!' " He put on his black hat and looked up suddenly and then away deep into the woods as if he were embarrassed again. "I'm sorry I don't have on a shirt before you ladies," he said, hunching his shoulders slightly. "We buried our clothes that we had on when we escaped and we're just making do until we can get better. We borrowed these from some folks we met," he explained.

"That's perfectly all right," the grandmother said. "Maybe Bailey has an extra shirt in his suitcase."

"I'll look and see terrectly," The Misfit said.

"Where are they taking him?" the children's mother screamed.

"Daddy was a card himself," The Misfit said. "You couldn't put anything over on him. He never got in trouble with the Authorities though. Just had the knack of handling them."

"You could be honest too if you'd only try," said the grandmother. "Think how wonderful it would be to settle down and live a comfortable life and not have to think about somebody chasing you all the time."

The Misfit kept scratching in the ground with the butt of his gun as if he were thinking about it. "Yes'm, somebody is always after you," he murmured.

The grandmother noticed how thin his shoulder blades were just behind his hat because she was standing up looking down on him. "Do you ever pray?" she asked.

He shook his head. All she saw was the black hat wiggle between his shoulder blades. "Nome," he said.

There was a pistol shot from the woods, followed closely by another. Then silence. The old lady's head jerked around. She could hear the wind move through the tree tops like a long satisfied insuck of breath. "Bailey Boy!" she called.

"I was a gospel singer for a while," The Misfit said. "I been most everything. Been in the arm service, both land and sea, at home and abroad, been twict married, been an undertaker, been with the railroads, plowed Mother Earth, been in a tornado, seen a man burnt alive oncet," and he looked up at the children's mother and the little girl who were sitting close together, their faces white and their eyes glassy; "I even seen a woman flogged," he said.

"Pray, pray," the grandmother began, "pray, pray . . ."

"I never was a bad boy that I remember of," The Misfit said in an almost dreamy voice, "but somewheres along the line I done something wrong and got sent to the penitentiary. I was buried alive," and he looked up and held her attention to him by a steady stare.

"That's when you should have started to pray," she said. "What did you do to get sent to the penitentiary that first time?"

"Turn to the right, it was a wall," The Misfit said, looking up again at the cloudless sky. "Turn to the left, it was a wall. Look up it was a ceiling, look down it was a floor. I forget what I done, lady. I set there and set there, trying to remember what it was I done and I ain't recalled it to this day. Oncet in a while, I would think it was coming to me, but it never come."

"Maybe they put you in by mistake," the old lady said vaguely.

"Nome," he said. "It wasn't no mistake. They had the papers on me."

"You must have stolen something," she said.

The Misfit sneered slightly. "Nobody had nothing I wanted," he said. "It was a head-doctor at the penitentiary said what I had done was kill my daddy but I known that for a lie. My daddy died in nineteen ought nineteen of the epidemic flu[5] and I never had a thing to do with it. He was buried in the Mount Hopewell Baptist churchyard and you can go there and see for yourself."

"If you would pray," the old lady said, "Jesus would help you."

"That's right," The Misfit said.

"Well then, why don't you pray?" she asked trembling with delight suddenly.

"I don't want no hep," he said. "I'm doing all right by myself."

Bobby Lee and Hiram came ambling back from the woods. Bobby Lee was dragging a yellow shirt with bright blue parrots in it.

"Throw me that shirt, Bobby Lee," The Misfit said. The shirt came flying at him and landed on his shoulder and he put it on. The grandmother couldn't name what the shirt reminded her of. "No, lady," The Misfit said while he was buttoning up, "I found out the crime don't matter. You can do one thing or you can do another, kill a man or take a tire off his car, because sooner or later you're going to forget what it was you done and just be punished for it."

The children's mother had begun to make heaving noises as if she couldn't get her breath. "Lady," he asked, "would you and that little girl like to step off yonder with Bobby Lee and Hiram and join your husband?"

"Yes, thank you," the mother said faintly. Her left arm dangled helplessly and she was holding the baby, who had gone to sleep, in

5. A deadly influenza spread through much of the world in 1918–19.

the other. "Hep that lady up, Hiram," The Misfit said as she struggled to climb out of the ditch, "and Bobby Lee, you hold onto that
little girl's hand."

"I don't want to hold hands with him," June Star said. "He reminds me of a pig."

The fat boy blushed and laughed and caught her by the arm and
pulled her off into the woods after Hiram and her mother.

Alone with The Misfit, the grandmother found that she had lost
her voice. There was not a cloud in the sky nor any sun. There was
nothing around her but woods. She wanted to tell him that he must
pray. She opened and closed her mouth several times before anything came out. Finally she found herself saying, "Jesus, Jesus,"
meaning, Jesus will help you, but the way she was saying it, it
sounded as if she might be cursing.

"Yes'm," The Misfit said as if he agreed. "Jesus thrown everything
off balance. It was the same case with Him as with me except He
hadn't committed any crime and they could prove I had committed
one because they had the papers on me. Of course," he said, "they
never shown me my papers. That's why I sign myself now. I said
long ago, you get you a signature and sign everything you do and
keep a copy of it. Then you'll know what you done and you can
hold up the crime to the punishment and see do they match and in
the end you'll have something to prove you ain't been treated right.
I call myself The Misfit," he said, "because I can't make what all I
done wrong fit what all I gone through in punishment."

There was a piercing scream from the woods, followed closely by
a pistol report. "Does it seem right to you, lady, that one is punished a heap and another ain't punished at all?"

"Jesus!" the old lady cried. "You've got good blood! I know you
wouldn't shoot a lady! I know you come from nice people! Pray! Jesus, you ought not to shoot a lady. I'll give you all the money I've
got!"

"Lady," The Misfit said, looking beyond her far into the woods,
"there never was a body that give the undertaker a tip."

There were two more pistol reports and the grandmother raised
her head like a parched old turkey hen crying for water and called,
"Bailey Boy, Bailey Boy!" as if her heart would break.

"Jesus was the only One that ever raised the dead," The Misfit continued, "and He shouldn't have done it. He thrown everything off balance. If He did what He said, then it's nothing for you to do but throw away everything and follow Him, and if He didn't then it's nothing for you to do but enjoy the few minutes you got left the best way you can—by killing somebody or burning down his house or doing some other meanness to him. No pleasure but meanness," he said and his voice had become almost a snarl.

"Maybe He didn't raise the dead," the old lady mumbled, not knowing what she was saying and feeling so dizzy that she sank down in the ditch with her legs twisted under her.

"I wasn't there so I can't say He didn't," The Misfit said, "I wisht I had of been there," he said, hitting the ground with his fist. "It ain't right I wasn't there because if I had of been there I would of known. Listen lady," he said in a high voice, "if I had of been there I would of known and I wouldn't be like I am now." His voice seemed about to crack and the grandmother's head cleared for an instant. She saw the man's face twisted close to her own as if he were going to cry and she murmured, "Why, you're one of my babies. You're one of my own children!" She reached out and touched him on the shoulder. The Misfit sprang back as if a snake had bitten him and shot her three times through the chest. Then he put his gun down on the ground and took off his glasses and began to clean them.

Hiram and Bobby Lee returned from the woods and stood over the ditch, looking down at the grandmother who half sat and half lay in a puddle of blood with her legs crossed under her like a child's and her face smiling up at the cloudless sky.

Without his glasses, The Misfit's eyes were red-rimmed and pale and defenseless-looking. "Take her off and throw her where you thrown the others," he said, picking up the cat that was rubbing itself against his leg.

"She was a talker, wasn't she?" Bobby Lee said, sliding down the ditch with a yodel.

"She would of been a good woman," The Misfit said, "if it had been somebody there to shoot her every minute of her life."

"Some fun!" Bobby Lee said.

"Shut up, Bobby Lee," The Misfit said. "It's no real pleasure in life."

1953

Frank O'Connor
1903–1966

> *O'Connor (born Michael O'Donovan) became active in the Irish Volunteers when he was fifteen. The Volunteers were a nationalist militia dedicated to freeing Ireland from English rule. After a treaty was concluded, he enlisted with the Irish Republican Army, which fought a civil war against the new native government rather than accept the exclusion of six northern counties from the Irish nation. At the age of nineteen, O'Connor resisted orders to shoot unarmed government soldiers. That incident probably inspired "Guests of the Nation," though the soldiers who were Irish in reality are English in the story. O'Connor was captured and interned in a prison camp, where he became thoroughly disgusted with war. O'Connor was a careful theorist of the short story as a genre. He distinguished it from novels on the basis of its ideology rather than its form. Novels, he wrote in* The Lonely Voice, *adhere to a belief that humans are living in a community, that society works or can work. The short story depicts people as romantics, as intransigent, individuals remote from a society that does not and cannot work.*

Guests of the Nation

I

At dusk the big Englishman, Belcher, would shift his long legs out of the ashes and say "Well, chums, what about it?" and Noble or me would say "All right, chum" (for we had picked up some of their curious expressions), and the little Englishman, Hawkins, would light the lamp and bring out the cards. Sometimes Jeremiah Donovan would come up and supervise the game and get excited over Hawkins's cards, which he always played badly, and shout at him as if he was one of our own "Ah, you divil, you, why didn't you play the tray?"

But ordinarily Jeremiah was a sober and contented poor devil like the big Englishman, Belcher, and was looked up to only because he was a fair hand at documents, though he was slow enough even with them. He wore a small cloth hat and big gaiters over his long pants; and you seldom saw him with his hands out of his pockets. He reddened when you talked to him, tilting from toe to heel and back, and looking down all the time at his big farmer's feet. Noble and me used to make fun of his broad accent, because we were from the town.

I couldn't at the time see the point of me and Noble guarding Belcher and Hawkins at all, for it was my belief that you could have planted that pair down anywhere from this to Claregalway and they'd have taken root there like a native weed. I never in my short experience seen two men to take to the country as they did.

They were handed on to us by the Second Battalion when the search[1] for them became too hot, and Noble and myself, being young, took over with a natural feeling of responsibility, but Hawkins made us look like fools when he showed that he knew the country better than we did.

"You're the bloke they calls Bonaparte," he says to me. "Mary Brigid O'Connell told me to ask you what you done with the pair of her brother's socks you borrowed."

For it seemed, as they explained it, that the Second used to have little evenings, and some of the girls of the neighbourhood turned in, and, seeing they were such decent chaps, our fellows couldn't leave the two Englishmen out of them. Hawkins learned to dance "The Walls of Limerick," "The Siege of Ennis," and "The Waves of Tory"[2] as well as any of them, though naturally, he couldn't return the compliment, because our lads at that time did not dance foreign dances on principle.

So whatever privileges Belcher and Hawkins had with the Second they just naturally took with us, and after the first day or two we gave up all pretence of keeping a close eye on them. Not that they could have got far, for they had accents you could cut with a knife and wore khaki tunics and overcoats with civilian pants and boots.

---

1. Belcher and Hawkins are British soldiers captured by Irish irregulars during the 1921 Anglo-Irish War.

2. These are Irish dances that, because they are nationalist, are implicitly anti-English.

But it's my belief that they never had any idea of escaping and were quite content to be where they were.

It was a treat to see how Belcher got off with the old woman of the house where we were staying. She was a great warrant to scold, and cranky even with us, but before ever she had a chance to giving our guests, as I may call them, a lick of her tongue, Belcher had made her his friend for life. She was breaking sticks, and Belcher, who hadn't been more than ten minutes in the house, jumped up from his seat and went over to her.

"Allow me, madam," he says, smiling his queer little smile, "please allow me"; and he takes the bloody hatchet. She was struck too paralytic to speak, and after that, Belcher would be at her heels, carrying a bucket, a basket, or a load of turf, as the case might be. As Noble said, he got into looking before she leapt, and hot water, or any little thing she wanted, Belcher would have it ready for her. For such a huge man (and though I am five foot ten myself I had to look up at him) he had an uncommon shortness—or should I say lack?—of speech. It took us some time to get used to him, walking in and out, like a ghost, without a word. Especially because Hawkins talked enough for a platoon, it was strange to hear big Belcher with his toes in the ashes come out with a solitary "Excuse me, chum," or "That's right, chum." His one and only passion was cards, and I will say for him that he was a good card-player. He could have fleeced myself and Noble, but whatever we lost to him Hawkins lost to us, and Hawkins played with the money Belcher gave him.

Hawkins lost to us because he had too much old gab, and we probably lost to Belcher for the same reason. Hawkins and Noble would spit at one another about religion into the early hours of the morning, and Hawkins worried the soul out of Noble, whose brother was a priest, with a string of questions that would puzzle a cardinal. To make it worse even in treating of holy subjects, Hawkins had a deplorable tongue. I never in all my career met a man who could mix such a variety of cursing and bad language into an argument. He was a terrible man, and a fright to argue. He never did a stroke of work, and when he had no one else to talk to, he got stuck in the old woman.

He met his match in her, for one day when he tried to get her to complain profanely of the drought, she gave him a great comedown by blaming it entirely on Jupiter Pluvius (a deity neither Hawkins nor I had ever heard of, though Noble said that among the pagans it was believed that he had something to do with the rain).[3] Another day he was swearing at the capitalists for starting the German war[4] when the old lady laid down her iron, puckered up her little crab's mouth, and said: "Mr. Hawkins, you can say what you like about the war, and think you'll deceive me because I'm only a simple poor countrywoman, but I know what started the war. It was the Italian Count that stole the heathen divinity out of the temple in Japan. Believe me, Mr. Hawkins, nothing but sorrow and want can follow the people that disturb the hidden powers."

A queer old girl, all right.

II

We had our tea one evening, and Hawkins lit the lamp and we all sat into cards. Jeremiah Donovan came in too, and sat down and watched us for a while, and it suddenly struck me that he had no great love for the two Englishmen. It came as a great surprise to me, because I hadn't noticed anything about him before.

Late in the evening a really terrible argument blew up between Hawkins and Noble, about capitalists and priests and love of your country.

"The capitalists," says Hawkins with an angry gulp, "pays the priests to tell you about the next world so as you won't notice what the bastards are up to in this."

"Nonsense, man!" says Noble, losing his temper. "Before ever a capitalist was thought of, people believed in the next world."

Hawkins stood up as though he was preaching a sermon.

"Oh, they did, did they?" he says with a sneer. "They believed all the things you believe, isn't that what you mean? And you believe that God created Adam, and Adam created Shem, and Shem cre-

---

3. Jupiter Pluvius is the rainmaker in Roman mythology.

4. World War I, in which England was at war with Germany.

ated Jehoshophat.[5] You believe all that silly old fairytale about Eve and Eden and the apple. Well, listen to me, chum. If you're entitled to hold a silly belief like that, I'm entitled to hold my silly belief—which is that the first thing your God created was a bleeding capitalist, with morality and Rolls-Royce complete. Am I right, chum?" he says to Belcher.

"You're right, chum," says Belcher with his amused smile, and got up from the table to stretch his long legs into the fire and stroke his moustache. So, seeing that Jeremiah Donovan was going, and that there was no knowing when the argument about religion would be over, I went out with him. We strolled down to the village together, and then he stopped and started blushing and mumbling and saying I ought to be behind, keeping guard on the prisoners. I didn't like the tone he took with me, and anyway I was bored with life in the cottage, so I replied by asking him what the hell we wanted guarding them at all for. I told him I'd talked it over with Noble, and that we'd both rather be out with a fighting column.

"What use are those fellows to us?" says I.

He looked at me in surprise and said: "I thought you knew we were keeping them as hostages."

"Hostages?" I said.

"The enemy have prisoners belonging to us," he says, "and now they're talking of shooting them. If they shoot our prisoners, we'll shoot theirs."

"Shoot them?" I said.

"What else did you think we were keeping them for?" he says.

"Wasn't it very unforeseen of you not to warn Noble and myself of that in the beginning?" I said.

"How was it?" says he. "You might have known it."

"We couldn't know it, Jeremiah Donovan," says I. "How could we when they were on our hands so long?"

"The enemy have our prisoners as long and longer," says he.

"That's not the same thing at all," says I.

"What difference is there?" says he.

I couldn't tell him, because I knew he wouldn't understand. If it

5. A condensation of Old Testament genealogy, since though Adam, Shem, and Jehoshophat appear in the Bible in that order, they lived many generations apart.

was only an old dog that was going to the vet's, you'd try and not get too fond of him, but Jeremiah Donovan wasn't a man that would ever be in danger of that.

"And when is this thing going to be decided?" says I.

"We might hear tonight," he says. "Or tomorrow or the next day at latest. So if it's only hanging round here that's a trouble to you, you'll be free soon enough."

It wasn't the hanging round that was a trouble to me at all by this time. I had worse things to worry about. When I got back to the cottage the argument was still on. Hawkins was holding forth in his best style, maintaining that there was no next world, and Noble was maintaining that there was; but I could see that Hawkins had had the best of it.

"Do you know what, chum?" he was saying with a saucy smile. "I think you're just as big a bleeding unbeliever as I am. You say you believe in the next world, and you know just as much about the next world as I do, which is sweet damn-all. What's heaven? You don't know. Where's heaven? You don't know. You know sweet damn-all! I ask you again, do they wear wings?"

"Very well, then," says Noble, "they do. Is that enough for you? They do wear wings."

"Where do they get them, then? Who makes them? Have they a factory for wings? Have they a sort of store where you hands in your chit and takes your bleeding wings?"

"You're an impossible man to argue with," says Noble. "Now, listen to me—" And they were off again.

It was long after midnight when we locked up and went to bed. As I blew out the candle I told Noble what Jeremiah Donovan was after telling me. Noble took it very quietly. When we'd been in bed about an hour he asked me did I think we ought to tell the Englishmen. I didn't think we should, because it was more than likely that the English wouldn't shoot our men, and even if they did, the brigade officers, who were always up and down with the Second Battalion and knew the Englishmen well, wouldn't be likely to want them plugged. "I think so too," says Noble. "It would be great cruelty to put the wind to them now."

"It was very unforeseen of Jeremiah Donovan anyhow," says I.

It was next morning that we found it so hard to face Belcher and

Hawkins. We went about the house all day scarcely saying a word. Belcher didn't seem to notice; he was stretched into the ashes as usual, with his look unusual of waiting in quietness for something unforeseen to happen, but Hawkins noticed and put it down to Noble's being beaten in the argument of the night before.

"Why can't you take a discussion in the proper spirit?" he says severely. "You and your Adam and Eve! I'm a Communist, that's what I am. Communist or anarchist, it all comes to much the same thing." And for hours he went round the house, muttering when the fit took him. "Adam and Eve! Adam and Eve! Nothing better to do with their time than picking bleeding apples!"

III

I don't know how we got through that day, but I was very glad when it was over, the tea things were cleared away, and Belcher said in his peaceable way: "Well, chums, what about it?" We sat round the table and Hawkins took out the cards, and just then I heard Jeremiah Donovan's footstep on the path and a dark presentiment crossed my mind. I rose from the table and caught him before he reached the door.

"What do you want?" I asked.

"I want those two soldier friends of yours," he says, getting red.

"Is that the way, Jeremiah Donovan?" I asked.

"That's the way. There were four of our lads shot this morning, one of them a boy of sixteen."

"That's bad," I said.

At that moment Noble followed me out, and the three of us walked down the path together, talking in whispers. Feeney, the local intelligence officer was standing by the gate.

"What are you going to do about it?" I asked Jeremiah Donovan.

"I want you and Noble to get them out; tell them they're being shifted again; that'll be the quietest way."

"Leave me out of that," says Noble under his breath.

Jeremiah Donovan looks at him hard.

"All right," he says. "You and Feeney get a few tools from the shed and dig a hole by the far end of the bog. Bonaparte and myself will be after you. Don't let anyone see you with the tools. I wouldn't like it to go beyond ourselves."

We saw Feeney and Noble go round to the shed and went in ourselves. I left Jeremiah Donovan to do the explanations. He told them that he had orders to send them back to the Second Battalion. Hawkins let out a mouthful of curses, and you could see that though Belcher didn't say anything, he was a bit upset too. The old woman was for having them stay in spite of us, and she didn't stop advising them until Jeremiah Donovan lost his temper and turned on her. He had a nasty temper, I noticed. It was pitch-dark in the cottage by this time, but no one thought of lighting the lamp, and in the darkness the two Englishmen fetched their topcoats and said good-bye to the old woman.

"Just as a man makes a home of a bleeding place, some bastard at headquarters thinks you're too cushy and shunts you off," says Hawkins, shaking her hand.

"A thousand thanks, madam," says Belcher. "A thousand thanks for everything"—as though he'd made it up.

We went round to the back of the house and down towards the bog. It was only then that Jeremiah Donovan told them. He was shaking with excitement.

"There were four of our fellows shot in Cork this morning and now you're to be shot as a reprisal."

"What are you talking about?" snaps Hawkins. "It's bad enough being mucked about as we are without having to put up with your funny jokes."

"It isn't a joke," says Donovan. "I'm sorry, Hawkins, but it's true," and begins on the usual rigmarole about duty and how unpleasant it is.

I never noticed that people who talk a lot about duty find it much of a trouble to them.

"Oh, cut it out!" says Hawkins.

"Ask Bonaparte," says Donovan, seeing that Hawkins isn't taking him seriously. "Isn't it true, Bonaparte?"

"It is," I say, and Hawkins stops.

"Ah, for Christ's sake, chum!"

"You don't sound as if you meant it."

"If he doesn't mean it, I do," says Donovan, working himself up.

"What have you against me, Jeremiah Donovan?"

"I never said I had anything against you. But why did your people take out four of our prisoners and shoot them in cold blood?"

He took Hawkins by the arm and dragged him on, but it was impossible to make him understand that we were in earnest. I had the Smith and Wesson[6] in my pocket and I kept fingering it and wondering what I'd do if they put up a fight for it or ran, and wishing to God they'd do one or the other. I knew if they did run for it, that I'd never fire on them. Hawkins wanted to know was Noble in it, and when we said yes, he asked us why Noble wanted to plug him. Why did any of us want to plug him? What had he done to us? Weren't we all chums? Didn't we understand him and didn't he understand us? Did we imagine for an instant that he'd shoot us for all the so-and-so officers in the so-and-so British Army?

By this time we'd reached the bog, and I was so sick I couldn't even answer him. We walked along the edge of it in the darkness, and every now and then Hawkins would call a halt and begin all over again, as if he was wound up, about our being chums, and I knew that nothing but the sight of the grave would convince him that we had to do it. And all the time I was hoping that something would happen; that they'd run for it or that Noble would take over the responsibility from me. I had the feeling that it was worse on Noble than on me.

IV

At last we saw the lantern in the distance and made towards it. Noble was carrying it, and Feeney was standing somewhere in the darkness behind him, and the picture of them so still and silent in the bogland brought it home to me that we were in earnest, and banished the last bit of hope I had.

Belcher, on recognizing Noble, said: "Hallo, chum," in his quiet way, but Hawkins flew at him at once, and the argument began all over again, only this time Noble had nothing to say for himself and stood with his head down, holding the lantern between his legs.

6. A revolver, as is the Webley, below.

It was Jeremiah Donovan who did the answering. For the twentieth time, as though it was haunting his mind, Hawkins asked if
anybody thought he'd shoot Noble.

"Yes, you would," says Jeremiah Donovan.

"No, I wouldn't, damn you!"

"You would, because you'd know you'd be shot for not doing
it."

"I wouldn't, not if I was to be shot twenty times over. I wouldn't
shoot a pal. And Belcher wouldn't—isn't that right, Belcher?"

"That's right, chum," Belcher said, but more by way of answering the question than of joining in the argument. Belcher sounded
as though whatever unforeseen thing he'd always been waiting for
had come at last.

"Anyway, who says Noble would be shot if I wasn't? What do you
think I'd do if I was in his place, out in the middle of a blasted
bog?"

"What would you do?" asks Donovan.

"I'd go with him wherever he was going, of course. Share my last
bob[7] with him and stick by him through thick and thin. No one
can ever say of me that I let down a pal."

"We had enough of this," says Jeremiah Donovan, cocking his revolver. "Is there any message you want to send?"

"No, there isn't."

"Do you want to say your prayers?"

Hawkins came out with a cold-blooded remark that even
shocked me and turned on Noble again.

"Listen to me, Noble," he says. "You and me are chums. You
can't come over to my side, so I'll come over to your side. That show
you I mean what I say? Give me a rifle and I'll go along with you
and the other lads."

Nobody answered him. We knew that was no way out.

"Hear what I'm saying?" he says. "I'm through with it. I'm a de-
serter or anything else you like. I don't believe in your stuff, but it's
no worse than mine. That satisfy you?"

Noble raised his head, but Donovan began to speak and he lowered it again without replying.

---

7. Shilling (British slang).

"For the last time, have you any messages to send?" says Donovan in a cold excited sort of voice.

"Shut up, Donovan! You don't understand me, but these lads do. They're not the sort to make a pal and kill a pal. They're not the tools of any capitalist."

I alone of the crowd saw Donovan raise his Webley to the back of Hawkins's neck, and as he did so I shut my eyes and tried to pray. Hawkins had begun to say something else when Donovan fired, and as I opened my eyes at the bang, I saw Hawkins stagger at the knees and lie out flat at Noble's feet, slowly and as quiet as a kid falling asleep, with the lantern-light on his lean legs and bright farmer's boots. We all stood very still, watching him settle out in the last agony.

Then Belcher took out a handkerchief and began to tie it about his own eyes (in our excitement we'd forgotten to do the same for Hawkins), and, seeing it wasn't big enough, turned and asked for the loan of mine. I gave it to him and he knotted the two together and pointed with his foot at Hawkins.

"He's not quite dead," he says. "Better give him another."

Sure enough, Hawkins's left knee is beginning to rise. I bend down and put my gun to his head; then, recollecting myself, I get up again. Belcher understands what's in my mind.

"Give him his first," he says. "I don't mind. Poor bastard, we don't know what's happening to him now."

I knelt and fired. By this time I didn't seem to know what I was doing. Belcher, who was fumbling a bit awkwardly with the handkerchiefs, came out with a laugh as he heard the shot. It was the first time I heard him laugh and it sent a shudder down my back; it sounded so unnatural.

"Poor bugger!" he said quietly. "And last night he was so curious about it all. It's very queer, chums, I always think. Now he knows as much about it as they'll ever let him know, and last night he was all in the dark."

Donovan helped him to tie the handkerchiefs about his eyes. "Thanks, chum," he said. Donovan asked if there were any messages he wanted sent.

"No, chum," he says. "Not for me. If any of you would like to write to Hawkins's mother, you'll find a letter from her in his pocket. He and his mother were great chums. But my missus left me eight years ago. Went away with another fellow and took the kid with her. I like the feeling of a home, as you may have noticed, but I couldn't start again after that."

It was an extraordinary thing, but in those few minutes Belcher said more than in all the weeks before. It was just as if the sound of the shot had started a flood of talk in him and he could go on the whole night like that, quite happily, talking about himself. We stood round like fools now that he couldn't see us any longer. Donovan looked at Noble, and Noble shook his head. Then Donovan raised his Webley, and at that moment Belcher gives his queer laugh again. He may have thought we were talking about him, or perhaps he noticed the same thing I'd noticed and couldn't understand it.

"Excuse me, chums," he says. "I feel I'm talking the hell of a lot, and so silly, about my being so handy about a house and things like that. But this thing came on me suddenly. You'll forgive me, I'm sure."

"You don't want to say a prayer?" asks Donovan.

"No, chum," he says. "I don't think it would help. I'm ready, and you boys want to get it over."

"You understand that we're only doing our duty?" says Donovan.

Belcher's head was raised like a blind man's so that you could only see his chin and the tip of his nose in the lantern-light.

"I never could make out what duty was myself," he said. "I think you're all good lads, if that's what you mean. I'm not complaining."

Noble, just as if he couldn't bear any more of it, raised his fist at Donovan, and in a flash Donovan raised his gun and fired. The big man went over like a sack of meal, and this time there was no need for a second shot.

I don't remember much about the burying, but that it was worse than all the rest because we had to carry them to the grave. It was all mad lonely with nothing but a patch of lantern light between ourselves and the dark, and birds hooting and screeching all round, disturbed by the guns. Noble went through Hawkins's belongings to find the letter from his mother, and then joined his hands together. He did the same with Belcher. Then, when we'd filled in the grave, we separated from Jeremiah Donovan and Feeney and took our tools back to the shed. All the way we didn't speak a word. The kitchen was dark and cold as we'd left it, and the old woman was sitting over the hearth, saying her beads. We walked past her into the room, and Noble struck a match to light the lamp. She rose quietly and came to the doorway with all her cantankerousness gone.

"What did ye do with them?" she asked in a whisper, and Noble started so that the match went out in his hand.

"What's that?" he asked without turning round.

"I heard ye," she said.

"What did you hear?" asked Noble.

"I heard ye. Do ye think I didn't hear ye, putting the spade back in the houseen?"[8]

Noble struck another match and this time the lamp lit for him.

"Was that what ye did to them?" she asked.

Then, by God, in the very doorway, she fell on her knees and began praying, and after looking at her for a minute or two Noble did the same by the fireplace. I pushed my way out past her and left them at it. I stood at the door, watching the stars and listening to the shrieking of the birds dying out over the bogs. It is so strange what you feel at times like that that you can't describe it. Noble says he saw everything ten times the size, as though there were nothing in the whole world but that little patch of bog with the two Englishmen stiffening into it, but with me it was as if the patch of bog where the Englishmen were was a million miles away, and even Noble and the old woman, mumbling behind me, and the birds and the bloody stars were all far away, and I was somehow very small and very lost and lonely like a child astray in the snow. And anything that happened to me afterwards, I never felt the same about again.

1930

---

8. "Een" is an Irish suffix meaning "little," hence "little house," or in this case, "shed."

Tillie Olsen

1913–

> The form of Olsen's stories, she says, "is dependent on . . . my personal
> situation, . . . both material and personal: that is, the writing time
> available to me; what is happening in my work and family life, and
> in the larger environment, in society." She wrote and rewrote "I
> Stand Here Ironing" on an ironing board, late at night, and the
> "back and forth movement as the iron moves" is reflected in the story
> itself. Her original impulse to write this story came from the situa-
> tion of a friend, whose teenage son had been arrested for drinking
> beer in a car. The friend was summoned to court to prove she was a
> fit mother; because she had a boyfriend who often slept over, the court
> considered her immoral. During this crisis, Olsen says that she
> "gagged at the difference between the way you're judged from the out-
> side and the true reality" of a single mother's life. She wrote the story
> to instruct "the kind of people who had the power to take away one's
> child." But in the writing, Olsen's own life took over the story: it is
> largely autobiographical. Olsen has complained that many of the an-
> thologies that include her story direct students to consider the narra-
> tor's feelings of guilt. "One is guilty," she explains, "only for what one
> oneself is responsible." Instead, the reader should focus on "society and
> its institutions" that force the narrator to suffer anguish.

I Stand Here Ironing

I stand here ironing, and what you asked me moves tormented
back and forth with the iron.

"I wish you would manage the time to come in and talk
with me about your daughter. I'm sure you can help me understand
her. She's a youngster who needs help and whom I'm deeply interested in helping."

"Who needs help." . . . Even if I came, what good would it do?
You think because I am her mother I have a key, or that in some
way you could use me as a key? She has lived for nineteen years.
There is all that life that has happened outside of me, beyond me.

And when is there time to remember, to sift, to weigh, to esti-
mate, to total? I will start and there will be an interruption and I

will have to gather it all together again. Or I will become engulfed with all I did or did not do, with what should have been and what cannot be helped.

She was a beautiful baby. The first and only one of our five that was beautiful at birth. You do not guess how new and uneasy her tenancy in her now-loveliness. You did not know her all those years she was thought homely, or see her poring over her baby pictures, making me tell her over and over how beautiful she had been—and would be, I would tell her—and was now, to the seeing eye. But the seeing eyes were few or non-existent. Including mine.

I nursed her. They feel that's important nowadays. I nursed all the children, but with her, with all the fierce rigidity of first motherhood, I did like the books then said. Though her cries battered me to trembling and my breasts ached with swollenness, I waited till the clock decreed.

Why do I put that first? I do not even know if it matters, or if it explains anything.

She was a beautiful baby. She blew shining bubbles of sound. She loved motion, loved light, loved color and music and textures. She would lie on the floor in her blue overalls patting the surface so hard in ecstasy her hands and feet would blur. She was a miracle to me, but when she was eight months old I had to leave her daytimes with the woman downstairs to whom she was no miracle at all, for I worked or looked for work and for Emily's father, who "could no longer endure" (he wrote in his good-bye note) "sharing want with us."

I was nineteen. It was the pre-relief, pre-WPA[1] world of the depression. I would start running as soon as I got off the streetcar, running up the stairs, the place smelling sour, and awake or asleep to startle awake, when she saw me she would break into a clogged weeping that could not be comforted, a weeping I can hear yet.

After a while I found a job hashing at night so I could be with her days, and it was better. But it came to where I had to bring her to his family and leave her.

It took a long time to raise the money for her fare back. Then she got chicken pox and I had to wait longer. When she finally came, I hardly knew her, walking quick and nervous like her father, looking

1. Works Progress Administration, a U.S. government agency established in 1935 to provide jobs, especially in public works; it was abolished in 1943.

like her father, thin, and dressed in a shoddy red that yellowed her skin and glared at the pockmarks. All the baby loveliness gone.

She was two. Old enough for nursery school they said, and I did not know then what I know now—the fatigue of the long day, and the lacerations of group life in the kinds of nurseries that are only parking places for children.

Except that it would have made no difference if I had known. It was the only place there was. It was the only way we could be together, the only way I could hold a job.

And even without knowing, I knew. I knew the teacher that was evil because all these years it has curdled into my memory, the little boy hunched in the corner, her rasp, "why aren't you outside, because Alvin hits you? that's no reason, go out, scaredy." I knew Emily hated it even if she did not clutch and implore "don't go Mommy" like the other children, mornings.

She always had a reason why we should stay home. Momma, you look sick, Momma. I feel sick. Momma, the teachers aren't there today, they're sick. Momma, we can't go, there was a fire there last night. Momma, it's a holiday today, no school, they told me.

But never a direct protest, never rebellion. I think of our others in their three-, four-year-oldness—the explosions, the tempers, the denunciations, the demands—and I feel suddenly ill. I put the iron down. What in me demanded that goodness in her? And what was the cost, the cost to her of such goodness?

The old man living in the back once said in his gentle way: "You should smile at Emily more when you look at her." What *was* in my face when I looked at her? I loved her. There were all the acts of love.

It was only with the others I remembered what he said, and it was the face of joy, and not of care or tightness or worry I turned to them—too late for Emily. She does not smile easily, let alone almost always as her brothers and sisters do. Her face is closed and sombre, but when she wants, how fluid. You must have seen it in her pantomimes, you spoke of her rare gift for comedy on the stage that rouses a laughter out of the audience so dear they applaud and applaud and do not want to let her go.

Where does it come from, that comedy? There was none of it in her when she came back to me that second time, after I had had to send her away again. She had a new daddy now to learn to love, and I think perhaps it was a better time.

Except when we left her alone nights, telling ourselves she was old enough.

"Can't you go some other time, Mommy, like tomorrow?" she would ask. "Will it be just a little while you'll be gone? Do you promise?"

The time we came back, the front door open, the clock on the floor in the hall. She rigid awake. "It wasn't just a little while. I didn't cry. Three times I called you, just three times, and then I ran downstairs to open the door so you could come faster. The clock talked loud. I threw it away, it scared me what it talked."

She said the clock talked loud again that night I went to the hospital to have Susan. She was delirious with the fever that comes before red measles, but she was fully conscious all the week I was gone and the week after we were home when she could not come near the new baby or me.

She did not get well. She stayed skeleton thin, not wanting to eat, and night after night she had nightmares. She would call for me, and I would rouse from exhaustion to sleepily call back: "You're all right, darling, go to sleep, it's just a dream," and if she still called, in a sterner voice, "now go to sleep, Emily, there's nothing to hurt you." Twice, only twice, when I had to get up for Susan anyhow, I went in to sit with her.

Now when it is too late (as if she would let me hold and comfort her like I do the others) I get up and go to her at once at her moan or restless stirring. "Are you awake, Emily? Can I get you something?" And the answer is always the same: "No, I'm all right, go back to sleep, Mother."

They persuaded me at the clinic to send her away to a convalescent home in the country where "she can have the kind of food and care you can't manage for her, and you'll be free to concentrate on the new baby." They still send children to that place. I see pictures on the society page of sleek young women planning affairs to raise money for it, or dancing at the affairs, or decorating Easter eggs or filling Christmas stockings for the children.

They never have a picture of the children so I do not know if the girls still wear those gigantic red bows and the ravaged looks on the every other Sunday when parents can come to visit "unless other-wise notified"—as we were notified the first six weeks.

Oh it is a handsome place, green lawns and tall trees and fluted flower beds. High up on the balconies of each cottage the children stand, the girls in their red bows and white dresses, the boys in white suits and giant red ties. The parents stand below shrieking up to be heard and the children shriek down to be heard, and between them the invisible wall "Not To Be Contaminated by Parental Germs or Physical Affection."

There was a tiny girl who always stood hand in hand with Emily. Her parents never came. One visit she was gone. "They moved her to Rose Cottage" Emily shouted in explanation. "They don't like you to love anybody here."

She wrote once a week, the labored writing of a seven-year-old. "I am fine. How is the baby. If I write my leter nicly I will have a star. Love." There never was a star. We wrote every other day, letters she could never hold or keep but only hear read—once. "We simply do not have room for children to keep any personal possessions," they patiently explained when we pieced one Sunday's shrieking together to plead how much it would mean to Emily, who loved so to keep things, to be allowed to keep her letters and cards.

Each visit she looked frailer. "She isn't eating," they told us.

(They had runny eggs for breakfast or mush with lumps, Emily said later, I'd hold it in my mouth and not swallow. Nothing ever tasted good, just when they had chicken.)

It took us eight months to get her released home, and only the fact that she gained back so little of her seven lost pounds convinced the social worker.

I used to try to hold and love her after she came back, but her body would stay stiff, and after a while she'd push away. She ate little. Food sickened her, and I think much of life too. Oh she had physical lightness and brightness, twinkling by on skates, bouncing like a ball up and down up and down over the jump rope, skimming over the hill; but these were momentary.

She fretted about her appearance, thin and dark and foreign-looking at a time when every little girl was supposed to look or thought she should look a chubby blonde replica of Shirley Temple.

The doorbell sometimes rang for her, but no one seemed to come and play in the house or be a best friend. Maybe because we moved so much.

There was a boy she loved painfully through two school semesters. Months later she told me how she had taken pennies from my purse to buy him candy. "Licorice was his favorite and I brought him some every day, but he still liked Jennifer better'n me. Why, Mommy?" The kind of question for which there is no answer.

School was a worry to her. She was not glib or quick in a world where glibness and quickness were easily confused with ability to learn. To her overworked and exasperated teachers she was an over-conscientious "slow learner" who kept trying to catch up and was absent entirely too often.

I let her be absent, though sometimes the illness was imaginary. How different from my now-strictness about attendance with the others. I wasn't working. We had a new baby, I was home anyhow. Sometimes, after Susan grew old enough, I would keep her home from school, too, to have them all together.

Mostly Emily had asthma, and her breathing, harsh and labored, would fill the house with a curiously tranquil sound. I would bring the two old dresser mirrors and her boxes of collections to her bed. She would select beads and single earrings, bottle tops and shells, dried flowers and pebbles, old postcards and scraps, all sorts of oddments; then she and Susan would play Kingdom, setting up landscapes and furniture, peopling them with action.

Those were the only times of peaceful companionship between her and Susan. I have edged away from it, that poisonous feeling between them, that terrible balancing of hurts and needs I had to do between the two, and did so badly, those earlier years.

Oh there are conflicts between the others too, each one human, needing, demanding, hurting, taking—but only between Emily and Susan, no, Emily toward Susan that corroding resentment. It seems so obvious on the surface, yet it is not obvious. Susan, the second child, Susan, golden- and curly-haired and chubby, quick and articulate and assured, everything in appearance and manner Emily was not; Susan, not able to resist Emily's precious things, losing or sometimes clumsily breaking them; Susan telling jokes and riddles to company for applause while Emily sat silent (to say to me later:

that was *my* riddle, Mother, I told it to Susan); Susan, who for all the five years' difference in age was just a year behind Emily in developing physically.

I am glad for that slow physical development that widened the difference between her and her contemporaries, though she suffered over it. She was too vulnerable for that terrible world of youthful competition, of preening and parading, of constant measuring of yourself against every other, of envy, "If I had that copper hair," "If I had that skin. . . ." She tormented herself enough about not looking like the others, there was enough of the unsureness, the having to be conscious of words before you speak, the constant caring— what are they thinking of me? without having it all magnified by the merciless physical drives.

Ronnie is calling. He is wet and I change him. It is rare there is such a cry now. That time of motherhood is almost behind me when the ear is not one's own but must always be racked and listening for the child cry, the child call. We sit for a while and I hold him, looking out over the city spread in charcoal with its soft aisles of light. *"Shoogily,"* he breathes and curls closer. I carry him back to bed, asleep. *Shoogily.* A funny word, a family word, inherited from Emily, invented by her to say: *comfort.*

In this and other ways she leaves her seal, I say aloud. And startle at my saying it. What do I mean? What did I start to gather together, to try and make coherent? I was at the terrible, growing years. War years. I do not remember them well. I was working, there were four smaller ones now, there was not time for her. She had to help be a mother, and housekeeper, and shopper. She had to set her seal. Mornings of crisis and near hysteria trying to get lunches packed, hair combed, coats and shoes found, everyone to school or Child Care on time, the baby ready for transportation. And always the paper scribbled on by a smaller one, the book looked at by Susan then mislaid, the homework not done. Running out to that huge school where she was one, she was lost, she was a drop; suffering over the unpreparedness, stammering and unsure in her classes.

There was so little time left at night after the kids were bedded down. She would struggle over books, always eating (it was in those years she developed her enormous appetite that is legendary in our family) and I would be ironing, or preparing food for the next day, or writing V-mail[2] to Bill, or tending the baby. Sometimes, to make me laugh, or out of her despair, she would imitate happenings or types at school.

I think I said once: "Why don't you do something like this in the school amateur show?" One morning she phoned me at work, hardly understandable through the weeping: "Mother, I did it. I won, I won; they gave me first prize; they clapped and clapped and wouldn't let me go."

Now suddenly she was Somebody, and as imprisoned in her difference as she had been in anonymity.

She began to be asked to perform at other high schools, even in colleges, then at city and statewide affairs. The first one we went to, I only recognized her that first moment when thin, shy, she almost drowned herself into the curtains. Then: Was this Emily? The control, the command, the convulsing and deadly clowning, the spell, then the roaring, stamping audience, unwilling to let this rare and precious laughter out of their lives.

Afterwards: You ought to do something about her with a gift like that—but without money or knowing how, what does one do? We have left it all to her, and the gift has as often eddied inside, clogged and clotted, as been used and growing.

She is coming. She runs up the stairs two at a time with her light graceful step, and I know she is happy tonight. Whatever it was that occasioned your call did not happen today.

"Aren't you ever going to finish the ironing, Mother? Whistler painted his mother in a rocker.[3] I'd have to paint mine standing over an ironing board." This is one of her communicative nights and she tells me everything and nothing as she fixes herself a plate of food out of the icebox.

She is so lovely. Why did you want me to come in at all? Why were you concerned? She will find her way.

She starts up the stairs to bed. "Don't get me up with the rest in the morning." "But I thought you were having midterms." "Oh, those," she comes back in, kisses me, and says quite lightly, "in a

---

2. Overseas mail service for the U.S. armed forces during World War II.

3. *Arrangement in Grey and Black* (1872),

by the American painter James Whistler (1834–1903).

couple of years when we'll all be atom-dead they won't matter a bit."

She has said it before. She *believes* it. But because I have been dredging the past, and all that compounds a human being is so heavy and meaningful in me, I cannot endure it tonight.

I will never total it all. I will never come in to say: She was a child seldom smiled at. Her father left me before she was a year old. I had to work her first six years when there was work, or I sent her home and to his relatives. There were years she had care she hated. She was dark and thin and foreign-looking in a world where the prestige went to blondeness and curly hair and dimples, she was slow where glibness was prized. She was a child of anxious, not proud, love. We were poor and could not afford for her the soil of easy growth. I was a young mother, I was a distracted mother. There were the other children pushing up, demanding. Her younger sister seemed all that she was not. There were years she did not want me to touch her. She kept too much in herself, her life was such she had to keep too much in herself. My wisdom came too late. She has much to her and probably little will come of it. She is a child of her age, of depression, of war, of fear.

Let her be. So all that is in her will not bloom—but in how many does it? There is still enough left to live by. Only help her to know—help make it so there is cause for her to know—that she is more than this dress on the ironing board, helpless before the iron.

1960

Edgar Allan Poe

1809–1849

> *Poe wrote "The Cask of Amontillado" relatively late in his career, in 1846. Though made famous the year before by his long poem "The Raven," Poe envied the successes of lesser writers and entangled himself in bitter battles with these rivals, which led to his banishment from the New York and New England literary circles. His ostracism and poverty may have inspired this tale of revenge, which, like Poe's other stories, is justly remembered for its weird grotesques.*

But Poe's stories continue to fascinate us because of their psychological complexities—the individual, unique psyche of his singular characters. In this vein, he distinguishes himself from his contemporary Hawthorne, whose allegories (such as "Young Goodman Brown") deal with the general *human psyche rather than with the* personal. *"The Cask of Amontillado" reaches this level of complexity when the reader remembers that it is told from Montresor's point of view. To sound the depths of the story, we must question everything he tells us, even about Fortunato's supposed offense. You might also consider to whom and why Montresor confesses this story.*

The Cask of Amontillado

The thousand injuries of Fortunato I had borne as I best could; but when he ventured upon insult, I vowed revenge. You, who so well know the nature of my soul, will not suppose, however, that I gave utterance to a threat. *At length* I would be avenged; this was a point definitively settled—but the very definitiveness with which it was resolved, precluded the idea of risk. I must not only punish, but punish with impunity. A wrong is unredressed when retribution overtakes its redresser. It is equally unredressed when the avenger fails to make himself felt as such to him who has done the wrong.

It must be understood, that neither by word nor deed had I given Fortunato cause to doubt my good-will. I continued, as was my wont, to smile in his face, and he did not perceive that my smile *now* was at the thought of his immolation.

He had a weak point—this Fortunato—although in other regards he was a man to be respected and even feared. He prided himself on his connoisseurship in wine. Few Italians have the true virtuoso spirit. For the most part their enthusiasm is adopted to suit the time and opportunity—to practise imposture upon the British and Austrian *millionnaires.* In painting and gemmary[1] Fortunato, like his countrymen, was a quack—but in the matter of old wines

---

1. Gems as objects of connoisseurship.

he was sincere. In this respect I did not differ from him materially: I was skilful in the Italian vintages myself, and bought largely whenever I could.

It was about dusk, one evening during the supreme madness of the carnival season,[2] that I encountered my friend. He accosted me with excessive warmth, for he had been drinking much. The man wore motley.[3] He had on a tight-fitting parti-striped dress, and his head was surmounted by the conical cap and bells. I was so pleased to see him, that I thought I should never have done wringing his hand.

I said to him: "My dear Fortunato, you are luckily met. How remarkably well you are looking to-day! But I have received a pipe of what passes for Amontillado,[4] and I have my doubts."

"How?" said he. "Amontillado? A pipe? Impossible! And in the middle of the carnival!"

"I have my doubts," I replied; "and I was silly enough to pay the full Amontillado price without consulting you in the matter. You were not to be found, and I was fearful of losing a bargain."

"Amontillado!"

"I have my doubts."

"Amontillado!"

"And I must satisfy them."

"Amontillado!"

"As you are engaged, I am on my way to Luchesi. If any one has a critical turn, it is he. He will tell me—"

"Luchesi cannot tell Amontillado from Sherry."

"And yet some fools will have it that his taste is a match for your own."

"Come, let us go."

"Whither?"

"To your vaults."

"My friend, no; I will not impose upon your good nature. I perceive you have an engagement. Luchesi—"

"I have no engagement;—come."

"My friend, no. It is not the engagement, but the severe cold

2. Time of feast and merrymaking just before Lent.

3. A suit of different colors, typically worn by old-time fools and jesters.

4. A type of Spanish sherry. A pipe is a large cask used to hold wine.

with which I perceive you are afflicted. The vaults are insufferably damp. They are encrusted with nitre."[5]

"Let us go, nevertheless. The cold is merely nothing. Amontillado! You have been imposed upon. And as for Luchesi, he cannot distinguish Sherry from Amontillado."

Thus speaking, Fortunato possessed himself of my arm. Putting on a mask of black silk, and drawing a *roquelaire*[6] closely about my person, I suffered him to hurry me to my palazzo.

There were no attendants at home; they had absconded to make merry in honor of the time. I had told them that I should not return until the morning, and had given them explicit orders not to stir from the house. These orders were sufficient, I well knew, to insure their immediate disappearance, one and all, as soon as my back was turned.

I took from their sconces two flambeaux, and giving one to Fortunato, bowed him through several suites of rooms to the archway that led into the vaults. I passed down a long and winding staircase, requesting him to be cautious as he followed. We came at length to the foot of the descent, and stood together on the damp ground of the catacombs of the Montresors.

The gait of my friend was unsteady, and the bells upon his cap jingled as he strode.

"The pipe?" said he.

"It is farther on," said I; "but observe the white web-work which gleams from these cavern walls."

He turned toward me, and looked into my eyes with two filmy orbs that distilled the rheum of intoxication.

"Nitre?" he asked, at length.

"Nitre," I replied. "How long have you had that cough?"

"Ugh! ugh! ugh!—ugh! ugh! ugh!—ugh! ugh! ugh!—ugh! ugh! ugh!—ugh! ugh! ugh!"

My poor friend found it impossible to reply for many minutes.

"It is nothing," he said, at last.

"Come," I said, with decision, "we will go back; your health is precious. You are rich, respected, admired, beloved; you are happy, as once I was. You are a man to be missed. For me it is no matter.

---

5. Naturally occurring sodium nitrate, often found in soil and encrusted on rock.

6. Cloak (French).

We will go back; you will be ill, and I cannot be responsible. Besides, there is Luchesi—"

"Enough," he said; "the cough is a mere nothing; it will not kill me. I shall not die of a cough."

"True—true," I replied; "and, indeed, I had no intention of alarming you unnecessarily; but you should use all proper caution. A draught of this Medoc[7] will defend us from the damps."

Here I knocked off the neck of a bottle which I drew from a long row of its fellows that lay upon the mould.

"Drink," I said, presenting him the wine.

He raised it to his lips with a leer. He paused and nodded to me familiarly, while his bells jingled.

"I drink," he said, "to the buried that repose around us."

"And I to your long life."

He again took my arm, and we proceeded.

"These vaults," he said, "are extensive."

"The Montresors," I replied, "were a great and numerous family."

"I forget your arms."

"A huge human foot d'or,[8] in a field azure; the foot crushes a serpent rampant whose fangs are imbedded in the heel."

"And the motto?"

"Nemo me impune lacessit."[9]

"Good!" he said.

The wine sparkled in his eyes and the bells jingled. My own fancy grew warm with the Medoc. We had passed through walls of piled bones, with casks and puncheons[10] intermingling, into the inmost recesses of the catacombs. I paused again, and this time I made bold to seize Fortunato by an arm above the elbow.

"The nitre!" I said; "see, it increases. It hangs like moss upon the vaults. We are below the river's bed. The drops of moisture trickle among the bones. Come, we will go back ere it is too late. Your cough—"

"It is nothing," he said; "let us go on. But first, another draught of the Medoc."

I broke and reached him a flagon of De Grâve.[11] He emptied it at

---

7. A red Bordeaux wine.
8. Of gold (French).
9. "No one attacks me with impunity" (Latin).

10. Another type of wine cask.
11. Wine from the Graves region in France.

a breath. His eyes flashed with a fierce light. He laughed and threw the bottle upward with a gesticulation I did not understand.

I looked at him in surprise. He repeated the movement—a grotesque one.

"You do not comprehend?" he said.

"Not I," I replied.

"Then you are not of the brotherhood."

"How?"

"You are not of the masons."[12]

"Yes, yes," I said; "yes, yes."

"You? Impossible! A mason?"

"A mason," I replied.

"A sign," he said.

"It is this," I answered, producing a trowel from beneath the folds of my *roquelaire*.

"You jest," he exclaimed, recoiling a few paces. "But let us proceed to the Amontillado."

"Be it so," I said, replacing the tool beneath the cloak, and again offering him my arm. He leaned upon it heavily. We continued our route in search of the Amontillado. We passed through a range of low arches, descended, passed on, and descending again, arrived at a deep crypt, in which the foulness of the air caused our flambeaux rather to glow than flame.

At the most remote end of the crypt there appeared another less spacious. Its walls had been lined with human remains, piled to the vault overhead, in the fashion of the great catacombs of Paris. Three sides of this interior crypt were still ornamented in this manner. From the fourth the bones had been thrown down, and lay promiscuously upon the earth, forming at one point a mound of some size. Within the wall thus exposed by the displacing of the bones, we perceived a still interior recess, in depth about four feet, in width three, in height six or seven. It seemed to have been constructed for no especial use within itself, but formed merely the interval between two of the colossal supports of the roof of the catacombs, and was backed by one of their circumscribing walls of solid granite.

It was in vain that Fortunato, uplifting his dull torch, endeavored

12. Freemasons.

to pry into the depth of the recess. Its termination the feeble light did not enable us to see.

"Proceed," I said; "herein is the Amontillado. As for Luchesi—"

"He is an ignoramus," interrupted my friend, as he stepped unsteadily forward, while I followed immediately at his heels. In an instant he had reached the extremity of the niche, and finding his progress arrested by the rock, stood stupidly bewildered. A moment more and I had fettered him to the granite. In its surface were two iron staples, distant from each other about two feet, horizontally. From one of these depended a short chain, from the other a padlock. Throwing the links about his waist, it was but the work of a few seconds to secure it. He was too much astounded to resist. Withdrawing the key I stepped back from the recess.

"Pass your hand," I said, "over the wall; you cannot help feeling the nitre. Indeed it is *very* damp. Once more let me *implore* you to return. No? Then I must positively leave you. But I must first render you all the little attentions in my power."

"The Amontillado!" ejaculated my friend, not yet recovered from his astonishment.

"True," I replied; "the Amontillado."

As I said these words I busied myself among the pile of bones of which I have before spoken. Throwing them aside, I soon uncovered a quantity of building stone and mortar. With these materials and with the aid of my trowel, I began vigorously to wall up the entrance of the niche.

I had scarcely laid the first tier of the masonry when I discovered that the intoxication of Fortunato had in a great measure worn off. The earliest indication I had of this was a low moaning cry from the depth of the recess. It was *not* the cry of a drunken man. There was then a long and obstinate silence. I laid the second tier, and the third, and the fourth; and then I heard the furious vibrations of the chain. The noise lasted for several minutes, during which, that I might hearken to it with the more satisfaction, I ceased my labors and sat down upon the bones. When at last the clanking subsided, I resumed the trowel, and finished without interruption the fifth, the sixth, and the seventh tier. The wall was now nearly upon a level with my breast. I again paused, and holding the flambeaux over the mason-work, threw a few feeble rays upon the figure within.

A succession of loud and shrill screams, bursting suddenly from the throat of the chained form, seemed to thrust me violently back. For a brief moment I hesitated—I trembled. Unsheathing my rapier,[13] I began to grope with it about the recess; but the thought of an instant reassured me. I placed my hand upon the solid fabric of the catacombs, and felt satisfied. I reapproached the wall. I replied to the yells of him who clamored. I re-echoed—I aided—I surpassed them in volume and in strength. I did this, and the clamorer grew still.

It was now midnight, and my task was drawing to a close. I had completed the eighth, the ninth, and the tenth tier. I had finished a portion of the last and the eleventh; there remained but a single stone to be fitted and plastered in. I struggled with its weight; I placed it partially in its destined position. But now there came from out the niche a low laugh that erected the hairs upon my head. It was succeeded by a sad voice, which I had difficulty in recognizing as that of the noble Fortunato. The voice said—

"Ha! ha! ha!—he! he!—a very good joke indeed—an excellent jest. We will have many a rich laugh about it at the palazzo—he! he! he!—over our wine—he! he! he!"

"The Amontillado!" I said.

"He! he! he!—he! he! he!—yes, the Amontillado. But is it not getting late? Will not they be awaiting us at the palazzo, the Lady Fortunato and the rest? Let us be gone."

"Yes," I said, "let us be gone."

"For the love of God, Montresor!"

"Yes," I said, "for the love of God!"

But to these words I hearkened in vain for a reply. I grew impatient. I called aloud:

"Fortunato!"

No answer. I called again:

"Fortunato!"

No answer still. I thrust a torch through the remaining aperture and let it fall within. There came forth in return only a jingling of the bells. My heart grew sick—on account of the dampness of the catacombs. I hastened to make an end of my labor. I forced the last

13. Sword.

stone into its position; I plastered it up. Against the new masonry I re-erected the old rampart of bones. For the half of a century no mortal has disturbed them. *In pace requiescat!* [14]

1846

Katherine Anne Porter
1890–1980

> *"The Jilting of Granny Weatherall" alludes to Jesus' parable of the ten virgins. Ten virgins kept vigil for a bridegroom, who was delayed. Five were wise and took flasks of oil for their lamps, but five were foolish and brought no oil. They fell asleep, and when the cry went out that the groom was approaching, the foolish virgins had to go out to buy more oil. In their absence, the groom arrived, went in to the marriage feast with the wise virgins, and shut the doors. When the foolish virgins returned, they called through the door, but the lord replied, "Verily, I say unto you, I know you not." The bridegroom is typically interpreted as Christ during the Second Coming and as a warning always to be prepared for the Judgment Day, and Granny confuses Christ and George in her distress. Granny's state of mind might make the story a bit difficult to untangle. Porter wrote the story using stream of consciousness. That technique always demands close attention from the reader, even more so here since Granny's consciousness is so distorting.*

The Jilting of Granny Weatherall

She flicked her wrist neatly out of Doctor Harry's pudgy careful fingers and pulled the sheet up to her chin. The brat ought to be in knee breeches. Doctoring around the country with spectacles on his nose! "Get along now, take your schoolbooks and go. There's nothing wrong with me."

Doctor Harry spread a warm paw like a cushion on her forehead where the forked green vein danced and made her eyelids

---

14. May he rest in peace! (Latin).

twitch. "Now, now, be a good girl, and we'll have you up in no time."

"That's no way to speak to a woman nearly eighty years old just because she's down. I'd have you respect your elders, young man."

"Well, Missy, excuse me." Doctor Harry patted her cheek. "But I've got to warn you, haven't I? You're a marvel, but you must be careful or you're going to be good and sorry."

"Don't tell me what I'm going to be. I'm on my feet now, morally speaking. It's Cornelia. I had to go to bed to get rid of her."

Her bones felt loose, and floated around in her skin, and Doctor Harry floated like a balloon around the foot of the bed. He floated and pulled down his waistcoat and swung his glasses on a cord. "Well, stay where you are, it certainly can't hurt you."

"Get along and doctor your sick," said Granny Weatherall. "Leave a well woman alone. I'll call for you when I want you. . . . Where were you forty years ago when I pulled through milk-leg and double pneumonia? You weren't even born. Don't let Cornelia lead you on," she shouted, because Doctor Harry appeared to float up to the ceiling and out. "I pay my own bills, and I don't throw my money away on nonsense!"

She meant to wave good-by, but it was too much trouble. Her eyes closed of themselves, it was like a dark curtain drawn around the bed. The pillow rose and floated under her, pleasant as a hammock in a light wind. She listened to the leaves rustling outside the window. No, somebody was swishing newspapers: no, Cornelia and Doctor Harry were whispering together. She leaped broad awake, thinking they whispered in her ear.

"She was never like this, *never* like this!" "Well, what can we expect?" "Yes, eighty years old. . . ."

Well, and what if she was? She still had ears. It was like Cornelia to whisper around doors. She always kept things secret in such a public way. She was always being tactful and kind. Cornelia was dutiful; that was the trouble with her. Dutiful and good: "So good and dutiful," said Granny, "that I'd like to spank her." She saw herself spanking Cornelia and making a fine job of it.

"What'd you say, Mother?"

Granny felt her face tying up in hard knots.

"Can't a body think, I'd like to know?"

"I thought you might want something."

"I do. I want a lot of things. First off, go away and don't whisper."

She lay and drowsed, hoping in her sleep that the children would keep out and let her rest a minute. It had been a long day. Not that she was tired. It was always pleasant to snatch a minute now and then. There was always so much to be done, let me see: tomorrow.

Tomorrow was far away and there was nothing to trouble about. Things were finished somehow when the time came; thank God there was always a little margin over for peace: then a person could spread out the plan of life and tuck in the edges orderly. It was good to have everything clean and folded away, with the hair brushes and tonic bottles sitting straight on the white embroidered linen: the day started without fuss and the pantry shelves laid out with rows of jelly glasses and brown jugs and white stone-china jars with blue whirligigs and words painted on them: coffee, tea, sugar, ginger, cinnamon, allspice: and the bronze clock with the lion on top nicely dusted off. The dust that lion could collect in twenty-four hours! The box in the attic with all those letters tied up, well, she'd have to go through that tomorrow. All those letters—George's letters and John's letters and her letters to them both—lying around for the children to find afterwards made her uneasy. Yes, that would be tomorrow's business. No use to let them know how silly she had been once.

While she was rummaging around she found death in her mind and it felt clammy and unfamiliar. She had spent so much time preparing for death there was no need for bringing it up again. Let it take care of itself now. When she was sixty she had felt very old, finished, and went around making farewell trips to see her children and grandchildren, with a secret in her mind: This is the very last of your mother, children! Then she made her will and came down with a long fever. That was all just a notion like a lot of other things, but it was lucky too, for she had once for all got over the idea of dying for a long time. Now she couldn't be worried. She hoped she had better sense now. Her father had lived to be one hundred and two years old and had drunk a noggin of strong hot toddy on his last birthday. He told the reporters it was his daily habit, and he owed his long life to that. He had made quite a scandal and was very pleased about it. She believed she'd just plague Cornelia a little.

"Cornelia! Cornelia!" No footsteps, but a sudden hand on her cheek. "Bless you, where have you been?"

"Here, mother."

"Well, Cornelia, I want a noggin of hot toddy."

"Are you cold, darling?"

"I'm chilly, Cornelia. Lying in bed stops the circulation. I must have told you that a thousand times."

Well, she could just hear Cornelia telling her husband that Mother was getting a little childish and they'd have to humor her. The thing that most annoyed her was that Cornelia thought she was deaf, dumb, and blind. Little hasty glances and tiny gestures tossed around her and over her head saying, "Don't cross her, let her have her way, she's eighty years old," and she sitting there as if she lived in a thin glass cage. Sometimes Granny almost made up her mind to pack up and move back to her own house where nobody could remind her every minute that she was old. Wait, wait, Cornelia, till your own children whisper behind your back!

In her day she had kept a better house and had got more work done. She wasn't too old yet for Lydia to be driving eighty miles for advice when one of the children jumped the track, and Jimmy still dropped in and talked things over: "Now, Mammy, you've a good business head, I want to know what you think of this? . . ." Old. Cornelia couldn't change the furniture around without asking. Little things, little things! They had been so sweet when they were little. Granny wished the old days were back again with the children young and everything to be done over. It had been a hard pull, but not too much for her. When she thought of all the food she had cooked, and all the clothes she had cut and sewed, and all the gardens she had made—well, the children showed it. There they were, made out of her, and they couldn't get away from that. Sometimes she wanted to see John again and point to them and say, Well, I didn't do so badly, did I? But that would have to wait. That was for tomorrow. She used to think of him as a man, but now all the children were older than their father, and he would be a child beside her if she saw him now. It seemed strange and there was something wrong in the idea. Why, he couldn't possibly recognize her. She had fenced in a hundred acres once, digging the post holes herself and clamping the wires with just a negro boy to help. That changed a woman. John would be looking for a young woman with the peaked Spanish comb in her hair and the painted fan. Digging post holes changed a woman. Riding country roads in the winter when women had their babies was another thing: sitting up nights with sick horses and sick negroes and sick children and hardly ever losing one. John, I hardly ever lost one of them! John would see that in a minute, that would be something he could understand, she wouldn't have to explain anything!

It made her feel like rolling up her sleeves and putting the whole place to rights again. No matter if Cornelia was determined to be everywhere at once, there were a great many things left undone on this place. She would start tomorrow and do them. It was good to be strong enough for everything, even if all you made melted and changed and slipped under your hands, so that by the time you finished you almost forgot what you were working for. What was it I set out to do? she asked herself intently, but she could not remember. A fog rose over the valley, she saw it marching across the creek swallowing the trees and moving up the hill like an army of ghosts. Soon it would be at the near edge of the orchard, and then it was time to go in and light the lamps. Come in, children, don't stay out in the night air.

Lighting the lamps had been beautiful. The children huddled up to her and breathed like little calves waiting at the bars in the twilight. Their eyes followed the match and watched the flame rise and settle in a blue curve, then they moved away from her. The lamp was lit, they didn't have to be scared and hang on to mother any more. Never, never, never more. God, for all my life I thank Thee. Without Thee, my God, I could never have done it. Hail, Mary, full of grace.

I want you to pick all the fruit this year and see that nothing is wasted. There's always someone who can use it. Don't let good things rot for want of using. You waste life when you waste good food. Don't let things get lost. It's bitter to lose things. Now, don't let me get to thinking, not when I am tired and taking a little nap before supper. . . .

The pillow rose about her shoulders and pressed against her heart and the memory was being squeezed out of it: oh, push down the pillow, somebody: it would smother her if she tried to hold it. Such a fresh breeze blowing and such a green day with no threats in it. But he had not come, just the same. What does a woman do when she has put on the white veil and set out the white cake for a man and he doesn't come? She tried to remember. No, I swear he never harmed me but in that. He never harmed me but in that . . . and what if he did? There was the day, the day, but a whirl of dark smoke rose and covered it, crept up and over into the bright field where everything was planted so carefully in orderly rows. That was hell, she knew hell when she saw it. For sixty years she had prayed against remembering him and against losing her soul in the deep pit of hell, and now the two things were mingled in one and the thought of him was a smoky cloud from hell that moved and crept in her head when she had just got rid of Doctor Harry and was trying to rest a minute. Wounded vanity, Ellen, said a sharp voice in the top of her mind. Don't let your wounded vanity get the upper hand of you. Plenty of girls get jilted. You were jilted, weren't you? Then stand up to it. Her eyelids wavered and let in streamers of blue-gray light like tissue paper over her eyes. She must get up and pull the shades down or she'd never sleep. She was in bed again and the shades were not down. How could that happen? Better turn over, hide from the light, sleeping in the light gave you nightmares. "Mother, how do you feel now?" and a stinging wetness on her forehead. But I don't like having my face washed in cold water!

Hapsy? George? Lydia? Jimmy? No, Cornelia, and her features were swollen and full of little puddles. "They're coming, darling, they'll all be here soon." Go wash your face, child, you look funny.

Instead of obeying, Cornelia knelt down and put her head on the pillow. She seemed to be talking but there was no sound. "Well, are you tongue-tied? Whose birthday is it? Are you going to give a party?"

Cornelia's mouth moved urgently in strange shapes. "Don't do that, you bother me, daughter."

"Oh, no, Mother. Oh, no. . . ."

Nonsense. It was strange about children. They disputed your every word. "No what, Cornelia?"

"Here's Doctor Harry."

"I won't see that boy again. He just left five minutes ago."

"That was this morning, Mother. It's night now. Here's the nurse."

"This is Doctor Harry, Mrs. Weatherall. I never saw you look so young and happy!"

"Ah, I'll never be young again—but I'd be happy if they'd let me lie in peace and get rested."

She thought she spoke up loudly, but no one answered. A warm weight on her forehead, a warm bracelet on her wrist, and a breeze went on whispering, trying to tell her something. A shuffle of leaves in the everlasting hand of God, He blew on them and they danced and rattled. "Mother, don't mind, we're going to give you a little hypodermic." "Look here, daughter, how do ants get in this bed? I saw sugar ants yesterday." Did you send for Hapsy too?

It was Hapsy she really wanted. She had to go a long way back through a great many rooms to find Hapsy standing with a baby on her arm. She seemed to herself to be Hapsy also, and the baby on Hapsy's arm was Hapsy and himself and herself, all at once, and there was no surprise in the meeting. Then Hapsy melted from within and turned flimsy as gray gauze and the baby was a gauzy shadow, and Hapsy came up close and said, "I thought you'd never come," and looked at her very searchingly and said, "You haven't changed a bit!" They leaned forward to kiss, when Cornelia began whispering from a long way off, "Oh, is there anything you want to tell me? Is there anything I can do for you?"

Yes, she had changed her mind after sixty years and she would like to see George. I want you to find George. Find him and be sure to tell him I forgot him. I want him to know I had my husband just the same and my children and my house like any other woman. A good house too and a good husband that I loved and fine children out of him. Better than I hoped for even. Tell him I was given back everything he took away and more. Oh, no, oh, God, no, there was something else besides the house and the man and the children. Oh, surely they were not all? What was it? Something not given back. . . . Her breath crowded down under her ribs and grew into a monstrous frightening shape with cutting edges; it bored up into her head, and the agony was unbelievable: Yes, John, get the Doctor now, no more talk, my time has come.

When this one was born it should be the last. The last. It should have been born first, for it was the one she had truly wanted. Everything came in good time. Nothing left out, left over. She was strong, in three days she would be as well as ever. Better. A woman needed milk in her to have her full health.

"Mother, do you hear me?"

"I've been telling you—"

"Mother, Father Connolly's here."

"I went to Holy Communion only last week. Tell him I'm not so sinful as all that."

"Father just wants to speak to you."

He could speak as much as he pleased. It was like him to drop in and inquire about her soul as if it were a teething baby, and then stay on for a cup of tea and a round of cards and gossip. He always had a funny story of some sort, usually about an Irishman who made his little mistakes and confessed them, and the point lay in some absurd thing he would blurt out in the confessional showing his struggles between native piety and original sin. Granny felt easy about her soul. Cornelia, where are your manners? Give Father Connolly a chair. She had her secret comfortable understanding with a few favorite saints who cleared a straight road to God for her. All as surely signed and sealed as the papers for the new Forty Acres. Forever . . . heirs and assigns forever. Since the day the wedding cake was not cut, but thrown out and wasted. The whole bottom dropped out of the world, and there she was blind and sweating with nothing under her feet and the walls falling away. His hand had caught her under the breast, she had not fallen, there was the freshly polished floor with the green rug on it, just as before. He had cursed like a sailor's parrot and said, "I'll kill him for you." Don't lay a hand on him, for my sake leave something to God. "Now, Ellen, you must believe what I tell you. . . ."

So there was nothing, nothing to worry about any more, except sometimes in the night one of the children screamed in a nightmare, and they both hustled out shaking and hunting for the matches and calling, "There, wait a minute, here we are!" John, get the doctor now, Hapsy's time has come. But there was Hapsy standing by the bed in a white cap. "Cornelia, tell Hapsy to take off her cap. I can't see her plain."

Her eyes opened very wide and the room stood out like a picture she had seen somewhere. Dark colors with the shadows rising towards the ceiling in long angles. The tall black dresser gleamed with nothing on it but John's picture, enlarged from a little one, with John's eyes very black when they should have been blue. You never saw him, so how do you know how he looked? But the man insisted the copy was perfect, it was very rich and handsome. For a picture, yes, but it's not my husband. The table by the bed had a linen cover and a candle and a crucifix. The light was blue from Cornelia's silk lampshades. No sort of light at all, just frippery. You had to live forty years with kerosene lamps to appreciate honest electricity. She felt very strong and she saw Doctor Harry with a rosy nimbus around him.

"You look like a saint, Doctor Harry, and I vow that's as near as you'll ever come to it."

"She's saying something."

"I heard you, Cornelia. What's all this carrying-on?"

"Father Connolly's saying—"

Cornelia's voice staggered and bumped like a cart in a bad road. It rounded corners and turned back again and arrived nowhere. Granny stepped up in the cart very lightly and reached for the reins, but a man sat beside her and she knew him by his hands, driving the cart. She did not look in his face, for she knew without seeing, but looked instead down the road where the trees leaned over and bowed to each other and a thousand birds were singing a Mass. She felt like singing too, but she put her hand in the bosom of her dress and pulled out a rosary, and Father Connolly murmured Latin in a very solemn voice and tickled her feet. My God, will you stop that nonsense? I'm a married woman. What if he did run away and leave me to face the priest by myself? I found another a whole world better. I wouldn't have exchanged my husband for anybody except St. Michael himself, and you may tell him that for me with a thank you in the bargain.

Light flashed on her closed eyelids, and a deep roaring shook her. Cornelia, is that lightning? I hear thunder. There's going to be a storm. Close all the windows. Call the children in. . . . "Mother, here we are, all of us." "Is that you, Hapsy?" "Oh, no, I'm Lydia. We drove as fast as we could." Their faces drifted above her, drifted away. The rosary fell out of her hands and Lydia put it back. Jimmy tried to help, their hands fumbled together, and Granny closed two fingers around Jimmy's thumb. Beads wouldn't do, it must be something alive. She was so amazed her thoughts ran round and round. So, my dear Lord, this is my death and I wasn't even thinking about it. My children have come to see me die. But I can't, it's not time. Oh, I always hated surprises. I wanted to give Cornelia the amethyst set—Cornelia, you're to have the amethyst set, but Hapsy's to wear it when she wants, and, Doctor Harry, do shut up. Nobody sent for you. Oh, my dear Lord, do wait a minute. I meant to do something about the Forty Acres, Jimmy doesn't need it and Lydia will later on, with that worthless husband of hers. I meant to finish the altar cloth and send six bottles of wine to Sister Borgia for her dyspepsia. I want to send six bottles of wine to Sister Borgia, Father Connolly, now don't let me forget.

Cornelia's voice made short turns and tilted over and crashed. "Oh, Mother, oh, Mother, oh, Mother. . . ."

"I'm not going, Cornelia. I'm taken by surprise. I can't go."

You'll see Hapsy again. What about her? "I thought you'd never come." Granny made a long journey outward, looking for Hapsy. What if I don't find her? What then? Her heart sank down and down, there was no bottom to death, she couldn't come to the end of it. The blue light from Cornelia's lampshade drew into a tiny point in the center of her brain, it flickered and winked like an eye, quietly it fluttered and dwindled. Granny lay curled down within herself, amazed and watchful, staring at the point of light that was herself; her body was now only a deeper mass of shadow in an endless darkness and this darkness would curl around the light and swallow it up. God, give a sign!

For the second time there was no sign. Again no bridegroom and the priest in the house. She could not remember any other sorrow because this grief wiped them all away. Oh, no, there's nothing more cruel than this—I'll never forgive it. She stretched herself with a deep breath and blew out the light.

1929

Leslie Marmon Silko
1948–

> *Silko is a Laguna Pueblo Indian from New Mexico. As "Yellow Woman" indicates, her writing derives from the lore and mythology of her tribe. This story comes from her book* Storyteller, *which mixes poetry, Silko's personal family folklore, short stories, myths, and photographs. The poems that follow this story in that book recount two of the stories the narrator's grandfather would have been fond of telling. In the first, Kochininako the Yellow Woman, with whom the narrator of this story identifies herself, abandons her three children and husband to live with the Sun, who appears to her as a human being. In the second story, Kochininako goes looking for water to relieve her drought-stricken people. She is kidnapped by Buffalo Man and taken far to the east. Her husband, Arrowboy, comes after her, steals her back, and slays all the Buffalo People who follow them. In this way, Kochininako's people have enough food to get them through the summer, and they learn where to hunt buffalo in the future. But Kochininako grieves because she wanted to stay with Buffalo Man, so Arrowboy kills her to reunite her with her dead lover. Another poem begins "The Laguna people / always begin their stories / with 'humma-hah': / that means 'long ago.'" An important theme in "Yellow Woman" is the presence of "long ago" in the "here and now."*

Yellow Woman

My thigh clung to his with dampness, and I watched the sun rising up through the tamaracks and willows. The small brown water birds came to the river and hopped across the mud, leaving brown scratches in the alkali-white crust. They bathed in the river silently. I could hear the water, almost at our feet where the narrow fast channel bubbled and washed green ragged moss and fern leaves. I looked at him beside me, rolled in the red blanket on the white river sand. I cleaned the sand out of the cracks between my toes, squinting because the sun was above the willow trees. I looked at him for the last time, sleeping on the white river sand.

I felt hungry and followed the river south the way we had come the afternoon before, following our footprints that were already blurred by lizard tracks and bug trails. The horses were still lying down, and the black one whinnied when he saw me but he did not get up—maybe it was because the corral was made out of thick cedar branches and the horses had not yet felt the sun like I had. I tried to look beyond the pale red mesas to the pueblo. I knew it was there, even if I could not see it, on the sandrock hill above the river, the same river that moved past me now and had reflected the moon last night.

The horse felt warm underneath me. He shook his head and pawed the sand. The bay whinnied and leaned against the gate trying to follow, and I remembered him asleep in the red blanket beside the river. I slid off the horse and tied him close to the other horse, I walked north with the river again, and the white sand broke loose in footprints over footprints.

"Wake up."

He moved in the blanket and turned his face to me with his eyes still closed. I knelt down to touch him.

"I'm leaving."

He smiled now, eyes still closed. "You are coming with me, remember?" He sat up now with his bare dark chest and belly in the sun.

"Where?"

"To my place."

"And will I come back?"

He pulled his pants on. I walked away from him, feeling him behind me and smelling the willows.

"Yellow Woman," he said.

I turned to face him. "Who are you?" I asked.

He laughed and knelt on the low, sandy bank, washing his face in the river. "Last night you guessed my name, and you knew why I had come."

I stared past him at the shallow moving water and tried to remember the night, but I could only see the moon in the water and remember his warmth around me.

"But I only said that you were him and that I was Yellow Woman—I'm not really her—I have my own name and I come from the pueblo on the other side of the mesa. Your name is Silva and you are a stranger I met by the river yesterday afternoon."

He laughed softly. "What happened yesterday has nothing to do with what you will do today, Yellow Woman."

"I know—that's what I'm saying—the old stories about the ka'tsina spirit and Yellow Woman can't mean us."

My old grandpa liked to tell those stories best. There is one about Badger and Coyote who went hunting and were gone all day, and when the sun was going down they found a house. There was a girl living there alone, and she had light hair and eyes and she told them that they could sleep with her. Coyote wanted to be with her all night so he sent Badger into a prairie-dog hole, telling him he thought he saw something in it. As soon as Badger crawled in, Coyote blocked up the entrance with rocks and hurried back to Yellow Woman.

"Come here," he said gently.

He touched my neck and I moved close to him to feel his breathing and to hear his heart. I was wondering if Yellow Woman had known who she was—if she knew that she would become part of the stories. Maybe she'd had another name that her husband and relatives called her so that only the ka'tsina from the north and the storytellers would know her as Yellow Woman. But I didn't go on; I felt him all around me, pushing me down into the white river sand.

Yellow Woman went away with the spirit from the north and lived with him and his relatives. She was gone for a long time, but then one day she came back and she brought twin boys.

"Do you know the story?"

"What story?" He smiled and pulled me close to him as he said this. I was afraid lying there on the red blanket. All I could know was the way he felt, warm, damp, his body beside me. This is the way it happens in the stories, I was thinking, with no thought beyond the moment she meets the ka'tsina spirit and they go.

"I don't have to go. What they tell in stories was real only then, back in time immemorial, like they say."

He stood up and pointed at my clothes tangled in the blanket. "Let's go," he said.

I walked beside him, breathing hard because he walked fast, his hand around my wrist. I had stopped trying to pull away from him, because his hand felt cool and the sun was high, drying the river bed into alkali. I will see someone, eventually I will see someone, and then I will be certain that he is only a man—some man from nearby—and I will be sure that I am not Yellow Woman. Because she is from out of time past and I live now and I've been to school and there are highways and pickup trucks that Yellow Woman never saw.

It was an easy ride north on horseback. I watched the change from the cottonwood trees along the river to the junipers that brushed past us in the foothills, and finally there were only piñons, and when I looked up at the rim of the mountain plateau I could see pine trees growing on the edge. Once I stopped to look down, but the pale sandstone had disappeared and the river was gone and the dark lava hills were all around. He touched my hand, not speaking, but always singing softly a mountain song and looking into my eyes.

I felt hungry and wondered what they were doing at home now—my mother, my grandmother, my husband, and the baby. Cooking breakfast, saying, "Where did she go?—maybe kidnapped." And Al going to the tribal police with the details: "She went walking along the river."

The house was made with black lava rock and red mud. It was high above the spreading miles of arroyos[1] and long mesas. I smelled a mountain smell of pitch and buck brush. I stood there beside the black horse, looking down on the small, dim country we had passed, and I shivered.

"Yellow Woman, come inside where it's warm." He lit a fire in the stove. It was an old stove with a round belly and an enamel coffeepot on top. There was only the stove, some faded Navajo blankets, and a bedroll and cardboard box. The floor was made of smooth adobe plaster, and there was one small window facing east. He pointed at the box.

"There's some potatoes and the frying pan." He sat on the floor with his arms around his knees pulling them close to his chest and he watched me fry the potatoes. I didn't mind him watching me because he was always watching me—he had been watching me since

---

1. Deep gulleys cut into the land by intermittent streams.

I came upon him sitting on the river bank trimming leaves from a willow twig with his knife. We ate from the pan and he wiped the grease from his fingers on his Levi's.

"Have you brought women here before?" He smiled and kept chewing, so I said, "Do you always use the same tricks?"

"What tricks?" He looked at me like he didn't understand.

"The story about being a ka'tsina from the mountains. The story about Yellow Woman."

Silva was silent; his face was calm.

"I don't believe it. Those stories couldn't happen now," I said.

He shook his head and said softly, "But someday they will talk about us, and they will say, 'Those two lived long ago when things like that happened.' "

He stood up and went out. I ate the rest of the potatoes and thought about things—about the noise the stove was making and the sound of the mountain wind outside. I remembered yesterday and the day before, and then I went outside.

I walked past the corral to the edge where the narrow trail cut through the black rim rock. I was standing in the sky with nothing around me but the wind that came down from the blue mountain peak behind me. I could see faint mountain images in the distance miles across the vast spread of mesas and valleys and plains. I wondered who was over there to feel the mountain wind on those sheer blue edges—who walks on the pine needles in those blue mountains.

"Can you see the pueblo?" Silva was standing behind me.

I shook my head. "We're too far away."

"From here I can see the world." He stepped out on the edge. "The Navajo reservation begins over there." He pointed to the east. "The Pueblo boundaries are over here." He looked below us to the south, where the narrow trail seemed to come from. "The Texans have their ranches over there, starting with that valley, the Concho Valley. The Mexicans run some cattle over there too."

"Do you ever work for them?"

"I steal from them," Silva answered. The sun was dropping behind us and the shadows were filling the land below. I turned away from the edge that dropped forever into the valleys below.

"I'm cold," I said, "I'm going inside." I started wondering about this man who could speak the Pueblo language so well but who lived on a mountain and rustled cattle. I decided that this man Silva must be Navajo, because Pueblo men didn't do things like that.

"You must be a Navajo."

Silva shook his head gently. "Little Yellow Woman," he said, "you never give up, do you? I have told you who I am. The Navajo people know me, too." He knelt down and unrolled the bedroll and spread the extra blankets out on a piece of canvas. The sun was down, and the only light in the house came from outside—the dim orange light from sundown.

I stood there and waited for him to crawl under the blankets.

"What are you waiting for?" he said, and I lay down beside him. He undressed me slowly like the night before beside the river—kissing my face gently and running his hands up and down my belly and legs. He took off my pants and then he laughed.

"Why are you laughing?"

"You are breathing so hard."

I pulled away from him and turned my back to him.

He pulled me around and pinned me down with his arms and chest. "You don't understand, do you, little Yellow Woman? You will do what I want."

And again he was all around me with his skin slippery against mine, and I was afraid because I understood that his strength could hurt me. I lay underneath him and I knew that he could destroy me. But later, while he slept beside me, I touched his face and I had a feeling—the kind of feeling for him that overcame me that morning along the river. I kissed him on the forehead and he reached out for me.

When I woke up in the morning he was gone. It gave me a strange feeling because for a long time I sat there on the blankets and looked around the little house for some object of his—some proof that he had been there or maybe that he was coming back. Only the blankets and the cardboard box remained. The .30-30 that had been leaning in the corner was gone, and so was the knife I had used the night before. He was gone, and I had my chance to go now. But first I had to eat, because I knew it would be a long walk home.

I found some dried apricots in the cardboard box, and I sat down on a rock at the edge of the plateau rim. There was no wind and the sun warmed me. I was surrounded by silence. I drowsed with apricots in my mouth, and I didn't believe that there were highways or railroads or cattle to steal.

When I woke up, I stared down at my feet in the black mountain dirt. Little black ants were swarming over the pine needles around my foot. They must have smelled the apricots. I thought about my family far below me. They would be wondering about me, because this had never happened to me before. The tribal police would file a report. But if old Grandpa weren't dead he would tell them what happened—he would laugh and say, "Stolen by a ka'tsina, a mountain spirit. She'll come home—they usually do." There are enough of them to handle things. My mother and grandmother will raise the baby like they raised me. Al will find someone else, and they will go on like before, except that there will be a story about the day I disappeared while I was walking along the river. Silva had come for me; he said he had. I did not decide to go. I just went. Moonflowers blossom in the sand hills before dawn, just as I followed him. That's what I was thinking as I wandered along the trail through the pine trees.

It was noon when I got back. When I saw the stone house I remembered that I had meant to go home. But that didn't seem important any more, maybe because there were little blue flowers growing in the meadow behind the stone house and the gray squirrels were playing in the pines next to the house. The horses were standing in the corral, and there was a beef carcass hanging on the shady side of a big pine in front of the house. Flies buzzed around the clotted blood that hung from the carcass. Silva was washing his hands in a bucket full of water. He must have heard me coming because he spoke to me without turning to face me.

"I've been waiting for you."

"I went walking in the big pine trees."

I looked into the bucket full of bloody water with brown-and-white animal hairs floating in it. Silva stood there letting his hand drip, examining me intently.

"Are you coming with me?"

"Where?" I asked him.

"To sell the meat in Marquez."

"If you're sure it's O.K."

"I wouldn't ask you if it wasn't," he answered.

He sloshed the water around in the bucket before he dumped it out and set the bucket upside down near the door. I followed him to the corral and watched him saddle the horses. Even beside the horses he looked tall, and I asked him again if he wasn't Navajo. He didn't say anything; he just shook his head and kept cinching up the saddle.

"But Navajos are tall."

"Get on the horse," he said, "and let's go."

The last thing he did before we started down the steep trail was to grab the .30-30 from the corner. He slid the rifle into the scabbard that hung from his saddle.

"Do they ever try to catch you?" I asked.

"They don't know who I am."

"Then why did you bring the rifle?"

"Because we are going to Marquez where the Mexicans live."

The trail leveled out on a narrow ridge that was steep on both sides like an animal spine. On one side I could see where the trail went around the rocky gray hills and disappeared into the southeast where the pale sandrock mesas stood in the distance near my home. On the other side was a trail that went west, and as I looked far into the distance I thought I saw the little town. But Silva said no, that I was looking in the wrong place, that I just thought I saw houses. After that I quit looking off into the distance; it was hot and the wildflowers were closing up their deep-yellow petals. Only the waxy cactus flowers bloomed in the bright sun, and I saw every color that a cactus blossom can be; the white ones and the red ones were still buds, but the purple and the yellow were blossoms, open full and the most beautiful of all.

Silva saw him before I did. The white man was riding a big gray horse, coming up the trail towards us. He was traveling fast and the gray horse's feet sent rocks rolling off the trail into the dry tumbleweeds. Silva motioned for me to stop and we watched the white man. He didn't see us right away, but finally his horse whinnied at our horses and he stopped. He looked at us briefly before he lapped the gray horse across the three hundred yards that separated us. He stopped his horse in front of Silva, and his young fat face was shad-owed by the brim of his hat. He didn't look mad, but his small, pale eyes moved from the blood-soaked gunny sacks hanging from my saddle to Silva's face and then back to my face.

"Where did you get the fresh meat?" the white man asked.

"I've been hunting," Silva said, and when he shifted his weight in the saddle the leather creaked.

"The hell you have, Indian. You've been rustling cattle. We've been looking for the thief for a long time."

The rancher was fat, and sweat began to soak through his white cowboy shirt and the wet cloth stuck to the thick rolls of belly fat. He almost seemed to be panting from the exertion of talking, and he smelled rancid, maybe because Silva scared him.

Silva turned to me and smiled. "Go back up the mountain, Yel-low Woman."

The white man got angry when he heard Silva speak in a lan-guage he couldn't understand. "Don't try anything, Indian. Just keep riding to Marquez. We'll call the state police from there."

The rancher must have been unarmed because he was very frightened and if he had a gun he would have pulled it out then. I turned my horse around and the rancher yelled, "Stop!" I looked at Silva for an instant and there was something ancient and dark—something I could feel in my stomach—in his eyes, and when I glanced at his hand I saw his finger on the trigger of the .30-30 that was still in the saddle scabbard. I slapped my horse across the flank and the sacks of raw meat swung against my knees as the horse leaped up the trail. It was hard to keep my balance, and once I thought I felt the saddle slipping backward; it was because of this that I could not look back.

I didn't stop until I reached the ridge where the trail forked. The horse was breathing deep gasps and there was a dark film of sweat on its neck. I looked down in the direction I had come from, but I couldn't see the place. I waited. The wind came up and pushed warm air past me. I looked up at the sky, pale blue and full of thin clouds and fading vapor trails left by jets.

I think four shots were fired—I remember hearing four hollow explosions that reminded me of deer hunting. There could have been more shots after that, but I couldn't have heard them because my horse was running again and the loose rocks were making too much noise as they scattered around his feet.

Horses have a hard time running downhill, but I went that way instead of uphill to the mountain because I thought it was safer. I felt better with the horse running southeast past the round gray hills that were covered with cedar trees and black lava rock. When I got to the plain in the distance I could see the dark green patches of tamaracks that grew along the river; and beyond the river I could see the beginning of the pale sandrock mesas. I stopped the horse and looked back to see if anyone was coming; then I got off the horse and turned the horse around, wondering if it would go back to its corral under the pines on the mountain. It looked back at me for a moment and then plucked a mouthful of green tumbleweeds before it trotted back up the trail with its ears pointed forward, carrying its head daintily to one side to avoid stepping on the dragging reins. When the horse disappeared over the last hill, the gunny sacks full of meat were still swinging and bouncing.

I walked toward the river on a wood-hauler's road that I knew would eventually lead to the paved road. I was thinking about waiting beside the road for someone to drive by, but by the time I got to the pavement I had decided it wasn't very far to walk if I followed the river back the way Silva and I had come.

The river water tasted good, and I sat in the shade under a cluster of silvery willows. I thought about Silva, and I felt sad at leaving him; still, there was something strange about him, and I tried to figure it out all the way back home.

I came back to the place on the river bank where he had been sitting the first time I saw him. The green willow leaves that he had trimmed from the branch were still lying there, wilted in the sand. I saw the leaves and I wanted to go back to him—to kiss him and to touch him—but the mountains were too far away now. And I told myself, because I believe it, he will come back sometime and be waiting again by the river.

I followed the path up from the river into the village. The sun was getting low, and I could smell supper cooking when I got to the screen door of my house. I could hear their voices inside—my mother was telling my grandmother how to fix the Jell-O and my husband, Al, was playing with the baby. I decided to tell them that some Navajo had kidnapped me, but I was sorry that old Grandpa wasn't alive to hear my story because it was the Yellow Woman stories he liked to tell best.

1974

John Steinbeck
1902–1968

> *Steinbeck wrote "The Chrysanthemums" in the early years of the Great Depression, and he published it in 1937, while he was writing his acclaimed novel* The Grapes of Wrath, *which criticizes the American economy and politics. But this story seems less political than personal. Steinbeck claimed that it was "designed to strike without the readers' knowledge. I mean he reads it casually and after it is finished feels that something profound has happened to him although he does not know what nor how." That profundity certainly concerns the change in Elisa's character, though what her character is at the story's end is often debated.*

The Chrysanthemums

The high grey-flannel fog of winter closed off the Salinas Valley from the sky and from all the rest of the world. On every side it sat like a lid on the mountains and made of the great valley a closed pot. On the broad, level land floor the gang ploughs bit deep and left the black earth shining like metal where the shares had cut. On the foot-hill ranches across the Salinas River, the yellow stubble fields seemed to be bathed in pale cold sunshine, but there was no sunshine in the valley now in December. The thick willow scrub along the river flamed with sharp and positive yellow leaves.

It was a time of quiet and of waiting. The air was cold and tender. A light wind blew up from the southwest so that the farmers were mildly hopeful of a good rain before long; but fog and rain do not go together.

Across the river, on Henry Allen's foot-hill ranch there was little work to be done, for the hay was cut and stored and the orchards were ploughed up to receive the rain deeply when it should come. The cattle on the higher slopes were becoming shaggy and rough-coated.

Elisa Allen, working in her flower garden, looked down across the yard and saw Henry, her husband, talking to two men in business suits. The three of them stood by the tractor-shed, each man with one foot on the side of the little Fordson. They smoked cigarettes and studied the machine as they talked.

Elisa watched them for a moment and then went back to her work. She was thirty-five. Her face was lean and strong and her eyes were as clear as water. Her figure looked blocked and heavy in her gardening costume, a man's black hat pulled low down over her eyes, clod-hopper shoes, a figured print dress almost completely covered by a big corduroy apron with four big pockets to hold the snips, the trowel and scratcher, the seeds and the knife she worked with. She wore heavy leather gloves to protect her hands while she worked.

She was cutting down the old year's chrysanthemum stalks with a pair of short and powerful scissors. She looked down toward the men by the tractor-shed now and then. Her face was eager and mature and handsome; even her work with the scissors was overeager, over-powerful. The chrysanthemum stems seemed too small and easy for her energy.

She brushed a cloud of hair out of her eyes with the back of her glove, and left a smudge of earth on her cheek in doing it. Behind her stood the neat white farmhouse with red geraniums close-banked around it as high as the windows. It was a hard-swept-looking little house, with hard-polished windows, and a clean mud-mat on the front steps.

Elisa cast another glance toward the tractor-shed. The strangers were getting into their Ford coupé. She took off a glove and put her strong fingers down into the forest of new green chrysanthemum sprouts that were growing around the old roots. She spread the leaves and looked down among the close-growing stems. No aphids were there, no sow bugs or snails or cutworms. Her terrier fingers destroyed such pests before they could get started.

Elisa started at the sound of her husband's voice. He had come near quietly, and he leaned over the wire fence that protected her flower garden from cattle and dogs and chickens.

"At it again," he said. "You've got a strong new crop coming."

Elisa straightened her back and pulled on the gardening glove again. "Yes. They'll be strong this coming year." In her tone and on her face there was a little smugness.

"You've got a gift with things," Henry observed. "Some of those yellow chrysanthemums you had this year were ten inches across. I wish you'd work out in the orchard and raise some apples that big."

Her eyes sharpened. "Maybe I could do it, too. I've a gift with things, all right. My mother had it. She could stick anything in the ground and make it grow. She said it was having planters' hands that knew how to do it."

"Well, it sure works with flowers," he said.

"Henry, who were those men you were talking to?"

"Why, sure, that's what I came to tell you. They were from the Western Meat Company. I sold those thirty head of three-year-old steers. Got nearly my own price, too."

"Good," she said. "Good for you."

"And I thought," he continued, "I thought how it's Saturday afternoon, and we might go into Salinas for dinner at a restaurant, and then to a picture show—to celebrate, you see."

"Good," she repeated. "Oh, yes. That will be good."

Henry put on his joking tone. "There's fights tonight. How'd you like to go to the fights?"

"Oh, no," she said breathlessly. "No, I wouldn't like fights."

"Just fooling, Elisa. We'll go to a movie. Let's see. It's two now. I'm going to take Scotty and bring down those steers from the hill. It'll take us maybe two hours. We'll go in town about five and have dinner at the Cominos Hotel. Like that?"

"Of course I'll like it. It's good to eat away from home."

"All right, then. I'll go get up a couple of horses."

She said: "I'll have plenty of time to transplant some of these sets, I guess."

She heard her husband calling Scotty down by the barn. And a little later she saw the two men ride up the pale yellow hillside in search of the steers.

There was a little square sandy bed kept for rooting the chrysanthemums. With her trowel she turned the soil over and over, and smoothed it and patted it firm. Then she dug ten parallel trenches to receive the sets. Back at the chrysanthemum bed she pulled out the little crisp shoots, trimmed off the leaves of each one with her scissors and laid it on a small orderly pile.

A squeak of wheels and plod of hoofs came from the road. Elisa looked up. The country road ran along the dense bank of willows and cottonwoods that bordered the river, and up this road came a curious vehicle, curiously drawn. It was an old spring-wagon, with a round canvas top on it like the cover of a prairie schooner. It was drawn by an old bay horse and a little grey-and-white burro. A big stubble-bearded man sat between the cover flaps and drove the crawling team. Underneath the wagon, between the hind wheels, a lean and rangy mongrel dog walked sedately. Words were painted on the canvas, in clumsy, crooked letters. "Pots, pans, knives, sisors, lawn mores, Fixed." Two rows of articles, and the triumphantly definitive "Fixed" below. The black paint had run down in little sharp points beneath each letter.

Elisa, squatting on the ground, watched to see the crazy, loose-jointed wagon pass by. But it didn't pass. It turned into the farm road in front of her house, crooked old wheels skirling and squeaking. The rangy dog darted from between the wheels and ran ahead. Instantly the two ranch shepherds flew out at him. Then all three stopped, and with stiff and quivering tails, with taut straight legs, with ambassadorial dignity, they slowly circled, sniffing daintily. The caravan pulled up to Elisa's wire fence and stopped. Now the newcomer dog, feeling out-numbered, lowered his tail and retired under the wagon with raised hackles and bared teeth.

The man on the wagon seat called out: "That's a bad dog in a fight when he gets started."

Elisa laughed. "I see he is. How soon does he generally get started?"

The man caught up her laughter and echoed it heartily. "Sometimes not for weeks and weeks," he said. He climbed stiffly down, over the wheel. The horse and the donkey drooped like unwatered flowers.

Elisa saw that he was a very big man. Although his hair and

beard were greying, he did not look old. His worn black suit was wrinkled and spotted with grease. The laughter had disappeared from his face and eyes the moment his laughing voice ceased. His eyes were dark, and they were full of the brooding that gets in the eyes of teamsters and of sailors. The calloused hands he rested on the wire fence were cracked, and every crack was a black line. He took off his battered hat.

"I'm off my general road, ma'am," he said. "Does this dirt road cut over across the river to the Los Angeles highway?"

Elisa stood up and shoved the thick scissors in her apron pocket. "Well, yes, it does, but it winds around and then fords the river. I don't think your team could pull through the sand."

He replied with some asperity: "It might surprise you what them beasts can pull through."

"When they get started?" she asked.

He smiled for a second. "Yes. When they get started."

"Well," said Elisa, "I think you'll save time if you go back to the Salinas road and pick up the highway there."

He drew a big finger down the chicken wire and made it sing. "I ain't in any hurry, ma'am. I go from Seattle to San Diego and back every year. Takes all my time. About six months each way. I aim to follow nice weather."

Elisa took off her gloves and stuffed them in the apron pocket with the scissors. She touched the under edge of her man's hat, searching for fugitive hairs. "That sounds like a nice kind of way to live," she said.

He leaned confidentially over the fence. "Maybe you noticed the writing on my wagon. I mend pots and sharpen knives and scissors. You got any of them things to do?"

"Oh, no," she said quickly. "Nothing like that." Her eyes hardened with resistance.

"Scissors is the worst thing," he explained. "Most people just ruin scissors trying to sharpen 'em, but I know how. I got a special tool. It's a little bobbit kind of thing, and patented. But it sure does the trick."

"No. My scissors are all sharp."

"All right, then. Take a pot," he continued earnestly, "a bent pot,

or a pot with a hole. I can make it like new so you don't have to buy
no new ones. That's a saving for you."

"No," she said shortly. "I tell you I have nothing like that for you
to do."

His face fell to an exaggerated sadness. His voice took on a whin-
ing undertone. "I ain't had a thing to do today. Maybe I won't have
no supper tonight. You see I'm off my regular road. I know folks on
the highway clear from Seattle to San Diego. They save their things
for me to sharpen up because they know I do it so good and save
them money."

"I'm sorry," Elisa said irritably. "I haven't anything for you to do."

His eyes left her face and fell to searching the ground. They
roamed about until they came to the chrysanthemum bed where she
had been working. "What's them plants, ma'am?"

The irritation and resistance melted from Elisa's face. "Oh, those
are chrysanthemums, giant whites and yellows. I raise them every
year, bigger than anybody around here."

"Kind of a long-stemmed flower? Looks like a quick puff of colored smoke?" he asked.

"That's it. What a nice way to describe them."

"They smell kind of nasty till you get used to them," he said.

"It's a good bitter smell," she retorted, "not nasty at all."

He changed his tone quickly. "I like the smell myself."

"I had ten-inch blooms this year," she said.

The man leaned farther over the fence. "Look. I know a lady
down the road a piece, has got the nicest garden you ever seen. Got
nearly every kind of flower but no chrysanthemums. Last time I was
mending a copper-bottom washtub for her (that's a hard job but I
do it good), she said to me: 'If you ever run acrost some nice
chrysanthemums I wish you'd try to get me a few seeds.' That's what
she told me."

Elisa's eyes grew alert and eager. "She couldn't have known much
about chrysanthemums. You *can* raise them from seed, but it's
much easier to root the little sprouts you see here."

"Oh," he said. "I s'pose I can't take none to her, then."

"Why yes you can," Elisa cried. "I can put some in damp sand,
and you can carry them right along with you. They'll take root in

the pot if you keep them damp. And then she can transplant them."

"She'd sure like to have some, ma'am. You say they're nice ones?"

"Beautiful," she said. "Oh, beautiful." Her eyes shone. She tore off the battered hat and shook out her dark pretty hair. "I'll put them in a flowerpot, and you can take them right with you. Come into the yard."

While the man came through the picket gate Elisa ran excitedly along the geranium-bordered path to the back of the house. And she returned carrying a big red flower-pot. The gloves were forgotten now. She kneeled on the ground by the starting bed and dug up the sandy soil with her fingers and scooped it into the bright new flower-pot. Then she picked up the little pile of shoots she had prepared. With her strong fingers she pressed them into the sand and tamped around them with her knuckles. The man stood over her. "I'll tell you what to do," she said. "You remember so you can tell the lady."

"Yes, I'll try to remember."

"Well, look. These will take root in about a month. Then she must set them out, about a foot apart in good rich earth like this, see?" She lifted a handful of dark soil for him to look at. "They'll grow fast and tall. Now remember this. In July tell her to cut them down, about eight inches from the ground."

"Before they bloom?" he asked.

"Yes, before they bloom." Her face was tight with eagerness. "They'll grow right up again. About the last of September the buds will start."

She stopped and seemed perplexed. "It's the budding that takes the most care," she said hesitantly. "I don't know how to tell you." She looked deep into his eyes, searchingly. Her mouth opened a little, and she seemed to be listening. "I'll try to tell you," she said. "Did you ever hear of planting hands?"

"Can't say I have, ma'am."

"Well, I can only tell you what it feels like. It's when you're picking off the buds you don't want. Everything goes right down into your fingertips. You watch your fingers work. They do it themselves. You can feel how it is. They pick and pick the buds. They never make a mistake. They're with the plant. Do you see? Your fingers and the plant. You can feel that, right up your arm. They know. They never make a mistake. You can feel it. When you're like that you can't do anything wrong. Do you see that? Can you understand that?"

She was kneeling on the ground looking up at him. Her breast swelled passionately.

The man's eyes narrowed. He looked away self-consciously.

"Maybe I know," he said. "Sometimes in the night in the wagon there——"

Elisa's voice grew husky. She broke in on him: "I've never lived as you do, but I know what you mean. When the night is dark—why, the stars are sharp-pointed, and there's quiet. Why, you rise up and up! Every pointed star gets driven into your body. It's like that. Hot and sharp and—lovely."

Kneeling there, her hand went out toward his legs in the greasy black trousers. Her hesitant fingers almost touched the cloth. Then her hand dropped to the ground. She crouched low like a fawning dog.

He said. "It's nice, just like you say. Only when you don't have no dinner it ain't."

She stood up then, very straight, and her face was ashamed. She held the flower-pot out to him and placed it gently in his arms. "Here. Put it in your wagon, on the seat, where you can watch it. Maybe I can find something for you to do."

At the back of the house she dug in the can pile and found two old and battered aluminum saucepans. She carried them back and gave them to him. "Here, maybe you can fix these."

His manner changed. He became professional. "Good as new I can fix them." At the back of his wagon he set a little anvil, and out of an oily tool-box dug a small machine hammer. Elisa came through the gate to watch him while he pounded out the dents in the kettles. His mouth grew sure and knowing. At a difficult part of the work he sucked his underlip.

"You sleep right in the wagon?" Elisa asked.

"Right in the wagon, ma'am. Rain or shine I'm dry as a cow in there."

"It must be nice," she said. "It must be very nice. I wish women could do such things."

"It ain't the right kind of a life for a woman."

Her upper lip raised a little, showing her teeth. "How do you know? How can you tell?" she said.

"I don't know, ma'am," he protested. "Of course I don't know. Now here's your kettles, done. You don't have to buy no new ones."

"How much?"

"Oh, fifty cents'll do. I keep my prices down and my work good. That's why I have all them satisfied customers up and down the highway."

Elisa brought him a fifty-cent piece from the house and dropped it in his hand. "You might be surprised to have a rival some time. I can sharpen scissors, too. And I can beat the dents out of little pots. I could show you what a woman might do."

He put his hammer back in the oily box and shoved the little anvil out of sight. "It would be a lonely life for a woman, ma'am, and a scarey life, too, with animals creeping under the wagon all night." He climbed over the single-tree, steadying himself with a hand on the burro's white rump. He settled himself in the seat, picked up the lines. "Thank you kindly ma'am," he said. "I'll do like you told me; I'll go back and catch the Salinas road."

"Mind," she called, "if you're long in getting there, keep the sand damp."

"Sand, ma'am? . . . Sand? Oh, sure. You mean around the chrysanthemums. Sure I will." He clucked his tongue. The beasts leaned luxuriously into their collars. The mongrel dog took his place between the back wheels. The wagon turned and crawled out the entrance road and back the way it had come, along the river.

Elisa stood in front of her wire fence watching the slow progress of the caravan. Her shoulders were straight, her head thrown back, her eyes half-closed, so that the scene came vaguely into them. Her lips moved silently, forming the words "Good-bye—good-bye." Then she whispered: "That's a bright direction. There's a glowing there." The sound of her whisper startled her. She shook herself free and looked about to see whether anyone had been listening. Only the dogs had heard. They lifted their heads toward her from their sleeping in the dust, and then stretched out their chins and settled asleep again. Elisa turned and ran hurriedly into the house.

In the kitchen she reached behind the stove and felt the water tank. It was full of hot water from the noonday cooking. In the bathroom she tore off her soiled clothes and flung them into the corner. And then she scrubbed herself with a little block of pumice, legs and thighs, loins and chest and arms, until her skin was scratched and red. When she had dried herself she stood in front of a mirror in her bedroom and looked at her body. She tightened her stomach and threw out her chest. She turned and looked over her shoulders at her back.

After a while she began to dress, slowly. She put on her newest underclothing and her nicest stockings and the dress which was the symbol of her prettiness. She worked carefully on her hair, pencilled her eyebrows and rouged her lips.

Before she was finished she heard the little thunder of hoofs and the shouts of Henry and his helper as they drove the red steers into the corral. She heard the gate bang shut and set herself for Henry's arrival.

His step sounded on the porch. He entered the house calling: "Elisa, where are you?"

"In my room, dressing. I'm not ready. There's hot water for your bath. Hurry up. It's getting late."

When she heard him splashing in the tub, Elisa laid his dark suit on the bed, and shirt and socks and tie beside it. She stood his polished shoes on the floor beside the bed. Then she went to the porch and sat primly and stiffly down. She looked toward the river road where the willow-line was still yellow with frosted leaves so that under the high grey fog they seemed a thin band of sunshine. This was the only color in the grey afternoon. She sat unmoving for a long time. Her eyes blinked rarely.

Henry came banging out of the door, shoving his tie inside his vest as he came. Elisa stiffened and her face grew tight. Henry stopped short and looked at her. "Why—why, Elisa. You look so nice!"

"Nice? You think I look nice? What do you mean by 'nice'?"

Henry blundered on. "I don't know. I mean you look different, strong and happy."

"I am strong? Yes, strong. What do you mean 'strong'?"

He looked bewildered. "You're playing some kind of a game," he said helplessly. "It's a kind of a play. You look strong enough to break a calf over your knee, happy enough to eat it like a water-melon."

For a second she lost her rigidity. "Henry! Don't talk like that. You didn't know what you said." She grew complete again. "I'm strong," she boasted. "I never knew before how strong."

Henry looked down toward the tractor-shed, and when he brought his eyes back to her, they were his own again. "I'll get out the car. You can put on your coat while I'm starting."

Elisa went into the house. She heard him drive to the gate and idle down his motor, and then she took a long time to put on her hat. She pulled it here and pressed it there. When Henry turned the motor off she slipped into her coat and went out.

The little roadster bounced along on the dirt road by the river, raising the birds and driving the rabbits into the brush. Two cranes flapped heavily over the willow-line and dropped into the river-bed.

Far ahead on the road Elisa saw a dark speck. She knew.

She tried not to look as they passed it, but her eyes would not obey. She whispered to herself sadly: "He might have thrown them off the road. That wouldn't have been much trouble, not very much. But he kept the pot," she explained. "He had to keep the pot. That's why he couldn't get them off the road."

The roadster turned a bend and she saw the caravan ahead. She swung full around toward her husband so she could not see the lit-tle covered wagon and the mis-matched team as the car passed them.

In a moment it was over. The thing was done. She did not look back.

She said loudly, to be heard above the motor: "It will be good, tonight, a good dinner."

"Now you've changed again," Henry complained. He took one hand from the wheel and patted her knee. "I ought to take you in to dinner oftener. It would be good for both of us. We get so heavy out on the ranch."

"Henry," she asked, "could we have wine at dinner?"

"Sure we could. Say! That will be fine."

She was silent for a while; then she said: "Henry, at those prize-fights, do the men hurt each other very much?"

"Sometimes a little, not often. Why?"

"Well, I've read how they break noses, and blood runs down their chests. I've read how the fighting gloves get heavy and soggy with blood."

He looked around at her. "What's the matter, Elisa? I didn't know you read things like that." He brought the car to a stop, then turned to the right over the Salinas River bridge.

"Do any women ever go to the fights?" she asked.

"Oh, sure, some. What's the matter, Elisa? Do you want to go? I don't think you'd like it, but I'll take you if you really want to go."

She relaxed limply in the seat. "Oh, no. No. I don't want to go. I'm sure I don't." Her face was turned away from him. "It will be enough if we can have wine. It will be plenty." She turned up her coat collar so he could not see that she was crying weakly—like an old woman.

1937

John Updike

1932–

> *"A & P" has spurred many contradictory interpretations, and no doubt its ambiguity contributes to its consistent popularity (it is one of the most often anthologized stories in North America). Some critics compare Sammy's final vision to the dark epiphany at the end of Joyce's "Araby." Some see Sammy's gesture as a triumphant rejection of American middle-class values. Others think he acquiesces to crass materialism by envying the girls' class status. It seems that Updike wanted to leave the story open-ended. In an early draft, Sammy walked home and drove to the water, ultimately idling his youth away at the beach waiting for the girls, who never reappear. You might begin your own interpretation of the story by imagining what Sammy will be doing the rest of the summer, and the rest of his days.*

A & P

In walks these three girls in nothing but bathing suits. I'm in the third checkout slot, with my back to the door, so I don't see them until they're over by the bread. The one that caught my eye first was the one in the plaid green two-piece. She was a chunky kid, with a good tan and a sweet broad soft-looking can with those two crescents of white just under it, where the sun never seems to hit, at the top of the backs of her legs. I stood there with my hand on a box of HiHo crackers trying to remember if I rang it up or not. I ring it up again and the customer starts giving me hell. She's one of these cash-register-watchers, a witch about fifty with rouge on her cheekbones and no eyebrows, and I know it made her day to trip me up. She'd been watching cash registers for fifty years and probably never seen a mistake before.

By the time I got her feathers smoothed and her goodies into a bag—she gives me a little snort in passing, if she'd been born at the right time they would have burned her over in Salem[1]—by the time I get her on her way the girls had circled around the bread and were coming back, without a pushcart, back my way along the counters, in the aisle between the checkouts and the Special bins. They didn't even have shoes on. There was this chunky one, with the two-piece—it was bright green and the seams on the bra were still sharp and her belly was still pretty pale so I guessed she just got it (the suit)—there was this one, with one of those chubby berry-faces, the lips all bunched together under her nose, this one, and a tall one, with black hair that hadn't quite frizzed right, and one of these sunburns right across under the eyes, and a chin that was too long—you know, the kind of girl other girls think is very "striking" and "attractive" but never quite makes it, as they very well know, which is why they like her so much—and then the third one, that wasn't quite so tall. She was the queen. She kind of led them, the other two peeking around and making their shoulders round. She didn't look around, not this queen, she just walked straight on slowly, on these

---

1. A city in Massachusetts, famous for the witch trials of 1692.

long white primadonna legs. She came down a little hard on her heels, as if she didn't walk in bare feet that much, putting down her heels and then letting the weight move along to her toes as if she was testing the floor with every step, putting a little deliberate extra action into it. You never know for sure how girls' minds work (do you really think it's a mind in there or just a little buzz like a bee in a glass jar?) but you got the idea she had talked the other two into coming here with her, and now she was showing them how to do it, walk slow and hold yourself straight.

She had on a kind of dirty-pink—beige maybe, I don't know— bathing suit with a little nubble all over it and, what got me, the straps were down. They were off her shoulders looped loose around the cool tops of her arms, and I guess as a result the suit had slipped a little on her, so all around the top of the cloth there was this shin- ing rim. If it hadn't been there you wouldn't have known there could have been anything whiter than those shoulders. With the straps pushed off, there was nothing between the top of the suit and the top of her head except just *her*, this clean bare plane of the top of her chest down from the shoulder bones like a dented sheet of metal tilted in the light. I mean, it was more than pretty.

She had a sort of oaky hair that the sun and salt had bleached, done up in a bun that was unravelling, and a kind of prim face. Walking into the A & P with your straps down, I suppose it's the only kind of face you *can* have. She held her head so high her neck, coming up out of those white shoulders, looked kind of stretched, but I didn't mind. The longer her neck was, the more of her there was.

She must have felt in the corner of her eye me and over my shoulder Stokesie in the second slot watching, but she didn't tip. Not this queen. She kept her eyes moving across the racks, and stopped, and turned so slow it made my stomach rub the inside of my apron, and buzzed to the other two, who kind of huddled against her for relief, and then they all three of them went up the cat-and-dog-food-breakfast-cereal-macaroni-rice-raisins-seasonings- spreads-spaghetti-soft-drinks-crackers-and-cookies aisle. From the third slot I look straight up this aisle to the meat counter, and I watched them all the way. The fat one with the tan sort of fumbled with the cookies, but on second thought she put the package back. The sheep pushing their carts down the aisle—the girls were walking against the usual traffic (not that we have one-way signs or anything)—were pretty hilarious. You could see them, when Queenie's white shoulders dawned on them, kind of jerk, or hop, or hiccup, but their eyes snapped back to their own baskets and on they pushed. I bet you could set off dynamite in an A & P and the people would by and large keep reaching and checking oatmeal off their lists and muttering "Let me see, there was a third thing, began with A, asparagus, no, ah, yes, applesauce!" or whatever it is they do mutter. But there was no doubt, this jiggled them. A few houseslaves in pin curlers even looked around after pushing their carts past to make sure what they had seen was correct.

You know, it's one thing to have a girl in a bathing suit down on the beach, where what with the glare nobody can look at each other much anyway, and another thing in the cool of the A & P, under the fluorescent lights, against all those stacked packages, with her feet paddling along naked over our checker-board green-and-cream rubber-tile floor.

"Oh Daddy," Stokesie said beside me. "I feel so faint."

"Darling," I said. "Hold me tight." Stokesie's married, with two babies chalked up on his fuselage already, but as far as I can tell that's the only difference. He's twenty-two, and I was nineteen this April.

"Is it done?" he asks, the responsible married man finding his voice. I forgot to say he thinks he's going to be manager some sunny day, maybe in 1990 when it's called the Great Alexandrov and Petrooshki Tea Company or something.

What he meant was, our town is five miles from a beach, with a big summer colony out on the Point, but we're right in the middle of town, and the women generally put on a shirt or shorts or something before they get out of the car into the street. And anyway these are usually women with six children and varicose veins mapping their legs and nobody, including them, could care less. As I say, we're right in the middle of town, and if you stand at our front doors you can see two banks and the Congregational church and the newspaper store and three real-estate offices and about twenty-seven old freeloaders tearing up Central Street because the sewer broke again. It's not as if we're on the Cape;[2] we're north of Boston and there's people in this town haven't seen the ocean for twenty years.

The girls had reached the meat counter and were asking McMahon something. He pointed, they pointed, and they shuffled out of sight behind a pyramid of Diet Delight peaches. All that was left for us to see was old McMahon patting his mouth and looking after them sizing up their joints. Poor kids, I began to feel sorry for them, they couldn't help it.

Now here comes the sad part of the story, at least my family says it's sad, but I don't think it's so sad myself. The store's pretty empty, it being Thursday afternoon, so there was nothing much to do except lean on the register and wait for the girls to show up again. The whole store was like a pinball machine and I didn't know which tunnel they'd come out of. After a while they come around out of the far aisle, around the light bulbs, records at discount of the Caribbean Six or Tony Martin Sings or some such gunk you wonder they waste the wax on, six-packs of candy bars, and plastic toys done up in cellophane that fall apart when a kid looks at them anyway. Around they come, Queenie still leading the way, and holding a little gray jar in her hand. Slots Three through Seven are unmanned and I could see her wondering between Stokes and me, but Stokesie with his usual luck draws an old party in baggy gray pants who stumbles up with four giant cans of pineapple juice (what do these bums *do* with all that pineapple juice? I've often asked myself) so the girls come to me. Queenie puts down the jar and I take it into my fingers icy cold. Kingfish Fancy Herring Snacks in Pure Sour Cream: 49¢. Now her hands are empty, not a ring or a bracelet; bare as God made them, and I wonder where the money's coming from. Still with that prim look she lifts a folded dollar bill out of the hollow at the center of her nubbled pink top. The jar went heavy in my hand. Really, I thought that was so cute.

Then everybody's luck begins to run out. Lengel comes in from hagging with a truck full of cabbages on the lot and is about to scuttle into that door marked MANAGER behind which he hides all day

2. Cape Cod, Massachusetts, a seaside resort area where dress is usually informal.

when the girls touch his eye. Lengel's pretty dreary, teaches Sunday school and the rest, but he doesn't miss that much. He comes over and says, "Girls, this isn't the beach."

Queenie blushes, though maybe it's just a brush of sunburn I was noticing for the first time, now that she was so close. "My mother asked me to pick up a jar of herring snacks." Her voice kind of startled me, the way voices do when you see the people first, coming out so flat and dumb yet kind of tony, too, the way it ticked over "pick up" and "snacks." All of a sudden I slid right down her voice into her living room. Her father and the other men were standing around in ice-cream coats and bow ties and the women were in sandals picking up herring snacks on toothpicks off a big glass plate and they were all holding drinks the color of water with olives and sprigs of mint in them. When my parents have somebody over they get lemonade and if it's a real racy affair Schlitz in tall glasses with "They'll Do It Every Time" cartoons stencilled on.

"That's all right," Lengel said. "But this isn't the beach." His repeating this struck me as funny as if it had just occurred to him, and he had been thinking all these years the A & P was a great big dune and he was the head lifeguard. He didn't like my smiling—as I say he doesn't miss much—but he concentrates on giving the girls that sad Sunday-school-superintendent stare.

Queenie's blush is no sunburn now, and the plump one in plaid, that I liked better from the back—a really sweet can—pipes up, "We weren't doing any shopping. We just came in for the one thing."

"That makes no difference," Lengel tells her and I could see from the way his eyes went that he hadn't noticed she was wearing a two-piece before. "We want you decently dressed when you come in here."

"We *are* decent," Queenie says suddenly her lower lip pushing, getting sore now that she remembers her place, a place from which the crowd that runs the A & P must look pretty crummy. Fancy Herring Snacks flashed in her very blue eyes.

"Girls, I don't want to argue with you. After this come in here with your shoulders covered. It's our policy." He turns his back. That's policy for you. Policy is what the kingpins want. What the others want is juvenile delinquency.

All this while, the customers had been showing up with their carts but, you know, sheep, seeing a scene, they had all bunched up on Stokesie, who shook open a paper bag as gently as peeling a peach, not wanting to miss a word. I could feel in the silence everybody getting nervous, most of all Lengel, who asks me, "Sammy, have you rung up their purchase?"

I thought and said "No" but it wasn't about that I was thinking. I go through the punches, 4, 9, GROC, TOT—it's more complicated than you think, and after you do it often enough, it begins to make a little song, that you hear words to, in my case "Hello (*bing*) there, you (*gung*) hap-py *pee*-pul (*splat*)!"—the *splat* being the drawer flying out. I uncrease the bill, tenderly as you may imagine, it just having come from between the two smoothest scoops of vanilla I had ever known there were, and pass a half and a penny into her narrow pink palm, and nestle the herrings in a bag and twist its neck and hand it over, all the time thinking.

The girls, and who'd blame them, are in a hurry to get out, so I say "I quit" to Lengel quick enough for them to hear, hoping they'll stop and watch me, their unsuspected hero. They keep right on going, into the electric eye; the door flies open and they flicker across the lot to their car, Queenie and Plaid and Big Tall Goony-Goony (not that as raw material she was so bad), leaving me with Lengel and a kink in his eyebrow.

"Did you say something, Sammy?"

"I said I quit."

"I thought you did."

"You didn't have to embarrass them."

"It was they who were embarassing us."

I started to say something that came out. "Fiddle-de-do." It's a saying of my grandmother's, and I know she would have been pleased.

"I don't think you know what you're saying," Lengel said.

"I know you don't," I said. "But I do." I pull the bow at the back of my apron and start shrugging it off my shoulders. A couple of customers that had been heading for my slot begin to knock against each other, liked scared pigs in a chute.

Lengel sighs and begins to look very patient and old and gray. He's been a friend of my parents for years. "Sammy, you don't want to do this to your Mom and Dad," he tells me. It's true, I don't. But it seems to me that once you begin a gesture it's fatal not to go through with it. I fold the apron, "Sammy" stitched in red on the pocket, and put it on the counter, and drop the bow tie on top of it. The bow tie is theirs, if you've ever wondered. "You'll feel this for the rest of your life," Lengel says, and I know that's true, too, but remembering how he made that pretty girl blush makes me so scrunchy inside I punch the No Sale tab and the machine whirs "pee-pul" and the drawer splats out. One advantage to this scene taking place in summer, I can follow this up with a clean exit, there's no fumbling around getting your coat and galoshes, I just saunter into the electric eye in my white shirt that my mother ironed the night before, and the door heaves itself open, and outside the sunshine is skating around on the asphalt.

I look around for my girls, but they're gone, of course. There wasn't anybody but some young married screaming with her children about some candy they didn't get by the door of a powder-blue Falcon station wagon. Looking back in the big windows, over the bags of peat moss and aluminum lawn furniture stacked on the pavement, I could see Lengel in my place in the slot, checking the sheep through. His face was dark gray and his back stiff, as if he's just had an injection of iron, and my stomach kind of fell as I felt how hard the world was going to be to me hereafter.

1962

Alice Walker

1944–

Much of Walker's inspiration for "Everyday Use" came from her own life in rural Georgia. Walker, like Maggie, grew up scarred and self-conscious: she was blinded in one eye by a BB gun at the age of eight. She also grew up poor, with a mother who made all her children's clothes, canned food in the summer, and made quilts to get through the winter. Her mother had an artist's soul, and she grew flowers that were famous in three countries. "Everyday Use" substitutes quilts for flowers. Walker was once transfixed by an old quilt she saw in the Smithsonian—throwaway rag pieces sewn to-

gether into Christ's crucifixion. Its author was an anonymous black woman who lived in the nineteenth century. Walker found in quilts, then, a rich and ready-made symbol representing the unrecorded tragedies and triumphs of black women like her mother. Even so, we shouldn't too easily congratulate Maggie on her victory at the end of this story. Though Dee is presented negatively as celebrating folk art while denigrating the folk who produce it, her character is haunted by Walker, too. Walker, like Dee, escaped the farm. She went to college, traveled, and with fellow protestors faced down mobs of white segregationists armed with ax handles and broken bottles in Atlanta. Would there have been a civil rights movement in the United States without women like Dee?

Everyday Use

for your grandmamma

I will wait for her in the yard that Maggie and I made so clean and wavy yesterday afternoon. A yard like this is more comfortable than most people know. It is not just a yard. It is like an extended living room. When the hard clay is swept clean as a floor and the fine sand around the edges lined with tiny, irregular grooves, anyone can come and sit and look up into the elm tree and wait for the breezes that never come inside the house.

Maggie will be nervous until after her sister goes: she will stand hopelessly in corners, homely and ashamed of the burn scars down her arms and legs, eying her sister with a mixture of envy and awe. She thinks her sister has held life always in the palm of one hand, that "no" is a word the world never learned to say to her.

You've no doubt seen those TV shows where the child who has "made it" is confronted, as a surprise, by her own mother and father, tottering in weakly from backstage. (A pleasant surprise, of course: What would they do if parent and child came on the show only to curse out and insult each other?) On TV mother and child embrace and smile into each other's faces. Sometimes the mother and father weep, the child wraps them in her arms and leans across the table to tell how she would not have made it without their help. I have seen these programs.

Sometimes I dream a dream in which Dee and I are suddenly brought together on a TV program of this sort. Out of a dark and soft-seated limousine I am ushered into a bright room filled with many people. There I meet a smiling, gray, sporty man like Johnny Carson who shakes my hand and tells me what a fine girl I have. Then we are on the stage and Dee is embracing me with tears in her eyes. She pins on my dress a large orchid, even though she has told me once that she thinks orchids are tacky flowers.

In real life I am a large, big-boned woman with rough, man-working hands. In the winter I wear flannel nightgowns to bed and overalls during the day. I can kill and clean a hog as mercilessly as a man. My fat keeps me hot in zero weather. I can work outside all day, breaking ice to get water for washing; I can eat pork liver cooked over the open fire minutes after it comes steaming from the hog. One winter I knocked a bull calf straight in the brain between the eyes with a sledge hammer and had the meat hung up to chill before nightfall. But of course all this does not show on television. I am the way my daughter would want me to be: a hundred pounds lighter, my skin like an uncooked barley pancake. My hair glistens in the hot bright lights. Johnny Carson has much to do to keep up with my quick and witty tongue.

But that is a mistake. I know even before I wake up. Who ever knew a Johnson with a quick tongue? Who can even imagine me looking a strange white man in the eye? It seems to me I have talked to them always with one foot raised in flight, with my head turned in whichever way is farthest from them. Dee, though. She would always look anyone in the eye. Hesitation was no part of her nature.

"How do I look, Mama?" Maggie says, showing just enough of her thin body enveloped in pink skirt and red blouse for me to know she's there, almost hidden by the door.

"Come out into the yard," I say.

Have you ever seen a lame animal, perhaps a dog run over by some careless person rich enough to own a car, sidle up to someone who is ignorant enough to be kind to them? That is the way my Maggie walks. She has been like this, chin on chest, eyes on ground, feet in shuffle, ever since the fire that burned the other house to the ground.

Dee is lighter than Maggie, with nicer hair and a fuller figure. She's a woman now, though sometimes I forget. How long ago was it that the other house burned? Ten, twelve years? Sometimes I can still hear the flames and feel Maggie's arms sticking to me, her hair smoking and her dress falling off her in little black papery flakes. Her eyes seemed stretched open, blazed open by the flames reflected in them. And Dee. I see her standing off under the sweet gum tree she used to dig gum out of; a look of concentration on her face as she watched the last dingy gray board of the house fall in toward the red-hot brick chimney. Why don't you do a dance around the ashes? I'd wanted to ask her. She had hated the house that much.

I used to think she hated Maggie, too. But that was before we raised the money, the church and me, to send her to Augusta to school. She used to read to us without pity; forcing words, lies, other folks' habits, whole lives upon us two, sitting trapped and ignorant underneath her voice. She washed us in a river of make-believe, burned us with a lot of knowledge we didn't necessarily need to know. Pressed us to her with the serious way she read, to shove us away at just the moment, like dimwits, we seemed about to understand.

Dee wanted nice things. A yellow organdy dress to wear to her graduation from high school; black pumps to match a green suit she'd made from an old suit somebody gave me. She was determined to stare down any disaster in her efforts. Her eyelids would not flicker for minutes at a time. Often I fought off the temptation to shake her. At sixteen she had a style of her own: and knew what style was.

I never had an education myself. After second grade the school was closed down. Don't ask me why: in 1927 colored asked fewer questions than they do now. Sometimes Maggie reads to me. She stumbles along good naturedly but can't see well. She knows she is not bright. Like good looks and money, quickness passed her by. She will marry John Thomas (who has mossy teeth in an earnest face) and then I'll be free to sit here and I guess just sing church songs to myself. Although I never was a good singer. Never could carry a tune. I was always better at a man's job. I used to love to milk till I was hooked[1] in the side in '49. Cows are soothing and slow and don't bother you, unless you try to milk them the wrong way.

I have deliberately turned my back on the house. It is three rooms, just like the one that burned, except the roof is tin; they don't make shingle roofs any more. There are no real windows, just some holes cut in the sides, like the portholes in a ship, but not round and not square, with rawhide holding the shutters up on the outside. This house is in a pasture, too, like the other one. No doubt when Dee sees it she will want to tear it down. She wrote me once that no matter where we "choose" to live, she will manage to come see us. But she will never bring her friends. Maggie and I thought about this and Maggie asked me, "Mama, when did Dee ever *have* any friends?"

She had a few. Furtive boys in pink shirts hanging about on washday after school. Nervous girls who never laughed. Impressed with her they worshiped the well-turned phrase, the cute shape, the scalding humor that erupted like bubbles in lye. She read to them.

When she was courting Jimmy T she didn't have much time to pay to us, but turned all her faultfinding power on him. He *flew* to marry a cheap city girl from a family of ignorant flashy people. She hardly had time to recompose herself.

When she comes I will meet—but there they are!

Maggie attempts to make a dash for the house, in her shuffling way, but I stay her with my hand. "Come back here," I say. And she stops and tries to dig a well in the sand with her toe.

It is hard to see them clearly through the strong sun. But even the first glimpse of leg out of the car tells me it is Dee. Her feet were always neat-looking, as if God himself had shaped them with a certain style. From the other side of the car comes a short, stocky man. Hair is all over his head a foot long and hanging from his chin like a kinky mule tail. I hear Maggie suck in her breath. "Uhnnnh," is what it sounds like. Like when you see the wriggling end of a snake just in front of your foot on the road. "Uhnnnh."

Dee next. A dress down to the ground, in this hot weather. A

---

1. I.e., gored by the horn of a cow.

dress so loud it hurts my eyes. There are yellows and oranges enough to throw back the light of the sun. I feel my whole face warming from the heat waves it throws out. Earrings gold, too, and hanging down to her shoulders. Bracelets dangling and making noises when she moves her arm up to shake the folds of the dress out of her armpits. The dress is loose and flows, and as she walks closer, I like it. I hear Maggie go "Uhnnnh" again. It is her sister's hair. It stands straight up like the wool on a sheep. It is black as night and around the edges are two long pigtails that rope about like small lizards disappearing behind her ears.

"Wa-su-zo-Tean-o!" she says, coming on in that gliding way the dress makes her move. The short stocky fellow with the hair to his navel is all grinning and he follows up with "Asalamalakim,[2] my mother and sister!" He moves to hug Maggie but she falls back, right up against the back of my chair. I feel her trembling there and when I look up I see the perspiration falling off her chin.

"Don't get up," says Dee. Since I am stout it takes something of a push. You can see me trying to move a second or two before I make it. She turns, showing white heels through her sandals, and goes back to the car. Out she peeks next with a Polaroid. She stoops down quickly and lines up picture after picture of me sitting there in front of the house with Maggie cowering behind me. She never takes a shot without making sure the house is included. When a cow comes nibbling around the edge of the yard she snaps it and me and Maggie *and* the house. Then she puts the Polaroid in the back seat of the car, and comes up and kisses me on the forehead.

Meanwhile Asalamalakim is going through motions with Maggie's hand. Maggie's hand is as limp as a fish, and probably as cold, despite the sweat, and she keeps trying to pull it back. It looks like Asalamalakim wants to shake hands but wants to do it fancy. Or maybe he don't know how people shake hands. Anyhow, he soon gives up on Maggie.

"Well," I say. "Dee."

"No, Mama," she says. "Not 'Dee,' Wangero Leewanika Kemanjo!"

---

2. Transliteration of a Muslim greeting; literally, "Peace be with you." "Wa-su-zo-Tean-o" is a similar rendering of an African salutation.

"What happened to 'Dee'?" I wanted to know.

"She's dead," Wangero said. "I couldn't bear it any longer, being named after the people who oppress me."

"You know as well as me you was named after your aunt Dicie," I said. Dicie is my sister. She named Dee. We called her "Big Dee" after Dee was born.

"But who was *she* named after?" asked Wangero.

"I guess after Grandma Dee," I said.

"And who was she named after?" asked Wangero.

"Her mother," I said, and saw Wangero was getting tired. "That's about as far back as I can trace it," I said. Though, in fact, I probably could have carried it back beyond the Civil War through the branches.

"Well," said Asalamalakim, "there you are."

"Uhnnnh," I heard Maggie say.

"There I was not," I said, "before 'Dicie' cropped up in our family, so why should I try to trace it that far back?"

He just stood there grinning, looking down on me like somebody inspecting a Model A car. Every once in a while he and Wangero sent eye signals over my head.

"How do you pronounce this name?" I asked.

"You don't have to call me by it if you don't want to," said Wangero.

"Why shouldn't I?" I asked. "If that's what you want us to call you, we'll call you."

"I know it might sound awkward at first," said Wangero.

"I'll get used to it," I said. "Ream it out again."

Well, soon we got the name out of the way. Asalamalakim had a name twice as long and three times as hard. After I tripped over it two or three times he told me to just call him Hakim-a-barber. I wanted to ask him was he a barber, but I didn't really think he was, so I didn't ask.

"You must belong to those beef-cattle peoples down the road," I said. They said "Asalamalakim" when they met you, too, but they didn't shake hands. Always too busy: feeding the cattle, fixing the fences, putting up salt-lick shelters, throwing down hay. When the white folks poisoned some of the herd the men stayed up all night with rifles in their hands. I walked a mile and a half just to see the sight.

Hakim-a-barber said, "I accept some of their doctrines, but farming and raising cattle is not my style." (They didn't tell me, and I didn't ask, whether Wangero (Dee) had really gone and married him.)

We sat down to eat and right away he said he didn't eat collards and pork was unclean. Wangero, though, went on through the chitlins and corn bread, the greens and everything else. She talked a blue streak over the sweet potatoes. Everything delighted her. Even the fact that we still used the benches her daddy made for the table when we couldn't afford to buy chairs.

"Oh, Mama!" she cried. Then turned to Hakim-a-barber. "I never knew how lovely these benches are. You can feel the rump prints," she said running her hands underneath her and along the bench. Then she gave a sigh and her hand closed over Grandma Dee's butter dish. "That's it!" she said. "I knew there was something I wanted to ask you if I could have." She jumped up from the table and went over in the corner where the churn stood, the milk in it clabber[3] by now. She looked at the churn and looked at it.

"This churn top is what I need," she said. "Didn't Uncle Buddy whittle it out of a tree you all used to have?"

"Yes," I said.

"Uh huh," she said happily. "And I want the dasher,[4] too."

"Uncle Buddy whittle that, too?" asked the barber.

Dee (Wangero) looked up at me.

"Aunt Dee's first husband whittled the dash," said Maggie so low you almost couldn't hear her. "His name was Henry, but they called him Stash."

"Maggie's brain is like an elephant's," Wangero said, laughing. "I can use the churn top as a centerpiece for the alcove table," she said, sliding a plate over the churn, "and I'll think of something artistic to do with the dasher."

When she finished wrapping the dasher the handle stuck out. I

---

3. Curdled.
4. A device for stirring the cream in a churn.

took it for a moment in my hands. You didn't even have to look close to see where hands pushing the dasher up and down to make butter had left a kind of sink in the wood. In fact, there were a lot of small sinks; you could see where thumbs and fingers had sunk into the wood. It was beautiful light yellow wood, from a tree that grew in the yard where Big Dee and Stash had lived.

After dinner Dee (Wangero) went to the trunk at the foot of my bed and started rifling through it. Maggie hung back in the kitchen over the dishpan. Out came Wangero with two quilts. They had been pieced by Grandma Dee and then Big Dee and me had hung them on the quilt frames on the front porch and quilted them. One was in the Lone Star pattern. The other was Walk Around the Mountain. In both of them were scraps of dresses Grandma Dee had worn fifty and more years ago. Bits and pieces of Grandpa Jarrell's Paisley shirts. And one teeny faded blue piece, about the size of a penny matchbox, that was from Great Grandpa Ezra's uniform that he wore in the Civil War.

"Mama," Wangero said sweet as a bird. "Can I have these old quilts?"

I heard something fall in the kitchen, and a minute later the kitchen door slammed.

"Why don't you take one or two of the others?" I asked. "These old things was just done by me and Big Dee from some tops your grandma pieced before she died."

"No," said Wangero. "I don't want those. They are stitched around the borders by machine."

"That'll make them last better," I said.

"That's not the point," said Wangero. "These are all pieces of dresses Grandma used to wear. She did all this stitching by hand. Imagine!" She held the quilts securely in her arms, stroking them.

"Some of the pieces, like those lavender ones, come from old clothes her mother handed down to her," I said, moving up to touch the quilts. Dee (Wangero) moved back just enough so that I couldn't reach the quilts. They already belonged to her.

"Imagine!" she breathed again, clutching them closely to her bosom.

"The truth is," I said, "I promised to give them quilts to Maggie, for when she marries John Thomas."

She gasped like a bee had stung her.

"Maggie can't appreciate these quilts!" she said. "She'd probably be backward enough to put them to everyday use."

"I reckon she would," I said. "God knows I been saving 'em for long enough with nobody using 'em. I hope she will!" I didn't want to bring up how I had offered Dee (Wangero) a quilt when she went away to college. Then she had told me they were old-fashioned, out of style.

"But they're *priceless*!" she was saying now, furiously; for she has a temper. "Maggie would put them on the bed and in five years they'd be in rags. Less than that!"

"She can always make some more," I said. "Maggie knows how to quilt."

Dee (Wangero) looked at me with hatred. "You just will not understand. The point is these quilts, *these* quilts!"

"Well," I said, stumped. "What would *you* do with them?"

"Hang them," she said. As if that was the only thing you *could* do with quilts.

Maggie by now was standing in the door. I could almost hear the sound her feet made as they scraped over each other.

"She can have them, Mama," she said, like somebody used to never winning anything, or having anything reserved for her. "I can 'member Grandma Dee without the quilts."

I looked at her hard. She had filled her bottom lip with checkerberry snuff and it gave her a face a kind of dopey, hangdog look. It was Grandma Dee and Big Dee who taught her how to quilt herself. She stood there with her scarred hands hidden in the folds of her skirt. She looked at her sister with something like fear but she wasn't mad at her. This was Maggie's portion. This was the way she knew God to work.

When I looked at her like that something hit me in the top of my head and ran down to the soles of my feet. Just like when I'm in church and the spirit of God touches me and I get happy and shout. I did something I never had done before: hugged Maggie to me, then dragged her on into the room, snatched the quilts out of Miss Wangero's hands and dumped them into Maggie's lap. Maggie just sat there on my bed with her mouth open.

"Take one or two of the others," I said to Dee.

But she turned without a word and went out to Hakim-a-barber.

"You just don't understand," she said, as Maggie and I came out to the car.

"What don't I understand?" I wanted to know.

"Your heritage," she said. And then she turned to Maggie, kissed her, and said, "You ought to try to make something of yourself, too, Maggie. It's really a new day for us. But from the way you and Mama still live you'd never know it."

She put on some sunglasses that hid everything above the tip of her nose and her chin.

Maggie smiled; maybe at the sunglasses. But a real smile, not scared. After we watched the car dust settle I asked Maggie to bring me a dip of snuff. And then the two of us sat there just enjoying, until it was time to go in the house and go to bed.

1973

Eudora Welty
1909–2001

> *Once, upon going out in the woods to keep a landscape painter company, Welty, a white writer from Mississippi, witnessed an old woman bent on some selfless errand crossing her field of vision. The woman appeared from and disappeared again into the woods. This simple event was the inspiration for "A Worn Path." That anecdote as well as the story's title tells us where to focus our attention. Welty often explained how she was continually bombarded with the same question from teachers and students alike: Is Phoenix Jackson's grandson really dead? Her answer: "Phoenix is alive." The story is told from Phoenix's unreliable point of view, but hers is the only perspective we have, and, Welty insisted, Phoenix's is the only point of view that Welty herself had. From that point of view, the boy is alive. Is the question of whether or not the boy is alive relevant to the story's meaning?*

A Worn Path

It was December—a bright frozen day in the early morning. Far out in the country there was an old Negro woman with her head tied in a red rag, coming along a path through the pinewoods. Her name was Phoenix Jackson. She was very old and small and she walked slowly in the dark pine shadows, moving a little from side to side in her steps, with the balanced heaviness and lightness of a pendulum in a grandfather clock. She carried a thin, small cane made from an umbrella, and with this she kept tapping the frozen earth in front of her. This made a grave and persistent noise in the still air, that seemed meditative like the chirping of a solitary little bird.

She wore a dark striped dress reaching down to her shoe tops, and an equally long apron of bleached sugar sacks, with a full pocket: all neat and tidy, but every time she took a step she might have fallen over her shoelaces, which dragged from her unlaced shoes. She looked straight ahead. Her eyes were blue with age. Her skin had a pattern all its own of numberless branching wrinkles and as though a whole little tree stood in the middle of her forehead, but a golden color ran underneath, and the two knobs of her cheeks were illumined by a yellow burning under the dark. Under the red rag her hair came down on her neck in the frailest of ringlets, still black, and with an odor like copper.

Now and then there was a quivering in the thicket. Old Phoenix said, "Out of my way, all you foxes, owls, beetles, jack rabbits, coons and wild animals! . . . Keep out from under these feet, little bob-whites. . . . Keep the big wild hogs out of my path. Don't let none of those come running my direction. I got a long way." Under her small black-freckled hand her cane, limber as a buggy whip, would switch at the brush as if to rouse up any hiding things.

On she went. The woods were deep and still. The sun made the pine needles almost too bright to look at, up where the wind rocked. The cones dropped as light as feathers. Down in the hollow was the mourning dove—it was not too late for him.

The path ran up a hill. "Seem like there is chains about my feet, time I get this far," she said, in the voice of argument old people keep to use with themselves. "Something always take a hold of me on this hill—pleads I should stay."

After she got to the top she turned and gave a full, severe look behind her where she had come. "Up through pines," she said at length. "Now down through oaks."

Her eyes opened their widest, and she started down gently. But before she got to the bottom of the hill a bush caught her dress.

Her fingers were busy and intent, but her skirts were full and long, so that before she could pull them free in one place they were caught in another. It was not possible to allow the dress to tear. "I in the thorny bush," she said. "Thorns, you doing your appointed work. Never want to let folks pass, no sir. Old eyes thought you was a pretty little *green* bush."

Finally, trembling all over, she stood free, and after a moment dared to stoop for her cane.

"Sun so high!" she cried, leaning back and looking, while the thick tears went over her eyes. "The time getting all gone here."

At the foot of this hill was a place where a log was laid across the creek.

"Now comes the trial," said Phoenix.

Putting her right foot out, she mounted the log and shut her eyes. Lifting her skirt, leveling her cane fiercely before her, like a festival figure in some parade, she began to march across. Then she opened her eyes and she was safe on the other side.

"I wasn't as old as I thought," she said.

But she sat down to rest. She spread her skirts on the bank around her and folded her hands over her knees. Up above her was a tree in a pearly cloud of mistletoe. She did not dare to close her eyes, and when a little boy brought her a plate with a slice of marble-cake on it she spoke to him. "That would be acceptable," she said. But when she went to take it there was just her own hand in the air.

So she left that tree, and had to go through a barbed-wire fence. There she had to creep and crawl, spreading her knees and stretching her fingers like a baby trying to climb the steps. But she talked loudly to herself: she could not let her dress be torn now, so late in the day, and she could not pay for having her arm or her leg sawed off if she got caught fast where she was.

At last she was safe through the fence and risen up out in the clearing. Big dead trees, like black men with one arm, were standing in the purple stalks of the withered cotton field. There sat a buzzard.

"Who you watching?"

In the furrow she made her way along.

"Glad this not the season for bulls," she said, looking sideways, "and the good Lord made his snakes to curl up and sleep in the winter. A pleasure I don't see no two-headed snake coming around that tree, where it come once. It took a while to get by him, back in the summer."

She passed through the old cotton and went into a field of dead corn. It whispered and shook and was taller than her head. "Through the maze now," she said, for there was no path.

Then there was something tall, black, and skinny there, moving before her.

At first she took it for a man. It could have been a man dancing in the field. But she stood still and listened, and it did not make a sound. It was as silent as a ghost.

"Ghost," she said sharply, "who be you the ghost of? For I have heard of nary death close by."

But there was no answer—only the ragged dancing in the wind.

She shut her eyes, reached out her hand, and touched a sleeve. She found a coat and inside that an emptiness, cold as ice.

"You scarecrow," she said. Her face lighted. "I ought to be shut up for good," she said with laughter. "My senses is gone. I too old. I the oldest people I ever know. Dance, old scarecrow," she said, "while I dancing with you."

She kicked her foot over the furrow, and with mouth drawn down, shook her head once or twice in a little strutting way. Some husks blew down and whirled in streamers about her skirts.

Then she went on, parting her way from side to side with the cane, through the whispering field. At last she came to the end, to a wagon track where the silver grass blew between the red ruts. The quail were walking around like pullets, seeming all dainty and unseen.

"Walk pretty," she said. "This the easy place. This the easy going."

She followed the track, swaying through the quiet bare fields, through the little strings of trees silver in their dead leaves, past cabins silver from weather, with the doors and windows boarded shut, all like old women under a spell sitting there. "I walking in their sleep," she said, nodding her head vigorously.

In a ravine she went where a spring was silently flowing through a hollow log. Old Phoenix bent and drank. "Sweet-gum makes the water sweet," she said, and drank more. "Nobody know who made this well, for it was here when I was born."

The track crossed a swampy part where the moss hung as white as lace from every limb. "Sleep on, alligators, and blow your bubbles." Then the track went into the road.

Deep, deep the road went down between the high green-colored banks, Overhead the live-oaks met, and it was as dark as a cave.

A black dog with a lolling tongue came up out of the weeds by the ditch. She was meditating, and not ready, and when he came at her she only hit him a little with her cane. Over she went in the ditch, like a little puff of milkweed.

Down there, her senses drifted away. A dream visited her, and she reached her hand up, but nothing reached down and gave her a pull. So she lay there and presently went to talking. "Old woman," she said to herself, "that black dog come up out of the weeds to stall you off, and now there he sitting on his fine tail, smiling at you."

A white man finally came along and found her—a hunter, a young man, with his dog on a chain.

"Well, Granny!" he laughed. "What are you doing there?"

"Lying on my back like a June-bug waiting to be turned over, mister," she said, reaching up her hand.

He lifted her up, gave her a swing in the air, and set her down. "Anything broken, Granny?"

"No sir, them old dead weeds is springy enough," said Phoenix, when she had got her breath. "I thank you for your trouble."

"Where do you live, Granny?" he asked, while the two dogs were growling at each other.

"Away back yonder, sir, behind the ridge. You can't even see it from here."

"On your way home?"

"No sir, I going to town."

"Why, that's too far! That's as far as I walk when I come out my-self, and I get something for my trouble." He patted the stuffed bag he carried, and there hung down a little closed claw. It was one of the bob-whites, with its beak hooked bitterly to show it was dead. "Now you go on home, Granny!"

"I bound to go to town, mister," said Phoenix. "The time come around."

He gave another laugh, filling the whole landscape. "I know you old colored people! Wouldn't miss going to town to see Santa Claus!"

But something held old Phoenix very still. The deep lines in her face went into a fierce and different radiation. Without warning, she had seen with her own eyes a flashing nickel fall out of the man's pocket onto the ground.

"How old are you, Granny?" he was saying.

"There's no telling, mister," she said, "no telling."

Then she gave a little cry and clapped her hands and said, "Git on away from here, dog! Look! Look at that dog!" She laughed as if in admiration. "He ain't scared of nobody. He a big black dog." She whispered, "Sic him!"

"Watch me get rid of that cur," said the man. "Sic him, Pete! Sic him!"

Phoenix heard the dogs fighting, and heard the man running and throwing sticks. She even heard a gunshot. But she was slowly bend-ing forward by that time, further and further forward, the lid stretched down over her eyes, as if she were doing this in her sleep. Her chin was lowered almost to her knees. The yellow palm of her hand came out from the fold of her apron. Her fingers slid down and along the ground under the piece of money with the grace and care they would have in lifting an egg from under a setting hen. Then she slowly straightened up, she stood erect, and the nickel was in her apron pocket. A bird flew by. Her lips moved. "God watching me the whole time. I come to stealing."

The man came back, and his own dog panted about them. "Well, I scared him off that time," he said, and then he laughed and lifted his gun and pointed it at Phoenix.

She stood straight and faced him.

"Doesn't the gun scare you?" he said, still pointing it.

"No, sir, I seen plenty go off closer by, in my day, and for less than what I done," she said, holding utterly still.

He smiled, and shouldered the gun. "Well, Granny," he said, "you must be a hundred years old, and scared of nothing. I'd give you a dime if I had any money with me. But you take my advice and stay home, and nothing will happen to you."

"I bound to go on my way, mister," said Phoenix. She inclined her head in the red rag. Then they went in different directions, but she could hear the gun shooting again and again over the hill.

She walked on. The shadows hung from the oak trees to the road like curtains. Then she smelled wood-smoke, and smelled the river, and she saw a steeple and the cabins on their steep steps. Dozens of little black children whirled around her. There ahead was Natchez[1] shining. Bells were ringing. She walked on.

In the paved city it was Christmas time. There were red and green electric lights strung and crisscrossed everywhere, and all turned on in the daytime. Old Phoenix would have been lost if she had not distrusted her eyesight and depended on her feet to know where to take her.

She paused quietly on the sidewalk where people were passing by. A lady came along in the crowd, carrying an armful of red-, green- and silver-wrapped presents; she gave off perfume like the red roses in hot summer, and Phoenix stopped her.

"Please, missy, will you lace up my shoe?" She held up her foot.

"What do you want, Grandma?"

"See my shoe," said Phoenix. "Do all right for out in the country, but wouldn't look right to go in a big building."

"Stand still then, Grandma," said the lady. She put her packages down on the sidewalk beside her and laced and tied both shoes tightly.

"Can't lace 'em with a cane," said Phoenix. "Thank you, missy. I doesn't mind asking a nice lady to tie up my shoe, when I gets out on the street."

Moving slowly and from side to side, she went into the big build-

1. A city in southwestern Mississippi, on the Mississippi River.

ing, and into the tower of steps, where she walked up and around and around and around until her feet knew to stop.

She entered a door, and there she saw nailed up on the wall the document that had been stamped with the gold seal and framed in the gold frame, which matched the dream that was hung up in her head.

"Here I be," she said. There was a fixed and ceremonial stiffness over her body.

"A charity case, I suppose," said an attendant who sat at the desk before her.

But Phoenix only looked above her head. There was a sweat on her face, the wrinkles in her skin shone like a bright net.

"Speak up, Grandma," the woman said. "What's your name? We must have your history, you know. Have you been here before? What seems to be the trouble with you?"

Old Phoenix only gave a twitch to her face as if a fly were bothering her.

"Are you deaf?" cried the attendant.

But then the nurse came in.

"Oh, that's just old Aunt Phoenix," she said. "She doesn't come for herself—she has a little grandson. She makes these trips just as regular as clockwork. She lives away back off the Old Natchez Trace." She bent down. "Well, Aunt Phoenix, why don't you just take a seat? We won't keep you standing after your long trip." She pointed.

The old woman sat down, bolt upright in the chair.

"Now, how is the boy?" asked the nurse.

Old Phoenix did not speak.

"I said, how is the boy?"

But Phoenix only waited and stared straight ahead, her face very solemn and withdrawn into rigidity.

"Is his throat any better?" asked the nurse. "Aunt Phoenix, don't you hear me? Is your grandson's throat any better since the last time you came for the medicine?"

With her hands on her knees, the old woman waited, silent, erect and motionless, just as if she were in armor.

"You mustn't take up our time this way, Aunt Phoenix," the nurse said. "Tell us quickly about your grandson, and get it over. He isn't dead, is he?"

At last there came a flicker and then a flame of comprehension across her face, and she spoke.

"My grandson. It was my memory had left me. There I sat and forgot why I made my long trip."

"Forgot?" The nurse frowned. "After you came so far?"

Then Phoenix was like an old woman begging a dignified forgiveness for waking up frightened in the night. "I never did go to school, I was too old at the Surrender,"[2] she said in a soft voice. "I'm an old woman without an education. It was my memory fail me. My little grandson, he is just the same, and I forgot it in the coming."

"Throat never heals, does it?" said the nurse, speaking in a loud, sure voice to old Phoenix. By now she had a card with something written on it, a little list. "Yes. Swallowed lye. When was it?—January—two-three years ago—"

Phoenix spoke unmasked now. "No, missy, he not dead, he just the same. Every little while his throat begin to close up again, and he not able to swallow. He not get his breath. He not able to help himself. So the time come around, and I go on another trip for the soothing medicine."

"All right. The doctor said as long as you came to get it, you could have it," said the nurse. "But it's an obstinate case."

"My little grandson, he sit up there in the house all wrapped up, waiting by himself," Phoenix went on. "We is the only two left in the world. He suffer and it don't seem to put him back at all. He got a sweet look. He going to last. He wear a little patch quilt and peep out holding his mouth open like a little bird. I remembers so plain now. I not going to forget him again, no, the whole enduring time. I could tell him from all the others in creation."

"All right." The nurse was trying to hush her now. She brought her a bottle of medicine. "Charity," she said, making a check mark in a book.

Old Phoenix held the bottle close to her eyes, and then carefully put it into her pocket.

---

2. The surrender of the Confederate general Robert E. Lee (1807–1870) to General Ulysses S. Grant (1822–1885) of the Union on April 9, 1865, which ended the American Civil War and slavery. Most Southern states had made it illegal to educate slaves, so Reconstruction opened the first schools for African Americans in the South in generations.

"I thank you," she said.

"It's Christmas time, Grandma," said the attendants. "Could I give you a few pennies out of my purse?"

"Five pennies is a nickel," said Phoenix stiffly.

"Here's a nickel," said the attendant.

Phoenix rose carefully and held out her hand. She received the nickel and then fished the other nickel out of her pocket and laid it beside the new one. She stared at her palm closely, with her head on one side.

Then she gave a tap with her cane on the floor.

"This is what come to me to do," she said. "I going to the store and buy my child a little windmill they sells, made out of paper. He going to find it hard to believe there such a thing in the world. I'll march myself back where he waiting, holding it straight up in this hand."

She lifted her free hand, gave a little nod, turned around, and walked out of the doctor's office. Then her slow step began on the stairs, going down.

1941

Edith Wharton
1862–1937

Like O. Henry's "The Furnished Room," "Roman Fever" depends on a surprise, ironic ending for its startling effect on the reader. But perhaps more important than the conflict between Mrs. Slade and Mrs. Ansley are the themes that reveal themselves repeatedly throughout the story. One is "the warm current of human communion" from which Mrs. Slade feels cut off. Another resides in the enveloping action: Wharton published "Roman Fever" in 1934, but the story is set in the mid-1920s. Though Mrs. Ansley and Mrs. Slade are considerably younger than Wharton herself, still they've lived to witness a revolution in social manners—accelerated by World War I—that parallels and amplifies the ever-present gap between generations. They are separated from the world of their youth by more than twenty-five years. The landscape spread out beneath this café perched on the Janiculum Hill in Rome—the vast ruins, even the Colosseum itself—is all symbolic.

Roman Fever

I

From the table at which they had been lunching two American ladies of ripe but well-cared-for middle age moved across the lofty terrace of the Roman restaurant and, leaning on its parapet, looked first at each other, and then down on the outspread glories of the Palatine and the Forum,[1] with the same expression of vague but benevolent approval.

As they leaned there a girlish voice echoed up gaily from the stairs leading to the court below. "Well, come along, then," it cried, not to them but to an invisible companion, "and let's leave the young things to their knitting"; and a voice as fresh laughed back; "Oh, look here, Babs, not actually knitting—" "Well, I mean figuratively," rejoined the first. "After all, we haven't left our poor parents much else to do . . ." and at that point the turn of the stairs engulfed the dialogue.

The two ladies looked at each other again, this time with a tinge of smiling embarrassment, and the smaller and paler one shook her head and coloured slightly.

"Barbara!" she murmured, sending an unheard rebuke after the mocking voice in the stairway.

The other lady, who was fuller, and higher in colour, with a small determined nose supported by vigorous black eyebrows, gave a good-humoured laugh. "That's what our daughters think of us!"

Her companion replied by a deprecating gesture. "Not of us individually. We must remember that. It's just the collective modern idea of Mothers. And you see—" Half guiltily she drew from her handsomely mounted black hand-bag a twist of crimson silk run through by two fine knitting needles. "One never knows," she murmured. "The new system has certainly given us a good deal of time to kill; and sometimes I get tired just looking—even at this." Her gesture was now addressed to the stupendous scene at their feet.

1. Ancient ruins in Rome.

The dark lady laughed again, and they both relapsed upon the view, contemplating it in silence, with a sort of diffused serenity which might have been borrowed from the spring effulgence of the Roman skies. The luncheon-hour was long past, and the two had their end of the vast terrace to themselves. At its opposite extremity a few groups, detained by a lingering look at the outspread city, were gathering up guide-books and fumbling for tips. The last of them scattered, and the two ladies were alone on the air-washed height.

"Well, I don't see why we shouldn't just stay here," said Mrs. Slade, the lady of the high colour and energetic brows. Two derelict basketchairs stood near, and she pushed them into the angle of the parapet, and settled herself in one, her gaze upon the Palatine. "After all, it's still the most beautiful view in the world."

"It always will be, to me," assented her friend Mrs. Ansley, with so slight a stress on the "me" that Mrs. Slade, though she noticed it, wondered if it were not merely accidental, like the random underlinings of old-fashioned letter-writers.

"Grace Ansley was always old-fashioned," she thought; and added aloud, with a retrospective smile: "It's a view we've both been familiar with for a good many years. When we first met here we were younger than our girls are now. You remember?"

"Oh, yes, I remember," murmured Mrs. Ansley, with the same undefinable stress.—"There's that head-waiter wondering," she interpolated. She was evidently far less sure than her companion of herself and of her rights in the world.

"I'll cure him of wondering," said Mrs. Slade, stretching her hand toward a bag as discreetly opulent-looking as Mrs. Ansley's. Signing to the head-waiter, she explained that she and her friend were old lovers of Rome, and would like to spend the end of the afternoon looking down on the view—that is, if it did not disturb the service? The head-waiter, bowing over her gratuity, assured her that the ladies were most welcome, and would be still more so if they would condescend to remain for dinner. A full moon night, they would remember . . .

Mrs. Slade's black brows drew together, as though references to the moon were out-of-place and even unwelcome. But she smiled away her frown as the head-waiter retreated. "Well, why not? We might do worse. There's no knowing, I suppose, when the girls will be back. Do you even know back from *where*? I don't!"

Mrs. Ansley again coloured slightly. "I think those young Italian aviators we met at the Embassy invited them to fly to Tarquinia[2] for tea. I suppose they'll want to wait and fly back by moonlight."

"Moonlight—moonlight! What a part it still plays. Do you suppose they're as sentimental as we were?"

"I've come to the conclusion that I don't in the least know what they are," said Mrs. Ansley. "And perhaps we didn't know much more about each other."

"No; perhaps we didn't."

Her friend gave her a shy glance. "I never should have supposed you were sentimental, Alida."

"Well, perhaps I wasn't." Mrs. Slade drew her lids together in retrospect; and for a few moments the two ladies, who had been intimate since childhood, reflected how little they knew each other. Each one, of course, had a label ready to attach to the other's name; Mrs. Delphin Slade, for instance, would have told herself, or any one who asked her, that Mrs. Horace Ansley, twenty-five years ago, had been exquisitely lovely—no, you wouldn't believe it, would you? . . . though, of course, still charming, distinguished . . . Well, as a girl she had been exquisite; far more beautiful than her daughter Barbara, though certainly Babs, according to the new standards at any rate, was more effective—had more *edge*, as they say. Funny where she got it, with those two nullities as parents. Yes; Horace Ansley was—well, just the duplicate of his wife. Museum specimens of old New York. Good-looking, irreproachable, exemplary. Mrs. Slade and Mrs. Ansley had lived opposite each other—actually as well as figuratively—for years. When the drawingroom curtains in No. 20 East 73rd Street were renewed, No. 23, across the way, was always aware of it. And of all the movings, buyings, travels, anniversaries, illnesses—the tame chronicle of an estimable pair. Little of it escaped Mrs. Slade. But she had grown bored with it by the time her husband made his big *coup* in Wall Street, and when they bought in upper Park Avenue had already begun to think: "I'd rather live op-

---

2. Ancient Etruscan town northeast of Rome.

posite a speak-easy[3] for a change; at least one might see it raided."
The idea of seeing Grace raided was so amusing that (before the
move) she launched it at a woman's lunch. It made a hit, and went
the rounds—she sometimes wondered if it had crossed the street,
and reached Mrs. Ansley. She hoped not, but didn't much mind.
Those were the days when respectability was at a discount, and it
did the irreproachable no harm to laugh at them a little.

A few years later, and not many months apart, both ladies lost
their husbands. There was an appropriate exchange of wreaths and
condolences, and a brief renewal of intimacy in the half-shadow of
their mourning; and now, after another interval, they had run across
each other in Rome, at the same hotel, each of them the modest ap-
pendage of a salient daughter. The similarity of their lot had again
drawn them together, lending itself to mild jokes, and the mutual
confession that, if in old days it must have been tiring to "keep up"
with daughters, it was now, at times, a little dull not to.

No doubt, Mrs. Slade reflected, she felt her unemployment more
than poor Grace ever would. It was a big drop from being the wife
of Delphin Slade to being his widow. She had always regarded herself (with a certain conjugal pride) as his equal in social gifts, as con-
tributing her full share to the making of the exceptional couple they
were: but the difference after his death was irremediable. As the wife
of the famous corporation lawyer, always with an international case
or two on hand, every day brought its exciting and unexpected
obligation: the impromptu entertaining of eminent colleagues from
abroad, the hurried dashes on legal business to London, Paris or
Rome, where the entertaining was so handsomely reciprocated; the
amusement of hearing in her wake: "What, that handsome woman
with the good clothes and the eyes is Mrs. Slade—*the* Slade's wife?
Really? Generally the wives of celebrities are such frumps."

Yes; being *the* Slade's widow was a dullish business after that. In
living up to such a husband all her faculties had been engaged; now
she had only her daughter to live up to, for the son who seemed to
have inherited his father's gifts had died suddenly in boyhood. She
had fought through that agony because her husband was there, to

3. A place where alcoholic beverages are illegally sold, especially such a place during Prohi-
bition.

be helped and to help; now, after the father's death, the thought of the boy had become unbearable. There was nothing left but to mother her daughter; and dear Jenny was such a perfect daughter that she needed no excessive mothering. "Now with Babs Ansley I don't know that I *should* be so quiet," Mrs. Slade sometimes half-enviously reflected; but Jenny, who was younger than her brilliant friend, was that rare accident, an extremely pretty girl who some-how made youth and prettiness seem as safe as their absence. It was all perplexing—and to Mrs. Slade a little boring. She wished that Jenny would fall in love—with the wrong man, even; that she might have to be watched, out-manoeuvred, rescued. And instead, it was Jenny who watched her mother, kept her out of draughts, made sure that she had taken her tonic . . .

Mrs. Ansley was much less articulate than her friend, and her mental portrait of Mrs. Slade was slighter, and drawn with fainter touches. "Alida Slade's awfully brilliant; but not as brilliant as she thinks," would have summed it up; though she would have added, for the enlightenment of strangers, that Mrs. Slade had been an extremely dashing girl; much more so than her daughter, who was pretty, of course, and clever in a way, but had none of her mother's—well, "vividness," some one had once called it. Mrs. Ansley would take up current words like this, and cite them in quotation marks, as unheard-of audacities. No; Jenny was not like her mother. Sometimes Mrs. Ansley thought Alida Slade was disappointed; on the whole she had had a sad life. Full of failures and mistakes; Mrs. Ansley had always been rather sorry for her . . .

So these two ladies visualized each other, each through the wrong end of her little telescope.

II

For a long time they continued to sit side by side without speaking. It seemed as though, to both, there was a relief in laying down their somewhat futile activities in the presence of the vast Memento Mori[4] which faced them. Mrs. Slade sat quite still, her eyes fixed on

---

4. Any object serving as a reminder of death; literally, "remember, you must die" (Latin).

the golden slope of the Palace of the Cæsars,[5] and after a while Mrs. Ansley ceased to fidget with her bag, and she too sank into meditation. Like many intimate friends, the two ladies had never before had occasion to be silent together, and Mrs. Ansley was slightly embarrassed by what seemed, after so many years, a new stage in their intimacy, and one with which she did not yet know how to deal.

Suddenly the air was full of that deep clangour of bells which periodically covers Rome with a roof of silver. Mrs. Slade glanced at her wrist-watch. "Five o'clock already," she said, as though surprised.

Mrs. Ansley suggested interrogatively: "There's bridge at the Embassy at five." For a long time Mrs. Slade did not answer. She appeared to be lost in contemplation, and Mrs. Ansley thought the remark had escaped her. But after a while she said, as if speaking out of a dream: "Bridge, did you say? Not unless you want to . . . But I don't think I will, you know."

"Oh, no," Mrs. Ansley hastened to assure her. "I don't care to at all. It's so lovely here; and so full of old memories, as you say." She settled herself in her chair, and almost furtively drew forth her knitting. Mrs. Slade took sideway note of this activity, but her own beautifully cared-for hands remained motionless on her knee.

"I was just thinking," she said slowly, "what different things Rome stands for to each generation of travellers. To our grandmothers, Roman fever; to our mothers, sentimental dangers—how we used to be guarded!—to our daughters, no more dangers than the middle of Main Street. They don't know it—but how much they're missing!"

The long golden light was beginning to pale, and Mrs. Ansley lifted her knitting a little closer to her eyes. "Yes; how we were guarded!"

"I always used to think," Mrs. Slade continued, "that our mothers had a much more difficult job than our grandmothers. When Roman fever stalked the streets it must have been comparatively easy to gather in the girls at the danger hour; but when you and I were young, with such beauty calling us, and the spice of disobedi-

5. On the Palatine Hill.

ence thrown in, and no worse risk than catching cold during the cool hour after sunset, the mothers used to be put to it to keep us in—didn't they?"

She turned again toward Mrs. Ansley, but the latter had reached a delicate point in her knitting. "One, two, three—slip two; yes, they must have been," she assented, without looking up.

Mrs. Slade's eyes rested on her with a deepened attention. "She can knit—in the face of *this*! How like her . . ."

Mrs. Slade leaned back, brooding, her eyes ranging from the ruins which faced her to the long green hollow of the Forum, the fading glow of the church fronts beyond it, and the outlying immensity of the Colosseum.[6] Suddenly she thought: "It's all very well to say that our girls have done away with sentiment and moonlight. But if Babs Ansley isn't out to catch that young aviator—the one who's a Marchese[7]—then I don't know anything. And Jenny has no chance beside her. I know that too. I wonder if that's why Grace Ansley likes the two girls to go everywhere together? My poor Jenny as a foil—!" Mrs. Slade gave a hardly audible laugh, and at the sound Mrs. Ansley dropped her knitting.

"Yes—?"

"I—oh, nothing. I was only thinking how your Babs carries everything before her. That Campolieri boy is one of the best matches in Rome. Don't look so innocent, my dear—you know he is. And I was wondering, ever so respectfully, you understand . . . wondering how two such exemplary characters as you and Horace had managed to produce anything quite so dynamic." Mrs. Slade laughed again, with a touch of asperity.

Mrs. Ansley's hands lay inert across her needles. She looked straight out at the great accumulated wreckage of passion and splendour at her feet. But her small profile was almost expressionless. At length she said: "I think you overrate Babs, my dear."

Mrs. Slade's tone grew easier. "No; I don't. I appreciate her. And perhaps envy you. Oh, my girl's perfect; if I were a chronic invalid I'd—well, I think I'd rather be in Jenny's hands. There must be

6. Ruined Roman amphitheater famous for its gladiatorial combats and hallowed by thousands of Christian martyrs.

7. A marquis, a nobleman ranking below a duke and above an earl or count.

times . . . but there! I always wanted a brilliant daughter . . . and never quite understood why I got an angel instead."

Mrs. Ansley echoed her laugh in a faint murmur. "Babs is an angel too."

"Of course—of course! But she's got rainbow wings. Well, they're wandering by the sea with their young men; and here we sit . . . and it all brings back the past a little too acutely."

Mrs. Ansley had resumed her knitting. One might almost have imagined (if one had known her less well, Mrs. Slade reflected) that, for her also, too many memories rose from the lengthening shadows of those august ruins. But no; she was simply absorbed in her work. What was there for her to worry about? She knew that Babs would almost certainly come back engaged to the extremely eligible Campolieri. "And she'll sell the New York house, and settle down near them in Rome, and never be in their way . . . she's much too tactful. But she'll have an excellent cook, and just the right people in for bridge and cocktails . . . and a perfectly peaceful old age among her grandchildren."

Mrs. Slade broke off this prophetic flight with a recoil of self-disgust. There was no one of whom she had less right to think unkindly than of Grace Ansley. Would she never cure herself of envying her? Perhaps she had begun too long ago.

She stood up and leaned against the parapet, filling her troubled eyes with the tranquillizing magic of the hour. But instead of tranquillizing her the sight seemed to increase her exasperation. Her gaze turned toward the Colosseum. Already its golden flank was drowned in purple shadow, and above it the sky curved crystal clear, without light or colour. It was the moment when afternoon and evening hang balanced in mid-heaven.

Mrs. Slade turned back and laid her hand on her friend's arm. The gesture was so abrupt that Mrs. Ansley looked up, startled.

"The sun's set. You're not afraid, my dear?"

"Afraid—"

"Of Roman fever or pneumonia? I remember how ill you were that winter. As a girl you had a very delicate throat, hadn't you?"

"Oh, we're all right up here. Down below, in the Forum, it does get deathly cold, all of a sudden . . . but not here."

"Ah, of course you know because you had to be so careful." Mrs.

Slade turned back to the parapet. She thought: "I must make one more effort not to hate her." Aloud she said: "Whenever I look at the Forum from up here, I remember that story about a great-aunt of yours, wasn't she? A dreadfully wicked great-aunt?"

"Oh, yes; Great-aunt Harriet. The one who was supposed to have sent her young sister out to the Forum after sunset to gather a night-blooming flower for her album. All our great-aunts and grand-mothers used to have albums of dried flowers."

Mrs. Slade nodded. "But she really sent her because they were in love with the same man—"

"Well, that was the family tradition. They said Aunt Harriet confessed it years afterward. At any rate, the poor little sister caught the fever and died. Mother used to frighten us with the story when we were children."

"And you frightened *me* with it, that winter when you and I were here as girls. The winter I was engaged to Delphin."

Mrs. Ansley gave a faint laugh. "Oh, did I? Really frightened you? I don't believe you're easily frightened."

"Not often; but I was then. I was easily frightened because I was too happy. I wonder if you know what that means?"

"I—yes . . . " Mrs. Ansley faltered.

"Well, I suppose that was why the story of your wicked aunt made such an impression on me. And I thought: 'There's no more Roman fever, but the Forum is deathly cold after sunset—especially after a hot day. And the Colosseum's even colder and damper.' "

"The Colosseum—?"

"Yes. It wasn't easy to get in, after the gates were locked for the night. Far from easy. Still, in those days it could be managed; it *was* managed, often. Lovers met there who couldn't meet elsewhere. You knew that?"

"I—I daresay. I don't remember."

"You don't remember? You don't remember going to visit some ruins or other one evening, just after dark, and catching a bad chill? You were supposed to have gone to see the moon rise. People always said that expedition was what caused your illness."

There was a moment's silence; then Mrs. Ansley rejoined: "Did they? It was all so long ago."

"Yes. And you got well again—so it didn't matter. But I suppose

it struck your friends—the reason given for your illness, I mean—
because everybody knew you were so prudent on account of your
throat, and your mother took such care of you . . . You *had* been out
late sight-seeing, hadn't you, that night?"

"Perhaps I had. The most prudent girls aren't always prudent.
What made you think of it now?"

Mrs. Slade seemed to have no answer ready. But after a moment
she broke out: "Because I simply can't bear it any longer—!"

Mrs. Ansley lifted her head quickly. Her eyes were wide and very
pale. "Can't bear what?"

"Why—your not knowing that I've always known why you
went."

"Why I went—?"

"Yes. You think I'm bluffing, don't you? Well, you went to meet
the man I was engaged to—and I can repeat every word of the letter
that took you there."

While Mrs. Slade spoke Mrs. Ansley had risen unsteadily to her
feet. Her bag, her knitting and gloves, slid in a panic-stricken heap
to the ground. She looked at Mrs. Slade as though she were looking
at a ghost.

"No, no—don't," she faltered out.

"Why not? Listen, if you don't believe me. 'My one darling,
things can't go on like this. I must see you alone. Come to the
Colosseum immediately after dark tomorrow. There will be somebody to let you in. No one whom you need fear will suspect'—but
perhaps you've forgotten what the letter said?"

Mrs. Ansley met the challenge with an unexpected composure.
Steadying herself against the chair she looked at her friend, and
replied: "No; I know it by heart too."

"And the signature? 'Only *your* D.S.' Was that it? I'm right, am I?
That was the letter that took you out that evening after dark?"

Mrs. Ansley was still looking at her. It seemed to Mrs. Slade that
a slow struggle was going on behind the voluntarily controlled mask
of her small quiet face. "I shouldn't have thought she had herself so
well in hand," Mrs. Slade reflected, almost resentfully. But at this
moment Mrs. Ansley spoke. "I don't know how you knew. I burnt
that letter at once."

"Yes; you would, naturally—you're so prudent!" The sneer was open now. "And if you burnt the letter you're wondering how on earth I know what was in it. That's it, isn't it?"

Mrs. Slade waited, but Mrs. Ansley did not speak.

"Well, my dear, I know what was in that letter because I wrote it!"

"You wrote it?"

"Yes."

The two women stood for a minute staring at each other in the last golden light. Then Mrs. Ansley dropped back into her chair. "Oh," she murmured, and covered her face with her hands.

Mrs. Slade waited nervously for another word or movement. None came, and at length she broke out: "I horrify you."

Mrs. Ansley's hands dropped to her knee. The face they uncovered was streaked with tears. "I wasn't thinking of you. I was thinking—it was the only letter I ever had from him!"

"And I wrote it. Yes; I wrote it! But I was the girl he was engaged to. Did you happen to remember that?"

Mrs. Ansley's head drooped again. "I'm not trying to excuse myself . . . I remembered . . ."

"And still you went?"

"Still I went."

Mrs. Slade stood looking down on the small bowed figure at her side. The flame of her wrath had already sunk, and she wondered why she had ever thought there would be any satisfaction in inflicting so purposeless a wound on her friend. But she had to justify herself.

"You do understand? I'd found out—and I hated you, hated you. I knew you were in love with Delphin—and I was afraid; afraid of you, of your quiet ways, your sweetness . . . your . . . well, I wanted you out of the way, that's all. Just for a few weeks; just till I was sure of him. So in a blind fury I wrote that letter . . . I don't know why I'm telling you now."

"I suppose," said Mrs. Ansley slowly, "it's because you've always gone on hating me."

"Perhaps. Or because I wanted to get the whole thing off my mind." She paused. "I'm glad you destroyed the letter. Of course I never thought you'd die."

Mrs. Ansley relapsed into silence, and Mrs. Slade, leaning above her, was conscious of a strange sense of isolation, of being cut off from the warm current of human communion. "You think me a monster!"

"I don't know . . . It was the only letter I had, and you say he didn't write it?"

"Ah, how you care for him still!"

"I cared for that memory," said Mrs. Ansley.

Mrs. Slade continued to look down on her. She seemed physically reduced by the blow—as if, when she got up, the wind might scatter her like a puff of dust. Mrs. Slade's jealousy suddenly leapt up again at the sight. All these years the woman had been living on that letter. How she must have loved him, to treasure the mere memory of its ashes! The letter of the man her friend was engaged to. Wasn't it she who was the monster?

"You tried your best to get him away from me, didn't you? But you failed; and I kept him. That's all."

"Yes. That's all."

"I wish now I hadn't told you. I'd no idea you'd feel about it as you do; I thought you'd be amused. It all happened so long ago, as you say; and you must do me the justice to remember that I had no reason to think you'd ever taken it seriously. How could I, when you were married to Horace Ansley two months afterward? As soon as you could get out of bed your mother rushed you off to Florence and married you. People were rather surprised—they wondered at its being done so quickly; but I thought I knew. I had an idea you did it out of *pique*—to be able to say you'd got ahead of Delphin and me. Girls have such silly reasons for doing the most serious things. And your marrying so soon convinced me that you'd never really cared."

"Yes. I suppose it would," Mrs. Ansley assented.

The clear heaven overhead was emptied of all its gold. Dusk spread over it, abruptly darkening the Seven Hills.[8] Here and there lights began to twinkle through the foliage at their feet. Steps were coming and going on the deserted terrace—waiters looking out of

---

8. Group of hills on which the ancient city of Rome was built.

the doorway at the head of the stairs, then reappearing with trays and napkins and flasks of wine. Tables were moved, chairs straightened. A feeble string of electric lights flickered out. Some vases of faded flowers were carried away, and brought back replenished. A stout lady in a dust-coat suddenly appeared, asking in broken Italian if any one had seen the elastic band which held together her tattered Baedeker.[9] She poked with her stick under the table at which she had lunched, the waiters assisting.

The corner where Mrs. Slade and Mrs. Ansley sat was still shadowy and deserted. For a long time neither of them spoke. At length Mrs. Slade began again: "I suppose I did it as a sort of joke—"

"A joke?"

"Well, girls are ferocious sometimes, you know. Girls in love especially. And I remember laughing to myself all that evening at the idea that you were waiting around there in the dark, dodging out of sight, listening for every sound, trying to get in—. Of course I was upset when I heard you were so ill afterward."

Mrs. Ansley had not moved for a long time. But now she turned slowly toward her companion. "But I didn't wait. He'd arranged everything. He was there. We were let in at once," she said.

Mrs. Slade sprang up from her leaning position. "Delphin there? They let you in?—Ah, now you're lying!" She burst out with violence.

Mrs. Ansley's voice grew clearer, and full of surprise. "But of course he was there. Naturally he came—"

"Came? How did he know he'd find you there? You must be raving!"

Mrs. Ansley hesitated, as though reflecting. "But I answered the letter. I told him I'd be there. So he came."

Mrs. Slade flung her hands up to her face. "Oh, God—you answered! I never thought of your answering . . ."

"It's odd you never thought of it, if you wrote the letter."

"Yes. I was blind with rage."

Mrs. Ansley rose, and drew her fur scarf about her. "It is cold here. We'd better go . . . I'm sorry for you," she said, as she clasped the fur about her throat.

9. Guidebook.

The unexpected words sent a pang through Mrs. Slade. "Yes; we'd better go." She gathered up her bag and cloak. "I don't know why you should be sorry for me," she muttered.

Mrs. Ansley stood looking away from her toward the dusky secret mass of the Colosseum. "Well—because I didn't have to wait that night."

Mrs. Slade gave an unquiet laugh. "Yes; I was beaten there. But I oughtn't to begrudge it to you, I suppose. At the end of all these years. After all, I had everything; I had him for twenty-five years. And you had nothing but that one letter that he didn't write."

Mrs. Ansley was again silent. At length she turned toward the door of the terrace. She took a step, and turned back, facing her companion.

"I had Barbara," she said, and began to move ahead of Mrs. Slade toward the stairway.

1934

Poems

What Is Poetry?

When we turn on the radio or put on a CD, we hear poetry's most popular form: song. In fact, lyrics that are set to music might be considered the most poetic of all poems because anything written in meter is poetry, and we can best define meter as music. In the lines of poetry, stressed and unstressed syllables rise and fall with a musical lilt. These rhythms are most obvious in songs: we've all sometimes felt the spell, the almost physical power, in the music of our favorite lyrics. When we replay the lyrics of a favorite song in our heads, we often remember the band's music and the singer's voice. And if we say the lines aloud, we often even mimic the rhythms given to them by the band and singer. If you're familiar with Bruce Springsteen's "The River," when you read his lyrics on pp. 566–68, the music of the recording will probably invade your mind. The song's power will reach you through the tones of the harmonica or through your memory of Springsteen's unique singing style.

Literary poems, including those reprinted here, have this disadvantage: no instruments play the rhythm, and no singer conveys the phrasing. The music can come to you only through your own voice. Try reading aloud these lines from the end of Alfred, Lord Tennyson's "Ulysses":

Though much is taken, much abides; and though
We are not now that strength which in old days
Moved earth and heaven; that which we are, we are,
One equal temper of heroic hearts,
Made weak by time and fate, but strong in will
To strive, to seek, to find, and not to yield.

Read it two or three more times, slowly, letting the rhythms settle themselves in your speech. Leaving aside any consideration of the words' meaning, their sound has a pleasure and a musical power. The meter directs you to say the lines a certain way. We can hear the difference from prose, even literary prose. Consider this passage for comparison:

> The *Nellie*, a cruising yawl, swung to her anchor without a flutter of the sails, and was at rest. The flood had made, the wind was nearly calm, and being bound down the river, the only thing for it was to come to and wait for the turn of the tide.

These lines, from the opening of Joseph Conrad's *Heart of Darkness*, capture the elegance and pleasure of natural speech at its best. But they are not musical, not in the way Tennyson's are.

If ever you've been moved to tears by a song, or if you have a favorite CD you blast in the car with the windows rolled down in the sun, if listening to a good song can change your mood, then you have a talent for poetry. And who does not? No matter how educated or unsophisticated, everyone knows the pleasure of listening to song. The root of that pleasure may be a mystery, but we all know it's true: that words wrestled into music have a charm and power ordinary language does not.

Like most descriptions of literary genres, this definition is fuzzy. Some prose writers do write in an almost musical style, while some poets consciously suppress the music in their poems. But roughly speaking, the definition will serve our needs: poetry is writing that sounds musical. A **lyric poem** is a short poem. There's no specific length requirement. We call a poem a lyric if it's about the size of a song. Of course, some songs are longer than others, so the division between lyrics and narratives can blur. And we can divide lyric poetry into other genres, like the **sonnet, dramatic monologue, elegy, ode,** and **ballad.** These special genres are defined in the section devoted to the structure of poetry.

How Do You Read Poems?

The literary forms that you know well, whether they're movies or TV shows or novels or popular songs, have laid the groundwork for reading poems. Songs, whose conventions you probably have been internalizing your whole life, are especially close to the poems in this volume. In studying poetry, you're not learning new skills so much as becoming more aware of what you already can do pretty well. But as you become more aware, you'll find yourself able to handle these analytical tools with more precision and confidence.

Speaker

Every lyric poem has a **speaker.** You should imagine that every poem is a little speech by a real person: the speaker. Sometimes the speaker's identity is a total mystery, but usually a poem will give you some clues. More often than not, it will tell you a lot about the speaker. The first thing to do when you analyze a poem is define the speaker as precisely as you can. For example, take this poem by William Wordsworth:

She Dwelt among the Untrodden Ways

She dwelt among the untrodden ways
  Beside the springs of Dove,
A Maid whom there were none to praise
  And very few to love;

A violet by a mossy stone
  Half hidden from the eye!

—Fair as a star, when only one
  Is shining in the sky.

She lived unknown, and few could know
  When Lucy ceased to be;
But she is in her grave, and, oh,
  The difference to me.

The speaker tells very little about himself, but we can speculate
about him. In fact, it's really speculation to say the speaker is male.
He sounds as if he was in love with Lucy and perhaps was courting
her. From the way he describes Lucy, we might further guess that he
was a little older than she; perhaps he is a bit cosmopolitan; probably he has seen something of the world. But even if he's seen something of the world, we might assume that he's lived near the Dove
River or that he's had a reason to spend some time on its "untrodden ways," or he never would have discovered Lucy.

We are often tempted to associate the speaker with the singer or
poet, and sometimes that works. Some poems are obviously autobiographical. Poems from the Romantic era especially often invite
us to equate the speaker with the poet. But it is good practice to assume that the speaker is a fictional persona unless you have evidence
to prove otherwise. In other words, don't say, "William Wordsworth
loved a girl named Lucy, but she died before he ever married her."
In this case, though Wordsworth is a Romantic poet and did write
many autobiographical poems, "She Dwelt among the Untrodden
Ways" does not tell a "true" story. We should always begin by assuming the poet is playing a role: "the speaker loved a girl named
Lucy, but she died before they married."

Audience and Rhetorical Situation

If every poem has a speaker, you might logically assume that every
poem also has a listener, or **audience.** Ultimately, of course, anyone
who reads the poem is the audience, just as anyone who hears a
song in concert or on a CD is its audience. But as a literary term,
audience has a specialized meaning: it is the character(s) or per-
sona(e) whom the speaker is addressing.

In Wordworth's poem, we have a much tougher time defining the audience than the speaker. This is not always the case. Most love poems, for example, are addressed to the speaker's lover. Turn to pp. 404–05 and look at Matthew Arnold's "Dover Beach." From clues in the poem, we can guess that the audience is the speaker's beloved.

We can also determine the **rhetorical situation** of "Dover Beach," what occasions the speaker to address the audience in these words. We might guess that the speaker and his audience are newlyweds because many English couples in the nineteenth century spent their wedding night at Dover and then took the ferry to the Continent for their honeymoon. Whether the speaker and his lover are embarking on a honeymoon or not, they seem to be on a vacation, because the speaker marvels at the seascape in a way that a local probably wouldn't. He and his lover may be in a cottage or a house or a hotel room. We can't be sure, but we know they are inside some building because they are looking out a window at the ocean.

In Wordsworth's poem, we don't have many clues about the rhetorical situation. The speaker's audience doesn't know Lucy, but he or she seems to be on fairly intimate terms with the speaker, since the speaker is unburdening his grief. Perhaps the audience is the speaker's close friend, someone from the city far from Lucy's home near Dove River. But where are they? Are they talking late at night before a hearth fire? Are they old men recounting their youth and their regrets? We don't know.

The first couple of times you read a poem, you should focus on these three elements: speaker, audience, and rhetorical situation. Try to figure out the story of the poem, who is speaking to whom on what occasion. If you read a poem that confuses you, guess who the speaker is. Then try out your hypothesis by rereading the poem. You'll probably have to adjust your idea. That's normal. Even professional critics have to reread poems to understand them. Keep rereading until you're confident you know who the speaker is and to whom he or she is talking.

Paraphrase

The next thing you should do is make sure you understand the literal level of the poem: the basic meaning of the speaker's words.

Some poems, like Wordsworth's, are so clear that you don't have to formulate a **paraphrase** at all. But most poems have at least a few lines that are challenging to figure out even on the literal level. Let's look again at Matthew Arnold's "Dover Beach," for example. The first eight lines are straightforward. If you read them slowly and carefully, you will probably understand the literal level. The following lines are a little more difficult:

> *Listen! you hear the grating roar*
> *Of pebbles which the waves draw back, and fling,*
> *At their return, up the high strand,*
> *Begin, and cease, and then again begin,*
> *With tremulous cadence slow, and bring*
> *The eternal note of sadness in.*

Arnold is taxing our sense of grammar to its limits. It helps, of course, to know that *strand* is an English word for "beach." A good dictionary would tell you that, and a good dictionary is an indispensable tool for reading poetry. But even knowing the meaning of *strand* doesn't clear things up totally. Where does that "Begin, and cease" belong, for example? Is the speaker telling his lover to begin and cease and then again begin?

By translating these lines into your own language, you can usually clear up those grammatical confusions. Here's one paraphrase of Arnold's lines:

> Listen to the loud noise of the pebbles. When the waves go out, they drag the pebbles out to sea, and when the waves come crashing back, they throw the pebbles up onto the beach. You can hear the noise of the pebbles begin and stop and begin again, almost as if they were beating out a slow rhythm. The sound they make makes me feel sad.

A paraphrase should be as straightforward as this. You should be able to read it aloud to your roommate, and your roommate should understand perfectly, without the slightest confusion, everything you say. If something in your paraphrase sounds unclear, then you should try again.

Note that this paraphrase used sixty-seven words to express in prose what Arnold said in forty-one words of poetry. That's typical. Poetry is economical. In a paraphrase, you should expect to use at least one and a half times as many words as the poet, and you should suspect you've omitted some important details if you use fewer. Notice also that this paraphrase broke Arnold's single sentence into four sentences. This technique of separating out the details can help you see the big picture. For instance, after paraphrasing the second and third lines of the selection from Arnold's poem, you may be able to see that "Begin, and cease" were not commands. They simply complete the thought that begins with these words: "you hear the grating roar / Of pebbles." Everything in between is an interruption. When you skip the interruption, the sentence makes more sense: "Listen! you can hear the grating roar / Of pebbles . . . / Begin, and cease, and then again begin."

You don't need to paraphrase every line of a poem. When you read through a poem, you should mark the parts that don't seem to make sense to you grammatically. Then go back and spend some time paraphrasing those lines. You don't have to write them down, but you should at least work them out in your head. When verbs seem to dangle by themselves, hunt down their subjects. When you see descriptive phrases, find out what thing they describe. Fill the margins of your book with the results so you'll remember them.

Sometimes you'll find that you do have to write down the paraphrase. Sometimes only by taking a pen to a blank piece of paper can you unravel the **syntax** of unclear lines. You should do this for any poem that you're writing a paper about, just to make sure that you understand the literal level perfectly, because the success of your interpretation hinges on accurately reading the poem's literal level. For example, to say that the speaker in "Dover Beach" is standing near the beach along the *French* coast rather than the *English* coast is just dead wrong. It would set your interpretation off in the wrong direction, and you would never get back on the right track.

After you've mastered the literal level of a poem, you should begin examining the **figurative levels.** As you read the poem over and over again, you'll begin to recognize how it communicates much more than what is conveyed by the literal meaning. Through metaphors and patterns of images and symbols, even through the physical sound of the words, a poem conveys meanings that deepen and amplify the literal level. What might have seemed a flat piece of writing suddenly explodes into a third dimension, and you'll find your emotions and your intellect caught up in the complexities. The following sections should help you see, understand, and feel that dimension.

Tone

Tone in a poem is the same as tone in speech. When someone is talking to you, you unconsciously determine the tone of his or her voice. By visual clues, like facial expression, you determine the emotion, and that information helps you to appreciate fully the meaning of the words. Take this dialogue, for example:

> "How are you doing?"
> "I'm doing all right, I guess."

Compare it with this version, which includes tonal clues:

> "How are you doing?" he asked lightly.
> "I'm doing all right," she said slowly, with a resigned look
> on her face. "I guess."

Sometimes tone does not just contribute to the meaning of the words: it also reverses the literal meaning. Someone asks you how you are doing, and you answer sarcastically, "I'm doing all right," and the inquirer knows that you are *not* doing all right. You convey the sarcasm through tonal qualities in your voice and maybe by rolling your eyes.

The text of a poem, of course, can use neither facial expression nor voice. Therefore, the tone of a poem is harder to detect than the tone of someone speaking to you. Nevertheless, with some careful attention, you should be able to determine the tone of the speaker in a poem, even though you cannot hear him or her.

Sometimes you might notice a difference between the speaker's tone and the poet's tone. In a poem like Gwendolyn Brooks's "We Real Cool," for example, we get a strong sense that the poet does not entirely approve of the speakers' swagger, especially when they nonchalantly conclude, "We / Die soon." Brooks's attitude is more knowing and more critical than the speakers'. When you recognize such a difference, you have detected **irony.** What the poet means is different from what the speaker means. Often the degree of irony in a poem is a matter of interpretation and debate. Does Ulysses speak for Tennyson in that dramatic monologue? Is Poe critical of the hypersensitive narrator in "The Raven"? These are matters that cannot be decided with finality, but it is nearly always useful to entertain the possibility that the speaker is ironized.

Imagery

An **image** is anything you see, hear, smell, touch, or taste in a work of literature. Anything "concrete" (to use a familiar metaphor) as opposed to "abstract" is an image. Images are the basic building blocks of just about any poem.

Consider these two poems, the first by A. E. Housman and the second by W. B. Yeats:

When I Was One-and-Twenty

When I was one and twenty
I heard a wise man say,
"Give crowns and pounds and guineas
But not your heart away;
Give pearls away and rubies
But keep your fancy free."
But I was one-and-twenty,
No use to talk to me.

When I was one-and-twenty
I heard him say again,
"The heart out of the bosom
Was never given in vain;
'Tis paid with sighs a plenty
And sold for endless rue."
And I am two-and-twenty,
And oh, 'tis true, 'tis true.

Down by the Salley Gardens

Down by the salley gardens my love and I did meet;
She passed the salley gardens with little snow-white feet.
She bid me take love easy, as the leaves grow on the tree;
But I, being young and foolish, with her would not agree.

In a field by the river my love and I did stand,
And on my leaning shoulder she laid her snow-white hand.
She bid me take life easy as the grass grows on the weirs;
But I was young and foolish, and now am full of tears.

The first poem doesn't give us many vivid images. Some vague pictures might come to your mind when you read it. You might picture a wise man speaking to a young man, though even that rhetorical situation is hardly described. There are some concrete nouns (currency and coins, hearts and bosoms), but for the most part the poem functions in the abstract. The lines do convey information (love leads to heartache), but they don't engage our imagination.

The second poem delivers the same information, but it conveys it through a series of evocative images: two young lovers meet under willow trees ("the salley gardens"); the woman is small, perhaps even frail in stature, with very white skin; we see the two argue, perhaps playfully; we see them by a river; we see the girl leaning her head on the speaker's shoulder; we see the speaker weeping. The final lines of the two poems will drive this point home: " 'The heart . . . / [is] sold for endless rue.' / And I am two-and-twenty, / And oh, 'tis true, 'tis true," compared with "But I was young and foolish, and now am full of tears." *Rue* is an abstraction; *tears* are an image.

If you read the two poems over and over again, you'll probably find yourself more attracted to the second. Housman's poem is pithy and witty, and though it's light verse, perhaps it is laced with serious undertones. Yeats's poem conveys the same information about young lovers, but it interests us more. It excites our imagination and draws out our emotions. That's why poets use images more than abstractions.

Most poems lay out their images in a pattern. Take this poem by
Robert Browning:

Home-Thoughts, from Abroad

I

Oh, to be in England
Now that April's there,
And whoever wakes in England
Sees, some morning, unaware,
That the lowest boughs and the brushwood sheaf
Round the elm-tree bole are in tiny leaf,
While the chaffinch sings on the orchard bough
In England—now!

2

And after April, when May follows,
And the whitethroat builds, and all the swallows!
Hark, where my blossomed peartree in the hedge
Leans to the field and scatters on the clover
Blossoms and dewdrops—at the bent spray's edge—
That's the wise thrush; he sings each song twice over,
Lest you should think he never could recapture
The first fine careless rapture!
And though the fields look rough with hoary dew,
All will be gay when noontide wakes anew
The buttercups, the little children's dower
—Far brighter than this gaudy melon-flower!

The speaker, living or vacationing abroad, feels nostalgia for the
springtime sights and sounds of his native country. It is a sentiment
anyone from *anywhere* might feel when abroad for a long time, and
it could be summed up by this short sentence: I miss home. But
if we examine the images in this poem—the details the speaker
chooses to mention—we can begin to see that the poem communicates much more than this universal statement of homesickness. We
can detect a moral judgment about England.

Here are the images:

low branches with tiny new leaves
dense underbrush with tiny leaves surrounding the trunk of an
   elm
a chaffinch singing from the branch of a tree in a (pear?)
   orchard
a whitethroat building a nest
many swallows
the little white blossoms of a pear tree
a hedge
clover, sprinkled with pear blossoms
dewdrops on clover
a thrush singing
fields all white with dew
buttercups in a yard reserved for children

When we list these images, we can begin to see some commonalities among them: All of the images are natural, and nearly are all small. Buttercups, pear blossoms, and clover blossoms are tiny flowers, yellow and white. We see small young leaves. The animals—a chaffinch, a whitethroat, swallows, and a thrush—are small song-birds. The only big image is an elm tree, and all we see of this is its trunk surrounded by bushes and its branches that hang down low. The combination of those images makes us feel as if England is a place where everything is on a small scale, unthreatening, and com-fortable. The only humans mentioned are children, and they along with the white flowers and young leaves and the little birds suggest an innocence, as if life in England were free of the complexities that plague grown-up life.

Contrasted to all of these images is the "gaudy melon-flower" that concludes the poem. From what we know of Robert Brown-ing's life, that flower is probably in Italy, but even without that knowledge we could guess that the speaker is in a semitropical locale where colors are brilliant, noises are loud, and the sun is blazing hot. If we think of the small, white pear blossom next to the colorful, big melon-flower, we might even detect some sexual connotations. If England is the place of childhood's prepubescent innocence, the semitropical place abroad is associated in the speaker's mind with sexual knowledge, perhaps even promiscuity.

The tropics themselves tend to have these connotations for people in colder climes, and Italy has long figured in the English imagination as a place where the staid, respectable English citizen can enjoy sensual pleasures. So the pattern of these concrete images—the generalizations that tie the specific images to one another—reveals an otherwise obscured theme in the poem.

It is especially important that you learn to track such patterns because they're working on your unconscious mind whether you know it or not. Even if you had not recognized the qualities that the images in "Home-Thoughts, from Abroad" have in common, on some level you would have been *feeling* England's innocence and youthful wholesomeness, and you would have sensed the corruption of the locale abroad. It is good to be able to recognize consciously these manipulations of your unconscious mind. Certainly, if you want to articulate how a poem affects you, you need to trace these patterns.

If you analyze the imagery of almost any poem, you're bound to find patterns like this. Obviously, you don't want to write out a column of images for every poem you read, nor should you. That would ruin the pleasure. But you should foster the habit of looking for these patterns. And for any poem you write about in an English class, you probably should write the images down.

Metaphors

A **metaphor** is a comparison. For example, "the ship plowed through the water" is a metaphor: a ship does not literally plow through water. The expression is a **figure of speech** that compares the way the ship's prow moves through water to the way a plow moves through soil. To interpret the metaphor, we imagine the work a plow does: it throws the earth up to the side in long ridges as it digs a straight, shallow furrow. The prow of the ship, then, must have been rolling up the water on either side in ridges higher than the level sea. And it must have left behind a shallow trough like a furrow in a plowed field.

Without even knowing it, your mind went through a shorthand version of this process when you first read the words "plowed through the water." In an instant, you pictured the water spurting up on either side of the ship's nose. More than likely, you skipped the step of picturing the plow in the earth. We've seen this metaphor so often in our lives that it has lost its ability to conjure up any comparison. The verb *plow* seems to have taken on a second literal meaning, so that it refers not only to what plows do but also to what prows do.

When a metaphor becomes so overused that it brings to our minds only one image rather than two, we call it a dead metaphor or a cliché. You could hardly utter a dozen words without using one. "The Yankees got slaughtered last night" and "I was just cruising home when out of nowhere this ambulance flies through a red light" and "I'm dying to get those tickets" all use metaphors. A baseball team's loss is compared to the butchering of cattle or swine; a car is compared to a boat; an ambulance is compared to an airplane; and a person's eagerness is compared to a fatal illness. But these metaphors might as well be literal, because they don't conjure up any figurative images anymore. *To be slaughtered* now literally means "to be beaten badly in a game." *To beat someone* is itself a dead metaphor: no one pictures one team punching or clubbing the other team into submission.

But new, fresh metaphors will conjure up *two* images in your mind. Take these famous lines from T. S. Eliot's "The Love Song of J. Alfred Prufrock":

> *Let us go then, you and I,*
> *When the evening is spread out against the sky*
> *Like a patient etherized upon a table[.]*

We see two images here: One is the evening sky (which is *literally* there in the poem). The other is a body anaesthetized and awaiting surgery (which is there in the poem *figuratively* but not literally). You might wonder how these two things could be compared. How can an evening be like a surgery patient? They seem to have nothing in common. By answering that question, you interpret the metaphor. Remember to ask the correct question: we're interested not in how a patient can be like a sky but in how a sky can be like a patient. The metaphor is about the literal term in the comparison, not about the figurative term.

So the first step is to think about the figurative image. What is an etherized patient like? An etherized patient is senseless, dulled to pain, horizontal, apparently lifeless though living, completely still though slightly breathing. Many of these ideas might apply to the evening sky. Perhaps the air is so still that there is only the slightest breath of wind or no wind at all. The clouds and the colors of twilight might stretch horizontally just above the horizon. There might not be any motion, not even a single bird, to suggest life.

We could develop the comparison even further by thinking about our associative responses to the image of the patient, even the emotions it arouses in us. We might recoil slightly from the image of the etherized patient as if it were something creepy. If we imagine the patient's cool, clammy, bloodless skin that's hardly more animate than a corpse's, we may get a difficult-to-define, unsavory feeling. Those are the feelings that the evening sky arouses in the speaker.

Some metaphors are easy to spot. Eliot's comparison is a **simile,** which is a metaphor that announces itself with the word *like* or *as* and is hard to miss. But some metaphors are so subtle that half the work of interpreting them is recognizing them in the first place. Take these lines from Eliot's poem: "And I have known the eyes already, known them all— / The eyes that fix you in a formulated phrase[.]" The speaker is remembering the way women look at him at tea parties: they "fix" him, which we know cannot be literally true. Even so, we might forget to ask, To what, exactly, are the eyes being compared? Have the eyes *repaired* the speaker? Have they *put him in a fix*? Or have they *fastened* him to something? In this case, the following lines leave no doubt: "And when I am formulated, sprawling on a pin, / When I am pinned and wriggling on the wall . . ." The eyes, then, are like a scientist fixing an insect specimen to a display with a needle. The woman's clever, withering phrase is the pin. And Prufrock, the speaker, is the not-yet-dead insect under scrutiny. This particular example is an **extended metaphor** because Eliot draws out the comparison over a few lines.

Symbols

A **symbol** is an object that represents something else, sometimes another object but more often an abstraction. For example, think about the Berlin Wall, which separated the Communist and democratic sections of the old German capital. It was a solid object, made of concrete and steel, but to Westerners it represented (among other things) the political repression for which the police states of Eastern Europe were notorious. After the European Communist governments fell, together East and West Germans attacked the wall with hammers and picks and anything that would chip away the concrete. By that time, the wall no longer functioned as a real barrier between East and West; nevertheless, it was an important symbolic target. Those who hammered at it symbolically attacked totalitarian governments and their policies of repression. As the citizens tore the wall down, they toppled the old regimes symbolically.

The Berlin Wall was a **conventional symbol:** its meaning derived from its special cultural context. Someone visiting Berlin from, say, Communist North Korea, who had been sheltered all her life from Western culture, would not understand its symbolic meaning. She would recognize it as a formidable barrier, for it was that *literally*. But she would not recognize its deeper meaning as a symbol of political repression. If that same person were to see thousands of ordinary people attacking the wall with sledgehammers, she'd wonder what was going on. It wouldn't make any sense to her. So a conventional symbol is a symbol that makes sense only within the context of the culture that authored it, so to speak.

Some conventional symbols are "authored." The Second Continental Congress decided on June 20, 1782, that the bald eagle would symbolize the United States. The board of directors of a new company adopts a logo, and immediately that symbol represents the company. But other conventional symbols seem to have been authored anonymously, as if the culture itself invented them. For example, if you saw a paddle-wheeled riverboat, you'd probably begin thinking about the antebellum American South. No one decided that the one would stand for the other; nevertheless, it does.

Another example is the rose. In North America and Great Britain, a red rose symbolizes love. But if you went to a town whose inhabitants had never read any Western literature, seen Hollywood movies, or heard of Hallmark cards, the citizens might look at a rose as they do a daffodil or tulip. The symbol is not universal: its meaning is a convention contrived by a particular population of people.

William Blake, whose cultural milieu overlaps somewhat with your own, counted on your knowing this when he wrote this poem:

The Sick Rose

O Rose, thou art sick.
The invisible worm
That flies in the night
In the howling storm

Has found out thy bed
Of crimson joy:
And his dark secret love
Does thy life destroy.

He also counted on your knowing that the rose—one white and the other red—represented the opposing factions in England's War of the Roses, and so he might have expected you to interpret the rose as the nation of England. If you're British or Canadian, you might be familiar with that symbolic association. If you're from the United States—whose culture overlaps less with Blake's—you might need to rely on a footnote, or you'd miss that association entirely.

Your ability to recognize conventional symbols is exactly proportional to your familiarity with a culture. You are probably adept at recognizing symbols that arise out of general North American culture, but the symbols of particular subcultures in America might escape your notice. And many of the poems in this book come from outside North America—many from England, a few from South America, Africa, Wales, and Ireland. Certainly, North Americans share a lot of culture with these continents and countries, but there might be some things that are symbols in, say, England that are not symbols in North America. For example, Dover means something to the English, as discussed above. It brings to mind newlyweds the way Niagara Falls might for Americans, and its tall chalk cliffs symbolize England the way the Statue of Liberty, which greets people arriving in New York Harbor, symbolizes the United States. But Dover may not mean anything to you. Likewise, quite a few of these poems were written generations ago, and objects that might have carried symbolic meaning three hundred years ago no longer do. In this case, only familiarity with the culture will help you recognize conventional symbols and their meanings. If you haven't lived in a culture, you might have seen enough movies or TV programs or read enough books or listened to enough music to recognize its symbols. Or you might study the culture or learn about it in a footnote. Otherwise, you'll need to treat these conventional symbols as if they were literary symbols, which I discuss below.

Other symbols are **universal.** They tend to carry the same meaning no matter the culture. The most obvious example is the sunrise. From North Korea to North Carolina, the sunrise symbolizes beginnings, fresh starts, new births. Similarly, the sunset will represent endings or death just about wherever you go. These are natural phenomena—rain, drought, a dense forest, the ocean's depths—whose traits seem to suggest their symbolic meanings. Look, for example, at William Butler Yeats's "The Lake Isle of Innisfree" (page 596). The island represents isolation not only in Yeats's native Ireland but the world round.

But universal symbols might go beyond the things of nature. Some poets—including Yeats—think that certain objects, even made-made objects, communicate symbolically to all humans. Yeats believed that the image of the Sphinx in his poem "The Second Coming" was such an object: an image residing in the universal *spiritus mundi*, the "spirit of the world," a repository similar to Carl Jung's "collective unconscious," to which we all have recourse, if we only dig deep enough into ourselves. Sigmund Freud's influential book *Interpretation of Dreams* is based on a similar concept: that certain objects carry the same symbolic meaning no matter who you are or where you grew up.

To come back to Blake's poem "The Sick Rose," we can detect at least one universal symbol. In cultures that bury their dead, worms (for obvious reasons) often bring to mind our mortality. So the worm that invades the rose's flower bed and attacks its roots might represent the diseases to which all living things are susceptible; or it might represent the aging process that inevitably blasts the bloom of youth and ultimately leads to death, what poets and philosophers sometimes call mutability. In the post-Freudian age, we might even say that the worm calls to mind a penis, in which case the poem is about a woman losing her "innocence" or virginity, an event that Blake likens to the progress of disease. I've found that students are admirably skeptical of such interpretations, but in this case the words "crimson joy," which might call to mind the bleeding typically associated with the loss of virginity, lend some credibility to the Freudian interpretation.

A third type of symbol is a **literary symbol,** which is an object that represents something else only within the context of a particular work of literature. Outside the poem, the object does not mean what it does inside the poem. Literary symbols, then, are not invented by nature or by any collective unconscious, nor by a culture. They are invented by a writer.

You need a good deal of ingenuity to recognize that an object in a poem not only is its literal self but also represents something else. There are a few clues you can count on to help you. If the title of a poem is a literal object in the poem, you can assume it also symbolizes something. That is the case in "Dover Beach" (Dover represents something), and it's true in most poems. For instance, the title of Elizabeth Bishop's poem "The Fish" tips us off to the fish's importance. We should expect the fish to carry meaning beyond the literal level of the poem. Right away you should be asking yourself, What could the fish represent? William Blake's "The Lamb" and "The Tyger" also call attention to important symbols.

For the most part, it is impossible to teach someone how to recognize which objects are symbolic and which are not. You have to trust your gut feelings. If you find your attention drawn to an object, if you suspect that something might have more than literal significance, you're probably right. The text itself will call attention to its literary symbols: listen to what the poem tells you. For example, "Dover Beach" tells us that the sea is a symbol. It appears in the first line of the poem ("The sea is calm tonight"), we hear its sound throughout the first stanza, and it figures again in the second stanza. The poem calls so much attention to the sea that, in a second or third read through the poem, we should guess that the sea is there to represent something other than its literal self. But what?

The second task in interpreting a literary symbol is to figure out what the object represents. Again, you have to trust your instincts. Read the poem a few times, and an idea will more than likely come to you: the object represents the speaker's love; it represents death; it represents the American dream; it represents hope. Usually, a symbol represents abstractions: love, death, dreams, hopes. And often it represents a range of things, not just one.

To come back to the "Dover Beach" example: we wonder, What could the sea represent? The speaker makes it easy for us when he says, "The Sea of Faith / Was once, too, at the full, and round earth's shore[.]" We know that it represents "faith." But we might further ask, Faith in what? Some possibilities: faith in God; faith in political institutions; faith in traditional mores and values; perhaps all of these. We'll have to see if any or all of these abstractions work in the poem.

Be prepared to revise your hypotheses. If you try to interpret an object symbolically and it just does not seem to work, maybe you were wrong. To paraphrase Sigmund Freud, sometimes a cigar is just a cigar. Or maybe you were wrong about what the object represents. Keep revising and refining your ideas until you think you've got it exactly right.

You can tell if you've got it right by interpreting the **symbolic action.** Look at what happens to the symbol in the poem; the same thing happens to what the symbol represents. Think of the symbol of the rose again. The morning after two college sophomores' first date, the young man gets up at dawn to bring a dozen roses to the apartment door of the woman. He knocks on the door and runs downstairs and around to the parking lot, where he can see without being seen. The young woman opens the door, finds the roses at her feet, picks them up, smells them. She knows that roses symbolize love, so she can interpret the symbolic action: The guy likes her a lot. By leaving these flowers at her door, he is offering his esteem, his affection, even his love. In short, he has given her his heart. Now the young man, from the parking lot, watches her pick up the flowers, smell them, think for a moment about what they mean. He sees her toss them on the ground. He watches in horror as she stomps them. She grinds the petals with her heel. She's grinding more than the flowers: she's stomping his love into the ground. And we know that he won't be calling her for a second date.

So interpreting a literary symbol takes three steps (the first two steps are automatic with universal and conventional symbols):

1. Identify which object(s) you think might be symbols.
2. Establish what the object(s) represent(s).
3. Interpret the symbolic action.

For example, let's consider the symbolic action of the sea in "Dover Beach." The tide is going out, and the speaker hears a note of sadness in its "long withdrawing roar." Similarly, then, faith is withdrawing from Europe, and its departure leaves people in misery. All of the earlier possibilities—faith in God, in political institutions, in traditional values—work in this context. According to Arnold, periods of faith and faithlessness go in cycles, like the tides, and the mid-nineteenth century was a low point in the cycle.

Structure

Prosody

Prosody is the study of poetry's **rhythms.** We can describe the rhythms of a poem by scanning its **meter.** To **scan** a poem, first read it aloud two or three times, until you can feel yourself using the rhythm dictated by the words. Then mark the stressed syllables by putting an ictus (´) above them. Mark the unstressed syllables with a mora (˘). A scanned line might look like this one from Shakespeare's Sonnet 73:

˘ ´ ˘ ´ ˘ ´ ˘ ´ ˘ ´

That time of year thou mayst in me behold

Once you've identified where the stresses fall, you should see a pattern. In this case, the pattern is unstressed/stressed. This repeated unit of unstressed/stressed syllables is called a **foot.** Feet are marked with slashes (/):

˘ ˊ / ˘ ˊ / ˘ ˊ / ˘ ˊ / ˘ ˊ
That time / of year / thou mayst / in me / behold

You can scan just about any line of poetry in English if you know six different kinds of feet:

iamb:	(˘ ˊ)	as in "the book"
trochee:	(ˊ ˘)	as in "printer"
anapest:	(˘ ˘ ˊ)	as in "intercede"
dactyl:	(ˊ ˘ ˘)	as in "willowy"
spondee:	(ˊ ˊ)	as in "big truck"
pyrrhic:	(˘ ˘)	as in "of the"

So the line from Sonnet 73 has five iambs. Our shorthand designation for lines of five iambs is "iambic pentameter." If the stresses had been reversed, the line would have been "trochaic pentameter." The names for the line lengths are

one foot:	monometer
two feet:	dimeter
three feet:	trimeter
four feet:	tetrameter
five feet:	pentameter
six feet:	hexameter
seven feet:	heptameter

By combining the names of the feet and the line lengths, you can describe the rhythm—the meter—of just about any line of poetry.

But don't get the idea that poets are thinking about spondees and iambs and heptameter when they compose their poems. Nearly all good poets know how to measure their lines, just as carpenters know how to measure the wood they work with. Yet poetry is unlike carpentry in this way: you do not measure the lines before you put them together. You do not work from a plan. Poets don't sit down and say to themselves, "All right, to complete this line, I need three more iambs." Poets trust their own ears to get the lines to sound right. In revision, they might scan their lines and tinker with the stresses with some conscious purpose. But for the most part, they just listen to the music. Prosody is a way of measuring lines *after* they have been composed.

Further, poetry violates regular rhythm all the time. For example, you will never find a poem written entirely in iambic pentameter. If you ever came across such a poem, say a sonnet, with fourteen lines of iambic pentameter, you'd be reading a hundred and forty straight syllables with the unstressed/stressed rhythm. It would sound like a metronome. Its music would be the unrelenting, steady beat of a drum, which is fine if you're marching, but otherwise it's pretty boring. Instead, the poet will substitute a spondee or a trochee or a pyrrhic here and there, or maybe an anapest, for a few iambs. For example, here is how we might scan the first four lines of Shakespeare's Sonnet 73:

˘   ʹ   ˘   ʹ   ˘   ʹ   ˘   ʹ   ˘   ʹ

That time / of year / thou mayst / in me / behold

˘   ʹ   ˘   ʹ   ˘   ʹ   ˘   ʹ   ˘   ʹ

When yel / low leaves, / or none, / or few, / do hang

˘   ʹ   ˘   ʹ   ˘   ʹ   ˘   ʹ   ˘   ʹ

Upon / those boughs / which shake / against / the cold,

ʹ   ʹ   ˘   ʹ   ˘   ʹ   ˘   ʹ   ʹ   ʹ

Bare ru / ined choirs, / where late / the sweet / birds sang.

Depending on how you read the poem, some of these lines could be scanned differently. Does "those boughs" have two stressed syllables? Is "which shake" a spondee? It's not certain. But the first and last feet of the fourth line are definitely spondees. It is completely unnatural to say "bare" without stressing it, just as it is impossible to say "birds" without a stress. By the fourth line of the poem, Shakespeare has disrupted the rhythm he laid down in the first two lines. Usually, the disruptions happen much sooner. Sometimes a poet disrupts the rhythm so often that it's hard to find a single line with a string of perfectly regular feet.

With so many disruptions to the rhythm, you might at first find it hard to scan poetry. Consider this tip: most monosyllabic nouns will take a stress, just as most articles (*a, an, the*) and one-syllable prepositions (*of, in, on,* and so on) will be unstressed. After scanning a few poems, you'll begin to get a feel for such shortcuts. But the best advice is to read the poem aloud again and again, and mark where you find yourself placing stresses. Listen for the rhythm. Mark where the stresses are trying to fall even if the effect doesn't quite work. More than likely, you'll find a lot of iambs. At least four out of five poems written in English use iambs as the basic foot. But whether you discover that the underlying rhythm is iambs or trochees or anapests, mark the whole poem as if it were perfectly regular. (Note: some poems might combine types of feet. The basic rhythm of a poem might begin each line with three iambs and conclude with an anapest.) Your goal at this stage is to recognize such regularities.

Then go back and find the spots that disrupt the rhythmic pattern. Properly mark those feet. The point to scanning a poem is not to figure out what the underlying rhythm is. Knowing that a poem is written in iambic pentameter doesn't help us understand it at all. We analyze a poem's regular rhythm only so we can figure out where it breaks the rhythm. In other words, we scan Shakespeare's sonnet not to see the iambs, which are all over the place, but to find the spondees.

What's the point of finding those irregularities? That's the toughest question to answer. It is not always possible to link such rhythmic irregularities to the meaning of a poem. Who can say with any confidence what the effect is on a reader of the spondee opening line 4 of Shakespeare's Sonnet 73?

Bare ru / ined choirs, / where late / the sweet / birds sang.

All we can say for sure is that such irregularities call attention to themselves. They add a bit of umph to the feet that contain them. The barrenness of those choirs might stick in our mind a little more emphatically than if we heard about them in another iamb.

Surely, the rhythms of a poem contribute to its tone, but, again, it is a delicate business to claim something like this: "the two spondees of line 4, following as they do on three lines of regular iambic pentameter, give us a sense of the echoing hollowness of the silent church ruins described in the line." The images convey this melancholic tone more ably than the rhythm. As you begin your study of poetry, then, you should make only the slightest claims about how the meter of a poem contributes to its meaning. Probably the best use of prosody is to help you compose your own poetry. It is the basic tools of the art—the brushstrokes and paints, if you will, of poetry. It is the most physical part of poetry.

Rhyme and Stanzas

Rhyme is the repetition of sound in different words. Usually, the repeated sound is in the end of the word. *Round, sound, ground,* and *profound* all rhyme. If a rhyme is in the middle of a line, it's called an **internal rhyme.**

Poets often use end rhymes to group the lines of their poems. We use a simple system of letters to describe the rhymes. The last sound of the first line is assigned the letter *a*, as are all subsequent lines ending with the same sound. Each line that introduces a new end-sound is assigned the next letter of the alphabet. So the **rhyme scheme** for the opening of Emily Dickinson's "Because I could not stop for Death—" looks like this:

Because I could not stop for Death—	a
He kindly stopped for me—	b
The Carriage held but just Ourselves—	c
And Immortality.	b
We slowly drove—He knew no haste	d
And I had put away	e
My labor and my leisure too,	f
For His Civility—	e

Away is not an exact rhyme for *civility,* so it's called an **off rhyme**. A **feminine rhyme** is a two-syllable rhyme with the stress falling on the next-to-last syllable, as in these lines from Anne Bradstreet's "A Letter to Her Husband":

> *So many steps, head from the heart to sever,*
> *If but a neck, soon should we be together.*

The end rhymes give a poem structure by dividing it into groups of lines, which are typically called **stanzas.** Notice in Dickinson's poem that the rhymes gather the lines into groups of four. Poets usually indicate the divisions between stanzas with a blank line on the page, but even if you don't see the text of a poem, when you hear it read aloud, the rhymes will tell you where each stanza ends. Like meter, rhymes establish a rhythm in our minds.

Often the literal meaning of the poem will divide into sections just as the stanzas do. It is not surprising, for example, that each of the stanzas in Dickinson's poem ends by finishing a sentence. In this way, the rhyme scheme will help you analyze a poem because it divides the poem into smaller coherent parts. Each stanza usually develops a single thought. Likewise, the rhyming end of each line usually mirrors a strong grammatical pause, as the ends do in Bradstreet's poems.

Just as with meter, you should be especially interested in irregularities in rhyme. In Dickinson's poem, for example, the rhyme suggests that we ought to pause after *away* in the sixth line, but the grammar of the sentence compels us to hurry on to line 7. Poets often use this technique. For example, Shakespeare disrupts our expectations in the opening lines of Sonnet 73:

> *That time of year thou mayst in me behold*
> *When yellow leaves, or none, or few, do hang*
> *Upon those boughs which shake against the cold,*

The first time you read the poem, you expect the rhyme at the end of the third line to mirror a strong grammatical pause. In that case, *cold* seems to be a noun rounding out the clause concerned with the tree boughs: the boughs seem to shake against the cold of winter. But the next line suggests that *cold* might be an adjective describing

> *Bare ruined choirs, where late the sweet birds sang.*

The line misled us: it does not designate a significant grammatical pause. When a line seems to pour over its natural boundary and spill into the next line, we call it **enjambment**. In this case, the confusion caused by the enjambment draws our attention to the image of the ruined choir, just as the spondee does. (An alternative reading does treat *cold* as a noun, in which case the bare ruined choirs are not literally the ruins of a church or abbey but a metaphoric reference to the leafless boughs. These competing interpretations depend upon whether or not you think the third and fourth lines are enjambed.)

Some subgenres of lyric poetry have fairly strict rules about rhyme schemes. By convention, certain rhyme schemes and certain stanzaic patterns have come to be associated with particular subjects. So stanzaic forms are linked to a poem's meaning by convention. Ballads, sonnets, and odes, each of which has a set of standard subjects, are defined by their stanzaic form.

Subgenres

Some poems have so many elements in common that they have created their own genres within the larger **genre** of lyric poems. Each of these **subgenres** calls up in the reader's mind certain expectations, just as the opening credits of a TV show will usually indicate whether you're watching a sitcom or a drama. When you recognize the subgenre, you expect certain things. The ballad, for example, has its own grammar, its own conventions. Below are descriptions of the subgenres that appear in this anthology, accompanied by some of the elements you should expect when you encounter each one.

Ballads

Ballads are the most popular form of lyric poetry. They were first sung in the city streets, at folk gatherings in the country, and at the fire's side. Now, most popular styles of music use ballads: rock, blues, pop, and particularly country. Ballads tell stories in short, terse narratives. The classic **ballad stanza** is four lines long with a rhyme scheme of *abab;* the *a* lines are tetrameter, and the *b* lines are trimeter. But just about any narrative lyric with four-line stanzas would be called a ballad today.

Dramatic Monologues

A **dramatic monologue** is a poem that seems as if it is a speech lifted right out of a play. It generally has one or a few long stanzas, usually unrhymed or in couplets, though the rhyme scheme can vary. Almost always in a dramatic monologue, the poet's beliefs do not exactly correspond to the speaker's beliefs. Robert Browning's "My Last Duchess" is a dramatic monologue, as is Alfred, Lord Tennyson's "Ulysses."

Elegies

Elegy used to designate poems written in alternating lines of hexameter and pentameter, usually on the theme of love. But a few hundred years ago, the genre began to deal exclusively with death. Sometimes an elegy might be a lament for a particular dead person, sometimes a complaint about mortality in general, often both. Though today elegies have no particular meter or rhyme, typically they are longish, meditative poems. Thomas Gray's "Elegy Written in a Country Churchyard" fits this description, as does W. H. Auden's "In Memory of W. B. Yeats," though that poem's stanzaic form suggests it is an irregular ode. Ben Jonson's two poems "On My First Daughter" and "On My First Son," which are short enough to be engraved on tombstones, are epitaphs rather than elegies.

Occasional Poems

An **occasional poem** is any poem written in response to a specific event: a death, an inauguration, a military victory or defeat, a marriage, and so on. Lynne Bryer's "The Way," which commemorates Nelson Mandela's release from prison, is an occasional poem.

Odes

John Keats's **odes** in this volume are modeled on the odes of the Roman poet Horace. These Horatian odes usually meditate on fairly abstract concepts or on objects that symbolize something abstract.

They use colloquial diction, and typically they are calm statements of praise or judgment. The stanzas can follow any invention of the poet, but every stanza must have the same meter and rhyme scheme.

Auden's "In Memory of W. B. Yeats" is an irregular ode: a meditation on some serious subject in stanzas of irregular length and rhyme scheme. This irregularity allows the tone of each stanza to mimic the varying mood and thoughts of the speaker, as if he were spontaneously thinking aloud in the poem.

Sonnets

Traditionally, the **sonnet** has been used to express the feelings that a beloved arouses in the speaker. Often sonnets come in sequences, or "cycles," that chronicle the speaker's varying emotions. The sentiment expressed in one poem might be contradicted in the very next poem, just as the moods of love can change quickly. Often the speaker's love is unrequited. William Shakespeare's, Elizabeth Barrett Browning's, and Edna St. Vincent Millay's sonnets in this anthology are from cycles of love poems.

In the Romantic era especially, but also in other ages, the sonnet has been used for different purposes, such as political commentary. Sonnets on such themes are usually not part of a sequence but stand alone.

There are two types of sonnets: the **Italian (or Petrarchan) sonnet,** and the **English (or Shakespearean) sonnet.** They each have fourteen lines, but the rhyme schemes divide the lines differently. An English sonnet has this rhyme scheme: *ababcdcdefefgg*. As a result, the poem is divided into four sections: three **quatrains** (stanzas of four lines) and a concluding **couplet** (two rhymed lines). An Italian sonnet has this rhyme scheme: *abbaabbacdecde*. As a result, the poem divides into an **octave** (a stanza of eight lines) and a **sestet** (a stanza of six lines). Sometimes the rhyme scheme of the sestet will vary, but an Italian sonnet always divides in two between the eighth and ninth lines. Recognizing these divisions, whether in an English or in an Italian sonnet, will help you interpret the poem: analyze it section by section.

Conclusion

After this long discussion of the parts of poems, of stanzaic forms and feminine rhymes and iambs, you may find yourself wondering if the pleasure of poetry has been ruined for you. Does analyzing poetry mean you can't enjoy it anymore? In a sense, Wordsworth *was* right in his poem "The Tables Turned": we do murder to dissect. The casual fan enjoys a figure skater's grace and agility with a simplicity and awe that the afficionado can only remember. The unlearned ear listens to a jazz ensemble with an innocence that the trained ear can never recapture. It is the same with poetry. As you discover how poems work, as you grow more adept at analysis, as you master the art of interpretation, something is lost.

But the loss is more than recovered by a different pleasure. The afficionado recognizes a thousand subtleties the casual observer can never notice, and each of those subtleties might occasion some analysis. The casual fan views a skater's jump, and her appreciation amounts to the awestruck phrase: "How can they do that?" The afficionado, who *knows* how the skater can do that, who knows the names of particular jumps, who knows the strength each requires and the technique, who can recognize the slight defect in the landing and notice the skater's smooth recovery, can appreciate each subtlety in the performance and the sum of them all. The learned observer's reaction is, perhaps, less pure but more profound.

But the most ardent claims on this regard cannot convince you of anything. Study, analyze, reread, recite like an afficionado of poetry, and confirm it for yourself.

Note on Dates

After each poem, we cite the date of first book publication on the right; in some instances, this date is followed by the date of a revised version for which the author was responsible. In a few instances (when the information may be relevant to the reading of a poem), we cite the date of composition on the left.

Anonymous

> "Western Wind" and "Sir Patrick Spens," two anonymous poems, were written in the early-sixteenth and mid-seventeenth centuries, respectively. "Western Wind," a short lyric, was originally set to music and was later incorporated into Mass services, despite its seemingly secular subject matter. "Sir Patrick Spens" is a ballad, a subgenre of lyric poetry that tells a story in a compact, yet detailed narrative. It recounts what may be the true experience of Spens, a Scottish nobleman sent against his will by the king to deliver a princess to her bridegroom in Norway. All members of the escort party drowned on the way home.

Western Wind

Western wind, when will thou blow,
    The small rain down can rain?
Christ, if my love were in my arms
    And I in my bed again!

Sir Patrick Spens

1

The king sits in Dumferling town,
    Drinking the blude-reid wine:
"O whar will I get guid sailor,
    To sail this ship of mine?"

2

Up and spak an eldern knicht,   5
    Sat at the king's richt knee:
"Sir Patrick Spens is the best sailor
    That sails upon the sea."

3

The king has written a braid[1] letter
   And signed it wi' his hand,   10
And sent it to Sir Patrick Spens,
   Was walking on the sand.

4

The first line that Sir Patrick read,
   A loud lauch lauched he;
The next line that Sir Patrick read,   15
   The tear blinded his ee.

5

"O wha is this has done this deed,
   This ill deed done to me,
To send me out this time o' the year,
   To sail upon the sea?   20

6

"Mak haste, mak haste, my mirry men all,
   Our guid ship sails the morn."
"O say na sae, my master dear,
   For I fear a deadly storm.

7

"Late, late yestre'en I saw the new moon   25
   Wi' the auld moon in hir arm,
And I fear, I fear, my dear master,
   That we will come to harm."

---

1. Broad, i.e., long.

8

O our Scots nobles were richt laith
  To weet their cork-heeled shoon,
But lang or a' the play were played
  Their hats they swam aboon.[2]   30

9

O lang, lang may their ladies sit,
  Wi' their fans into their hand,
Or ere they see Sir Patrick Spens   35
  Come sailing to the land.

10

O lang, lang may the ladies stand
  Wi' their gold kems in their hair,
Waiting for their ain dear lords,
  For they'll see them na mair.   40

11

Half o'er, half o'er to Aberdour
  It's fifty fadom deep,
And there lies guid Sir Patrick Spens
  Wi' the Scots lords at his feet.

1765

---

2. I.e., their hats swam above (them).

John Agard
1945–

Agard was born in Guyana, which was once a British colony on the Caribbean coast of South America. Like most Guyanans, Agard descended from black slaves imported by whites to work the rich mines and plantations. In this poem, Agard writes in the local creole dialect, and you might consider the degree to which the speaker is "putting it on," so to speak.

Palm Tree King

Because I come from the West Indies
certain people in England seem to think
I is a expert on palm trees

So not wanting to sever dis link
with me native roots (know what ah mean?)   5
or to disappoint dese culture vulture
I does smile cool as seabreeze

and say to dem
which specimen
you interested in   10
cause you talking
to the right man
I is palm tree king
I know palm tree history
like de palm o me hand   15
In fact me navel string
bury under a palm tree

If you think de queen could wave
you ain't see nothing yet
till you see the Roystonea Regia   20
—that is the royal palm—
with she crown of leaves

waving calm-calm
over the blue Caribbean carpet
nearly 100 feet of royal highness   25

But let we get down to business
Tell me what you want to know
How tall a palm tree does grow?
What is the biggest coconut I ever see?
What is the average length of the leaf?   30

Don't expect me to be brief
cause palm tree history
is a long-long story

Anyway why you so interested
in length and circumference?   35
That kind of talk so ordinary
That don't touch the essence
of palm tree mystery
That is no challenge
to a palm tree historian like me   40

If you insist on statistics
why you don't pose a question
with some mathematical profundity?

Ask me something more tricky
like if a American tourist with a camera   45
take 9 minutes to climb a coconut tree
how long a English tourist without a camera
would take to climb the same coconut tree?

That is problem pardner
Now ah coming harder   50

If 6 straw hat
and half a dozen bikini
multiply by the same number of coconut tree

equal one postcard
how many square miles of straw hat   55
you need to make a tourist industry?

That is problem pardner
Find the solution
and you got a revolution

But before you say anything   60
let I palm tree king
give you dis warning
Ah want de answer in metric
it kind of rhyme with tropic
Besides it sound more exotic   65

                              1985—

Paul Allen
1945—

> *"The Man with the Hardest Belly" is a narrative poem, so we read*
> *it with some of the same tools we use to read a story, looking for a*
> *conflict and resolution. It is also a study in irony. Readers, as well as*
> *the characters in the poem, view the preacher and his sermon dif-*
> *ferently than he expects to be viewed. Thus his similarities to Christ*
> *are undercut. But in the last three lines of the poem we discover a*
> *possible conflict and the role the preacher played in resolving the*
> *conflict. With these last three lines in mind, you might reread the*
> *poem and consider the irony once again.*

The Man with the Hardest Belly

I

THE MAN WITH THE HARDEST BELLY knows God
compensates his loss of limbs—legs

to knee, nub arms—with a gift
to titillate the congregations when he is delivered
from Ocala in his motor home to call us to Christ.   5
This handsome chunk of what was left
after he'd been shucked, he says, at 14
found God by serving himself on our tables
if we had canned corn at all in 19 and 55.

We are not members here. As Dad said, we   10
have our own faith. But someone spirit-filled
made Mother promise. So we're here cross-legged
on the cool ground at the river,
and my father is chosen. The Youth Director
is chosen. The man high up in Amway   15
is chosen. The three of them hang
THE MAN WITH THE HARDEST BELLY over the first branch
of the maple like a sandbag on the levee.
He pops his torso, flips, chins
to the next branch, flips, grabs a limb   20
with his thighs. Left nub for leverage,
he hooks another V with the back
of his head, walks on stumps up the trunk
to the next limb, flips to his belly, bends,
flips, holds with his teeth. He maneuvers   25
like something stained and mating
toward the top of our slide in godless biology,
or like the little dots we see inside our own eyes
on days we're morose. The thing
we've come to watch we can't watch   30
directly as he works toward the sun. The higher
he goes, the more we must look down to save
our eyes. We pull grass, look up and squint
to check his progress, kill an ant climbing our shoe.
Some stand to change the angle,   35
to keep him closer to the shaded cars.
Settling high, balanced and swaying, he preaches
from the texts painted on his motor home
under the faded "DOUBT AND DELIVERY."

II

. . . so look with me now at Genesis, whole people, Genesis 15:1–6.   40
Abram. Abram was a cripple in bed, had no standing among
men. Listen to me, had no standing among men, praise God, and
Moses, who said no, not me, not me, God gave Moses what he
needed. And Joshua at their first real trial? Joshua didn't think he
could do nothing. Joshua 7:1–10. I thank God my arms and legs   45
went to your soft tummies in '55. I was born again in that
shucking machine, look at my belly, my hard and strong belly, you
could park a truck on my belly praise God, God gives you what
you need. I need a strong belly and a lithe neck to climb trees and
show you the Holy Spirit at work, and show you the   50
compensations of our precious Lord. Praise you, Lord. The Holy
Spirit turns my pages for me. Look at Joshua splashing dirt up in
his face. I'm here to tell you people there's no dirt in my face, no
Lord. And Gideon. It's right there in your book. Judges 6:1–14.
What does God say to that worthless garment of feces? (Excuse me,   55
ladies, but the compensations of God is nothing to be delicate
about.) Says to Gideon, go in your power. Go in your power.
Listen to me now: Go in your power and save my people. Read it.
Isn't that what it says? Your power. Don't look at me, I know I'm
pretty. Look at your book, look at your own Holy Word. Now   60
examine, if you will, First Corinthians 10:13. See? God won't give
you nothing wrong without a correlational power to get out of it.
. . . Jesus himself, his wonderment self, take this cup from my lips,
listen now, take this cup from my lips, take this cup. . . .

III

We pull off the road to let the other cars by.   65
The Youth Director finds a wide place.
And the man high up in Amway finds a wide place.
The three of us wait, our hazard lights blinking,
while the born again wave and the kids shout
from their windows that Jesus is the One   70
and fathers honk (Honk If You Love Jesus).

My father nods occasionally. My sister starts
it. We are arguing about whether
THE MAN WITH THE HARDEST BELLY crawls on all
four nubs around the rooms of his scriptural   75
motor home, or slithers like something run over.
Crawls. Slithers. My father hushes us. My sister hits
me, says, "For unto you is born *a child*." I hit
my sister: "Let the women keep silent
in the Chevrolet." My mother has had enough.   80
She separates us. We aren't to speak. We aren't
to utter a peep. Each of us must look out our own window.

IV

The cars are thinning. We can hear the hazards now.
The road is dark and the dust is settling.
"I told her we'd go, and we went," my mother says.   85
"I told you we'd come, and we came," my father says.
"I thought it a bit much, though," she says, "when
he stood on his perch, spread those arms
and screamed, 'Nail me. Nail me.' "
"Me too," my father says, "nails wouldn't work."   90
My mother is looking at him. He says,
"Toggle bolts might work."
"Go help him down," my mother says, "and let's go home."

My father joins the other two on the road. They walk
back toward the river. My mother tells us it will   95
turn cool; we don't need to bathe when we get home,
but we do need to wash our feet. My father appears.
He eases us between the Youth Director and the man
high up in Amway. When we're on the main road
and the others have turned off, my mother says,   100
"I thought we'd have your mother over tomorrow.
Remind me to get a ham out when we get home."
"And corn?" my father says. "Whatever," she says.

V

Tonight down the cold upstairs hall we hear
them laughing, my mother and father.   105
Tonight we hear them making love again.

1997

Matthew Arnold
1822–1888

> *Because Dover is the spot on the English coast closest to France,*
> *newlyweds often would spend their wedding night there before sail-*
> *ing for the Continent, and some evidence indicates that Arnold first*
> *drafted this poem on his honeymoon in 1851. The poem was not*
> *published until 1867, so it made its debut in the midst of the reli-*
> *gious doubts fomented by Darwin's* Origin of Species *(1859). In the*
> *wake of what he considered religion's failure, Arnold imagined that*
> *poetry would do the work religion no longer could.*

Dover Beach

The sea is calm tonight.
The tide is full, the moon lies fair
Upon the straits; on the French coast the light
Gleams and is gone; the cliffs of England stand,
Glimmering and vast, out in the tranquil bay.   5
Come to the window, sweet is the night-air!
Only, from the long line of spray
Where the sea meets the moon-blanched land,
Listen! you hear the grating roar
Of pebbles which the waves draw back, and fling,   10
At their return, up the high strand,
Begin, and cease, and then again begin,
With tremulous cadence slow, and bring
The eternal note of sadness in.

Sophocles long ago   15
Heard it on the Aegean, and it brought
Into his mind the turbid ebb and flow
Of human misery; we
Find also in the sound a thought,
Hearing it by this distant northern sea.   20

The Sea of Faith
Was once, too, at the full, and round earth's shore
Lay like the folds of a bright girdle furled.
But now I only hear
Its melancholy, long withdrawing roar,   25
Retreating, to the breath
Of the night-wind, down the vast edges drear
And naked shingles¹ of the world.

Ah, love, let us be true
To one another! for the world, which seems   30
To lie before us like a land of dreams,
So various, so beautiful, so new,
Hath really neither joy, nor love, nor light,
Nor certitude, nor peace, nor help for pain;
And we are here as on a darkling plain   35
Swept with confused alarms of struggle and flight,
Where ignorant armies clash by night.

                                    1867

---

1. Beaches of smooth pebbles.

Margaret Atwood
1939–

> *"You Fit into Me" is the first poem in Atwood's* Power Politics *(1971).*
> *This book tells the story of a relationship between a female speaker*
> *and her male lover, who is the audience. As it follows the pair going*
> *to the movies, going out to dinner, doing all the things courting cou-*
> *ples do,* Power Politics *demythologizes the romance of domestic love.*
> *The book's title echoes that of Kate Millett's* Sexual Politics *(1970), a*
> *landmark volume that demonstrates that political power is exercised*
> *through domestic and romantic relations between men and women.*

You Fit into Me

you fit into me
like a hook into an eye

a fish hook
an open eye

1971

W. H. (Wystan Hugh) Auden
1907–1973

> *Auden, a political liberal and homosexual, wrote "Musée des Beaux*
> *Arts" (Museum of Fine Arts) while staying in Paris in December 1938.*
> *He believed that Western democracies were doing nothing as fascists in*
> *Spain, Germany, and Italy violently oppressed communists, homosexu-*
> *als, Jews, and others. The first stanza describes Pieter Brueghel's paint-*
> *ing* The Massacre of the Innocents, *which depicts Herod's attempt to*
> *kill the infant Jesus by slaughtering all young Jewish children. The sec-*
> *ond stanza refers to Brueghel's* The Fall of Icarus, *in which that myth-*
> *ical figure, who flew too near the sun wearing wings of feathers and*
> *wax, falls from the sky in a corner of the painting, almost unnoticed.*
> *In early 1939, Auden wrote "In Memory of W. B. Yeats" to commemo-*
> *rate the death of the Irish poet. The poem surprised Auden's contempo-*
> *raries because it seems to declare that poetry cannot change society.*

Musée des Beaux Arts

About suffering they were never wrong,
The Old Masters: how well they understood
Its human position; how it takes place
While someone else is eating or opening a window or just
    walking dully along;
How, when the aged are reverently, passionately waiting   5
For the miraculous birth, there always must be
Children who did not specially want it to happen, skating
On a pond at the edge of the wood:
They never forgot
That even the dreadful martyrdom must run its course   10
Anyhow in a corner, some untidy spot
Where the dogs go on with their doggy life and the torturer's
    horse
Scratches its innocent behind on a tree.

In Brueghel's *Icarus*, for instance: how everything turns away
Quite leisurely from the disaster; the ploughman may   15
Have heard the splash, the forsaken cry,
But for him it was not an important failure; the sun shone
As it had to on the white legs disappearing into the green
Water; and the expensive delicate ship that must have seen
Something amazing, a boy falling out of the sky,
Had somewhere to get to and sailed calmly on.

                                    1938

In Memory of W. B. Yeats

   (d. Jan. 1939)

                   I

He disappeared in the dead of winter:
The brooks were frozen, the airports almost deserted,
And snow disfigured the public statues;

The mercury sank in the mouth of the dying day.
What instruments we have agree   5
The day of his death was a dark cold day.

Far from his illness
The wolves ran on through the evergreen forests,
The peasant river was untempted by the fashionable quays;
By mourning tongues   10
The death of the poet was kept from his poems.

But for him it was his last afternoon as himself,
An afternoon of nurses and rumours;
The provinces of his body revolted,
The squares of his mind were empty,   15
Silence invaded the suburbs,
The current of his feeling failed: he became his admirers.

Now he is scattered among a hundred cities
And wholly given over to unfamiliar affections;
To find his happiness in another kind of wood   20
And be punished under a foreign code of conscience.
The words of a dead man
Are modified in the guts of the living.[1]

But in the importance and noise of to-morrow
When the brokers are roaring like beasts on the floor of the
    Bourse,[2]   25
And the poor have the sufferings to which they are fairly
    accustomed,
And each in the cell of himself is almost convinced of his
    freedom,
A few thousand will think of this day
As one thinks of a day when one did something slightly
    unusual.

---

1. Auden suggests here that after death poets live only through their poems; Yeats, whose politics approached fascism, might suffer from this condition.   2. Stock exchange.

What instruments we have agree   30
The day of his death was a dark cold day.

2

You were silly like us: your gift survived it all:
The parish of rich women,[3] physical decay,
Yourself. Mad Ireland hurt you into poetry.
Now Ireland has her madness and her weather still,   35
For poetry makes nothing happen: it survives
In the valley of its making where executives
Would never want to tamper, flows on south
From ranches of isolation and the busy griefs,
Raw towns that we believe and die in; it survives,   40
A way of happening, a mouth.

3

Earth, receive an honoured guest:
William Yeats is laid to rest.
Let the Irish vessel lie
Emptied of its poetry.[4]   45

In the nightmare of the dark
All the dogs of Europe bark,[5]
And the living nations wait,
Each sequestered in its hate;

3. Yeats was often supported by rich women, especially Lady Augusta Gregory (1851–1932), the owner of an estate in the west of Ireland.

4. Three stanzas that originally followed this were omitted in the 1966 edition of Auden's *Collected Shorter Poems* and thereafter: "Time that is intolerant / Of the brave and innocent, / And indifferent in a week / To a beautiful physique, // Worships language and forgives / Everyone by whom it lives; / Pardons cowardice, conceit, / Lays its honours at their feet. // Time that with this strange excuse / Pardoned Kipling and his views, / And will pardon Paul Claudel, / Pardons him for writing well." Rudyard Kipling's views were imperialistic. Paul Claudel (1868–1955), French poet, dramatist, and diplomat, was extremely right-wing in his political ideas. Yeats's own politics were at times antidemocratic and appeared to favor dictatorship.

5. Perhaps a reference to the heated political rhetoric that preceded World War II.

Intellectual disgrace   50
Stares from every human face,
And the seas of pity lie
Locked and frozen in each eye.

Follow, poet, follow right
To the bottom of the night,   55
With your unconstraining voice
Still persuade us to rejoice;

With the farming of a verse
Make a vineyard of the curse,
Sing of human unsuccess   60
In a rapture of distress;

In the deserts of the heart
Let the healing fountain start,
In the prison of his days
Teach the free man how to praise.   65

Feb. 1939   *1940, 1966*

Elizabeth Bishop
1911–1979

> Bishop spent most of 1940 in Key West, where she caught a giant
> Caribbean jewfish, the subject of "The Fish." Partisan Review
> published the poem in March 1940 and launched Bishop's career.
> Readers often take the speakers in Bishop's poems to be the poet her-
> self. In "Sestina" Bishop writes about her own childhood, just as
> "One Art," a villanelle written in 1975, was inspired by her battle
> with alcohol. When reading Bishop, consider whether the strict for-
> mal requirements of the sestina and villanelle increase or diminish
> the emotions expressed in her poems.

The Fish

I caught a tremendous fish
and held him beside the boat
half out of water, with my hook
fast in a corner of his mouth.
He didn't fight.   5
He hadn't fought at all.
He hung a grunting weight,
battered and venerable
and homely. Here and there
his brown skin hung in strips   10
like ancient wallpaper,
and its pattern of darker brown
was like wallpaper:
shapes like full-blown roses
stained and lost through age.   15
He was speckled with barnacles,
fine rosettes of lime,
and infested
with tiny white sea-lice,
and underneath two or three   20
rags of green weed hung down.
While his gills were breathing in
the terrible oxygen
—the frightening gills,
fresh and crisp with blood,   25
that can cut so badly—
I thought of the coarse white flesh
packed in like feathers,
the big bones and the little bones,
the dramatic reds and blacks   30
of his shiny entrails,
and the pink swim-bladder
like a big peony.
I looked into his eyes
which were far larger than mine   35

but shallower, and yellowed,
the irises backed and packed
with tarnished tinfoil
seen through the lenses
of old scratched isinglass.[1]   40
They shifted a little, but not
to return my stare.
—It was more like the tipping
of an object toward the light.
I admired his sullen face,   45
the mechanism of his jaw,
and then I saw
that from his lower lip
—if you could call it a lip—
grim, wet, and weaponlike,   50
hung five old pieces of fish-line,
or four and a wire leader
with the swivel still attached,
with all their five big hooks
grown firmly in his mouth.   55
A green line, frayed at the end
where he broke it, two heavier lines,
and a fine black thread
still crimped from the strain and snap
when it broke and he got away.   60
Like medals with their ribbons
frayed and wavering,
a five-haired beard of wisdom
trailing from his aching jaw.
I stared and stared   65
and victory filled up
the little rented boat,
from the pool of bilge
where oil had spread a rainbow
around the rusted engine   70
to the bailer rusted orange,

---

1. A transparent gelatin made from the air bladders of some fish.

the sun-cracked thwarts,
the oarlocks on their strings,
the gunnels—until everything
was rainbow, rainbow, rainbow!   75
And I let the fish go.

                          1946

Sestina

September rain falls on the house.
In the failing light, the old grandmother
sits in the kitchen with the child
beside the Little Marvel Stove,
reading the jokes from the almanac,   5
laughing and talking to hide her tears.

She thinks that her equinoctial tears
and the rain that beats on the roof of the house
were both foretold by the almanac,
but only known to a grandmother.   10
The iron kettle sings on the stove.
She cuts some bread and says to the child,

It's time for tea now; but the child
is watching the teakettle's small hard tears
dance like mad on the hot black stove,   15
the way the rain must dance on the house.
Tidying up, the old grandmother
hangs up the clever almanac

on its string. Birdlike, the almanac
hovers half open above the child,   20
hovers above the old grandmother
and her teacup full of dark brown tears.
She shivers and says she thinks the house
feels chilly, and puts more wood in the stove.

It was to be, says the Marvel Stove.   25
I know what I know, says the almanac.
With crayons the child draws a rigid house
and a winding pathway. Then the child
puts in a man with buttons like tears
and shows it proudly to the grandmother.   30

But secretly, while the grandmother
busies herself about the stove,
the little moons fall down like tears
from between the pages of the almanac
into the flower bed the child   35
has carefully placed in the front of the house.

Time to plant tears, says the almanac.
The grandmother sings to the marvelous stove
and the child draws another inscrutable house.

                                              1965

One Art

The art of losing isn't hard to master;
so many things seem filled with the intent
to be lost that their loss is no disaster.

Lose something every day. Accept the fluster
of lost door keys, the hour badly spent.   5
The art of losing isn't hard to master.

Then practice losing farther, losing faster:
places, and names, and where it was you meant
to travel. None of these will bring disaster.

I lost my mother's watch. And look! my last, or   10
next-to-last, of three loved houses went.
The art of losing isn't hard to master.

I lost two cities, lovely ones. And, vaster,
some realms I owned, two rivers, a continent.
I miss them, but it wasn't a disaster.   15

—Even losing you (the joking voice, a gesture
I love) I shan't have lied. It's evident
the art of losing's not too hard to master
though it may look like (*Write* it!) like disaster.

                                                        1976

William Blake
1757–1827

> Blake, an Englishman sympathetic to political and social revolu-
> tion, was an engraver, and his books included his own illustrations.
> In 1789, the year of the French Revolution, Blake published Songs
> of Innocence, *which he expanded five years later to include his*
> Songs of Experience. *The two sections of this book were meant to*
> display "the two Contrary States of the Human Soul," as his title
> page announces. The "innocent" poems are prefaced by a picture of
> an angelic child and a rustic musician. The child asks the musician
> to "Pipe a song about a Lamb," and the musician sings the "songs of
> innocence" in response. Of the six poems here, "The Lamb" and the
> first "The Chimney Sweeper" come from the Songs of Innocence.
> *The poems of "experience," "The Sick Rose," "The Tyger," "Lon-*
> don," and the second "The Chimney Sweeper," are "earth's answer"
> to the heavenly "innocence."

The Lamb

   Little Lamb, who made thee?
   Dost thou know who made thee?
Gave thee life & bid thee feed,
By the stream & o'er the mead;
Gave thee clothing of delight,   5

Softest clothing wooly bright;
Gave thee such a tender voice,
Making all the vales rejoice!
   Little Lamb who made thee?
   Dost thou know who made thee?   10

   Little Lamb I'll tell thee,
   Little Lamb I'll tell thee!
He is calléd by thy name,
For he calls himself a Lamb:
He is meek & he is mild,   15
He became a little child:
I a child & thou a lamb,
We are calléd by his name.
   Little Lamb God bless thee.
   Little Lamb God bless thee.   20

1789

The Chimney Sweeper

When my mother died I was very young,
And my father sold me while yet my tongue,
Could scarcely cry weep weep weep weep.
So your chimneys I sweep & in soot I sleep.

Theres little Tom Dacre, who cried when his head   5
That curl'd like a lambs back, was shav'd, so I said.
Hush Tom never mind it, for when your head's bare,
You know that the soot cannot spoil your white hair.

And so he was quiet, & that very night,
As Tom was a sleeping he had such a sight,   10
That thousands of sweepers Dick, Joe, Ned & Jack
Were all of them lock'd up in coffins of black,

And by came an Angel who had a bright key,
And he open'd the coffins & set them all free.

Then down a green plain leaping laughing they run   15
And wash in a river and shine in the Sun.

Then naked & white, all their bags left behind,
They rise upon clouds, and sport in the wind.
And the Angel told Tom if he'd be a good boy,
He'd have God for his father & never want joy.   20

And so Tom awoke and we rose in the dark
And got with our bags & our brushes to work.
Tho' the morning was cold, Tom was happy & warm,
So if all do their duty, they need not fear harm.

1789

The Sick Rose

O Rose, thou art sick.
The invisible worm
That flies in the night
In the howling storm

Has found out thy bed   5
Of crimson joy,
And his dark secret love
Does thy life destroy.

1794

The Tyger

Tyger! Tyger! burning bright
In the forests of the night,
What immortal hand or eye
Could frame thy fearful symmetry?

In what distant deeps or skies   5
Burnt the fire of thine eyes?

On what wings dare he aspire?
What the hand, dare seize the fire?

And what shoulder, & what art,
Could twist the sinews of thy heart?   10
And when thy heart began to beat,
What dread hand? & what dread feet?

What the hammer? what the chain?
In what furnace was thy brain?
What the anvil? what dread grasp   15
Dare its deadly terrors clasp?

When the stars threw down their spears,
And water'd heaven with their tears,
Did he smile his work to see?
Did he who made the Lamb make thee?   20

Tyger! Tyger! burning bright
In the forests of the night,
What immortal hand or eye
Dare frame thy fearful symmetry?

                                        1794

London

I wander thro' each charter'd[1] street,
Near where the charter'd Thames does flow,
And mark in every face I meet
Marks of weakness, marks of woe.

In every cry of every man,   5
In every Infant's cry of fear,
In every voice, in every ban,[2]
The mind-forg'd manacles I hear.

---

1. Within the city limits of London.
2. A law or notice commanding or forbidding; a published penalty.

How the Chimney-sweeper's cry
Every blackning Church appalls;   10
And the hapless Soldier's sigh
Runs in blood down Palace walls.

But most thro' midnight streets I hear
How the youthful Harlot's curse
Blasts the new-born Infant's tear,   15
And blights with plagues the Marriage hearse.

1794

The Chimney Sweeper

A little black thing among the snow:
Crying weep, weep, in notes of woe!
Where are thy father & mother? say?
They are both gone up to the church to pray.

Because I was happy upon the heath,   5
And smil'd among the winter's snow:
They clothed me in the clothes of death,
And taught me to sing the notes of woe.

And because I am happy, & dance & sing,
They think they have done me no injury: 10
And are gone to praise God & his Priest & King
Who make up a heaven of our misery.

1794

Anne Bradstreet
1612 or 1613–1672

The primitive conditions of colonial America contrasted with the delicacy of Bradstreet's life in England, but she prospered and raised eight children, all the while writing poetry. These two love poems to her husband were not published until the posthumous, second edi-

tion of her one book, The Tenth Muse, *in 1678. They were written
after she settled in Andover in a comfortable, three-story house, the
privations of pioneering behind her. In these poems, Bradstreet addresses her husband, Simon, who was once governor of the colony
and ambassador to the court of England. In many interesting ways,
Bradstreet contradicts the stereotype we have of the Puritan ethic of
fleshly denial.*

To My Dear and Loving Husband

If ever two were one, then surely we.
If ever man were loved by wife, then thee;
If ever wife was happy in a man,
Compare with me, ye women, if you can.
I prize thy love more than whole mines of gold   5
Or all the riches that the East doth hold.
My love is such that rivers cannot quench,
Nor ought but love from thee, give recompense.
Thy love is such I can no way repay,
The heavens reward thee manifold, I pray.   10
Then while we live, in love let's so persevere
That when we live no more, we may live ever.

                                                        1678

A Letter to Her Husband, Absent upon Public Employment

My head, my heart, mine eyes, my life, nay, more,
My joy, my magazine[1] of earthly store,
If two be one, as surely thou and I,
How stayest thou there, whilst I at Ipswich lie?
So many steps, head from the heart to sever,   5
If but a neck, soon should we be together.
I, like the Earth this season, mourn in black,

---

1. Warehouse, storehouse.

My Sun is gone so far in's zodiac,
Whom whilst I 'joyed, nor storms, nor frost I felt,
His warmth such frigid colds did cause to melt.   10
My chilled limbs now numbed lie forlorn;
Return, return, sweet Sol, from Capricorn;[2]
In this dead time, alas, what can I more
Than view those fruits which through thy heat I bore?
Which sweet contentment yield me for a space,   15
True living pictures of their father's face.
O strange effect! now thou art southward gone,
I weary grow the tedious day so long;
But when thou northward to me shalt return,
I wish my Sun may never set, but burn   20
Within the Cancer[3] of my glowing breast,
The welcome house of him my dearest guest.
Where ever, ever stay, and go not thence,
Till nature's sad decree shall call thee hence;
Flesh of thy flesh, bone of thy bone,   25
I here, thou there, yet both but one.

                                                    1678

Gwendolyn Brooks
1917–2000

> *Though Brooks's early poems dealt with racial injustice, her work was initially recognized more for its fine craftmanship. "The Mother" is from her first book of poems,* A Street in Bronzeville *(1945), which recorded in realistic detail some of the experiences of Chicago's African American community. Brooks won the Pulitzer Prize in 1950, the first African American to do so, which expanded her audience considerably. "We Real Cool" and "The Bean Eaters" were published in* The Bean Eaters *(1960), which overtly criticized racial discrimination in America. Some critics attacked Brooks for abandoning the lyricism of her earlier work in favor of political rhetoric. The dropouts in "We*

2. Capricorn, the tenth sign of the zodiac, represents winter. "Sol": sun.
3. Cancer, the fourth sign of the zodiac, represents summer.

Real Cool," she explained, *"are people who are essentially saying, 'Kil-roy is here. We are.' But they're a little uncertain of the strength of their identity. . . . I want to represent their basic uncertainty."*

the mother

Abortions will not let you forget.
You remember the children you got that you did not get,
The damp small pulps with a little or with no hair,
The singers and workers that never handled the air.
You will never neglect or beat   5
Them, or silence or buy with a sweet.
You will never wind up the sucking-thumb
Or scuttle off ghosts that come.
You will never leave them, controlling your luscious sigh,
Return for a snack of them, with gobbling mother-eye.   10

I have heard in the voices of the wind the voices of my dim
        killed children.
I have contracted. I have eased
My dim dears at the breasts they could never suck.
I have said, Sweets, if I sinned, if I seized
Your luck   15
And your lives from your unfinished reach,
If I stole your births and your names,
Your straight baby tears and your games,
Your stilted or lovely loves, your tumults, your marriages,
        aches, and your deaths,
If I poisoned the beginnings of your breaths,   20
Believe that even in my deliberateness I was not deliberate.
Though why should I whine,
Whine that the crime was other than mine?—
Since anyhow you are dead.
Or rather, or instead,   25
You were never made.
But that too, I am afraid,
Is faulty: oh, what shall I say, how is the truth to be said?

You were born, you had body, you died.
It is just that you never giggled or planned or cried.   30

Believe me, I loved you all.
Believe me, I knew you, though faintly, and I loved, I loved
        you
All.

1945

We Real Cool

THE POOL PLAYERS.
SEVEN AT THE GOLDEN SHOVEL.

We real cool. We
Left school. We

Lurk late. We
Strike straight. We

Sing sin. We   5
Thin gin. We

Jazz June. We
Die soon.

1960

The Bean Eaters

They eat beans mostly, this old yellow pair.
Dinner is a casual affair.
Plain chipware on a plain and creaking wood,
Tin flatware.

Two who are Mostly Good.   5
Two who have lived their day,

But keep on putting on their clothes
And putting things away.

And remembering . . .
Remembering, with twinklings and twinges,   10
As they lean over the beans in their rented back room that is
    full of beads and receipts and dolls and clothes, tobacco
    crumbs, vases and fringes.

1960

Elizabeth Barrett Browning
1806–1861

> *Barrett was a famous poet and invalid when, in 1846, the young*
> *playwright, Robert Browning, secretly courted her. Barrett recorded*
> *her feelings of excitement, doubt, and ecstasy in a series of forty-four*
> *sonnets. "How Do I Love Thee" is the penultimate poem in the se-*
> *quence. The curious title,* Sonnets from the Portuguese, *was*
> *meant to disguise the autobiographical nature of the poems, but to-*
> *day they are considered an accurate portrait of Barrett's feelings for*
> *Browning. Though it is tempting to dismiss this poem as sentimen-*
> *tal, in the context of the great religious doubts of the nineteenth*
> *century, assigning one's lover the role of savior was provocative*
> *rather than conventional.*

Sonnets from the Portuguese

43

How do I love thee? Let me count the ways.
I love thee to the depth and breadth and height
My soul can reach, when feeling out of sight
For the ends of Being and ideal Grace.
I love thee to the level of everyday's   5
Most quiet need, by sun and candle-light.

I love thee freely, as men strive for Right;
I love thee purely, as they turn from Praise.
I love thee with the passion put to use
In my old griefs, and with my childhood's faith.   10
I love thee with a love I seemed to lose
With my lost saints—I love thee with the breath,
Smiles, tears, of all my life!—and, if God choose,
I shall but love thee better after death.

1850

Robert Browning
1812–1889

"My Last Duchess" was first published in the collection Dramatic
Lyrics *in 1842. It breaks with the Romantic tendency to equate the
speaker in the poem with the poet. Rather, "My Last Duchess" is a
dramatic monologue: the situation of the poem is a fiction, and the
speaker and his listener are characters. Though the Duke was suggested to Browning by a real, historical figure, this poem says as
much about gender relations in Victorian England as in sixteenth-
century Italy.*

My Last Duchess[1]

Ferrara

That's my last duchess painted on the wall,
Looking as if she were alive. I call
That piece a wonder, now: Frà Pandolf's hands
Worked busily a day, and there she stands.
Will't please you sit and look at her? I said   5

---

1. Alfonso II d'Este, the duke of Ferrara in the sixteenth century, married the fourteen-
year-old daughter of the duke of Florence in 1558. Three years later she died suspiciously, and
Alfonso soon began negotiating for the daughter of the count of Tyrol.

"Frà Pandolf" by design, for never read
Strangers like you that pictured countenance,
The depth and passion of its earnest glance,
But to myself they turned (since none puts by
The curtain I have drawn for you, but I)　　　　　　　10
And seemed as they would ask me, if they durst,
How such a glance came there; so, not the first
Are you to turn and ask thus. Sir, 'twas not
Her husband's presence only, called that spot
Of joy into the Duchess' cheek: perhaps　　　　　　15
Frà Pandolf chanced to say "Her mantle laps
Over my lady's wrist too much," or "Paint
Must never hope to reproduce the faint
Half-flush that dies along her throat": such stuff
Was courtesy, she thought, and cause enough　　　20
For calling up that spot of joy. She had
A heart—how shall I say?—too soon made glad,
Too easily impressed; she liked whate'er
She looked on, and her looks went everywhere.
Sir, 'twas all one! My favor at her breast,　　　　　25
The dropping of the daylight in the West,
The bough of cherries some officious fool
Broke in the orchard for her, the white mule
She rode with round the terrace—all and each
Would draw from her alike the approving speech,　30
Or blush, at least. She thanked men—good! but thanked
Somehow—I know not how—as if she ranked
My gift of a nine-hundred-years-old name
With anybody's gift. Who'd stoop to blame
This sort of trifling? Even had you skill　　　　　35
In speech—(which I have not)—to make your will
Quite clear to such an one, and say, "Just this
Or that in you disgusts me; here you miss,
Or there exceed the mark"—and if she let
Herself be lessoned so, nor plainly set　　　　　40
Her wits to yours, forsooth, and made excuse,
—E'en then would be some stooping; and I choose
Never to stoop. Oh sir, she smiled, no doubt,

Whene'er I passed her; but who passed without
Much the same smile? This grew; I gave commands;   45
Then all smiles stopped together. There she stands
As if alive. Will 't please you rise? We'll meet
The company below, then. I repeat,
The Count your master's known munificence
Is ample warrant that no just pretense   50
Of mine for dowry will be disallowed;
Though his fair daughter's self, as I avowed
At starting, is my object. Nay, we'll go
Together down, sir. Notice Neptune, though,
Taming a sea-horse, thought a rarity,   55
Which Claus of Innsbruck cast in bronze for me!

1842

Lynne Bryer

1946–1994

"The Way" was first published in Illuminations, *an international magazine of contemporary writing. Later, when Bryer republished it in a popular anthology of South African poets, she changed the title to "Release, February 1990," making no doubt that the subject of the poem is Nelson Mandela. The speaker, like Bryer herself, is white. Note the allusion to Zecchaeus, the tax collector in Luke's Gospel, who climbed a tree to catch a glimpse of Christ walking by.*

The Way

He came out, walked free
looking like an ordinary, sweet grandfather
from the Eastern Cape:
those lovely old men we children knew
were wise and saintly   5
when we saw them walking down the streets
in ancient suits, greatcoats
from the First World War. We always

greeted, an exchange both
courteous and right.   10

So now, grown older, we salute
Mandela. Not the bogeyman whose face
was a forbidden sight (abroad,
we looked in libraries): nor charismatic
warrior, giving tongue in blood and flame.   15
The heavens did not fall.
But then, for days before, the mountain
(struck by lightning) burned,
the dark alive with crimson snakes
writhing on air, black elevation of the night.   20

Omens alone foretold the change.
And confirmation came
less from our eyes, watching the images that flew
about the world, than from the way we felt:
elated, cool, not doubting this was true,   25
the destined time and place.

This is the way messiahs come—
when time can stand no more delay,
and people walk the streets, mill in the square,
climb trees to see. Even the soldiers,   30
nervous in the mob (since they alone are armed,
and hence not free) are part of the rightness,
the dislocated, sudden calm of knowing:
This was the way it had to be.

                                        1990

Lewis Carroll [*Charles Lutwidge Dodgson*]
1832–1898

Carroll is remembered today for his pair of challenging children's
books, Alice in Wonderland *(1865) and* Through the Looking-
Glass *(1871). Alice reads "Jabberwocky" in the first chapter of the*
second book, but Carroll began writing the poem much earlier and
even published the first stanza, with his own glosses, in 1855.
Humpty Dumpty explains to Alice that "slithy" is a combination of
"slimy" and "lithe," and thus the "toves" have slick, limber, nimble
bodies. But what is a "tove"? According to Humpty Dumpty, a tove
is a type of badger with long back legs and horns and a hunger for
cheese. And "bryllyg," Humpty explains, comes from the verb
"broiling" and means late afternoon, that time of day when dinner
is broiled. Obviously, we cannot even guess the meaning of some
words—they exist only in Carroll's imagination. Nevertheless, as
this poem demonstrates, even nonsense syllables have connotations
for readers and listeners.

Jabberwocky

'Twas brillig, and the slithy toves
  Did gyre and gimble in the wabe:
All mimsy were the borogoves,
  And the mome raths outgrabe.

"Beware the Jabberwock, my son!   5
  The jaws that bite, the claws that catch!
Beware the Jubjub bird, and shun
  The frumious Bandersnatch!"

He took his vorpal sword in hand:
  Long time the manxome foe he sought—   10
So rested he by the Tumtum tree,
  And stood awhile in thought.

And, as in uffish thought he stood,
   The Jabberwock, with eyes of flame,
Came whiffling through the tulgey wood,   15
   And burbled as it came!

One, two! One, two! And through and through
   The vorpal blade went snicker-snack!
He left it dead, and with its head
   He went galumphing back.   20

"And hast thou slain the Jabberwock?
   Come to my arms, my beamish boy!
O frabjous day! Callooh! Callay!"
   He chortled in his joy.

'Twas brillig, and the slithy toves   25
   Did gyre and gimble in the wabe:
All mimsy were the borogoves,
   And the mome raths outgrabe.

1871

Samuel Taylor Coleridge
1772–1834

> *In his preface to "Kubla Khan," Coleridge describes how he composed two or three hundred lines of the poem in an opium reverie, writing them down upon waking until he was interrupted. Coleridge was habituated to opium by October 1797, but his claims about his method of composition are part of the fiction of the poem itself. In fact, his pose is characteristic of that of Romantic poets, who abhorred artifice and believed poetry should flow naturally from the artist. Probably, Coleridge labored long over the poem, and even if he dreamed the images in 1797, most likely he did not write the poem until much later. He did not publish it until 1816. Likewise, his claim to have no special understanding of the symbolism in the poem, as if it originated in something other than his own consciousness, is Romantic. In modern terms, we might say that Coleridge's subconscious authored the symbols.*

Kubla Khan

In Xanadu did Kubla Khan
A stately pleasure-dome decree:
Where Alph, the sacred river, ran
Through caverns measureless to man
   Down to a sunless sea.   5
So twice five miles of fertile ground
With walls and towers were girdled round:
And there were gardens bright with sinuous rills
Where blossomed many an incense-bearing tree;
And here were forests ancient as the hills,   10
Enfolding sunny spots of greenery.

But oh! that deep romantic chasm which slanted
Down the green hill athwart a cedarn cover!
A savage place! as holy and enchanted
As e'er beneath a waning moon was haunted   15
By woman wailing for her demon-lover!
And from this chasm, with ceaseless turmoil seething,
As if this earth in fast thick pants were breathing,
A mighty fountain momently was forced:
Amid whose swift half-intermitted burst   20
Huge fragments vaulted like rebounding hail,
Or chaffy grain beneath the thresher's flail:
And 'mid these dancing rocks at once and ever
It flung up momently the sacred river.
Five miles meandering with a mazy motion   25
Through wood and dale the sacred river ran,
Then reached the caverns measureless to man,
And sank in tumult to a lifeless ocean:
And 'mid this tumult Kubla heard from far
Ancestral voices prophesying war!   30

   The shadow of the dome of pleasure
   Floated midway on the waves;
   Where was heard the mingled measure

From the fountain and the caves.
It was a miracle of rare device,   35
A sunny pleasure-dome with caves of ice!
   A damsel with a dulcimer
   In a vision once I saw:
   It was an Abyssinian maid,
   And on her dulcimer she played,   40
   Singing of Mount Abora.
   Could I revive within me
   Her symphony and song,
   To such a deep delight 'twould win me,
That with music loud and long,   45
I would build that dome in air,
That sunny dome! those caves of ice!
And all who heard should see them there,
And all should cry, Beware! Beware!
His flashing eyes, his floating hair!   50
Weave a circle round him thrice,[1]
And close your eyes with holy dread,
For he on honey-dew hath fed,
And drunk the milk of Paradise.

                      1816

Billy Collins

1941–

> *To understand "Picnic, Lightning," you might find it useful to compare it to Philip Larkin's "Aubade." Both consider the inescapable truth that we all will someday die, but the effect that this knowledge has on Collins's speaker is quite different than the effect it has on Larkin's. "On Turning Ten" comically alludes to Shelley's "Ode to the West Wind" in its last lines (Shelley's statement, meant to be taken quite seriously, reads "I fall upon the thorns of life! I bleed!"). Collins's meditation on growing up, then, gently satirizes poems like Dylan Thomas's "Fern Hill," which regrets what is lost*

---

1. A magic ritual, to protect the inspired poet from intrusion.

when we take on the knowledge of maturity. Collins is famous for these deceptively serious parodies. "Sonnet," for example, pokes fun at the formula of the Petrarchan sonnet. But by the end of the poem Collins turns the parody into a genuine love poem, and he comments on the idealized, Platonic love relations typical of sonnet cycles.

Picnic, Lightning

"My very photogenic mother died in a freak accident (picnic, lightning) when I was three." —Lolita

It is possible to be struck by a meteor
or a single-engine plane
while reading in a chair at home.
Safes drop from rooftops
and flatten the odd pedestrian   5
mostly within the panels of the comics,
but still, we know it is possible,
as well as the flash of summer lightning,
the thermos toppling over,
spilling out on the grass.   10

And we know the message
can be delivered from within.
The heart, no valentine,
decides to quit after lunch,
the power shut off like a switch,   15
or a tiny dark ship is unmoored
into the flow of the body's rivers,
the brain a monastery,
defenseless on the shore.

This is what I think about   20
when I shovel compost
into a wheelbarrow,

and when I fill the long flower boxes,
then press into rows
the limp roots of red impatiens—   25
the instant hand of Death
always ready to burst forth
from the sleeve of his voluminous cloak.

Then the soil is full of marvels,
bits of leaf like flakes off a fresco,   30
red-brown pine needles, a beetle quick
to burrow back under the loam.
Then the wheelbarrow is a wilder blue,
the clouds a brighter white,

and all I hear is the rasp of the steel edge   35
against a round stone,
the small plants singing
with lifted faces, and the click
of the sundial
as one hour sweeps into the next.   40

                                             1998

On Turning Ten

The whole idea of it makes me feel
like I'm coming down with something,
something worse than any stomach ache
or the headaches I get from reading in bad light—
a kind of measles of the spirit,   5
a mumps of the psyche,
a disfiguring chicken pox of the soul.

You tell me it is too early to be looking back,
but that is because you have forgotten
the perfect simplicity of being one   10
and the beautiful complexity introduced by two.
But I can lie on my bed and remember every digit.

At four I was an Arabian wizard.
I could make myself invisible
by drinking a glass of milk a certain way.   15
At seven I was a soldier, at nine a prince.

But now I am mostly at the window
watching the late afternoon light.
Back then it never fell so solemnly
against the side of my tree house,   20
and my bicycle never leaned against the garage
as it does today,
all the dark blue speed drained out of it.

This is the beginning of sadness, I say to myself,
as I walk through the universe in my sneakers.   25
It is time to say good-bye to my imaginary friends,
time to turn the first big number.
It seems only yesterday I used to believe
there was nothing under my skin but light.
If you cut me I would shine.   30
But now when I fall upon the sidewalks of life,
I skin my knees. I bleed.

                                        1998

Sonnet

All we need is fourteen lines, well, thirteen now,
and after this next one just a dozen
to launch a little ship on love's storm-tossed seas,
then only ten more left like rows of beans.
How easily it goes unless you get Elizabethan   5
and insist the iambic bongos must be played
and rhymes positioned at the ends of lines,
one for every station of the cross.
But hang on here while we make the turn
into the final six where all will be resolved,   10
where longing and heartache will find an end,

where Laura will tell Petrarch to put down his pen,
take off those crazy medieval tights,
blow out the lights, and come at last to bed.

1999

E. E. (Edward Estlin) Cummings
1894–1962

"Buffalo Bill 's" and "in Just-" appeared in Cummings's first book,
Tulips and Chimneys *(1923). They are both among the "tulips,"
or organic poems, in contrast to the sonnets that make up the
"chimneys" section. "Buffalo Bill 's" appeared in a subsection called
"Portraits," while "in Just-" was the first of three "Chansons Inno-
centes," or songs of innocence. The title calls to mind Blake's* Songs
of Innocence and Experience. *Immediately reviewers fixed on the
unique typography of Cummings's poems, which garnered him considerable criticism and recognition.*

Buffalo Bill 's

Buffalo Bill 's
defunct
         who used to
         ride a watersmooth-silver

                              stallion   5
and break onetwothreefourfive pigeonsjustlikethat
                                        Jesus

he was a handsome man
                    and what i want to know is
how do you like your blueeyed boy   10
Mister Death

1920, 1923

in Just-

                in Just-
spring   when the world is mud-
luscious the little
lame balloonman

whistles   far   and wee   5

and eddieandbill come
running from marbles and
piracies and it's
spring

when the world is puddle-wonderful   10

the queer
old balloonman whistles
far   and   wee
and bettyandisbel come dancing

from hop-scotch and jump-rope and   15

it's
spring
and
    the

          goat-footed[1]   20

balloonMan   whistles
far
and
wee

1920, 1923

1. An allusion to satyrs, the lewd forest gods of Greek mythology.

Emily Dickinson
1830–1886

> Only a handful of Dickinson's poems were published in her lifetime. "Because I could not stop for Death—," "The Soul Selects Her Own Society—," and "I heard a Fly buzz—when I died—" were written during the Civil War, but they were not published until the 1890s. "After great pain" was first published in 1929. A rare exception is "A narrow Fellow in the Grass," written in 1865 and published in the Springfield Daily Republican in February 1866 under the title "The Snake," which links the poem to the biblical Garden of Eden. Four years after Dickinson died, an editor for the Atlantic Monthly smoothed and regularized some of her poems and published them in a book, which critics instantly praised. But editors did not restore her idiosyncratic punctuation and expressions until the twentieth century. Written in 1861, "Wild Nights—Wild Nights!" worried Dickinson's literary executor, who feared that readers would see in the poem more than the "virgin recluse" put there. Most readers today do not so easily dismiss the sexual suggestiveness of her poems. Similarly, the poems are ambiguous about religious beliefs, including the immortality of the soul. Dickinson is notoriously difficult to pin down: her poems often support entirely contradictory interpretations.

249

Wild Nights—Wild Nights!
Were I with thee
Wild Nights should be
Our luxury!

Futile—the Winds—
To a Heart in port—
Done with the Compass—
Done with the Chart!

5

Rowing in Eden—
Ah, the Sea!   10
Might I but moor—Tonight—
In Thee!

              1891

303

The Soul selects her own Society—
Then—shuts the Door—
To her divine Majority—
Present no more—

Unmoved—she notes the Chariots—pausing—   5
At her low Gate—
Unmoved—an Emperor be kneeling
Upon her Mat—

I've known her—from an ample nation—
Choose One—   10
Then—close the Valves of her attention—
Like Stone—

              1890

341

After great pain, a formal feeling comes—
The Nerves sit ceremonious, like Tombs—
The stiff Heart questions was it He, that bore,
And Yesterday, or Centuries before?

The Feet, mechanical, go round—   5
Of Ground, or Air, or Ought[1]—
A Wooden way

1. Nothing, or anything.

Regardless grown,
A Quartz contentment, like a stone—

This is the Hour of Lead—   10
Remembered, if outlived,
As Freezing persons, recollect the Snow—
First—Chill—then Stupor—then the letting go—

1929

465

I heard a Fly buzz—when I died—
The Stillness in the Room
Was like the Stillness in the Air—
Between the Heaves of Storm—

The Eyes around—had wrung them dry—   5
And Breaths were gathering firm
For that last Onset—when the King
Be witnessed—in the Room—

I willed my Keepsakes—Signed away
What portion of me be   10
Assignable—and then it was
There interposed a Fly—

With Blue—uncertain stumbling Buzz—
Between the light—and me—
And then the Windows failed—and then   15
I could not see to see—

1896

712

Because I could not stop for Death—
He kindly stopped for me—

The Carriage held but just Ourselves—
And Immortality.

We slowly drove—He knew no haste   5
And I had put away
My labor and my leisure too,
For His Civility—

We passed the School, where Children strove
At Recess—in the Ring—   10
We passed the Fields of Gazing Grain—
We passed the Setting Sun—

Or rather—He passed Us—
The Dews drew quivering and chill—
For only Gossamer, my Gown—   15
My Tippet—only Tulle[1]—

We paused before a House that seemed
A Swelling of the Ground—
The Roof was scarcely visible—
The Cornice—in the Ground—   20

Since then—'tis Centuries—and yet
Feels shorter than the Day
I first surmised the Horses' Heads
Were toward Eternity—

1890

986

A narrow Fellow in the Grass
Occasionally rides—
You may have met Him—did you not
His notice sudden is—

---

1. Thin silk. "Tippet": a shawl.

The Grass divides as with a Comb—   5
A spotted shaft is seen—
And then it closes at your feet
And opens further on—

He likes a Boggy Acre
A Floor too cool for Corn—   10
Yet when a Boy, and Barefoot—
I more than once at Noon

Have passed, I thought, a Whip lash
Unbraiding in the Sun
When stooping to secure it   15
It wrinkled, and was gone—

Several of Nature's People
I know, and they know me—
I feel for them a transport
Of cordiality—   20

But never met this Fellow
Attended, or alone
Without a tighter breathing
And Zero at the Bone—

                                             1866

John Donne
1572–1631

> *Donne wrote poems for a coterie of friends, an elite society, and cir-*
> *culated them only in manuscript. Those included here were not*
> *published until two years after his death. Donne's poems "The Sun*
> *Rising," "The Canonization," and "The Flea" all depict a love af-*
> *fair remarkable for the age, perhaps for any age, and their bawdy*
> *conceits are striking even today. "A Valediction Forbidding Mourn-*
> *ing" is less cheerful but equally suggestive and intricate. To under-*
> *stand these "metaphysical" poems, as Donne's style of startling,*
> *extended metaphors (or conceits) came to be called, you must pa-*

*tiently unravel the intricate comparisons. His Holy Sonnets, in-
cluding "Death be not proud" and "Batter my heart," express a
piety belied by the love poems, though they were possibly written
around the same time.*

The Sun Rising

    Busy old fool, unruly sun,
      Why dost thou thus,
Through windows, and through curtains call on us?
Must to thy motions lovers' seasons run?
      Saucy pedantic wretch, go chide   5
      Late school boys and sour prentices,
   Go tell court huntsmen that the king will ride,
   Call country ants to harvest offices;
Love, all alike, no season knows nor clime,
Nor hours, days, months, which are the rags of time.   10

    Thy beams, so reverend and strong
      Why shouldst thou think?[1]
I could eclipse and cloud them with a wink,
But that I would not lose her sight so long;
      If her eyes have not blinded thine,   15
      Look, and tomorrow late, tell me,
   Whether both th' Indias of spice and mine
   Be where thou leftst them, or lie here with me.
Ask for those kings whom thou saw'st yesterday,
And thou shalt hear, All here in one bed lay.   20
      She's all states, and all princess, I,
      Nothing else is.
Princes do but play us; compared to this,
All honor's mimic, all wealth alchemy.
      Thou, sun, art half as happy as we,   25
      In that the world's contracted thus.
    Thine age asks ease, and since thy duties be

1. Reverse these two lines and they will make sense.

To warm the world, that's done in warming us.
Shine here to us, and thou art everywhere;
This bed thy center is, these walls, thy sphere.[2]　　　　30

1633

The Canonization[3]

　　For God's sake hold your tongue, and let me love,
　Or chide my palsy, or my gout,
My five gray hairs, or ruined fortune, flout,
　With wealth your state, your mind with arts improve,
　　Take you a course, get you a place,[4]　　　　5
　　Observe his honor, or his grace,
Or the King's real, or his stampèd face
　Contemplate; what you will, approve,
　So you will let me love.

Alas, alas, who's injured by my love?　　　　10
　What merchant's ships have my sighs drowned?
Who says my tears have overflowed his ground?
　When did my colds a forward spring remove?[5]
　　When did the heats which my veins fill
　　Add one more to the plaguy bill?[6]　　　　15
Soldiers find wars, and lawyers find out still
　Litigious men, which quarrels move,
　Though she and I do love.

---

2. Though Donne was Galileo's contemporary, this conceit presumes that the sun revolves around the earth. The bed, like the earth, is the center of the sun's orbit; the walls are the region or "sphere" through which the sun passes.

3. Candidates for sainthood are canonized only after they have undergone a rigorous scrutiny in which a "devil's advocate" exposes all the defects that might undermine such a pronouncement.

4. A "place" is an appointment; "take you a course" means pursue a career.

5. The speaker's "colds" have not robbed the early spring of its warmth; "colds" might refer to the chill a rejected lover feels when given a "cold shoulder."

6. A public list of plague victims during an epidemic.

Call us what you will, we are made such by love;
 Call her one, me another fly,   20
We're tapers too, and at our own cost die,[7]
 And we in us find the eagle and the dove.
  The phoenix riddle hath more wit
  By us: we two being one, are it.
So, to one neutral thing both sexes fit.   25
 We die and rise the same, and prove
 Mysterious by this love.

We can die by it, if not live by love,
 And if unfit for tombs and hearse
Our legend be, it will be fit for verse;   30
 And if no piece of chronicle we prove,
  We'll build in sonnets pretty rooms;[8]
  As well a well-wrought urn becomes
The greatest ashes, as half-acre tombs;
 And by these hymns, all shall approve   35
 Us canonized for love.

And thus invoke us: You whom reverend love
 Made one another's hermitage;
You, to whom love was peace, that now is rage;[9]
 Who did the whole world's soul contract, and drove   40
  Into the glasses of your eyes
  (So made such mirrors, and such spies,
That they did all to you epitomize)[1]
 Countries, towns, courts: Beg from above
 A pattern of your love!   45

                                            1633

7. "To die" was a conventional metaphor for orgasm, and superstition in Donne's day held that each ejaculation cost a man one day of life.

8. I.e., the pretty sonnets will contain their story, just as urns store ashes as well as giant mausoleums do.

9. I.e., lust.

1. Putting "epitomize" between "did" and "all" will help make sense of this line: a too-simple paraphrase of this and the preceding three lines might read, "whose eyes have seen it all."

The Flea[2]

Mark but this flea, and mark in this,
How little that which thou deniest me is;
It sucked me first, and now sucks thee,
And in this flea, our two bloods mingled be;
Thou know'st that this cannot be said   5
A sin, nor shame nor loss of maidenhead,
    Yet this enjoys before it woo,[3]
    And pampered swells with one blood made of two,[4]
    And this, alas, is more than we would do.

Oh stay, three lives in one flea spare,   10
Where we almost, yea more than married are.
This flea is you and I, and this
Our marriage bed, and marriage temple is;
Though parents grudge, and you, we are met,
And cloistered in these living walls of jet.[5]   15
    Though use make you apt to kill me,
    Let not to that, self murder added be,
    And sacrilege, three sins in killing three.

Cruel and sudden, hast thou since
Purpled thy nail, in blood of innocence?   20
Wherein could this flea guilty be,
Except in that drop which it sucked from thee?
Yet thou triumph'st, and say'st that thou
Find'st not thy self, nor me the weaker now;
    'Tis true, then learn how false, fears be;   25
    Just so much honor, when thou yield'st to me,
        Will waste, as this flea's death took life from thee.[6]

1633

---

2. Fleas were a conventional item in Renaissance love poetry. Typically, the speaker envies the flea for its ability to roam the beloved's body at will, a liberty denied the speaker.

3. I.e., the flea does not have to court the woman before he "enjoys" her.

4. In the Renaissance, doctors believed that pregnancy resulted from the man's blood mixing with the woman's during intercourse.

5. I.e., the black body of the flea.

6. I.e., having sex with the speaker will hurt the woman's honor about as much as the flea's death lessened her life.

A Valediction: Forbidding Mourning[7]

As virtuous men pass mildly away,
   And whisper to their souls to go,
Whilst some of their sad friends do say
   The breath goes now, and some say, no;

So let us melt, and make no noise,   5
   No tear-floods, nor sigh-tempests move,
'Twere profanation of our joys
   To tell the laity our love.

Moving of th' earth brings harms and fears,
   Men reckon what it did and meant;   10
But trepidation of the spheres,[8]
   Though greater far, is innocent.

Dull sublunary[9] lovers' love
   (Whose soul is sense) cannot admit
Absence, because it doth remove   15
   Those things which elemented[1] it.

But we by a love so much refined
   That our selves know not what it is,
Inter-assurèd of the mind,
   Care less, eyes, lips, and hands to miss.   20

Our two souls therefore, which are one,
   Though I must go, endure not yet
A breach, but an expansion,
   Like gold to airy thinness beat.

7. Some evidence suggests that Donne wrote this poem in 1611 when he had to leave his wife to take a trip to the Continent.

8. Geocentric astronomers trying to explain why the planets did not orbit the earth in perfect circles like the stars suggested that they periodically and suddenly stopped themselves and reversed their direction.

9. Beneath the moon's orbit, and thus earthly as opposed to heavenly; in other words, subject to decay and corruption.

1. I.e., composed.

If they be two, they are two so   25
    As stiff twin compasses² are two;
Thy soul, the fixed foot, makes no show
    To move, but doth, if th' other do.

And though it in the center sit,
    Yet when the other far doth roam,   30
It leans and hearkens after it,
    And grows erect, as that comes home.

Such wilt thou be to me, who must
    Like th' other foot, obliquely run.
Thy firmness makes my circle just,   35
    And makes me end where I begun.

                                        1633

Holy Sonnet

10

Death, be not proud, though some have callèd thee
Mighty and dreadful, for thou are not so;
For those whom thou think'st thou dost overthrow
Die not, poor Death, nor yet canst thou kill me.
From rest and sleep, which but thy pictures be,   5
Much pleasure; then from thee much more must flow,
And soonest our best men with thee do go,
Rest of their bones, and soul's delivery.
Thou art slave to fate, chance, kings, and desperate men,
And dost with poison, war, and sickness dwell,   10
And poppy or charms can make us sleep as well
And better than thy stroke; why swell'st thou then?
One short sleep past, we wake eternally,
And death shall be no more; Death, thou shalt die.

                                        1633

2. I.e., compasses used to draw circles, not to find magnetic north.

Holy Sonnet

14

Batter my heart, three-personed God;[3] for you
As yet but knock, breathe, shine, and seek to mend;
That I may rise and stand, o'erthrow me, and bend
Your force to break, blow, burn, and make me new.
I, like an usurped town, to another due,   5
Labor to admit you, but O, to no end;
Reason, your viceroy in me, me should defend,
But is captived, and proves weak or untrue.
Yet dearly I love you, and would be loved fain,[4]
But am betrothed unto your enemy.   10
Divorce me, untie or break that knot again;
Take me to you, imprison me, for I,
Except you enthrall me, never shall be free,
Nor ever chaste, except you ravish me.

1633

Rita Dove
1952–

> "The House Slave" explores the ambiguous position of plantation
> slaves who worked in the master's "big house" rather than the fields
> in the pre–Civil War South. The life of a house slave was often less
> difficult and dangerous than the field hand's, and sometimes al-
> lowed for a measure of education. House workers enjoyed a high
> status among slaves, but because their ascendency depended on their
> closeness to their aristocratic owners, it was often accompanied by
> feelings of guilt. Perhaps this poem suggests an analogue in the
> status of the economically successful, modern day African Ameri-
> can. Dove based her poetry sequence Thomas and Beulah (1987),
> which won the Pulitzer Prize and the wide general audience that

---

3. God the Father, Son, and Holy Spirit.   4. I.e., with pleasure.

*follows such recognition, on the lives of her grandparents. "Daystar"
is one of the* Beulah *poems in the collection.*

The House Slave

The first horn lifts its arm over the dew-lit grass
and in the slave quarters there is a rustling—
children are bundled into aprons, cornbread

and water gourds grabbed, a salt pork breakfast taken.
I watch them driven into the vague before-dawn   5
while their mistress sleeps like an ivory toothpick

and Massa dreams of asses, rum and slave-funk.
I cannot fall asleep again. At the second horn,
the whip curls across the backs of the laggards—

sometimes my sister's voice, unmistaken, among them.   10
"Oh! pray," she cries. "Oh! pray!" Those days
I lie on my cot, shivering in the early heat,

and as the fields unfold to whiteness,
and they spill like bees among the fat flowers,
I weep. It is not yet daylight.   15

1987

Daystar

She wanted a little room for thinking:
but she saw diapers steaming on the line,
a doll slumped behind the door.

So she lugged a chair behind the garage
to sit out the children's naps.   5

Sometimes there were things to watch—
the pinched armor of a vanished cricket,
a floating maple leaf. Other days
she stared until she was assured
when she closed her eyes   10
she'd see only her own vivid blood.

She had an hour, at best, before Liza appeared
pouting from the top of the stairs.
And just *what* was mother doing
out back with the field mice? Why,   15

building a palace. Later
that night when Thomas rolled over and
lurched into her, she would open her eyes
and think of the place that was hers
for an hour—where   20
she was nothing,
pure nothing, in the middle of the day.

                                                    1987

T. S. (Thomas Stearns) Eliot
1888–1965

Eliot was working on his Ph.D. in philosophy at Harvard when he began writing "The Love Song of J. Alfred Prufrock." When he traveled to London, he met Ezra Pound, who persuaded the Chicago Poetry *magazine to publish "Prufrock" in 1915. The poem established Eliot as one of the new poets using a "modern" style that refused to make any concessions to what we might call the "common reader." "Prufrock," like most of Eliot's poetry, is characterized by striking conceits (like the simile in lines 2–3) and allusions to literary tradition (such as* Hamlet *and the Bible). Eliot's poetry may be disconcerting on a first read: because he leaves out logical links and signposts between images, it can be hard to figure out the literal level of "Prufrock." Even so, the poem is easier to understand than*

*it first appears. Gauging Prufrock's character will give you a fair es-
timate of the "modern" or "anti-hero" Eliot helped define: the sensitive figure crippled by his insight into human character.*

The Love Song of J. Alfred Prufrock

*S'io credesse che mia risposta fosse
A persona che mai tornasse al mondo,
Questa fiamma staria senza piu scosse.
Ma perciocche giammai di questo fondo
Non torno vivo alcun, s'i'odo il vero,
Senza tema d'infamia ti rispondo.*[1]

Let us go then, you and I,
When the evening is spread out against the sky
Like a patient etherised upon a table;
Let us go, through certain half-deserted streets,
The muttering retreats   5
Of restless nights in one-night cheap hotels
And sawdust restaurants with oyster-shells:
Streets that follow like a tedious argument
Of insidious intent
To lead you to an overwhelming question . . .   10
Oh, do not ask, "What is it?"
Let us go and make our visit.

In the room the women come and go
Talking of Michelangelo.

The yellow fog that rubs its back upon the window-panes,   15
The yellow smoke that rubs its muzzle on the window-panes
Licked its tongue into the corners of the evening,

---

1. Dante, *Inferno* 27.61–66; spoken by Guido da Montefeltro, whom Dante and Virgil find
among the false counselors (each spirit is concealed within a flame): "If I thought my answer
were given / to anyone who would ever return to the world, / this flame would stand still
without moving any further. / But since never from this abyss / has anyone ever returned
alive, if what I hear is true, / without fear of infamy I answer you."

Lingered upon the pools that stand in drains,
Let fall upon its back the soot that falls from chimneys,
Slipped by the terrace, made a sudden leap, 20
And seeing that it was a soft October night,
Curled once about the house, and fell asleep.

And indeed there will be time
For the yellow smoke that slides along the street,
Rubbing its back upon the window-panes; 25
There will be time, there will be time
To prepare a face to meet the faces that you meet;
There will be time to murder and create,
And time for all the works and days of hands
That lift and drop a question on your plate; 30
Time for you and time for me,
And time yet for a hundred indecisions,
And for a hundred visions and revisions,
Before the taking of a toast and tea.

In the room the women come and go 35
Talking of Michelangelo.

And indeed there will be time
To wonder, "Do I dare?" and, "Do I dare?"
Time to turn back and descend the stair,
With a bald spot in the middle of my hair— 40
(They will say: "How his hair is growing thin!")
My morning coat, my collar mounting firmly to the chin,
My necktie rich and modest, but asserted by a simple pin—
(They will say: "But how his arms and legs are thin!")
Do I dare 45
Disturb the universe?
In a minute there is time
For decisions and revisions which a minute will reverse.

For I have known them all already, known them all—
Have known the evenings, mornings, afternoons, 50

I have measured out my life with coffee spoons;
I know the voices dying with a dying fall[2]
Beneath the music from a farther room.
　　So how should I presume?

And I have known the eyes already, known them all—   55
The eyes that fix you in a formulated phrase,
And when I am formulated, sprawling on a pin,
When I am pinned and wriggling on the wall,
Then how should I begin
To spit out all the butt-ends of my days and ways?   60
　　And how should I presume?

And I have known the arms already, known them all—
Arms that are braceleted and white and bare
(But in the lamplight, downed with light brown hair!)
Is it perfume from a dress   65
That makes me so digress?
Arms that lie along a table, or wrap about a shawl.
　　And should I then presume?
　　And how should I begin?

． ． ． ． ． ．

Shall I say, I have gone at dusk through narrow streets   70
And watched the smoke that rises from the pipes
Of lonely men in shirt-sleeves, leaning out of windows? . . .

I should have been a pair of ragged claws
Scuttling across the floors of silent seas.

． ． ． ． ． ．

And the afternoon, the evening, sleeps so peacefully!   75
Smoothed by long fingers,
Asleep . . . tired . . . or it malingers,
Stretched on the floor, here beside you and me.
Should I, after tea and cakes and ices,
Have the strength to force the moment to its crisis?   80
But though I have wept and fasted, wept and prayed,

---

2. An echo of Shakespeare's *Twelfth Night* (1.1.1–4): "If music be the food of love, play on.
. . . That strain again, it had a dying fall."

Though I have seen my head (grown slightly bald) brought in
    upon a platter,[3]
I am no prophet—and here's no great matter;
I have seen the moment of my greatness flicker,
And I have seen the eternal Footman hold my coat, and snicker, 85
And in short, I was afraid.

And would it have been worth it, after all,
After the cups, the marmalade, the tea,
Among the porcelain, among some talk of you and me,
Would it have been worth while,   90
To have bitten off the matter with a smile,
To have squeezed the universe into a ball
To roll it toward some overwhelming question,
To say: "I am Lazarus, come from the dead,
Come back to tell you all, I shall tell you all"—   95
If one, settling a pillow by her head,
    Should say: "That is not what I meant at all.
    That is not it, at all."

And would it have been worth it, after all,
Would it have been worth while,   100
After the sunsets and the dooryards and the sprinkled streets,
After the novels, after the teacups, after the skirts that trail
    along the floor—
And this, and so much more?—
It is impossible to say just what I mean!
But as if a magic lantern threw the nerves in patterns on a
    screen: 105
Would it have been worth while
If one, settling a pillow or throwing off a shawl,
And turning toward the window, should say:
    "That is not it at all,
    That is not what I meant, at all."   110
   · · · · · ·

3. At her request, King Herod gave his daughter, Salome, the head of John the Baptist on
a serving plate (Matthew 14.1–12).

No! I am not Prince Hamlet, nor was meant to be;
Am an attendant lord, one that will do
To swell a progress,[4] start a scene or two,
Advise the prince; no doubt, an easy tool,
Deferential, glad to be of use,   115
Politic, cautious, and meticulous;
Full of high sentence, but a bit obtuse;
At times, indeed, almost ridiculous—
Almost, at times, the Fool.

I grow old . . . I grow old . . .   120
I shall wear the bottoms of my trousers rolled.

Shall I part my hair behind? Do I dare to eat a peach?
I shall wear white flannel trousers, and walk upon the beach.
I have heard the mermaids singing, each to each.

I do not think that they will sing to me.   125

I have seen them riding seaward on the waves
Combing the white hair of the waves blown back
When the wind blows the water white and black.

We have lingered in the chambers of the sea
By sea-girls wreathed with seaweed red and brown   130
Till human voices wake us, and we drown.

                                                                1917

Louise Erdrich

1954–

> *In an interview, Erdrich explained that the children speaking in
> "Indian Boarding School: The Runaways" have "been taken from
> their homes [and] their cultures by the Bureau of Indian Affairs."*

---

4. I.e., to enlarge the group accompanying a lord with one more body, as might be done
with bit actors on the Elizabethan stage.

Earlier in this century, such schools attempted to acclimate Native American children to mainstream American life by obliterating their culture. The speaker in "Captivity" is a European woman captured by Native Americans. While you might think that her natural reaction to being rescued would be relief, the speaker's response is more complex. She is suspended between cultures, and her dream suggests some ambivalence. Erdrich herself has one foot in each culture: she has both German and Chippewa ancestors.

Indian Boarding School: The Runaways

Home's the place we head for in our sleep.
Boxcars stumbling north in dreams
don't wait for us. We catch them on the run.
The rails, old lacerations that we love,
shoot parallel across the face and break   5
just under Turtle Mountains. Riding scars
you can't get lost. Home is the place they cross.

The lame guard strikes a match and makes the dark
less tolerant. We watch through cracks in boards
as the land starts rolling, rolling till it hurts   10
to be here, cold in regulation clothes.
We know the sheriff's waiting at midrun
to take us back. His car is dumb and warm.
The highway doesn't rock, it only hums
like a wing of long insults. The worn-down welts   15
of ancient punishments lead back and forth.

All runaways wear dresses, long green ones,
the color you would think shame was. We scrub
the sidewalks down because it's shameful work.
Our brushes cut the stone in watered arcs   20
and in the soak frail outlines shiver clear
a moment, things us kids pressed on the dark

face before it hardened, pale, remembering
delicate old injuries, the spines of names and leaves.

1987

Captivity

> *He (my captor) gave me a bisquit, which I put in my pocket, and not dar-*
> *ing to eat it, buried it under a log, fearing he had put something in it to*
> *make me love him.*
>
> —from the narrative of the captivity of Mrs. Mary Rowlandson,
> who was taken prisoner by the Wampanoag when Lancaster,
> Massachusetts, was destroyed, in the year 1676

The stream was swift, and so cold
I thought I would be sliced in two.
But he dragged me from the flood
by the ends of my hair.
I had grown to recognize his face.   5
I could distinguish it from the others.
There were times I feared I understood
his language, which was not human,
and I knelt to pray for strength.

We were pursued! By God's agents   10
or pitch devils I did not know.
Only that we must march.
Their guns were loaded with swan shot.
I could not suckle and my child's wail
put them in danger.   15
He had a woman
with teeth black and glittering.
She fed the child milk of acorns.
The forest closed, the light deepened.

I told myself that I would starve   20
before I took food from his hands

but I did not starve.
One night
he killed a deer with a young one in her
and gave me to eat of the fawn.   25
It was so tender,
the bones like the stems of flowers,
that I followed where he took me.
The night was thick. He cut the cord
that bound me to the tree.   30

After that the birds mocked.
Shadows gaped and roared
and the trees flung down
their sharpened lashes.
He did not notice God's wrath.   35
God blasted fire from half-buried stumps.
I hid my face in my dress, fearing He would burn us all
but this, too, passed.

Rescued, I see no truth in things.
My husband drives a thick wedge   40
through the earth, still it shuts
to him year after year.
My child is fed of the first wheat.
I lay myself to sleep
on a Holland-laced pillowbeer.   45
I lay to sleep.
And in the dark I see myself
as I was outside their circle.

They knelt on deerskins, some with sticks,
and he led his company in the noise   50
until I could no longer bear
the thought of how I was.
I stripped a branch
and struck the earth,
in time, begging it to open   55

to admit me
as he was
and feed me honey from the rock.

1989

Carolyn Forché
1950–

> In 1978, supported by a Guggenheim Fellowship, Forché traveled to
> El Salvador and produced her award-winning The Country Be-
> tween Us (1981), which included "The Colonel." Beginning in
> 1960, El Salvador was ruled by a series of repressive military gov-
> ernments, and the country was in civil war by the late 1970s.
> Colonel Arturo Armando Molina ruled until 1977, when he was re-
> placed by the extremely repressive General Carlos Humberto
> Romero, who, in turn, was ousted by a coup in 1979. When the
> colonel in this poem says, "As for the rights of anyone, tell your peo-
> ple to go fuck themselves," he is probably referring to the new em-
> phasis on human rights in American foreign policy that President
> Jimmy Carter instituted. That policy was reversed in 1981 by
> Ronald Reagan, who spent millions of American dollars helping the
> newly elected Salvadorian government combat a coalition of leftist
> revolutionaries.

The Colonel

What you have heard is true. I was in his house. His wife carried
a tray of coffee and sugar. His daughter filed her nails, his son went
out for the night. There were daily papers, pet dogs, a pistol on the
cushion beside him. The moon swung bare on its black cord over
the house. On the television was a cop show. It was in English. Broken bottles were embedded in the walls around the house to scoop
the kneecaps from a man's legs or cut his hands to lace. On the windows there were gratings like those in liquor stores. We had dinner,
rack of lamb, good wine, a gold bell was on the table for calling the

maid. The maid brought green mangoes, salt, a type of bread. I was asked how I enjoyed the country. There was a brief commercial in Spanish. His wife took everything away. There was some talk of how difficult it had become to govern. The parrot said hello on the terrace. The colonel told it to shut up, and pushed himself from the table. My friend said to me with his eyes: say nothing. The colonel returned with a sack used to bring groceries home. He spilled many human ears on the table. They were like dried peach halves. There is no other way to say this. He took one of them in his hands, shook it in our faces, dropped it into a water glass. It came alive there. I am tired of fooling around he said. As for the rights of anyone, tell your people they can go fuck themselves. He swept the ears to the floor with his arm and held the last of his wine in the air.

Something for your poetry, no? he said. Some of the ears on the floor caught this scrap of his voice. Some of the ears on the floor were pressed to the ground.

1978

Robert Frost
1874–1963

Frost's formal style and rural subjects helped make his poetry particularly accessible to a popular reading audience. Even so, you must be careful to gauge the tone of these eight selections: Frost's poems are darker than his reputation might suggest. Many deal with the isolation and loneliness of the human condition. For instance, Frost's oldest child died in 1900, an event that probably inspired "Home Burial." And do not forget that the memorable line in "Mending Wall," "Good fences make good neighbors," is uttered by "an old-stone savage armed . . . [and moving] in darkness." Likewise, you may have seen the last three lines of "The Road Not Taken" quoted on a poster in high school, where it exhorted you to be an individual. But be careful to consider the context of those lines, and ask yourself, will the speaker, in "ages hence," be lying to himself? Though his rural subjects, as in "After Apple-Picking," "Out, Out—," and "Birches," often spark comparisons to those of the Romantic poets a hundred years earlier, Frost was no worshipper of Nature (it is interesting to think about his relationship to Nature when reading the "city" poem "Acquainted with the Night"). "Design," which Frost wrote when he was sixty-two, is a Petrarchan sonnet that could only be written in the post-Darwinian age since it takes seriously the possibility that the complexity of the natural world is random.

Home Burial

He saw her from the bottom of the stairs
Before she saw him. She was starting down,
Looking back over her shoulder at some fear.
She took a doubtful step and then undid it
To raise herself and look again. He spoke   5
Advancing toward her: "What is it you see
From up there always?—for I want to know."
She turned and sank upon her skirts at that,
And her face changed from terrified to dull.
He said to gain time: "What is it you see?"   10
Mounting until she cowered under him.
"I will find out now—you must tell me, dear."
She, in her place, refused him any help,
With the least stiffening of her neck and silence.
She let him look, sure that he wouldn't see,   15
Blind creature; and awhile he didn't see.
But at last he murmured, "Oh," and again, "Oh."

"What is it—what?" she said.

                              "Just that I see."

"You don't," she challenged. "Tell me what it is."

"The wonder is I didn't see at once.   20
I never noticed it from here before.
I must be wonted to it—that's the reason.

The little graveyard where my people are!
So small the window frames the whole of it.
Not so much larger than a bedroom, is it?   25

There are three stones of slate and one of marble,
Broad-shouldered little slabs there in the sunlight
On the sidehill. We haven't to mind *those*.
But I understand: it is not the stones,
But the child's mound——"

                              "Don't, don't, don't,
    don't," she cried.   30

She withdrew, shrinking from beneath his arm
That rested on the banister, and slid downstairs;
And turned on him with such a daunting look,
He said twice over before he knew himself:
"Can't a man speak of his own child he's lost?"   35

"Not you!—Oh, where's my hat? Oh, I don't need it!
I must get out of here. I must get air.—
I don't know rightly whether any man can."

"Amy! Don't go to someone else this time.
Listen to me. I won't come down the stairs."   40
He sat and fixed his chin between his fists.
"There's something I should like to ask you, dear."

"You don't know how to ask it."

                              "Help me, then."

Her fingers moved the latch for all reply.

"My words are nearly always an offense.   45
I don't know how to speak of anything
So as to please you. But I might be taught,
I should suppose. I can't say I see how.

A man must partly give up being a man
With womenfolk. We could have some arrangement   50
By which I'd bind myself to keep hands off
Anything special you're a-mind to name.
Though I don't like such things, 'twixt those that love.
Two that don't love can't live together without them.
But two that do can't live together with them."   55
She moved the latch a little. "Don't—don't go.
Don't carry it to someone else this time.
Tell me about it if it's something human.
Let me into your grief. I'm not so much
Unlike other folks as your standing there   60
Apart would make me out. Give me my chance.
I do think, though, you overdo it a little.
What was it brought you up to think it the thing
To take your mother-loss of a first child
So inconsolably—in the face of love.   65
You'd think his memory might be satisfied——"

"There you go sneering now!"

                        "I'm not, I'm not!
You make me angry. I'll come down to you.
God, what a woman! And it's come to this,
A man can't speak of his own child that's dead."   70

"You can't because you don't know how to speak.
If you had any feelings, you that dug
With your own hand—how could you?—his little grave;
I saw you from that very window there,
Making the gravel leap and leap in air,   75
Leap up, like that, like that, and land so lightly
And roll back down the mound beside the hole.
I thought, Who is that man? I didn't know you.
And I crept down the stairs and up the stairs
To look again, and still your spade kept lifting.   80
Then you came in. I heard your rumbling voice

Out in the kitchen, and I don't know why,
But I went near to see with my own eyes.
You could sit there with the stains on your shoes
Of the fresh earth from your own baby's grave   85
And talk about your everyday concerns.
You had stood the spade up against the wall
Outside there in the entry, for I saw it."

"I shall laugh the worst laugh I ever laughed.
I'm cursed. God, if I don't believe I'm cursed."   90

"I can repeat the very words you were saying:
'Three foggy mornings and one rainy day
Will rot the best birch fence a man can build.'
Think of it, talk like that at such a time!
What had how long it takes a birch to rot   95
To do with what was in the darkened parlor?
You *couldn't* care! The nearest friends can go
With anyone to death, comes so far short
They might as well not try to go at all.
No, from the time when one is sick to death,   100
One is alone, and he dies more alone.
Friends make pretense of following to the grave,
But before one is in it, their minds are turned
And making the best of their way back to life
And living people, and things they understand.   105
But the world's evil. I won't have grief so
If I can change it. Oh, I won't, I won't!"

"There, you have said it all and you feel better.
You won't go now. You're crying. Close the door.
The heart's gone out of it: why keep it up?   110
Amy! There's someone coming down the road!"

"*You*—oh, you think the talk is all. I must go—
Somewhere out of this house. How can I make you——"

"If—you—do!" She was opening the door wider.
"Where do you mean to go? First tell me that.   115
I'll follow and bring you back by force. I *will!*—"

1914

After Apple-Picking

My long two-pointed ladder's sticking through a tree
Toward heaven still,
And there's a barrel that I didn't fill
Beside it, and there may be two or three
Apples I didn't pick upon some bough.   5
But I am done with apple-picking now.
Essence of winter sleep is on the night,
The scent of apples: I am drowsing off.
I cannot rub the strangeness from my sight
I got from looking through a pane of glass   10
I skimmed this morning from the drinking trough
And held against the world of hoary grass.
It melted, and I let it fall and break.
But I was well
Upon my way to sleep before it fell,   15
And I could tell
What form my dreaming was about to take.
Magnified apples appear and disappear,
Stem end and blossom end,
And every fleck of russet showing clear.   20
My instep arch not only keeps the ache,
It keeps the pressure of a ladder-round.
I feel the ladder sway as the boughs bend.
And I keep hearing from the cellar bin
The rumbling sound   25
Of load on load of apples coming in.
For I have had too much
Of apple-picking: I am overtired
Of the great harvest I myself desired.
There were ten thousand thousand fruit to touch,   30

Cherish in hand, lift down, and not let fall.
For all
That struck the earth,
No matter if not bruised or spiked with stubble,
Went surely to the cider-apple heap   35
As of no worth.
One can see what will trouble
This sleep of mine, whatever sleep it is.
Were he not gone,
The woodchuck could say whether it's like his   40
Long sleep, as I describe its coming on,
Or just some human sleep.

                                                        1914

Mending Wall

Something there is that doesn't love a wall,
That sends the frozen-ground-swell under it,
And spills the upper boulders in the sun;
And makes gaps even two can pass abreast.
The work of hunters is another thing: 5
I have come after them and made repair
Where they have left not one stone on a stone,
But they would have the rabbit out of hiding,
To please the yelping dogs. The gaps I mean,
No one has seen them made or heard them made,   10
But at spring mending-time we find them there.
I let my neighbor know beyond the hill;
And on a day we meet to walk the line
And set the wall between us once again.
We keep the wall between us as we go.   15
To each the boulders that have fallen to each.
And some are loaves and some so nearly balls
We have to use a spell to make them balance:
'Stay where you are until our backs are turned!'
We wear our fingers rough with handling them.   20
Oh, just another kind of outdoor game,

One on a side. It comes to little more:
There where it is we do not need the wall:
He is all pine and I am apple orchard.
My apple trees will never get across   25
And eat the cones under his pines, I tell him.
He only says, 'Good fences make good neighbors.'
Spring is the mischief in me, and I wonder
If I could put a notion in his head:
'*Why* do they make good neighbors? Isn't it   30
Where there are cows? But here there are no cows.
Before I built a wall I'd ask to know
What I was walling in or walling out,
And to whom I was like to give offense.
Something there is that doesn't love a wall,   35
That wants it down.' I could say 'Elves' to him,
But it's not elves exactly, and I'd rather
He said it for himself. I see him there
Bringing a stone grasped firmly by the top
In each hand, like an old-stone savage armed.   40
He moves in darkness as it seems to me,
Not of woods only and the shade of trees.
He will not go behind his father's saying,
And he likes having thought of it so well
He says again, 'Good fences make good neighbors.'   45

                                        1914

"Out, Out—"

The buzz saw snarled and rattled in the yard
And made dust and dropped stove-length sticks of wood,
Sweet-scented stuff when the breeze drew across it.
And from there those that lifted eyes could count
Five mountain ranges one behind the other   5
Under the sunset far into Vermont.
And the saw snarled and rattled, snarled and rattled,
As it ran light, or had to bear a load.
And nothing happened: day was all but done.

Call it a day, I wish they might have said   10
To please the boy by giving him the half hour
That a boy counts so much when saved from work.
His sister stood beside them in her apron
To tell them "Supper." At the word, the saw,
As if to prove saws knew what supper meant,   15
Leaped out at the boy's hand, or seemed to leap—
He must have given the hand. However it was,
Neither refused the meeting. But the hand!
The boy's first outcry was a rueful laugh,
As he swung toward them holding up the hand,   20
Half in appeal, but half as if to keep
The life from spilling. Then the boy saw all—
Since he was old enough to know, big boy
Doing a man's work, though a child at heart—
He saw all spoiled. "Don't let him cut my hand off—   25
The doctor, when he comes. Don't let him, sister!"
So. But the hand was gone already.
The doctor put him in the dark of ether.
He lay and puffed his lips out with his breath.
And then—the watcher at his pulse took fright.   30
No one believed. They listened at his heart.
Little—less—nothing!—and that ended it.
No more to build on there. And they, since they
Were not the one dead, turned to their affairs.

                                            1916

The Road Not Taken

Two roads diverged in a yellow wood,
And sorry I could not travel both
And be one traveler, long I stood
And looked down one as far as I could
To where it bent in the undergrowth;   5

Then took the other, as just as fair,
And having perhaps the better claim,

Because it was grassy and wanted wear;
Though as for that the passing there
Had worn them really about the same,   10

And both that morning equally lay
In leaves no step had trodden black.
Oh, I kept the first for another day!
Yet knowing how way leads on to way,
I doubted if I should ever come back.   15

I shall be telling this with a sigh
Somewhere ages and ages hence:
Two roads diverged in a wood, and I—
I took the one less traveled by,
And that has made all the difference.   20

1916

Birches

When I see birches bend to left and right
Across the lines of straighter darker trees,
I like to think some boy's been swinging them.
But swinging doesn't bend them down to stay
As ice-storms do. Often you must have seen them   5
Loaded with ice a sunny winter morning
After a rain. They click upon themselves
As the breeze rises, and turn many-colored
As the stir cracks and crazes their enamel.
Soon the sun's warmth makes them shed crystal shells   10
Shattering and avalanching on the snow-crust—
Such heaps of broken glass to sweep away
You'd think the inner dome of heaven had fallen.
They are dragged to the withered bracken by the load,
And they seem not to break; though once they are bowed   15
So low for long, they never right themselves:
You may see their trunks arching in the woods
Years afterwards, trailing their leaves on the ground

Like girls on hands and knees that throw their hair
Before them over their heads to dry in the sun.   20
But I was going to say when Truth broke in
With all her matter-of-fact about the ice-storm
I should prefer to have some boy bend them
As he went out and in to fetch the cows—
Some boy too far from town to learn baseball,   25
Whose only play was what he found himself,
Summer or winter, and could play alone.
One by one he subdued his father's trees
By riding them down over and over again
Until he took the stiffness out of them,   30
And not one but hung limp, not one was left
For him to conquer. He learned all there was
To learn about not launching out too soon
And so not carrying the tree away
Clear to the ground. He always kept his poise   35
To the top branches, climbing carefully
With the same pains you use to fill a cup
Up to the brim, and even above the brim.
Then he flung outward, feet first, with a swish,
Kicking his way down through the air to the ground.   40
So was I once myself a swinger of birches.
And so I dream of going back to be.
It's when I'm weary of considerations,
And life is too much like a pathless wood
Where your face burns and tickles with the cobwebs   45
Broken across it, and one eye is weeping
From a twig's having lashed across it open.
I'd like to get away from earth awhile
And then come back to it and begin over.
May no fate willfully misunderstand me   50
And half grant what I wish and snatch me away
Not to return. Earth's the right place for love:
I don't know where it's likely to go better.
I'd like to go by climbing a birch tree,
And climb black branches up a snow-white trunk   55
Toward heaven, till the tree could bear no more,

But dipped its top and set me down again.
That would be good both going and coming back.
One could do worse than be a swinger of birches.

1916

Stopping by Woods on a Snowy Evening

Whose woods these are I think I know.
His house is in the village though;
He will not see me stopping here
To watch his woods fill up with snow.

My little horse must think it queer   5
To stop without a farmhouse near
Between the woods and frozen lake
The darkest evening of the year.

He gives his harness bells a shake
To ask if there is some mistake.   10
The only other sound's the sweep
Of easy wind and downy flake.

The woods are lovely, dark and deep,
But I have promises to keep,
And miles to go before I sleep,   15
And miles to go before I sleep.

1923

Acquainted with the Night

I have been one acquainted with the night.
I have walked out in rain—and back in rain.
I have outwalked the furthest city light.

I have looked down the saddest city lane.
I have passed by the watchman on his beat   5
And dropped my eyes, unwilling to explain.

I have stood still and stopped the sound of feet
When far away an interrupted cry
Came over houses from another street,

But not to call me back or say good-by;   10
And further still at an unearthly height,
One luminary clock against the sky

Proclaimed the time was neither wrong nor right.
I have been one acquainted with the night.

1928

Design

I found a dimpled spider, fat and white,
On a white heal-all,[1] holding up a moth
Like a white piece of rigid satin cloth—
Assorted characters of death and blight
Mixed ready to begin the morning right,   5
Like the ingredients of a witches' broth—
A snow-drop spider, a flower like a froth,
And dead wings carried like a paper kite.

What had that flower to do with being white,
The wayside blue and innocent heal-all?   10
What brought the kindred spider to that height,
Then steered the white moth thither in the night?
What but design of darkness to appall?—
If design govern in a thing so small.

1936

---

1. One of a variety of plants in the mint family; the flowers are usually violet-blue.

Allen Ginsberg
1926–1998

> *"A Supermarket in California" appeared in Ginsberg's provocative*
> Howl and Other Poems *(1956), a volume that made Ginsberg fa-*
> *mous at least partly because its publisher was tried for obscenity*
> *and acquitted. That book put him in the company of Jack Kerouac*
> *and the other Beat writers centered in San Francisco. In the 1960s*
> *he became a well-known figure among hippies and one of the voices*
> *of the counterculture generation: Ginsberg coined the term "flower*
> *power." As this poem makes clear, Ginsberg consciously echoes Walt*
> *Whitman and assumed for himself the long beard and sandals of*
> *the prophet. Here he questions whether the consumer society of*
> *modern America is the same country Whitman celebrated a hun-*
> *dred years earlier.*

A Supermarket in California

What thoughts I have of you tonight, Walt Whitman, for I
walked down the sidestreets under the trees with a headache
self-conscious looking at the full moon.

In my hungry fatigue, and shopping for images, I went
into the neon fruit supermarket, dreaming of your
enumerations!

What peaches and what penumbras! Whole families
shopping at night! Aisles full of husbands! Wives in the
avocados, babies in the tomatoes!—and you, García Lorca,
what were you doing down by the watermelons?

I saw you, Walt Whitman, childless, lonely old grubber,
poking among the meats in the refrigerator and eyeing the
grocery boys.

I heard you asking questions of each: Who killed the pork
chops? What price bananas? Are you my Angel?   5

I wandered in and out of the brilliant stacks of cans
following you, and followed in my imagination by the store
detective.

We strode down the open corridors together in our solitary
fancy tasting artichokes, possessing every frozen delicacy, and
never passing the cashier.

Where are we going, Walt Whitman? The doors close in an
hour. Which way does your beard point tonight?
(I touch your book and dream of our odyssey in the
supermarket and feel absurd.)
Will we walk all night through solitary streets? The trees add
shade to shade, lights out in the houses, we'll both be lonely.   10
Will we stroll dreaming of the lost America of love past blue
automobiles in driveways, home to our silent cottage?
Ah, dear father, graybeard, lonely old courage-teacher, what
America did you have when Charon quit poling his ferry and
you got out on a smoking bank and stood watching the boat
disappear on the black waters of Lethe?

1956

Thomas Gray
1716–1771
*"Elegy Written in a Country Churchyard," Gray's best-known poem,
was written to mourn the death of Gray's close friend, Richard West,
who died of tuberculosis in 1742. Though "Elegy" represents one of
Gray's earliest efforts at writing poetry, it was revised for five years
before publication. When the public finally read "Elegy," Gray became an immediate celebrity. This elegy is unusual in that it considers not the death of an individual nor human mortality in general,
but the deaths of a particular group of people: commoners.*

Elegy Written in a Country Churchyard

The curfew tolls the knell of parting day,
    The lowing herd wind slowly o'er the lea,
The plowman homeward plods his weary way,
    And leaves the world to darkness and to me.

Now fades the glimmering landscape on the sight,   5
    And all the air a solemn stillness holds,
Save where the beetle wheels his droning flight,
    And drowsy tinklings lull the distant folds;

Save that from yonder ivy-mantled tower
    The moping owl does to the moon complain   10
Of such, as wandering near her secret bower,
    Molest her ancient solitary reign.

Beneath those rugged elms, that yew tree's shade,
    Where heaves the turf in many a moldering heap,
Each in his narrow cell forever laid,   15
    The rude forefathers of the hamlet sleep.

The breezy call of incense-breathing morn,
    The swallow twittering from the straw-built shed,
The cock's shrill clarion, or the echoing horn,
    No more shall rouse them from their lowly bed.   20

For them no more the blazing hearth shall burn,
    Or busy housewife ply her evening care;
No children run to lisp their sire's return,
    Or climb his knees the envied kiss to share.

Oft did the harvest to their sickle yield,   25
    Their furrow oft the stubborn glebe has broke;
How jocund did they drive their team afield!
    How bowed the woods beneath their sturdy stroke!

Let not Ambition mock their useful toil,
    Their homely joys, and destiny obscure;   30
Nor Grandeur hear with a disdainful smile
    The short and simple annals of the poor.

The boast of heraldry, the pomp of power,
  And all that beauty, all that wealth e'er gave,
Awaits alike the inevitable hour.   35
  The paths of glory lead but to the grave.

Nor you, ye proud, impute to these the fault,
  If Memory o'er their tomb no trophies raise,
Where through the long-drawn aisle and fretted vault
  The pealing anthem swells the note of praise.   40

Can storied urn or animated bust
  Back to its mansion call the fleeting breath?
Can Honor's voice provoke the silent dust,
  Or Flattery soothe the dull cold ear of Death?

Perhaps in this neglected spot is laid   45
  Some heart once pregnant with celestial fire;
Hands that the rod of empire might have swayed,
  Or waked to ecstasy the living lyre.

But Knowledge to their eyes her ample page
  Rich with the spoils of time did ne'er unroll;   50
Chill Penury repressed their noble rage,
  And froze the genial current of the soul.

Full many a gem of purest ray serene,
  The dark unfathomed caves of ocean bear:
Full many a flower is born to blush unseen,   55
  And waste its sweetness on the desert air.

Some village Hampden¹ that with dauntless breast
  The little tyrant of his fields withstood;
Some mute inglorious Milton here may rest,
  Some Cromwell guiltless of his country's blood.   60

---

1. Leader of the opposition to Charles I in the controversy over ship money; killed in battle in the civil wars.

The applause of listening senates to command,
    The threats of pain and ruin to despise,
To scatter plenty o'er a smiling land,
    And read their history in a nation's eyes,

Their lot forbade; nor circumscribed alone   65
    Their growing virtues, but their crimes confined;
Forbade to wade through slaughter to a throne,
    And shut the gates of mercy on mankind,

The struggling pangs of conscious truth to hide,
    To quench the blushes of ingenuous shame,   70
Or heap the shrine of Luxury and Pride
    With incense kindled at the Muse's flame.

Far from the madding crowd's ignoble strife,
    Their sober wishes never learned to stray;
Along the cool sequestered vale of life   75
    They kept the noiseless tenor of their way.

Yet even these bones from insult to protect
    Some frail memorial still erected nigh,
With uncouth rhymes and shapeless sculpture decked,
    Implores the passing tribute of a sigh.   80

Their name, their years, spelt by the unlettered Muse,
    The place of fame and elegy supply:
And many a holy text around she strews,
    That teach the rustic moralist to die.

For who to dumb Forgetfulness a prey,   85
    This pleasing anxious being e'er resigned,
Left the warm precincts of the cheerful day,
    Nor cast one longing lingering look behind?

On some fond breast the parting soul relies,
   Some pious drops the closing eye requires;   90
Even from the tomb the voice of Nature cries,
   Even in our ashes live their wonted fires.

For thee, who mindful of the unhonored dead
   Dost in these lines their artless tale relate;
If chance, by lonely contemplation led,   95
   Some kindred spirit shall inquire thy fate,

Haply some hoary-headed swain may say,
   "Oft have we seen him at the peep of dawn
Brushing with hasty steps the dews away
   To meet the sun upon the upland lawn.   100

"There at the foot of yonder nodding beech
   That wreathes its old fantastic roots so high,
His listless length at noontide would he stretch,
   And pore upon the brook that babbles by.

"Hard by yon wood, now smiling as in scorn,   105
   Muttering his wayward fancies he would rove,
Now drooping, woeful wan, like one forlorn,
   Or crazed with care, or crossed in hopeless love.

"One morn I missed him on the customed hill,
   Along the heath and near his favorite tree;   110
Another came; nor yet beside the rill,
   Nor up the lawn, nor at the wood was he;

"The next with dirges due in sad array
   Slow through the churchway path we saw him borne.
Approach and read (for thou canst read) the lay,   115
   Graved on the stone beneath yon aged thorn."

THE EPITAPH

Here rests his head upon the lap of Earth
  A youth to Fortune and to Fame unknown.
Fair Science frowned not on his humble birth,
  And Melancholy marked him for her own.   120

Large was his bounty, and his soul sincere,
  Heaven did a recompense as largely send:
He gave to Misery all he had, a tear,
  He gained from Heaven ('twas all he wished) a friend.

No farther seek his merits to disclose,   125
  Or draw his frailties from their dread abode
(There they alike in trembling hope repose),
  The bosom of his Father and his God.

                                1751

Thomas Hardy
1840–1928

> *Hardy wrote "Hap" in 1866, just seven years after Darwin's* Origin of Species, *though the poem was not published until 1898. Clearly, this Petrarchan sonnet is inspired by Darwin's theory that human beings are the result of random, natural forces rather than a divine plan. "Hap" is short for "happenstance," or chance. "Convergence of the Twain" and "Channel Firing" are both occasional poems, or poems triggered by historical events. The sinking of the* Titanic *in 1912 gave Western society reason to reflect on its place in the universe and relation to God. "Channel Firing" comments on the English Navy's gunnery practice in April 1914, just four months before the war everyone expected, World War I, finally erupted.*

Hap

If but some vengeful god would call to me
From up the sky, and laugh: "Thou suffering thing,
Know that thy sorrow is my ecstasy,
That thy love's loss is my hate's profiting!"

Then would I bear it, clench myself, and die,   5
Steeled by the sense of ire unmerited;
Half-eased in that a Powerfuller than I
Had willed and meted me the tears I shed.

But not so. How arrives it joy lies slain,
And why unblooms the best hope ever sown?   10
—Crass Casualty obstructs the sun and rain,
And dicing Time for gladness casts a moan. . . .
These purblind Doomsters had as readily strown
Blisses about my pilgrimage as pain.

1898

The Convergence of the Twain
Lines on the Loss of the Titanic[1]

I

In a solitude of the sea
Deep from human vanity,
And the Pride of Life that planned her, stilly couches she.

---

1. On April 15, 1912, the R.M.S. *Titanic* sank on its maiden voyage from Southampton to New York. The ship was thought to be unsinkable because it was constructed with many water-tight sections. It struck an iceberg, which tore a long gash in its side, and quickly sank.

2

Steel chambers, late the pyres
Of her salamandrine fires,[2]   5
Cold currents thrid,[3] and turn to rhythmic tidal lyres.

3

Over the mirrors meant
To glass the opulent
The sea-worm crawls—grotesque, slimed, dumb, indifferent.

4

Jewels in joy designed   10
To ravish the sensuous mind
Lie lightless, all their sparkles bleared and black and blind.

5

Dim moon-eyed fishes near
Gaze at the gilded gear
And query: "What does this vaingloriousness down here?"   15

6

Well: while was fashioning
This creature of cleaving wing,
The Immanent Will that stirs and urges everything

7

Prepared a sinister mate
For her—so gaily great—   20
A Shape of Ice, for the time far and dissociate.

2. According to legend, salamanders can
live in fire. The boilers of the *Titanic* were
similarly remarkable for burning though
they were under water, so to speak.
3. I.e., thread.

8

And as the smart ship grew
In stature, grace, and hue,
In shadowy silent distance grew the Iceberg too.

9

Alien they seemed to be: 25
No mortal eye could see
The intimate welding of their later history.

10

Or sign that they were bent
By paths coincident
On being anon twin halves of one august event,   30

11

'Till the Spinner of the Years
Said "Now!" And each one hears,
And consummation comes, and jars two hemispheres.

1912

Channel Firing

That night your great guns, unawares,
Shook all our coffins as we lay,
And broke the chancel window-squares,
We thought it was the Judgment-day.

And sat upright. While drearisome   5
Arose the howl of wakened hounds:
The mouse let fall the altar-crumb,
The worms drew back into the mounds,

The glebe cow drooled. Till God called, "No;
It's gunnery practice out at sea   10
Just as before you went below;
The world is as it used to be:

"All nations striving strong to make
Red war yet redder. Mad as hatters
They do no more for Christés sake   15
Than you who are helpless in such matters.

"That this is not the judgment-hour
For some of them's a blessed thing,
For if it were they'd have to scour
Hell's floor for so much threatening. . . .   20

"Ha, ha. It will be warmer when
I blow the trumpet (if indeed
I ever do; for you are men,
And rest eternal sorely need)."

So down we lay again. "I wonder,   25
Will the world ever saner be,"
Said one, "than when He sent us under
In our indifferent century!"

And many a skeleton shook his head.
"Instead of preaching forty year,"   30
My neighbour Parson Thirdly said,
"I wish I had stuck to pipes and beer."

Again the guns disturbed the hour,
Roaring their readiness to avenge,
As far inland as Stourton Tower,   35
And Camelot, and starlit Stonehenge.

1914

Robert Hayden
1913–1980

> *Hayden's birth parents gave him up for adoption when he was two years old, and "Those Winter Sundays" recounts his youth growing up in the working-class, Detroit home of his adoptive family. Much of Hayden's work deals with racial injustice in America, but, as he declared, he wanted to be a black poet "the way [W. B.] Yeats was an Irish poet." That is, he wanted his sensibility to be suffused with a racial awareness, and his work to be political in a broad sense of that word, but he allows neither to narrow the scope of his work. No reader of the 1962 book in which Hayden published "Those Winter Sundays" could ignore the racial injustices that kept this family poor. But at the same time Hayden does not reserve "love's austere and lonely offices" for the working-class, black American.*

Those Winter Sundays

Sundays too my father got up early
and put his clothes on in the blueblack cold,
then with cracked hands that ached
from labor in the weekday weather made
banked fires blaze. No one ever thanked him.   5

I'd wake and hear the cold splintering, breaking.
When the rooms were warm, he'd call,
and slowly I would rise and dress,
fearing the chronic angers of that house,

Speaking indifferently to him,   10
who had driven out the cold
and polished my good shoes as well.
What did I know, what did I know
of love's austere and lonely offices?

1962

Seamus Heaney
1939–

Heaney put "Digging" on the first page of his first book in 1966, suggesting he meant it to inaugurate and justify his vocation. For Ireland's Catholics, potatoes are rich symbols: they represent both the sustenance of the earth and the terrible famines in the 1840s under England's colonial rule. The Irish cut "turf" from peat bogs to burn in their stoves and fireplaces like coal. By the mid-1970s, the public recognized Heaney as Ireland's chief poet, but he was criticized for not taking a stand against England's oppression of Irish Catholics. Heaney responded with North in 1975, but it hardly endorsed militant nationalism. In North, the bogs figure as the racial memory bank of Celts: the bog woman in "Punishment" is an ancient Celt unearthed in modern times. The archeological evidence suggests that she was ritually executed for adultery. The women chained to the rails are contemporary Catholics who were tarred, shaved, and stripped naked by soldiers in the Irish Republican Army for the crime of dating British soldiers.

Digging

Between my finger and my thumb
The squat pen rests; snug as a gun.

Under my window, a clean rasping sound
When the spade sinks into gravelly ground:
My father, digging. I look down   5

Till his straining rump among the flowerbeds
Bends low, comes up twenty years away
Stooping in rhythm through potato drills[1]
Where he was digging.

The coarse boot nestled on the lug, the shaft   10
Against the inside knee was levered firmly.

---

1. Small furrows in which seeds are sown.

He rooted out tall tops, buried the bright edge deep
To scatter new potatoes that we picked
Loving their cool hardness in our hands.

By god, the old man could handle a spade.   15
Just like his old man.

My grandfather cut more turf in a day
Than any other man on Toner's bog.
Once I carried him milk in a bottle
Corked sloppily with paper. He straightened up   20
To drink it, then fell to right away
Nicking and slicing neatly, heaving sods
Over his shoulder, going down and down
For the good turf. Digging.

The cold smell of potato mould, the squelch and slap   25
Of soggy peat, the curt cuts of an edge
Through living roots awaken in my head.
But I've no spade to follow men like them.

Between my finger and my thumb
The squat pen rests.   30
I'll dig with it.

1966

Punishment

I can feel the tug
of the halter at the nape
of her neck, the wind
on her naked front.

It blows her nipples   5
to amber beads,
it shakes the frail rigging
of her ribs.

I can see her drowned
body in the bog,   10
the weighing stone,
the floating rods and boughs.

Under which at first
she was a barked sapling
that is dug up   15
oak-bone, brain-firkin:[1]

her shaved head
like a stubble of black corn,
her blindfold a soiled bandage,
her noose a ring   20

to store
the memories of love.
Little adulteress,
before they punished you

you were flaxen-haired,   25
undernourished, and your
tar-black face was beautiful.
My poor scapegoat,

I almost love you
but would have cast, I know,   30
the stones of silence.
I am the artful voyeur

of your brain's exposed
and darkened combs,
your muscles' webbing   35
and all your numbered bones:

---

1. A small wooden cask or vessel.

I who have stood dumb
when your betraying sisters,
cauled in tar,
wept by the railings,   40

who would connive
in civilized outrage
yet understand the exact
and tribal, intimate revenge.

1975

Robert Herrick

1591–1674

> *Herrick carried on a slow life as a country minister until the Puri-*
> *tans took over England in the 1640s. Then he was deprived of his*
> *parish and forced to return to London, where he prepared his verse*
> *for publication. More than fourteen hundred poems—including*
> *the three here—came out at once in 1648. Public opinion during*
> *the Puritan regime was not likely to praise his poems "of youth, of*
> *love, and . . . of cleanly wantonness," as Herrick described his own*
> *work. Actually, no one noticed his poems, not even to condemn*
> *their salaciousness. He was ignored until the nineteenth century.*
> *"To the Virgins to Make Much of Time" is a seduction poem using*
> *the conventional* carpe diem *strategy, just as "Upon Julia's Clothes"*
> *is a typical poem in praise of the speaker's beloved. But "Delight in*
> *Disorder" suggests that underlying these conventions is a distinct*
> *philosophy of life. In the mind of a seventeenth-century reader, the*
> *word "precise" in the last line would have called up images of Puri-*
> *tans and their ethic.*

Delight in Disorder

A sweet disorder in the dress
Kindles in clothes a wantonness.
A lawn about the shoulders thrown

Into a fine distractiòn;
An erring lace, which here and there   5
Enthralls the crimson stomacher;
A cuff neglectful, and thereby
Ribbons to flow confusedly;
A winning wave, deserving note,
In the tempestuous petticoat;   10
A careless shoestring, in whose tie
I see a wild civility;
Do more bewitch me than when art
Is too precise in every part.

1648

To the Virgins, to Make Much of Time

Gather ye rosebuds while ye may,
    Old time is still a-flying;
And this same flower that smiles today
    Tomorrow will be dying.

The glorious lamp of heaven, the sun,   5
    The higher he's a-getting,
The sooner will his race be run,
    And nearer he's to setting.

That age is best which is the first,
    When youth and blood are warmer;   10
But being spent, the worse, and worst
    Times still succeed the former.

Then be not coy, but use your time,
    And, while ye may, go marry;
For, having lost but once your prime,   15
    You may forever tarry.

1648

Upon Julia's Clothes

Whenas in silks my Julia goes,
Then, then, methinks, how sweetly flows
That liquefaction of her clothes.

Next, when I cast mine eyes, and see
That brave vibration, each way free,   5
O, how that glittering taketh me!

1648

Gerard Manley Hopkins
1844–1889

> *At twenty-two years old, against his parents' will, Hopkins con-
> verted to Catholicism, and a few years later he joined the Jesuit or-
> der and burned all his poems. With his rector's blessing he composed
> ten sonnets on nature in 1877, including "God's Grandeur" and
> "The Windhover," each remarkable for its striking rhythms. Hop-
> kins called it "sprung rhythm," which he developed from ancient
> Welsh verse that combines in each line any number of lightly
> stressed syllables with a set number of stressed syllables. Yet more
> striking are Hopkins's conceits, which were like nothing anyone else
> was writing in Victorian England. In fact, the poems were not pub-
> lished until 1918, when they found proper companions with modern
> poems, like Eliot's and Pound's. "Margaret" in "Spring and Fall" is
> not based on a real girl; Hopkins invented her when he wrote the
> poem on September 7, 1880. "God's Grandeur," "The Windhover,"
> and "Spring and Fall" all come to us from letters Hopkins sent to
> Robert Bridges, a fellow poet, who saved them for posterity.*

God's Grandeur

The world is charged with the grandeur of God.
　It will flame out, like shining from shook foil;[1]
　It gathers to a greatness, like the ooze of oil
Crushed. Why do men then now not reck his rod?
Generations have trod, have trod, have trod;   5
　And all is seared with trade; bleared, smeared with toil;
　And wears man's smudge and shares man's smell: the soil
Is bare now, nor can foot feel, being shod.

And for all this, nature is never spent;
　There lives the dearest freshness deep down things;   10
And though the last lights off the black West went
　Oh, morning, at the brown brink eastward, springs—
Because the Holy Ghost over the bent
　World broods with warm breast and with ah! bright wings.
1877   *1918*

The Windhover[2]

To Christ Our Lord

I caught this morning morning's minion, king-
　dom of daylight's dauphin, dapple-dawn-drawn Falcon, in
　　his riding
Of the rolling level underneath him steady air, and striding
High there, how he rung upon the rein of a wimpling wing
In his ecstasy! then off, off forth on swing,   5
　As a skate's heel sweeps smooth on a bow-bend: the hurl
　　and gliding

1. In a letter to Robert Bridges (January 4, 1883), Hopkins says: "I mean foil in its sense of leaf or tinsel, and no other word whatever will give the effect I want. Shaken goldfoil gives off broad glares like sheet lightning and also, and this is true of noth-ing else, owing to its zigzag dints and cross-ings and network of small many cornered facets, a sort of fork lightning too."

2. "A name for the kestrel [a species of small hawk], from its habit of hovering or hanging with its head to the wind" [O.E.D.].

Rebuffed the big wind. My heart in hiding
Stirred for a bird,—the achieve of, the mastery of the thing!

Brute beauty and valour and act, oh, air, pride, plume, here
    Buckle!³ AND the fire that breaks from thee then, a billion   10
Times told lovelier, more dangerous, O my chevalier!

    No wonder of it; shéer plód makes plough down sillion
Shine, and blue-bleak embers, ah my dear,
    Fall, gall themselves, and gash gold-vermilion.
1877   *1918*

Spring and Fall

To a Young Child

Márgarét, áre you gríeving
Over Goldengrove unleaving?
Leáves, líke the things of man, you
With your fresh thoughts care for, can you?
Áh! ás the heart grows older   5
It will come to such sights colder
By and by, nor spare a sigh
Though worlds of wanwood leafmeal lie;
And yet you *will* weep and know why.
Now no matter, child, the name: 10
Sórrow's spríngs áre the same.
Nor mouth had, no nor mind, expressed
What heart heard of, ghost guessed:
It ís the blight man was born for,
It is Margaret you mourn for.   15
1880   *1918*

---

3. "Buckle" can be understood two ways: either the elements in line 9 are fastened together as if by a buckle, or they crumble as a support might buckle. The verb also can be read as an indicative or an imperative, as if the speaker were either describing an action or commanding it.

A. E. (Alfred Edward) Housman
1859–1936

Housman was tormented for years by his love for his college room-mate and close friend, Moses Jackson. When Jackson went to India to make his fortune and marry, Housman transferred his affections to Jackson's brother, who died unexpectedly. This event might have triggered Housman's burst of creative energy in the mid-1890s, which produced all of these poems. The speaker in these poems is Terence Hearsay, a youth from Shropshire, a county that figures in the English imagination the way the states Iowa or Nebraska might in the American. "1887" commemorates the fiftieth anniversary of Queen Victoria's reign, and its apparent endorsement of Empire made Housman's book popular when England went to war against the Boers in South Africa. English soldiers dead in the foreign fields had these poems buttoned in their pockets. Housman was an athe-ist, as "The Immortal Part" suggests, which calls into question the advice Terence gives in "To An Athlete Dying Young" and "Shot? So Quick, So Clean an Ending?" (Housman wrote these about the same time that Oscar Wilde was convicted of homosexuality in a sensational trial and sentenced to two years of hard labor, which makes Terence's approval of the suicide more understandable.) These celebrations of the dead should be read in the context of "Terence, This Is Stupid Stuff . . . ," which suggests that the speaker might not be entirely sincere.

1887

From Clee to heaven the beacon burns,
 The shires have seen it plain,
From north and south the sign returns
 And beacons burn again.

Look left, look right, the hills are bright,   5
 The dales are light between,
Because 'tis fifty years to-night
 That God has saved the Queen.

Now, when the flame they watch not towers
    About the soil they trod,   10
Lads, we'll remember friends of ours
    Who shared the work with God.

To skies that knit their heartstrings right,
    To fields that bred them brave,
The saviours come not home to-night: 15
    Themselves they could not save.

It dawns in Asia, tombstones show
    And Shropshire names are read;
And the Nile spills his overflow
    Beside the Severn's[1] dead.   20

We pledge in peace by farm and town
    The Queen they served in war,
And fire the beacons up and down
    The land they perished for.

"God save the Queen" we living sing,   25
    From height to height 'tis heard;
And with the rest your voices ring,
    Lads of the Fifty-third.

Oh, God will save her, fear you not:
    Be you the men you've been,   30
Get you the sons your fathers got,
    And God will save the Queen.

                          1896

---

1. The Severn River divides England from Wales.

To an Athlete Dying Young

The time you won your town the race
We chaired you through the market-place;
Man and boy stood cheering by,
And home we brought you shoulder-high.

Today, the road all runners come,   5
Shoulder-high we bring you home,
And set you at your threshold down,
Townsman of a stiller town.

Smart lad, to slip betimes away
From fields where glory does not stay   10
And early though the laurel grows
It withers quicker than the rose.

Eyes the shady night has shut
Cannot see the record cut,
And silence sounds no worse than cheers   15
After earth has stopped the ears:

Now you will not swell the rout
Of lads that wore their honours out,
Runners whom renown outran
And the name died before the man.   20

So set, before its echoes fade,
The fleet foot on the sill of shade,
And hold to the low lintel up
The still-defended challenge-cup.

And round that early-laurelled head   25
Will flock to gaze the strengthless dead,
And find unwithered on its curls
The garland briefer than a girl's.

1896

The Immortal Part

When I meet the morning beam,
Or lay me down at night to dream,
I hear my bones within me say,
"Another night, another day.

"When shall this slough of sense be cast,   5
This dust of thoughts be laid at last,
The man of flesh and soul be slain
And the man of bone remain?

"This tongue that talks, these lungs that shout,
These thews that hustle us about,   10
This brain that fills the skull with schemes,
And its humming hive of dreams,—

"These to-day are proud in power
And lord it in their little hour:
The immortal bones obey control   15
Of dying flesh and dying soul.

" 'Tis long till eve and morn are gone:
Slow the endless night comes on,
And late to fulness grows the birth
That shall last as long as earth.   20

"Wanderers eastward, wanderers west,
Know you why you cannot rest?
'Tis that every mother's son
Travails with a skeleton.

"Lie down in the bed of dust;   25
Bear the fruit that bear you must;
Bring the eternal seed to light,
And morn is all the same as night.

"Rest you so from trouble sore,
Fear the heat o' the sun no more,   30
Nor the snowing winter wild,
Now you labor not with child.

"Empty vessel, garment cast,
We that wore you long shall last.
—Another night, another day."   35
So my bones within me say.

Therefore they shall do my will
To-day while I am master still,
And flesh and soul, now both are strong,
Shall hale the sullen slaves along,   40

Before this fire of sense decay,
This smoke of thought blow clean away,
And leave with ancient night alone
The stedfast and enduring bone.

                              1896

Shot? So quick, so clean an ending?

Shot? so quick, so clean an ending?
    Oh that was right, lad, that was brave:
Yours was not an ill for mending,
    'Twas best to take it to the grave.

Oh you had forethought, you could reason,   5
    And saw your road and where it led,
And early wise and brave in season
    Put the pistol to your head.

Oh soon, and better so than later
    After long disgrace and scorn,   10
You shot dead the household traitor,
    The soul that should not have been born.

Right you guessed the rising morrow
   And scorned to tread the mire you must:
Dust's your wages, son of sorrow,   15
   But men may come to worse than dust.

Souls undone, undoing others,—
   Long time since the tale began.
You would not live to wrong your brothers:
   Oh lad, you died as fits a man.   20

Now to your grave shall friend and stranger
   With ruth and some with envy come:
Undishonoured, clear of danger,
   Clean of guilt, pass hence and home.

Turn safe to rest, no dreams, no waking;   25
   And here, man, here's the wreath I've made.
'Tis not a gift that's worth the taking,
   But wear it and it will not fade.

1896

"Terence, this is stupid stuff . . ."

   "Terence, this is stupid stuff:
You eat your victuals fast enough;
There can't be much amiss, 'tis clear,
To see the rate you drink your beer.
But oh, good Lord, the verse you make,   5
It gives a chap the belly-ache.
The cow, the old cow, she is dead;
It sleeps well, the hornéd head:
We poor lads, 'tis our turn now
To hear such tunes as killed the cow.   10
Pretty friendship 'tis to rhyme
Your friends to death before their time
Moping melancholy mad:
Come, pipe a tune to dance to, lad."

Why, if 'tis dancing you would be,   15
There's brisker pipes than poetry.
Say, for what were hop-yards meant,
Or why was Burton built on Trent?
Oh many a peer of England brews
Livelier liquor than the Muse,   20
And malt does more than Milton can
To justify God's ways to man.
Ale, man, ale's the stuff to drink
For fellows whom it hurts to think:
Look into the pewter pot   25
To see the world as the world's not.
And faith, 'tis pleasant till 'tis past:
The mischief is that 'twill not last.
Oh I have been to Ludlow fair
And left my necktie God knows where,   30
And carried halfway home, or near,
Pints and quarts of Ludlow beer:
Then the world seemed none so bad,
And I myself a sterling lad;
And down in lovely muck I've lain,   35
Happy till I woke again.
Then I saw the morning sky:
Heigho, the tale was all a lie;
The world, it was the old world yet,
I was I, my things were wet,   40
And nothing now remained to do
But begin the game anew.

    Therefore, since the world has still
Much good, but much less good than ill,
And while the sun and moon endure   45
Luck's a chance, but trouble's sure,
I'd face it as a wise man would,
And train for ill and not for good.
'Tis true, the stuff I bring for sale
Is not so brisk a brew as ale: 50
Out of a stem that scored the hand

I wrung it in a weary land.
But take it: if the smack is sour,
The better for the embittered hour;
It should do good to heart and head   55
When your soul is in my soul's stead;
And I will friend you, if I may,
In the dark and cloudy day.

    There was a king reigned in the East:
There, when kings will sit to feast,   60
They get their fill before they think
With poisoned meat and poisoned drink.
He gathered all that springs to birth
From the many-venomed earth;
First a little, thence to more,   65
He sampled all her killing store;
And easy, smiling, seasoned sound,
Sate the king when healths went round.
They put arsenic in his meat
And stared aghast to watch him eat;   70
They poured strychnine in his cup
And shook to see him drink it up:
They shook, they stared as white's their shirt:
Them it was their poison hurt.
—I tell the tale that I heard told.   75
Mithridates, he died old.[1]

                                        1896

---

    1. In the first century B.C.E., King Mithridates VI took small doses of poison until he developed an immunity to it.

Langston Hughes
1902–1967

> *Not long after he graduated from high school, Hughes published "The Negro Speaks of Rivers" in the political magazine* The Crisis. *The poem counters white views of blacks as a primitive race without history by linking African Americans to ancient black civilizations. Hughes went to Columbia University, where he began meeting the leaders of the Harlem Renaissance, a movement among African American artists in literature, music, painting, dance, and the like. In 1926, at just twenty-four years old, Hughes published an essay in the widely circulated, leftist paper* The Nation, *which argued that African Americans should create a "racial art." That concept was controversial in the 1920s because many intellectuals, black and white, thought that subcultures should dissolve themselves in the American mainstream. "Harlem" and "Theme for English B" came much later in Hughes's career, after he had established himself as one of America's most successful poets, but both illustrate what he called for in 1926. Hughes wanted these and the other poems in* Montage of a Dream Deferred (1951) *to express contemporary Harlem by borrowing from the "current of Afro-American popular music . . . jazz, ragtime, swing, blues, boogie-woogie, and bebop."*

The Negro Speaks of Rivers

(To W. E. B. Du Bois)[1]

I've known rivers:
I've known rivers ancient as the world and older than the
    flow of human blood in human veins.
My soul has grown deep like the rivers.

---

1. (1868–1963); American historian, educator, and activist; one of the founders of the NAACP.

I bathed in the Euphrates when dawns were young.
I built my hut near the Congo and it lulled me to sleep.   5
I looked upon the Nile and raised the pyramids above it.
I heard the singing of the Mississippi when Abe Lincoln
      went down to New Orleans, and I've seen its muddy
      bosom turn all golden in the sunset.

I've known rivers:
Ancient, dusky rivers.

My soul has grown deep like the rivers.   10

1926

Harlem

What happens to a dream deferred?

Does it dry up
like a raisin in the sun?
Or fester like a sore—
And then run?   5
Does it stink like rotten meat?
Or crust and sugar over—
like a syrupy sweet?

Maybe it just sags
like a heavy load.   10

Or does it explode?

1951

Theme for English B

The instructor said,

> Go home and write
> a page tonight.
> And let that page come out of you—
> Then, it will be true.   5

I wonder if it's that simple?
I am twenty-two, colored, born in Winston-Salem.
I went to school there, then Durham, then here
to this college on the hill above Harlem.
I am the only colored student in my class.   10
The steps from the hill lead down into Harlem,
through a park, then I cross St. Nicholas,
Eighth Avenue, Seventh, and I come to the Y,
the Harlem Branch Y, where I take the elevator
up to my room, sit down, and write this page: 15

It's not easy to know what is true for you or me
at twenty-two, my age. But I guess I'm what
I feel and see and hear, Harlem, I hear you:
hear you, hear me—we two—you, me, talk on this page.
(I hear New York, too.) Me—who?   20
Well, I like to eat, sleep, drink, and be in love.
I like to work, read, learn, and understand life.
I like a pipe for a Christmas present,
or records—Bessie,[2] bop, or Bach.
I guess being colored doesn't make me *not* like   25
the same things other folks like who are other races.
So will my page be colored that I write?
Being me, it will not be white.
But it will be
a part of you, instructor.   30

---

2. Bessie Smith (1894?–1937), American blues singer.

You are white—
yet a part of me, as I am a part of you.
That's American.
Sometimes perhaps you don't want to be a part of me.
Nor do I often want to be a part of you.   35
But we are, that's true!
I guess you learn from me—
although you're older—and white—
and somewhat more free.

This is my page for English B.   40

1951

Randall Jarrell
1914–1965

> *In 1942 Jarrell joined the Army Air Force and spent World War II teaching celestial navigation to flyers in Arizona. During these years, he wrote "The Death of the Ball Turret Gunner," which he published in 1945. Jarrell explained that the machine gunner in the plexiglass sphere attached to the underside of a World War II bomber reminded him of a fetus still in its mother's womb. The hose in the last line, Jarrell noted, would have been a steam hose.*

The Death of the Ball Turret Gunner

From my mother's sleep I fell into the State,
And I hunched in its belly till my wet fur froze.
Six miles from earth, loosed from its dream of life,
I woke to black flak and the nightmare fighters.
When I died they washed me out of the turret with a hose.   5

1945

Ben Jonson
1572–1637

> Jonson, a colleague of Shakespeare, gathered around himself England's first "school" of literature, the Cavaliers, characterized by their classical learning and frank, playful treatment of sexual themes, a direct challenge to the Puritan ethic of seventeenth-century England. "Song: To Celia" is a translation stitched together from various parts of the Epistles of Philostratus, an ancient Greek philosopher. The key to the poem is how the speaker (and you) interpret the symbolic action in lines 9–16. "On My First Daughter" and "On My First Son" are epitaphs: poems that might have been carved on tombstones. We do not know if Jonson really had a daughter, but his son, Benjamin ("child of the right hand" is what the name means in Hebrew), died in 1603 on his seventh birthday.

Song: To Celia

Drink to me only with thine eyes,
And I will pledge with mine;
Or leave a kiss but in the cup,
And I'll not look for wine.
The thirst that from the soul doth rise,　　　　　5
Doth ask a drink divine:
But might I of Jove's nectar sup,
I would not change for thine.
I sent thee late a rosy wreath,
Not so much honoring thee,　　　　　10
As giving it a hope, that there
It could not withered be.
But thou thereon did'st only breathe,
And sent'st it back to me;
Since when it grows and smells, I swear,　　　　　15
Not of itself, but thee.

1616

On My First Daughter

Here lies, to each her parents' ruth,
Mary, the daughter of their youth;
Yet all heaven's gifts being heaven's due,
It makes the father less to rue.
At six months' end she parted hence   5
With safety of her innocence;
Whose soul heaven's queen, whose name she bears,
In comfort of her mother's tears,
Hath placed amongst her virgin-train:
Where, while that severed doth remain,[1]   10
This grave partakes the fleshly birth;
Which cover lightly, gentle earth!

                                                    1616

On My First Son

Farewell, thou child of my right hand, and joy;
My sin was too much hope of thee, loved boy:
Seven years thou wert lent to me, and I thee pay,
Exacted by thy fate, on the just day.
O could I lose all father now! for why   5
Will man lament the state he should envy,
To have so soon 'scaped world's and flesh's rage,
And, if no other misery, yet age?
Rest in soft peace, and asked, say, "Here doth lie
Ben Jonson his best piece of poetry."   10
For whose sake henceforth all his vows be such
As what he loves may never like too much.

                                                    1616

---

1. The severing of the soul from the body is only temporary, according to orthodoxy. They will reunite at the end of time.

John Keats
1795–1821

> One evening in October 1816, the twenty-one-year-old Keats stayed
> up late with his former teacher reading George Chapman's trans-
> lation of Homer. The vigor of the Elizabethan poetry astonished
> Keats, who had known Homer only through Alexander Pope's for-
> mal, abstract translations. After walking home at dawn, Keats
> wrote "On First Looking into Chapman's Homer" in about an hour
> and sent it to his teacher, who found the Petrarchan sonnet waiting
> for him at breakfast. Sir William Herschel's discovery of Uranus in
> 1781 probably inspired the first simile in the sestet. In the second
> simile, Keats confused Cortez with Balboa, who was the first Euro-
> pean to see the Pacific Ocean. The foreboding of his own death ex-
> pressed in "When I Have Fears," written in January 1818, intensified
> later that year, when Keats nursed his younger brother through the
> final stages of tuberculosis. Then came the great burst of writing
> that produced the other poems here. In them you can trace Keats's
> evolving attitude toward death: first "La Belle Dame sans Merci";
> then "Ode to a Nightingale" and "Ode on a Grecian Urn," written
> about the same time; finally "To Autumn." "La Belle Dame sans
> Merci," a pseudo-medieval poem, means "The beautiful woman
> without pity." The nightingale is a conventional symbol of immor-
> tality. Inside the Grecian urn, perhaps, are the cremated remains of
> a person; on its outside are the scenes described in the first four stan-
> zas of the poem. Autumn, of course, is a conventional symbol for
> the end of life; in this poem Keats may be reconciling himself to
> death.

On First Looking into Chapman's Homer

Much have I traveled in the realms of gold,
  And many goodly states and kingdoms seen;
  Round many western islands have I been
Which bards in fealty to Apollo[1] hold.
Oft of one wide expanse had I been told   5

---

1. God of poetic inspiration.

That deep-browed Homer ruled as his demesne;[2]
   Yet did I never breathe its pure serene
Till I heard Chapman speak out loud and bold:
Then felt I like some watcher of the skies
   When a new planet swims into his ken;   10
Or like stout Cortez when with eagle eyes
   He stared at the Pacific—and all his men
Looked at each other with a wild surmise—
   Silent, upon a peak in Darien.

                             1816

When I Have Fears

When I have fears that I may cease to be
   Before my pen has gleaned my teeming brain,
Before high-piléd books, in charact'ry,
   Hold like rich garners the full-ripened grain;
When I behold, upon the night's starred face,   5
   Huge cloudy symbols of a high romance,
And think that I may never live to trace
   Their shadows, with the magic hand of chance;
And when I feel, fair creature of an hour,
   That I shall never look upon thee more,   10
Never have relish in the faery power
   Of unreflecting love!—then on the shore
Of the wide world I stand alone, and think
Till Love and Fame to nothingness do sink.
1818   *1848*

La Belle Dame sans Merci

O what can ail thee, Knight at arms,
   Alone and palely loitering?
The sedge has withered from the Lake
   And no birds sing!

2. I.e., domain.

O what can ail thee, Knight at arms,   5
   So haggard, and so woebegone?
The squirrel's granary is full
   And the harvest's done.

I see a lily on thy brow
   With anguish moist and fever dew,   10
And on thy cheeks a fading rose
   Fast withereth too.

"I met a Lady in the Meads,
   Full beautiful, a faery's child,
Her hair was long, her foot was light   15
   And her eyes were wild.

"I made a Garland for her head,
   And bracelets too, and fragrant Zone;[3]
She looked at me as she did love
   And made sweet moan.   20

"I set her on my pacing steed
   And nothing else saw all day long,
For sidelong would she bend and sing
   A faery's song.

"She found me roots of relish sweet,   25
   And honey wild, and manna dew,
And sure in language strange she said
   'I love thee true.'

"She took me to her elfin grot
   And there she wept and sighed full sore,   30
And there I shut her wild wild eyes
   With kisses four.

3. I.e., girdle.

"And there she lulléd me asleep,
  And there I dreamed, Ah Woe betide!
The latest dream I ever dreamt   35
  On the cold hill side.

"I saw pale Kings, and Princes too,
  Pale warriors, death-pale were they all;
They cried, 'La belle dame sans merci
  Hath thee in thrall!'   40

"I saw their starved lips in the gloam
  With horrid warning gapéd wide,
And I awoke, and found me here
  On the cold hill's side.

"And this is why I sojourn here,   45
  Alone and palely loitering;
Though the sedge is withered from the Lake
  And no birds sing."

                         1820

Ode to a Nightingale

I

My heart aches, and a drowsy numbness pains
  My sense, as though of hemlock I had drunk,
Or emptied some dull opiate to the drains
  One minute past, and Lethe-wards[4] had sunk:
'Tis not through envy of thy happy lot,   5
  But being too happy in thine happiness—
    That thou, light-wingéd Dryad of the trees,
      In some melodious plot
  Of beechen green, and shadows numberless,
    Singest of summer in full-throated ease.   10

---

4. Toward the river Lethe, whose waters in Hades bring the dead forgetfulness.

2

O, for a draught of vintage! that hath been
  Cooled a long age in the deep-delvéd earth,
Tasting of Flora and the country green,
  Dance, and Provençal song, and sunburnt mirth!
O for a beaker full of the warm South,   15
  Full of the true, the blushful Hippocrene,[5]
    With beaded bubbles winking at the brim,
      And purple-stainéd mouth;
  That I might drink, and leave the world unseen,
    And with thee fade away into the forest dim: 20

3

Fade far away, dissolve, and quite forget
  What thou among the leaves hast never known,
The weariness, the fever, and the fret
  Here, where men sit and hear each other groan;
Where palsy shakes a few, sad, last gray hairs,   25
  Where youth grows pale, and specter-thin, and dies,
    Where but to think is to be full of sorrow
      And leaden-eyed despairs,
  Where Beauty cannot keep her lustrous eyes,
    Or new Love pine at them beyond tomorrow.   30

4

Away! away! for I will fly to thee,
  Not charioted by Bacchus and his pards,[6]
But on the viewless wings of Poesy,
  Though the dull brain perplexes and retards:
Already with thee! tender is the night,   35
  And haply the Queen-Moon is on her throne,

5. The fountain of the Muses (goddesses of poetry and the arts) on Mt. Helicon in Greece; its waters inspire poets.

6. "Bacchus": god of wine, often depicted in a chariot drawn by leopards ("pards").

Clustered around by all her starry Fays;
  But here there is no light,
Save what from heaven is with the breezes blown
  Through verdurous glooms and winding mossy ways.   40

                    5

I cannot see what flowers are at my feet,
  Nor what soft incense hangs upon the boughs,
But, in embalméd darkness, guess each sweet
  Wherewith the seasonable month endows
The grass, the thicket, and the fruit tree wild;   45
  White hawthorn, and the pastoral eglantine;
    Fast fading violets covered up in leaves;
      And mid-May's eldest child,
The coming musk-rose, full of dewy wine,
  The murmurous haunt of flies on summer eves.   50

                    6

Darkling I listen; and for many a time
  I have been half in love with easeful Death,
Called him soft names in many a muséd rhyme,
  To take into the air my quiet breath;
Now more than ever seems it rich to die,   55
  To cease upon the midnight with no pain,
    While thou art pouring forth thy soul abroad
      In such an ecstasy!
Still wouldst thou sing, and I have ears in vain—
  To thy high requiem become a sod.   60

                    7

Thou wast not born for death, immortal Bird!
  No hungry generations tread thee down;
The voice I hear this passing night was heard
  In ancient days by emperor and clown:

Perhaps the selfsame song that found a path   65
    Through the sad heart of Ruth,[7] when, sick for home,
        She stood in tears amid the alien corn;
            The same that ofttimes hath
    Charmed magic casements, opening on the foam
        Of perilous seas, in faery lands forlorn.   70

                                    8

Forlorn! the very word is like a bell
    To toll me back from thee to my sole self!
Adieu! the fancy cannot cheat so well
    As she is famed to do, deceiving elf.
Adieu! adieu! thy plaintive anthem fades   75
    Past the near meadows, over the still stream,
        Up the hill side; and now 'tis buried deep
            In the next valley-glades:
    Was it a vision, or a waking dream?
        Fled is that music:—Do I wake or sleep?   80

                                            1820

Ode on a Grecian Urn

                                    I

Thou still unravished bride of quietness,
    Thou foster child of silence and slow time,
Sylvan historian, who canst thus express
    A flowery tale more sweetly than our rhyme:
What leaf-fringed legend haunts about thy shape   5
    Of deities or mortals, or of both,
        In Tempe or the dales of Arcady?[8]
    What men or gods are these? What maidens loath?

---

7. In the Old Testament, a woman of great loyalty and modesty who, as a stranger in Judah, won a husband while gleaning in the barley fields ("the alien corn," line 67).

8. The Greeks considered Tempe and Arcadia to be perfect examples of rural landscapes.

What mad pursuit? What struggle to escape?
    What pipes and timbrels? What wild ecstasy?   10

2

Heard melodies are sweet, but those unheard
    Are sweeter; therefore, ye soft pipes, play on;
Not to the sensual ear, but, more endeared,
    Pipe to the spirit ditties of no tone:
Fair youth, beneath the trees, thou canst not leave   15
    Thy song, nor ever can those trees be bare;
        Bold Lover, never, never canst thou kiss,
Though winning near the goal—yet, do not grieve;
        She cannot fade, though thou hast not thy bliss,
    Forever wilt thou love, and she be fair!   20

3

Ah, happy, happy boughs! that cannot shed
    Your leaves, nor ever bid the Spring adieu;
And, happy melodist, unwearièd,
    Forever piping songs forever new;
More happy love! more happy, happy love!   25
    Forever warm and still to be enjoyed,
        Forever panting, and forever young;
All breathing human passion far above,
    That leaves a heart high-sorrowful and cloyed,
        A burning forehead, and a parching tongue.   30

4

Who are these coming to the sacrifice?
    To what green altar, O mysterious priest,
Lead'st thou that heifer lowing at the skies,
    And all her silken flanks with garlands dressed?
What little town by river or sea shore,   35
    Or mountain-built with peaceful citadel,
        Is emptied of this folk, this pious morn?

And, little town, thy streets forevermore
　　Will silent be; and not a soul to tell
　　　Why thou art desolate, can e'er return.　　　　　　　40

5

O Attic[9] shape! Fair attitude! with brede[1]
　　Of marble men and maidens overwrought,
With forest branches and the trodden weed;
　　Thou, silent form, dost tease us out of thought
As doth eternity: Cold Pastoral!　　　　　　　　　　45
　　When old age shall this generation waste,
　　　Thou shalt remain, in midst of other woe
　　Than ours, a friend to man, to whom thou say'st,
"Beauty is truth, truth beauty,"—that is all
　　Ye know on earth, and all ye need to know.　　　50

1820

To Autumn

1

Season of mists and mellow fruitfulness,
　　Close bosom-friend of the maturing sun;
Conspiring with him how to load and bless
　　With fruit the vines that round the thatch-eaves run;
To bend with apples the mossed cottage-trees,　　　5
　　And fill all fruit with ripeness to the core;
　　　To swell the gourd, and plump the hazel shells
　　With a sweet kernel; to set budding more,
And still more, later flowers for the bees,
Until they think warm days will never cease,　　　10
　　　For Summer has o'er-brimmed their clammy cells.

---

9. Greek, especially Athenian.　　　　　1. I.e., woven pattern.

2

Who hath not seen thee oft amid thy store?
  Sometimes whoever seeks abroad may find
Thee sitting careless on a granary floor,
    Thy hair soft-lifted by the winnowing wind;   15
Or on a half-reaped furrow sound asleep,
    Drowsed with the fume of poppies, while thy hook
      Spares the next swath and all its twinéd flowers:
And sometimes like a gleaner thou dost keep
    Steady thy laden head across a brook;   20
    Or by a cider-press, with patient look,
      Thou watchest the last oozings hours by hours.

3

Where are the songs of Spring? Aye, where are they?
  Think not of them, thou hast thy music too—
While barréd clouds bloom the soft-dying day,   25
    And touch the stubble-plains with rosy hue;
Then in a wailful choir the small gnats mourn
    Among the river sallows, borne aloft
      Or sinking as the light wind lives or dies;
And full-grown lambs loud bleat from hilly bourn;   30
    Hedge crickets sing; and now with treble soft
    The redbreast whistles from a garden-croft;
      And gathering swallows twitter in the skies.

1820

Galway Kinnell

1927–

    *Kinnell is known for both his political poetry, which addresses the
    destructive capacity of technology, and for poems that explore the
    natural world on a number of levels. The selection here, "Black-
    berry Eating," literally describes eating blackberries right off the
    vine. But lines 9–13 compare the blackberries to "certain peculiar*

words" and, presumably, eating the blackberries is like writing a poem with these words. Carrying out the logic of this analogy leads to some interesting questions: Why would writing poems with words like "strengths" and "squinched" be a "black art"? And why are these long, monosyllabic words "black language"? What's the meaning of the thorns? Is this poem itself an example of "black art"?

Blackberry Eating

I love to go out in late September
among the fat, overripe, icy, black blackberries
to eat blackberries for breakfast,
the stalks very prickly, a penalty
they earn for knowing the black art   5
of blackberry making; and as I stand among them
lifting the stalks to my mouth, the ripest berries
fall almost unbidden to my tongue,
as words sometimes do, certain peculiar words
like *strengths* or *squinched* or *broughamed,*   10
many-lettered, one-syllabled lumps,
which I squeeze, squinch open, and splurge well
in the silent, startled, icy, black language
of blackberry eating in late September.

                                                    1980

Yusef Komunyakaa
1947–

Komunyakaa was an army correspondent during the Vietnam War. The speaker in "Facing It" is visiting the Vietnam Veterans Memorial in Washington, D.C., two long, low arms of polished black granite on which are engraved the names of the American dead. Compare the African American speaker's reflection in the granite to the white veteran's image, which floats toward the speaker. "We Never Know" describes in disturbingly sexual terms the experience of killing someone. The speaker is an American soldier; the dead man is either

*North Vietnamese or a Viet Cong soldier. To make sense of this poem,
you might determine how this experience has affected the American.*

Facing It

My black face fades,
hiding inside the black granite.
I said I wouldn't,
dammit: No tears.
I'm stone. I'm flesh.   5
My clouded reflection eyes me
like a bird of prey, the profile of night
slanted against morning. I turn
this way—the stone lets me go.
I turn that way—I'm inside   10
the Vietnam Veterans Memorial
again, depending on the light
to make a difference.
I go down the 58,022 names,
half-expecting to find   15
my own in letters like smoke.
I touch the name Andrew Johnson;
I see the booby trap's white flash.
Names shimmer on a woman's blouse
but when she walks away   20
the names stay on the wall.
Brushstrokes flash, a red bird's
wings cutting across my stare.
The sky. A plane in the sky.
A white vet's image floats   25
closer to me, then his pale eyes
look through mine. I'm a window.
He's lost his right arm
inside the stone. In the black mirror
a woman's trying to erase names: 30
No, she's brushing a boy's hair.

1988

We Never Know

He danced with tall grass
for a moment, like he was swaying
with a woman. Our gun barrels
glowed white-hot.
When I got to him,   5
a blue halo
of flies had already claimed him.
I pulled the crumbled photograph
from his fingers.
There's no other way   10
to say this: I fell in love.
The morning cleared again,
except for a distant mortar
& somewhere choppers taking off.
I slid the wallet into his pocket   15
& turned him over, so he wouldn't be
kissing the ground.

1988

Maxine Kumin
1925–

> *Kumin won the Pulitzer Prize in 1973 for* Up Country: Poems of
> New England, *her fourth book of poems, which included "Wood-*
> *chucks." The first group of poems in the book was inspired by her*
> *property in rural New Hampshire. She creates the persona of the*
> *hermit, the person fleeing human society and, like Henry David*
> *Thoreau, taking up residence among the plants and animals of a*
> *country place. The speaker in "Woodchucks" is all the more surpris-*
> *ing given the cluster of nature-loving poems within which it dwells.*

Woodchucks

Gassing the woodchucks didn't turn out right.
The knockout bomb from the Feed and Grain Exchange
was featured as merciful, quick at the bone
and the case we had against them was airtight,
both exits shoehorned shut with puddingstone,   5
but they had a sub-sub-basement out of range.

Next morning they turned up again, no worse
for the cyanide than we for our cigarettes
and state-store Scotch, all of us up to scratch.
They brought down the marigolds as a matter of course   10
and then took over the vegetable patch
nipping the broccoli shoots, beheading the carrots.

The food from our mouths, I said, righteously thrilling
to the feel of the .22, the bullets' neat noses.
I, a lapsed pacifist fallen from grace   15
puffed with Darwinian pieties for killing,
now drew a bead on the littlest woodchuck's face.
He died down in the everbearing roses.

Ten minutes later I dropped the mother. She
flipflopped in the air and fell, her needle teeth   20
still hooked in a leaf of early Swiss chard.
Another baby next. O one-two-three
the murderer inside me rose up hard,
the hawkeye killer came on stage forthwith.

There's one chuck left. Old wily fellow, he keeps   25
me cocked and ready day after day after day.
All night I hunt his humped-up form. I dream
I sight along the barrel in my sleep.
If only they'd all consented to die unseen
gassed underground the quiet Nazi way.   30

1973

Philip Larkin
1922–1985

Larkin was part of a wave of English writers who, in the 1950s and after, reacted against modernists like T. S. Eliot and Ezra Pound and strove to write in an easier, less academic style. An "aubade" celebrates the coming of dawn, but clearly Larkin uses the term ironically, since the coming of another sunrise terrifies the speaker. You might consider why this fear leads to indecision, as the speaker declares in the fourth stanza. The theme of this poem is the particular concern of existentialist philosophers who were burdened by the terrible experience of World War II. But ever since Darwin first suggested we shared an ancestor with apes, many men and women have had to confront and somehow resolve the dilemma explored here.

Aubade

I work all day, and get half-drunk at night.
Waking at four to soundless dark, I stare.
In time the curtain-edges will grow light.
Till then I see what's really always there:
Unresting death, a whole day nearer now,   5
Making all thought impossible but how
And where and when I shall myself die.
Arid interrogation: yet the dread
Of dying, and being dead,
Flashes afresh to hold and horrify.   10

The mind blanks at the glare. Not in remorse
—The good not done, the love not given, time
Torn off unused—nor wretchedly because
An only life can take so long to climb
Clear of its wrong beginnings, and may never;   15
But at the total emptiness for ever,
The sure extinction that we travel to
And shall be lost in always. Not to be here,

Not to be anywhere,
And soon; nothing more terrible, nothing more true.   20

This is a special way of being afraid
No trick dispels. Religion used to try,
That vast moth-eaten musical brocade
Created to pretend we never die,
And specious stuff that says *No rational being*   25
Can fear a thing it will not feel, not seeing
That this is what we fear—no sight, no sound,
No touch or taste or smell, nothing to think with,
Nothing to love or link with,
The anaesthetic from which none come round.   30

And so it stays just on the edge of vision,
A small unfocused blur, a standing chill
That slows each impulse down to indecision.
Most things may never happen: this one will,
And realisation of it rages out   35
In furnace-fear when we are caught without
People or drink. Courage is no good:
It means not scaring others. Being brave
Lets no one off the grave.
Death is no different whined at than withstood.   40

Slowly light strengthens, and the room takes shape.
It stands plain as a wardrobe, what we know,
Have always known, know that we can't escape,
Yet can't accept. One side will have to go.
Meanwhile telephones crouch, getting ready to ring   45
In locked-up offices, and all the uncaring
Intricate rented world begins to rouse.
The sky is white as clay, with no sun.
Work has to be done.
Postmen like doctors go from house to house.   50

1977

Li-Young Lee
1957–

> Lee combines a variety of traditions, from Chinese poetry to Walt
> Whitman, to whom he is often compared. For the Chinese influ-
> ence, you might compare the concluding stanzas of "Visions and
> Interpretations" to Pound's translation of the Chinese poem "The
> River-Merchant's Wife." Despite this affinity with old forms, "Vi-
> sions and Interpretations" is one of the few examples of postmodern
> poetry in this volume. One of the poem's main concerns is the na-
> ture of poetry and its relation to real experience. This poem is,
> among other things, about writing poems. "The Gift" is an excel-
> lent example of the emotive power of simple diction and mundane
> incident. Among the poem's striking features is the juxtaposition of
> a son's love for his father with a husband's love for his wife.

Visions and Interpretations

Because this graveyard is a hill,
I must climb up to see my dead,
stopping once midway to rest
beside this tree.

It was here, between the anticipation   5
of exhaustion, and exhaustion,
between vale and peak,
my father came down to me

and we climbed arm in arm to the top.
He cradled the bouquet I'd brought,   10
and I, a good son, never mentioned his grave,
erect like a door behind him.

And it was here, one summer day, I sat down
to read an old book. When I looked up
from the noon-lit page, I saw a vision   15
of a world about to come, and a world about to go.

Truth is, I've not seen my father
since he died, and, no, the dead
do not walk arm in arm with me.

If I carry flowers to them, I do so without their help,   20
the blossoms not always bright, torch-like,
but often heavy as sodden newspaper.

Truth is, I came here with my son one day,
and we rested against this tree,
and I fell asleep, and dreamed   25

a dream which, upon my boy waking me, I told.
Neither of us understood.
Then we went up.

Even this is not accurate.
Let me begin again: 30

Between two griefs, a tree.
Between my hands, white chrysanthemums, yellow
    chrysanthemums.

The old book I finished reading
I've since read again and again.

And what was far grows near,   35
and what is near grows more dear,

and all of my visions and interpretations
depend on what I see,

and between my eyes is always
the rain, the migrant rain.   40

1986

The Gift

To pull the metal splinter from my palm
my father recited a story in a low voice.
I watched his lovely face and not the blade.
Before the story ended, he'd removed
the iron sliver I thought I'd die from.   5

I can't remember the tale,
but hear his voice still, a well
of dark water, a prayer.
And I recall his hands,
two measures of tenderness   10
he laid against my face,
the flames of discipline
he raised above my head.

Had you entered that afternoon
you would have thought you saw a man   15
planting something in a boy's palm,
a silver tear, a tiny flame.
Had you followed that boy
you would have arrived here,
where I bend over my wife's right hand.   20

Look how I shave her thumbnail down
so carefully she feels no pain.
Watch as I lift the splinter out.
I was seven when my father
took my hand like this,   25
and I did not hold that shard
between my fingers and think,
Metal that will bury me,
christen it Little Assassin,
Ore Going Deep for My Heart.   30
And I did not lift up my wound and cry,

Death visited here!
I did what a child does
when he's given something to keep.
I kissed my father.   35

1986

Robert Lowell
1917–1977
> *"Skunk Hour"* contrasts the human and natural worlds in Castine,
> Maine, where Lowell had a summer residence. He composed it in
> the summer of 1957, after Elizabeth Bishop encouraged him to write
> in a looser, less formal style. The poem breaks with the impersonal
> style instituted by T. S. Eliot, a style that was still popular among
> many prominent American poets in the 1950s. In fact, Lowell's
> poem could in some sense be considered confessional: Lowell had
> bipolar disorder, also known as manic depression, and in the fall of
> 1957, extremely manic, he checked himself into a psychiatric hospi-
> tal in Boston.

Skunk Hour

(For Elizabeth Bishop)

Nautilus Island's hermit
heiress still lives through winter in her Spartan cottage;
her sheep still graze above the sea.
Her son's a bishop. Her farmer
is first selectman in our village;   5
she's in her dotage.

Thirsting for
the hierarchic privacy
of Queen Victoria's century,
she buys up all   10

the eyesores facing her shore,
and lets them fall.

The season's ill—
we've lost our summer millionaire,
who seemed to leap from an L. L. Bean   15
catalogue. His nine-knot yawl
was auctioned off to lobstermen.
A red fox stain covers Blue Hill.

And now our fairy
decorator brightens his shop for fall;   20
his fishnet's filled with orange cork,
orange, his cobbler's bench and awl;
there is no money in his work,
he'd rather marry.

One dark night,   25
my Tudor Ford climbed the hill's skull;
I watched for love-cars. Lights turned down,
they lay together, hull to hull,
where the graveyard shelves on the town. . . .
My mind's not right.   30

A car radio bleats,
"Love, O careless Love. . . ." I hear
my ill-spirit sob in each blood cell,
as if my hand were at its throat. . . .
I myself am hell;   35
nobody's here—

only skunks, that search
in the moonlight for a bite to eat.
They march on their soles up Main Street:
white stripes, moonstruck eyes' red fire   40
under the chalk-dry and spar spire
of the Trinitarian Church.

I stand on top
of our back steps and breathe the rich air—
a mother skunk with her column of kittens swills the garbage
      pail.   45
She jabs her wedge-head in a cup
of sour cream, drops her ostrich tail,
and will not scare.

                     1959

Susan Ludvigson
1942–

> Ludvigson says that the images in her poetry come from her child-
> hood and her dreams and credits "learning to listen to one's inner
> ear and trusting to the unconscious." "After Love" was published in
> Everything Winged Must Be Dreaming *(1993). Winged creatures
> appear in many of the poems, either on the literal level or, as here,
> in a metaphor. That context emphasizes Ludvigson's decision to
> compare reason to a* moth *rather than some other animal. You
> might ask yourself: Why not a pheasant or a peacock or a swallow
> or an angel, which appear in her other poems?*

After Love

She remembers how reason
escaped from the body,
flew out with a sigh,
went winging up
to a corner of the ceiling   5
and fluttered there,
a moth, a translucence,
waiting.

She did not hear it
return, did not see   10
but felt its brush

against her breasts
quieter, quieter,
until it slipped
back in, powdered   15
wings intact.

      1993

Archibald MacLeish
1892–1982

> *When MacLeish published "Ars Poetica" (the art of poetry), it be-*
> *came a sort of manifesto for the American, mid-century poets asso-*
> *ciated with New Criticism (represented in this volume by Williams,*
> *Moore, Lowell, Bishop, Ransom, Stevens, and Jarrell). "Ars Poetica"*
> *erects the pillars of New Critical aesthetics: that poetry, because it is*
> *experienced rather than interpreted, is something completely differ-*
> *ent from ordinary language (and therefore does not convey a mean-*
> *ing the way we think of, for example, a political speech meaning*
> *something); that the proper subject matter of poetry is the univer-*
> *sal, timeless truths of the human heart, like grief and love; and that*
> *these truths are conveyed through images (an "empty doorway" for*
> *"grief "). Reforming society, then, according to MacLeish and the*
> *New Critics, is not the business of poetry. For this reason, some of*
> *the more political poets in this volume would dispute the philosophy*
> *presented in "Ars Poetica."*

Ars Poetica

A poem should be palpable and mute
As a globed fruit,

Dumb
As old medallions to the thumb,

Silent as the sleeve-worn stone   5
Of casement ledges where the moss has grown—

A poem should be wordless
As the flight of birds.

*

A poem should be motionless in time
As the moon climbs,   10

Leaving, as the moon releases
Twig by twig the night-entangled trees,

Leaving, as the moon behind the winter leaves,
Memory by memory the mind—

A poem should be motionless in time   15
As the moon climbs.

*

A poem should be equal to:
Not true.

For all the history of grief
An empty doorway and a maple leaf.   20

For love
The leaning grasses and two lights above the sea—

A poem should not mean
But be.

1926

Christopher Marlowe
1564–1593

> *Marlowe was Shakespeare's contemporary and his chief rival as playwright. "The Passionate Shepherd to His Love" circulated in manuscript throughout London's literary circles, as was the case with many poems in the Elizabethan era (it was not published until eight years after Marlowe's untimely death in a bar fight). Its original audience, then, was aristocrats (both men and women)*

*and well-educated men of letters, and it was widely read by these
groups. "The Passionate Shepherd" is the best example in this volume of the pastoral lyric—a popular form in the Elizabethan age.
No one would mistake the shepherds for real people.*

The Passionate Shepherd to His Love

Come live with me and be my love,
And we will all the pleasures prove
That valleys, groves, hills, and fields,
Woods, or steepy mountain yields.

And we will sit upon the rocks,   5
Seeing the shepherds feed their flocks,
By shallow rivers to whose falls
Melodious birds sing madrigals.

And I will make thee beds of roses
And a thousand fragrant posies,   10
A cap of flowers, and a kirtle
Embroidered all with leaves of myrtle;

A gown made of the finest wool
Which from our pretty lambs we pull;
Fair lined slippers for the cold,   15
With buckles of the purest gold;

A belt of straw and ivy buds,
With coral clasps and amber studs:
And if these pleasures may thee move,
Come live with me, and be my love.   20

The shepherds' swains shall dance and sing
For thy delight each May morning:
If these delights thy mind may move,
Then live with me and be my love.

                    1599, 1600

Andrew Marvell
1621–1678

> *Marvell, a friend of John Milton, published little during his life-time: his housekeeper, who represented herself as his widow, brought out a collection of his poems after his death. The speaker in "To His Coy Mistress" is the persona speaking in a conventional* carpe diem *poem: the artful seducer. In fact, this poem is probably the most famous example of its kind in the English language. Note how the poem breaks down into a logical, three-point argument: "If," "but," "therefore."*

To His Coy Mistress

Had we but world enough, and time,
This coyness, lady, were no crime.
We would sit down, and think which way
To walk, and pass our long love's day.
Thou by the Indian Ganges' side   5
Shouldst rubies[1] find; I by the tide
Of Humber would complain. I would
Love you ten years before the flood,
And you should, if you please, refuse
Till the conversion of the Jews.   10
My vegetable[2] love should grow
Vaster than empires and more slow;
An hundred years should go to praise
Thine eyes, and on thy forehead gaze;
Two hundred to adore each breast,   15
But thirty thousand to the rest;
An age at least to every part,
And the last age should show your heart.
For, lady, you deserve this state,
Nor would I love at lower rate.   20

---

1. Rubies were thought to help preserve virginity. "Ganges": the Ganges River.

2. I.e., characterized by plantlike growth.

But at my back I always hear
Time's wingèd chariot hurrying near;
And yonder all before us lie
Deserts of vast eternity.
Thy beauty shall no more be found;   25
Nor, in thy marble vault, shall sound
My echoing song; then worms shall try
That long-preserved virginity,
And your quaint[3] honor turn to dust,
And into ashes all my lust: 30
The grave's a fine and private place,
But none, I think, do there embrace.
  Now therefore, while the youthful hue
Sits on thy skin like morning dew,
And while thy willing soul transpires   35
At every pore with instant fires,
Now let us sport us while we may,
And now, like amorous birds of prey,
Rather at once our time devour
Than languish in his slow-chapped power.   40
Let us roll all our strength and all
Our sweetness up into one ball,
And tear our pleasures with rough strife
Through the iron gates of life:
Thus, though we cannot make our sun   45
Stand still, yet we will make him run.

1681

Edna St. Vincent Millay
1892–1950

> *Millay exemplified the rakish free spirit of Greenwich Village in
> the years during and after World War I. She took many lovers and
> wrote frankly about them in her verse. "What Lips My Lips Have*

---

3. Has several meanings, including: fine, elegant, fastidious, and oversubtle; also with a
pun on the Middle English noun "queynte," meaning a woman's genitals.

Kissed" was the fifth of a sequence of eight sonnets that helped win her the Pulitzer Prize in 1922. The season motif appears throughout the sequence: the third sonnet begins with these lines: "I know I am but summer to your heart, / And not the full four seasons of the year[.]" "Love Is Not All" was part of a 1931 sequence, Fatal Interview. *Though its rhyme scheme indicates it is a Shakespearean sonnet, the poem seems to divide like a Petrarchan sonnet. Part of the poem's subtlety derives from the last line: is the speaker unsure or confident?*

What Lips My Lips Have Kissed

What lips my lips have kissed, and where, and why,
I have forgotten, and what arms have lain
Under my head till morning; but the rain
Is full of ghosts tonight, that tap and sigh
Upon the glass and listen for reply,   5
And in my heart there stirs a quiet pain
For unremembered lads that not again
Will turn to me at midnight with a cry.
Thus in the winter stands the lonely tree,
Nor knows what birds have vanished one by one,   10
Yet knows its boughs more silent than before:
I cannot say what loves have come and gone,
I only know that summer sang in me
A little while, that in me sings no more.

                        1922

Love Is Not All: It Is Not Meat Nor Drink

Love is not all: it is not meat nor drink
Nor slumber nor a roof against the rain;
Nor yet a floating spar to men that sink
And rise and sink and rise and sink again;
Love can not fill the thickened lung with breath,   5
Nor clean the blood, nor set the fractured bone;

Yet many a man is making friends with death
Even as I speak, for lack of love alone.
It well may be that in a difficult hour,
Pinned down by pain and moaning for release,   10
Or nagged by want past resolution's power,
I might be driven to sell your love for peace,
Or trade the memory of this night for food.
It well may be. I do not think I would.

                                        1931

John Milton
1608–1674

> *Milton wrote "When I Consider How My Light Is Spent" after go-
> ing blind around 1651. His eyesight deteriorated while he was writ-
> ing political pamphlets defending Parliament's 1649 execution of
> King Charles I, though it would be fair to say he considered the
> king's downfall to be God's work, since Charles was overthrown by
> a Puritan revolution that was as much religious and cultural as it
> was political. For example, the Puritan government closed down
> England's theaters. Milton's fortunes fell when the monarchy was
> restored in 1660. Blind and poor, he wrote his greatest work, the
> epic* Paradise Lost, *which was instantly recognized by English au-
> diences as a work worthy of Homer or Virgil when it was published
> in 1667. When his short lyrics—including this one—were first pub-
> lished in 1673, readers would have known Milton as England's fa-
> mous, blind epic poet.*

When I Consider How My Light Is Spent

When I consider how my light is spent
  Ere half my days, in this dark world and wide,
  And that one talent which is death to hide
  Lodged with me useless, though my soul more bent
To serve therewith my Maker, and present   5

My true account, lest he returning chide;
"Doth God exact day-labor, light denied?"
I fondly ask; but Patience to prevent
That murmur, soon replies, "God doth not need
  Either man's work or his own gifts; who best   10
  Bear his mild yoke, they serve him best. His state
Is kingly. Thousands at his bidding speed
  And post o'er land and ocean without rest:
They also serve who only stand and wait."

                                1673

Marianne Moore
1887–1972

> *Moore's career paralleled Pound's and Eliot's, and as editor of the influential* Dial *magazine, she mentored many of America's mid-century poets—people like Elizabeth Bishop. The way she frames her question about poetry's importance is, then, somewhat surprising, especially when you consider "Poetry" alongside a work like MacLeish's "Ars Poetica." It is difficult to gauge her attitude toward those things "that we do not admire" because we can't understand them: the "immovable critic" of course is a figure of some contempt, but Moore's famous love of the Dodgers suggests that the frivolity and inutility of the baseball fan is something the speaker admires.*

Poetry

I, too, dislike it: there are things that are important beyond all
      this fiddle.
  Reading it, however, with a perfect contempt for it, one
      discovers in
it after all, a place for the genuine.
    Hands that can grasp, eyes
      that can dilate, hair that can rise   5
        if it must, these things are important not because a

high-sounding interpretation can be put upon them but
      because they are
useful. When they become so derivative as to become
      unintelligible,
the same thing may be said for all of us, that we
    do not admire what   10
    we cannot understand: the bat
      holding on upside down or in quest of something to

eat, elephants pushing, a wild horse taking a roll, a tireless wolf under
    a tree, the immovable critic twitching his skin like a horse
      that feels a flea, the base-
ball fan, the statistician—   15
    nor is it valid
      to discriminate against "business documents and

school-books"; all these phenomena are important. One must
    make a distinction
however: when dragged into prominence by half poets, the
    result is not poetry,
nor till the poets among us can be   20
    "literalists of
    the imagination"—above
      insolence and triviality and can present

for inspection, "imaginary gardens with real toads in them,"
    shall we have
it. In the meantime, if you demand on the one hand,   25
the raw material of poetry in
    all its rawness and
    that which is on the other hand
      genuine, then you are interested in poetry.

                    1921, 1935

Sharon Olds
1942–

> Both of these poems appeared in Olds's second volume, The Dead
> and the Living. *The book is a sort of biography of its speaker, who
> seems to be Olds herself. We learn of the speaker's alcoholic, abusive
> father, her suffering mother and sister, her miscarriage and abor-
> tion. Both selections here are among the "Poems for the Living."
> "Sex Without Love," in a sequence called "The Men," is sand-
> wiched between two poems describing sexual ecstasy between the
> speaker and her husband—that is, sex with love—which should
> help you determine the speaker's tone. "The One Girl at the Boys'
> Party" is one of twenty poems about "The Children": Consider here
> the relationship between mathematics and female sexuality, mathe-
> matics and female power.*

Sex Without Love

How do they do it, the ones who make love
without love? Beautiful as dancers,
gliding over each other like ice-skaters
over the ice, fingers hooked
inside each other's bodies, faces   5
red as steak, wine, wet as the
children at birth whose mothers are going to
give them away. How do they come to the
come to the come to the God come to the
still waters, and not love   10
the one who came there with them, light
rising slowly as steam off their joined
skin? These are the true religious,
the purists, the pros, the ones who will not
accept a false Messiah, love the   15
priest instead of the God. They do not
mistake the lover for their own pleasure,
they are like great runners: they know they are alone
with the road surface, the cold, the wind,

the fit of their shoes, their over-all cardio-   20
vascular health—just factors, like the partner
in the bed, and not the truth, which is the
single body alone in the universe
against its own best time.

1984

The One Girl at the Boys' Party

When I take our girl to the swimming party
I set her down among the boys. They tower and
bristle, she stands there smooth and sleek,
her math scores unfolding in the air around her.
They will strip to their suits, her body hard and   5
indivisible as a prime number,
they'll plunge in the deep end, she'll subtract
her height from ten feet, divide it into
hundreds of gallons of water, the numbers
bouncing in her mind like molecules of chlorine   10
in the bright blue pool. When they climb out,
her ponytail will hand its pencil lead
down her back, her narrow silk suit
with hamburgers and french fries printed on it
will glisten in the brilliant air, and they will   15
see her sweet face, solemn and
sealed, a factor of one, and she will
see their eyes, two each,
their legs, two each, and the curves of their sexes,
one each, and in her head she'll be doing her   20
wild multiplying, as the drops
sparkle and fall to the power of a thousand from her body.

1984

Wilfred Owen
1893–1918

> *Owen enlisted in the British Army to fight the Germans in World War I, was dispatched to the front, sickened, and was sent to Scotland to recuperate, where he wrote "Dulce Et Decorum Est" in October 1917. Originally he dedicated it to Jessie Pope, an author of children's books and editor of patriotic war poems; Pope is probably the "friend" in line 25. Owen translated the title, a popular motto, thus: "It is sweet and meet to die for one's country. Sweet! and decorous!" He was returned to the front and killed a week before the cease-fire. This poem was not published until 1920, when it came to be heard as, essentially, the plea of a dead soldier.*

Dulce Et Decorum Est

Bent double, like old beggars under sacks,
Knock-kneed, coughing like hags, we cursed through sludge,
Till on the haunting flares we turned our backs
And towards our distant rest began to trudge.
Men marched asleep. Many had lost their boots   5
But limped on, blood-shod. All went lame; all blind;
Drunk with fatigue; deaf even to the hoots
Of tired, outstripped Five-Nines[1] that dropped behind.

Gas! GAS! Quick, boys!—An ecstasy of fumbling,
Fitting the clumsy helmets just in time;   10
But someone still was yelling out and stumbling,
And flound'ring like a man in fire or lime . . .
Dim, through the misty panes[2] and thick green light,
As under a green sea, I saw him drowning.

In all my dreams, before my helpless sight,   15
He plunges at me, guttering, choking, drowning.

---

1. I.e., 5.9-inch caliber shells.   2. Of the gas mask's celluloid window.

If in smothering dreams you too could pace
Behind the wagon that we flung him in,
And watch the white eyes writhing in his face,
His hanging face, like a devil's sick of sin;   20
If you could hear, at every jolt, the blood
Come gargling from the froth-corrupted lungs,
Obscene as cancer, bitter as the cud
Of vile, incurable sores on innocent tongues,—
My friend, you would not tell with such high zest   25
To children ardent for some desperate glory,
The old Lie: Dulce et decorum est
Pro patria mori.

1920

Marge Piercy
1936—

> In her poetry and prose, Piercy engages with social myths that she
> believes inform the behavior of women and men. She has rewritten
> traditional stories and, in "Barbie doll," offers a critical look at a
> female icon. "Barbie doll" eschews subtlety in favor of shock, but
> this poem is more complex than you might at first think. For exam-
> ple, it seems obvious that we are meant to read the last two lines
> ironically. But why does Piercy use the word "consummation"
> rather than "ending"? The third stanza compares the woman's good
> nature to a fan belt—a striking metaphor. How are the two simi-
> lar? What does a fan belt do? How does it wear out?

Barbie doll

This girlchild was born as usual
and presented dolls that did pee-pee
and miniature GE stoves and irons
and wee lipsticks the color of cherry candy.
Then in the magic of puberty, a classmate said: 5
You have a great big nose and fat legs.

She was healthy, tested intelligent,
possessed strong arms and back,
abundant sexual drive and manual dexterity.
She went to and fro apologizing.   10
Everyone saw a fat nose on thick legs.

She was advised to play coy,
exhorted to come on hearty,
exercise, diet, smile and wheedle.
Her good nature wore out   15
like a fan belt.
So she cut off her nose and her legs
and offered them up.

In the casket displayed on satin she lay
with the undertaker's cosmetics painted on,   20
a turned-up putty nose,
dressed in a pink and white nightie.
Doesn't she look pretty? everyone said.
Consummation at last.
To every woman a happy ending.   25

                              1973

Sylvia Plath
1932–1963

> *In England on a Fulbright scholarship, at twenty-four years old, Plath*
> *married the British poet Ted Hughes. She finished writing "Metaphors"*
> *on March 20, 1959, just after she discovered to her disappointment that*
> *she wasn't pregnant. "Daddy" was written on October 12, 1962, shortly*
> *after she decided to divorce Hughes. Though it is* emotionally *autobi-*
> *ographical it is not* factual, *at least not the parts about her father. Otto*
> *Plath was not a Nazi and was not abusive. Nevertheless, when she fin-*
> *ished the poem, Plath declared, "It is over. . . . My life can begin." But*
> *before "Daddy" appeared in print, Plath, who was living in London*
> *with her two young children, committed suicide. She was thirty. She*
> *died on the verge of the feminist movement, and women have turned*
> *to her life and poems to voice their own struggles since the 1960s.*

Metaphors

I'm a riddle in nine syllables,
An elephant, a ponderous house,
A melon strolling on two tendrils.
O red fruit, ivory, fine timbers!
This loaf's big with its yeasty rising.   5
Money's new-minted in this fat purse.
I'm a means, a stage, a cow in calf.
I've eaten a bag of green apples,
Boarded the train there's no getting off.

                                        1961

Daddy

You do not do, you do not do
Any more, black shoe
In which I have lived like a foot
For thirty years, poor and white,
Barely daring to breathe or Achoo.   5

Daddy, I have had to kill you.
You died before I had time——
Marble-heavy, a bag full of God,
Ghastly statue with one gray toe[1]
Big as a Frisco seal   10

And a head in the freakish Atlantic
Where it pours bean green over blue
In the waters off beautiful Nauset.
I used to pray to recover you.
Ach, du.[2]   15

---

1. Plath's father's toe turned black from gangrene.   2. "Ah, you" (German).

In the German tongue, in the Polish town
Scraped flat by the roller
Of wars, wars, wars.
But the name of the town is common.
My Polack friend   20

Says there are a dozen or two.
So I never could tell where you
Put your foot, your root,
I never could talk to you.
The tongue stuck in my jaw.   25

It stuck in a barb wire snare.
Ich, ich, ich, ich,³
I could hardly speak.
I thought every German was you.
And the language obscene   30

An engine, an engine
Chuffing me off like a Jew.
A Jew to Dachau, Auschwitz, Belsen.⁴
I began to talk like a Jew.
I think I may well be a Jew.   35

The snows of the Tyrol, the clear beer of Vienna
Are not very pure or true.
With my gypsy ancestress and my weird luck
And my Taroc pack and my Taroc pack⁵
I may be a bit of a Jew.   40

I have always been scared of *you*,
With your Luftwaffe,⁶ your gobbledygoo.
And your neat moustache

3. "I, I, I, I" (German).
4. German concentration camps where
millions of Jews were murdered during
World War II.

5. Tarot cards, used for fortune-telling.
6. The German air force.

And your Aryan eye, bright blue.
Panzer[7]-man, panzer-man, O You—   45

Not God but a swastika
So black no sky could squeak through.
Every woman adores a Fascist,
The boot in the face, the brute
Brute heart of a brute like you.   50

You stand at the blackboard, daddy,
In the picture I have of you,
A cleft in your chin instead of your foot
But no less a devil for that, no not
Any less the black man who   55

Bit my pretty red heart in two.
I was ten when they buried you.
At twenty I tried to die
And get back, back, back to you.
I thought even the bones would do.   60

But they pulled me out of the sack,
And they stuck me together with glue,
And then I knew what to do.
I made a model of you,
A man in black with a Meinkampf[8] look   65

And a love of the rack and the screw.
And I said I do, I do.
So daddy, I'm finally through.
The black telephone's off at the root,
The voices just can't worm through.   70

If I've killed one man, I've killed two—
The vampire who said he was you

---

7. "Armor" (German), especially, during World War II, referring to the German armored tank corps.   8. *Mein Kampf* ("My Struggle") is the title of Hitler's political autobiography and Nazi polemic, written before his rise to power.

And drank my blood for a year,
Seven years, if you want to know.
Daddy, you can lie back now.   75

There's a stake in your fat black heart
And the villagers never liked you.
They are dancing and stamping on you.
They always *knew* it was you.
Daddy, daddy, you bastard, I'm through.   80

                    1965

Edgar Allan Poe
1809–1849

> *Poe wrote "The Raven" in a deliberate attempt to become famous.
> He didn't want the poem to be too high for popular or too low for
> critical taste, so it is not surprising that between January and
> March 1845, it was published both in a New York newspaper and
> in two literary journals. "The Raven" earned him little money, but
> it did establish Poe as a celebrity. Though ravens are conventionally
> associated with evil, Poe's symbolism, like Coleridge's, is psychologi-
> cal. Poe attempts to convey in the* sound *of the words the melan-
> choly and foreboding felt by the speaker.*

The Raven

Once upon a midnight dreary, while I pondered, weak and weary,
Over many a quaint and curious volume of forgotten lore—
While I nodded, nearly napping, suddenly there came a tapping,
As of some one gently rapping, rapping at my chamber door.
" 'Tis some visiter," I muttered, "tapping at my chamber door—   5
                    Only this and nothing more."

Ah, distinctly I remember it was in the bleak December;
And each separate dying ember wrought its ghost upon the floor.
Eagerly I wished the morrow;—vainly I had sought to borrow
From my books surcease of sorrow—sorrow for the lost
    Lenore—   10
For the rare and radiant maiden whom the angels name
    Lenore—
                       Nameless *here* for evermore.

And the silken, sad, uncertain rustling of each purple curtain
Thrilled me—filled me with fantastic terrors never felt before;
So that now, to still the beating of my heart, I stood repeating   15
" 'Tis some visiter entreating entrance at my chamber door—
Some late visiter entreating entrance at my chamber door;—
                  This it is and nothing more."

Presently my soul grew stronger; hesitating then no longer,
"Sir," said I, "or Madam, truly your forgiveness I implore;   20
But the fact is I was napping, and so gently you came rapping,
And so faintly you came tapping, tapping at my chamber door,
That I scarce was sure I heard you"—here I opened wide the
    door;—
                Darkness there and nothing more.

Deep into that darkness peering, long I stood there wondering,
    fearing,   25
Doubting, dreaming dreams no mortal ever dared to dream
    before;
But the silence was unbroken, and the stillness gave no token,
And the only word there spoken was the whispered word,
    "Lenore?"
This I whispered, and an echo murmured back the word,
    "Lenore!"
              Merely this and nothing more.   30

Back into the chamber turning, all my soul within me burning,
Soon again I heard a tapping somewhat louder than before.
"Surely," said I, "surely that is something at my window lattice;

Let me see, then, what thereat is, and this mystery explore—
Let my heart be still a moment and this mystery explore;—   35
            'Tis the wind and nothing more!"

Open here I flung the shutter, when, with many a flirt and
    flutter,
In there stepped a stately Raven of the saintly days of yore;
Not the least obeisance made he; not a minute stopped or
    stayed he;
But, with mien of lord or lady, perched above my chamber
    door—   40
Perched upon a bust of Pallas[1] just above my chamber door—
          Perched, and sat, and nothing more.

Then this ebony bird beguiling my sad fancy into smiling,
By the grave and stern decorum of the countenance it wore,
"Though thy crest be shorn and shaven, thou," I said, "art sure
    no craven,   45
Ghastly grim and ancient Raven wandering from the Nightly
    shore—
Tell me what thy lordly name is on the Night's Plutonian[2]
    shore!"
          Quoth the Raven "Nevermore."

Much I marvelled this ungainly fowl to hear discourse so plainly,
Though its answer little meaning—little relevancy bore;   50
For we cannot help agreeing that no living human being
Ever yet was blessed with seeing bird above his chamber door—
Bird or beast upon the sculptured bust above his chamber door,
          With such name as "Nevermore."

But the Raven, sitting lonely on the placid bust, spoke only   55
That one word, as if his soul in that one word he did outpour.
Nothing farther then he uttered—not a feather then he
    fluttered—

---

1. Athena, Greek goddess of wisdom and the arts.

2. Black; Pluto was the Greek god of the underworld.

Till I scarcely more than muttered "Other friends have flown
    before—
On the morrow *he* will leave me, as my Hopes have flown
    before."
           Then the bird said "Nevermore."   60

Startled at the stillness broken by reply so aptly spoken,
"Doubtless," said I, "what it utters is its only stock and store
Caught from some unhappy master whom unmerciful Disaster
Followed fast and followed faster till his songs one burden bore—
Till the dirges of his Hope that melancholy burden bore   65
           Of 'Never—nevermore.' "

But the Raven still beguiling my sad fancy into smiling,
Straight I wheeled a cushioned seat in front of bird, and bust
    and door;
Then, upon the velvet sinking, I betook myself to linking
Fancy unto fancy, thinking what this ominous bird of yore—   70
What this grim, ungainly, ghastly, gaunt, and ominous bird of
    yore
           Meant in croaking "Nevermore."

This I sat engaged in guessing, but no syllable expressing
To the fowl whose fiery eyes now burned into my bosom's core;
This and more I sat divining, with my head at ease reclining   75
On the cushion's velvet lining that the lamp-light gloated o'er,
But whose velvet-violet lining with the lamp-light gloating o'er,
           She shall press, ah, nevermore!

Then, methought, the air grew denser, perfumed from an
    unseen censer
Swung by seraphim whose foot-falls tinkled on the tufted
    floor.   80
"Wretch," I cried, "thy God hath lent thee—by these angels he
    hath sent thee
Respite—respite and nepenthe[3] from thy memories of Lenore;

---

3. Oblivion-inducing drug.

Quaff, oh quaff this kind nepenthe and forget this lost Lenore!"
    Quoth the Raven "Nevermore."

"Prophet!"said I, "thing of evil!—prophet still, if bird or
  devil!—   85
Whether Tempter sent, or whether tempest tossed thee here
  ashore,
Desolate yet all undaunted, on this desert land enchanted—
On this home by Horror haunted—tell me truly, I implore—
Is there—*is* there balm in Gilead?—tell me—tell me, I
  implore!"
    Quoth the Raven "Nevermore." 90

"Prophet!" said I, "thing of evil!—prophet still, if bird or devil!
By that Heaven that bends above us—by that God we both
  adore—
Tell this soul with sorrow laden if, within the distant Aidenn,
It shall clasp a sainted maiden whom the angels name
  Lenore—
Clasp a rare and radiant maiden whom the angels name
  Lenore."   95
    Quoth the Raven "Nevermore."

"Be that word our sign of parting, bird or fiend!" I shrieked,
  upstarting—
"Get thee back into the tempest and the Night's Plutonian
  shore!
Leave no black plume as a token of that lie thy soul hath
  spoken!
Leave my loneliness unbroken!—quit the bust above my door! 100
Take thy beak from out my heart, and take thy form from off
  my door!"
    Quoth the Raven "Nevermore."

And the Raven, never flitting, still is sitting, *still* is sitting
On the pallid bust of Pallas just above my chamber door;
And his eyes have all the seeming of a demon's that is
  dreaming,   105

And the lamp-light o'er him streaming throws his shadow on
  the floor;
And my soul from out that shadow that lies floating on the
  floor
                              Shall be lifted—nevermore!
                                                    1845

Ezra Pound
1885–1972

> *In 1915, Pound translated a number of poems from Chinese ideo-graphs, and with these poems—which deposit all meaning in concrete images—he meant to release himself from what he considered the tyranny of iambic pentameter. The rhythm of "The River-Merchant's Wife: A Letter," which is a translation of an eighth-century poem by Li Po, is based on syntax, not meter. The rhythmic unit is the sentence, not the foot, and it typically comprises a single line. For "In a Station of the Metro," Pound borrowed the technique of juxtaposed images from Japanese* haiku *(a three-line poem of five, seven, and five syllables). He attempted to express through the image of the petals what he felt watching beautiful faces, one after another, emerge from the La Concorde station of the Paris subway. The image of the petals is meant to be equivalent to the emotion he wanted to express.*

The River-Merchant's Wife: A Letter

While my hair was still cut straight across my forehead
I played about the front gate, pulling flowers.
You came by on bamboo stilts, playing horse,
You walked about my seat, playing with blue plums.
And we went on living in the village of Chokan: 5
Two small people, without dislike or suspicion.
At fourteen I married My Lord you.
I never laughed, being bashful.
Lowering my head, I looked at the wall.
Called to, a thousand times, I never looked back.   10

At fifteen I stopped scowling,
I desired my dust to be mingled with yours
Forever and forever and forever.
Why should I climb the look out?

At sixteen you departed,   15
You went into far Ku-to-yen, by the river of swirling eddies,
And you have been gone five months.
The monkeys make sorrowful noise overhead.

You dragged your feet when you went out.
By the gate now, the moss is grown, the different mosses,   20
Too deep to clear them away!
The leaves fall early this autumn, in wind.
The paired butterflies are already yellow with August
Over the grass in the West garden;
They hurt me. I grow older.   25
If you are coming down through the narrows of the river
        Kiang,
Please let me know beforehand,
And I will come out to meet you
                As far as Cho-fu-Sa.

                                                        By *Rihaku*
                                                            1915

In a Station of the Metro

The apparition of these faces in the crowd;
Petals on a wet, black bough.

                                1916

John Crowe Ransom
1888–1974

> *As a college professor, Ransom trained a generation of southern writers who formed the core of the New Critical movement in literature. Aristocratic and traditional in politics and culture, the New Critics*

*instituted the methods of close reading still taught in most English
departments, though their insistence on a poem's autonomy from its
poet and from its cultural context is largely rejected today. Ransom
wrote "Bells for John Whiteside's Daughter" in the spring of 1924 after he watched a neighbor's daughter playing outside and imagined
the aftermath of her death. You will probably find yourself perplexed
by the repeated phrase "brown study." There is no clear meaning to
the phrase: by interpreting it, you will interpret the poem.*

Bells for John Whiteside's Daughter

There was such speed in her little body,
And such lightness in her footfall,
It is no wonder her brown study
Astonishes us all.

Her wars were bruited[1] in our high window.   5
We looked among orchard trees and beyond
Where she took arms against her shadow,
Or harried unto the pond

The lazy geese, like a snow cloud
Dripping their snow on the green grass,   10
Tricking and stopping, sleepy and proud,
Who cried in goose, Alas,

For the tireless heart within the little
Lady with rod that made them rise
From their noon apple-dreams and scuttle   15
Goose-fashion under the skies!

But now go the bells, and we are ready,
In one house we are sternly stopped
To say we are vexed at her brown study,
Lying so primly propped.   20

1924

1. I.e., loudly voiced.

Edwin Arlington Robinson
1869–1935

In 1897 Robinson published at his own expense The Children of
the Night, *which included "Richard Cory." The book was largely
ignored until President Theodore Roosevelt happened across a copy
and, attracted by what he considered a masculine style and progressive sentiments, started promoting Robinson—to the chagrin of
some members of the literary community, who thought Robinson
was second-rate. Many poets in the twentieth century, following the
lead of Eliot and Pound, thought that if a poem was straightforward and appealed to the mass market, it must be bad. Thus
"Richard Cory" provides a good opportunity to reflect on poetry's
purpose and definition.*

Richard Cory

Whenever Richard Cory went down town,
We people on the pavement looked at him:
He was a gentleman from sole to crown,
Clean favored, and imperially slim.

And he was always quietly arrayed,   5
And he was always human when he talked;
But still he fluttered pulses when he said,
"Good-morning," and he glittered when he walked.

And he was rich—yes, richer than a king—
And admirably schooled in every grace: 10
In fine, we thought that he was everything
To make us wish that we were in his place.

So on we worked, and waited for the light,
And went without the meat, and cursed the bread;
And Richard Cory, one calm summer night,   15
Went home and put a bullet through his head.

1869

Theodore Roethke

1908–1963

> Roethke's "Greenhouse Poems," which include "Root Cellar," reflect
> his childhood observations in Saginaw, Michigan, where his father
> owned a greenhouse. The bulbs and shoots are some of those "mini-
> mal creatures" in which Roethke delighted and which characterize
> most of his poetry. What raises this poem above mere (though vivid)
> description is that it joins "evil" to these things that would not "give
> up life." "My Papa's Waltz" initiated a group of seven autobio-
> graphical poems that express the poet's dissatisfaction with human
> society. Even so, it is very difficult to determine the speaker's atti-
> tude toward his father. In 1958 Roethke won the National Book
> Award for Words for the Wind, which reprinted his best work
> and added new poems, like "I Knew A Woman." That poem is in a
> section titled "Love Poems." Perhaps the most difficult part of this
> poem is to figure out the speaker's relation to this woman. Is he a
> child, she a mother? Is she a teacher? Is he a young man and she the
> older lover? "Turn, and Counter-turn, and Stand" are the stanzas
> in a Pindaric ode, which were sung and danced by the chorus in a
> Greek play, so this line suggests the woman taught the speaker po-
> etry and dance.

Root Cellar

Nothing would sleep in that cellar, dank as a ditch,
Bulbs broke out of boxes hunting for chinks in the dark,
Shoots dangled and drooped,
Lolling obscenely from mildewed crates,
Hung down long yellow evil necks, like tropical snakes.   5
And what a congress of stinks!
Roots ripe as old bait,
Pulpy stems, rank, silo-rich,
Leaf-mold, manure, lime, piled against slippery planks.
Nothing would give up life: 10
Even the dirt kept breathing a small breath.

                              1948

My Papa's Waltz

The whiskey on your breath
Could make a small boy dizzy;
But I hung on like death:
Such waltzing was not easy.

We romped until the pans   5
Slid from the kitchen shelf;
My mother's countenance
Could not unfrown itself.

The hand that held my wrist
Was battered on one knuckle;   10
At every step you missed
My right ear scraped a buckle.

You beat time on my head
With a palm caked hard by dirt,
Then waltzed me off to bed   15
Still clinging to your shirt.

1948

I Knew a Woman

I knew a woman, lovely in her bones,
When small birds sighed, she would sigh back at them;
Ah, when she moved, she moved more ways than one:
The shapes a bright container can contain!
Of her choice virtues only gods should speak,   5
Or English poets who grew up on Greek
(I'd have them sing in chorus, cheek to cheek).

How well her wishes went! She stroked my chin,
She taught me Turn, and Counter-turn, and Stand;
She taught me Touch, that undulant white skin;   10

I nibbled meekly from her proffered hand;
She was the sickle; I, poor I, the rake,
Coming behind her for her pretty sake
(But what prodigious mowing we did make).

Love likes a gander, and adores a goose: 15
Her full lips pursed, the errant note to seize;
She played it quick, she played it light and loose,
My eyes, they dazzled at her flowing knees;
Her several parts could keep a pure repose,
Or one hip quiver with a mobile nose   20
(She moved in circles, and those circles moved).

Let seed be grass, and grass turn into hay:
I'm martyr to a motion not my own;
What's freedom for? To know eternity.
I swear she cast a shadow white as stone.   25
But who would count eternity in days?
These old bones live to learn her wanton ways:
(I measure time by how a body sways).

                                                              1958

William Shakespeare
1564–1616

> *Readers have long argued the identities of the speaker and listener
> in these sonnets, but with so little evidence of Shakespeare's life no
> one can prove or disprove that the poems are autobiographical. The
> 1609 edition is dedicated "TO THE ONLIE BEGETTER OF THESE
> INSUING SONNETS MR W. H.," whose identity has eluded the
> most careful scholars. Many candidates have been suggested, but
> none have been proven. It is clear that in the first 126 sonnets
> an older man addresses a younger man and urges him to marry.
> The relationship between these two men is intimate—some readers
> think they are sexually intimate, others do not. Sonnet 18 gives us
> Shakespeare's version of a conventional poetic boast: that the poet
> bestows immortality on his subject. In Sonnet 29 Shakespeare con-*

tinues lauding the young man. Here, his friendship refreshes the poet. *Sonnet 73 is a fine example of how a Shakespearean sonnet can develop an idea in successive, related images, each expressed in a quatrain. Sonnet 116 speaks to the enduring quality of love. In Sonnets 127–152, the speaker addresses a female persona who has come to be called "the dark lady" on account of her complexion and bawdy habits. Sonnet 130 satirizes the conventions of love poetry that exaggerate the beloved's beauty. The mistress is not necessarily ugly; these terms seem so negative merely because they are realistic. You might consider whether this poem is more flattering than, say, the first two quatrains of Sonnet 18.*

18

Shall I compare thee to a summer's day?
Thou art more lovely and more temperate:
Rough winds do shake the darling buds of May,
And summer's lease hath all too short a date;
Sometimes too hot the eye of heaven shines,   5
And often is his gold complexion dimmed;
And every fair from fair sometimes declines,
By chance or nature's changing course untrimmed;[1]
But thy eternal summer shall not fade,
Nor lose possession of that fair thou ow'st;   10
Nor shall death brag thou wand'rest in his shade,
When in eternal lines to Time thou grow'st:[2]
   So long as men can breathe, or eyes can see,
   So long lives this, and this gives life to thee.

1609

1. Divested of its beauty.
2. I.e., when you are grafted to Time in this immortal poetry.

29

When, in disgrace with fortune and men's eyes,
I all alone beweep my outcast state,
And trouble deaf heaven with my bootless[3] cries,
And look upon myself, and curse my fate,
Wishing me like to one more rich in hope,　　　　　　　　5
Featured like him, like him with friends possessed,
Desiring this man's art and that man's scope,
With what I most enjoy contented least;
Yet in these thoughts myself almost despising,
Haply I think on thee—and then my state,　　　　　　　10
Like to the lark at break of day arising
From sullen earth, sings hymns at heaven's gate;
　　For thy sweet love rememb'red such wealth brings
　　That then I scorn to change my state with kings.

1609

73

That time of year thou mayst in me behold
When yellow leaves, or none, or few, do hang
Upon those boughs which shake against the cold,
Bare ruined choirs, where late the sweet birds sang.
In me thou see'st the twilight of such day　　　　　　5
As after sunset fadeth in the west;
Which by and by black night doth take away,
Death's second self, that seals up all in rest.
In me thou see'st the glowing of such fire,
That on the ashes of his youth doth lie,　　　　　　　10
As the deathbed whereon it must expire,
Consumed with that which it was nourished by.
　　This thou perceiv'st, which makes thy love more strong,
　　To love that well which thou must leave ere long.

1609

3. I.e., futile.

116

Let me not to the marriage of true minds
Admit impediments. Love is not love
Which alters when it alteration finds,
Or bends with the remover to remove:
Oh, no! it is an ever-fixèd mark,   5
That looks on tempests and is never shaken;
It is the star to every wandering bark,
Whose worth's unknown, although his height be taken.
Love's not Time's fool, though rosy lips and cheeks
Within his bending sickle's compass come;   10
Love alters not with his brief hours and weeks,
But bears it out even to the edge of doom.
   If this be error and upon me proved,
   I never writ, nor no man ever loved.

1609

130

My mistress' eyes are nothing like the sun;
Coral is far more red than her lips' red;
If snow be white, why then her breasts are dun;[4]
If hairs be wires, black wires grow on her head.
I have seen roses damasked, red and white,   5
But no such roses see I in her cheeks;
And in some perfumes is there more delight
Than in the breath that from my mistress reeks.
I love to hear her speak, yet well I know
That music hath a far more pleasing sound;   10
I grant I never saw a goddess go;
My mistress, when she walks, treads on the ground.
   And yet, by heaven, I think my love as rare
   As any she belied with false compare.

1609

4. I.e., dull grayish brown.

Percy Bysshe Shelley
1792–1822

> *In late 1817, Shelley and another poet, Horace Smith, challenged each other to write a poem about a statue of Ramses II, the Egyptian pharoah whom Moses and the Jews escaped in Exodus ("Ozymandias" is his Greek name). Shelley's poem, with obvious implications for contemporary politics (England had recently defeated Napoleon and so dominated Europe), was published in Leigh Hunt's radical newspaper* The Examiner *in February 1818. "Ode to the West Wind" was inspired by an autumn storm Shelley witnessed on the edge of a wood near Florence. The last lines might refer to Shelley's labors on behalf of the working classes; though an aristocrat himself, he hoped for the overthrow of the privileged classes. He concluded his "Defense of Poetry" with these lines: "Poets are . . . the trumpets which sing to battle, and feel not what they inspire: the influence which is moved not, but moves. Poets are the unacknowledged legislators of the World."*

Ozymandias

I met a traveler from an antique land
Who said: Two vast and trunkless legs of stone
Stand in the desert . . . Near them, on the sand,
Half sunk, a shattered visage lies, whose frown,
And wrinkled lip, and sneer of cold command,   5
Tell that its sculptor well those passions read
Which yet survive, stamped on these lifeless things,
The hand that mocked them, and the heart that fed:
And on the pedestal these words appear:
"My name is Ozymandias, king of kings: 10
Look on my works, ye Mighty, and despair!"
Nothing beside remains. Round the decay
Of that colossal wreck, boundless and bare
The lone and level sands stretch far away.

1818

Ode to the West Wind

1

O wild West Wind, thou breath of Autumn's being,
Thou, from whose unseen presence the leaves dead
Are driven, like ghosts from an enchanter fleeing,

Yellow, and black, and pale, and hectic red,
Pestilence-stricken multitudes: O thou,   5
Who chariotest to their dark wintry bed

The wingéd seeds, where they lie cold and low,
Each like a corpse within its grave, until
Thine azure sister of the Spring shall blow

Her clarion[1] o'er the dreaming earth, and fill   10
(Driving sweet buds like flocks to feed in air)
With living hues and odors plain and hill:

Wild Spirit, which art moving everywhere;
Destroyer and preserver; hear, oh, hear!

2

Thou on whose stream, mid the steep sky's commotion,   15
Loose clouds like earth's decaying leaves are shed,
Shook from the tangled boughs of Heaven and Ocean,

Angels of rain and lightning: there are spread
On the blue surface of thine aëry surge,
Like the bright hair uplifted from the head   20

---

1. Melodious trumpet-call.

Of some fierce Maenad,[2] even from the dim verge
Of the horizon to the zenith's height,
The locks of the approaching storm. Thou dirge

Of the dying year, to which this closing night
Will be the dome of a vast sepulcher,   25
Vaulted with all thy congregated might

Of vapors, from whose solid atmosphere
Black rain, and fire, and hail will burst: oh, hear!

3

Thou who didst waken from his summer dreams
The blue Mediterranean, where he lay,   30
Lulled by the coil of his crystálline streams,

Beside a pumice isle in Baiae's bay,
And saw in sleep old palaces and towers
Quivering within the wave's intenser day,

All overgrown with azure moss and flowers   35
So sweet, the sense faints picturing them! Thou
For whose path the Atlantic's level powers

Cleave themselves into chasms, while far below
The sea-blooms and the oozy woods which wear
The sapless foliage of the ocean, know   40

Thy voice, and suddenly grow gray with fear,
And tremble and despoil themselves: oh, hear!

---

2. Frenzied dancer, worshiper of Dionysus (Greek god of wine and fertility).

4

If I were a dead leaf thou mightest bear;
If I were a swift cloud to fly with thee;
A wave to pant beneath thy power, and share   45

The impulse of thy strength, only less free
Than thou, O uncontrollable! If even
I were as in my boyhood, and could be

The comrade of thy wanderings over Heaven,
As then, when to outstrip thy skyey speed   50
Scarce seemed a vision; I would ne'er have striven

As thus with thee in prayer in my sore need.
Oh, lift me as a wave, a leaf, a cloud!
I fall upon the thorns of life! I bleed!

A heavy weight of hours has chained and bowed   ·   55
One too like thee: tameless, and swift, and proud.

5

Make me thy lyre,³ even as the forest is:
What if my leaves are falling like its own!
The tumult of thy mighty harmonies

Will take from both a deep, autumnal tone,   60
Sweet though in sadness. Be thou, Spirit fierce,
My spirit! Be thou me, impetuous one!

Drive my dead thoughts over the universe
Like withered leaves to quicken a new birth!
And, by the incantation of this verse,   65

---

3. Small harp traditionally used to accompany songs and recited poems.

Scatter, as from an unextinguished hearth
Ashes and sparks, my words among mankind!
Be through my lips to unawakened earth

The trumpet of a prophecy! O Wind,
If Winter comes, can Spring be far behind?   70

1820

Bruce Springsteen
1949–

> *Springsteen's songs celebrate the outcast, the working-class dreamer. "The River," the title song to Springsteen's acclaimed 1980 album, is an excellent example of a contemporary ballad, and, like "Sir Patrick Spens," it tells a story with terse details. But each detail suggests so much that you can flesh out the picture with little effort. For example, the fields of green to which the speaker and Mary, flush with their young love and lust, escape, represent a way of life. And by contrast, though the speaker doesn't tell us, we can imagine that the valley is smothered in the gray, industrial dinginess that gave the Rust Belt its name. Likewise, the Johnstown Company alludes to Johnstown, Pennsylvania, the site of a terrible flood caused by a breaking dam. In the valley below the dam was the working-class, factory town; above was a picturesque lake and the yachting resorts of the factory owners.*

The River

I come from down in the valley
Where mister, when you're young
They bring you up to do
Like your daddy done

Me and Mary we met in high school   5
When she was just seventeen
We'd drive out of this valley
Down to where the fields were green

We'd go down to the river
And into the river we'd dive   10
Oh down to the river we'd ride

Then I got Mary pregnant
And, man, that was all she wrote
And for my 19th birthday
I got a union card and a wedding coat   15

We went down to the courthouse
And the judge put it all to rest
No wedding day smiles, no walk down the aisle
No flowers, no wedding dress

That night we went down to the river   20
And into the river we'd dive
Oh down to the river we did ride

I got a job working construction
For the Johnstown Company
But lately there ain't been much work   25
On account of the economy

Now all them things that seemed so important
Well, mister they vanished right into the air
Now I just act like I don't remember
Mary acts like she don't care   30

But I remember us riding in my brother's car
Her body tan and wet down at the reservoir
At night on them banks I'd lie awake
And pull her close just to feel each breath she'd take

Now those memories come back to haunt me   35
They haunt me like a curse
Is a dream a lie if it don't come true
Or is it something worse

That sends me down to the river
Though I know the river is dry   40
That sends me down to the river tonight
Down to the river
My baby and I
Oh down to the river we ride

                                        1980

William Stafford
1914–1993

> *After Stafford published his first book at age forty-six, readers
> quickly recognized and noted his extraordinary moral authority.
> "Traveling through the Dark" tells the story of something that actu-
> ally happened to Stafford while he was driving the seventy-mile
> mountain road home from a Wednesday night class in Oregon.
> Stafford said he wanted to "deliver for the reader something of
> the loneliness and the minimum scope for action we all have in ex-
> treme situations." Note the literal and metaphoric uses of "swerve"
> in lines 4 and 17.*

Traveling through the Dark

Traveling through the dark I found a deer
dead on the edge of the Wilson River road.
It is usually best to roll them into the canyon:
that road is narrow; to swerve might make more dead.

By glow of the tail-light I stumbled back of the car   5
and stood by the heap, a doe, a recent killing;
she had stiffened already, almost cold.
I dragged her off; she was large in the belly.

My fingers touching her side brought me the reason—
her side was warm; her fawn lay there waiting,   10
alive, still, never to be born.
Beside that mountain road I hesitated.

The car aimed ahead its lowered parking lights;
under the hood purred the steady engine.
I stood in the glare of the warm exhaust turning red;   15
around our group I could hear the wilderness listen.

I thought hard for us all—my only swerving—,
then pushed her over the edge into the river.

1962

Wallace Stevens

1879–1955

*Stevens is famous for the beautiful sounds his lines produce: read
these aloud without worrying about meaning, and you'll hear the
fine rhythms. "Anecdote of the Jar" displays the kind of contrast between the human and natural worlds that is typical of Romantic
poetry, like Wordsworth's "Nutting." A good way into this poem is
to decide whether or not the speaker, like a Romantic, regrets what
the "gray and bare" jar does to the "slovenly wilderness." In a letter,
Stevens explained that "Sunday Morning" is "simply an expression
of paganism, although, of course, I did not think that I was expressing paganism when I wrote it." Likewise, "The Emperor of
Ice-Cream" seems to deny the orthodox, Christian view of life and
death. While it is difficult to determine what the ice-cream man
symbolizes in line 8, the last line seems to be unambiguous: there is
no God.*

Anecdote of the Jar

I placed a jar in Tennessee,
And round it was, upon a hill.
It made the slovenly wilderness
Surround that hill.

The wilderness rose up to it, 5
And sprawled around, no longer wild.
The jar was round upon the ground
And tall and of a port in air.

It took dominion everywhere.
The jar was gray and bare. 10
It did not give of bird or bush,
Like nothing else in Tennessee.

1923

Sunday Morning

I

Complacencies of the peignoir, and late
Coffee and oranges in a sunny chair,
And the green freedom of a cockatoo
Upon a rug mingle to dissipate
The holy hush of ancient sacrifice. 5
She dreams a little, and she feels the dark
Encroachment of that old catastrophe,
As a calm darkens among water-lights.
The pungent oranges and bright, green wings
Seem things in some procession of the dead, 10
Winding across wide water, without sound.
The day is like wide water, without sound,
Stilled for the passing of her dreaming feet

Over the seas, to silent Palestine,
Dominion of the blood and sepulchre.[1]   15

2

Why should she give her bounty to the dead?
What is divinity if it can come
Only in silent shadows and in dreams?
Shall she not find in comforts of the sun,
In pungent fruit and bright, green wings, or else   20
In any balm or beauty of the earth,
Things to be cherished like the thought of heaven?
Divinity must live within herself:
Passions of rain, or moods in falling snow;
Grievings in loneliness, or unsubdued   25
Elations when the forest blooms; gusty
Emotions on wet roads on autumn nights;
All pleasures and all pains, remembering
The bough of summer and the winter branch.
These are the measures destined for her soul.   30

3

Jove in the clouds had his inhuman birth.
No mother suckled him, no sweet land gave
Large-mannered motions to his mythy mind
He moved among us, as a muttering king,
Magnificent, would move among his hinds,   35
Until our blood, commingling, virginal,
With heaven, brought such requital to desire
The very hinds discerned it, in a star.
Shall our blood fail? Or shall it come to be
The blood of paradise? And shall the earth   40
Seem all of paradise that we shall know?

---

1. I.e., the holy sepulcher, the cave in Jerusalem where Jesus was entombed; much blood
was shed during the Crusades (eleventh–thirteenth centuries) as Christians attempted to gain
control of Palestine.

The sky will be much friendlier then than now,
A part of labor and a part of pain,
And next in glory to enduring love,
Not this dividing and indifferent blue. 45

4

She says, "I am content when wakened birds,
Before they fly, test the reality
Of misty fields, by their sweet questionings;
But when the birds are gone, and their warm fields
Return no more, where, then, is paradise?" 50
There is not any haunt of prophecy,
Nor any old chimera[2] of the grave,
Neither the golden underground, nor isle
Melodious, where spirits gat them home,
Nor visionary south, nor cloudy palm 55
Remote on heaven's hill, that has endured
As April's green endures; or will endure
Like her remembrance of awakened birds,
Or her desire for June and evening, tipped
By the consummation of the swallow's wings. 60

5

She says, "But in contentment I still feel
The need of some imperishable bliss."
Death is the mother of beauty; hence from her,
Alone, shall come fulfilment to our dreams
And our desires. Although she strews the leaves 65
Of sure obliteration on our paths,
The path sick sorrow took, the many paths
Where triumph rang its brassy phrase, or love
Whispered a little out of tenderness,
She makes the willow shiver in the sun 70

2. In Greek mythology, a monster with a lion's head, goat's body, and serpent's tail. Also, an illusion or fabrication of the mind.

For maidens who were wont to sit and gaze
Upon the grass, relinquished to their feet.
She causes boys to pile new plums and pears
On disregarded plate. The maidens taste
And stray impassioned in the littering leaves.   75

6

Is there no change of death in paradise?
Does ripe fruit never fall? Or do the boughs
Hang always heavy in that perfect sky,
Unchanging, yet so like our perishing earth,
With rivers like our own that seek for seas   80
They never find, the same receding shores
That never touch with inarticulate pang?
Why set the pear upon those river-banks
Or spice the shores with odors of the plum?
Alas, that they should wear our colors there,   85
The silken weavings of our afternoons,
And pick the strings of our insipid lutes!
Death is the mother of beauty, mystical,
Within whose burning bosom we devise
Our earthly mothers waiting, sleeplessly.   90

7

Supple and turbulent, a ring of men
Shall chant in orgy on a summer morn
Their boisterous devotion to the sun,
Not as a god, but as a god might be,
Naked among them, like a savage source.   95
Their chant shall be a chant of paradise,
Out of their blood, returning to the sky;
And in their chant shall enter, voice by voice,
The windy lake wherein their lord delights,
The trees, like serafin, and echoing hills,   100
That choir among themselves long afterward.
They shall know well the heavenly fellowship

Of men that perish and of summer morn.
And whence they came and whither they shall go
The dew upon their feet shall manifest.   105

                                   8

She hears, upon that water without sound,
A voice that cries, "The tomb in Palestine
Is not the porch of spirits lingering.
It is the grave of Jesus, where he lay."
We live in an old chaos of the sun,   110
Or old dependency of day and night,
Or island solitude, unsponsored, free,
Of that wide water, inescapable.
Deer walk upon our mountains, and the quail
Whistle about us their spontaneous cries;   115
Sweet berries ripen in the wilderness;
And, in the isolation of the sky,
At evening, casual flocks of pigeons make
Ambiguous undulations as they sink,
Downward to darkness, on extended wings.   120

1923

The Emperor of Ice-Cream

Call the roller of big cigars,
The muscular one, and bid him whip
In kitchen cups concupiscent curds.
Let the wenches dawdle in such dress
As they are used to wear, and let the boys   5
Bring flowers in last month's newspapers.
Let be be finale of seem
The only emperor is the emperor of ice-cream.

Take from the dresser of deal[3]
Lacking the three glass knobs, that sheet   10

_____
3. I.e., pine or firwood.

On which she embroidered fantails once
And spread it so as to cover her face.
If her horny feet protrude, they come
To show how cold she is, and dumb.
Let the lamp affix its beam.   15
The only emperor is the emperor of ice-cream.

1923

Leon Stokesbury

1945–

This meditation on death and dying comes from a book called The
Drifting Away *(1986), which is prefaced by a passage from* Huck-
leberry Finn*: "I heard an owl, away off, who-whooing about
somebody that was dead, and a whippowill and a dog crying about
somebody that was going to die, and the wind was trying to whisper something to me and I couldn't make out what it was . . ." This
passage suggests that the speaker in "Unsent Message to My Brother
in His Pain" is, like Huck, the sensible, good-hearted, innocent bewildered by the mysteries of this world. The metaphor in the last
two lines derives from this innocence.*

Unsent Message to My Brother in His Pain

Please do not die now. Listen.
Yesterday, storm clouds rolled
out of the west like thick muscles.
Lightning bloomed. Such a sideshow
of colors. You should have seen it.   5
A woman watched with me, then we slept.
Then, when I woke first, I saw
in her face that rest is possible.
The sky, it suddenly seems
important to tell you, the sky   10
was pink as a shell. Listen

to me. People orbit the moon now.
They must look like flies around
Fatty Arbuckle's head, that new
and that strange. My fellow American,   15
I bought a French cookbook. In it
are hundreds and hundreds of recipes.
If you come to see me, I shit you not,
we will cook with wine. Listen
to me. Listen to me, my brother,   20
please don't go. Take a later flight,
a later train. Another look around.

1986

Alfred, Lord Tennyson
1809–1892

> *"Ulysses" broke with the Romantic practice of autobiographical po-
> etry—the speaker is a character and the poem is a dramatic mono-
> logue. What Ulysses thinks is not necessarily what Tennyson thinks.
> Nevertheless, many critics think Tennyson's friend, Arthur Hallam,
> who died in 1833, inspired the lines about Achilles, and the rousing
> conclusion to the poem was taken at face value by Tennyson's Victo-
> rian readers. The poem alludes to Dante's version of Ulysses' final
> journey: he sailed across the Atlantic toward Purgatory, and God sank
> his ship to punish him for the impudence of the act. In the 1830s, sci-
> entific advancements and engineering feats like the railroad did in-
> deed make some think that humanity "strove with gods." "Crossing
> the Bar" was written in 1889, near the end of Tennyson's life, and he
> left instructions that it should conclude all posthumous collections of
> his poetry. The "bar" is the sandbar that forms naturally at the mouth
> of a harbor; it can be crossed safely only at high tide.*

Ulysses

It little profits that an idle king,
By this still hearth, among these barren crags,
Matched with an aged wife, I mete and dole

Unequal laws unto a savage race,
That hoard, and sleep, and feed, and know not me.   5

   I cannot rest from travel: I will drink
Life to the lees: all times I have enjoyed
Greatly, have suffered greatly, both with those
That loved me, and alone; on shore, and when
Through scudding drifts the rainy Hyades[1]   10
Vext the dim sea: I am become a name;
For always roaming with a hungry heart
Much have I seen and known; cities of men
And manners, climates, councils, governments,
Myself not least, but honored of them all;   15
And drunk delight of battle with my peers,
Far on the ringing plains of windy Troy.
I am a part of all that I have met;
Yet all experience is an arch wherethrough
Gleams that untravelled world whose margin fades   20
For ever and for ever when I move.
How dull it is to pause, to make an end,
To rust unburnished, not to shine in use!
As though to breathe were life! Life piled on life
Were all too little, and of one to me   25
Little remains: but every hour is saved
From that eternal silence, something more,
A bringer of new things; and vile it were
For some three suns to store and hoard myself,
And this gray spirit yearning in desire   30
To follow knowledge like a sinking star,
Beyond the utmost bound of human thought.

   This is my son, mine own Telemachus,
To whom I leave the scepter and the isle—
Well-loved of me, discerning to fulfill   35
This labor, by slow prudence to make mild

---

1. A group of stars in the constellation Taurus, believed to foretell the coming of rain when they rose with the sun.

A rugged people, and through soft degrees
Subdue them to the useful and the good.
Most blameless is he, centered in the sphere
Of common duties, decent not to fail   40
In offices of tenderness, and pay
Meet adoration to my household gods,
When I am gone. He works his work, I mine.

    There lies the port; the vessel puffs her sail:
There gloom the dark, broad seas. My mariners,   45
Souls that have toiled, and wrought, and thought with me—
That ever with a frolic welcome took
The thunder and the sunshine, and opposed
Free hearts, free foreheads—you and I are old;
Old age hath yet his honor and his toil;   50
Death closes all: but something ere the end,
Some work of noble note, may yet be done,
Not unbecoming men that strove with Gods.
The lights begin to twinkle from the rocks:
The long day wanes: the slow moon climbs: the deep   55
Moans round with many voices. Come, my friends,
'Tis not too late to seek a newer world.
Push off, and sitting well in order smite
The sounding furrows; for my purpose holds
To sail beyond the sunset, and the baths   60
Of all the western stars, until I die.
It may be that the gulfs will wash us down:
It may be we shall touch the Happy Isles,[2]
And see the great Achilles, whom we knew.
Though much is taken, much abides; and though   65
We are not now that strength which in old days
Moved earth and heaven; that which we are, we are,
One equal temper of heroic hearts,
Made weak by time and fate, but strong in will
To strive, to seek, to find, and not to yield.   70

                             1842

---

2. The Islands of the Blessed, the abode after death of those favored by the gods, especially
heroes and patriots.

Crossing the Bar

Sunset and evening star,
   And one clear call for me!
And may there be no moaning of the bar,
   When I put out to sea,

But such a tide as moving seems asleep,   5
   Too full for sound and foam,
When that which drew from out the boundless deep
   Turns again home.

Twilight and evening bell,
   And after that the dark!   10
And may there be no sadness of farewell,
   When I embark;

For though from out our bourne of Time and Place
   The flood may bear me far,
I hope to see my Pilot face to face   15
   When I have crossed the bar.

1889

Dylan Thomas
1914–1953

> *Fern Hill was a country farm, a largish, peasant plot with a damp, dark, creaky house on the side of a hill, rented by an aunt and uncle. Thomas spent summers there in childhood, and remembered it as an Edenic farm in "Fern Hill." Thomas personifies "Time" in the first stanza and carries the metaphor through to the last: one way to enter the poem is to trace "Time's" character. Thomas wrote "Do Not Go Gentle into That Good Night" while watching his father, the once proud and fiery schoolteacher "who had a violent and quite personal dislike for God," wither, grow powerless, then die. "Do Not Go Gentle" is a villanelle; you might hypothesize*

why Thomas chose to write this poem in such a tightly structured form.

Fern Hill

Now as I was young and easy under the apple boughs
About the lilting house and happy as the grass was green,
    The night above the dingle[1] starry,
       Time let me hail and climb
      Golden in the heydays of his eyes,   5
And honoured among wagons I was prince of the apple towns
And once below a time I lordly had the trees and leaves
       Trail with daisies and barley
      Down the rivers of the windfall light.

And as I was green and carefree, famous among the barns   10
About the happy yard and singing as the farm was home,
    In the sun that is young once only,
       Time let me play and be
      Golden in the mercy of his means,
And green and golden I was huntsman and herdsman, the
    calves   15
Sang to my horn, the foxes on the hills barked clear and cold,
       And the sabbath rang slowly
      In the pebbles of the holy streams.

All the sun long it was running, it was lovely, the hay
Fields high as the house, the tunes from the chimneys, it was
    air   20
       And playing, lovely and watery
          And fire green as grass.
        And nightly under the simple stars
As I rode to sleep the owls were bearing the farm away,
All the moon long I heard, blessed among stables, the night-
    jars[2]   25

---

1. Small wooded valley.   2. Nocturnal birds.

Flying with the ricks,[3] and the horses
Flashing into the dark.

And then to awake, and the farm, like a wanderer white
With the dew, come back, the cock on his shoulder: it was all
Shining, it was Adam and maiden,   30
The sky gathered again
And the sun grew round that very day.
So it must have been after the birth of the simple light
In the first, spinning place, the spellbound horses walking warm
Out of the whinnying green stable   35
On to the fields of praise.

And honoured among foxes and pheasants by the gay house
Under the new made clouds and happy as the heart was long,
In the sun born over and over,
I ran my heedless ways,   40
My wishes raced through the house high hay
And nothing I cared, at my sky blue trades, that time allows
In all his tuneful turning so few and such morning songs
Before the children green and golden
Follow him out of grace,   45

Nothing I cared, in the lamb white days, that time would take me
Up to the swallow thronged loft by the shadow of my hand,
In the moon that is always rising,
Nor that riding to sleep
I should hear him fly with the high fields   50
And wake to the farm forever fled from the childless land.
Oh as I was young and easy in the mercy of his means,
Time held me green and dying
Though I sang in my chains like the sea.

1946

---

3. Haystacks.

Do Not Go Gentle into That Good Night

Do not go gentle into that good night,
Old age should burn and rave at close of day;
Rage, rage against the dying of the light.

Though wise men at their end know dark is right,
Because their words had forked no lightning they   5
Do not go gentle into that good night.

Good men, the last wave by, crying how bright
Their frail deeds might have danced in a green bay,
Rage, rage against the dying of the light.

Wild men who caught and sang the sun in flight,   10
And learn, too late, they grieved it on its way,
Do not go gentle into that good night.

Grave men, near death, who see with blinding sight
Blind eyes could blaze like meteors and be gay,
Rage, rage against the dying of the light.   15

And you, my father, there on the sad height,
Curse, bless, me now with your fierce tears, I pray.
Do not go gentle into that good night.
Rage, rage against the dying of the light.

                                                        1952

Walt Whitman
1819–1892

> *Whitman popularized free verse in American and British poetry,*
> *but "A Noiseless Patient Spider" demonstrates that "free" does not*
> *mean "random." For example, note the similar syntax in lines 4*
> *and 8, which connects the action of the spider to that of the*
> *speaker's soul. This poem is an apostrophe: the speaker is talking to*

his soul. Its meaning depends on the comparison of the soul to the spider. You should ask yourself why Whitman chose a spider and not, say, a bird building a nest or a lion stalking its prey. "When I Heard the Learn'd Astronomer" is a latter-day Romantic poem, very similar in theme to Wordsworth's "The Tables Turned" and its pronouncement on science: "We murder to dissect."

A Noiseless Patient Spider

A noiseless patient spider,
I mark'd where on a little promontory it stood isolated,
Mark'd how to explore the vacant vast surrounding,
It launch'd forth filament, filament, filament, out of itself,
Ever unreeling them, ever tirelessly speeding them.   5

And you O my soul where you stand,
Surrounded, detached, in measureless oceans of space,
Ceaselessly musing, venturing, throwing, seeking the spheres
     to connect them,
Till the bridge you will need be form'd, till the ductile anchor
     hold,
Till the gossamer thread you fling catch somewhere, O my
     soul.   10

                                                              1881

When I Heard the Learn'd Astronomer

When I heard the learn'd astronomer,
When the proofs, the figures, were ranged in columns before
     me,
When I was shown the charts and diagrams, to add, divide,
     and measure them,
When I sitting heard the astronomer where he lectured with
     much applause in the lecture-room,
How soon unaccountable I became tired and sick,   5
Till rising and gliding out I wander'd off by myself,

In the mystical moist night-air, and from time to time,
Look'd up in perfect silence at the stars.

1865

Richard Wilbur
1921–

> *Influenced by the seventeenth-century metaphysical poets and the*
> *ironic stances of his contemporaries, Wilbur composes poetry with*
> *precision, wit, and a keen attention to meter. Of "Love Calls Us to*
> *the Things of This World" Wilbur wrote, "You must imagine the*
> *poem as occurring at perhaps seven-thirty in the morning; the scene*
> *is a bedroom high up in a city apartment building; outside the bed-*
> *room window, the first laundry of the day is being yanked across*
> *the sky and one has been awakened by the squeaking pulleys of the*
> *laundry-line." Pay particular attention to the soul: where it is in*
> *the beginning of the poem, how the laundry on the line is like the*
> *soul, and why the soul finally "accepts the waking body."*

Love Calls Us to the Things of This World

The eyes open to a cry of pulleys,
And spirited from sleep, the astounded soul
Hangs for a moment bodiless and simple
As false dawn.
                              Outside the open window
The morning air is all awash with angels.   5

Some are in bed-sheets, some are in blouses,
Some are in smocks: but truly there they are.
Now they are rising together in calm swells
Of halcyon feeling, filling whatever they wear
With the deep joy of their impersonal breathing;   10

Now they are flying in place, conveying
The terrible speed of their omnipresence, moving
And staying like white water; and now of a sudden
They swoon down into so rapt a quiet
That nobody seems to be there.
       The soul shrinks   15

 From all that it is about to remember,
From the punctual rape of every blessèd day
And cries,
   "Oh, let there be nothing on earth but laundry,
Nothing but rosy hands in the rising steam
And clear dances done in the sight of heaven."   20

 Yet, as the sun acknowledges
With a warm look the world's hunks and colors,
The soul descends once more in bitter love
To accept the waking body, saying now
In a changed voice as the man yawns and rises,   25

 "Bring them down from their ruddy gallows;
Let there be clean linen for the backs of thieves;
Let lovers go fresh and sweet to be undone,
And the heaviest nuns walk in a pure floating
Of dark habits,
    keeping their difficult balance."   30

         1956

William Carlos Williams
1883–1963

> *In 1923 Williams broke with his fellow modern poets by publishing* Spring and All, *perhaps in response to what he considered T. S. Eliot's great catastrophe,* The Waste Land. *"Spring and All," the first poem in the volume, seems to comment on the opening of Eliot's poem, "April is the cruelest month." But Williams explained that he did not want his poems to communicate ideas. They were*

"[t]o refine, to clarify, to intensify that eternal moment in which we alone live" through contact with things. "The Red Wheelbarrow," the twenty-second poem (none had titles in the original book), is, perhaps, his best attempt to achieve that intensity. What depends on our seeing the wheelbarrow (on our really experiencing the things around us) is life. In such moments of heightened perception, time stops, and we are immortal even if, paradoxically, only for a short interval. "This Is Just to Say" challenges our notions of what is and is not poetry. As you read it, you should ask yourself what a text must contain to be a poem.

Spring and All

By the road to the contagious hospital
under the surge of the blue
mottled clouds driven from the
northeast—a cold wind. Beyond, the
waste of broad, muddy fields   5
brown with dried weeds, standing and fallen

patches of standing water
the scattering of tall trees

All along the road the reddish
purplish, forked, upstanding, twiggy   10
stuff of bushes and small trees
with dead, brown leaves under them
leafless vines—

Lifeless in appearance, sluggish
dazed spring approaches—   15

They enter the new world naked,
cold, uncertain of all

save that they enter. All about them
the cold, familiar wind—

Now the grass, tomorrow   20
the stiff curl of wildcarrot leaf
One by one objects are defined—
It quickens: clarity, outline of leaf

But now the stark dignity of
entrance—Still, the profound change   25
has come upon them: rooted, they
grip down and begin to awaken

1923

The Red Wheelbarrow

so much depends
upon

a red wheel
barrow

glazed with rain   5
water

beside the white
chickens.

1923

This Is Just to Say

I have eaten
the plums
that were in
the icebox

and which   5
you were probably
saving
for breakfast

Forgive me
they were delicious   10
so sweet
and so cold
              1934

William Wordsworth
1770–1850

> *Wordsworth's 1798* Lyrical Ballads *revolutionized English poetry by lowering poetic diction to simple, ordinary language and by widening poetic subjects to include farmers, flowers, children, and the poet's spontaneous thoughts as they interact with the world. "The Tables Turned" celebrates the effect of this interaction. Wordsworth deplored how the Industrial Revolution was moving whole populations from the country to the cities, removing us from the rhythms of the natural world and leaving us in an increasingly artificial and inhumane environment. Likewise, he hated the modern attitude that the natural world is raw material waiting to be exploited. Much of our current love and respect for wilderness was first articulated by Wordsworth. "Nutting" compares the harvesting of nuts to a rape. Keeping the final lines of "Nutting" in mind helps explain Wordsworth's high regard for nature. "The World Is Too Much With Us" compares the modern, urbane, civilized, sensible unbelief of an Englishman in 1807 to paganism, which was popularly thought of as the superstitious, unlearned myths of half-savage country folk. Underlying the poem is Wordsworth's belief that civilization corrupts our natural nobility and our capacity to perceive the divine.*

The Tables Turned

Up! up! my Friend, and quit your books;
Or surely you'll grow double:
Up! up! my Friend, and clear your looks;
Why all this toil and trouble?

The sun, above the mountain's head,   5
A freshening lustre mellow
Through all the long green fields has spread,
His first sweet evening yellow.

Books! 'tis a dull and endless strife:
Come, hear the woodland linnet,   10
How sweet his music! on my life,
There's more of wisdom in it.

And hark! how blithe the throstle sings!
He, too, is no mean preacher:
Come forth into the light of things,   15
Let Nature be your Teacher.

She has a world of ready wealth,
Our minds and hearts to bless—
Spontaneous wisdom breathed by health,
Truth breathed by cheerfulness.   20

One impulse from a vernal wood
May teach you more of man,
Of moral evil and of good,
Than all the sages can.

Sweet is the lore which Nature brings;   25
Our meddling intellect
Mis-shapes the beauteous forms of things:—
We murder to dissect.

Enough of Science and of Art;
Close up those barren leaves;   30
Come forth, and bring with you a heart
That watches and receives.

1798

Nutting

——————————It seems a day
(I speak of one from many singled out)
One of those heavenly days that cannot die;
When, in the eagerness of boyish hope,
I left our cottage-threshold, sallying forth   5
With a huge wallet o'er my shoulder slung,
A nutting-crook in hand; and turned my steps
Tow'rd some far-distant wood, a Figure quaint,
Tricked out in proud disguise of cast-off weeds[1]
Which for that service had been husbanded,   10
By exhortation of my frugal Dame[2]—
Motley accoutrement, of power to smile
At thorns, and brakes, and brambles,—and, in truth,
More ragged than need was! O'er pathless rocks,
Through beds of matted fern, and tangled thickets,   15
Forcing my way, I came to one dear nook
Unvisited, where not a broken bough
Drooped with its withered leaves, ungracious sign
Of devastation; but the hazels rose
Tall and erect, with tempting clusters hung,   20
A virgin scene!—A little while I stood,
Breathing with such suppression of the heart
As joy delights in; and, with wise restraint
Voluptuous, fearless of a rival, eyed
The banquet;—or beneath the trees I sate   25
Among the flowers, and with the flowers I played;

1. Clothes.   lodged   while   at   Hawkshead   grammar
2. Ann Tyson, with whom Wordsworth   school.

A temper known to those, who, after long
And weary expectation, have been blest
With sudden happiness beyond all hope.
Perhaps it was a bower beneath whose leaves   30
The violets of five seasons re-appear
And fade, unseen by any human eye;
Where fairy water-breaks[3] do murmur on
For ever; and I saw the sparkling foam,
And—with my cheek on one of those green stones   35
That, fleeced with moss, under the shady trees,
Lay round me, scattered like a flock of sheep—
I heard the murmur and the murmuring sound,
In that sweet mood when pleasure loves to pay
Tribute to ease; and, of its joy secure,   40
The heart luxuriates with indifferent things,
Wasting its kindliness on stocks and stones,
And on the vacant air. Then up I rose,
And dragged to earth both branch and bough, with crash
And merciless ravage: and the shady nook   45
Of hazels, and the green and mossy bower,
Deformed and sullied, patiently gave up
Their quiet being: and, unless I now
Confound my present feelings with the past,
Ere from the mutilated bower I turned   50
Exulting, rich beyond the wealth of kings,
I felt a sense of pain when I beheld
The silent trees, and saw the intruding sky.—
Then, dearest Maiden, move along these shades
In gentleness of heart; with gentle hand   55
Touch—for there is a spirit in the woods.

1800

3. Places where rocks break a stream's flow.

The World Is Too Much with Us

The world is too much with us; late and soon,
Getting and spending, we lay waste our powers;
Little we see in Nature that is ours;
We have given our hearts away, a sordid boon!
This Sea that bares her bosom to the moon,   5
The winds that will be howling at all hours,
And are up-gathered now like sleeping flowers,
For this, for everything, we are out of tune;
It moves us not.—Great God! I'd rather be
A Pagan suckled in a creed outworn;   10
So might I, standing on this pleasant lea,[1]
Have glimpses that would make me less forlorn;
Have sight of Proteus rising from the sea;
Or hear old Triton blow his wreathèd horn.[2]

1807

James Wright
1927–1980

In his poetry, Wright often grapples with the tension between two visions of midwestern America: the social forces that can cripple individuals and the natural forces that have a restorative power. Like many poems since the Romantic era, "A Blessing" describes a moment of heightened awareness or perception during which the things of the world seem to harmonize in unusual splendor. (Twilight seems to be the appropriate time for such moments.) What distinguishes Wright's poem is the comparison of the slender pony to a girl: what does this metaphor suggest about the speaker's relationship to the phenomena he perceives?

1. I.e., open meadow.
2. In Greek myth Proteus, the "Old Man of the Sea," rises from the sea at midday and can be forced to read the future by anyone who holds him while he takes many frightening shapes. Triton is the son of the sea god, Neptune; the sound of his conch-shell horn calms the waves.

A Blessing

Just off the highway to Rochester, Minnesota,
Twilight bounds softly forth on the grass.
And the eyes of those two Indian ponies
Darken with kindness.
They have come gladly out of the willows   5
To welcome my friend and me.
We step over the barbed wire into the pasture
Where they have been grazing all day, alone.
They ripple tensely, they can hardly contain their happiness
That we have come.   10
They bow shyly as wet swans. They love each other.
There is no loneliness like theirs.
At home once more,
They begin munching the young tufts of spring in the darkness.
I would like to hold the slenderer one in my arms,   15
For she has walked over to me
And nuzzled my left hand.
She is black and white,
Her mane falls wild on her forehead,
And the light breeze moves me to caress her long ear   20
That is delicate as the skin over a girl's wrist.
Suddenly I realize
That if I stepped out of my body I would break
Into blossom.

                                                       1963

Sir Thomas Wyatt the Elder
1503–1542

> *Wyatt introduced the sonnet into English and first modified the Pe-*
> *trarchan or Italian rhyme scheme into the English scheme adopted*
> *and popularized by Shakespeare generations later. "My Galley" is*
> *a translation of one of Petrarch's sonnets. The speaker, as in most*
> *sonnets of the sixteenth and seventeenth centuries, is a male lover*

pining over his beloved's cold indifference. "They Flee from Me" introduces an interesting comparison between the speaker's lover and a wild animal in the first stanza. Part of this poem's continuing appeal is the range of emotions expressed: try to trace the speaker's vacillating attitudes toward this fickle woman, which are reflected in subtle changes in tone.

My Galley

My galley charged[1] with forgetfulness
   Thorough sharp seas in winter nights doth pass
   'Tween rock and rock; and eke mine enemy,[2] alas,
   That is my lord, steereth with cruelness;
And every oar a thought in readiness,   5
   As though that death were light in such a case.
   An endless wind doth tear the sail apace
   Of forced sighs and trusty fearfulness.
A rain of tears, a cloud of dark disdain,
   Hath done the wearied cords[3] great hinderance;   10
   Wreathed with error and eke with ignorance.
The stars be hid[4] that led me to this pain;
   Drowned is reason that should me consort,
   And I remain despairing of the port.

They Flee from Me

They flee from me that sometime did me seek
   With naked foot stalking in my chamber.
I have seen them gentle tame and meek
   That now are wild and do not remember
   That sometime they put themselves in danger   5
To take bread at my hand; and now they range
Busily seeking with a continual change.

1. I.e., laden.
2. I.e., love. "Eke": also.
3. The worn lines of the sail, with a possible pun on the Latin for heart *(cor, cordis)*.
4. I.e., the lady's eyes.

Thanked be fortune, it hath been otherwise
   Twenty times better; but once in special,
In thin array after a pleasant guise,[5]   10
   When her loose gown from her shoulders did fall,
   And she me caught in her arms long and small;
And therewithal sweetly did me kiss,
And softly said, *Dear heart,*[6] *how like you this?*

It was no dream, I lay broad waking.   15
   But all is turned thorough my gentleness
Into a strange fashion of forsaking;
   And I have leave to go of her goodness
   And she also to use newfangleness.
But since that I so kindely[7] am served,   20
I would fain know what she hath deserved.

William Butler Yeats

1865–1939

> *Born into an old Irish family, Yeats cherished "the ambition . . . of living in imitation of Thoreau on Innisfree, a small island in Lough Gill," a lake on Ireland's west coast. In his autobiography, Yeats tells us that once, on the streets of London, he saw in a shop-window a display with a little spout of water, and he thought of writing "The Lake Isle of Innisfree." "The Second Coming" was written just after World War I, and its apocalyptic images were pro-voked by the Bolshevik Revolution in Russia. Later, Yeats claimed that the poem foresaw the rise of fascism in Italy and Nazism in Germany. Some critics think he made this comment to distance himself from the nearly fascist politics he espoused in the 1920s. The image of the falcon and falconer symbolizes Yeats's view that history can be depicted by a gyre, or cone. The point of the cone is the birth of Christ, which initiated a two-thousand-year era of individual-*

---

5. In a thin gown, made in a pleasing fashion.

6. With a pun on "heart" and "hart" (as deer).

7. I.e., in the way typical of female nature, or "kind"; with kindness (ironic).

*ism that reached its best moment in the Renaissance and was now
spinning out of control in the mass politics of the twentieth century:
democracy and communism. At this widest point of the cone, a new
era would be initiated, reversing the last. Yeats originally titled
"Leda and the Swan" "The Annunciation." The poem's depiction of
a god, who appears as a swan, raping a mortal woman deliberately
insulted Catholic readers, who saw in the poem a comment on the
Virgin Mary's impregnation. Yeats meant the violent and obscene
imagery to defy the censorship laws of the increasingly conservative
and Catholic government in Ireland. "Sailing to Byzantium" was
published when Yeats was sixty-three years old and felt there was
little place for old men like himself in the young country. The first
stanza, though universalized, describes Ireland. Byzantium was,
for Yeats, an admired place of timeless, unchanging culture.*

The Lake Isle of Innisfree

I will arise and go now, and go to Innisfree,
And a small cabin build there, of clay and wattles made:
Nine bean-rows will I have there, a hive for the honey-bee,
And live alone in the bee-loud glade.

And I shall have some peace there, for peace comes dropping
    slow,   5
Dropping from the veils of the morning to where the cricket
    sings;
There midnight's all a glimmer, and noon a purple glow,
And evening full of the linnet's wings.

I will arise and go now, for always night and day
I hear lake water lapping with low sounds by the shore;   10
While I stand on the roadway, or on the pavements grey,
I hear it in the deep heart's core.

1892

The Second Coming

Turning and turning in the widening gyre
The falcon cannot hear the falconer;
Things fall apart; the centre cannot hold;
Mere anarchy is loosed upon the world,
The blood-dimmed tide is loosed, and everywhere   5
The ceremony of innocence is drowned;
The best lack all conviction, while the worst
Are full of passionate intensity.

Surely some revelation is at hand;
Surely the Second Coming is at hand: 10
The Second Coming! Hardly are those words out
When a vast image out of *Spiritus Mundi*
Troubles my sight: somewhere in sands of the desert
A shape with lion body and the head of a man,
A gaze blank and pitiless as the sun,   15
Is moving its slow thighs, while all about it
Reel shadows of the indignant desert birds.
The darkness drops again; but now I know
That twenty centuries of stony sleep
Were vexed to nightmare by a rocking cradle,   20
And what rough beast, its hour come round at last,
Slouches towards Bethlehem to be born?

1921

Leda and the Swan[1]

A sudden blow: the great wings beating still
Above the staggering girl, her thighs caressed
By the dark webs, her nape caught in his bill,
He holds her helpless breast upon his breast.

How can those terrified vague fingers push   5
The feathered glory from her loosening thighs?
And how can body, laid in that white rush,
But feel the strange heart beating where it lies?

A shudder in the loins engenders there
The broken wall, the burning roof and tower   10
And Agamemnon dead.
                              Being so caught up,
So mastered by the brute blood of the air,
Did she put on his knowledge with his power
Before the indifferent beak could let her drop?

1924

1. In Greek mythology, Leda, a human woman, was raped by the god Zeus, who appeared in the form of a swan. Leda gave birth to Helen, who eventually married Menelaus, a Greek king. When Paris of Troy kidnapped Helen, the Greeks, led by Menelaus's brother Agamemnon (who was married to Helen's sister, Clytemnestra), banded together to invade Troy and retrieve Helen. The long history of the Trojan War, including Clytemnestra's murdering Agamemnon upon his return, was engendered by this rape. Yeats considered this story to be an analogue of the Christian annunciation, when God, in the form of a dove, impregnated Mary. In Yeats's idiosyncratic theory of history, the birth of Jesus initiated a two-thousand-year epoch that culminated in the mass politics and wars of the twentieth century.

Sailing to Byzantium[2]

I

That is no country for old men. The young
In one another's arms, birds in the trees
—Those dying generations—at their song,
The salmon-falls, the mackerel-crowded seas,
Fish, flesh, or fowl, commend all summer long   5
Whatever is begotten, born, and dies.
Caught in that sensual music all neglect
Monuments of unaging intellect.

2

An aged man is but a paltry thing,
A tattered coat upon a stick, unless   10
Soul clap its hands and sing, and louder sing
For every tatter in its mortal dress,
Nor is there singing school but studying
Monuments of its own magnificence;
And therefore I have sailed the seas and come   15
To the holy city of Byzantium.

3

O sages standing in God's holy fire
As in the gold mosaic of a wall,
Come from the holy fire, perne in a gyre,[3]

2. Byzantium (now Istanbul) was for centuries the capital of the Eastern Roman Empire.
Yeats saw in its mosaics the prototype of an artificial, symbolic art that made no attempt at
realism. Byzantium became, in his imagination, a country of unchanging, undeveloping artifice, and this permanence he contrasted with the mutability of a young country, like Ireland,
which had gained its independence just six years before he wrote this poem.
3. The speaker is asking the sages to come down as if out of the golden mosaics painted on
the inside of a dome and inspire him. "Perne" is Yeats's coinage. It refers to thread pulled
from a bobbin; the unwinding thread would appear to make a conical shape. In this comparison, the thread would be the sages, and the point of the cone would be the speaker into
whom these sages are descending.

And be the singing-masters of my soul.　　　　　20
Consume my heart away; sick with desire
And fastened to a dying animal
It knows not what it is; and gather me
Into the artifice of eternity.

4

Once out of nature I shall never take　　　　　25
My bodily form from any natural thing,
But such a form as Grecian goldsmiths make
Of hammered gold and gold enamelling
To keep a drowsy Emperor awake;
Or set upon a golden bough to sing　　　　　30
To lords and ladies of Byzantium
Of what is past, or passing, or to come.

1927

Plays

What Is Drama?

Even if you have never read a play before, you have probably spent your life absorbing the skills necessary to read one. Anyone who has grown up going to the movies and watching television learned the common language of drama long ago. When your pulse races during a tense scene in a movie or when you laugh at a pratfall in a sitcom, you're responding as you should when you read a play: exercising your best judgment of character, following and reacting to the manipulations of plot, and staying alert to underlying meanings.

As if by instinct, you most likely react to drama with the "correct" emotions. These reactions don't happen accidentally, of course. Directors, scriptwriters, and playwrights avidly study human nature, and they use their knowledge of instinctual responses to push emotional buttons. For example, they count on your responding in a particular way when you see a child in danger, in a different way when you see an attractive person disrobing by candlelight. But instinct is only half the story; many of your responses are shaped not by your instincts but by **dramatic conventions**—devices, phrases, or actions that have, over time, become so common that their meaning is immediately apparent. Without knowing it, you've internalized dozens of dramatic conventions. When you hear a violin playing in a minor key on a movie sound track, you, like most people, probably feel melancholy. That's not so much instinct at work as a learned response, even if you are not consciously aware of it. You don't need to *know* you've been conditioned to feel sad when you hear a violin in the background for your emotions to respond "correctly." The process is automatic.

Dramatic Conventions Then and Now

While familiar dramatic conventions produce responses automatically (or nearly so), unfamiliar ones can seem strange and can interfere with your emotional responses. If you've ever struggled through Shakespeare or puzzled over Sophocles, your confusion might have resulted from unfamiliar conventions. The use of a **chorus**—in ancient Greek theater, a group of singers and dancers who participate in or comment on the action—is a good example. When you first read Greek tragedy, the chorus's pronouncements can seem odd— unrealistic and alienating. Once you absorb the rules of this particular dramatic convention, however, the strangeness disappears.

Contemporary dramas don't use choruses unless they're self-consciously, perhaps ironically, borrowing the ancient device. But the conventions of long-ago theater have modern counterparts. What these now-strange conventions accomplished for their audiences are accomplished today by other means, conventions that contemporary audiences feel perfectly comfortable with and interpret without even noticing. One such convention is the "voiceover" narration common in movies. The voiceover would no doubt strike someone completely unfamiliar with film or television as a very odd convention. Where, after all, is that voice *coming from*? Whose voice is it? And where, exactly, is the speaking supposed to be occurring? To the person asking questions such as these, the voiceover would be just as strange as the Greek chorus is to you today.

By learning about some of the older conventions of drama and keeping in mind that contemporary forms of cultural expression have their own peculiar conventions, you should be able to overcome many of the difficulties inherent in reading plays written for past societies, even ones that have long since perished.

Cultural Context

Another possible confusion when reading plays written in the past has to do with cultural differences between you, the reader (or theater-goer), and the characters inhabiting the play (and the playwright who created those characters). In all the plays reprinted in this book, the characters struggle with questions that remain pertinent: What is the meaning of existence? What constitutes a good life? How can men and women get along? Why must children contest their parents? Why is there suffering and injustice? As universal as these questions may be, however, the ways they are presented, and the assumptions that guide the characters' actions and words as they seek to answer them, are often rooted in a specific time and place—in a **cultural context**—that can seem unfamiliar and confusing now. But just as frequent exposure to dramatic conventions can make them seem more and more familiar, so too can learning about the time and place in which a play was written help you respond to the work in a more direct and meaningful way.

Take an example from Shakespeare's *Hamlet*. Near the end of act 2, his fellow students Rosencrantz and Guildenstern inform Prince Hamlet about the late difficulties of a group of traveling tragic actors. In subsequent scenes, Hamlet digresses on the proper way to perform a play. Though the whole issue of acting troupes occupies hundreds of lines, it is so tangential to the main line of the play's action that modern directors, looking for places to cut this long play, often dispense with them altogether. To modern readers, Hamlet's long speeches on acting may prove confusing or, worse, intrusive and boring. But to Shakespeare's contemporaries, the lines must have made perfect sense, as a reference to a particular theatrical controversy with which they were all familiar.

Theaters like the Globe, which Shakespeare co-owned and where most of his plays were performed, dominated theatrical London until about 1600, when a more exclusive type of theater developed. The Globe was an open-air structure in which people from different social classes took in popular entertainments that mixed verbiage with physicality and were performed entirely by men and boys. In the alternative, private type of theater, the venues were smaller and enclosed. Admission was expensive, so the clientele tended to exclude the lower orders. Because the actors were children, the plays tended to be less raucous and bawdy (a company of boys could hardly have acted many scenes in a play like *Hamlet*); and they were seen as more erudite than the lowbrow affairs Shakespeare wrote. So the strange digressions about theater in the second and third acts of *Hamlet* can be seen as Shakespeare's contribution to the bitter dispute among competing acting companies.

Henrik Ibsen's *A Doll House* provides another type of cultural dissonance between an older play—this one from nineteenth-century Europe—and contemporary readers. The plot hinges on a bit of contractual fraud that most readers today find fairly trivial. Whenever I teach the play, my students wonder why the characters make such a fuss about a course of events that would pretty well meet their own ethical standards. To feel any of the tension Ibsen meant you to feel, you have to understand how important public reputation was to a business career at the time and how even a small slip could ruin a reputation.

Throughout this book, I keep footnotes to a minimum, but I use them to explain cultural differences like these, which would otherwise make the plays harder to understand.

Page Versus Stage

Unlike a short story or a novel, a play is written not primarily for *reading* but instead as the guiding text for *performing* onstage. When reciting lines, actors provide all sorts of physical cues—facial expressions and body language and tone of voice—that make the words more understandable, that deliver to their audience a thousand subtleties latent in the written words. For example:

MAN: I'm through with everything here. I want peace. I want to see if somewhere there is something left in life with charm and grace. Do you know what I'm talking about?
WOMAN: No. I only know that I love you.
MAN: That's your misfortune.
WOMAN: If you go, where shall I go? What shall I do?
MAN: Frankly, my dear, I don't give a damn.

Once you reached the last line, you might have realized that this dialogue comes from the last scene of Victor Fleming's film *Gone with the Wind* (1939), where Rhett Butler (Clark Gable) abandons a sobbing Scarlett O'Hara (Vivien Leigh) on the staircase of their mansion. If you've seen the film, you can probably conjure images of Gable and Leigh, he delivering his lines with cold disdain, she delivering hers with panicked desperation. But if you *haven't* seen the movie, you might wonder, reading the lines above, what all the fuss has been about—why some people claim that the final scene of *Gone with the Wind* is one of the most powerful and memorable movie endings they've ever seen. Without the actors' intonations and gestures, without the sets and lighting, without dozens of contextual cues, the dialogue can seem dry.

Although plays can be enjoyed and studied as texts, fundamentally they are written guides for other artists—directors, actors, set designers, and many others—to create artistic performances. When you read a play on the page, those other artists are not present to help you imagine all aspects of the performance, as they would be if you saw the play performed. Therefore, your imagination needs to be fully engaged when you read—at every turn, you essentially decide how you would stage the play if you were the director.

After you've read a play once, you should try to see it performed—not as a *substitute* for your reading, of course, but as a *supplement*. If you have access to live theater, see the play onstage. If not, try to find a performance on video or DVD. Watching the lines being brought to life often reveals subtleties of meaning barely perceptible in the text. This is especially true of Shakespeare. I often show my students scenes from Franco Zeffirelli's 1990 film adaptation of *Hamlet* (starring Mel Gibson, Glenn Close, and Helena Bonham Carter), and only then do they realize that Polonius is something of a fool; only then do they understand how betrayed Hamlet feels by Ophelia and recognize the barely submerged sexual tension between Hamlet and his mother. But even more recent plays—plays with characters whose speech patterns are closer to our own or with detailed stage directions—become more accessible when experienced in performance.

Perhaps more important, a performance helps you see that the very act of putting a play into action involves interpretation and analysis on the part of the director, the actors, and every other artist involved in the production—activities very similar to your own interpretative and analytical work when you read the play on the page and form a version in your mind's eye. Each performance of a play, even one that follows the text to the letter, differs from every other performance, and the differences among performances reveal interesting differences of opinions about the play's meanings.

Before you can fully appreciate the differences among performances, though, you need to understand what is familiar—the elements common to all drama. Let's turn to those elements now.

The Parts of a Play

Analysis means "a breaking down into parts." You are analyzing whenever you come out of a movie arguing with your friends about one thing or another, whenever you ask, Did the main character deserve what he got? Did you like or dislike so-and-so? and other questions of that nature. To answer those questions, you analyze the film, meaning you break it into parts and scrutinize these parts in some detail.

People have been breaking plays down into parts for over two thousand years. Aristotle, a Greek philosopher of the fourth century B.C.E., wrote the first great work of literary criticism, *Poetics,* not long after Sophocles wrote *Oedipus the King.* In fact, the *Poetics* drew on *Oedipus* for most of its examples. Aristotle invented the first list of parts to drama: spectacle, (moral) character, plot, diction, melody, and thought. Over the centuries, these have been modified somewhat, but most discussions of dramatic form owe a debt to Aristotle's acute analysis of Greek theater.

Plot

The **plot** is the sequence of things that happen in a play. Generally, a play acts out a story before the eyes of its audience, so that people in the audience feel as though they are witnessing the events. (Some specialized forms of drama, such as Samuel Beckett's extremely minimal monologues, do not work this way, but those genres are beyond the scope of this book.) And so a play includes all the elements you expect of a story:

1. It begins in some state of **equilibrium,** which is stable and often (though not necessarily) more or less pleasant.
2. A **conflict** is introduced into this state of equilibrium by some event (the **complication**).
3. Over the course of the play, the conflict grows in a sequence of events (**rising action**).
4. The conflict comes to a head (the **climax**), which ends the conflict.
5. The climactic event brings about a sequence of consequences (**falling action**).
6. Finally, the plot reaches its **resolution,** a concluding situation that rests in another state of equilibrium, though the condition of the characters is probably different from what it was at the story's beginning.

These elements constitute just about any plot. The story in nearly every mainstream movie, television drama, short story, novel, narrative poem, or play can be broken down into these parts.

Let's take a simple fairy tale for an example—say, the story of "The Three Little Pigs." The initial state of equilibrium exists when the story begins, with the three pigs building and moving into their houses of straw, sticks, and brick. Everything is stable at this point in the story. But this initial condition of stability is disrupted by the arrival of a wolf, who threatens to eat the pigs. This event is the complication, because it introduces into the story a conflict: pig versus wolf.

Conflict can always be expressed as one force struggling against another. Sometimes these forces are people: in *Hamlet,* Hamlet struggles against Claudius; in *A Doll House,* Nora opposes Helmer. Sometimes the "forces" battle within one character: Hamlet fights against his own tendency to overanalyze the situation and procrastinate rather than act; Nora fights against her motherly instincts. And as the preceding examples make clear, typically several conflicts occur in any play.

Most plays don't devote much time to the original state of things before the complication. They tend to begin **in medias res** (literally, "in the midst of things"), after the action has started and the complication has occurred, when the conflict is in its beginning stages. Typically, a dramatist will provide some sort of background information in the opening scene to give viewers an understanding of the early stages of the plot. This information is called **exposition.**

The rising action depicts the escalating struggle of the conflict. In our example, the rising action plays out in the huffs and puffs of the wolf. He threatens the first pig, then blows down the house of straw; but this pig escapes to the house of sticks, and the wolf renews his threats and blows down that house too. The rising action is often compared to the slope of a mountain, and you've probably seen graphs of plots in the shape of a pyramid:

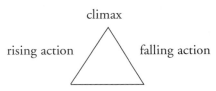

This metaphor is apt. As the play moves toward the climax, the conflict grows more and more acute, and so the audience tends to feel more and more anxiety about the outcome.

The climax of "The Three Little Pigs" is that scene in which the wolf fails to blow down the brick house and resorts to climbing down the inside of the chimney. The clever pigs, of course, have a hot cauldron on the fire, and the wolf gets cooked or, in less gruesome versions, runs away. No matter the version, the wolf clearly won't come back anytime soon; the pigs have won the struggle. The climax has resolved the conflict. One side wins, so to speak, and the other side loses. You can speak in terms of a contest even when the conflict happens within one character, as if two impulses or sides within that character were fighting for control. At the climax, one impulse or side "wins" and the other "loses."

The falling action is the sequence of events that cascade in consequence of the climax. In movies and television dramas, the falling action tends to be very brief, but in plays it often occupies a fairly substantial portion of the drama. "The Three Little Pigs" contains practically no falling action. Once the pigs win, the wolf disappears without further incident. You're launched immediately into the resolution: that final situation in which order and stability are restored. Usually, the fairy tale ends with a scene depicting the "happy ever after" of the pigs as they dance around, feast, and live the high life in their brick house.

In most of the plays in this book, the resolution is a state considerably less attractive than the original state of equilibrium. The characters enjoy no happy ever after. That's because most of these plays either are tragedies, which tend to depict the fall of the main character, or owe a debt to tragedy. We'll talk more about tragedy a little further below.

Character

A **character,** of course, is a person on the stage, a personage being acted for the audience. Time has proved character to be the element of drama that distinguishes great plays from the rest. Plays that rely on interesting plots but superficial characters often become popular for a short time, but they burn out quickly and are forgotten. An entire genre of drama, the **well-made play** of the nineteenth century, exploited the crowd-pleasing elements of plot, like surprise revelations and dramatic climaxes—while purposely neglecting to develop memorable characters. The formulaic nature of Hollywood **genre** movies—westerns, crime films, horror movies, the *Rambo* series, and so on—makes them the modern versions of plot-driven drama. Some movies made in these genres rise above the others and join the ranks of classic films, but they always do so by adding depth of character to their exciting plots. In fact, fascinating characters enable even plays, television shows, and films with straightforward or simple plots to live beyond their first seasons or initial releases. Obviously, the best combinations wed interesting plots to interesting characters, but of the two, character seems more important.

You analyze characters in a play much the same way you analyze people in life. At first, you react to them spontaneously. Gradually, as each character acts, speaks, and develops (or doesn't develop), you modify your first impression to create a more complex sense of each character's nature. Throughout, you should trust your instincts but remain open to new information and new impressions. Be cautious about personal likes and dislikes—you might hate redheads, for instance, for no good (or a very personal) reason and thus fail to sympathize with a character with whom the playwright intends you to sympathize. As long as you're mindful of your prejudices and idiosyncrasies, you'll probably have little trouble judging characters. Of all parts of analysis, analyzing characters will come most naturally.

At the most basic level, you should identify which characters you like and which you dislike. As in real life, characters tend to be a mixture of good and bad, but typically the play will lead you to sympathize with some over others—to wish them well and feel sorry for them when they suffer. Such characters are called **sympathetic characters.** Characters with whom you are not meant to sympathize are called **unsympathetic characters.** Sometimes a play will ask you to do more than sympathize. In fact, according to Aristotle, tragedy works only if the play gets you to **identify** with the protagonist. To identify with a character is to imagine yourself in the character's place.

No one can call your responses to characters wrong, but you should cultivate an ability to justify your spontaneous reactions. Rather than merely judging characters—saying you like this person or dislike that one—try to explain why you have made these judgments. Again, your reasons may be the same as they would be in real life. As you watch a play, all sorts of things influence your spontaneous impressions: the costumes, the actors' body language and **diction,** and so on. If you're reading the play, you have fewer cues. You will be able to judge the characters mostly by what they say and do but also by how the other characters react to them. So the process of analyzing characters, while fairly easy, might require you to slow down and become conscious of how your affinities have been manipulated by the writer. You might keep in mind these very simple questions: Why do I like so-and-so? What is it about so-and-so that rubs me the wrong way? Simple questions like these will lead to sophisticated answers about character.

You should also note certain roles played by characters. Every play, if it has a conflict, will have a **protagonist.** The protagonist is the character that the play focuses on—logically enough, it is Hamlet in *Hamlet* and Oedipus in *Oedipus the King*. Though the protagonist is usually a good person, he or she does not have to be (it is not sufficient to define *protagonist* as the "good guy"). In most plays, the protagonist faces some physical or psychological challenge, and the play dramatizes his or her grappling with that challenge. If the protagonist struggles against another character, that character is called the **antagonist.**

Generally, the struggle (or conflict) causes some change in the protagonist. Any character who changes through the course of the play is called a **dynamic character.** A character who does not change is called a **static character.** A static character may be so two-dimensional, even one-dimensional, that he or she is called a **stock character,** as if the playwright just rummaged around in the stockroom to find a character to perform a particular function. The gravediggers in *Hamlet* might be called stock characters—in this case, witty stereotypes of the working class often found in Elizabethan plays.

Spectacle

Spectacle was Aristotle's term for what the audience sees—the play as a physical reality. We might amplify this category to include all the material aspects of the play, including the **set (scenery, props)**, costumes, music, sound effects, and so on. These elements contribute much to your experience of a play. Think, for example, of scenery. The lights come up on a deserted stage. You see nothing but the setting: an *"apartment . . . in the rear of the building, one of those vast hive-like conglomerations of cellular living-units that flower as warty growths in overcrowded urban centers of lower middle-class population."* This is the scene for Tennessee Williams's *The Glass Menagerie,* and immediately upon seeing it you will feel (though perhaps without realizing that you do) how the setting suffocates each character, stifling each individual's capacity for happiness.

Thus, the spectacle establishes the **atmosphere** for the play. The production manipulates your attitude and mood. Essentially, as a viewer, you are told how to regard the action you are about to see. A good production uses spectacle to communicate to you on a non-verbal level, and you begin "interpreting" the spectacle before you even hear any words. Your gut reacts to it.

To a large extent, then, *reading* a play rather than *viewing* it puts you at a disadvantage. When you read a play, of course, you have to picture the scene in your mind, so the process is somewhat lengthened. For plays as old as those of Sophocles and Shakespeare, that imaginative work puts you on a level playing field with the original audiences: the playwrights don't provide elaborate directions for how to set the scenes because their theaters didn't use much scenery or costuming; you have to pay careful attention to the dialogue, which is often encumbered by descriptions of the setting and the weather. These verbal cues enable you, like the plays' original audiences, to visualize the spectacle.

Contemporary plays, of course, often use fairly elaborate scenery, which you won't see if you just read the plays. But the play texts tend to give detailed descriptions of that scenery, usually at the very beginning. In fact, by reading contemporary plays, you might have an advantage over theatergoers, because playwrights often go beyond mere description and actually interpret scenes for you. For example, after he describes the setting of *The Glass Menagerie*, Williams goes on to say that the apartment is "*symptomatic of the impulse of this largest and fundamentally enslaved section of American society* [the lower-middle-class population] *to avoid fluidity and differentiation and to exist and function as one interfused mass of automatism.*" So you learn that the apartment manifests a disease, that the host of the disease is a fundamentally enslaved portion of our society, and that the disease mainly destroys individuality. Even the most talented set designer would have trouble conveying all that to the theatergoer. A set design might convey a feeling of claustrophobia, for example, but the symbolic import of that feeling might remain vague. Reading Williams's stage directions is, perhaps, a shallower experience than viewing the set, but it makes up for that deficiency in intellectual precision. Such a precise meaning is impossible to convey through stage scenery alone.

Music works in a similar fashion. Music typically creates atmosphere in the theater and a mood in the viewer. Reading a text cannot re-create in you the physical reaction you might have to music, but usually you can approximate the experience intellectually. And sometimes the playwright will tell you flat out how the sound should affect you.

The spectacle necessarily raises another important element in drama: symbolism.

Symbolism

A **symbol** is a thing that represents something else. In a play, it will be something you can see—a prop, an aspect of the set, a costume, a character himself or herself. This physical object functions as its literal self in the action of the play, but it also represents something other than itself, usually some abstract concept. Take Yorick's skull in the fifth act of Shakespeare's *Hamlet,* for example, which reminds Hamlet of the jester and his vivacious antics. The contrast between the memory and the bones becomes an occasion for ruminating on mortality, on the mutability of all living things. The skull, a memento mori, or "reminder of death," is a symbol, an object that represents something else.

Some objects are **universal symbols:** their representations are the same in many cultures. The sunrise, for example, symbolizes rebirth or new beginnings in just about all cultures. Many universal symbols derive from the natural world—the sunset, a dense forest, a ferocious predator, a soaring bird—and so they are not so common in plays, which are limited by the practicalities of stagecraft. Even a short lyric poem, which can place before the reader's eyes an image of any object, has more symbolic possibilities than a play, which is limited to the physical objects it can present on stage. For example, William Blake's short poem "The Tyger" makes that animal into a symbol—something that is practically impossible to do in a stage play. Nevertheless, you will find some universal symbols in the plays. Yorick's skull is one—a natural reminder of human mortality.

More common are **conventional symbols.** These are objects that represent something else only within the context of a particular culture. In any culture acquainted with Christianity, for example, the cross represents Jesus's crucifixion, his redemption of humanity, and all the religious sects that believe in his divinity. But if you erected a cross in some distant town whose inhabitants had never heard of the Christian Gospels, the villagers might hang their laundry from it, never thinking they were dishonoring someone's god. A cross would have no symbolic meaning for them; it carries meaning only within the context of cultures familiar with Christianity. Rather than being universal, the symbol has a meaning that is agreed on by a particular group of people.

Sometimes the symbolic meanings of conventional symbols have obviously been contrived by particular people. The regalia of clubs and political organizations are good examples. In the 1870s, the caricaturist Thomas Nast depicted the Republicans and Democrats as an elephant and a donkey, and thereafter these beasts symbolize these American political parties. A committee adopts the flag sewn by Betsy Ross, and thereafter the Stars and Stripes symbolizes a nation.

But most conventional symbols seem to grow right out of their cultures, with no identifiable "author." For example, imagine you're watching a film, and the main character drives up in a Volkswagen Beetle, one of the old ones, all beat up and patched with unmatching colors. Immediately, you'll make some assumptions about the character based on the symbolic meaning of the car: more than likely, the object will call to mind associations with hippies, or at least it will suggest that the driver is part of the counterculture. She's hardly likely to vote Republican in the next election. Who decided that a Volkswagen Beetle would call to mind these things? No one person did. It was the American culture in the 1960s and '70s that authored the symbol.

Anyone familiar with the culture from which a symbol derives will be perfectly able to interpret it. If you meet someone sporting a pink ribbon on his shirt, you'll know that he supports gay rights. Having grown up in our culture tells you that. But recognizing and interpeting conventional symbols from other cultures can be tricky. In the opening sequence of *Oedipus the King,* Creon, returning from a visit to the oracle, wears a wreath of laurel branches on his head. To the typical twenty-first-century reader, this object is meaningless. But any Greek citizen in antiquity would have seen the laurel crown as indicating that Creon's trip was a success. He was bringing good news. Sometimes a footnote will help you interpret such conventional symbols. But more often than not, you'll need to figure them out yourself. In such cases, you should treat conventional symbols as if they were literary symbols.

A **literary symbol** is an object that represents something else only within the context of a particular literary work. Outside the play or story or poem, the object does not carry the same symbolic meaning. A literary symbol, then, is authored neither by nature nor by a culture, but by the individual writer. For example, near the end of *The Glass Menagerie,* Laura hands Jim a broken glass figurine of a unicorn. You might guess at some symbolic meaning here—after all, in Western culture, unicorns are associated with virgins. But you can't understand the full meaning of Laura's gesture unless you read the play. The writer, Tennessee Williams, has given the glass figurines symbolic meaning that they don't carry outside his play.

How do you recognize that an object in a play is not just its literal self but also represents something else? Identifying literary symbols is an art, but a few tricks will help you hone your interpretive skills. If a play title refers to an object, for example, you can be pretty sure the object symbolizes something. Pay careful attention, then, to the fence in *Fences.* By calling attention to the fence through his title, Wilson tips us off to its importance. On your first reading of the play, you should be asking yourself, What could the fence represent? Meanwhile, watch for textual references to it. Repeated references are another good indication that something has symbolic significance.

No foolproof way exists, though, to recognize immediately which objects are symbolic and which are not. Again, trust your instincts. If you find your attention drawn to an object, if you suspect that something might have more than literal significance, you're probably right. The text will guide you to its literary symbols. Even if Wilson had called his play *The Tragedy of Troy Maxson,* you still could figure out that the fence is symbolic because the characters draw your attention to it.

After you've identified a potential symbol, you still have the tougher task of figuring out what the symbol represents. You might have to read scenes or passages a few times until an idea comes to you. Usually, a symbol represents an abstraction: love, death, dreams, hope, and so on.

Trust your gut, but be prepared to revise your gut feelings. If you try to interpret an object symbolically and it doesn't seem to work, maybe you were wrong. Maybe the object is not a symbol. Or maybe you were wrong about what the object represents. Keep revising and refining your idea until you have it right—until your interpretation of the symbol's meaning and importance fits your sense of the play as a whole.

With universal symbols and conventional symbols (at least with conventional symbols from your culture), you won't have to go through this interpretive process. You'll recognize the objects that are symbols, and you'll know what they represent. But with all symbols—universal, conventional, and literary—you need to go through this final stage of interpretation. You need to pay careful attention to what happens to the object in the play because whatever happens to the object *literally* happens to what it represents *symbolically*. For example, you might figure out that the little caged bird in Susan Glaspell's *Trifles* represents the hopes and aspirations for a freer, happier life. But you mustn't stop there. You must look at what happens to the bird, for what happens to it also happens to those hopes and aspirations. Such events are what we might call **symbolic action,** and you haven't fully understood a symbol until you have interpreted the action that involves it.

Tragedy

Everything we've considered so far applies to plays in general. But now we need to focus on one particular genre of plays: **tragedy.** *Oedipus, Hamlet,* and *Fences* are tragedies, and many other plays in this collection share some elements of tragedy. So an understanding of how tragedy affects plot and character will prove useful in much of your reading here.

The plot of tragedy follows the general pattern of all plots, but some aspects are unique to tragedy. Tragedy always begins with the protagonist in a state of **prosperity.** Sometimes you can take this term literally: the character is rich, well liked, and admired, a figure of some prominence in the community. Other times, especially in modern plays, the character displays a metaphoric prosperity based on a different measure of success. For example, at the beginning of *Fences,* Troy Maxson, despite his modest economic status, enjoys stature among his friends and relations. He is a success in their eyes, even a leader among them.

The conflict in a tragedy usually occurs between the protagonist and some larger force, like the gods or fate in Greek tragedy or like a social imperative in modern plays. This force is so powerful that it overwhelms the protagonist, who nonetheless gains nobility in the struggle. For example, in *Fences,* Troy defies the insults and indignities that segregation imposed on African Americans. He is doomed to fail, but in his determined attempt he anticipates the civil rights activists of the 1960s.

The conflict reaches its breaking point at the climax, and in tragedy the climax always enacts a **reversal.** In the plainest terms, the hero's original prosperity turns into poverty. In Greek tragedy, this is a literal reversal: Oedipus, king of Thebes at the play's beginning, becomes a beggar by the play's end. But for works from other ages, these terms apply figuratively: after the reversal, the protagonist somehow falls from his or her metaphorical prosperity. At the play's end, the protagonist has a lower status than at the beginning, having lost something crucial to that earlier success and happiness.

The falling action of tragedy typically reveals that the protagonist has gained some self-understanding. Aristotle called this element **recognition** and considered it crucial to tragedy. Tragic heroes must face up to their own complicity in reversal. They have to take responsibility for the events that bring them to the point of poverty.

The term **tragic hero** merits some explanation. The protagonist in a tragedy is, by definition, a tragic hero. But over the ages, such protagonists have tended to share certain character traits. For example, tragic heroes generally have been drawn from the higher classes—even from royalty, as in *Oedipus the King* and *Hamlet.* This exalted status ensures that audiences view the heroes as, in some ways, larger, even better, than themselves and their fates as more important than ordinary people's fates. In the modern world, especially in democratic societies, this imbalance seems anachronistic, even offensive, so dramatists convey largeness of character in other ways. In *Fences,* for example, Troy transcends his job as a sanitation worker by carrying himself like the sports hero he once was. He fills the stage when he walks onto it.

The audience must admire the hero to some extent, whatever his or her faults, for a tragedy to work properly. Viewers must feel **pity** as they watch the hero go from a position above them to a position below them. They must feel sorry for the hero. And so the character's final state of poverty must appear out of proportion. The punishment cannot fit the crime. If the plot depicted a wicked person (someone visibly worse than the audience) receiving just deserts, viewers probably would feel satisfaction rather than pity or sorrow.

Still, the protagonist must have earned some punishment. The tragic hero cannot be a saint, someone too good and exalted to make a mistake. High school textbooks often label this aspect of the hero a tragic flaw, and they typically identify overweening pride (or **hubris**) as the most common tragic flaw. These ideas derive from Aristotle's *Poetics,* but they are a bit too loosely translated and are too reductive to describe complex heroes. It would be a mistake, for example, to try to figure out Hamlet's "flaw" merely because a tragic hero "must" have one. Instead, think of the proverb "To err is human." The tragic hero must be as imperfect, perhaps as full of contradictions, as any human being.

If the hero were a god or good beyond reason, the audience would not be able to identify with the hero, and this sense of identification lies at the heart of tragedy. Viewers must be able to see themselves in the hero, to think that they are not all that different from the hero, to recognize shared human traits in even a large or exalted character. Not many people will identify with a saint, but most people will identify with a character who is mostly but not entirely good because that is how they think of themselves. Once people put themselves in the hero's shoes, they can experience the second of the tragic emotions, what Aristotle somewhat grandly called **terror.**

After first pitying the hero, viewers realize that they, who are not fundamentally different from the hero, can or do share the character's fate, that they are, in fact, pitying themselves. And it should be a bit terrifying to contemplate suffering the same fate as the hero, to realize that the hero's struggle could be anyone's, and to conclude that a massive reversal of fortune may be part of the human condition.

You might wonder why anyone would go to a tragedy if seeing one just leads to feelings of pity and terror. Who would pay money to experience those emotions? The answer is a bit elusive. Aristotle thought tragedies were valuable, even popular, because they not only make people feel pity and terror, but they ultimately flush those emotions out of people. It is almost as if tragedies inoculate viewers against the effects of those emotions in real life. This purgation is sometimes called **catharsis.** But whatever the reason, throughout history, audiences have enjoyed watching, and vicariously experiencing, tragic events onstage.

Comedy

Comedy's popularity presents no such mystery. As a genre or subgenre, however, comedy is much more difficult to describe and define than tragedy (Aristotle's thoughts on the subject are lost to the ages). We all can recognize a comedy when we see one, and perhaps the common understanding of the term is the best—a comedy is a play that makes people laugh a lot. Just as to be successful, tragedy must elicit feelings of pity and terror in viewers, so comedy must make viewers happy. And just as tragedy makes viewers experience (at least vicariously) the difficulties and frailties of the human condition, so comedy celebrates humanity in all its sloppy, raucous, robust fertility.

The comedic plot is generally the reverse of the tragic plot: the protagonist begins in a state of relative poverty and ends in a state of prosperity. But these terms must be taken even more metaphorically than they are in tragedy, because the poverty often consists of nothing more than the protagonist's feelings of loneliness or emptiness in not having a mate. That is certainly the case in the thousands of **romantic comedies** that have been forever popular (Oscar Wilde's *The Importance of Being Earnest* is a good example). You might describe the standard plot reductively but pretty accurately as "Boy is alone; boy meets girl; boy is separated from girl; boy and girl re-unite." (For many contemporary examples, substitute *boy* for *girl* or *girl* for *boy* as necessary.) While tragedies often end in death, romantic comedies usually end in betrothal or marriage, a symbol of human renewal and fecundity.

This description is not meant to trivialize comedy. The most famous comedies of all time, including Shakespeare's, basically tell boy-meets-girl stories. The genius of such plays resides never in the plot itself but in the playwright's handling of the characters. Ingenuity enables comedians to still delight and entertain audiences as they tell the same basic story time and time again.

Major Moments in the History of Theater

I mentioned above that the conventions of theater have changed throughout the ages, and that the strange conventions of long-past civilizations might make it harder to enjoy reading their plays. What follows here is a very brief discussion of the types of theater represented in this volume. You should not take it as a comprehensive history—nor even an outline of theater history. I focus only on the contexts of the plays in this book: eight nearly discrete points in a time line. I've skipped everything between those points, even the evolutionary connections between the different epochs. But this sketch should help you appreciate the plays. I recommend that you read it through from beginning to end now, then return to an individual section when (before, after, while) you read the corresponding play.

Greek Theater

The Greeks invented drama. Jackie Chan and Halle Berry and Antonio Banderas earn millions today because of what the Greeks did twenty-five centuries ago. This is not to say Greek theater much resembled movies. Drama grew out of religious festivals devoted to the worship of Dionysus, the god of wine. Raised to the pantheon of gods fairly late in Greek history, Dionysus was a social leveler. His rites first became popular in Athens during the antiaristocratic reign of Peisistratus (d. 527 B.C.E.), so drama, from its very beginnings, was linked to democratic traditions. In ecstatic dances and songs, choruses took on the identities of historical figures (soldiers of Argos, for example) and satyrs. They sometimes retold traditional epic stories in song, but they did not dramatize the events.

Spoken dialogue became possible after a man named Thespis (sixth century B.C.E.), from whose name comes the word *thespian,* added an actor to these choral dances and songs. The earliest tragedy (by Aeschylus, 525–456 B.C.E.) includes three choruses, who dance and sing for 603 of 1,073 lines. In performances, an actor playing a character would give speeches that interacted with the chorus's songs. When Aeschylus added a second actor to subsequent plays, the songs and speeches began to dramatize stories. Having two actors enabled Aeschylus to introduce conflicts between people, and conflict is the essential element of plot. So drama as the playing out of a story really began with Aeschylus. Sophocles (ca. 496–406 B.C.E.) added a third actor and was thus able to increase the complexities of the stories. He retained the chorus but diminished its role to a supporting function, such as representing the people (the citizens of Thebes in *Oedipus the King*); and he used its songs to punctuate the action, commenting on and sometimes interpreting for the audience what the characters do and say. In *Oedipus,* the chorus sings only 317 lines out of 1,530. The performance focuses not on the lyric songs but on the story unfolded by the characters.

Greek plays were performed during daytime in immense outdoor amphitheaters, with semicircular rows of stone bleachers rising up hillsides. These theaters could seat up to fifteen thousand spectators—as many people as can fit into sports arenas today. At the base of the bleachers was a circular floor, the **orchestra,** where the chorus danced and sang its odes. Behind this level space stood a slightly raised, uncurtained stage area, where the actors performed in front of a wooden facade. The actors could change costumes in a backstage area behind the facade. They made their entrances through doors in this structure—a door might represent, for example, the entrance to a palace, as it does in *Oedipus*. Sophocles introduced painted scenery to the stage, but otherwise these productions employed no sets.

The actors could use their voices expressively thanks to the theaters' acoustics. Even in the largest theaters, whispers could project to the audience. As an undergraduate, I went on a school trip to Greece, where we visited the theater at Epidaurus, one of the best-preserved Greek amphitheaters. I sat in the very back row and looked down on my teacher, who stood on a stone that marked the exact center of the theater. I could barely see his face. He removed from his pocket a bus ticket, a flimsy thing about as thick as the tissue paper we stuff in gift boxes. When he tore this little piece of paper in half, I could barely see the thing in his fingers, but I could hear it rip. Such subtleties, of volume and vocal tone, will of course be lost when you read a play, so you'll have to imagine how each speech should be delivered.

The size of the Greek theaters made it impossible for actors to use anything but the grandest gestures. Actors today—on television, in movies, and even in smaller theaters—can communicate through facial expressions like raised eyebrows or slight frowns, but these expressions would be lost in theaters the size of sports arenas. So Greek actors wore large masks, carved and painted with realistic faces, that could be seen even from the back rows of the theaters. These masks provided one way for the audience to distinguish one character from another (remember: only three actors played all the roles in Sophocles' plays; Sophocles expanded the repertoire of dramatic masks). Because these masks were stiff, the actors had to rely on their voices and the words themselves to convey subtleties of emotion and attitude. So a *reader* (as opposed to a *viewer*) might find it relatively easy to imagine the characters' inner lives. Because the playwrights couldn't rely on the actors' facial expressions to convey emotions, they put a lot of emotional cues into the texts. Contemporary plays sometimes read much flatter than ancient Greek plays because actors now perform the work of those cues.

Even so, contemporary audiences tend to find Greek drama a bit stiff, even boring. That's because contemporary culture is dominated by the visual. If something dramatic happens, people want to *see* it. They're much more interested in watching people *do* something than in listening to them *talk* about something. Even when they read fiction—consumed through the eyes, but not in the same visual way movies are consumed—the text must involve them vicariously in the action, to make them feel as though they are part of what's happening.

Greek culture was much more aural. Greek drama, then, unfolds in verbal exchanges. Not much *happens*. While a lot of blood spills in *Oedipus,* it spills offstage, away from the audience's eyes, and is reported by messengers. And the real drama of the play doesn't reside in the bloody scenes anyway: it's in the verbal battles between Oedipus and Creon and Tiresias. This convention can be a barrier to modern readers, but because you come to the play prepared, you should be able to bypass the problem.

No doubt some conventions of ancient Greek drama have been lost forever. But the ones I've discussed should help you approximate in your imagination what Sophocles wanted his audience to experience when they saw *Oedipus* performed.

Elizabethan Theater

The term *Elizabethan* refers to the first Queen Elizabeth of England, who ruled from 1558 to 1603. During her reign, England rose to the level of superpower among the nations of Europe, and London was the continent's largest city, a sprawling, gangly octopus of narrow, filthy streets, bustling docksides, grand palaces, lively bars, spectacular churches, and a vibrant mix of European tongues and English dialects.

Some of Shakespeare's contemporaries—more learned men like Ben Jonson—were influenced by Roman drama (itself indebted to Greek theater), but for the most part early Elizabethan theater was a homegrown phenomenon. Entertainers performed modest scenes from wagons at fairs or, sometimes, in the banquet halls of the rich. But those dramatists hardly seem related to the energetic, industrious, and glamorous London play companies in Shakespeare's time. Theater struck London in the 1580s as suddenly as movies hit America in the 1920s and television did in the 1950s. Coming out of nowhere, it completely reshaped the cultural landscape.

The theaters and the life surrounding them were seen as disreputable. Onstage and offstage, actors and playwrights excited the public with the prospect of love affairs, villainy, and swordplay. People from all social levels came together in audiences to witness murder, mayhem, and sex. (Because women were not allowed to act, boys in drag played all the female roles.) The phenomenon seemed uncontrollable, and government figures feared the effects on the people. When the Puritans came to power, in 1642, they closed the theaters outright rather than try to moralize them. You might think of the theatrical explosion in Elizabethan England as the Internet revolution of its day. In each case, a new medium becomes immensely popular and seems able to democratically influence politics and, perhaps, undermine morals. In Shakespeare's chaotic, raucous world, theater companies were every bit as entrepreneurial as today's dot-coms. They schemed against each other, stole each other's talent, and jealously guarded their material. Fortunes were made nearly overnight, especially by those who built the theater buildings. (Fortunes were also lost nearly overnight, especially when the Puritans closed the theaters.)

Shakespeare's Globe was built on the south side of the River Thames in 1599. *Hamlet* most likely was first played in this theater, probably around 1600. The theater was shaped like a doughnut. Its empty center was open to the sky and contained no seats; like the Greeks, the Elizabethans performed plays only during the daytime. The common people, or **groundlings,** each paid a penny, or about a day's wage, to enter this yard, where they stood and chewed their sausages and watched the action onstage. The stage, uncurtained though canopied with an elaborate roof, stood on five-foot-high trestles and jutted into this open-air space, so the players would have been acting practically in the midst of the groundlings, their feet in the faces of the poor. People who could afford more expensive tickets (about three pence) sat in the tiers of roofed seats that made up the outside of the doughnut. All together, these audiences represented a broad range of London's one hundred thousand citizens, from nobility down to artisans and shopkeepers. As many as three thousand people could fit into the theater at once, making it large by contemporary standards but much more intimate than the Greek theaters.

At the back of the stage stood a facade with, perhaps, three curtained doors that led into the backstage area, or **tiring-house.** Above these doors were box seats for wealthy spectators, making the stage almost a theater-in-the-round. The actors also appeared in these boxes during some rare scenes, like the famous balcony scene in *Romeo and Juliet.* A trapdoor in the stage enabled actors to appear or disappear suddenly, as, for example, when playing the ghost in the first act of *Hamlet.*

The Elizabethans used few props and, like the Greeks, no scenery, so audiences had to imagine the setting from clues in the dialogue. Despite similarities like this, Elizabethans experienced the theater very differently than did the Greeks. The Elizabethan actors' physical proximity to the groundlings more than likely led to a fair amount of give-and-take between the two sides. The play texts sometimes call for characters to whisper confidences to the audience about the other characters, and playwrights seem to have expected actors to interact with the audience almost the way stand-up comics play to their audiences today. In the last act of *Hamlet,* for example, the gravediggers certainly played to the groundlings, who must have delighted while their counterparts onstage outwitted their "betters."

You will probably find *Hamlet* more immediately interesting than *Oedipus,* because it employs nearly contemporary plot conventions. The action might seem a bit tame to a reader conditioned by the *Terminator* series and kung-fu movies, but the play is still fairly busy. In fact, the multiple scene changes and time shifts, the swords drawn and people killed onstage, would all have seemed quite dizzying to an ancient Athenian.

But you will also find more speeches than you are used to. Contemporary dialogue tends to sound close to natural speech—with informal vocabulary, rough grammar, clipped sentences—to provide the illusion of reality. In real life, people generally don't talk to each other in paragraphs; one interlocutor hardly completes a sentence before the other speaker responds. Some dialogue in *Hamlet* doesn't work this way. Even in the midst of informal exchanges, like Hamlet's famous harangue of Ophelia, the characters go on much longer than people would in real life. This is not to say Shakespeare had a bad ear for real conversation (the dialogue in the opening scene will sound remarkably real even to contemporary ears). It is just that Elizabethan audiences tolerated much longer exchanges without any

insult to their sense of reality. Indeed, Elizabethan audiences tolerated much longer stretches of sustained drama, for the actors didn't
pause between scenes and acts. Scene and act numbers were added
by later editors, not by Shakespeare.

Nineteenth-Century Middle-Class Theater

Henrik Ibsen's *A Doll House* was staged in a new type of theater that
corresponded (more or less) to what most people today think of
when they hear the word *theater*. With the advent of good artificial
lighting, first gas and later electric, the theater became a decidedly
indoor activity. People attended the theater at night, to fill their
leisure hours. Actors no longer performed in the midst of the audience—they acted in a space removed from the theater seats, as if an
invisible fourth wall separated them from the audience. Curtains
could be drawn to close the stage from view, enabling theater companies to divide one scene from another and change sets. The sets
became far more elaborate and important than in Shakespeare's day,
and set designers took full advantage of innovations in engineering to create special effects. In general, the *spectacle* of the theater
became nearly as important as the actors. Sometimes it even over-
whelmed the actors, as when, for example, in productions of *Ben-
Hur,* an epic set in ancient Rome, live horses on treadmills
re-created chariot races onstage.

The nineteenth-century theater also sharply divided audiences
according to economic status. The music hall variety show (akin to
what became, in twentieth-century America, vaudeville) catered to
the lower classes, who watched, cheered, and heckled these performances in penny theaters—cheap, no-frills playhouses with tables
and chairs that ran perpendicular to the stage. People could drink,
facing each other, with the show going on to the left or right, over
their shoulders. Other theaters—the ones we are concerned with
here—catered to the middle class. They used the auditorium seating
still in use today: rows of individual seats facing a stage, which was
usually crowned by what came to be known as the **proscenium
arch.** The seats sported cushions, which encouraged audiences to be
more passive than those in the music halls were (or than the
groundlings in Shakespeare's Globe had been). Going to a play be-

gan to resemble your experience today—you pay for your ticket, find your seat, settle back in the darkness, then quietly witness what happens on the lighted stage.

The new style of theater separated audiences from the actors decisively. Actors no longer confided in the audience with knowing winks or clever asides. Watching scenes played out in elaborate sets and with authentic costumes, audiences began to feel like flies on the wall, eavesdropping on real life. They lost themselves in the drama—forgot they were in a theater at all. Thus the current custom of studied silence in the audience established itself in these theaters. To make noise was considered impolite. It disturbed the illusion of reality.

In general, nineteenth-century theater demanded a much higher degree of realism than had been present in either Greek or Elizabethan drama. In plays like *A Doll House* and (to a degree) Oscar Wilde's *The Importance of Being Earnest,* theatergoers expected to see people like themselves moving about in rooms that resembled their own houses. And the style of acting grew progressively less exaggerated, quieter, and more subtle.

Audiences still demanded to be entertained, however, and most of the plays that thrilled the middle class then would probably be called melodramatic today. Most popular of all were the well-made plays, a tradition that Ibsen reacted against with his serious social dramas and that Wilde made fun of with his highly unserious social comedy.

The Provincetown Players

By the early twentieth century, Broadway in New York City had become the established center of theater in America, and most of the productions there could be described as well-made plays. These plays often made a lot of money, but they seemed superficial and lightweight to a coterie of disaffected intellectuals, many of whom lived in New York's Greenwich Village. It was a heady time for radical thinkers, and the Village was full of revolutionaries who challenged the inherited social institutions (like monogamous marriage) and the inherited economic structures and political structures of American society. These progressives firmly opposed, for example, the exclusion of women from politics (women still could not vote in America) and the near-exclusion of women from higher education and the professions. From the art of painting to the art of politics, these bohemian artists and activists were ready to remake the world.

They came largely from the middle and upper-middle classes but repudiated the paths provided for them by their social status—jobs as lawyers or stockbrokers or doctors for the men, roles as socialites for the women—to pursue what they saw as more vital and meaningful lives. As one member of the group, Susan Glaspell, put it, "Most of us were from families who had other ideas—who wanted to make money, played bridge, voted the Republican ticket, went to church, thinking one should be like everyone else." Glaspell's husband, George Cook, came from a wealthy, stolid Iowa family, whom he shocked by divorcing two wives; the second divorce freed him to marry Glaspell.

Cook and Glaspell (among others) established a new kind of theater that was decidedly uncommercial. They didn't care whether the typical Broadway audience was interested. They set about writing and staging plays they were interested in seeing: theater that would examine and interpret the national character and present to audiences intelligent plays regardless of commercial concerns.

In summers, Glaspell, Cook, and a number of their friends would escape the heat of New York City and gather in the fishing village of Provincetown, Massachusetts, where they could rent cheap cottages and discuss their ideas late into the night. In 1915, Cook converted a small warehouse on a fishing wharf into a crude theater, and the group of New Yorkers wrote some short plays to present to themselves—a fairly informal and certainly uncommercial beginning for what would blossom into the Provincetown Players, an amateur troupe of actors with a bona fide theater in New York City. Their notion of theater was purposely stripped-down: gone were the elaborate sets and the spectacle of nineteenth-century tradition. The focus was on character. This serious, intellectual theater scorned easy entertainment, and it helped produce America's first acknowledged great dramatist: Eugene O'Neill.

Because the Provincetown Players scorned spectacle, you won't be missing too much visually by reading rather than viewing

Glaspell's play *Trifles*. You will lose, of course, the actors' interpretations of their lines (which you should try to imagine). Glaspell wrote her play for an intimate theater in which the slightest gesture onstage could be seen by the audience. Consequently, a fair amount of subtlety was conveyed by the actors. The trend toward realistic dialogue and gesture that dominated the nineteenth century was extended even further.

Contemporary American Theater

Unsurprisingly, theater companies like the Provincetown Players never became hugely popular. They cultivated a sophisticated, perhaps even elite audience. Meanwhile, Broadway chugged merrily along. In the 1920s, the kind of theater that Glaspell was reacting against grew even more successful. Nevertheless, its days were numbered, because live theater faced the challenge of a new medium— movies—that easily outdid the best spectacles and well-made plots that the commercial theaters produced. After the 1920s, plays would never again occupy the central cultural role they enjoyed in previous centuries because they could never hope to compete with the popularity of movies—which drew from not only the lower classes but also the middle classes. After the stock market crash of 1929, live theater declined.

In 1944, serious American theater was still much influenced by old traditions, and plays that made it to the stage tended toward the style popularized by Henrik Ibsen. The stories and characters on the American stage in the difficult years of the Great Depression exposed and diagnosed problems in modern society the way, for example, *A Doll House* examines the limitations to the domestic role assigned women by the expanding middle class. Glaspell's *Trifles* helped bring this tradition of serious, realistic drama to America, where it reached its peak of importance in the 1930s.

Tennessee Williams cut against this tradition, experimenting with new techniques, many of which he borrowed from the film industry, which in turn had borrowed from the melodramatic drama vilified by Ibsen and Glaspell. In fact, *The Glass Menagerie* began first as a short story ("Portrait of a Girl in Glass") that Williams adapted into a screenplay (*The Gentleman Caller*) for MGM. The movie was never produced, but the play retained many elements of film. The music, for example, more closely resembles the sound track to a movie than it does the sound effects typically used by realistic plays. The peculiar lighting effects in *The Glass Menagerie* also owe more to filmmaking than to stagecraft. Perhaps the most notable borrowing from film is Williams's use of the **flashback.**

When Williams's next play, *A Streetcar Named Desire,* opened on Broadway, in 1947, the director was Elia Kazan, who revolutionized stage acting in America. Earlier that year, Kazan had helped establish the Actors Studio to train actors in a style known as **method acting.** Appropriate for dramas like Williams's and for film, "the method" relied less on stock gestures and more on subtleties like facial and tonal expression. This style encouraged actors to draw on their own emotional memories in embodying their roles, to *become* their characters and let their bodies act accordingly. Some of the most successful film actors to come out of the 1940s and '50s, like Marlon Brando and Paul Newman, made their names in conjunction with Kazan and Tennessee Williams.

The increased emotional dimension of actors' expressions enabled Williams to attempt onstage what had been attempted only in movies—a drama more akin to the memory of life than to life as experienced. The set of *The Glass Menagerie* is more psychological than it is real. The scenes played for the audience represent not actual events but events filtered and distorted by Tom's psyche as he remembers his life. Critics have often described Williams's influence on the theater as a turning inward, a move away from the realistic drama then preferred by audiences toward a more psychological drama.

By the mid–twentieth century, writers like Williams understood that more people would probably read their plays than see them, and so they produced, essentially, two different versions—one for actors to use in production and another to be published for general readers. In the latter, the playwrights provided far more commentary—descriptions of setting, for example—than had previously been customary. For the last fifty years, reading plays has moved much closer to the experience of reading fiction. In the text of *Fences,* for example, August Wilson provides a far greater wealth of detail than any viewing audience could ever get.

Regional Theaters

Though August Wilson has certainly found success on Broadway, it might be more appropriate to associate him with the regional theater movement. Regional theaters have grown in cities all across North America, and they vary so widely that it is difficult to generalize about them. Often they're subsidized by cadres of patrons: private individuals who donate money to keep the theaters afloat. So they typically do not depend on developing a viable commercial market for live theater.

This type of funding would seem to make theater the domain of the wealthier classes of society. But the regional theaters tend to customize their repertoires to the needs and interests of their local populations, and they usually cut against the economic grain—bringing theater to groups excluded by the highbrow nature of most contemporary theater. Many regional theaters have specific missions, like the Kuntu Repertory Theater at the University of Pittsburgh, which is committed to educating audiences about the black experience and moving them to social action.

Because they are uncommercial, regional theaters do not often produce theatrical spectaculars. Typically, their plays take place in single settings so that only one set has to be built for each production. A contemporary work derived from that world, *Fences* employs no difficult or arcane theatrical conventions.

Conclusion

After all of this prefatory material, it would be easy to lose sight of an important goal in reading these plays: to have fun. Ultimately, increasing your reading pleasure is the purpose of this introduction. You should enjoy reading these plays (your level of enjoyment being a good index of your level of understanding) just as your instructor and I delight in introducing you to plays that we continue to enjoy reading.

Sophocles

CA. 496–406 B.C.E.

OEDIPUS THE KING

The ancient Athenians who saw Oedipus the King *first performed would have gone into the theater knowing the outline of Oedipus's story: The king and queen of Thebes, Laïos and Iocaste, had a son. When they asked one of the oracles at Delphi to prophesy about this boy, the oracle told them that their son would kill his father. So Laïos gave the infant to a shepherd, who was supposed to destroy him. The shepherd pinned the child's ankles together and left him on a remote hillside. A peasant from Corinth found the boy, rescued him, and brought him back to the king and queen of that city, who, having no child of their own, adopted him. That child was Oedipus.*

As a young man, not knowing his true origins, Oedipus met Laïos on a road. Both were driving chariots, and neither would yield the right of way. Laïos's attendant killed one of Oedipus's horses, enraging Oedipus, who killed both the attendant and his own father, Laïos.

Not long after that, Thebes was beseiged by the Sphinx, a monster with the body of a lion and the head of a woman. The Sphinx would ask travelers a riddle, and when they could not answer it, she would eat them. Oedipus boldly went out to face the monster and was challenged with this question: what walks on four legs in the morning, two legs in the afternoon, and three legs in the evening? He answered that man does—meaning that a human being crawls on all fours as an infant, walks upright as an adult, and leans on a cane in old age. In despair over Oedipus's success, the Sphinx jumped off a cliff to its death.

The people of Thebes were so grateful and so impressed by Oedipus's courage and ability, they made him king. He married the widowed queen, Iocaste, his own mother. They had four children, Polyneices, Eteocles, Antigone, and Ismene. But later, during a plague, Oedipus's true parentage was revealed, Iocaste killed herself, and Oedipus, driven mad by the knowledge that Iocaste was his mother, blinded himself and left his native city to wander as a beggar.

Sophocles changed the story in some places and added a number of elements. For example, Oedipus's initial anxiety about sleeping with his mother (and Iocaste's response to his anxieties) may be Sophocles' addition to or at least his amplification of the story. This anxiety inspired Sigmund Freud's great interest in the myth and his coining of the term Oedipus complex *(in his* Interpretation of Dreams *[1900]).*

Sophocles almost certainly did not intend a psychological interpretation of his play—at least not consciously. In its original context, the play's concerns are more obvious, especially its treatment of politics (the obligations of a citizen and a ruler to his city) and religion (the role of the gods in the lives of humans). So the political and religious history of Athens will help you understand the play.

Oedipus the King *probably was first performed in 430* B.C.E., *when Sophocles was about sixty-five. For a generation, the city-state of Athens had enjoyed unparalleled prestige and influence in the Greek world, as it expanded its political dominion and championed its self-consciously superior civic institutions. But in the year before Sophocles wrote* Oedipus, *Athens was shaken to its foundations. The city of Sparta had invaded Attica, the region of Greece attached to Athens. Refugees filled Athens; the crowded people suffered plagues for the next few years (the opening scene of this play would have seemed all too close to home to Sophocles' audience). Thebes and Corinth allied themselves with Sparta against Athens. Though Oedipus was reared in Corinth and ruled Thebes, Sophocles' audience would have recognized in him the traits that Athenians liked to see in themselves—respect for practical experience, trust in logical reasoning, and decisiveness of action. Apparently, Sophocles meant for Oedipus to embody the prototypical Athenian. As you read, you might consider Sophocles' insights into this character type. Does Sophocles blame Athens for its crises? Does he criticize the Athenian "character"?*

The theological questions in the play were topics of fiery debate in Sophocles' Athens. The great intellectual explosion in this century, which produced thinkers such as Socrates and Plato, Pericles and Euripides, brought with it a conflict between free thought and religion. *Apollo's oracles at Delphi were the central religious institu-tion among the Greek cities, and their influence dominated policy and manners. The younger generation of Athenians included free thinkers who openly attacked the prophets' claim to unique knowl-edge, even going so far as to suggest that the prophets were frauds. That suggestion threatened the whole structure of the Greek pan-theon. The conflict between fate and free will, then, had an imme-diate urgency for Sophocles' audience.*

These issues are more than historical curiosities. Indeed, Sopho-cles' play, despite its antiquity, remains amazingly topical. In this post-Darwinian age, we ask ourselves some of the same religious and political questions that the ancient Athenians asked themselves.

Oedipus the King*

PERSONS REPRESENTED:

OEDIPUS	MESSENGER
A PRIEST	SHEPHERD OF LAÏOS
CREON	SECOND MESSENGER
TEIRESIAS	CHORUS OF THEBAN ELDERS
IOCASTE	

THE SCENE: *Before the palace of Oedipus, King of Thebes. A central door and two lateral doors open onto a platform which runs the length of the façade. On the platform, right and left, are altars; and three steps lead down into the "orchestra," or chorus-ground. At the beginning of the action these steps are crowded by suppliants who have brought branches and chaplets of olive leaves and who lie in various attitudes of despair.* OEDIPUS *enters.*

PROLOGUE[1]

OEDIPUS: My children, generations of the living
  In the line of Kadmos,[2] nursed at his ancient hearth:

---

* Translated by Dudley Fitts and Robert Fitzgerald.

1. Introductory scene that establishes the setting, conflct, themes, and main characters of the play.

2. Or Cadmus, legendary founder of Thebes.

Why have you strewn yourselves before these altars
In supplication, with your boughs and garlands?
The breath of incense rises from the city   5
With a sound of prayer and lamentation.
                                        Children,
I would not have you speak through messengers,
And therefore I have come myself to hear you—
I, Oedipus, who bear the famous name.
[*To a* PRIEST.] You, there, since you are eldest in the company,   10
    Speak for them all, tell me what preys upon you,
    Whether you come in dread, or crave some blessing:
    Tell me, and never doubt that I will help you
    In every way I can; I should be heartless
    Were I not moved to find you suppliant here.   15
PRIEST: Great Oedipus, O powerful King of Thebes!
    You see how all the ages of our people
    Cling to your altar steps: here are boys
    Who can barely stand alone, and here are priests
    By weight of age, as I am a priest of God,   20
    And young men chosen from those yet unmarried;
    As for the others, all that multitude.
    They wait with olive chaplets in the squares,
    At the two shrines of Pallas,³ and where Apollo
    Speaks in the glowing embers.
                                    Your own eyes   25
    Must tell you: Thebes is tossed on a murdering sea
    And cannot lift her head from the death surge.
    A rust consumes the buds and fruits of the earth;
    The herds are sick; children die unborn,
    And labor is vain. The god of plague and pyre   30
    Raids like detestable lightning through the city,
    And all the house of Kadmos is laid waste,
    All emptied, and all darkened: Death alone
    Battens⁴ upon the misery of Thebes.
    You are not one of the immortal gods, we know;   35

3. Athena, goddess of wisdom.
4. Fattens.

Yet we have come to you to make our prayer
As to the man surest in mortal ways
And wisest in the ways of God. You saved us
From the Sphinx, that flinty singer, and the tribute
We paid to her so long; yet you were never   40
Better informed than we, nor could we teach you:
It was some god breathed in you to set us free.

Therefore, O mighty King, we turn to you:
Find us our safety, find us a remedy,
Whether by counsel of the gods or men.   45
A king of wisdom tested in the past
Can act in a time of troubles, and act well.
Noblest of men, restore
Life to your city! Think how all men call you
Liberator for your triumph long ago;   50
Ah, when your years of kingship are remembered,
Let them not say *We rose, but later fell—*
Keep the State from going down in the storm!
Once, years ago, with happy augury,[5]
You brought us fortune; be the same again!   55
No man questions your power to rule the land:
But rule over men, not over a dead city!
Ships are only hulls, citadels are nothing,
When no life moves in the empty passageways.
OEDIPUS: Poor children! You may be sure I know   60
All that you longed for in your coming here.
I know that you are deathly sick; and yet,
Sick as you are, not one is as sick as I.
Each of you suffers in himself alone
His anguish, not another's; but my spirit   65
Groans for the city, for myself, for you.
I was not sleeping, you are not waking me.
No, I have been in tears for a long while
And in my restless thought walked many ways.
In all my search, I found one helpful course,   70

---

5. Oedipus saved Thebes by solving the riddle of the Sphinx.

And that I have taken: I have sent Creon,
Son of Menoikeus, brother of the Queen,
To Delphi, Apollo's place of revelation,
To learn there, if he can,
What act or pledge of mine may save the city.   75
I have counted the days, and now, this very day,
I am troubled, for he has overstayed his time.
What is he doing? He has been gone too long.
Yet whenever he comes back, I should do ill
To scant whatever duty God reveals.   80
PRIEST: It is a timely promise. At this instant
   They tell me Creon is here.
OEDIPUS: O Lord Apollo!
   May his news be fair as his face is radiant!
PRIEST: It could not be otherwise: he is crowned with bay,
   The chaplet is thick with berries.
OEDIPUS: We shall soon know;   85
   He is near enough to hear us now.
      [*Enter* CREON.]
                              O Prince:
   Brother: son of Menoikeus:
   What answer do you bring us from the god?
CREON: A strong one. I can tell you, great afflictions
   Will turn out well, if they are taken well.   90
OEDIPUS: What was the oracle? These vague words
   Leave me still hanging between hope and fear.
CREON: Is it your pleasure to hear me with all these
   Gathered around us? I am prepared to speak,
   But should we not go in?
OEDIPUS: Let them all hear it.   95
   It is for them I suffer, more than for myself.
CREON: Then I will tell you what I heard at Delphi.

   In plain words
   The god commands us to expel from the land of Thebes
   An old defilement we are sheltering.   100
   It is a deathly thing, beyond cure;
   We must not let it feed upon us longer.

OEDIPUS: What defilement? How shall we rid ourselves of it?
CREON: By exile or death, blood for blood. It was
    Murder that brought the plague-wind on the city.   105
OEDIPUS: Murder of whom? Surely the god has named him?
CREON: My lord: long ago Laïos was our king,
    Before you came to govern us.
OEDIPUS: I know;
    I learned of him from others; I never saw him.
CREON: He was murdered; and Apollo commands us now   110
    To take revenge upon whoever killed him.
OEDIPUS: Upon whom? Where are they? Where shall we find a clue
    To solve that crime, after so many years?
CREON: Here in this land, he said.
                        If we make enquiry,
    We may touch things that otherwise escape us.   115
OEDIPUS: Tell me: Was Laïos murdered in his house,
    Or in the fields, or in some foreign country?
CREON: He said he planned to make a pilgrimage.
    He did not come home again.   And was there no one,
    No witness, no companion, to tell what happened?   120
CREON: They were all killed but one, and he got away
    So frightened that he could remember one thing only.
OEDIPUS: What was that one thing? One may be the key
    To everything, if we resolve to use it.
CREON: He said that a band of highwaymen attacked them,   125
    Outnumbered them, and overwhelmed the King.
OEDIPUS: Strange, that a highwayman should be so daring—
    Unless some faction here bribed him to do it.
CREON: We thought of that. But after Laïos' death
    New troubles arose and we had no avenger.   130
OEDIPUS: What troubles could prevent your hunting down the
    killers?
CREON: The riddling Sphinx's song
    Made us deaf to all mysteries but her own.
OEDIPUS: Then once more I must bring what is dark to light.
    It is most fitting that Apollo shows,   135
    As you do, this compunction for the dead.

You shall see how I stand by you, as I should,
To avenge the city and the city's god,
And not as though it were for some distant friend,
But for my own sake, to be rid of evil. 140
Whoever killed King Laïos might—who knows?—
Decide at any moment to kill me as well.
By avenging the murdered king I protect myself.

Come, then, my children: leave the altar steps,
Lift up your olive boughs!
                    One of you go 145
And summon the people of Kadmos to gather here.
I will do all that I can; you may tell them that. [*Exit a* PAGE.]
So, with the help of God,
We shall be saved—or else indeed we are lost.
PRIEST: Let us rise, children. It was for this we came, 150
And now the King has promised it himself.
Phoibos has sent us an oracle; may he descend
Himself to save us and drive out the plague.
> [*Exeunt* OEDIPUS *and* CREON *into the palace by the central door.*
> *The* PRIEST *and the* SUPPLIANTS *disperse. After a short pause the*
> CHORUS *enters the orchestra.*]

PÁRODOS[1]
CHORUS: [*Strophe 1.*] What is God singing in his profound
  Delphi of gold and shadow? 155
  What oracle for Thebes, the sunwhipped city?

Fear unjoints me, the roots of my heart tremble.

Now I remember, O Healer, your power, and wonder:
Will you send doom like a sudden cloud, or weave it
Like nightfall of the past? 160

Speak, speak to us, issue of holy sound:
Dearest to our expectancy: be tender!

---
1. Entrance of the chorus. The chorus moves in one direction while chanting the strophe and reverses its direction during the antistrophe.

[*Antistrophe 1.*] Let me pray to Athenê, the immortal daughter
    of Zeus,
And to Artemis her sister
Who keeps her famous throne in the market ring,   165
And to Apollo, bowman at the far butts[2] of heaven—

O gods, descend! Like three streams leap against
The fires of our grief, the fires of darkness;
Be swift to bring us rest!

As in the old time from the brilliant house   170
Of air you stepped to save us, come again!

[*Strophe 2.*] Now our afflictions have no end,
Now all our stricken host lies down
And no man fights off death with his mind;

The noble plowland bears no grain,   175
And groaning mothers cannot bear—

See, how our lives like birds take wing,
Like sparks that fly when a fire soars,
To the shore of the god of evening.

[*Antistrophe 2.*] The plague burns on, it is pitiless,   180
Though pallid children laden with death
Lie unwept in the stony ways,

And old gray women by every path
Flock to the strand about the altars

There to strike their breasts and cry   185
Worship of Phoibos[3] in wailing prayers:
Be kind, God's golden child!

---

2. Places where shooting is practiced.   3. Or Phoebus, Apollo.
Zeus: king of the gods. *Artemis:* moon god-
dess, often depicted as a virgin huntress.

[*Strophe 3.*] There are no swords in this attack by fire,
No shields, but we are ringed with cries.

Send the besieger plunging from our homes   190
Into the vast sea-room of the Atlantic
Or into the waves that foam eastward of Thrace—

For the day ravages what the night spares—

Destroy our enemy, lord of the thunder!
Let him be riven by lightning from heaven!   195

[*Antistrophe 3.*] Phoibos Apollo, stretch the sun's bowstring,
That golden cord, until it sing for us,
Flashing arrows in heaven!
                    Artemis, Huntress,
Race with flaring lights upon our mountains!

O scarlet god, O golden-banded brow,   200
O Theban Bacchos in a storm of Maenads,[4]
    [*Enter* OEDIPUS.]
Whirl upon Death, that all the Undying hate!
Come with blinding torches, come in joy!

SCENE I
OEDIPUS: Is this your prayer? It may be answered. Come,
Listen to me, act as the crisis demands.   205
And you shall have relief from all these evils.

Until now I was a stranger to this tale,
As I had been a stranger to the crime.
Could I track down the murderer without a clue?
But now, friends,   210
As one who became a citizen after the murder,
I make this proclamation to all Thebans:
If any man knows by whose hand Laïos, son of Labdakos,

4. Priestesses or followers of Bacchos, or Bacchus, god of wine and fertility.

Met his death, I direct that man to tell me everything,
No matter what he fears for having so long withheld it.   215
Let it stand as promised that no further trouble
Will come to him, but he may leave the land in safety.

Moreover: If anyone knows the murderer to be foreign,
Let him not keep silent: he shall have his reward from me.
However, if he does conceal it; if any man   220
Fearing for his friend or for himself disobeys this edict,
Hear what I propose to do:

I solemnly forbid the people of this country,
Where power and throne are mine, ever to receive that man
Or speak to him, no matter who he is, or let him   225
Join in sacrifice, lustration, or in prayer.
I decree that he be driven from every house,
Being, as he is, corruption itself to us: the Delphic
Voice of Zeus has pronounced this revelation.
Thus I associate myself with the oracle   230
And take the side of the murdered king.

As for the criminal, I pray to God—
Whether it be a lurking thief, or one of a number—
I pray that that man's life be consumed in evil and
    wretchedness.
And as for me, this curse applies no less   235
If it should turn out that the culprit is my guest here,
Sharing my hearth.
                    You have heard the penalty.
I lay it on you now to attend to this
For my sake, for Apollo's, for the sick
Sterile city that heaven has abandoned.   240
Suppose the oracle had given you no command:
Should this defilement go uncleansed for ever?
You should have found the murderer: your king,
A noble king, had been destroyed!
                    Now I,
Having the power that he held before me,   245

Having his bed, begetting children there
Upon his wife, as he would have, had he lived—
Their son would have been my children's brother,
If Laïos had had luck in fatherhood!
(But surely ill luck rushed upon his reign)—   250
I say I take the son's part, just as though
I were his son, to press the fight for him
And see it won! I'll find the hand that brought
Death to Labdakos' and Polydoros' child,
Heir of Kadmos' and Agenor's line.   255
And as for those who fail me,
May the gods deny them the fruit of the earth,
Fruit of the womb, and may they rot utterly!
Let them be wretched as we are wretched, and worse!

For you, for loyal Thebans, and for all   260
Who find my actions right, I pray the favor
Of justice, and of all the immortal gods.
CHORAGOS:[1] Since I am under oath, my lord, I swear
I did not do the murder, I cannot name
The murderer. Might not the oracle   265
That has ordained the search tell where to find him?
OEDIPUS: An honest question. But no man in the world
Can make the gods do more than the gods will.
CHORAGOS: There is one last expedient—
OEDIPUS: Tell me what it is.
Though it seem slight, you must not hold it back.   270
CHORAGOS: A lord clairvoyant to the lord Apollo,
As we all know, is the skilled Teiresias.
One might learn much about this from him, Oedipus.
OEDIPUS: I am not wasting time:
Creon spoke of this, and I have sent for him—   275
Twice, in fact; it is strange that he is not here.
CHORAGOS: The other matter—that old report—seems useless.
OEDIPUS: Tell me. I am interested in all reports.
CHORAGOS: The King was said to have been killed by highway-men.

1. Leader of the chorus.

OEDIPUS: I know. But we have no witnesses to that.   280
CHORAGOS: If the killer can feel a particle of dread,
    Your curse will bring him out of hiding!
OEDIPUS: No.
    The man who dared that act will fear no curse.
    [*Enter the blind seer* TEIRESIAS, *led by a* PAGE.]
CHORAGOS: But there is one man who may detect the criminal.
    This is Teiresias, this is the holy prophet   285
    In whom, alone of all men, truth was born.
OEDIPUS: Teiresias: seer: student of mysteries,
    Of all that's taught and all that no man tells,
    Secrets of Heaven and secrets of the earth:
    Blind though you are, you know the city lies   290
    Sick with plague; and from this plague, my lord,
    We find that you alone can guard or save us.
    Possibly you did not hear the messengers?
    Apollo, when we sent to him,
    Sent us back word that this great pestilence   295
    Would lift, but only if we established clearly
    The identity of those who murdered Laïos.
    They must be killed or exiled.
                       Can you use
    Birdflight or any art of divination
    To purify yourself, and Thebes, and me   300
    From this contagion? We are in your hands.
    There is no fairer duty
    Than that of helping others in distress.
TEIRESIAS: How dreadful knowledge of the truth can be
    When there's no help in truth! I knew this well,   305
    But made myself forget. I should not have come.
OEDIPUS: What is troubling you? Why are your eyes so cold?
TEIRESIAS: Let me go home. Bear your own fate, and I'll
    Bear mine. It is better so: trust what I say.
OEDIPUS: What you say is ungracious and unhelpful   310
    To your native country. Do not refuse to speak.
TEIRESIAS: When it comes to speech, your own is neither
      temperate
    Nor opportune. I wish to be more prudent.

OEDIPUS: In God's name, we all beg you—
TEIRESIAS: You are all ignorant.
    No; I will never tell you what I know.   315
    Now it is my misery; then, it would be yours.
OEDIPUS: What! You do know something, and will not tell us?
    You would betray us all and wreck the State?
TEIRESIAS: I do not intend to torture myself, or you.
    Why persist in asking? You will not persuade me.   320
OEDIPUS: What a wicked old man you are! You'd try a stone's
    Patience! Out with it! Have you no feeling at all?
TEIRESIAS: You call me unfeeling. If you could only see
    The nature of your own feelings . . .
OEDIPUS: Why,
    Who would not feel as I do? Who could endure   325
    Your arrogance toward the city?
TEIRESIAS: What does it matter!
    Whether I speak or not, it is bound to come.
OEDIPUS: Then, if "it" is bound to come, you are bound to
        tell me.
TEIRESIAS: No, I will not go on. Rage as you please.
OEDIPUS: Rage? Why not!
                        And I'll tell you what I think: 330
    You planned it, you had it done, you all but
    Killed him with your own hands: if you had eyes,
    I'd say the crime was yours, and yours alone.
TEIRESIAS: So? I charge you, then,
    Abide by the proclamation you have made: 335
    From this day forth
    Never speak again to these men or to me;
    You yourself are the pollution of this country.
OEDIPUS: You dare say that! Can you possibly think you have
    Some way of going free, after such insolence?   340
TEIRESIAS: I have gone free. It is the truth sustains me.
OEDIPUS: Who taught you shamelessness? It was not your craft.
TEIRESIAS: You did. You made me speak. I did not want to.
OEDIPUS: Speak what? Let me hear it again more clearly.
TEIRESIAS: Was it not clear before? Are you tempting me?   345
OEDIPUS: I did not understand it. Say it again.

TEIRESIAS: I say that you are the murderer whom you seek.

OEDIPUS: Now twice you have spat out infamy. You'll pay for it!

TEIRESIAS: Would you care for more? Do you wish to be really
    angry?

OEDIPUS: Say what you will. Whatever you say is worthless.   350

TEIRESIAS: I say you live in hideous shame with those
  Most dear to you. You cannot see the evil.

OEDIPUS: It seems you can go on mouthing like this for ever.

TEIRESIAS: I can, if there is power in truth.

OEDIPUS: There is:
  But not for you, not for you,   355
  You sightless, witless, senseless, mad old man!

TEIRESIAS: You are the madman. There is no one here
  Who will not curse you soon, as you curse me.

OEDIPUS: You child of endless night! You cannot hurt me
  Or any other man who sees the sun.   360

TEIRESIAS: True: it is not from me your fate will come.
  That lies within Apollo's competence,
    As it is his concern.

OEDIPUS: Tell me:
  Are you speaking for Creon, or for yourself?

TEIRESIAS: Creon is no threat. You weave your own doom.   365

OEDIPUS: Wealth, power, craft of statesmanship!
  Kingly position, everywhere admired!
  What savage envy is stored up against these,
  If Creon, whom I trusted, Creon my friend,
  For this great office which the city once   370
  Put in my hands unsought—if for this power
  Creon desires in secret to destroy me!

  He has bought this decrepit fortune-teller, this
  Collector of dirty pennies, this prophet fraud—
  Why, he is no more clairvoyant than I am!
                           Tell us: 375
  Has your mystic mummery ever approached the truth?
  When that hellcat the Sphinx was performing here,
  What help were you to these people?
  Her magic was not for the first man who came along:

It demanded a real exorcist. Your birds—   380
What good were they? or the gods, for the matter of that?
But I came by,
Oedipus, the simple man, who knows nothing—
I thought it out for myself, no birds helped me!
And this is the man you think you can destroy,   385
That you may be close to Creon when he's king!
Well, you and your friend Creon, it seems to me,
Will suffer most. If you were not an old man,
You would have paid already for your plot.

CHORAGOS: We cannot see that his words or yours   390
Have been spoken except in anger, Oedipus,
And of anger we have no need. How can God's will
Be accomplished best? That is what most concerns us.

TEIRESIAS: You are a king. But where argument's concerned
I am your man, as much a king as you.   395
I am not your servant, but Apollo's.
I have no need of Creon to speak for me.

Listen to me. You mock my blindness, do you?
But I say that you, with both your eyes, are blind:
You cannot see the wretchedness of your life,   400
Nor in whose house you live, no, nor with whom.
Who are your father and mother? Can you tell me?
You do not even know the blind wrongs
That you have done them, on earth and in the world below.
But the double lash of your parents' curse will whip you   405
Out of this land some day, with only night
Upon your precious eyes.
Your cries then—where will they not be heard?
What fastness of Kithairon² will not echo them?
And that bridal-descant of yours—you'll know it then,   410
The song they sang when you came here to Thebes
And found your misguided berthing.
All this, and more, that you cannot guess at now,
Will bring you to yourself among your children.

---

2. Mountain range between Corinth and Thebes.

Be angry, then. Curse Creon. Curse my words.   415
I tell you, no man that walks upon the earth
Shall be rooted out more horribly than you.
OEDIPUS: Am I to bear this from him?—Damnation
Take you! Out of this place! Out of my sight!
TEIRESIAS: I would not have come at all if you had not asked me.   420
OEDIPUS: Could I have told that you'd talk nonsense, that
You'd come here to make a fool of yourself, and of me?
TEIRESIAS: A fool? Your parents thought me sane enough.
OEDIPUS: My parents again!—Wait: who were my parents?
TEIRESIAS: This day will give you a father, and break your heart.   425
OEDIPUS: Your infantile riddles! Your damned abracadabra!
TEIRESIAS: You were a great man once at solving riddles.
OEDIPUS: Mock me with that if you like; you will find it true.
TEIRESIAS: It was true enough. It brought about your ruin.
OEDIPUS: But if it saved this town?
TEIRESIAS: [*To the* PAGE.] Boy, give me
your hand.   430
OEDIPUS: Yes, boy; lead him away.
                                        —While you are here
We can do nothing. Go; leave us in peace.
TEIRESIAS: I will go when I have said what I have to say.
How can you hurt me? And I tell you again:
The man you have been looking for all this time,   435
The damned man, the murderer of Laïos,
That man is in Thebes. To your mind he is foreign-born,
But it will soon be shown that he is a Theban,
A revelation that will fail to please.
                                        A blind man,
Who has his eyes now; a penniless man, who is rich now;   440
And he will go tapping the strange earth with his staff
To the children with whom he lives now he will be
Brother and father—the very same; to her
Who bore him, son and husband—the very same
Who came to his father's bed, wet with his father's blood.   445

Enough. Go think that over.
If later you find error in what I have said,

You may say that I have no skill in prophecy.
[*Exit* TEIRESIAS, *led by his* PAGE, OEDIPUS *goes into the palace.*]

ODE I
CHORUS: [*Strophe 1.*] The Delphic stone of prophecies
    Remembers ancient regicide   450
    And a still bloody hand.
    That killer's hour of flight has come.
    He must be stronger than riderless
    Coursers of untiring wind,
    For the son of Zeus armed with his father's thunder   455
    Leaps in lightning after him;
    And the Furies[1] follow him, the sad Furies.

    [*Antistrophe 1.*] Holy Parnassos[2] peak of snow
    Flashes and blinds that secret man.
    That all shall hunt him down: 460
    Though he may roam the forest shade
    Like a bull gone wild from pasture
    To rage through glooms of stone.
    Doom comes down on him; flight will not avail him;
    For the world's heart calls him desolate,   465
    And the immortal Furies follow, for ever follow.

    [*Strophe 2.*] But now a wilder thing is heard
    From the old man skilled at hearing Fate in the wingbeat of
        a bird.
    Bewildered as a blown bird, my soul hovers and cannot find
    Foothold in this debate, or any reason or rest of mind.   470
    But no man ever brought—none can bring
    Proof of strife between Thebes' royal house,
    Labdakos' line, and the son of Polybos;
    And never until now has any man brought word
    Of Laïos' dark death staining Oedipus the King.   475

---

1. Supernatural avengers.   2. Mountain on which the oracle at Delphi is located.

[*Antistrophe 2.*] Divine Zeus and Apollo hold
Perfect intelligence alone of all tales ever told;
And well though this diviner works, he works in his own
    night;
No man can judge that rough unknown or trust in second
    sight,
For wisdom changes hands among the wise.   480
Shall I believe my great lord criminal
At a raging word that a blind old man let fall?
I saw him, when the carrion woman faced him of old,
Prove his heroic mind! These evil words are lies.

SCENE II
CREON: Men of Thebes: 485
    I am told that heavy accusations
    Have been brought against me by King Oedipus.

    I am not the kind of man to bear this tamely.

    If in these present difficulties
    He holds me accountable for any harm to him   490
    Through anything I have said or done—why, then,
    I do not value life in this dishonor.
    It is not as though this rumor touched upon
    Some private indiscretion. The matter is grave.
    The fact is that I am being called disloyal   495
    To the State, to my fellow citizens, to my friends.
CHORAGOS: He may have spoken in anger, not from his mind.
CREON: But did you not hear him say I was the one
    Who seduced the old prophet into lying?
CHORAGOS: The thing was said; I do not know how seriously.   500
CREON: But you were watching him! Were his eyes steady?
    Did he look like a man in his right mind?
CHORAGOS: I do not know.
    I cannot judge the behavior of great men.
    But here is the King himself.
        [*Enter* OEDIPUS.]
OEDIPUS: So you dared come back.

Why? How brazen of you to come to my house, 505
You murderer!
    Do you think I do not know
That you plotted to kill me, plotted to steal my throne?
Tell me, in God's name: am I coward, a fool,
That you should dream you could accomplish this?
A fool who could not see your slippery game? 510
A coward, not to fight back when I saw it?
You are the fool, Creon, are you not? hoping
Without support or friends to get a throne?
Thrones may be won or bought: you could do neither.

CREON: Now listen to me. You have talked; let me talk, too. 515
 You cannot judge unless you know the facts.

OEDIPUS: You speak well: there is one fact; but I find it hard
 To learn from the deadliest enemy I have.

CREON: That above all I must dispute with you.

OEDIPUS: That above all I will not hear you deny. 520

CREON: If you think there is anything good in being stubborn
 Against all reason, then I say you are wrong.

OEDIPUS: If you think a man can sin against his own kind
 And not be punished for it, I say you are mad.

CREON: I agree. But tell me: what have I done to you? 525

OEDIPUS: You advised me to send for that wizard, did you not?

CREON: I did. I should do it again.

OEDIPUS: Very well. Now tell me:
 How long has it been since Laïos—

CREON: What of Laïos?

OEDIPUS: Since he vanished in that onset by the road?

CREON: It was long ago, a long time.

OEDIPUS: And this prophet, 530
 Was he practicing here then?

CREON: He was; and with honor, as now.

OEDIPUS: Did he speak of me at that time?

CREON: He never did;
 At least, not when I was present.

OEDIPUS: But . . . the enquiry?
 I suppose you held one?

CREON: We did, but we learned nothing.

OEDIPUS: Why did the prophet not speak against me then?   535
CREON: I do not know; and I am the kind of man
  Who holds his tongue when he has no facts to go on.
OEDIPUS: There's one fact that you know, and you could tell it.
CREON: What fact is that? If I know it, you shall have it.
OEDIPUS: If he were not involved with you, he could not say   540
  That it was I who murdered Laïos.
CREON: If he says that, you are the one that knows it!—
  But now it is my turn to question you.
OEDIPUS: Put your questions. I am no murderer.
CREON: First, then: You married my sister?
OEDIPUS: I married your sister.   545
CREON: And you rule the kingdom equally with her?
OEDIPUS: Everything that she wants she has from me.
CREON: And I am the third, equal to both of you?
OEDIPUS: That is why I call you a bad friend.
CREON: No. Reason it out, as I have done.   550
  Think of this first: Would any sane man prefer
  Power, with all a king's anxieties,
  To that same power and the grace of sleep?
  Certainly not I.
  I have never longed for the king's power—only his rights.   555
  Would any wise man differ from me in this?
  As matters stand, I have my way in everything
  With your consent, and no responsibilities.
  If I were king, I should be a slave to policy.

  How could I desire a scepter more   560
  Than what is now mine—untroubled influence?
  No, I have not gone mad; I need no honors,
  Except those with the perquisites I have now.
  I am welcome everywhere; every man salutes me,
  And those who want your favor seek my ear,   565
  Since I know how to manage what they ask.
  Should I exchange this ease for that anxiety?
  Besides, no sober mind is treasonable.
  I hate anarchy
  And never would deal with any man who likes it.   570

Test what I have said. Go to the priestess
At Delphi, ask if I quoted her correctly.
And as for this other thing: if I am found
Guilty of treason with Teiresias,
Then sentence me to death! You have my word   575
It is a sentence I should cast my vote for—
But not without evidence!
                          You do wrong
When you take good men for bad, bad men for good.
A true friend thrown aside—why, life itself
Is not more precious!
                          In time you will know this well: 580
For time, and time alone, will show the just man,
Though scoundrels are discovered in a day.
CHORAGOS: This is well said, and a prudent man would
     ponder it.
Judgments too quickly formed are dangerous.
OEDIPUS: But is he not quick in his duplicity?   585
     And shall I not be quick to parry him?
     Would you have me stand still, hold my peace, and let
     This man win everything, through my inaction?
CREON: And you want—what is it, then? To banish me?
OEDIPUS: No, not exile. It is your death I want,   590
     So that all the world may see what treason means.
CREON: You will persist, then? You will not believe me?
OEDIPUS: How can I believe you?
CREON: Then you are a fool.
OEDIPUS: To save myself?
CREON: In justice, think of me.
OEDIPUS: You are evil incarnate.
CREON: But suppose that you are
     wrong?   595
OEDIPUS: Still I must rule.
CREON: But not if you rule badly.
OEDIPUS: O city, city!
CREON: It is my city, too!
CHORAGOS: Now, my lords, be still. I see the Queen,
     Iocastê, coming from her palace chambers;

And it is time she came, for the sake of you both.   600
This dreadful quarrel can be resolved through her.
    [*Enter* IOCASTE.]
IOCASTE: Poor foolish men, what wicked din is this?
With Thebes sick to death, is it not shameful
That you should rake some private quarrel up?
[*To* OEDIPUS.] Come into the house.
                      —And you, Creon, go
    now: 605
Let us have no more of this tumult over nothing.
CREON: Nothing? No, sister: what your husband plans for me
Is one of two great evils: exile or death.
OEDIPUS: He is right.
                Why, woman I have caught him squarely
Plotting against my life.
CREON: No! Let me die   610
Accurst if ever I have wished you harm!
IOCASTE: Ah, believe it, Oedipus!
In the name of the gods, respect this oath of his
For my sake, for the sake of these people here!
CHORAGOS: [*Strophe 1.*] Open your mind to her, my lord. Be
    ruled by her, I beg you!   615
OEDIPUS: What would you have me do?
CHORAGOS: Respect Creon's word. He has never spoken like
    a fool,
And now he has sworn an oath.
OEDIPUS: You know what you ask?
CHORAGOS: I do.
OEDIPUS: Speak on, then.
CHORAGOS: A friend so sworn should not be baited so,
In blind malice, and without final proof.   620
OEDIPUS: You are aware, I hope, that what you say
Means death for me, or exile at the least.
CHORAGOS: [*Strophe 2.*] No, I swear by Helios,[1] first in Heaven!
    May I die friendless and accurst,
The worst of deaths, if ever I meant that!   625

---

1. The sun god.

It is the withering fields
      That hurt my sick heart:
      Must we bear all these ills,
      And now your bad blood as well?
OEDIPUS: Then let him go. And let me die, if I must,   630
  Or be driven by him in shame from the land of Thebes.
  It is your unhappiness, and not his talk,
  That touches me.
            As for him—
  Wherever he goes, hatred will follow him.
CREON: Ugly in yielding, as you were ugly in rage!   635
  Natures like yours chiefly torment themselves.
OEDIPUS: Can you not go? Can you not leave me?
CREON: I can.
  You do not know me; but the city knows me,
  And in its eyes I am just, if not in yours.   [*Exit* CREON.]
CHORAGOS: [*Antistrophe 1.*] Lady Locastê, did you not ask the
      King to go to his chambers?   640
IOCASTE: First tell me what has happened.
CHORAGOS: There was suspicion without evidence; yet it rankled
  As even false charges will.
IOCASTE: On both sides?
CHORAGOS: On both.
IOCASTE: But what was said?
CHORAGOS: Oh let it rest, let it be done with!
  Have we not suffered enough?   645
OEDIPUS: You see to what your decency has brought you:
  You have made difficulties where my heart saw none.
CHORAGOS: [*Antistrophe 2.*] Oedipus, it is not once only I have
      told you—
  You must know I should count myself unwise
  To the point of madness, should I now forsake you—   650
            You, under whose hand,
            In the storm of another time,
            Our dear land sailed out free.
            But now stand fast at the helm!
IOCASTE: In God's name, Oedipus, inform your wife as well: 655
  Why are you so set in this hard anger?

OEDIPUS: I will tell you, for none of these men deserves
   My confidence as you do. It is Creon's work,
   His treachery, his plotting against me.
IOCASTE: Go on, if you can make this clear to me.   660
OEDIPUS: He charges me with the murder of Laïos.
IOCASTE: Has he some knowledge? Or does he speak from hearsay?
OEDIPUS: He would not commit himself to such a charge,
   But he has brought in that damnable soothsayer
   To tell his story.
IOCASTE: Set your mind at rest.   665
   If it is a question of soothsayers, I tell you
   That you will find no man whose craft gives knowledge
   Of the unknowable.

                     Here is my proof:

An oracle was reported to Laïos once
(I will not say from Phoibos himself, but from   670
His appointed ministers, at any rate)
That his doom would be death at the hands of his own son—
His son, born of his flesh and of mine!

Now, you remember the story: Laïos was killed
By marauding strangers where three highways meet;   675
But his child had not been three days in this world
Before the King had pierced the baby's ankles
And left him to die on a lonely mountainside.

Thus, Apollo never caused that child
To kill his father, and it was not Laïos' fate   680
To die at the hands of his son, as he had feared.
This is what prophets and prophecies are worth!
Have no dread of them.
                     It is God himself
Who can show us what he wills, in his own way.
OEDIPUS: How strange a shadowy memory crossed my mind,   685
   Just now while you were speaking: it chilled my heart.
IOCASTE: What do you mean? What memory do you speak of?

OEDIPUS: If I understand you, Laïos was killed
   At a place where three roads meet.
IOCASTE: So it was said;
   We have no later story.
OEDIPUS: Where did it happen?   690
IOCASTE: Phokis, it is called: at a place where the Theban Way
   Divides into the roads toward Delphi and Daulia.
OEDIPUS: When?
IOCASTE: We had the news not long before you came
   And proved the right to your succession here.
OEDIPUS: Ah, what net has God been weaving for me?   695
IOCASTE: Oedipus! Why does this trouble you?
OEDIPUS: Do not ask me yet.
   First, tell me how Laïos looked, and tell me
   How old he was.
IOCASTE: He was tall, his hair just touched
   With white; his form was not unlike your own.
OEDIPUS: I think that I myself may be accurst   700
   By my own ignorant edict.
IOCASTE: You speak strangely.
   It makes me tremble to look at you, my King.
OEDIPUS: I am not sure that the blind man cannot see.
   But I should know better if you were to tell me—
IOCASTE: Anything—though I dread to hear you ask it.   705
OEDIPUS: Was the King lightly escorted, or did he ride
   With a large company, as a ruler should?
IOCASTE: There were five men with him in all: one was a
      herald,
   And a single chariot, which he was driving.
OEDIPUS: Alas, that makes it plain enough!
                          But who—   710
   Who told you how it happened?
IOCASTE: A household servant,
   The only one to escape.
OEDIPUS: And is he still
   A servant of ours?
IOCASTE: No; for when he came back at last
   And found you enthroned in the place of the dead king,

He came to me, touched my hand with his, and begged   715
That I would send him away to the frontier district
Where only the shepherds go—
As far away from the city as I could send him.
I granted his prayer; for although the man was a slave,
He had earned more than this favor at my hands.   720
OEDIPUS: Can he be called back quickly?
IOCASTE: Easily.
  But why?
OEDIPUS: I have taken too much upon myself
  Without enquiry; therefore I wish to consult him.
IOCASTE: Then he shall come.
                        But am I not one also
  To whom you might confide these fears of yours?   725
OEDIPUS: That is your right; it will not be denied you,
  Now least of all; for I have reached a pitch
  Of wild foreboding. Is there anyone
  To whom I should sooner speak?

  Polybos of Corinth is my father.   730
  My mother is a Dorian: Meropê.
  I grew up chief among the men of Corinth
  Until a strange thing happened—
  Not worth my passion, it may be, but strange.

  At a feast, a drunken man maundering in his cups   735
  Cries out that I am not my father's son!

  I contained myself that night, though I felt anger
  And a sinking heart. The next day I visited
  My father and mother, and questioned them. They stormed,
  Calling it all the slanderous rant of a fool;   740
  And this relieved me. Yet the suspicion
  Remained always aching in my mind;
  I knew there was talk; I could not rest;
  And finally, saying nothing to my parents,
  I went to the shrine at Delphi.   745
  The god dismissed my question without reply;

He spoke of other things.
                    Some were clear,
Full of wretchedness, dreadful, unbearable:
As, that I should lie with my own mother, breed
Children from whom all men would turn their eyes;   750
And that I should be my father's murderer.

I heard all this, and fled. And from that day
Corinth to me was only in the stars
Descending in that quarter of the sky,
As I wandered farther and farther on my way   755
To a land where I should never see the evil
Sung by the oracle. And I came to this country
Where, so you say, King Laïos was killed.

I will tell you all that happened there, my lady.

There were three highways   760
Coming together at a place I passed;
And there a herald came towards me, and a chariot
Drawn by horses, with a man such as you describe
Seated in it. The groom leading the horses
Forced me off the road at his lord's command;   765
But as this charioteer lurched over towards me
I struck him in my rage. The old man saw me
And brought his double goad down upon my head
As I came abreast.
                    He was paid back, and more!
Swinging my club in this right hand I knocked him   770
Out of his car, and he rolled on the ground.
                                        I killed him.
I killed them all.
Now if that stranger and Laïos were—kin,
Where is a man more miserable than I?
More hated by the gods? Citizen and alien alike   775
Must never shelter me or speak to me—
I must be shunned by all.

And I myself
Pronounced this malediction upon myself!

Think of it: I have touched you with these hands,
These hands that killed your husband. What defilement!   780

Am I all evil, then? It must be so,
Since I must flee from Thebes, yet never again
See my own countrymen, my own country,
For fear of joining my mother in marriage
And killing Polybos, my father.
                                        Ah.   785
If I was created so, born to this fate,
Who could deny the savagery of God?

O holy majesty of heavenly powers!
May I never see that day! Never!
Rather let me vanish from the race of men   790
Than know the abomination destined me!
CHORAGOS: We too, my lord, have felt dismay at this.
    But there is hope: you have yet to hear the shepherd.
OEDIPUS: Indeed, I fear no other hope is left me.
IOCASTE: What do you hope from him when he comes?
OEDIPUS: This much: 795
    If his account of the murder tallies with yours,
    Then I am cleared.
IOCASTE: What was it that I said
    Of such importance?
OEDIPUS: Why, "marauders," you said,
    Killed the King, according to this man's story.
    If he maintains that still, if there were several,   800
    Clearly the guilt is not mine: I was alone.
    But if he says one man, singlehanded, did it,
    Then the evidence all points to me.
IOCASTE: You may be sure that he said there were several;
    And can he call back that story now? He cannot.   805
    The whole city heard it as plainly as I.

But suppose he alters some detail of it:
He cannot ever show that Laïos' death
Fulfilled the oracle: for Apollo said
My child was doomed to kill him; and my child—   810
Poor baby!—it was my child that died first.

No. From now on, where oracles are concerned,
I would not waste a second thought on any.
OEDIPUS: You may be right.
                          But come: let someone go
For the shepherd at once. This matter must be settled.   815
IOCASTE: I will send for him.
I would not wish to cross you in anything:
And surely not in this.—Let us go in. [*Exeunt into the
    palace.*]

ODE II

CHORUS: [*Strophe 1.*] Let me be reverent in the ways of right,
    Lowly the paths I journey on;   820
    Let all my words and actions keep
    The laws of the pure universe
    From highest Heaven handed down.
    For Heaven is their bright nurse,
    Those generations of the realms of light;   825
    Ah, never of mortal kind were they begot,
    Nor are they slaves of memory, lost in sleep:
    Their Father is greater than Time, and ages not.

[*Antistrophe 1.*] The tyrant is a child of Pride
    Who drinks from his great sickening cup   830
    Recklessness and vanity,
    Until from his high crest headlong
    He plummets to the dust of hope.
    That strong man is not strong.
    But let no fair ambition be denied;   835
    May God protect the wrestler for the State
    In government, in comely policy,
    Who will fear God, and on His ordinance wait.

[*Strophe 2.*] Haughtiness and the high hand of disdain
Tempt and outrage God's holy law;   840
And any mortal who dares hold
No immortal Power in awe
Will be caught up in a net of pain:
The price for which his levity is sold.
Let each man take due earnings, then,   845
And keep his hands from holy things,
And from blasphemy stand apart—
Else the crackling blast of heaven
Blows on his head, and on his desperate heart;
Though fools will honor impious men,   850
In their cities no tragic poet sings.

[*Antistrophe 2.*] Shall we lose faith in Delphi's obscurities,
We who have heard the world's core
Discredited, and the sacred wood
Of Zeus at Elis praised no more?   855
The deeds and the strange prophecies
Must make a pattern yet to be understood.
Zeus, if indeed you are lord of all,
Throned in light over night and day,
Mirror this in your endless mind: 860
Our masters call the oracle
Words on the wind, and the Delphic vision blind!
Their hearts no longer know Apollo,
And reverence for the gods has died away.

SCENE III
    [*Enter* IOCASTE.]
IOCASTE: Princes of Thebes, it has occurred to me   865
    To visit the altars of the gods, bearing
    These branches as a suppliant, and this incense.
    Our King is not himself: his noble soul
    Is overwrought with fantasies of dread,
    Else he would consider   870
    The new prophecies in the light of the old.
    He will listen to any voice that speaks disaster,

And my advice goes for nothing. [*She approaches the altar.*]
                                                To you, then, Apollo,
Lycean[1] lord, since you are nearest, I turn in prayer.
Receive these offerings, and grant us deliverance   875
From defilement. Our hearts are heavy with fear
When we see our leader distracted, as helpless sailors
Are terrified by the confusion of their helmsman.
        [*Enter* MESSENGER.]
MESSENGER: Friends, no doubt you can direct me:
        Where shall I find the house of Oedipus,   880
        Or, better still, where is the King himself?
CHORAGOS: It is this very place, stranger; he is inside.
        This is his wife and mother of his children.
MESSENGER: I wish her happiness in a happy house,
        Blest in all the fulfillment of her marriage.   885
IOCASTE: I wish as much for you: your courtesy
        Deserves a like good fortune. But now, tell me:
        Why have you come? What have you to say to us?
MESSENGER: Good news, my lady, for your house and your
            husband.
IOCASTE: What news? Who sent you here?
MESSENGER: I am from Corinth.   890
        The news I bring ought to mean joy for you,
        Though it may be you will find some grief in it.
IOCASTE: What is it? How can it touch us in both ways?
MESSENGER: The word is that the people of the Isthmus
        Intend to call Oedipus to be their king.   895
IOCASTE: But old King Polybos—is he not reigning still?
MESSENGER: No. Death holds him in his sepulchre.
IOCASTE: What are you saying? Polybos is dead?
MESSENGER: If I am not telling the truth, may I die myself.
IOCASTE: [*To a* MAIDSERVANT.] Go in, go quickly; tell this to
        your master.   900

O riddlers of God's will, where are you now!
This was the man whom Oedipus, long ago,

---

1. Of Lycia, an ancient region in Asia Minor.

Feared so, fled so, in dread of destroying him—
But it was another fate by which he died.
    [*Enter* OEDIPUS.]
OEDIPUS: Dearest Iocastê, why have you sent for me?   905
IOCASTE: Listen to what this man says, and then tell me
    What has become of the solemn prophecies.
OEDIPUS: Who is this man? What is his news for me?
IOCASTE: He has come from Corinth to announce your father's
    death!
OEDIPUS: Is it true, stranger? Tell me in your own words.   910
MESSENGER: I cannot say it more clearly: the King is dead.
OEDIPUS: Was it by treason? Or by an attack of illness?
MESSENGER: A little thing brings old men to their rest.
OEDIPUS: It was sickness, then?
MESSENGER: Yes, and his many years.
OEDIPUS: Ah!   915
    Why should a man respect the Pythian hearth, or
    Give heed to the birds that jangle above his head?
    They prophesied that I should kill Polybos.
    Kill my own father; but he is dead and buried.
    And I am here—I never touched him, never,   920
    Unless he died of grief for my departure,
    And thus, in a sense, through me. No. Polybos
    Has packed the oracles off with him underground.
    They are empty words.
IOCASTE: Had I not told you so?
OEDIPUS: You had; it was my faint heart that betrayed me.   925
IOCASTE: From now on never think of those things again.
OEDIPUS: And yet—must I not fear my mother's bed?
IOCASTE: Why should anyone in this world be afraid,
    Since Fate rules us and nothing can be foreseen?
    A man should live only for the present day.   930

    Have no more fear of sleeping with your mother:
    How many men, in dreams, have lain with their
        mothers!
    No reasonable man is troubled by such things.
OEDIPUS: That is true; only—

If only my mother were not still alive!   935
   But she is alive. I cannot help my dread.
IOCASTE: Yet this news of your father's death is wonderful.
OEDIPUS: Wonderful. But I fear the living woman.
MESSENGER: Tell me, who is this woman that you fear?
OEDIPUS: It is Meropê, man; the wife of King Polybos.   940
MESSENGER: Meropê? Why should you be afraid of her?
OEDIPUS: An oracle of the gods, a dreadful saying.
MESSENGER: Can you tell me about it or are you sworn to silence?
OEDIPUS: I can tell you, and I will.
   Apollo said through his prophet that I was the man   945
   Who should marry his own mother, shed his father's blood
   With his own hands. And so, for all these years
   I have kept clear of Corinth, and no harm has come—
   Though it would have been sweet to see my parents again.
MESSENGER: And is this the fear that drove you out of
      Corinth?   950
OEDIPUS: Would you have me kill my father?
MESSENGER: As for that
   You must be reassured by the news I gave you.
OEDIPUS: If you could reassure me, I would reward you.
MESSENGER: I had that in mind, I will confess: I thought
   I could count on you when you returned to Corinth.   955
OEDIPUS: No: I will never go near my parents again.
MESSENGER: Ah, son, you still do not know what you are
      doing—
OEDIPUS: What do you mean? In the name of God tell me!
MESSENGER:—If these are your reasons for not going home.
OEDIPUS: I tell you, I fear the oracle may come true.   960
MESSENGER: And guilt may come upon you through your
      parents?
OEDIPUS: That is the dread that is always in my heart.
MESSENGER: Can you not see that all your fears are groundless?
OEDIPUS: How can you say that? They are my parents, surely?
MESSENGER: Polybos was not your father.
OEDIPUS: Not my father?   965
MESSENGER: No more your father than the man speaking
      to you.

OEDIPUS: But you are nothing to me!

MESSENGER: Neither was he.

OEDIPUS: Then why did he call me son?

MESSENGER: I will tell you:
Long ago he had you from my hands, as a gift.

OEDIPUS: Then how could he love me so, if I was not his?   970

MESSENGER: He had no children, and his heart turned to you.

OEDIPUS: What of you? Did you buy me? Did you find me by
   chance?

MESSENGER: I came upon you in the crooked pass of Kithairon.

OEDIPUS: And what were you doing there?

MESSENGER: Tending my flocks.

OEDIPUS: A wandering shepherd?

MESSENGER: But your savior, son, that day.   975

OEDIPUS: From what did you save me?

MESSENGER: Your ankles should tell
  you that.

OEDIPUS: Ah, stranger, why do you speak of that childhood
  pain?

MESSENGER: I cut the bonds that tied your ankles together.

OEDIPUS: I have had the mark as long as I can remember.

MESSENGER: That was why you were given the name you bear.[1] 980

OEDIPUS: God! Was it my father, or my mother who did it?
  Tell me!

MESSENGER: I do not know. The man who gave you to me
  Can tell you better than I.

OEDIPUS: It was not you that found me, but another?

MESSENGER: It was another shepherd gave you to me.   985

OEDIPUS: Who was he? Can you tell me who he was?

MESSENGER: I think he was said to be one of Laïos' people.

OEDIPUS: You mean the Laïos who was king here years ago?

MESSENGER: Yes; King Laïos; and the man was one of his
  herdsmen.

OEDIPUS: Is he still alive? Can I see him?

MESSENGER: These men here   990
  Know best about such things.

---

1. The name *Oedipus* means "swollen foot."

OEDIPUS: Does anyone here
  Know this shepherd that he is talking about?
  Have you seen him in the fields, or in the town?
  If you have, tell me. It is time things were made plain.
CHORAGOS: I think the man he means is that same shepherd   995
  You have already asked to see. Iocastê perhaps
  Could tell you something.
OEDIPUS: Do you know anything
  About him, Lady? Is he the man we have summoned?
  Is that the man this shepherd means?
IOCASTE: Why think of him?
  Forget this herdsman. Forget it all.   1000
  This talk is a waste of time.
OEDIPUS: How can you say that.
  When the clues to my true birth are in my hands?
IOCASTE: For God's love, let us have no more questioning!
  Is your life nothing to you?
  My own is pain enough for me to bear.   1005
OEDIPUS: You need not worry. Suppose my mother a slave,
  And born of slaves: no baseness can touch you.
IOCASTE: Listen to me, I beg you: do not do this thing!
OEDIPUS: I will not listen; the truth must be made known.
IOCASTE: Everything that I say is for your own good!
OEDIPUS: My own
  good   1010
  Snaps my patience, then; I want none of it.
IOCASTE: You are fatally wrong! May you never learn who
  you are!
OEDIPUS: Go, one of you, and bring the shepherd here.
  Let us leave this woman to brag of her royal name.
IOCASTE: Ah, miserable!   1015
  That is the only word I have for you now.
  That is the only word I can ever have. [*Exit into the palace.*]
CHORAGOS: Why has she left us, Oedipus? Why has she gone
  In such a passion of sorrow? I fear this silence:
  Something dreadful may come of it.
OEDIPUS: Let it come!   1020
  However base my birth, I must know about it.

The Queen, like a woman, is perhaps ashamed
To think of my low origin. But I
Am a child of Luck; I cannot be dishonored.
Luck is my mother; the passing months, my brothers,   1025
Have seen me rich and poor.
                    If this is so,
How could I wish that I were someone else?
How could I not be glad to know my birth?

ODE III

CHORUS: [*Strophe.*] If ever the coming time were known
    To my heart's pondering,   1030
Kithairon, now by Heaven I see the torches
At the festival of the next full moon,
And see the dance, and hear the choir sing
A grace to your gentle shade:
Mountain where Oedipus was found,   1035
O mountain guard of a noble race!
May the god who heals us lend his aid,
And let that glory come to pass
For our king's cradling-ground.

[*Antistrophe.*] Of the nymphs that flower beyond the years,   1040
Who bore you, royal child,
To Pan of the hills or the timberline Apollo,
Cold in delight where the upland clears,
Or Hermês for whom Kyllenê's heights are piled?[1]
Or flushed as evening cloud,   1045
Great Dionysos, roamer of mountains,
He—was it he who found you there,
And caught you up in his own proud
Arms from the sweet god-ravisher
Who laughed by the Muses' fountains?[2]   1050

1. Mount Kyllene, his birthplace, is sacred to Hermes, a multifaceted god. *Nymphs:* maiden goddesses who live in nature. *Pan:* god of pastures, flocks, and shepherds.

2. The Muses, sister goddesses, dwelled near fountains on Mount Helicon. *Dionysos:* Or Dionysus, also known as Bacchos/Bacchus, here posited as having taken Oedipus from Oedipus's "mother," a nymph.

SCENE IV

OEDIPUS: Sirs: though I do not know the man,
  I think I see him coming, this shepherd we want:
  He is old, like our friend here, and the men
  Bringing him seem to be servants of my house.
  But you can tell, if you have ever seen him.   1055
    [*Enter* SHEPHERD *escorted by servants.*]
CHORAGOS: I know him, he was Laïos' man. You can trust him.
OEDIPUS: Tell me first, you from Corinth: is this the shepherd
  We were discussing?
MESSENGER: This is the very man.
OEDIPUS: [*To* SHEPHERD.] Come here. No, look at me. You
    must answer
  Everything I ask.—You belonged to Laïos: 1060
SHEPHERD: Yes: born his slave, brought up in his house.
OEDIPUS: Tell me: what kind of work did you do for him?
SHEPHERD: I was a shepherd of his, most of my life.
OEDIPUS: Where mainly did you go for pasturage?
SHEPHERD: Sometimes Kithairon, sometimes the hills near-by.   1065
OEDIPUS: Do you remember ever seeing this man out there?
SHEPHERD: What would he be doing there? This man?
OEDIPUS: This man standing here. Have you ever seen him
    before?
SHEPHERD: No. At least, not to my recollection.
MESSENGER: And that is not strange, my lord. But I'll refresh   1070
  His memory: he must remember when we two
  Spent three whole seasons together, March to September,
  On Kithairon or thereabouts. He had two flocks:
  I had one. Each autumn I'd drive mine home
  And he would go back with his to Laïos' sheepfold.—   1075
  Is this not true, just as I have described it?
SHEPHERD: True, yes; but it was all so long ago.
MESSENGER: Well, then: do you remember, back in those days,
  That you gave me a baby boy to bring up as my own?
SHEPHERD: What if I did? What are you trying to say?   1080
MESSENGER: King Oedipus was once that little child.
SHEPHERD: Damn you, hold your tongue!

OEDIPUS: No more of that!
     It is your tongue needs watching, not this man's.
SHEPHERD: My King, my Master, what is it I have done wrong?
OEDIPUS: You have not answered his question about the boy.   1085
SHEPHERD: He does not know . . . He is only making
     trouble . . .
OEDIPUS: Come, speak plainly, or it will go hard with you.
SHEPHERD: In God's name, do not torture an old man!
OEDIPUS: Come here, one of you; bind his arms behind him.
SHEPHERD: Unhappy king! What more do you wish to learn?   1090
OEDIPUS: Did you give this man the child he speaks of?
SHEPHERD: I did.
     And I would to God I had died that very day,
OEDIPUS: You will die now unless you speak the truth.
SHEPHERD: Yet if I speak the truth, I am worse than dead.
OEDIPUS: Very well; since you insist upon delaying—   1095
SHEPHERD: No! I have told you already that I gave him the
     boy.
OEDIPUS: Where did you get him? From your house? From
     somewhere else?
SHEPHERD: Not from mine, no. A man gave him to me.
OEDIPUS: Is that man here? Do you know whose slave he was?
SHEPHERD: For God's love, my King, do not ask me any more!   1100
OEDIPUS: You are a dead man if I have to ask you again.
SHEPHERD: Then . . . Then the child was from the palace of
     Laïos.
OEDIPUS: A slave child? or a child of his own line?
SHEPHERD: Ah, I am on the brink of dreadful speech!
OEDIPUS: And I of dreadful hearing. Yet I must hear.   1105
SHEPHERD: If you must be told, then . . .
                                    They said it was
     Laïos' child;
     But it is your wife who can tell you about that.
OEDIPUS: My wife!—Did she give it to you?
SHEPHERD: My lord, she did.
OEDIPUS: Do you know why?
SHEPHERD: I was told to get rid of it.

OEDIPUS: An unspeakable mother!

SHEPHERD: There had been

    prophecies . . .   1110

OEDIPUS: Tell me.

SHEPHERD: It was said that the boy would kill his own father.

OEDIPUS: Then why did you give him over to this old man?

SHEPHERD: I pitied the baby, my King,

    And I thought that this man would take him far away   1115

    To his own country.

                 He saved him—but for what a fate!

    For if you are what this man says you are,

    No man living is more wretched than Oedipus.

OEDIPUS: Ah God!

    It was true!

          All the prophecies!

                  —Now,   1120

    O Light, may I look on you for the last time!

    I, Oedipus,

    Oedipus, damned in his birth, in his marriage damned,

    Damned in the blood he shed with his own hand! [*He rushes*

      into the palace.]

ODE IV

CHORUS: [*Strophe 1.*] Alas for the seed of men.   1125

    What measure shall I give these generations

    That breathe on the void and are void

    And exist and do not exist?

    Who bears more weight of joy

    Than mass of sunlight shifting in images,   1130

    Or who shall make his thought stay on

    That down time drifts away?

    Your splendor is all fallen.

    O naked brow of wrath and tears,

    O change of Oedipus!   1135

I who saw your days call no man blest—
Your great days like ghósts góne.

[*Antistrophe 1.*] That mind was a strong bow.

Deep, how deep you drew it then, hard archer,
At a dim fearful range,   1140
And brought dear glory down!

You overcame the stranger—
The virgin with her hooking lion claws—
And though death sang, stood like a tower
To make pale Thebes take heart.   1145

Fortress against our sorrow!

True king, giver of laws,
Majestic Oedipus!
No prince in Thebes had ever such renown,
No prince won such grace of power.   1150

[*Strophe 2.*] And now of all men ever known
Most pitiful is this man's story:
His fortunes are most changed, his state
Fallen to a low slave's
Ground under bitter fate.   1155

O Oedipus, most royal one!
The great door that expelled you to the light
Gave at night—ah, gave night to your glory:
As to the father, to the fathering son.

All understood too late.   1160

How could that queen whom Laïos won,
The garden that he harrowed at his height,
Be silent when that act was done?

[*Antistrophe 2.*] But all eyes fail before time's eye,
All actions come to justice there.   1165
Though never willed, though far down the deep past,
Your bed, your dread sirings,
Are brought to book at last.

Child by Laïos doomed to die,
Then doomed to lose that fortunate little death,   1170
Would God you never took breath in this air
That with my wailing lips I take to cry:

For I weep the world's outcast.

I was blind, and now I can tell why:
Asleep, for you had given ease of breath   1175
To Thebes, while the false years went by.

ÉXODOS[1]

[*Enter, from the palace,* SECOND MESSENGER.]
SECOND MESSENGER: Elders of Thebes, most honored in this
    land,
What horrors are yours to see and hear, what weight
Of sorrow to be endured, if, true to your birth,
You venerate the line of Labdakos!   1180
I think neither Istros nor Phasis, those great rivers,
Could purify this place of the corruption
It shelters now, or soon must bring to light—
Evil not done unconsciously, but willed.

The greatest griefs are those we cause ourselves.   1185
CHORAGOS: Surely, friend, we have grief enough already;
    What new sorrow do you mean?
SECOND MESSENGER: The Queen is dead.
CHORAGOS: Iocastê? Dead? But at whose hand?
SECOND MESSENGER: Her own.
    The full horror of what happened you cannot know,

1. The final scene, which includes the chorus's exit.

For you did not see it; but I, who did will tell you   1190
As clearly as I can how she met her death.

When she had left us,
In passionate silence, passing through the court,
She ran to her apartment in the house,
Her hair clutched by the fingers of both hands.   1195
She closed the doors behind her; then, by that bed
Where long ago the fatal son was conceived—
That son who should bring about his father's death—
We heard her call upon Laïos, dead so many years,
And heard her wail for the double fruit of her marriage,   1200
A husband by her husband, children by her child.

Exactly how she died I do not know:
For Oedipus burst in moaning and would not let us
Keep vigil to the end: it was by him
As he stormed about the room that our eyes were
       caught.   1205
From one to another of us he went, begging a sword.
Cursing the wife who was not his wife, the mother
Whose womb had carried his own children and himself.
I do not know: it was none of us aided him,
But surely one of the gods was in control!   1210
For with a dreadful cry
He hurled his weight, as though wrenched out of himself,
At the twin doors: the bolts gave, and he rushed in.
And there we saw her hanging, her body swaying
From the cruel cord she had noosed about her neck.   1215
A great sob broke from him, heartbreaking to hear,
As he loosed the rope and lowered her to the ground.

I would blot out from my mind what happened next!
For the King ripped from her gown the golden brooches
That were her ornament, and raised them, and plunged
       them down   1220
Straight into his own eyeballs, crying, "No more,
No more shall you look on the misery about me,

The horrors of my own doing! Too long you have known
The faces of those whom I should never have seen,
Too long been blind to those for whom I was searching!   1225
From this hour, go in darkness!" And as he spoke,
He struck at his eyes—not once, but many times;
And the blood spattered his beard,
Bursting from his ruined sockets like red hail.

So from the unhappiness of two this evil has sprung.   1230
A curse on the man and woman alike. The old
Happiness of the house of Labdakos
Was happiness enough: where is it today?
It is all wailing and ruin, disgrace, death—all
The misery of mankind that has a name—   1235
And it is wholly and for ever theirs.

CHORAGOS: Is he in agony still? Is there no rest for him?
SECOND MESSENGER: He is calling for someone to lead him to
       the gates
So that all the children of Kadmos may look upon
His father's murderer, his mother's—no,   1240
I cannot say it!
                   And then he will leave Thebes.
Self-exiled, in order that the curse
Which he himself pronounced may depart from the house.
He is weak, and there is none to lead him,
So terrible is his suffering.
                            But you will see: 1245
Look, the doors are opening; in a moment
You will see a thing that would crush a heart of stone.
   [*The central door is opened;* OEDIPUS, *blinded, is led in.*]
CHORAGOS: Dreadful indeed for men to see.
   Never have my own eyes
   Looked on a sight so full of fear.   1250

Oedipus!
What madness came upon you, what daemon
Leaped on your life with heavier
Punishment than a mortal man can bear?

No: I cannot even   1255
Look at you, poor ruined one.
And I would speak, question, ponder,
If I were able. No.
You make me shudder.

OEDIPUS: God.   God.   1260
Is there a sorrow greater?
Where shall I find harbor in this world?
My voice is hurled far on a dark wind.
What has God done to me?

CHORAGOS: Too terrible to think of, or to see.   1265

OEDIPUS: [*Strophe 1.*] O cloud of night,
Never to be turned away: night coming on,
I cannot tell how: night like a shroud!

My fair winds brought me here.
                            O God. Again
The pain of the spikes where I had sight,   1270
The flooding pain
Of memory, never to be gouged out.

CHORAGOS: This is not strange.
You suffer it all twice over, remorse in pain,
Pain in remorse.   1275

OEDIPUS: [*Antistrophe 1.*] Ah dear friend
Are you faithful even yet, you alone?
Are you still standing near me, will you stay here,
Patient, to care for the blind?
                            The blind man!
Yet even blind I know who it is attends me,   1280
By the voice's tone—
Though my new darkness hide the comforter.

CHORAGOS: Oh fearful act!
What god was it drove you to rake black
Night across your eyes?   1285

OEDIPUS: [*Strophe 2.*] Apollo. Apollo. Dear
Children, the god was Apollo.
He brought my sick, sick fate upon me.
But the blinding hand was my own!

How could I bear to see   1290
  When all my sight was horror everywhere?
CHORAGOS: Everywhere; that is true.
OEDIPUS: And now what is left?
  Images? Love? A greeting even,
  Sweet to the senses? Is there anything?   1295
  Ah, no, friends: lead me away.
  Lead me away from Thebes.
                           Lead the great wreck
  And hell of Oedipus, whom the gods hate.
CHORAGOS: Your fate is clear, you are not blind to that.
  Would God you had never found it out!   1300
OEDIPUS: [*Antistrophe 2.*] Death take the man who unbound
  My feet on that hillside
  And delivered me from death to life! What life?
  If only I had died,
  This weight of monstrous doom   1305
  Could not have dragged me and my darlings down.
  CHORAGOS: I would have wished the same.
OEDIPUS: Oh never to have come here
  With my father's blood upon me! Never
  To have been the man they call his mother's husband!   1310
  Oh accurst! Oh child of evil,
  To have entered that wretched bed—
                             the selfsame one!
  More primal than sin itself, this fell to me.
CHORAGOS: I do not know how I can answer you.
  You were better dead than alive and blind.   1315
OEDIPUS: Do not counsel me any more. This punishment
  That I have laid upon myself is just.
  If I had eyes,
  I do not know how I could hear the sight
  Of my father, when I came to the house of Death,   1320
  Or my mother: for I have sinned against them both
  So vilely that I could not make my peace
  By strangling my own life.
                  Or do you think my children,
  Born as they were born, would be sweet to my eyes?

Ah never, never! Nor this town with its high walls,   1325
Nor the holy images of the gods.
                              For I,
Thrice miserable—Oedipus, noblest of all the line
Of Kadmos, have condemned myself to enjoy
These things no more, by my own malediction
Expelling that man whom the gods declared   1330
To be a defilement in the house of Laïos.
After exposing the rankness of my own guilt,
How could I look men frankly in the eyes?
No, I swear it,
If I could have stifled my hearing at its source,   1335
I would have done it and made all this body
A tight cell of misery, blank to light and sound:
So I should have been safe in a dark agony
Beyond all recollection.
                              Ah Kithairon!
Why did you shelter me? When I was cast upon you,   1340
Why did I not die? Then I should never
Have shown the world my execrable birth.

Ah Polybos! Corinth, city that I believed
The ancient seat of my ancestors: how fair
I seemed, your child! And all the while this evil   1345
Was cancerous within me!
                              For I am sick
In my daily life, sick in my origin.

O three roads, dark ravine, woodland and way
Where three roads met: you, drinking my father's blood,
My own blood, spilled by my own hand: can you remember   1350
The unspeakable things I did there, and the things
I went on from there to do?
                              O marriage, marriage!
The act that engendered me, and again the act
Performed by the son in the same bed—
                              Ah, the net
Of incest, mingling fathers, brothers, sons,   1355

With brides, wives, mothers: the last evil
That can be known by men: no tongue can say
How evil!
            No. For the love of God, conceal me
Somewhere far from Thebes; or kill me; or hurl me
Into the sea, away from men's eyes for ever.   1360

Come, lead me. You need not fear to touch me.
Of all men, I alone can bear this guilt.
    [*Enter* CREON.]
CHORAGOS: We are not the ones to decide; but Creon here
    May fitly judge of what you ask. He only
    Is left to protect the city in your place.   1365
OEDIPUS: Alas, how can I speak to him? What right have I
    To beg his courtesy whom I have deeply wronged?
CREON: I have not come to mock you, Oedipus,
    Or to reproach you, either.
                    [*To* ATTENDANTS.]—You, standing
        there:
    If you have lost all respect for man's dignity,   1370
    At least respect the flame of Lord Helios:
    Do not allow this pollution to show itself
    Openly here, an affront to the earth
    And Heaven's rain and the light of day. No, take him
    Into the house as quickly as you can.   1375
    For it is proper
    That only the close kindred see his grief.
OEDIPUS: I pray you in God's name, since your courtesy
    Ignores my dark expectation, visiting
    With mercy this man of all men most execrable: 1380
    Give me what I ask—for your good, not for mine.
CREON: And what is it that you would have me do?
OEDIPUS: Drive me out of this country as quickly as may be
    To a place where no human voice can ever greet me.
CREON: I should have done that before now—only,   1385
    God's will had not been wholly revealed to me.
OEDIPUS: But his command is plain: the parricide
    Must be destroyed. I am that evil man.

CREON: That is the sense of it, yes; but as things are,
　We had best discover clearly what is to be done.　　　　1390
OEDIPUS: You would learn more about a man like me?
CREON: You are ready now to listen to the god.
OEDIPUS: I will listen. But it is to you
　That I must turn for help. I beg you, hear me.

　The woman in there—　　　　1395
　Give her whatever funeral you think proper:
　She is your sister.
　　　　　—But let me go, Creon!
　Let me purge my father's Thebes of the pollution
　Of my living here, and go out to the wild hills,
　To Kithairon, that has won such fame with me,　　　　1400
　The tomb my mother and father appointed for me,
　And let me die there, as they willed I should.
　And yet I know
　Death will not ever come to me through sickness
　Or in any natural way: I have been preserved　　　　1405
　For some unthinkable fate. But let that be.

　As for my sons, you need not care for them.
　They are men, they will find some way to live.
　But my poor daughters, who have shared my table,
　Who never before have been parted from their father—　　　　1410
　Take care of them, Creon; do this for me.
　And will you let me touch them with my hands
　A last time, and let us weep together?
　Be kind, my lord,
　Great prince, be kind!
　　　　　Could I but touch them,　　　　1415
　They would be mine again, as when I had my eyes.
　　　[Enter ANTIGONE and ISMENE, attended.]
　Ah, God!
　Is it my dearest children I hear weeping?
　Has Creon pitied me and sent my daughters?
CREON: Yes, Oedipus: I knew that they were dear to you　　　　1420
　In the old days, and know you must love them still.

OEDIPUS: May God bless you for this—and be a friendlier
Guardian to you than he has been to me!

Children, where are you?
Come quickly to my hands: they are your brother's—   1425
Hands that have brought your father's once clear eyes
To this way of seeing—
      Ah dearest ones,
I had neither sight nor knowledge then, your father
By the woman who was the source of his own life!
And I weep for you—having no strength to see
  you—,   1430
I weep for you when I think of the bitterness
That men will visit upon you all your lives.
What homes, what festivals can you attend
Without being forced to depart again in tears?
And when you come to marriageable age,   1435
Where is the man, my daughters, who would dare
Risk the bane that lies on all my children?
Is there any evil wanting? Your father killed
His father; sowed the womb of her who bore him;
Engendered you at the fount of his own existence!   1440
That is what they will say of you.

       Then, whom
Can you ever marry? There are no bridegrooms for you,
And your lives must wither away in sterile dreaming.

O Creon, son of Menoikeus!
You are the only father my daughters have,   1445
Since we, their parents, are both of us gone for ever.
They are your own blood: you will not let them
Fall into beggary and loneliness;
You will keep them from the miseries that are mine!
Take pity on them; see, they are only children,   1450
Friendless except for you. Promise me this,
Great Prince, and give me your hand in token of it.
 [CREON *clasps his right hand.*]

Children:
I could say much, if you could understand me,
But as it is, I have only this prayer for you: 1455
Live where you can, be as happy as you can—
Happier, please God, than God has made your father!
CREON: Enough. You have wept enough. Now go within.
OEDIPUS: I must; but it is hard.
CREON: Time eases all things.
OEDIPUS: But you must promise—
CREON: Say what you desire.   1460
OEDIPUS: Send me from Thebes!
CREON: God grant that I may!
OEDIPUS: But since God hates me . . .
CREON: No, he will grant your
        wish.
OEDIPUS: You promise?
CREON: I cannot speak beyond my knowledge.
OEDIPUS: Then lead me in.
CREON: Come now, and leave your children.
OEDIPUS: No! Do not take them from me!
CREON: Think no longer   1465
    That you are in command here, but rather think
    How, when you were, you served your own destruction.
        [*Exeunt into the house all but the* CHORUS; *the* CHORAGOS
        chants directly to the audience.]
CHORAGOS: Men of Thebes: look upon Oedipus.

    This is the king who solved the famous riddle
    And towered up, most powerful of men.   1470
    No mortal eyes but looked on him with envy,
    Yet in the end ruin swept over him.

    Let every man in mankind's frailty
    Consider his last day; and let none
    Presume on his good fortune until he find   1475
    Life, at his death, a memory without pain.

ca. 430 B.C.E.

William Shakespeare
1564–1616

HAMLET

Sometime in the late 1580s, William Shakespeare, then in his early twenties, traveled the muddy roads that connected the picturesque country town of Stratford-on-Avon to England's metropolis, the London of Queen Elizabeth. No one knows how Shakespeare made his living in Stratford, nor why he left. But most Shakespeare scholars believe he joined an acting company in London and learned the business of theater from the bottom up. When he started writing plays, Shakespeare broke the mold—playwrights were typically men of much higher education. His plays were undeniably popular, but to those in polite English society, Shakespeare and his fans were somewhat lowbrow.

As he did for many of his plays, Shakespeare borrowed the story for Hamlet. *At least four hundred years old when Shakespeare adapted it, the story of Hamlet had its roots in Norse legend. Its earliest written version was nearly a hundred years old by 1600, when Shakespeare based his play on another Elizabethan* Hamlet, *perhaps by John Kyd. Staged in the late 1580s, this first version had helped popularize the genre known as **revenge tragedy**, which is roughly equivalent to today's action thriller. In the typical revenge tragedy, the main character commits acts of terrible violence to avenge some murdered relative. Catering to unsophisticated tastes, the revenge tragedy fills the stage with bloody bodies.*

Shakespeare's Hamlet, *too, ends in carnage, but in other respects it differs from its immediate predecessor and from the earlier versions of the Hamlet story. In the previous incarnations, for example, Claudius's regicide is well known, not a secret, and Ophelia is indubitably Hamlet's mistress. This organic quality to the Hamlet story—its changing and growing in each new telling—probably accounts for the many inconsistencies in Shakespeare's version. In act 3, for example, Hamlet spies on Claudius and leaves him praying, then goes directly to Gertrude's chamber, where he thinks he finds Claudius hiding. The play presents dozens of such problems,* which seem to derive from Shakespeare's rewriting of an existing tale for his own purposes, purposes that in some ways contradict the conventions of the revenge tragedy.

The most important of these changes involves Hamlet's character—and audiences' responses to it. Shakespeare's audience would have known Hamlet's basic story, and they would have expected Hamlet to be a swashbuckling hothead. They would have been surprised by the brooding, introspective character Shakespeare gave them. Even so, Hamlet's long delays, apparently, did not much affect them. Not until the Romantic period, in the early 1800s, did critics remark on Hamlet's slow execution of revenge. The Romantics, perhaps seeing themselves in Shakespeare's hero, attributed his procrastinating to a fatal introspection, which drains his will of energy for action. In the twentieth century, after the advent of Freud's theories of human psychology, critics added an Oedipal complex to Hamlet's problems. Some contemporary readers hear in Hamlet's ravings what would become the angst of the existential philosophers. You should consider for yourself why Hamlet takes so long to act and what his delays mean.

How the play is staged can radically change your interpretation of such issues. For example, is Hamlet's madness real or fake? Of course, he tells Horatio in the first act that he will pretend to be mad, but this plot device might have been one of those awkward holdovers from Shakespeare's sources. There, the feigned madness protects Hamlet from Claudius's suspicions; it doesn't seem to have that effect here, nor does Hamlet seem too careful to hide his enmity for Claudius. Consider his treatment of Ophelia in act 3: does he rave so angrily because her sudden, inexplicable coldness has driven him to the edge of sanity, or because he knows she's a pawn in a plot against himself? Franco Zeffirelli's 1990 film adaptation of Hamlet presents the second version: Hamlet secretly watches Polonius manipulate Ophelia, and so he knows she's in league with her father and the king. Mel Gibson's Hamlet, though distraught, is clearly sane.

In making the story of Hamlet his own, Shakespeare created a huge, linguistically rich drama, one that addresses themes too complex and varied to fit within a conventional telling of the same story. He crafted a protagonist large enough—spiritually, intellectu-

ally, emotionally—to continue fascinating audiences four hundred years later. Whether you see yourself in that character, become engrossed in his predicament and his contradictory responses to it, or find some other route into the play's many inner chambers, Hamlet *should leave you feeling as though you've witnessed an expansion of the theater's possibilities. When the Danish prince tells his friend Horatio that "There are more things in heaven and earth . . . / Than are dreamt of in your philosophy" (1.5.165–66), his wisdom about life could easily apply to the work in which he appears.*

Hamlet

CHARACTERS

CLAUDIUS, *King of Denmark*
HAMLET, *son of the former and*
　nephew to the present King
POLONIUS, *Lord Chamberlain*
HORATIO, *friend of Hamlet*
LAERTES, *son of Polonius*
VOLTEMAND ⎤
CORNELIUS ⎟
ROSENCRANTZ ⎬ *courtiers*
GUILDENSTERN ⎟
OSRIC ⎟
A GENTLEMAN ⎦
A PRIEST

MARCELLUS ⎤ *officers*
BERNARDO ⎦
FRANCISCO, *a soldier*
REYNALDO, *servant to Polonius*
PLAYERS
TWO CLOWNS, *gravediggers*
FORTINBRAS, *Prince of Norway*
A NORWEGIAN CAPTAIN
ENGLISH AMBASSADORS
GERTRUDE, *Queen of Denmark,*
　and mother of Hamlet
OPHELIA, *daughter of Polonius*
GHOST OF HAMLET'S FATHER

LORDS, LADIES, OFFICERS, SOLDIERS, SAILORS, MESSENGERS,
　AND ATTENDANTS

SCENE: *The action takes place in or near the royal castle of Denmark at Elsinore.*

ACT I
SCENE 1

A guard station atop the castle. Enter BERNARDO *and* FRANCISCO, *two sentinels.*

BERNARDO: Who's there?

FRANCISCO: Nay, answer me. Stand and unfold yourself.

BERNARDO: Long live the king!

FRANCISCO: Bernardo?

BERNARDO: He.   5

FRANCISCO: You come most carefully upon your hour.

BERNARDO: 'Tis now struck twelve. Get thee to bed, Francisco.

FRANCISCO: For this relief much thanks. 'Tis bitter cold,
    And I am sick at heart.

BERNARDO: Have you had quiet guard?

FRANCISCO: Not a mouse stirring.   10

BERNARDO: Well, good night.
    If you do meet Horatio and Marcellus,
    The rivals[1] of my watch, bid them make haste.
        [*Enter* HORATIO *and* MARCELLUS.]

FRANCISCO: I think I hear them. Stand, ho! Who is there?

HORATIO: Friends to this ground.

MARCELLUS: And liegemen to the Dane.[2]   15

FRANCISCO: Give you good night.

MARCELLUS: O, farewell, honest soldier!
    Who hath relieved you?

FRANCISCO: Bernardo hath my place.
    Give you good night.   [*Exit* FRANCISCO.]

MARCELLUS: Holla, Bernardo!

BERNARDO: Say—
    What, is Horatio there?

HORATIO: A piece of him.

BERNARDO: Welcome, Horatio. Welcome, good Marcellus.   20

HORATIO: What, has this thing appeared again tonight?

BERNARDO: I have seen nothing.

MARCELLUS: Horatio says 'tis but our fantasy,
    And will not let belief take hold of him
    Touching this dreaded sight twice seen of us.   25
    Therefore I have entreated him along
    With us to watch the minutes of this night,

---

1. Companions.

2. The king of Denmark, also called
"Denmark," as in line 48 of this scene.

That if again this apparition come,
He may approve[3] our eyes and speak to it.
HORATIO: Tush, tush, 'twill not appear.
BERNARDO: Sit down awhile,   30
    And let us once again assail your ears,
    That are so fortified against our story,
    What we have two nights seen.
HORATIO: Well, sit we down.
    And let us hear Bernardo speak of this.
BERNARDO: Last night of all,   35
    When yond same star that's westward from the pole[4]
    Had made his course t' illume that part of heaven
    Where now it burns, Marcellus and myself,
    The bell then beating one—
        [*Enter* GHOST.]
MARCELLUS: Peace, break thee off. Look where it comes again.   40
BERNARDO: In the same figure like the king that's dead.
MARCELLUS: Thou art a scholar; speak to it, Horatio.
BERNARDO: Looks 'a[5] not like the king? Mark it, Horatio.
HORATIO: Most like. It harrows me with fear and wonder.
BERNARDO: It would be spoke to.
MARCELLUS: Speak to it, Horatio.   45
HORATIO: What art thou that usurp'st this time of night
    Together with that fair and warlike form
    In which the majesty of buried Denmark
    Did sometimes march? By heaven I charge thee, speak.
MARCELLUS: It is offended.
BERNARDO: See, it stalks away.   50
HORATIO: Stay. Speak, speak. I charge thee, speak.
                                        [*Exit* GHOST.]
MARCELLUS: 'Tis gone and will not answer.
BERNARDO: How now, Horatio! You tremble and look pale.
    Is not this something more than fantasy?
    What think you on't?   55
HORATIO: Before my God, I might not this believe

---

3. Confirm the testimony of.   5. He.
4. Polestar.

Without the sensible[6] and true avouch
Of mine own eyes.

MARCELLUS: Is it not like the king?

HORATIO: As thou art to thyself.

Such was the very armor he had on   60
When he the ambitious Norway combated.
So frowned he once when, in an angry parle,[7]
He smote the sledded Polacks on the ice.
'Tis strange.

MARCELLUS: Thus twice before, and jump[8] at this dead hour,
With martial stalk hath he gone by our watch.   65

HORATIO: In what particular thought to work I know not,
But in the gross and scope of mine opinion,
This bodes some strange eruption to our state.

MARCELLUS: Good now, sit down, and tell me he that knows,
Why this same strict and most observant watch   70
So nightly toils the subject[9] of the land,
And why such daily cast of brazen cannon
And foreign mart for implements of war;
Why such impress of shipwrights, whose sore task
Does not divide the Sunday from the week.   75
What might be toward that this sweaty haste
Doth make the night joint-laborer with the day?
Who is't that can inform me?

HORATIO: That can I.
At last, the whisper goes so. Our last king,
Whose image even but now appeared to us,   80
Was as you know by Fortinbras of Norway,
Thereto pricked on by a most emulate pride,
Dared to the combat; in which our valiant Hamlet
(For so this side of our known world esteemed him)
Did slay this Fortinbras; who by a sealed compact   85
Well ratified by law and heraldry,
Did forfeit, with his life, all those his lands
Which he stood seized of,[1] to the conqueror;

---

6. Perceptible.
7. Parley, debate.
8. Precisely.

9. People.
1. Possessed.

Against the which a moiety competent[2]
Was gagéd[3] by our king; which had returned   90
To the inheritance of Fortinbras,
Had he been vanquisher; as, by the same covenant
And carriage of the article designed,
His fell to Hamlet. Now, sir, young Fortinbras,
Of unimprovéd[4] mettle hot and full,   95
Hath in the skirts of Norway here and there
Sharked up a list of lawless resolutes
For food and diet to some enterprise
That hath a stomach in't; which is no other,
As it doth well appear unto our state,   100
But to recover of us by strong hand
And terms compulsatory, those foresaid lands
So by his father lost; and this, I take it,
Is the main motive of our preparations,
The source of this our watch, and the chief head   105
Of this post-haste and romage[5] in the land.
BERNARDO: I think it be no other but e'en so.
    Well may it sort[6] that this portentous figure
    Comes arméd through our watch so like the king
    That was and is the question of these wars.   110
HORATIO: A mote[7] it is to trouble the mind's eye.
    In the most high and palmy state of Rome,
    A little ere the mightiest Julius fell,
    The graves stood tenantless, and the sheeted dead
    Did squeak and gibber in the Roman streets;   115
    As stars with trains of fire, and dews of blood,
    Disasters in the sun; and the moist star,[8]
    Upon whose influence Neptune's empire stands,
    Was sick almost to doomsday with eclipse.
    And even the like precurse[9] of feared events,   120
    As harbingers preceding still the fates

2. Portion of similar value.   6. Chance.
3. Pledged.   7. Speck of dust.
4. Unproved.   8. The moon.
5. Stir.   9. Precursor.

And prologue to the omen coming on,
Have heaven and earth together demonstrated
Unto our climatures[1] and countrymen.
    [*Ente*r GHOST.]
But soft, behold, lo where it comes again!   125
I'll cross it though it blast me.—Stay, illusion.
    [*It spreads (its) arms.*]
If thou hast any sound or use of voice,
Speak to me.
If there be any good thing to be done,
That may to thee do ease, and grace to me,   130
Speak to me.
If thou art privy to thy country's fate,
Which happily foreknowing may avoid,
O, speak!
Or if thou hast uphoarded in thy life   135
Extorted treasure in the womb of earth,
For which, they say, you spirits oft walk in death,
    [*The cock crows.*]
Speak of it. Stay, and speak. Stop it, Marcellus.
MARCELLUS: Shall I strike at it with my partisan?[2]
HORATIO: Do, if it will not stand.
BERNARDO: 'Tis here.
HORATIO: 'Tis here.   140
MARCELLUS: 'Tis gone.   [*Exit* GHOST.]
We do it wrong, being so majestical,
To offer it the show of violence;
For it is as the air, invulnerable,
And our vain blows malicious mockery.   145
BERNARDO: It was about to speak when the cock crew.
HORATIO: And then it started like a guilty thing
Upon a fearful summons. I have heard
The cock, that is the trumpet to the morn;
Doth with his lofty and shrill-sounding throat   150
Awake the god of day, and at his warning,
Whether in sea or fire, in earth or air,

---

1. Regions.   2. Halberd.

Th' extravagant and erring[3] spirit hies
To his confine; and of the truth herein
This present object made probation.[4]   155
MARCELLUS: It faded on the crowing of the cock.
Some say that ever 'gainst that season comes
Wherein our Savior's birth is celebrated,
This bird of dawning singeth all night long,
And then, they say, no spirit dare stir abroad,   160
The nights are wholesome, then no planets strike,
No fairy takes,[5] nor witch hath power to charm,
So hallowed and so gracious is that time.
HORATIO: So have I heard and do in part believe it.
But look, the morn in russet mantle clad   165
Walks o'er the dew of yon high eastward hill.
Break we our watch up, and by my advice
Let us impart what we have seen tonight
Unto young Hamlet, for upon my life
This spirit, dumb to us, will speak to him.   170
Do you consent we shall acquaint him with it,
As needful in our loves, fitting our duty?
MARCELLUS: Let's do't, I pray, and I this morning know
Where we shall find him most conveniently.   [*Exeunt.*]

SCENE 2

A chamber of state. Enter KING CLAUDIUS, QUEEN GERTRUDE, HAMLET, POLONIUS, LAERTES, VOLTEMAND, CORNELIUS *and other members of the court.*

KING: Though yet of Hamlet our dear brother's death
The memory be green, and that it us befitted
To bear our hearts in grief, and our whole kingdom
To be contracted in one brow of woe,
Yet so far hath discretion fought with nature   5
That we with wisest sorrow think on him,
Together with remembrance of ourselves.
Therefore our sometime sister, now our queen,

---

3. Wandering out of bounds.   5. Enchants.
4. Proof.

Th' imperial jointress[1] to this warlike state,
Have we, as 'twere with a defeated joy,   10
With an auspicious and a dropping eye,
With mirth in funeral, and with dirge in marriage,
In equal scale weighing delight and dole,
Taken to wife; nor have we herein barred
Your better wisdoms, which have freely gone   15
With this affair along. For all, our thanks.
Now follows that you know young Fortinbras,
Holding a weak supposal of our worth,
Or thinking by our late dear brother's death
Our state to be disjoint and out of frame,   20
Colleaguéd with this dream of his advantage,
He hath not failed to pester us with message
Importing the surrender of those lands
Lost by his father, with all bonds of law,
To our most valiant brother. So much for him.   25
Now for ourself, and for this time of meeting,
Thus much the business is: we have here writ
To Norway, uncle of young Fortinbras—
Who, impotent and bedrid, scarcely hears
Of this his nephew's purpose—to suppress   30
His further gait[2] herein, in that the levies,
The lists, and full proportions are all made
Out of his subject; and we here dispatch
You, good Cornelius, and you, Voltemand,
For bearers of this greeting to old Norway,   35
Giving to you no further personal power
To business with the king, more than the scope
Of these dilated[3] articles allow.
Farewell, and let your haste commend your duty.
CORNELIUS: } In that, and all things will we show our duty.   40
VOLTEMAND: }
KING: We doubt it nothing, heartily farewell.

---

1. A widow who holds a *jointure*, or life interest, in the estate of her deceased husband.

2. Progress.

3. Fully expressed.

[Exeunt VOLTEMAND *and* CORNELIUS.]
And now, Laertes, what's the news with you?
You told us of some suit. What is't, Laertes?
You cannot speak of reason to the Dane
And lose your voice. What wouldst thou beg, Laertes,   45
That shall not be my offer, not thy asking?
The head is not more native to the heart,
The hand more instrumental[4] to the mouth,
Than is the throne of Denmark to thy father.
What wouldst thou have, Laertes?

LAERTES: My dread lord,   50
Your leave and favor to return to France,
From whence, though willingly, I came to Denmark
To show my duty in your coronation,
Yet now I must confess, that duty done,
My thoughts and wishes bend again toward France,   55
And bow them to your gracious leave and pardon.

KING: Have you your father's leave? What says Polonius?

POLONIUS: He hath, my lord, wrung from me my slow leave
By laborsome petition, and at last
Upon his will I sealed my hard consent.   60
I do beseech you give him leave to go.

KING: Take thy fair hour, Laertes. Time be thine,
And thy best graces spend it at thy will.
But now, my cousin[5] Hamlet, and my son—

HAMLET: *[Aside.]* A little more than kin, and less than kind.   65

KING: How is it that the clouds still hang on you?

HAMLET: Not so, my lord. I am too much in the sun.

QUEEN: Good Hamlet, cast thy nighted color off,
And let thine eye look like a friend on Denmark.
Do not for ever with thy vailéd lids[6]   70
Seek for thy noble father in the dust.
Thou know'st 'tis common—all that lives must die,
Passing through nature to eternity.

HAMLET: Ay, madam, it is common.

4. Serviceable.
5. Used here as a general term of kinship.
6. Lowered eyes.

QUEEN: If it be,
  Why seems it so particular with thee?   75
HAMLET: Seems, madam? Nay, it is. I know not "seems."
  'Tis not alone my inky cloak, good mother,
  Nor customary suits of solemn black,
  Nor windy suspiration of forced breath,
  No, nor the fruitful river in the eye,   80
  Nor the dejected havior[7] of the visage,
  Together with all forms, moods, shapes of grief,
  That can denote me truly. These indeed seem,
  For they are actions that a man might play,
  But I have that within which passes show—   85
  These but the trappings and the suits of woe.
KING: 'Tis sweet and commendable in your nature, Hamlet,
  To give these mourning duties to your father,
  But you must know your father lost a father,
  That father lost, lost his, and the survivor bound   90
  In filial obligation for some term
  To do obsequious sorrow. But to persever[8]
  In obstinate condolement is a course
  Of impious stubbornness. 'Tis unmanly grief.
  It shows a will most incorrect to heaven,   95
  A heart unfortified, a mind impatient,
  An understanding simple and unschooled.
  For what we know must be, and is as common
  As any the most vulgar thing to sense,
  Why should we in our peevish opposition   100
  Take it to heart? Fie, 'tis a fault[9] to heaven,
  A fault against the dead, a fault to nature,
  To reason most absurd, whose common theme
  Is death of fathers, and who still hath cried,
  From the first corse[1] till he that died today,   105
  "This must be so." We pray you throw to earth
  This unprevailing woe and think of us
  As of a father, for let the world take note

7. Appearance.
8. Persevere. *Obsequious:* Suited for funeral obsequies, or ceremonies.

9. Insult.
1. Corpse.

You are the most immediate[2] to our throne,
And with no less nobility of love   110
Than that which dearest father hears his son
Do I impart toward you. For your intent
In going back to School in Wittenberg,
It is most retrograde[3] to out desire,
And we beseech you, bend you to remain   115
Here in the cheer and comfort of our eye,
Our chiefest courtier, cousin, and our son

QUEEN: Let not they mother lose her prayers, Hamlet.
    I pray thee stay with us, go not to Wittenberg.

HAMLET: I shall in all my best obey you madam.   120

KING: Why, 'tis a loving and a fair reply.
    Be as ourself in Denmark. Madam, come.
    This gentle and unforced accord of Hamlet
    Sits smiling to my heart, in grace whereof,
    No jocund health that Denmark drinks today   125
    But the great cannon to the clouds shall tell,
    And the king's rouse the heaven shall bruit[4] again,
    Respeaking earthly thunder. Come away.

               [Flourish. Exeunt all but HAMLET.]

HAMLET: O, that this too too solid flesh would melt,
    Thaw, and resolve itself into a dew,   130
    Or that the Everlasting had not fixed
    His canon[5] 'gainst self-slaughter. O God, God,
    How weary, stale, flat, and unprofitable
    Seem to me all the uses of this world!
    Fie on't, ah, fie, 'tis an unweeded garden   135
    That grows to seed. Things rank and gross in nature
    Possess it merely.[6] That it should come to this,
    But two months dead, nay, not so much, not two.
    So excellent a king, that was to this
    Hyperion to a satyr,[7] so loving to my mother,   140

---

2. Next in line.
3. Contrary.
4. Echo. *Rouse:* carousal.
5. Law.

6. Entirely.
7. In Greek mythology, a lecherous creature, half man and half goat, in contrast to Hyperion, a god.

That he might not beteem[8] the winds of heaven
Visit her face too roughly. Heaven and earth,
Must I remember? Why, she would hang on him
As if increase of appetite had grown
By what it fed on, and yet, within a month—   145
Let me not think on't. Frailty, thy name is woman—
A little month, or ere those shoes were old
With which she followed my poor father's body
Like Niobe,[9] all tears, why she, even she—
O God, a beast that wants discourse of reason   150
Would have mourned longer—married with my uncle,
My father's brother, but no more like my father
Than I to Hercules.[1] Within a month,
Ere yet the salt of most unrighteous tears
Had left the flushing in her gallèd eyes,   155
She married. O, most wicked speed, to post
With such dexterity to incestuous sheets!
It is not, nor it cannot come to good.
But break my heart, for I must hold my tongue.
    [*Enter* HORATIO, MARCELLUS, *and* BERNARDO.]
HORATIO: Hail to your lordship!
HAMLET: I am glad to see you well.   160
    Horatio—or I do forget myself.
HORATIO: The same, my lord, and your poor servant ever.
HAMLET: Sir, my good friend, I'll change[2] that name with you.
    And what make you from Wittenberg, Horatio?
    Marcellus?   165
MARCELLUS: My good lord!
HAMLET: I am very glad to see you. [*To* BERNARDO.] Good
    even, sir.—
    But what, in faith, make you from Wittenberg?
HORATIO: A truant disposition, good my lord.
HAMLET: I would not hear your enemy say so,   170
    Nor shall you do my ear that violence

8. Permit.
9. In Greek mythology, Niobe was turned to stone while weeping over the death of her fourteen children.

1. The demigod Hercules was noted for his strength and a series of spectacular labors.
2. Exchange.

To make it truster of your own report
Against yourself. I know you are no truant.
But what is you affair in Elsinore?
We'll teach you to drink deep ere you depart.   175
HORATIO: My lord, I came to see your father's funeral.
HAMLET: I prithee do not mock me, fellow-student,
   I think it was to see my mother's wedding.
HORATIO: Indeed, my lord, it followed hard upon.
HAMLET: Thrift, thrift, Horatio. The funeral-baked meats   180
   Did coldly furnish forth the marriage tables.
   Would I had met my dearest[3] foe in heaven
   Or ever I had seen that day, Horatio!
   My father—methinks I see my father.
HORATIO: Where, my lord?
HAMLET: In my mind's eye, Horatio.   185
HORATIO: I saw him once, 'a was a goodly king.
HAMLET: 'A was a man, take him for all in all,
   I shall not look upon his like again.
HORATIO: My lord, I think I saw him yesternight.
HAMLET: Saw who?   190
HORATIO: My lord, the king your father.
HAMLET: The king my father?
HORATIO: Season your admiration[4] for a while
   With an attent ear till I may deliver[5]
   Upon the witness of these gentlemen
   This marvel to you.
HAMLET: For God's love, let me hear!   195
HORATIO: Two nights together had these gentlemen,
   Marcellus and Bernardo, on their watch
   In the dead waste and middle of the night
   Been thus encountered. A figure like your father,
   Arméd at point exactly, cap-a-pe,[6]   200
   Appears before them, and with solemn march
   Goes slow and stately by them. Thrice he walked
   By their oppressed and fear-surpriséd eyes

3. Bitterest.
4. Moderate your wonder.

5. Relate. *Attent:* attentive.
6. From head to toe. *Exactly:* completely.

Within his truncheon's[7] length, whilst they, distilled
Almost to jelly with the act of fear,   205
Stand dumb and speak not to him. This to me
In dreadful secrecy impart they did,
And I with them the third night kept the watch,
Where, as they had delivered, both in time,
Form of the thing, each word made true and good,   210
The apparition comes. I knew your father.
These hands are not more like.
HAMLET: But where was this?
MARCELLUS: My lord, upon the platform where we watch.
HAMLET: Did you not speak to it?
HORATIO: My lord, I did,
But answer made it none. Yet once methought   215
It lifted up it head and did address
Itself to motion, like as it would speak;
But even then the morning cock crew loud,
And at the sound it shrunk in haste away
And vanished from our sight.
HAMLET: 'Tis very strange.   220
HORATIO: As I do live, my honored lord, 'tis true,
And we did think it writ down in our duty
To let you know of it.
HAMLET: Indeed, sirs, but
This troubles me. Hold you the watch tonight?
ALL: We do, my lord.
HAMLET: Armed, say you?
ALL: Armed, my lord.   225
HAMLET: From top to toe?
ALL: My lord, from head to foot.
HAMLET: Then saw you not his face.
HORATIO: O yes, my lord, he wore his beaver[8] up.
HAMLET: What, looked he frowningly?
HORATIO: A countenance more in sorrow than in anger.   230
HAMLET: Pale or red?
HORATIO: Nay, very pale.

---

7. His baton of office.   8. His helmet's visor.

HAMLET: And fixed his eyes upon you?

HORATIO: Most constantly.

HAMLET: I would I had been there.

HORATIO: It would have much amazed you.

HAMLET: Very like.
   Stayed it long? 235

HORATIO: While one with moderate haste might tell a hundred.

BOTH: Longer, longer.

HORATIO: Not when I saw't.

HAMLET: His beard was grizzled, no?

HORATIO: It was as I have seen it in his life,
   A sable silvered.

HAMLET: I will watch tonight. 240
   Perchance 'twill walk again.

HORATIO: I warr'nt it will.

HAMLET: If it assume my noble father's person,
   I'll speak to it though hell itself should gape⁹
   And bid me hold my peace. I pray you all,
   If you have hitherto concealed this sight, 245
   Let it be tenable¹ in your silence still,
   And whatsomever else shall hap tonight,
   Give it an understanding but no tongue.
   I will requite your loves. So fare you well.
   Upon the platform 'twixt eleven and twelve 250
   I'll visit you.

ALL: Our duty to your honor.

HAMLET: Your loves, as mine to you. Farewell.

[Exeunt all but HAMLET.]
   My father's spirit in arms? All is not well.
   I doubt² some foul play. Would the night were come!
   Till then sit still, my soul. Foul deeds will rise, 255
   Though all the earth o'erwhelm them, to men's eyes.

[Exit.]

---

9. Open (its mouth) wide.   2. Suspect.
1. Held.

SCENE 3
The dwelling of POLONIUS. *Enter* LAERTES *and* OPHELIA.

LAERTES: My necessaries are embarked. Farewell.
   And, sister, as the winds give benefit
   And convoy is assistant,[1] do not sleep,
   But let me hear from you.
OPHELIA: Do you doubt that?
LAERTES: For Hamlet, and the trifling of his favor,   5
   Hold it a fashion and a toy in blood,
   A violet in the youth of primy[2] nature,
   Forward, not permanent, sweet, not lasting,
   The perfume and suppliance of a minute,
   No more.
OPHELIA: No more but so?
LAERTES: Think it no more.   10
   For nature crescent[3] does not grow alone
   In thews and bulk, but as this temple[4] waxes
   The inward service of the mind and soul
   Grows wide withal. Perhaps he loves you now,
   And now no soil nor cautel[5] doth besmirch   15
   The virtue of his will, but you must fear,
   His greatness weighted,[6] his will is not his own,
   For he himself is subject to his birth.
   He may not, as unvalued persons do,
   Carve for himself, for on his choice depends   20
   The safety and health of this whole state,
   And therefore must his choice be circumscribed
   Unto the voice[7] and yielding of that body
   Whereof he is the head. Then if he says he loves you,
   It fits your wisdom so far to believe it   25
   As he in his particular act and place
   May give his saying deed,[8] which is no further

---

1. Means of transport is available.
2. Of the spring.
3. Growing.
4. Body.
5. Deceit.

6. Rank considered.
7. Assent.
8. *May give . . . deed:* can do what he
promises (that is, marry Ophelia).

Than the main voice of Denmark goes withal.
Then weigh what loss your honor may sustain
If with too credent ear you list[9] his songs,   30
Or lose your heart, or your chaste treasure open
To his unmastered importunity.
Fear it, Ophelia, fear it, my dear sister,
And keep you in the rear of your affection,
Out of the shot and danger of desire.   35
The chariest[1] maid is prodigal enough
If she unmask her beauty to the moon.
Virtue itself scapes not calumnious strokes.
The canker galls the infants[2] of the spring
Too oft before their buttons be disclosed,[3]   40
And in the morn and liquid dew of youth
Contagious blastments[4] are most imminent.
Be wary then; best safety lies in fear.
Youth to itself rebels, though none else near.
OPHELIA: I shall the effect of this good lesson keep   45
    As watchman to my heart. But, good my brother,
    Do not as some ungracious pastors do,
    Show me the steep and thorny way to heaven,
    Whiles like a puffed and reckless libertine
    Himself the primrose path of dalliance treads   50
    And recks not his own rede.[5]
LAERTES: O, fear me not.
        [*Enter* POLONIUS.]
    I stay too long. But here my father comes.
    A double blessing is a double grace;
    Occasion smiles upon a second leave.
POLONIUS: Yet here, Laertes? Aboard, aboard, for shame!   55
    The wind sits in the shoulder of your sail,
    And you are stayed for. There—my blessing with thee,
    And these few precepts in thy memory
    Look thou character.[6] Give thy thoughts no tongue,

9. Too credulous an ear you listen to.   4. Blights.
1. Most circumspect.   5. Heeds not his own advice.
2. The rose caterpillar injures the shoots.   6. Write.
3. Before the buds blossom.

Nor any unproportioned thought his act. 60
Be thou familiar, but by no means vulgar.
Those friends thou hast, and their adoption tried,
Grapple them unto thy soul with hoops of steel;
But do not dull[7] thy palm with entertainment
Of each new-hatched, unfledged comrade. Beware 65
Of entrance to a quarrel, but being in,
Bear't that th' opposéd[8] may beware of thee.
Give every man thy ear, but few thy voice;[9]
Take each man's censure, but reserve thy judgment.
Costly thy habit as thy purse can buy, 70
But not expressed in fancy; rich not gaudy,
For the apparel oft proclaims the man,
And they in France of the best rank and station
Are of a most select and generous chief[1] in that.
Neither a borrower nor a lender be, 75
For loan oft loses both itself and friend,
And borrowing dulls th' edge of husbandry.
This above all, to thine own self be true,
And it must follow as the night the day
Thou canst not then be false to any man. 80
Farewell. My blessing season this in thee!
LAERTES: Most humbly do I take my leave, my lord.
POLONIUS: The time invests you. Go, your servants tend.[2]
LAERTES: Farewell, Ophelia, and remember well
    What I have said to you.
OPHELIA: 'Tis in my memory locked, 85
    And you yourself shall keep the key of it.
LAERTES: Farewell.   [*Exit.*]
POLONIUS: What is't, Ophelia, he hath said to you?
OPHELIA: So please you, something touching the Lord Hamlet.
POLONIUS: Marry, well bethought. 90
    'Tis told me he hath very oft of late
    Given private time to you, and you yourself
    Have of your audience been most free and bounteous.

7. Make callous.   1. Eminence.
8. Conduct it so that the opponent.   2. Await.
9. Approval.

If it be so—as so 'tis put on me,
And that in way of caution—I must tell you,   95
You do not understand yourself so clearly
As it behooves my daughter and your honor.
What is between you? Give me up the truth.
OPHELIA: He hath, my lord, of late made many tenders
Of his affection to me.   100
POLONIUS: Affection? Pooh! You speak like a green girl,
Unsifted in such perilous circumstance.
Do you believe his tenders, as you call them?
OPHELIA: I do not know, my lord, what I should think.
POLONIUS: Marry, I will teach you. Think yourself a baby   105
That you have ta'en these tenders for true pay
Which are not sterling. Tender yourself more dearly,
Or (not to crack the wind of the poor phrase,
Running it thus) you'll tender me a fool.
OPHELIA: My lord, he hath importuned me with love   110
In honorable fashion.
POLONIUS: Ay, fashion you may call it. Go to, go to.
OPHELIA: And hath given countenance[3] to his speech, my lord,
With almost all the holy vows of heaven.
POLONIUS: Ay, springes to catch woodcocks.[4] I do know,   115
When the blood burns, how prodigal the soul
Lends the tongue vows. These blazes, daughter,
Giving more light than heat, extinct in both
Even in their promise, as it is a-making,
You must not take for fire. From this time   120
Be something scanter of your maiden presence.
Set your entreatments[5] at a higher rate
Than a command to parle. For Lord Hamlet,
Believe so much in him that he is young,
And with a larger tether may he walk   125
Than may be given you. In few, Ophelia,
Do not believe his vows, for they are brokers,[6]
Not of that dye which their investments[7] show,

3. Confirmation.   6. Panderers.
4. Snares to catch gullible birds.   7. Garments.
5. Negotiations before a surrender.

But mere implorators[8] of unholy suits,
Breathing like sanctified and pious bawds,   130
The better to beguile. This is for all:
I would not, in plain terms, from this time forth
Have you so slander any moment leisure
As to give words or talk with the Lord Hamlet.
Look to't, I charge you. Come your ways.   135
OPHELIA: I shall obey, my lord.   [*Exeunt.*]

SCENE 4
The guard station. Enter HAMLET, HORATIO *and* MARCELLUS.

HAMLET: The air bites shrewdly;[1] it is very cold.
HORATIO: It is a nipping and an eager[2] air.
HAMLET: What hour now?
HORATIO: I think it lacks of twelve.
MARCELLUS: No, it is struck.
HORATIO: Indeed? I heard it not.
  It then draws near the season   5
  Wherein the spirit held his wont to walk.
    [*A flourish of trumpets, and two pieces go off.*]
  What does this mean, my lord?
HAMLET: The king doth wake tonight and takes his rouse,
  Keeps wassail, and the swagg'ring up-spring[3] reels,
  And as he drains his draughts of Rhenish[4] down,   10
  The kettledrum and trumpet thus bray out
  The triumph of his pledge.
HORATIO: Is it a custom?
HAMLET: Ay, marry, is't,
  But to my mind, though I am native here
  And to the manner born, it is a custom   15
  More honored in the breach than the observance.
  This heavy-headed revel east and west
  Makes us traduced and taxed of other nations.
  They clepe[5] us drunkards, and with swinish phrase

8. Solicitors.   3. A German dance.
1. Sharply.   4. Rhine wine.
2. Keen.   5. Call.

Soil our addition,[6] and indeed it takes   20
From our achievements, though performed at height,
The pith and marrow of our attribute.[7]
So oft it chances in particular men,
That for some vicious mole of nature[8] in them,
As in their birth, wherein they are not guilty   25
(Since nature cannot choose his origin),
By their o'ergrowth of some complexion,
Oft breaking down the pales[9] and forts of reason,
Or by some habit that too much o'er-leavens
The form of plausive[1] manners—that these men,   30
Carrying, I say, the stamp of one defect,
Being nature's livery or fortune's star,
His virtues else, be they as pure as grace,
As infinite as man may undergo,
Shall in the general censure take corruption   35
From that particular fault. The dram of evil
Doth all the noble substance often doubt[2]
To his own scandal.
        [*Enter* GHOST.]
HORATIO: Look, my lord, it comes.
HAMLET: Angels and ministers of grace defend us!
    Be thou a spirit of health or goblin damned,   40
    Bring with thee airs from heaven or blasts from hell,
    Be thy intents wicked or charitable,
    Thou com'st in such a questionable[3] shape
    That I will speak to thee. I'll call thee Hamlet,
    King, father, royal Dane. O, answer me!   45
    Let me not burst in ignorance, but tell
    Why thy canonized[4] bones, hearsèd in death,
    Have burst their cerements;[5] why the sepulchre
    Wherein we saw thee quietly inurned
    Hath oped his ponderous and marble jaws   50

6. Reputation.
7. Honor.
8. Some natural, vice-related blemish.
9. Defensive palisade or fence.
1. Pleasing.
2. Extinguish.
3. Prompting question.
4. Buried in accordance with church canons.
5. Burial cloths.

To cast thee up again. What may this mean
That thou, dead corse, again in complete steel[6]
Revisits thus the glimpses of the moon,
Making night hideous, and we fools of nature
So horridly to shake our disposition   55
With thoughts beyond the reaches of our souls?
Say, why is this? wherefore? What should we do?
    [GHOST *beckons.*]
HORATIO: It beckons you to go away with it,
  As if it some impartment[7] did desire
  To you alone.
MARCELLUS: Look with what courteous action   60
  It waves you to a more removéd[8] ground.
  But do not go with it.
HORATIO: No, by no means.
HAMLET: It will not speak; then I will follow it.
HORATIO: Do not, my lord.
HAMLET: Why, what should be the fear?
  I do not set my life at a pin's fee,[9]   65
  And for my soul, what can it do to that,
  Being a thing immortal as itself?
  It waves me forth again. I'll follow it
HORATIO: What if it tempt you toward the flood, my lord,
  Or to the dreadful summit of the cliff   70
  That beetles[1] o'er his base into the sea,
  And there assume some other horrible form,
  Which might deprive your sovereignty of reason
  And draw you into madness? Think of it.
  The very place puts toys of desperation,[2]   75
  Without more motive, into every brain
  That looks so many fathoms to the sea
  And hears it roar beneath.
HAMLET: It wafts me still.
  Go on. I'll follow thee.
MARCELLUS: You shall not go, my lord.

---

6. Armor.
7. Communication.
8. Beckons you to a more distant.

9. Price.
1. Juts out.
2. Desperate fancies.

HAMLET: Hold off your hands.   80
HORATIO: Be ruled. You shall not go.
HAMLET: My fate cries out
  And makes each petty artere[3] in this body
  As hardy as the Nemean lion's[4] nerve.
  Still am I called. Unhand me, gentlemen.
  By heaven, I'll make a ghost of him that lets[5] me.   85
  I say, away! Go on. I'll follow thee.
                    [*Exeunt* GHOST *and* HAMLET.]
HORATIO: He waxes desperate with imagination.
MARCELLUS: Let's follow. 'Tis not fit thus to obey him.
HORATIO: Have after. To what issue will this come?
MARCELLUS: Something is rotten in the state of Denmark.   90
HORATIO: Heaven will direct it.
MARCELLUS: Nay, let's follow him.
                                        [*Exeunt.*]

Scene 5

Near the guard station. Enter GHOST *and* HAMLET.

HAMLET: Whither wilt thou lead me? Speak. I'll go no further.
GHOST: Mark me.
HAMLET: I will.
GHOST: My hour is almost come,
  When I to sulph'rous and tormenting flames
  Must render up myself.
HAMLET: Alas, poor ghost!
GHOST: Pity me not, but lend thy serious hearing   5
  To what I shall unfold.
HAMLET: Speak. I am bound to hear.
GHOST: So art thou to revenge, when thou shalt hear.
HAMLET: What?
GHOST: I am thy father's spirit,
  Doomed for a certain term to walk the night,
  And for the day confined to fast[1] in fires,   10

---

3. Artery.   5. Hinders.
4. A mythological lion slain by Hercules.   1. Do penance.

Till the foul crimes done in my days of nature[2]
Are burnt and purged away. But that I am forbid
To tell the secrets of my prison house,
I could a tale unfold whose lightest word   15
Would harrow up thy soul, freeze thy young blood,
Make thy two eyes like stars start from their spheres,
Thy knotted and combinéd[3] locks to part,
And each particular hair to stand an end,
Like quills upon the fretful porpentine.[4]   20
But this eternal blazon[5] must not be
To ears of flesh and blood. List, list, O, list!
If thou didst every thy dear father love—

HAMLET: O God!

GHOST: Revenge his foul and most unnatural murder.   25

HAMLET: Murder!

GHOST: Murder most foul, as in the best it is,
But this most foul, strange, and unnatural.

HAMLET: Haste me to know't, that I, with wings as swift
As meditation or the thoughts of love,   30
May sweep to my revenge.

GHOST: I find thee apt.
And duller shouldst thou be than the fat weed
That rots itself in ease on Lethe wharf,—[6]
Wouldst thou not stir in this. Now, Hamlet, hear.
'Tis given out that, sleeping in my orchard,   35
A serpent stung me. So the whole ear of Denmark
Is by a forgéd process[7] of my death
Rankly abused. But know, thou noble youth,
The serpent that did sting thy father's life
Now wears his crown.

HAMLET: O my prophetic soul!   40
My uncle!

GHOST: Ay, that incestuous, that adulterate beast,
With witchcraft of his wits, with traitorous gifts—

2. That is, while I was alive.
3. Tangled.
4. Porcupine.
5. Description of eternity.

6. The asphodel that rots on the bank of Lethe, the river of forgetfulness in the classical underworld.
7. False report.

O wicked wit and gifts that have the power
So to seduce!—won to his shameful lust 45
The will of my most seeming virtuous queen.
O Hamlet, what a falling off was there,
From me, whose love was of that dignity
That it went hand in hand even with the vow
I made to her in marriage, and to decline[8] 50
Upon a wretch whose natural gifts were poor
To those of mine!
But virtue as it never will be moved,
Though lewdness court it in a shape of heaven,
So lust, though to a radiant angel linked, 55
Will sate itself in a celestial bed
And prey on garbage.
But soft, methinks I scent the morning air.
Brief let me be. Sleeping within my orchard,
My custom always of the afternoon, 60
Upon my secure hour thy uncle stole,
With juice of cursed hebona[9] in a vial,
And in the porches of my ears did pour
The leperous distilment, whose effect
Holds such an enmity with blood of man 65
That swift as quicksilver it courses through
The natural gates and alleys of the body,
And with a sudden vigor it doth posset[1]
And curd, like eager[2] droppings into milk,
The thin and wholesome blood. So did it mine, 70
And a most instant tetter barked about[3]
Most lazar-like[4] with vile and loathsome crust
All my smooth body.
Thus was I sleeping by a brother's hand
Of life, of crown, of queen at once dispatched, 75
Cut off even in the blossoms of my sin,
Unhouseled, disappointed, unaneled,[5]

8. Sink.
9. A poison.
1. Coagulate.
2. Acid. *Curd:* curdle.
3. Covered like bark. *Tetter:* a skin disease.
4. Leperlike.
5. Without having received the Eucharist, made a final confession, or been given last rites.

No reck'ning made, but sent to my account
With all my imperfections on my head.
O, horrible! O, horrible! most horrible!   80
If thou hast nature in thee, bear it not.
Let not the royal bed of Denmark be
A couch of luxury[6] and damnéd incest.
But howsomever thou pursues this act,
Taint not thy mind, nor let thy soul contrive   85
Against thy mother aught. Leave her to heaven,
And to those thorns that in her bosom lodge
To prick and sting her. Fare thee well at once.
The glowworm shows the matin[7] to be near,
And gins to pale his uneffectual fire.   90
Adieu, adieu, adieu. Remember me.   [*Exit.*]
HAMLET: O all you host of heaven! O earth! What else?
And shall I couple hell? O, fie! Hold, hold, my heart,
And you, my sinews, grow not instant old,
But bear me stiffly up. Remember thee?   95
Ay, thou poor ghost, whiles memory holds a seat
In this distracted globe.[8] Remember thee?
Yea, from the table[9] of my memory
I'll wipe away all trivial fond[1] records,
All saws of books, all forms, all pressures past   100
That youth and observation copied there,
And thy commandment all alone shall live
Within the book and volume of my brain,
Unmixed with baser matter. Yes, by heaven!
O most pernicious woman!   105
O villain, villain, smiling, damnéd villain!
My tables—meet it is I set it down
That one may smile, and smile, and be a villain.
At least I am sure it may be so in Denmark.
So, uncle, there you are. Now to my word:[2]   110
It is "Adieu, adieu. Remember me."
I have sworn't.

6. Lust.   9. Writing tablet.
7. Morning.   1. Foolish.
8. Skull.   2. For my motto.

[*Enter* HORATIO *and* MARCELLUS.]

HORATIO: My lord, my lord!

MARCELLUS: Lord Hamlet!

HORATIO: Heavens secure him!

HAMLET: So be it!

MARCELLUS: Illo, ho, ho, my lord!   115

HAMLET: Hillo, ho, ho, boy![3] Come, bird, come.

MARCELLUS: How is't, my noble lord?

HORATIO: What news, my lord?

HAMLET: O, wonderful!

HORATIO: Good my lord, tell it.

HAMLET: No, you will reveal it.

HORATIO: Not I, my lord, by heaven.

MARCELLUS: Nor I, my lord.   120

HAMLET: How say you then, would heart of man once think it?
     But you'll be secret?

BOTH: Ay, by heaven, my lord.

HAMLET: There's never a villain dwelling in all Denmark
     But he's an arrant knave.

HORATIO: There needs no ghost, my lord, come from the grave   125
     To tell us this.

HAMLET: Why, right, you are in the right,
     And so without more circumstance at all
     I hold it fit that we shake hands and part,
     You, as your business and desire shall point you,
     For every man hath business and desire   130
     Such as it is, and for my own poor part,
     Look you, I'll go pray.

HORATIO: These are but wild and whirling words, my lord.

HAMLET: I am sorry they offend you, heartily;
     Yes, faith, heartily.

HORATIO: There's no offence, my lord.   135

HAMLET: Yes, by Saint Patrick, but there is, Horatio,
     And much offence too. Touching this vision here,
     It is an honest ghost, that let me tell you.
     For your desire to know what is between us,

3. A falconer's cry.

O'ermaster't as you may. And now, good friends,   140
As you are friends, scholars, and soldiers,
Give me one poor request.
HORATIO: What is't, my lord? We will.
HAMLET: Never make known what you have seen tonight.
BOTH: My lord, we will not.
HAMLET: Nay, but swear't.
HORATIO: In faith,   145
My lord, not I.
MARCELLUS: Nor I, my lord, in faith.
HAMLET: Upon my sword.
MARCELLUS: We have sworn, my lord, already.
HAMLET: Indeed, upon my sword, indeed.
     [GHOST *cries under the stage.*]
GHOST: Swear.
HAMLET: Ha, ha, boy, say'st thou so? Art thou there,
     truepenny?⁴
     Come on. You hear this fellow in the cellarage.⁵   150
     Consent to swear.
HORATIO: Propose the oath, my lord.
HAMLET: Never to speak of this that you have seen,
     Swear by my sword.
GHOST: [*Beneath.*] Swear.
HAMLET: Hic et ubique?⁶ Then we'll shift our ground.   155
     Come hither, gentlemen,
     And lay your hands again upon my sword.
     Swear by my sword
     Never to speak of this that you have heard.
GHOST: [*Beneath.*] Swear by his sword.   160
HAMLET: Well said, old mole! Canst work i' th' earth so fast?
     A worthy pioneer!⁷ Once more remove, good friends.
HORATIO: O day and night, but this is wondrous strange!
HAMLET: And therefore as a stranger give it welcome.
     There are more things in heaven and earth, Horatio,   165
     Than are dreamt of in your philosophy.

4. Trusty fellow.   6. Here and everywhere?
5. Below.   7. Soldier who digs trenches.

But come.
Here as before, never, so help you mercy,
How strange or odd some'er I bear myself
(As I perchance hereafter shall think meet   170
To put an antic[8] disposition on),
That you, at such times, seeing me, never shall,
With arms encumbered[9] thus, or this head-shake,
Or by pronouncing of some doubtful phrase,
As "Well, we know," or "We could, and if we would"   175
Or "If we list to speak," or "There be, and if they might"
Or such ambiguous giving out, to note
That you know aught of me—this do swear,
So grace and mercy at your most need help you.
GHOST: [*Beneath.*] Swear.   180
   [*They swear.*]
HAMLET: Rest, rest, perturbéd spirit! So, gentlemen,
  With all my love I do commend me to you,
  And what so poor a man as Hamlet is
  May do t'express his love and friending[1] to you,
  God willing, shall not lack. Let us go in together,   185
  And still your fingers on your lips, I pray.
  The time is out of joint. O cursèd spite
  That ever I was born to set it right!
  Nay, come, let's go together.   [*Exeunt.*]

ACT II
SCENE 1
The dwelling of POLONIUS. *Enter* POLONIUS *and* REYNALDO.

POLONIUS: Give him this money and these notes, Reynaldo.
REYNALDO: I will, my lord.
POLONIUS: You shall do marvellous wisely, good Reynaldo,
  Before you visit him, to make inquire[1]
  Of his behavior.
REYNALDO: My lord, I did intend it.   5

---

8. Mad.   1. Friendship.
9. Folded.   1. Inquiry.

POLONIUS: Marry, well said, very well said. Look you, sir.
  Enquire me first what Danskers[2] are in Paris,
  And how, and who, what means, and where they keep,[3]
  What company, at what expense; and finding
  By this encompassment[4] and drift of question   10
  That they do know my son, come you more nearer
  Than your particular demands[5] will touch it.
  Take you as 'twere some distant knowledge of him,
  As thus, "I know his father and his friends,
  And in part him." Do you mark this, Reynaldo?   15
REYNALDO: Ay, very well, my lord.
POLONIUS: "And in part him, but," you may say, "not well,
  But if't be he I mean, he's very wild,
  Addicted so and so." And there put on him
  What forgeries you please; marry, none so rank[6]   20
  As may dishonor him. Take heed of that.
  But, sir, such wanton, wild, and usual slips
  As are companions noted and most known
  To youth and liberty.
REYNALDO: As gaming, my lord.
POLONIUS: Ay, or drinking, fencing, swearing,   25
  Quarrelling, drabbing[7]—you may go so far.
REYNALDO: My lord, that would dishonor him.
POLONIUS: Faith, no, as you may season it in the charge.[8]
  You must not put another scandal on him,
  That he is open to incontinency.[9]   30
  That's not my meaning. But breathe his faults so quaintly[1]
  That they may seem the taints of liberty,[2]
  The flash and outbreak of a fiery mind,
  A savageness in unreclaiméd[3] blood,
  Of general assault.[4]
REYNALDO: But, my good lord—   35

---

2. Danes.
3. Live.
4. Indirect means.
5. Direct questions.
6. Foul. *Forgeries:* lies.
7. Whoring.

8. Soften the accusation.
9. Sexual excess.
1. With delicacy.
2. Faults of freedom.
3. Untamed.
4. Touching everyone.

POLONIUS: Wherefore should you do this?
REYNALDO: Ay, my lord,
  I would know that.
POLONIUS: Marry, sir, here's my drift,
  And I believe it is a fetch of warrant.[5]
  You laying these slight sullies on my son,
  As 'twere a thing a little soiled wi' th' working,   40
  Mark you,
  Your party in converse,[6] him you would sound,
  Having ever seen in the prenominate[7] crimes
  The youth you breathe[8] of guilty, be assured
  He closes with you in this consequence,   45
  "Good sir," or so, or "friend," or "gentleman,"
  According to the phrase or the addition
  Of man and country.
REYNALDO: Very good, my lord.
POLONIUS: And then, sir, does 'a this—'a does—What was I
    about to say?
  By the mass, I was about to say something.   50
  Where did I leave?
REYNALDO: At "closes in the consequence."
POLONIUS: At "closes in the consequence"—ay, marry,
  He closes thus: "I know the gentleman.
  I saw him yesterday, or th' other day,   55
  Or then, or then, with such, or such, and as you say,
  There was 'a gaming, there o'ertook in's rouse,[9]
  There falling out at tennis," or perchance
  "I saw him enter such a house of sale,"
  Videlicet,[1] a brothel, or so forth.   60
  See you, now—
  Your bait of falsehood takes this carp of truth,
  And thus do we of wisdom and of reach,[2]
  With windlasses and with assays of bias,[3]
  By indirections find directions out;   65

5. Permissible trick.
6. Conversation.
7. Already named.
8. Speak.

9. Carousing.
1. Namely.
2. Ability.
3. Indirect tests.

So by my former lecture and advice
Shall you my son. You have me, have you not?
REYNALDO: My lord, I have.
POLONIUS: God b'wi' ye; fare ye well.
REYNALDO: Good my lord.
POLONIUS: Observe his inclination in yourself.   70
REYNALDO: I shall, my lord.
POLONIUS: And let him ply⁴ his music.
REYNALDO: Well, my lord.
POLONIUS: Farewell.   [*Exit* REYNALDO.]
        [*Enter* OPHELIA.]
                          How now, Ophelia, what's the matter?
OPHELIA: O my lord, my lord, I have been so affrighted!
POLONIUS: With what, i' th' name of God?   75
OPHELIA: My lord, as I was sewing in my closet,⁵
    Lord Hamlet with his doublet all unbraced,⁶
    No hat upon his head, his stockings fouled,
    Ungartered and down-gyvéd⁷ to his ankle,
    Pale as his shirt, his knees knocking each other,   80
    And with a look so piteous in purport
    As if he had been looséd out of hell
    To speak of horrors—he comes before me.
POLONIUS: Mad for thy love?
OPHELIA: My lord, I do not know,
    But truly I do fear it.
POLONIUS: What said he?   85
OPHELIA: He took me by the wrist, and held me hard,
    Then goes he to the length of all his arm,
    And with his other hand thus o'er his brow,
    He falls to such perusal of my face
    As 'a would draw it. Long stayed he so.   90
    At last, a little shaking of mine arm,
    And thrice his head thus waving up and down,
    He raised a sigh so piteous and profound
    As it did seem to shatter all his bulk,⁸

4. Practice.   7. Fallen down like fetters.
5. Chamber.   8. Body.
6. Jacket all unlaced.

And end his being. That done, he lets me go,   95
And with his head over his shoulder turned
He seemed to find his way without his eyes,
For out adoors he went without their helps,
And to the last bended[9] their light on me.
POLONIUS: Come, go with me. I will go seek the king.   100
This is the very ecstasy of love,
Whose violent property fordoes[1] itself,
And leads the will to desperate undertakings
As oft as any passion under heaven
That does afflict our natures. I am sorry.   105
What, have you given him any hard words of late?
OPHELIA: No, my good lord, but as you did command
I did repel[2] his letters, and denied
His access to me.
POLONIUS: That hath made him mad.
I am sorry that with better heed and judgment   110
I had not quoted[3] him. I feared he did but trifle,
And meant to wrack[4] thee; but beshrew my jealousy.
By heaven, it is as proper to our age
To cast beyond ourselves in our opinions
As it is common for the younger sort   115
To lack discretion. Come, go we to the king.
This must be known,[5] which being kept close, might move
More grief to hide than hate to utter love.
Come.   [*Exeunt.*]

Scene 2

A public room. Enter KING, QUEEN, ROSENCRANTZ *and* GUILDEN-
STERN.

KING: Welcome, dear Rosencrantz and Guildenstern.
Moreover that[1] we much did long to see you,
The need we have to use you did provoke
Our hasty sending. Something have you heard

9. Directed.   4. Harm.
1. Character destroys.   5. Revealed (to the king).
2. Refuse.   1. In addition to the fact that.
3. Observed.

Of Hamlet's transformation—so call it, 5
Sith² nor th' exterior nor the inward man
Resembles that it was. What it should be,
More than his father's death, that thus hath put him
So much from th' understanding of himself,
I cannot deem of, I entreat you both 10
That, being of so young days³ brought up with him,
And sith so neighbored to his youth and havior,⁴
That you vouchsafe your rest here in our court
Some little time, so by your companies
To draw him on to pleasures, and to gather 15
So much as from occasion you may glean,
Whether aught to us unknown afflicts him thus,
That opened lies within our remedy.
QUEEN: Good gentlemen, he hath much talked of you,
And sure I am two men there are not living 20
To whom he more adheres. If it will please you
To show us so much gentry⁵ and good will
As to expend your time with us awhile
For the supply and profit of our hope,
Your visitation shall receive such thanks 25
As fits a king's remembrance.
ROSENCRANTZ: Both your majesties
Might, by the sovereign power you have of us,
Put your dread pleasures more into command
Than to entreaty.
GUILDENSTERN: But we both obey,
And here give up ourselves in the full bent⁶ 30
To lay our service freely at your feet,
To be commanded.
KING: Thanks, Rosencrantz and gentle Guildenstern.
QUEEN: Thanks, Guildenstern and gentle Rosencrantz.
And I beseech you instantly to visit 35
My too much changed son. Go, some of you,
And bring these gentlemen where Hamlet is.

---

2. Since.
3. From childhood.
4. Behavior. *Neighbored:* closely allied.

5. Courtesy.
6. Completely.

GUILDENSTERN: Heavens make our presence and our practices
    Pleasant and helpful to him!
QUEEN: Ay, amen!
            [*Exeunt* ROSENCRANTZ *and* GUILDENSTERN.]
        [*Enter* POLONIUS.]
POLONIUS: Th' ambassadors from Norway, my good lord,   40
    Are joyfully returned.
KING: Thou still⁷ hast been the father of good news.
POLONIUS: Have I, my lord? I assure you, my good liege,
    I hold my duty as I hold my soul,
    Both to my God and to my gracious king;   45
    And I do think—or else this brain of mine
    Hunts not the trail of policy⁸ so sure
    As it hath used to do—that I have found
    The very cause of Hamlet's lunacy.
KING: O, speak of that, that do I long to hear.   50
POLONIUS: Give first admittance to th' ambassadors.
    My news shall be the fruit⁹ to that great feast.
KING: Thyself do grace to them, and bring them in.
                              [*Exit* POLONIUS.]
    He tells me, my dear Gertrude, he hath found
    The head and source of all your son's distemper.   55
QUEEN: I doubt it is no other but the main,
    His father's death and our o'erhasty marriage.
KING: Well, we shall sift¹ him.
        [*Enter Ambassadors* (VOLTEMAND *and* CORNELIUS) *with*
        POLONIUS.]
                              Welcome, my good friends,
    Say, Voltemand, what from our brother Norway?
VOLTEMAND: Most fair return of greetings and desires.   60
    Upon our first,² he sent out to suppress
    His nephew's levies, which to him appeared
    To be a preparation 'gainst the Polack,³
    But better looked into, he truly found
    It was against your highness, whereat grieved,   65

7. Ever.   1. Examine.
8. Statecraft.   2. That is, first appearance.
9. Dessert.   3. King of Poland.

That so his sickness, age, and impotence
Was falsely borne in hand, sends out arrests[4]
On Fortinbras, which he in brief obeys,
Receives rebuke from Norway, and in fine,
Makes vow before his uncle never more   70
To give th' assay[5] of arms against your majesty.
Whereon old Norway, overcome with joy,
Gives him three thousand crowns in annual fee,
And his commission to employ those soldiers,
So levied as before, against the Polack,   75
With an entreaty, herein further shown, [*Gives* CLAUDIUS *a
     paper.*]
That it might please you to give quiet pass[6]
Through your dominions for this enterprise,
On such regards of safety and allowance
As therein are set down.
KING: It likes[7] us well,   80
And at our more considered time[8] we'll read,
Answer, and think upon this business.
Meantime we thank you for your well-took[9] labor.
Go to your rest; at night we'll feast together.
Most welcome home!   [*Exeunt* AMBASSADORS.]
POLONIUS: This business is well ended.   85
My liege and madam, to expostulate[1]
What majesty should be, what duty is,
Why day is day, night night, and time is time,
Were nothing but to waste night, day, and time.
Therefore, since brevity is the soul of wit,   90
And tediousness the limbs and outward flourishes,[2]
I will be brief. Your noble son is mad.
Mad call I it, for to define true madness,
What is't but to be nothing else but mad?
But let that go.

4. Orders to stop. *Falsely borne in hand:*
deceived.
  5. Trial.
  6. Safe conduct.
  7. Pleases.

8. Time for more consideration.
9. Successful.
1. Discuss.
2. Adornments.

QUEEN: More matter with less art.   95
POLONIUS: Madam, I swear I use no art at all.
  That he is mad, 'tis true: 'tis true 'tis pity,
  And pity 'tis 'tis true. A foolish figure,
  But farewell it, for I will use no art.
  Mad let us grant him, then, and now remains   100
  That we find out the cause of this effect,
  Or rather say the cause of this defect,
  For this effect defective comes by cause.
  Thus it remains, and the remainder thus.
  Perpend.[3]   105
  I have a daughter—have while she is mine—
  Who in her duty and obedience, mark,
  Hath given me this. Now gather, and surmise.
  "To the celestial, and my soul's idol, the most beautified
    Ophelia."—That's an ill phrase, a vile phrase, "beautified" 110
    is a vile phrase. But you shall hear. Thus:
  "In her excellent white bosom, these, etc."
QUEEN: Came this from Hamlet to her?
POLONIUS: Good madam, stay awhile. I will be faithful.
  "Doubt thou the stars are fire,   115
    Doubt that the sun doth move;
  Doubt truth to be a liar;
    But never doubt I love.
  O dear Ophella, I am ill at these numbers.[4] I have not art
    to reckon my groans, but that I love thee best, O most   120
    best, believe it. Adieu.
  Thine evermore, most dear lady, whilst this machine[5] is to
    him, Hamlet."
  This in obedience hath my daughter shown me,
  And more above, hath his solicitings,   125
  As they fell out by time, by means, and place,
  All given to mine ear.
KING: But how hath she
  Received his love?
POLONIUS: What do you think of me?

3. Consider.   5. Body.
4. Verses.

KING: As of a man faithful and honorable.
POLONIUS: I would fain prove so. But what might you think,   130
  When I had seen this hot love on the wing.
  (As I perceived it, I must tell you that,
  Before my daughter told me), what might you,
  Or my dear majesty your queen here, think,
  If I had played the desk or table-book,   135
  Or given my heart a winking, mute and dumb,
  Or looked upon this love with idle sight,[6]
  What might you think? No, I went round[7] to work,
  And my young mistress thus I did bespeak:
  "Lord Hamlet is a prince out of thy star.[8]   140
  This must not be." And then I prescripts[9] gave her,
  That she should lock herself from his resort,
  Admit no messengers, receive no tokens.
  Which done, she took[1] the fruits of my advice;
  And he repelled, a short tale to make,   145
  Fell into a sadness, then into a fast,
  Thence to a watch,[2] thence into a weakness,
  Thence to a lightness, and by this declension,
  Into the madness wherein now he raves,
  And all we mourn for.
KING: Do you think 'tis this?   150
QUEEN: It may be, very like.
POLONIUS: Hath there been such a time—I would fain know
    that—
  That I have positively said "Tis so,"
  When it proved otherwise?
KING: Not that I know.
POLONIUS: [*Pointing to his head and shoulder.*] Take this from
  this, if this be otherwise.   155
  If circumstances lead me, I will find
  Where truth is hid, though it were hid indeed
  Within the centre.[3]

---

6. If he had remained silent and kept the information to himself.
7. Directly.
8. Beyond your sphere.
9. Orders.
1. Followed.
2. An insomnia.
3. Of the earth.

KING: How may we try it further?

POLONIUS: You know sometimes he walks four hours together
  Here in the lobby.

QUEEN: So he does, indeed.   160

POLONIUS: At such a time I'll loose[4] my daughter to him.
  Be you and I behind an arras[5] then.
  Mark the encounter. If he love her not,
  And be not from his reason fall'n thereon,
  Let me be no assistant for a state,   165
  But keep a farm and carters.

KING: We will try it.
  [Enter HAMLET reading a book.]

QUEEN: But look where sadly the poor wretch comes
  reading.

POLONIUS: Away, I do beseech you both away,
  I'll board[6] him presently.   [Exeunt KING and QUEEN.]
                    O, give me leave.
  How does my good Lord Hamlet?   170

HAMLET: Well, God-a-mercy.

POLONIUS: Do you know me, my lord?

HAMLET: Excellent well, you are a fishmonger.

POLONIUS: Not I, my lord.

HAMLET: Then I would you were so honest a man.   175

POLONIUS: Honest, my lord?

HAMLET: Ay, sir, to be honest as this world goes, is to be one
  man picked out of ten thousand.

POLONIUS: That's very true, my lord.

HAMLET: For if the sun breed maggots in a dead dog, being a   180
  god kissing carrion[7]—Have you a daughter?

POLONIUS: I have, my lord.

HAMLET: Let her not walk i' th' sun. Conception is a blessing,
  but as your daughter may conceive—friend, look to't.

POLONIUS: How say you by that? [Aside.] Still harping on my   185
  daughter. Yet he knew me not at first. 'A said I was a fishmonger. 'A is far gone. And truly in my youth I suffered

---

4. Let loose.
5. Tapestry.
6. Accost.

7. The Elizabethans believed that sunshine on dead flesh produced maggots.

much extremity for love. Very near this. I'll speak to him
again.—What do you read, my lord?

HAMLET: Words, words, words.   190

POLONIUS: What is the matter, my lord?

HAMLET: Between who?

POLONIUS: I mean the matter that you read, my lord.

HAMLET: Slanders, sir; for the satirical rogue says here that old
men have grey beards, that their faces are wrinkled, their   195
eyes purging thick amber and plum-tree gum, and that
they have a plentiful lack of wit, together with most weak
hams[8]—all which, sir, though I most powerfully and po-
tently believe, yet I hold it not honesty to have it thus set
down, for yourself, sir shall grow old as I am, if like a crab   200
you could go backward.

POLONIUS: [Aside.] Though this be madness, yet there is
method in't.—Will you walk out of the air, my lord?

HAMLET: Into my grave?

POLONIUS: [Aside.] Indeed, that's out of the air. How pregnant   205
sometime his replies are! a happiness that often madness
hits on, which reason and sanity could not so prosperously
be delivered of. I will leave him, and suddenly contrive the
means of meeting between him and my daughter.—My
honorable lord. I will most humbly take my leave of you.   210

HAMLET: You cannot take from me anything that I will more
willingly part withal—except my life, except my life, except
my life.

[Enter GUILDENSTERN and ROSENCRANTZ.]

POLONIUS: Fare you well, my lord.

HAMLET: These tedious old fools!   215

POLONIUS: You go to seek the Lord Hamlet. There he is.

ROSENCRANTZ: [To POLONIUS.] God save you, sir!

[Exit POLONIUS.]

GUILDENSTERN: My honored lord!

ROSENCRANTZ: My most dear lord!

HAMLET: My excellent good friends! How dost thou,
Guildenstern?   220

8. Limbs.

Ah, Rosencrantz! Good lads, how do you both?

ROSENCRANTZ: As the indifferent[9] children of the earth.

GUILDENSTERN: Happy in that we are not over-happy;
On Fortune's cap we are not the very button.[1]

HAMLET: Not the soles of her shoe?   225

ROSENCRANTZ: Neither, my lord.

HAMLET: Then you live about her waist, or in the middle of
her favors?

GUILDENSTERN: Faith, her privates[2] we.

HAMLET: In the secret parts of Fortune? O, most true, she is a   230
strumpet.[3] What news?

ROSENCRANTZ: None, my lord, but that the world's grown
honest.

HAMLET: Then is doomsday near. But your news is not true.
Let me question more in particular. What have you, my   235
good friends, deserved at the hands of Fortune, that she
sends you to prison hither?

GUILDENSTERN: Prison, my lord?

HAMLET: Denmark's a prison.

ROSENCRANTZ: Then is the world one.   240

HAMLET: A goodly one, in which there are many confines,
wards[4] and dungeons. Denmark being one o' th' worst.

ROSENCRANTZ: We think not so, my lord.

HAMLET: Why then 'tis none to you; for there is nothing
either good or bad, but thinking makes it so. To me it is a   245
prison.

ROSENCRANTZ: Why then your ambition makes it one. 'Tis
too narrow for your mind.

HAMLET: O God, I could be bounded in a nutshell and count
myself a king of infinite space, were it not that I have bad   250
dreams.

GUILDENSTERN: Which dreams indeed are ambition; for the very
substance of the ambitious is merely the shadow of a dream.

HAMLET: A dream itself is but a shadow.

---

9. Ordinary.
1. That is, on top.
2. Ordinary citizens, but also private parts (sexual organs).

3. Prostitute.
4. Cells.

ROSENCRANTZ: Truly, and I hold ambition of so airy and light 255
a quality that it is but a shadow's shadow.

HAMLET: Then are our beggars bodies, and our monarchs and
outstretched heroes the beggars' shadows. Shall we to th'
court? for, by my fay,[5] I cannot reason.

BOTH: We'll wait upon you. 260

HAMLET: No such matter. I will not sort[6] you with the rest of
my servants; for to speak to you like an honest man, I am
most dreadfully attended. But in the beaten way of friendship, what make you at Elsinore?

ROSENCRANTZ: To visit you, my lord; no other occasion. 265

HAMLET: Beggar that I am, I am even poor in thanks, but I
thank you; and sure, dear friends, my thanks are too dear a
halfpenny.[7] Were you not sent for? Is it your own inclining?
Is it a free visitation? Come, come, deal justly with me.
Come, come, nay speak. 270

GUILDENSTERN: What should we say, my lord?

HAMLET: Anything but to th' purpose. You were sent for, and
there is a kind of confession in your looks, which your
modesties have not craft enough to color. I know the good
king and queen have sent for you. 275

ROSENCRANTZ: To what end, my lord?

HAMLET: That you must teach me. But let me conjure you by
the rights of our fellowship, by the consonancy of our
youth, by the obligation of our ever-preserved love, and by
what more dear a better proposer can charge you withal, be 280
even and direct with me whether you were sent for or no.

ROSENCRANTZ: [*Aside to* GUILDENSTERN.] What say you?

HAMLET: [*Aside.*] Nay, then, I have an eye of you.—If you love
me, hold not off.

GUILDENSTERN: My lord, we were sent for. 285

HAMLET: I will tell you why; so shall my anticipation prevent
your discovery,[8] and your secrecy to the king and queen
moult no feather. I have of late—but wherefore I know
not—lost all my mirth, forgone all custom of exercises; and

---

5. Faith.
6. Include.

7. Not worth a halfpenny.
8. Disclosure.

indeed it goes so heavily with my disposition, that this   290
goodly frame the earth seems to me a sterile promontory,
this most excellent canopy the air, look you, this brave
o'er-hanging firmament, this majestical roof fretted[9] with
golden fire, why it appeareth nothing to me but a foul and
pestilent congregation of vapors. What a piece of work is a   295
man, how noble in reason, how infinite in faculties, in
form and moving, how express[1] and admirable in action,
how like an angel in apprehension, how like a god: the
beauty of the world, the paragon of animals. And yet to
me; what is this quintessence of dust? Man delights not me,   300
nor woman neither, though by your smiling you seem to
say so.

ROSENCRANTZ: My lord, there was no such stuff in my thoughts.

HAMLET: Why did ye laugh, then, when I said "Man delights
not me"?   305

ROSENCRANTZ: To think, my lord, if you delight not in man,
what lenten entertainment the players shall receive from
you. We coted[2] them on the way, and hither are they coming to offer you service.

HAMLET: He that plays the king shall be welcome—his   310
majesty shall have tribute of me; the adventurous knight
shall use his foil and target; the lover shall not sigh gratis;
the humorous[3] man shall end his part in peace; the clown
shall make those laugh whose lungs are tickle o' th' sere;[4]
and the lady shall say her mind freely, or the blank verse   315
shall halt for't. What players are they?

ROSENCRANTZ: Even those you were wont to take such delight
in, the tragedians of the city.

HAMLET: How chances it they travel? Their residence,[5] both in
reputation and profit, was better both ways.   320

ROSENCRANTZ: I think their inhibition comes by the means of
the late innovation.

---

9. Ornamented with fretwork.
1. Well built.
2. Passed. *Lenten entertainment:* scanty reception.

3. Eccentric. *Foil and target:* sword and shield.
4. Easily set off.
5. Permanent or home theater.

HAMLET: Do they hold the same estimation they did when I was in the city? Are they so followed?

ROSENCRANTZ: No, indeed, are they not.   325

HAMLET: How comes it? Do they grow rusty?

ROSENCRANTZ: Nay, their endeavor keeps in the wonted pace; but there is, sir, an eyrie of children, little eyases,[6] that cry out on the top of question,[7] and are most tyrannically clapped for't. These are now the fashion, and so berattle the   330 common stages (so they call them) that many wearing rapiers are afraid of goose quills[8] and dare scarce come thither.

HAMLET: What, are they children? Who maintains 'em? How are they escoted?[9] Will they pursue the quality no longer   335 than they can sing? Will they not say afterwards, if they should grow themselves to common players (as it is most like, if their means are no better), their writers do them wrong to make them exclaim against their own succession?[1]

ROSENCRANTZ: Faith, there has been much todo on both sides;   340 and the nation holds it no sin to tarre[2] them to controversy. There was for a while no money bid for argument,[3] unless the poet and the player went to cuffs[4] in the question.

HAMLET: Is't possible?

GUILDENSTERN: O, there has been much throwing about of   345 brains.

HAMLET: Do the boys carry it away?

ROSENCRANTZ: Ay, that they do, my lord. Hercules and his load too.[5]

HAMLET: It is not very strange, for my uncle is King of Den-   350 mark, and those that would make mouths[6] at him while

---

6. Little hawks; an allusion to the boy-actor companies that rivaled the Globe theater.

7. With a loud, high delivery.

8. Many noblemen fear the pens of satirical writers.

9. Supported.

1. Future careers.

2. Urge.

3. Paid for a play plot.

4. Blows.

5. During one of his labors, Hercules assumed for a time the burden of the Titan Atlas, who supported the heavens on his shoulders. Also a reference to the effect on business at Shakespeare's theater, the Globe.

6. Sneer.

my father lived give twenty, forty, fifty, a hundred ducats apiece for his picture in little.[7] 'Sblood,[8] there is something in this more than natural, if philosophy could find it out.
    [*A flourish.*]

GUILDENSTERN: There are the players.   355

HAMLET: Gentlemen, you are welcome to Elsinore. Your hands. Come then, th' appurtenance of welcome is fashion and ceremony. Let me comply with you in this garb, lest my extent[9] to the players, which I tell you must show fairly outwards should more appear like entertainment[1] than   360
    yours. You are welcome. But my uncle-father and aunt-mother are deceived.

GUILDENSTERN: In what, my dear lord?

HAMLET: I am but mad north-north-west; when the wind is southerly I know a hawk from a handsaw.[2]   365
    [*Enter* POLONIUS.]

POLONIUS: Well be with you, gentlemen.

HAMLET: Hark you, Guildenstern—and you too—at each ear a hearer. That great baby you see there is not yet out of his swaddling clouts.[3]

ROSENCRANTZ: Happily he is the second time come to them,   370
    for they say an old man is twice a child.

HAMLET: I will prophesy he comes to tell me of the players.
    Mark it.
    —You say right, sir, a Monday morning, 'twas then indeed.

POLONIUS: My lord, I have news to tell you.

HAMLET: My lord, I have news to tell you.   375
    When Roscius was an actor in Rome—[4]

POLONIUS: The actors are come hither, my lord.

HAMLET: Buzz, buzz.

POLONIUS: Upon my honor—

HAMLET: Then came each actor on his ass—   380

POLONIUS: The best actors in the world, either for tragedy,

---

7. Miniature.
8. By God's blood.
9. Fashion. *Comply with:* welcome.
1. Cordiality.
2. That is, I know a plasterer's tool from (perhaps) a hernshaw, or heron.

3. Wrappings for an infant.
4. Roscius was the most famous actor of classical Rome.

comedy, history, pastoral, pastoral-comical, historical-pastoral, tragical-historical, tragical-comical-historical-pastoral, scene individable, or poem unlimited. Seneca cannot be too heavy nor Plautus too light. For the law of writ and the liberty, these are the only men.[5]

HAMLET: O Jephtha, judge of Israel, what a treasure hadst thou![6]

POLONIUS: What a treasure had he, my lord?

HAMLET: Why—

"One fair daughter, and no more,

The which he loved passing well."

POLONIUS: [*Aside.*] Still on my daughter.

HAMLET: Am I not i' th' right, old Jephtha?

POLONIUS: If you call me Jephtha, my lord, I have a daughter that I love passing well.

HAMLET: Nay, that follows not.

POLONIUS: What follows then, my lord?

HAMLET: Why—

"As by lot, God wot"

and then, you know,

"It came to pass, as most like it was."

The first row of the pious chanson[7] will show you more, for look where my abridgement comes.

[*Enter* the PLAYERS.]

You are welcome, masters; welcome, all—I am glad to see thee well.—Welcome, good friends.—O, old friend! Why thy face is valanced since I saw thee last. Com'st thou to beard[8] me in Denmark?—What, my young lady and mistress? By'r lady, your ladyship is nearer to heaven than when I saw you last by the altitude of a chopine.[9] Pray God your voice, like a piece of uncurrent gold, be

385

390

395

400

405

410

5. Seneca and Plautus were Roman writers of tragedy and comedy, respectively. The "law of writ" refers to plays written according to classical rules; the "liberty," to those written otherwise.

6. In the Bible, Jephtha asked God for victory and vowed to sacrifice the first crea-

ture he encountered upon his return. His only daughter became the victim of his vow.

7. Song. *Row:* stanza.

8. Defy. *Valanced:* Fringed (with a beard).

9. The height of a woman's thick-soled shoe.

not cracked within the ring.[1]—Masters, you are all welcome. We'll e'en to't like French falconers, fly at anything we see. We'll have a speech straight. Come give us
a taste of your quality,[2] come a passionate speech.

FIRST PLAYER: What speech, my good lord?   415

HAMLET: I heard thee speak me a speech once, but it was never
acted, or if it was, not above once, for the play, I remember,
pleased not the million; 'twas caviary to the general.[3] But it
was—as I received it, and others whose judgments in such
matters cried in the top of[4] mine—an excellent play, well   420
digested[5] in the scenes, set down with as much modesty as
cunning. I remember one said there were no sallets[6] in the
lines to make the matter savory, nor no matter in the
phrase that might indict the author of affectation, but
called it an honest method, as wholesome as sweet, and by   425
very much more handsome than fine. One speech in't I
chiefly loved. 'Twas Æneas' tale to Dido, and thereabout of
it especially where he speaks of Priam's slaughter.[7] If it live
in your memory, begin at this line—let me see, let me see:
"The rugged Pyrrhus, like th' Hyrcanian beast"[8]—   430
'tis not so; it begins with Pyrrhus—
"The rugged Pyrrhus, he whose sable arms,
Black as his purpose, did the night resemble
When he lay couchéd in th' ominous horse,[9]
Hath now this dread and black complexion smeared   435
With heraldry more dismal; head to foot
Now is he total gules, horridly tricked[1]
With blood of fathers, mothers, daughters, sons,
Baked and impasted with the parching[2] streets,

---

1. *Pray God . . . ring:* a reference to
the Elizabethan theatrical practice of using boys to play women's roles; Hamlet
hopes that this boy has not matured to
the point at which his voice might
change.
2. Trade.
3. Caviar to the masses.
4. Were weightier than.
5. Arranged.

6. Spicy passages.
7. In Virgil's *Aeneid*, Aeneas tells Dido,
the queen of Carthage, about the fall of
Troy. Here he describes Pyrrhus's killing of
Priam, the aged king of Troy, also known
(like his city) as Ilium.
8. Tiger.
9. That is, the Trojan horse.
1. Adorned. *Total gules:* completely red.
2. Burning. *Impasted:* crusted.

That lend a tyrannous and a damnéd light   440
To their lord's murder. Roasted in wrath and fire,
And thus o'er-sizéd with coagulate³ gore,
With eyes like carbuncles, the hellish Pyrrhus
Old grandsire Priam seeks."
So proceed you.   445
POLONIUS: Fore God, my lord, well spoken, with good accent
   and good discretion.
FIRST PLAYER: "Anon he finds him⁴
   Striking too short at Greeks. His antique⁵ sword,
   Rebellious⁶ to his arm, lies where it falls,   450
   Repugnant to command. Unequal matched,
   Pyrrhus at Priam drives, in rage strikes wide.
   But with the whiff and wind of his fell sword
   Th' unnervéd father falls. Then senseless⁷ Ilium,
   Seeming to feel this blow, with flaming top   455
   Stoops⁸ to his base, and with a hideous crash
   Takes prisoner Pyrrhus' ear. For, lo! his sword,
   Which was declining⁹ on the milky head
   Of reverend Priam, seemed i' th' air to stick.
   So as a painted tyrant Pyrrhus stood,   460
   And like a neutral to his will and matter,¹
   Did nothing.
   But as we often see, against some storm,
   A silence in the heavens, the rack² stand still,
   The bold winds speechless, and the orb below   465
   As hush as death, anon the dreadful thunder
   Doth rend the region; so, after Pyrrhus' pause,
   A rouséd vengeance sets him new awork,³
   And never did the Cyclops' hammers fall
   On Mars's armor, forged for proof eterne,⁴   470
   With less remorse than Pyrrhus' bleeding sword

---

3. Clotted. *O'er-sizéd:* glued over.
4. That is, Pyrrhus finds Priam.
5. Which he used when young.
6. Unmanageable.
7. Without feeling.
8. Falls.
9. About to fall.

1. Between his will and the fulfillment of it.
2. Clouds.
3. To work.
4. Mars, the Roman war god, had impenetrable armor made for him by the blacksmith god, Vulcan, and his assistants, the Cyclopes.

Now falls on Priam.
Out, out, thou strumpet, Fortune! All you gods,
In general synod take away her power,
Break all the spokes and fellies[5] from her wheel,   475
And bowl the round nave[6] down the hill of heaven
As low as to the fiends."
POLONIUS: This is too long.
HAMLET: It shall to the barber's with your beard.—Prithee
say on. He's for a jig,[7] or a tale of bawdry, or he sleeps.   480
Say on; come to Hecuba.[8]
FIRST PLAYER: "But who, ah woe! had seen the mobléd[9]
    queen—"
HAMLET: "The mobléd queen"?
POLONIUS: That's good. "Mobléd queen" is good.
FIRST PLAYER: "Run barefoot up and down, threat'ning the
    flames   485
With bisson rheum, a clout[1] upon that head
Where late the diadem stood, and for a robe,
About her lank and all o'er-teeméd loins.
A blanket, in the alarm of fear caught up—
Who this had seen, with tongue in venom steeped,   490
'Gainst Fortune's state[2] would treason have pronounced.
But if the gods themselves did see her then,
When she saw Pyrrhus make malicious sport
In mincing[3] with his sword her husband's limbs,
The instant burst of clamor that she made,   495
Unless things mortal move them not at all,
Would have made milch[4] the burning eyes of heaven,
And passion in the gods."
POLONIUS: Look whe'r[5] he has not turned his color, and has
tears in's eyes. Prithee no more.   500
HAMLET: 'Tis well. I'll have thee speak out the rest of this

---

5. Parts of the rim.
6. Roll the round hub.
7. A comic act.
8. Wife of Priam and queen of Troy. Her "loins" are described below as "o'er-teeméd" because of her celebrated fertility.

9. Muffled (in a hood).
1. With blinding tears, a cloth.
2. Government.
3. Cutting up.
4. Tearful (literally, milk-giving).
5. Whether.

soon.—Good my lord, will you see the players well bestowed?[6] Do you hear, let them be well used, for they are
the abstract[7] and brief chronicles of the time; after your
death you were better have a bad epitaph than their ill re-   505
port while you live.

POLONIUS: My lord, I will use them according to their desert.

HAMLET: God's bodkin,[8] man, much better. Use every man after his desert, and who shall 'scape whipping? Use them after your own honor and dignity. The less they deserve, the   510
more merit is in your bounty. Take them in.

POLONIUS: Come, sirs.

HAMLET: Follow him, friends. We'll hear a play tomorrow.
[*Aside to* FIRST PLAYER.] Dost thou hear me, old friend, can
you play "The Murder of Gonzago"?   515

FIRST PLAYER: Ay, my lord.

HAMLET: We'll ha't tomorrow night. You could for a need
study a speech of some dozen or sixteen lines which I
would set down and insert in't, could you not?

FIRST PLAYER: Ay, my lord.   520

HAMLET: Very well. Follow that lord, and look you mock him
not.   [*Exeunt* POLONIUS *and* PLAYERS.]
My good friends, I'll leave you till night. You are welcome
to Elsinore.

ROSENCRANTZ: Good my lord.   525

                [*Exeunt* ROSENCRANTZ *and* GUILDENSTERN.]

HAMLET: Ay, so God b'wi'ye. Now I am alone.
O, what a rogue and peasant slave am I!
Is it not monstrous that this player here,
But in a fiction, in a dream of passion,
Could force his soul so to his own conceit[9]   530
That from her working all his visage wanned;[1]
Tears in his eyes, distraction in his aspect[2]
A broken voice, and his whole function suiting
With forms to his conceit? And all for nothing,

6. Provided for.
7. Summary.
8. Dear body.
9. Imagination.
1. Grew pale.
2. Face.

For Hecuba!   535
What's Hecuba to him or he to Hecuba,
That he should weep for her? What would he do
Had he the motive and the cue for passion
That I have? He would drown the stage with tears,
And cleave the general ear with horrid speech,   540
Make mad the guilty, and appal the free,
Confound the ignorant, and amaze indeed
The very faculties of eyes and ears.
Yet I,
A dull and muddy-mettled rascal, peak[3]   545
Like John-a-dreams, unpregnant of[4] my cause,
And can say nothing; no, not for a king
Upon whose property and most dear life
A damned defeat was made. Am I a coward?
Who calls me villain, breaks my pate across,   550
Plucks off my beard and blows it in my face,
Tweaks me by the nose, gives me the lie i' th' throat
As deep as to the lungs? Who does me this?
Ha, 'swounds,[5] I should take it; for it cannot be
But I am pigeon-livered and lack gall[6]   555
To make oppression bitter, or ere this
I should 'a fatted all the region kites[7]
With this slave's offal. Bloody, bawdy villain!
Remorseless, treacherous, lecherous, kindless[8] villain!
O, vengeance!   560
Why, what an ass am I! This is most brave,
That I, the son of a dear father murdered,
Prompted to my revenge by heaven and hell,
Must like a whore unpack[9] my heart with words,
And fall a-cursing like a very drab,   565
A scullion! Fie upon't! foh!
About, my brains. Hum—I have heard
That guilty creatures sitting at a play,

3. Mope. *Muddy-mettled:* dull-spirited.　　6. Bitterness.
4. Unenlivened by. *John-a-dreams:* a　　7. Vultures of the area.
loafer.　　8. Unnatural.
5. By God's wounds.　　9. Relieve.

Have by the very cunning of the scene
Been struck so to the soul that presently   570
They have proclaimed[1] their malefactions;
For murder, though it have no tongue, will speak
With most miraculous organ. I'll have these players
Play something like the murder of my father
Before mine uncle. I'll observe his looks.   575
I'll tent him to the quick. If 'a do blench,[2]
I know my course. The spirit that I have seen
May be a devil, and the devil hath power
T' assume a pleasing shape, yea, and perhaps
Out of my weakness and my melancholy,   580
As he is very potent with such spirits,
Abuses me to damn me. I'll have grounds
More relative[3] than this. The play's the thing
Wherein I'll catch the conscience of the king.   [*Exit.*]

ACT III

SCENE 1

A room in the castle. Enter KING, QUEEN, POLONIUS, OPHELIA,
ROSENCRANTZ *and* GUILDENSTERN.

KING: And can you by no drift of conference[1]
  Get from him why he puts on this confusion,
  Grating so harshly all his days of quiet
  With turbulent and dangerous lunacy?
ROSENCRANTZ: He does confess he feels himself distracted,   5
  But from what cause 'a will by no means speak.
GUILDENSTERN: Nor do we find him forward to be sounded,[2]
  But with a crafty madness keeps aloof
  When we would bring him on to some confession
  Of his true state.
QUEEN: Did he receive you well?   10
ROSENCRANTZ: Most like a gentleman.

---

1. Admitted.   1. Line of conversation.
2. Turn pale. *Tent:* try.   2. Eager to be questioned.
3. Conclusive.

GUILDENSTERN: But with much forcing of his disposition.³
ROSENCRANTZ: Niggard of question, but of our demands⁴
  Most free in his reply.
QUEEN: Did you assay⁵ him
  To any pastime?   15
ROSENCRANTZ: Madam, it so fell out that certain players
  We o'er-raught⁶ on the way. Of these we told him,
  And there did seem in him a kind of joy
  To hear of it. They are here about the court,
  And as I think, they have already order   20
  This night to play before him.
POLONIUS: 'Tis most true,
  And he beseeched me to entreat your majesties
  To hear and see the matter.⁷
KING: With all my heart, and it doth much content me
  To hear him so inclined.   25
  Good gentlemen, give him a further edge,⁸
  And drive his purpose into these delights.
ROSENCRANTZ: We shall, my lord.
          [*Exeunt* ROSENCRANTZ *and* GUILDENSTERN.]
KING: Sweet Gertrude, leave us too,
  For we have closely sent for Hamlet hither,
  That he, as 'twere by accident, may here   30
  Affront⁹ Ophelia.
  Her father and myself (lawful espials¹)
  Will so bestow ourselves that, seeing unseen,
  We may of their encounter frankly judge,
  And gather by him, as he is behaved,   35
  If't be th' affliction of his love or no
  That thus he suffers for.
QUEEN: I shall obey you.—
  And for your part, Ophelia, I do wish
  That your good beauties be the happy cause
  Of Hamlet's wildness. So shall I hope your virtues 40

3. Mood.
4. To our questions.
5. Tempt.
6. Passed.
7. Performance.
8. Sharpen his intention.
9. Confront.
1. Justified spies.

Will bring him to his wonted[2] way again,
To both your honors.

OPHELIA: Madam, I wish it may.

                                    [*Exit* QUEEN.]

POLONIUS: Ophelia, walk you here—Gracious,[3] so please you,
We will bestow ourselves.—[*To* OPHELIA.] Read on this
    book,[4]
That show of such an exercise may color[5]   45
Your loneliness.—We are oft to blame in this,
'Tis too much proved, that with devotion's visage
And pious action we do sugar o'er
The devil himself.

KING: [*Aside.*]   O, 'tis too true.
How smart a lash that speech doth give my conscience!   50
The harlot's cheek, beautied with plast'ring[6] art,
Is not more ugly to the thing that helps it
Than is my deed to my most painted word.
O heavy burden!

POLONIUS: I hear him coming. Let's withdraw, my lord.   55

                        [*Exeunt* KING *and* POLONIUS.]

        [*Enter* HAMLET.]

HAMLET: To be, or not to be, that is the question:
Whether 'tis nobler in the mind to suffer
The slings and arrows of outrageous fortune,
Or to take arms against a sea of troubles,
And by opposing end them. To die, to sleep—   60
No more; and by a sleep to say we end
The heartache, and the thousand natural shocks
That flesh is heir to. 'Tis a consummation
Devoutly to be wished—to die, to sleep—
To sleep, perchance to dream, ay there's the rub;   65
For in that sleep of death what dreams may come
When we have shuffled off this mortal coil[7]
Must give us pause—there's the respect[8]

2. Usual.   6. Thickly painted.
3. Majesty.   7. Turmoil.
4. Prayer book or devotional text. 8. Consideration.
5. Act of devotion may explain.

That makes calamity of so long life.
For who would bear the whips and scorns of time,   70
Th' oppressor's wrong, the proud man's contumely,[9]
The pangs of despised love, the law's delay,
The insolence of office, and the spurns[1]
That patient merit of th' unworthy takes,
When he himself might his quietus[2] make   75
With a bare bodkin? Who would fardels[3] bear,
To grunt and sweat under a weary life,
But that the dread of something after death,
The undiscovered country, from whose bourn[4]
No traveller returns, puzzles the will,   80
And makes us rather bear those ills we have
Than fly to others that we know not of?
Thus conscience does make cowards of us all;
And thus the native[5] hue of resolution
Is sicklied o'er with the pale cast of thought,   85
And enterprises of great pitch and moment[6]
With this regard their currents turn awry
And lose the name of action.—Soft you now,
The fair Ophelia.—Nymph, in thy orisons[7]
Be all my sins remembered.
OPHELIA: Good my lord,   90
How does your honor for this many a day?
HAMLET: I humbly thank you, well, well, well.
OPHELIA: My lord, I have remembrances of yours
That I have longéd long to re-deliver.
I pray you now receive them.
HAMLET: No, not I,   95
I never gave you aught.
OPHELIA: My honored lord, you know right well you did,
And with them words of so sweet breath composed

---

9. Insulting behavior.
1. Rejections.
2. Settlement, as in the paying off of a debt.
3. Burdens. *Bare bodkin:* an unsheathed dagger.

4. Boundary.
5. Natural.
6. Great height and importance.
7. Prayers.

As made the things more rich. Their perfume lost,
Take these again, for to the noble mind   100
Rich gifts wax[8] poor when givers prove unkind.
There, my lord.

HAMLET: Ha, ha! are you honest?[9]

OPHELIA: My lord?

HAMLET: Are you fair?   105

OPHELIA: What means your lordship?

HAMLET: That if you be honest and fair, your honesty should
admit no discourse to your beauty.

OPHELIA: Could beauty, my lord, have better commerce[1] than
with honesty?   110

HAMLET: Ay, truly, for the power of beauty will sooner transform honesty from what it is to a bawd than the force of
honesty can translate beauty into his likeness. This was
sometimes a paradox, but now the time gives it proof. I did
love you once.   115

OPHELIA: Indeed, my lord, you made me believe so.

HAMLET: You should not have believed me, for virtue cannot
so inoculate[2] our old stock but we shall relish of it. I loved
you not.

OPHELIA: I was the more deceived.   120

HAMLET: Get thee to a nunnery.[3] Why wouldst thou be a
breeder of sinners? I am myself indifferent[4] honest, but yet
I could accuse me of such things that it were better my
mother had not borne me: I am very proud, revengeful,
ambitious, with more offences at my beck[5] than I have   125
thoughts to put them in, imagination to give them shape,
or time to act them in. What should such fellows as I do
crawling between earth and heaven? We are arrant[6] knaves
all; believe none of us. Go thy ways to a nunnery. Where's
your father?   130

OPHELIA: At home, my lord.

8. Become.
9. Chaste.
1. Dealings.
2. Change by grafting.
3. Both a convent of nuns and, in Elizabethan slang, a brothel.

4. Moderately.
5. Command.
6. Thorough.

HAMLET: Let the doors be shut upon him, that he may play
the fool nowhere but in's own house. Farewell.

OPHELIA: O, help him, you sweet heavens!

HAMLET: If thou dost marry, I'll give thee this plague for thy   135
dowry: be thou as chaste as ice, as pure as snow, thou shalt
not escape calumny. Get thee to a nunnery, farewell. Or if
thou wilt needs marry, marry a fool, for wise men know
well enough what monsters[7] you make of them. To a nunnery, go, and quickly too. Farewell.   140

OPHELIA: Heavenly powers, restore him!

HAMLET: I have heard of your paintings, too, well enough.
God hath given you one face, and you make yourselves another. You jig, you amble, and you lisp;[8] you nickname
God's creatures, and make your wantonness your igno-   145
rance.[9] Go to, I'll no more on't, it hath made me mad. I say
we will have no more marriage. Those that are married already, all but one, shall live. The rest shall keep as they are.
To a nunnery, go.   [Exit.]

OPHELIA: O, what a noble mind is here o'erthrown!   150
The courtier's, soldier's, scholar's, eye, tongue, sword,
Th' expectancy and rose[1] of the fair state,
The glass of fashion and the mould[2] of form,
Th' observed of all observers, quite quite down!
And I of ladies most deject and wretched,   155
That sucked the honey of his music[3] vows,
Now see that noble and most sovereign reason
Like sweet bells jangled, out of time and harsh;
That unmatched form and feature of blown[4] youth
Blasted with ecstasy. O, woe is me   160
T' have seen what I have seen, see what I see!
[Enter KING and POLONIUS.]

KING: Love! His affections do not that way tend,
Nor what he spake, though it lacked form a little,
Was not like madness. There's something in his soul

---

7. Horned because cuckolded.
8. Walk and talk affectedly.
9. Call things by pet names and then
blame the affectation on ignorance.

1. The hope and ornament.
2. Model. *Glass:* mirror.
3. Musical.
4. Full-blown.

O'er which his melancholy sits on brood,[5]   165
And I do doubt the hatch and the disclose[6]
Will be some danger; which to prevent,
I have in quick determination
Thus set it down: he shall with speed to England
For the demand of our neglected tribute.   170
Haply the seas and countries different,
With variable objects, shall expel
This something-settled matter in his heart
Whereon his brains still beating puts him thus
From fashion of himself. What think you on't?   175
POLONIUS: It shall do well. But yet do I believe
The origin and commencement of his grief
Sprung from neglected love.—How now, Ophelia?
You need not tell us what Lord Hamlet said,
We heard it all.—My lord, do as you please,   180
But if you hold it fit, after the play
Let his queen-mother all alone entreat him
To show his grief. Let her be round[7] with him,
And I'll be placed, so please you, in the ear[8]
Of all their conference. If she find him not,[9]   185
To England send him; or confine him where
Your wisdom best shall think.
KING: It shall be so.
Madness in great ones must not unwatched go.
                                                [*Exeunt.*]

SCENE 2

A public room in the castle. Enter HAMLET *and three of the*
PLAYERS.

HAMLET: Speak the speech, I pray you, as I pronounced it to
   you, trippingly on the tongue; but if you mouth it as many
   of our players do, I had as lief the town-crier spoke my

---

5. That is, like a hen.   8. Hearing.
6. Result. *Doubt:* fear.   9. Does not discover the cause of his be-
7. Direct.   havior.

lines. Nor do not saw the air too much with your hand
thus, but use all gently, for in the very torrent, tempest, and   305
as I may say, whirlwind of your passion, you must acquire
and beget a temperance that may give it smoothness. O, it
offends me to the soul to hear a robustious periwig-pated[1]
fellow tear a passion to tatters, to very rags, to split the ears
of the groundlings, who for the most part are capable of[2]   310
nothing but inexplicable dumb shows and noise. I would
have such a fellow whipped for o'erdoing Termagant. It
out-herods Herod.[3] Pray you avoid it.

FIRST PLAYER: I warrant your honor.

HAMLET: Be not too tame neither, but let your own discretion   315
be your tutor. Suit the action to the word, the word to
the action, with this special observance, that you o'erstep
not the modesty of nature; for anything so o'erdone is
from[4] the purpose of playing, whose end both at the first,
and now, was and is, to hold as 'twere the mirror up to na-   320
ture, to show virtue her own feature, scorn her own image,
and the very age and body of the time his form and pressure.[5] Now this overdone, or come tardy off, though it
makes the unskilful[6] laugh, cannot but make the judicious
grieve, the censure[7] of the which one must in your al-   325
lowance o'erweigh a whole theatre of others. O, there
be players that I have seen play—and heard others praise,
and that highly—not to speak it profanely, that neither
having th' accent of Christians, nor the gait of Christian,
pagan, nor man, have so strutted and bellowed that I   330
have thought some of nature's journeymen[8] had made
men, and not made them well, they imitated humanity so
abominably.

FIRST PLAYER: I hope we have reformed that indifferently[9] with
us, sir.   335

---

1. A noisy bewigged.

2. That is, capable of understanding.
Groundlings: the spectators in the cheapest
area.

3. Termagant, an imaginary deity, and
the biblical Herod were violent and loud
stock characters in popular drama.

4. Contrary to.

5. His shape and likeness.

6. Ignorant.

7. Judgment.

8. Inferior craftsmen.

9. Somewhat.

HAMLET: O, reform it altogether. And let those that play
your clowns speak no more than is set down for them,
for there be of them that will themselves laugh, to set on
some quantity of barren[1] spectators to laugh too, though
in the meantime some necessary question of the play be   340
then to be considered. That's villainous, and shows a most
pitiful ambition in the fool that uses it. Go, make you
ready.
                                                  [*Exeunt* PLAYERS.]
            [*Enter* POLONIUS, GUILDENSTERN, *and* ROSENCRANTZ.]
    How now my lord? Will the king hear this piece of work?
POLONIUS: And the queen too, and that presently.   345
HAMLET: Bid the players make haste.   [*Exit* POLONIUS.]
    Will you two help to hasten them?
ROSENCRANTZ: Ay, my lord.   [*Exeunt they two.*]
HAMLET: What, ho, Horatio!
            [*Enter* HORATIO.]
HORATIO: Here, sweet lord, at your service.   350
HAMLET: Horatio, thou art e'en as just a man
    As e'er my conversation coped[2] withal.
HORATIO: O my dear lord!
HAMLET: Nay, do not think I flatter,
    For what advancement may I hope from thee,
    That no revenue hast but thy good spirits   355
    To feed and clothe thee? Why should the poor be flattered?
    No, let the candied tongue lick absurd pomp,
    And crook the pregnant[3] hinges of the knee
    Where thrift[4] may follow fawning. Dost thou hear?
    Since my dear soul was mistress of her choice   360
    And could of men distinguish her election,
    S'hath sealed thee for herself, for thou hast been
    As one in suff'ring all that suffers nothing,
    A man that Fortune's buffets and rewards
    Hast ta'en with equal thanks; and blest are those   365
    Whose blood and judgment are so well commingled

1. Dull-witted.   3. Quick to bend.
2. Encountered.   4. Profit.

That they are not a pipe[5] for Fortune's finger
To sound what stop[6] she please. Give me that man
That is not passion's slave, and I will wear him
In my heart's core, ay, in my heart of heart,   370
As I do thee. Something too much of this.
There is a play tonight before the king.
One scene of it comes near the circumstance
Which I have told thee of my father's death.
I prithee, when thou seest that act afoot,   375
Even with the very comment[7] of thy soul
Observe my uncle. If his occulted[8] guilt
Do not itself unkennel[9] in one speech,
It is a damnéd ghost that we have seen,
And my imaginations are as foul   380
As Vulcan's stithy. Give him heedful note,[1]
For I mine eyes will rivet to his face,
And after we will both our judgments join
In censure of his seeming.[2]

HORATIO: Well, my lord.
If 'a[3] steal aught the whilst this play in playing,   385
And 'scape detecting, I will pay[4] the theft.

  [*Enter Trumpets and Kettledrums,* KING, QUEEN, POLO-
  NIUS, OPHELIA, ROSENCRANTZ, GUILDENSTERN, *and other*
  LORDS *attendant.*]

HAMLET: They are coming to the play. I must be idle.
 Get you a place.

KING: How fares our cousin Hamlet?

HAMLET: Excellent, i' faith, of the chameleon's dish.[5] I eat the   390
 air, promise-crammed. You cannot feed capons so.

KING: I have nothing with this answer, Hamlet. These words
 are not mine.

---

5. Musical instrument.   2. Manner.
6. To play what note.   3. He.
7. Keenest observation.   4. Repay.
8. Hidden.   5. Chameleons were popularly believed
9. Break loose.   to eat nothing but air.
1. Careful attention. *Stithy:* smithy, forge.

HAMLET: No, nor mine now. [*To* POLONIUS.] My lord, you
    played once i' th' university, you say?   395

POLONIUS: That did I, my lord, and was accounted a good
    actor.

HAMLET: What did you enact?

POLONIUS: I did enact Julius Cæsar. I was killed i' th' Capitol;
    Brutus killed me.[6]   400

HAMLET: It was a brute part of him to kill so capital a calf
    there. Be the players ready?

ROSENCRANTZ: Ay, my lord, they stay upon your patience.[7]

QUEEN: Come hither, my dear Hamlet, sit by me.

HAMLET: No, good mother, here's metal more attractive.   405

POLONIUS: [*To the* KING.] O, ho! do you mark that?

HAMLET: Lady, shall I lie in your lap? [*Lying down at* OPHELIA*'s*
    feet.]

OPHELIA: No, my lord.

HAMLET: I mean, my head upon your lap?

OPHELIA: Ay, my lord.   410

HAMLET: Do you think I meant country matters?[8]

OPHELIA: I think nothing, my lord.

HAMLET: That's a fair thought to lie between maids' legs.

OPHELIA: What is, my lord?

HAMLET: Nothing.   415

OPHELIA: You are merry, my lord.

HAMLET: Who, I?

OPHELIA: Ay, my lord.

HAMLET: O God, your only jig-maker![9] What should a man
    do but be merry? For look you how cheerfully my mother   420
    looks, and my father died within's two hours.

OPHELIA: Nay, 'tis twice two months, my lord.

HAMLET: So long? Nay then, let the devil wear black, for I'll
    have a suit of sables.[1] O heavens! die two months ago, and

---

6. Perhaps an allusion to Shakespeare's
Julius Caesar, which dramatizes the assassi-
nation of Julius Caesar by Brutus and others.

7. Leisure. *Stay:* wait.

8. Here and elsewhere in this exchange
Hamlet intends some ribald double meanings.

9. Writer of comic scenes.

1. Fur; also, black.

not forgotten yet? Then there's hope a great man's memory   425
may outlive his life half a year, but by'r lady 'a must build
churches then, or else shall 'a suffer not thinking on, with
the hobby-horse, whose epitaph is "For O, for O, the
hobby-horse is forgot!"[2]

> *The trumpets sound. Dumb Show follows. Enter a* KING
> *and a* QUEEN *very lovingly; the* QUEEN *embracing him and*
> *he her. She kneels, and makes show of protestation unto*
> *him. He takes her up, and declines[3] his head upon her neck.*
> *He lies him down upon a bank of flowers; she, seeing him*
> *asleep, leaves him. Anon come in another man, takes off his*
> *crown, kisses it, pours poison in the sleeper's ears, and leaves*
> *him. The* QUEEN *returns, finds the* KING *dead, makes pas-*
> *sionate action. The* POISONER *with some three or four come*
> *in again, seem to condole with her. The dead body is carried*
> *away. The* POISONER *woos the* QUEEN *with gifts; she seems*
> *harsh awhile, but in the end accepts love.*
>
> [Exeunt.]

OPHELIA: What means this, my lord?   430
HAMLET: Marry, this is miching mallecho;[4] it means mischief.
OPHELIA: Belike this show imports the argument[5] of the play.

> [*Enter* PROLOGUE.]

HAMLET: We shall know by this fellow. The players cannot
keep counsel; they'll tell all.
OPHELIA: Will 'a tell us what this show meant?   435
HAMLET: Ay, or any show that you will show him. Be not
you ashamed to show, he'll not shame to tell you what it
means.
OPHELIA: You are naught, you are naught. I'll mark[6] the play.
PROLOGUE: *For us, and for our tragedy,*   440
    Here stooping to your clemency,
    We beg your hearing patiently.   [*Exit.*]
HAMLET: Is this a prologue, or the posy[7] of a ring?
OPHELIA: 'Tis brief, my lord.

---

2. An Elizabethan ballad refrain. In traditional games and dances one of the characters was a man represented as riding a horse.
    3. Lays.

4. Sneaking crime.
5. Explains the plot.
6. Attend to. *Naught:* obscene.
7. Motto engraved inside.

HAMLET: As woman's love.   445

[*Enter the* PLAYER KING *and* QUEEN.]

PLAYER KING: *Full thirty times hath Phœbus' cart gone round*
    Neptune's salt wash and Tellus' orbéd ground,
    And thirty dozen moons with borrowed sheen[8]
    About the world have times twelve thirties been,
    Since love our hearts and Hymen did our hands   450
    Unite comutual in most sacred bands.[9]

PLAYER QUEEN: *So many journeys may the sun and moon*
    Make us again count o'er ere love be done!
    But woe is nie, you are so sick of late,
    So far from cheer and from your former state,   455
    That I distrust[1] *you. Yet though I distrust,*
    Discomfort you, my lord, it nothing must.
    For women's fear and love hold quantity,[2]
    In neither aught, or in extremity.[3]
    Now what my love is proof hath made you know,   460
    And as my love is sized,[4] *my fear is so.*
    Where love is great, the littlest doubts are fear;
    Where little fears grow great, great love grows there.

PLAYER KING: *Faith, I must leave thee, love, and shortly too;*
    My operant powers their functions leave[5] *to do.*   465
    And thou shalt live in this fair world behind,
    Honored, beloved, and haply one as kind
    For husband shalt thou—

PLAYER QUEEN: *O, confound the rest!*
    Such love must needs be treason in my breast.
    In second husband let me be accurst!   470
    None wed the second but who killed the first.

HAMLET: That's wormwood.

PLAYER QUEEN: *The instances*[6] *that second marriage move*

8. Light.

9. The speech contains several references to Greek and Roman mythology. Phoebus was the sun god; his chariot, or "cart," is the sun. Neptune was the sea god; his "salt wash" is the ocean. Tellus was an earth goddess; her "orbed ground" is Earth, or the globe. Hymen was the god of marriage. *Comutual:* mutually.

1. Fear for.

2. Agree in weight.

3. Without regard to too much or too little.

4. In size.

5. Cease. *Operant powers:* active forces.

6. Causes.

Are base respects[7] of thrift, but none of love.
A second time I kill my husband dead,   475
When second husband kisses me in bed.
PLAYER KING: *I do believe you think what now you speak,*
But what we do determine oft we break.
Purpose is but the slave to memory,
Of violent birth, but poor validity;   480
Which now, like fruit unripe, sticks on the tree,
But fall unshaken when they mellow be.
Most necessary 'tis that we forget
To pay ourselves what to ourselves is debt.
What to ourselves in passion we propose,   485
The passion ending, doth the purpose lose.
The violence of either grief or joy
Their own enactures[8] with themselves destroy.
Where joy most revels, grief doth most lament;
Grief joys, joy grieves, on slender accident.   490
This world is not for aye,[9] nor 'tis not strange
That even our loves should with our fortunes change;
For 'tis a question left us yet to prove,
Whether love lead fortune, or else fortune love.
The great man down, you mark his favorite flies;   495
The poor advanced makes friends of enemies;
And hitherto doth love on fortune tend,
For who not needs shall never lack a friend,
And who in want a hollow[1] friend doth try,
Directly seasons him[2] his enemy.   500
But orderly to end where I begun,
Our wills and fates do so contrary run
That our devices[3] still are overthrown;
Our thoughts are ours, their ends none of our own.
So think thou wilt no second husband wed,   505
But die thy thoughts when thy first lord is dead.
PLAYER QUEEN: *Nor earth to me give food, nor heaven light,*

---

7. Concerns.
8. Actions.
9. Eternal.

1. False.
2. Ripens him into.
3. Plans.

Sport and repose lock from me day and night,
To desperation turn my trust and hope,
An anchor's cheer[4] *in prison be my scope,*   510
Each opposite that blanks[5] *the face of joy*
Meet what I would have well, and it destroy,
Both here and hence[6] *pursue me lasting strife,*
If once a widow, ever I be wife!

HAMLET: If she should break it now!   515

PLAYER KING: *'Tis deeply sworn. Sweet, leave me here awhile.*
My spirits grow dull, and fain I would beguile
The tedious day with sleep. [*Sleeps.*]

PLAYER QUEEN: *Sleep rock thy brain,*
And never come mischance between us twain!   [*Exit.*]

HAMLET: Madam, how like you this play?   520

QUEEN: The lady doth protest too much, methinks.

HAMLET: O, but she'll keep her word.

KING: Have you heard the argument? Is there no offence in't?

HAMLET: No, no, they do but jest, poison in jest; no offence i'
th' world.   525

KING: What do you call the play?

HAMLET: "The Mouse-trap." Marry, how? Tropically.[7] This
play is the image of a murder done in Vienna. Gonzago is
the duke's name; his wife, Baptista. You shall see anon. 'Tis
a knavish piece of work, but what of that? Your majesty,   530
and we that have free souls, it touches us not. Let the galled
jade wince, our withers are unwrung.[8]

[*Enter* LUCIANUS.]

This is one Lucianus, nephew to the king.

OPHELIA: You are as good as a chorus, my lord.

HAMLET: I could interpret between you and your love, if I   535
could see the puppets dallying.

OPHELIA: You are keen, my lord, you are keen.

HAMLET: It would cost you a groaning to take off mine edge.

OPHELIA: Still better, and worse.

4. Anchorite's food.
5. Blanches.
6. In the next world.
7. Figuratively.

8. Let the horse with the sore back
wince. Our shoulders are not chafed by the
harness.

HAMLET: So you mistake your husbands.—Begin, murderer.   540
Leave thy damnable faces and begin. Come, the croaking
raven doth bellow for revenge.

LUCIANUS: *Thoughts black, hands apt, drugs fit, and time*
agreeing,
Confederate season,⁹ else no creature seeing,
Thou mixture rank, of midnight weeds collected,   545
With Hecate's¹ ban thrice blasted, thrice infected,
Thy natural magic² and dire property
On wholesome life usurp immediately.

[*Pours the poison in his ears.*]

HAMLET: 'A poisons him i' th' garden for his estate. His name's
Gonzago. The story is extant, and written in very choice   550
Italian. You shall see anon how the murderer gets the love
of Gonzago's wife.

OPHELIA: The king rises.

HAMLET: What, frighted with false fire?

QUEEN: How fares my lord?   555

POLONIUS: Give o'er the play.

KING: Give me some light. Away!

POLONIUS: Lights, lights, lights!

[*Exeunt all but* HAMLET *and* HORATIO.]

HAMLET: Why; let the strucken deer go weep,
The hart ungallèd³ play.   560
For some must watch while some must sleep;
Thus runs the world away.
Would not this, sir, and a forest of feathers⁴—if the rest of
my fortunes turn Turk with⁵ me—with two Provincial
roses on my razed shoes, get me a fellowship in a cry⁶ of   565
players?

HORATIO: Half a share.

HAMLET: A whole one, I.
For thou dost know, O Damon dear,⁷

---

9. Helpful time for the crime.
1. Classical goddess of witchcraft.
2. Native power.
3. Uninjured.
4. Plumes.

5. Turn against.
6. Partnership in a company.
7. *Damon:* a common name in ancient
lyric poetry. Also, a legendary friend.

This realm dismantled was   570
Of Jove[8] himself, and now reigns here
A very, very—peacock.
HORATIO: You might have rhymed.[9]
HAMLET: O good Horatio, I'll take the ghost's word for a
    thousand pound. Didst perceive?   575
HORATIO: Very well, my lord.
HAMLET: Upon the talk of the poisoning.
HORATIO: I did very well note him.
HAMLET: Ah, ha! Come, some music. Come, the recorders.
    For if the king like not the comedy.   580
    Why then, belike he likes it not, perdy.[1]
    Come, some music.
        [*Enter* ROSENCRANTZ *and* GUILDENSTERN.]
GUILDENSTERN: Good my lord, vouchsafe me a word with
    you.
HAMLET: Sir, a whole history.   585
GUILDENSTERN: The king, sir—
HAMLET: Ay, sir, what of him?
GUILDENSTERN: Is in his retirement marvellous distempered.
HAMLET: With drink, sir?
GUILDENSTERN: No, my lord, with choler.[2]   590
HAMLET: Your wisdom should show itself more richer to
    signify this to the doctor, for for me to put him to his
    purgation[3] would perhaps plunge him into more
    choler.
GUILDENSTERN: Good my lord, put your discourse into some   595
    frame,[4] and start not so wildly from my affair.
HAMLET: I am tame, sir. Pronounce.
GUILDENSTERN: The queen your mother, in most great afflic-
    tion of spirit, hath sent me to you.
HAMLET: You are welcome.   600
GUILDENSTERN: Nay, good my lord, this courtesy is not of the
    right breed. If it shall please you to make me a wholesome[5]

---

8. Chief Roman god.   2. Bile.
9. "Ass," for example, would have com-   3. Treatment with a laxative.
pleted the rhyme.   4. Speech into some order.
1. *Par Dieu* (by God).   5. Reasonable.

answer, I will do your mother's commandment. If not, your
pardon and my return[6] shall be the end of my business.

HAMLET: Sir, I cannot. 605

ROSENCRANTZ: What, my lord?

hamlet: Make you a wholesome answer; my wit's diseased.
But, sir, such answer as I can make, you shall command, or
rather, as you say, my mother. Therefore no more, but to
the matter. My mother, you say— 610

ROSENCRANTZ: Then thus she says: your behavior hath struck
her into amazement and admiration.[7]

HAMLET: O wonderful son, that can so stonish[8] a mother! But
is there no sequel at the heels of his mother's admiration?
Impart. 615

ROSENCRANTZ: She desires to speak with you in her closet[9] ere
you go to bed.

HAMLET: We shall obey, were she ten times our mother. Have
you any further trade with us?

ROSENCRANTZ: My lord, you once did love me. 620

HAMLET: And do still, by these pickers and stealers.[1]

ROSENCRANTZ: Good my lord, what is your cause of distemper? You do surely bar the door upon your own liberty, if
you deny your griefs to your friend.

HAMLET: Sir, I lack advancement. 625

ROSENCRANTZ: How can that be, when you have the voice of
the king himself for your succession in Denmark?

HAMLET: Ay, sir, but "while the grass grows"—the proverb[2] is
something musty.

[Enter the PLAYERS with recorders.]

O, the recorders! Let me see one. To withdraw with you[3]— 630
why do you go about to recover the wind of me, as if you
would drive me into a toil?[4]

GUILDENSTERN: O my lord, if my duty be too bold, my love is
too unmannerly.

6. That is, to the queen.
7. Wonder.
8. Astonish.
9. Bedroom.
1. These hands.
2. The proverb ends "the horse starves."

3. Let me step aside.
4. The figure is from hunting. Hamlet
asks why Guildenstern is attempting to get
windward of him, as if he would drive him
into a net.

HAMLET: I do not well understand that. Will you play upon 635
this pipe?[5]

GUILDENSTERN: My lord, I cannot.

HAMLET: I pray you.

GUILDENSTERN: Believe me, I cannot.

HAMLET: I do beseech you. 640

GUILDENSTERN: I know no touch of it,[6] my lord.

HAMLET: It is as easy as lying. Govern these ventages[7] with
your fingers and thumb, give it breath with your mouth,
and it will discourse most eloquent music. Look you, these
are the stops. 645

GUILDENSTERN: But these cannot I command to any utt'rance
of harmony. I have not the skill.

HAMLET: Why, look you now, how unworthy a thing you
make of me! You would play upon me, you would seem to
know my stops, you would pluck out the heart of my mys- 650
tery, you would sound[8] me from my lowest note to the top
of my compass;[9] and there is much music, excellent voice,
in this little organ, yet cannot you make it speak. 'Sblood,
do you think I am easier to be played on than a pipe? Call
me what instrument you will, though you can fret[1] me, you 655
cannot play upon me.

[*Enter* POLONIUS.]

God bless you, sir!

POLONIUS: My lord, the queen would speak with you, and
presently.

HAMLET: Do you see yonder cloud that's almost in shape of a 660
camel?

POLONIUS: By th' mass, and 'tis like a camel indeed.

HAMLET: Methinks it is like a weasel.

POLONIUS: It is backed like a weasel.

HAMLET: Or like a whale. 665

POLONIUS: Very like a whale.

5. Recorder.
6. Have no ability.
7. Cover and uncover these holes, or stops.
8. Play.
9. Range.
1. To annoy; also, to play a guitar or similar instrument using the "frets," or small bars on the neck.

HAMLET: Then I will come to my mother by and by. [*Aside.*]
  They fool me to the top of my bent.[2]—I will come by and
  by.
POLONIUS: I will say so.   [*Exit.*]   670
HAMLET: "By and by" is easily said. Leave me, friends.
                              [*Exeunt all but* HAMLET.]
  'Tis now the very witching time of night,
  When churchyards yawn, and hell itself breathes out
  Contagion to this world. Now could I drink hot blood,
  And do such bitter business as the day   675
  Would quake to look on. Soft, now to my mother.
  O heart, lose not thy nature; let not ever
  The soul of Nero[3] enter this firm bosom.
  Let me be cruel, not unnatural;
  I will speak daggers to her, but use none.   680
  My tongue and soul in this be hypocrites—
  How in my words somever she be shent,[4]
  To give them seals[5] never, my soul, consent!   [*Exit.*]

SCENE 3

A room in the castle. Enter KING, ROSENCRANTZ *and* GUILDEN-
STERN.

KING: I like him not, nor stands it safe with us
  To let his madness range. Therefore prepare you.
  I your commission will forthwith dispatch,
  And he to England shall along with you.
  The terms of our estate[1] may not endure   5
  Hazard so near 's as doth hourly grow
  Out of his brows.
GUILDENSTERN: We will ourselves provide,[2]
  Most holy and religious fear[3] it is
  To keep those many many bodies safe

2. Treat me as an utter fool.
3. Roman emperor who reputedly mur-dered his mother.
4. However much by my words she is shamed.
5. Fulfillment in action.
1. Condition of the state.
2. Equip (for the journey).
3. Care.

That live and feed upon your majesty. 10
ROSENCRANTZ: The single and peculiar[4] life is bound
With all the strength and armor of the mind
To keep itself from noyance,[5] but much more
That spirit upon whose weal[6] depends and rests
The lives of many. The cess[7] of majesty 15
Dies not alone, but like a gulf[8] doth draw
What's near it with it. It is a massy[9] wheel
Fixed on the summit of the highest mount,
To whose huge spokes ten thousand lesser things
Are mortised and adjoined,[1] which when it falls, 20
Each small annexment, petty consequence,
Attends[2] the boist'rous ruin. Never alone
Did the king sigh, but with a general groan.
KING: Arm[3] you, I pray you, to this speedy voyage,
For we will fetters put about this fear, 25
Which now goes too free-footed.
ROSENCRANTZ: We will haste us.
          [*Exeunt* ROSENCRANTZ *and* GUILDENSTERN.]
          [*Enter* POLONIUS.]
POLONIUS: My lord, he's going to his mother's closet.
Behind the arras I'll convey myself
To hear the process. I'll warrant she'll tax him home,[4]
And as you said, and wisely was it said, 30
'Tis meet that some more audience than a mother,
Since nature makes them partial, should o'erhear
The speech, of vantage.[5] Fare you well, my liege.
I'll call upon you ere you go to bed,
And tell you what I know.
KING: Thanks, dear my lord. 35
          [*Exit* POLONIUS.]
O, my offence is rank, it smells to heaven;

---

4. The individual and private.   1. Are attached.
5. Harm.   2. Joins in.
6. Welfare.   3. Prepare.
7. Cessation.   4. Sharply. *Process:* proceedings.
8. Whirlpool.   5. From a position of vantage.
9. Massive.

It hath the primal eldest curse[6] upon't,
A brother's murder. Pray can I not,
Though inclination be as sharp as will.
My stronger guilt defeats my strong intent,   40
And like a man to double business[7] bound,
I stand in pause where I shall first begin,
And both neglect. What if this cursèd hand
Were thicker than itself with brother's blood,
Is there not rain enough in the sweet heavens   45
To wash it white as snow? Whereto serves mercy
But to confront the visage of offence?
And what's in prayer but this twofold force,
To be forestallèd[8] ere we come to fall,
Or pardoned being down?[9] Then I'll look up.   50
My fault is past. But, O, what form of prayer
Can serve my turn? "Forgive me my foul murder"?
That cannot be, since I am still possessed
Of those effects[1] for which I did the murder—
My crown, mine own ambition, and my queen.   55
May one be pardoned and retain th' offence?[2]
In the corrupted currents of this world
Offence's gilded[3] hand may shove by justice,
And oft 'tis seen the wicked prize itself
Buys out the law. But 'tis not so above.   60
There is no shuffling; there the action[4] lies
In his true nature, and we ourselves compelled,
Even to the teeth and forehead of[5] our faults,
To give in evidence. What then? What rests?[6]
Try what repentance can. What can it not?   65
Yet what can it when one cannot repent?
O wretched state! O bosom black as death!
O limèd[7] soul, that struggling to be free

---

6. That is, of Cain (the biblical figure
who murdered his brother, Abel).
    7. Two mutually opposed interests.
    8. Prevented (from sin).
    9. Having sinned.
    1. Gains.

2. That is, benefits of the offense.
3. Bearing gold as a bribe.
4. Legal case.
5. Face-to-face with.
6. Remains.
7. Caught as with birdlime.

Art more engaged! Help, angels! Make assay.
Bow, stubborn knees, and heart with strings of steel,   70
Be soft as sinews of the new-born babe.
All may be well. [*He kneels.*]
     [*Enter* HAMLET.]
HAMLET: Now might I do it pat,[8] now 'a is a-praying,
And now I'll do't—and so 'a goes to heaven,
And so am I revenged. That would be scanned.[9]   75
A villain kills my father, and for that,
I, his sole son, do this same villain send
To heaven.
Why, this is hire and salary, not revenge.
'A took my father grossly, full of bread,[1]   80
With all his crimes broad blown, as flush[2] as May;
And how his audit stands who knows save heaven?
But in our circumstance and course of thought
'Tis heavy with him; and am I then revenged
To take him in the purging of his soul,   85
When he is fit and seasoned[3] for his passage?
No.
Up, sword, and know thou a more horrid hent.[4]
When he is drunk, asleep, or in his rage,
Or in th' incestuous pleasure of his bed,   90
At game a-swearing, or about some act
That has no relish[5] of salvation in't—
Then trip him, that his heels may kick at heaven,
And that his soul may be as damned and black
As hell, whereto it goes. My mother stays.   95
This physic[6] but prolongs thy sickly days.   [*Exit.*]
KING: [*Rising.*] My words fly up, my thoughts remain below.
Words without thoughts never to heaven go.   [*Exit.*]

8. Easily.   3. Ready.
9. Calls for evaluation.   4. Opportunity.
1. In a state of sin and without fasting.   5. Flavor.
2. Full-blown, as vigorous.   6. Medicine.

SCENE 4

The Queen's chamber. Enter QUEEN *and* POLONIUS.

POLONIUS: 'A will come straight. Look you lay home to[1] him.
　Tell him his pranks have been too broad[2] to bear with,
　And that your grace hath screen'd and stood between
　Much heat and him. I'll silence me even here.
　Pray you be round[3] with him.　　　　　　　　　　　　　5
HAMLET: [*Within.*] Mother, mother, mother!
QUEEN: I'll warrant you. Fear[4] me not.
　Withdraw, I hear him coming.
　　　　[POLONIUS *goes behind the arras. Enter* HAMLET.]
HAMLET: Now, mother, what's the matter?
QUEEN: Hamlet, thou hast thy father much offended.　　　10
HAMLET: Mother, you have my father much offended.
HAMLET: Come, come, you answer with an idle tongue.
HAMLET: Go, go, you question with a wicked tongue.
QUEEN: Why, how now, Hamlet?
HAMLET:　　　　　　　　　　　　What's the matter now?
QUEEN: Have you forgot me?
HAMLET:　　　　　　　　　　No, by the rood,[5] not so.　　15
　You are the queen, your husband's brother's wife,
　And would it were not so, you are my mother.
QUEEN: Nay, then I'll set those to you that can speak.
HAMLET: Come, come, and sit you down. You shall not budge.
　You go not till I set you up a glass[6]　　　　　　　　　20
　Where you may see the inmost part of you.
QUEEN: What wilt thou do? Thou wilt not murder me?
　Help, ho!
POLONIUS: [*Behind.*] What, ho! help!
HAMLET: [*Draws.*] How now, a rat?　　　　　　　　　　25
　Dead for a ducat, dead![7] [*Kills* POLONIUS *with a pass
　　through the arras.*]
POLONIUS: [*Behind.*] O, I am slain!

---

1. Be sharp with.
2. Outrageous.
3. Direct forthright.
4. Doubt.

5. Cross.
6. Mirror.
7. I bet a gold coin he's dead.

QUEEN: O me, what hast thou done?

HAMLET: Nay, I know not.
  Is it the king?

QUEEN: O, what a rash and bloody deed is this!   30

HAMLET: A bloody deed!—almost as bad, good mother,
  As kill a king and marry with his brother.

QUEEN: As kill a king?

HAMLET: Ay, lady, it was my word.
  [*Parting the arras.*] Thou wretched, rash, intruding fool,
      farewell!
  I took thee for thy better. Take thy fortune.   35
  Thou find'st to be too busy[8] is some danger.—
  Leave wringing of your hands. Peace, sit you down
  And let me wring your heart, for so I shall
  If it be made of penetrable stuff,
  If damnéd custom have not brazed it[9] so   40
  That it be proof and bulwark against sense.[1]

QUEEN: What have I done that thou dar'st wag thy tongue
  In noise so rude against me?

HAMLET: Such an act
  That blurs the grace and blush of modesty,
  Calls virtue hypocrite, takes off the rose   45
  From the fair forehead of an innocent love
  And sets a blister[2] there, makes marriage-vows
  As false as dicers' oaths. O, such a deed
  As from the body of contraction[3] plucks
  The very soul, and sweet religion makes   50
  A rhapsody of words. Heaven's face does glow
  O'er this solidity and compound mass[4]
  With heated visage, as against the doom[5]—
  Is thought-sick at the act.

QUEEN: Ay me, what act
  That roars so loud and thunders in the index?[6]   55

HAMLET: Look here upon this picture and on this,

---

8. Officious.
9. Plated it with brass.
1. Feeling. *Proof:* armor.
2. Brand.

3. The marriage contract.
4. Meaningless mass (Earth).
5. Judgment Day.
6. Table of contents.

The counterfeit presentment[7] of two brothers.
See what a grace was seated on this brow:
Hyperion's curls, the front[8] of Jove himself,
An eye like Mars, to threaten and command,   60
A station like the herald Mercury[9]
New lighted[1] on a heaven-kissing hill—
A combination and a form indeed
Where every god did seem to set his seal,
To give the world assurance of a man.   65
This was your husband. Look you now what follows.
Here is your husband, like a mildewed ear
Blasting[2] his wholesome brother. Have you eyes?
Could you on this fair mountain leave to feed,
And batten[3] on this moor? Ha! have you eyes?   70
You cannot call it love, for at your age
The heyday in the blood is tame, it's humble,
And waits upon the judgment, and what judgment
Would step from this to this? Sense sure you have
Else could you not have motion, but sure that sense   75
Is apoplexed[4] for madness would not err,
Nor sense to ecstacy was ne'er so thralled
But it reserved some quantity of choice
To serve in such a difference.[5] What devil was't
That thus hath cozened you at hoodman-blind?[6]   80
Eyes without feeling, feeling without sight,
Ears without hands or eyes, smelling sans[7] all,
Or but a sickly part of one true sense
Could not so mope.[8] O shame! where is thy blush?
Rebellious hell,   85
If thou canst mutine[9] in a matron's bones,
To flaming youth let virtue be as wax

---

7. Portrait.
8. Forehead.
9. A bearing like that of the messenger of the gods.
1. Newly alighted.
2. Infecting. *Ear:* of corn.
3. Fatten.

4. Paralyzed.
5. The power to choose between such different men.
6. Blindman's buff. *Cozened:* cheated.
7. Without.
8. Be stupid.
9. Commit mutiny.

And melt in her own fire. Proclaim no shame
When the compulsive ardor gives the charge,[1]
Since frost itself as actively doth burn,   90
And reason panders[2] will.
QUEEN: O Hamlet, speak no more!
Thou turn'st my eyes into my very soul;
And there I see such black and grainéd[3] spots
As will not leave their tinct.[4]
HAMLET: Nay, but to live
In the rank sweat of an enseaméd[5] bed,   95
Stewed in curruption, honeying and making love
Over the nasty sty—
QUEEN: O, speak to me no more!
These words like daggers enter in my ears;
No more, sweet Hamlet.
HAMLET: A murderer and a villain,
A slave that is not twentieth part the tithe[6]   100
Of your precedent lord, a vice[7] of kings,
A cutpurse[8] of the empire and the rule,
That from a shelf the precious diadem stole
And put it in his pocket—
QUEEN: No more.   105
        [*Enter* GHOST.]
HAMLET: A king of shreds and patches—
Save me and hover o'er me with your wings,
You heavenly guards! What would your gracious figure?
QUEEN: Alas, he's mad.
HAMLET: Do you not come your tardy[9] son to chide,   110
That lapsed in time and passion lets go by
Th' important acting of your dread command?
O, say!
GHOST: Do not forget. This visitation
Is but to whet thy almost blunted purpose.   115

1. Attacks.   6. One-tenth.
2. Pimps for.   7. The "Vice" was a clown or buffoon in
3. Ingrained.   morality plays. *Precedent lord:* first husband.
4. Lose their color.   8. Pickpocket.
5. Greasy.   9. Slow to act.

But look, amazement on thy mother sits.
O, step between her and her fighting soul!
Conceit[1] in weakest bodies strongest works.
Speak to her, Hamlet.

HAMLET: How is it with you, lady?

QUEEN: Alas, how is't with you,   120
That you do bend[2] your eye on vacancy,
And with th' incorporal[3] air do hold discourse?
Forth at your eyes your spirits wildly peep,
And as the sleeping soldiers in th' alarm,
Your bedded hairs like life in excrements[4]   125
Start up and stand an end. O gentle son,
Upon the heat and flame of thy distemper
Sprinkle cool patience. Whereon do you look?

HAMLET: On him, on him! Look you how pale he glares.
His form and cause conjoined,[5] preaching to stones,   130
Would make them capable.[6]—Do not look upon me,
Lest with this piteous action you convert
My stern effects.[7] Then what I have to do
Will want true color—tears perchance for blood.

QUEEN: To whom do you speak this?   135

HAMLET: Do you see nothing there?

QUEEN: Nothing at all, yet all that is I see.

HAMLET: Nor did you nothing hear?

QUEEN: No, nothing but ourselves.

HAMLET: Why, look you there. Look how it steals away.   140
My father, in his habit[8] as he lived!
Look where he goes even now out at the portal.

                                        [*Exit* GHOST.]

QUEEN: This is the very coinage[9] of your brain.
The bodiless creation ecstasy[1]
Is very cunning[2] in.

---

1. Imagination.   7. Deeds.
2. Turn.   8. Costume.
3. Incorporeal.   9. Invention.
4. Nails and hair.   1. Madness.
5. Working together.   2. Skilled.
6. Of responding.

HAMLET: Ecstasy?   145
  My pulse as yours doth temperately keep time,
  And makes as healthful music. It is not madness
  That I have uttered. Bring me to the test,
  And I the matter will re-word, which madness
  Would gambol[3] from. Mother, for love of grace,   150
  Lay not that flattering unction[4] to your soul,
  That not your trespass but my madness speaks.
  It will but skin and film the ulcerous place
  Whiles rank corruption, mining[5] all within,
  Infects unseen. Confess yourself to heaven,   155
  Repent what's past, avoid what is to come.
  And do not spread the compost on the weeds,
  To make them ranker. Forgive me this my virtue,
  For in the fatness of these pursy[6] times
  Virtue itself of vice must pardon beg,   160
  Yea, curb[7] and woo for leave to do him good.
QUEEN: O Hamlet, thou hast cleft my heart in twain.
HAMLET: O, throw away the worser part of it,
  And live the purer with the other half.
  Good night—but go not to my uncle's bed.   165
  Assume a virtue, if you have it not.
  That monster custom[8] who all sense doth eat,
  Of habits devil, is angel yet in this,
  That to the use of actions fair and good
  He likewise gives a frock or livery   170
  That aptly[9] is put on. Refrain tonight,
  And that shall lend a kind of easiness
  To the next abstinence; the next more easy;
  For use almost can change the stamp of nature,
  And either curb the devil, or throw him out   175
  With wondrous potency. Once more, good night,
  And when you are desirous to be blest,
  I'll blessing beg of you. For this same lord

---

3. Shy away.   7. Bow.
4. Ointment.   8. Habit.
5. Undermining.   9. Easily.
6. Bloated.

I do repent; but heaven hath pleased it so,
To punish me with this, and this with me,   180
That I must be their scourge and minister.
I will bestow[1] him and will answer well
The death I gave him. So, again, good night.
I must be cruel only to be kind.
Thus bad begins and worse remains behind.   185
One word more, good lady.

QUEEN: What shall I do?

HAMLET: Not this, by no means, that I bid you do:
Let the bloat[2] king tempt you again to bed,
Pinch wanton[3] on your cheek, call you his mouse,
And let him, for a pair of reechy[4] kisses,   190
Or paddling in your neck with his damned fingers,
Make you to ravel[5] all this matter out,
That I essentially am not in madness,
But mad in craft. 'Twere good you let him know,
For who that's but a queen, fair, sober, wise,   195
Would from a paddock, from a bat, a gib,[6]
Such dear concernings hide? Who would so do?
No, in despite of sense and secrecy,
Unpeg the basket on the house's top,
Let the birds fly, and like the famous ape,   200
To try conclusions, in the basket creep
And break your own neck down.[7]

QUEEN: Be thou assured, if words be made of breath
And breath of life, I have no life to breathe
What thou hast said to me.   205

HAMLET: I must to England; you know that?

QUEEN: Alack,
I had forgot. 'Tis so concluded on.

HAMLET: There's letters sealed, and my two school-fellows,
Whom I will trust as I will adders fanged,

1. Dispose of.
2. Bloated.
3. Lewdly.
4. Foul.
5. Reveal.
6. Tomcat. *Paddock:* toad.

7. Apparently a reference to a now-lost fable in which an ape, finding a basket containing a cage of birds on a housetop, opens the cage. The birds fly away. The ape, thinking that if he were in the basket he too could fly, enters, jumps out, and breaks his neck.

They bear the mandate; they must sweep[8] my way   210
And marshal me to knavery. Let it work,
For 'tis the sport to have the enginer
Hoist with his own petard;[9] and't shall go hard
But I will delve[1] one yard below their mines
And blow them at the moon. O, 'tis most sweet   215
When in one line two crafts directly meet.
This man shall set me packing.
I'll lug the guts into the neighbor room.
Mother, good night. Indeed, this counsellor
Is now most still, most secret, and most grave,   220
Who was in life a foolish prating knave.
Come sir, to draw toward an end with you.
Good night, mother.
    [*Exit the* QUEEN. *Then exit* HAMLET *tugging* POLONIUS.]

ACT IV
SCENE 1
 A room in the castle. Enter KING, QUEEN, ROSENCRANTZ *and*
GUILDENSTERN.

KING: There's matter in these sighs, these profound heaves,
 You must translate;[1] 'tis fit we understand them.
 Where is your son?
QUEEN: Bestow this place on us a little while.
    [*Exeunt* ROSENCRANTZ *and* GUILDENSTERN.]
 Ah, mine own lord, what have I seen tonight!   5
KING: What, Gertrude? How does Hamlet?
QUEEN: Mad as the sea and wind when both contend
 Which is the mightier. In his lawless fit,
 Behind the arras hearing something stir,
 Whips out his rapier, cries "A rat, a rat!"   10
 And in this brainish apprehension[2] kills
 The unseen good old man.
KING: O heavy deed!

---

8. Prepare. *Mandate:* command.   1. Explain.
9. Blown up by his own bomb.   2. Insane notion.
1. Dig.

It had been so with us had we been there.
His liberty is full of threats to all—
To you yourself, to us, to every one.   15
Alas, how shall this bloody deed be answered?
It will be laid to us, whose providence[3]
Should have kept short, restrained, and out of haunt,[4]
This mad young man. But so much was our love,
We would not understand what was most fit;   20
But, like the owner of a foul disease,
To keep it from divulging, let it feed
Even on the pith of life. Where is he gone?
QUEEN: To draw apart the body he hath killed,
    O'er whom his very madness, like some ore   25
    Among a mineral of metals base,
    Shows itself pure: 'a weeps for what is done.
KING: O Gertrude, come away!
    The sun no sooner shall the mountains touch
    But we will ship him hence, and this vile deed   30
    We must with all our majesty and skill
    Both countenance and excuse. Ho, Guildenstern!
        [*Enter* ROSENCRANTZ *and* GUILDENSTERN.]
    Friends both, go join you with some further aid.
    Hamlet in madness hath Polonius slain,
    And from his mother's closet hath he dragged him.   35
    Go seek him out; speak fair, and bring the body
    Into the chapel. I pray you haste in this.
        [*Exeunt* ROSENCRANTZ *and* GUILDENSTERN.]
    Come, Gertrude, we'll call up our wisest friends
    And let them know both what we mean to do
    And what's untimely done;   40
    Whose whisper o'er the world's diameter,
    As level as the cannon to his blank,[5]
    Transports his poisoned shot—may miss our name,
    And hit the woundless air. O, come away!
    My soul is full of discord and dismay.   45
                                                        [*Exeunt.*]

3. Prudence.   5. Mark. *Level:* direct.
4. Away from court.

SCENE 2

A passageway. Enter HAMLET.

HAMLET: Safely stowed.

ROSENCRANTZ *and* GUILDENSTERN: [*Within.*] Hamlet! Lord
  Hamlet!

HAMLET: But soft, what noise? Who calls on Hamlet? O, here
  they come.   5

  [*Enter* ROSENCRANTZ, GUILDENSTERN, *and* OTHERS.]

ROSENCRANTZ: What have you done, my lord, with the dead
  body?

HAMLET: Compounded it with dust, whereto 'tis kin.

ROSENCRANTZ: Tell us where 'tis, that we may take it thence
  And bear it to the chapel.   10

HAMLET: Do not believe it.

ROSENCRANTZ: Believe what?

HAMLET: That I can keep your counsel and not mine own.
  Besides, to be demanded of a sponge—what replication[1]
  should be made by the son of a king?   15

ROSENCRANTZ: Take you me for a sponge, my lord?

HAMLET: Ay, sir, that soaks up the king's countenance,[2] his re-
  wards, his authorities. But such officers do the king best
  service in the end. He keeps them like an apple in the corner of his jaw, first mouthed to be last swallowed. When he   20
  needs what you have gleaned, it is but squeezing you and,
  sponge, you shall be dry again.

ROSENCRANTZ: I understand you not, my lord.

HAMLET: I am glad of it. A knavish speech sleeps in a foolish ear.

ROSENCRANTZ: My lord, you must tell us where the body is,   25
  and go with us to the king.

HAMLET: The body is with the king, but the king is not with
  the body.
  The king is a thing—

GUILDENSTERN: A thing, my lord!

HAMLET: Of nothing. Bring me to him. Hide fox, and all   30
  after.[3]   [*Exeunt.*]

---

1. Answer. *Demanded of:* questioned by.   3. Apparently a reference to a children's
2. Favor.   game like hide-and-seek.

SCENE 3
A room in the castle. Enter KING.

KING: I have sent to seek him, and to find the body.
   How dangerous is it that this man goes loose!
   Yet must not we put the strong law on him.
   He's loved of the distracted[1] multitude,
   Who like not in their judgment but their eyes,   5
   And where 'tis so, th' offender's scourge[2] is weighed,
   But never the offence. To bear all smooth and even,
   This sudden sending him away must seem
   Deliberate pause.[3] Diseases desperate grown
   By desperate appliance are relieved,   10
   Or not at all.
      [*Enter* ROSENCRANTZ, GUILDENSTERN, *and all the rest.*]
               How now! what hath befall'n?
ROSENCRANTZ: Where the dead body is bestowed, my lord,
   We cannot get from him.
KING: But where is he?
ROSENCRANTZ: Without, my lord; guarded, to know[4] your
      pleasure.
KING: Bring him before us.
ROSENCRANTZ: Ho! bring in the lord.   15
      [*They enter with* HAMLET.]
KING: Now, Hamlet, where's Polonius?
HAMLET: At supper.
KING: At supper? Where?
HAMLET: Not where he eats, but where 'a is eaten. A certain
   convocation of politic worms are e'en[5] at him. Your worm   20
   is your only emperor for diet. We fat all creatures else to fat
   us, and we fat ourselves for maggots. Your fat king and your
   lean beggar is but variable service—two dishes, but to one
   table. That's the end.
KING: Alas, alas!   25

---

1. Confused.
2. Punishment.
3. That is, not an impulse.

4. Await.
5. Now. *Convocation of politic:* gathering
of scheming (or cunning).

HAMLET: A man may fish with the worm that hath eat of a
king, and eat of the fish that hath fed of that worm.

KING: What dost thou mean by this?

HAMLET: Nothing but to show you how a king may go a
progress through the guts of a beggar.   30

KING: Where is Polonius?

HAMLET: In heaven. Send thither to see. If your messenger
find him not there, seek him i' th' other place yourself. But
if, indeed, you find him not within this month, you shall
nose[6] him as you go up the stairs into the lobby.   35

KING: [*To* ATTENDANTS.] Go seek him there.

HAMLET: 'A will stay till you come.

                              [*Exeunt* ATTENDANTS.]

KING: Hamlet, this deed, for thine especial safety—
Which we do tender, as we dearly[7] grieve
For that which thou hast done—must sent thee hence   40
With fiery quickness. Therefore prepare thyself.
The bark is ready, and the wind at help,
Th' associates tend, and everything is bent
For England.

HAMLET: For England?

KING: Ay, Hamlet.

HAMLET: Good.

KING: So it is, if thou knew'st our purposes.   45

HAMLET: I see a cherub that sees them. But come, for
England!
Farewell, dear mother.

KING: Thy loving father, Hamlet.

HAMLET: My mother. Father and mother is man and wife,
man and wife is one flesh. So, my mother. Come, for   50
England.   [*Exit.*]

KING: Follow him at foot;[8] tempt him with speed aboard.
Delay it not; I'll have him hence tonight.
Away! for everything is sealed and done
                  [*Exeunt all but the* KING.]

6. Smell.
7. Deeply. *Tender:* consider.
8. Closely.

That else leans on th' affair. Pray you make haste.   55
And, England, if my love thou hold'st at aught—
As my great power thereof may give thee sense,[9]
Since yet thy cicatrice[1] looks raw and red
After the Danish sword, and thy free awe
Pays homage to us—thou mayst not coldly set[2]   60
Our sovereign process,[3] which imports at full
By letters congruing[4] to that effect
The present death of Hamlet. Do it, England,
For like the hectic[5] in my blood he rages,
And thou must cure me. Till I know 'tis done,   65
Howe'er my haps, my joys were ne'er begun.   [*Exit.*]

SCENE 4

Near Elsinore. Enter FORTINBRAS *with his army.*

FORTINBRAS: Go, captain, from me greet the Danish king.
  Tell him that by his license Fortinbras
  Craves the conveyance[1] of a promised march
  Over his kingdom. You know the rendezvous.
  If that his majesty would aught with us,   5
  We shall express our duty in his eye,[2]
  And let him know so.
CAPTAIN: I will do't, my lord.
FORTINBRAS: Go softly on.   [*Exeunt all but the* CAPTAIN.]
    [*Enter* HAMLET, ROSENCRANTZ, GUILDENSTERN, *and*
    OTHERS.]
HAMLET: Good sir, whose powers are these?
CAPTAIN: They are of Norway, sir.   10
HAMLET: How purposed, sir, I pray you?
CAPTAIN: Against some part of Poland.
HAMLET: Who commands them, sir?
CAPTAIN: The nephew to old Norway, Fortinbras.

---

9. Of its value.   4. Agreeing.
1. Scar.   5. Chronic fever.
2. Set aside.   1. Escort.
3. Mandate.   2. Presence.

HAMLET: Goes it against the main³ of Poland, sir,   15
  Or for some frontier?
CAPTAIN: Truly to speak, and with no addition,⁴
  We go to gain a little patch of ground
  That hath in it no profit but the name.
  To pay five ducats,⁵ five, I would not farm it;   20
  Nor will it yield to Norway or the Pole
  A ranker rate should it be sold in fee.⁶
HAMLET: Why, then the Polack never will defend it.
CAPTAIN: Yes, it is already garrisoned.
HAMLET: Two thousand souls and twenty thousand ducats   25
  Will not debate the question of this straw.
  This is th' imposthume⁷ of much wealth and peace,
  That inward breaks, and shows no cause without
  Why the man dies. I humbly thank you, sir.
CAPTAIN: God b'wi'ye, sir.   [*Exit.*]
ROSENCRANTZ: Will't please you go, my lord?   30
HAMLET: I'll be with you straight. Go a little before.
            [*Exeunt all but* HAMLET.]
  How all occasions do inform against me,
  And spur my dull revenge! What is a man,
  If his chief good and market⁸ of his time
  Be but to sleep and feed? A beast, no more.   35
  Sure he that made us with such large discourse,⁹
  Looking before and after, gave us not
  That capability and godlike reason
  To fust¹ in us unused. Now, whether it be
  Bestial oblivion, or some craven scruple   40
  Of thinking too precisely on th' event²—
  A thought which, quartered, hath but one part wisdom
  And ever three parts coward—I do not know
  Why yet I live to say "This thing's to do,"
  Sith³ I have cause, and will, and strength, and means,   45

3. Central part.
4. Exaggeration.
5. That is, in rent.
6. Outright. *Ranker:* higher.
7. Abscess.

8. Occupation.
9. Ample reasoning power.
1. Grow musty.
2. Outcome.
3. Since.

To do't. Examples gross as earth exhort me.
Witness this army of such mass and charge,[4]
Led by a delicate and tender prince,
Whose spirit, with divine ambition puffed,
Makes mouths at[5] the invisible event,   50
Exposing what is mortal and unsure
To all that fortune, death, and danger dare,
Even for an eggshell. Rightly to be great
Is not to stir without great argument,
But greatly to find quarrel in a straw   55
When honor's at the stake. How stand I then,
That have a father killed, a mother stained,
Excitements of my reason and my blood,
And let all sleep, while to my shame I see
The imminent death of twenty thousand men   60
That for a fantasy and trick of fame
Go to their graves like beds, fight for a plot
Whereon the numbers cannot try the cause,
Which is not tomb enough and continent
To hide the slain?[6] O, from this time forth,   65
My thoughts be bloody, or be nothing worth!   [*Exit.*]

Scene 5

A room in the castle. Enter QUEEN, HORATIO *and a* GENTLEMAN.

QUEEN: I will not speak with her.
GENTLEMAN: She is importunate, indeed distract.
  Her mood will needs to be pitied.
QUEEN: What would she have?
GENTLEMAN: She speaks much of her father, says she hears
  There's tricks i' th' world, and hems, and beats her heart,   5
  Spurns enviously at straws,[1] speaks things in doubt
  That carry but half sense. Her speech is nothing,
  Yet the unshapéd use of it doth move

4. Expense.
5. Scorns.
6. The plot of ground involved is so small that it cannot contain the number of

men involved in fighting or furnish burial space for the number of those who will die.

1. Takes offense at trifles.

The hearers to collection;² they yawn at it,
And botch the words up fit to their own thoughts,   10
Which, as her winks and nods and gestures yield them,
Indeed would make one think there might be thought,
Though nothing sure, yet much unhappily.
HORATIO: 'Twere good she were spoken with, for she may
    strew
Dangerous conjectures in ill-breeding minds.   15
QUEEN: Let her come in.   [*Exit* GENTLEMAN.]
    [*Aside.*] To my sick soul, as sin's true nature is,
Each toy seems prologue to some great amiss.³
So full of artless jealousy is guilt,
It spills itself in fearing to be spilt.   20
    [*Enter* OPHELIA *distracted.*]
OPHELIA: Where is the beauteous majesty of Denmark?
QUEEN: How now, Ophelia!
OPHELIA: [*Sings.*]
    How should I your true love know
        From another one?
    By his cockle hat and staff,⁴   25
        And his sandal shoon.⁵
QUEEN: Alas, sweet lady, what imports this song?
OPHELIA: Say you? Nay, pray you mark. [*Sings.*]
    He is dead and gone, lady,
        He is dead and gone;   30
    At his head a grass-green turf,
        At his heels a stone.
      O, ho!
QUEEN: Nay, but Ophelia—
OPHELIA: Pray you mark. [*Sings.*]
    White his shroud as the mountain snow—
    [*Enter* KING.]
QUEEN: Alas, look here, my lord.   35
OPHELIA: [*Sings.*]
    Larded all with sweet flowers;

2. To decipher her meaning.
3. Catastrophe. *Toy:* trifle.
4. Things associated with a pilgrimage.
5. Shoes.

Which bewept to the grave did not go
    With true-love showers.
KING: How do you, pretty lady?
OPHELIA: Well, God dild[6] you! They say the owl was a baker's   40
    daughter. Lord, we know what we are, but know not what
    we may be. God be at your table!
KING: Conceit[7] upon her father.
OPHELIA: Pray let's have no words of this, but when they ask
    you what it means, say you this: [*Sings.*]   45
        Tomorrow is Saint Valentine's day,
            All in the morning betime,
        And I a maid at your window,
            To be your Valentine.

        Then up he rose, and donn'd his clo'es,   50
            And dupped the chamber-door,
        Let in the maid, that out a maid[8]
            Never departed more.
KING: Pretty Ophelia!
OPHELIA: Indeed, without an oath, I'll make an end on't.   55
    [*Sings.*]
        By Gis[9] and by Saint Charity,
            Alack, and fie for shame!
        Young men will do't, if they come to't;
            By Cock,[1] they are to blame.
        Quoth she "before you tumbled me,   60
            You promised me to wed."
    He answers:
        "So would I'a done, by yonder sun,
            An thou hadst not come to my bed."
KING: How long hath she been thus?   65
OPHELIA: I hope all will be well. We must be patient, but I
    cannot choose but weep to think they would lay him i'
    th' cold ground. My brother shall know of it, and so I
    thank you for your good counsel. Come, my coach! Good

6. Yield.   9. Jesus.
7. Thought.   1. God.
8. Virgin. *Dupped:* opened.

night, ladies, good night. Sweet ladies, good night, good   70
night.

                                                    [*Exit.*]
KING: Follow her close; give her good watch, I pray you.

                    [*Exeunt* HORATIO *and* GENTLEMAN.]
O, this is the poison of deep grief; it springs
All from her father's death, and now behold!
O Gertrude, Gertrude!   75
When sorrows come, they come not single spies,
But in battalions: first, her father slain;
Next, your son gone, and he most violent author
Of his own just remove; the people muddied,[2]
Thick and unwholesome in their thoughts and whispers   80
For good Polonius' death; and we have done but greenly[3]
In hugger-mugger[4] to inter him; poor Ophelia
Divided from herself and her fair judgment,
Without the which we are pictures, or mere beasts;
Last, and as much containing as all these,   85
Her brother is in secret come from France,
Feeds on his wonder, keeps himself in clouds,
And wants not buzzers[5] to infect his ear
With pestilent speeches of his father's death,
Wherein necessity, of matter beggared,[6]   90
Will nothing stick our person to arraign[7]
In ear and ear.[8] O my dear Gertrude, this,
Like to a murd'ring piece,[9] in many places
Gives me superfluous death.

            [*A noise within.*]
QUEEN: Alack, what noise is this?   95
KING: Attend!
Where are my Switzers?[1] Let them guard the door.
What is the matter?

---

2. Disturbed.   7. Accuse. *Stick:* hesitate.
3. Without judgment.   8. From both sides.
4. Haste.   9. A cannon that fires grapeshot so as to
5. And doesn't lack scandal mongers.   kill as many soldiers as possible.
Couds: rumors, suspicions.   1. Swiss guards.
6. Short on facts.

MESSENGER: Save yourself, my lord.
 The ocean, overpeering of his list,[2]
 Eats not the flats with more impiteous[3] haste   100
 Then young Laertes, in a riotous head,[4]
 O'erbears your officers. The rabble call him lord,
 And as the world were now but to begin,
 Antiquity forgot, custom not known,
 The ratifiers and props of every word,   105
 They cry "Choose we, Laertes shall be king."
 Caps, hands, and tongues, applaud it to the clouds,
 "Laertes shall be king, Laertes king."
QUEEN: How cheerfully on the false trail they cry![5]
 [*A noise within.*]
 O, this is counter,[6] you false Danish dogs!   110
KING: The doors are broke.
 [*Enter* LAERTES, *with* OTHERS.]
LAERTES: Where is this king?—Sirs, stand you all without.
ALL: No, let's come in.
LAERTES: I pray you give me leave.
ALL: We will, we will.
LAERTES: I thank you. Keep[7] the door.
         [*Exeunt his followers.*]
       O thou vile king,   115
 Give me my father!
QUEEN: Calmly, good Laertes.
LAERTES: That drop of blood that's calm proclaims me bastard,
 Cries cuckold to my father, brands the harlot
 Even here between the chaste unsmirchéd brow
 Of my true mother.
KING: What is the cause, Laertes,   120
 That thy rebellion looks so giant-like?
 Let him go, Gertrude. Do not fear[8] our person.
 There's such divinity doth hedge a king

---

2. Towering above its limits.   6. Backward.
3. Pitiless.   7. Guard.
4. With an armed band.   8. Fear for.
5. As if following the scent.

That treason can but peep to[9] what it would,
Acts little of his will. Tell me, Laertes. 125
Why thou art thus incensed. Let him go, Gertrude.
Speak, man.
LAERTES: Where is my father?
KING: Dead.
QUEEN: But not by him.
KING: Let him demand[1] his fill.
LAERTES: How came he dead? I'll not be juggled with.
To hell allegiance, vows to the blackest devil, 130
Conscience and grace to the profoundest pit!
I dare damnation. To this point I stand,
That both the worlds I give to negligence,[2]
Let come what comes, only I'll be revenged
Most throughly[3] for my father. 135
KING: Who shall stay you?
LAERTES: My will, not all the world's.
And for my means, I'll husband[4] them so well
They shall go far with little.
KING: Good Laertes,
If you desire to know the certainty
Of your dear father, is't writ in your revenge 140
That, swoopstake,[5] you will draw both friend and foe,
Winner and loser?
LAERTES: None but his enemies.
KING: Will you know them, then?
LAERTES: To his good friends thus wide I'll ope my arms,
And like the kind life-rend'ring pelican,[6] 145
Repast them with my blood.
KING: Why, now you speak
Like a good child and a true gentleman.
That I am guiltless of your father's death,

---

9. See over or through a barrier.
1. Question.
2. That I disregard this world and the next.
3. Thoroughly.
4. Manage.
5. Sweeping the board.
6. The pelican was believed to feed her young with her own blood.

And am most sensibly in grief for it,
It shall as level[7] to your judgment 'pear   150
As day does to your eye.
    [*A noise within*: "Let her come in."]
LAERTES: How now? What noise is that?
    [*Enter* OPHELIA.]
    O, heat dry up my brains! tears seven times salt
Burn out the sense and virtue[8] of mine eye!
By heaven, thy madness shall be paid with weight   155
Till our scale turn the beam. O rose of May,
Dear maid, kind sister, sweet Ophelia!
O heavens! is't possible a young maid's wits
Should be as mortal as an old man's life?
Nature is fine[9] in love, and where 'tis fine   160
It sends some precious instances of itself
After the thing it loves.
OPHELIA: [*Sings.*]
    They bore him barefac'd on the bier;
      Hey non nonny, nonny, hey nonny;
    And in his grave rain'd many a tear—   165
Fare you well, my dove!
LAERTES: Hadst thou thy wits, and didst persuade revenge,
    It could not move thus.
OPHELIA: You must sing "A-down, a-down, and you call him
a-down-a." O, how the wheel becomes it! It is the false   170
steward, that stole his master's daughter.
LAERTES: This nothing's more than matter.
OPHELIA: There's a rosemary, that's for remembrance. Pray
you, love, remember. And there is pansies, that's for
thoughts.   175
LAERTES: A document[1] in madness, thoughts and remembrance fitted.
OPHELIA: There's fennel for you, and columbines. There's rue
for you, and here's some for me. We may call it herb of
grace a Sundays. O, you must wear your rue with a differ-   180

---

7. Plain.   9. Refined.
8. The feeling and function.   1. Lesson

ence. There's a daisy. I would give you some violets,[2] but
they withered all when my father died. They say 'a made a
good end. [*Sings.*]
  For bonny sweet Robin is all my joy.
LAERTES: Thought and affliction, passion, hell itself,   185
  She turns to favor[3] and to prettiness.
OPHELIA: [*Sings.*]
  And will 'a not come again?
  And will 'a not come again?
    No, no, he is dead,
    Go to thy death-bed,   190
  He never will come again.

  His beard was as white as snow,
  All flaxen was his poll;[4]
    He is gone, he is gone,
    And we cast away moan: 195
  God-a-mercy on his soul!
And of all Christian souls, I pray God. God b'wi'you.
                                                     [*Exit.*]
LAERTES: Do you see this, O God?
KING: Laertes, I must commune with your grief,
  Or you deny me right. Go but apart,   200
  Make choice of whom your wisest friends you will,
  And they shall hear and judge 'twixt you and me.
  If by direct or by collateral[5] hand
  They find us touched,[6] we will our kingdom give,
  Our crown, our life, and all that we call ours,   205
  To you in satisfaction; but if not,
  Be you content to lend your patience to us,
  And we shall jointly labor with your soul
  To give it due content.
LAERTES: Let this be so.
  His means of death, his obscure funeral—   210

---

2. Fennel symbolized flattery; columbines,   4. Head.
ungratefulness; rue, grief; daisies, lies; and   5. Indirect.
violets, loyalty.   6. By guilt.
  3. Beauty.

No trophy, sword, nor hatchment,⁷ o'er his bones,
No noble rite nor formal ostentation⁸—
Cry to be heard, as 'twere from heaven to earth,
That I must call't in question.
KING: So you shall;
And where th' offence is, let the great axe fall.   215
I pray you go with me.   [*Exeunt.*]

SCENE 6
Another room in the castle. Enter HORATIO *and a* GENTLEMAN.

HORATIO: What are they that would speak with me?
GENTLEMAN: Sea-faring men, sir. They say they have letters for
you.
HORATIO: Let them come in.   [*Exit* GENTLEMAN.]
I do not know from what part of the world   5
I should be greeted, if not from Lord Hamlet.
    [*Enter* SAILORS.]
SAILOR: God bless you, sir.
HORATIO: Let him bless thee too.
SAILOR: 'A shall, sir, an't please him. There's a letter for you,
sir—it came from th' ambassador that was bound for En-   10
gland—if your name be Horatio, as I am let to know¹
it is.
HORATIO: [*Reads.*] "Horatio, when thou shalt have over-
looked² this, give these fellows some means³ to the king.
They have letters for him. Ere we were two days old at sea, 15
a pirate of very warlike appointment⁴ gave us chase. Finding ourselves too slow of sail, we put on a compelled valor,
and in the grapple I boarded them. On the instant they got
clear of our ship, so I alone became their prisoner. They
have dealt with me like thieves of mercy, but they knew   20
what they did; I am to do a good turn for them. Let the
king have the letters I have sent, and repair thou to me with

7. Coat of arms.
8. Pomp.
1. Informed.

2. Read through.
3. Access.
4. Equipment.

as much speed as thou wouldest fly death. I have words to
speak in thine ear will make thee dumb; yet are they much
too light for the bore of the matter.[5] These good fellows   25
will bring thee where I am. Rosencrantz and Guildenstern
hold their course for England. Of them I have much to tell
thee. Farewell.

He that thou knowest thine, Hamlet."

Come, I will give you way[6] for these your letters,   30
And do't the speedier that you may direct me
To him from whom you brought them.   [*Exeunt.*]

SCENE 7

Another room in the castle. Enter KING *and* LAERTES.

KING: Now must your conscience my acquittance seal,[1]
And you must put me in your heart for friend,
Sith you have heard, and with a knowing ear,
That he which hath your noble father slain
Pursued my life.
LAERTES: It well appears. But tell me   5
Why you proceeded not against these feats,
So criminal and so capital in nature,
As by your safety, greatness, wisdom, all things else,
You mainly were stirred up.
KING: O, for two special reasons,
Which may to you, perhaps, seem much unsinewed,[2]   10
But yet to me th' are strong. The queen his mother
Lives almost by his looks, and for myself—
My virtue or my plague, be it either which—
She is so conjunctive[3] to my life and soul
That, as the star moves not but in his sphere,[4]   15
I could not but by her. The other motive,

5. A figure from gunnery, referring to
shot that is too small for the size of the
weapons to be fired.
6. Means of delivery.
1. Grant me innocent.
2. Weak.

3. Closely joined.
4. A reference to the Ptolemaic cosmol-
ogy, in which planets and stars were believed
to revolve in crystalline spheres concentri-
cally about Earth.

Why to a public count⁵ I might not go,
Is the great love the general gender⁶ bear him,
Who, dipping all his faults in their affection,
Work like the spring that turneth wood to stone,⁷   20
Convert his gyves⁸ to graces; so that my arrows,
Too slightly timbered⁹ for so loud a wind,
Would have reverted to my bow again,
But not where I had aimed them.

LAERTES: And so have I a noble father lost,   25
A sister driven into desp'rate terms,
Whose worth, if praises may go back again,
Stood challenger on mount of all the age
For her perfections.¹ But my revenge will come.

KING: Break not your sleeps for that. You must not think   30
That we are made of stuff so flat and dull
That we can let our beard be shook with danger,
And think it pastime. You shortly shall hear more.
I loved you father, and we love our self,
And that, I hope, will teach you to imagine—   35
    [*Enter a* MESSENGER *with letters.*]
How now? What news?

MESSENGER: Letters, my lord, from Hamlet.
These to your majesty; this to the queen.

KING: From Hamlet! Who brought them?

MESSENGER: Sailors, my lord, they say. I saw them not.
They were given me by Claudio; he received them   40
Of him that brought them.

KING: Laertes, you shall hear them.—
Leave us.   [*Exit* MESSENGER.]
[*Reads.*] "High and mighty, you shall know I am set naked
on your kingdom. Tomorrow shall I beg leave to see your
kingly eyes; when I shall, first asking your pardon there-   45

---

5. Reckoning.
6. Common people.
7. Certain English springs contain so
much lime that a lime covering will be deposited on a log that sits in one of them long
enough.

8. Shackles, that is, faults.
9. Shafted.
1. Challenged the world to match her
perfections.

unto, recount the occasion of my sudden and more strange
return.

Hamlet."

What should this mean? Are all the rest come back?
Or is it some abuse,[2] and no such thing?   50
LAERTES: Know you the hand?
KING: 'Tis Hamlet's character.[3] "Naked"!
  And in a postscript here, he says "alone."
  Can you devise[4] me?
LAERTES: I am lost in it, my lord. But let him come.   55
  It warms the very sickness in my heart
  That I shall live and tell him to his teeth
  "Thus didest thou."
KING: If it be so, Laertes—
  As how should it be so, how otherwise?—
  Will you be ruled by me?
LAERTES: Ay, my lord,   60
  So you will not o'errule me to a peace.
KING: To thine own peace. If he be now returned,
  As checking at[5] his voyage, and that he means
  No more to undertake it, I will work him
  To an exploit now ripe in my device,   65
  Under the which he shall not choose but fall;
  And for his death no wind of blame shall breathe
  But even his mother shall uncharge[6] the practice
  And call it accident.
LAERTES: My lord, I will be ruled;
  The rather if you could devise it so   70
  That I might be the organ.[7]
KING: It falls right.
  You have been talked of since your travel much,
  And that in Hamlet's hearing, for a quality
  Wherein they say you shine. Your sum of parts
  Did not together pluck such envy from him   75

2. Trick.
3. Handwriting.
4. Explain it to.
5. Turning aside from.
6. Not find villainy in.
7. Instrument.

As did that one, and that, in my regard,
Of the unworthiest siege.[8]
LAERTES: What part is that, my lord?
KING: A very riband in the cap of youth,
   Yet needful too, for youth no less becomes
   The light and careless livery that it wears   80
   Than settled age his sables and his weeds,[9]
   Importing health and graveness. Two months since
   Here was a gentleman of Normandy.
   I have seen myself, and served against, the French,
   And they can[1] well on horseback, but this gallant   85
   Had witchcraft in't. He grew unto his seat,
   And to such wondrous doing brought his horse,
   As had he been incorpsed and demi-natured[2]
   With the brave beast. So far he topped my thought
   That I, in forgery[3] of shapes and tricks,   90
   Come short of what he did.
LAERTES: A Norman was't?
KING: A Norman.
LAERTES: Upon my life, Lamord.
KING: The very same.
LAERTES: I know him well. He is the brooch indeed
   And gem of all the nation.   95
KING: He made confession[4] of you,
   And gave you such a masterly report
   For art and exercise in your defence,[5]
   And for your rapier most especial,
   That he cried out 'twould be a sight indeed   100
   If one could match you. The scrimers[6] of their nation
   He swore had neither motion, guard, nor eye,
   If you opposed them. Sir, this report of his
   Did Hamlet so envenom with his envy
   That he could nothing do but wish and beg   105

8. Rank.   3. Imagination.
9. Dignified clothing.   4. Gave a report.
1. Perform.   5. Skill in fencing.
2. Shared a body and a nature.   6. Swordsmen.

Your sudden coming o'er, to play with you.
Now out of this—
LAERTES: What out of this, my lord?
KING: Laertes, was your father dear to you?
  Or are you like the painting of a sorrow,
  A face without a heart?
LAERTES: Why ask you this?   110
KING: Not that I think you did not love your father,
  But that I know love is begun by time,
  And that I see in passages of proof,[7]
  Time qualifies the spark and fire of it.
  There lives within the very flame of love   115
  A kind of wick or snuff that will abate it,
  And nothing is at a like goodness still,
  For goodness, growing to a plurisy,[8]
  Dies in his own too much.[9] That we would do,
  We should do when we would; for this "would" changes,   120
  And hath abatements and delays as many
  As there are tongues, are hands, are accidents,
  And then this "should" is like a spendthrift's sigh
  That hurts by easing. But to the quick of th' ulcer—
  Hamlet comes back; what would you undertake   125
  To show yourself in deed your father's son
  More than in words?
LAERTES: To cut his throat i' th' church.
KING: No place indeed should murder sanctuarize;[1]
  Revenge should have no bounds. But, good Laertes,
  Will you do this? Keep close within your chamber.   130
  Hamlet returned shall know you are come home.
  We'll put on those shall praise your excellence,
  And set a double varnish[2] on the fame
  The Frenchman gave you, bring you in fine[3] together,
  And wager on your heads. He, being remiss,[4]   135

---

7. Tests of experience.
8. Fullness.
9. Excess.
1. Provide sanctuary for murder.

2. Gloss.
3. In short.
4. Careless.

Most generous, and free from all contriving,
Will not peruse⁵ the foils, so that with ease,
Or with a little shuffling, you may choose
A sword unbated,⁶ and in a pass of practice
Requite him for your father.

LAERTES: I will do't,   140
And for that purpose I'll anoint my sword.
I bought an unction of a mountebank
So mortal that but dip a knife in it,
Where it draws blood no cataplasm⁷ so rare,
Collected from all simples⁸ that have virtue   145
Under the moon, can save the thing from death
That is but scratched withal. I'll touch my point
With this contagion, that if I gall⁹ him slightly,
It may be death.

KING: Let's further think of this,
Weigh what convenience both of time and means   150
May fit us to our shape. If this should fail,
And that our drift look¹ through our bad performance,
'Twere better not assayed. Therefore this project
Should have a back or second that might hold
If this did blast in proof.² Soft, let me see.   155
We'll make a solemn wager on your cunnings—
I ha't.
When in your motion you are hot and dry—
As make your bouts more violent to that end—
And that he calls for drink, I'll have prepared him   160
A chalice for the nonce, whereon but sipping,
If he by chance escape your venomed stuck,³
Our purpose may hold there.—But stay, what noise?
    [*Enter* QUEEN.]

QUEEN: One woe doth tread upon another's heel,
So fast they follow. Your sister's drowned, Laertes.   165

LAERTES: Drowned? O, where?

---

5. Examine.
6. Not blunted.
7. Poultice.
8. Herbs.

9. Scratch.
1. Intent become obvious.
2. Fail when tried.
3. Thrust.

QUEEN: There is a willow grows aslant the brook
    That shows his hoar leaves in the glassy stream.
    Therewith fantastic garlands did she make
    Of crowflowers, nettles, daisies, and long purples   170
    That liberal shepherds give a grosser[4] name,
    But our cold[5] maids do dead men's fingers call them.
    There on the pendent boughs her coronet weeds
    Clamb'ring to hang, an envious[6] sliver broke,
    When down her weedy trophies and herself   175
    Fell in the weeping brook. Her clothes spread wide,
    And mermaid-like awhile they bore her up,
    Which time she chanted snatches of old tunes,
    As one incapable[7] of her own distress,
    Or like a creature native and indued[8]   180
    Unto that element. But long it could not be
    Till that her garments, heavy with their drink,
    Pulled the poor wretch from her melodious lay
    To muddy death.
LAERTES: Alas, then she is drowned?
QUEEN: Drowned, drowned.   185
LAERTES: Too much of water hast thou, poor Ophelia,
    And therefore I forbid my tears; but yet
    It is our trick; nature her custom holds,
    Let shame say what it will. When these[9] are gone,
    The woman will be out. Adieu, my lord.   190
    I have a speech o' fire that fain would blaze
    But that this folly drowns it.   [Exit.]
KING: Let's follow, Gertrude.
    How much I had to do to calm his rage!
    Now fear I this will give it start again;
    Therefore let's follow.   [Exeunt.] 195

---

4. Coarser. *Liberal:* vulgar.   7. Unaware.
5. Chaste.   8. Habituated.
6. Malicious.   9. His tears.

ACT V

SCENE 1

A churchyard. Enter two CLOWNS.[1]

CLOWN: Is she to be buried in Christian burial when she wilfully seeks her own salvation?

OTHER: I tell thee she is. Therefore make her grave straight. The crowner hath sat on her,[2] and finds it Christian burial.   5

CLOWN: How can that be, unless she drowned herself in her own defence?

OTHER: Why, 'tis found so.

CLOWN: It must be "se offendendo";[3] it cannot be else. For here lies the point: if I drown myself wittingly, it argues an   10
act, and an act hath three branches— it is to act, to do, to perform; argal,[4] she drowned herself wittingly.

OTHER: Nay, but hear you, Goodman Delver.

CLOWN: Give me leave. Here lies the water; good. Here stands the man; good. If the man go to this water and drown himself, it is, will he, nill he, he goes—mark you that. But if   15
the water come to him and drown him, he drowns not himself. Argal, he that is not guilty of his own death shortens not his own life.

OTHER: But is this law?   20

CLOWN: Ay, marry, is't; crowner's quest law.

OTHER: Will you ha' the truth on't? If this had not been a gentlewoman, she should have been buried out o' Christian burial.

CLOWN: Why, there thou say'st. And the more pity that great   25
folk should have count'nance[5] in this world to drown or hang themselves more than their even-Christen.[6] Come, my spade. There is no ancient gentlemen but gard'ners, ditchers, and grave-makers. They hold up Adam's profession.   30

---

1. Rustics.
2. Coroner held an inquest (below, "quest").
3. An error for *se defendendo*, "in self-defense."
4. An error for *ergo*.
5. Approval.
6. Fellow Christians.

OTHER: Was he a gentleman?

CLOWN: 'A was the first that ever bore arms.

OTHER: Why, he had none.

CLOWN: What, art a heathen? How dost thou understand the
Scripture? The Scripture says Adam digged. Could he dig   35
without arms? I'll put another question to thee. If thou an-
swerest me not to the purpose, confess thyself—

OTHER: Go to.

CLOWN: What is he that builds stronger than either the mason, the shipwright, or the carpenter?   40

OTHER: The gallows-maker, for that frame outlives a thousand
tenants.

CLOWN: I like thy wit well, in good faith. The gallows does
well. But how does it well? It does well to those that do ill.
Now thou dost ill to say the gallows is built stronger than   45
the church. Argal, the gallows may do well to thee. To't
again,[7] come.

OTHER: Who builds stronger than a mason, a shipwright, or a
carpenter?

CLOWN: Ay tell me that, and unyoke.[8]   50

OTHER: Marry, now I can tell.

CLOWN: To't.

OTHER: Mass, I cannot tell.

CLOWN: Cudgel thy brains no more about it, for your dull ass
will not mend his pace with beating. And when you are   55
asked this question next, say "a grave maker." The houses
he makes lasts till doomsday. Go, get thee in, and fetch me
a stoup[9] of liquor.   [*Exit* OTHER CLOWN.]
    [*Enter* HAMLET *and* HORATIO *as* CLOWN *digs and sings.*]
    In youth, when I did love, did love,
        Methought it was very sweet,   60
    To contract the time for-a my behove,[1]
        O, methought there-a was nothing-a meet.

HAMLET: Has this fellow no feeling of his business, that 'a
sings in grave-making?

---

7. Guess again.   9. Mug.
8. Finish the matter.   1. Advantage. *Contract:* shorten.

HORATIO: Custom hath made it in him a property of easiness.   65
HAMLET: 'Tis e'en so. The band of little employment hath the
    daintier sense.
CLOWN: [*Sings.*]
    But age, with his stealing steps,
        Hath clawed me in his clutch,
    And hath shipped me into the land,   70
        As if I had never been such. [*Throws up a skull.*]
HAMLET: That skull had a tongue in it, and could sing once.
    How the knave jowls[2] it to the ground, as if 'twere Cain's
    jawbone, that did the first murder! This might be the pate
    of a politician, which this ass now o'erreaches;[3] one that   75
    would circumvent God, might it not?
HORATIO: It might, my lord.
HAMLET: Or of a courtier, which could say, "Good morrow,
    sweet lord! How does thou, sweet lord?" This might be my
    Lord Such-a-one, that praised my Lord Such-a-one's horse,   80
    when 'a meant to beg it, might it not?
HORATIO: Ay, my lord.
HAMLET: Why, e'en so, and now my Lady Worm's, chapless,[4]
    and knock'd about the mazzard[5] with a sexton's spade.
    Here's fine revolution, an[6] we had the trick to see't. Did   85
    these bones cost no more the breeding but to play at
    loggets[7] with them? Mine ache to think on't.
CLOWN: [*Sings.*]
    A pick-axe and a spade, a spade,
        For and a shrouding sheet:
    O, a pit of clay for to be made   90
        For such a guest is meet. [*Throws up another skull.*]
HAMLET: There's another. Why may not that be the skull of a
    lawyer? Where be his quiddities now, his quillets, his cases,
    his tenures, and his tricks?[8] Why does he suffer this mad
    knave now to knock him about the sconce[9] with a dirty   95

2. Hurls.
3. Gets the better of.
4. Lacking a lower jaw.
5. Head.
6. Reversal of fortune, if.

7. Small pieces of wood thrown as part of a game.
8. In this speech Hamlet lists legal terms relating to property transactions.
9. Head.

shovel, and will not tell him of his action of battery? Hum! This fellow might be in's time a great buyer of land, with his statutes, his recognizances, his fines, his double vouchers, his recoveries. Is this the fine[1] of his fines, and the recovery of his recoveries, to have his fine pate full of fine dirt? Will his vouchers vouch him no more of his purchases, and double ones too, than the length and breadth of a pair of indentures?[2] The very conveyances of his lands will scarcely lie in this box, and must th' inheritor himself have no more, ha?

HORATIO: Not a jot more, my lord.

HAMLET: Is not parchment made of sheepskins?

HORATIO: Ay, my lord, and of calves' skins too.

HAMLET: They are sheep and calves which seek out assurance in that. I will speak to this fellow. Whose grave's this, sirrah?

CLOWN: Mine, sir. [*Sings.*]
        O, a pit of clay for to be made
            For such a guest is meet.

HAMLET: I think it be thine indeed, for thou liest in't.

CLOWN: You lie out on't, sir, and therefore 'tis not yours. For my part, I do not lie in't, yet it is mine.

HAMLET: Thou dost lie in't, to be in't and say it is thine. 'Tis for the dead, not for the quick;[3] therefore thou liest.

CLOWN: 'Tis a quick lie, sir; 'twill away again from me to you.

HAMLET: What man dost thou dig it for?

CLOWN: For no man, sir.

HAMLET: What woman, then?

CLOWN: For none neither.

HAMLET: Who is to be buried in't?

CLOWN: One that was a woman, sir; but, rest her soul, she's dead.

HAMLET: How absolute the knave is! We must speak by the card,[4] or equivocation will undo us. By the Lord, Horatio, this three years I have took note of it, the age is grown so

100

105

110

115

120

125

130

---

1. End.
2. Contracts.

3. Living.
4. Exactly. *Absolute:* literal.

picked[5] that the toe of the peasant comes so near the heel of the courtier, he galls his kibe.[6] How long hast thou been a grave-maker?

CLOWN: Of all the days i' th' year, I came to't that day that our last King Hamlet overcame Fortinbras.   135

HAMLET: How long is that since?

CLOWN: Cannot you tell that? Every fool can tell that. It was that very day that young Hamlet was born—he that is mad, and sent into England.

HAMLET: Ay, marry, why was he sent into England?   140

CLOWN: Why, because 'a was mad. 'A shall recover his wits there; or, if 'a do not, 'tis no great matter there.

HAMLET: Why?

CLOWN: 'Twill not be seen in him there. There the men are as mad as he.   145

HAMLET: How came he mad?

CLOWN: Very strangely, they say.

HAMLET: How strangely?

CLOWN: Faith, e'en with losing his wits.

HAMLET: Upon what ground?   150

CLOWN: Why, here in Denmark. I have been sexton here, man and boy, thirty years.

HAMLET: How long will a man lie i' th' earth ere he rot?

CLOWN: Faith, if 'a be not rotten before 'a die—as we have many pocky[7] corses now-a-days that will scarce hold the   155
laying in—'a will last you some eight year or nine year. A tanner will last you nine year.

HAMLET: Why he more than another?

CLOWN: Why, sir, his hide is so tanned with his trade that 'a will keep out water a great while; and your water is a sore   160
decayer of your whoreson dead body. Here's a skull now hath lien[8] you i' th' earth three and twenty years.

HAMLET: Whose was it?

CLOWN: A whoreson mad fellow's it was. Whose do you think it was?   165

HAMLET: Nay, I know not.

---

5. Refined.
6. Rubs a blister on his heel.

7. Riddled with pox (syphilis).
8. Lain. *Whoreson:* bastard (figuratively).

CLOWN: A pestilence on him for a mad rogue! 'A poured a flagon of Rhenish on my head once. This same skull, sir, was, sir, Yorick's skull, the king's jester.

HAMLET: [*Takes the skull.*] This?   170

CLOWN: E'en that.

HAMLET: Alas, poor Yorick! I knew him, Horatio—a fellow of infinite jest, of most excellent fancy. He hath bore me on his back a thousand times, and now how abhorred in my imagination it is! My gorge[9] rises at it. Here hung those lips   175
that I have kissed I know not how oft. Where be your gibes now, your gambols, your songs, your flashes of merriment that were wont to set the table on a roar? Not one now to mock your own grinning? Quite chap-fall'n?[1] Now get you to my lady's chamber, and tell her, let her paint an inch   180
thick, to this favor[2] she must come. Make her laugh at that. Prithee, Horatio, tell me one thing.

HORATIO: What's that, my lord?

HAMLET: Dost thou think Alexander looked o' this fashion i' th' earth?   185

HORATIO: E'en so.

HAMLET: And smelt so? Pah! [*Throws down the skull.*]

HORATIO: E'en so, my lord.

HAMLET: To what base uses we may return, Horatio! Why may not imagination trace the noble dust of Alexander till 'a   190
find it stopping a bung-hole?

HORATIO: 'Twere to consider too curiously[3] to consider so.

HAMLET: No, faith, not a jot, but to follow him thither with modesty[4] enough, and likelihood to lead it. Alexander died, Alexander was buried, Alexander returneth to dust; the   195
dust is earth; of earth we make loam; and why of that loam whereto he was converted might they not stop a beer-barrel?

    Imperious Cæsar, dead and turned to clay,
    Might stop a hole to keep the wind away.   200
    O, that that earth which kept the world in awe

---

9. Throat.   3. Precisely.
1. Lacking a lower jaw.   4. Moderation.
2. Appearance.

Should patch a wall t'expel the winter's flaw!⁵
But soft, but soft awhile! Here comes the king,
The queen, the courtiers.
    [*Enter* KING, QUEEN, LAERTES, *and the Corse with a* PRIEST
    and LORDS *attendant.*]
                      Who is this they follow?
And with such maiméd⁶ rites? This doth betoken   205
The corse they follow did with desperate hand
Fordo its own life. 'Twas of some estate.⁷
Couch we⁸ awhile and mark. [*Retires with* HORATIO.]
LAERTES: What ceremony else?⁹
HAMLET: That is Laertes, a very noble youth. Mark.   210
LAERTES: What ceremony else?
PRIEST: Here obsequies have been as far enlarged¹
    As we have warranty. Her death was doubtful,
    And but that great command o'ersways the order,²
    She should in ground unsanctified been lodged   215
    Till the last trumpet. For charitable prayers,
    Shards, flints, and pebbles, should be thrown on her.
    Yet here she is allowed her virgin crants,³
    Her maiden strewments,⁴ and the bringing home
    Of bell and burial.   220
LAERTES: Must there no more be done?
PRIEST: No more be done.
    We should profane the service of the dead
    To sing a requiem and such rest to her
    As to peace-parted souls.
LAERTES: Lay her i' th' earth,
    And from her fair and unpolluted flesh   225
    May violets spring! I tell thee, churlish priest,
    A minist'ring angel shall my sister be
    When thou liest howling.⁵
HAMLET: What, the fair Ophelia!

---

5. Gusty wind.
6. Abbreviated.
7. Rank. *Fordo:* destroy.
8. Conceal ourselves.
9. More.

1. Extended.
2. Usual rules.
3. Wreaths.
4. Flowers strewn on the grave.
5. In Hell.

QUEEN: Sweets to the sweet. Farewell! [*Scatters flowers.*]
    I hoped thou shouldst have been my Hamlet's wife.   230
    I thought thy bride-bed to have decked, sweet maid,
    And not t' have strewed thy grave.
LAERTES: O, treble woe
    Fall ten times treble on that cursèd head
    Whose wicked deed thy most ingenious sense[6]
    Deprived thee of! Hold off the earth awhile,   235
    Till I have caught her once more in mine arms. [*Leaps into*
       the grave.]
    Now pile your dust upon the quick and dead,
    Till of this flat a mountain you have made
    T' o'er-top old Pelion or the skyish head
    Of blue Olympus.[7]   240
HAMLET: [*Coming forward.*] What is he whose grief
    Bears such an emphasis, whose phrase of sorrow
    Conjures[8] the wand'ring stars, and makes them stand
    Like wonder-wounded hearers? This is I,
    Hamlet the Dane. [HAMLET *leaps into the grave and they*   245
      grapple.]
LAERTES: The devil take thy soul!
HAMLET: Thou pray'st not well.
    I prithee take thy fingers from my throat,
    For though I am not splenitive[9] and rash,
    Yet have I in me something dangerous,
    Which let thy wisdom fear. Hold off thy hand.   250
KING: Pluck them asunder.
QUEEN: Hamlet! Hamlet!
ALL: Gentlemen!
HORATIO: Good my lord, be quiet.
    [*The* ATTENDANTS *part them, and they come out of the*
    grave.]
HAMLET: Why, I will fight with him upon this theme   255
    Until my eyelids will no longer wag.[1]
QUEEN: O my son, what theme?

---

6. Lively mind.   9. Hot-tempered.
7. Like Pelion, mountain in Greece.   1. Move.
8. Casts a spell on.

HAMLET: I loved Ophelia. Forty thousand brothers
    Could not with all their quantity of love
    Make up my sum. What wilt thou do for her?   260
KING: O, he is mad, Laertes.
QUEEN: For love of God, forbear[2] him.
HAMLET: 'Swounds, show me what th'owt do.
    Woo't[3] weep, woo't fight, woo't fast, woo't tear thyself,
    Woo't drink up eisel,[4] eat a crocodile?   265
    I'll do't. Dost come here to whine?
    To outface[5] me with leaping in her grave?
    Be buried quick with her, and so will I.
    And if thou prate of mountains, let them throw
    Millions of acres on us, till our ground,   270
    Singeing his pate against the burning zone,[6]
    Make Ossa[7] like a wart! Nay, an thou'lt mouth,
    I'll rant as well as thou.
QUEEN: This is mere madness;
    And thus awhile the fit will work on him.
    Anon, as patient as the female dove   275
    When that her golden couplets[8] are disclosed,
    His silence will sit drooping.
HAMLET: Hear you, sir.
    What is the reason that you use me thus?
    I loved you ever. But it is no matter.
    Let Hercules himself do what he may,   280
    The cat will mew, and dog will have his day.   [*Exit.*]
KING: I pray thee, good Horatio, wait upon[9] him.
                      [*Exit* HORATIO.]
    [*To* LAERTES.] Strengthen your patience in our last night's
        speech.
    We'll put the matter to the present push.[1]—
    Good Gertrude, set some watch over your son.—   285
    This grave shall have a living monument.

2. Bear with.
3. Will you.
4. Vinegar.
5. Get the best of.
6. Sky in the torrid zone.
7. Mountain in Greece.
8. Pair of eggs.
9. Attend.
1. Immediate trial.

An hour of quiet shortly shall we see;
Till then in patience our proceeding be.   *[Exeunt.]*

SCENE 2

A hall or public room. Enter HAMLET *and* HORATIO.

HAMLET: So much for this, sir; now shall you see the other.
   You do remember all the circumstance?
HORATIO: Remember it, my lord!
HAMLET: Sir, in my heart there was a kind of fighting
   That would not let me sleep. Methought I lay   5
   Worse than the mutines in the bilboes.[1] Rashly,
   And praised be rashness for it—let us know,
   Our indiscretion sometime serves us well,
   When our deep plots do pall; and that should learn[2] us
   There's a divinity that shapes our ends,   10
   Rough-hew them how we will—
HORATIO: That is most certain.
HAMLET: Up from my cabin,
   My sea-gown scarfed[3] about me, in the dark
   Groped I to find out them,[4] had my desire,
   Fingered their packet, and in fine[5] withdrew   15
   To mine own room again, making so bold,
   My fears forgetting manners, to unseal
   Their grand commission; where I found, Horatio—
   Ah, royal knavery!—an exact command,
   Larded[6] with many several sorts of reasons,   20
   Importing Denmark's health, and England's too,
   With, ho! such bugs and goblins in my life,[7]
   That on the supervise, no leisure bated,[8]
   No, not to stay the grinding of the axe,
   My head should be struck off.
HORATIO: Is't possible?   25

---

1. Mutineers in the stocks.
2. Teach. *Pall:* weaken and die.
3. Wrapped.
4. That is, Rosencrantz and Guildenstern.

5. Quickly. *Fingered:* stole.
6. Garnished.
7. Such dangers if I remained alive.
8. As soon as the commission was read,
no pause allowed.

HAMLET: Here's the commission; read it at more leisure.
    But wilt thou hear now how I did proceed?
HORATIO: I beseech you.
HAMLET: Being thus benetted round with villainies,
    Ere I could make a prologue to my brains,   30
    They had begun the play. I sat me down,
    Devised a new commission, wrote it fair.[9]
    I once did hold it, as our statists[1] do,
    A baseness to write fair, and labored much
    How to forget that learning; but sir, now   35
    It did me yeoman's service. Wilt thou know
    Th' effect[2] of what I wrote?
HORATIO: Ay, good my lord.
HAMLET: An earnest conjuration[3] from the king,
    As England was his faithful tributary,
    As love between them like the palm might flourish,   40
    As peace should still her wheaten garland wear
    And stand a comma 'tween their amities[4]
    And many such like as's of great charge,[5]
    That on the view and knowing of these contents,
    Without debatement further more or less,   45
    He should those bearers put to sudden death,
    Not shriving-time allowed.[6]
HORATIO: How was this sealed?
HAMLET: Why, even in that was heaven ordinant,[7]
    I had my father's signet in my purse,
    Which was the model of that Danish seal,   50
    Folded the writ up in the form of th' other,
    Subscribed it, gave't th' impression,[8] placed it safely,
    The changeling[9] never known. Now, the next day
    Was our sea-fight, and what to this was sequent[1]
    Thou knowest already.   55

9. Legibly. *Devised:* made.
1. Politicians.
2. Contents.
3. Appeal.
4. And link their friendships.
5. Important clauses beginning with "as";
also, asses bearing heavy burdens.

6. Without time for confession.
7. Operative.
8. Of the seal.
9. Alteration.
1. Followed.

HORATIO: So Guildenstern and Rosencrantz go to't.

HAMLET: Why, man, they did make love to this employment.
They are not near my conscience; their defeat[2]
Does by their own insinuation grow.
'Tis dangerous when the baser nature comes   60
Between the pass and fell incensèd points[3]
Of mighty opposites.

HORATIO: Why, what a king is this!

HAMLET: Does it not, think thee, stand me now upon—
He that hath killed my king and whored my mother,
Popped in between th' election and my hopes,[4]   65
Thrown out his angle[5] for my proper life,
And with such coz'nage[6]—is't not perfect conscience
To quit[7] him with this arm? And is't not to be damned
To let this canker of our nature come
In further evil?   70

HORATIO: It must be shortly known to him from England
What is the issue of the business there.

HAMLET: It will be short; the interim is mine.
And a man's life's no more than to say "one."
But I am very sorry, good Horatio,   75
That to Laertes I forgot myself;
For by the image of my cause I see
The portraiture of his. I'll court his favors.
But sure the bravery[8] of his grief did put me
Into a tow'ring passion.

HORATIO: Peace; who comes here?   80

[*Enter* OSRIC.]

OSRIC: Your lordship is right welcome back to Denmark.

HAMLET: I humbly thank you, sir. [*Aside to* HORATIO.] Dost
know this water-fly?

HORATIO: [*Aside to* HAMLET.] No, my good lord.

HAMLET: [*Aside to* HORATIO.] Thy state is the more gracious,   85
for 'tis a vice to know him. He hath much land, and fertile.

---

2. Death. *Are not near:* do not touch.   5. Fishhook.
3. That is, amidst dangerous swordplay.   6. Trickery.
4. Between the selection of the next king   7. Repay.
and Hamlet's desire for the throne.   8. Exaggerated display.

Let a beast be lord of beasts, and his crib shall stand at the king's mess. 'Tis a chough,[9] but as I say, spacious in the possession of dirt.

OSRIC: Sweet lord, if your lordship were at leisure, I should impart a thing to you from his majesty.   90

HAMLET: I will receive it, sir, with all diligence of spirit. Put your bonnet to his right use. 'Tis for the head.

OSRIC: I thank your lordship, it is very hot.

HAMLET: No, believe me, 'tis very cold; the wind is northerly.   95

OSRIC: It is indifferent[1] cold, my lord, indeed.

HAMLET: But yet methinks it is very sultry and hot for my complexion.[2]

OSRIC: Exceedingly, my lord; it is very sultry, as 'twere—I cannot tell how. My lord, his majesty bade me signify to you   100 that 'a has laid a great wager on your head. Sir, this is the matter—

HAMLET: I beseech you, remember. [*Moves him to put on his hat.*]

OSRIC: Nay, good my lord; for my ease, in good faith. Sir, here is newly come to court Laertes; believe me, an absolute   105 gentleman, full of most excellent differences,[3] of very soft society and great showing.[4] Indeed, to speak feelingly of him, he is the card or calendar of gentry, for you shall find in him the continent[5] of what part a gentleman would see.   110

HAMLET: Sir, his definement[6] suffers no perdition in you, though I know to divide him inventorially would dozy[7] th' arithmetic of memory, and yet but yaw[8] neither in respect of his quick sail. But in the verity of extolment, I take him to be a soul of great article, and his infusion[9] of such dearth   115 and rareness as, to make true diction of him, his semblage[1]

9. Jackdaw, a bird.
1. Moderately.
2. Temperament.
3. Qualities.
4. Good manners.
5. Sum total. *Calendar:* measure.

6. Description.
7. To examine him bit by bit would daze.
8. Steer wildly.
9. Great scope, and his nature.
1. To speak truly about him, his likeness.

is his mirror, and who else would trace him, his umbrage,[2]
nothing more.

OSRIC: Your lordship speaks most infallibly of him.

HAMLET: The concernancy,[3] sir? Why do we wrap the gentle-   120
man in our more rawer breath?[4]

OSRIC: Sir?

HORATIO: Is't not possible to understand in another tongue?
You will to't, sir, really.

HAMLET: What imports the nomination[5] of this gentleman?   125

OSRIC: Of Laertes?

HORATIO: [*Aside.*] His purse is empty already. All's golden
words are spent.

HAMLET: Of him, sir.

OSRIC: I know you are not ignorant—   130

HAMLET: I would you did, sir; yet, in faith, if you did, it would
not much approve me. Well, sir.

OSRIC: You are not ignorant of what excellence Laertes is—

HAMLET: I dare not confess that, lest I should compare[6] with
him in excellence; but to know a man well were to know   135
himself.

OSRIC: I mean, sir, for his weapon; but in the imputation[7] laid
on him by them, in his meed he's unfellowed.[8]

HAMLET: What's his weapon?

OSRIC: Rapier and dagger.   140

HAMLET: That's two of his weapons—but well.

OSRIC: The king, sir, hath wagered with him six Barbary
horses, against the which he has impawned,[9] as I take it, six
French rapiers and poniards, with their assigns, as girdle,
hangers,[1] and so. Three of the carriages, in faith, are very   145
dear to fancy,[2] very responsive to the hilts, most delicate
carriages, and of very liberal conceit.[3]

---

2. Would keep pace with him, his shadow.
3. Meaning.
4. Cruder words.
5. Naming.
6. That is, compare myself.
7. Reputation.

8. Unequaled in his excellence.
9. Staked.
1. Belts from which swords hang. *Assigns:* accessories.
2. Finely designed.
3. Intricately decorated. *Delicate:* well adjusted.

HAMLET: What call you the carriages?

HORATIO: [*Aside to* HAMLET.] I knew you must be edified by
the margent[4] ere you had done.   150

OSRIC: The carriages, sir, are the hangers.

HAMLET: The phrase would be more germane to the matter if
we could carry a cannon by our sides. I would it might be
hangers till then. But on! Six Barbary horses against six
French swords, their assigns, and three liberal conceited   155
carriages; that's the French bet against the Danish. Why is
this all impawned, as you call it?

OSRIC: The king, sir, hath laid, sir, that in a dozen passes between yourself and him he shall not exceed you three hits;
he hath laid on twelve for nine, and it would come to im-   160
mediate trial if your lordship would vouchsafe the answer.

HAMLET: How if I answer no?

OSRIC: I mean, my lord, the opposition of your person in
trial.[5]

HAMLET: Sir, I will walk here in the hall. If it please his   165
majesty, it is the breathing time[6] of day with me. Let the
foils be brought, the gentleman willing, and the king hold
his purpose; I will win for him an I can. If not, I will gain
nothing but my shame and the odd hits.

OSRIC: Shall I deliver you so?   170

HAMLET: To this effect, sir, after what flourish your nature will.

OSRIC: I commend my duty to your lordship.

HAMLET: Yours, yours. [*Exit* OSRIC.] He does well to commend
it himself; there are no tongues else for's turn.

HORATIO: This lapwing runs away with the shell on his head.[7]   175

HAMLET: 'A did comply, sir, with his dug[8] before 'a sucked it.
Thus has he, and many more of the same bevy that I know
the drossy age dotes on, only got the tune of the time; and
out of an habit of encounter, a king of yesty[9] collection
which carries them through and through the most fanned   180

---

4. Marginal gloss.
5. Your participation in the contest.
6. Time for exercise.
7. The lapwing was thought to be so pre-
cocious that it could run immediately after

being hatched, even, as here, with bits of the
shell still on its head.
8. Deal formally . . . with his mother's
breast.
9. Yeasty.

and winnowed opinions; and do but blow them to their trial, the bubbles are out.

    [*Enter a* LORD.]

LORD: My lord, his majesty commended him to you by young Osric, who brings back to him that you attend him in the hall. He sends to know if your pleasure hold to play with Laertes, or that you will take longer time.

HAMLET: I am constant to my purposes; they follow the king's pleasure. If his fitness speaks, mine is ready; now or whensoever, provided I be so able as now.

LORD: The king and queen and all are coming down.

HAMLET: In happy time.

LORD: The queen desires you to use some gentle entertainment[1] to Laertes before you fall to play.

HAMLET: She well instructs me.   [*Exit* LORD.]

HORATIO: You will lose this wager, my lord.

HAMLET: I do not think so. Since he went into France I have been in continual practice. I shall win at the odds. But thou wouldst not think how ill[2] all's here about my heart. But it's no matter.

HORATIO: Nay, good my lord—

HAMLET: It is but foolery, but it is such a kind of gaingiving[3] as would perhaps trouble a woman.

HORATIO: If your mind dislike anything, obey it. I will forestall their repair[4] hither, and say you are not fit.

HAMLET: Not a whit, we defy augury. There is special providence in the fall of a sparrow. If it be now, 'tis not to come; if it be not to come, it will be now; if it be not now, yet it will come. The readiness is all. Since no man of aught he leaves knows, what is't to leave betimes? Let be.

    [*A table prepared. Enter* TRUMPETS, DRUMS, *and* OFFICERS *with cushions;* KING, QUEEN, OSRIC *and* ATTENDANTS *with foils, daggers, and* LAERTES.]

KING: Come, Hamlet, come and take this hand from me. [*The* KING *puts* LAERTES' *hand into* HAMLET'S.]

---

1. Cordiality.
2. Uneasy.

3. Misgiving.
4. Coming.

HAMLET: Give me your pardon, sir. I have done you wrong,
　　But pardon 't as you are a gentleman.
　　This presence[5] knows, and you must needs have heard,
　　How I am punished with a sore distraction.
　　What I have done   215
　　That might your nature, honor, and exception[6]
　　Roughly awake, I here proclaim was madness.
　　Was't Hamlet wronged Laertes? Never Hamlet.
　　If Hamlet from himself be ta'en away,
　　And when he's not himself does wrong Laertes,   220
　　Then Hamlet does it not, Hamlet denies it.
　　Who does it then? His madness. If't be so,
　　Hamlet is of the faction that is wronged;
　　His madness is poor Hamlet's enemy.
　　Sir, in this audience,   225
　　Let my disclaiming from[7] a purposed evil
　　Free[8] me so far in your most generous thoughts
　　That I have shot my arrow o'er the house
　　And hurt my brother.
LAERTES: I am satisfied in nature,
　　Whose motive in this case should stir me most   230
　　To my revenge. But in my terms of honor
　　I stand aloof, and will no reconcilement
　　Till by some elder masters of known honor
　　I have a voice[9] and precedent of peace.
　　To keep my name ungored.[1] But till that time   235
　　I do receive your offered love like love,
　　And will not wrong it.
HAMLET: I embrace it freely,
　　And will this brother's wager frankly[2] play.
　　Give us the foils. Come on.
LAERTES: Come, one for me.
HAMLET: I'll be your foil, Laertes. In mine ignorance   240

5. Company.
6. Resentment.
7. Denying of.
8. Absolve.

9. Authority.
1. Unshamed.
2. Without rancor.

Your skill shall, like a star i' th' darkest night,
  Stick fiery off³ indeed.
LAERTES: You mock me, sir.
HAMLET: No, by this hand.
KING: Give them the foils, young Osric. Cousin Hamlet,
  You know the wager?
HAMLET: Very well, my lord;   245
  Your Grace has laid the odds o' th' weaker side.
KING: I do not fear it, I have seen you both;
  But since he is bettered⁴ we have therefore odds.
LAERTES: This is too heavy; let me see another.
HAMLET: This likes me well. These foils have all a⁵ length?   250
  [*They prepare to play.*]
OSRIC: Ay, my good lord.
KING: Set me the stoups of wine upon that table.
  If Hamlet give the first or second hit,
  Or quit in answer of⁶ the third exchange,
  Let all the battlements their ordnance fire.   255
  The king shall drink to Hamlet's better breath,
  And in the cup an union⁷ shall he throw,
  Richer than that which four successive kings
  In Denmark's crown have worn. Give me the cups,
  And let the kettle⁸ to the trumpet speak,   260
  The trumpet to the cannoneer without,
  The cannons to the heavens, the heaven to earth,
  "Now the king drinks to Hamlet." Come, begin—
  [*Trumpets the while.*]
  And you, the judges, bear a wary eye.
HAMLET: Come on, sir.
LAERTES: Come, my lord.
  [*They play.*]
HAMLET: One.
LAERTES: No.
HAMLET: Judgment?   265

---

3. Shine brightly.
4. Reported better.
5. The same. *Likes:* suits.
6. Or repay.
7. Pearl.
8. Kettledrum.

OSRIC: A hit, a very palpable hit.
  [*Drums, trumpets, and shot. Flourish; a piece goes off.*]
LAERTES: Well, again.
KING: Stay, give me drink. Hamlet, this pearl is thine.
  Here's to thy health. Give him the cup.
HAMLET: I'll play this bout first; set it by awhile.   270
  Come.
  [*They play.*]
  Another hit; what say you?
LAERTES: A touch, a touch, I do confess't.
KING: Our son shall win.
QUEEN: He's fat,[9] and scant of breath.
  Here, Hamlet, take my napkin, rub thy brows.   275
  The queen carouses to thy fortune, Hamlet.
HAMLET: Good madam!
KING: Gertrude, do not drink.
QUEEN: I will, my lord; I pray you pardon me.
KING: [*Aside.*] It is the poisoned cup; it is too late.   280
HAMLET: I dare not drink yet, madam; by and by.
QUEEN: Come, let me wipe thy face.
LAERTES: My lord, I'll hit him now.
KING: I do not think't.
LAERTES: [*Aside.*] And yet it is almost against my conscience.
HAMLET: Come, for the third, Laertes. You do but dally.   285
  I pray you pass[1] with your best violence;
  I am afeard you make a wanton of me.[2]
LAERTES: Say you so? Come on.
  [*They play.*]
OSRIC: Nothing, neither way.
LAERTES: Have at you now!   290
  [LAERTES *wounds* HAMLET: *then, in scuffling, they change*
  rapiers, and HAMLET *wounds* LAERTES.]
KING: Part them. They are incensed.
HAMLET: Nay, come again.
  [*The* QUEEN *falls.*]

---

9. Out of shape.   2. Trifle with me.
1. Attack.

OSRIC: Look to the queen there, ho!

HORATIO: They bleed on both sides. How is it, my lord?

OSRIC: How is't, Laertes?   295

LAERTES: Why, as a woodcock to mine own springe,[3] Osric.
    I am justly killed with mine own treachery.

HAMLET: How does the queen?

KING: She swoons to see them bleed.

QUEEN: No, no, the drink, the drink! O my dear Hamlet!
    The drink, the drink! I am poisoned. [*Dies.*]   300

HAMLET: O, villainy! Ho! let the door be locked.
    Treachery! seek it out.

LAERTES: It is here, Hamlet. Hamlet, thou art slain;
    No med'cine in the world can do thee good.
    In thee there is not half an hour's life.   305
    The treacherous instrument is in thy hand,
    Unbated[4] and envenomed. The foul practice
    Hath turned itself on me. Lo, here I lie,
    Never to rise again. Thy mother's poisoned.
    I can no more. The king, the king's to blame.   310

HAMLET: The point envenomed too?
    Then, venom, to thy work. [*Hurts the* KING.]

ALL: Treason! treason!

KING: O, yet defend me, friends. I am but hurt.[5]

HAMLET: Here, thou incestuous, murd'rous, damnéd Dane,   315
    Drink off this potion. Is thy union here?
    Follow my mother.
        [*The* KING *dies.*]

LAERTES: He is justly served.
    It is a poison tempered[6] by himself.
    Exchange forgiveness with me, noble Hamlet.
    Mine and my father's death come not upon thee,   320
    Nor thine on me! [*Dies.*]

HAMLET: Heaven make thee free of it! I follow thee.
    I am dead, Horatio. Wretched queen, adieu!
    You that look pale and tremble at this chance,[7]

---

3. Snare.   6. Mixed.
4. Unblunted.   7. Circumstance.
5. Wounded.

That are but mutes or audience to this act,   325
Had I but time, as this fell sergeant Death
Is strict in his arrest,[8] O, I could tell you—
But let it be. Horatio, I am dead:
Thou livest; report me and my cause aright
To the unsatisfied.[9]
HORATIO: Never believe it.   330
I am more an antique Roman than a Dane.[1]
Here's yet some liquor left.
HAMLET: As th'art a man,
Give me the cup. Let go. By heaven; I'll ha't.
O God, Horatio, what a wounded name,
Things standing thus unknown, shall live behind me!   335
If thou didst ever hold me in thy heart,
Absent thee from felicity awhile,
And in this harsh world draw thy breath in pain,
To tell my story.
    [*A march afar off.*]
                    What warlike noise is this?
OSRIC: Young Fortinbras, with conquest come from Poland,   340
To th' ambassadors of England gives
This warlike volley.
HAMLET: O, I die, Horatio!
The potent poison quite o'er-crows[2] my spirit.
I cannot live to hear the news from England,
But I do prophesy th' election lights   345
On Fortinbras. He has my dying voice.[3]
So tell him, with th' occurrents,[4] more and less,
Which have solicited[5]—the rest is silence. [*Dies.*]
HORATIO: Now cracks a noble heart. Good night, sweet
    prince,
And flights of angels sing thee to thy rest!   350
    [*March within.*]

---

8. Summons to court.   2. Overcomes.
9. Uninformed.   3. Support.
  1. Horatio proposes to kill himself, as an   4. Circumstances.
ancient Roman might in similar circum-   5. Brought about this scene.
stances.

Why does the drum come hither?
[*Enter* FORTINBRAS, *with the* AMBASSADORS *and with drum,*
colors, and ATTENDANTS.]
FORTINBRAS: Where is this sight?
HORATIO: What is it you would see?
  If aught of woe or wonder, cease your search.
FORTINBRAS: This quarry cries on havoc.[6] O proud death,
  What feast is toward[7] in thine eternal cell   355
  That thou so many princes at a shot
  So bloodily hast struck?
AMBASSADORS: The sight is dismal;
  And our affairs from England come too late.
  The ears are senseless[8] that should give us hearing
  To tell him his commandment is fulfilled,   360
  That Rosencrantz and Guildenstern are dead.
  Where should we have our thanks?
HORATIO: Not from his[9] mouth,
  Had it th' ability of life to thank you.
  He never gave commandment for their death.
  But since, so jump[1] upon this bloody question,   365
  You from the Polack wars, and you from England,
  Are here arrived, give orders that these bodies
  High on a stage be placéd to the view,
  And let me speak to th' yet unknowing world
  How these things came about. So shall you hear   370
  Of carnal, bloody, and unnatural acts;
  Of accidental judgments, casual[2] slaughters;
  Of deaths put on by cunning and forced cause;
  And, in this upshot,[3] purposes mistook
  Fall'n on th' inventors' heads. All this can I   375
  Truly deliver.
FORTINBRAS: Let us haste to hear it,
  And call the noblest to the audience.[4]

---

6. The game killed in the hunt proclaims
a slaughter.
  7. In preparation.
  8. Without sense of hearing.
  9. That is, Claudius's.

1. Exactly.
2. Brought about by apparent accident.
3. Result.
4. Hearing.

For me, with sorrow I embrace my fortune.
I have some rights of memory[5] in this kingdom,
Which now to claim my vantage[6] doth invite me.   380
HORATIO: Of that I shall have also cause to speak,
And from his mouth whose voice will draw on more.
But let this same be presently performed,
Even while men's minds are wild, lest more mischance
On plots and errors happen.
FORTINBRAS: Let four captains   385
Bear Hamlet like a soldier to the stage,
For he was likely, had he been put on,[7]
To have proved most royal; and for his passage
The soldier's music and the rite of war
Speak loudly for him.   390
Take up the bodies. Such a sight as this
Becomes the field, but here shows much amiss.
Go, bid the soldiers shoot.
           [*Exeunt marching. A peal of ordinance shot off.*]

ca. 1600

Henrik Ibsen
1828–1906

A DOLL HOUSE

Ibsen's early plays, beginning in 1850, were poetic, mythic, and ro-
mantic. But in the late 1860s he began writing in plain language
about the struggles of ordinary, middle-class people. Theatergoers
saw on the stage for the first time people just like themselves, who
talked as they did, dealt with the same issues they dealt with, and
lived the same kinds of lives. The people in the audience became the
subjects of the stories dramatized on stage. These plays are some-
times called "social dramas" because they tend to reveal defects in
society and the ways those defects hindered the individual's personal

5. Succession.   7. Elected king.
6. Position.

growth. The route to the individual's full and unchained growth became Ibsen's most persistent theme, and A Doll House *represented the centerpiece of his realistic period.*

The rise of the middle class during this time intensified the subjection of women. Women of all classes exercised no political power in the European democracies until they gained the vote in the twentieth century. They had unequal rights in marriage: a husband owned what today would be joint property, and a wife surrendered property she owned even before marriage to her husband's absolute control. Women had unequal rights to divorce and risked losing their children if they pressed for a separation from even an abusive husband. And mainstream attitudes—often based on scientific mistakes, like the comparison of brain sizes between men and women— took for granted that women were mentally inferior to men.

Such attitudes, coupled with the middle class's fetish for home life, left few roles for women other than wife and mother and domestic ornament. Not until late in the nineteenth century could women attend university, and even then they rarely did so. They were systematically excluded from the professions, like medicine and law. Married middle-class women seldom worked outside their homes, so as not to embarrass their husbands. Unmarried middle-class women had very narrow career choices. Middle-class women generally were trained to perform subservient roles, learning, for example, to converse, to entertain, to play a musical instrument, to sketch (but not to paint with oils), to read French or Italian (but not Latin or Greek, the languages that prepared one for the professions), and so on.

As you might expect, many people, men and women alike, were dissatisfied with these conditions, so the "woman question" became a vital social issue. In 1869, John Stuart Mill's revolutionary book The Subjection of Women, *which argued that society ought to extend equal rights to women, was translated into German. Ibsen read the translation, and though he continued to believe that women were mentally inferior to men, he began to realize that both sexes held the right to individualism. And he recognized that Victorian society's compulsory domestication of women made it especially hard for them to fully realize their potential.*

Ironically, Ibsen did not consider himself a feminist. He saw his plays as chronicling the struggles of the individual—any individ-

ual, man or woman, artist or schoolteacher, mythic hero or house-wife—against the forces of banality, mediocrity, and philistinism. Nora Helmer's story, in A Doll House, is one of these chronicles.

Nora is based on someone Ibsen knew. In 1869, by then a famous playwright in his forties, he became a mentor to a twenty-year-old writer named Laura Peterson, who lived in Copenhagen. Taken by her personality, Ibsen called her "lark" and "songbird," and their friendship grew even after Peterson married a poor schoolteacher in Denmark. The husband fell ill and was advised to travel south to warmer climates; Peterson secretly borrowed the money for the trip, could not pay off the loan, and resorted to forging a note. She confided in Ibsen, who indignantly advised her to confess to her husband. But when she did confess, her husband, enraged, divorced her. This cruel treatment broke the woman, who ended up in an asylum. Laura Peterson's story—and the poor role he played in it—affected Ibsen deeply.

In the summer of 1878, he sent A Doll House to Copenhagen, where it was first produced. An immediate success, the play quickly swept through Scandinavia, Germany, Finland, Poland, Russia, Italy, and England. Audiences were attracted to Nora; some sympathized with her, and others were revolted by her. The play constituted the biggest literary controversy of its generation, inspiring ardent defenders and troubled detractors.

It also reinvented the theater. Realistic social drama would remain on the European stage for generations. In England, the great playwright George Bernard Shaw considered himself the direct descendent of Ibsen, and Shaw's social dramas dominated London's theatrical tastes well into the twentieth century. To get a feel for this "realism," you might contrast Ibsen's domestic drama with the plays preceding this one by Sophocles and Shakespeare, comparing the characters, the scope of the stories, and the uses of language.

A good way to engage yourself in this play is to debate Nora's choice. Did she do the right thing? What else might she have done? Can you envision a marriage like hers today? You shouldn't need much imagination to recognize similar cruxes in contemporary lives—struggles between people's obligations to others, the impulse to conform to middle-class standards of behavior, and individuals' duties to themselves.

A Doll House[*]

THE CHARACTERS

TORVALD HELMER, *a lawyer*

NORA, *his wife*

DR. RANK

MRS. LINDE

NILS KROGSTAD, *a bank clerk*

THE HELMERS' THREE SMALL
CHILDREN

ANNE-MARIE, *their nurse*

HELENE, *a maid*

A DELIVERY BOY

The action takes place in HELMER's *residence.*

ACT ONE

*A comfortable room, tastefully but not expensively furnished. A door
to the right in the back wall leads to the entryway; another to the left
leads to* HELMER's *study. Between these doors, a piano. Midway in the
left-hand wall a door, and farther down a window. Near the window a
round table with an armchair and a small sofa. In the right-hand wall,
toward the rear, a door, and nearer the foreground a porcelain stove
with two armchairs and a rocking chair beside it. Between the stove
and the side door, a small table. Engravings on the walls. An* etagère[1]
*with china figures and other small art objects; a small bookcase with
richly bound books; the floor carpeted; a fire burning in the stove. It is a
winter day.*

*A bell rings in the entryway; shortly after we hear the door being un-
locked.* NORA *comes into the room, humming happily to herself; she is
wearing street clothes and carries an armload of packages, which she
puts down on the table to the right. She has left the hall door open; and
through it a* DELIVERY BOY *is seen, holding a Christmas tree and a basket, which he gives to the* MAID *who let them in.*

NORA: Hide the tree well, Helene. The children mustn't get a
glimpse of it till this evening, after it's trimmed. [*To the* DELIVERY
BOY, *taking out her purse.*] How much?

DELIVERY BOY: Fifty, ma'am.

NORA: There's a crown. No, keep the change. [*The* BOY *thanks her*

---

[*]Translated by Rolf Fjelde.

1. Small piece of furniture with shelves
for displaying small articles.

and leaves. NORA *shuts the door. She laughs softly to herself while taking off her street things. Drawing a bag of macaroons from her pocket, she eats a couple, then steals over and listens at her husband's study door.*] Yes, he's home. [*Hums again as she moves to the table right.*]

HELMER: [*From the study.*] Is that my little lark twittering out there?

NORA: [*Busy opening some packages.*] Yes, it is.

HELMER: Is that my squirrel rummaging around?

NORA: Yes!

HELMER: When did my squirrel get in?

NORA: Just now. [*Putting the macaroon bag in her pocket and wiping her mouth.*] Do come in, Torvald, and see what I've bought.

HELMER: Can't be disturbed. [*After a moment he opens the door and peers in, pen in hand.*] Bought, you say? All that there? Has the little spendthrift been out throwing money around again?

NORA: Oh, but Torvald, this year we really should let ourselves go a bit. It's the first Christmas we haven't had to economize.

HELMER: But you know we can't go squandering.

NORA: Oh yes, Torvald, we can squander a little now. Can't we? Just a tiny, wee bit. Now that you've got a big salary and are going to make piles and piles of money.

HELMER: Yes—starting New Year's. But then it's a full three months till the raise comes through.

NORA: Pooh! We can borrow that long.

HELMER: Nora! [*Goes over and playfully takes her by the ear.*] Are your scatterbrains off again? What if today I borrowed a thousand crowns, and you squandered them over Christmas week, and then on New Year's Eve a roof tile fell on my head, and I lay there—

NORA: [*Putting her hand on his mouth.*] Oh! Don't say such things!

HELMER: Yes, but what if it happened—then what?

NORA: If anything so awful happened, then it just wouldn't matter if I had debts or not.

HELMER: Well, but the people I'd borrowed from?

NORA: Them? Who cares about them! They're strangers.

HELMER: Nora, Nora, how like a woman! No, but seriously, Nora, you know what I think about that. No debts! Never borrow!

Something of freedom's lost—and something of beauty, too—
from a home that's founded on borrowing and debt. We've made
a brave stand up to now, the two of us; and we'll go right on like
that the little while we have to.

NORA: [*Going toward the stove.*] Yes, whatever you say, Torvald.

HELMER: [*Following her.*] Now, now, the little lark's wings mustn't
droop. Come on, don't be a sulky squirrel. [*Taking out his wallet.*]
Nora, guess what I have here.

NORA: [*Turning quickly.*] Money!

HELMER: There, see. [*Hands her some note.*] Good grief, I know how
costs go up in a house at Christmastime.

NORA: Ten—twenty—thirty—forty. Oh, thank you, Torvald; I can
manage no end on this.

HELMER: You really will have to.

NORA: Oh yes, I promise I will! But come here so I can show you
everything I bought. And so cheap! Look, new clothes for Ivar
here—and a sword. Here a horse and a trumpet for Bob. And a
doll and a doll's bed here for Emmy; they're nothing much, but
she'll tear them to bits in no time anyway. And here I have dress
material and handkerchiefs for the maids. Old Anne-Marie really
deserves something more.

HELMER: And what's in that package there?

NORA: [*With a cry.*] Torvald, no! You can't see that till tonight!

HELMER: I see. But tell me now, you little prodigal, what have you
thought of for yourself?

NORA: For myself? Oh, I don't want anything at all.

HELMER: Of course you do. Tell me just what—within reason—
you'd most like to have.

NORA: I honestly don't know. Oh, listen, Torvald—

HELMER: Well?

NORA: [*Fumbling at his coat buttons, without looking at him.*] If you
want to give me something, then maybe you could—you
could—

HELMER: Come on, out with it.

NORA: [*Hurriedly.*] You could give me money, Torvald. No more
than you think you can spare; then one of these days I'll buy
something with it.

HELMER: But Nora—

NORA: Oh, please, Torvald darling, do that! I beg you, please. Then I could hang the bills in pretty gilt paper on the Christmas tree. Wouldn't that be fun?

HELMER: What are those little birds called that always fly through their fortunes?

NORA: Oh yes, spendthrifts; I know all that. But let's do as I say, Torvald; then I'll have time to decide what I really need most. That's very sensible, isn't it?

HELMER: [*Smiling.*] Yes, very—that is, if you actually hung onto the money I give you, and you actually used it to buy yourself something. But it goes for the house and for all sorts of foolish things, and then I only have to lay out some more.

NORA: Oh, but Torvald—

HELMER: Don't deny it, my dear little Nora. [*Putting his arm around her waist.*] Spendthrifts are sweet, but they use up a frightful amount of money. It's incredible what it costs a man to feed such birds.

NORA: Oh, how can you say that! Really, I save everything I can.

HELMER: [*Laughing.*] Yes, that's the truth. Everything you can. But that's nothing at all.

NORA: [*Humming, with a smile of quiet satisfaction.*] Hm, if you only knew what expenses we larks and squirrels have, Torvald.

HELMER: You're an odd little one. Exactly the way your father was. You're never at a loss for scaring up money; but the moment you have it, it runs right out through your fingers; you never know what you've done with it. Well, one takes you as you are. It's deep in your blood. Yes, these things are hereditary, Nora.

NORA: Ah, I could wish I'd inherited many of Papa's qualities.

HELMER: And I couldn't wish you anything but just what you are, my sweet little lark. But wait; it seems to me you have a very— what should I call it?—a very suspicious look today—

NORA: I do?

HELMER: You certainly do. Look me straight in the eye.

NORA: [*Looking at him.*] Well?

HELMER: [*Shaking an admonitory finger.*] Surely my sweet tooth hasn't been running riot in town today, has she?

NORA: No. Why do you imagine that?

HELMER: My sweet tooth really didn't make a little detour through the confectioner's?

NORA: No, I assure you, Torvald—

HELMER: Hasn't nibbled some pastry?

NORA: No, not at all.

HELMER: Not even munched a macaroon or two?

NORA: No, Torvald, I assure you, really—

HELMER: There, there now. Of course I'm only joking.

NORA: [*Going to the table, right.*] You know I could never think of going against you.

HELMER: No, I understand that; and you *have* given me your word. [*Going over to her.*] Well, you keep your little Christmas secrets to yourself, Nora darling. I expect they'll come to light this evening, when the tree is lit.

NORA: Did you remember to ask Dr. Rank?

HELMER: No. But there's no need for that; it's assumed he'll be dining with us. All the same, I'll ask him when he stops by here this morning. I've ordered some fine wine. Nora, you can't imagine how I'm looking forward to this evening.

NORA: So am I. And what fun for the children, Torvald!

HELMER: Ah, it's so gratifying to know that one's gotten a safe, secure job, and with a comfortable salary. It's a great satisfaction, isn't it?

NORA: Oh, it's wonderful!

HELMER: Remember last Christmas? Three whole weeks before, you shut yourself in every evening till long after midnight, making flowers for the Christmas tree, and all the other decorations to surprise us. Ugh, that was the dullest time I've ever lived through.

NORA: It wasn't at all dull for me.

HELMER: [*Smiling.*] But the outcome *was* pretty sorry, Nora.

NORA: Oh, don't tease me with that again. How could I help it that the cat came in and tore everything to shreds.

HELMER: No, poor thing, you certainly couldn't. You wanted so much to please us all, and that's what counts. But it's just as well that the hard times are past.

NORA: Yes, it's really wonderful.

HELMER: Now I don't have to sit here alone, boring myself, and you don't have to tire your precious eyes and your fair little delicate hands—

NORA: [*Clapping her hands.*] No, is it really true, Torvald, I don't have to? Oh, how wonderfully lovely to hear! [*Taking his arm.*] Now I'll tell you just how I've thought we should plan things. Right after Christmas— [*The doorbell rings.*] Oh, the bell. [*Straightening the room up a bit.*] Somebody would have to come. What a bore!

HELMER: I'm not at home to visitors, don't forget.

MAID: [*From the hall doorway.*] Ma'am, a lady to see you—

NORA: All right, let her come in.

MAID: [*To* HELMER.] And the doctor's just come too.

HELMER: Did he go right to my study?

MAID: Yes, he did.

> [HELMER *goes into his room. The* MAID *shows in* MRS. LINDE, *dressed in traveling clothes, and shuts the door after her.*]

MRS. LINDE: [*In a dispirited and somewhat hesitant voice.*] Hello, Nora.

NORA: [*Uncertain.*] Hello—

MRS. LINDE: You don't recognize me.

NORA: No, I don't know—but wait, I think— [*Exclaiming.*] What! Kristine! Is it really you?

MRS. LINDE: Yes, it's me.

NORA: Kristine! To think I didn't recognize you. But then, how could I? [*More quietly.*] How you've changed, Kristine!

MRS. LINDE: Yes, no doubt I have. In nine—ten long years.

NORA: Is it so long since we met! Yes, it's all of that. Oh, these last eight years have been a happy time, believe me. And so now you've come in to town, too. Made the long trip in the winter. That took courage.

MRS. LINDE: I just got here by ship this morning.

NORA: To enjoy yourself over Christmas, of course. Oh, how lovely! Yes, enjoy ourselves, we'll do that. But take your coat off. You're not still cold? [*Helping her.*] There now, let's get cozy here by the stove. No, the easy chair there! I'll take the rocker here. [*Seizing her hands.*] Yes, now you have your old look again; it was only in that first moment. You're a bit more pale, Kristine—and maybe a bit thinner.

MRS. LINDE: And much, much older, Nora.

NORA: Yes, perhaps a bit older; a tiny, tiny bit; not much at all. [*Stopping short; suddenly serious.*] Oh, but thoughtless me, to sit here, chattering away. Sweet, good Kristine, can you forgive me?

MRS. LINDE: What do you mean, Nora?

NORA: [*Softly.*] Poor Kristine, you've become a widow.

MRS. LINDE: Yes, three years ago.

NORA: Oh, I knew it, of course; I read it in the papers. Oh, Kristine, you must believe me; I often thought of writing you then, but I kept postponing it, and something always interfered.

MRS. LINDE: Nora dear, I understand completely.

NORA: No, it was awful of me, Kristine. You poor thing, how much you must have gone through. And he left you nothing?

MRS. LINDE: No.

NORA: And no children?

MRS. LINDE: No.

NORA: Nothing at all, then?

MRS. LINDE: Not even a sense of loss to feed on.

NORA: [*Looking incredulously at her.*] But Kristine, how could that be?

MRS. LINDE: [*Smiling wearily and smoothing her hair.*] Oh, sometimes it happens, Nora.

NORA: So completely alone. How terribly hard that must be for you. I have three lovely children. You can't see them now; they're out with the maid. But now you must tell me everything—

MRS. LINDE: No, no, no, tell me about yourself.

NORA: No, you begin. Today I don't want to be selfish. I want to think only of you today. But there *is* something I must tell you, Did you hear of the wonderful luck we had recently?

MRS. LINDE: No, what's that?

NORA: My husband's been made manager in the bank, just think!

MRS. LINDE: Your husband? How marvelous!

NORA: Isn't it? Being a lawyer is such an uncertain living, you know, especially if one won't touch any cases that aren't clean and decent. And of course Torvald would never do that, and I'm with him completely there. Oh, we're simply delighted, believe me! He'll join the bank right after New Year's and start getting a huge salary and lots of commissions. From now on we can live quite differently—just as we want. Oh, Kristine, I feel so light and happy! Won't it be lovely to have stacks of money and not a care in the world?

MRS. LINDE: Well, anyway, it would be lovely to have enough for necessities.

NORA: No, not just for necessities, but stacks and stacks of money!

MRS. LINDE: [*Smiling.*] Nora, Nora, aren't you sensible yet? Back in school you were such a free spender.

NORA: [*With a quiet laugh.*] Yes, that's what Torvald still says. [*Shaking her finger.*] But "Nora, Nora" isn't as silly as you all think. Really, we've been in no position for me to go squandering. We've had to work, both of us.

MRS. LINDE: You too?

NORA: Yes, at odd jobs—needlework, crocheting, embroidery, and such—[*Casually.*] and other things too. You remember that Torvald left the department when we were married? There was no chance of promotion in his office, and of course he needed to earn more money. But that first year he drove himself terribly. He took on all kinds of extra work that kept him going morning and night. It wore him down, and then he fell deathly ill. The doctors said it was essential for him to travel south.

MRS. LINDE: Yes, didn't you spend a whole year in Italy?

NORA: That's right. It wasn't easy to get away, you know. Ivar had just been born. But of course we had to go. Oh, that was a beautiful trip, and it saved Torvald's life. But it cost a frightful sum, Kristine.

MRS. LINDE: I can well imagine.

NORA: Four thousand, eight hundred crowns it cost. That's really a lot of money.

MRS. LINDE: But it's lucky you had it when you needed it.

NORA: Well, as it was, we got it from Papa.

MRS. LINDE: I see. It was just about the time your father died.

NORA: Yes, just about then. And, you know, I couldn't make that trip out to nurse him. I had to stay here, expecting Ivar any moment, and with my poor sick Torvald to care for. Dearest Papa, I never saw him again, Kristine. Oh, that was the worst time, I've known in all my marriage.

MRS. LINDE: I know how you loved him. And then you went off to Italy?

NORA: Yes. We had the means now, and the doctors urged us. So we left a month after.

MRS. LINDE: And your husband came back completely cured?

NORA: Sound as a drum!

MRS. LINDE: But—the doctor?

NORA: Who?

MRS. LINDE: I thought the maid said he was a doctor, the man who came in with me.

NORA: Yes, that was Dr. Rank—but he's not making a sick call. He's our closest friend, and he stops by at least once a day. No, Torvald hasn't had a sick moment since, and the children are fit and strong, and I am, too. [*Jumping up and clapping her hands.*] Oh, dear God, Kristine, what a lovely thing to live and be happy! But how disgusting of me—I'm talking of nothing but my own affairs. [*Sits on a stool close by* KRISTINE, *arms resting across her knees.*] Oh, don't be angry with me! Tell me, is it really true that you weren't in love with your husband? Why did you marry him, then?

MRS. LINDE: My mother was still alive, but bedridden and helpless—and I had my two younger brothers to look after. In all conscience, I didn't think I could turn him down.

NORA: No, you were right there. But was he rich at the time?

MRS. LINDE: He was very well off, I'd say. But the business was shaky, Nora. When he died, it all fell apart, and nothing was left.

NORA: And, then—?

MRS. LINDE: Yes, so I had to scrape up a living with a little shop and a little teaching and whatever else I could find. The last three years have been like one endless workday without a rest for me. Now it's over, Nora. My poor mother doesn't need me, for she's passed on. Nor the boys, either; they're working now and can take care of themselves.

NORA: How free you must feel—

MRS. LINDE: No—only unspeakably empty. Nothing to live for now. [*Standing up anxiously.*] That's why I couldn't take it any longer out in that desolate hole. Maybe here it'll be easier to find something to do and keep my mind occupied. If I could only be lucky enough to get a steady job, some office work—

NORA: Oh, but Kristine, that's so dreadfully tiring, and you already look so tired. It would be much better for you if you could go off to a bathing resort.

MRS. LINDE: [*Going toward the window.*] I have no father to give me travel money, Nora.

NORA: [*Rising.*] Oh, don't be angry with me.

MRS. LINDE: [*Going to her.*] Nora dear, don't you be angry with me. The worst of my kind of situation is all the bitterness that's stored away. No one to work for, and yet you're always having to snap up your opportunities. You have to live; and so you grow selfish. When you told me the happy change in your lot, do you know I was delighted less for your sakes than for mine?

NORA: How so? Oh, I see. You think maybe Torvald could do something for you.

MRS. LINDE: Yes, that's what I thought.

NORA: And he will, Kristine! Just leave it to me; I'll bring it up so delicately—find something attractive to humor him with. Oh, I'm so eager to help you.

MRS. LINDE: How very kind of you, Nora, to be so concerned over me—doubly kind, considering you really know so little of life's burdens yourself.

NORA: I—? I know so little—?

MRS. LINDE: [*Smiling.*] Well, my heavens—a little needlework and such—Nora, you're just a child.

NORA: [*Tossing her head and pacing the floor.*] You don't have to act so superior.

MRS. LINDE: Oh?

NORA: You're just like the others. You all think I'm incapable of anything serious—

MRS. LINDE: Come now—

NORA: That I've never had to face the raw world.

MRS. LINDE: Nora dear, you've just been telling me all your troubles.

NORA: Hm! Trivia! [*Quietly.*] I haven't told you the big thing.

MRS. LINDE: Big thing? What do you mean?

NORA: You look down on me so, Kristine, but you shouldn't. You're proud that you worked so long and hard for your mother.

MRS. LINDE: I don't look down on a soul. But it *is* true: I'm proud—
and happy, too—to think it was given to me to make my
mother's last days almost free of care.

NORA: And you're also proud thinking of what you've done for your
brothers.

MRS. LINDE: I feel I've a right to be.

NORA: I agree. But listen to this, Kristine—I've also got something
to be proud and happy for.

MRS. LINDE: I don't doubt it. But whatever do you mean?

NORA: Not so loud. What if Torvald heard! He mustn't, not for anything in the world. Nobody must know, Kristine. No one but
you.

MRS. LINDE: But what is it, then?

NORA: Come here. [*Drawing her down beside her on the sofa.*] It's
true—I've also got something to be proud and happy for. I'm the
one who saved Torvald's life.

MRS. LINDE: Saved—? Saved how?

NORA: I told you about the trip to Italy. Torvald never would have
lived if he hadn't gone south—

MRS. LINDE: Of course; your father gave you the means—

NORA: [*Smiling.*] That's what Torvald and all the rest think, but—

MRS. LINDE: But—?

NORA: Papa didn't give us a pin. I was the one who raised the
money.

MRS. LINDE: You? That whole amount?

NORA: Four thousand, eight hundred crowns. What do you say to
that?

MRS. LINDE: But Nora, how was it possible? Did you win the lottery?

NORA: [*Disdainfully.*] The lottery? Pooh! No art to that.

MRS. LINDE: But where did you get it from then?

NORA: [*Humming, with a mysterious smile.*] Hmm, tra-la-la-la.

MRS. LINDE: Because you couldn't have borrowed it.

NORA: No? Why not?

MRS. LINDE: A wife can't borrow without her husband's consent.

NORA: [*Tossing her head.*] Oh, but a wife with a little business sense,
a wife who knows how to manage—

MRS. LINDE: Nora, I simply don't understand—

NORA: You don't have to. Whoever said I *borrowed* the money? I could have gotten it other ways. [*Throwing herself back on the sofa.*] I could have gotten it from some admirer or other. After all, a girl with my ravishing appeal—

MRS. LINDE: You lunatic.

NORA: I'll bet you're eaten up with curiosity, Kristine.

MRS. LINDE: Now listen here, Nora—you haven't done something indiscreet?

NORA: [*Sitting up again.*] Is it indiscreet to save your husband's life?

MRS. LINDE: I think it's indiscreet that without his knowledge you—

NORA: But that's the point: he mustn't know! My Lord, can't you understand? He mustn't ever know the close call he had. It was to *me* the doctors came to say his life was in danger—that nothing could save him but a stay in the south. Didn't I try strategy then! I began talking about how lovely it would be for me to travel abroad like other young wives; I begged and I cried; I told him please to remember my condition, to be kind and indulge me; and then I dropped a hint that he could easily take out a loan. But at that, Kristine, he nearly exploded. He said I was frivolous, and it was his duty as man of the house not to indulge me in whims and fancies—as I think he called them. Aha, I thought, now you'll just have to be saved—and that's when I saw my chance.

MRS. LINDE: And your father never told Torvald the money wasn't from him?

NORA: No, never. Papa died right about then. I'd considered bringing him into my secret and begging him never to tell. But he was too sick at the time—and then, sadly, it didn't matter.

MRS. LINDE: And you've never confided in your husband since?

NORA: For heaven's sake, no! Are you serious? He's so strict on that subject. Besides—Torvald, with all his masculine pride—how painfully humiliating for him if he ever found out he was in debt to me. That would just ruin our relationship. Our beautiful, happy home would never be the same.

MRS. LINDE: Won't you ever tell him?

NORA: [*Thoughtfully, half smiling.*] Yes—maybe sometime, years from now, when I'm no longer so attractive. Don't laugh! I only mean when Torvald loves me less than now, when he stops enjoying my dancing and dressing up and reciting for him. Then it might be wise to have something in reserve— [*Breaking off.*] How ridiculous! That'll never happen— Well, Kristine, what do you think of my big secret? I'm capable of something too, hm? You can imagine, of course, how this thing hangs over me. It really hasn't been easy meeting the payments on time. In the business world there's what they call quarterly interest and what they call amortization, and these are always so terribly hard to manage. I've had to skimp a little here and there, wherever I could, you know. I could hardly spare anything from my house allowance, because Torvald has to live well. I couldn't let the children go poorly dressed; whatever I got for them, I felt I had to use up completely—the darlings!

MRS. LINDE: Poor Nora, so it had to come out of your own budget, then?

NORA: Yes, of course. But I was the one most responsible, too. Every time Torvald gave me money for new clothes and such, I never used more than half; always bought the simplest, cheapest outfits. It was a godsend that everything looks so well on me that Torvald never noticed. But it did weigh me down at times, Kristine. It *is* such a joy to wear fine things. You understand.

MRS. LINDE: Oh, of course.

NORA: And then I found other ways of making money. Last winter I was lucky enough to get a lot of copying to do. I locked myself in and sat writing every evening till late in the night. Ah, I was tired so often, dead tired. But still it was wonderful fun, sitting and working like that, earning money. It was almost like being a man.

MRS. LINDE: But how much have you paid off this way so far?

NORA: That's hard to say, exactly. These accounts, you know, aren't easy to figure. I only know that I've paid out all I could scrape together. Time and again I haven't known where to turn. [*Smiling.*] Then I'd sit here dreaming of a rich old gentleman who had fallen in love with me—

MRS. LINDE: What! Who is he?

NORA: Oh, really! And that he'd died, and when his will was opened, there in big letters it said, "All my fortune shall be paid over in cash, immediately, to that enchanting Mrs. Nora Helmer."

MRS. LINDE: But Nora dear—who *was* this gentleman?

NORA: Good grief, can't you understand? The old man never existed; that was only something I'd dream up time and again whenever I was at my wits' end for money. But it makes no difference now; the old fossil can go where he pleases for all I care; I don't need him or his will—because now I'm free. [*Jumping up.*] Oh, how lovely to think of that, Kristine! Carefree! To know you're carefree, utterly carefree; to be able to romp and play with the children, and to keep up a beautiful, charming home—everything just the way Torvald likes it! And think, spring is coming, with big blue skies. Maybe we can travel a little then. Maybe I'll see the ocean again. Oh yes, it *is* so marvelous to live and be happy!

[*The front doorbell rings.*]

MRS. LINDE: [*Rising.*] There's the bell. It's probably best that I go.

NORA: No, stay. No one's expected. It must be for Torvald.

MAID: [*From the hall doorway.*] Excuse me, ma'am—there's a gentleman here to see Mr. Helmer, but I didn't know—since the doctor's with him—

NORA: Who is the gentleman?

KROGSTAD: [*From the doorway.*] It's me, Mrs. Helmer.

[MRS. LINDE *starts and turns away toward the window.*]

NORA: [*Stepping toward him, tense, her voice a whisper.*] You? What is it? Why do you want to speak to my husband?

KROGSTAD: Bank business—after a fashion. I have a small job in the investment bank, and I hear now your husband is going to be our chief—

NORA: In other words, it's—

KROGSTAD: Just dry business, Mrs. Helmer. Nothing but that.

NORA: Yes, then please be good enough to step into the study. [*She nods indifferently as she sees him out by the hall door, then returns and begins stirring up the stove.*]

MRS. LINDE: Nora—who was that man?

NORA: That was a Mr. Krogstad—a lawyer.

MRS. LINDE: Then it really was him.

NORA: Do you know that person?

MRS. LINDE: I did once—many years ago. For a time he was a law clerk in our town.

NORA: Yes, he's been that.

MRS. LINDE: How he's changed.

NORA: I understand he had a very unhappy marriage.

MRS. LINDE: He's a widower now.

NORA: With a number of children. There now, it's burning. [*She closes the stove door and moves the rocker a bit to one side.*]

MRS. LINDE: They say he has a hand in all kinds of business.

NORA: Oh? That may be true; I wouldn't know. But let's not think about business. It's so dull.

[DR. RANK *enters from* HELMER'S *study.*]

RANK: [*Still in the doorway.*] No, no, really—I don't want to intrude, I'd just as soon talk a little while with your wife. [*Shuts the door, then notices* MRS. LINDE.] Oh, beg pardon. I'm intruding here too.

NORA: No, not at all. [*Introducing him.*] Dr. Rank, Mrs. Linde.

RANK: Well now, that's a name much heard in this house. I believe I passed the lady on the stairs as I came.

MRS. LINDE: Yes, I take the stairs very slowly. They're rather hard on me.

RANK: Uh-hm, some touch of internal weakness?

MRS. LINDE: More overexertion, I'd say.

RANK: Nothing else? Then you're probably here in town to rest up in a round of parties?

MRS. LINDE: I'm here to look for work.

RANK: Is that the best cure for overexertion?

MRS. LINDE: One has to live, Doctor.

RANK: Yes, there's a common prejudice to that effect.

NORA: Oh, come on, Dr. Rank—you really do want to live yourself.

RANK: Yes, I really do. Wretched as I am, I'll gladly prolong my torment indefinitely. All my patients feel like that. And it's quite the same, too, with the morally sick. Right at this moment there's one of those moral invalids in there with Helmer—

MRS. LINDE: [*Softly.*] Ah!

NORA: Who do you mean?

RANK: Oh, it's a lawyer, Krogstad, a type you wouldn't know. His character is rotten to the root—but even he began chattering all-importantly about how he had to *live.*

NORA: Oh? What did he want to talk to Torvald about?

RANK: I really don't know. I only heard something about the bank.

NORA: I didn't know that Krog—that this man Krogstad had anything to do with the bank.

RANK: Yes, he's gotten some kind of berth down there. [*To* MRS. LINDE.] I don't know if you also have, in your neck of the woods, a type of person who scuttles about breathlessly, sniffing out hints of moral corruption, and then maneuvers his victim into some sort of key position where he can keep an eye on him. It's the healthy these days that are out in the cold.

MRS. LINDE: All the same, it's the sick who most need to be taken in.

RANK: [*With a shrug.*] Yes, there we have it. That's the concept that's turning society into a sanatorium.

[NORA, *lost in her thoughts, breaks out into quiet laughter and claps her hands.*]

RANK: Why do you laugh at that? Do you have any real idea of what society is?

NORA: What do I care about dreary old society? I was laughing at something quite different—something terribly funny. Tell me, Doctor—is everyone who works in the bank dependent now on Torvald?

RANK: Is that what you find so terribly funny?

NORA: [*Smiling and humming.*] Never mind, never mind! [*Pacing the floor.*] Yes, that's really immensely amusing: that we—that Torvald has so much power now over all those people. [*Taking the bag out of her pocket.*] Dr. Rank, a little macaroon on that?

RANK: See here, macaroons! I thought they were contraband here.

NORA: Yes, but these are some that Kristine gave me.

MRS. LINDE: What? I—?

NORA: Now, now, don't be afraid. You couldn't possibly know that Torvald had forbidden them. You see, he's worried they'll ruin my teeth. But hmp! Just this once! Isn't that so, Dr. Rank? Help yourself! [*Puts a macaroon in his mouth.*] And you too, Kristine. And I'll also have one, only a little one—or two, at the most. [*Walking about again.*] Now I'm really tremendously happy. Now there's just one last thing in the world that I have an enormous desire to do.

RANK: Well! And what's that?

NORA: It's something I have such a consuming desire to say so Torvald could hear.

RANK: And why can't you say it?

NORA: I don't dare. It's quite shocking.

MRS. LINDE: Shocking?

RANK: Well, then it isn't advisable. But in front of us you certainly can. What do you have such a desire to say so Torvald could hear?

NORA: I have such a huge desire to say—to hell and be damned!

RANK: Are you crazy?

MRS. LINDE: My goodness, Nora!

RANK: Go on, say it. Here he is.

NORA: [*Hiding the macaroon bag.*] Shh, shh, shh!

[HELMER *comes in from his study, hat in hand, overcoat over his arm.*]

NORA: [*Going toward him.*] Well, Torvald dear, are you through with him?

HELMER: Yes, he just left.

NORA: Let me introduce you—this is Kristine, who's arrived here in town.

HELMER: Kristine—? I'm sorry, but I don't know—

NORA: Mrs. Linde, Torvald dear. Mrs. Kristine Linde.

HELMER: Of course. A childhood friend of my wife's, no doubt?

MRS. LINDE: Yes, we knew each other in those days.

NORA: And just think, she made the long trip down here in order to talk with you.

HELMER: What's this?

MRS. LINDE: Well, not exactly—

NORA: You see, Kristine is remarkably clever in office work, and so she's terribly eager to come under a capable man's supervision and add more to what she already knows—

HELMER: Very wise, Mrs. Linde.

NORA: And then when she heard that you'd become a bank manager—the story was wired out to the papers—then she came in as fast as she could and— Really, Torvald, for my sake you can do a little something for Kristine, can't you?

HELMER: Yes, it's not at all impossible. Mrs. Linde, I suppose you're a widow?

MRS. LINDE: Yes.

HELMER: Any experience in office work?

MRS. LINDE: Yes, a good deal.

HELMER: Well, it's quite likely that I can make an opening for you—

NORA: [*Clapping her hands.*] You see, you see!

HELMER: You've come at a lucky moment, Mrs. Linde.

MRS. LINDE: Oh, how can I thank you?

HELMER: Not necessary. [*Putting his overcoat on.*] But today you'll have to excuse me—

RANK: Wait, I'll go with you. [*He fetches his coat from the hall and warms it at the stove.*]

NORA: Don't stay out long, dear.

HELMER: An hour; no more.

NORA: Are you going too, Kristine?

MRS. LINDE: [*Putting on her winter garments.*] Yes, I have to see about a room now.

HELMER: Then perhaps we can all walk together.

NORA: [*Helping her.*] What a shame we're so cramped here, but it's quite impossible for us to—

MRS. LINDE: Oh, don't even think of it! Good-bye, Nora dear, and thanks for everything.

NORA: Good-bye for now. Of course you'll be back this evening. And you too, Dr. Rank. What? If you're well enough? Oh, you've got to be! Wrap up tight now.

[*In a ripple of small talk the company moves out into the hall; children's voices are heard outside on the steps.*]

NORA: There they are! There they are! [*She runs to open the door. The children come in with their nurse,* ANNE-MARIE.] Come in, come in! [*Bends down and kisses them.*] Oh, you darlings—! Look at them, Kristine. Aren't they lovely!

RANK: No loitering in the draft here.

HELMER: Come, Mrs. Linde—this place is unbearable now for anyone but mothers.

[DR. RANK, HELMER, *and* MRS. LINDE *go down the stairs.* ANNE-MARIE *goes into the living room with the children.* NORA *follows, after closing the hall door.*]

NORA: How fresh and strong you look. Oh, such red cheeks you have! Like apples and roses. [*The children interrupt her throughout the following.*] And it was so much fun? That's wonderful. Really? You pulled both Emmy and Bob on the sled? Imagine, all to-

gether! Yes, you're a clever boy, Ivar. Oh, let me hold her a bit,
Anne-Marie. My sweet little doll baby! [*Takes the smallest from the
nurse and dances with her.*] Yes, yes, Mama will dance with Bob as
well. What? Did you throw snowballs? Oh, if I'd only been there!
No, don't bother, Anne-Marie—I'll undress them myself. Oh yes,
let me. It's such fun. Go in and rest; you look half frozen. There's
hot coffee waiting for you on the stove. [*The nurse goes into the
room to the left.* NORA *takes the children's winter things off, throwing
them about, while the children talk to her all at once.*] Is that so? A
big dog chased you? But it didn't bite? No, dogs never bite little,
lovely doll babies. Don't peek in the packages, Ivar! What is it?
Yes, wouldn't you like to know. No, no, it's an ugly something.
Well? Shall we play? What shall we play? Hide-and-seek? Yes, let's
play hide-and-seek. Bob must hide first. I must? Yes, let me hide
first. [*Laughing and shouting, she and the children play in and out
of the living room and the adjoining room to the right. At last* NORA
*hides under the table. The children come storming in, search, but
cannot find her, then hear her muffled laughter, dash over to the
table, lift the cloth up and find her. Wild shouting. She creeps forward as if to scare them. More shouts. Meanwhile, a knock at the
hall door; no one has noticed it. Now the door half opens, and*
KROGSTAD *appears. He waits a moment; the game goes on.*]
KROGSTAD: Beg pardon, Mrs. Helmer—
NORA: [*With a strangled cry, turning and scrambling to her knees.*] Oh!
What do you want?
KROGSTAD: Excuse me. The outer door was ajar; it must be someone
forgot to shut it—
NORA: [*Rising.*] My husband isn't home, Mr. Krogstad.
KROGSTAD: I know that.
NORA: Yes—then what do you want here?
KROGSTAD: A word with you.
NORA: With—? [*To the children, quietly.*] Go in to Anne-Marie.
What? No, the strange man won't hurt Mama. When he's gone,
we'll play some more. [*She leads the children into the room to the
left and shuts the door after them. Then, tense and nervous.*] You
want to speak to me?
KROGSTAD: Yes, I want to.
NORA: Today? But it's not yet the first of the month—

KROGSTAD: No, it's Christmas Eve. It's going to be up to you how merry a Christmas you have.

NORA: What is it you want? Today I absolutely can't—

KROGSTAD: We won't talk about that till later. This is something else. You do have a moment to spare, I suppose?

NORA: Oh yes, of course—I do, except—

KROGSTAD: Good. I was sitting over at Olsen's Restaurant when I saw your husband go down the street—

NORA: Yes?

KROGSTAD: With a lady.

NORA: Yes. So?

KROGSTAD: If you'll pardon my asking: wasn't that lady a Mrs. Linde?

NORA: Yes.

KROGSTAD: Just now come into town?

NORA: Yes, today.

KROGSTAD: She's a good friend of yours?

NORA: Yes, she is. But I don't see—

KROGSTAD: I also knew her once.

NORA: I'm aware of that.

KROGSTAD: Oh? You know all about it. I thought so. Well, then let me ask you short and sweet: is Mrs. Linde getting a job in the bank?

NORA: What makes you think you can cross-examine me, Mr. Krogstad—you, one of my husband's employees? But since you ask, you might as well know—yes, Mrs. Linde's going to be taken on at the bank. And I'm the one who spoke for her, Mr. Krogstad. Now you know.

KROGSTAD: So I guessed right.

NORA: [*Pacing up and down.*] Oh, one does have a tiny bit of influence, I should hope. Just because I am a woman, don't think it means that— When one has a subordinate position, Mr. Krogstad, one really ought to be careful about pushing somebody who—hm—

KROGSTAD: Who has influence?

NORA: That's right.

KROGSTAD: [*In a different tone.*] Mrs. Helmer, would you be good enough to use your influence on my behalf?

NORA: What? What do you mean?

KROGSTAD: Would you please make sure that I keep my subordinate position in the bank?

NORA: What does that mean? Who's thinking of taking away your position?

KROGSTAD: Oh, don't play the innocent with me. I'm quite aware that your friend would hardly relish the chance of running into me again; and I'm also aware now whom I can thank for being turned out.

NORA: But I promise you—

KROGSTAD: Yes, yes, yes, to the point: there's still time, and I'm advising you to use your influence to prevent it.

NORA: But Mr. Krogstad, I have absolutely no influence.

KROGSTAD: You haven't? I thought you were just saying—

NORA: You shouldn't take me so literally. I! How can you believe that I have any such influence over my husband?

KROGSTAD: Oh, I've known your husband from our student days. I don't think the great bank manager's more steadfast than any other married man.

NORA: You speak insolently about my husband, and I'll show you the door.

KROGSTAD: The lady has spirit.

NORA: I'm not afraid of you any longer. After New Year's, I'll soon be done with the whole business.

KROGSTAD: [*Restraining himself.*] Now listen to me, Mrs. Helmer. If necessary, I'll fight for my little job in the bank as if it were life itself.

NORA: Yes, so it seems.

KROGSTAD: It's not just a matter of income; that's the least of it. It's something else— All right, out with it! Look, this is the thing. You know, just like all the others, of course, that once, a good many years ago, I did something rather rash.

NORA: I've heard rumors to that effect.

KROGSTAD: The case never got into court; but all the same, every door was closed in my face from then on. So I took up those various activities you know about. I had to grab hold somewhere; and I dare say I haven't been among the worst. But now I want to drop all that. My boys are growing up. For their sakes, I'll have to win back as much respect as possible here in town. That job in the bank was like the first rung in my ladder. And now your husband wants to kick me right back down in the mud again.

NORA: But for heaven's sake, Mr. Krogstad, it's simply not in my power to help you.

KROGSTAD: That's because you haven't the will to—but I have the means to make you.

NORA: You certainly won't tell my husband that I owe you money?

KROGSTAD: Hm—what if I told him that?

NORA: That would be shameful of you. [*Nearly in tears.*] This secret—my joy and my pride—that he should learn it in such a crude and disgusting way—learn it from you. You'd expose me to the most horrible unpleasantness—

KROGSTAD: Only unpleasantness?

NORA: [*Vehemently.*] But go on and try. It'll turn out the worse for you, because then my husband will really see what a crook you are, and then you'll *never* be able to hold your job.

KROGSTAD: I asked if it was just domestic unpleasantness you were afraid of?

NORA: If my husband finds out, then of course he'll pay what I owe at once, and then we'd be through with you for good.

KROGSTAD: [*A step closer.*] Listen, Mrs. Helmer—you've either got a very bad memory, or else no head at all for business. I'd better put you a little more in touch with the facts.

NORA: What do you mean?

KROGSTAD: When your husband was sick, you came to me for a loan of four thousand, eight hundred crowns.

NORA: Where else could I go?

KROGSTAD: I promised to get you that sum—

NORA: And you got it.

KROGSTAD: I promised to get you that sum, on certain conditions. You were so involved in your husband's illness, and so eager to finance your trip, that I guess you didn't think out all the details. It might just be a good idea to remind you. I promised you the money on the strength of a note I drew up.

NORA: Yes, and that I signed.

KROGSTAD: Right. But at the bottom I added some lines for your father to guarantee the loan. He was supposed to sign down there.

NORA: Supposed to? He did sign.

KROGSTAD: I left the date blank. In other words, your father would have dated his signature himself. Do you remember that?

NORA: Yes, I think—

KROGSTAD: Then I gave you the note for you to mail to your father. Isn't that so?

NORA: Yes.

KROGSTAD: And naturally you sent it at once—because only some five, six days later you brought me the note, properly signed. And with that, the money was yours.

NORA: Well, then; I've made my payments regularly, haven't I?

KROGSTAD: More or less. But—getting back to the point—those were hard times for you then, Mrs. Helmer.

NORA: Yes, they were.

KROGSTAD: Your father was very ill, I believe.

NORA: He was near the end.

KROGSTAD: He died soon after?

NORA: Yes.

KROGSTAD: Tell me, Mrs. Helmer, do you happen to recall the date of your father's death? The day of the month, I mean.

NORA: Papa died the twenty-ninth of September.

KROGSTAD: That's quite correct; I've already looked into that. And now we come to a curious thing— [*Taking out a paper.*] which I simply cannot comprehend.

NORA: Curious thing? I don't know—

KROGSTAD: This is the curious thing: that your father co-signed the note for your loan three days after his death.

NORA: How—? I don't understand.

KROGSTAD: Your father died the twenty-ninth of September. But look. Here your father dated his signature October second. Isn't that curious, Mrs. Helmer? [NORA *is silent.*] Can you explain it to me? [NORA *remains silent.*] It's also remarkable that the words "October second" and the year aren't written in your father's hand, but rather in one that I think I know. Well, it's easy to understand. Your father forgot perhaps to date his signature, and then someone or other added it, a bit sloppily, before anyone knew of his death. There's nothing wrong in that. It all comes down to the signature. And there's no question about *that*, Mrs.

HELMER. It really *was* your father who signed his own name here, wasn't it?

NORA: [*After a short silence, throwing her head back and looking squarely at him.*] No, it wasn't. *I* signed Papa's name.

KROGSTAD: Wait, now—are you fully aware that this is a dangerous confession?

NORA: Why? You'll soon get your money.

KROGSTAD: Let me ask you a question—why didn't you send the paper to your father?

NORA: That was impossible. Papa was so sick. If I'd asked him for his signature, I also would have had to tell him what the money was for. But I couldn't tell him, sick as he was, that my husband's life was in danger. That was just impossible.

KROGSTAD: Then it would have been better if you'd given up the trip abroad.

NORA: I couldn't possibly. The trip was to save my husband's life. I couldn't give that up.

KROGSTAD: But didn't you ever consider that this was a fraud against me?

NORA: I couldn't let myself be bothered by that. You weren't any concern of mine. I couldn't stand you, with all those cold complications you made, even though you knew how badly off my husband was.

KROGSTAD: Mrs. Helmer, obviously you haven't the vaguest idea of what you've involved yourself in. But I can tell you this: it was nothing more and nothing worse that I once did—and it wrecked my whole reputation.

NORA: You? Do you expect me to believe that you ever acted bravely to save your wife's life?

KROGSTAD: Laws don't inquire into motives.

NORA: Then they must be very poor laws.

KROGSTAD: Poor or not—if I introduce this paper in court, you'll be judged according to law.

NORA: This I refuse to believe. A daughter hasn't a right to protect her dying father from anxiety and care? A wife hasn't a right to save her husband's life? I don't know much about laws, but I'm sure that somewhere in the books these things are allowed. And

you don't know anything about it—you who practice the law?
You must be an awful lawyer, Mr. Krogstad.

KROGSTAD: Could be. But business—the kind of business we two
are mixed up in—don't you think I know about that? All right.
Do what you want now. But I'm telling you *this*: if I get shoved
down a second time, you're going to keep me company. [*He bows
and goes out through the hall.*]

NORA: [*Pensive for a moment, then tossing her head.*] Oh, really! Trying to frighten me! I'm not so silly as all that. [*Begins gathering up
the children's clothes, but soon stops.*] But—? No, but that's impossible! I did it out of love.

THE CHILDREN: [*In the doorway, left.*] Mama, that strange man's
gone out the door.

NORA: Yes, yes, I know it. But don't tell anyone about the strange
man. Do you hear? Not even Papa!

THE CHILDREN: No, Mama. But now will you play again?

NORA: No, not now.

THE CHILDREN: Oh, but Mama, you promised.

NORA: Yes, but I can't now. Go inside; I have too much to do. Go
in, go in, my sweet darlings. [*She herds them gently back in the
room and shuts the door after them. Settling on the sofa, she takes up
a piece of embroidery and makes some stitches, but soon stops
abruptly.*] No! [*Throws the work aside, rises, goes to the hall door
and calls out.*] Helene! Let me have the tree in here. [*Goes to the
table, left, opens the table drawer, and stops again.*] No, but that's
utterly impossible!

MAID: [*With the Christmas tree.*] Where should I put it, ma'am?

NORA: There. The middle of the floor.

MAID: Should I bring anything else?

NORA: No, thanks. I have what I need.

[*The* MAID, *who has set the tree down, goes out.*]

NORA: [*Absorbed in trimming the tree.*] Candles here—and flowers
here. That terrible creature! Talk, talk, talk! There's nothing to it
at all. The tree's going to be lovely. I'll do anything to please you,
Torvald. I'll sing for you, dance for you—

[HELMER *comes in from the hall, with a sheaf of papers under his
arm.*]

NORA: Oh! You're back so soon?

HELMER: Yes. Has anyone been here?

NORA: Here? No.

HELMER: That's odd. I saw Krogstad leaving the front door.

NORA: So? Oh yes, that's true. Krogstad was here a moment.

HELMER: Nora, I can see by your face that he's been here, begging you to put in a good word for him.

NORA: Yes.

HELMER: And it was supposed to seem like your own idea? You were to hide it from me that he'd been here. He asked you that, too, didn't he?

NORA: Yes, Torvald, but—

HELMER: Nora, Nora, and you could fall for that? Talk with that sort of person and promise him anything? And then in the bargain, tell me an untruth.

NORA: An untruth—?

HELMER: Didn't you say that no one had been here? [*Wagging his finger.*] My little songbird must never do that again. A songbird needs a clean beak to warble with. No false notes. [*Putting his arm about her waist.*] That's the way it should be, isn't it? Yes, I'm sure of it. [*Releasing her.*] And so, enough of that. [*Sitting by the stove.*] Ah, how snug and cozy it is here. [*Leafing among his papers.*]

NORA: [*Busy with the tree, after a short pause.*] Torvald!

HELMER: Yes.

NORA: I'm so much looking forward to the Stenborgs' costume party, day after tomorrow.

HELMER: And I can't wait to see what you'll surprise me with.

NORA: Oh, that stupid business!

HELMER: What?

NORA: I can't find anything that's right. Everything seems so ridiculous, so inane.

HELMER: So my little Nora's come to *that* recognition?

NORA: [*Going behind his chair, her arms resting on its back.*] Are you very busy, Torvald?

HELMER: Oh—

NORA: What papers are those?

HELMER: Bank matters.

NORA: Already?

HELMER: I've gotten full authority from the retiring management to make all necessary changes in personnel and procedure. I'll need Christmas week for that. I want to have everything in order by New Year's.

NORA: So that was the reason this poor Krogstad—

HELMER: Hm.

NORA: [*Still leaning on the chair and slowly stroking the nape of his neck.*] If you weren't so very busy, I would have asked you an enormous favor, Torvald.

HELMER: Let's hear. What is it?

NORA: You know, there isn't anyone who has your good taste—and I want so much to look well at the costume party. Torvald, couldn't you take over and decide what I should be and plan my costume?

HELMER: Ah, is my stubborn little creature calling for a lifeguard?

NORA: Yes, Torvald, I can't get anywhere without your help.

HELMER: All right—I'll think it over. We'll hit on something.

NORA: Oh, how sweet of you. [*Goes to the tree again. Pause.*] Aren't the red flowers pretty—? But tell me, was it really such a crime that this Krogstad committed?

HELMER: Forgery. Do you have any idea what that means?

NORA: Couldn't he have done it out of need?

HELMER: Yes, or thoughtlessness, like so many others. I'm not so heartless that I'd condemn a man categorically for just one mistake.

NORA: No, of course not, Torvald!

HELMER: Plenty of men have redeemed themselves by openly confessing their crimes and taking their punishment.

NORA: Punishment—?

HELMER: But now Krogstad didn't go that way. He got himself out by sharp practices, and that's the real cause of his moral breakdown.

NORA: Do you really think that would—?

HELMER: Just imagine how a man with that sort of guilt in him has to lie and cheat and deceive on all sides, has to wear a mask even with the nearest and dearest he has, even with his own wife and children. And with the children, Nora—that's where it's most horrible.

NORA: Why?

HELMER: Because that kind of atmosphere of lies infects the whole life of a home. Every breath the children take in is filled with the germs of something degenerate.

NORA: [*Coming closer behind him.*] Are you sure of that?

HELMER: Oh, I've seen it often enough as a lawyer. Almost everyone who goes bad early in life has a mother who's a chronic liar.

NORA: Why just—the mother?

HELMER: It's usually the mother's influence that's dominant, but the father's works in the same way, of course. Every lawyer is quite familiar with it. And still this Krogstad's been going home year in, year out, poisoning his own children with lies and pretense; that's why I call him morally lost. [*Reaching his hands out toward her.*] So my sweet little Nora must promise me never to plead his cause. Your hand on it. Come, come, what's this? Give me your hand. There, now. All settled. I can tell you it'd be impossible for me to work alongside of him. I literally feel physically revolted when I'm anywhere near such a person.

NORA: [*Withdraws her hand and goes to the other side of the Christmas tree.*] How hot it is here! And I've got so much to do.

HELMER: [*Getting up and gathering his papers.*] Yes, and I have to think about getting some of these read through before dinner. I'll think about your costume, too. And something to hang on the tree in gilt paper, I may even see about that. [*Putting his hand on her head.*] Oh you, my darling little songbird. [*He goes into his study and closes the door after him.*]

NORA: [*Softly, after a silence.*] Oh, really! It isn't so. It's impossible. It must be impossible.

ANNE-MARIE: [*In the doorway, left.*] The children are begging so hard to come in to Mama.

NORA: No, no, no, don't let them in to me! You stay with them, Anne-Marie.

ANNE-MARIE: Of course, ma'am. [*Closes the door.*]

NORA: [*Pale with terror.*] Hurt my children—! Poison my home? [*A moment's pause; then she tosses her head.*] That's not true. Never. Never in all the world.

ACT TWO

Same room. Beside the piano the Christmas tree now stands stripped of ornament, burned-down candle stubs on its ragged branches. NORA'*s street clothes lie on the sofa.* NORA, *alone in the room, moves restlessly about; at last she stops at the sofa and picks up her coat.*

NORA: [*Dropping the coat again.*] Someone's coming! [*Goes toward the door, listens.*] No—there's no one. Of course—nobody's coming today, Christmas Day—or tomorrow, either. But maybe— [*Opens the door and looks out.*] No, nothing in the mailbox. Quite empty. [*Coming forward.*] What nonsense! He won't do anything serious. Nothing terrible could happen. It's impossible. Why, I have three small children.

[ANNE-MARIE, *with a large carton, comes in from the room to the left.*]

ANNE-MARIE: Well, at last I found the box with the masquerade clothes.

NORA: Thanks. Put it on the table.

ANNE-MARIE: [*Does so.*] But they're all pretty much of a mess.

NORA: Ahh! I'd love to rip them in a million pieces!

ANNE-MARIE: Oh, mercy, they can be fixed right up. Just a little patience.

NORA: Yes, I'll go get Mrs. Linde to help me.

ANNE-MARIE: Out again now? In this nasty weather? Miss Nora will catch cold—get sick.

NORA: Oh, worse things could happen— How are the children?

ANNE-MARIE: The poor mites are playing with their Christmas presents, but—

NORA: Do they ask for me much?

ANNE-MARIE: They're so used to having Mama around, you know.

NORA: Yes, but Anne-Marie, I *can't* be together with them as much as I was.

ANNE-MARIE: Well, small children get used to anything.

NORA: You think so? Do you think they'd forget their mother if she was gone for good?

ANNE-MARIE: Oh, mercy—gone for good!

NORA: Wait, tell me, Anne-Marie—I've wondered so often—how could you ever have the heart to give your child over to strangers?

ANNE-MARIE: But I had to, you know, to become little Nora's nurse.

NORA: Yes, but how could you *do* it?

ANNE-MARIE: When I could get such a good place? A girl who's poor and who's gotten in trouble is glad enough for that. Because that slippery fish, he didn't do a thing for me, you know.

NORA: But your daughter's surely forgotten you.

ANNE-MARIE: Oh, she certainly has not. She's written to me, both when she was confirmed and when she was married.

NORA: [*Clasping her about the neck.*] You old Anne-Marie, you were a good mother for me when I was little.

ANNE-MARIE: Poor little Nora, with no other mother but me.

NORA: And if the babies didn't have one, then I know that you'd— What silly talk! [*Opening the carton.*] Go in to them. Now I'll have to— Tomorrow you can see how lovely I'll look.

ANNE-MARIE: Oh, there won't be anyone at the party as lovely as Miss Nora. [*She goes off into the room, left.*]

NORA: [*Begins unpacking the box, but soon throws it aside.*] Oh, if I dared to go out. If only nobody would come. If only nothing would happen here while I'm out. What craziness—nobody's coming. Just don't think. This muff—needs a brushing. Beautiful gloves, beautiful gloves. Let it go. Let it go! One, two, three, four, five, six— [*With a cry.*] Oh, there they are! [*Poises to move toward the door, but remains irresolutely standing.* MRS. LINDE *enters from the hall, where she has removed her street clothes.*]

NORA: Oh, it's you, Kristine. There's no one else out there? How good that you've come.

MRS. LINDE: I hear you were up asking for me.

NORA: Yes, I just stopped by. There's something you really can help me with. Let's get settled on the sofa. Look, there's going to be a costume party tomorrow evening at the Stenborgs' right above us, and now Torvald wants me to go as a Neapolitan peasant girl and dance the tarantella that I learned in Capri.

MRS. LINDE: Really, are you giving a whole performance?

NORA: Torvald says yes, I should. See, here's the dress. Torvald had it made for me down there; but now it's all so tattered that I just don't know—

MRS. LINDE: Oh, we'll fix that up in no time. It's nothing more than the trimmings—they're a bit loose here and there. Needle and thread? Good, now we have what we need.

NORA: Oh, how sweet of you!

MRS. LINDE: [*Sewing.*] So you'll be in disguise tomorrow, Nora. You know what? I'll stop by then for a moment and have a look at you all dressed up. But listen, I've absolutely forgotten to thank you for that pleasant evening yesterday.

NORA: [*Getting up and walking about.*] I don't think it was as pleasant as usual yesterday. You should have come to town a bit sooner, Kristine— Yes, Torvald really knows how to give a home elegance and charm.

MRS. LINDE: And you do, too, if you ask me. You're not your father's daughter for nothing. But tell me, is Dr. Rank always so down in the mouth as yesterday?

NORA: No, that was quite an exception. But he goes around critically ill all the time—tuberculosis of the spine, poor man. You know, his father was a disgusting thing who kept mistresses and so on—and that's why the son's been sickly from birth.[1]

MRS. LINDE: [*Lets her sewing fall to her lap.*] But my dearest Nora, how do you know about such things?

NORA: [*Walking more jauntily.*] Hmp! When you've had three children, then you've had a few visits from—from women who know something of medicine, and they tell you this and that.

MRS. LINDE: [*Resumes sewing; a short pause.*] Does Dr. Rank come here every day?

NORA: Every blessed day. He's Torvald's best friend from childhood, and *my* good friend, too. Dr. Rank almost belongs to this house.

MRS. LINDE: But tell me—is he quite sincere? I mean, doesn't he rather enjoy flattering people?

NORA: Just the opposite. Why do you think that?

MRS. LINDE: When you introduced us yesterday, he was proclaiming that he'd often heard my name in this house; but later I noticed that your husband hadn't the slightest idea who I really was. So how could Dr. Rank—?

NORA: But it's all true, Kristine. You see, Torvald loves me beyond words, and, as he puts it, he'd like to keep me all to himself. For a

---

1. Dr. Rank suffers from congenital syphilis.

long time he'd almost be jealous if I even mentioned any of my old friends back home. So of course I dropped that. But with Dr. Rank I talk a lot about such things, because he likes hearing about them.

MRS. LINDE: Now listen, Nora; in many ways you're still like a child. I'm a good deal older than you, with a little more experience. I'll tell you something: you ought to put an end to all this with Dr. Rank.

NORA: What should I put an end to?

MRS. LINDE: Both parts of it, I think. Yesterday you said something about a rich admirer who'd provide you with money—

NORA: Yes, one who doesn't exist—worse luck. So?

MRS. LINDE: Is Dr. Rank well off?

NORA: Yes, he is.

MRS. LINDE: With no dependents?

NORA: No, no one. But—

MRS. LINDE: And he's over here every day?

NORA: Yes, I told you that.

MRS. LINDE: How can a man of such refinement be so grasping?

NORA: I don't follow you at all.

MRS. LINDE: Now don't try to hide it, Nora. You think I can't guess who loaned you the forty-eight hundred crowns?

NORA: Are you out of your mind? How could you think such a thing! A friend of ours, who comes here every single day. What an intolerable situation that would have been!

MRS. LINDE: Then it really wasn't him.

NORA: No, absolutely not. It never even crossed my mind for a moment— And he had nothing to lend in those days; his inheritance came later.

MRS. LINDE: Well, I think that was a stroke of luck for you, Nora dear.

NORA: No, it never would have occurred to me to ask Dr. Rank— Still, I'm quite sure that if I had asked him—

MRS. LINDE: Which you won't, of course.

NORA: No, of course not. I can't see that I'd ever need to. But I'm quite positive that if I talked to Dr. Rank—

MRS. LINDE: Behind your husband's back?

NORA: I've got to clear up this other thing; *that's* also behind his back. I've *got* to clear it all up.

MRS. LINDE: Yes, I was saying that yesterday, but—

NORA: [*Pacing up and down.*] A man handles these problems so much better than a woman—

MRS. LINDE: One's husband does, yes.

NORA: Nonsense. [*Stopping.*] When you pay everything you owe, then you get your note back, right?

MRS. LINDE: Yes, naturally.

NORA: And can rip it into a million pieces and burn it up—that filthy scrap of paper!

MRS. LINDE: [*Looking hard at her, laying her sewing aside, and rising slowly.*] Nora, you're hiding something from me.

NORA: You can see it in my face?

MRS. LINDE: Something's happened to you since yesterday morning. Nora, what is it?

NORA: [*Hurrying toward her.*] Kristine! [*Listening.*] Shh! Torvald's home. Look, go in with the children a while. Torvald can't bear all this snipping and stitching. Let Anne-Marie help you.

MRS. LINDE: [*Gathering up some of the things.*] All right, but I'm not leaving here until we've talked this out. [*She disappears into the room, left, as* TORVALD *enters from the hall.*]

NORA: Oh, how I've been waiting for you, Torvald dear.

HELMER: Was that the dressmaker?

NORA: No, that was Kristine. She's helping me fix up my costume. You know, it's going to be quite attractive.

HELMER: Yes, wasn't that a bright idea I had?

NORA: Brilliant! But then wasn't I good as well to give in to you?

HELMER: Good—because you give in to your husband's judgment? All right, you little goose, I know you didn't mean it like that. But I won't disturb you. You'll want to have a fitting, I suppose.

NORA: And you'll be working?

HELMER: Yes. [*Indicating a bundle of papers.*] See. I've been down to the bank. [*Starts toward his study.*]

NORA: Torvald.

HELMER: [*Stops.*] Yes.

NORA: If your little squirrel begged you, with all her heart and soul, for something—?

HELMER: What's that?

NORA: Then would you do it?

HELMER: First, naturally, I'd have to know what it was.

NORA: Your squirrel would scamper about and do tricks, if you'd only be sweet and give in.

HELMER: Out with it.

NORA: Your lark would be singing high and low in every room—

HELMER: Come on, she does that anyway.

NORA: I'd be a wood nymph[2] and dance for you in the moonlight.

HELMER: Nora—don't tell me it's that same business from this morning?

NORA: [*Coming closer.*] Yes, Torvald, I beg you, please!

HELMER: And you actually have the nerve to drag that up again?

NORA: Yes, yes, you've got to give in to me; you *have* to let Krogstad keep his job in the bank.

HELMER: My dear Nora, I've slated his job for Mrs. Linde.

NORA: That's awfully kind of you. But you could just fire another clerk instead of Krogstad.

HELMER: This is the most incredible stubbornness! Because you go and give an impulsive promise to speak up for him, I'm expected to—

NORA: That's not the reason, Torvald. It's for your own sake. That man does writing for the worst papers; you said it yourself. He could do you any amount of harm. I'm scared to death of him—

HELMER: Ah, I understand. It's the old memories haunting you.

NORA: What do you mean by that?

HELMER: Of course, you're thinking about your father.

NORA: Yes, all right. Just remember how those nasty gossips wrote in the papers about Papa and slandered him so cruelly. I think they'd have had him dismissed if the department hadn't sent you up to investigate, and if you hadn't been so kind and open-minded toward him.

HELMER: My dear Nora, there's a notable difference between your father and me. Your father's official career was hardly above reproach. But mine is; and I hope it'll stay that way as long as I hold my position.

NORA: Oh, who can ever tell what vicious minds can invent? We

---

2. In Greek mythology, a maiden goddess who lives in nature.

could be so snug and happy now in our quiet, carefree home—
you and I and the children, Torvald! That's why I'm pleading
with you so—

HELMER: And just by pleading for him you make it impossible for
me to keep him on. It's already known at the bank that I'm firing
Krogstad. What if it's rumored around now that the new bank
manager was vetoed by his wife—

NORA: Yes, what then—?

HELMER: Oh yes—as long as our little bundle of stubbornness
gets her way—! I should go and make myself ridiculous in front
of the whole office—give people the idea I can be swayed by
all kinds of outside pressure. Oh, you can bet I'd feel the effects
of that soon enough! Besides—there's something that rules
Krogstad right out at the bank as long as I'm the manager.

NORA: What's that?

HELMER: His moral failings I could maybe overlook if I had to—

NORA: Yes, Torvald, why not?

HELMER: And I hear he's quite efficient on the job. But he was a
crony of mine back in my teens—one of those rash friendships
that crop up again and again to embarrass you later in life. Well,
I might as well say it straight out: we're on a first-name basis.
And that tactless fool makes no effort at all to hide it in front of
others. Quite the contrary—he thinks that entitles him to take a
familiar air around me, and so every other second he comes
booming out with his "Yes, Torvald!" and "Sure thing, Torvald!"
I tell you, it's been excruciating for me. He's out to make my
place in the bank unbearable.

NORA: Torvald, you can't be serious about all this.

HELMER: Oh no? Why not?

NORA: Because these are such petty considerations.

HELMER: What are you saying? Petty? You think I'm petty!

NORA: No, just the opposite, Torvald dear. That's exactly why—

HELMER: Never mind. You call my motives petty; then I might as
well be just that. Petty! All right! We'll put a stop to this for good.
[*Goes to the hall door and calls.*] Helene!

NORA: What do you want?

HELMER: [*Searching among his papers.*] A decision. [*The* MAID *comes in.*] Look here; take this letter; go out with it at once. Get hold of a messenger and have him deliver it. Quick now. It's already addressed. Wait, here's some money.

MAID: Yes, sir. [*She leaves with the letter.*]

HELMER: [*Straightening his papers.*] There, now, little Miss Willful.

NORA: [*Breathlessly.*] Torvald, what was that letter?

HELMER: Krogstad's notice.

NORA: Call it back, Torvald! There's still time. Oh, Torvald, call it back! Do it for my sake—for your sake, for the children's sake! Do you hear, Torvald; do it! You don't know how this can harm us.

HELMER: Too late.

NORA: Yes, too late.

HELMER: Nora dear, I can forgive you this panic, even though basically you're insulting me. Yes, you are! Or isn't it an insult to think that *I* should be afraid of a courtroom hack's revenge? But I forgive you anyway, because this shows so beautifully how much you love me. [*Takes her in his arms.*] This is the way it should be, my darling Nora. Whatever comes, you'll see: when it really counts, I have strength and courage enough as a man to take on the whole weight myself.

NORA: [*Terrified.*] What do you mean by that?

HELMER: The whole weight, I said.

NORA: [*Resolutely.*] No, never in all the world.

HELMER: Good. So we'll share it, Nora, as man and wife. That's as it should be. [*Fondling her.*] Are you happy now? There, there, there—not these frightened dove's eyes. It's nothing at all but empty fantasies— Now you should run through your tarantella and practice your tambourine. I'll go to the inner office and shut both doors, so I won't hear a thing; you can make all the noise you like. [*Turning in the doorway.*] And when Rank comes, just tell him where he can find me. [*He nods to her and goes with his papers into the study, closing the door.*]

NORA: [*Standing as though rooted, dazed with fright, in a whisper.*] He really could do it. He will do it. He'll do it in spite of everything. No, not that, never, never! Anything but that! Escape! A way out— [*The doorbell rings.*] Dr. Rank! Anything but that! *Anything*, whatever it is! [*Her hands pass over her face, smoothing*

it; she pulls herself together, goes over and opens the hall door. DR.
RANK *stands outside, hanging his fur coat up. During the following
scene, it begins getting dark.*]

NORA: Hello, Dr. Rank. I recognized your ring. But you mustn't go
in to Torvald yet; I believe he's working.

RANK: And you?

NORA: For you, I always have an hour to spare—you know that. [*He
has entered, and she shuts the door after him.*]

RANK: Many thanks. I'll make use of these hours while I can.

NORA: What do you mean by that? While you can?

RANK: Does that disturb you?

NORA: Well, it's such an odd phrase. Is anything going to happen?

RANK: What's going to happen is what I've been expecting so long—
but I honestly didn't think it would come so soon.

NORA: [*Gripping his arm.*] What is it you've found out? Dr. Rank,
you have to tell me!

RANK: [*Sitting by the stove.*] It's all over with me. There's nothing to
be done about it.

NORA: [*Breathing easier.*] Is it you—then—?

RANK: Who else? There's no point in lying to one's self. I'm the most
miserable of all my patients, Mrs. Helmer. These past few days
I've been auditing my internal accounts. Bankrupt! Within a
month I'll probably be laid out and rotting in the churchyard.

NORA: Oh, what a horrible thing to say.

RANK: The thing itself is horrible. But the worst of it is all the other
horror before it's over. There's only one final examination left;
when I'm finished with that, I'll know about when my disinte-
gration will begin. There's something I want to say. Helmer with
his sensitivity has such a sharp distaste for anything ugly. I don't
want him near my sickroom.

NORA: Oh, but Dr. Rank—

RANK: I won't have him in there. Under no condition. I'll lock my
door to him— As soon as I'm completely sure of the worst, I'll
send you my calling card marked with a black cross, and you'll
know then the wreck has started to come apart.

NORA: No, today you're completely unreasonable. And I wanted you
so much to be in a really good humor.

RANK: With death up my sleeve? And then to suffer this way for somebody else's sins. Is there any justice in that? And in every single family, in some way or another, this inevitable retribution of nature goes on—

NORA: [*Her hands pressed over her ears.*] Oh, stuff! Cheer up! Please—be gay!

RANK: Yes, I'd just as soon laugh at it all. My poor, innocent spine, serving time for my father's gay army days.

NORA: [*By the table, left.*] He was so infatuated with asparagus tips and *pâté de foie gras*, wasn't that it?

RANK: Yes—and with truffles.

NORA: Truffles, yes. And then with oysters, I suppose?

RANK: Yes, tons of oysters, naturally.

NORA: And then the port and champagne to go with it. It's so sad that all these delectable things have to strike at our bones.

RANK: Especially when they strike at the unhappy bones that never shared in the fun.

NORA: Ah, that's the saddest of all.

RANK: [*Looks searchingly at her.*] Hm.

NORA: [*After a moment.*] Why did you smile?

RANK: No, it was you who laughed.

NORA: No, it was you who smiled, Dr. Rank!

RANK: [*Getting up.*] You're even a bigger tease than I'd thought.

NORA: I'm full of wild ideas today.

RANK: That's obvious.

NORA: [*Putting both hands on his shoulders.*] Dear, dear Dr. Rank, you'll never die for Torvald and me.

RANK: Oh, that loss you'll easily get over. Those who go away are soon forgotten.

NORA: [*Looks fearfully at him.*] You believe that?

RANK: One makes new connections, and then—

NORA: Who makes new connections?

RANK: Both you and Torvald will when I'm gone. I'd say you're well under way already. What was that Mrs. Linde doing here last evening?

NORA: Oh, come—you can't be jealous of poor Kristine?

RANK: Oh yes, I am. She'll be my successor here in the house. When I'm down under, that woman will probably—

NORA: Shh! Not so loud. She's right in there.

RANK: Today as well. So you see.

NORA: Only to sew on my dress. Good gracious, how unreasonable you are. [*Sitting on the sofa.*] Be nice now, Dr. Rank. Tomorrow you'll see how beautifully I'll dance; and you can imagine then that I'm dancing only for you—yes, and of course for Torvald, too—that's understood. [*Takes various items out of the carton.*] Dr. Rank, sit over here and I'll show you something.

RANK: [*Sitting.*] What's that?

NORA: Look here. Look.

RANK: Silk stockings.

NORA: Flesh-colored. Aren't they lovely? Now it's so dark here, but tomorrow— No, no, no, just look at the feet. Oh well, you might as well look at the rest.

RANK: Hm—

NORA: Why do you look so critical? Don't you believe they'll fit?

RANK: I've never had any chance to form an opinion on that.

NORA: [*Glancing at him a moment.*] Shame on you. [*Hits him lightly on the ear with the stockings.*] That's for you. [*Puts them away again.*]

RANK: And what other splendors am I going to see now?

NORA: Not the least bit more, because you've been naughty. [*She hums a little and rummages among her things.*]

RANK: [*After a short silence.*] When I sit here together with you like this, completely easy and open, then I don't know—I simply can't imagine—whatever would have become of me if I'd never come into this house.

NORA: [*Smiling.*] Yes, I really think you feel completely at ease with us.

RANK: [*More quietly, staring straight ahead.*] And then to have to go away from it all—

NORA: Nonsense, you're not going away.

RANK: [*His voice unchanged.*] —and not even be able to leave some poor show of gratitude behind, scarcely a fleeting regret—no more than a vacant place that anyone can fill.

NORA: And if I asked you now for—? No—

RANK: For what?

NORA: For a great proof of your friendship—

RANK: Yes, yes?

NORA: No, I mean—for an exceptionally big favor—

RANK: Would you really, for once, make me so happy?

NORA: Oh, you haven't the vaguest idea what it is.

RANK: All right, then tell me.

NORA: No, but I can't, Dr. Rank—it's all out of reason. It's advice and help, too—and a favor—

RANK: So much the better. I can't fathom what you're hinting at. Just speak out. Don't you trust me?

NORA: Of course. More than anyone else. You're my best and truest friend, I'm sure. That's why I want to talk to you. All right, then, Dr. Rank: there's something you can help me prevent. You know how deeply, how inexpressibly dearly Torvald loves me; he'd never hesitate a second to give up his life for me.

RANK: [*Leaning close to her.*] Nora—do you think he's the only one—

NORA: [*With a slight start.*] Who—?

RANK: Who'd gladly give up his life for you.

NORA: [*Heavily.*] I see.

RANK: I swore to myself you should know this before I'm gone. I'll never find a better chance. Yes, Nora, now you know. And also you know now that you can trust me beyond anyone else.

NORA: [*Rising, natural and calm.*] Let me by.

RANK: [*Making room for her, but still sitting.*] Nora—

NORA: [*In the hall doorway.*] Helene, bring the lamp in. [*Goes over to the stove.*] Ah, dear Dr. Rank, that was really mean of you.

RANK: [*Getting up.*] That I've loved you just as deeply as somebody else? Was *that* mean?

NORA: No, but that you came out and told me. That was quite unnecessary—

RANK: What do you mean? Have you known—?

[*The* MAID *comes in with the lamp, sets it on the table, and goes out again.*]

RANK: Nora—Mrs. Helmer—I'm asking you: have you known about it?

NORA: Oh, how can I tell what I know or don't know? Really, I don't know what to say— Why did you have to be so clumsy, Dr. Rank! Everything was so good.

RANK: Well, in any case, you now have the knowledge that my body and soul are at your command. So won't you speak out?

NORA: [*Looking at him.*] After that?

RANK: Please, just let me know what it is.

NORA: You can't know anything now.

RANK: I have to. You mustn't punish me like this. Give me the chance to do whatever is humanly possible for you.

NORA: Now there's nothing you can do for me. Besides, actually, I don't need any help. You'll see—it's only my fantasies. That's what it is. Of course! [*Sits in the rocker, looks at him, and smiles.*] What a nice one you are, Dr. Rank. Aren't you a little bit ashamed, now that the lamp is here?

RANK: No, not exactly. But perhaps I'd better go—for good?

NORA: No, you certainly can't do that. You must come here just as you always have. You know Torvald can't do without you.

RANK: Yes, but *you?*

NORA: You know how much I enjoy it when you're here.

RANK: That's precisely what threw me off. You're a mystery to me. So many times I've felt you'd almost rather be with me than with Helmer.

NORA: Yes—you see, there are some people that one loves most and other people that one would almost prefer being with.

RANK: Yes, there's something to that.

NORA: When I was back home, of course I loved Papa most. But I always thought it was so much fun when I could sneak down to the maids' quarters, because they never tried to improve me, and it was always so amusing, the way they talked to each other.

RANK: Aha, so it's *their* place that I've filled.

NORA: [*Jumping up and going to him.*] Oh, dear, sweet Dr. Rank, that's not what I meant at all. But you can understand that with Torvald it's just the same as with Papa—

[*The* MAID *enters from the hall.*]

MAID: Ma'am—please! [*She whispers to* NORA *and hands her a calling card.*]

NORA: [*Glancing at the card.*] Ah! [*Slips it into her pocket.*]

RANK: Anything wrong?

NORA: No, no, not at all. It's only some—it's my new dress—

RANK: Really? But—there's your dress.

NORA: Oh, that. But this is another one—I ordered it—Torvald mustn't know—

RANK: Ah, now we have the big secret.

NORA: That's right. Just go in with him—he's back in the inner study. Keep him there as long as—

RANK: Don't worry. He won't get away. [*Goes into the study.*]

NORA: [*To the* MAID.] And he's standing waiting in the kitchen?

MAID: Yes, he came up by the back stairs.

NORA: But didn't you tell him somebody was here?

MAID: Yes, but that didn't do any good.

NORA: He won't leave?

MAID: No, he won't go till he's talked with you, ma'am.

NORA: Let him come in, then—but quietly. Helene, don't breathe a word about this. It's a surprise for my husband.

MAID: Yes, yes, I understand— [*Goes out.*]

NORA: This horror—it's going to happen. No, no, no, it can't happen, it mustn't. [*She goes and bolts* HELMER's *door. The* MAID *opens the hall door for* KROGSTAD *and shuts it behind him. He is dressed for travel in a fur coat, boots, and a fur cap.*]

NORA: [*Going toward him.*] Talk softly. My husband's home.

KROGSTAD: Well, good for him.

NORA: What do you want?

KROGSTAD: Some information.

NORA: Hurry up, then. What is it?

KROGSTAD: You know, of course, that I got my notice.

NORA: I couldn't prevent it, Mr. Krogstad. I fought for you to the bitter end, but nothing worked.

KROGSTAD: Does your husband's love for you run so thin? He knows everything I can expose you to, and all the same he dares to—

NORA: How can you imagine he knows anything about this?

KROGSTAD: Ah, no—I can't imagine it either, now. It's not at all like my fine Torvald Helmer to have so much guts—

NORA: Mr. Krogstad, I demand respect for my husband!

KROGSTAD: Why, of course—all due respect. But since the lady's keeping it so carefully hidden, may I presume to ask if you're also a bit better informed than yesterday about what you've actually done?

NORA: More than you ever could teach me.

KROGSTAD: Yes, I *am* such an awful lawyer.

NORA: What is it you want from me?

KROGSTAD: Just a glimpse of how you are, Mrs. Helmer. I've been thinking about you all day long. A cashier, a night-court scribbler, a—well, a type like me also has a little of what they call a heart, you know.

NORA: Then show it. Think of my children.

KROGSTAD: Did you or your husband ever think of mine? But never mind. I simply wanted to tell you that you don't need to take this thing too seriously. For the present, I'm not proceeding with any action.

NORA: Oh no, really! Well—I knew that.

KROGSTAD: Everything can be settled in a friendly spirit. It doesn't have to get around town at all; it can stay just among us three.

NORA: My husband must never know anything of this.

KROGSTAD: How can you manage that? Perhaps you can pay me the balance?

NORA: No, not right now.

KROGSTAD: Or you know some way of raising the money in a day or two?

NORA: No way that I'm willing to use.

KROGSTAD: Well, it wouldn't have done you any good, anyway. If you stood in front of me with a fistful of bills, you still couldn't buy your signature back.

NORA: Then tell me what you're going to do with it.

KROGSTAD: I'll just hold onto it—keep it on file. There's no outsider who'll even get wind of it. So if you've been thinking of taking some desperate step—

NORA: I have.

KROGSTAD: Been thinking of running away from home—

NORA: I have!

KROGSTAD: Or even of something worse—

NORA: How could you guess that?

KROGSTAD: You can drop those thoughts.

NORA: How could you guess I was thinking of *that*?

KROGSTAD: Most of us think about *that* at first. I thought about it too, but I discovered I hadn't the courage—

NORA: [*Lifelessly.*] I don't either.

KROGSTAD: [*Relieved.*] That's true, you haven't the courage? You too?

NORA: I don't have it—I don't have it.

KROGSTAD: It would be terribly stupid, anyway. After that first storm at home blows out, why, then— I have here in my pocket a letter for your husband—

NORA: Telling everything?

KROGSTAD: As charitably as possible.

NORA: [*Quickly.*] He mustn't ever get that letter. Tear it up. I'll find some way to get money.

KROGSTAD: Beg pardon, Mrs. Helmer, but I think I just told you—

NORA: Oh, I don't mean the money I owe you. Let me know how much you want from my husband, and I'll manage it.

KROGSTAD: I don't want any money from your husband.

NORA: What do you want, then?

KROGSTAD: I'll tell you what. I want to recoup, Mrs. Helmer; I want to get on in the world—and there's where your husband can help me. For a year and a half I've kept myself clean of anything disreputable—all that time struggling with the worst conditions; but I was satisfied, working my way up step by step. Now I've been written right off, and I'm just not in the mood to come crawling back. I tell you, I want to move on. I want to get back in the bank—in a better position. Your husband can set up a job for me—

NORA: He'll never do that!

KROGSTAD: He'll do it. I know him. He won't dare breathe a word of protest. And once I'm in there together with him, you just wait and see! Inside of a year, I'll be the manager's right-hand man. It'll be Nils Krogstad, not Torvald Helmer, who runs the bank.

NORA: You'll never see the day!

KROGSTAD: Maybe you think you can—

NORA: I have the courage now—for *that.*

KROGSTAD: Oh, you don't scare me. A smart, spoiled lady like you—

NORA: You'll see; you'll see!

KROGSTAD: Under the ice, maybe? Down in the freezing, coal-black water? There, till you float up in the spring, ugly, unrecognizable, with your hair falling out—

NORA: You don't frighten me.

KROGSTAD: Nor do you frighten me. One doesn't do these things, Mrs. Helmer. Besides, what good would it be? I'd still have him safe in my pocket.

NORA: Afterwards? When I'm no longer—?

KROGSTAD: Are you forgetting that *I'll* be in control then over your final reputation? [NORA *stands speechless, staring at him.*] Good; now I've warned you. Don't do anything stupid. When Helmer's read my letter, I'll be waiting for his reply. And bear in mind that it's your husband himself who's forced me back to my old ways. I'll never forgive him for that. Good-bye, Mrs. Helmer. [*He goes out through the hall.*]

NORA: [*Goes to the hall door, opens it a crack, and listens.*] He's gone. Didn't leave the letter. Oh no, no, that's impossible too! [*Opening the door more and more.*] What's that? He's standing outside—not going downstairs. He's thinking it over? Maybe he'll—? [*A letter falls in the mailbox; then* KROGSTAD'S *footsteps are heard, dying away down a flight of stairs.* NORA *gives a muffled cry and runs over toward the sofa table. A short pause.*] In the mailbox. [*Slips warily over to the hall door.*] It's lying there. Torvald, Torvald—now we're lost!

MRS. LINDE: [*Entering with the costume from the room, left.*] There now, I can't see anything else to mend. Perhaps you'd like to try—

NORA: [*In a hoarse whisper.*] Kristine, come here.

MRS. LINDE: [*Tossing the dress on the sofa.*] What's wrong? You look upset.

NORA: Come here. See that letter? *There!* Look—through the glass in the mailbox.

MRS. LINDE: Yes, yes, I see it.

NORA: That letter's from Krogstad—

MRS. LINDE: Nora—it's Krogstad who loaned you the money!

NORA: Yes, and now Torvald will find out everything.

MRS. LINDE: Believe me, Nora, it's best for both of you.

NORA: There's more you don't know. I forged a name.

MRS. LINDE: But for heaven's sake—?

NORA: I only want to tell you that, Kristine, so that you can be my witness.

MRS. LINDE: Witness? Why should I—?

NORA: If I should go out of my mind—it could easily happen—

MRS. LINDE: Nora!

NORA: Or anything else occurred—so I couldn't be present here—

MRS. LINDE: Nora, Nora, you aren't yourself at all!

NORA: And someone should try to take on the whole weight, all of the guilt, you follow me—

MRS. LINDE: Yes, of course, but why do you think—?

NORA: Then you're the witness that it isn't true, Kristine. I'm very much myself; my mind right now is perfectly clear; and I'm telling you: nobody else has known about this; I alone did everything. Remember that.

MRS. LINDE: I will. But I don't understand all this.

NORA: Oh, how could you ever understand it? It's the miracle now that's going to take place.

MRS. LINDE: The miracle?

NORA: Yes, the miracle. But it's so awful, Kristine. It mustn't take place, not for anything in the world.

MRS. LINDE: I'm going right over and talk with Krogstad.

NORA: Don't go near him; he'll do you some terrible harm!

MRS. LINDE: There was a time once when he'd gladly have done anything for me.

NORA: He?

MRS. LINDE: Where does he live?

NORA: Oh, how do I know? Yes. [*Searches in her pocket.*] Here's his card. But the letter, the letter—!

HELMER: [*From the study, knocking on the door.*] Nora!

NORA: [*With a cry of fear.*] Oh! What is it? What do you want?

HELMER: Now, now, don't be so frightened. We're not coming in. You locked the door—are you trying on the dress?

NORA: Yes, I'm trying it. I'll look just beautiful, Torvald.

MRS. LINDE: [*Who has read the card.*] He's living right around the corner.

NORA: Yes, but what's the use? We're lost. The letter's in the box.

MRS. LINDE: And your husband has the key?

NORA: Yes, always.

MRS. LINDE: Krogstad can ask for his letter back unread; he can find some excuse—

NORA: But it's just this time that Torvald usually—

MRS. LINDE: Stall him. Keep him in there. I'll be back as quick as I can. [*She hurries out through the hall entrance.*]

NORA: [*Goes to* HELMER's *door, opens it, and peers in.*] Torvald!

HELMER: [*From the inner study.*] Well—does one dare set foot in one's own living room at last? Come on, Rank, now we'll get a look— [*In the doorway.*] But what's this?

NORA: What, Torvald dear?

HELMER: Rank had me expecting some grand masquerade.

RANK: [*In the doorway.*] That was my impression, but I must have been wrong.

NORA: No one can admire me in my splendor—not till tomorrow.

HELMER: But Nora dear, you look so exhausted. Have you practiced too hard?

NORA: No, I haven't practiced at all yet.

HELMER: You know, it's necessary—

NORA: Oh, it's absolutely necessary, Torvald. But I can't get anywhere without your help. I've forgotten the whole thing completely.

HELMER: Ah, we'll soon take care of that.

NORA: Yes, take care of me, Torvald, please! Promise me that? Oh, I'm so nervous. That big party— You must give up everything this evening for me. No business—don't even touch your pen. Yes? Dear Torvald, promise?

HELMER: It's a promise. Tonight I'm totally at your service—you little helpless thing. Hm—but first there's one thing I want to— [*Goes toward the hall door.*]

NORA: What are you looking for?

HELMER: Just to see if there's any mail.

NORA: No, no, don't do that, Torvald!

HELMER: Now what?

NORA: Torvald, please. There isn't any.

HELMER: Let me look, though. [*Starts out.* NORA, *at the piano, strikes the first notes of the tarantella.* HELMER, *at the door, stops.*] Aha!

NORA: I can't dance tomorrow if I don't practice with you.

HELMER: [*Going over to her.*] Nora dear, are you really so frightened?

NORA: Yes, so terribly frightened. Let me practice right now; there's still time before dinner. Oh, sit down and play for me, Torvald. Direct me. Teach me, the way you always have.

HELMER: Gladly, if it's what you want. [*Sits at the piano.*]

NORA: [*Snatches the tambourine up from the box, then a long, varicolored shawl, which she throws around herself, whereupon she springs forward and cries out.*] Play for me now! Now I'll dance!

[HELMER *plays and* NORA *dances.* RANK *stands behind* HELMER *at the piano and looks on.*]

HELMER: [*As he plays.*] Slower. Slow down.

NORA: Can't change it.

HELMER: Not so violent, Nora!

NORA: Has to be just like this.

HELMER: [*Stopping.*] No, no, that won't do at all.

NORA: [*Laughing and swinging her tambourine.*] Isn't that what I told you?

RANK: Let me play for her.

HELMER: [*Getting up.*] Yes, go on. I can teach her more easily then.

[RANK *sits at the piano and plays;* NORA *dances more and more wildly.* HELMER *has stationed himself by the stove and repeatedly gives her directions; she seems not to hear them; her hair loosens and falls over her shoulders; she does not notice, but goes on dancing.* MRS. LINDE *enters.*]

MRS. LINDE: [*Standing dumbfounded at the door.*] Ah——!

NORA: [*Still dancing.*] See what fun, Kristine!

HELMER: But Nora darling, you dance as if your life were at stake.

NORA: And it is.

HELMER: Rank, stop! This is pure madness. Stop it, I say!

[RANK *breaks off playing, and* NORA *halts abruptly.*]

HELMER: [*Going over to her.*] I never would have believed it. You've forgotten everything I taught you.

NORA: [*Throwing away the tambourine.*] You see for yourself.

HELMER: Well, there's certainly room for instruction here.

NORA: Yes, you see how important it is. You've got to teach me to the very last minute. Promise me that, Torvald?

HELMER: You can bet on it.

NORA: You mustn't, either today or tomorrow, think about anything else but me; you mustn't open any letters—or the mailbox—

HELMER: Ah, it's still the fear of that man—

NORA: Oh yes, yes, that too.

HELMER: Nora, it's written all over you—there's already a letter from him out there.

NORA: I don't know. I guess so. But you mustn't read such things now; there mustn't be anything ugly between us before it's all over.

RANK: [*Quietly to* HELMER.] You shouldn't deny her.

HELMER: [*Putting his arm around her.*] The child can have her way. But tomorrow night, after you've danced—

NORA: Then you'll be free.

MAID: [*In the doorway, right.*] Ma'am, dinner is served.

NORA: We'll be wanting champagne, Helene.

MAID: Very good, ma'am. [*Goes out.*]

HELMER: So—a regular banquet, hm?

NORA: Yes, a banquet—champagne till daybreak! [*Calling out.*] And some macaroons, Helene. Heaps of them—just this once.

HELMER: [*Taking her hands.*] Now, now, now—no hysterics. Be my own little lark again.

NORA: Oh, I will soon enough. But go on in—and you, Dr. Rank. Kristine, help me put up my hair.

RANK: [*Whispering, as they go.*] There's nothing wrong—really wrong, is there?

HELMER: Oh, of course not. It's nothing more than this childish anxiety I was telling you about. [*They go out, right.*]

NORA: Well?

MRS. LINDE: Left town.

NORA: I could see by your face.

MRS. LINDE: He'll be home tomorrow evening. I wrote him a note.

NORA: You shouldn't have. Don't try to stop anything now. After all, it's a wonderful joy, this waiting here for the miracle.

MRS. LINDE: What is it you're waiting for?

NORA: Oh, you can't understand that. Go in to them; I'll be along in a moment.

[MRS. LINDE *goes into the dining room.* NORA *stands a short while as if composing herself; then she looks at her watch.*]

NORA: Five. Seven hours to midnight. Twenty-four hours to the midnight after, and then the tarantella's done. Seven and twenty-four? Thirty-one hours to live.

HELMER: [*In the doorway, right.*] What's become of the little lark?

NORA: [*Going toward him with open arms.*] Here's your lark!

ACT THREE

Same scene. The table, with chairs around it, has been moved to the center of the room. A lamp on the table is lit. The hall door stands open.

Dance music drifts down from the floor above. MRS. LINDE *sits at the table, absently paging through a book, trying to read, but apparently unable to focus her thoughts. Once or twice she pauses, tensely listening for a sound at the outer entrance.*

MRS. LINDE: [*Glancing at her watch.*] Not yet—and there's hardly any time left. If only he's not— [*Listening again.*] Ah, there he is. [*She goes out in the hall and cautiously opens the outer door. Quiet footsteps are heard on the stairs. She whispers.*] Come in. Nobody's here.

KROGSTAD: [*In the doorway.*] I found a note from you at home. What's back of all this?

MRS. LINDE: I just *had* to talk to you.

KROGSTAD: Oh? And it just *had* to be here in this house?

MRS. LINDE: At my place it was impossible; my room hasn't a private entrance. Come in; we're all alone. The maid's asleep, and the Helmers are at the dance upstairs.

KROGSTAD: [*Entering the room.*] Well, well, the Helmers are dancing tonight? Really?

MRS. LINDE: Yes, why not?

KROGSTAD: How true—why not?

MRS. LINDE: All right, Krogstad, let's talk.

KROGSTAD: Do we two have anything more to talk about?

MRS. LINDE: We have a great deal to talk about.

KROGSTAD: I wouldn't have thought so.

MRS. LINDE: No, because you've never understood me, really.

KROGSTAD: Was there anything more to understand—except what's all too common in life? A calculating woman throws over a man the moment a better catch comes by.

MRS. LINDE: You think I'm so thoroughly calculating? You think I broke it off lightly?

KROGSTAD: Didn't you?

MRS. LINDE: Nils—is that what you really thought?

KROGSTAD: If you cared, then why did you write me the way you did?

MRS. LINDE: What else could I do? If I had to break off with you, then it was my job as well to root out everything you felt for me.

KROGSTAD: [*Wringing his hands.*] So that was it. And this—all this, simply for money!

MRS. LINDE: Don't forget I had a helpless mother and two small brothers. We couldn't wait for you, Nils; you had such a long road ahead of you then.

KROGSTAD: That may be; but you still hadn't the right to abandon me for somebody else's sake.

MRS. LINDE: Yes—I don't know. So many, many times I've asked myself if I did have that right.

KROGSTAD: [*More softly.*] When I lost you, it was as if all the solid ground dissolved from under my feet. Look at me; I'm a half-drowned man now, hanging onto a wreck.

MRS. LINDE: Help may be near.

KROGSTAD: It was near—but then you came and blocked it off.

MRS. LINDE: Without my knowing it, Nils. Today for the first time I learned that it's you I'm replacing at the bank.

KROGSTAD: All right—I believe you. But now that you know, will you step aside?

MRS. LINDE: No, because that wouldn't benefit you in the slightest.

KROGSTAD: Not "benefit" me, hm! I'd step aside anyway.

MRS. LINDE: I've learned to be realistic. Life and hard, bitter necessity have taught me that.

KROGSTAD: And life's taught me never to trust fine phrases.

MRS. LINDE: Then life's taught you a very sound thing. But you do have to trust in actions, don't you?

KROGSTAD: What does that mean?

MRS. LINDE: You said you were hanging on like a half-drowned man to a wreck.

KROGSTAD: I've good reason to say that.

MRS. LINDE: I'm also like a half-drowned woman on a wreck. No one to suffer with; no one to care for.

KROGSTAD: You made your choice.

MRS. LINDE: There wasn't any choice then.

KROGSTAD: So—what of it?

MRS. LINDE: Nils, if only we two shipwrecked people could reach across to each other.

KROGSTAD: What are you saying?

MRS. LINDE: Two on one wreck are at least better off than each on his own.

KROGSTAD: Kristine!

MRS. LINDE: Why do you think I came into town?

KROGSTAD: Did you really have some thought of me?

MRS. LINDE: I have to work to go on living. All my born days, as long as I can remember, I've worked, and it's been my best and my only joy. But now I'm completely alone in the world; it frightens me to be so empty and lost. To work for yourself—there's no joy in that. Nils, give me something—someone to work for.

KROGSTAD: I don't believe all this. It's just some hysterical feminine urge to go out and make a noble sacrifice.

MRS. LINDE: Have you ever found me to be hysterical?

KROGSTAD: Can you honestly mean this? Tell me—do you know everything about my past?

MRS. LINDE: Yes.

KROGSTAD: And you know what they think I'm worth around here.

MRS. LINDE: From what you were saying before, it would seem that with me you could have been another person.

KROGSTAD: I'm positive of that.

MRS. LINDE: Couldn't it happen still?

KROGSTAD: Kristine—you're saying this in all seriousness? Yes, you are! I can see it in you. And do you really have the courage, then—?

MRS. LINDE: I need to have someone to care for; and your children need a mother. We both need each other. Nils, I have faith that you're good at heart—I'll risk everything together with you.

KROGSTAD: [*Gripping her hands.*] Kristine, thank you, thank you—Now I know I can win back a place in their eyes. Yes—but I forgot—

MRS. LINDE: [*Listening.*] Shh! The tarantella. Go now! Go on!

KROGSTAD: Why? What is it?

MRS. LINDE: Hear the dance up there? When that's over, they'll be coming down.

KROGSTAD: Oh, then I'll go. But—it's all pointless. Of course, you don't know the move I made against the Helmers.

MRS. LINDE: Yes, Nils, I know.

KROGSTAD: And all the same, you have the courage to—?

MRS. LINDE: I know how far despair can drive a man like you.

KROGSTAD: Oh, if I only could take it all back.

MRS. LINDE: You easily could—your letter's still lying in the mailbox.

KROGSTAD: Are you sure of that?

MRS. LINDE: Positive. But—

KROGSTAD: [*Looks at her searchingly.*] Is that the meaning of it, then? You'll save your friend at any price. Tell me straight out. Is that it?

MRS. LINDE: Nils—anyone who's sold herself for somebody else once isn't going to do it again.

KROGSTAD: I'll demand my letter back.

MRS. LINDE: No, no.

KROGSTAD: Yes, of course. I'll stay here till Helmer comes down; I'll tell him to give me my letter again—that it only involves my dismissal—that he shouldn't read it—

MRS. LINDE: No, Nils, don't call the letter back.

KROGSTAD: But wasn't that exactly why you wrote me to come here?

MRS. LINDE: Yes, in that first panic. But it's been a whole day and night since then, and in that time I've seen such incredible things in this house. Helmer's got to learn everything; this dreadful secret has to be aired; those two have to come to a full understanding; all these lies and evasions can't go on.

KROGSTAD: Well, then, if you want to chance it. But at least there's one thing I can do, and do right away—

MRS. LINDE: [*Listening.*] Go now, go, quick! The dance is over. We're not safe another second.

KROGSTAD: I'll wait for you downstairs.

MRS. LINDE: Yes, please do; take me home.

KROGSTAD: I can't believe it; I've never been so happy. [*He leaves by way of the outer door; the door between the room and the hall stays open.*]

MRS. LINDE: [*Straightening up a bit and getting together her street clothes.*] How different now! How different! Someone to work for, to live for—a home to build. Well, it is worth the try! Oh, if they'd only come! [*Listening.*] Ah, there they are. Bundle up. [*She picks up her hat and coat.* NORA's *and* HELMER's *voices can be heard outside; a key turns in the lock, and* HELMER *brings* NORA *into the hall almost by force. She is wearing the Italian costume with a large black shawl about her; he has on evening dress, with a black domino*[1] *open over it.*]

---

1. A loose cloak fitted with a mask, used at masquerades.

NORA: [*Struggling in the doorway.*] No, no, no, not inside! I'm going up again. I don't want to leave so soon.

HELMER: But Nora dear—

NORA: Oh, I beg you, please, Torvald. From the bottom of my heart, *please*—only an hour more!

HELMER: Not a single minute, Nora darling. You know our agreement. Come on, in we go; you'll catch cold out here. [*In spite of her resistance, he gently draws her into the room.*]

MRS. LINDE: Good evening.

NORA: Kristine!

HELMER: Why, Mrs. Linde—are you here so late?

MRS. LINDE: Yes, I'm sorry, but I did want to see Nora in costume.

NORA: Have you been sitting here, waiting for me?

MRS. LINDE: Yes. I didn't come early enough; you were all upstairs; and then I thought I really couldn't leave without seeing you.

HELMER: [*Removing NORA's shawl.*] Yes, take a good look. She's worth looking at, I can tell you that, Mrs. Linde. Isn't she lovely?

MRS. LINDE: Yes, I should say—

HELMER: A dream of loveliness, isn't she? That's what everyone thought at the party, too. But she's horribly stubborn—this sweet little thing. What's to be done with her? Can you imagine, I almost had to use force to pry her away.

NORA: Oh, Torvald, you're going to regret you didn't indulge me, even for just a half hour more.

HELMER: There, you see. She danced her tarantella and got a tumultuous hand—which was well earned, although the performance may have been a bit too naturalistic—I mean it rather overstepped the proprieties of art. But never mind—what's important is, she made a success, an overwhelming success. You think I could let her stay on after that and spoil the effect? Oh no; I took my lovely little Capri girl—my capricious little Capri girl, I should say—took her under my arm; one quick tour of the ballroom, a curtsy to every side, and then—as they say in novels—the beautiful vision disappeared. An exit should always be effective, Mrs. Linde, but that's what I can't get Nora to grasp. Phew, it's hot in here. [*Flings the domino on a chair and opens the door to his room.*] Why's it dark in here? Oh yes, of course. Excuse me. [*He goes in and lights a couple of candles.*]

NORA: [*In a sharp, breathless whisper.*] So?

MRS. LINDE: [*Quietly.*] I talked with him.

NORA: And—?

MRS. LINDE: Nora—you must tell your husband everything.

NORA: [*Dully.*] I knew it.

MRS. LINDE: You've got nothing to fear from Krogstad, but you have to speak out.

NORA: I won't tell.

MRS. LINDE: Then the letter will.

NORA: Thanks, Kristine. I know now what's to be done. Shh!

HELMER: [*Reentering.*] Well, then, Mrs. Linde—have you admired her?

MRS. LINDE: Yes, and now I'll say good night.

HELMER: Oh, come, so soon? Is this yours, this knitting?

MRS. LINDE: Yes, thanks. I nearly forgot it.

HELMER: Do you knit, then?

MRS. LINDE: Oh yes.

HELMER: You know what? You should embroider instead.

MRS. LINDE: Really? Why?

HELMER: Yes, because it's a lot prettier. See here, one holds the embroidery so, in the left hand, and then one guides the needle with the right—so—in an easy, sweeping curve—right?

MRS. LINDE: Yes, I guess that's—

HELMER: But, on the other hand, knitting—it can never be anything but ugly. Look, see here, the arms tucked in, the knitting needles going up and down—there's something Chinese about it. Ah, that was really a glorious champagne they served.

MRS. LINDE: Yes, good night, Nora, and don't be stubborn anymore.

HELMER: Well put, Mrs. Linde!

MRS. LINDE: Good night, Mr. Helmer.

HELMER: [*Accompanying her to the door.*] Good night, good night. I hope you get home all right. I'd be very happy to—but you don't have far to go. Good night, good night. [*She leaves. He shuts the door after her and returns.*] There, now, at last we got her out the door. She's a deadly bore, that creature.

NORA: Aren't you pretty tired, Torvald?

HELMER: No, not a bit.

NORA: You're not sleepy?

HELMER: Not at all. On the contrary, I'm feeling quite exhilarated. But you? Yes, you really look tired and sleepy.

NORA: Yes, I'm very tired. Soon now I'll sleep.

HELMER: See! You see! I was right all along that we shouldn't stay longer.

NORA: Whatever you do is always right.

HELMER: [*Kissing her brow.*] Now my little lark talks sense. Say, did you notice what a time Rank was having tonight?

NORA: Oh, was he? I didn't get to speak with him.

HELMER: I scarcely did either, but it's a long time since I've seen him in such high spirits. [*Gazes at her a moment, then comes nearer her.*] Hm—it's marvelous, though, to be back home again—to be completely alone with you. Oh, you bewitchingly lovely young woman!

NORA: Torvald, don't look at me like that!

HELMER: Can't I look at my richest treasure? At all that beauty that's mine, mine alone—completely and utterly.

NORA: [*Moving around to the other side of the table.*] You mustn't talk to me that way tonight.

HELMER: [*Following her.*] The tarantella is still in your blood, I can see—and it makes you even more enticing. Listen. The guests are beginning to go. [*Dropping his voice.*] Nora—it'll soon be quiet through this whole house.

NORA: Yes, I hope so.

HELMER: You do, don't you, my love? Do you realize—when I'm out at a party like this with you—do you know why I talk to you so little, and keep such a distance away; just send you a stolen look now and then—you know why I do it? It's because I'm imagining then that you're my secret darling, my secret young bride-to-be, and that no one suspects there's anything between us.

NORA: Yes, yes; oh, yes, I know you're always thinking of me.

HELMER: And then when we leave and I place the shawl over those fine young rounded shoulders—over that wonderful curving neck—then I pretend that you're my young bride, that we're just coming from the wedding, that for the first time I'm bringing you into my house—that for the first time I'm alone with you—completely alone with you, your trembling young beauty! All this evening I've longed for nothing but you. When I saw you turn and sway in the tarantella—my blood was pounding till I couldn't stand it—that's why I brought you down here so early—

NORA: Go away, Torvald! Leave me alone. I don't want all this.

HELMER: What do you mean? Nora, you're teasing me. You will, won't you? Aren't I your husband—?

[*A knock at the outside door.*]

NORA: [*Startled.*] What's that?

HELMER: [*Going toward the hall.*] Who is it?

RANK: [*Outside.*] It's me. May I come in a moment?

HELMER: [*With quiet irritation.*] Oh, what does he want now? [*Aloud.*] Hold on. [*Goes and opens the door.*] Oh, how nice that you didn't just pass us by!

RANK: I thought I heard your voice, and then I wanted so badly to have a look in. [*Lightly glancing about.*] Ah, me, these old familiar haunts. You have it snug and cozy in here, you two.

HELMER: You seemed to be having it pretty cozy upstairs, too.

RANK: Absolutely. Why shouldn't I? Why not take in everything in life? As much as you can, anyway, and as long as you can. The wine was superb—

HELMER: The champagne especially.

RANK: You noticed that too? It's amazing how much I could guzzle down.

NORA: Torvald also drank a lot of champagne this evening.

RANK: Oh?

NORA: Yes, and that always makes him so entertaining.

RANK: Well, why shouldn't one have a pleasant evening after a well-spent day?

HELMER: Well spent? I'm afraid I can't claim that.

RANK: [*Slapping him on the back.*] But I can, you see!

NORA: Dr. Rank, you must have done some scientific research today.

RANK: Quite so.

HELMER: Come now—little Nora talking about scientific research!

NORA: And can I congratulate you on the results?

RANK: Indeed you may.

NORA: Then they were good?

RANK: The best possible for both doctor and patient—certainty.

NORA: [*Quickly and searchingly.*] Certainty?

RANK: Complete certainty. So don't I owe myself a gay evening afterwards?

NORA: Yes, you're right, Dr. Rank.

HELMER: I'm with you—just so long as you don't have to suffer for it in the morning.

RANK: Well, one never gets something for nothing in life.

NORA: Dr. Rank—are you very fond of masquerade parties?

RANK: Yes, if there's a good array of odd disguises—

NORA: Tell me, what should we two go as at the next masquerade?

HELMER: You little featherhead—already thinking of the next!

RANK: We two? I'll tell you what: you must go as Charmed Life—

HELMER: Yes, but find a costume for *that*!

RANK: Your wife can appear just as she looks every day.

HELMER: That was nicely put. But don't you know what you're going to be?

RANK: Yes, Helmer, I've made up my mind.

HELMER: Well?

RANK: At the next masquerade I'm going to be invisible.

HELMER: That's a funny idea.

RANK: They say there's a hat—black, huge—have you never heard of the hat that makes you invisible? You put it on, and then no one on earth can see you.

HELMER: [*Suppressing a smile.*] Ah, of course.

RANK: But I'm quite forgetting what I came for. Helmer, give me a cigar, one of the dark Havanas.

HELMER: With the greatest pleasure. [*Holds out his case.*]

RANK: Thanks. [*Takes one and cuts off the tip.*]

NORA: [*Striking a match.*] Let me give you a light.

RANK: Thank you. [*She holds the match for him; he lights the cigar.*] And now good-bye.

HELMER: Good-bye, good-bye, old friend.

NORA: Sleep well, Doctor.

RANK: Thanks for that wish.

NORA: Wish me the same.

RANK: You? All right, if you like— Sleep well. And thanks for the light. [*He nods to them both and leaves.*]

HELMER: [*His voice subdued.*] He's been drinking heavily.

NORA: [*Absently.*] Could be. [HELMER *takes his keys from his pocket and goes out in the hall.*] Torvald—what are you after?

HELMER: Got to empty the mailbox; it's nearly full. There won't be room for the morning papers.

NORA: Are you working tonight?

HELMER: You know I'm not. Why—what's this? Someone's been at the lock.

NORA: At the lock—?

HELMER: Yes, I'm positive. What do you suppose—? I can't imagine one of the maids—? Here's a broken hairpin. Nora, it's yours—

NORA: [*Quickly.*] Then it must be the children—

HELMER: You'd better break them of that. Hm, hm—well, opened it after all. [*Takes the contents out and calls into the kitchen.*] Helene! Helene, would you put out the lamp in the hall. [*He returns to the room, shutting the hall door, then displays the handful of mail.*] Look how it's piled up. [*Sorting through them.*] Now what's this?

NORA: [*At the window.*] The letter! Oh, Torvald, no!

HELMER: Two calling cards—from Rank.

NORA: From Dr. Rank?

HELMER: [*Examining them.*] "Dr. Rank, Consulting Physician." They were on top. He must have dropped them in as he left.

NORA: Is there anything on them?

HELMER: There's a black cross over the name. See? That's a gruesome notion. He could almost be announcing his own death.

NORA: That's just what he's doing.

HELMER: What! You've heard something? Something he's told you?

NORA: Yes. That when those cards came, he'd be taking his leave of us. He'll shut himself in now and die.

HELMER: Ah, my poor friend! Of course I knew he wouldn't be here much longer. But so soon— And then to hide himself away like a wounded animal.

NORA: If it has to happen, then it's best it happens in silence—don't you think so, Torvald?

HELMER: [*Pacing up and down.*] He'd grown right into our lives. I simply can't imagine him gone. He with his suffering and loneliness—like a dark cloud setting off our sunlit happiness. Well, maybe it's best this way. For him, at least. [*Standing still.*] And maybe for us too, Nora. Now we're thrown back on each other, completely. [*Embracing her.*] Oh you, my darling wife, how can I hold you close enough? You know what, Nora—time and again I've wished you were in some terrible danger, just so I could stake my life and soul and everything, for your sake.

NORA: [*Tearing herself away, her voice firm and decisive.*] Now you must read your mail, Torvald.

HELMER: No, no, not tonight. I want to stay with you, dearest.

NORA: With a dying friend on your mind?

HELMER: You're right. We've both had a shock. There's ugliness between us—these thoughts of death and corruption. We'll have to get free of them first. Until then—we'll stay apart.

NORA: [*Clinging about his neck.*] Torvald—good night! Good night!

HELMER: [*Kissing her on the cheek.*] Good night, little songbird. Sleep well, Nora. I'll be reading my mail now. [*He takes the letters into his room and shuts the door after him.*]

NORA: [*With bewildered glances, groping about, seizing* HELMER's *domino, throwing it around her, and speaking in short, hoarse, broken whispers.*] Never see him again. Never, never. [*Putting her shawl over her head.*] Never see the children either—them, too. Never, never. Oh, the freezing black water! The depths—down— Oh, I wish it were over— He has it now; he's reading it—now. Oh no, no, not yet. Torvald, good-bye, you and the children— [*She starts for the hall; as she does,* HELMER *throws open his door and stands with an open letter in his hand.*]

HELMER: Nora!

NORA: [*Screams.*] Oh—!

HELMER: What is this? You know what's in this letter?

NORA: Yes, I know. Let me go! Let me out!

HELMER: [*Holding her back.*] Where are you going?

NORA: [*Struggling to break loose.*] You can't save me, Torvald!

HELMER: [*Slumping back.*] True! Then it's true what he writes? How horrible! No, no, it's impossible—it can't be true.

NORA: It *is* true. I've loved you more than all this world.

HELMER: Ah, none of your slippery tricks.

NORA: [*Taking one step toward him.*] Torvald—!

HELMER: What *is* this you've blundered into!

NORA: Just let me loose. You're not going to suffer for my sake. You're not going to take on my guilt.

HELMER: No more playacting. [*Locks the hall door.*] You stay right
here and give me a reckoning. You understand what you've done?
Answer! You understand?

NORA: [*Looking squarely at him, her face hardening.*] Yes. I'm beginning to understand everything now.

HELMER: [*Striding about.*] Oh, what an awful awakening! In all these
eight years—she who was my pride and joy—a hypocrite, a
liar—worse, worse—a criminal! How infinitely disgusting it all
is! The shame! [NORA *says nothing and goes on looking straight at
him. He stops in front of her.*] I should have suspected something
of the kind. I should have known. All your father's flimsy values— Be still! All your father's flimsy values have come out in
you. No religion, no morals, no sense of duty— Oh, how I'm
punished for letting him off! I did it for your sake, and you repay
me like this.

NORA: Yes, like this.

HELMER: Now you've wrecked all my happiness—ruined my whole
future. Oh, it's awful to think of. I'm in a cheap little grafter's[2]
hands; he can do anything he wants with me, ask for anything,
play with me like a puppet—and I can't breathe a word. I'll be
swept down miserably into the depths on account of a feather-
brained woman.

NORA: When I'm gone from this world, you'll be free.

HELMER: Oh, quit posing. Your father had a mess of those speeches
too. What good would that ever do me if you were gone from
this world, as you say? Not the slightest. He can still make the
whole thing known; and if he does, I could be falsely suspected
as your accomplice. They might even think that I was behind
it—that I put you up to it. And all that I can thank you for—
you that I've coddled the whole of our marriage. Can you see
now what you've done to me?

NORA: [*Icily calm.*] Yes.

HELMER: It's so incredible, I just can't grasp it. But we'll have to
patch up whatever we can. Take off the shawl. I said, take it off!
I've got to appease him somehow or other. The thing has to be
hushed up at any cost. And as for you and me, it's got to seem

---

2. Swindler's; in this usage, blackmailer's.

like everything between us is just as it was—to the outside world, that is. You'll go right on living in this house, of course. But you can't be allowed to bring up the children; I don't dare trust you with them— Oh, to have to say this to someone I've loved so much, and that I still—! Well, that's done with. From now on happiness doesn't matter; all that matters is saving the bits and pieces, the appearance— [*The doorbell rings.* HELMER *starts.*] What's that? And so late. Maybe the worst—? You think he'd—? Hide, Nora! Say you're sick. [NORA *remains standing motionless.* HELMER *goes and opens the door.*]

MAID: [*Half dressed, in the hall.*] A letter for Mrs. Helmer.

HELMER: I'll take it. [*Snatches the letter and shuts the door.*] Yes, it's from him. You don't get it; I'm reading it myself.

NORA: Then read it.

HELMER: [*By the lamp.*] I hardly dare. We may be ruined, you and I. But—I've got to know. [*Rips open the letter, skims through a few lines, glances at an enclosure, then cries out joyfully.*] Nora! [NORA *looks inquiringly at him.*] Nora! Wait—better check it again— Yes, yes, it's true. I'm saved. Nora, I'm saved!

NORA: And I?

HELMER: You too, of course. We're both saved, both of us. Look. He's sent back your note. He says he's sorry and ashamed—that a happy development in his life—oh, who cares what he says! Nora, we're saved! No one can hurt you. Oh, Nora, Nora—but first, this ugliness all has to go. Let me see— [*Takes a look at the note.*] No, I don't want to see it; I want the whole thing to fade like a dream. [*Tears the note and both letters to pieces, throws them into the stove and watches them burn.*] There—now there's nothing left— He wrote that since Christmas Eve you— Oh, they must have been three terrible days for you, Nora.

NORA: I fought a hard fight.

HELMER: And suffered pain and saw no escape but— No, we're not going to dwell on anything unpleasant. We'll just be grateful and keep on repeating: it's over now, it's over! You hear me, Nora? You don't seem to realize—it's over. What's it mean—that frozen look? Oh, poor little Nora, I understand. You can't believe I've forgiven you. But I have, Nora; I swear I have. I know that what you did, you did out of love for me.

NORA: That's true.

HELMER: You loved me the way a wife ought to love her husband. It's simply the means that you couldn't judge. But you think I love you any the less for not knowing how to handle your affairs? No, no—just lean on me; I'll guide you and teach you. I wouldn't be a man if this feminine helplessness didn't make you twice as attractive to me. You mustn't mind those sharp words I said—that was all in the first confusion of thinking my world had collapsed. I've forgiven you, Nora; I swear I've forgiven you.

NORA: My thanks for your forgiveness. [*She goes out through the door, right.*]

HELMER: No, wait— [*Peers in.*] What are you doing in there?

NORA: [*Inside.*] Getting out of my costume.

HELMER: [*By the open door.*] Yes, do that. Try to calm yourself and collect your thoughts again, my frightened little songbird. You can rest easy now; I've got wide wings to shelter you with. [*Walking about close by the door.*] How snug and nice our home is, Nora. You're safe here; I'll keep you like a hunted dove I've rescued out of a hawk's claws. I'll bring peace to your poor, shuddering heart. Gradually it'll happen, Nora; you'll see. Tomorrow all this will look different to you; then everything will be as it was. I won't have to go on repeating I forgive you; you'll feel it for yourself. How can you imagine I'd ever conceivably want to disown you—or even blame you in any way? Ah, you don't know a man's heart, Nora. For a man there's something indescribably sweet and satisfying in knowing he's forgiven his wife—and forgiven her out of a full and open heart. It's as if she belongs to him in two ways now: in a sense he's given her fresh into the world again, and she's become his wife and his child as well. From now on that's what you'll be to me—you little, bewildered, helpless thing. Don't be afraid of anything, Nora; just open your heart to me, and I'll be conscience and will to you both— [NORA *enters in her regular clothes.*] What's this? Not in bed? You've changed your dress?

NORA: Yes, Torvald, I've changed my dress.

HELMER: But why now, so late?

NORA: Tonight I'm not sleeping.

HELMER: But Nora dear—

NORA: [*Looking at her watch.*] It's still not so very late. Sit down, Torvald; we have a lot to talk over. [*She sits at one side of the table.*]

HELMER: Nora—what is this? That hard expression—

NORA: Sit down. This'll take some time. I have a lot to say.

HELMER: [*Sitting at the table directly opposite her.*] You worry me, Nora. And I don't understand you.

NORA: No, that's exactly it. You don't understand me. And I've never understood you either—until tonight. No, don't interrupt. You can just listen to what I say. We're closing out accounts, Torvald.

HELMER: How do you mean that?

NORA: [*After a short pause.*] Doesn't anything strike you about our sitting here like this?

HELMER: What's that?

NORA: We've been married now eight years. Doesn't it occur to you that this is the first time we two, you and I, man and wife, have ever talked seriously together?

HELMER: What do you mean—seriously?

NORA: In eight whole years—longer even—right from our first acquaintance, we've never exchanged a serious word on any serious thing.

HELMER: You mean I should constantly go and involve you in problems you couldn't possibly help me with?

NORA: I'm not talking of problems. I'm saying that we've never sat down seriously together and tried to get to the bottom of anything.

HELMER: But dearest, what good would that ever do you?

NORA: That's the point right there: you've never understood me. I've been wronged greatly, Torvald—first by Papa, and then by you.

HELMER: What! By us—the two people who've loved you more than anyone else?

NORA: [*Shaking her head.*] You never loved me. You've thought it fun to be in love with me, that's all.

HELMER: Nora, what a thing to say!

NORA: Yes, it's true now, Torvald. When I lived at home with Papa, he told me all his opinions, so I had the same ones too; or if they were different I hid them, since he wouldn't have cared for that. He used to call me his doll-child, and he played with me the way I played with my dolls. Then I came into your house—

HELMER: How can you speak of our marriage like that?

NORA: [*Unperturbed.*] I mean, then I went from Papa's hands into yours. You arranged everything to your own taste, and so I got the same taste as you—or I pretended to; I can't remember. I guess a little of both, first one, then the other. Now when I look back, it seems as if I'd lived here like a beggar—just from hand to mouth. I've lived by doing tricks for you, Torvald. But that's the way you wanted it. It's a great sin what you and Papa did to me. You're to blame that nothing's become of me.

HELMER: Nora, how unfair and ungrateful you are! Haven't you been happy here?

NORA: No, never. I thought so—but I never have.

HELMER: Not—not happy!

NORA: No, only lighthearted. And you've always been so kind to me. But our home's been nothing but a playpen. I've been your doll-wife here, just as at home I was Papa's doll-child. And in turn the children have been my dolls. I thought it was fun when you played with me, just as they thought it fun when I played with them. That's been our marriage, Torvald.

HELMER: There's some truth in what you're saying—under all the raving exaggeration. But it'll all be different after this. Playtime's over; now for the schooling.

NORA: Whose schooling—mine or the children's?

HELMER: Both yours and the children's, dearest.

NORA: Oh, Torvald, you're not the man to teach me to be a good wife to you.

HELMER: And you can say that?

NORA: And I—how am I equipped to bring up children?

HELMER: Nora!

NORA: Didn't you say a moment ago that that was no job to trust me with?

HELMER: In a flare of temper! Why fasten on that?

NORA: Yes, but you were so very right. I'm not up to the job. There's another job I have to do first. I have to try to educate myself. You can't help me with that. I've got to do it alone. And that's why I'm leaving you now.

HELMER: [*Jumping up.*] What's that?

NORA: I have to stand completely alone, if I'm ever going to discover myself and the world out there. So I can't go on living with you.

HELMER: Nora, Nora!

NORA: I want to leave right away. Kristine should put me up for the night—

HELMER: You're insane! You've no right! I forbid you!

NORA: From here on, there's no use forbidding me anything. I'll take with me whatever is mine. I don't want a thing from you, either now or later.

HELMER: What kind of madness is this!

NORA: Tomorrow I'm going home—I mean, home where I came from. It'll be easier up there to find something to do.

HELMER: Oh, you blind, incompetent child!

NORA: I must learn to be competent, Torvald.

HELMER: Abandon your home, your husband, your children! And you're not even thinking what people will say.

NORA: I can't be concerned about that. I only know how essential this is.

HELMER: Oh, it's outrageous. So you'll run out like this on your most sacred vows.

NORA: What do you think are my most sacred vows?

HELMER: And I have to tell you that! Aren't they your duties to your husband and children?

NORA: I have other duties equally sacred.

HELMER: That isn't true. What duties are they?

NORA: Duties to myself.

HELMER: Before all else, you're a wife and a mother.

NORA: I don't believe in that anymore. I believe that, before all else, I'm a human being, no less than you—or anyway, I ought to try to become one. I know the majority thinks you're right, Torvald, and plenty of books agree with you, too. But I can't go on believing what the majority says, or what's written in books. I have to think over these things myself and try to understand them.

HELMER: Why can't you understand your place in your own home? On a point like that, isn't there one everlasting guide you can turn to? Where's your religion?

NORA: Oh, Torvald, I'm really not sure what religion is.

HELMER: What—?

NORA: I only know what the minister said when I was confirmed. He told me religion was this thing and that. When I get clear and away by myself, I'll go into that problem too. I'll see if what the minister said was right, or, in any case, if it's right for me.

HELMER: A young woman your age shouldn't talk like that. If religion can't move you, I can try to rouse your conscience. You do have some moral feeling? Or, tell me—has that gone too?

NORA: It's not easy to answer that, Torvald. I simply don't know. I'm all confused about these things. I just know I see them so differently from you. I find out, for one thing, that the law's not at all what I'd thought—but I can't get it through my head that the law is fair. A woman hasn't a right to protect her dying father or save her husband's life! I can't believe that.

HELMER: You talk like a child. You don't know anything of the world you live in.

NORA: No, I don't. But now I'll begin to learn for myself. I'll try to discover who's right, the world or I.

HELMER: Nora, you're sick; you've got a fever. I almost think you're out of your head.

NORA: I've never felt more clearheaded and sure in my life.

HELMER: And—clearheaded and sure—you're leaving your husband and children?

NORA: Yes.

HELMER: Then there's only one possible reason.

NORA: What?

HELMER: You no longer love me.

NORA: No. That's exactly it.

HELMER: Nora! You can't be serious!

NORA: Oh, this is so hard, Torvald—you've been so kind to me always. But I can't help it. I don't love you anymore.

HELMER: [Struggling for composure.] Are you also clearheaded and sure about that?

NORA: Yes, completely. That's why I can't go on staying here.

HELMER: Can you tell me what I did to lose your love?

NORA: Yes, I can tell you. It was this evening when the miraculous thing didn't come—then I knew you weren't the man I'd imagined.

HELMER: Be more explicit; I don't follow you.

NORA: I've waited now so patiently eight long years—for, my Lord, I know miracles don't come every day. Then this crisis broke over me, and such a certainty filled me: *now* the miraculous event would occur. While Krogstad's letter was lying out there, I never for an instant dreamed that you could give in to his terms. I was so utterly sure you'd say to him: go on, tell your tale to the whole wide world. And when he'd done that—

HELMER: Yes, what then? When I'd delivered my own wife into shame and disgrace—!

NORA: When he'd done that, I was so utterly sure that you'd step forward, take the blame on yourself and say: I am the guilty one.

HELMER: Nora—!

NORA: You're thinking I'd never accept such a sacrifice from you? No, of course not. But what good would my protests be against you? That was the miracle I was waiting for, in terror and hope. And to stave that off, I would have taken my life.

HELMER: I'd gladly work for you day and night, Nora—and take on pain and deprivation. But there's no one who gives up honor for love.

NORA: Millions of women have done just that.

HELMER: Oh, you think and talk like a silly child.

NORA: Perhaps. But you neither think nor talk like the man I could join myself to. When your big fright was over—and it wasn't from any threat against me, only for what might damage you—when all the danger was past, for you it was just as if nothing had happened. I was exactly the same, your little lark, your doll, that you'd have to handle with double care now that I'd turned out so brittle and frail. [*Gets up.*] Torvald—in that instant it dawned on me that for eight years I've been living here with a stranger, and that I'd even conceived three children—oh, I can't stand the thought of it! I could tear myself to bits.

HELMER: [*Heavily.*] I see. There's a gulf that's opened between us— that's clear. Oh, but Nora, can't we bridge it somehow?

NORA: The way I am now, I'm no wife for you.

HELMER: I have the strength to make myself over.

NORA: Maybe—if your doll gets taken away.

HELMER: But to part! To part from you! No, Nora, no—I can't imagine it.

NORA: [*Going out, right.*] All the more reason why it has to be. [*She reenters with her coat and a small overnight bag, which she puts on a chair by the table.*]

HELMER: Nora, Nora, not now! Wait till tomorrow.

NORA: I can't spend the night in a strange man's room.

HELMER: But couldn't we live here like brother and sister—

NORA: You know very well how long that would last. [*Throws her shawl about her.*] Good-bye, Torvald. I won't look in on the children. I know they're in better hands than mine. The way I am now, I'm no use to them.

HELMER: But someday, Nora—someday—?

NORA: How can I tell? I haven't the least idea what'll become of me.

HELMER: But you're my wife, now and wherever you go.

NORA: Listen, Torvald—I've heard that when a wife deserts her husband's house just as I'm doing, then the law frees him from all responsibility. In any case, I'm freeing you from being responsible. Don't feel yourself bound, any more than I will. There has to be absolute freedom for us both. Here, take your ring back. Give me mine.

HELMER: That too?

NORA: That too.

HELMER: There it is.

NORA: Good. Well, now it's all over. I'm putting the keys here. The maids know all about keeping up the house—better than I do. Tomorrow, after I've left town, Kristine will stop by to pack up everything that's mine from home. I'd like those things shipped up to me.

HELMER: Over! All over! Nora, won't you ever think about me?

NORA: I'm sure I'll think of you often, and about the children and the house here.

HELMER: May I write you?

NORA: No—never. You're not to do that.

HELMER: Oh, but let me send you—

NORA: Nothing. Nothing.

HELMER: Or help you if you need it.

NORA: No. I accept nothing from strangers.

HELMER: Nora—can I never be more than a stranger to you?

NORA: [*Picking up the overnight bag.*] Ah, Torvald—it would take the greatest miracle of all—

HELMER: Tell me the greatest miracle!

NORA: You and I both would have to transform ourselves to the point that— Oh, Torvald, I've stopped believing in miracles.

HELMER: But I'll believe. Tell me! Transform ourselves to the point that—?

NORA: That our living together could be a true marriage. [*She goes out down the hall.*]

HELMER: [*Sinks down on a chair by the door, face buried in his hands.*] Nora! Nora! [*Looking about and rising.*] Empty. She's gone. [*A sudden hope leaps in him.*] The greatest miracle—?
   [*From below, the sound of a door slamming shut.*]

1878   *1879*

Oscar Wilde
1854–1900

THE IMPORTANCE OF BEING EARNEST

Oscar Wilde, an Irishman schooled at Oxford and living in London, embodied the Aesthetic movement, which made its way through English literary society in the 1880s and 1890s. Based on the epicurean philosophy of the essayist and critic Walter Pater, the movement promoted a cult of the beautiful. Its slogan, "Art for art's sake," repudiated the more characteristically Victorian notion that art ought to serve a good and edifying purpose.

This undercutting of values is evident in the title of Wilde's best-known play. Victorians prized "earnestness" in their men more than nearly any other virtue. This old and complex word betokens bravery in battle, a seriousness in demeanor (and, of course, an aversion to tomfoolery), zealousness in religious convictions, and confidence in one's purpose. The English generally associated these traits with the middle class, which rose to economic and political power in the nineteenth century. Indeed, the English middle class relied on "earnestness" and its accompanying traits for so many accomplishments in that century—the erection of elaborate systems of railroads, the building of the world's greatest fleets of steam-powered ships, extraordinary feats of engineering (bridges, canals), in short, the whole might and energy and work ethic of the industrial age.

The industrial age had replaced the antiquated structures of an agricultural society, and so the earnest bourgeoisie disdained the lifestyle and ideology of the landed aristocracy. To the prudish Victorians, the old aristocracy often seemed not only obsolete but lazy and decadent.

Wilde deflated this high tide of stuffy and self-important Victorianism through **satire**, a comedic genre that encourages audiences to laugh at and even ridicule human (and societal) vices and follies. Indeed, this play helped generate a cultural shift in England, a shift that undermined the "truths" and values on which the sense of proper Victorian behavior had been erected. Wilde also made fun of himself and the aristocrats he found so congenial. Audiences would have recognized the playwright in the characterization of Algernon: the cynical, effeminate aesthete who cannot take anything seriously. And the portrait of Lady Bracknell exposes how ready the old aristocrats were to sell their sense of exclusivity for a few thousand pounds.

If he did not introduce the English to the well-made play (at that time in vogue in France), Wilde succeeded with the form better than anyone else. His plays delighted in the plot intrigues and the devices of mistaken identity that were codified in the French theater. His characters, drawn from types, seem less like real people than do the characters in other plays. But audiences approach comedy with different expectations than they bring to serious drama, and satire works by exaggeration. Earnest presents cynicism, craven greed, and vacuousness in proportions not likely to be found in real life. In fact, the one characteristic not exaggerated in the play is earnestness, which often comes in greater concentrations than it does in Jack.

Wilde wanted to make his audiences laugh, and the London public proved happy to oblige. The play was a hit in the early months of 1895. As in all great comedies, though, the laughs came not just for their own sake—the jokes bit like hyenas. In fact, just months after the premiere, audiences viewed the play in light of Wilde's dramatic, scandalous private life, which suddenly became public. Though married with two children, Wilde had conducted a homosexual affair with an aristocrat, whose father, upset by the relationship, publicly accused Wilde of being a sodomite. Wilde, encouraged by his lover, sued for libel. The result of the suit was Wilde's conviction for homosexuality. To many contemporaries, London's profligate society, and much of the sentiment expressed in his play, was tried and convicted also. Certainly, the trial chilled the increasingly libertine late-Victorian Londoners and dampened the play's accomplishments.

To some extent, because it satirizes its time, The Importance of Being Earnest *is a period piece. The Victorians it mocks are no longer with us, nor do we have the vestige of even an obsolescent aristocracy. But we, like the Victorians, live in an age dominated by middle-class values and morality, in a society that still attaches importance to earnestness. To what extent is this play apropos today? Is it irrelevant to your life, or do its bites still sting?*

The Importance of Being Earnest

CHARACTERS

JOHN WORTHING, J.P.
ALGERNON MONCRIEFF
REV. CANON CHASUBLE, D.D.
MERRIMAN (*Butler*)
LANE (*Manservant*)

LADY BRACKNELL
HON. GWENDOLEN FAIRFAX
CECILY CARDEW
MISS PRISM (*Governess*)

THE SCENES OF THE PLAY

ACT I. *Algernon Moncrieff's Flat in Half-Moon Street, W.*
ACT II. *The Garden at the Manor House, Woolton.*
ACT III. *Drawing-Room of the Manor House, Woolton.*

TIME.—*The Present.* PLACE.—*London.*

ACT I

SCENE.—*Morning-room in* ALGERNON'*s flat in Half-Moon Street. The room is luxuriously and artistically furnished. The sound of a piano is heard in the adjoining room.* LANE *is arranging afternoon tea on the table, and after the music has ceased,* ALGERNON *enters.*

ALGERNON: Did you hear what I was playing, Lane?

LANE: I didn't think it polite to listen, sir.

ALGERNON: I'm sorry for that, for your sake. I don't play accurately—anyone can play accurately—but I play with wonderful expression. As far as the piano is concerned, sentiment is my forte. I keep science for Life.

LANE: Yes, sir.

ALGERNON: And, speaking of the science of Life, have you got the cucumber sandwiches cut for Lady Bracknell?

LANE: Yes, sir. [*Hands them on a salver.*]

ALGERNON: [*Inspects them, takes two, and sits down on the sofa.*] Oh! . . . by the way, Lane, I see from your book that on Thursday night, when Lord Shoreman and Mr. Worthing were dining with me, eight bottles of champagne are entered as having been consumed.

LANE: Yes, sir; eight bottles and a pint.

ALGERNON: Why is it that at a bachelor's establishment the servants invariably drink the champagne? I ask merely for information.

LANE: I attribute it to the superior quality of the wine, sir. I have often observed that in married households the champagne is rarely of a first-rate brand.

ALGERNON: Good Heavens! Is marriage so demoralizing as that?

LANE: I believe it *is* a very pleasant state, sir. I have had very little experience of it myself up to the present. I have only been married once. That was in consequence of a misunderstanding between myself and a young woman.

ALGERNON: [*Languidly.*] I don't know that I am much interested in your family life, Lane.

LANE: No, sir; it is not a very interesting subject. I never think of it myself.

ALGERNON: Very natural, I am sure. That will do, Lane, thank you.

LANE: Thank you, sir. [LANE *goes out.*]

ALGERNON: Lane's views on marriage seem somewhat lax. Really, if the lower orders don't set us a good example, what on earth is the use of them? They seem, as a class, to have absolutely no sense of moral responsibility.

[*Enter* LANE.]

LANE: Mr. Ernest Worthing.

[*Enter* JACK. LANE *goes out.*]

ALGERNON: How are you, my dear Ernest? What brings you up to town?

JACK: Oh, pleasure, pleasure! What else should bring one anywhere? Eating as usual, I see, Algy!

ALGERNON: [*Stiffly.*] I believe it is customary in good society to take some slight refreshment at five o'clock. Where have you been since last Thursday?

JACK: [*Sitting down on the sofa.*] In the country.

ALGERNON: What on earth do you do there?

JACK: [*Pulling off his gloves.*] When one is in town one amuses oneself. When one is in the country one amuses other people. It is excessively boring.

ALGERNON: And who are the people you amuse?

JACK: [*Airily.*] Oh, neighbours, neighbours.

ALGERNON: Got nice neighbours in your part of Shropshire?[1]

JACK: Perfectly horrid! Never speak to one of them.

ALGERNON: How immensely you must amuse them! [*Goes over and takes sandwich.*] By the way, Shropshire is your county, is it not?

JACK: Eh? Shropshire? Yes, of course. Hallo! Why all these cups? Why cucumber sandwiches? Why such reckless extravagance in one so young? Who is coming to tea?

ALGERNON: Oh! merely Aunt Augusta and Gwendolen.

JACK: How perfectly delightful!

ALGERNON: Yes, that is all very well; but I am afraid Aunt Augusta won't quite approve of your being here.

JACK: May I ask why?

ALGERNON: My dear fellow, the way you flirt with Gwendolen is perfectly disgraceful. It is almost as bad as the way Gwendolen flirts with you.

JACK: I am in love with Gwendolen. I have come up to town expressly to propose to her.

ALGERNON: I thought you had come up for pleasure? . . . I call that business.

JACK: How utterly unromantic you are!

ALGERNON: I really don't see anything romantic in proposing. It is

---

1. Rural county in the west of England, remote from metropolitan London.

very romantic to be in love. But there is nothing romantic about a definite proposal. Why, one may be accepted. One usually is, I believe. Then the excitement is all over. The very essence of romance is uncertainty. If ever I get married, I'll certainly try to forget the fact.

JACK: I have no doubt about that, dear Algy. The Divorce Court was specially invented for people whose memories are so curiously constituted.

ALGERNON: Oh! there is no use speculating on that subject. Divorces are made in Heaven— [JACK *puts out his hand to take a sandwich.* ALGERNON *at once interferes.*] Please don't touch the cucumber sandwiches. They are ordered specially for Aunt Augusta. [*Takes one and eats it.*]

JACK: Well, you have been eating them all the time.

ALGERNON: That is quite a different matter. She is my aunt. [*Takes plate from below.*] Have some bread and butter. The bread and butter is for Gwendolen. Gwendolen is devoted to bread and butter.

JACK: [*Advancing to table and helping himself.*] And very good bread and butter it is, too.

ALGERNON: Well, my dear fellow, you need not eat as if you were going to eat it all. You behave as if you were married to her already. You are not married to her already, and I don't think you ever will be.

JACK: Why on earth do you say that?

ALGERNON: Well, in the first place girls never marry the men they flirt with. Girls don't think it right.

JACK: Oh, that is nonsense!

ALGERNON: It isn't. It is a great truth. It accounts for the extraordinary number of bachelors that one sees all over the place. In the second place, I don't give my consent.

JACK: Your consent!

ALGERNON: My dear fellow, Gwendolen is my first cousin. And before I allow you to marry her, you will have to clear up the whole question of Cecily. [*Rings bell.*]

JACK: Cecily! What on earth do you mean? What do you mean, Algy, by Cecily? I don't know anyone of the name of Cecily.

[*Enter* LANE.]

ALGERNON: Bring me that cigarette case Mr. Worthing left in the smoking-room the last time he dined here.

LANE: Yes, sir. [LANE *goes out.*]

JACK: Do you mean to say you have had my cigarette case all this time? I wish to goodness you had let me know. I have been writing frantic letters to Scotland Yard about it. I was very nearly offering a large reward.

ALGERNON: Well, I wish you would offer one. I happen to be more than usually hard up.

JACK: There is no good offering a large reward now that the thing is found.

[*Enter* LANE *with the cigarette case on a salver.* ALGERNON *takes it at once.* LANE *goes out.*]

ALGERNON: I think that is rather mean of you, Ernest, I must say. [*Opens case and examines it.*] However, it makes no matter, for, now that I look at the inscription, I find that the thing isn't yours after all.

JACK: Of course it's mine. [*Moving to him.*] You have seen me with it a hundred times, and you have no right whatsoever to read what is written inside. It is a very ungentlemanly thing to read a private cigarette case.

ALGERNON: Oh! it is absurd to have a hard-and-fast rule about what one should read and what one shouldn't. More than half of modern culture depends on what one shouldn't read.

JACK: I am quite aware of the fact, and I don't propose to discuss modern culture. It isn't the sort of thing one should talk of in private. I simply want my cigarette case back.

ALGERNON: Yes; but this isn't your cigarette case. This cigarette case is a present from someone of the name of Cecily, and you said you didn't know anyone of that name.

JACK: Well, if you want to know, Cecily happens to be my aunt.

ALGERNON: Your aunt!

JACK: Yes. Charming old lady she is, too. Lives at Tunbridge Wells. Just give it back to me, Algy.

ALGERNON: [*Retreating to back of sofa.*] But why does she call herself little Cecily if she is your aunt and lives at Tunbridge Wells? [*Reading.*] "From little Cecily with her fondest love."

JACK: [*Moving to sofa and kneeling upon it.*] My dear fellow, what on earth is there in that? Some aunts are tall, some aunts are not tall. That is a matter that surely an aunt may be allowed to decide for herself. You seem to think that every aunt should be exactly like your aunt! That is absurd! For Heaven's sake give me back my cigarette case. [*Follows* ALGERNON *round the room.*]

ALGERNON: Yes. But why does your aunt call you her uncle? "From little Cecily, with her fondest love to her dear Uncle Jack." There is no objection, I admit, to an aunt being a small aunt, but why an aunt, no matter what her size may be, should call her own nephew her uncle, I can't quite make out. Besides, your name isn't Jack at all; it is Ernest.

JACK: It isn't Ernest; it's Jack.

ALGERNON: You have always told me it was Ernest. I have introduced you to everyone as Ernest. You answer to the name of Ernest. You look as if your name was Ernest. You are the most ernest looking person I ever saw in my life. It is perfectly absurd your saying that your name isn't Ernest. It's on your cards. Here is one of them. [*Taking it from case.*] "Mr. Ernest Worthing, B 4, The Albany." I'll keep this as a proof your name is Ernest if ever you attempt to deny it to me, or to Gwendolen, or to anyone else. [*Puts the card in his pocket.*]

JACK: Well, my name is Ernest in town and Jack in the country, and the cigarette case was given to me in the country.

ALGERNON: Yes, but that does not account for the fact that your small Aunt Cecily, who lives at Tumbridge Wells, calls you her dear uncle. Come, old boy, you had much better have the thing out at once.

JACK: My dear Algy, you talk exactly as if you were a dentist. It is very vulgar to talk like a dentist when one isn't a dentist. It produces a false impression.

ALGERNON: Well, that is exactly what dentists always do. Now, go on! Tell me the whole thing. I may mention that I have always suspected you of being a confirmed and secret Bunburyist; and I am quite sure of it now.

JACK: Bunburyist? What on earth do you mean by a Bunburyist?

ALGERNON: I'll reveal to you the meaning of that incomparable expression as soon as you are kind enough to inform me why you are Ernest in town and Jack in the country.

JACK: Well, produce my cigarette case first.

ALGERNON: Here it is. [*Hands cigarette case.*] Now produce your explanation, and pray make it improbable. [*Sits on sofa.*]

JACK: My dear fellow, there is nothing improbable about my explanation at all. In fact it's perfectly ordinary. Old Mr. Thomas Cardew, who adopted me when I was a little boy, made me in his will guardian to his granddaughter, Miss Cecily Cardew. Cecily, who addresses me as her uncle from motives of respect that you could not possibly appreciate, lives at my place in the country under the charge of her admirable governess, Miss Prism.

ALGERNON: Where is that place in the country, by the way?

JACK: That is nothing to you, dear boy. You are not going to be invited. . . . I may tell you candidly that the place is not in Shropshire.

ALGERNON: I suspected that, my dear fellow! I have Bunburyed all over Shropshire on two separate occasions. Now, go on. Why are you Ernest in town and Jack in the country?

JACK: My dear Algy, I don't know whether you will be able to understand my real motives. You are hardly serious enough. When one is placed in the position of guardian, one has to adopt a very high moral tone on all subjects. It's one's duty to do so. And as a high moral tone can hardly be said to conduce very much to either one's health or one's happiness, in order to get up to town I have always pretended to have a younger brother of the name of Ernest, who lives in the Albany, and gets into the most dreadful scrapes. That, my dear Algy, is the whole truth pure and simple.

ALGERNON: The truth is rarely pure and never simple. Modern life would be very tedious if it were either, and modern literature a complete impossibility!

JACK: That wouldn't be at all a bad thing.

ALGERNON: Literary criticism is not your forte, my dear fellow. Don't try it. You should leave that to people who haven't been at a University. They do it so well in the daily papers. What you really are is a Bunburyist. I was quite right in saying you were a Bunburyist. You are one of the most advanced Bunburyists I know.

JACK: What on earth do you mean?

ALGERNON: You have invented a very useful younger brother called

Ernest, in order that you may be able to come up to town as often as you like. I have invented an invaluable permanent invalid called Bunbury, in order that I may be able to go down into the country whenever I choose. Bunbury is perfectly invaluable. If it wasn't for Bunbury's extraordinary bad health, for instance, I wouldn't be able to dine with you at Willis's to-night, for I have been really engaged to Aunt Augusta for more than a week.

JACK: I haven't asked you to dine with me anywhere tonight.

ALGERNON: I know. You are absolutely careless about sending out invitations. It is very foolish of you. Nothing annoys people so much as not receiving invitations.

JACK: You had much better dine with your Aunt Augusta.

ALGERNON: I haven't the smallest intention of doing anything of the kind. To begin with, I dined there on Monday, and once a week is quite enough to dine with one's own relatives. In the second place, whenever I do dine there I am always treated as a member of the family, and sent down with either no woman at all, or two. In the third place, I know perfectly well whom she will place me next to, to-night. She will place me next Mary Farquhar, who always flirts with her own husband across the dinner-table. That is not very pleasant. Indeed, it is not even decent . . . and that sort of thing is enormously on the increase. The amount of women in London who flirt with their own husbands is perfectly scandalous. It looks so bad. It is simply washing one's clean linen in public. Besides, now that I know you to be a confirmed Bunburyist I naturally want to talk to you about Bunburying. I want to tell you the rules.

JACK: I'm not a Bunburyist at all. If Gwendolen accepts me, I am going to kill my brother, indeed I think I'll kill him in any case. Cecily is a little too much interested in him. It is rather a bore. So I am going to get rid of Ernest. And I strongly advise you to do the same with Mr. . . . with your invalid friend who has the absurd name.

ALGERNON: Nothing will induce me to part with Bunbury, and if you ever get married, which seems to me extremely problematic, you will be very glad to know Bunbury. A man who marries without knowing Bunbury has a very tedious time of it.

JACK: That is nonsense. If I marry a charming girl like Gwendolen, and she is the only girl I ever saw in my life that I would marry, I certainly won't want to know Bunbury.

ALGERNON: Then your wife will. You don't seem to realize, that in married life three is company and two is none.

JACK: [*Sententiously.*] That, my dear young friend, is the theory that the corrupt French Drama[2] has been propounding for the last fifty years.

ALGERNON: Yes; and that the happy English home has proved in half the time.

JACK: For heaven's sake, don't try to be cynical. It's perfectly easy to be cynical.

ALGERNON: My dear fellow, it isn't easy to be anything now-a-days. There's such a lot of beastly competition about. [*The sound of an electric bell is heard.*] Ah! that must be Aunt Augusta. Only relatives, or creditors, ever ring in that Wagnerian manner. Now, if I get her out of the way for ten minutes, so that you can have an opportunity for proposing to Gwendolen, may I dine with you to-night at Willis's?

JACK: I suppose so if you want to.

ALGERNON: Yes, but you must be serious about it. I hate people who are not serious about meals. It is so shallow of them.

　　　[*Enter* LANE.]

LANE: Lady Bracknell and Miss Fairfax.

　　　[ALGERNON *goes forward to meet them. Enter* LADY BRACKNELL *and* GWENDOLEN.]

LADY BRACKNELL: Good afternoon, dear Algernon, I hope you are behaving very well.

ALGERNON: I'm feeling very well, Aunt Augusta.

LADY BRACKNELL: That's not quite the same thing. In fact the two things rarely go together. [*Sees* JACK *and bows to him with icy coldness.*]

ALGERNON: [*To* GWENDOLEN.] Dear me, you are smart!

GWENDOLEN: I am always smart! Aren't I, Mr. Worthing?

JACK: You're quite perfect, Miss Fairfax.

GWENDOLEN: Oh! I hope I am not that. It would leave no room

---

2. With its irreverent and often comical treatment of real life, the French theater seemed libertine to the English.

for developments, and I intend to develop in *many directions.*
[GWENDOLEN *and* JACK *sit down together in the corner.*]

LADY BRACKNELL: I'm sorry if we are a little late, Algernon, but I was obliged to call on dear Lady Harbury. I hadn't been there since her poor husband's death. I never saw a woman so altered; she looks quite twenty years younger. And now I'll have a cup of tea, and one of those nice cucumber sandwiches you promised me.

ALGERNON: Certainly, Aunt Augusta. [*Goes over to tea-table.*]

LADY BRACKNELL: Won't you come and sit here, Gwendolen?

GWENDOLEN: Thanks, mamma, I'm quite comfortable where I am.

ALGERNON: [*Picking up empty plate in horror.*] Good heavens! Lane! Why are there no cucumber sandwiches? I ordered them specially.

LANE: [*Gravely.*] There were no cucumbers in the market this morning, sir. I went down twice.

ALGERNON: No cucumbers!

LANE: No, sir. Not even for ready money.

ALGERNON: That will do, Lane, thank you.

LANE: Thank you sir. [*Goes out.*]

ALGERNON: I am greatly distressed, Aunt Augusta, about there being no cucumbers, not even for ready money.

LADY BRACKNELL: It really makes no matter, Algernon. I had some crumpets with Lady Harbury, who seems to me to be living entirely for pleasure now.

ALGERNON: I hear her hair has turned quite gold from grief.

LADY BRACKNELL: It certainly has changed its colour. From what cause I, of course, cannot say. [ALGERNON *crosses and hands tea.*] Thank you. I've quite a treat for you to-night, Algernon. I am going to send you down with Mary Farquhar. She is such a nice woman, and so attentive to her husband. It's delightful to watch them.

ALGERNON: I am afraid, Aunt Augusta, I shall have to give up the pleasure of dining with you to-night after all.

LADY BRACKNELL: [*Frowning.*] I hope not, Algernon. It would put my table completely out. Your uncle would have to dine upstairs. Fortunately he is accustomed to that.

ALGERNON: It is a great bore, and, I need hardly say, a terrible disappointment to me, but the fact is I have just had a telegram to say that my poor friend Bunbury is very ill again. [*Exchanges glances with* JACK.] They seem to think I should be with him.

LADY BRACKNELL: It is very strange. This Mr. Bunbury seems to suffer from curiously bad health.

ALGERNON: Yes; poor Bunbury is a dreadful invalid.

LADY BRACKNELL: Well, I must say, Algernon, that I think it is high time that Mr. Bunbury made up his mind whether he was going to live or to die. This shilly-shallying with the question is absurd. Nor do I in any way approve of the modern sympathy with invalids. I consider it morbid. Illness of any kind is hardly a thing to be encouraged in others. Health is the primary duty of life. I am always telling that to your poor uncle, but he never seems to take much notice . . . as far as any improvement in his ailments goes. I should be much obliged if you would ask Mr. Bunbury, from me, to be kind enough not to have a relapse on Saturday, for I rely on you to arrange my music for me. It is my last reception and one wants something that will encourage conversation, particularly at the end of the season when everyone has practically said whatever they had to say, which, in most cases, was probably not much.

ALGERNON: I'll speak to Bunbury, Aunt Augusta, if he is still conscious, and I think I can promise you he'll be all right by Saturday. You see, if one plays good music, people don't listen, and if one plays bad music people don't talk. But I'll run over the programme I've drawn out, if you will kindly come into the next room for a moment.

LADY BRACKNELL: Thank you, Algernon. It is very thoughtful of you. [*Rising, and following* ALGERNON.] I'm sure the programme will be delightful, after a few expurgations. French songs I cannot possibly allow. People always seem to think that they are improper, and either look shocked, which is vulgar, or laugh, which is worse. But German sounds a thoroughly respectable language, and indeed, I believe is so.[3] Gwendolen, you will accompany me.

GWENDOLEN: Certainly, mamma.

[LADY BRACKNELL *and* ALGERNON *go into the music-room,* GWENDOLEN *remains behind.*]

---

3. To the English, French culture seemed racy; German culture, staid.

JACK: Charming day it has been, Miss Fairfax.

GWENDOLEN: Pray don't talk to me about the weather, Mr. Worthing. Whenever people talk to me about the weather, I always feel quite certain that they mean something else. And that makes me so nervous.

JACK: I do mean something else.

GWENDOLEN: I thought so. In fact, I am never wrong.

JACK: And I would like to be allowed to take advantage of Lady Bracknell's temporary absence . . .

GWENDOLEN: I would certainly advise you to do so. Mamma has a way of coming back suddenly into a room that I have often had to speak to her about.

JACK: [*Nervously.*] Miss Fairfax, ever since I met you I have admired you more than any girl . . . I have ever met since . . . I met you.

GWENDOLEN: Yes, I am quite aware of the fact. And I often wish that in public, at any rate, you had been more demonstrative. For me you have always had an irresistible fascination. Even before I met you I was far from indifferent to you. [JACK *looks at her in amazement.*] We live, as I hope you know, Mr. Worthing, in an age of ideals. The fact is constantly mentioned in the more expensive monthly magazines, and has reached the provincial pulpits I am told: and my ideal has always been to love some one of the name of Ernest. There is something in that name that inspires absolute confidence. The moment Algernon first mentioned to me that he had a friend called Ernest, I knew I was destined to love you.

JACK: You really love me, Gwendolen?

GWENDOLEN: Passionately!

JACK: Darling! You don't know how happy you've made me.

GWENDOLEN: My own Ernest!

JACK: But you don't really mean to say that you couldn't love me if my name wasn't Ernest?

GWENDOLEN: But your name is Ernest.

JACK: Yes, I know it is. But supposing it was something else? Do you mean to say you couldn't love me then?

GWENDOLEN: [*Glibly.*] Ah! that is clearly a metaphysical speculation, and like most metaphysical speculations has very little reference at all to the actual facts of real life, as we know them.

JACK: Personally, darling, to speak quite candidly, I don't much care about the name of Ernest . . . I don't think that name suits me at all.

GWENDOLEN: It suits you perfectly. It is a divine name. It has a music of its own. It produces vibrations.

JACK: Well, really, Gwendolen, I must say that I think there are lots of other much nicer names. I think, Jack, for instance, a charming name.

GWENDOLEN: Jack? . . . No, there is very little music in the name Jack, if any at all, indeed. It does not thrill. It produces absolutely no vibration. . . . I have known several Jacks, and they all, without exception, were more than usually plain. Besides, Jack is a notorious domesticity for John! And I pity any woman who is married to a man called John. She would probably never be allowed to know the entrancing pleasure of a single moment's solitude. The only really safe name is Ernest.

JACK: Gwendolen, I must get christened at once—I mean we must get married at once. There is no time to be lost.

GWENDOLEN: Married, Mr. Worthing?

JACK: [*Astounded.*] Well . . . surely. You know that I love you, and you led me to believe, Miss Fairfax, that you were not absolutely indifferent to me.

GWENDOLEN: I adore you. But you haven't proposed to me yet. Nothing has been said at all about marriage. The subject has not even been touched on.

JACK: Well . . . may I propose to you now?

GWENDOLEN: I think it would be an admirable opportunity. And to spare you any possible disappointment, Mr. Worthing, I think it only fair to tell you quite frankly beforehand that I am fully determined to accept you.

JACK: Gwendolen!

GWENDOLEN: Yes, Mr. Worthing, what have you got to say to me?

JACK: You know what I have got to say to you.

GWENDOLEN: Yes, but you don't say it.

JACK: Gwendolen, will you marry me? [*Goes on his knees.*]

GWENDOLEN: Of course I will, darling. How long you have been about it! I am afraid you have had very little experience in how to propose.

JACK: My own one, I have never loved anyone in the world but you.

GWENDOLEN: Yes, but men often propose for practice. I know my brother Gerald does. All my girl-friends tell me so. What wonderfully blue eyes you have, Ernest! They are quite, quite blue. I hope you will always look at me just like that, especially when there are other people present.

[*Enter* LADY BRACKNELL.]

LADY BRACKNELL: Mr. Worthing! Rise, sir, from this semi-recumbent posture. It is most indecorous.

GWENDOLEN: Mamma! [*He tries to rise; she restrains him.*] I must beg you to retire. This is no place for you, besides, Mr. Worthing has not quite finished yet.

LADY BRACKNELL: Finished what, may I ask?

GWENDOLEN: I am engaged to Mr. Worthing, mamma. [*They rise together.*]

LADY BRACKNELL: Pardon me, you are not engaged to anyone. When you do become engaged to some one, I, or your father, should his health permit him, will inform you of the fact. An engagement should come on a young girl as a surprise, pleasant or unpleasant, as the case may be. It is hardly a matter that she could be allowed to arrange for herself[4] . . . And now I have a few questions to put to you, Mr. Worthing. While I am making these inquiries, you, Gwendolen, will wait for me below in the carriage.

GWENDOLEN: [*Reproachfully.*] Mamma!

LADY BRACKNELL: In the carriage, Gwendolen! [GWENDOLEN *goes to the door. She and* JACK *blow kisses to each other behind* LADY BRACKNELL'*s back.* LADY BRACKNELL *looks vaguely about as if she could not understand what the noise was. Finally turns round.*] Gwendolen, the carriage!

GWENDOLEN: Yes, mamma. [*Goes out, looking back at* JACK.]

LADY BRACKNELL: [*Sitting down.*] You can take a seat, Mr. Worthing. [*Looks in her pocket for note-book and pencil.*]

JACK: Thank you, Lady Bracknell, I prefer standing.

LADY BRACKNELL: [*Pencil and notebook in hand.*] I feel bound to tell you that you are not down on my list of eligible young men, al-

---

4. By the 1890s, marriages in England, even among the aristocracy, were no longer "arranged."

though I have the same list as the dear Duchess of Bolton has. We work together, in fact. However, I am quite ready to enter your name, should your answers be what a really affectionate mother requires. Do you smoke?

JACK: Well, yes, I must admit I smoke.

LADY BRACKNELL: I am glad to hear it. A man should always have an occupation of some kind.[5] There are far too many idle men in London as it is. How old are you?

JACK: Twenty-nine.

LADY BRACKNELL: A very good age to be married at. I have always been of opinion that a man who desires to get married should know either everything or nothing. Which do you know?

JACK: [*After some hesitation.*] I know nothing, Lady Bracknell.

LADY BRACKNELL: I am pleased to hear it. I do not approve of anything that tampers with natural ignorance. Ignorance is like a delicate exotic fruit; touch it and the bloom is gone. The whole theory of modern education is radically unsound. Fortunately in England, at any rate, education produces no effect whatsoever. If it did, it would prove a serious danger to the upper classes, and probably lead to acts of violence in Grosvenor Square.[6] What is your income?

JACK: Between seven and eight thousand a year.

LADY BRACKNELL: [*Makes a note in her book.*] In land, or in investments?

JACK: In investments, chiefly.[7]

LADY BRACKNELL: That is satisfactory. What between the duties expected of one during one's life-time, and the duties exacted from one after one's death, land has ceased to be either a profit or a pleasure. It gives one position, and prevents one from keeping it up.[8] That's all that can be said about land.

JACK: I have a country house with some land, of course, attached to

---

5. Not having to work for a living often distinguished true aristocrats from pretenders; even so, the rise of middle-class ethics in the Victorian age promoted a work ethic even among the rich.

6. Wealthy residential district in London.

7. Jack's income is considerable, and its deriving from investments links him with the newly rich rather than the landed aristocracy.

8. Land was the mark of an old family, but by the 1890s it was already obsolete as a source of wealth—in fact, owning a lot of land drained one's finances.

it, about fifteen hundred acres, I believe; but I don't depend on that for my real income. In fact, as far as I can make out, the poachers are the only people who make anything out of it.

LADY BRACKNELL: A country house! How many bedrooms? Well, that point can be cleared up afterwards. You have a town house, I hope? A girl with a simple, unspoiled nature, like Gwendolen, could hardly be expected to reside in the country.

JACK: Well, I own a house in Belgrave Square, but it is let by the year to Lady Bloxham. Of course, I can get it back whenever I like, at six months' notice.

LADY BRACKNELL: Lady Bloxham? I don't know her.

JACK: Oh, she goes about very little. She is a lady considerably advanced in years.

LADY BRACKNELL: Ah, now-a-days that is no guarantee of respectability of character. What number in Belgrave Square?

JACK: 149.

LADY BRACKNELL: [*Shaking her head.*] The unfashionable side. I thought there was something. However, that could easily be altered.

JACK: Do you mean the fashion, or the side?

LADY BRACKNELL: [*Sternly.*] Both, if necessary, I presume. What are your politics?

JACK: Well, I am afraid I really have none. I am a Liberal Unionist.[9]

LADY BRACKNELL: Oh, they count as Tories.[1] They dine with us. Or come in the evening, at any rate. Now to minor matters. Are your parents living?

JACK: I have lost both my parents.

LADY BRACKNELL: Both? . . . That seems like carelessness. Who was your father? He was evidently a man of some wealth. Was he born in what the Radical papers call the purple of commerce, or did he rise from the ranks of the aristocracy?

JACK: I am afraid I really don't know. The fact is, Lady Bracknell, I said I had lost my parents. It would be nearer the truth to say that my parents seem to have lost me . . . I don't actually know who I am by birth. I was . . . well, I was found.

9. An English political party that split from the Liberal Party in 1886 and, by the turn of the century, effectively merged with the Conservative Party.

1. A political party linked to the landed aristocracy; forerunner of the Conservative Party.

LADY BRACKNELL: Found!

JACK: The late Mr. Thomas Cardew, an old gentleman of a very charitable and kindly disposition, found me, and gave me the name of Worthing, because he happened to have a first-class ticket for Worthing in his pocket at the time. Worthing is a place in Sussex. It is a seaside resort.

LADY BRACKNELL: Where did the charitable gentleman who had a first-class ticket for this seaside resort find you?

JACK: [*Gravely.*] In a hand-bag.

LADY BRACKNELL: A hand-bag?

JACK: [*Very seriously.*] Yes, Lady Bracknell. I was in a hand-bag—a somewhat large, black leather hand-bag, with handles to it—an ordinary hand-bag in fact.

LADY BRACKNELL: In what locality did Mr. James, or Thomas, Cardew come across this ordinary hand-bag?

JACK: In the cloak-room at Victoria Station. It was given to him in mistake for his own.

LADY BRACKNELL: The cloak-room at Victoria Station?

JACK: Yes. The Brighton line.

LADY BRACKNELL: The line is immaterial. Mr. Worthing, I confess I feel somewhat bewildered by what you have just told me. To be born, or at any rate bred, in a hand-bag, whether it had handles or not, seems to me to display a contempt for the ordinary decencies of family life that remind one of the worst excesses of the French Revolution.[2] And I presume you know what that unfortunate movement led to? As for the particular locality in which the hand-bag was found, a cloak-room at a railway station might serve to conceal a social indiscretion—has probably, indeed, been used for the purpose before now—but it could hardly be regarded as an assured basis for a recognized position in good society.

JACK: May I ask you then what you would advise me to do? I need hardly say I would do anything in the world to ensure Gwendolen's happiness.

LADY BRACKNELL: I would strongly advise you, Mr. Worthing, to try

---

2. The French Revolution dissolved many of the legal privileges given aristocrats by virtue of their "noble" blood.

and acquire some relations as soon as possible, and to make a definite effort to produce at any rate one parent, of either sex, before the season is quite over.

JACK: Well, I don't see how I could possibly manage to do that. I can produce the hand-bag at any moment. It is in my dressing-room at home. I really think that should satisfy you, Lady Bracknell.

LADY BRACKNELL: Me, sir! What has it to do with me? You can hardly imagine that I and Lord Bracknell would dream of allowing our only daughter—a girl brought up with the utmost care—to marry into a cloak-room, and form an alliance with a parcel? Good morning, Mr. Worthing! [LADY BRACKNELL *sweeps out in majestic indignation.*]

JACK: Good morning! [ALGERNON, *from the other room, strikes up the Wedding March.* JACK *looks perfectly furious, and goes to the door.*] For goodness' sake don't play that ghastly tune, Algy! How idiotic you are!

[*The music stops, and* ALGERNON *enters cheerily.*]

ALGERNON: Didn't it go off all right, old boy? You don't mean to say Gwendolen refused you? I know it is a way she has. She is always refusing people. I think it is most ill-natured of her.

JACK: Oh, Gwendolen is as right as a trivet. As far as she is concerned, we are engaged. Her mother is perfectly unbearable. Never met such a Gorgon[3] . . . I don't really know what a Gorgon is like, but I am quite sure that Lady Bracknell is one. In any case, she is a monster, without being a myth, which is rather unfair. . . . I beg your pardon, Algy, I suppose I shouldn't talk about your own aunt in that way before you.

ALGERNON: My dear boy, I love hearing my relations abused. It is the only thing that makes me put up with them at all. Relations are simply a tedious pack of people, who haven't got the remotest knowledge of how to live, nor the smallest instinct about when to die.

JACK: Oh, that is nonsense!

ALGERNON: It isn't!

JACK: Well, I won't argue about the matter. You always want to argue about things.

---

3. One of three snake-haired sisters in Greek mythology; to look at a Gorgon would turn a person to stone.

ALGERNON: That is exactly what things were originally made for.

JACK: Upon my word, if I thought that, I'd shoot myself . . . [*A pause.*] You don't think there is any chance of Gwendolen becoming like her mother in about a hundred and fifty years, do you, Algy?

ALGERNON: All women become like their mothers. That is their tragedy. No man does. That's his.

JACK: Is that clever?

ALGERNON: It is perfectly phrased! and quite as true as any observation in civilized life should be.

JACK: I am sick to death of cleverness. Everybody is clever now-a-days. You can't go anywhere without meeting clever people. The thing has become an absolute public nuisance. I wish to goodness we had a few fools left.

ALGERNON: We have.

JACK: I should extremely like to meet them. What do they talk about?

ALGERNON: The fools? Oh! about the clever people, of course.

JACK: What fools!

ALGERNON: By the way, did you tell Gwendolen the truth about your being Ernest in town, and Jack in the country?

JACK: [*In a very patronising manner.*] My dear fellow, the truth isn't quite the sort of thing one tells to a nice, sweet, refined girl. What extraordinary ideas you have about the way to behave to a woman!

ALGERNON: The only way to behave to a woman is to make love to[4] her, if she is pretty, and to someone else if she is plain.

JACK: Oh, that is nonsense.

ALGERNON: What about your brother? What about the profligate Ernest?

JACK: Oh, before the end of the week I shall have got rid of him. I'll say he died in Paris of apoplexy. Lots of people die of apoplexy, quite suddenly, don't they?

ALGERNON: Yes, but it's hereditary, my dear fellow. It's a sort of thing that runs in families. You had much better say a severe chill.

---

4. *Make love to:* court.

JACK: You are sure a severe chill isn't hereditary, or anything of that kind?

ALGERNON: Of course it isn't!

JACK: Very well, then. My poor brother Ernest is carried off suddenly in Paris, by a severe chill. That gets rid of him.

ALGERNON: But I thought you said that . . . Miss Cardew was a little too much interested in your poor brother Ernest? Won't she feel his loss a good deal?

JACK: Oh, that is all right. Cecily is not a silly, romantic girl, I am glad to say. She has got a capital appetite, goes for long walks, and pays no attention at all to her lessons.

ALGERNON: I would rather like to see Cecily.

JACK: I will take very good care you never do. She is excessively pretty, and she is only just eighteen.

ALGERNON: Have you told Gwendolen yet that you have an excessively pretty ward who is only just eighteen?

JACK: Oh! one doesn't blurt these things out to people. Cecily and Gwendolen are perfectly certain to be extremely great friends. I'll bet you anything you like that half an hour after they have met, they will be calling each other sister.

ALGERNON: Women only do that when they have called each other a lot of other things first. Now, my dear boy, if we want to get a good table at Willis's, we really must go and dress. Do you know it is nearly seven?

JACK: [*Irritably.*] Oh! it always is nearly seven.

ALGERNON: Well, I'm hungry.

JACK: I never knew you when you weren't. . . .

ALGERNON: What shall we do after dinner? Go to a theatre?

JACK: Oh, no! I loathe listening.

ALGERNON: Well, let us go to the Club?

JACK: Oh, no! I hate talking.

ALGERNON: Well, we might trot round to the Empire[5] at ten?

JACK: Oh, no! can't bear looking at things. It is so silly.

ALGERNON: Well, what shall we do?

JACK: Nothing!

ALGERNON: It is awfully hard work doing nothing. However, I

5. The Empire Theatre of Varieties, a music hall.

don't mind hard work where there is no definite object of any kind.

[*Enter* LANE.]

LANE: Miss Fairfax.

[*Enter* GWENDOLEN. LANE *goes out.*]

ALGERNON: Gwendolen, upon my word!

GWENDOLEN: Algy, kindly turn your back. I have something very particular to say to Mr. Worthing.

ALGERNON: Really, Gwendolen, I don't think I can allow this at all.

GWENDOLEN: Algy, you always adopt a strictly immoral attitude towards life. You are not quite old enough to do that.

[ALGERNON *retires to the fireplace.*]

JACK: My own darling!

GWENDOLEN: Ernest, we may never be married. From the expression on mamma's face I fear we never shall. Few parents now-a-days pay any regard to what their children say to them. The old-fashioned respect for the young is fast dying out. Whatever influence I ever had over mamma, I lost at the age of three. But although she may prevent us from becoming man and wife, and I may marry someone else, and marry often, nothing that she can possibly do can alter my eternal devotion to you.

JACK: Dear Gwendolen.

GWENDOLEN: The story of your romantic origin, as related to me by mamma, with unpleasing comments, has naturally stirred the deeper fibers of my nature. Your Christian name has an irresistible fascination. The simplicity of your character makes you exquisitely incomprehensible to me. Your town address at the Albany I have. What is your address in the country?

JACK: The Manor House, Woolton, Hertfordshire.

[ALGERNON, *who has been carefully listening, smiles to himself, and writes the address on his shirt-cuff. Then picks up the Railway Guide.*]

GWENDOLEN: There is a good postal service, I suppose? It may be necessary to do something desperate. That, of course, will require serious consideration. I will communicate with you daily.

JACK: My own one!

GWENDOLEN: How long do you remain in town?

JACK: Till Monday.

GWENDOLEN: Good! Algy, you may turn round now.

ALGERNON: Thanks, I've turned round already.

GWENDOLEN: You may also ring the bell.

JACK: You will let me see you to your carriage, my own darling?

GWENDOLEN: Certainly.

JACK: [*To* LANE, *who now enters.*] I will see Miss Fairfax out.

LANE: Yes, sir.

> [JACK *and* GWENDOLEN *go off.* LANE *presents several letters on a salver to* ALGERNON. *It is to be surmised that they are bills, as* AL-GERNON, *after looking at the envelopes, tears them up.*]

ALGERNON: A glass of sherry, Lane.

LANE: Yes, sir.

ALGERNON: To-morrow, Lane, I'm going Bunburying.

LANE: Yes, sir.

ALGERNON: I shall probably not be back till Monday. You can put up my dress clothes, my smoking jacket, and all the Bunbury suits . . .

LANE: Yes, sir. [*Handing sherry.*]

ALGERNON: I hope to-morrow will be a fine day, Lane.

LANE: It never is, sir.

ALGERNON: Lane, you're a perfect pessimist.

LANE: I do my best to give satisfaction, sir.

> [*Enter* JACK. LANE *goes off.*]

JACK: There's a sensible, intellectual girl! the only girl I ever cared for in my life. [ALGERNON *is laughing immoderately.*] What on earth are you so amused at?

ALGERNON: Oh, I'm a little anxious about poor Bunbury, that's all.

JACK: If you don't take care, your friend Bunbury will get you into a serious scrape some day.

ALGERNON: I love scrapes. They are the only things that are never serious.

JACK: Oh, that's nonsense, Algy. You never talk anything but nonsense.

ALGERNON: Nobody ever does.

> [JACK *looks indignantly at him, and leaves the room.* ALGERNON *lights a cigarette, reads his shirt-cuff and smiles.*]

[*Curtain.*]

ACT II

SCENE.—*Garden at the Manor House. A flight of gray stone steps leads up to the house. The garden, an old-fashioned one, full of roses. Time of year, July. Basket chairs, and a table covered with books are set under a large yew tree.* MISS PRISM *discovered seated at the table.* CE-CILY *is at the back watering flowers.*

MISS PRISM: [*Calling.*] Cecily, Cecily! Surely such a utilitarian occupation as the watering of flowers is rather Moulton's duty than yours? Especially at a moment when intellectual pleasures await you. Your German grammar is on the table. Pray open it at page fifteen. We will repeat yesterday's lesson.

CECILY: [*Coming over very slowly.*] But I don't like German. It isn't at all a becoming language. I know perfectly well that I look quite plain after my German lesson.

MISS PRISM: Child, you know how anxious your guardian is that you should improve yourself in every way. He laid particular stress on your German, as he was leaving for town yesterday. Indeed, he always lays stress on your German when he is leaving for town.

CECILY: Dear Uncle Jack is so very serious! Sometimes he is so serious that I think he cannot be quite well.

MISS PRISM: [*Drawing herself up.*] Your guardian enjoys the best of health, and his gravity of demeanour is especially to be commended in one so comparatively young as he is. I know no one who has a higher sense of duty and responsibility.

CECILY: I suppose that is why he often looks a little bored when we three are together.

MISS PRISM: Cecily! I am surprised at you. Mr. Worthing has many troubles in his life. Idle merriment and triviality would be out of place in his conversation. You must remember his constant anxiety about that unfortunate young man, his brother.

CECILY: I wish Uncle Jack would allow the unfortunate young man, his brother, to come down here sometimes. We might have a good influence over him, Miss Prism. I am sure you certainly would. You know German, and geology, and things of that kind influence a man very much. [CECILY *begins to write in her diary.*]

MISS PRISM: [*Shaking her head.*] I do not think that even I could produce any effect on a character that, according to his own brother's admission, is irretrievably weak and vacillating. Indeed, I am not sure that I would desire to reclaim him. I am not in favour of this modern mania for turning bad people into good people at a moment's notice. As a man sows so let him reap. You must put away your diary, Cecily. I really don't see why you should keep a diary at all.

CECILY: I keep a diary in order to enter the wonderful secrets of my life. If I didn't write them down I should probably forget all about them.

MISS PRISM: Memory, my dear Cecily, is the diary that we all carry about with us.

CECILY: Yes, but it usually chronicles the things that have never happened, and couldn't possibly have happened. I believe that Memory is responsible for nearly all the three-volume novels that Mudie sends us.[1]

MISS PRISM: Do not speak slightingly of the three-volume novel, Cecily. I wrote one myself in earlier days.

CECILY: Did you really, Miss Prism? How wonderfully clever you are! I hope it did not end happily? I don't like novels that end happily. They depress me so much.

MISS PRISM: The good ended happily, and the bad unhappily. That is what Fiction means.

CECILY: I suppose so. But it seems very unfair. And was your novel ever published?

MISS PRISM: Alas! no. The manuscript unfortunately was abandoned. I use the word in the sense of lost or mislaid. To your work, child, these speculations are profitless.

CECILY: [Smiling.] But I see dear Dr. Chasuble coming up through the garden.

MISS PRISM: [Rising and advancing.] Dr. Chasuble! This is indeed a pleasure.

[Enter CANON CHASUBLE.]

CHASUBLE: And how are we this morning? Miss Prism, you are, I trust, well?

---

1. Three-volume novels were the standard format for novelists of an earlier generation, like Dickens and Thackeray, but people like Wilde considered them old-fashioned and their contents unrealistic. *Mudie:* Mudie's, a lending library.

CECILY: Miss Prism has just been complaining of a slight headache. I think it would do her so much good to have a short stroll with you in the park, Dr. Chasuble.

MISS PRISM: Cecily, I have not mentioned anything about a headache.

CECILY: No, dear Miss Prism, I know that, but I felt instinctively that you had a headache. Indeed I was thinking about that, and not about my German lesson, when the Rector came in.

CHASUBLE: I hope, Cecily, you are not inattentive.

CECILY: Oh, I am afraid I am.

CHASUBLE: That is strange. Were I fortunate enough to be Miss Prism's pupil, I would hang upon her lips. [MISS PRISM *glares.*] I spoke metaphorically.—My metaphor was drawn from bees. Ahem! Mr. Worthing, I suppose, has not returned from town yet?

MISS PRISM: We do not expect him till Monday afternoon.

CHASUBLE: Ah, yes, he usually likes to spend his Sunday in London. He is not one of those whose sole aim is enjoyment, as by all accounts, that unfortunate young man, his brother, seems to be. But I must not disturb Egeria[2] and her pupil any longer.

MISS PRISM: Egeria? My name is Lætitia, Doctor.

CHASUBLE: [*Bowing.*] A classical allusion merely, drawn from the Pagan authors. I shall see you both no doubt at Evensong.

MISS PRISM: I think, dear Doctor, I will have a stroll with you. I find I have a headache after all, and a walk might do it good.

CHASUBLE: With pleasure, Miss Prism, with pleasure. We might go as far as the schools and back.

MISS PRISM: That would be delightful. Cecily, you will read your Political Economy in my absence. The chapter on the Fall of the Rupee[3] you may omit. It is somewhat too sensational. Even these metallic problems have their melodramatic side. [*Goes down the garden with* DR. CHASUBLE.]

CECILY: [*Picks up books and throws them back on table.*] Horrid Political Economy! Horrid Geography! Horrid, horrid German!

[*Enter* MERRIMAN *with a card on a salver.*]

---

2. In Roman mythology, a wood nymph (maiden goddess) who advised a king of Rome until his death, after which she pined for him.

3. Standard coin of India; in the early 1890s, it suffered such a devaluation that the mints were closed to try to break its fall.

MERRIMAN: Mr. Ernest Worthing has just driven over from the station. He has brought his luggage with him.

CECILY: [*Takes the card and reads it.*] "Mr. Ernest Worthing, B 4 The Albany, W." Uncle Jack's brother! Did you tell him Mr. Worthing was in town?

MERRIMAN: Yes, Miss. He seemed very much disappointed. I mentioned that you and Miss Prism were in the garden. He said he was anxious to speak to you privately for a moment.

CECILY: Ask Mr. Ernest Worthing to come here. I suppose you had better talk to the housekeeper about a room for him.

MERRIMAN: Yes, Miss. [MERRIMAN *goes off.*]

CECILY: I have never met any really wicked person before. I feel rather frightened. I am so afraid he will look just like everyone else.

    [*Enter* ALGERNON, *very gay and debonair.*]

He does!

ALGERNON: [*Raising his hat.*] You are my little cousin Cecily, I'm sure.

CECILY: You are under some strange mistake. I am not little. In fact, I am more than usually tall for my age. [ALGERNON *is rather taken aback.*] But I am your cousin Cecily. You, I see from your card, are Uncle Jack's brother, my cousin Ernest, my wicked cousin Ernest.

ALGERNON: Oh! I am not really wicked at all, cousin Cecily. You mustn't think that I am wicked.

CECILY: If you are not, then you have certainly been deceiving us all in a very inexcusable manner. I hope you have not been leading a double life, pretending to be wicked and being really good all the time. That would be hypocrisy.

ALGERNON: [*Looks at her in amazement.*] Oh! of course I have been rather reckless.

CECILY: I am glad to hear it.

ALGERNON: In fact, now you mention the subject, I have been very bad in my own small way.

CECILY: I don't think you should be so proud of that, though I am sure it must have been very pleasant.

ALGERNON: It is much pleasanter being here with you.

CECILY: I can't understand how you are here at all. Uncle Jack won't be back till Monday afternoon.

ALGERNON: That is a great disappointment. I am obliged to go up by the first train on Monday morning. I have a business appointment that I am anxious . . . to miss.

CECILY: Couldn't you miss it anywhere but in London?

ALGERNON: No; the appointment is in London.

CECILY: Well, I know, of course, how important it is not to keep a business engagement, if one wants to retain any sense of the beauty of life, but still I think you had better wait till Uncle Jack arrives. I know he wants to speak to you about your emigrating.

ALGERNON: About my what?

CECILY: Your emigrating. He has gone up to buy your outfit.

ALGERNON: I certainly wouldn't let Jack buy my outfit. He has no taste in neckties at all.

CECILY: I don't think you will require neckties. Uncle Jack is sending you to Australia.

ALGERNON: Australia! I'd sooner die.

CECILY: Well, he said at dinner on Wednesday night, that you would have to choose between this world, the next world, and Australia.

ALGERNON: Oh, well! The accounts I have received of Australia and the next world are not particularly encouraging. This world is good enough for me, cousin Cecily.

CECILY: Yes, but are you good enough for it?

ALGERNON: I'm afraid I'm not that. That is why I want you to reform me. You might make that your mission, if you don't mind, cousin Cecily.

CECILY: I'm afraid I've not time, this afternoon.

ALGERNON: Well, would you mind my reforming myself this afternoon?

CECILY: That is rather Quixotic of you. But I think you should try.

ALGERNON: I will. I feel better already.

CECILY: You are looking a little worse.

ALGERNON: That is because I am hungry.

CECILY: How thoughtless of me. I should have remembered that when one is going to lead an entirely new life, one requires regular and wholesome meals. Won't you come in?

ALGERNON: Thank you. Might I have a button-hole first? I never have any appetite unless I have a button-hole first.

CECILY: A Maréchal Niel?[4] [*Picks up scissors.*]

ALGERNON: No, I'd sooner have a pink rose.

CECILY: Why? [*Cuts a flower.*]

ALGERNON: Because you are like a pink rose, cousin Cecily.

CECILY: I don't think it can be right for you to talk to me like that. Miss Prism never says such things to me.

ALGERNON: Then Miss Prism is a short-sighted old lady. [CECILY *puts the rose in his button-hole.*] You are the prettiest girl I ever saw.

CECILY: Miss Prism says that all good looks are a snare.

ALGERNON: They are a snare that every sensible man would like to be caught in.

CECILY: Oh! I don't think I would care to catch a sensible man. I shouldn't know what to talk to him about.

[*They pass into the house.* MISS PRISM *and* DR. CHASUBLE *return.*]

MISS PRISM: You are too much alone, dear Dr. Chasuble. You should get married. A misanthrope I can understand—a womanthrope, never!

CHASUBLE: [*With a scholar's shudder.*] Believe me, I do not deserve so neologistic a phrase. The precept as well as the practice of the Primitive Church was distinctly against matrimony.

MISS PRISM: [*Sententiously.*] That is obviously the reason why the Primitive Church has not lasted up to the present day. And you do not seem to realize, dear Doctor, that by persistently remaining single, a man converts himself into a permanent public temptation. Men should be careful; this very celibacy leads weaker vessels astray.

CHASUBLE: But is a man not equally attractive when married?

MISS PRISM: No married man is ever attractive except to his wife.

CHASUBLE: And often, I've been told, not even to her.

MISS PRISM: That depends on the intellectual sympathies of the woman. Maturity can always be depended on. Ripeness can be trusted. Young women are green. [DR. CHASUBLE *starts.*] I spoke horticulturally. My metaphor was drawn from fruits. But where is Cecily?

4. A popular yellow rose of the period, here to be worn on Algernon's lapel.

CHASUBLE: Perhaps she followed us to the schools.

[*Enter* JACK *slowly from the back of the garden. He is dressed in the deepest mourning, with crepe hatband and black gloves.*]

MISS PRISM: Mr. Worthing!

CHASUBLE: Mr. Worthing?

MISS PRISM: This is indeed a surprise. We did not look for you till Monday afternoon.

JACK: [*Shakes* MISS PRISM'*s hand in a tragic manner.*] I have returned sooner than I expected. Dr. Chasuble, I hope you are well?

CHASUBLE: Dear Mr. Worthing, I trust this garb of woe does not betoken some terrible calamity?

JACK: My brother.

MISS PRISM: More shameful debts and extravagance?

CHASUBLE: Still leading his life of pleasure?

JACK: [*Shaking his head.*] Dead!

CHASUBLE: Your brother Ernest dead?

JACK: Quite dead.

MISS PRISM: What a lesson for him! I trust he will profit by it.

CHASUBLE: Mr. Worthing, I offer you my sincere condolence. You have at least the consolation of knowing that you were always the most generous and forgiving of brothers.

JACK: Poor Ernest! He had many faults, but it is a sad, sad blow.

CHASUBLE: Very sad indeed. Were you with him at the end?

JACK: No. He died abroad; in Paris, in fact. I had a telegram last night from the manager of the Grand Hotel.

CHASUBLE: Was the cause of death mentioned?

JACK: A severe chill, it seems.

MISS PRISM: As a man sows, so shall he reap.

CHASUBLE: [*Raising his hand.*] Charity, dear Miss Prism, charity! None of us are perfect. I myself am peculiarly susceptible to draughts. Will the interment take place here?

JACK: No. He seems to have expressed a desire to be buried in Paris.

CHASUBLE: In Paris! [*Shakes his head.*] I fear that hardly points to any very serious state of mind at the last. You would no doubt wish me to make some slight allusion to this tragic domestic affliction next Sunday. [JACK *presses his hand convulsively.*] My sermon on the meaning of the manna in the wilderness can be adapted to almost any occasion, joyful, or, as in the present case, distressing.

[*All sigh.*] I have preached it at harvest celebrations, christenings, confirmations, on days of humiliation and festal days. The last time I delivered it was in the Cathedral, as a charity sermon on behalf of the Society for the Prevention of Discontentment among the Upper Orders. The Bishop, who was present, was much struck by some of the analogies I drew.

JACK: Ah, that reminds me, you mentioned christenings I think, Dr. Chasuble? I suppose you know how to christen all right? [DR. CHASUBLE *looks astounded.*] I mean, of course, you are continually christening, aren't you?

MISS PRISM: It is, I regret to say, one of the Rector's most constant duties in this parish. I have often spoken to the poorer classes on the subject. But they don't seem to know what thrift is.

CHASUBLE: But is there any particular infant in whom you are interested, Mr. Worthing? Your brother was, I believe, unmarried, was he not?

JACK: Oh, yes.

MISS PRISM: [*Bitterly.*] People who live entirely for pleasure usually are.

JACK: But it is not for any child, dear Doctor. I am very fond of children. No! the fact is, I would like to be christened myself, this afternoon, if you have nothing better to do.

CHASUBLE: But surely, Mr. Worthing, you have been christened already?

JACK: I don't remember anything about it.

CHASUBLE: But have you any grave doubts on the subject?

JACK: I certainly intend to have. Of course, I don't know if the thing would bother you in any way, or if you think I am a little too old now.

CHASUBLE: Not at all. The sprinkling, and, indeed, the immersion of adults is a perfectly canonical practice.

JACK: Immersion!

CHASUBLE: You need have no apprehensions. Sprinkling is all that is necessary, or indeed I think advisable. Our weather is so changeable. At what hour would you wish the ceremony performed?

JACK: Oh, I might trot around about five if that would suit you.

CHASUBLE: Perfectly, perfectly! In fact I have two similar ceremonies to perform at that time. A case of twins that occurred recently in one of the outlying cottages on your own estate. Poor Jenkins the carter, a most hard-working man.

JACK: Oh! I don't see much fun in being christened along with other babies. It would be childish. Would half-past five do?

CHASUBLE: Admirably! Admirably! [*Takes out watch.*] And now, dear Mr. Worthing, I will not intrude any longer into a house of sorrow. I would merely beg you not to be too much bowed down by grief. What seem to us bitter trials at the moment are often blessings in disguise.

MISS PRISM: This seems to me a blessing of an extremely obvious kind.

[*Enter* CECILY *from the house.*]

CECILY: Uncle Jack! Oh, I am pleased to see you back. But what horrid clothes you have on! Do go and change them.

MISS PRISM: Cecily!

CHASUBLE: My child! my child!

[CECILY *goes towards* JACK; *he kisses her brow in a melancholy manner.*]

CECILY: What is the matter, Uncle Jack? Do look happy! You look as if you had a toothache and I have such a surprise for you. Who do you think is in the dining-room? Your brother!

JACK: Who?

CECILY: Your brother Ernest. He arrived about half an hour ago.

JACK: What nonsense! I haven't got a brother.

CECILY: Oh, don't say that. However badly he may have behaved to you in the past he is still your brother. You couldn't be so heartless as to disown him. I'll tell him to come out. And you will shake hands with him, won't you, Uncle Jack? [*Runs back into the house.*]

CHASUBLE: There are very joyful tidings.

MISS PRISM: After we had all been resigned to his loss, his sudden return seems to me peculiarly distressing.

JACK: My brother is in the dining-room? I don't know what it all means. I think it is perfectly absurd.

[*Enter* ALGERNON *and* CECILY *hand in hand. They come slowly up to* JACK.]

JACK: Good heavens! [*Motions* ALGERNON *away.*]

ALGERNON: Brother John, I have come down from town to tell you that I am very sorry for all the trouble I have given you, and that I intend to lead a better life in the future. [JACK *glares at him and does not take his hand.*]

CECILY: Uncle Jack, you are not going to refuse your own brother's hand.

JACK: Nothing will induce me to take his hand. I think his coming down here disgraceful. He knows perfectly well why.

CECILY: Uncle Jack, do be nice. There is good in everyone. Ernest has just been telling me about his poor invalid friend, Mr. Bunbury, whom he goes to visit so often. And surely there must be much good in one who is kind to an invalid, and leaves the pleasures of London to sit by a bed of pain.

JACK: Oh, he has been talking about Bunbury, has he?

CECILY: Yes, he has told me all about poor Mr. Bunbury, and his terrible state of health.

JACK: Bunbury! Well, I won't have him talk to you about Bunbury or about anything else. It is enough to drive one perfectly frantic.

ALGERNON: Of course I admit that the faults were all on my side. But I must say that I think that Brother John's coldness to me is peculiarly painful. I expected a more enthusiastic welcome, especially considering it is the first time I have come here.

CECILY: Uncle Jack, if you don't shake hands with Ernest I will never forgive you.

JACK: Never forgive me?

CECILY: Never, never, never!

JACK: Well, this is the last time I shall ever do it. [*Shakes hands with* ALGERNON *and glares.*]

CHASUBLE: It's pleasant, is it not, to see so perfect a reconciliation? I think we might leave the two brothers together.

MISS PRISM: Cecily, you will come with us.

CECILY: Certainly, Miss Prism. My little task of reconciliation is over.

CHASUBLE: You have done a beautiful action to-day, dear child.

MISS PRISM: We must not be premature in our judgments.

CECILY: I feel very happy. [*They all go off.*]

JACK: You young scoundrel, Algy, you must get out of this place as soon as possible. I don't allow any Bunburying here.

[*Enter* MERRIMAN.]

MERRIMAN: I have put Mr. Ernest's things in the room next to yours, sir. I suppose that is all right?

JACK: What?

MERRIMAN: Mr. Ernest's luggage, sir. I have unpacked it and put it in the room next to your own.

JACK: His luggage?

MERRIMAN: Yes, sir. Three portmanteaus, a dressing-case, two hat-boxes, and a large luncheon-basket.

ALGERNON: I am afraid I can't stay more than a week this time.

JACK: Merriman, order the dog-cart at once. Mr. Ernest has been suddenly called back to town.

MERRIMAN: Yes, sir. [*Goes back into the house.*]

ALGERNON: What a fearful liar you are, Jack. I have not been called back to town at all.

JACK: Yes, you have.

ALGERNON: I haven't heard anyone call me.

JACK: Your duty as a gentleman calls you back.

ALGERNON: My duty as a gentleman has never interfered with my pleasures in the smallest degree.

JACK: I can quite understand that.

ALGERNON: Well, Cecily is a darling.

JACK: You are not to talk of Miss Cardew like that. I don't like it.

ALGERNON: Well, I don't like your clothes. You look perfectly ridiculous in them. Why on earth don't you go up and change? It is perfectly childish to be in deep mourning for a man who is actually staying for a whole week with you in your house as a guest. I call it grotesque.

JACK: You are certainly not staying with me for a whole week as a guest or anything else. You have got to leave . . . by the four-five train.

ALGERNON: I certainly won't leave you so long as you are in mourning. It would be most unfriendly. If I were in mourning you would stay with me, I suppose. I should think it very unkind if you didn't.

JACK: Well, will you go if I change my clothes?

ALGERNON: Yes, if you are not too long. I never saw anybody take so long to dress, and with such little result.

JACK: Well, at any rate, that is better than being always over-dressed as you are.

ALGERNON: If I am occasionally a little over-dressed, I make up for it by being always immensely over-educated.

JACK: Your vanity is ridiculous, your conduct an outrage, and your presence in my garden utterly absurd. However, you have got to catch the four-five, and I hope you will have a pleasant journey back to town. This Bunburying, as you call it, has not been a great success for you. [*Goes into the house.*]

ALGERNON: I think it has been a great success. I'm in love with Cecily, and that is everything. [*Enter* CECILY *at the back of the garden. She picks up the can and begins to water the flowers.*] But I must see her before I go, and make arrangements for another Bunbury. Ah, there she is.

CECILY: Oh, I merely came back to water the roses. I thought you were with Uncle Jack.

ALGERNON: He's gone to order the dog-cart for me.

CECILY: Oh, is he going to take you for a nice drive?

ALGERNON: He's going to send me away.

CECILY: Then have we got to part?

ALGERNON: I am afraid so. It's a very painful parting.

CECILY: It is always painful to part from people whom one has known for a very brief space of time. The absence of old friends one can endure with equanimity. But even a momentary separation from anyone to whom one has just been introduced is almost unbearable.

ALGERNON: Thank you.

[*Enter* MERRIMAN.]

MERRIMAN: The dog-cart is at the door, sir. [ALGERNON *looking appealingly at* CECILY.]

CECILY: It can wait, Merriman . . . for . . . five minutes.

MERRIMAN: Yes, miss. [*Exit* MERRIMAN.]

ALGERNON: I hope, Cecily, I shall not offend you if I state quite frankly and openly that you seem to me to be in every way the visible personification of absolute perfection.

CECILY: I think your frankness does you great credit, Ernest. If you will allow me I will copy your remarks into my diary. [*Goes over to table and begins writing in diary.*]

ALGERNON: Do you really keep a diary? I'd give any thing to look at it. May I?

CECILY: Oh, no. [*Puts her hand over it.*] You see, it is simply a very young girl's record of her own thoughts and impressions, and consequently meant for publication. When it appears in volume form I hope you will order a copy. But pray, Ernest, don't stop. I delight in taking down from dictation. I have reached "absolute perfection." You can go on. I am quite ready for more.

ALGERNON: [*Somewhat taken aback.*] Ahem! Ahem!

CECILY: Oh, don't cough, Ernest. When one is dictating one should speak fluently and not cough. Besides, I don't know how to spell a cough. [*Writes as* ALGERNON *speaks.*]

ALGERNON: [*Speaking very rapidly.*] Cecily, ever since I first looked upon your wonderful and incomparable beauty, I have dared to love you wildly, passionately, devotedly, hopelessly.

CECILY: I don't think that you should tell me that you love me wildly, passionately, devotedly, hopelessly. Hopelessly doesn't seem to make much sense, does it?

ALGERNON: Cecily!

[*Enter* MERRIMAN.]

MERRIMAN: The dog-cart is waiting, sir.

ALGERNON: Tell it to come round next week, at the same hour.

MERRIMAN: [*Looks at* CECILY, *who makes no sign.*] Yes, sir. [MERRIMAN *retires.*]

CECILY: Uncle Jack would be very much annoyed if he knew you were staying on till next week, at the same hour.

ALGERNON: Oh, I don't care about Jack. I don't care for anybody in the whole world but you. I love you, Cecily. You will marry me, won't you?

CECILY: You silly you! Of course. Why, we have been engaged for the last three months.

ALGERNON: For the last three months?

CECILY: Yes, it will be exactly three months on Thursday.

ALGERNON: But how did we become engaged?

CECILY: Well, ever since dear Uncle Jack first confessed to us that he had a younger brother who was very wicked and bad, you of course have formed the chief topic of conversation between my-self and Miss Prism. And of course a man who is much talked about is always very attractive. One feels there must be some-thing in him after all. I daresay it was foolish of me, but I fell in love with you, Ernest.

ALGERNON: Darling! And when was the engagement actually settled?

CECILY: On the 14th of February last. Worn out by your entire igno-rance of my existence, I determined to end the matter one way or the other, and after a long struggle with myself I accepted you under this dear old tree here. The next day I bought this little ring in your name, and this is the little bangle with the true lovers' knot I promised you always to wear.

ALGERNON: Did I give you this? It's very pretty, isn't it?

CECILY: Yes, you've wonderfully good taste, Ernest. It's the excuse I've always given for your leading such a bad life. And this is the box in which I keep all your dear letters. [*Kneels at table, opens box, and produces letters tied up with blue ribbon.*]

ALGERNON: My letters! But my own sweet Cecily, I have never writ-ten you any letters.

CECILY: You need hardly remind me of that, Ernest. I remember only too well that I was forced to write your letters for you. I wrote always three times a week, and sometimes oftener.

ALGERNON: Oh, do let me read them, Cecily?

CECILY: Oh, I couldn't possibly. They would make you far too con-ceited. [*Replaces box.*] The three you wrote me after I had broken off the engagement are so beautiful, and so badly spelled, that even now I can hardly read them without crying a little.

ALGERNON: But was our engagement ever broken off?

CECILY: Of course it was. On the 22nd of last March. You can see the entry if you like. [*Shows diary.*] "Today I broke off my en-gagement with Ernest. I feel it is better to do so. The weather still continues charming."

ALGERNON: But why on earth did you break it off? What had I done? I had done nothing at all, Cecily. I am very much hurt in-deed to hear you broke it off. Particularly when the weather was so charming.

CECILY: It would hardly have been a really serious engagement if it hadn't been broken off at least once. But I forgave you before the week was out.

ALGERNON: [*Crossing to her, and kneeling.*] What a perfect angel you are, Cecily.

CECILY: You dear romantic boy. [*He kisses her, she puts her fingers through his hair.*] I hope your hair curls naturally, does it?

ALGERNON: Yes, darling, with a little help from others.

CECILY: I am so glad.

ALGERNON: You'll never break off our engagement again, Cecily?

CECILY: I don't think I could break it off now that I have actually met you. Besides, of course, that is the question of your name.

ALGERNON: Yes, of course. [*Nervously.*]

CECILY: You must not laugh at me, darling, but it had always been a girlish dream of mine to love some one whose name was Ernest. [ALGERNON *rises*, CECILY *also.*] There is something in that name that seems to inspire absolute confidence. I pity any poor married woman whose husband is not called Ernest.

ALGERNON: But, my dear child, do you mean to say you could not love me if I had some other name?

CECILY: But what name?

ALGERNON: Oh, any name you like—Algernon, for instance. . . .

CECILY: But I don't like the name of Algernon.

ALGERNON: Well, my own dear, sweet, loving little darling, I really can't see why you should object to the name of Algernon. It is not at all a bad name. In fact, it is rather an aristocratic name. Half of the chaps who get into the Bankruptcy Court are called Algernon. But seriously, Cecily . . . [*Moving to her*] . . . if my name was Algy, couldn't you love me?

CECILY: [*Rising.*] I might respect you, Ernest, I might admire your character, but I fear that I should not be able to give you my undivided attention.

ALGERNON: Ahem! Cecily! [*Picking up hat.*] Your Rector here is, I suppose, thoroughly experienced in the practice of all the rites and ceremonials of the church?

CECILY: Oh, yes. Dr. Chasuble is a most learned man. He has never written a single book, so you can imagine how much he knows.

ALGERNON: I must see him at once on a most important christening—I mean on most important business.

CECILY: Oh!

ALGERNON: I sha'n't be away more than half an hour.

CECILY: Considering that we have been engaged since February the 14th, and that I only met you to-day for the first time, I think it is rather hard that you should leave me for so long a period as half an hour. Couldn't you make it twenty minutes?

ALGERNON: I'll be back in no time. [*Kisses her and rushes down the garden.*]

CECILY: What an impetuous boy he is. I like his hair so much. I must enter his proposal in my diary.

[*Enter* MERRIMAN.]

MERRIMAN: A Miss Fairfax has just called to see Mr. Worthing. On very important business, Miss Fairfax states.

CECILY: Isn't Mr. Worthing in his library?

MERRIMAN: Mr. Worthing went over in the direction of the Rectory some time ago.

CECILY: Pray ask the lady to come out here; Mr. Worthing is sure to be back soon. And you can bring tea.

MERRIMAN: Yes, miss. [*Goes out.*]

CECILY: Miss Fairfax! I suppose one of the many good elderly women who are associated with Uncle Jack in some of his philanthropic work in London. I don't quite like women who are interested in philanthropic work. I think it is so forward of them.

[*Enter* MERRIMAN.]

MERRIMAN: Miss Fairfax.

[*Enter* GWENDOLEN. *Exit* MERRIMAN.]

CECILY: [*Advancing to meet her.*] Pray let me introduce myself to you. My name is Cecily Cardew.

GWENDOLEN: Cecily Cardew? [*Moving to her and shaking hands.*] What a very sweet name! Something tells me that we are going to be great friends. I like you already more than I can say. My first impressions of people are never wrong.

CECILY: How nice of you to like me so much after we have known each other such a comparatively short time. Pray sit down.

GWENDOLEN: [*Still standing up.*] I may call you Cecily, may I not?

CECILY: With pleasure!

GWENDOLEN: And you will always call me Gwendolen, won't you?

CECILY: If you wish.

GWENDOLEN: Then that is all quite settled, is it not?

CECILY: I hope so. [*A pause. They both sit down together.*]

GWENDOLEN: Perhaps this might be a favourable opportunity for my mentioning who I am. My father is Lord Bracknell. You have never heard of papa, I suppose?

CECILY: I don't think so.

GWENDOLEN: Outside the family circle, papa, I am glad to say, is entirely unknown. I think that is quite as it should be. The home seems to me to be the proper sphere for the man. And certainly once a man begins to neglect his domestic duties he becomes painfully effeminate, does he not? And I don't like that. It makes men so very attractive. Cecily, mamma, whose views on education are remarkably strict, has brought me up to be extremely short-sighted; it is part of her system; so do you mind my looking at you through my glasses?

CECILY: Oh, not at all, Gwendolen. I am very fond of being looked at.

GWENDOLEN: [*After examining* CECILY *carefully through a lorgnette.*] You are here on a short visit, I suppose.

CECILY: Oh, no, I live here.

GWENDOLEN: [*Severely.*] Really? Your mother, no doubt, or some female relative of advanced years, resides here also?

CECILY: Oh, no. I have no mother, nor, in fact, any relations.

GWENDOLEN: Indeed?

CECILY: My dear guardian, with the assistance of Miss Prism, has the arduous task of looking after me.

GWENDOLEN: Your guardian?

CECILY: Yes, I am Mr. Worthing's ward.

GWENDOLEN: Oh! It is strange he never mentioned to me that he had a ward. How secretive of him! He grows more interesting hourly. I am not sure, however, that the news inspires me with feelings of unmixed delight. [*Rising and going to her.*] I am very fond of you, Cecily; I have liked you ever since I met you. But I am bound to state that now that I know that you are Mr. Worthing's ward, I cannot help expressing a wish you were— well, just a little older than you seem to be—and not quite so very alluring in appearance. In fact, if I may speak candidly—

CECILY: Pray do! I think that whenever one has anything unpleasant to say, one should always be quite candid.

GWENDOLEN: Well, to speak with perfect candour, Cecily, I wish that you were fully forty-two, and more than usually plain for your age. Ernest has a strong upright nature. He is the very soul of truth and honour. Disloyalty would be as impossible to him as deception. But even men of the noblest possible moral character are extremely susceptible to the influence of the physical charms of others. Modern, no less than Ancient History, supplies us with many most painful examples of what I refer to. If it were not so, indeed, History would be quite unreadable.

CECILY: I beg your pardon, Gwendolen, did you say Ernest?

GWENDOLEN: Yes.

CECILY: Oh, but it is not Mr. Ernest Worthing who is my guardian. It is his brother—his elder brother.

GWENDOLEN: [*Sitting down again.*] Ernest never mentioned to me that he had a brother.

CECILY: I am sorry to say they have not been on good terms for a long time.

GWENDOLEN: Ah! that accounts for it. And now that I think of it I have never heard any man mention his brother. The subject seems distasteful to most men. Cecily, you have lifted a load from my mind. I was growing almost anxious. It would have been terrible if any cloud had come across a friendship like ours, would it not? Of course you are quite, quite sure that it is not Mr. Ernest Worthing who is your guardian?

CECILY: Quite sure. [*A pause.*] In fact, I am going to be his.

GWENDOLEN: [*Enquiringly.*] I beg your pardon?

CECILY: [*Rather shy and confidingly.*] Dearest Gwendolen, there is no reason why I should make a secret of it to you. Our little county newspaper is sure to chronicle the fact next week. Mr. Ernest Worthing and I are engaged to be married.

GWENDOLEN: [*Quite politely, rising.*] My darling Cecily, I think there must be some slight error. Mr. Ernest Worthing is engaged to me. The announcement will appear in the *Morning Post* on Saturday at the latest.

CECILY: [*Very politely, rising.*] I am afraid you must be under some misconception. Ernest proposed to me exactly ten minutes ago. [*Shows diary.*]

GWENDOLEN: [*Examines diary through her lorgnette carefully.*] It is certainly very curious, for he asked me to be his wife yesterday afternoon at 5.30. If you would care to verify the incident, pray do so. [*Produces diary of her own.*] I never travel without my diary. One should always have something sensational to read in the train. I am so sorry, dear Cecily, if it is any disappointment to you, but I am afraid *I* have the prior claim.

CECILY: It would distress me more than I can tell you, dear Gwendolen, if it caused you any mental or physical anguish, but I feel bound to point out that since Ernest proposed to you he clearly has changed his mind.

GWENDOLEN: [*Meditatively.*] If the poor fellow has been entrapped into any foolish promise I shall consider it my duty to rescue him at once, and with a firm hand.

CECILY: [*Thoughtfully and sadly.*] Whatever unfortunate entanglement my dear boy may have got into, I will never reproach him with it after we are married.

GWENDOLEN: Do you allude to me, Miss Cardew, as an entanglement? You are presumptuous. On an occasion of this kind it becomes more than a moral duty to speak one's mind. It becomes a pleasure.

CECILY: Do you suggest, Miss Fairfax, that I entrapped Ernest into an engagement? How dare you? This is no time for wearing the shallow mask of manners. When I see a spade I call it a spade.

GWENDOLEN: [*Satirically.*] I am glad to say that I have never seen a spade. It is obvious that our social spheres have been widely different.

[*Enter* MERRIMAN, *followed by the footman. He carries a salver, tablecloth, and plate-stand.* CECILY *is about to retort. The presence of the servants exercises a restraining influence, under which both girls chafe.*]

MERRIMAN: Shall I lay tea here as usual, miss?

CECILY: [*Sternly, in a calm voice.*] Yes, as usual.

[MERRIMAN *begins to clear and lay cloth. A long pause.* CECILY *and* GWENDOLYN *glare at each other.*]

GWENDOLEN: Are there many interesting walks in the vicinity, Miss Cardew?

CECILY: Oh, yes, a great many. From the top of one of the hills quite close one can see five counties.

GWENDOLEN: Five counties! I don't think I should like that. I hate crowds.

CECILY: [*Sweetly.*] I suppose that is why you live in town?

[GWENDOLEN *bites her lip, and beats her foot nervously with her parasol.*]

GWENDOLEN: [*Looking round.*] Quite a well-kept garden this is, Miss Cardew.

CECILY: So glad you like it, Miss Fairfax.

GWENDOLEN: I had no idea there were any flowers in the country.

CECILY: Oh, flowers are as common here, Miss Fairfax, as people are in London.

GWENDOLEN: Personally I cannot understand how anybody manages to exist in the country, if anybody who is anybody does. The country always bores me to death.

CECILY: Ah! This is what the newspapers call agricultural depression, is it not? I believe the aristocracy are suffering very much from it just at present. It is almost an epidemic amongst them, I have been told. May I offer you some tea, Miss Fairfax?

GWENDOLEN: [*With elaborate politeness.*] Thank you. [*Aside.*] Detestable girl! But I require tea!

CECILY: [*Sweetly.*] Sugar?

GWENDOLEN: [*Superciliously.*] No, thank you. Sugar is not fashionable any more.

[CECILY *looks angrily at her, takes up the tongs and puts four lumps of sugar into the cup.*]

CECILY: [*Severely.*] Cake or bread and butter?

GWENDOLEN: [*In a bored manner.*] Bread and butter, please. Cake is rarely seen at the best houses nowadays.

CECILY: [*Cuts a very large slice of cake, and puts it on the tray.*] Hand that to Miss Fairfax.

[MERRIMAN *does so, and goes out with footman.* GWENDOLEN *drinks the tea and makes a grimace. Puts down cup at once, reaches out her hand to the bread and butter, looks at it, and finds it is cake. Rises in indignation.*]

GWENDOLEN: You have filled my tea with lumps of sugar, and

though I asked most distinctly for bread and butter, you have given me cake. I am known for the gentleness of my disposition, and the extraordinary sweetness of my nature, but I warn you, Miss Cardew, you may go too far.

CECILY: [*Rising.*] To save my poor, innocent, trusting boy from the machinations of any other girl there are no lengths to which I would not go.

GWENDOLEN: From the moment I saw you I distrusted you. I felt that you were false and deceitful. I am never deceived in such matters. My first impressions of people are invariably right.

CECILY: It seems to me, Miss Fairfax, that I am trespassing on your valuable time. No doubt you have many other calls of a similar character to make in the neighbourhood.

[*Enter* JACK.]

GWENDOLEN: [*Catching sight of him.*] Ernest! My own Ernest!

JACK: Gwendolen! Darling! [*Offers to kiss her.*]

GWENDOLEN: [*Drawing back.*] A moment! May I ask if you are en-gaged to be married to this young lady? [*Points to* CECILY.]

JACK: [*Laughing.*] To dear little Cecily! Of course not! What could have put such an idea into your pretty little head?

GWENDOLEN: Thank you. You may. [*Offers her cheek.*]

CECILY: [*Very sweetly.*] I knew there must be some misunderstanding, Miss Fairfax. The gentleman whose arm is at present around your waist is my dear guardian, Mr. John Worthing.

GWENDOLEN: I beg your pardon?

CECILY: This is Uncle Jack.

GWENDOLEN: [*Receding.*] Jack! Oh!

[*Enter* ALGERNON.]

CECILY: Here is Ernest.

ALGERNON: [*Goes straight over to* CECILY *without noticing anyone else.*] My own love! [*Offers to kiss her.*]

CECILY: [*Drawing back.*] A moment, Ernest! May I ask you—are you engaged to be married to this young lady?

ALGERNON: [*Looking round.*] To what young lady? Good heavens! Gwendolen!

CECILY: Yes, to good heavens, Gwendolen, I mean to Gwendolen.

ALGERNON: [*Laughing.*] Of course not! What could have put such an idea into your pretty little head?

CECILY: Thank you. [*Presenting her cheek to be kissed.*] You may. [AL-GERNON *kisses her.*]

GWENDOLEN: I felt there was some slight error, Miss Cardew. The gentleman who is now embracing you is my cousin, Mr. Algernon Moncrieff.

CECILY: [*Breaking away from* ALGERNON.] Algernon Moncrieff! Oh! [*The two girls move towards each other and put their arms round each other's waists as if for protection.*] Are you called Algernon?

ALGERNON: I cannot deny it.

CECILY: Oh!

GWENDOLEN: Is your name really John?

JACK: [*Standing rather proudly.*] I could deny it if I liked. I could deny anything if I liked. But my name certainly is John. It has been John for years.

CECILY: [*To* GWENDOLEN.] A gross deception has been practised on both of us.

GWENDOLEN: My poor wounded Cecily!

CECILY: My sweet, wronged Gwendolen!

GWENDOLEN: [*Slowing and seriously.*] You will call me sister, will you not?

> [*They embrace.* JACK *and* ALGERNON *groan and walk up and down.*]

CECILY: [*Rather brightly.*] There is just one question I would like to be allowed to ask my guardian.

GWENDOLEN: An admirable idea! Mr. Worthing, there is just one question I would like to be permitted to put to you. Where is your brother Ernest? We are both engaged to be married to your brother Ernest, so it is a matter of some importance to us to know where your brother Ernest is at present.

JACK: [*Slowly and hesitatingly.*] Gwendolen—Cecily—it is very painful for me to be forced to speak the truth. It is the first time in my life that I have ever been reduced to such a painful position, and I am really quite inexperienced in doing anything of the kind. However I will tell you quite frankly that I have no brother Ernest. I have no brother at all. I never had a brother in my life, and I certainly have not the smallest intention of ever having one in the future.

CECILY: [*Surprised.*] No brother at all?

JACK: [*Cheerily.*] None!

GWENDOLEN: [*Severely.*] Had you never a brother of any kind?

JACK: [*Pleasantly.*] Never. Not even of any kind.

GWENDOLEN: I am afraid it is quite clear, Cecily, that neither of us is engaged to be married to anyone.

CECILY: It is not a very pleasant position for a young girl suddenly to find herself in. Is it?

GWENDOLEN: Let us go into the house. They will hardly venture to come after us there.

CECILY: No, men are so cowardly, aren't they?

[*They retire into the house with scornful looks.*]

JACK: This ghastly state of things is what you call Bunburying, I suppose?

ALGERNON: Yes, and a perfectly wonderful Bunbury it is. The most wonderful Bunbury I have ever had in my life.

JACK: Well, you've no right whatsoever to Bunbury here.

ALGERNON: That is absurd. One has a right to Bunbury anywhere one chooses. Every serious Bunburyist knows that.

JACK: Serious Bunburyist! Good heavens!

ALGERNON: Well, one must be serious about something, if one wants to have any amusement in life. I happen to be serious about Bunburying. What on earth you are serious about I haven't got the remotest idea. About everything, I should fancy. You have such an absolutely trivial nature.

JACK: Well, the only small satisfaction I have in the whole of this wretched business is that your friend Bunbury is quite exploded. You won't be able to run down to the country quite so often as you used to do, dear Algy. And a very good thing, too.

ALGERNON: Your brother is a little off colour, isn't he, dear Jack? You won't be able to disappear to London quite so frequently as your wicked custom was. And not a bad thing, either.

JACK: As for your conduct towards Miss Cardew, I must say that your taking in a sweet, simple, innocent girl like that is quite inexcusable. To say nothing of the fact that she is my ward.

ALGERNON: I can see no possible defence at all for your deceiving a brilliant, clever, thoroughly experienced young lady like Miss Fairfax. To say nothing of the fact that she is my cousin.

JACK: I wanted to be engaged to Gwendolen, that is all. I love her.

ALGERNON: Well, I simply wanted to be engaged to Cecily. I adore her.

JACK: There is certainly no chance of your marrying Miss Cardew.

ALGERNON: I don't think there is much likelihood, Jack, of you and Miss Fairfax being united.

JACK: Well, that is no business of yours.

ALGERNON: If it was my business, I wouldn't talk about it. [*Begins to eat muffins.*] It is very vulgar to talk about one's business. Only people like stock-brokers do that, and then merely at dinner parties.

JACK: How you can sit there, calmly eating muffins, when we are in this horrible trouble, I can't make out. You seem to me to be perfectly heartless.

ALGERNON: Well, I can't eat muffins in an agitated manner. The butter would probably get on my cuffs. One should always eat muffins quite calmly. It is the only way to eat them.

JACK: I say it's perfectly heartless your eating muffins at all, under the circumstances.

ALGERNON: When I am in trouble, eating is the only thing that consoles me. Indeed, when I am in really great trouble, as anyone who knows me intimately will tell you, I refuse everything except food and drink. At the present moment I am eating muffins because I am unhappy. Besides, I am particularly fond of muffins. [*Rising.*]

JACK: [*Rising.*] Well, that is no reason why you should eat them all in that greedy way. [*Takes muffin from* ALGERNON.]

ALGERNON: [*Offering tea-cake.*] I wish you would have tea-cake instead. I don't like tea-cake.

JACK: Good heavens! I suppose a man may eat his own muffins in his own garden.

ALGERNON: But you have just said it was perfectly heartless to eat muffins.

JACK: I said it was perfectly heartless of you, under the circumstances. That is a very different thing.

ALGERNON: That may be. But the muffins are the same. [*He seizes the muffin dish from* JACK.]

JACK: Algy, I wish to goodness you would go.

ALGERNON: You can't possibly ask me to go without having some dinner. It's absurd. I never go without my dinner. No one ever does, except vegetarians and people like that. Besides I have just made arrangements with Dr. Chasuble to be christened at a quarter to six under the name of Ernest.

JACK: My dear fellow, the sooner you give up that nonsense the better. I made arrangements this morning with Chasuble to be christened myself at 5.30, and I naturally will take the name of Ernest. Gwendolen would wish it. We can't both be christened Ernest. It's absurd. Besides, I have a perfect right to be christened if I like. There is no evidence at all that I ever have been christened by anybody. I should think it extremely probable I never was, and so does Dr. Chasuble. It is entirely different in your case. You have been christened already.

ALGERNON: Yes, but I have not been christened for years.

JACK: Yes, but you have been christened. That is the important thing.

ALGERNON: Quite so. So I know my constitution can stand it. If you are not quite sure about your ever having been christened, I must say I think it rather dangerous your venturing on it now. It might make you very unwell. You can hardly have forgotten that someone very closely connected with you was very nearly carried off this week in Paris by a severe chill.

JACK: Yes, but you said yourself that a severe chill was not hereditary.

ALGERNON: It usedn't to be, I know—but I daresay it is now. Science is always making wonderful improvements in things.

JACK: [*Picking up the muffin-dish.*] Oh, that is nonsense; you are always talking nonsense.

ALGERNON: Jack, you are at the muffins again! I wish you wouldn't. There are only two left. [*Takes them.*] I told you I was particularly fond of muffins.

JACK: But I hate tea-cake.

ALGERNON: Why on earth then do you allow tea-cake to be served up for your guests? What ideas you have of hospitality!

JACK: Algernon! I have already told you to go. I don't want you here. Why don't you go?

ALGERNON: I haven't quite finished my tea yet, and there is still one muffin left.

[JACK *groans, and sinks into a chair.* ALGERNON *still continues eating.*]

[*Curtain.*]

ACT III

SCENE.—*Morning-room at the Manor House.* GWENDOLEN *and* CECILY *are at the window, looking out into the garden.*

GWENDOLEN: The fact that they did not follow us at once into the house, as anyone else would have done, seems to me to show that they have some sense of shame left.

CECILY: They have been eating muffins. That looks like repentance.

GWENDOLEN: [*After a pause.*] They don't seem to notice us at all. Couldn't you cough?

GWENDOLEN: They're looking at us. What effrontery!

CECILY: They're approaching. That's very forward of them.

GWENDOLEN: Let us preserve a dignified silence.

CECILY: Certainly, it's the only thing to do now.

　　[*Enter* JACK, *followed by* ALGERNON. *They whistle some dreadful popular air from a British opera.*]

GWENDOLEN: This dignified silence seems to produce an unpleasant effect.

CECILY: A most distasteful one.

GWENDOLEN: But we will not be the first to speak.

CECILY: Certainly not.

GWENDOLEN: Mr. Worthing, I have something very particular to ask you. Much depends on your reply.

CECILY: Gwendolen, your common sense is invaluable. Mr. Moncrieff, kindly answer me the following question. Why did you pretend to be my guardian's brother?

ALGERNON: In order that I might have an opportunity of meeting you.

CECILY: [*To* GWENDOLEN.] That certainly seems a satisfactory explanation, does it not?

GWENDOLEN: Yes, dear, if you can believe him.

CECILY: I don't. But that does not affect the wonderful beauty of his answer.

GWENDOLEN: True. In matters of grave importance, style, not sincerity, is the vital thing. Mr. Worthing, what explanation can you offer to me for pretending to have a brother? Was it in order that you might have an opportunity of coming up to town to see me as often as possible?

JACK: Can you doubt it, Miss Fairfax?

GWENDOLEN: I have the gravest doubts upon the subject. But I intend to crush them. This is not the moment for German scepticism.[1] [*Moving to* CECILY.] Their explanations appear to be quite satisfactory, especially Mr. Worthing's. That seems to me to have the stamp of truth upon it.

CECILY: I am more than content with what Mr. Moncrieff said. His voice alone inspires one with absolute credulity.

GWENDOLEN: Then you think we should forgive them?

CECILY: Yes. I mean no.

GWENDOLEN: True! I had forgotten. There are principles at stake that one cannot surrender. Which of us should tell them? The task is not a pleasant one.

CECILY: Could we not both speak at the same time?

GWENDOLEN: An excellent ideal I nearly always speak at the same time as other people. Will you take the time from me?

CECILY: Certainly. [GWENDOLEN *beats time with uplifted finger.*]

GWENDOLEN *and* CECILY: [*Speaking together.*] Your Christian names are still an insuperable barrier. That is all!

JACK *and* ALGERNON: [*Speaking together.*] Our Christian names! Is that all? But we are going to be christened this afternoon.

GWENDOLEN: [*To* JACK.] For my sake you are prepared to do this terrible thing?

JACK: I am.

CECILY: [*To* ALGERNON.] To please me you are ready to face this fearful ordeal?

ALGERNON: I am!

GWENDOLEN: How absurd to talk of the equality of the sexes! Where questions of self-sacrifice are concerned, men are infinitely beyond us.

JACK: We are. [*Clasps hands with* ALGERNON.]

CECILY: They have moments of physical courage of which we women know absolutely nothing.

GWENDOLEN: [*To* JACK.] Darling!

ALGERNON: [*To* CECILY.] Darling! [*They fall into each other's arms.*]

---

1. A reference to theological movements such as the "Higher Criticism," which subjected the Bible to the kind of study accorded other books.

[*Enter* MERRIMAN. *When he enters he coughs loudly seeing the situation.*]

MERRIMAN: Ahem! Ahem! Lady Bracknell!

JACK: Good heavens!

[*Enter* LADY BRACKNELL. *The couples separate in alarm. Exit* MERRIMAN.]

LADY BRACKNELL: Gwendolen! What does this mean?

GWENDOLEN: Merely that I am engaged to be married to Mr. Worthing, Mamma.

LADY BRACKNELL: Come here. Sit down. Sit down immediately. Hesitation of any kind is a sign of mental decay in the young, of physical weakness in the old. [*Turns to* JACK.] Apprised, sir, of my daughter's sudden flight by her trusty maid, whose confidence I purchased by means of a small coin, I followed her at once by a luggage train. Her unhappy father is, I am glad to say, under the impression that she is attending a more than usually lengthy lecture by the University Extension Scheme on the Influence of a Permanent Income on Thought. I do not propose to undeceive him. Indeed I have never undeceived him on any question. I would consider it wrong. But of course, you will clearly understand that all communication between yourself and my daughter must cease immediately from this moment. On this point, as indeed on all points, I am firm.

JACK: I am engaged to be married to Gwendolen, Lady Bracknell!

LADY BRACKNELL: You are nothing of the kind, sir. And now, as regards Algernon! . . . Algernon!

ALGERNON: Yes, Aunt Augusta.

LADY BRACKNELL: May I ask if it is in this house that your invalid friend Mr. Bunbury resides?

ALGERNON: [*Stammering.*] Oh no! Bunbury doesn't live here. Bunbury is somewhere else at present. In fact, Bunbury is dead.

LADY BRACKNELL: Dead! When did Mr. Bunbury die? His death must have been extremely sudden.

ALGERNON: [*Airily.*] Oh, I killed Bunbury this afternoon. I mean poor Bunbury died this afternoon.

LADY BRACKNELL: What did he die of?

ALGERNON: Bunbury? Oh, he was quite exploded.

LADY BRACKNELL: Exploded! Was he the victim of a revolutionary

938   ★   O s c a r   W i l d e

outrage? I was not aware that Mr. Bunbury was interested in social legislation. If so, he is well punished for his morbidity.

ALGERNON: My dear Aunt Augusta, I mean he was found out! The
doctors found out that Bunbury could not live, that is what I
mean—so Bunbury died.

LADY BRACKNELL: He seems to have had great confidence in the
opinion of his physicians. I am glad, however, that he made up
his mind at the last to some definite course of action, and acted
under proper medical advice. And now that we have finally got
rid of this Mr. Bunbury, may I ask, Mr. Worthing, who is that
young person whose hand my nephew Algernon is now holding
in what seems to me a peculiarly unnecessary manner?

JACK: That lady is Miss Cecily Cardew, my ward.

[LADY BRACKNELL *bows coldly to* CECILY.]

ALGERNON: I am engaged to be married to Cecily, Aunt Augusta.

LADY BRACKNELL: I beg your pardon?

CECILY: Mr. Moncrieff and I are engaged to be married, Lady
Bracknell.

LADY BRACKNELL: [*With a shiver, crossing to the sofa and sitting
down.*] I do not know whether there is anything peculiarly exciting in the air of this particular part of Hertfordshire, but the
number of engagements that go on seems to me considerably
above the proper average that statistics have laid down for our
guidance. I think some preliminary enquiry on my part would
not be out of place. Mr. Worthing, is Miss Cardew at all connected with any of the larger railway stations in London? I
merely desire information. Until yesterday I had no idea that
there were any families or persons whose origin was a Terminus.

[JACK *looks perfectly furious, but restrains himself.*]

JACK: [*In a clear, cold voice.*] Miss Cardew is the granddaughter of
the late Mr. Thomas Cardew of 149, Belgrave Square, S.W.; Ger-
vase Park, Dorking, Surrey; and the Sporran, Fifeshire, N.B.

LADY BRACKNELL: That sounds not unsatisfactory. Three addresses
always inspire confidence, even in tradesmen. But what proof
have I of their authenticity?

JACK: I have carefully preserved the Court Guide[2] of the period.

---

2. A registry of aristocratic genealogy.

They are open to your inspection, Lady Bracknell.

LADY BRACKNELL: [*Grimly.*] I have known strange errors in that publication.

JACK: Miss Cardews's family solicitors are Messrs. Markby, Markby, and Markby.

LADY BRACKNELL: Markby, Markby, and Markby? A firm of the very highest position in their profession. Indeed I am told that one of the Mr. Markbys is occasionally to be seen at dinner parties. So far I am satisfied.

JACK: [*Very irritably.*] How extremely kind of you, Lady Bracknell! I have also in my possession, you will be pleased to hear, certificates of Miss Cardew's birth, baptism, whooping cough, registration, vaccination, confirmation, and the measles; both the German and the English variety.

LADY BRACKNELL: Ah! A life crowded with incident, I see; though perhaps somewhat too exciting for a young girl. I am not myself in favor of premature experiences. [*Rises, looks at her watch.*] Gwendolen! the time approaches for our departure. We have not a moment to lose. As a matter of form, Mr. Worthing, I had better ask you if Miss Cardew has any little fortune?

JACK: Oh, about a hundred and thirty thousand pounds in the Funds.³ That is all. Good-bye, Lady Bracknell. So pleased to have seen you.

LADY BRACKNELL: [*Sitting down again.*] A moment, Mr. Worthing. A hundred and thirty thousand pounds! And in the Funds! Miss Cardew seems to me a most attractive young lady, now that I look at her. Few girls of the present day have any really solid qualities, any of the qualities that last, and improve with time. We live, I regret to say, in an age of surfaces. [*To* CECILY.] Come over here, dear. [CECILY *goes across.*] Pretty child! your dress is sadly simple, and your hair seems almost as Nature might have left it. But we can soon alter all that. A thoroughly experienced French maid produces a really marvellous result in a very brief space of time. I remember recommending one to young Lady Lancing, and after three months her own husband did not know her.

---

3. Government stocks.

JACK: [*Aside.*] And after six months nobody knew her.

LADY BRACKNELL: [*Glares at* JACK *for a few moments. Then bends, with a practised smile, to* CECILY.] Kindly turn round, sweet child. [CECILY *turns completely round.*] No, the side view is what I want. [CECILY *presents her profile.*] Yes, quite as I expected. There are distinct social possibilities in your profile. The two weak points in our age are its want of principle and its want of profile. The chin a little higher, dear. Style largely depends on the way the chin is worn. They are worn very high, just at present. Algernon!

ALGERNON: Yes, Aunt Augusta!

LADY BRACKNELL: There are distinct social possibilities in Miss Cardew's profile.

ALGERNON: Cecily is the sweetest, dearest, prettiest girl in the whole world. And I don't care twopence about social possibilities.

LADY BRACKNELL: Never speak disrespectfully of society,[4] Algernon. Only people who can't get into it do that. [*To* CECILY.] Dear child, of course you know that Algernon has nothing but his debts to depend upon. But I do not approve of mercenary marriages. When I married Lord Bracknell I had no fortune of any kind. But I never dreamed for a moment of allowing that to stand in my way. Well, I suppose I must give my consent.

ALGERNON: Thank you, Aunt Augusta.

LADY BRACKNELL: Cecily, you may kiss me!

CECILY: [*Kisses her.*] Thank you, Lady Bracknell.

LADY BRACKNELL: You may also address me as Aunt Augusta for the future.

CECILY: Thank you, Aunt Augusta.

LADY BRACKNELL: The marriage, I think, had better take place quite soon.

ALGERNON: Thank you, Aunt Augusta.

CECILY: Thank you, Aunt Augusta.

LADY BRACKNELL: To speak frankly, I am not in favour of long engagements. They give people the opportunity of finding out each other's character before marriage, which I think is never advisable.

JACK: I beg your pardon for interrupting you, Lady Bracknell, but

4. The exclusive circle of the aristocracy.

this engagement is quite out of the question. I am Miss Cardew's guardian, and she cannot marry without my consent until she comes of age. That consent I absolutely decline to give.

LADY BRACKNELL: Upon what grounds, may I ask? Algernon is an extremely, I may almost say an ostentatiously, eligible young man. He has nothing, but he looks everything. What more can one desire?

JACK: It pains me very much to have to speak frankly to you, Lady Bracknell, about your nephew, but the fact is that I do not approve at all of his moral character. I suspect him of being untruthful.

[ALGERNON *and* CECILY *look at him in indignant amazement.*]

LADY BRACKNELL: Untruthful! My nephew Algernon? Impossible! He is an Oxonian.[5]

JACK: I fear there can be no possible doubt about the matter. This afternoon, during my temporary absence in London on an important question of romance, he obtained admission to my house by means of the false pretense of being my brother. Under an assumed name he drank, I've just been informed by my butler, an entire pint bottle of my Perrier-Jouet, Brut, '89; a wine I was specially reserving for myself. Continuing his disgraceful deception, he succeeded in the course of the afternoon in alienating the affections of my only ward. He subsequently stayed to tea, and devoured every single muffin. And what makes his conduct all the more heartless is, that he was perfectly well aware from the first that I have no brother, that I never had a brother, and that I don't intend to have a brother, not even of any kind. I distinctly told him so myself yesterday afternoon.

LADY BRACKNELL: Ahem! Mr. Worthing, after careful consideration I have decided entirely to overlook my nephew's conduct to you.

JACK: That is very generous of you, Lady Bracknell. My own decision, however, is unalterable. I decline to give my consent.

LADY BRACKNELL: [*To* CECILY.] Come here, sweet child. [CECILY *goes over.*] How old are you, dear?

CECILY: Well, I am really only eighteen, but I always admit to twenty when I go to evening parties.

5. Someone who has attended Oxford University.

LADY BRACKNELL: You are perfectly right in making some slight alteration. Indeed, no woman should ever be quite accurate about her age. It looks so calculating. . . . [*In meditative manner.*] Eighteen, but admitting to twenty at evening parties. Well, it will not be very long before you are of age and free from the restraints of tutelage. So I don't think your guardian's consent is, after all, a matter of any importance.

JACK: Pray excuse me, Lady Bracknell, for interrupting you again, but it is only fair to tell you that according to the terms of her grandfather's will Miss Cardew does not come legally of age till she is thirty-five.

LADY BRACKNELL: That does not seem to me to be a grave objection. Thirty-five is a very attractive age. London society is full of women of the very highest birth who have, of their own free choice, remained thirty-five for years. Lady Dumbleton is an instance in point. To my own knowledge she has been thirty-five ever since she arrived at the age of forty, which was many years ago now. I see no reason why our dear Cecily should not be even still more attractive at the age you mention than she is at present. There will be a large accumulation of property.

CECILY: Algy, could you wait for me till I was thirty-five?

ALGERNON: Of course I could, Cecily. You know I could.

CECILY: Yes, I felt it instinctively, but I couldn't wait all that time. I hate waiting even five minutes for anybody. It always makes me rather cross. I am not punctual myself, I know, but I do like punctuality in others, and waiting, even to be married, is quite out of the question.

ALGERNON: Then what is to be done, Cecily?

CECILY: I don't know, Mr. Moncrieff.

LADY BRACKNELL: My dear Mr. Worthing, as Miss Cardew states positively that she cannot wait till she is thirty-five—a remark which I am bound to say seems to me to show a somewhat impatient nature—I would beg of you to reconsider your decision.

JACK: But my dear Lady Bracknell, the matter is entirely in your own hands. The moment you consent to my marriage with Gwendolen, I will most gladly allow your nephew to form an alliance with my ward.

LADY BRACKNELL: [*Rising and drawing herself up.*] You must be quite aware that what you propose is out of the question.

JACK: Then a passionate celibacy is all that any of us can look forward to.

LADY BRACKNELL: That is not the destiny I propose for Gwendolen. Algernon, of course, can choose for himself. [*Pulls out her watch.*] Come, dear; [GWENDOLEN *rises.*] we have already missed five, if not six, trains. To miss any more might expose us to comment on the platform.

[*Enter* DR. CHASUBLE.]

CHASUBLE: Everything is quite ready for the christenings.

LADY BRACKNELL: The christenings, sir! Is not that somewhat premature?

CHASUBLE: [*Looking rather puzzled, and pointing to* JACK *and* ALGERNON.] Both these gentlemen have expressed a desire for immediate baptism.

LADY BRACKNELL: At their age? The idea is grotesque and irreligious! Algernon, I forbid you to be baptised. I will not hear of such excesses. Lord Bracknell would be highly displeased if he learned that that was the way in which you wasted your time and money.

CHASUBLE: Am I to understand then that there are to be no christenings at all this afternoon?

JACK: I don't think that, as things are now, it would be of much practical value to either of us, Dr. Chasuble.

CHASUBLE: I am grieved to hear such sentiments from you, Mr. Worthing. They savour of the heretical views of the Anabaptists,[6] views that I have completely refuted in four of my unpublished sermons. However, as your present mood seems to be one peculiarly secular, I will return to the church at once. Indeed, I have just been informed by the pew-opener that for the last hour and a half Miss Prism has been waiting for me in the vestry.

LADY BRACKNELL: [*Starting.*] Miss Prism! Did I hear you mention a Miss Prism?

CHASUBLE: Yes, Lady Bracknell. I am on my way to join her.

LADY BRACKNELL: Pray allow me to detain you for a moment. This

---

6. A Christian sect distinguished by its opposition to baptism.

matter may prove to be one of vital importance to Lord Bracknell and myself. Is this Miss Prism a female of repellent aspect,
remotely connected with education?

CHASUBLE: [*Somewhat indignantly.*] She is the most cultivated of
ladies, and the very picture of respectability.

LADY BRACKNELL: It is obviously the same person. May I ask what
position she holds in your household?

CHASUBLE: [*Severely.*] I am a celibate, madam.

JACK: [*Interposing.*] Miss Prism, Lady Bracknell, has been for the last
three years Miss Cardew's esteemed governess and valued companion.

LADY BRACKNELL: In spite of what I hear of her, I must see her at
once. Let her be sent for.

CHASUBLE: [*Looking off.*] She approaches; she is nigh.
[*Enter* MISS PRISM *hurriedly.*]

MISS PRISM: I was told you expected me in the vestry, dear Canon. I
have been waiting for you there for an hour and three-quarters.
[*Catches sight of* LADY BRACKNELL, *who has fixed her with a stony
glare.* MISS PRISM *grows pale and quails. She looks anxiously round
as if desirous to escape.*]

LADY BRACKNELL: [*In a severe, judicial voice.*] Prism! [MISS PRISM
bows her head in shame.] Come here, Prism! [MISS PRISM *approaches in a humble manner.*] Where is that baby? [*General con-
sternation. The Canon starts back in horror.* ALGERNON *and* JACK
pretend to be anxious to shield CECILY *and* GWENDOLEN *from hearing the details of a terrible public scandal.*] Twenty-eight years ago,
Prism, you left Lord Bracknell's house, Number 104, Upper
Grosvenor Street, in charge of a perambulator that contained a
baby, of the male sex. You never returned. A few weeks later,
through the elaborate investigations of the Metropolitan police,
the perambulator was discovered at midnight, standing by itself
in a remote corner of Bayswater. It contained the manuscript of a
three-volume novel of more than usually revolting sentimentality.
[MISS PRISM *starts in involuntary indignation.*] But the baby was
not there! [*Everyone looks at* MISS PRISM.] Prism, where is that
baby? [*A pause.*]

MISS PRISM: Lady Bracknell, I admit with shame that I do not know.
I only wish I did. The plain facts of the case are these. On the

morning of the day you mention, a day that is forever branded on my memory, I prepared as usual to take the baby out in its perambulator. I had also with me a somewhat old but capacious hand-bag in which I had intended to place the manuscript of a work of fiction that I had written during my few unoccupied hours. In a moment of mental abstraction, for which I never can forgive myself, I deposited the manuscript in the bassinette, and placed the baby in the hand-bag.

JACK: [*Who had been listening attentively.*] But where did you deposit the hand-bag?

MISS PRISM: Do not ask me, Mr. Worthing.

JACK: Miss Prism, this is a matter of no small importance to me. I insist on knowing where you deposited the hand-bag that contained that infant.

MISS PRISM: I left it in the cloak-room of one of the larger railway stations in London.

JACK: What railway station?

MISS PRISM: [*Quite crushed.*] Victoria. The Brighton line. [*Sinks into a chair.*]

JACK: I must retire to my room for a moment. Gwendolen, wait here for me.

GWENDOLEN: If you are not too long, I will wait here for you all my life.

[*Exit* JACK *in great excitement.*]

CHASUBLE: What do you think this means, Lady Bracknell?

LADY BRACKNELL: I dare not even suspect, Dr. Chasuble. I need hardly tell you that in families of high position strange coincidences are not supposed to occur. They are hardly considered the thing.

[*Noises heard overhead as if someone was throwing trunks about. Everybody looks up.*]

CECILY: Uncle Jack seems strangely agitated.

CHASUBLE: Your guardian has a very emotional nature.

LADY BRACKNELL: This noise is extremely unpleasant. It sounds as if he was having an argument. I dislike arguments of any kind. They are always vulgar, and often convincing.

CHASUBLE: [*Looking up.*] It has stopped now.

[*The noise is redoubled.*]

LADY BRACKNELL: I wish he would arrive at some conclusion.

GWENDOLEN: The suspense is terrible. I hope it will last.

[*Enter* JACK *with a hand-bag of black leather in his hand.*]

JACK: [*Rushing over to* MISS PRISM.] Is this the hand-bag, Miss Prism? Examine it carefully before you speak. The happiness of more than one life depends on your answers.

MISS PRISM: [*Calmly.*] It seems to be mine. Yes, here is the injury it received through the upsetting of a Gower Street omnibus in younger and happier days. Here is the stain on the lining caused by the explosion of a temperance beverage,[1] an incident that occurred at Leamington. And here, on the lock, are my initials. I had forgotten that in an extravagant mood I had had them placed there. The bag is undoubtedly mine. I am delighted to have it so unexpectedly restored to me. It has been a great inconvenience being without it all these years.

JACK: [*In a pathetic voice.*] Miss Prism, more is restored to you than this hand-bag. I was the baby you placed in it.

MISS PRISM: [*Amazed.*] You?

JACK: [*Embracing her.*] Yes . . . mother!

MISS PRISM: [*Recoiling in indignant astonishment.*] Mr. Worthing! I am unmarried!

JACK: Unmarried! I do not deny that is a serious blow. But after all, who has the right to cast a stone against one who has suffered? Cannot repentance wipe out an act of folly? Why should there be one law for men and another for women? Mother, I forgive you. [*Tries to embrace her again.*]

MISS PRISM: [*Still more indignant.*] Mr. Worthing, there is some error. [*Pointing to* LADY BRACKNELL.] There is the lady who can tell you who you really are.

JACK: [*After a pause.*] Lady Bracknell, I hate to seem inquisitive, but would you kindly inform me who I am?

LADY BRACKNELL: I am afraid that the news I have to give you will not altogether please you. You are the son of my poor sister, Mrs. Moncrieff, and consequently Algernon's elder brother.

JACK: Algy's elder brother! Then I have a brother after all. I knew I

[1]Soft drink.

had a brother! I always said I had a brother! Cecily,—how could you have ever doubted that I had a brother? [*Seizes hold of* AL-GERNON.] Dr. Chasuble, my unfortunate brother. Miss Prism, my unfortunate brother. Gwendolen, my unfortunate brother. Algy, you young scoundrel, you will have to treat me with more respect in the future. You have never behaved to me like a brother in all your life.

ALGERNON: Well, not till to-day, old boy, I admit. I did my best, however, though I was out of practice. [*Shakes hands.*]

GWENDOLEN: [*To* JACK.] My own! But what own are you? What is your Christian name, now that you have become someone else?

JACK: Good heavens! . . . I had quite forgotten that point. Your decision on the subject of my name is irrevocable, I suppose?

GWENDOLEN: I never change, except in my affections.

CECILY: What a noble nature you have, Gwendolen!

JACK: Then the question had better be cleared up at once. Aunt Augusta, a moment. At the time when Miss Prism left me in the hand-bag, had I been christened already?

LADY BRACKNELL: Every luxury that money could buy, including christening, had been lavished on you by your fond and doting parents.

JACK: Then I was christened! That is settled. Now, what name was I given? Let me know the worst.

LADY BRACKNELL: Being the eldest son you were naturally christened after your father.

JACK: [*Irritably.*] Yes, but what was my father's Christian name?

LADY BRACKNELL: [*Meditatively.*] I cannot at the present moment recall what the General's Christian name was. But I have no doubt he had one. He was eccentric, I admit. But only in later years. And that was the result of the Indian climate, and marriage, and indigestion, and other things of that kind.

JACK: Algy! Can't you recollect what our father's Christian name was?

ALGERNON: My dear boy, we were never even on speaking terms. He died before I was a year old.

JACK: His name would appear in the Army Lists of the period, I suppose, Aunt Augusta?

LADY BRACKNELL: The general was essentially a man of peace, except in his domestic life. But I have no doubt his name would appear in any military directory.

JACK: The Army Lists of the last forty years are here. These delightful records should have been my constant study. [*Rushes to bookcase and tears the books out.*] M. Generals . . . Mallham, Maxbohm, Magley, what ghastly names they have—Markby, Migsby, Mobbs, Moncrieff! Lieutenant 1840, Captain, Lieutenant-Colonel, Colonel, General 1869, Christian names, Ernest John. [*Puts book very quietly down and speaks quite calmly.*] I always told you, Gwendolen, my name was Ernest, didn't I? Well, it is Ernest after all, I mean it naturally is Ernest.

LADY BRACKNELL: Yes, I remember the General was called Ernest. I knew I had some particular reason for disliking the name.

GWENDOLEN: Ernest! My own Ernest! I felt from the first that you could have no other name!

JACK: Gwendolen, it is a terrible thing for a man to find out suddenly that all his life he has been speaking nothing but the truth. Can you forgive me?

GWENDOLEN: I can. For I feel sure that you are sure to change.

JACK: My own one!

CHASUBLE: [*To* MISS PRISM.] Lætitia! [*Embraces her.*]

MISS PRISM: [*Enthusiastically.*] Frederick! At last!

ALGERNON: Cecily! [*Embraces her.*] At last!

JACK: Gwendolen! [*Embraces her.*] At last!

LADY BRACKNELL: My nephew, you seem to be displaying signs of triviality.

JACK: On the contrary, Aunt Augusta, I've now realized for the first time in my life the vital Importance of Being Earnest.

[*Tableau.*]

[*Curtain.*]

1895

Susan Glaspell
1882–1948

TRIFLES

Trifles *is based on a real-life murder. On a cold December night, in an Iowa farmhouse, John Hossack was sleeping in his bed when someone struck him in the head with an axe. His wife, Margaret, claimed she was awakened by the noise of the blows, which sounded like one block of wood striking another one, but evidence suggested she was the murderer. Her motive, according to the authorities, was unhappiness within a bad marriage.*

Susan Glaspell, a young reporter for the Des Moines Daily News, *covered the case. At first, she led readers down a familiar, lurid path of indignation and outrage, appealing to her readers' prejudices, sensationalizing the crime, and portraying Margaret Hossack as a monster. But after visiting the Hossacks' kitchen in the company of investigators, she came to regard the wife not as a criminal but as a victim, and her newspaper stories began to describe the horrific life Margaret Hassock suffered during thirty-three years of marriage to an oppressive and abusive husband. The trial proved a great public entertainment; the courthouse was packed to overflowing, with more women in attendance than men. Although Hassock was convicted of murder and sentenced to life at hard labor, her lawyers appealed the verdict and won; in a retrial, the jury couldn't reach a consensus, so Hassock was released.*

The story lay dormant in Glaspell's imagination for a dozen years. When her husband, the writer George Cook, announced to their friends that Glaspell would provide a new play for the 1916 "season" of the Provincetown Players, a modest theatrical company the couple had cofounded in Provincetown, Massachusetts, Glaspell, who was really a fiction writer, settled down to write a play. In the heat of summer days, she sat in the empty space of the Wharf Theater until, as she put it, the "bare little stage" began to take on the features of Margaret Hassock's kitchen. She wrote the play in two weeks, and it opened on August 8, 1916, with Cook and Glaspell in the roles of Mr. and Mrs. Hale. Some critics have seen features of the young Glaspell, as she was when she reported the Hassock case, in Mrs. Hale.

The play was picked up by New York City's Washington Square Players, a group midway between the Provincetown Players and the mainstream, commercial theaters on Broadway. The New York production gave Glaspell a wider audience, and soon she was a famous figure in the New York theater world, with the New York Times *printing feature stories about her.*

Like her fellow Provincetowners, including playwright Eugene O'Neill, Glaspell sought to give America a serious theater predicated on a repudiation of the melodrama and sentimentality that dominated the popular stage. She did not, however, disdain common theatergoers or think that her proper audience was the elite intellectuals among whom she worked and lived. A socialist, Glaspell wanted her work to affect people beyond her circle, to entertain a popular audience at the same time that it improved Americans' lives.

Within Trifles, *you'll find many insights into relations between men and women in America. If you look carefully, you'll also detect Glaspell's social commentary on class distinctions, in the different characterizations of Mrs. Hale and Mrs. Peters, who have different class status.*

Trifles

CHARACTERS

SHERIFF	MRS. PETERS, *Sheriff's wife*
COUNTY ATTORNEY	MRS. HALE
HALE	

SCENE: *The kitchen in the now abandoned farmhouse of* JOHN WRIGHT, *a gloomy kitchen, and left without having been put in order—unwashed pans under the sink, a loaf of bread outside the breadbox, a dish-towel on the table—other signs of incompleted work. At the rear the outer door opens and the* SHERIFF *comes in followed by the* COUNTY ATTORNEY *and* HALE. *The* SHERIFF *and* HALE *are men in middle life, the* COUNTY ATTORNEY *is a young man; all are much bundled up and go at once to the stove. They are followed by the two women—the* SHERIFF's *wife first; she is a slight wiry woman, a thin nervous face.* MRS. HALE *is larger and would ordinarily be called more comfortable looking, but she is disturbed now and looks fearfully about as she enters. The women have come in slowly, and stand close together near the door.*

COUNTY ATTORNEY: [*Rubbing his hands.*] This feels good. Come up to the fire, ladies.

MRS. PETERS: [*After taking a step forward.*] I'm not—cold.

SHERIFF: [*Unbuttoning his overcoat and stepping away from the stove as if to mark the beginning of official business.*] Now, Mr. Hale, before we move things about, you explain to Mr. Henderson just what you saw when you came here yesterday morning.

COUNTY ATTORNEY: By the way, has anything been moved? Are things just as you left them yesterday?

SHERIFF: [*Looking about.*] It's just the same. When it dropped below zero last night I thought I'd better send Frank out this morning to make a fire for us—no use getting pneumonia with a big case on, but I told him not to touch anything except the stove—and you know Frank.

COUNTY ATTORNEY: Somebody should have been left here yesterday.

SHERIFF: Oh—yesterday. When I had to send Frank to Morris Center for that man who went crazy—I want you to know I had my hands full yesterday. I knew you could get back from Omaha by today and as long as I went over everything here myself—

COUNTY ATTORNEY: Well, Mr. Hale, tell just what happened when you came here yesterday morning.

HALE: Harry and I had started to town with a load of potatoes. We came along the road from my place and as I got here I said, "I'm going to see if I can't get John Wright to go in with me on a party telephone."[1] I spoke to Wright about it once before and he put me off, saying folks talked too much anyway, and all he asked was peace and quiet—I guess you know about how much he talked himself; but I thought maybe if I went to the house and talked about it before his wife, though I said to Harry that I didn't know as what his wife wanted made much difference to John—

_____

1. One telephone line shared by a number of houses.

COUNTY ATTORNEY: Let's talk about that later, Mr. Hale. I do want to talk about that, but tell now just what happened when you got to the house.

HALE: I didn't hear or see anything; I knocked at the door, and still it was all quiet inside. I knew they must be up, it was past eight o'clock. So I knocked again, and I thought I heard somebody say, "Come in." I wasn't sure, I'm not sure yet, but I opened the door— this door [*Indicating the door by which the two women are still standing.*] and there in that rocker— [*Pointing to it.*] sat Mrs. Wright.
[*They all look at the rocker.*]

COUNTY ATTORNEY: What—was she doing?

HALE: She was rockin' back and forth. She had her apron in her hand and was kind of—pleating it.

COUNTY ATTORNEY: And how did she—look?

HALE: Well, she looked queer.

COUNTY ATTORNEY: How do you mean—queer?

HALE: Well, as if she didn't know what she was going to do next. And kind of done up.

COUNTY ATTORNEY: How did she seem to feel about your coming?

HALE: Why, I don't think she minded—one way or other. She didn't pay much attention. I said, "How do, Mrs. Wright, it's cold, ain't it?" And she said, "Is it?"—and went on kind of pleating at her apron. Well, I was surprised; she didn't ask me to come up to the stove, or to set down, but just sat there, not even looking at me, so I said, "I want to see John." And then she—laughed. I guess you would call it a laugh. I thought of Harry and the team outside, so I said a little sharp: "Can't I see John?" "No," she says, kind o' dull like. "Ain't he home?" says I. "Yes," says she, "he's home." "Then why can't I see him?" I asked her, out of patience." 'Cause he's dead," says she. "*Dead?*" says I. She just nodded her head, not getting a bit excited, but rockin' back and forth. "Why—where is he?" says I, not knowing what to say. She just pointed upstairs—like that. [*Himself pointing to the room above.*] I got up, with the idea of going up there. I walked from there to here—then I says, "Why, what did he die of?" "He died of a rope round his neck," says she, and just went on pleatin' at her apron. Well, I went out and called Harry. I thought I might—need help. We went upstairs and there he was lyin'—

COUNTY ATTORNEY: I think I'd rather have you go into that upstairs, where you can point it all out. Just go on now with the rest of the story.

HALE: Well, my first thought was to get that rope off. It looked . . . [*Stops, his face twitches.*] . . . but Harry, he went up to him, and he said, "No, he's dead all right, and we'd better not touch anything." So we went back down stairs. She was still sitting that same way. "Has anybody been notified?" I asked. "No," says she unconcerned. "Who did this, Mrs. Wright?" said Harry. He said it business-like—and she stopped pleatin' of her apron. "I don't know," she says. "You don't *know?*" says Harry. "No," says she. "Weren't you sleepin' in the bed with him?" says Harry. "Yes," says she, "but I was on the inside." "Somebody slipped a rope round his neck and strangled him and you didn't wake up?" says Harry. "I didn't wake up," she said after him. We must 'a looked as if we didn't see how that could be, for after a minute she said, "I sleep sound." Harry was going to ask her more questions but I said maybe we ought to let her tell her story first to the coroner, or the sheriff, so Harry went fast as he could to Rivers' place, where there's a telephone.

COUNTY ATTORNEY: And what did Mrs. Wright do when she knew that you had gone for the coroner?

HALE: She moved from that chair to this one over here [*Pointing to a small chair in the corner.*] and just sat there with her hands held together and looking down. I got a feeling that I ought to make some conversation, so I said I had come in to see if John wanted to put in a telephone, and at that she started to laugh, and then she stopped and looked at me—scared. [*The* COUNTY ATTORNEY, *who has had his notebook out, makes a note.*] I dunno, maybe it wasn't scared. I wouldn't like to say it was. Soon Harry got back, and then Dr. Lloyd came, and you, Mr. Peters, and so I guess that's all I know that you don't.

COUNTY ATTORNEY: [*Looking around.*] I guess we'll go upstairs first—and then out to the barn and around there. [*To the* SHERIFF.] You're convinced that there was nothing important here— nothing that would point to any motive?

SHERIFF: Nothing here but kitchen things.

[*The* COUNTY ATTORNEY, *after again looking around the*

kitchen, opens the door of a cupboard closet. He gets up on a chair and looks on a shelf. Pulls his hand away, sticky.]

COUNTY ATTORNEY: Here's a nice mess.

[*The women draw nearer.*]

MRS. PETERS: [*To the other woman.*] Oh, her fruit; it did freeze. [*To the* LAWYER.] She worried about that when it turned so cold. She said the fire'd go out and her jars would break.

SHERIFF: Well, can you beat the women! Held for murder and worryin' about her preserves.

COUNTY ATTORNEY: I guess before we're through she may have something more serious than preserves to worry about.

HALE: Well, women are used to worrying over trifles.

[*The two women move a little closer together.*]

COUNTY ATTORNEY: [*With the gallantry of a young politician.*] And yet, for all their worries, what would we do without the ladies? [*The women do not unbend. He goes to the sink, takes a dipperful of water from the pail, and pouring it into a basin, washes his hands. Starts to wipe them on the roller-towel, turns it for a cleaner place.*] Dirty towels! [*Kicks his foot against the pans under the sink.*] Not much of a housekeeper, would you say, ladies?

MRS. HALE: [*Stiffly.*] There's a great deal of work to be done on a farm.

COUNTY ATTORNEY: To be sure. And yet [*With a little bow to her.*] I know there are some Dickson county farmhouses which do not have such roller towels. [*He gives it a pull to expose its length again.*]

MRS. HALE: Those towels get dirty awful quick. Men's hands aren't always as clean as they might be.

COUNTY ATTORNEY: Ah, loyal to your sex, I see. But you and Mrs. Wright were neighbors. I suppose you were friends, too.

MRS. HALE: [*Shaking her head.*] I've not seen much of her of late years. I've not been in this house—it's more than a year.

COUNTY ATTORNEY: And why was that? You didn't like her?

MRS. HALE: I liked her all well enough. Farmers' wives have their hands full, Mr. Henderson. And then—

COUNTY ATTORNEY: Yes—?

MRS. HALE: [*Looking about.*] It never seemed a very cheerful place.

COUNTY ATTORNEY: No—it's not cheerful. I shouldn't say she had the homemaking instinct.

MRS. HALE: Well, I don't know as Wright had, either.

COUNTY ATTORNEY: You mean that they didn't get on very well?

MRS. HALE: No, I don't mean anything. But I don't think a place'd be any cheerfuller for John Wright's being in it.

COUNTY ATTORNEY: I'd like to talk more of that a little later. I want to get the lay of things upstairs now. [*He goes to the left, where three steps lead to a stair door.*]

SHERIFF: I suppose anything Mrs. Peters does'll be all right. She was to take in some clothes for her, you know, and a few little things. We left in such a hurry yesterday.

COUNTY ATTORNEY: Yes, but I would like to see what you take, Mrs. Peters, and keep an eye out for anything that might be of use to us.

MRS. PETERS: Yes, Mr. Henderson. [*The women listen to the men's steps on the stairs, then look about the kitchen.*]

MRS. HALE: I'd hate to have men coming into my kitchen, snooping around and criticizing. [*She arranges the pans under sink which the* LAWYER *had shoved out of place.*]

MRS. PETERS: Of course it's no more than their duty.

MRS. HALE: Duty's all right, but I guess that deputy sheriff that came out to make the fire might have got a little of this on. [*Gives the roller towel a pull.*] Wish I'd thought of that sooner. Seems mean to talk about her for not having things slicked up when she had to come away in such a hurry.

MRS. PETERS: [*Who has gone to a small table in the left rear corner of the room, and lifted one end of a towel that covers a pan.*] She had bread set. [*Stands still.*]

MRS. HALF: [*Eyes fixed on a loaf of bread beside the bread box, which is on a low shelf at the other side of the room. Moves slowly toward it.*] She was going to put this in there. [*Picks up loaf, then abruptly drops it. In a manner of returning to familiar things.*] It's a shame about her fruit. I wonder if it's all gone. [*Gets up on the chair and looks.*] I think there's some here that's all right, Mrs. Peters. Yes— here; [*Holding it toward the window.*] this is cherries, too. [*Looking again.*] I declare I believe that's the only one. [*Gets down, bottle in her hand. Goes to the sink and wipes it off on the outside.*] She'll feel awful bad after all her hard work in the hot weather. I remember the afternoon I put up my cherries last summer. [*She puts the bottle on the big kitchen table, center of the room. With a sigh, is about to sit down in the rocking-chair. Before she is seated realizes what chair it is; with a slow look at it, steps back. The chair, which she has touched, rocks back and forth.*]

MRS. PETERS: Well, I must get those things from the front room closet. [*She goes to the door at the right, but after looking into the other room, steps back.*] You coming with me, Mrs. Hale? You could help me carry them. [*They go in the other room; reappear,* MRS. PETERS *carrying a dress and skirt,* MRS. HALE *following with a pair of shoes.*] My, it's cold in there. [*She puts the clothes on the big table, and hurries to the stove.*]

MRS. HALE: [*Examining the skirt.*] Wright was close. I think maybe that's why she kept so much to herself. She didn't even belong to the Ladies Aid.[2] I suppose she felt she couldn't do her part, and then you don't enjoy things when you feel shabby. She used to wear pretty clothes and be lively, when she was Minnie Foster, one of the town girls singing in the choir. But that—oh, that was thirty years ago. This all you was to take in?

MRS. PETERS: She said she wanted an apron. Funny thing to want, for there isn't much to get you dirty in jail, goodness knows. But I suppose just to make her feel more natural. She said they was in the top drawer in this cupboard. Yes, here. And then her little shawl that always hung behind the door. [*Opens stair door and looks.*] Yes, here it is. [*Quickly shuts door leading upstairs.*]

MRS. HALE: [*Abruptly moving toward her.*] Mrs. Peters?

MRS. PETERS: Yes, Mrs. Hale?

MRS. HALE: Do you think she did it?

MRS. PETERS: [*In a frightened voice.*] Oh, I don't know.

MRS. HALE: Well, I don't think she did. Asking for an apron and her little shawl. Worrying about her fruit.

MRS. PETERS: [*Starts to speak, glances up, where footsteps are heard in the room above. In a low voice.*] Mr. Peters says it looks bad for

---

2. A volunteer benevolence society.

her. Mr. Henderson is awful sarcastic in a speech and he'll make fun of her sayin' she didn't wake up.

MRS. HALE: Well, I guess John Wright didn't wake when they was slipping that rope under his neck.

MRS. PETERS: No, it's strange. It must have been done awful crafty and still. They say it was such a—funny way to kill a man, rigging it all up like that.

MRS. HALE: That's just what Mr. Hale said. There was a gun in the house. He says that's what he can't understand.

MRS. PETERS: Mr. Henderson said coming out that what was needed for the case was a motive; something to show anger, or—sudden feeling.

MRS. HALE: [*Who is standing by the table.*] Well, I don't see any signs of anger around here. [*She puts her hand on the dish towel which lies on the table, stands looking down at table, one half of which is clean, the other half messy.*] It's wiped to here. [*Makes a move as if to finish work, then turns and looks at loaf of bread outside the bread box. Drops towel. In that voice of coming back to familiar things.*] Wonder how they are finding things upstairs. I hope she had it a little more red-up[3] up there. You know, it seems kind of *sneaking.* Locking her up in town and then coming out here and trying to get her own house to turn against her!

MRS. PETERS: But Mrs. Hale, the law is the law.

MRS. HALE: I s'pose 'tis. [*Unbuttoning her coat.*] Better loosen up your things, Mrs. Peters. You won't feel them when you go out.

[MRS. PETERS *takes off her fur tippet,[4] goes to hang it on hook at back of room, stands looking at the under part of the small corner table.*]

MRS. PETERS: She was piecing a quilt. [*She brings the large sewing basket and they look at the bright pieces.*]

MRS. HALE: It's log cabin pattern. Pretty, isn't it? I wonder if she was goin' to quilt it or just knot it?[5]

[*Footsteps have been heard coming down the stairs. The* SHERIFF *enters followed by* HALE *and the* COUNTY ATTORNEY.]

---

3. Tidied up.
4. Shoulder covering, like a full scarf.
5. The top of a quilt can be attached to the backing by sewing, which is a laborious process, or by knotting thick yarn, which is much quicker and easier.

SHERIFF: They wonder if she was going to quilt it or just knot it!

[*The men laugh, the women look abashed.*]

COUNTY ATTORNEY: [*Rubbing his hands over the stove.*] Frank's fire didn't do much up there, did it? Well, let's go out to the barn and get that cleared up.

[*The men go outside.*]

MRS. HALE: [*Resentfully.*] I don't know as there's anything so strange, our takin' up our time with little things while we're waiting for them to get the evidence. [*She sits down at the big table smoothing out a block with decision.*] I don't see as it's anything to laugh about.

MRS. PETERS: [*Apologetically.*] Of course they've got awful important things on their minds. [*Pulls up a chair and joins* MRS. HALE *at the table.*]

MRS. HALE: [*Examining another block.*] Mrs. Peters, look at this one. Here, this is the one she was working on, and look at the sewing! All the rest of it has been so nice and even. And look at this! It's all over the place! Why, it looks as if she didn't know what she was about! [*After she has said this they look at each other, then start to glance back at the door. After an instant* MRS. HALE *has pulled at a knot and ripped the sewing.*]

MRS. PETERS: Oh, what are you doing, Mrs. Hale?

MRS. HALE: [*Mildly.*] Just pulling out a stitch or two that's not sewed very good. [*Threading the needle.*] Bad sewing always made me fidgety.

MRS. PETERS: [*Nervously.*] I don't think we ought to touch things.

MRS. HALE: I'll just finish up this end. [*Suddenly stopping and leaning forward.*] Mrs. Peters?

MRS. PETERS: Yes, Mrs. Hale?

MRS. HALE: What do you suppose she was so nervous about?

MRS. PETERS: Oh—I don't know. I don't know as she was nervous. I sometimes sew awful queer when I'm just tired. [MRS. HALE *starts to say something, looks at* MRS. PETERS, *then goes on sewing.*] Well I must get these things wrapped up. They may be through sooner than we think. [*Putting apron and other things together.*] I wonder where I can find a piece of paper, and string.

MRS. HALE: In that cupboard, maybe.

MRS. PETERS: [*Looking in cupboard.*] Why, here's a bird-cage. [*Holds it up.*] Did she have a bird, Mrs. Hale?

MRS. HALE: Why, I don't know whether she did or not—I've not been here for so long. There was a man around last year selling canaries cheap, but I don't know as she took one; maybe she did. She used to sing real pretty herself.

MRS. PETERS: [*Glancing around.*] Seems funny to think of a bird here. But she must have had one, or why would she have a cage? I wonder what happened to it.

MRS. HALE: I s'pose maybe the cat got it.

MRS. PETERS: No, she didn't have a cat. She's got that feeling some people have about cats—being afraid of them. My cat got in her room and she was real upset and asked me to take it out.

MRS. HALE: My sister Bessie was like that. Queer, ain't it?

MRS. PETERS: [*Examining the cage.*] Why, look at this door. It's broke. One hinge is pulled apart.

MRS. HALE: [*Looking too.*] Looks as if someone must have been rough with it.

MRS. PETERS: Why, yes. [*She brings the cage forward and puts it on the table.*]

MRS. HALE: I wish if they're going to find any evidence they'd be about it. I don't like this place.

MRS. PETERS: But I'm awful glad you came with me, Mrs. Hale. It would be lonesome for me sitting here alone.

MRS. HALE: It would, wouldn't it? [*Dropping her sewing.*] But I tell you what I do wish, Mrs. Peters. I wish I had come over sometimes when *she* was here. I— [*Looking around the room.*] —wish I had.

MRS. PETERS: But of course you were awful busy, Mrs. Hale—your house and your children.

MRS. HALE: I could've come. I stayed away because it weren't cheerful—and that's why I ought to have come. I—I've never liked this place. Maybe because it's down in a hollow and you don't see the road. I dunno what it is, but it's a lonesome place and always was. I wish I had come over to see Minnie Foster sometimes. I can see now— [*Shakes her head.*]

MRS. PETERS: Well, you mustn't reproach yourself, Mrs. Hale. Somehow we just don't see how it is with other folks until—something comes up.

MRS. HALE: Not having children makes less work—but it makes a quiet house, and Wright out to work all day, and no company when he did come in. Did you know John Wright, Mrs. Peters?

MRS. PETERS: Not to know him; I've seen him in town. They say he was a good man.

MRS. HALE: Yes—good; he didn't drink, and kept his word as well as most, I guess, and paid his debts. But he was a hard man, Mrs. Peters. Just to pass the time of day with him— [*Shivers.*] Like a raw wind that gets to the bone. [*Pauses, her eye falling on the cage.*] I should think she would 'a wanted a bird. But what do you suppose went with it?

MRS. PETERS: I don't know, unless it got sick and died. [*She reaches over and swings the broken door, swings it again, both women watch it.*]

MRS. HALE: You weren't raised round here, were you? [MRS. PETERS *shakes her head.*] You didn't know—her?

MRS. PETERS: Not till they brought her yesterday.

MRS. HALE: She—come to think of it, she was kind of like a bird herself—real sweet and pretty, but kind of timid and—fluttery. How—she—did—change. [*Silence; then as if struck by a happy thought and relieved to get back to everyday things.*] Tell you what, Mrs. Peters, why don't you take the quilt in with you? It might take up her mind.

MRS. PETERS: Why, I think that's a real nice idea, Mrs. Hale. There couldn't possibly be any objection to it, could there? Now, just what would I take? I wonder if her patches are in here—and her things. [*They look in the sewing basket.*]

MRS. HALE: Here's some red. I expect this has got sewing things in it. [*Brings out a fancy box.*] What a pretty box. Looks like something somebody would give you. Maybe her scissors are in here. [*Opens box. Suddenly puts her hand to her nose.*] Why— [MRS. PETERS *bends nearer, then turns her face away.*] There's something wrapped up in this piece of silk.

MRS. PETERS: Why, this isn't her scissors.

MRS. HALE: [*Lifting the silk.*] Oh, Mrs. Peters—it's—

[MRS. PETERS *bends closer.*]

MRS. PETERS: It's the bird.

MRS. HALE: [*Jumping up.*] But, Mrs. Peters—look at it! Its neck! Look at its neck! It's all—other side *to.*

MRS. PETERS: Somebody—wrung—its—neck.

> [*Their eyes meet. A look of growing comprehension, of horror. Steps are heard outside.* MRS. HALE *slips box under quilt pieces, and sinks into her chair. Enter* SHERIFF *and* COUNTY ATTORNEY. MRS. PETERS *rises.*]

COUNTY ATTORNEY: [*As one turning from serious things to little pleasantries.*] Well ladies, have you decided whether she was going to quilt it or knot it?

MRS. PETERS: We think she was going to—knot it.

COUNTY ATTORNEY: Well, that's interesting, I'm sure. [*Seeing the bird-cage.*] Has the bird flown?

MRS. HALE: [*Putting more quilt pieces over the box.*] We think the—cat got it.

COUNTY ATTORNEY: [*Preoccupied.*] Is there a cat?

> [MRS. HALE *glances in a quick covert way at* MRS. PETERS.]

MRS. PETERS: Well not *now.* They're superstitious, you know. They leave.

COUNTY ATTORNEY: [*To* SHERIFF PETERS, *continuing an interrupted conversation.*] No sign at all of anyone having come from the outside. Their own rope. Now let's go up again and go over it piece by piece. [*They start upstairs.*] It would have to have been someone who knew just the—

> [MRS. PETERS *sits down. The two women sit there not looking at one another, but as if peering into something and at the same time holding back. When they talk now it is in the manner of feeling their way over strange ground, as if afraid of what they are saying, but as if they cannot help saying it.*]

MRS. HALE: She liked the bird. She was going to bury it in that pretty box.

MRS. PETERS: [*In a whisper.*] When I was a girl—my kitten—there was a boy took a hatchet, and before my eyes—and before I could get there— [*Covers her face an instant.*] If they hadn't held me back I would have— [*Catches herself, looks upstairs where steps are heard, falters weakly.*] —hurt him.

MRS. HALE: [*With a slow look around her.*] I wonder how it would seem never to have had any children around. [*Pause.*] No, Wright wouldn't like the bird—a thing that sang. She used to sing. He killed that, too.

MRS. PETERS: [*Moving uneasily.*] We don't know who killed the bird.

MRS. HALE: I knew John Wright.

MRS. PETERS: It was an awful thing was done in this house that night, Mrs. Hale. Killing a man while he slept, slipping a rope around his neck that choked the life out of him.

MRS. HALE: His neck. Choked the life out of him. [*Her hand goes out and rests on the bird-cage.*]

MRS. PETERS: [*With rising voice.*] We don't know who killed him. We don't *know.*

MRS. HALE: [*Her own feeling not interrupted.*] If there's been years and years of nothing, then a bird to sing to you, it would be awful—still, after the bird was still.

MRS. PETERS: [*Something within her speaking.*] I know what stillness is. When we homesteaded in Dakota, and my first baby died—after he was two years old, and me with no other then—

MRS. HALE: [*Moving.*] How soon do you suppose they'll be through, looking for the evidence?

MRS. PETERS: I know what stillness is. [*Pulling herself back.*] The law has got to punish crime, Mrs. Hale.

MRS. HALE: [*Not as if answering that.*] I wish you'd seen Minnie Foster when she wore a white dress with blue ribbons and stood up there in the choir and sang. [*A look around the room.*] Oh, I *wish* I'd come over here once in a while! That was a crime! That was a crime! Who's going to punish that?

MRS. PETERS: [*Looking upstairs.*] We mustn't—take on.

MRS. HALE: I might have known she needed help! I know how things can be—for women. I tell you, it's queer, Mrs. Peters. We live close together and we live far apart. We all go through the same things—it's all just a different kind of the same thing. [*Brushes her eyes, noticing the bottle of fruit, reaches out for it.*] If I was you, I wouldn't tell her her fruit was gone. Tell her it *ain't.* Tell her it's all right. Take this in to prove it to her. She—she may never know whether it was broke or not.

MRS. PETERS: [*Takes the bottle, looks about for something to wrap it in; takes petticoat from the clothes brought from the other room, very nervously begins winding this around the bottle. In a false voice.*] My, it's a good thing the men couldn't hear us. Wouldn't they just laugh! Getting all stirred up over a little thing like a—dead canary. As if that could have anything to do with—with—wouldn't they *laugh!*

[*The men are heard coming down stairs.*]

MRS. HALE: [*Under her breath.*] Maybe they would—maybe they wouldn't.

COUNTY ATTORNEY: No, Peters, it's all perfectly clear except a reason for doing it. But you know juries when it comes to women. If there was some definite thing. Something to show—something to make a story about—a thing that would connect up with this strange way of doing it—

[*The women's eyes meet for an instant. Enter* HALE *from outer door.*]

HALE: Well, I've got the team around. Pretty cold out there.

COUNTY ATTORNEY: I'm going to stay here a while by myself. [*To the* SHERIFF.] You can send Frank out for me, can't you? I want to go over everything. I'm not satisfied that we can't do better.

SHERIFF: Do you want to see what Mrs. Peters is going to take in?

[*The* LAWYER *goes to the table, picks up the apron, laughs.*]

COUNTY ATTORNEY: Oh, I guess they're not very dangerous things the ladies have picked out. [*Moves a few things about, disturbing the quilt pieces which cover the box. Steps back.*] No, Mrs. Peters doesn't need supervising. For that matter, a sheriff's wife is married to the law. Ever think of it that way, Mrs. Peters?

MRS. PETERS: Not—just that way.

SHERIFF: [*Chuckling.*] Married to the law. [*Moves toward the other room.*] I just want you to come in here a minute, George. We ought to take a look at these windows.

COUNTY ATTORNEY: [*Scoffingly.*] Oh, windows!

SHERIFF: We'll be right out, Mr. Hale.

[HALE *goes outside. The* SHERIFF *follows the* COUNTY ATTORNEY *into the other room. Then* MRS. HALE *rises, hands tight together, looking intensely at* MRS. PETERS, *whose eyes make a slow turn, finally meeting* MRS. HALE's. *A moment* MRS. HALE *holds her, then her own eyes point the way to where the box is concealed. Suddenly* MRS. PETERS *throws back quilt pieces and tries to put the box in the bag she is wearing. It is too big. She opens box, starts to take bird out, cannot touch it, goes to pieces, stands there helpless. Sound of a knob turning in the other room.* MRS. HALE *snatches*

the box and puts it in the pocket of her big coat. Enter COUNTY
ATTORNEY *and* SHERIFF.]

COUNTY ATTORNEY: [*Facetiously.*] Well, Henry, at least we found out
that she was not going to quilt it. She was going to—what is it
you call it, ladies?

MRS. HALE: [*Her hand against her pocket.*] We call it—knot it, Mr.
Henderson.

[*Curtain.*]

1916   *1920*

Tennessee Williams
1911–1983

THE GLASS MENAGERIE

Much of The Glass Menagerie *is, at least on the surface, autobiographical. The life of the play's "narrator," Tom, originates in
Williams's early life, and the play's characters and psychological
complexity derive from Williams's own family drama. Like Tom's
sister, Laura, for example, Williams's sister, Rose, suffered from a
mental disorder. Increasingly unbalanced, she was diagnosed as
schizophrenic. The last of her many breakdowns resulted from a
traumatic episode involving their chronically drunk and abusive
father, who on this occasion beat their mother and, perhaps, made
a sexual advance toward Rose. Her treatment ended with a pre-
frontal lobotomy, a radical procedure that decimated her personality and consigned her to sanitoriums for most of her life. Rose had
been Williams's closest childhood companion, and he remained
haunted by her tragedy. In his will, he left his millions to her.*

    *Despite the explosive and heartbreaking nature of this story,
Laura is not the central figure in this play. Instead, actors and
audiences focus on Amanda, who is loosely based on Williams's
mother, a southern belle known as Miss Edwina. On stage, film,
and television, major actors such as Helen Hayes, Maureen Staple-*

ton, Kathryn Hepburn, and Jessica Tandy have interpreted the role, which older female actors covet the way young male actors covet, say, Hamlet.

Because The Glass Menagerie is a "memory play," however, its characters seem less like realistic people than like images in dreams, rising up from some storehouse of the conscious and the unconscious. Williams aimed to create a kind of symbolic theatrical language that would communicate overwise inexpressible psychological dimensions. The glass figurines from which the play takes its title provide a richer symbolism than that found in, say, the Ibsenite dramas of the previous few generations—as, for example, when Williams invokes the associations that medieval artists attached to unicorns. And this rich symbolism seems to come from what the post-Freudian audience recognizes as human beings' highly sexualized, secret psyche. As a reader, you must be ready to look beyond the literal, linguistic surface.

In employing his new language, Williams was one among many prominent American writers who chronicled and reinterpreted the South for the twentieth century. Like William Faulkner, Allen Tate, and Robert Penn Warren, Williams came from a generation that did not experience the Civil War, but experienced rather the crushing nostalgia of parents and grandparents who pined for an idealized fantasy of the antebellum Old South. Margaret Mitchell's novel Gone With the Wind (1936) expresses this nostalgia, and Williams's play was written and performed only a few years after that best-seller was made into a blockbuster movie. Williams and his fellow southern writers accepted the burden of interpreting the South's past and to some extent tried to chart a path for the New South in the modern world.

As you ask yourself what The Glass Menagerie says about the South, remember that the play takes place in the late 1930s. America has suffered through the Great Depression, and the economic prospects of young men like Tom still look very dim. In Europe, the Spanish Civil War is raging. Within a couple of years, World War II will have begun, and Tom will probably be in the army or navy fighting Japan or Germany. In fact, when this play was first staged, the war was still being fought, and though Americans were *reasonably assured of their eventual victory, the end was not in sight. The great optimism and prosperity of the postwar period was not yet even dimly glimpsed over the horizon.*

Note that the script reprinted here represents a "reading" version of the play, first published in 1945. Stage productions generally use a different text, not published until 1948. The stage script dampens some of the more unrealistic effects of the play. As a result, stage productions tend to be less strange than this reading text suggests. They often omit the projected words, for example.

The Glass Menagerie

SCENE: *An alley in St. Louis*

Part I. Preparation for a Gentleman Caller.
Part II. The Gentleman calls.

TIME: *Now and the Past*

THE CHARACTERS
AMANDA WINGFIELD *(the mother)*
A little woman of great but confused vitality clinging frantically to another time and place. Her characterization must be carefully created, not copied from type. She is not paranoiac, but her life is paranoia. There is much to admire in Amanda, and as much to love and pity as there is to laugh at. Certainly she has endurance and a kind of heroism, and though her foolishness makes her unwittingly cruel at times, there is tenderness in her slight person.

LAURA WINGFIELD *(her daughter)*
Amanda, having failed to establish contact with reality, continues to live vitally in her illusions, but Laura's situation is even graver. A childhood illness has left her crippled, one leg slightly shorter than the other, and held in a brace. This defect need not be more than suggested on the stage. Stemming from this, Laura's separation increases till she is like a piece of her own glass collection, too exquisitely fragile to move from the shelf.

TOM WINGFIELD *(her son)*

And the narrator of the play. A poet with a job in a warehouse. His nature is not remorseless, but to escape from a trap he has to act without pity.

JIM O'CONNOR *(the gentleman caller)*

A nice, ordinary, young man.

PRODUCTION NOTES

Being a "memory play," *The Glass Menagerie* can be presented with unusual freedom of convention. Because of its considerably delicate or tenuous material, atmospheric touches and subtleties of direction play a particularly important part. Expressionism and all other un-conventional techniques in drama have only one valid aim, and that is a closer approach to truth. When a play employs unconventional techniques, it is not, or certainly shouldn't be, trying to escape its responsibility of dealing with reality, or interpreting experience, but is actually or should be attempting to find a closer approach, a more penetrating and vivid expression of things as they are. The straight realistic play with its genuine Frigidaire and authentic ice-cubes, its characters who speak exactly as its audience speaks, corresponds to the academic landscape and has the same virtue of a photographic likeness. Everyone should know nowadays the unimportance of the photographic in art: that truth, life, or reality is an organic thing which the poetic imagination can represent or suggest, in essence, only through transformation, through changing into other forms than those which were merely present in appearance.

These remarks are not meant as a preface only to this particular play. They have to do with a conception of a new, plastic theatre which must take the place of the exhausted theatre of realistic con-ventions if the theatre is to resume vitality as a part of our culture.

THE SCREEN DEVICE: There is *only one important difference between the original and the acting version of the play* and that is the *omission* in the latter of the device that I tentatively included in my *original* script. This device was the use of a screen on which were projected magic-lantern slides bearing images or titles. I do not regret the omission of this device from the original Broadway production. The extraordinary power of Miss Taylor's performance made it suitable to have the utmost simplicity in the physical production. But I think it may be interesting to some readers to see how this device was conceived. So I am putting it into the published manuscript. These images and legends, projected from behind, were cast on a section of wall between the front-room and dining-room areas, which should be indistinguishable from the rest when not in use.

The purpose of this will probably be apparent. It is to give accent to certain values in each scene. Each scene contains a particular point (or several) which is structurally the most important. In an episodic play, such as this, the basic structure or narrative line may be obscured from the audience; the effect may seem fragmentary rather than architectural. This may not be the fault of the play so much as a lack of attention in the audience. The legend or image upon the screen will strengthen the effect of what is merely allusion in the writing and allow the primary point to be made more simply and lightly than if the entire responsibility were on the spoken lines. Aside from this structural value, I think the screen will have a definite emotional appeal, less definable but just as important. An imaginative producer or director may invent many other uses for this device than those indicated in the present script. In fact the possibilities of the device seem much larger to me than the instance of this play can possibly utilize.

THE MUSIC: Another extra-literary accent in this play is provided by the use of music. A single recurring tune, "The Glass Menagerie," is used to give emotional emphasis to suitable passages. This tune is like circus music, not when you are on the grounds or in the immediate vicinity of the parade, but when you are at some distance and very likely thinking of something else. It seems under those circumstances to continue almost interminably and it weaves in and out of your preoccupied consciousness; then it is the lightest, most delicate music in the world and perhaps the saddest. It expresses the surface vivacity of life with the underlying strain of immutable and inexpressible sorrow. When you look at a piece of delicately spun glass you think of two things: how beautiful it is and how easily it can be broken. Both of those ideas should be woven into the recurring tune, which dips in and out of the play as if it were carried on a wind that changes. It serves as a thread of connection and allusion between the narrator with his separate point in time and space and the subject of his story. Between each episode it returns as reference to the emotion, nostalgia, which is the first condition of the play. It is primarily Laura's music and therefore comes out most clearly when the play focuses upon her and the lovely fragility of glass which is her image.

THE LIGHTING: The lighting in the play is not realistic. In keeping with the atmosphere of memory, the stage is dim. Shafts of light are focused on selected areas or actors, sometimes in contradistinction to what is the apparent center. For instance, in the quarrel scene between Tom and Amanda, in which Laura has no active part, the clearest pool of light is on her figure. This is also true of the supper scene, when her silent figure on the sofa should remain the visual center. The light upon Laura should be distinct from the others, having a peculiar pristine clarity such as light used in early religious portraits of female saints or madonnas. A certain correspondence to light in religious paintings, such as El Greco's,[1] where the figures are radiant in atmosphere that is relatively dusky, could be effectively used throughout the play. (It will also permit a more effective use of the screen.) A free, imaginative use of light can be of enormous value in giving a mobile, plastic quality to plays of a more or less static nature.

Tennessee Williams

SCENE ONE

The Wingfield apartment is in the rear of the building, one of those vast hive-like conglomerations of cellular living-units that flower as warty growths in overcrowded urban centers of lower middle-class population and are symptomatic of the impulse of this largest and fundamentally enslaved section of American society to avoid fluidity and differentiation and to exist and function as one interfused mass of automatism.

The apartment faces an alley and is entered by a fire escape, a struc-

1. Sixteenth-century Spanish (Cretan-born) painter known for his dramatic, dreamy style.

ture whose name is a touch of accidental poetic truth, for all of these huge buildings are always burning with the slow and implacable fires of human desperation. The fire escape is part of what we see—that is, the landing of it and steps descending from it.

The scene is memory and is therefore nonrealistic. Memory takes a lot of poetic license. It omits some details; others are exaggerated, according to the emotional value of the articles it touches, for memory is seated predominantly in the heart. The interior is therefore rather dim and poetic.

At the rise of the curtain, the audience is faced with the dark, grim rear wall of the Wingfield tenement. This building is flanked on both sides by dark, narrow alleys which run into murky canyons of tangled clotheslines, garbage cans, and the sinister latticework of neighboring fire escapes. It is up and down these side alleys that exterior entrances and exits are made during the play. At the end of TOM's opening commentary, the dark tenement wall slowly becomes transparent and reveals the interior of the ground-floor Windfield apartment.

Nearest the audience is the living room, which also serves as a sleeping room for LAURA, the sofa unfolding to make her bed. Just beyond, separated from the living room by a wide arch or second proscenium with transparent faded portieres (or second curtain), is the dining room. In an old-fashioned whatnot[1] in the living room are seen scores of transparent glass animals. A blown-up photograph of the father hangs on the wall of the living room, to the left of the archway. It is the face of a very handsome young man in a doughboy's First World War cap. He is gallantly smiling, ineluctably smiling, as if to say "I will be smiling forever."

Also hanging on the wall, near the photograph, are a typewriter keyboard chart and a Gregg shorthand diagram.[2] An upright typewriter on a small table stands beneath the charts.

The audience hears and sees the opening scene in the dining room through both the transparent fourth wall of the building and the transparent gauze portieres of the dining-room arch. It is during this revealing scene that the fourth wall slowly ascends, out of sight. This transparent exterior wall is not brought down again until the very end of the play, during TOM's final speech.

---

1. A shelved stand used to display decorative items.

2. John Robert Gregg (1864–1948) invented a popular stenography system.

The narrator is an undisguised convention of the play. He takes whatever license with dramatic convention is convenient to his purposes.

TOM *enters, dressed as a merchant sailor, and strolls across to the fire escape. There he stops and lights a cigarette. He addresses the audience.*

TOM: Yes, I have tricks in my pocket, I have things up my sleeve. But I am the opposite of a stage magician. He gives you illusion that has the appearance of truth. I give you truth in the pleasant disguise of illusion.

To begin with, I turn back time. I reverse it to that quaint period, the thirties, when the huge middle class of America was matriculating in a school for the blind. Their eyes had failed them, or they had failed their eyes, and so they were having their fingers pressed forcibly down on the fiery Braille alphabet of a dissolving economy.

In Spain there was revolution. Here there was only shouting and confusion. In Spain there was Guernica.[3] Here there were disturbances of labor, sometimes pretty violent, in otherwise peaceful cities such as Chicago, Cleveland, Saint Louis. . . . This is the social background of the play. [*Music begins to play.*]

The play is memory. Being a memory play, it is dimly lighted, it is sentimental, it is not realistic. In memory everything seems to happen to music. That explains the fiddle in the wings.

I am the narrator of the play, and also a character in it. The other characters are my mother, Amanda, my sister, Laura, and a gentleman caller who appears in the final scenes. He is the most realistic character in the play, being an emissary from a world of reality that we were somehow set apart from. But since I have a poet's weakness for symbols, I am using this character also as a symbol; he is the long-delayed but always expected something that we live for.

There is a fifth character in the play who doesn't appear except in this larger-than-life-size photograph over the mantel. This is our

---

3. A small mountain town brutally bombed by Nazi Germany during the Spanish Civil War, waged between the Fascists, aided by Germany, and the Communists, aided by Stalinist Russia.

father who left us a long time ago. He was a telephone man who fell in love with long distances; he gave up his job with the telephone company and skipped the light fantastic out of town . . .

The last we heard of him was a picture postcard from Mazatlan, on the Pacific coast of Mexico, containing a message of two words: "Hello—Goodbye!" and no address.

I think the rest of the play will explain itself. . . .

[AMANDA's *voice becomes audible through the portieres.*]

[*Legend on screen:* "Ou sont les neiges."[4]]

[TOM *divides the portieres and enters the dining room.* AMANDA *and* LAURA *are seated at a drop-leaf table. Eating is indicated by gestures without food or utensils.* AMANDA *faces the audience.* TOM *and* LAURA *are seated in profile. The interior has lit up softly and through the scrim we see* AMANDA *and* LAURA *seated at the table.*]

AMANDA: [*Calling.*] Tom?

TOM: Yes, Mother.

AMANDA: We can't say grace until you come to the table!

TOM: Coming, Mother. [*He bows slightly and withdraws, reappearing a few moments later in his place at the table.*]

AMANDA: [*To her son.*] Honey, don't *push* with your *fingers.* If you have to push with something, the thing to push with is a crust of bread. And chew—chew! Animals have secretions in their stomachs which enable them to digest food without mastication, but human beings are supposed to chew their food before they swallow it down. Eat food leisurely, son, and really enjoy it. A well-cooked meal has lots of delicate flavors that have to be held in the mouth for appreciation. So chew your food and give your salivary glands a chance to function!

[TOM *deliberately lays his imaginary fork down and pushes his chair back from the table.*]

TOM: I haven't enjoyed one bite of this dinner because of your constant directions on how to eat it. It's you that make me rush through meals with your hawklike attention to every bite I take. Sickening—spoils my appetite—all this discussion of—animals' secretion—salivary glands—mastication!

4. Where are the snows? (French).

AMANDA: [*Lightly.*] Temperament like a Metropolitan[5] star! [TOM *rises and walks toward the living room.*]
  You're not excused from the table.
TOM: I'm getting a cigarette.
AMANDA: You smoke too much.
  [LAURA *rises.*]
LAURA: I'll bring in the blanc mange.
  [TOM *remains standing with his cigarette by the portieres.*]
AMANDA: [*Rising.*] No, sister, no, sister—you be the lady this time and I'll be the darky.[6]
LAURA: I'm already up.
AMANDA: Resume your seat, little sister—I want you to stay fresh and pretty—for gentlemen callers!
LAURA: [*Sitting down.*] I'm not expecting any gentlemen callers.
AMANDA: [*Crossing out to the kitchenette, airily.*] Sometimes they come when they are least expected! Why, I remember one Sunday afternoon in Blue Mountain— [*She enters the kitchenette.*]
TOM: I know what's coming!
LAURA: Yes. But let her tell it.
TOM: Again?
LAURA: She loves to tell it.
  [AMANDA *returns with a bowl of dessert.*]
AMANDA: One Sunday afternoon in Blue Mountain—your mother received—*seventeen!*—gentlemen callers! Why, sometimes there weren't chairs enough to accommodate them all. We had to send the nigger[7] over to bring in folding chairs from the parish house.
TOM: [*Remaining at the portieres.*] How did you entertain those gentlemen callers?
AMANDA: I understood the art of conversation!
TOM: I bet you could talk.
AMANDA: Girls in those days *knew* how to talk, I can tell you.
TOM: Yes?
  [*Image on screen:* AMANDA *as a girl on a porch, greeting callers.*]

---

  5. New York City's Metropolitan Opera.
  6. African American (here, servant); a degrading term.
  7. Though obviously insulting to African Americans, this term would not necessarily mark Amanda an extraordinary bigot. Her bigotry is quite ordinary among white southerners in the 1930s.

AMANDA: They knew how to entertain their gentlemen callers. It wasn't enough for a girl to be possessed of a pretty face and a graceful figure—although I wasn't slighted in either respect. She also needed to have a nimble wit and a tongue to meet all occasions.

TOM: What did you talk about?

AMANDA: Things of importance going on in the world! Never anything coarse or common or vulgar. [*She addresses* TOM *as though he were seated in the vacant chair at the table though he remains by the portieres. He plays this scene as though reading from a script.*] My callers were gentlemen—all! Among my callers were some of the most prominent young planters of the Mississippi Delta— planters and sons of planters!

[TOM *motions for music and a spot of light on* AMANDA. *Her eyes lift, her face glows, her voice becomes rich and elegiac.*]

[*Screen legend:* "Ou sont les neiges d'antan?"][8]

There was young Champ Laughlin who later became vice-president of the Delta Planters Bank. Hadley Stevenson who was drowned in Moon Lake and left his widow one hundred and fifty thousand in Government bonds. There were the Cutrere brothers, Wesley and Bates. Bates was one of my bright particular beaux! He got in a quarrel with that wild Wainwright boy. They shot it out on the floor of Moon Lake Casino. Bates was shot through the stomach. Died in the ambulance on his way to Memphis. His widow was also well provided-for, came into eight or ten thousand acres, that's all. She married him on the rebound—never loved her—carried my picture on him the night he died! And there was that boy that every girl in the Delta had set her cap for! That beautiful, brilliant young Fitzhugh boy from Greene County!

TOM: What did he leave his widow?

AMANDA: He never married! Gracious, you talk as though all of my old admirers had turned up their toes to the daisies!

TOM: Isn't this the first you've mentioned that still survives?

AMANDA: That Fitzhugh boy went North and made a fortune— came to be known as the Wolf of Wall Street! He had the Midas

8. Where are the snows of yesteryear? (French).

touch, whatever he touched turned to gold! And I could have been Mrs. Duncan J. Fitzhugh, mind you! But—I picked your *father!*

LAURA: [*Rising.*] Mother, let me clear the table.

AMANDA: No, dear, you go in front and study your typewriter chart. Or practice your shorthand a little. Stay fresh and pretty!—It's almost time for our gentlemen callers to start arriving. [*She flounces girlishly toward the kitchenette.*] How many do you suppose we're going to entertain this afternoon?

[TOM *throws down the paper and jumps up with a groan.*]

LAURA: [*Alone in the dining room.*] I don't believe we're going to receive any, Mother.

AMANDA: [*Reappearing, airily.*] What? No one—not one? You must be joking! [LAURA *nervously echoes her laugh. She slips in a fugitive manner through the half-open portieres and draws them gently behind her. A shaft of very clear light is thrown on her face against the faded tapestry of the curtains. Faintly the music of "The Glass Menagerie" is heard as she continues, lightly.*]

Not one gentleman caller? It can't be true! There must be a flood, there must have been a tornado!

LAURA: It isn't a flood, it's not a tornado, Mother. I'm just not popular like you were in Blue Mountain. . . . [TOM *utters another groan.* LAURA *glances at him with a faint, apologetic smile. Her voice catches a little.*] Mother's afraid I'm going to be an old maid.

[*The scene dims out with the "Glass Menagerie" music.*]

SCENE TWO

On the dark stage the screen is lighted with the image of blue roses. Gradually LAURA's *figure becomes apparent and the screen goes out. The music subsides.*

LAURA *is seated in the delicate ivory chair at the small claw-foot table. She wears a dress of soft violet material for a kimono—her hair is tied back from her forehead with a ribbon. She is washing and polishing her collection of glass.* AMANDA *appears on the fire escape steps. At the sound of her ascent,* LAURA *catches her breath, thrusts the bowl of ornaments away, and seats herself stiffly before the diagram of the typewriter keyboard as though it held her spellbound. Something has happened to* AMANDA. *It is written in her face as she climbs to the landing:*

a look that is grim and hopeless and a little absurd. She has on one of those cheap or imitation velvety-looking cloth coats with imitation fur collar. Her hat is five or six years old, one of those dreadful cloche hats that were worn in the late Twenties, and she is clutching an enormous black patent-leather pocketbook with nickel clasps and initials. This is her full-dress outfit, the one she usually wears to the D.A.R.[1] Before entering she looks through the door. She purses her lips, opens her eyes very wide, rolls them upward and shakes her head. Then she slowly lets herself in the door. Seeing her mother's expression LAURA *touches her lips with a nervous gesture.*

LAURA: Hello, Mother, I was— [*She makes a nervous gesture toward the chart on the wall.* AMANDA *leans against the shut door and stares at* LAURA *with a martyred look.*]

AMANDA: Deception? Deception? [*She slowly removes her hat and gloves, continuing the sweet suffering stare. She lets the hat and gloves fall on the floor—a bit of acting.*]

LAURA: [*Shakily.*] How was the D.A.R. meeting? [AMANDA *slowly opens her purse and removes a dainty white handkerchief which she shakes out delicately and delicately touches to her lips and nostrils.*] Didn't you go to the D.A.R. meeting, Mother?

AMANDA: [*Faintly, almost inaudibly.*] —No. —No. [*Then more forcibly.*] I did not have the strength—to go to the D.A.R. In fact, I did not have the courage! I wanted to find a hole in the ground and hide myself in it forever! [*She crosses slowly to the wall and removes the diagram of the typewriter keyboard. She holds it in front of her for a second, staring at it sweetly and sorrowfully—then bites her lips and tears it in two pieces.*]

LAURA: [*Faintly.*] Why did you do that, Mother? [AMANDA *repeats the same procedure with the chart of the Gregg Alphabet.*] Why are you—

AMANDA: Why? Why? How old are you, Laura?

LAURA: Mother, you know my age.

AMANDA: I thought that you were an adult; it seems that I was mistaken. [*She crosses slowly to the sofa and sinks down and stares at* LAURA.]

---

1. Daughters of the American Revolution; exclusive volunteer society for women descended from patriots of the Revolution.

LAURA: Please don't stare at me, Mother.

[AMANDA *closes her eyes and lowers her head. There is a ten-second pause.*]

AMANDA: What are we going to do, what is going to become of us, what is the future?

[*There is another pause.*]

LAURA: Has something happened, Mother? [AMANDA *draws a long breath, takes out the handkerchief again, goes through the dabbing process.*] Mother, has—something happened?

AMANDA: I'll be all right in a minute, I'm just bewildered— [*She hesitates.*] —by life. . . .

LAURA: Mother, I wish that you would tell me what's happened!

AMANDA: As you know, I was supposed to be inducted into my office at the D.A.R. this afternoon. [*Screen image*: A swarm of typewriters.] But I stopped off at Rubicam's Business College to speak to your teachers about your having a cold and ask them what progress they thought you were making down there.

LAURA: Oh. . . .

AMANDA: I went to the typing instructor and introduced myself as your mother. She didn't know who you were. "Wingfield," she said, "We don't have any such student enrolled at the school!"

I assured her she did, that you had been going to classes since early in January.

"I wonder," she said, "If you could be talking about that terribly shy little girl who dropped out of school after only a few days' attendance?"

"No," I said, "Laura, my daughter, has been going to school every day for the past six weeks!"

"Excuse me," she said. She took the attendance book out and there was your name, unmistakably printed, and all the dates you were absent until they decided that you had dropped out of school.

I still said, "No, there must have been some mistake! There must have been some mix-up in the records!"

And she said, "No—I remember her perfectly now. Her hands shook so that she couldn't hit the right keys! The first time we gave a speed test, she broke down completely—was sick at the stomach and almost had to be carried into the wash room! After that morning she never showed up any more. We phoned the house but never got any answer"—While I was working at Famous–Barr, I suppose, demonstrating those— [*She indicates a brassiere with her hands.*] Oh! I felt so weak I could barely keep on my feet! I had to sit down while they got me a glass of water! Fifty dollars' tuition, all of our plans—my hopes and ambitions for you—just gone up the spout, just gone up the spout like that. [LAURA *draws a long breath and gets awkwardly to her feet. She crosses to the Victrola and winds it up.*] What are you doing?

LAURA: Oh! [*She releases the handle and returns to her seat.*]

AMANDA: Laura, where have you been going when you've gone out pretending that you were going to business college?

LAURA: I've just been going out walking.

AMANDA: That's not true.

LAURA: It is. I just went walking.

AMANDA: Walking? Walking? In winter? Deliberately courting pneumonia in that light coat? Where did you walk to, Laura?

LAURA: All sorts of places—mostly in the park.

AMANDA: Even after you'd started catching that cold?

LAURA: It was the lesser of two evils, Mother. [*Screen image*: Winter scene in a park.] I couldn't go back there. I—threw up—on the floor!

AMANDA: From half past seven till after five every day you mean to tell me you walked around in the park, because you wanted to make me think that you were still going to Rubicam's Business College?

LAURA: It wasn't as bad as it sounds. I went inside places to get warmed up.

AMANDA: Inside where?

LAURA: I went in the art museum and the bird houses at the Zoo. I visited the penguins every day! Sometimes I did without lunch and went to the movies. Lately I've been spending most of my afternoons in the Jewel Box, that big glass house where they raise the tropical flowers.

AMANDA: You did all this to deceive me, just for deception? [LAURA *looks down.*] Why?

LAURA: Mother, when you're disappointed, you get that awful suffering look on your face, like the picture of Jesus' mother in the museum!

AMANDA: Hush!

LAURA: I couldn't face it.

[*There is a pause. A whisper of strings is heard. Legend on screen:* "The Crust of Humility."]

AMANDA: [*Hopelessly fingering the huge pocketbook.*] So what are we going to do the rest of our lives? Stay home and watch the parades go by? Amuse ourselves with the glass menagerie, darling? Eternally play those worn-out phonograph records your father left as a painful reminder of him? We won't have a business career—we've given that up because it gave us nervous indigestion! [*She laughs wearily.*] What is there left but dependency all our lives? I know so well what becomes of unmarried women who aren't prepared to occupy a position. I've seen such pitiful cases in the South—barely tolerated spinsters living upon the grudging patronage of sister's husband or brother's wife!—stuck away in some little mousetrap of a room—encouraged by one in-law to visit another—little birdlike women without any nest—eating the crust of humility all their life!

Is that the future that we've mapped out for ourselves? I swear it's the only alternative I can think of! [*She pauses.*] It isn't a very pleasant alternative, is it? [*She pauses again.*] Of course—some girls *do marry.* [LAURA *twists her hands nervously.*] Haven't you ever liked some boy?

LAURA: Yes, I liked one once. [*She rises.*] I came across his picture a while ago.

AMANDA: [*With some interest.*] He gave you his picture?

LAURA: No, it's in the yearbook.

AMANDA: [*Disappointed.*] Oh—a high school boy.

[*Screen image:* Jim as the high school hero bearing a silver cup.]

LAURA: Yes. His name was Jim. [*She lifts the heavy annual from the claw-foot table.*] Here he is in *The Pirates of Penzance.*

AMANDA: [*Absently.*] The what?

LAURA: The operetta the senior class put on. He had a wonderful voice and we sat across the aisle from each other Mondays,

Wednesday and Fridays in the Aud. Here he is with the silver cup for debating! See his grin?

AMANDA: [*Absently.*] He must have had a jolly disposition.

LAURA: He used to call me—Blue Roses.

[*Screen image: Blue roses.*]

AMANDA: Why did he call you such a name as that?

LAURA: When I had that attack of pleurosis[2]—he asked me what was the matter when I came back. I said pleurosis—he thought that I said Blue Roses! So that's what he always called me after that. Whenever he saw me, he'd holler, "Hello, Blue Roses!" I didn't care for the girl that he went out with. Emily Meisenbach. Emily was the best-dressed girl at Soldan. She never struck me, though, as being sincere. . . . It says in the Personal Section—they're engaged. That's—six years ago! They must be married by now.

AMANDA: Girls that aren't cut out for business careers usually wind up married to some nice man. [*She gets up with a spark of revival.*] Sister, that's what you'll do!

[LAURA *utters a startled, doubtful laugh. She reaches quickly for a piece of glass.*]

LAURA: But, Mother—

AMANDA: Yes? [*She goes over to the photograph.*]

LAURA: [*In a tone of frightened apology.*] I'm—crippled!

AMANDA: Nonsense! Laura, I've told you never, never to use that word. Why, you're not crippled, you just have a little defect—hardly noticeable, even! When people have some slight disadvantage like that, they cultivate other things to make up for it—develop charm—and vivacity—and—*charm!* That's all you have to do! [*She turns again to the photograph.*] One thing your father had *plenty of*—*was charm!*

[*The scene fades out with music.*]

SCENE THREE

Legend on screen: "After the fiasco—"

TOM *speaks from the fire escape landing.*

TOM: After the fiasco at Rubicam's Business College, the idea of getting a gentleman caller for Laura began to play a more and more

---

2. A lung condition.

important part in Mother's calculations. It became an obsession. Like some archetype of the universal unconscious, the image of the gentleman caller haunted our small apartment. . . . [*Screen image*: A young man at the door of a house with flowers.] An evening at home rarely passed without some allusion to this image, this specter, this hope. . . . Even when he wasn't mentioned, his presence hung in Mother's preoccupied look and in my sister's frightened, apologetic manner—hung like a sentence passed upon the Wingfields!

Mother was a woman of action as well as words. She began to take logical steps in the planned direction. Late that winter and in the early spring—realizing that extra money would be needed to properly feather the nest and plume the bird—she conducted a vigorous campaign on the telephone, roping in subscribers to one of those magazines for matrons called *The Homemaker's Companion*, the type of journal that features the serialized sublimations of ladies of letters who think in terms of delicate cuplike breasts, slim, tapering waists, rich, creamy thighs, eyes like wood smoke in autumn, fingers that soothe and caress like strains of music, bodies as powerful as Etruscan sculpture.[1]

[*Screen image:* The cover of a glamor magazine.]

[AMANDA *enters with the telephone on a long extension cord. She is spotlighted in the dim stage.*]

AMANDA: Ida Scott? This is Amanda Wingfield! We *missed* you at the D.A.R. last Monday! I said to myself: She's probably suffering with that sinus condition! How is that sinus condition?

Horrors! Heaven have mercy!—You're a Christian martyr, yes, that's what you are, a Christian martyr!

Well, I just now happened to notice that your subscription to the *Companion's* about to expire! Yes, it expires with the next issue, honey!—just when that wonderful new serial by Bessie Mae Hopper is getting off to such an exciting start. Oh, honey, it's something that you can't miss! You remember how *Gone with the Wind* took everybody by storm? You simply couldn't go out if you hadn't read it. All everybody *talked* was Scarlett O'Hara. Well, this is a book that critics already compare to *Gone with the Wind*. It's the

1. Stolid style of sculpture characteristic of pre-Roman Italy.

Gone with the Wind of the post-World-War generation!—What?—
Burning?—Oh, honey, don't let them burn, go take a look in the
oven and I'll hold the wire! Heavens—I think she's hung up!

[*The scene dims out.*]

[*Legend on screen*: "You think I'm in love with Continental
Shoemakers?"]

[*Before the lights come up again, the violent voices of* TOM *and*
AMANDA *are heard. They are quarreling behind the portieres. In
front of them stands* LAURA *with clenched hands and panicky expression. A clear pool of light is on her figure throughout this scene.*]

TOM: What in Christ's name am I—

AMANDA: [*Shrilly.*] Don't you use that—

TOM: —supposed to do!

AMANDA: —expression! Not in my—

TOM: Ohhh!

AMANDA: —presence! Have you gone out of your senses?

TOM: I have, that's true, *driven* out!

AMANDA: What is the matter with you, you—big—big—IDIOT!

TOM: Look!—I've got *no thing*, no single thing—

AMANDA: Lower your voice!

TOM: —in my life here that I can call my OWN! Everything is—

AMANDA: Stop that shouting!

TOM: Yesterday you confiscated my books! You had the nerve to—

AMANDA: I took that horrible novel back to the library—yes! That
hideous book by that insane Mr. Lawrence.[2] [TOM *laughs wildly.*]
I cannot control the output of diseased minds or people who
cater to them— [TOM *laughs still more wildly.*] BUT I WON'T AL-
LOW SUCH FILTH BROUGHT INTO MY HOUSE! No, no, no, no, no!

TOM: House, house! Who pays rent on it, who makes a slave of
himself to—

AMANDA: [*Fairly screeching.*] Don't you DARE to—

TOM: No, no, *I* mustn't say things! *I've* got to just—

AMANDA: Let me tell you—

TOM: I don't want to hear any more! [*He tears the portieres open. The
dining-room area is lit with a turgid smoky red glow. Now we see*

---

2. D(avid) H(erbert) Lawrence (1885–1930), English novelist notorious for his frank treatment of sex. *Lady Chatterley's Lover* (1928) was banned in America at the time Williams wrote
this play.

AMANDA; *her hair is in metal curlers and she is wearing a very old bathrobe, much too large for her slight figure, a relic of the faithless Mr. Wingfield. The upright typewriter now stands on the drop-leaf table, along with a wild disarray of manuscripts. The quarrel was probably precipitated by* AMANDA's *interruption of* TOM's *creative labor. A chair lies overthrown on the floor. Their gesticulating shadows are cast on the ceiling by the fiery glow.*]

AMANDA: You *will* hear more, you—

TOM: No, I won't hear more, I'm going out!

AMANDA: You come right back in—

TOM: Out, out, out! Because I'm—

AMANDA: Come back here, Tom Wingfield! I'm not through talking to you!

TOM: Oh, go—

LAURA: [*Desperately.*]—Tom!

AMANDA: You're going to listen, and no more insolence from you! I'm at the end of my patience!

    [*He comes back toward her.*]

TOM: What do you think I'm at? Aren't I supposed to have any patience to reach the end of, Mother? I know, I know. It seems unimportant to you, what I'm *doing*—what I *want* to do—having a little *difference* between them! You don't think that—

AMANDA: I think you've been doing things that you're ashamed of. That's why you act like this. I don't believe that you go every night to the movies. Nobody goes to the movies night after night. Nobody in their right minds goes to the movies as often as you pretend to. People don't go to the movies at nearly midnight, and movies don't let out at two A.M. Come in stumbling. Muttering to yourself like a maniac! You get three hours' sleep and then go to work. Oh, I can picture the way you're doing down there. Moping, doping, because you're in no condition.

TOM: [*Wildly.*] No, I'm in no condition!

AMANDA: What right have you got to jeopardize your job? Jeopardize the security of us all? How do you think we'd manage if you were—

TOM: Listen! You think I'm crazy about the *warehouse?* [*He bends fiercely toward her slight figure.*] You think I'm in love with the Continental Shoemakers? You think I want to spend fifty-five *years* down there in that—*celotex interior!* with—*fluorescent*— *tubes!* Look! I'd rather somebody picked up a crowbar and battered out my brains—than go back mornings! I *go!* Every time you come in yelling that Goddamn *"Rise and Shine!" "Rise and Shine!"* I say to myself, "How *lucky dead* people are!" But I get up. I *go!* For sixty-five dollars a month I give up all that I dream of doing and being *ever!* And you say self—*self's* all I ever think of. Why, listen, if self is what I thought of, Mother, I'd be where he is—GONE! [*He points to his father's picture.*] As far as the system of transportation reaches! [*He starts past her. She grabs his arm.*] Don't grab at me, Mother!

AMANDA: Where are you going?

TOM: I'm going to the *movies!*

AMANDA: I don't believe that lie!

    [TOM *crouches toward her, overtowering her tiny figure. She backs away, gasping.*]

TOM: I'm going to opium dens! Yes, opium dens, dens of vice and criminals' hangouts, Mother. I've joined the Hogan Gang, I'm a hired assassin, I carry a tommy gun in a violin case! I run a string of cat houses in the Valley! They call me Killer, Killer Wingfield, I'm leading a double-life, a simple, honest warehouse worker by day, by night a dynamic *czar* of the *underworld, Mother.* I go to gambling casinos, I spin away fortunes on the roulette table! I wear a patch over one eye and a false mustache, sometimes I put on green whiskers. On those occasions they call me—*El Diablo!* Oh, I could tell you many things to make you sleepless! My enemies plan to dynamite this place. They're going to blow us all sky-high some night! I'll be glad, very happy, and so will you! You'll go up, up on a broomstick, over Blue Mountain with seventeen gentlemen callers! You ugly—babbling old—*witch. . . .* [*He goes through a series of violent, clumsy movements, seizing his overcoat, lunging to the door, pulling it fiercely open. The women watch him, aghast. His arm catches in the sleeve of the coat as he struggles to pull it on. For a moment he is pinioned by the bulky garment. With an outraged groan he tears the coat off again, splitting the shoulder of it, and hurls it across the room. It strikes against the shelf of* LAURA's *glass collection, and there is a tinkle of shattering glass.* LAURA *cries out as if wounded.*]

    [*Music.*]

[*Screen legend:* "The Glass Menagerie."]

LAURA: [*Shrilly.*] *My glass!*—menagerie. . . . [*She covers her face and turns away.*]

[*But* AMANDA *is still stunned and stupefied by the "ugly witch" so that she barely notices this occurrence. Now she recovers her speech.*]

AMANDA: [*In an awful voice.*] I won't speak to you—until you apologize! [*She crosses through the portieres and draws them together behind her.* TOM *is left with* LAURA. LAURA *clings weakly to the mantel with her face averted.* TOM *stares at her stupidly for a moment. Then he crosses to the shelf. He drops awkwardly on his knees to collect the fallen glass, glancing at* LAURA *as if he would speak but couldn't.*]

[*"The Glass Menagerie" music steals in as the scene dims out.*]

SCENE FOUR

The interior of the apartment is dark. There is a faint light in the alley. A deep-voiced bell in a church is tolling the hour of five.

TOM *appears at the top of the alley. After each solemn boom of the bell in the tower, he shakes a little noisemaker or rattle as if to express the tiny spasm of man in contrast to the sustained power and dignity of the Almighty. This and the unsteadiness of his advance make it evident that he has been drinking. As he climbs the few steps to the fire escape landing light steals up inside.* LAURA *appears in the front room in a nightdress. She notices that* TOM's *bed is empty.* TOM *fishes in his pockets for his door key, removing a motley assortment of articles in the search, including a shower of movie ticket stubs and an empty bottle. At last he finds the key, but just as he is about to insert it, it slips from his fingers. He strikes a match and crouches below the door.*

TOM: [*Bitterly.*] One crack—and it falls through!

[LAURA *opens the door.*]

LAURA: Tom! Tom, what are you doing?

TOM: Looking for a door key.

LAURA: Where have you been all this time?

TOM: I have been to the movies.

LAURA: All this time at the movies?

TOM: There was a very long program. There was a Garbo[1] picture and a Mickey Mouse and a travelogue and a newsreel and a pre-

---

1. Greta Garbo (1905–1990), American (Swedish-born) movie actor.

view of coming attractions. And there was an organ solo and a collection for the Milk Fund—simultaneously—which ended up in a terrible fight between a fat lady and an usher!

LAURA: [*Innocently.*] Did you have to stay through everything?

TOM: Of course! And, oh, I forgot! There was a big stage show! The headliner on this stage show was Malvolio the Magician. He performed wonderful tricks, many of them, such as pouring water back and forth between pitchers. First it turned to wine and then it turned to beer and then it turned to whisky. I know it was whisky it finally turned into because he needed somebody to come up out of the audience to help him, and I came up—both shows! It was Kentucky Straight Bourbon. A very generous fellow, he gave souvenirs. [*He pulls from his back pocket a shimmering rainbow-colored scarf.*] He gave me this. This is his magic scarf. You can have it, Laura. You wave it over a canary cage and you get a bowl of goldfish. You wave it over the goldfish bowl and they fly away canaries. . . . But the wonderfullest trick of all was the coffin trick. We nailed him into a coffin and he got out of the coffin without removing one nail. [*He has come inside.*] There is a trick that would come in handy for me—get me out of this two-by-four situation! [*He flops onto the bed and starts removing his shoes.*]

LAURA: Tom—shhh!

TOM: What're you shushing me for?

LAURA: You'll wake up Mother.

TOM: Goody, goody! Pay 'er back for all those "Rise an' Shines." [*He lies down, groaning.*] You know it don't take much intelligence to get yourself into a nailed-up coffin, Laura. But who in hell ever got himself out of one without removing one nail?

[*As if in answer, the father's grinning photograph lights up. The scene dims out.*]

[*Immediately following, the church bell is heard striking six. At the sixth stroke the alarm clock goes off in* AMANDA's *room, and after a few moments we hear her calling: "Rise and Shine! Rise and Shine! Laura, go tell your brother to rise and shine!"*]

TOM: [*Sitting up slowly.*] I'll rise—but I won't shine.

[*The light increases.*]

AMANDA: Laura, tell your brother his coffee is ready.

[LAURA *slips into the front room.*]

LAURA: Tom!—It's nearly seven. Don't make Mother nervous. [*He stares at her stupidly.*] [*Beseechingly.*] Tom, speak to Mother this morning. Make up with her, apologize, speak to her!

TOM: She won't to me. It's her that started not speaking.

LAURA: If you just say you're sorry she'll start speaking.

TOM: Her not speaking—is that such a tragedy?

LAURA: Please—please!

AMANDA: [*Calling from the kitchenette.*] Laura, are you going to do what I asked you to do, or do I have to get dressed and go out myself?

LAURA: Going, going—soon as I get on my coat! [*She pulls on a shapeless felt hat with a nervous, jerky movement, pleadingly glancing at* TOM. *She rushes awkwardly for her coat. The coat is one of* AMANDA*'s, inaccurately made-over, the sleeves too short for* LAURA.] Butter and what else?

AMANDA: [*Entering from the kitchenette.*] Just butter. Tell them to charge it.

LAURA: Mother, they make such faces when I do that.

AMANDA: Sticks and stones can break our bones, but the expression on Mr. Garfinkel's face won't harm us! Tell your brother his coffee is getting cold.

LAURA: [*At the door.*] Do what I asked you, will you, will you, Tom? [*He looks sullenly away.*]

AMANDA: Laura, go now or just don't go at all!

LAURA: [*Rushing out.*] Going—going! [*A second later she cries out.* TOM *springs up and crosses to the door.* TOM *opens the door.*]

TOM: Laura?

LAURA: I'm all right. I slipped, but I'm all right.

AMANDA: [*Peering anxiously after her.*] If anyone breaks a leg on those fire-escape steps, the landlord ought to be sued for every cent he possesses! [*She shuts the door. Now she remembers she isn't speaking to* TOM *and returns to the other room.*]

   [*As* TOM *comes listlessly for his coffee, she turns her back to him and stands rigidly facing the window on the gloomy gray vault of the areaway. Its light on her face with its aged but childish features is cruelly sharp, satirical as a Daumier[2] print.*]

___

2. Honoré Daumier, nineteenth-century French caricaturist and painter.

[*The music of "Ave Maria" is heard softly.*]

[TOM *glances sheepishly but sullenly at her averted figure and slumps at the table. The coffee is scalding hot; he sips it and gasps and spits it back in the cup. At his gasp,* AMANDA *catches her breath and half turns. Then she catches herself and turns back to the window.* TOM *blows on his coffee, glancing sidewise at his mother. She clears her throat.* TOM *clears his. He starts to rise, sinks back down again, scratches his head, clears his throat again.* AMANDA *coughs.* TOM *raises his cup in both hands to blow on it, his eyes staring over the rim of it at his mother for several moments. Then he slowly sets the cup down and awkwardly and hesitantly rises from the chair.*]

TOM: [*Hoarsely.*] Mother. I—I apologize, Mother.

[AMANDA *draws a quick, shuddering breath. Her face works grotesquely. She breaks into childlike tears.*] I'm sorry for what I said, for everything that I said, I didn't mean it.

AMANDA: [*Sobbingly.*] *My devotion has made me a witch and so I make myself hateful to my children!*

TOM: *No*, you *don't.*

AMANDA: I worry so much, don't sleep, it makes me nervous!

TOM: [*Gently.*] I understand that.

AMANDA: I've had to put up a solitary battle all these years. But you're my right-hand bower! Don't fall down, don't fail!

TOM: [*Gently.*] I try, Mother.

AMANDA: [*With great enthusiasm.*] Try and you will *succeed*! [*The notion makes her breathless.*] Why, you—you're just *full* of natural endowments! Both of my children—they're *unusual* children! Don't you think I know it? I'm so—*proud*! Happy and—feel I've—so much to be thankful for but—promise me one thing, son!

TOM: What, Mother?

AMANDA: Promise, son, you'll—never be a drunkard!

TOM: [*Turns to her grinning.*] I will never be a drunkard, Mother.

AMANDA: That's what frightened me so, that you'd be drinking! Eat a bowl of Purina!

TOM: Just coffee, Mother.

AMANDA: Shredded wheat biscuit?

TOM: No. No, Mother, just coffee.

AMANDA: You can't put in a day's work on an empty stomach. You've got ten minutes—don't gulp! Drinking too-hot liquids makes cancer of the stomach. . . . Put cream in.

TOM: No, thank you.

AMANDA: To cool it.

TOM: No! No, thank you, I want it black.

AMANDA: I know, but it's not good for you. We have to do all that we can to build ourselves up. In these trying times we live in, all that we have to cling to is—each other. . . . That's why it's so important to—Tom, I—I sent out your sister so I could discuss something with you. If you hadn't spoken I would have spoken to you. [*She sits down.*]

TOM: [*gently.*] What is it, Mother, that you want to discuss?

AMANDA: *Laura!*

[TOM *puts his cup down slowly.*]
[*Legend on screen:* "Laura." *Music:* "*The Glass Menagerie.*"]

TOM:—Oh.—Laura . . .

AMANDA: [*Touching his sleeve.*] You know how Laura is. So quiet but—still water runs deep! She notices things and I think she—broods about them. [*Tom looks up.*] A few days ago I came in and she was crying.

TOM: What about?

AMANDA: You.

TOM: Me?

AMANDA: She has an idea that you're not happy here.

TOM: What gave her that idea?

AMANDA: What gives her any idea? However, you do act strangely. I—I'm not criticizing, understand *that*! I know your ambitions do not lie in the warehouse, that like everybody in the whole wide world—you've had to—make sacrifices, but—Tom—Tom—life's not easy, it calls for—Spartan endurance! There's so many things in my heart that I cannot describe to you! I've never told you but I—*loved* your father. . . .

TOM: [*Gently.*] I know that, Mother.

AMANDA: And you—when I see you taking after his ways! Staying out late—and—well, you *had* been drinking the night you were in that—terrifying condition! Laura says that you hate the apartment and that you go out nights to get away from it! Is that true, Tom?

TOM: No. You say there's so much in your heart that you can't describe to me. That's true of me, too. There's so much in my heart that I can't describe to *you*! So let's respect each other's—

AMANDA: But, why—*why*, Tom—are you always so *restless*? Where do you *go* to, nights?

TOM: I—go to the movies.

AMANDA: Why do you go to the movies so much, Tom?

TOM: I go to the movies because—I like adventure. Adventure is something I don't have much of at work, so I go to the movies.

AMANDA: But, Tom, you go to the movies *entirely* too *much*!

TOM: I like a lot of adventure.

> [AMANDA *looks baffled, then hurt. As the familiar inquisition resumes,* TOM *becomes hard and impatient again.* AMANDA *slips back into her querulous attitude toward him.*]
> [*Image on screen*: A sailing vessel with Jolly Roger.]

AMANDA: Most young men find adventure in their careers.

TOM: Then most young men are not employed in a warehouse.

AMANDA: The world is full of young men employed in warehouses and offices and factories.

TOM: Do all of them find adventure in their careers?

AMANDA: They do or they do without it! Not everybody has a craze for adventure.

TOM: Man is by instinct a lover, a hunter, a fighter, and none of those instincts are given much play at the warehouse!

AMANDA: Man is by instinct! Don't quote instinct to me! Instinct is something that people have got away from! It belongs to animals! Christian adults don't want it!

TOM: What do Christian adults want, then, Mother?

AMANDA: Superior things! Things of the mind and the spirit! Only animals have to satisfy instincts! Surely your aims are somewhat higher than theirs! Than monkeys—pigs—

TOM: I reckon they're not.

AMANDA: You're joking. However, that isn't what I wanted to discuss.

TOM: [*Rising.*] I haven't much time.

AMANDA: [*Pushing his shoulders.*] Sit down.

TOM: You want me to punch in red at the warehouse, Mother?

AMANDA: You have five minutes. I want to talk about Laura.

[*Screen legend:* "Plans and Provisions."]

TOM: All right! What about Laura?

AMANDA: We have to be making some plans and provisions for her. She's older than you, two years, and nothing has happened. She just drifts along doing nothing. It frightens me terribly how she just drifts along.

TOM: I guess she's the type that people call home girls.

AMANDA: There's no such type, and if there is, it's a pity! That is unless the home is hers, with a husband!

TOM: What?

AMANDA: Oh, I can see the handwriting on the wall as plain as I see the nose in front of my face! It's terrifying! More and more you remind me of your father! He was out all hours without explanation!—Then *left*! *Goodbye!* And me with the bag to hold. I saw that letter you got from the Merchant Marine. I know what you're dreaming of. I'm not standing here blindfolded. [*She pauses.*] Very well, then. Then *do* it! But not till there's somebody to take your place.

TOM: What do you mean?

AMANDA: I mean that as soon as Laura has got somebody to take care of her, married, a home of her own, independent—why, then you'll be free to go wherever you please, on land, on sea, whichever way the wind blows you! But until that time you've got to look out for your sister. I don't say me because I'm old and don't matter! I say for your sister because she's young and dependent.

I put her in business college—a dismal failure! Frightened her so it made her sick at the stomach. I took her over to the Young People's League at the church. Another fiasco. She spoke to nobody, nobody spoke to her. Now all she does is fool with those pieces of glass and play those worn-out records. What kind of a life is that for a girl to lead?

TOM: What can I do about it?

AMANDA: Overcome selfishness! Self, self, self is all that you ever think of! [TOM *springs up and crosses to get his coat. It is ugly and bulky. He pulls on a cap with earmuffs.*] Where is your muffler? Put your wool muffler on! [*He snatches it angrily from the closet, tosses it around his neck and pulls both ends tight.*] Tom! I haven't said what I had in mind to ask you.

TOM: I'm too late to—

AMANDA: [*Catching his arm—very importunately; then shyly.*] Down at the warehouse, aren't there some—nice young men?

TOM: No!

AMANDA: There *must* be—*some . . .*

TOM: Mother— [*He gestures.*]

AMANDA: Find out one that's clean-living—doesn't drink and ask him out for sister!

TOM: What?

AMANDA: For *sister!* To *meet!* Get *acquainted!*

TOM: [*Stamping to the door.*] Oh, my *go-osh!*

AMANDA: Will you? [*He opens the door. She says, imploringly.*] Will you? [*He starts down the fire escape.*] Will you? *Will* you, dear?

TOM: [*Calling back.*] Yes!

[AMANDA *closes the door hesitantly and with a troubled but faintly hopeful expression.*]

[*Screen image*: The cover of a glamor magazine.]

[*The spotlight picks up* AMANDA *at the phone.*]

AMANDA: Ella Cartwright? This is Amanda Wingfield! How are you, honey? How is that kidney condition? [*There is a five-second pause.*] Horrors! [*There is another pause.*] You're a Christian martyr, yes, honey, that's what you are, a Christian martyr! Well, I just now happened to notice in my little red book that your subscription to the *Companion* has just run out! I knew that you wouldn't want to miss out on the wonderful serial starting in this new issue. It's by Bessie Mae Hopper, the first thing she's written since *Honeymoon for Three.* Wasn't that a strange and interesting story? Well, this one is even lovelier, I believe. It has a sophisticated, society background. It's all about the horsey set on Long Island!

[*The light fades out.*]

SCENE FIVE

Legend on the screen: "Annunciation."[1]

Music is heard as the light slowly comes on.

It is early dusk of a spring evening. Supper has just been finished in the Wingfield apartment. AMANDA *and* LAURA *in light-colored dresses, are removing dishes from the table in the dining room, which is shad-*

---

1. In Christianity, the Virgin Mary's acceptance of God's plan for her to give birth to Jesus.

owy, *their movements formalized almost as a dance or ritual, their moving forms as pale and silent as moths.* TOM, *in white shirt and trousers, rises from the table and crosses toward the fire escape.*

AMANDA: [*As he passes her.*] Son, will you do me a favor?

TOM: What?

AMANDA: Comb your hair! You look so pretty when your hair is combed! [TOM *slouches on the sofa with the evening paper. Its enormous headline reads: "Franco[2] Triumphs."*] There is only one respect in which I would like you to emulate your father.

TOM: What respect is that?

AMANDA: The care he always took of his appearance. He never allowed himself to look untidy. [*He throws down the paper and crosses to the fire escape.*] Where are you going?

TOM: I'm going out to smoke.

AMANDA: You smoke too much. A pack a day at fifteen cents a pack. How much would that amount to in a month? Thirty times fifteen is how much, Tom? Figure it out and you will be astounded at what you could save. Enough to give you a night-school course in accounting at Washington U.! Just think what a wonderful thing that would be for you, son!

[TOM *is unmoved by the thought.*]

TOM: I'd rather smoke. [*He steps out on the landing, letting the screen door slam.*]

AMANDA: [*Sharply.*] I know! That's the tragedy of it. . . . [*Alone, she turns to look at her husband's picture.*]

[*Dance music: "The World Is Waiting for the Sunrise!"*]

TOM: [*To the audience.*] Across the alley from us was the Paradise Dance Hall. On evenings in spring the windows and doors were open and the music came outdoors. Sometimes the lights were turned out except for a large glass sphere that hung from the ceiling. It would turn slowly about and filter the dusk with delicate rainbow colors. Then the orchestra played a waltz or a tango, something that had a slow and sensuous rhythm. Couples would come outside, to the relative privacy of the alley. You could see them kissing behind ash pits[3] and telephone poles. This was the

---

2. General Francisco Franco (1892–1975)   3. Garbage receptacles.
led the Fascists in the Spanish Civil War.

compensation for lives that passed like mine, without any change or adventure. Adventure and change were imminent in this year. They were waiting around the corner for all these kids. Suspended in the mist over Berchtesgaden, caught in the folds of Chamberlain's[4] umbrella. In Spain there was Guernica! But here there was only hot swing music and liquor, dance halls, bars, and movies, and sex that hung in the gloom like a chandelier and flooded the world with brief, deceptive rainbows. . . . All the world was waiting for bombardments!

[AMANDA *turns from the picture and comes outside.*]

AMANDA: [*Sighing.*] A fire escape landing's a poor excuse for a porch. [*She spreads a newspaper on a step and sits down, gracefully and demurely as if she were settling into a swing on a Mississippi veranda.*] What are you looking at?

TOM: The moon.

AMANDA: Is there a moon this evening?

TOM: It's rising over Garfinkel's Delicatessen.

AMANDA: So it is! A little silver slipper of a moon. Have you made a wish on it yet?

TOM: Um-hum.

AMANDA: What did you wish for?

TOM: That's a secret.

AMANDA: A secret, huh? Well, I won't tell mine either. I will be just as mysterious as you.

TOM: I bet I can guess what yours is.

AMANDA: Is my head so transparent?

TOM: You're not a sphinx.

AMANDA: No, I don't have secrets. I'll tell you what I wished for on the moon. Success and happiness for my precious children! I wish for that whenever there's a moon, and when there isn't a moon, I wish for it, too.

TOM: I thought perhaps you wished for a gentleman caller.

AMANDA: Why do you say that?

TOM: Don't you remember asking me to fetch one?

AMANDA: I remember suggesting that it would be nice for your sis-

4. Neville Chamberlain (1869–1940), prime minister of Great Britain, best known for capitulating to Adolf Hitler's expansionist policies. *Berchtesgaden:* resort town in Southern Germany favored by Hitler.

ter if you brought home some nice young man from the warehouse. I think that I've made that suggestion more than once.

TOM: Yes, you have made it repeatedly.

AMANDA: Well?

TOM: We are going to have one.

AMANDA: *What?*

TOM: A gentleman caller!

[*The annunciation is celebrated with music.*]

[AMANDA *rises.*]

[*Image on screen*: A caller with a bouquet.]

AMANDA: You mean you have asked some nice young man to come
over?

TOM: Yep. I've asked him to dinner.

AMANDA: You really did?

TOM: I did!

AMANDA: You did, and did he—*accept?*

TOM: He did!

AMANDA: Well, well—well, well! That's—lovely!

TOM: I thought that you would be pleased.

AMANDA: It's definite then?

TOM: Very definite.

AMANDA: Soon?

TOM: Very soon.

AMANDA: For heaven's sake, stop putting on and tell me some
things, will you?

TOM: What things do you want me to tell you?

AMANDA: *Naturally* I would like to know when he's *coming!*

TOM: He's coming tomorrow.

AMANDA: *Tomorrow?*

TOM: Yep. Tomorrow.

AMANDA: But, Tom!

TOM: Yes, Mother?

AMANDA: Tomorrow gives me no time!

TOM: Time for what?

AMANDA: Preparations! Why didn't you phone me at once, as soon
as you asked him, the minute that he accepted? Then, don't you
see, I could have been getting ready!

TOM: You don't have to make any fuss.

AMANDA: Oh, Tom, Tom, Tom, of course I have to make a fuss! I want things nice, not sloppy! Not thrown together. I'll certainly have to do some fast thinking, won't I?

TOM: I don't see why you have to think at all.

AMANDA: You just don't know. We can't have a gentleman caller in a pigsty! All my wedding silver has to be polished, the monogrammed table linen ought to be laundered! The windows have to be washed and fresh curtains put up. And how about clothes? We have to *wear* something, don't we?

TOM: Mother, this boy is no one to make a fuss over!

AMANDA: Do you realize he's the first young man we've introduced to your sister? It's terrible, dreadful, disgraceful that poor little sister has never received a single gentleman caller! Tom, come inside! [*She opens the screen door.*]

TOM: What for?

AMANDA: I want to ask you some things.

TOM: If you're going to make such a fuss, I'll call it off, I'll tell him not to come!

AMANDA: You certainly won't do anything of the kind. Nothing offends people worse than broken engagements. It simply means I'll have to work like a Turk! We won't be brilliant, but we will pass inspection. Come on inside. [TOM *follows her inside, groaming.*] Sit down.

TOM: Any particular place you would like me to sit?

AMANDA: Thank heavens I've got that new sofa! I'm also making payments on a floor lamp I'll have sent out! And put the chintz covers on, they'll brighten things up! Of course I'd hoped to have these walls re-papered. . . . What is the young man's name?

TOM: His name is O'Connor.

AMANDA: That, of course, means fish—tomorrow is Friday![5] I'll have that salmon loaf—with Durkee's dressing! What does he do? He works at the warehouse?

TOM: Of course! How else would I—

AMANDA: Tom, he—doesn't drink?

TOM: Why do you ask me that?

5. O'Connor, an Irish name, suggests that Tom's friend is Catholic. Before the 1960s, many Catholics abstained from meat on Fridays.

AMANDA: Your father *did*!

TOM: Don't get started on that!

AMANDA: He *does* drink, then?

TOM: Not that I know of!

AMANDA: Make sure, be certain! The last thing I want for my daughter's a boy who drinks!

TOM: Aren't you being a little bit premature? Mr. O'Connor has not yet appeared on the scene!

AMANDA: But will tomorrow. To meet your sister, and what do I know about his character? Nothing! Old maids are better off than wives of drunkards!

TOM: Oh, my God!

AMANDA: Be still!

TOM: [*Leaning forward to whispers.*] Lots of fellows meet girls whom they don't marry!

AMANDA: Oh, talk sensibly, Tom—and don't be sarcastic! [*She has gotten a hairbrush.*]

TOM: What are you doing?

AMANDA: I'm brushing that cowlick down! [*She attacks his hair with the brush.*] What is this young man's position at the warehouse?

TOM: [*Submitting grimly to the brush and the interrogation.*] This young man's position is that of a shipping clerk, Mother.

AMANDA: Sounds to me like a fairly responsible job, the sort of a job *you* would be in if you just had more *get-up*. What is his salary? Have you any idea?

TOM: I would judge it to be approximately eighty-five dollars a month.

AMANDA: Well—not princely, but—

TOM: Twenty more than I make.

AMANDA: Yes, how well I know! But for a family man, eighty-five dollars a month is not much more than you can just get by on. . . .

TOM: Yes, but Mr. O'Connor is not a family man.

AMANDA: He might be, mightn't he? Some time in the future?

TOM: I see. Plans and provisions.

AMANDA: You are the only young man that I know of who ignores the fact that the future becomes the present, the present the past, and the past turns into everlasting regret if you don't plan for it!

TOM: I will think that over and see what I can make of it.

AMANDA: Don't be supercilious with your mother! Tell me some more about this—what do you call him?

TOM: James D. O'Connor. The D. is for Delaney.

AMANDA: Irish on *both* sides! *Gracious!* And doesn't drink?

TOM: Shall I call him up and ask him right this minute?

AMANDA: The only way to find out about those things is to make discreet inquiries at the proper moment. When I was a girl in Blue Mountain and it was suspected that a young man drank, the girl whose attentions he had been receiving, if any girl *was*, would sometimes speak to the minister of his church, or rather her father would if her father was living, and sort of feel him out on the young man's character. That is the way such things are discreetly handled to keep a young woman from making a tragic mistake!

TOM: Then how did you happen to make a tragic mistake?

AMANDA: That innocent look of your father's had everyone fooled! He *smiled*—the world was *enchanted*! No girl can do worse than put herself at the mercy of a handsome appearance! I hope that Mr. O'Connor is not too good-looking.

TOM: No, he's not too good-looking. He's covered with freckles and hasn't too much of a nose.

AMANDA: He's not right-down homely, though?

TOM: Not right-down homely. Just medium homely, I'd say.

AMANDA: Character's what to look for in a man.

TOM: That's what I've always said, Mother.

AMANDA: You've never said anything of the kind and I suspect you would never give it a thought.

TOM: Don't be so suspicious of me.

AMANDA: At least I hope he's the type that's up and coming.

TOM: I think he really goes in for self-improvement.

AMANDA: What reason have you to think so?

TOM: He goes to night school.

AMANDA: [*Beaming.*] Splendid! What does he do, I mean study?

TOM: Radio engineering and public speaking!

AMANDA: Then he has visions of being advanced in the world! Any young man who studies public speaking is aiming to have an executive job some day! And radio engineering? A thing for the future! Both of these facts are very illuminating. Those are the sort of things that a mother should know concerning any young man who comes to call on her daughter. Seriously or—not.

TOM: One little warning. He doesn't know about Laura. I didn't let on that we had dark ulterior motives. I just said, why don't you come and have dinner with us? He said okay and that was the whole conversation.

AMANDA: I bet it was! You're eloquent as an oyster. However, he'll know about Laura when he gets here. When he sees how lovely and sweet and pretty she is, he'll thank his lucky stars he was asked to dinner.

TOM: Mother, you mustn't expect too much of Laura.

AMANDA: What do you mean?

TOM: Laura seems all those things to you and me because she's ours and we love her. We don't even notice she's crippled any more.

AMANDA: Don't say crippled! You know that I never allow that word to be used!

TOM: But face facts, Mother. She is and—that's not all—

AMANDA: What do you mean "not all"?

TOM: Laura is very different from other girls.

AMANDA: I think the difference is all to her advantage.

TOM: Not quite all—in the eyes of others—strangers—she's terribly shy and lives in a world of her own and those things make her seem a little peculiar to people outside the house.

AMANDA: Don't say peculiar.

TOM: Face the facts. She is.

[*The dance hall music changes to a tango that has a minor and somewhat ominous tone.*]

AMANDA: In what way is she peculiar—may I ask?

TOM: [*Gently.*] She lives in a world of her own—a world of little glass ornaments, Mother. . . . [*He gets up.* AMANDA *remains holding the brush, looking at him, troubled.*] She plays old phonograph records and—that's about all— [*He glances at himself in the mirror and crosses to the door.*]

AMANDA: [*Sharply.*] Where are you going?

TOM: I'm going to the movies. [*He goes out the screen door.*]

AMANDA: Not to the movies, every night to the movies! [*She follows quickly to the screen door.*] I don't believe you always go to the movies! [*He is gone.* AMANDA *looks worriedly after him for a mo-*

ment. Then vitality and optimism return and she turns from the door, crossing to the portieres.] Laura! Laura! [LAURA *answers from the kitchenette.*]

LAURA: Yes, Mother.

AMANDA: Let those dishes go and come in front! [LAURA *appears with a dish towel.* AMANDA *speaks to her gaily.*] Laura, come here and make a wish on the moon!

[*Screen image:* The Moon.]

LAURA: [*Entering.*] Moon—moon?

AMANDA: A little silver slipper of a moon. Look over your left shoulder, Laura, and make a wish! [LAURA *looks faintly puzzled as if called out of sleep.* AMANDA *seizes her shoulders and turns her at an angle by the door.*] Now! Now, darling, *wish*!

LAURA: What shall I wish for, Mother?

AMANDA: [*Her voice trembling and her eyes suddenly filling with tears.*] Happiness! Good fortune!

[*The sound of the violin rises and the stage dims out.*]

SCENE SIX

The light comes up on the fire escape landing. TOM *is leaning against the grill, smoking.*

[*Screen image:* The high school hero.]

TOM: And so the following evening I brought Jim home to dinner. I had known Jim slightly in high school. In high school Jim was a hero. He had tremendous Irish good nature and vitality with the scrubbed and polished look of white chinaware. He seemed to move in a continual spotlight. He was a star in basketball, captain of the debating club, president of the senior class and the glee club and he sang the male lead in the annual light operas. He was always running or bounding, never just walking. He seemed always at the point of defeating the law of gravity. He was shooting with such velocity through his adolescence that you would logically expect him to arrive at nothing short of the White House by the time he was thirty. But Jim apparently ran into more interference after his graduation from Soldan. His speed had definitely slowed. Six years after he left high school he was holding a job that wasn't much better than mine. [*Screen image*: The Clerk.] He was the only one at the warehouse with whom I was on friendly terms. I was valuable to him as someone who could remember his former glory, who had seen him win basketball games and the silver cup in debating. He knew of my secret practice of retiring to a cabinet of the washroom to work on poems when business was slack in the warehouse. He called me Shakespeare. And while the other boys in the warehouse regarded me with suspicious hostility, Jim took a humorous attitude toward me. Gradually his attitude affected the others, their hostility wore off and they also began to smile at me as people smile at an oddly fashioned dog who trots across their path at some distance.

I knew that Jim and Laura had known each other at Soldan, and I had heard Laura speak admiringly of his voice. I didn't know if Jim remembered her or not. In high school Laura had been as unobtrusive as Jim had been astonishing. If he did remember Laura, it was not as my sister, for when I asked him to dinner, he grinned and said, "You know, Shakespeare, I never thought of you as having folks!"

He was about to discover that I did. . . .

[*Legend on screen:* "The accent of a coming foot."]

[*The light dims out on* TOM *and comes up in the Wingfield living room—a delicate lemony light. It is about five on a Friday evening of late spring which comes "scattering poems in the sky."*]

[AMANDA *has worked like a Turk in preparation for the gentleman caller. The results are astonishing. The new floor lamp with its rose silk shade is in place, a colored paper lantern conceals the broken light fixture in the ceiling, new billowing white curtains are at the windows, chintz[1] covers are on the chairs and sofa, a pair of new sofa pillows make their initial appearance. Open boxes and tissue paper are scattered on the floor.*]

[LAURA *stands in the middle of the room with lifted arms while* AMANDA *crouches before her, adjusting the hem of a new dress, devout and ritualistic. The dress is colored and designed by memory. The arrangement of* LAURA'S *hair is changed; it is softer and more becoming. A fragile, unearthly prettiness has come out in* LAURA: *she is like a piece of translucent glass touched by light, given a momentary radiance, not actual, not lasting.*]

---

1. A colorful, printed fabric, often glazed.

AMANDA: [*Impatiently.*] Why are you trembling?

LAURA: Mother, you've made me so nervous!

AMANDA: How have I made you nervous?

LAURA: By all this fuss! You make it seem so important!

AMANDA: I don't understand you, Laura. You couldn't be satisfied with just sitting home, and yet whenever I try to arrange something for you, you seem to resist it. [*She gets up.*] Now take a look at yourself. No, wait! Wait just a moment—I have an idea!

LAURA: What is it now?

[AMANDA *produces two powder puffs which she wraps in handkerchiefs and stuffs in* LAURA's *bosom.*]

LAURA: Mother, what are you doing?

AMANDA: They call them "Gay Deceivers"!

LAURA: I won't wear them!

AMANDA: You will!

LAURA: Why should I?

AMANDA: Because, to be painfully honest, your chest is flat.

LAURA: You make it seem like we were setting a trap.

AMANDA: All pretty girls are a trap, a pretty trap, and men expect them to be. [*Legend on screen:* "A pretty trap."] Now look at yourself, young lady. This is the prettiest you will ever be! [*She stands back to admire* LAURA.] I've got to fix myself now! You're going to be surprised by your mother's appearance! [AMANDA *crosses through the portieres, humming gaily.* LAURA *moves slowly to the long mirror and stares solemnly at herself. A wind blows the white curtains inward in a slow, graceful motion and with a faint, sorrowful, sighing.*]

AMANDA: [*From somewhere behind the portieres.*] It isn't dark enough yet.

[LAURA *turns slowly before the mirror with a troubled look.*]

[*Legend on screen:* "This is my sister: Celebrate her with strings!" *Music plays.*]

AMANDA: [*Laughing, still not visible.*] I'm going to show you something. I'm going to make a spectacular appearance!

LAURA: What is it, Mother?

AMANDA: Possess your soul in patience—you will see! Something I've resurrected from that old trunk! Styles haven't changed so terribly much after all. . . . [*She parts the portieres.*] Now just look at your mother! [*She wears a girlish frock of yellowed voile with a blue silk sash. She carries a bunch of jonquils—the legend of her youth is nearly revived. Now she speaks feverishly.*] This is the dress in which I led the cotillion. Won the cakewalk twice at Sunset Hill, wore one Spring to the Governor's Ball in Jackson! See how I sashayed around the ballroom, Laura? [*She raises her skirt and does a mincing step around the room.*] I wore it on Sundays for my gentlemen callers! I had it on the day I met your father. . . . I had malaria fever all that Spring. The change of climate from East Tennessee to the Delta—weakened resistance. I had a little temperature all the time—not enough to be serious—just enough to make me restless and giddy! Invitations poured in—parties all over the Delta! "Stay in bed," said Mother, "you have a fever!"—but I just wouldn't. I took quinine[2] but kept on going, going! Evenings, dances! Afternoons, long, long rides! Picnics—lovely! So lovely, that country in May—all lacy with dogwood, literally flooded with jonquils! That was the spring I had the craze for jonquils. Jonquils became an absolute obsession. Mother said, "Honey, there's no more room for jonquils." And still I kept on bringing in more jonquils. Whenever, wherever I saw them, I'd say, "Stop! Stop! I see jonquils!" I made the young men help me gather the jonquils! It was a joke, Amanda and her jonquils. Finally there were no more vases to hold them, every available space was filled with jonquils. No vases to hold them? All right, I'll hold them myself! And then I— [*She stops in front of the picture. Music plays.*] met your father! Malaria fever and jonquils and then—this—boy. . . . [*She switches on the rose-colored lamp.*] I hope they get here before it starts to rain. [*She crosses the room and places the jonquils in a bowl on the table.*] I gave your brother a little extra change so he and Mr. O'Connor could take the service car home.

LAURA: [*With an altered look.*] What did you say his name was?

AMANDA: O'Connor.

LAURA: What is his first name?

AMANDA: I don't remember. Oh, yes, I do. It was—Jim!

[LAURA *sways slightly and catches hold of a chair.*]

[*Legend on screen*: "Not Jim!"]

---

2. A drug used against malaria.

LAURA: [*Faintly.*] Not—Jim!

AMANDA: Yes, that was it, it was Jim! I've never known a Jim that wasn't nice!

[*The music becomes ominous.*]

LAURA: Are you sure his name is Jim O'Connor?

AMANDA: Yes. Why?

LAURA: Is he the one that Tom used to know in high school?

AMANDA: He didn't say so. I think he just got to know him at the warehouse.

LAURA: There was a Jim O'Connor we both knew in high school— [*Then, with effort.*] If that is the one that Tom is bringing to dinner—you'll have to excuse me, I won't come to the table.

AMANDA: What sort of nonsense is this?

LAURA: You asked me once if I'd ever liked a boy. Don't you remember I showed you this boy's picture?

AMANDA: You mean the boy you showed me in the yearbook?

LAURA: Yes, that boy.

AMANDA: Laura, Laura, were you in love with that boy?

LAURA: I don't know, Mother. All I know is I couldn't sit at the table if it was him!

AMANDA: It won't be him! It isn't the least bit likely. But whether it is or not, you will come to the table. You will not be excused.

LAURA: I'll have to be, Mother.

AMANDA: I don't intend to humor your silliness, Laura. I've had too much from you and your brother, both! So just sit down and compose yourself till they come. Tom has forgotten his key so you'll have to let them in, when they arrive.

LAURA: [*Panicky.*] Oh, Mother—*you* answer the door!

AMANDA: [*Lightly.*] I'll be in the kitchen—busy!

LAURA: Oh, Mother, please answer the door, don't make me do it!

AMANDA: [*Crossing into the kitchenette.*] I've got to fix the dressing for the salmon. Fuss, fuss—silliness!—over a gentleman caller!

[*The door swings shut.* LAURA *is left alone.*]

[*Legend on screen:* "Terror!"]

[*She utters a low moan and turns off the lamp—sits stiffly on the edge of the sofa, knotting her fingers together.*]

[*Legend on screen:* "The Opening of a Door!"]

[TOM *and* JIM *appear on the fire escape steps and climb to the landing. Hearing their approach,* LAURA *rises with a panicky gesture. She retreats to the portieres. The doorbell rings.* LAURA *catches her breath and touches her throat. Low drums sound.*]

AMANDA: [*Calling.*] Laura, sweetheart! The door!

[LAURA *stares at it without moving.*]

JIM: I think we just beat the rain.

TOM: Uh-huh. [*He rings again, nervously.* JIM *whistles and fishes for a cigarette.*]

AMANDA: [*Very, very gaily.*] Laura, that is your brother and Mr. O'Connor! Will you let them in, darling?

[LAURA *crosses toward the kitchenette door.*]

LAURA: [*Breathlessly.*] Mother—you go to the door!

[AMANDA *steps out of the kitchenette and stares furiously at* LAURA. *She points imperiously at the door.*]

LAURA: Please, please!

AMANDA: [*In a fierce whisper.*] What is the matter with you, you silly thing?

LAURA: [*Desperately.*] Please, you answer it, *please*!

AMANDA: I told you I wasn't going to humor you, Laura. Why have you chosen this moment to lose your mind?

LAURA: Please, please, please, you go!

AMANDA: You'll have to go to the door because I can't!

LAURA: [*Despairingly.*] I can't either!

AMANDA: *Why?*

LAURA: I'm *sick*!

AMANDA: I'm sick, too—of your nonsense! Why can't you and your brother be normal people? Fantastic whims and behavior! [TOM *gives a long ring.*] Preposterous goings on! Can you give me one reason.— [*She calls out lyrically.*] Coming! Just one second!—why you should be afraid to open a door? Now you answer it, Laura!

LAURA: Oh, oh, oh . . . [*She returns through the portieres, darts to the Victrola, winds it frantically and turns it on.*]

AMANDA: Laura Wingfield, you march right to that door!

LAURA: *Yes—yes, Mother!*

[*A faraway, scratchy rendition of "Dardanella" softens the air and gives her strength to move through it. She slips to the door and draws it cautiously open.* TOM *enters with the caller,* JIM O'CONNOR.]

TOM: Laura, this is Jim. Jim, this is my sister, Laura.

JIM: [*Stepping inside.*] I didn't know that Shakespeare had a sister!

LAURA: [*Retreating, stiff and trembling, from the door.*] How—how do you do?

JIM: [*Heartily, extending his hand.*] Okay!

[LAURA *touches it hesitantly with hers.*]

JIM: Your hand's *cold*, Laura!

LAURA: Yes, well—I've been playing the Victrola. . . .

JIM: Must have been playing classical music on it! You ought to play a little hot swing music to warm you up!

LAURA: Excuse me—I haven't finished playing the Victrola. . . . [*She turns awkwardly and hurries into the front room. She pauses a second by the Victrola. Then she catches her breath and darts through the portieres like a frightened deer.*]

JIM: [*Grinning.*] What was the matter?

TOM: Oh—with Laura? Laura is—terribly shy.

JIM: Shy, huh? It's unusual to meet a shy girl nowadays. I don't believe you ever mentioned you had a sister.

TOM: Well, now you know. I have one. Here is the *Post Dispatch.* You want a piece of it?

JIM: Uh-huh.

TOM: What piece? The comics?

JIM: Sports! [*He glances at it.*] Ole Dizzy Dean[3] is on his bad behavior.

TOM: [*Uninterested.*] Yeah? [*He lights a cigarette and goes over to the fire-escape door.*]

JIM: Where are *you* going?

TOM: I'm going out on the terrace.

JIM: [*Going after him.*] You know, Shakespeare—I'm going to sell you a bill of goods!

TOM: What goods?

JIM: A course I'm taking.

TOM: Huh?

JIM: In public speaking! You and me, we're not the warehouse type.

TOM: Thanks—that's good news. But what has public speaking got to do with it?

JIM: It fits you for—executive positions!

3. Star pitcher for the St. Louis Cardinals, a successful baseball team in the 1930s.

TOM: Awww.

JIM: I tell you it's done a helluva lot for me.

[*Image on screen:* Executive at his desk.]

TOM: In what respect?

JIM: In every! Ask yourself what is the difference between you an' me and men in the office down front? Brains?—No!—Ability?—No! Then what? Just one little thing—

TOM: What is that one little thing?

JIM: Primarily it amounts to—social poise! Being able to square up to people and hold your own on any social level!

AMANDA: [*From the kitchenette.*] Tom?

TOM: Yes, Mother?

AMANDA: Is that you and Mr. O'Connor?

TOM: Yes, Mother.

AMANDA: Well, you just make yourselves comfortable in there.

TOM: Yes, Mother.

AMANDA: Ask Mr. O'Connor if he would like to wash his hands.

JIM: Aw, no—no—thank you—I took care of that at the warehouse. Tom—

TOM: Yes?

JIM: Mr. Mendoza was speaking to me about you.

TOM: Favorably?

JIM: What do you think?

TOM: Well—

JIM: You're going to be out of a job if you don't wake up.

TOM: I am waking up—

JIM: You show no signs.

TOM: The signs are interior.

[*Image on screen:* The sailing vessel with the Jolly Roger again.]

TOM: I'm planning to change. [*He leans over the fire-escape rail, speaking with quiet exhilaration. The incandescent marquees and signs of the first-run movie houses light his face from across the alley. He looks like a voyager.*] I'm right at the point of committing myself to a future that doesn't include the warehouse and Mr. Mendoza or even a night-school course in public speaking.

JIM: What are you gassing about?

TOM: I'm tired of the movies.

JIM: Movies!

TOM: Yes, movies! Look at them— [*A wave toward the marvels of Grand Avenue.*] All of those glamorous people—having adventures—hogging it all, gobbling the whole thing up! You know what happens? People go to the *movies* instead of *moving*! Hollywood characters are supposed to have all the adventures for everybody in America, while everybody in America sits in a dark room and watches them have them! Yes, until there's a war. That's when adventure becomes available to the masses! *Everyone's* dish, not only Gable's![4] Then the people in the dark room come out of the dark room to have some adventures themselves—goody, goody! It's our turn now, to go to the South Sea Island—to make a safari—to be exotic, far-off! But I'm not patient. I don't want to wait till then. I'm tired of the *movies* and I am *about* to *move*!

JIM: [*Incredulously.*] Move?

TOM: Yes.

JIM: When?

TOM: Soon!

JIM: Where? Where?

[*The music seems to answer the question, while* TOM *thinks it over. He searches in his pockets.*]

TOM: I'm starting to boil inside. I know I seem dreamy, but inside—well, I'm boiling! Whenever I pick up a shoe, I shudder a little thinking how short life is and what I am doing! Whatever that means, I know it doesn't mean shoes—except as something to wear on a traveler's feet! [*He finds what he has been searching for in his pockets and holds out a paper to* JIM.] Look—

JIM: What?

TOM: I'm a member.

JIM: [*Reading.*] The Union of Merchant Seamen.

TOM: I paid my dues this month, instead of the light bill.

JIM: You will regret it when they turn the lights off.

TOM: I won't be here.

JIM: How about your mother?

TOM: I'm like my father. The bastard son of a bastard! Did you notice how he's grinning in his picture in there? And he's been absent going on sixteen years!

---

4. Clark Gable (1901–1960), American movie actor.

JIM: You're just talking, you drip. How does your mother feel about it?

TOM: Shhh! Here comes Mother! Mother is not acquainted with my plans!

AMANDA: [*Coming through the portieres.*] Where are you all?

TOM: On the terrace, Mother.

[*They start inside. She advances to them.* TOM *is distinctly shocked at her appearance. Even* JIM *blinks a little. He is making his first contact with girlish Southern vivacity and in spite of the night-school course in public speaking is somewhat thrown off the beam by the unexpected outlay of social charm. Certain responses are attempted by* JIM *but are swept aside by* AMANDA's *gay laughter and chatter.* TOM *is embarrassed but after the first shock* JIM *reacts very warmly. He grins and chuckles, is altogether won over.*]

[*Image on screen*: Amanda as a girl.]

AMANDA: [*Coyly smiling, shaking her girlish ringlets.*] Well, well, well, so this is Mr. O'Connor. Introductions entirely unnecessary. I've heard so much about you from my boy. I finally said to him, Tom—good gracious!—why don't you bring this paragon to supper? I'd like to meet this nice young man at the warehouse!—instead of just hearing him sing your praises so much! I don't know why my son is so stand-offish—that's not Southern behavior!

Let's sit down and—I think we could stand a little more air in here! Tom, leave the door open. I felt a nice fresh breeze a moment ago. Where has it gone to? Mmm, so warm already! And not quite summer, even. We're going to burn up when summer really gets started. However, we're having—we're having a very light supper. I think light things are better fo' this time of year. The same as light clothes are. Light clothes an' light food are what warm weather calls fo'. You know our blood gets so thick during th' winter—it takes a while fo' us to *adjust* ou'selves!— when the season changes. . . . It's come so quick this year. I wasn't prepared. All of a sudden—heavens! Already summer! I ran to the trunk an' pulled out this light dress—terribly old! Historical almost! But feels so good—so good an' co-ol, y' know. . . .

TOM: Mother—

AMANDA: Yes, honey?

TOM: How about—supper?

AMANDA: Honey, you go ask Sister if supper is ready! You know that Sister is in full charge of supper! Tell her you hungry boys are waiting for it. [*To* JIM.] Have you met Laura?

JIM: She—

AMANDA: Let you in? Oh, good, you've met already! It's rare for a girl as sweet an' pretty as Laura to be domestic! But Laura is, thank heavens, not only pretty but also very domestic. I'm not at all. I never was a bit. I never could make a thing but angel-food cake. Well, in the South we had so many servants. Gone, gone, gone. All vestige of gracious living! Gone completely! I wasn't prepared for what the future brought me. All of my gentlemen callers were sons of planters and so of course I assumed that I would be married to one and raise my family on a large piece of land with plenty of servants. But man proposes—and woman accepts the proposal! To vary that old, old saying a little bit—I married no planter! I married a man who worked for the telephone company! That gallantly smiling gentleman over there! [*She points to the picture.*] A telephone man who—fell in love with long-distance! Now he travels and I don't even know where! But what am I going on for about my—tribulations? Tell me yours—I hope you don't have any! Tom?

TOM: [*Returning.*] Yes, Mother?

AMANDA: Is supper nearly ready?

TOM: It looks to me like supper is on the table.

AMANDA: Let me look— [*She rises prettily and looks through the portieres.*] Oh, lovely! But where is Sister?

TOM: Laura is not feeling well and she says that she thinks she'd better not come to the table.

AMANDA: What? Nonsense! Laura? Oh, Laura!

LAURA: [*From the kitchenette, faintly.*] Yes, Mother.

AMANDA: You really must come to the table. We won't be seated until you come to the table! Come in, Mr. O'Connor. You sit over there, and I'll. . . . Laura? Laura Wingfield! You're keeping us waiting, honey! We can't say grace until you come to the table!

[*The kitchenette door is pushed weakly open and* LAURA *comes in. She is obviously quite faint, her lips trembling, her eyes wide and staring. She moves unsteadily toward the table.*]

[*Screen legend:* "Terror!"]

[*Outside a summer storm is coming on abruptly. The white curtains billow inward at the windows and there is a sorrowful murmur from the deep blue dusk.*]

[LAURA *suddenly stumbles; she catches at a chair with a faint moan.*]

TOM: Laura!

AMANDA: Laura! [*There is a clap of thunder.*] [*Screen legend*: "Ah!"]

[*Despairingly.*] Why, Laura, you *are* ill, darling! Tom, help your sister into the living room, dear! Sit in the living room, Laura— rest on the sofa. Well! [*To* JIM *as* TOM *helps his sister to the sofa in the living room.*] Standing over the hot stove made her ill! I told her that it was just too warm this evening, but— [TOM *comes back to the table.*] Is Laura all right now?

TOM: Yes.

AMANDA: What *is* that? Rain? A nice cool rain has come up! [*She give* JIM *a frightened look.*] I think we may—have grace—now. . . . [TOM *looks at her stupidly.*] Tom, honey—you say grace!

TOM: Oh . . . "For these and all thy mercies—" [*They bow their heads,* AMANDA *stealing a nervous glance at* JIM. *In the living room* LAURA, *stretched on the sofa, clenches her hand to her lips, to hold back a shuddering sob.*] God's Holy Name be praised—

[*The scene dims out.*]

SCENE SEVEN

It is half an hour later. Dinner is just being finished in the dining room, LAURA *is still huddled upon the sofa, her feet drawn under her, her head resting on a pale blue pillow, her eyes wide and mysteriously watchful. The new floor lamp with its shade of rose-colored silk gives a soft, becoming light to her face, bringing out the fragile, unearthly prettiness which usually escapes attention. From outside there is a steady murmur of rain, but it is slackening and soon stops; the air outside becomes pale and luminous as the moon breaks through the clouds. A moment after the curtain rises, the lights in both rooms flicker and go out.*

JIM: Hey, there, Mr. Light Bulb!

[AMANDA *laughs nervously.*]

[*Legend on screen*: "Suspension of a public service."]

AMANDA: Where was Moses when the lights went out? Ha-ha. Do you know the answer to that one, Mr. O'Connor?

JIM: No, Ma'am, what's the answer?

AMANDA: In the dark! [JIM *laughs appreciatively.*] Everybody sit still. I'll light the candles. Isn't it lucky we have them on the table? Where's a match? Which of you gentlemen can provide a match?

JIM: Here.

AMANDA: Thank you, Sir.

JIM: Not at all, Ma'am!

AMANDA: [*As she lights the candles.*] I guess the fuse has burnt out. Mr. O'Connor, can you tell a burnt-out fuse? I know I can't and Tom is a total loss when it comes to mechanics. [*They rise from the table and go into the kitchenette, from where their voices are heard.*] Oh, be careful you don't bump into something. We don't want our gentleman caller to break his neck. Now wouldn't that be a fine howdy-do?

JIM: Ha-ha! Where is the fuse-box?

AMANDA: Right here next to the stove. Can you see anything?

JIM: Just a minute.

AMANDA: Isn't electricity a mysterious thing? Wasn't it Benjamin Franklin who tied a key to a kite? We live in such a mysterious universe, don't we? Some people say that science clears up all the mysteries for us. In my opinion it only creates more! Have you found it yet?

JIM: No, Ma'am. All these fuses look okay to me.

AMANDA: Tom!

TOM: Yes, Mother?

AMANDA: That light bill I gave you several days ago. The one I told you we got the notices about?

[*Legend on screen:* "Ha!"]

TOM: Oh—yeah.

AMANDA: You didn't neglect to pay it by any chance?

TOM: Why, I—

AMANDA: Didn't! I might have known it!

JIM: Shakespeare probably wrote a poem on that light bill, Mrs. Wingfield.

AMANDA: I might have known better than to trust him with it! There's such a high price for negligence in this world!

JIM: Maybe the poem will win a ten-dollar prize.

AMANDA: We'll just have to spend the remainder of the evening in the nineteenth century, before Mr. Edison made the Mazda lamp![1]

JIM: Candlelight is my favorite kind of light.

AMANDA: That shows you're romantic! But that's no excuse for Tom. Well, we got through dinner. Very considerate of them to let us get through dinner before they plunged us into everlasting darkness, wasn't it, Mr. O'Connor?

JIM: Ha-ha!

AMANDA: Tom, as a penalty for your carelessness you can help me with the dishes.

JIM: Let me give you a hand.

AMANDA: Indeed you will not!

JIM: I ought to be good for something.

AMANDA: Good for something? [*Her tone is rhapsodic.*] *You?* Why, Mr. O'Connor, nobody, *nobody's* given me this much entertainment in years—as you have!

JIM: Aw, now, Mrs. Wingfield!

AMANDA: I'm not exaggerating, not one bit! But Sister is all by her lonesome. You go keep her company in the parlor! I'll give you this lovely old candelabrum that used to be on the altar at the Church of the Heavenly Rest. It was melted a little out of shape when the church burnt down. Lightning struck it one spring. Gypsy Jones was holding a revival at the time and he intimated that the church was destroyed because the Episcopalians gave card parties.

JIM: Ha-ha.

AMANDA: And how about you coaxing Sister to drink a little wine? I think it would be good for her! Can you carry both at once?

JIM: Sure. I'm Superman!

AMANDA: Now, Thomas, get into this apron!

> [JIM *comes into the dining room, carrying the candelabrum, its candles lighted, in one hand and a glass of wine in the other. The door of the kitchenette swings closed on* AMANDA's *gay laughter; the flickering light approaches the portieres.* LAURA *sits up ner-*

---

1. A lightbulb patented in 1910.

vously as JIM *enters. She can hardly speak from the almost intolerable strain of being alone with a stranger.*]

[*Screen legend:* "I don't suppose you remember me at all!"]

[*At first, before* JIM'S *warmth overcomes her paralyzing shyness,* LAURA'S *voice is thin and breathless, as though she had just run up a steep flight of stairs.* JIM'S *attitude is gently humorous. While the incident is apparently unimportant, it is to* LAURA *the climax of her secret life.*]

JIM: Hello there, Laura.

LAURA: [*Faintly.*] Hello. [*She clears her throat.*]

JIM: How are you feeling now? Better?

LAURA: Yes. Yes, thank you.

JIM: This is for you. A little dandelion wine. [*He extends the glass toward her with extravagant gallantry.*]

LAURA: Thank you.

JIM: Drink it—but don't get drunk! [*He laughs heartily.* LAURA *takes the glass uncertainly; she laughs shyly.*] Where shall I set the candles?

LAURA: Oh—oh, anywhere . . .

JIM: How about here on the floor? Any objections?

LAURA: No.

JIM: I'll spread a newspaper under to catch the drippings. I like to sit on the floor. Mind if I do?

LAURA: Oh, no.

JIM: Give me a pillow?

LAURA: What?

JIM: A pillow!

LAURA: Oh . . . [*She hands him one quickly.*]

JIM: How about you? Don't you like to sit on the floor?

LAURA: Oh—yes.

JIM: Why don't you, then?

LAURA: I—will.

JIM: Take a pillow! [LAURA *does. She sits on the floor on the other side of the candelabrum.* JIM *crosses his legs and smiles engagingly at her.*] I can't hardly see you sitting way over there.

LAURA: I can—see you.

JIM: I know, but that's not fair, I'm in the limelight. [LAURA *moves her pillow closer.*] Good! Now I can see you! Comfortable?

LAURA: Yes.

JIM: So am I. Comfortable as a cow! Will you have some gum?

LAURA: No, thank you.

JIM: I think that I will indulge, with your permission. [*He musingly unwraps a stick of gum and holds it up.*] Think of the fortune made by the guy that invented the first piece of chewing gum. Amazing, huh? The Wrigley Building is one of the sights of Chicago—I saw it when I went up to the Century of Progress. Did you take in the Century of Progress?[2]

LAURA: No, I didn't.

JIM: Well, it was quite a wonderful exposition. What impressed me most was the Hall of Science. Gives you an idea of what the future will be in America, even more wonderful than the present time is! [*There is a pause.* JIM *smiles at her.*] Your brother tells me you're shy. Is that right, Laura?

LAURA: I—don't know.

JIM: I judge you to be an old-fashioned type of girl. Well, I think that's a pretty good type to be. Hope you don't think I'm being too personal—do you?

LAURA: [*Hastily, out of embarrassment.*] I believe I *will* take a piece of gum, if you—don't mind. [*Clearing her throat.*] Mr. O'Connor, have you—kept up with your singing?

JIM: Singing? Me?

LAURA: Yes. I remember what a beautiful voice you had.

JIM: When did you hear me sing?

[LAURA *does not answer, and in the long pause which follows a man's voice is heard singing offstage.*]

VOICE:
O blow, ye winds, heigh-ho,
A-roving I will go!
    I'm off to my love
      With a boxing glove—
Ten thousand miles away!

JIM: You say you've heard me sing?

LAURA: Oh, yes! Yes, very often . . . I—don't suppose—you remember me—at all?

JIM: [*Smiling doubtfully.*] You know I have an idea I've seen you

---

2. The world's fair held in Chicago in 1933–34.

before. I had that idea soon as you opened the door. It seemed almost like I was about to remember your name. But the name that I started to call you—wasn't a name! And so I stopped myself before I said it.

LAURA: Wasn't it—Blue Roses?

JIM: [*Springing up, grinning.*] Blue Roses! My gosh, yes—Blue Roses! That's what I had on my tongue when you opened the door! Isn't it funny what tricks your memory plays? I didn't connect you with high school somehow or other. But that's where it was; it was high school. I didn't even know you were Shakespeare's sister! Gosh, I'm sorry.

LAURA: I didn't expect you to. You—barely knew me!

JIM: But we did have a speaking acquaintance, huh?

LAURA: Yes, we—spoke to each other.

JIM: When did you recognize me?

LAURA: Oh, right away!

JIM: Soon as I came in the door?

LAURA: When I heard your name I thought it was probably you. I knew that Tom used to know you a little in high school. So when you came in the door—well, then I was—sure.

JIM: Why didn't you *say* something, then?

LAURA: [*Breathlessly.*] I didn't know what to say, I was—too surprised!

JIM: For goodness' sakes! You know, this sure is funny!

LAURA: Yes! Yes, isn't it, though . . .

JIM: Didn't we have a class in something together?

LAURA: Yes, we did.

JIM: What class was that?

LAURA: It was—singing—chorus!

JIM: Aw!

LAURA: I sat across the aisle from you in the Aud.

JIM: Aw.

LAURA: Mondays, Wednesdays, and Fridays.

JIM: Now I remember—you always came in late.

LAURA: Yes, it was so hard for me, getting upstairs. I had that brace on my leg—it clumped so loud!

JIM: I never heard any clumping.

LAURA: [*Wincing at the recollection.*] To me it sounded like—thunder!

JIM: Well, well, well, I never even noticed.

LAURA: And everybody was seated before I came in. I had to walk in front of all those people. My seat was in the back row. I had to go clumping all the way up the aisle with everyone watching!

JIM: You shouldn't have been self-conscious.

LAURA: I know, but I was. It was always such a relief when the singing started.

JIM: Aw, yes, I've placed you now! I used to call you Blue Roses. How was it that I got started calling you that?

LAURA: I was out of school a little while with pleurosis. When I came back you asked me what was the matter. I said I had pleurosis—you thought I said *Blue Roses*. That's what you always called me after that!

JIM: I hope you didn't mind.

LAURA: Oh, no—I liked it. You see, I wasn't acquainted with many—people. . . .

JIM: As I remember you sort of stuck by yourself.

LAURA: I—I—never have had much luck at—making friends.

JIM: I don't see why you wouldn't.

LAURA: Well, I—started out badly.

JIM: You mean being—

LAURA: Yes, it sort of—stood between me—

JIM: You shouldn't have let it!

LAURA: I know, but it did, and—

JIM: You were shy with people!

LAURA: I tried not to be but never could—

JIM: Overcome it?

LAURA: No, I—I never could!

JIM: I guess being shy is something you have to work out of kind of gradually.

LAURA: [*Sorrowfully.*] Yes—I guess it—

JIM: Takes time!

LAURA: Yes—

JIM: People are not so dreadful when you know them. That's what you have to remember! And everybody has problems, not just you, but practically everybody has got some problems. You think of yourself as having the only problems, as being the only one who is disappointed. But just look around you and you will see lots of people as disappointed as you are. For instance, I hoped when I was going to high school that I would be further along at this time, six years later, than I am now. You remember that wonderful write-up I had in *The Torch*?

LAURA: Yes! [*She rises and crosses to the table.*]

JIM: It said I was bound to succeed in anything I went into! [LAURA *returns with the high school yearbook.*] Holy Jeez! *The Torch!* [*He accepts it reverently. They smile across the book with mutual wonder. LAURA crouches beside him and they begin to turn the pages. LAURA's shyness is dissolving in his warmth.*]

LAURA: Here you are in *The Pirates of Penzance*!

JIM: [*Wistfully.*] I sang the baritone lead in that operetta.

LAURA: [*Raptly.*] So—*beautifully*!

JIM: [*Protesting.*] Aw—

LAURA: Yes, yes—beautifully—beautifully!

JIM: You heard me?

LAURA: All three times!

JIM: No!

LAURA: Yes!

JIM: All three performances?

LAURA: [*Looking down.*] Yes.

JIM: Why?

LAURA: I—wanted to ask you to—autograph my program. [*She takes the program from the back of the yearbook and shows it to him.*]

JIM: Why didn't you ask me to?

LAURA: You were always surrounded by your own friends so much that I never had a chance to.

JIM: You should have just—

LAURA: Well, I—thought you might think I was—

JIM: Thought I might think you was—what?

LAURA: Oh—

JIM: [*With reflective relish.*] I was beleaguered by females in those days.

LAURA: You were terribly popular!

JIM: Yeah—

LAURA: You had such a—friendly way—

JIM: I was spoiled in high school.

LAURA: Everybody—liked you!

JIM: Including you?

LAURA: I—yes, I—did, too— [*She gently closes the book in her lap.*]

JIM: Well, well, well! Give me that program, Laura. [*She hands it to him. He signs it with a flourish.*] There you are—better late than never!

LAURA: Oh, I—what a—surprise!

JIM: My signature isn't worth very much right now. But some day— maybe—it will increase in value! Being disappointed is one thing and being discouraged is something else. I am disappointed but I am not discouraged. I'm twenty-three years old. How old are you?

LAURA: I'll be twenty-four in June.

JIM: That's not old age!

LAURA: No, but—

JIM: You finished high school?

LAURA: [*With difficulty.*] I didn't go back.

JIM: You mean you dropped out?

LAURA: I made bad grades in my final examinations. [*She rises and replaces the book and the program on the table. Her voice is strained.*] How is—Emily Meisenbach getting along?

JIM: Oh, that kraut-head![3]

LAURA: Why do you call her that?

JIM: That's what she was.

LAURA: You're not still—going with her?

JIM: I never see her.

LAURA: It said in the "Personal" section that you were—engaged!

JIM: I know, but I wasn't impressed by that—propaganda!

LAURA: It wasn't—the truth?

JIM: Only in Emily's optimistic opinion!

LAURA: Oh—

[*Legend:* "What have you done since high school?"]

[JIM *lights a cigarette and leans indolently back on his elbows smiling at* LAURA *with a warmth and charm which lights her inwardly with altar candles. She remains by the table, picks up a piece from the glass menagerie collection, and turns it in her hands to cover her tumult.*]

---

3. Derogatory term for a German.

JIM: [*After several reflective puffs on his cigarette.*] What have you done since high school? [*She seems not to hear him.*] Huh? [LAURA *looks up.*] I said what have you done since high school, Laura?

LAURA: Nothing much.

JIM: You must have been doing something these six long years.

LAURA: Yes.

JIM: Well, then, such as what?

LAURA: I took a business course at business college—

JIM: How did that work out?

LAURA: Well, not very—well—I had to drop out, it gave me—indigestion—

[JIM *laughs gently.*]

JIM: What are you doing now?

LAURA: I don't do anything—much. Oh, please don't think I sit around doing nothing! My glass collection takes up a good deal of time. Glass is something you have to take good care of.

JIM: What did you say—about glass?

LAURA: Collection I said—I have one— [*She clears her throat and turns away again, acutely shy.*]

JIM: [*Abruptly.*] You know what I judge to be the trouble with you? Inferiority complex! Know what that is? That's what they call it when someone low-rates himself! I understand it because I had it, too. Although my case was not so aggravated as yours seems to be. I had it until I took up public speaking, developed my voice, and learned that I had an aptitude for science. Before that time I never thought of myself as being outstanding in any way whatsoever! Now I've never made a regular study of it, but I have a friend who says I can analyze people better than doctors that make a profession of it. I don't claim that to be necessarily true, but I can sure guess a person's psychology, Laura! [*He takes out his gum.*] Excuse me, Laura. I always take it out when the flavor is gone. I'll use this scrap of paper to wrap it in. I know how it is to get it stuck on a shoe. [*He wraps the gum in paper and puts it in his pocket.*] Yep—that's what I judge to be your principal trouble. A lack of confidence in yourself as a person. You don't have the proper amount of faith in yourself. I'm basing that fact on a number of your remarks and also on certain observations I've made. For instance that clumping you thought was so awful in high school. You say that you even dreaded to walk into class. You see what you did? You dropped out of school, you gave up an education because of a clump, which as far as I know was practically non-existent! A little physical defect is what you have. Hardly noticeable even! Magnified thousands of times by imagination! You know what my strong advice to you is? Think of yourself as *superior* in some way!

LAURA: In what way would I think?

JIM: Why, man alive, Laura! Just look about you a little. What do you see? A world full of common people! All of 'em born and all of 'em going to to die! Which of them has one-tenth of your good points! Or mine! Or anyone else's, as far as that goes—gosh! Everybody excels in some one thing. Some in many! [*He unconsciously glances at himself in the mirror.*] All you've got to do is discover in *what*! Take me, for instance. [*He adjusts his tie at the mirror.*] My interest happens to lie in electro-dynamics. I'm taking a course in radio engineering at night school, Laura, on top of a fairly responsible job at the warehouse. I'm taking that course and studying public speaking.

LAURA: Ohhhh.

JIM: Because I believe in the future of television! [*Turning his back to her.*] I wish to be ready to go up right along with it. Therefore I'm planning to get in on the ground floor. In fact I've already made the right connections and all that remains is for the industry itself to get under way! Full steam— [*His eyes are starry.*] Knowledge—Zzzzzp! *Money*—Zzzzzp!—*Power!* That's the cycle democracy is built on! [*His attitude is convincingly dynamic.* LAURA *stares at him, even her shyness eclipsed in her absolute wonder. He suddenly grins.*] I guess you think I think a lot of myself!

LAURA: No—o-o-o, I—

JIM: Now how about you? Isn't there something you take more interest in than anything else?

LAURA: Well, I do—as I said—have my—glass collection—
[*A peal of girlish laughter rings from the kitchenette.*]

JIM: I'm not right sure I know what you're talking about. What kind of glass is it?

LAURA: Little articles of it, they're ornaments mostly! Most of them are little animals made out of glass, the tiniest little animals in

the world. Mother calls them a glass menagerie! Here's an example of one, if you'd like to see it! This one is one of the oldest. It's
nearly thirteen. [*Music*: "The Glass Menagerie."] [*He stretches out
his hand.*] Oh, be careful—if you breathe, it breaks!

JIM: I'd better not take it. I'm pretty clumsy with things.

LAURA: Go on, I trust you with him! [*She places the piece in his
palm.*] There now—you're holding him gently! Hold him over
the light, he loves the light! You see how the light shines through
him?

JIM: It sure does shine!

LAURA: I shouldn't be partial, but he is my favorite one.

JIM: What kind of a thing is this one supposed to be?

LAURA: Haven't you noticed the single horn on his forehead?

JIM: A unicorn,[4] huh?

LAURA: Mmmm-hmmm!

JIM: Unicorns—aren't they extinct in the modern world?

LAURA: I know!

JIM: Poor little fellow, he must feel sort of lonesome.

LAURA: [*Smiling.*] Well, if he does, he doesn't complain about it. He
stays on a shelf with some horses that don't have horns and all of
them seem to get along nicely together.

JIM: How do you know?

LAURA: [*Lightly.*] I haven't heard any arguments among them!

JIM: [*Grinning.*] No arguments, huh? Well, that's a pretty good sign!
Where shall I set him?

LAURA: Put him on the table. They all like a change of scenery once
in a while!

JIM: Well, well, well, well— [*He places the glass piece on the table,
then raises his arms and stretches.*] Look how big my shadow is
when I stretch!

LAURA: Oh, oh, yes—it stretches across the ceiling!

JIM: [*Crossing to the door.*] I think it's stopped raining. [*He opens the
fire-escape door and the background music changes to a dance tune.*]
Where does the music come from?

LAURA: From the Paradise Dance Hall across the alley.

JIM: How about cutting the rug a little, Miss Wingfield?

---

4. Legendary beast charmed by virgins but otherwise impossible to catch.

LAURA: Oh, I—

JIM: Or is your program filled up? Let me have a look at it. [*He grasps an imaginary card.*] Why, every dance is taken! I'll just have to scratch some out. [*Waltz music:* "La Golondrina."]

Ahhh, a waltz! [*He executes some sweeping turns by himself, then holds his arms toward* LAURA.]

LAURA: [*Breathlessly.*] I—can't dance!

JIM: There you go, that inferiority stuff!

LAURA: I've never danced in my life!

JIM: Come on, try!

LAURA: Oh, but I'd step on you!

JIM: I'm not made out of glass.

LAURA: How—how—how do we start?

JIM: Just leave it to me. You hold your arms out a little.

LAURA: Like this?

JIM: [*Taking her in his arms.*] A little bit higher. Right. Now don't tighten up, that's the main thing about it—relax.

LAURA: [*Laughing breathlessly.*] It's hard not to.

JIM: Okay.

LAURA: I'm afraid you can't budge me.

JIM: What do you bet I can't? [*He swings her into motion.*]

LAURA: Goodness, yes, you can!

JIM: Let yourself go, now, Laura, just let yourself go.

LAURA: I'm—

JIM: Come on!

LAURA: —trying!

JIM: Not so stiff—easy does it!

LAURA: I know but I'm—

JIM: Loosen th' backbone! There now, that's a lot better.

LAURA: Am I?

JIM: Lots, lots better! [*He moves her about the room in a clumsy waltz.*]

LAURA: Oh, my!

JIM: Ha-ha!

LAURA: Oh, my goodness!

JIM: Ha-ha-ha! [*They suddenly bump into the table, and the glass piece on it falls to the floor.* JIM *stops the dance.*] What did we hit on?

LAURA: Table.

JIM: Did something fall off it? I think—

LAURA: Yes.

JIM: I hope that it wasn't the little glass horse with the horn!

LAURA: Yes. [*She stoops to pick it up.*]

JIM: Aw, aw, aw. Is it broken?

LAURA: Now it is just like all the other horses.

JIM: It's lost its—

LAURA: Horn! It doesn't matter. Maybe it's a blessing in disguise.

JIM: You'll never forgive me. I bet that that was your favorite piece of glass.

LAURA: I don't have favorites much. It's no tragedy, Freckles. Glass breaks so easily. No matter how careful you are. The traffic jars the shelves and things fall off them.

JIM: Still I'm awfully sorry that I was the cause.

LAURA: [*Smiling.*] I'll just imagine he had an operation. The horn was removed to make him feel less—freakish! [*They both laugh.*]

Now he will feel more at home with the other horses, the ones that don't have horns. . . .

JIM: Ha-ha, that's very funny! [*Suddenly he is serious.*] I'm glad to see that you have a sense of humor. You know—you're—well—very different! Surprisingly different from anyone else I know! [*His voice becomes soft and hesitant with a genuine feeling.*] Do you mind me telling you that? [LAURA *is abashed beyond speech.*] I mean it in a nice way— [LAURA *nods shyly, looking away.*] You make me feel sort of—I don't know how to put it! I'm usually pretty good at expressing things, but—this is something that I don't know how to say! [LAURA *touches her throat and clears it— turns the broken unicorn in her hands. His voice becomes softer.*]

Has anyone ever told you that you were pretty? [*There is a pause, and the music rises slightly.* LAURA *looks up slowly, with wonder, and shakes her head.*]

Well, you are! In a very different way from anyone else. And all the nicer because of the difference, too. [*His voice becomes low and husky.* LAURA *turns away, nearly faint with the novelty of her emotions.*]

I wish that you were my sister. I'd teach you to have some confidence in yourself. The different people are not like other people, but being different is nothing to be ashamed of. Because other people are not such wonderful people. They're one hundred times one thousand. You're one times one! They walk all over the earth. You just stay here. They're common as—weeds, but—you—well, you're—*Blue Roses!*

[*Image on screen:* Blue Roses.]

[*The music changes.*]

LAURA: But blue is wrong for—roses. . . .

JIM: It's right for you! You're—pretty!

LAURA: In what respect am I pretty?

JIM: In all respects—believe me! Your eyes—your hair—are pretty! Your hands are pretty! [*He catches hold of her hand.*] You think I'm making this up because I'm invited to dinner and have to be nice. Oh, I could do that! I could put on an act for you, Laura, and say lots of things without being very sincere. But this time I am. I'm talking to you sincerely. I happened to notice you had this inferiority complex that keeps you from feeling comfortable with people. Somebody needs to build your confidence up and make you proud instead of shy and turning away and—blushing. Somebody—ought to—*kiss* you, Laura! [*His hand slips slowly up her arm to her shoulder as the music swells tumultuously. He suddenly turns her about and kisses her on the lips. When he releases her,* LAURA *sinks on the sofa with a bright, dazed look.* JIM *backs away and fishes in his pocket for a cigarette.*] [*Legend on screen:* "A souvenir."]

   Stumblejohn![5] [*He lights the cigarette, avoiding her look. There is a peal of girlish laughter from* AMANDA *in the kitchenette.* LAURA *slowly raises and opens her hand. It still contains the little broken glass animal. She looks at it with a tender, bewildered expression.*]

   Stumblejohn! I shouldn't have done that—that was way off the beam. You don't smoke, do you? [*She looks up, smiling, not hearing the question. He sits beside her rather gingerly. She looks at him speechlessly—waiting. He coughs decorously and moves a little farther aside as he considers the situation and senses her feelings, dimly, with perturbation. He speaks gently.*]

   Would you—care for a—mint? [*She doesn't seem to hear him but her look grows brighter even.*]

   Peppermint? Life Saver? My pocket's a regular drugstore—

---

5. Stumblebum, a clumsy or inept person.

wherever I go. . . . [*He pops a mint in his mouth. Then he gulps and decides to make a clean breast of it. He speaks slowly and gingerly.*] Laura, you know, if I had a sister like you, I'd do the same thing as Tom. I'd bring out fellows and—introduce her to them. The right type of boys—of a type to—appreciate her. Only—well—he made a mistake about me. Maybe I've got no call to be saying this. That may not have been the idea in having me over. But what if it was? There's nothing wrong about that. The only trouble is that in my case—I'm not in a situation to—do the right thing. I can't take down your number and say I'll phone. I can't call up next week and—ask for a date. I thought I had better explain the situation in case you—misunderstood it and—I hurt your feelings. . . .

> [*There is a pause. Slowly, very slowly,* LAURA's *look changes, her eyes returning slowly from his to the glass figure in her palm.* AMANDA *utters another gay laugh in the kitchenette.*]

LAURA: [*Faintly.*] You—won't—call again?

JIM: No, Laura, I can't. [*He rises from the sofa.*] As I was just explaining, I've—got strings on me. Laura, I've—been going steady! I go out all the time with a girl named Betty. She's a home-girl like you, and Catholic, and Irish, and in a great many ways we—get along fine. I met her last summer on a moonlight boat trip up the river to Alton, on the *Majestic*. Well—right away from the start it was—love! [*Legend:* Love!] [LAURA *sways slightly forward and grips the arm of the sofa. He fails to notice, now enrapt in his own comfortable being.*]

Being in love has made a new man of me! [*Leaning stiffly forward, clutching the arm of the sofa,* LAURA *struggles visibly with her storm. But* JIM *is oblivious; she is a long way off.*]

The power of love is really pretty tremendous! Love is something that—changes the whole world, Laura! [*The storm abates a little and* LAURA *leans back. He notices her again.*]

It happened that Betty's aunt took sick, she got a wire and had to go to Centralia. So Tom—when he asked me to dinner—I naturally just accepted the invitation, not knowing that you—that he—that I— [*He stops awkwardly.*] Huh—I'm a stumble-john! [*He flops back on the sofa. The holy candles on the altar of*

LAURA's *face have been snuffed out. There is a look of almost infinite desolation.* JIM *glances at her uneasily.*]

I wish that you would—say something. [*She bites her lip which was trembling and then bravely smiles. She opens her hand again on the broken glass figure. Then she gently takes his hand and raises it level with her own. She carefully places the unicorn in the palm of his hand, then pushes his fingers closed upon it.*]

What are you—doing that for? You want me to have him? Laura? [*She nods.*]

What for?

LAURA: A—souvenir. . . . [*She rises unsteadily and crouches beside the Victrola to wind it up.*]

[*Legend on screen:* "Things have a way of turning out so badly!" *Or image:* "Gentleman caller waving goodbye—gaily."]

[*At this moment* AMANDA *rushes brightly back into the living room. She bears a pitcher of fruit punch in an old-fashioned cut-glass pitcher, and a plate of macaroons. The plate has a gold border and poppies painted on it.*]

AMANDA: Well, well, well! Isn't the air delightful after the shower? I've made you children a little liquid refreshment.

[*She turns gaily to* JIM.] Jim, do you know that song about lemonade?

"Lemonade, lemonade
Made in the shade and stirred with a spade—
Good enough for any old maid!"

JIM: [*Uneasily.*] Ha-ha! No—I never heard it.

AMANDA: Why, Laura! You look so serious!

JIM: We were having a serious conversation.

AMANDA: Good! Now you're better acquainted!

JIM: [*Uncertainly.*] Ha-ha! Yes.

AMANDA: You modern young people are much more serious-minded than my generation. I was so gay as a girl!

JIM: You haven't changed, Mrs. Wingfield.

AMANDA: Tonight I'm rejuvenated! The gaiety of the occasion, Mr. O'Connor! [*She tosses her head with a peal of laughter, spilling some lemonade.*] Oooo! I'm baptizing myself!

JIM: Here—let me—

AMANDA: [*Setting the pitcher down.*] There now. I discovered we had some maraschino cherries. I dumped them in, juice and all!

JIM: You shouldn't have gone to that trouble, Mrs. Wingfield.

AMANDA: Trouble, trouble? Why, it was loads of fun! Didn't you hear me cutting up in the kitchen? I bet your ears were burning! I told Tom how outdone with him I was for keeping you to himself so long a time! He should have brought you over much, much sooner! Well, now that you've found your way, I want you to be a very frequent caller! Not just occasional but all the time. Oh, we're going to have a lot of gay times together! I see them coming! Mmm, just breathe that air! So fresh, and the moon's so pretty! I'll skip back out—I know where my place is when young folks are having a—serious conversation!

JIM: Oh, don't go out, Mrs. Wingfield. The fact of the matter is I've got to be going.

AMANDA: Going, now? You're joking! Why, it's only the shank of the evening, Mr. O'Connor!

JIM: Well, you know how it is.

AMANDA: You mean you're a young workingman and have to keep workingmen's hours. We'll let you off early tonight. But only on the condition that next time you stay later. What's the best night for you? Isn't Saturday night the best night for you workingmen?

JIM: I have a couple of time-clocks to punch, Mrs. Wingfield. One at morning, another one at night!

AMANDA: My, but you *are* ambitious! You work at night, too?

JIM: No, Ma'am, not work but—Betty! [*He crosses deliberately to pick up his hat. The band at the Paradise Dance Hall goes into a tender waltz.*]

AMANDA: Betty? Betty? Who's—Betty!

[*There is an ominous cracking sound in the sky.*]

JIM: Oh, just a girl. The girl I go steady with! [*He smiles charmingly. The sky falls.*]

[*Legend: "The Sky Falls."*]

AMANDA: [*A long-drawn exhalation.*] Ohhhh . . . Is it a serious romance, Mr. O'Connor?

JIM: We're going to be married the second Sunday in June.

AMANDA: Ohhhh—how nice! Tom didn't mention that you were engaged to be married.

JIM: The cat's not out of the bag at the warehouse yet. You know how they are. They call you Romeo and stuff like that. [*He stops at the oval mirror to put on his hat. He carefully shapes the brim and the crown to give a discreetly dashing effect.*] It's been a wonderful evening, Mrs. Wingfield. I guess this is what they mean by Southern hospitality.

AMANDA: It really wasn't anything at all.

JIM: I hope it don't seem like I'm rushing off. But I promised Betty I'd pick her up at the Wabash depot, an' by the time I get my jalopy down there her train'll be in. Some women are pretty upset if you keep 'em waiting.

AMANDA: Yes, I know—the tyranny of women! [*She extends her hand.*] Goodbye, Mr. O'Connor. I wish you luck—and happiness—and success! All three of them, and so does Laura! Don't you, Laura?

LAURA: Yes!

JIM: [*Taking* LAURA'*s hand.*] Goodbye, Laura. I'm certainly going to treasure that souvenir. And don't you forget the good advice I gave you. [*He raises his voice to a cheery shout.*] So long, Shakespeare! Thanks again, ladies. Good night! [*He grins and ducks jauntily out. Still bravely grimacing, Amanda closes the door on the gentleman caller. Then she turns back to the room with a puzzled expression. She and* LAURA *don't dare to face each other.* LAURA *crouches beside the Victrola to wind it.*]

AMANDA: [*Faintly.*] Things have a way of turning out so badly. I don't believe that I would play the Victrola. Well, well—well! Our gentleman caller was engaged to be married! [*She raises her voice.*] Tom!

TOM: [*From the kitchenette.*] Yes, Mother?

AMANDA: Come in here a minute. I want to tell you something awfully funny.

TOM: [*Entering with a macaroon and a glass of the lemonade.*] Has the gentleman caller gotten away already?

AMANDA: The gentleman caller has made an early departure. What a wonderful joke you played on us!

TOM: How do you mean?

AMANDA: You didn't mention that he was engaged to be married.

TOM: Jim? Engaged?

AMANDA: That's what he just informed us.

TOM: I'll be jiggered! I didn't know about that.

AMANDA: That seems very peculiar.

TOM: What's peculiar about it?

AMANDA: Didn't you call him your best friend down at the warehouse?

TOM: He is, but how did I know?

AMANDA: It seems extremely peculiar that you wouldn't know your best friend was going to be married!

TOM: The warehouse is where I work, not where I know things about people!

AMANDA: You don't know things anywhere! You live in a dream; you manufacture illusions! [*He crosses to the door.*] Where are you going?

TOM: I'm going to the movies.

AMANDA: That's right, now that you've had us make such fools of ourselves. The effort, the preparations, all the expense! The new floor lamp, the rug, the clothes for Laura! All for what? To entertain some other girl's fiancé! Go to the movies, go! Don't think about us, a mother deserted, an unmarried sister who's crippled and has no job! Don't let anything interfere with your selfish pleasure! Just go, go, go—to the movies!

TOM: All right, I will! The more you shout about my selfishness to me the quicker I'll go, and I won't go to the movies!

AMANDA: Go, then! Go to the moon—you selfish dreamer!

[TOM *smashes his glass on the floor. He plunges out on the fire escape, slamming the door.* LAURA *screams in fright. The dance-hall music becomes louder.* TOM *stands on the fire escape, gripping the rail. The moon breaks through the storm clouds, illuminating his face.*]

[*Legend on screen:* "And so goodbye . . ."]

[TOM'*s closing speech is timed with what is happening inside the house. We see, as though through soundproof glass, that* AMANDA *appears to be making a comforting speech to* LAURA, *who is huddled upon the sofa. Now that we cannot hear the mother's speech, her silliness is gone and she has dignity and tragic beauty.* LAURA'*s hair hides her face until, at the end of the speech, she lifts her head to smile at her mother.* AMANDA's *gestures are slow and graceful, almost dancelike, as she comforts her daughter. At the end of her speech she glances a moment at the father's picture— then withdraws through the portieres. At the close of* TOM's *speech,* LAURA *blows out the candles, ending the play.*]

TOM: I didn't go to the moon, I went much further—for time is the longest distance between two places. Not long after that I was fired for writing a poem on the lid of a shoe-box. I left Saint Louis. I descended the steps of this fire escape for a last time and followed, from then on, in my father's footsteps, attempting to find in motion what was lost in space. I traveled around a great deal. The cities swept about me like dead leaves, leaves that were brightly colored but torn away from the branches. I would have stopped, but I was pursued by something. It always came upon me unawares, taking me altogether by surprise. Perhaps it was a familiar bit of music. Perhaps it was only a piece of transparent glass. Perhaps I am walking along a street at night, in some strange city, before I have found companions. I pass the lighted window of a shop where perfume is sold. The window is filled with pieces of colored glass, tiny transparent bottles in delicate colors, like bits of a shattered rainbow. Then all at once my sister touches my shoulder. I turn around and look into her eyes. Oh, Laura, Laura, I tried to leave you behind me, but I am more faithful than I intended to be! I reach for a cigarette, I cross the street, I run into the movies or a bar, I buy a drink, I speak to the nearest stranger—anything that can blow your candles out! [LAURA *bends over the candles.*]

For nowadays the world is lit by lightning! Blow out your candles, Laura—and so goodbye. . . .

[*She blows the candles out.*]

1944   *1945*

August Wilson
1945–

FENCES

All of August Wilson's plays dramatize the experiences of African Americans in a racist society. Most of them focus on life in an African American neighborhood of Pittsburgh, the "Hill," during particular decades of the twentieth century. Fences, the second play in this historical cycle, takes place during the 1950s and derives partly from Wilson's family history. Like the play's main character, Troy Maxson, Wilson's stepfather, David Bedford, had been an exceptional high school athlete in the 1930s. He was poor, however, and at that time few colleges would offer a scholarship to a black man. Bedford turned to crime, and in a robbery gone wrong he killed someone. He served over two decades in prison before he was released and married Wilson's mother.

While he drew on Bedford for some details of Maxson's biography, Wilson's portrait of a proud soul battered by racism needed no model other than himself. As an African American growing up in a largely white suburb, he saw and experienced the effects of an environment hostile to its inhabitants' success, especially to their intellectual success. In response, Wilson later affiliated himself with the Nation of Islam, especially with the civil rights leader Malcolm X and his message of black self-reliance and independence.

Another model for Troy Maxson is the baseball legend Josh Gibson. Born in Georgia in 1911, Gibson moved with his family to Pittsburgh, Pennsylvania, in the early 1920s. He studied to be an electrician, but had to drop out of school after the ninth grade to work in a factory. He started playing for a Negro League baseball team, the Pittsburgh Crawfords, in 1929, and for the next seventeen years he played for the Crawfords, for the Homestead Grays (also in Pittsburgh), and in the Mexican League. He was a prodigious slugger, the black Babe Ruth (as many called him, though it might have been more accurate to call Ruth the white Josh Gibson). His accomplishments are incredible: 962 home runs, a lifetime batting average of .354, and an amazing 84 home runs in one season in 1936.

In the mid-1940s, the Washington Senators (a Major League team) flirted with the idea of signing Gibson, but the owner, Clark

Griffith, lacked the courage to break the color barrier. Gibson's last season was 1946. He died of a stroke in early 1947. His health had been declining for four years, and he was always a hard drinker, but legend contends that he died of a broken heart, for by 1946, Jackie Robinson was headed for the Major Leagues and Gibson knew that he was too old to join him. Though Gibson made decent money in the Negro Leagues and even more in the Mexican League, he was so poor when he died that donations had to be collected to pay for his funeral. You might consider Troy Maxson to be a portrait of Josh Gibson had he lived another ten years.

Maxson's experience as a garbage man, especially his fights with the sanitation workers' union, reflects Wilson's interest in the rise of the American labor movement. Of all American cities, Pittsburgh probably has been the most important to the political cause of labor, and Homestead, on the outskirts of the city, was the battleground of the most notorious assault on workers in American history. In 1892, industrialist Andrew Carnegie, assiduously denying steel workers the right to unionize and refusing them a decent wage, triggered a long and bloody battle between labor and capital.

Until fairly recently, however, unions were just as racist as the rest of American society. Though all laborers had the same interest in wresting decent pay and humane working conditions from corporations, whites typically refused to close ranks with their black coworkers. African Americans had to fight for equal treatment by the labor movement just as they fought for equal treatment by the law. In fact, Martin Luther King Jr. was helping black sanitation workers unionize when he was assassinated in Memphis in 1968.

As he chronicles such changes, Wilson also notes what the black communities lost when America integrated. Though few people today would argue for the ghettoizing of any single race of Americans, such enforced isolation fostered a sense of community and allowed for an economic independence that integration undermined. For example, integrating the Major Leagues destroyed the Negro Leagues, and with the Negro Leagues went the only black-owned ball clubs in America. Only now, more than half a century after Jackie Robinson started to play for the Dodgers, are African Americans breaking into the upper ranks of management and ownership in the Major Leagues.

> *The first generation of integrated minorities must experience a sense of loss even as it gains so much. Wilson has been accused of sentimentalizing that loss and even of supporting separatism, the belief that African Americans must sustain their own communities and cultural institutions apart from the white-dominated mainstream. Certainly, he has worked to improve opportunities for black actors, black theaters, and black directors, staunchly supporting regional theaters that cater to black audiences. Indeed, Paramount Pictures' plans to make a movie out of* Fences *stalled because of Wilson's insistence on using a black director.*
>
> *Even as you read the play in light of these issues, however, don't forget that it is also about family—about fathers and sons, wives and husbands. Like the best "problem" plays in the Ibsen tradition,* Fences *can stand as well outside as it stands inside its historical and cultural context.*

Fences

CHARACTERS

TROY MAXSON	
JIM BONO	TROY's *friend*
ROSE	TROY's *wife*
LYONS	TROY's *oldest son by previous marriage*
GABRIEL	TROY's *brother*
CORY	TROY *and* ROSE's *son*
RAYNELL	TROY's *daughter*

SETTING

The setting is the yard which fronts the only entrance to the MAXSON household, an ancient two-story brick house set back off a small alley in a big-city neighborhood. The entrance to the house is gained by two or three steps leading to a wooden porch badly in need of paint.

A relatively recent addition to the house and running its full width, the porch lacks congruence. It is a sturdy porch with a flat roof. One or two chairs of dubious value sit at one end where the kitchen window opens onto the porch. An old-fashioned icebox stands silent guard at the opposite end.

The yard is a small dirt yard, partially fenced, except for the last scene, with a wooden sawhorse, a pile of lumber, and other fence-building equipment set off to the side. Opposite is a tree from which hangs a ball made of rags. A baseball bat leans against the tree. Two oil drums serve as garbage receptacles and sit near the house at right to complete the setting.

THE PLAY

Near the turn of the century, the destitute of Europe sprang on the city with tenacious claws and an honest and solid dream. The city devoured them. They swelled its belly until it burst into a thousand furnaces and sewing machines, a thousand butcher shops and bakers' ovens, a thousand churches and hospitals and funeral parlors and moneylenders. The city grew. It nourished itself and offered each man a partnership limited only by his talent, his guile, and his willingness and capacity for hard work. For the immigrants of Europe, a dream dared and won true.

The descendants of African slaves were offered no such welcome or participation. They came from places called the Carolinas and the Virginias, Georgia, Alabama, Mississippi, and Tennessee. They came strong, eager, searching. The city rejected them and they fled and settled along the riverbanks and under bridges in shallow, ramshackle houses made of sticks and tar-paper. They collected rags and wood. They sold the use of their muscles and their bodies. They cleaned houses and washed clothes, they shined shoes, and in quiet desperation and vengeful pride, they stole, and lived in pursuit of their own dream. That they could breathe free, finally, and stand to meet life with the force of dignity and whatever eloquence the heart could call upon.

By 1957, the hard-won victories of the European immigrants had solidified the industrial might of America. War had been confronted and won with new energies that used loyalty and patriotism as its fuel. Life was rich, full, and flourishing. The Milwaukee Braves won the World Series, and the hot winds of change that would make the sixties a turbulent, racing, dangerous, and provocative decade had not yet begun to blow full.

ACT ONE
Scene One

It is 1957. TROY *and* BONO *enter the yard, engaged in conversation.* TROY *is fifty-three years old, a large man with thick, heavy hands; it is this largeness that he strives to fill out and make an accommodation with. Together with his blackness, his largeness informs his sensibilities and the choices he has made in his life.*

Of the two men, BONO *is obviously the follower. His commitment to their friendship of thirty-odd years is rooted in his admiration of* TROY'S *honesty, capacity for hard work, and strength, which* BONO *seeks to emulate.*

It is Friday night, payday, and the one night of the week the two men engage in a ritual of talk and drink. TROY *is usually the most talkative and at times he can be crude and almost vulgar, though he is capable of rising to profound heights of expression. The men carry lunch buckets and wear or carry burlap aprons and are dressed in clothes suitable to their jobs as garbage collectors.*

BONO: Troy, you ought to stop that lying!

TROY: I ain't lying! The nigger had a watermelon this big. [*He indicates with his hands.*] Talking about . . . "What watermelon, Mr. Rand?" I liked to fell out! "What watermelon, Mr. Rand?" . . . And it sitting there big as life.

BONO: What did Mr. Rand say?

TROY: Ain't said nothing. Figure if the nigger too dumb to know he carrying a watermelon, he wasn't gonna get much sense out of him. Trying to hide that great big old watermelon under his coat. Afraid to let the white man see him carry it home.

BONO: I'm like you. . . . I ain't got no time for them kind of people.

TROY: Now what he look like getting mad cause he see the man from the union talking to Mr. Rand?

BONO: He come to me talking about . . . "Maxson gonna get us fired." I told him to get away from me with that. He walked away from me calling you a troublemaker. What Mr. Rand say?

TROY: Ain't said nothing. He told me to go down the Commissioner's office next Friday. They called me down there to see them.

BONO: Well, as long as you got your complaint filed, they can't fire you. That's what one of them white fellows tell me.

TROY: I ain't worried about them firing me. They gonna fire me cause I asked a question? That's all I did. I went to Mr. Rand and asked him, "Why? Why you got the white mens driving and the colored lifting?" Told him, "What's the matter, don't I count? You think only white fellows got sense enough to drive a truck. That ain't no paper job! Hell, anybody can drive a truck. How come you got all whites driving and the colored lifting? He told me "take it to the union." Well, hell, that's what I done! Now they wanna come up with this pack of lies.

BONO: I told Brownie if the man come and ask him any questions . . . just tell the truth! It ain't nothing but something they done trumped up on you cause you filed a complaint on them.

TROY: Brownie don't understand nothing. All I want them to do is change the job description. Give everybody a chance to drive the truck. Brownie can't see that. He ain't got that much sense.

BONO: How you figure he be making out with that gal be up at Taylors' all the time . . . that Alberta gal?

TROY: Same as you and me. Getting just as much as we is. Which is to say, nothing.

BONO: It is, huh? I figure you doing a little better than me . . . and I ain't saying what I'm doing.

TROY: Aw, nigger, look here . . . I know you. If you had got anywhere near that gal, twenty minutes later you be looking to tell somebody. And the first one you gonna tell . . . that you gonna want to brag to . . . is gonna be me.

BONO: I ain't saying that. I see where you be eyeing her.

TROY: I eye all the women. I don't miss nothing. Don't never let nobody tell you Troy Maxson don't eye the women.

BONO: You been doing more than eyeing her. You done bought her a drink or two.

TROY: Hell yeah, I bought her a drink! What that mean? I bought you one, too. What that mean cause I buy her a drink? I'm just being polite.

BONO: It's alright to buy her one drink. That's what you call being polite. But when you wanna be buying two or three . . . that's what you call eyeing her.

TROY: Look here, as long as you known me . . . you ever known me to chase after women?

BONO: Hell yeah! Long as I done known you. You forgetting I knew you when.

TROY: Naw, I'm talking about since I been married to Rose?

BONO: Oh, not since you been married to Rose. Now, that's the truth, there. I can say that.

TROY: Alright then! Case closed.

BONO: I see you be walking up around Alberta's house. You supposed to be at Taylors' and you be walking up around there.

TROY: What you watching where I'm walking for? I ain't watching after you.

BONO: I seen you walking around there more than once.

TROY: Hell, you liable to see me walking anywhere! That don't mean nothing cause you see me walking around there.

BONO: Where she come from anyway? She just kinda showed up one day.

TROY: Tallahassee. You can look at her and tell she one of them Florida gals. They got some big healthy women down there. Grow them right up out the ground. Got a little bit of Indian in her. Most of them niggers down in Florida got some Indian in them.

BONO: I don't know about that Indian part. But she damn sure big and healthy. Woman wear some big stockings. Got them great big old legs and hips as wide as the Mississippi River.

TROY: Legs don't mean nothing. You don't do nothing but push them out of the way. But them hips cushion the ride!

BONO: Troy, you ain't got no sense.

TROY: It's the truth! Like you riding on Goodyears!

[ROSE *enters from the house. She is ten years younger than* TROY, *her devotion to him stems from her recognition of the possibilities of her life without him: a succession of abusive men and their babies, a life of partying and running the streets, the Church, or aloneness with its attendant pain and frustration. She recognizes* TROY's *spirit as a fine and illuminating one and she either ignores or forgives his faults, only some of which she recognizes. Though she doesn't drink, her presence is an integral part of the Friday night rituals. She alternates between the porch and the kitchen, where supper preparations are under way.*]

ROSE: What you all out here getting into?

TROY: What you worried about what we getting into for? This is men talk, woman.

ROSE: What I care what you all talking about? Bono, you gonna stay for supper?

BONO: No, I thank you, Rose. But Lucille say she cooking up a pot of pigfeet.

TROY: Pigfeet! Hell, I'm going home with you! Might even stay the night if you got some pigfeet. You got something in there to top them pigfeet, Rose?

ROSE: I'm cooking up some chicken. I got some chicken and collard greens.

TROY: Well, go on back in the house and let me and Bono finish what we was talking about. This is men talk. I got some talk for you later. You know what kind of talk I mean. You go on and powder it up.

ROSE: Troy Maxson, don't you start that now!

TROY: [*Puts his arm around her.*] Aw, woman . . . come here. Look here, Bono . . . when I met this woman . . . I got out that place, say, "Hitch up my pony, saddle up my mare . . . there's a woman out there for me somewhere. I looked here. Looked there. Saw Rose and latched on to her." I latched on to her and told her— I'm gonna tell you the truth—I told her, "Baby, I don't wanna marry, I just wanna be your man." Rose told me . . . tell him what you told me, Rose.

ROSE: I told him if he wasn't the marrying kind, then move out the way so the marrying kind could find me.

TROY: That's what she told me. "Nigger, you in my way. You blocking the view! Move out the way so I can find me a husband." I thought it over two or three days. Come back—

ROSE: Ain't no two or three days nothing. You was back the same night.

TROY: Come back, told her . . . "Okay, baby . . . but I'm gonna buy me a banty rooster and put him out there in the backyard . . . and when he see a stranger come, he'll flap his wings and crow . . ."

Look here, Bono, I could watch the front door by myself . . . it was that back door I was worried about.

ROSE: Troy, you ought not talk like that. Troy ain't doing nothing but telling a lie.

TROY: Only thing is . . . when we first got married . . . forget the rooster . . . we ain't had no yard!

BONO: I hear you tell it. Me and Lucille was staying down there on Logan Street. Had two rooms with the outhouse in the back. I ain't mind the outhouse none. But when that goddamn wind blow through there in the winter . . . that's what I'm talking about! To this day I wonder why in the hell I ever stayed down there for six long years. But see, I didn't know I could do no better. I thought only white folks had inside toilets and things.

ROSE: There's a lot of people don't know they can do no better than they doing now. That's just something you got to learn. A lot of folks still shop at Bella's.

TROY: Ain't nothing wrong with shopping at Bella's. She got fresh food.

ROSE: I ain't said nothing about if she got fresh food. I'm talking about what she charge. She charge ten cents more than the A&P.

TROY: The A&P ain't never done nothing for me. I spends my money where I'm treated right. I go down to Bella, say, "I need a loaf of bread, I'll pay you Friday." She give it to me. What sense that make when I got money to go and spend it somewhere else and ignore the person who done right by me? That ain't in the Bible.

ROSE: We ain't talking about what's in the Bible. What sense it make to shop there when she overcharge?

TROY: You shop where you want to. I'll do my shopping where the people been good to me.

ROSE: Well, I don't think it's right for her to overcharge. That's all I was saying.

BONO: Look here . . . I got to get on. Lucille going be raising all kind of hell.

TROY: Where you going, nigger? We ain't finished this pint. Come here, finish this pint.

BONO: Well, hell, I am . . . if you ever turn the bottle loose.

TROY: [Hands him the bottle.] The only thing I say about the A&P is

I'm glad Cory got that job down there. Help him take care of his school clothes and things. Gabe done moved out and things getting tight around here. He got that job. . . . He can start to look out for himself.

ROSE: Cory done went and got recruited by a college football team.

TROY: I told that boy about that football stuff. The white man ain't gonna let him get nowhere with that football. I told him when he first come to me with it. Now you come telling me he done went and got more tied up in it. He ought to go and get recruited in how to fix cars or something where he can make a living.

ROSE: He ain't talking about making no living playing football. It's just something the boys in school do. They gonna send a recruiter by to talk to you. He'll tell you he ain't talking about making no living playing football. It's a honor to be recruited.

TROY: It ain't gonna get him nowhere. Bono'll tell you that.

BONO: If he be like you in the sports . . . he's gonna be alright. Ain't but two men ever played baseball as good as you. That's Babe Ruth and Josh Gibson.[1] Them's the only two men ever hit more home runs than you.

TROY: What it ever get me? Ain't got a pot to piss in or a window to throw it out of.

ROSE: Times have changed since you was playing baseball, Troy. That was before the war.[2] Times have changed a lot since then.

TROY: How in hell they done changed?

ROSE: They got lots of colored boys playing ball now. Baseball and football.

BONO: You right about that, Rose. Times have changed, Troy. You just come along too early.

TROY: There ought not never have been no time called too early! Now you take that fellow . . . what's that fellow they had playing right field for the Yankees back then? You know who I'm talking about, Bono. Used to play right field for the Yankees.

ROSE: Selkirk?

TROY: Selkirk! That's it! Man batting .269, understand? .269. What

1. See headnote (p. 1032) for a discussion of Josh Gibson.

2. World War II, which ended in 1945.

kind of sense that make? I was hitting .432 with thirty-seven home runs! Man batting .269 and playing right field for the Yankees! I saw Josh Gibson's daughter yesterday. She walking around with raggedy shoes on her feet. Now I bet you Selkirk's daughter ain't walking around with raggedy shoes on her feet! I bet you that!

ROSE: They got a lot of colored baseball players now. Jackie Robinson was the first. Folks had to wait for Jackie Robinson.

TROY: I done seen a hundred niggers play baseball better than Jackie Robinson. Hell, I know some teams Jackie Robinson couldn't even make! What you talking about Jackie Robinson. Jackie Robinson wasn't nobody. I'm talking about if you could play ball then they ought to have let you play. Don't care what color you were. Come telling me I come along too early. If you could play . . . then they ought to have let you play. [TROY *takes a long drink from the bottle.*]

ROSE: You gonna drink yourself to death. You don't need to be drinking like that.

TROY: Death ain't nothing. I done seen him. Done wrassled with him. You can't tell me nothing about death. Death ain't nothing but a fastball on the outside corner. And you know what I'll do to that! Lookee here, Bono . . . am I lying? You get one of them fastballs, about waist high, over the outside corner of the plate where you can get the meat of the bat on it . . . and good God! You can kiss it goodbye. Now, am I lying?

BONO: Naw, you telling the truth there. I seen you do it.

TROY: If I'm lying . . . that 450 feet worth of lying! [*Pause.*] That's all death is to me. A fastball on the outside corner.

ROSE: I don't know why you want to get on talking about death.

TROY: Ain't nothing wrong with talking about death. That's part of life. Everybody gonna die. You gonna die, I'm gonna die. Bono's gonna die. Hell, we all gonna die.

ROSE: But you ain't got to talk about it. I don't like to talk about it.

TROY: You the one brought it up. Me and Bono was talking about baseball . . . you tell me I'm gonna drink myself to death. Ain't that right, Bono? You know I don't drink this but one night out of the week. That's Friday night. I'm gonna drink just enough to where I can handle it. Then I cuts it loose. I leave it alone. So don't you worry about me drinking myself to death. 'Cause I ain't worried about Death. I done seen him. I done wrestled with him.

Look here, Bono . . . I looked up one day and Death was marching straight at me. Like Soldiers on Parade! The Army of Death was marching straight at me. The middle of July, 1941. It got real cold just like it be winter. It seem like Death himself reached out and touched me on the shoulder. He touch me just like I touch you. I got cold as ice and Death standing there grinning at me.

ROSE: Troy, why don't you hush that talk.

TROY: I say . . . What you want, Mr. Death? You be wanting me? You done brought your army to be getting me? I looked him dead in the eye. I wasn't fearing nothing. I was ready to tangle. Just like I'm ready to tangle now. The Bible say be ever vigilant. That's why I don't get but so drunk. I got to keep watch.

ROSE: Troy was right down there in Mercy Hospital. You remember he had pneumonia? Laying there with a fever talking plumb out of his head.

TROY: Death standing there staring at me . . . carrying that sickle in his hand. Finally he say, "You want bound over for another year?" See, just like that . . . "You want bound over for another year?" I told him, "Bound over hell! Let's settle this now!"

It seem like he kinda fell back when I said that, and all the cold went out of me. I reached down and grabbed that sickle and threw it just as far as I could throw it . . . and me and him commenced to wrestling.

We wrestled for three days and three nights. I can't say where I found the strength from. Every time it seemed like he was gonna get the best of me, I'd reach way down deep inside myself and find the strength to do him one better.

ROSE: Every time Troy tell that story he find different ways to tell it. Different things to make up about it.

TROY: I ain't making up nothing. I'm telling you the facts of what happened. I wrestled with Death for three days and three nights and I'm standing here to tell you about it. [*Pause.*] Alright. At the end of the third night we done weakened each other to where we can't hardly move. Death stood up, throwed on his robe . . . had him a white robe with a hood on it. He throwed on that robe and went off to look for his sickle. Say, "I'll be back." Just like that. "I'll be back." I told him, say, "Yeah, but . . . you gonna have to find me!" I wasn't no fool. I wasn't going looking for him. Death ain't nothing to play with. And I know he's gonna get me. I know I got to join his army . . . his camp followers. But as long as I keep my strength and see him coming . . . as long as I keep up my vigilance . . . he's gonna have to fight to get me. I ain't going easy.

BONO: Well, look here, since you got to keep up your vigilance . . . let me have the bottle.

TROY: Aw hell, I shouldn't have told you that part. I should have left out that part.

ROSE: Troy be talking that stuff and half the time don't even know what he be talking about.

TROY: Bono know me better than that.

BONO: That's right. I know you. I know you got some Uncle Remus[3] in your blood. You got more stories than the devil got sinners.

TROY: Aw hell, I done seen him too! Done talked with the devil.

ROSE: Troy, don't nobody wanna be hearing all that stuff.

> [LYONS *enters the yard from the street. Thirty-four years old,* TROY's *son by a previous marriage, he sports a neatly trimmed goatee, sport coat, white shirt, tieless and buttoned at the collar. Though he fancies himself a musician, he is more caught up in the rituals and "idea" of being a musician than in the actual practice of the music. He has come to borrow money from* TROY, *and while he knows he will be successful, he is uncertain as to what extent his lifestyle will be held up to scrutiny and ridicule.*]

LYONS: Hey, Pop.

TROY: What you come "Hey, Popping" me for?

LYONS: How you doing, Rose? [*He kisses her.*] Mr. Bono. How you doing?

BONO: Hey, Lyons . . . how you been?

TROY: He must have been doing alright. I ain't seen him around here last week.

---

3. The wise, old, black narrator of a series of stories about Brer Rabbit and Brer Fox, written by Joel Chandler Harris (1848–1908).

ROSE: Troy, leave your boy alone. He come by to see you and you wanna start all that nonsense.

TROY: I ain't bothering Lyons. [*Offers him the bottle.*] Here . . . get you a drink. We got an understanding. I know why he come by to see me and he know I know.

LYONS: Come on, Pop . . . I just stopped by to say hi . . . see how you was doing.

TROY: You ain't stopped by yesterday.

ROSE: You gonna stay for supper, Lyons? I got some chicken cooking in the oven.

LYONS: No, Rose . . . thanks. I was just in the neighborhood and thought I'd stop by for a minute.

TROY: You was in the neighborhood alright, nigger. You telling the truth there. You was in the neighborhood cause it's my payday.

LYONS: Well, hell, since you mentioned it . . . let me have ten dollars.

TROY: I'll be damned! I'll die and go to hell and play blackjack with the devil before I give you ten dollars.

BONO: That's what I wanna know about . . . that devil you done seen.

LYONS: What . . . Pop done seen the devil? You too much, Pops.

TROY: Yeah, I done seen him. Talked to him too!

ROSE: You ain't seen no devil. I done told you that man ain't had nothing to do with the devil. Anything you can't understand, you want to call it the devil.

TROY: Look here, Bono . . . I went down to see Hertzberger about some furniture. Got three rooms for two-ninety-eight. That what it say on the radio. "Three rooms . . . two-ninety-eight." Even made up a little song about it. Go down there . . . man tell me I can't get no credit. I'm working every day and can't get no credit. What to do? I got an empty house with some raggedy furniture in it. Cory ain't got no bed. He's sleeping on a pile of rags on the floor. Working every day and can't get no credit. Come back here—Rose'll tell you—madder than hell. Sit down . . . try to figure what I'm gonna do. Come a knock on the door. Ain't been living here but three days. Who know I'm here? Open the door . . . devil standing there bigger than life. White fellow . . . got on good clothes and everything. Standing there with a clipboard in his hand. I ain't had to say nothing. First words come out of his mouth was . . . "I understand you need some furniture and can't get no credit." I liked to fell over. He say "I'll give you all the credit you want, but you got to pay the interest on it." I told him, "Give me three rooms' worth and charge whatever you want." Next day a truck pulled up here and two men unloaded them three rooms. Man what drove the truck give me a book. Say send ten dollars, first of every month to the address in the book and everything will be alright. Say if I miss a payment the devil was coming back and it'll be hell to pay. That was fifteen years ago. To this day . . . the first of the month I send my ten dollars, Rose'll tell you.

ROSE: Troy lying.

TROY: I ain't never seen that man since. Now you tell me who else that could have been but the devil? I ain't sold my soul or nothing like that, you understand. Naw, I wouldn't have truck with the devil about nothing like that. I got my furniture and pays my ten dollars the first of the month just like clockwork.

BONO: How long you say you been paying this ten dollars a month?

TROY: Fifteen years!

BONO: Hell, ain't you finished paying for it yet? How much the man done charged you.

TROY: Aw hell, I done paid for it. I done paid for it ten times over! The fact is I'm scared to stop paying it.

ROSE: Troy lying. We got that furniture from Mr. Glickman. He ain't paying no ten dollars a month to nobody.

TROY: Aw hell, woman. Bono know I ain't that big a fool.

LYONS: I was just getting ready to say . . . I know where there's a bridge for sale.

TROY: Look here, I'll tell you this . . . it don't matter to me if he was the devil. It don't matter if the devil give credit. Somebody has got to give it.

ROSE: It ought to matter. You going around talking about having truck with the devil . . . God's the one you gonna have to answer to. He's the one gonna be at the Judgment.

LYONS: Yeah, well, look here, Pop . . . let me have that ten dollars. I'll give it back to you. Bonnie got a job working at the hospital.

TROY: What I tell you, Bono? The only time I see this nigger is when he wants something. That's the only time I see him.

LYONS: Come on, Pop, Mr. Bono don't want to hear all that. Let me have the ten dollars. I told you Bonnie working.

TROY: What that mean to me? "Bonnie working." I don't care if she working. Go ask her for the ten dollars if she working. Talking about "Bonnie working." Why ain't you working?

LYONS: Aw, Pop, you know I can't find no decent job. Where am I gonna get a job at? You know I can't get no job.

TROY: I told you I know some people down there. I can get you on the rubbish if you want to work. I told you that the last time you came by here asking me for something.

LYONS: Naw, Pop . . . thanks. That ain't for me. I don't wanna be carrying nobody's rubbish. I don't wanna be punching nobody's time clock.

TROY: What's the matter, you too good to carry people's rubbish? Where you think that ten dollars you talking about come from? I'm just supposed to haul people's rubbish and give my money to you cause you too lazy to work. You too lazy to work and wanna know why you ain't got what I got.

ROSE: What hospital Bonnie working at? Mercy?

LYONS: She's down at Passavant working in the laundry.

TROY: I ain't got nothing as it is. I give you that ten dollars and I got to eat beans the rest of the week. Naw . . . you ain't getting no ten dollars here.

LYONS: You ain't got to be eating no beans. I don't know why you wanna say that.

TROY: I ain't got no extra money. Gabe done moved over to Miss Pearl's paying her the rent and things done got tight around here. I can't afford to be giving you every payday.

LYONS: I ain't asked you to give me nothing. I asked you to loan me ten dollars. I know you got ten dollars.

TROY: Yeah, I got it. You know why I got it? Cause I don't throw my money away out there in the streets. You living the fast life . . . wanna be a musician . . . running around in them clubs and things . . . then, you learn to take care of yourself. You ain't gonna find me going and asking nobody for nothing. I done spent too many years without.

LYONS: You and me is two different people, Pop.

TROY: I done learned my mistake and learned to do what's right by it. You still trying to get something for nothing. Life don't owe you nothing. You owe it to yourself. Ask Bono. He'll tell you I'm right.

LYONS: You got your way of dealing with the world . . . I got mine. The only thing that matters to me is the music.

TROY: Yeah, I can see that! It don't matter how you gonna eat . . . where your next dollar is coming from. You telling the truth there.

LYONS: I know I got to eat. But I got to live too. I need something that gonna help me to get out of the bed in the morning. Make me feel like I belong in the world. I don't bother nobody. I just stay with my music cause that's the only way I can find to live in the world. Otherwise there ain't no telling what I might do. Now I don't come criticizing you and how you live. I just come by to ask you for ten dollars. I don't wanna hear all that about how I live.

TROY: Boy, your mama did a hell of a job raising you.

LYONS: You can't change me, Pop. I'm thirty-four years old. If you wanted to change me, you should have been there when I was growing up. I come by to see you . . . ask for ten dollars and you want to talk about how I was raised. You don't know nothing about how I was raised.

ROSE: Let the boy have ten dollars, Troy.

TROY: [To LYONS.] What the hell you looking at me for? I ain't got no ten dollars. You know what I do with my money. [To ROSE.] Give him ten dollars if you want him to have it.

ROSE: I will. Just as soon as you turn it loose.

TROY: [Handing ROSE the money.] There it is. Seventy-six dollars and forty-two cents. You see this, Bono? Now, I ain't gonna get but six of that back.

ROSE: You ought to stop telling that lie. Here, Lyons. [She hands him the money.]

LYONS: Thanks, Rose. Look . . . I got to run. . . . I'll see you later.

TROY: Wait a minute. You gonna say, "Thanks, Rose" and ain't gonna look to see where she got that ten dollars from? See how they do me, Bono?

LYONS: I know she got it from you, Pop. Thanks. I'll give it back to you.

TROY: There he go telling another lie. Time I see that ten dollars . . . he'll be owing me thirty more.

LYONS: See you, Mr. Bono.

BONO: Take care, Lyons!

LYONS: Thanks, Pop. I'll see you again. [LYONS *exits the yard.*]

TROY: I don't know why he don't go and get him a decent job and take care of that woman he got.

BONO: He'll be alright, Troy. The boy is still young.

TROY: The *boy* is thirty-four years old.

ROSE: Let's not get off into all that.

BONO: Look here . . . I got to be going. I got to be getting on. Lucille gonna be waiting.

TROY: [*Puts his arm around* ROSE.] See this woman, Bono? I love this woman. I love this woman so much it hurts. I love her so much . . . I done run out of ways of loving her. So I got to go back to basics. Don't you come by my house Monday morning talking about time to go to work . . . 'cause I'm still gonna be stroking!

ROSE: Troy! Stop it now!

BONO: I ain't paying him no mind, Rose. That ain't nothing but gin-talk. Go on, Troy. I'll see you Monday.

TROY: Don't you come by my house, nigger! I done told you what I'm gonna be doing.

[*The lights go down to black.*]

SCENE TWO

The lights come up on ROSE *hanging up clothes. She hums and sings softly to herself. It is the following morning.*

ROSE: [*Sings.*] Jesus, be a fence all around me every day.
   Jesus, I want you to protect me as I travel on my way.
   Jesus, be a fence all around me every day.
   [TROY *enters from the house.*]
   Jesus, I want you to protect me
   As I travel on my way.
   [*To* TROY.] 'Morning. You ready for breakfast? I can fix it soon as I finish hanging up these clothes.

TROY: I got the coffee on. That'll be alright. I'll just drink some of that this morning.

ROSE: That 651 hit yesterday. That's the second time this month. Miss Pearl hit for a dollar . . . seem like those that need the least always get lucky. Poor folks can't get nothing.

TROY: Them numbers don't know nobody. I don't know why you fool with them. You and Lyons both.

ROSE: It's something to do.

TROY: You ain't doing nothing but throwing your money away.

ROSE: Troy, you know I don't play foolishly. I just play a nickel here and a nickel there.

TROY: That's two nickels you done thrown away.

ROSE: Now I hit sometimes . . . that makes up for it. It always comes in handy when I do hit. I don't hear you complaining then.

TROY: I ain't complaining now. I just say it's foolish. Trying to guess out of six hundred ways which way the number gonna come. If I had all the money niggers, these Negroes, throw away on numbers for one week—just one week—I'd be a rich man.

ROSE: Well, you wishing and calling it foolish ain't gonna stop folks from playing numbers. That's one thing for sure. Besides . . . some good things come from playing numbers. Look where Pope done bought him that restaurant off of numbers.

TROY: I can't stand niggers like that. Man ain't had two dimes to rub together. He walking around with his shoes all run over bumming money for cigarettes. Alright. Got lucky there and hit the numbers. . . .

ROSE: Troy, I know all about it.

TROY: Had good sense, I'll say that for him. He ain't throwed his money away. I seen niggers hit the numbers and go through two thousand dollars in four days. Man brought him that restaurant down there . . . fixed it up real nice . . . and then didn't want nobody to come in it! A Negro go in there and can't get no kind of service. I seen a white fellow come in there and order a bowl of stew. Pope picked all the meat out the pot for him. Man ain't had nothing but a bowl of meat! Negro come behind him and ain't got nothing but the potatoes and carrots. Talking about what numbers do for people, you picked a wrong example. Ain't done nothing but make a worser fool out of him than he was before.

ROSE: Troy, you ought to stop worrying about what happened at work yesterday.

TROY: I ain't worried. Just told me to be down there at the Commissioner's office on Friday. Everybody think they gonna fire me. I ain't worried about them firing me. You ain't got to worry about that. [*Pause.*] Where's Cory? Cory in the house? [*Calls.*] Cory?

ROSE: He gone out.

TROY: Out, huh? He gone out 'cause he know I want him to help me with this fence. I know how he is. That boy scared of work. [GABRIEL *enters. He comes halfway down the alley and, hearing* TROY's *voice, stops.*] He ain't done a lick of work in his life.

ROSE: He had to go to football practice. Coach wanted them to get in a little extra practice before the season start.

TROY: I got his practice . . . running out of here before he get his chores done.

ROSE: Troy, what is wrong with you this morning? Don't nothing set right with you. Go on back in there and go to bed . . . get up on the other side.

TROY: Why something got to be wrong with me? I ain't said nothing wrong with me.

ROSE: You got something to say about everything. First it's the numbers . . . then it's the way the man runs his restaurant . . . then you done got on Cory. What's it gonna be next? Take a look up there and see if the weather suits you . . . or is it gonna be how you gonna put up the fence with the clothes hanging in the yard.

TROY: You hit the nail on the head then.

ROSE: I know you like I know the back of my hand. Go on in there and get you some coffee . . . see if that straighten you up. 'Cause you ain't right this morning.

[TROY *starts into the house and sees* GABRIEL. GABRIEL *starts singing.* TROY's *brother, he is seven years younger than* TROY. *Injured in World War II, he has a metal plate in his head. He carries an old trumpet tied around his waist and believes with every fiber of his being that he is the Archangel Gabriel.*[1] *He carries a chipped*

---

1. In Christianity, God's messenger who announced the births of John the Baptist and Jesus.

*basket with an assortment of discarded fruits and vegetables he has
picked up in the strip district and which he attempts to sell.*]

GABRIEL: [*Singing.*] Yes, ma'am, I got plums
You ask me how I sell them
Oh ten cents apiece
Three for a quarter
Come and buy now
'Cause I'm here today
And tomorrow I'll be gone
[GABRIEL *enters.*] Hey, Rose!

ROSE: How you doing, Gabe?

GABRIEL: There's Troy. . . . Hey, Troy!

TROY: Hey, Gabe. [*Exit into kitchen.*]

ROSE: [*To* GABRIEL.] What you got there?

GABRIEL: You know what I got, Rose. I got fruits and vegetables.

ROSE: [*Looking in basket.*] Where's all these plums you talking
about?

GABRIEL: I ain't got no plums today, Rose. I was just singing that.
Have some tomorrow. Put me in a big order for plums. Have
enough plums tomorrow for St. Peter and everybody. [TROY *reenters from kitchen, crosses to steps.*] [*To* ROSE.] Troy's mad at me.

TROY: I ain't mad at you. What I got to be mad at you about? You
ain't done nothing to me.

GABRIEL: I just moved over to Miss Pearl's to keep out from in your
way. I ain't mean no harm by it.

TROY: Who said anything about that? I ain't said anything about
that.

GABRIEL: You ain't mad at me, is you?

TROY: Naw . . . I ain't mad at you, Gabe. If I was mad at you I'd tell
you about it.

GABRIEL: Got me two rooms. In the basement. Got my own door
too. Wanna see my key? [*He holds up a key.*] That's my own key!
Ain't nobody else got a key like that. That's my key! My two
rooms!

TROY: Well, that's good, Gabe. You got your own key . . . that's
good.

ROSE: You hungry, Gabe? I was just fixing to cook Troy his breakfast.

GABRIEL: I'll take some biscuits. You got some biscuits? Did you know when I was in heaven . . . every morning me and St. Peter would sit down by the gate and eat some big fat biscuits? Oh, yeah! We had us a good time. We'd sit there and eat us them biscuits and then St. Peter would go off to sleep and tell me to wake him up when it's time to open the gates for the judgment.

ROSE: Well, come on . . . I'll make up a batch of biscuits. [ROSE *exits into the house.*]

GABRIEL: Troy . . . St. Peter got your name in the book. I seen it. It say . . . Troy Maxson. I say . . . I know him! He got the same name like what I got. That's my brother!

TROY: How many times you gonna tell me that, Gabe?

GABRIEL: Ain't got my name in the book. Don't have to have my name. I done died and went to heaven. He got your name though. One morning St. Peter was looking at his book . . . marking it up for the judgment . . . and he let me see your name. Got it in there under M. Got Rose's name. . . . I ain't seen it like I seen yours . . . but I know it's in there. He got a great big book. Got everybody's name what was ever been born. That's what he told me. But I seen your name. Seen it with my own eyes.

TROY: Go on in the house there. Rose going to fix you something to eat.

GABRIEL: Oh, I ain't hungry. I done had breakfast with Aunt Jemimah. She come by and cooked me up a whole mess of flapjacks. Remember how we used to eat them flapjacks?

TROY: Go on in the house and get you something to eat now.

GABRIEL: I got to go sell my plums. I done sold some tomatoes. Got me two quarters. Wanna see? [*He shows* TROY *his quarters.*] I'm gonna save them and buy me a new horn so St. Peter can hear me when it's time to open the gates. [GABRIEL *stops suddenly. Listens.*] Hear that? That's the hellhounds. I got to chase them out of here. Go on get out of here! Get out! [GABRIEL *exits singing.*]

Better get ready for the judgment
Better get ready for the judgment
My Lord is coming down
[ROSE *enters from the house.*]

TROY: He gone off somewhere.

GABRIEL: [*Offstage.*] Better get ready for the judgment
Better get ready for the judgment morning

  Better get ready for the judgment
  My God is coming down

ROSE: He ain't eating right. Miss Pearl say she can't get him to eat nothing.

TROY: What you want me to do about it, Rose? I done did everything I can for the man. I can't make him get well. Man got half his head blown away . . . what you expect?

ROSE: Seem like something ought to be done to help him.

TROY: Man don't bother nobody. He just mixed up from that metal plate he got in his head. Ain't no sense for him to go back into the hospital.

ROSE: Least he be eating right. They can help him take care of himself.

TROY: Don't nobody wanna be locked up, Rose. What you wanna lock him up for? Man go over there and fight the war . . . messin' around with them Japs, get half his head blown off . . . and they give him a lousy three thousand dollars. And I had to swoop down on that.

ROSE: Is you fixing to go into that again?

TROY: That's the only way I got a roof over my head . . . 'cause of that metal plate.

ROSE: Ain't no sense you blaming yourself for nothing. Gabe wasn't in no condition to manage that money. You done what was right by him. Can't nobody say you ain't done what was right by him. Look how long you took care of him . . . till he wanted to have his own place and moved over there with Miss Pearl.

TROY: That ain't what I'm saying, woman! I'm just stating the facts. If my brother didn't have that metal plate in his head . . . I wouldn't have a pot to piss in or a window to throw it out of. And I'm fifty-three years old. Now see if you can understand that! [TROY *gets up from the porch and starts to exit the yard.*]

ROSE: Where you going off to? You been running out of here every Saturday for weeks. I thought you was gonna work on this fence?

TROY: I'm gonna walk down to Taylors'. Listen to the ball game. I'll be back in a bit. I'll work on it when I get back. [*He exits the yard. The lights go to black.*]

SCENE THREE

The lights come up on the yard. It is four hours later. ROSE *is taking down the clothes from the line.* CORY *enters carrying his football equipment.*

ROSE: Your daddy like to had a fit with you running out of here this morning without doing your chores.

CORY: I told you I had to go to practice.

ROSE: He say you were supposed to help him with this fence.

CORY: He been saying that the last four or five Saturdays, and then he don't never do nothing, but go down to Taylors'. Did you tell him about the recruiter?

ROSE: Yeah, I told him.

CORY: What he say?

ROSE: He ain't said nothing too much. You get in there and get started on your chores before he gets back. Go on and scrub down them steps before he gets back here hollering and carrying on.

CORY: I'm hungry. What you got to eat, Mama?

ROSE: Go on and get started on your chores. I got some meat loaf in there. Go on and make you a sandwich . . . and don't leave no mess in there. [CORY *exits into the house.* ROSE *continues to take down the clothes.* TROY *enters the yard and sneaks up and grabs her from behind.*] Troy! Go on, now. You liked to scared me to death. What was the score of the game? Lucille had me on the phone and I couldn't keep up with it.

TROY: What I care about the game? Come here, woman. [*He tries to kiss her.*]

ROSE: I thought you went down Taylors' to listen to the game. Go on, Troy! You supposed to be putting up this fence.

TROY: [*Attempting to kiss her again.*] I'll put it up when I finish with what is at hand.

ROSE: Go on, Troy. I ain't studying you.

TROY: [*Chasing after her.*] I'm studying you . . . fixing to do my homework!

ROSE: Troy, you better leave me alone.

TROY: Where's Cory? That boy brought his butt home yet?

ROSE: He's in the house doing his chores.

TROY: [*Calling.*] Cory! Get your butt out here, boy!

[ROSE *exits into the house with the laundry.* TROY *goes over to the pile of wood, picks up a board, and starts sawing.* CORY *enters from the house.*]

TROY: You just now coming in here from leaving this morning?

CORY: Yeah, I had to go to football practice.

TROY: Yeah, what?

CORY: Yessir.

TROY: I ain't but two seconds off you noway. The garbage sitting in there overflowing . . . you ain't done none of your chores . . . and you come in here talking about "Yeah."

CORY: I was just getting ready to do my chores now, Pop. . . .

TROY: Your first chore is to help me with this fence on Saturday. Everything else come after that. Now get that saw and cut them boards.

[CORY *takes the saw and begins cutting the boards.* TROY *continues working. There is a long pause.*]

CORY: Hey, Pop . . . why don't you buy a TV?

TROY: What I want with a TV? What I want one of them for?

CORY: Everybody got one. Earl, Ba Bra . . . Jesse!

TROY: I ain't asked you who had one. I say what I want with one?

CORY: So you can watch it. They got lots of things on TV. Baseball games and everything. We could watch the World Series.

TROY: Yeah . . . and how much this TV cost?

CORY: I don't know. They got them on sale for around two hundred dollars.

TROY: Two hundred dollars, huh?

CORY: That ain't that much, Pop.

TROY: Naw, it's just two hundred dollars. See that roof you got over your head at night? Let me tell you something about that roof. It's been over ten years since that roof was last tarred. See now . . . the snow come this winter and sit up there on that roof like it is . . . and it's gonna seep inside. It's just gonna be a little bit . . . ain't gonna hardly notice it. Then the next thing you know, it's gonna be leaking all over the house. Then the wood rot from all that water and you gonna need a whole new roof. Now, how much you think it cost to get that roof tarred?

CORY: I don't know.

TROY: Two hundred and sixty-four dollars . . . cash money. While

you thinking about a TV, I got to be thinking about the roof . . .
and whatever else go wrong around here. Now if you had two
hundred dollars, what would you do . . . fix the roof or buy a TV?

CORY: I'd buy a TV. Then when the roof started to leak . . . when it
needed fixing . . . I'd fix it.

TROY: Where you gonna get the money from? You done spent it for
a TV. You gonna sit up and watch the water run all over your
brand new TV.

CORY: Aw, Pop. You got money. I know you do.

TROY: Where I got it at, huh?

CORY: You got it in the bank.

TROY: You wanna see my bankbook? You wanna see that seventy-
three dollars and twenty-two cents I got sitting up in there.

CORY: You ain't got to pay for it all at one time. You can put a down
payment on it and carry it on home with you.

TROY: Not me. I ain't gonna owe nobody nothing if I can help it.
Miss a payment and they come and snatch it right out your
house. Then what you got? Now, soon as I get two hundred dollars clear, then I'll buy a TV. Right now, as soon as I get two hundred and sixty-four dollars, I'm gonna have this roof tarred.

CORY: Aw . . . Pop!

TROY: You go on and get you two hundred dollars and buy one if ya
want it. I got better things to do with my money.

CORY: I can't get no two hundred dollars. I ain't never seen two hundred dollars.

TROY: I'll tell you what . . . you get you a hundred dollars and I'll
put the other hundred with it.

CORY: Alright, I'm gonna show you.

TROY: You gonna show me how you can cut them boards right now.

[CORY *begins to cut the boards. There is a long pause.*]

CORY: The Pirates won today. That makes five in a row.

TROY: I ain't thinking about the Pirates. Got an all-white team. Got
that boy . . . that Puerto Rican boy . . . Clemente.[1] Don't even
half-play him. That boy could be something if they give him
a chance. Play him one day and sit him on the bench the next.

---

1. Roberto Clemente (1934–1972), Hall of Fame right fielder for the Pittsburgh Pirates
from 1955 until his death, in a plane crash en route to Nicaragua, where he intended to help
victims of an earthquake.

CORY: He gets a lot of chances to play.

TROY: I'm talking about playing regular. Playing every day so you can get your timing. That's what I'm talking about.

CORY: They got some white guys on the team that don't play every day. You can't play everybody at the same time.

TROY: If they got a white fellow sitting on the bench . . . you can bet your last dollar he can't play! The colored guy got to be twice as good before he get on the team. That's why I don't want you to get all tied up in them sports. Man on the team and what it get him? They got colored on the team and don't use them. Same as not having them. All them teams the same.

CORY: The Braves got Hank Aaron and Wes Covington.[2] Hank Aaron hit two home runs today. That makes forty-three.

TROY: Hank Aaron ain't nobody. That's what you supposed to do. That's how you supposed to play the game. Ain't nothing to it. It's just a matter of timing . . . getting the right follow-through. Hell, I can hit forty-three home runs right now!

CORY: Not off no major-league pitching, you couldn't.

TROY: We had better pitching in the Negro leagues. I hit seven home runs off of Satchel Paige.[3] You can't get no better than that!

CORY: Sandy Koufax.[4] He's leading the league in strikeouts.

TROY: I ain't thinking of no Sandy Koufax.

CORY: You got Warren Spahn and Lew Burdette.[5] I bet you couldn't hit no home runs off of Warren Spahn.

TROY: I'm through with it now. You go on and cut them boards. [*Pause.*] Your mama tell me you done got recruited by a college football team? Is that right?

CORY: Yeah. Coach Zellman say the recruiter gonna be coming by to talk to you. Get you to sign the permission papers.

TROY: I thought you supposed to be working down there at the A&P. Ain't you suppose to be working down there after school?

2. John Wesley Covington (1932–1956), outfielder, and Henry Louis Aaron (1934–), infielder and outfielder, helped the Milwaukee Braves win the World Series in 1957. Aaron holds the all-time home-run record.

3. Leroy Robert Paige (1906?–1982), considered by many the best pitcher in baseball history, played in the Negro Leagues for over twenty years before the Cleveland Indians hired him in 1948.

4. Sanford Koufax (1935–   ) pitched for the Brooklyn Dodgers in 1957.

5. Selva Lewis Burdette Jr. (1926–   ) and Warren Edward Spahn (1921–2003) were star pitchers for the Braves in 1957.

CORY: Mr. Stawicki say he gonna hold my job for me until after the football season. Say starting next week I can work weekends.

TROY: I thought we had an understanding about this football stuff? You suppose to keep up with your chores and hold that job down at the A&P. Ain't been around here all day on a Saturday. Ain't none of your chores done . . . and now you telling me you done quit your job.

CORY: I'm gonna be working weekends.

TROY: You damn right you are! And ain't no need for nobody coming around here to talk to me about signing nothing.

CORY: Hey, Pop . . . you can't do that. He's coming all the way from North Carolina.

TROY: I don't care where he coming from. The white man ain't gonna let you get nowhere with that football noway. You go on and get your book-learning so you can work yourself up in that A&P or learn how to fix cars or build houses or something, get you a trade. That way you have something can't nobody take away from you. You go on and learn how to put your hands to some good use. Besides hauling people's garbage.

CORY: I get good grades, Pop. That's why the recruiter wants to talk with you. You got to keep up your grades to get recruited. This way I'll be going to college. I'll get a chance. . . .

TROY: First you gonna get your butt down there to the A&P and get your job back.

CORY: Mr. Stawicki done already hired somebody else 'cause I told him I was playing football.

TROY: You a bigger fool than I thought . . . to let somebody take away your job so you can play some football. Where you gonna get your money to take out your girlfriend and whatnot? What kind of foolishness is that to let somebody take away your job?

CORY: I'm still gonna be working weekends.

TROY: Naw . . . naw. You getting your butt out of here and finding you another job.

CORY: Come on, Pop! I got to practice. I can't work after school and play football too. The team needs me. That's what Coach Zellman say. . . .

TROY: I don't care what nobody else say. I'm the boss . . . you understand? I'm the boss around here. I do the only saying what counts.

CORY: Come on, Pop!

TROY: I asked you . . . did you understand?

CORY: Yeah . . .

TROY: What?!

CORY: Yessir.

TROY: You go on down there to that A&P and see if you can get your job back. If you can't do both . . . then you quit the football team. You've got to take the crookeds with the straights.

CORY: Yessir. [*Pause.*] Can I ask you a question?

TROY: What the hell you wanna ask me? Mr. Stawicki the one you got the questions for.

CORY: How come you ain't never liked me?

TROY: Liked you? Who the hell say I got to like you? What law is there say I got to like you? Wanna stand up in my face and ask a damn fool-ass question like that. Talking about liking somebody. Come here, boy, when I talk to you. [CORY *comes over to where* TROY *is working. He stands slouched over and* TROY *shoves him on his shoulder.*] Straighten up, goddammit! I asked you a question . . . what law is there say I got to like you?

CORY: None.

TROY: Well, alright then! Don't you eat every day? [*Pause.*] Answer me when I talk to you! Don't you eat every day?

CORY: Yeah.

TROY: Nigger, as long as you in my house, you put that sir on the end of it when you talk to me!

CORY: Yes . . . sir.

TROY: You eat every day.

CORY: Yessir!

TROY: Got a roof over your head.

CORY: Yessir!

TROY: Got clothes on your back.

CORY: Yessir.

TROY: Why you think that is?

CORY: 'Cause of you.

TROY: Aw, hell I know it's 'cause of me . . . but why do you think that is?

CORY: [*Hesitant.*] 'Cause you like me.

TROY: Like you? I go out of here every morning . . . bust my butt . . .

putting up with them crackers every day . . . cause I like you? You about the biggest fool I ever saw. [*Pause.*] It's my job. It's my responsibility! You understand that? A man got to take care of his family. You live in my house . . . sleep you behind on my bed-clothes . . . fill you belly up with my food . . . 'cause you my son. You my flesh and blood. Not 'cause I like you! 'Cause it's my duty to take care of you. I owe a responsibility to you!

Let's get this straight right here . . . before it go along any further. . . . I ain't got to like you. Mr. Rand don't give me my money come payday cause he likes me. He gives me cause he owe me. I done give you everything I had to give you. I gave you your life! Me and your mama worked that out between us. And liking your black ass wasn't part of the bargain. Don't you try and go through life worrying about if somebody like you or not. You best be making sure they doing right by you. You understand what I'm saying, boy?

CORY: Yessir.

TROY: Then get the hell out of my face, and get on down to that A&P.

[ROSE *has been standing behind the screen door for much of the scene. She enters as* CORY *exits.*]

ROSE: Why don't you let the boy go ahead and play football, Troy? Ain't no harm in that. He's just trying to be like you with the sports.

TROY: I don't want him to be like me! I want him to move as far away from my life as he can get. You the only decent thing that ever happened to me. I wish him that. But I don't wish him a thing else from my life. I decided seventeen years ago that boy wasn't getting involved in no sports. Not after what they did to me in the sports.

ROSE: Troy, why don't you admit you was too old to play in the major leagues? For once . . . why don't you admit that?

TROY: What do you mean too old? Don't come telling me I was too old. I just wasn't the right color. Hell, I'm fifty-three years old and can do better than Selkirk's .269 right now!

ROSE: How's was you gonna play ball when you were over forty? Sometimes I can't get no sense out of you.

TROY: I got good sense, woman. I got sense enough not to let my boy get hurt over playing no sports. You been mothering that boy too much. Worried about if people like him.

ROSE: Everything that boy do . . . he do for you. He wants you to say "Good job, son." That's all.

TROY: Rose, I ain't got time for that. He's alive. He's healthy. He's got to make his own way. I made mine. Ain't nobody gonna hold his hand when he get out there in that world.

ROSE: Times have changed from when you was young, Troy. People change. The world's changing around you and you can't even see it.

TROY: [*Slow, methodical.*] Woman . . . I do the best I can do. I come in here every Friday. I carry a sack of potatoes and a bucket of lard. You all line up at the door with your hands out. I give you the lint from my pockets. I give you my sweat and my blood. I ain't got no tears. I done spent them. We go upstairs in that room at night . . . and I fall down on you and try to blast a hole into forever. I get up Monday morning . . . find my lunch on the table. I go out. Make my way. Find my strength to carry me through to the next Friday. [*Pause.*] That's all I got, Rose. That's all I got to give. I can't give nothing else. [TROY *exits into the house. The lights go down to black.*]

SCENE FOUR

It is Friday. Two weeks later. CORY *starts out of the house with his football equipment. The phone rings.*

CORY: [*Calling.*] I got it! [*He answers the phone and stands in the screen door talking.*] Hello? Hey, Jesse. Naw . . . I was just getting ready to leave now.

ROSE: [*Calling.*] Cory!

CORY: I told you, man, them spikes is all tore up. You can use them if you want, but they ain't no good. Earl got some spikes.

ROSE: [*Calling.*] Cory!

CORY: [*Calling to* ROSE.] Mam? I'm talking to Jesse. [*Into phone.*] When she say that? [*Pause.*] Aw, you lying, man. I'm gonna tell her you said that.

ROSE: [*Calling.*] Cory, don't you go nowhere!

CORY: I got to go to the game, Ma! [*Into the phone.*] Yeah, hey, look,

I'll talk to you later. Yeah, I'll meet you over Earl's house. Later. Bye, Ma. [CORY *exits the house and starts out the yard.*]

ROSE: Cory, where you going off to? You got that stuff all pulled out and thrown all over your room.

CORY: [*In the yard.*] I was looking for my spikes. Jesse wanted to borrow my spikes.

ROSE: Get up there and get that cleaned up before your daddy get back in here.

CORY: I got to go to the game! I'll clean it up *when I get back.* [CORY *exits.*]

ROSE: That's all he need to do is see that room all messed up.

[ROSE *exits into the house.* TROY *and* BONO *enter the yard.* TROY *is dressed in clothes other than his work clothes.*]

BONO: He told him the same thing he told you. Take it to the union.

TROY: Brownie ain't got that much sense. Man wasn't thinking about nothing. He wait until I confront them on it . . . then he wanna come crying seniority. [*Calls.*] Hey, Rose!

BONO: I wish I could have seen Mr. Rand's face when he told you.

TROY: He couldn't get it out of his mouth! Liked to bit his tongue! When they called me down there to the Commissioner's office . . . he thought they was gonna fire me. Like everybody else.

BONO: I didn't think they was gonna fire you. I thought they was gonna put you on the warning paper.

TROY: Hey, Rose! [*To* BONO.] Yeah, Mr. Rand like to bit his tongue. [TROY *breaks the seal on the bottle, takes a drink, and hands it to* BONO.]

BONO: I see you run right down to Taylors' and told that Alberta gal.

TROY: [*Calling.*] Hey, Rose! [*To* BONO.] I told everybody. Hey, Rose! I went down there to cash my check.

ROSE: [*Entering from the house.*] Hush all that hollering, man! I know you out here. What they say down there at the Commissioner's office?

TROY: You supposed to come when I call you, woman. Bono'll tell you that. [*To* BONO.] Don't Lucille come when you call her?

ROSE: Man, hush your mouth. I ain't no dog . . . talk about "come when you call me."

TROY: [*Puts his arm around* ROSE.] You hear this, Bono? I had me an

old dog used to get uppity like that. You say, "C'mere, Blue!" . . .
and he just lay there and look at you. End up getting a stick and
chasing him away trying to make him come.

ROSE: I ain't studying you and your dog. I remember you used to
sing that old song.

TROY: [*He sings.*] Hear it ring! Hear it ring!
   I had a dog his name was Blue.

ROSE: Don't nobody wanna hear you sing that old song.

TROY: [*Sings.*] You know Blue was mighty true.

ROSE: Used to have Cory running around here singing that song.

BONO: Hell, I remember that song myself.

TROY: [*Sings.*] You know Blue was a good old dog.
      Blue treed a possum in a hollow log.
   That was my daddy's song. My daddy made up that song.

ROSE: I don't care who made it up. Don't nobody wanna hear you
sing it.

TROY: [*Makes a song like calling a dog.*] Come here, woman.

ROSE: You come in here carrying on, I reckon they ain't fired you.
What they say down there at the Commissioner's office?

TROY: Look here, Rose . . . Mr. Rand called me into his office today
when I got back from talking to them people down there . . . it
come from up top . . . he called me in and told me they was
making me a driver.

ROSE: Troy, you kidding!

TROY: No I ain't. Ask Bono.

ROSE: Well, that's great, Troy. Now you don't have to hassle them
people no more.

   [LYONS *enters from the street.*]

TROY: Aw hell, I wasn't looking to see you today. I thought you was
in jail. Got it all over the front page of the *Courier* about them
raiding Sefus' place . . . where you be hanging out with all them
thugs.

LYONS: Hey, Pop . . . that ain't got nothing to do with me. I don't go
down there gambling. I go down there to sit in with the band. I
ain't got nothing to do with the gambling part. They got some
good music down there.

TROY: They got some rogues . . . is what they got.

LYONS: How you been, Mr. Bono? Hi, Rose.

BONO: I see where you playing down at the Crawford Grill tonight.

ROSE: How come you ain't brought Bonnie like I told you. You should have brought Bonnie with you, she ain't been over in a month of Sundays.

LYONS: I was just in the neighborhood . . . thought I'd stop by.

TROY: Here he come. . . .

BONO: Your daddy got a promotion on the rubbish. He's gonna be the first colored driver. Ain't got to do nothing but sit up there and read the paper like them white fellows.

LYONS: Hey, Pop . . . if you knew how to read you'd be alright.

BONO: Naw . . . naw . . . you mean if the nigger knew how to *drive* he'd be all right. Been fighting with them people about driving and ain't even got a license. Mr. Rand know you ain't got no driver's license?

TROY: Driving ain't nothing. All you do is point the truck where you want it to go. Driving ain't nothing.

BONO: Do Mr. Rand know you ain't got no driver's license? That's what I'm talking about. I ain't asked if driving was easy. I asked if Mr. Rand know you ain't got no driver's license.

TROY: He ain't got to know. The man ain't got to know my business. Time he find out, I have two or three driver's licenses.

LYONS: [*Going into his pocket.*] Say, look here, Pop . . .

TROY: I knew it was coming. Didn't I tell you, Bono? I know what kind of "Look here, Pop" that was. The nigger fixing to ask me for some money. It's Friday night. It's my payday. All them rogues down there on the avenue . . . the ones that ain't in jail . . . and Lyons is hopping in his shoes to get down there with them.

LYONS: See, Pop . . . if you give somebody else a chance to talk sometime, you'd see that I was fixing to pay you back your ten dollars like I told you. Here . . . I told you I'd pay you when Bonnie got paid.

TROY: Naw . . . you go ahead and keep that ten dollars. Put it in the bank. The next time you feel like you wanna come by here and ask me for something . . . you go on down there and get that.

LYONS: Here's your ten dollars, Pop. I told you I don't want you to give me nothing. I just wanted to borrow ten dollars.

TROY: Naw . . . you go on and keep that for the next time you want to ask me.

LYONS: Come on, Pop . . . here go your ten dollars.

ROSE: Why don't you go on and let the boy pay you back, Troy?

LYONS: Here you go, Rose. If you don't take it I'm gonna have to hear about it for the next six months. [*He hands her the money.*]

ROSE: You can hand yours over here too, Troy.

TROY: You see this, Bono. You see how they do me.

BONO: Yeah, Lucille do me the same way.

[GABRIEL *is heard singing offstage. He enters.*]

GABRIEL: Better get ready for the Judgment! Better get ready for . . . Hey! . . . Hey! . . . There's Troy's boy!

LYONS: How you doing, Uncle Gabe?

GABRIEL: Lyons . . . The King of the Jungle! Rose . . . hey, Rose. Got a flower for you. [*He takes a rose from his pocket.*] Picked it myself. That's the same rose like you is!

ROSE: That's right nice of you, Gabe.

LYONS: What you been doing, Uncle Gabe?

GABRIEL: Oh, I been chasing hellhounds and waiting on the time to tell St. Peter to open the gates.

LYONS: You been chasing hellhounds, huh? Well . . . you doing the right thing, Uncle Gabe. Somebody got to chase them.

GABRIEL: Oh, yeah . . . I know it. The devil's strong. The devil ain't no pushover. Hellhounds snipping at everybody's heels. But I got my trumpet waiting on the judgment time.

LYONS: Waiting on the Battle of Armageddon, huh?

GABRIEL: Ain't gonna be too much of a battle when God get to waving that Judgment sword. But the people's gonna have a hell of a time trying to get into heaven if them gates ain't open.

LYONS: [*Putting his arm around* GABRIEL.] You hear this, Pop. Uncle Gabe, you alright!

GABRIEL: [*Laughing with* LYONS.] Lyons! King of the Jungle.

ROSE: You gonna stay for supper, Gabe. Want me to fix you a plate?

GABRIEL: I'll take a sandwich, Rose. Don't want no plate. Just wanna eat with my hands. I'll take a sandwich.

ROSE: How about you, Lyons? You staying? Got some short ribs cooking.

LYONS: Naw, I won't eat nothing till after we finished playing. [*Pause.*] You ought to come down and listen to me play, Pop.

TROY: I don't like that Chinese music. All that noise.

ROSE: Go on in the house and wash up, Gabe. . . . I'll fix you a sandwich.

GABRIEL: [*To* LYONS, *as he exits.*] Troy's mad at me.

LYONS: What you mad at Uncle Gabe for, Pop.

ROSE: He thinks Troy's mad at him cause he moved over to Miss Pearl's.

TROY: I ain't mad at the man. He can live where he want to live at.

LYONS: What he move over there for? Miss Pearl don't like nobody.

ROSE: She don't mind him none. She treats him real nice. She just don't allow all that singing.

TROY: She don't mind that rent he be paying . . . that's what she don't mind.

ROSE: Troy, I ain't going through that with you no more. He's over there cause he want to have his own place. He can come and go as he please.

TROY: Hell, he could come and go as he please here. I wasn't stopping him. I ain't put no rules on him.

ROSE: It ain't the same thing, Troy. And you know it. [GABRIEL *comes to the door.*] Now, that's the last I wanna hear about that. I don't wanna hear nothing else about Gabe and Miss Pearl. And next week . . .

GABRIEL: I'm ready for my sandwich, Rose.

ROSE: And next week . . . when that recruiter come from that school . . . I want you to sign that paper and go on and let Cory play football. Then that'll be the last I have to hear about that.

TROY: [*To* ROSE *as she exits into the house.*] I ain't thinking about Cory nothing.

LYONS: What . . . Cory got recruited? What school he going to?

TROY: That boy walking around here smelling his piss . . . thinking he's grown. Thinking he's gonna do what he want, irrespective of what I say. Look here, Bono . . . I left the Commissioner's office and went down to the A&P . . . that boy ain't working down there. He lying to me. Telling me he got his job back . . . telling me he working weekends . . . telling me he working after school. . . . Mr. Stawicki tell me he ain't working down there at all!

LYONS: Cory just growing up. He's just busting at the seams trying to fill out your shoes.

TROY: I don't care what he's doing. When he get to the point where he wanna disobey me . . . then it's time for him to move on. Bono'll tell you that. I bet he ain't never disobeyed his daddy without paying the consequences.

BONO: I ain't never had a chance. My daddy came on through . . . but I ain't never knew him to see him . . . or what he had on his mind or where he went. Just moving on through. Searching out the New Land. That's what the old folks used to call it. See a fellow moving around from place to place . . . woman to woman . . . called it searching out the New Land. I can't say if he ever found it. I come along, didn't want no kids. Didn't know if I was gonna be in one place long enough to fix on them right as their daddy. I figured I was going searching too. As it turned out I been hooked up with Lucille near about as long as your daddy been with Rose. Going on sixteen years.

TROY: Sometimes I wish I hadn't known my daddy. He ain't cared nothing about no kids. A kid to him wasn't nothing. All he wanted was for you to learn how to walk so he could start you to working. When it come time for eating . . . he ate first. If there was anything left over, that's what you got. Man would sit down and eat two chickens and give you the wing.

LYONS: You ought to stop that, Pop. Everybody feed their kids. No matter how hard times is . . . everybody care about their kids. Make sure they have something to eat.

TROY: The only thing my daddy cared about was getting them bales of cotton in to Mr. Lubin. That's the only thing that mattered to him. Sometimes I used to wonder why he was living. Wonder why the devil hadn't come and got him. "Get them bales of cotton in to Mr. Lubin" and find out he owe him money. . . .

LYONS: He should have just went on and left when he saw he couldn't get nowhere. That's what I would have done.

TROY: How he gonna leave with eleven kids? And where he gonna go? He ain't knew how to do nothing but farm. No, he was trapped and I think he knew it. But I'll say this for him . . . he felt a responsibility toward us. Maybe he ain't treated us the way I felt he should have . . . but without that responsibility he could have walked off and left us . . . made his own way.

BONO: A lot of them did. Back in those days what you talking about

. . . they walk out their front door and just take on down one road or another and keep on walking.

LYONS: There you go! That's what I'm talking about.

BONO: Just keep on walking till you come to something else. Ain't you never heard of nobody having the walking blues? Well, that's what you call it when you just take off like that.

TROY: My daddy ain't had them walking blues! What you talking about? He stayed right there with his family. But he was just as evil as he could be. My mama couldn't stand him. Couldn't stand that evilness. She run off when I was about eight. She sneaked off one night after he had gone to sleep. Told me she was coming back for me. I ain't never seen her no more. All his women run off and left him. He wasn't good for nobody.

When my turn come to head out, I was fourteen and got to sniffing around Joe Canewell's daughter. Had us an old mule we called Greyboy. My daddy sent me out to do some plowing and I tied up Greyboy and went to fooling around with Joe Canewell's daughter. We done found us a nice little spot, got real cozy with each other. She about thirteen and we done figured we was grown anyway . . . so we down there enjoying ourselves . . . ain't thinking about nothing. We didn't know Greyboy had got loose and wandered back to the house and my daddy was looking for me. We down there by the creek enjoying ourselves when my daddy come up on us. Surprised us. He had them leather straps off the mule and commenced to whupping me like there was no tomorrow. I jumped up, mad and embarrassed. I was scared of my daddy. When he commenced to whupping on me . . . quite naturally I run to get out of the way. [*Pause.*]

Now I thought he was mad cause I ain't done my work. But I see where he was chasing me off so he could have the gal for himself. When I see what the matter of it was, I lost all fear of my daddy. Right there is where I become a man . . . at fourteen years of age. [*Pause.*]

Now it was my turn to run him off. I picked up them same reins that he had used on me. I picked up them reins and commenced to whupping on him. The gal jumped up and run off . . . and when my daddy turned to face me, I could see why the devil had never come to get him . . . 'cause he was the devil himself. I don't know what happened. When I woke up, I was laying right there by the creek, and Blue . . . this old dog we had . . . was licking my face. I thought I was blind. I couldn't see nothing. Both my eyes were swollen shut. I layed there and cried. I didn't know what I was gonna do. The only thing I knew was the time had come for me to leave my daddy's house. And right there the world suddenly got big. And it was a long time before I could cut it down to where I could handle it.

Part of that cutting down was when I got to the place where I could feel him kicking in my blood and knew that the only thing that separated us was the matter of a few years.

[GABRIEL *enters from the house with a sandwich.*]

LYONS: What you got there, Uncle Gabe?

GABRIEL: Got me a ham sandwich. Rose gave me a ham sandwich.

TROY: I don't know what happened to him. I done lost touch with everybody except Gabriel. But I hope he's dead. I hope he found some peace.

LYONS: That's a heavy story, Pop. I didn't know you left home when you was fourteen.

TROY: And didn't know nothing. The only part of the world I knew was the forty-two acres of Mr. Lubin's land. That's all I knew about life.

LYONS: Fourteen's kinda young to be out on your own. [*Phone rings.*] I don't even think I was ready to be out on my own at fourteen. I don't know what I would have done.

TROY: I got up from the creek and walked on down to Mobile. I was through with farming. Figured I could do better in the city. So I walked the two hundred miles to Mobile.

LYONS: Wait a minute . . . you ain't walked no two hundred miles, Pop. Ain't nobody gonna walk no two hundred miles. You talking about some walking there.

BONO: That's the only way you got anywhere back in them days.

LYONS: Shhh. Damn if I wouldn't have hitched a ride with somebody!

TROY: Who you gonna hitch it with? They ain't had no cars and things like they got now. We talking about 1918.

ROSE: [*Entering.*] What you all out here getting into?

TROY: [*To* ROSE.] I'm telling Lyons how good he got it. He don't know nothing about this I'm talking.

ROSE: Lyons, that was Bonnie on the phone. She say you supposed to pick her up.

LYONS: Yeah, okay, Rose.

TROY: I walked on down to Mobile and hitched up with some of them fellows that was heading this way. Got up here and found out . . . not only couldn't you get a job . . . you couldn't find no place to live. I thought I was in freedom. Shhh. Colored folks living down there on the riverbanks in whatever kind of shelter they could find for themselves. Right down there under the Brady Street Bridge. Living in shacks made of sticks and tarpaper. Messed around there and went from bad to worse. Started stealing. First it was food. Then I figured, hell, if I steal money I can buy me some food. Buy me some shoes too! One thing led to another. Met your mama. I was young and anxious to be a man. Met your mama and had you. What I do that for? Now I got to worry about feeding you and her. Got to steal three times as much. Went out one day looking for somebody to rob . . . that's what I was, a robber. I'll tell you the truth. I'm ashamed of it today. But it's the truth. Went to rob this fellow . . . pulled out my knife . . . and he pulled out a gun. Shot me in the chest. It felt just like somebody had taken a hot branding iron and laid it on me. When he shot me I jumped at him with my knife. They told me I killed him and they put me in the penitentiary and locked me up for fifteen years. That's where I met Bono. That's where I learned how to play baseball. Got out that place and your mama had taken you and went on to make life without me. Fifteen years was a long time for her to wait. But that fifteen years cured me of that robbing stuff. Rose'll tell you. She asked me when I met her if I had gotten all that foolishness out of my system. And I told her, "Baby, it's you and baseball all what count with me." You hear me, Bono? I meant it too. She say, "Which one comes first?" I told her, "Baby, ain't no doubt it's baseball . . . but you stick and get old with me and we'll both outlive this baseball." Am I right, Rose? And it's true.

ROSE: Man, hush your mouth. You ain't said no such thing. Talking

about, "Baby, you know you'll always be number one with me."
That's what you was talking.

TROY: You hear that, Bono. That's why I love her.

BONO: Rose'll keep you straight. You get off the track, she'll straighten you up.

ROSE: Lyons, you better get on up and get Bonnie. She waiting on you.

LYONS: [*Gets up to go.*] Hey, Pop, why don't you come on down to the Grill and hear me play?

TROY: I ain't going down there. I'm too old to be sitting around in them clubs.

BONO: You got to be good to play down at the Grill.

LYONS: Come on, Pop . . .

TROY: I got to get up in the morning.

LYONS: You ain't got to stay long.

TROY: Naw, I'm gonna get my supper and go on to bed.

LYONS: Well, I got to go. I'll see you again.

TROY: Don't you come around my house on my payday.

ROSE: Pick up the phone and let somebody know you coming. And bring Bonnie with you. You know I'm always glad to see her.

LYONS: Yeah, I'll do that, Rose. You take care now. See you, Pop. See you, Mr. Bono. See you, Uncle Gabe.

GABRIEL: Lyons! King of the Jungle!

[LYONS *exits.*]

TROY: Is supper ready, woman? Me and you got some business to take care of. I'm gonna tear it up too.

ROSE: Troy, I done told you now!

TROY: [*Puts his arm around* BONO.] Aw hell, woman . . . this is Bono. Bono like family. I done known this nigger since . . . how long I done know you?

BONO: It's been a long time.

TROY: I done known this nigger since Skippy was a pup. Me and him done been through some times.

BONO: You sure right about that.

TROY: Hell, I done know him longer than I known you. And we still standing shoulder to shoulder. Hey, look here, Bono . . . a man can't ask for no more than that. [*Drinks to him.*] I love you, nigger.

BONO: Hell, I love you too . . . but I got to get home see my woman. You got yours in hand. I got to go get mine.

[BONO *starts to exit as* CORY *enters the yard, dressed in his football uniform. He gives* TROY *a hard, uncompromising look.*]

CORY: What you do that for, Pop? [*He throws his helmet down in the direction of* TROY.]

ROSE: What's the matter? Cory . . . what's the matter?

CORY: Papa done went up to the school and told Coach Zellman I can't play football no more. Wouldn't even let me play the game. Told him to tell the recruiter not to come.

ROSE: Troy . . .

TROY: What you Troying me for. Yeah, I did it. And the boy know why I did it.

CORY: Why you wanna do that to me? That was the one chance I had.

ROSE: Ain't nothing wrong with Cory playing football, Troy.

TROY: The boy lied to me. I told the nigger if he wanna play football . . . to keep up his chores and hold down that job at the A&P. That was the conditions. Stopped down there to see Mr. Stawicki . . .

CORY: I can't work after school during the football season, Pop! I tried to tell you that Mr. Stawicki's holding my job for me. You don't never want to listen to nobody. And then you wanna go and do this to me!

TROY: I ain't done nothing to you. You done it to yourself.

CORY: Just cause you didn't have a chance! You just scared I'm gonna be better than you, that's all.

TROY: Come here.

ROSE: Troy . . .

[CORY *reluctantly crosses over to* TROY.]

TROY: Alright! See. You done made a mistake.

CORY: I didn't even do nothing!

TROY: I'm gonna tell you what your mistake was. See . . . you swung at the ball and didn't hit it. That's strike one. See, you in the batter's box now. You swung and you missed. That's strike one. Don't you strike out!

[*Lights fade to black.*]

ACT TWO
SCENE ONE

The following morning. CORY *is at the tree hitting the ball with the bat. He tries to mimic* TROY, *but his swing is awkward, less sure.* ROSE *enters from the house.*

ROSE: Cory, I want you to help me with this cupboard.

CORY: I ain't quitting the team. I don't care what Poppa say.

ROSE: I'll talk to him when he gets back. He had to go see about your Uncle Gabe. The police done arrested him. Say he was disturbing the peace. He'll be back directly. Come on in here and help me clean out the top of this cupboard. [CORY *exits into the house.* ROSE *sees* TROY *and* BONO *coming down the alley.*] Troy . . . what they say down there?

TROY: Ain't said nothing. I give them fifty dollars and they let him go. I'll talk to you about it. Where's Cory?

ROSE: He's in there helping me clean out these cupboards.

TROY: Tell him to get his butt out here.

[TROY *and* BONO *go over to the pile of wood.* BONO *picks up the saw and begins sawing.*]

TROY: [*To* BONO.] All they want is the money. That makes six or seven times I done went down there and got him. See me coming they stick out their *hands.*

BONO: Yeah. I know what you mean. That's all they care about . . . that money. They don't care about what's right. [*Pause.*] Nigger, why you got to go and get some hard wood? You ain't doing nothing but building a little old fence. Get you some soft pine wood. That's all you need.

TROY: I know what I'm doing. This is outside wood. You put pine wood inside the house. Pine wood is inside wood. This here is outside wood. Now you tell me where the fence is gonna be?

BONO: You don't need this wood. You can put it up with pine wood and it'll stand as long as you gonna be here looking at it.

TROY: How you know how long I'm gonna be here, nigger? Hell, I might just live forever. Live longer than old man Horsely.

BONO: That's what Magee used to say.

TROY: Magee's a damn fool. Now you tell me who you ever heard of gonna pull their own teeth with a pair of rusty pliers.

BONO: The old folks . . . my granddaddy used to pull his teeth with pliers. They ain't had no dentists for the colored folks back then.

TROY: Get clean pliers! You understand? Clean pliers! Sterilize them! Besides we ain't living back then. All Magee had to do was walk over to Doc Goldblums.

BONO: I see where you and that Tallahassee gal . . . that Alberta . . . I see where you all done got tight.

TROY: What you mean "got tight"?

BONO: I see where you be laughing and joking with her all the time.

TROY: I laughs and jokes with all of them, Bono. You know me.

BONO: That ain't the kind of laughing and joking I'm talking about.

[CORY *enters from the house.*]

CORY: How you doing, Mr. Bono?

TROY: Cory? Get that saw from Bono and cut some wood. He talking about the wood's too hard to cut. Stand back there, Jim, and let that young boy show you how it's done.

BONO: He's sure welcome to it. [CORY *takes the saw and begins to cut the wood.*] Whew-e-e! Look at that. Big old strong boy. Look like Joe Louis.[1] Hell, must be getting old the way I'm watching that boy whip through that wood.

CORY: I don't see why Mama want a fence around the yard noways.

TROY: Damn if I know either. What the hell she keeping out with it? She ain't got nothing nobody want.

BONO: Some people build fences to keep people out . . . and other people build fences to keep people in. Rose wants to hold on to you all. She loves you.

TROY: Hell, nigger, I don't need nobody to tell me my wife loves me, Cory . . . go on in the house and see if you can find that other saw.

CORY: Where's it at?

TROY: I said find it! Look for it till you find it! [CORY *exits into the house.*] What's that supposed to mean? Wanna keep us in?

BONO: Troy . . . I done known you seem like damn near my whole life. You and Rose both. I done know both of you all for a long time. I remember when you met Rose. When you was hitting them baseball out the park. A lot of them old gals was after you

---

1. Boxer (1914–1981), heavyweight champion of the world from 1937 to 1949.

then. You had the pick of the litter. When you picked Rose, I was happy for you. That was the first time I knew you had any sense. I said . . . My man Troy knows what he's doing . . . I'm gonna follow this nigger . . . he might take me somewhere. I been following you too. I done learned a whole heap of things about life watching you. I done learned how to tell where the shit lies. How to tell it from the alfalfa. You done learned me a lot of things. You showed me how to not make the same mistakes . . . to take life as it comes along and keep putting one foot in front of the other. [*Pause.*] Rose a good woman, Troy.

TROY: Hell, nigger, I know she a good woman. I been married to her for eighteen years. What you got on your mind, Bono?

BONO: I just say she a good woman. Just like I say anything. I ain't got to have nothing on my mind.

TROY: You just gonna say she a good woman and leave it hanging out there like that? Why you telling me she a good woman?

BONO: She loves you, Troy. Rose loves you.

TROY: You saying I don't measure up. That's what you trying to say. I don't measure up cause I'm seeing this other gal. I know what you trying to say.

BONO: I know what Rose means to you, Troy. I'm just trying to say I don't want to see you mess up.

TROY: Yeah, I appreciate that, Bono. If you was messing around on Lucille I'd be telling you the same thing.

BONO: Well, that's all I got to say. I just say that because I love you both.

TROY: Hell, you know me. . . . I wasn't out there looking for nothing. You can't find a better woman than Rose. I know that. But seems like this woman just stuck onto me where I can't shake her loose. I done wrestled with it, tried to throw her off me . . . but she just stuck on tighter. Now she's stuck on for good.

BONO: You's in control . . . that's what you tell me all the time. You responsible for what you do.

TROY: I ain't ducking the responsibility of it. As long as it sets right in my heart . . . then I'm okay. 'Cause that's all I listen to. It'll tell me right from wrong every time. And I ain't talking about doing Rose no bad turn. I love Rose. She done carried me a long ways and I love and respect her for that.

BONO: I know you do. That's why I don't want to see you hurt her. But what you gonna do when she find out? What you got then? If you try and juggle both of them . . . sooner or later you gonna drop one of them. That's common sense.

TROY: Yeah, I hear what you saying, Bono. I been trying to figure a way to work it out.

BONO: Work it out right, Troy. I don't want to be getting all up between you and Rose's business . . . but work it so it come out right.

TROY: Aw hell, I get all up between you and Lucille's business. When you gonna get that woman that refrigerator she been wanting? Don't tell me you ain't got no money now. I know who your banker is. Mellon don't need that money bad as Lucille want that refrigerator. I'll tell you that.

BONO: Tell you what I'll do . . . when you finish building this fence for Rose . . . I'll buy Lucille that refrigerator.

TROY: You done stuck your foot in your mouth now! [TROY *grabs up a board and begins to saw.* BONO *starts to walk out the yard.*] Hey, nigger . . . where you going?

BONO: I'm going home. I know you don't expect me to help you now. I'm protecting my money. I wanna see you put that fence up by yourself. That's what I want to see. You'll be here another six months without me.

TROY: Nigger, you ain't right.

BONO: When it comes to my money . . . I'm right as fireworks on the Fourth of July.

TROY: Alright, we gonna see now. You better get out your bankbook. [BONO *exits, and* TROY *continues to work.* ROSE *enters from the house.*]

ROSE: What they say down there? What's happening with Gabe?

TROY: I went down there and got him out. Cost me fifty dollars. Say he was disturbing the peace. Judge set up a hearing for him in three weeks. Say to show cause why he shouldn't be recommitted.

ROSE: What was he doing that cause them to arrest him?

TROY: Some kids was teasing him and he run them off home. Say he was howling and carrying on. Some folks seen him and called the police. That's all it was.

ROSE: Well, what's you say? What'd you tell the judge?

TROY: Told him I'd look after him. It didn't make no sense to recommit the man. He stuck out his big greasy palm and told me to give him fifty dollars and take him on home.

ROSE: Where's he at now? Where'd he go off to?

TROY: He's gone on about his business. He don't need nobody to hold his hand.

ROSE: Well, I don't know. Seem like that would be the best place for him if they did put him into the hospital. I know what you're gonna say. But that's what I think would be best.

TROY: The man done had his life ruined fighting for what? And they wanna take and lock him up. Let him be free. He don't bother nobody.

ROSE: Well, everybody got their own way of looking at it, I guess. Come on and get your lunch. I got a bowl of lima beans and some cornbread in the oven. Come on get something to eat. Ain't no sense you fretting over Gabe. [ROSE *turns to go into the house.*]

TROY: Rose . . . got something to tell you.

ROSE: Well, come on . . . wait till I get this food on the table.

TROY: Rose! [*She stops and turns around.*] I don't know how to say this. [*Pause.*] I can't explain it none. It just sort of grows on you till it gets out of hand. It starts out like a little bush . . . and the next think you know it's a whole forest.

ROSE: Troy . . . what is you talking about?

TROY: I'm talking, woman, let me talk. I'm trying to find a way to tell you . . . I'm gonna be a daddy. I'm gonna be somebody's daddy.

ROSE: Troy . . . you're not telling me this? You're gonna be . . . what?

TROY: Rose . . . now . . . see . . .

ROSE: You telling me you gonna be somebody's daddy? You telling your *wife* this?

[GABRIEL *enters from the street. He carries a rose in his hand.*]

GABRIEL: Hey, Troy! Hey, Rose!

ROSE: I have to wait eighteen years to hear something like this.

GABRIEL: Hey, Rose . . . I got a flower for you. [*He hands it to her.*] That's a rose. Same rose like you is.

ROSE: Thanks, Gabe.

GABRIEL: Troy, you ain't mad at me, is you? Them bad mens come and put me away. You ain't mad at me, is you?

TROY: Naw, Gabe, I ain't mad at you.

ROSE: Eighteen years and you wanna come with this.

GABRIEL: [*Takes a quarter out of his pocket.*] See what I got? Got a brand new quarter.

TROY: Rose . . . it's just . . .

ROSE: Ain't nothing you can say, Troy. Ain't no way of explaining that.

GABRIEL: Fellow that give me this quarter had a whole mess of them. I'm gonna keep this quarter till it stop shining.

ROSE: Gabe, go on in the house there. I got some watermelon in the frigidaire. Go on and get you a piece.

GABRIEL: Say, Rose . . . you know I was chasing hellhounds and them bad mens come and get me and take me away. Troy helped me. He come down there and told them they better let me go before he beat them up. Yeah, he did!

ROSE: You go on and get you a piece of watermelon, Gabe. Them bad mens is gone now.

GABRIEL: Okay, Rose . . . gonna get me some watermelon. The kind with the stripes on it. [GABRIEL *exits into the house.*]

ROSE: Why, Troy? Why? After all these years to come dragging this in to me now. It don't make no sense at your age. I could have expected this ten or fifteen years ago, but not now.

TROY: Age ain't got nothing to do with it, Rose.

ROSE: I done tried to be everything a wife should be. Everything a wife could be. Been married eighteen years and I got to live to see the day you tell me you been seeing another woman and done fathered a child by her. And you know I ain't never wanted no half nothing in my family. My whole family is half. Everybody got different fathers and mothers . . . my two sisters and my brother. Can't hardly tell who's who. Can't never sit down and talk about Papa and Mama. It's your papa and your mama and my papa and my mama . . .

TROY: Rose . . . stop it now.

ROSE: I ain't never wanted that for none of my children. And now you wanna drag your behind in here and tell me something like this.

TROY: You ought to know. It's time for you to know.

ROSE: Well, I don't want to know, goddamn it!

TROY: I can't just make it go away. It's done now. I can't wish the circumstance of the thing away.

ROSE: And you don't want to either. Maybe you want to wish me and my boy away. Maybe that's what you want? Well, you can't wish us away. I've got eighteen years of my life invested in you. You ought to have stayed upstairs in my bed where you belong.

TROY: Rose . . . now listen to me . . . we can get a handle on this thing. We can talk this out . . . come to an understanding.

ROSE: All of a sudden it's "we." Where was "we" at when you was down there rolling around with some godforsaken woman? "We" should have come to an understanding before you started making a damn fool of yourself. You're a day late and a dollar short when it comes to an understanding with me.

TROY: It's just . . . She gives me a different idea . . . a different understanding about myself. I can step out of this house and get away from the pressures and problems . . . be a different man. I ain't got to wonder how I'm gonna pay the bills or get the roof fixed. I can just be a part of myself that I ain't never been.

ROSE: What I want to know . . . is do you plan to continue seeing her. That's all you can say to me.

TROY: I can sit up in her house and laugh. Do you understand what I'm saying. I can laugh out loud . . . and it feels good. It reaches all the way down to the bottom of my shoes. [*Pause.*] Rose, I can't give that up.

ROSE: Maybe you ought to go on and stay down there with her . . . if she a better woman than me.

TROY: It ain't about nobody being a better woman or nothing. Rose, you ain't the blame. A man couldn't ask for no woman to be a better wife than you've been. I'm responsible for it. I done locked myself into a pattern trying to take care of you all that I forgot about myself.

ROSE: What the hell was I there for? That was my job, not somebody else's.

TROY: Rose, I done tried all my life to live decent . . . to live a clean . . . hard . . . useful life. I tried to be a good husband to you. In every way I knew how. Maybe I come into the world backwards, I don't know. But . . . you born with two strikes on you before you come to the plate. You got to guard it closely . . . always looking for the curve-ball on the inside corner. You can't afford to let none get past you. You can't afford a call strike. If you going down . . . you going down swinging. Everything lined up against you. What you gonna do. I fooled them, Rose. I bunted. When I found you and Cory and a halfway decent job . . . I was safe. Couldn't nothing touch me. I wasn't gonna strike out no more. I wasn't going back to the penitentiary. I wasn't gonna lay in the streets with a bottle of wine. I was safe. I had me a family. A job. I wasn't gonna get that last strike. I was on first looking for one of them boys to knock me in. To get me home.

ROSE: You should have stayed in my bed, Troy.

TROY: Then when I saw that gal . . . she firmed up my backbone. And I got to thinking that if I tried . . . I just might be able to steal second. Do you understand after eighteen years I wanted to steal second.

ROSE: You should have held me tight. You should have grabbed me and held on.

TROY: I stood on first base for eighteen years and I thought . . . well, goddamn it . . . go on for it!

ROSE: We're not talking about baseball! We're talking about you going off to lay in bed with another woman . . . and then bring it home to me. That's what we're talking about. We ain't talking about no baseball.

TROY: Rose, you're not listening to me. I'm trying the best I can to explain it to you. It's not easy for me to admit that I been standing in the same place for eighteen years.

ROSE: I been standing with you! I been right here with you, Troy. I got a life too. I gave eighteen years of my life to stand in the same spot with you. Don't you think I ever wanted other things? Don't you think I had dreams and hopes? What about my life? What about me. Don't you think it ever crossed my mind to want to know other men? That I wanted to lay up somewhere and forget about my responsibilities? That I wanted someone to make me laugh so I could feel good? You not the only one who's got wants and needs. But I held on to you, Troy. I took all my feelings, my wants and needs, my dreams . . . and I buried them inside you. I planted a seed and watched and prayed over it. I planted myself inside you and waited to bloom. And it didn't take me no eighteen years to find out the soil was hard and rocky and it wasn't never gonna bloom.

But I held on to you, Troy. I held you tighter. You was my husband. I owed you everything I had. Every part of me I could find to give you. And upstairs in that room . . . with the darkness falling in on me . . . I gave everything I had to try and erase the doubt that you wasn't the finest man in the world. And wherever you was going . . . I wanted to be there with you. 'Cause you was my husband. 'Cause that's the only way I was gonna survive as your wife. You always talking about what you give . . . and what you don't have to give. But you take too. You take . . . and don't even know nobody's giving!

[ROSE *turns to exit into the house;* TROY *grabs her arm.*]

TROY: You say I take and don't give!

ROSE: Troy! You're hurting me!

TROY: You say I take and don't give.

ROSE: Troy . . . you're hurting my arm! Let go!

TROY: I done give you everything I got. Don't you tell that lie on me.

ROSE: Troy!

TROY: Don't you tell that lie on me!

[CORY *enters from the house.*]

CORY: Mama!

ROSE: Troy. You're hurting me.

TROY: Don't you tell me about no taking and giving.

[CORY *comes up behind* TROY *and grabs him.* TROY, *surprised, is thrown off balance just as* CORY *throws a glancing blow that catches him on the chest and knocks him down.* TROY *is stunned, as is* CORY.]

ROSE: Troy. Troy. No! [TROY *gets to his feet and starts at* CORY.] Troy . . . no. Please! Troy! [ROSE *pulls on* TROY *to hold him back.* TROY *stops himself.*]

TROY: [*To* CORY] Alright. That's strike two. You stay away from around me, boy. Don't you strike out. You living with a full count. Don't you strike out. [TROY *exits out the yard as the lights go down.*]

SCENE TWO

It is six months later, early afternoon. TROY *enters from the house and starts to exit the yard.* ROSE *enters from the house.*

ROSE: Troy, I want to talk to you.

TROY: All of a sudden, after all this time, you want to talk to me, huh? You ain't wanted to talk to me for months. You ain't wanted to talk to me last night. You ain't wanted no part of me then. What you wanna talk to me about now?

ROSE: Tomorrow's Friday.

TROY: I know what day tomorrow is. You think I don't know tomorrow's Friday? My whole life I ain't done nothing but look to see Friday coming and you got to tell me it's Friday.

ROSE: I want to know if you're coming home.

TROY: I always come home, Rose. You know that. There ain't never been a night I ain't come home.

ROSE: That ain't what I mean . . . and you know it. I want to know if you're coming straight home after work.

TROY: I figure I'd cash my check . . . hang out at Taylors' with the boys . . . maybe play a game of checkers. . . .

ROSE: Troy, I can't live like this. I won't live like this. You livin' on borrowed time with me. It's been going on six months now you ain't been coming home.

TROY: I be here every night. Every night of the year. That's 365 days.

ROSE: I want you to come home tomorrow after work.

TROY: Rose . . . I don't mess up my pay. You know that now. I take my pay and I give it to you. I don't have no money but what you give me back. I just want to have a little time to myself . . . a little time to enjoy life.

ROSE: What about me? When's my time to enjoy life?

TROY: I don't know what to tell you, Rose. I'm doing the best I can.

ROSE: You ain't been home from work but time enough to change your clothes and run out . . . and you wanna call that the best you can do?

TROY: I'm going over to the hospital to see Alberta. She went into the hospital this afternoon. Look like she might have the baby early. I won't be gone long.

ROSE: Well, you ought to know. They went over to Miss Pearl's and got Gabe today. She said you told them to go ahead and lock him up.

TROY: I ain't said no such thing. Whoever told you that is telling a lie. Pearl ain't doing nothing but telling a big fat lie.

ROSE: She ain't had to tell me. I read it on the papers.

TROY: I ain't told them nothing of the kind.

ROSE: I saw it right there on the papers.

TROY: What it say, huh?

ROSE: It said you told them to take him.

TROY: Then they screwed that up, just the way they screw up everything. I ain't worried about what they got on the paper.

ROSE: Say the government send part of his check to the hospital and the other part to you.

TROY: I ain't got nothing to do with that if that's the way it works. I ain't made up the rules about how it work.

ROSE: You did Gabe just like you did Cory. You wouldn't sign the paper for Cory . . . but you signed for Gabe. You signed that paper.

[The telephone is heard ringing inside the house.]

TROY: I told you I ain't signed nothing, woman! The only thing I signed was the release form. Hell, I can't read, I don't know what they had on that paper! I ain't signed nothing about sending Gabe away.

ROSE: I said send him to the hospital . . . you said let him be free . . . now you done went down there and signed him to the hospital for half his money. You went back on yourself, Troy. You gonna have to answer for that.

TROY: See now . . . you been over there talking to Miss Pearl. She done got mad cause she ain't getting Gabe's rent money. That's all it is. She's liable to say anything.

ROSE: Troy, I seen where you signed the paper.

TROY: You ain't seen nothing I signed. What she doing got papers on my brother anyway? Miss Pearl telling a big fat lie. And I'm gonna tell her about it too! You ain't seen nothing I signed. Say . . . you ain't seen nothing I signed.

[ROSE exits into the house to answer the telephone. Presently she returns.]

ROSE: Troy . . . that was the hospital. Alberta had the baby.

TROY: What she have? What is it?

ROSE: It's a girl.

TROY: I better get on down to the hospital to see her.

ROSE: Troy . . .

TROY: Rose . . . I got to go see her now. That's only right . . . what's the matter . . . the baby's alright, ain't it?

ROSE: Alberta died having the baby.

TROY: Died . . . you say she's dead? Alberta's dead?

ROSE: They said they done all they could. They couldn't do nothing for her.

TROY: The baby? How's the baby?

ROSE: They say it's healthy. I wonder who's gonna bury her.

TROY: She had family, Rose. She wasn't living in the world by herself.

ROSE: I know she wasn't living in the world by herself.

TROY: Next thing you gonna want to know if she had any insurance.

ROSE: Troy, you ain't got to talk like that.

TROY: That's the first thing that jumped out your mouth. "Who's gonna bury her?" Like I'm fixing to take on that task for myself.

ROSE: I am your wife. Don't push me away.

TROY: I ain't pushing nobody away. Just give me some space. That's all. Just give me some room to breathe.

[ROSE *exits into the house.* TROY *walks about the yard.*]

TROY: [*With a quiet rage that threatens to consume him.*] Alright . . . Mr. Death. See now . . . I'm gonna tell you what I'm gonna do. I'm gonna take and build me a fence around this yard. See? I'm gonna build me a fence around what belongs to me. And then I want you to stay on the other side. See? You stay over there until you're ready for me. Then you come on. Bring your army. Bring your sickle. Bring your wrestling clothes. I ain't gonna fall down on my vigilance this time. You ain't gonna sneak up on me no more. When you ready for me . . . when the top of your list say Troy Maxson . . . that's when you come around here. You come up and knock on the front door. Ain't nobody else got nothing to do with this. This is between you and me. Man to man. You stay on the other side of that fence until you ready for me. Then you come up and knock on the front door. Anytime you want. I'll be ready for you.

[*The lights go down to black.*]

SCENE THREE

The lights come up on the porch. It is late evening three days later.
ROSE *sits listening to the ball game waiting for* TROY. *The final out of
the game is made and* ROSE *switches off the radio.* TROY *enters the yard
carrying an infant wrapped in blankets. He stands back from the house
and calls.*

> [ROSE *enters and stands on the porch. There is a long, awkward
> silence, the weight of which grows heavier with each passing
> second.*]

TROY: Rose . . . I'm standing here with my daughter in my arms.
She ain't but a wee bittie little old thing. She don't know nothing
about grownups' business. She innocent . . . and she ain't got no
mama.

ROSE: What you telling me for, Troy? [*She turns and exits into the
house.*]

TROY: Well . . . I guess we'll just sit out here on the porch. [*He sits
down on the porch. There is an awkward indelicateness about the
way he handles the baby. His largeness engulfs and seems to swallow
it. He speaks loud enough for* ROSE *to hear.*] A man's got to do
what's right for him. I ain't sorry for nothing I done. It felt right
in my heart.

[*To the baby.*] What you smiling at? Your daddy's a big man.
Got these great big old hands. But sometimes he's scared. And
right now your daddy's scared cause we sitting out here and ain't
got no home. Oh, I been homeless before. I ain't had no little
baby with me. But I been homeless. You just be out on the road
by your lonesome and you see one of them trains coming and
you just kinda go like this . . .

[*He sings as a lullaby.*] Please, Mr. Engineer let a man ride the
line

Please, Mr. Engineer let a man ride the line
I ain't got no ticket please let me ride the blinds
[ROSE *enters from the house.* TROY, *hearing her steps behind him,
stands and faces her.*]

She's my daughter, Rose. My own flesh and blood. I can't deny
her no more than I can deny them boys. [*Pause.*] You and them
boys is my family. You and them and this child is all I got in the

world. So I guess what I'm saying is . . . I'd appreciate it if you'd help me take care of her.

ROSE: Okay, Troy . . . you're right. I'll take care of your baby for you . . . 'cause . . . like you say . . . she's innocent . . . and you can't visit the sins of the father upon the child. A motherless child has got a hard time. [*She takes the baby from him.*] From right now . . . this child got a mother. But you a womanless man.

[ROSE *turns and exits into the house with the baby. Lights go down to black.*]

SCENE FOUR

It is two months later. LYONS *enters from the street. He knocks on the door and calls.*

LYONS: Hey, Rose! [*Pause.*] Rose!

ROSE: [*From inside the house.*] Stop that yelling. You gonna wake up Raynell. I just got her to sleep.

LYONS: I just stopped by to pay Papa this twenty dollars I owe him. Where's Papa at?

ROSE: He should be here in a minute. I'm getting ready to go down to the church. Sit down and wait on him.

LYONS: I got to go pick up Bonnie over her mother's house.

ROSE: Well, sit it down there on the table. He'll get it.

LYONS: [*Enters the house and sets the money on the table.*] Tell Papa I said thanks. I'll see you again.

ROSE: Alright, Lyons. We'll see you.

[LYONS *starts to exit as* CORY *enters.*]

CORY: Hey, Lyons.

LYONS: What's happening, Cory. Say, man, I'm sorry I missed your graduation. You know I had a gig and couldn't get away. Otherwise, I would have been there, man. So what you doing?

CORY: I'm trying to find a job.

LYONS: Yeah I know how that go, man. It's rough out here. Jobs are scarce.

CORY: Yeah, I know.

LYONS: Look here, I got to run. Talk to Papa . . . he know some people. He'll be able to help get you a job. Talk to him . . . see what he say.

CORY: Yeah . . . alright, Lyons.

LYONS: You take care. I'll talk to you soon. We'll find some time to talk.

[LYONS *exits the yard.* CORY *wanders over to the tree, picks up the bat and assumes a batting stance. He studies an imaginary pitcher and swings. Dissatisfied with the result, he tries again.* TROY *enters. They eye each other for a beat.* CORY *puts the bat down and exits the yard.* TROY *starts into the house as* ROSE *exits with* RAYNELL. *She is carrying a cake.*]

TROY: I'm coming in and everybody's going out.

ROSE: I'm taking this cake down to the church for the bakesale. Lyons was by to see you. He stopped by to pay you your twenty dollars. It's laying in there on the table.

TROY: [*Going into his pocket.*] Well . . . here go this money.

ROSE: Put in there on the table, Troy. I'll get it.

TROY: What time you coming back?

ROSE: Ain't no use in you studying me. It don't matter what time I come back.

TROY: I just asked you a question, woman. What's the matter . . . can't I ask you a question?

ROSE: Troy, I don't want to go into it. Your dinner's in there on the stove. All you got to do is heat it up. And don't you be eating the rest of them cakes in there. I'm coming back for them. We having a bakesale at the church tomorrow.

[ROSE *exits the yard.* TROY *sits down on the steps, takes a pint bottle from his pocket, opens it and drinks. He begins to sing.*]

TROY: Hear it ring! Hear it ring!
Had an old dog his name was Blue
You know Blue was mighty true
You know Blue as a good old dog
Blue trees a possum in a hollow log
You know from that he was a good old dog
[BONO *enters the yard.*]

BONO: Hey, Troy.

TROY: Hey, what's happening, Bono?

BONO: I just thought I'd stop by to see you.

TROY: What you stop by and see me for? You ain't stopped by in a month of Sundays. Hell, I must owe you money or something.

BONO: Since you got your promotion I can't keep up with you. Used to see you everyday. Now I don't even know what route you working.

TROY: They keep switching me around. Got me out in Greentree now . . . hauling white folks' garbage.

BONO: Greentree, huh? You lucky, at least you ain't got to be lifting them barrels. Damn if they ain't getting heavier. I'm gonna put in my two years and call it quits.

TROY: I'm thinking about retiring myself.

BONO: You got it easy. You can *drive* for another five years.

TROY: It ain't the same, Bono. It ain't like working the back of the truck. Ain't got nobody to talk to . . . feel like you working by yourself. Naw, I'm thinking about retiring. How's Lucille?

BONO: She alright. Her arthritis get to acting up on her sometime. Saw Rose on my way in. She going down to the church, huh?

TROY: Yeah, she took up going down there. All them preachers looking for somebody to fatten their pockets. [*Pause.*] Got some gin here.

BONO: Naw, thanks. I just stopped by to say hello.

TROY: Hell, nigger . . . you can take a drink. I ain't never known you to say no to a drink. You ain't got to work tomorrow.

BONO: I just stopped by. I'm fixing to go over to Skinner's. We got us a domino game going over his house every Friday.

TROY: Nigger, you can't play no dominoes. I used to whup you four games out of five.

BONO: Well, that learned me. I'm getting better.

TROY: Yeah? Well, that's alright.

BONO: Look here . . . I got to be getting on. Stop by sometime, huh?

TROY: Yeah, I'll do that, Bono. Lucille told Rose you bought her a new refrigerator.

BONO: Yeah, Rose told Lucille you had finally built your fence . . . so I figured we'd call it even.

TROY: I knew you would.

BONO: Yeah . . . okay. I'll be talking to you.

TROY: Yeah, take care, Bono. Good to see you. I'm gonna stop over.

BONO: Yeah. Okay, Troy. [BONO *exits.* TROY *drinks from the bottle.*]

TROY: Old Blue died and I dig his grave

Let him down with a golden chain
Every night when I hear old Blue bark
I know Blue treed a possum in Noah's Ark.
Hear it ring! Hear it ring!
[CORY *enters the yard. They eye each other for a beat.* TROY *is sitting in the middle of the steps.* CORY *walks over.*]

CORY: I got to get by.

TROY: Say what? What's you say?

CORY: You in my way. I got to get by.

TROY: You got to get by where? This is my house. Bought and paid for. In full. Took me fifteen years. And if you wanna go in my house and I'm sitting on the steps . . . you say excuse me. Like your mama taught you.

CORY: Come on, Pop . . . I got to get by.

[CORY *starts to maneuver his way past* TROY. TROY *grabs his leg and shoves him back.*]

TROY: You just gonna walk over top of me?

CORY: I live here too!

TROY: [*Advancing toward him.*] You just gonna walk over top of me in my own house?

CORY: I ain't scared of you.

TROY: I ain't asked if you was scared of me. I asked you if you was fixing to walk over top of me in my own house? That's the question. You ain't gonna say excuse me? You just gonna walk over top of me?

CORY: If you wanna put it like that.

TROY: How else am I gonna put it?

CORY: I was walking by you to go into the house cause you sitting on the steps drunk, singing to yourself. You can put it like that.

TROY: Without saying excuse me??? [CORY *doesn't respond.*] I asked you a question. Without saying excuse me???

CORY: I ain't got to say excuse me to you. You don't count around here no more.

TROY: Oh, I see, . . . I don't count around here no more. You ain't got to say excuse me to your daddy. All of a sudden you done got so grown that your daddy don't count around here no more. . . . Around here in his own house and yard that he done paid for with the sweat of his brow. You done got so grown to where you gonna take over. You gonna take over my house. Is that right? You gonna wear my pants. You gonna go in there and stretch out on my bed. You ain't got to say excuse me cause I don't count around here no more. Is that right?

CORY: That's right. You always talking this dumb stuff. Now, why don't you just get out my way.

TROY: I guess you got someplace to sleep and something to put in your belly. You got that, huh? You got that? That's what you need. You got that, huh?

CORY: You don't know what I got. You ain't got to worry about what I got.

TROY: You right! You one hundred percent right! I done spent the last seventeen years worrying about what you got. Now it's your turn, see? I'll tell you what to do. You grown . . . we done established that. You a man. Now, let's see you act like one. Turn your behind around and walk out this yard. And when you get out there in the alley . . . you can forget about this house. See? 'Cause this is my house. You go on and be a man and get your own house. You can forget about this. 'Cause this is mine. You go on and get yours 'cause I'm through with doing for you.

CORY: You talking about what you did for me . . . what'd you ever give me?

TROY: Them feet and bones! That pumping heart, nigger! I give you more than anybody else is ever gonna give you.

CORY: You ain't never gave me nothing! You ain't never done nothing but hold me back. Afraid I was gonna be better than you. All you ever did was try and make me scared of you. I used to tremble every time you called my name. Every time I heard your footsteps in the house. Wondering all the time . . . what's Papa gonna say if I do this? . . . What's he gonna say if I do that? . . . What's Papa gonna say if I turn on the radio? And Mama, too . . . she tries . . . but she's scared of you.

TROY: You leave your mama out of this. She ain't got nothing to do with this.

CORY: I don't know how she stand you . . . after what you did to her.

TROY: I told you to leave your mama out of this! [*He advances toward* CORY.]

CORY: What you gonna do . . . give me a whupping? You can't whup me no more. You're too old. You just an old man.

TROY: [*Shoves him on his shoulder.*] Nigger! That's what you are. You just another nigger on the street to me!

CORY: You crazy! You know that?

TROY: Go on now! You got the devil in you. Get on away from me!

CORY: You just a crazy old man . . . talking about I got the devil in me.

TROY: Yeah, I'm crazy! If you don't get on the other side of that yard . . . I'm gonna show you how crazy I am! Go on . . . get the hell out of my yard.

CORY: It ain't your yard. You took Uncle Gabe's money he got from the army to buy this house and then you put him out.

TROY: [TROY *advances on* CORY.] Get your black ass out of my yard!
[TROY'*s advance backs* CORY *up against the tree.* CORY *grabs up the bat.*]

CORY: I ain't going nowhere! Come on . . . put me out! I ain't scared of you.

TROY: That's my bat!

CORY: Come on!

TROY: Put my bat down!

CORY: Come on, put me out. [CORY *swings at* TROY, *who backs across the yard.*] What's the matter? You so bad . . . put me out!
[TROY *advances toward* CORY.]

CORY: [*Backing up.*] Come on! Come on!

TROY: You're gonna have to use it! You wanna draw that bat back on me . . . you're gonna have to use it.

CORY: Come on! . . . Come on!
[CORY *swings the bat at* TROY *a second time. He misses.* TROY *continues to advance toward him.*]

TROY: You're gonna have to kill me! You wanna draw that bat back on me. You're gonna have to kill me.
[CORY, *backed up against the tree, can go no farther.* TROY *taunts him. He sticks out his head and offers him a target.*]
Come on! Come on!
[CORY *is unable to swing the bat.* TROY *grabs it.*]

TROY: Then I'll show you.
[CORY *and* TROY *struggle over the bat. The struggle is fierce and*

fully engaged. TROY *ultimately is the stronger, and takes the bat from* CORY *and stands over him ready to swing. He stops himself.*]
Go on and get away from around my house.
[CORY, *stung by his defeat, picks himself up, walks slowly out of the yard and up the alley.*]

CORY: Tell Mama I'll be back for my things.

TROY: They'll be on the other side of that fence.

[CORY *exits.*]

TROY: I can't taste nothing. Helluljah! I can't taste nothing no more.

[TROY *assumes a batting posture and begins to taunt Death, the fastball in the outside corner.*] Come on! It's between you and me now! Come on! Anytime you want! Come on! I be ready for you . . . but I ain't gonna be easy.

[*The lights go down on the scene.*]

SCENE FIVE

The time is 1965. The lights come up in the yard. It is the morning of TROY'*s funeral. A funeral plaque with a light hangs beside the door. There is a small garden plot off to the side. There is noise and activity in the house as* ROSE, GABRIEL *and* BONO *have gathered. The door opens and* RAYNELL, *seven years old, enters dressed in a flannel nightgown. She crosses to the garden and pokes around with a stick.* ROSE *calls from the house.*

ROSE: Raynell!

RAYNELL: Mam?

ROSE: What you doing out there?

RAYNELL: Nothing.

[ROSE *comes to the door.*]

ROSE: Girl, get in here and get dressed. What you doing?

RAYNELL: Seeing if my garden growed.

ROSE: I told you it ain't gonna grow overnight. You got to wait.

RAYNELL: It don't look like it never gonna grow. Dag!

ROSE: I told you a watched pot never boils. Get in here and get dressed.

RAYNELL: This ain't even no pot, Mama.

ROSE: You just have to give it a chance. It'll grow. Now you come on and do what I told you. We got to be getting ready. This ain't no morning to be playing around. You hear me?

RAYNELL: Yes, mam.

[ROSE *exits into the house.* RAYNELL *continues to poke at her garden with a stick.* CORY *enters. He is dressed in a Marine corporal's uniform, and carries a duffel bag. His posture is that of a military man, and his speech has a clipped sternness.*]

CORY: [*To* RAYNELL.] Hi. [*Pause.*] I bet your name is Raynell.

RAYNELL: Uh huh.

CORY: Is your mama home?

[RAYNELL *runs up on the porch and calls through the screendoor.*]

RAYNELL: Mama . . . there's some man out here. Mama?

[ROSE *comes to the door.*]

ROSE: Cory? Lord have mercy! Look here, you all!

[ROSE *and* CORY *embrace in a tearful reunion as* BONO *and* LYONS *enter from the house dressed in funeral clothes.*]

BONO: Aw, looka here . . .

ROSE: Done got all grown up!

CORY: Don't cry, Mama. What you crying about?

ROSE: I'm just so glad you made it.

CORY: Hey, Lyons. How you doing, Mr. Bono.

[LYONS *goes to embrace* CORY.]

LYONS: Look at you, man. Look at you. Don't he look good, Rose. Got them Corporal stripes.

ROSE: What took you so long.

CORY: You know how the Marines are, Mama. They got to get all their paperwork straight before they let you do anything.

ROSE: Well, I'm sure glad you made it. They let Lyons come. Your Uncle Gabe's still in the hospital. They don't know if they gonna let him out or not. I just talked to them a little while ago.

LYONS: A Corporal in the United States Marines.

BONO: Your daddy knew you had it in you. He used to tell me all the time.

LYONS: Don't he look good, Mr. Bono?

BONO: Yeah, he remind me of Troy when I first met him. [*Pause.*]
Say, Rose, Lucille's down at the church with the choir. I'm gonna go down and get the pallbearers lined up. I'll be back to get you all.

ROSE: Thanks, Jim.

CORY: See you, Mr. Bono.

LYONS: [*With his arm around* RAYNELL.] Cory . . . look at Raynell. Ain't she precious? She gonna break a whole lot of hearts.

ROSE: Raynell, come and say hello to your brother. This is your brother, Cory. You remember Cory.

RAYNELL: No, Mam.

CORY: She don't remember me, Mama.

ROSE: Well, we talk about you. She heard us talk about you. [*To* RAYNELL.] This is your brother, Cory. Come on and say hello.

RAYNELL: Hi.

CORY: Hi. So you're Raynell. Mama told me a lot about you.

ROSE: You all come on into the house and let me fix you some breakfast. Keep up your strength.

CORY: I ain't hungry, Mama.

LYONS: You can fix me something, Rose. I'll be in there in a minute.

ROSE: Cory, you sure you don't want nothing. I know they ain't feeding you right.

CORY: No, Mama . . . thanks. I don't feel like eating. I'll get something later.

ROSE: Raynell . . . get on upstairs and get that dress on like I told you.

[ROSE *and* RAYNELL *exit into the house.*]

LYONS: So . . . I hear you thinking about getting married.

CORY: Yeah, I done found the right one, Lyons. It's about time.

LYONS: Me and Bonnie been split up about four years now. About the time Papa retired. I guess she just got tired of all them changes I was putting her through. [*Pause.*] I always knew you was gonna make something out yourself. Your head was always in the right direction. So . . . you gonna stay in . . . make it a career . . . put in your twenty years?

CORY: I don't know. I got six already, I think that's enough.

LYONS: Stick with Uncle Sam and retire early. Ain't nothing out here. I guess Rose told you what happened with me. They got me down the workhouse. I thought I was being slick cashing other people's checks.

CORY: How much time you doing?

LYONS: They give me three years. I got that beat now. I ain't got but nine more months. It ain't so bad. You learn to deal with it like anything else. You got to take the crookeds with the straights.

That's what Papa used to say. He used to say that when he struck out. I seen him strike out three times in a row . . . and the next time up he hit the ball over the grandstand. Right out there in Homestead Field. He wasn't satisfied hitting in the seats . . . he want to hit it over everything! After the game he had two hundred people standing around waiting to shake his hand. You got to take the crookeds with the straights. Yeah, Papa was something else.

CORY: You still playing?

LYONS: Cory . . . you know I'm gonna do that. There's some fellows down there we got us a band . . . we gonna try and stay together when we get out . . . but yeah, I'm still playing. It still helps me to get out of bed in the morning. As long as it do that I'm gonna be right there playing and trying to make some sense out of it.

ROSE: [*Calling.*] Lyons, I got these eggs in the pan.

LYONS: Let me go on and get these eggs, man. Get ready to go bury Papa. [*Pause.*] How you doing? You doing alright?

[CORY *nods.* LYONS *touches him on the shoulder and they share a moment of silent grief.* LYONS *exits into the house.* CORY *wanders about the yard.* RAYNELL *enters.*]

RAYNELL: Hi.

CORY: Hi.

RAYNELL: Did you used to sleep in my room?

CORY: Yeah . . . that used to be my room.

RAYNELL: That's what Papa call it. "Cory's room." It got your football in the closet.

[ROSE *comes to the door.*]

ROSE: Raynell, get in there and get them good shoes on.

RAYNELL: Mama, can't I wear these. Them other one hurt my feet.

ROSE: Well, they just gonna have to hurt your feet for a while. You ain't said they hurt your feet when you went down to the store and got them.

RAYNELL: They didn't hurt then. My feet done got bigger.

ROSE: Don't you give me no backtalk now. You get in there and get them shoes on. [RAYNELL *exits into the house.*] Ain't too much changed. He still got that piece of rag tied to that tree. He was out here swinging that bat. I was just ready to go back in the house. He swung that bat and then he just fell over. Seem like he swung it and stood there with this grin on his face . . . and then he just fell over. They carried him on down to the hospital, but I knew there wasn't no need . . . why don't you come on in the house?

CORY: Mama . . . I got something to tell you. I don't know how to tell you this . . . but I've got to tell you . . . I'm not going to Papa's funeral.

ROSE: Boy, hush your mouth. That's your daddy you talking about. I don't want hear that kind of talk this morning. I done raised you to come to this? You standing there all healthy and grown talking about you ain't going to your daddy's funeral?

CORY: Mama . . . listen . . .

ROSE: I don't want to hear it, Cory. You just get that thought out of your head.

CORY: I can't drag Papa with me everywhere I go. I've got to say no to him. One time in my life I've got to say no.

ROSE: Don't nobody have to listen to nothing like that. I know you and your daddy ain't seen eye to eye, but I ain't got to listen to that kind of talk this morning. Whatever was between you and your daddy . . . the time has come to put it aside. Just take it and set it over there on the shelf and forget about it. Disrespecting your daddy ain't gonna make you a man, Cory. You got to find a way to come to that on your own. Not going to your daddy's funeral ain't gonna make you a man.

CORY: The whole time I was growing up . . . living in his house . . . Papa was like a shadow that followed you everywhere. It weighed on you and sunk into your flesh. It would wrap around you and lay there until you couldn't tell which one was you anymore. That shadow digging in your flesh. Trying to crawl in. Trying to live through you. Everywhere I looked, Troy Maxson was staring back at me . . . hiding under the bed . . . in the closet. I'm just saying I've got to find a way to get rid of that shadow, Mama.

ROSE: You just like him. You got him in you good.

CORY: Don't tell me that, Mama.

ROSE: You Troy Maxson all over again.

CORY: I don't want to be Troy Maxson. I want to be me.

ROSE: You can't be nobody but who you are, Cory. That shadow wasn't nothing but you growing into yourself. You either got to grow into it or cut it down to fit you. But that's all you got to make life with. That's all you got to measure yourself against that world out there. Your daddy wanted you to be everything he wasn't . . . and at the same time he tried to make you into everything he was. I don't know if he was right or wrong . . . but I do know he meant to do more good than he meant to do harm. He wasn't always right. Sometimes when he touched he bruised. And sometimes when he took me in his arms he cut.

When I first met your daddy I thought . . . Here is a man I can lay down with and make a baby. That's the first thing I thought when I seen him. I was thirty years old and had done seen my share of men. But when he walked up to me and said, "I can dance a waltz that'll make you dizzy," I thought, Rose Lee, here is a man that you can open yourself up to and be filled to bursting. Here is a man that can fill all them empty spaces you been tipping around the edges of. One of them empty spaces was being somebody's mother.

I married your daddy and settled down to cooking his supper and keeping clean sheets on the bed. When your daddy walked through the house he was so big he filled it up. That was my first mistake. Not to make him leave some room for me. For my part in the matter. But at that time I wanted that. I wanted a house that I could sing in. And that's what your daddy gave me. I didn't know to keep up his strength. I had to give up little pieces of mine. I did that. I took on his life as mine and mixed up the pieces so that you couldn't hardly tell which was which anymore. It was my choice. It was my life and I didn't have to live it like that. But that's what life offered me in the way of being a woman and I took it. I grabbed hold of it with both hands.

By the time Raynell came into the house, me and your daddy had done lost touch with one another. I didn't want to make my blessing off of nobody's misfortune . . . but I took on to Raynell like she was all them babies I had wanted and never had. [*The phone rings.*] Like I'd been blessed to relive a part of my life. And if the Lord see fit to keep up my strength . . . I'm gonna do her just like your daddy did you . . . I'm gonna give her the best of what's in me.

RAYNELL: [*Entering, still with her old shoes.*] Mama . . . Reverend Tollivier on the phone.

[ROSE *exits into the house.*]

RAYNELL: Hi.

CORY: Hi.

RAYNELL: You in the Army or the Marines?

CORY: Marines.

RAYNELL: Papa said it was the Army. Did you know Blue?

CORY: Blue? Who's Blue?

RAYNELL: Papa's dog what he sing about all the time.

CORY: [*Singing.*] Hear it ring! Hear it ring!
> I had a dog his name was Blue
> You know Blue was mighty true
> You know Blue was a good old dog
> Blue treed a possum in a hollow log
> You know from that he was a good old dog.
> Hear it ring! Hear it ring!
> [RAYNELL *joins in singing.*]

CORY and RAYNELL: Blue treed a possum out on a limb
> Blue looked at me and I looked at him
> Grabbed that possum and put him in a sack
> Blue stayed there till I came back
> Old Blue's feets was big and round
> Never allowed a possum to touch the ground.
>
> Old Blue died and I dug his grave
> I dug his grave with a silver spade
> Let him down with a golden chain
> And every night I call his name
> Go on Blue, you good dog you
> Go on Blue, you good dog you

RAYNELL: Blue laid down and died like a man
> Blue laid down and died . . .

BOTH: Blue laid down and died like a man
> Now he's treeing possums in the Promised Land
> I'm gonna tell you this to let you know
> Blue's gone where the good dogs go
> When I hear old Blue bark
> When I hear old Blue bark
> Blue treed a possum in Noah's Ark
> Blue treed a possum in Noah's Ark.

[ROSE *comes to the screen door.*]

ROSE: Cory, we gonna be ready to go in a minute.

CORY: [*To* RAYNELL.] You go on in the house and change them shoes like Mama told you so we can go to Papa's funeral.

RAYNELL: Okay, I'll be back.

[RAYNELL *exits into the house.* CORY *gets up and crosses over to the tree.* ROSE *stands in the screen door watching him.* GABRIEL *enters from the alley.*]

GABRIEL: [*Calling.*] Hey, Rose!

ROSE: Gabe?

GABRIEL: I'm here, Rose. Hey, Rose, I'm here!

[ROSE *enters from the house.*]

ROSE: Lord . . . Look here, Lyons!

LYONS: See, I told you, Rose . . . I told you they'd let him come.

CORY: How you doing, Uncle Gabe?

LYONS: How you doing, Uncle Gabe?

GABRIEL: Hey, Rose. It's time. It's time to tell St. Peter to open the gates. Troy, you ready? You ready, Troy. I'm gonna tell St. Peter to open the gates. You get ready now. [GABRIEL, *with great fanfare, braces himself to blow. The trumpet is without a mouthpiece. He puts the end of it into his mouth and blows with great force, like a man who has been waiting some twenty-odd years for this single moment. No sound comes out of the trumpet. He braces himself and blows again with the same result. A third time he blows. There is a weight of impossible description that falls away and leaves him bare and exposed to a frightful realization. It is a trauma that a sane and normal mind would be unable to withstand. He begins to dance. A slow, strange dance, eerie and lifegiving. A dance of atavistic signature and ritual.* LYONS *attempts to embrace him.* GABRIEL *pushes* LYONS *away. He begins to howl in what is an attempt at song, or perhaps a song turning back into itself in an attempt at speech. He finishes his dance and the gates of heaven stand open as wide as God's closet.*] That's the way that go!

[*Blackout.*]

1983   *1986*

David Henry Hwang
1957–

M . BUTTERFLY

M. Butterfly *is based on a true story. Beginning in 1960, Bernard Boursicot, a French diplomat in China, carried on a clandestine affair with a Chinese woman, Shi Pei Pu, who claimed to have had his son. During the Cultural Revolution—Chinese leader Mao Tsetung's tyrannical and often violent attempt, roughly from 1966 through 1976, to restore the ethos of the Communist Revolution by purging China of Western influences—Shi Pei Pu was in danger. To protect his lover, Boursicot agreed to deliver photographs of French documents to a Chinese operative. The lovers eventually were caught in Paris in 1986. The ensuing investigation revealed that Shi Pei Pu, despite Boursicot's strenuous denials, was actually a man.*

After reading a two-paragraph newspaper article, Hwang immediately decided to write a play about the story. He purposely did no further research, to keep his treatment of the story's themes free from the particulars of Boursicot and Shi Pei Pu's case.

Hwang sought a truth larger than any single encounter between an Asian and a Westerner. He was dramatizing a pattern of behavior and a habit of representation that were, perhaps, best explained by the late Palestinian American scholar Edward Said, who long studied the portrayal of Arabs in Western literature. In his hugely influential book Orientalism *(1978, rev. 2003), Said delineates how Western cultures depict their contact with the "exotic" cultures they colonized in the last three hundred years. Western artists—of both high and low culture—have been remarkably consistent in how they present themselves and the colonized "native" peoples of the East in their novels, plays, operas, cartoons, even advertisements.*

Colonizers typically present themselves as male, rational, practical, capable, and able to exercise the adult capacities of self-denial and service to abstractions like "God" and "nation." They depict colonized peoples as female, irrational, impractical, incapable of governing themselves, childlike, even animalistic, and mysterious. When a colonizer depicts "native" men, he tends either to feminize or bestialize them.

These stereotypes repeat themselves whenever one people domi-

nates another. If you doubt that "orientalism" exists, just think of the stereotypes that stubbornly remain within our culture. As apparently innocuous a "truth" as "White men can't jump" is a myth borne out of orientalism. It supposes the physical (almost animal) superiority of blacks, while it implies the mental superiority of whites. African Americans are good at things like jumping, so they ought to do sports (or the mundane counterpart to sports, physical labor); Caucasians are good at something else, which generally means something cerebral.

Given the West's willingness to indulge its myths about the East (and about itself), and men's myths about women (and about themselves), Boursicot's colossal mistake seems as inevitable as it is absurd. In deconstructing these myths, Hwang offered a "plea to all sides [West and East, men and women] to cut through our respective layers of cultural and sexual misperception, to deal with one another truthfully for our mutual good, from the common and equal ground we share as human beings."

Into this mix he added Madame Butterfly. This work began life as a novella written by an American, John Luther Long, then became a Broadway play, and finally was adapted by the Italian composer Giacomo Puccini into a popular opera premiering in Milan in 1904. The story is very simple: an American sailor, Pinkerton, temporarily stationed in Nagasaki, Japan, brokers a marriage with a young woman, Cio-Cio-San. The audience never doubts that Pinkerton is a cad, for he has a girl in every port and wants to add Cio-Cio-San to his international plunder. Nevertheless, despite plenty of evidence of his true motives, Cio-Cio-San falls in love with Pinkerton, marries him, and bears his son. Pinkerton aptly compares her to a frail and beautiful butterfly, whose wings he will crush even as he captures her. Pinkerton leaves Japan for three years, during which time he marries an American woman. When he returns to Nagasaki with his new wife, Cio-Cio-San faces the incontrovertible evidence of Pinkerton's disloyalty. She says goodbye to her son and kills herself.

Cio-Cio-San's character is so memorable that her nickname has become slang in Asian American communities. When a woman "pulls a Butterfly," she pretends to be the shy, retiring, "bowing, blushing flower," as Hwang puts it, that Westerners expect Asian *women to be. Asian Americans like Hwang know how fake such a personality is. The term is similar to "Uncle Tom," which African Americans apply to anyone acting subserviently like the title character in Harriet Beecher Stowe's famous novel,* Uncle Tom's Cabin.

The belief that Asian women are submissive and obedient has its larger implications. The political relationships imposed by the West on the East reflect this domestic arrangement: "good natives serve Whites," Hwang explains, while "bad natives rebel."

This theme percolates behind the scenes of Hwang's play in the form of the Vietnam War. Vietnam was a French colony at the beginning of World War II, when it was invaded and conquered by Japan. A native partisan resistance, led by Ho Chi Minh and supplied by the Allies, fought the Japanese heroically. After the Japanese withdrew, Ho Chi Minh opposed the return of the French. But because Ho was also a communist, the United States, first under President Truman, then under President Eisenhower, helped France recolonize the country. When the communists soundly defeated the French in 1954, a cease-fire agreement divided the country into the North, controlled by Ho, and the South, nominally a democracy but really a dictatorship under Ngo Dinh Diem and propped up by the United States. During John Kennedy's presidency, American military "advisors" tacitly allowed a coup d'etat, in which Diem was assassinated, but the South became further destabilized, and by 1965 the United States had sent hundreds of thousands of soldiers to fight the Communists. Over fifty thousand Americans died and three hundred thousand were wounded before the United States withdrew from Vietnam in 1973, and the South fell to the North in 1975.

M. Butterfly

CHARACTERS

KUROGO	GIRL IN MAGAZINE
RENE GALLIMARD	COMRADE CHIN
SONG LILING	SUZUKI
MARC	SHU-FANG
MAN #2	HELGA
CONSUL SHARPLESS	M. TOULON

RENEE   MAN #1
WOMAN AT PARTY   JUDGE

SETTING

The action of the play takes place in a Paris prison in the present, and in recall, during the decade 1960 to 1970 in Beijing, and from 1966 to the present in Paris.

ACT ONE
SCENE 1

M. GALLIMARD's *prison cell. Paris. Present.*

Lights fade up to reveal RENE GALLIMARD, *65, in a prison cell. He wears a comfortable bathrobe, and looks old and tired. The sparsely furnished cell contains a wooden crate upon which sits a hot plate with a kettle, and a portable tape recorder.* GALLIMARD *sits on the crate staring at the recorder, a sad smile on his face.*

Upstage SONG, *who appears as a beautiful woman in traditional Chinese garb, dances a traditional piece from the Peking Opera, surrounded by the percussive clatter of Chinese music.*

Then, slowly, lights and sound cross-fade; the Chinese opera music dissolves into a Western opera, the "Love Duet" from Puccini's Madame Butterfly. SONG *continues dancing, now to the Western accompaniment. Though her movements are the same, the difference in music now gives them a balletic quality.*

GALLIMARD *rises, and turns upstage towards the figure of* SONG, *who dances without acknowledging him.*

GALLIMARD: Butterfly, Butterfly . . .

[*He forces himself to turn away, as the image of* SONG *fades out, and talks to us.*]

GALLIMARD: The limits of my cell are as such: four-and-a-half meters by five. There's one window against the far wall; a door, very strong, to protect me from autograph hounds. I'm responsible for the tape recorder, the hot plate, and this charming coffee table.

When I want to eat, I'm marched off to the dining room—hot, steaming slop appears on my plate. When I want to sleep, the light bulb turns itself off—the work of fairies. It's an enchanted space I occupy. The French—we know how to run a prison.

But, to be honest, I'm not treated like an ordinary prisoner. Why? Because I'm a celebrity. You see, I make people laugh.

I never dreamed this day would arrive. I've never been considered witty or clever. In fact, as a young boy, in an informal poll among my grammar school classmates, I was voted "least likely to be invited to a party." It's a title I managed to hold onto for many years. Despite some stiff competition.

But now, how the tables turn! Look at me: the life of every social function in Paris. Paris? Why be modest? My fame has spread to Amsterdam, London, New York. Listen to them! In the world's smartest parlors. I'm the one who lifts their spirits!

[*With a flourish,* GALLIMARD *directs our attention to another part of the stage.*]

SCENE 2

A party. Present.

Lights go up on a chic-looking parlor, where a well-dressed trio, two men and one woman, make conversation. GALLIMARD *also remains lit; he observes them from his cell.*

WOMAN: And what of Gallimard?

MAN 1: Gallimard?

MAN 2: Gallimard!

GALLIMARD: [*To us.*] You see? They're all determined to say my name, as if it were some new dance.

WOMAN: He still claims not to believe the truth.

MAN 1: What? Still? Even since the trial?

WOMAN: Yes, Isn't it mad?

MAN 2: [*Laughing.*] He says . . . it was dark . . . and she was very modest!

[*The trio break into laughter.*]

MAN 1: So—what? He never touched her with his hands?

MAN 2: Perhaps he did, and simply misidentified the equipment. A compelling case for sex education in the schools.

WOMAN: To protect the National Security—the Church can't argue with that.

MAN 1: That's impossible! How could he not know?

MAN 2: Simple ignorance.

MAN 1: For twenty years?

MAN 2: Time flies when you're being stupid.

WOMAN: Well, I thought the French were ladies' men.

MAN 2: It seems Monsieur Gallimard was overly anxious to live up to his national reputation.

WOMAN: Well, he's not very good-looking.

MAN 1: No, he's not.

MAN 2: Certainly not.

WOMAN: Actually, I feel sorry for him.

MAN 2: A toast! To Monsieur Gallimard!

WOMAN: Yes! To Gallimard!

MAN 1: To Gallimard!

MAN 2: Vive la différence!

[*They toast, laughing. Lights down on them.*]

Scene 3

M. GALLIMARD'*s cell.*

GALLIMARD: [*Smiling.*] You see? They toast me. I've become patron saint of the socially inept. Can they really be so foolish? Men like that—they should be scratching at my door, begging to learn my secrets! For I, Rene Gallimard, you see, I have known, and been loved by . . . the Perfect Woman.

Alone in this cell, I sit night after night, watching our story play through my head, always searching for a new ending, one which redeems my honor, where she returns at last to my arms. And I imagine you—my ideal audience—who come to understand and even, perhaps just a little, to envy me.

[*He turns on his tape recorder. Over the house speakers, we hear the opening phrases of* Madame Butterfly.]

GALLIMARD: In order for you to understand what I did and why, I must introduce you to my favorite opera: *Madame Butterfly.* By Giacomo Puccini. First produced at La Scala, Milan, in 1904, it is now beloved throughout the Western world.

[*As* GALLIMARD *describes the opera, the tape segues in and out to sections he may be describing.*]

GALLIMARD: And why not? Its heroine, Cio-Cio-San, also known as Butterfly, is a feminine ideal, beautiful and brave. And its hero, the man for whom she gives up everything, is—[*He pulls out a naval officer's cap from under his crate, pops it on his head, and struts about.*]—not very good-looking, not too bright, and pretty much a wimp: Benjamin Franklin Pinkerton of the U.S. Navy. As the curtain rises, he's just closed on two great bargains: one on a house, the other on a woman—call it a package deal.

Pinkerton purchased the rights to Butterfly for one hundred yen—in modern currency, equivalent to about . . . sixty-six cents. So, he's feeling pretty pleased with himself as Sharpless, the American consul, arrives to witness the marriage.

[MARC, *wearing an official cap to designate* SHARPLESS, *enters and plays the character.*]

SHARPLESS/MARC: Pinkerton!

PINKERTON/GALLIMARD: Sharpless! How's it hangin'? It's a great day, just great. Between my house, my wife, and the rickshaw ride in from town, I've saved nineteen cents just this morning.

SHARPLESS: Wonderful. I can see the inscription on your tombstone already: "I saved a dollar, here I lie." [*He looks around.*] Nice house.

PINKERTON: It's artistic. Artistic, don't you think? Like the way the shoji screens slide open to reveal the wet bar and disco mirror ball? Classy, huh? Great for impressing the chicks.

SHARPLESS: "Chicks"? Pinkerton, you're going to be a married man!

PINKERTON: Well, sort of.

SHARPLESS: What do you mean?

PINKERTON: This country—Sharpless, it is okay. You got all these geisha girls running around—

SHARPLESS: I know! I live here!

PINKERTON: Then, you know the marriage laws, right? I split for one month, it's annulled!

SHARPLESS: Leave it to you to read the fine print. Who's the lucky girl?

PINKERTON: Cio-Cio-San. Her friends call her Butterfly. Sharpless, she eats out of my hand!

SHARPLESS: She's probably very hungry.

PINKERTON: Not like American girls. It's true what they say about Oriental girls. They want to be treated bad!

SHARPLESS: Oh, please!

PINKERTON: It's true!

SHARPLESS: Are you serious about this girl?

PINKERTON: I'm marrying her, aren't I?

SHARPLESS: Yes—with generous trade-in terms.

PINKERTON: When I leave, she'll know what it's like to have loved a real man. And I'll even buy her a few nylons.

SHARPLESS: You aren't planning to take her with you?

PINKERTON: Huh? Where?

SHARPLESS: Home!

PINKERTON: You mean, America? Are you crazy? Can you see her trying to buy rice in St. Louis?

SHARPLESS: So, you're not serious.

[Pause.]

PINKERTON/GALLIMARD: [As PINKERTON.] Consul, I am a sailor in port. [As GALLIMARD.] They then proceed to sing the famous duet, "The Whole World Over."

[The duet plays on the speakers. GALLIMARD, as PINKERTON, lip-syncs his lines from the opera.]

GALLIMARD: To give a rough translation: "The whole world over, the Yankee travels, casting his anchor wherever he wants. Life's not worth living unless he can win the hearts of the fairest maidens, then hotfoot it off the premises ASAP." [He turns towards MARC.] In the preceding scene, I played Pinkerton, the womanizing cad, and my friend Marc from school . . . [MARC bows grandly for our benefit.] played Sharpless, the sensitive soul of reason. In life, however, our positions were usually—no, always—reversed.

SCENE 4

Ecole Nationale.[1] *Aix-en-Provence. 1947.*

GALLIMARD: No, Marc, I think I'd rather stay home.

MARC: Are you crazy?! We are going to Dad's condo in Marseille![2] You know what happened last time?

---

1. French national (high) school of arts and trades. 2. City on the Mediterranean coast.

GALLIMARD: Of course I do.

MARC: Of course you don't! You never know. . . . They stripped, Rene!

GALLIMARD: Who stripped?

MARC: The girls!

GALLIMARD: Girls? Who said anything about girls?

MARC: Rene, we're a buncha university guys goin' up to the woods. What are we gonna do—talk philosophy?

GALLIMARD: What girls? Where do you get them?

MARC: Who cares? The point is, they come. On trucks. Packed in like sardines. The back flips open, babes hop out, we're ready to roll.

GALLIMARD: You mean, they just—?

MARC: Before you know it, every last one of them—they're stripped and splashing around my pool. There's no moon out, they can't see what's going on, their boobs are flapping, right? You close your eyes, reach out—it's grab bag, get it? Doesn't matter whose ass is between whose legs, whose teeth are sinking into who. You're just in there, going at it, eyes closed, on and on for as long as you can stand. [*Pause.*] Some fun, huh?

GALLIMARD: What happens in the morning?

MARC: In the morning, you're ready to talk some philosophy. [*Beat.*] So how 'bout it?

GALLIMARD: Marc, I can't. . . . I'm afraid they'll say no—the girls. So I never ask.

MARC: You don't have to ask! That's the beauty—don't you see? They don't have to say yes. It's perfect for a guy like you, really.

GALLIMARD: You go ahead. . . . I may come later.

MARC: Hey, Rene—it doesn't matter that you're clumsy and got zits—they're not looking!

GALLIMARD: Thank you very much.

MARC: Wimp.

> [MARC *walks over to the other side of the stage, and starts waving and smiling at women in the audience.*]

GALLIMARD: [*To us.*] We now return to my version of *Madame Butterfly* and the events leading to my recent conviction for treason.

> [GALLIMARD *notices* MARC *making lewd gestures.*]

GALLIMARD: Marc, what are you doing?

MARC: Huh? [*Sotto voce.*[3]] Rene, there're a lotta great babes out there. They're probably lookin' at me and thinking. "What a dangerous guy."

GALLIMARD: Yes—how could they help but be impressed by your cool sophistication?

> [GALLIMARD *pops the* SHARPLESS *cap on* MARC*'s head, and points him offstage.* MARC *exits, leering.*]

Scene 5

M. GALLIMARD*'s cell.*

GALLIMARD: Next, Butterfly makes her entrance. We learn her age—fifteen . . . but very mature for her years.

> [*Lights come up on the area where we saw* SONG *dancing at the top of the play. She appears there again, now dressed as Madame Butterfly, moving to the "Love Duet."* GALLIMARD *turns upstage slightly to watch, transfixed.*]

GALLIMARD: But as she glides past him, beautiful, laughing softly behind her fan, don't we who are men sigh with hope? We, who are not handsome, nor brave, nor powerful, yet somehow believe, like Pinkerton, that we deserve a Butterfly. She arrives with all her possessions in the folds of her sleeves, lays them all out, for her man to do with as he pleases. Even her life itself—she bows her head as she whispers that she's not even worth the hundred yen he paid for her. He's already given too much, when we know he's really had to give nothing at all.

> [*Music and lights on* SONG *out.* GALLIMARD *sits at his crate.*]

GALLIMARD: In real life, women who put their total worth at less than sixty-six cents are quite hard to find. The closest we come is in the pages of these magazines. [*He reaches into his crate, pulls out a stack of girlie magazines, and begins flipping through them.*] Quite a necessity in prison. For three or four dollars, you get seven or eight women.

I first discovered these magazines at my uncle's house. One day, as a boy of twelve. The first time I saw them in his closet . . . all

---

3. A low, conspiratorial tone (Italian for "under the voice").

lined up—my body shook. Not with lust—no, with power. Here were women—a shelfful—who would do exactly as I wanted.

[*The "Love Duet" creeps in over the speakers. Special[1] comes up, revealing, not* SONG *this time, but a* PINUP GIRL *in a sexy negligee, her back to us.* GALLIMARD *turns upstage and looks at her.*]

GIRL: I know you're watching me.

GALLIMARD: My throat . . . it's dry.

GIRL: I leave my blinds open every night before I go to bed.

GALLIMARD: I can't move.

GIRL: I leave my blinds open and the lights on.

GALLIMARD: I'm shaking. My skin is hot, but my penis is soft. Why?

GIRL: I stand in front of the window.

GALLIMARD: What is she going to do?

GIRL: I toss my hair, and I let my lips part . . . barely.

GALLIMARD: I shouldn't be seeing this. It's so dirty. I'm so bad.

GIRL: Then, slowly, I lift off my nightdress.

GALLIMARD: Oh, god. I can't believe it. I can't—

GIRL: I toss it to the ground.

GALLIMARD: Now, she's going to walk away. She's going to—

GIRL: I stand there, in the light, displaying myself.

GALLIMARD: No. She's—why is she naked?

GIRL: To you.

GALLIMARD: In front of a window? This is wrong. No—

GIRL: Without shame.

GALLIMARD: No, she must . . . like it.

GIRL: I like it.

GALLIMARD: She . . . she wants me to see.

GIRL: I want you to see.

GALLIMARD: I can't believe it! She's getting excited!

GIRL: I can't see you. You can do whatever you want.

GALLIMARD: I can't do a thing. Why?

GIRL: What would you like me to do . . . next?

[*Light go down on her. Music off. Silence, as* GALLIMARD *puts away his magazines. Then he resumes talking to us.*]

GALLIMARD: Act Two begins with Butterfly staring at the ocean. Pinkerton's been called back to the U.S., and he's given his wife a

---

1. Spotlight; as used elsewhere, also refers to a spotlighted area of the stage.

detailed schedule of his plans. In the column marked "return date," he's written "when the robins nest." This failed to ignite her suspicions. Now, three years have passed without a peep from him. Which brings a response from her faithful servant, Suzuki.

[COMRADE CHIN *enters, playing* SUZUKI.]

SUZUKI: Girl, he's a loser. What'd he ever give you? Nineteen cents and those ugly Day-Glo stockings? Look, it's finished! Kaput! Done! And you should be glad! I mean, the guy was a woofer! He tried before, you know—before he met you, he went down to geisha central and plunked down his spare change in front of the usual candidates—everyone else gagged! These are hungry prostitutes, and they were not interested, get the picture? Now, stop slathering when an American ship sails in, and let's make some bucks—I mean, yen! We are broke!

Now, what about Yamadori? Hey, hey—don't look away—the man is a prince—figuratively, and, what's even better, literally. He's rich, he's handsome, he says he'll die if you don't marry him—and he's even willing to overlook the little fact that you've been deflowered all over the place by a foreign devil. What do you mean, "But he's Japanese?" You're Japanese! You think you've been touched by the whitey god? He was a sailor with dirty hands!

[SUZUKI *stalks offstage.*]

GALLIMARD: She's also visited by Consul Sharpless, sent by Pinkerton on a minor errand.

[MARC *enters, as* SHARPLESS.]

SHARPLESS: I hate this job.

GALLIMARD: This Pinkerton—he doesn't show up personally to tell his wife he's abandoning her. No, he sends a government diplomat . . . at taxpayer's expense.

SHARPLESS: Butterfly? Butterfly? I have some bad—I'm going to be ill. Butterfly, I came to tell you—

GALLIMARD: Butterfly says she knows he'll return and if he doesn't she'll kill herself rather than go back to her own people. [*Beat.*] This causes a lull in the conversation.

SHARPLESS: Let's put it this way . . .

GALLIMARD: Butterfly runs into the next room, and returns holding—

[*Sound cue: a baby crying.* SHARPLESS, *"seeing" this, backs away.*]

SHARPLESS: Well, good. Happy to see things going so well. I suppose I'll be going now. Ta ta. Ciao. [*He turns away. Sound cue out.*] I hate this job. [*He exits.*]

GALLIMARD: At that moment, Butterfly spots in the harbor an American ship—the *Abramo Lincoln!*

[*Music cue: "The Flower Duet."* SONG, *still dressed as Butterfly, changes into a wedding kimono, moving to the music.*]

GALLIMARD: This is the moment that redeems her years of waiting. With Suzuki's help, they cover the room with flowers—

[CHIN, *as* SUZUKI, *trudges onstage and drops a lone flower without much enthusiasm.*]

GALLIMARD: —and she changes into her wedding dress to prepare for Pinkerton's arrival.

[SUZUKI *helps Butterfly change.* HELGA *enters, and helps* GALLIMARD *change into a tuxedo.*]

GALLIMARD: I married a woman older than myself—Helga.

HELGA: My father was ambassador to Australia. I grew up among criminals and kangaroos.

GALLIMARD: Hearing that brought me to the altar—

[HELGA *exits.*]

GALLIMARD: —where I took a vow renouncing love. No fantasy woman would ever want me, so, yes, I would settle for a quick leap up the career ladder. Passion, I banish, and in its place—practicality!

But my vows had long since lost their charm by the time we arrived in China. The sad truth is that all men want a beautiful woman, and the uglier the man, the greater the want.

[SUZUKI *makes final adjustments of Butterfly's costume, as does* GALLIMARD *of his tuxedo.*]

GALLIMARD: I married late, at age thirty-one. I was faithful to my marriage for eight years. Until the day when, as a junior-level diplomat in puritanical Peking, in a parlor at the German ambassador's house, during the "Reign of a Hundred Flowers,"[2] I first saw her . . . singing the death scene from *Madame Butterfly.*

[SUZUKI *runs offstage.*]

2. Campaign (1956–57) during which the Chinese Communist Party encouraged citizens to criticize the Party.

SCENE 6

German ambassador's house. Beijing. 1960.

The upstage special area now becomes a stage. Several chairs face upstage, representing seating for some twenty guests in the parlor. A few "diplomats"—RENEE, MARC, TOULON—in formal dress enter and take seats.

GALLIMARD also sits down, but turns towards us and continues to talk. Orchestral accompaniment on the tape is now replaced by a simple piano. SONG *picks up the death scene from the point where Butterfly uncovers the hara-kiri knife.*

GALLIMARD: The ending is pitiful. Pinkerton, in an act of great courage, stays home and sends his American wife to pick up Butterfly's child. The truth, long deferred, has come up to her door.
[SONG, *playing Butterfly, sings the lines from the opera in her own voice—which, though not classical, should be decent.*]
SONG: "Con onor muore/ chi non puo serbar/ vita con onore."
GALLIMARD: [*Simultaneously.*] "Death with honor/ Is better than life/ Life with dishonor."
[*The stage is illuminated; we are now completely within an elegant diplomat's residence.* SONG *proceeds to play out an abbreviated death scene. Everyone in the room applauds.* SONG, *shyly, takes her bows. Others in the room rush to congratulate her.* GALLIMARD *remains with us.*]
GALLIMARD: They say in opera the voice is everything. That's probably why I'd never before enjoyed opera. Here . . . here was a Butterfly with little or no voice—but she had the grace, the delicacy. . . . I believed this girl. I believed her suffering. I wanted to take her in my arms—so delicate, even I could protect her, take her home, pamper her until she smiled.
[*Over the course of the preceeding speech,* SONG *has broken from the upstage crowd and moved directly upstage of* GALLIMARD.]
SONG: Excuse me. Monsieur . . . ?
[GALLIMARD *turns upstage, shocked.*]
GALLIMARD: Oh! Gallimard. Mademoiselle . . . ? A beautiful . . .
SONG: Song Liling.
GALLIMARD: A beautiful performance.
SONG: Oh, please.
GALLIMARD: I usually—

SONG: You make me blush. I'm no opera singer at all.

GALLIMARD: I usually don't like *Butterfly*.

SONG: I can't blame you in the least.

GALLIMARD: I mean, the story—

SONG: Ridiculous.

GALLIMARD: I like the story, but . . . what?

SONG: Oh, you like it?

GALLIMARD: I . . . what I mean is, I've always seen it played by huge women in so much bad makeup.

SONG: Bad makeup is not unique to the West.

GALLIMARD: But, who can believe them?

SONG: And you believe me?

GALLIMARD: Absolutely. You were utterly convincing. It's the first time—

SONG: Convincing? As a Japanese woman? The Japanese used hundreds of our people for medical experiments during the war,[1] you know. But I gather such an irony is lost on you.

GALLIMARD: No! I was about to say, it's the first time I've seen the beauty of the story.

SONG: Really?

GALLIMARD: Of her death. It's a . . . a pure sacrifice. He's unworthy, but what can she do? She loves him . . . so much. It's a very beautiful story.

SONG: Well, yes, to a Westerner.

GALLIMARD: Excuse me?

SONG: It's one of your favorite fantasies, isn't it? The submissive Oriental woman and the cruel white man.

GALLIMARD: Well, I didn't quite mean . . .

SONG: Consider it this way: what would you say if a blonde homecoming queen fell in love with a short Japanese businessman? He treats her cruelly, then goes home for three years, during which time she prays to his picture and turns down marriage from a young Kennedy. Then, when she learns he has remarried, she kills herself. Now, I believe you would consider this girl to be a deranged idiot, correct? But because it's an Oriental who kills herself for a Westerner—ah!—you find it beautiful. [*Silence.*]

---

1. World War II, during which Japan invaded and occupied much of China.

GALLIMARD: Yes . . . well . . . I see your point. . . .

SONG: I will never do Butterfly again, Monsieur Gallimard. If you wish to see some real theatre, come to the Peking Opera sometime. Expand your mind. [SONG *walks offstage.*]

GALLIMARD: [*To us.*] So much for protecting her in my big Western arms.

SCENE 7

  M. GALLIMARD's *apartment. Beijing. 1960.*
  GALLIMARD *changes from his tux into a casual suit.* HELGA *enters.*

GALLIMARD: The Chinese are an incredibly arrogant people.

HELGA: They warned us about that in Paris, remember?

GALLIMARD: Even Parisians consider them arrogant. That's a switch.

HELGA: What is it that Madame Su says? "We are a very old civilization." I never know if she's talking about her country or herself.

GALLIMARD: I walk around here, all I hear every day, everywhere is how *old* this culture is. The fact that "old" may be synonymous with "senile" doesn't occur to them.

HELGA: You're not going to change them. "East is east, west is west, and . . ." whatever that guy said.

GALLIMARD: It's just that—silly. I met . . . at Ambassador Koening's tonight—you should've been there.

HELGA: Koening? Oh god, no. Did he enchant you all again with the history of Bavaria?

GALLIMARD: No. I met, I suppose, the Chinese equivalent of a diva. She's a singer in the Chinese opera.

HELGA: They have an opera, too? Do they sing in Chinese? Or maybe—in Italian?

GALLIMARD: Tonight, she did sing in Italian.

HELGA: How'd she manage that?

GALLIMARD: She must've been educated in the West before the Revolution.[1] Her French is very good also. Anyway, she sang the death scene from *Madame Butterfly.*

HELGA: *Madame Butterfly!* Then I should have come. [*She begins*

1. A civil war (1945–49) that brought the Communists to power by the defeat of the Nationalists, who were allied with the West.

humming, floating around the room as if dragging long kimono sleeves.] Did she have a nice costume? I think it's a classic piece of music.

GALLIMARD: That's what *I* thought, too. Don't let her hear you say that.

HELGA: What's wrong?

GALLIMARD: Evidently the Chinese hate it.

HELGA: She hated it, but she performed it anyway? Is she perverse?

GALLIMARD: They hate it because the white man gets the girl. Sour grapes if you ask me.

HELGA: Politics again? Why can't they just hear it as a piece of beautiful music? So, what's in their opera?

GALLIMARD: I don't know. But, whatever it is, I'm sure it must be *old*.

[HELGA *exits.*]

Scene 8

Chinese opera house and the streets of Beijing, 1960.
The sound of gongs clanging fills the stage.

GALLIMARD: My wife's innocent question kept ringing in my ears. I asked around, but no one knew anything about the Chinese opera. It took four weeks, but my curiosity overcame my cowardice. This Chinese diva—this unwilling Butterfly—what did she do to make her so proud?

The room was hot, and full of smoke. Wrinkled faces, old women, teeth missing—a man with a growth on his neck, like a human toad. All smiling, pipes falling from their mouths, cracking nuts between their teeth, a live chicken pecking at my foot— all looking, screaming, gawking . . . at her.

The upstage area is suddenly hit with a harsh white light. It has become the stage for the Chinese opera performance. Two dancers enter, along with SONG. GALLIMARD *stands apart, watching.* SONG *glides gracefully amidst the two dancers. Drums suddenly slam to a halt.* SONG *strikes a pose, looking straight at* GALLIMARD. *Dancers exit. Light change. Pause, then* SONG *walks right off the stage and straight up to* GALLIMARD.

SONG: Yes. You. White man. I'm looking straight at you.

GALLIMARD: Me?

SONG: You see any other white men? It was too easy to spot you. How often does a man in my audience come in a tie?

[SONG *starts to remove her costume. Underneath, she wears simple baggy clothes. They are now backstage. The show is over.*]

SONG: So, you are an adventurous imperialist?

GALLIMARD: I . . . thought it would further my education.

SONG: It took you four weeks. Why?

GALLIMARD: I've been busy.

SONG: Well, education has always been undervalued in the West, hasn't it?

GALLIMARD: [*Laughing.*] I don't think it's true.

SONG: No, you wouldn't. You're a Westerner. How can you objectively judge your own values?

GALLIMARD: I think it's possible to achieve some distance.

SONG: Do you? [*Pause.*] It stinks in here. Let's go.

GALLIMARD: These are the smells of your loyal fans.

SONG: I love them for being my fans, I hate the smell they leave behind. I too can distance myself from my people. [*She looks around, then whispers in his ear.*] "Art for the masses" is a shitty excuse to keep artists poor. [*She pops a cigarette in her mouth.*] Be a gentleman, will you? And light my cigarette.

[*Gallimard fumbles for a match.*]

GALLIMARD: I don't . . . smoke.

SONG: [*Lighting her own.*] Your loss. Had you lit my cigarette, I might have blown a puff of smoke right between your eyes. Come.

[*They start to walk about the stage. It is a summer night on the Beijing streets. Sounds of the city play on the house speakers.*]

SONG: How I wish there were even a tiny cafe to sit in. With cappuccinos, and men in tuxedos and bad expatriate jazz.

GALLIMARD: If my history serves me correctly, you weren't even allowed into the clubs in Shanghai before the Revolution.

SONG: Your history serves you poorly, Monsieur Gallimard. True, there were signs reading "No dogs and Chinamen." But a woman, especially a delicate Oriental woman—we always go where we please. Could you imagine it otherwise? Clubs in China filled with pasty, big-thighed white women, while thou-

sands of slender lotus blossoms wait just outside the door? Never.
The clubs would be empty. [*Beat.*] We have always held a certain
fascination for you Caucasian men, have we not?

GALLIMARD: But . . . that fascination is imperialist, or so you tell me.

SONG: Do you believe everything I tell you? Yes. It is always imperialist. But sometimes . . . sometimes, it is also mutual. Oh—this is
my flat.

GALLIMARD: I didn't even—

SONG: Thank you. Come another time and we will further expand
your mind.

> [SONG *exits.* GALLIMARD *continues roaming the streets as he
> speaks to us.*]

GALLIMARD: What was that? What did she mean, "Sometimes . . . it
is mutual?" Women do not flirt with me. And I normally can't
talk to them. But tonight, I held up my end of the conversation.

SCENE 9

> GALLIMARD'*s bedroom. Beijing. 1960.* HELGA *enters.*

HELGA: You didn't tell me you'd be home late.

GALLIMARD: I didn't intend to. Something came up.

HELGA: Oh? Like what?

GALLIMARD: I went to the . . . to the Dutch ambassador's home.

HELGA: Again?

GALLIMARD: There was a reception for a visiting scholar. He's writing a six-volume treatise on the Chinese revolution. We all gathered that meant he'd have to live here long enough to actually
write six volumes, and we all expressed our deepest sympathies.

HELGA: Well, I had a good night too. I went with the ladies to a
martial arts demonstration. Some of those men—when they
break those thick boards— [*She mimes fanning herself.*] whoo-
whoo! [HELGA *exits. Lights dim.*]

GALLIMARD: I lied to my wife. Why? I've never had any reason to lie
before. But what reason did I have tonight? I didn't do anything
wrong. That night, I had a dream. Other people, I've been told,
have dreams where angels appear. Or dragons, or Sophia Loren
in a towel. In my dream, Marc from school appeared.

> [MARC *enters, in a nightshirt and cap.*]

MARC: Rene! You met a girl!

[GALLIMARD *and* MARC *stumble down the Beijing streets. Night sounds over the speakers.*]

GALLIMARD: It's not that amazing, thank you.

MARC: No! It's so monumental, I heard about it halfway around the world in my sleep!

GALLIMARD: I've met girls before, you know.

MARC: Name one. I've come across time and space to congratulate you. [*He hands* GALLIMARD *a bottle of wine.*]

GALLIMARD: Marc, this is expensive.

MARC: On those rare occasions when you become a formless spirit, why not steal the best?

[MARC *pops open the bottle, begins to share it with* GALLIMARD.]

GALLIMARD: You embarrass me. She . . . there's no reason to think she likes me.

MARC: "Sometimes, it is mutual"?

GALLIMARD: Oh.

MARC: "Mutual"? "Mutual"? What does that mean?

GALLIMARD: You heard!

MARC: It means the money is in the bank, you only have to write the check!

GALLIMARD: I am a married man!

MARC: And an excellent one too. I cheated after . . . six months. Then again and again, until now—three hundred girls in twelve years.

GALLIMARD: I don't think we should hold that up as a model.

MARC: Of course not! My life—it is disgusting! Phooey! Phooey! But, you—you are the model husband.

GALLIMARD: Anyway, it's impossible. I'm a foreigner.

MARC: Ah, yes. She cannot love you, it is taboo, but something deep inside her heart . . . she cannot help herself . . . she must surrender to you. It is her destiny.

GALLIMARD: How do you imagine all this?

MARC: The same way you do. It's an old story. It's in our blood. They fear us, Rene. Their women fear us. And their men—their men hate us. And, you know something? They are all correct.

[*They spot a light in a window.*]

MARC: There! There, Rene!

GALLIMARD: It's her window.

MARC: Late at night—it burns. The light—it burns for you.

GALLIMARD: I won't look. It's not respectful.

MARC: We don't have to be respectful. We're foreign devils.

[*Enter* SONG, *in a sheer robe. The "One Fine Day" aria creeps in over the speakers. With her back to us,* SONG *mimes attending to her toilette. Her robe comes loose, revealing her white shoulders.*]

MARC: All your life you've waited for a beautiful girl who would lay down for you. All your life you've smiled like a saint when it's happened to every other man you know. And you see them in magazines and you see them in movies. And you wonder, what's wrong with me? Will anyone beautiful ever want me? As the years pass, your hair thins and you struggle to hold onto even your hopes. Stop struggling, Rene. The wait is over. [*He exits.*]

GALLIMARD: Marc? Marc?

[*At that moment,* SONG, *her back still towards us, drops her robe. A second of her naked back, then a sound cue: a phone ringing, very loud. Blackout, followed in the next beat by a special up on the bedroom area, where a phone now sits.* GALLIMARD *stumbles across the stage and picks up the phone. Sound cue out. Over the course of his conversation, area lights fill in the vicinity of his bed. It is the following morning.*]

GALLIMARD: Yes? Hello?

SONG: [*Offstage.*] Is it very early?

GALLIMARD: Why, yes.

SONG: [*Offstage.*] How early?

GALLIMARD: It's . . . it's 5:30. Why are you—?

SONG: [*Offstage.*] But it's light outside. Already.

GALLIMARD: It is. The sun must be in confusion today.

[*Over the course of* SONG's *next speech, her upstage special comes up again. She sits in a chair, legs crossed, in a robe, telephone to her ear.*]

SONG: I waited until I saw the sun. That was as much discipline as I could manage for one night. Do you forgive me?

GALLIMARD: Of course . . . for what?

SONG: Then I'll ask you quickly. Are you really interested in the opera?

GALLIMARD: Why, yes. Yes, I am.

SONG: Then come again next Thursday. I am playing *The Drunken Beauty.* May I count on you?

GALLIMARD: Yes. You may.

SONG: Perfect. Well, I must be getting to bed. I'm exhausted. It's been a very long night for me.

> [SONG *hangs up; special on her goes off.* GALLIMARD *begins to dress for work.*]

SCENE 10

SONG LILING'*s apartment. Beijing. 1960.*

GALLIMARD: I returned to the opera that next week, and the week after that . . . she keeps our meetings so short—perhaps fifteen, twenty minutes at most. So I am left each week with a thirst which is intensified. In this way, fifteen weeks have gone by. I am starting to doubt the words of my friend Marc. But no, not really. In my heart, I know she has . . . an interest in me. I suspect this is her way. She is outwardly bold and outspoken, yet her heart is shy and afraid. It is the Oriental in her at war with her Western education.

SONG: [*Offstage.*] I will be out in an instant. Ask the servant for anything you want.

GALLIMARD: Tonight, I have finally been invited to enter her apartment. Though the idea is almost beyond belief, I believe she is afraid of me.

> [GALLIMARD *looks around the room. He picks up a picture in a frame, studies it. Without his noticing,* SONG *enters, dressed elegantly in a black gown from the twenties. She stands in the doorway looking like Anna May Wong.*[1]]

SONG: That is my father.

GALLIMARD: [*Surprised.*] Mademoiselle Song . . .

> [*She glides up to him, snatches away the picture.*]

SONG: It is very good that he did not live to see the Revolution. They would, no doubt, have made him kneel on broken glass. Not that he didn't deserve such a punishment. But he is my father. I would've hated to see it happen.

---

1. Chinese American movie actor (1905–1962), known for her beauty, her trademark bangs, and her characteristically Asian clothing.

GALLIMARD: I'm very honored that you've allowed me to visit your home.

[SONG *curtsys.*]

SONG: Thank you. Oh! Haven't you been poured any tea?

GALLIMARD: I'm really not—

SONG: [*To her offstage servant.*] Shu-Fang! Cha! Kwai-lah! [*To* GALLI-MARD.] I'm sorry. You want everything to be perfect—

GALLIMARD: Please.

SONG: —and before the evening even begins—

GALLIMARD: I'm really not thirsty.

SONG: —it's ruined.

GALLIMARD: [*Sharply.*] Mademoiselle Song!

[SONG *sits down.*]

SONG: I'm sorry.

GALLIMARD: What are you apologizing for now?

[*Pause;* SONG *starts to giggle.*]

SONG: I don't know!

[GALLIMARD *laughs.*]

GALLIMARD: Exactly my point.

SONG: Oh, I am silly. Lightheaded. I promise not to apologize for anything else tonight, do you hear me?

GALLIMARD: That's a good girl.

[SHU-FANG, *a servant girl, comes out with a tea tray and starts to pour.*]

SONG: [*To* SHU-FANG.] No! I'll pour myself for the gentleman!

[SHU-FANG, *staring at* GALLIMARD, *exits.*]

SONG: No, I . . . I don't even know why I invited you up.

GALLIMARD: Well, I'm glad you did.

[SONG *looks around the room.*]

SONG: There is an element of danger to your presence.

GALLIMARD: Oh?

SONG: You must know.

GALLIMARD: It doesn't concern me. We both know why I'm here.

SONG: It doesn't concern me either. No . . . well, perhaps.

GALLIMARD: What?

SONG: Perhaps I am slightly afraid of scandal.

GALLIMARD: What are we doing?

SONG: I'm entertaining you. In my parlor.

GALLIMARD: In France, that would hardly—

SONG: France. France is a country living in the modern era. Perhaps even ahead of it. China is a nation whose soul is firmly rooted two thousand years in the past. What I do, even pouring the tea for you now . . . it has . . . implications. The walls and windows say so. Even my own heart, strapped inside this Western dress . . . even it says things—things I don't care to hear.

[SONG *hands* GALLIMARD *a cup of tea.* GALLIMARD *puts his hand over both the teacup and* SONG's *hand.*]

GALLIMARD: This is a beautiful dress.

SONG: Don't.

GALLIMARD: What?

SONG: I don't even know if it looks right on me.

GALLIMARD: Believe me—

SONG: You are from France. You see so many beautiful women.

GALLIMARD: France? Since when are the European women—?

SONG: Oh! What am I trying to do, anyway?!

[SONG *runs to the door, composes herself, then turns towards* GALLIMARD.]

SONG: Monsieur Gallimard, perhaps you should go.

GALLIMARD: But . . . why?

SONG: There's something wrong about this.

GALLIMARD: I don't see what.

SONG: I feel . . . I am not myself.

GALLIMARD: No. You're nervous.

SONG: Please. Hard as I try to be modern, to speak like a man, to hold a Western woman's strong face up to my own . . . in the end, I fail. A small, frightened heart beats too quickly and gives me away. Monsieur Gallimard, I'm a Chinese girl. I've never . . . never invited a man up to my flat before. The forwardness of my actions makes my skin burn.

GALLIMARD: What are you afraid of? Certainly not me, I hope.

SONG: I'm a modest girl.

GALLIMARD: I know. And very beautiful. [*He touches her hair.*]

SONG: Please—go now. The next time you see me, I shall again be myself.

GALLIMARD: I like you the way you are right now.

SONG: You are a cad.

GALLIMARD: What do you expect? I'm a foreign devil.

[GALLIMARD *walks downstage.* SONG *exits.*]

GALLIMARD: [*To us.*] Did you hear the way she talked about Western women? Much differently than the first night. She does—she feels inferior to them—and to me.

SCENE 11

The French embassy. Beijing. 1960.
GALLIMARD *moves towards a desk.*

GALLIMARD: I determined to try an experiment. In *Madame Butterfly,* Cio-Cio-San fears that the Western man who catches a butterfly will pierce its heart with a needle, then leave it to perish. I began to wonder: had I, too, caught a butterfly who would writhe on a needle?

[MARC *enters, dressed as a bureaucrat, holding a stack of papers. As* GALLIMARD *speaks,* MARC *hands papers to him. He peruses, then signs, stamps or rejects them.*]

GALLIMARD: Over the next five weeks, I worked like a dynamo. I stopped going to the opera, I didn't phone or write her. I knew this little flower was waiting for me to call, and, as I wickedly refused to do so, I felt for the first time that rush of power—the absolute power of a man.

[MARC *continues acting as the bureaucrat, but he now speaks as himself.*]

MARC: Rene! It's me!

GALLIMARD: Marc—I hear your voice everywhere now. Even in the midst of work.

MARC: That's because I'm watching you—all the time.

GALLIMARD: You were always the most popular guy in school.

MARC: Well, there's no guarantee of failure in life like happiness in high school. Somehow I knew I'd end up in the suburbs working for Renault and you'd be in the Orient picking exotic women off the trees. And they say there's no justice.

GALLIMARD: That's why you were my friend?

MARC: I gave you a little of my life, so that now you can give me some of yours. [*Pause.*] Remember Isabelle?

GALLIMARD: Of course I remember! She was my first experience.

MARC: We all wanted to ball her. But she only wanted me.

GALLIMARD: I had her.

MARC: Right. You balled her.

GALLIMARD: You were the only one who ever believed me.

MARC: Well, there's a good reason for that. [*Beat.*] C'mon. You must've guessed.

GALLIMARD: You told me to wait in the bushes by the cafeteria that night. The next thing I knew, she was on me. Dress up in the air.

MARC: She never wore underwear.

GALLIMARD: My arms were pinned to the dirt.

MARC: She loved the superior position. A girl ahead of her time.

GALLIMARD: I looked up, and there was this woman . . . bouncing up and down on my loins.

MARC: Screaming, right?

GALLIMARD: Screaming, and breaking off the branches all around me, and pounding my butt up and down into the dirt.

MARC: Huffing and puffing like a locomotive.

GALLIMARD: And in the middle of all this, the leaves were getting into my mouth, my legs were losing circulation, I thought, "God. So this is *it?*"

MARC: You thought that?

GALLIMARD: Well, I was worried about my legs falling off.

MARC: You didn't have a good time?

GALLIMARD: No, that's not what I—I had a great time!

MARC: You're sure?

GALLIMARD: Yeah. Really.

MARC: 'Cuz I wanted you to have a good time.

GALLIMARD: I did. [*Pause.*]

MARC: Shit. [*Pause.*] When all is said and done, she was kind of a lousy lay, wasn't she? I mean, there was a lot of energy there, but you never knew what she was doing with it. Like when she yelled "I'm coming!"—hell, it was so loud, you wanted to go "Look, it's not that big a deal."

GALLIMARD: I got scared. I thought she meant someone was actually coming. [*Pause.*] But, Marc?

MARC: What?

GALLIMARD: Thanks.

MARC: Oh, don't mention it.

GALLIMARD: It was my first experience.

MARC: Yeah. You got her.

GALLIMARD: I got her.

MARC: Wait! Look at that letter again!

> [GALLIMARD *picks up one of the papers he's been stamping, and rereads it.*]

GALLIMARD: [*To us.*] After six weeks, they began to arrive. The letters.

> [*Upstage special on* SONG, *as Madame Butterfly. The scene is underscored by the "Love Duet."*]

SONG: Did we fight? I do not know. Is the opera no longer of interest to you? Please come—my audiences miss the white devil in their midst.

> [GALLIMARD *looks up from the letter, towards us.*]

GALLIMARD: [*To us.*] A concession, but much too dignified. [*Beat; he discards the letter.*] I skipped the opera again that week to complete a position paper on trade.

> [*The bureaucrat hands him another letter.*]

SONG: Six weeks have passed since last we met. Is this your practice—to leave friends in the lurch? Sometimes I hate you, sometimes I hate myself, but always I miss you.

GALLIMARD: [*To us.*] Better, but I don't like the way she calls me "friend." When a woman calls a man her "friend," she's calling him a eunuch or a homosexual. [*Beat; he discards the letter.*] I was absent from the opera for the seventh week, feeling a sudden urge to clean out my files.

> [*Bureaucrat hands him another letter.*]

SONG: Your rudeness is beyond belief. I don't deserve this cruelty. Don't bother to call. I'll have you turned away at the door.

GALLIMARD: [*To us.*] I didn't. [*He discards the letter; bureaucrat hands him another.*] And then finally, the letter that concluded my experiment.

SONG: I am out of words. I can hide behind dignity no longer. What do you want? I have already given you my shame.

> [GALLIMARD *gives the letter back to* MARC, *slowly. Special on* SONG *fades out.*]

GALLIMARD: [*To us.*] Reading it, I became suddenly ashamed. Yes, my experiment had been a success. She was turning on my needle. But the victory seemed hollow.

MARC: Hollow?! Are you crazy?

GALLIMARD: Nothing, Marc. Please go away.

MARC: [*Exiting, with papers.*] Haven't I taught you anything?

GALLIMARD: "I have already given you my shame." I had to attend a reception that evening. On the way, I felt sick. If there is a God, surely he would punish me now. I had finally gained power over a beautiful woman, only to abuse it cruelly. There must be justice in the world. I had the strange feeling that the ax would fall this very evening.

SCENE 12

Ambassador Toulon's residence. Beijing. 1960.

Sound cue: party noises. Light change. We are now in a spacious residence. TOULON, *the French ambassador, enters and taps* GALLIMARD *on the shoulder.*

TOULON: Gallimard? Can I have a word? Over here.

GALLIMARD: [*To us.*] Manuel Toulon. French ambassador to China. He likes to think of us all as his children. Rather like God.

TOULON: Look, Gallimard, there's not much to say. I've liked you. From the day you walked in. You were no leader, but you were tidy and efficient.

GALLIMARD: Thank you, sir.

TOULON: Don't jump the gun. Okay, our needs in China are changing. It's embarrassing that we lost Indochina.[1] Someone just wasn't on the ball there. I don't mean you personally, of course.

GALLIMARD: Thank you, sir.

TOULON: We're going to be doing a lot more information-gathering in the future. The nature of our work here is changing. Some people are just going to have to go. It's nothing personal.

GALLIMARD: Oh.

TOULON: Want to know a secret? Vice-Consul LeBon is being transferred.

GALLIMARD: [*To us.*] My immediate superior!

TOULON: And most of his department.

GALLIMARD: [*To us.*] Just as I feared! God has seen my evil heart—

1. Vietnam, Cambodia, Laos.

TOULON: But not you.

GALLIMARD: [*To us.*]—and he's taking her away just as . . . [*To Toulon.*] Excuse me, sir?

TOULON: Scare you? I think I did. Cheer up, Gallimard. I want you to replace LeBon as vice-consul.

GALLIMARD: You—? Yes, well, thank you, sir.

TOULON: Anytime.

GALLIMARD: I . . . accept with great humility.

TOULON: Humility won't be part of the job. You're going to coordinate the revamped intelligence division. Want to know a secret? A year ago, you would've been out. But the past few months, I don't know how it happened, you've become this new aggressive confident . . . thing. And they also tell me you get along with the Chinese. So I think you're a lucky man, Gallimard. Congratulations.

[*They shake hands.* TOULON *exits. Party noises out.* GALLIMARD *stumbles across a darkened stage.*]

GALLIMARD: Vice-consul? Impossible! As I stumbled out of the party, I saw it written across the sky: There is no God. Or, no— say that there is a God. But that God . . . understands. Of course! God who creates Eve to serve Adam, who blesses Solomon with his harem but ties Jezebel[2] to a burning bed—that God is a man. And he understands! At age thirty-nine, I was suddenly initiated into the way of the world.

SCENE 13

SONG LILING's *apartment. Beijing. 1960.*
SONG *enters, in a sheer dressing gown.*

SONG: Are you crazy?

GALLIMARD: Mademoiselle Song—

SONG: To come here—at this hour? After . . . after eight weeks?

GALLIMARD: It's the most amazing—

SONG: You bang on my door? Scare my servants, scandalize the neighbors?

2. In the Bible, wife of Ahab; she comes to a gruesome end. Colloquially, a jezebel is a painted woman, wicked and impudent. *Solomon:* king of Israel, renowned for his wisdom. The Song of Solomon, a collection of love poems, is the most sexually provocative book in the Bible.

GALLIMARD: I've been promoted. To vice-consul. [*Pause.*]

SONG: And what is that supposed to mean to me?

GALLIMARD: Are you my Butterfly?

SONG: What are you saying?

GALLIMARD: I've come tonight for an answer: are you my Butterfly?

SONG: Don't you know already?

GALLIMARD: I want you to say it.

SONG: I don't want to say it.

GALLIMARD: So, that is your answer?

SONG: You know how I feel about—

GALLIMARD: I do remember one thing.

SONG: What?

GALLIMARD: In the letter I received today.

SONG: Don't.

GALLIMARD: "I have already given you my shame."

SONG: It's enough that I even wrote it.

GALLIMARD: Well, then—

SONG: I shouldn't have it splashed across my face.

GALLIMARD: —if that's all true—

SONG: Stop!

GALLIMARD: Then what is one more short answer?

SONG: I don't want to!

GALLIMARD: Are you my Butterfly? [*Silence; he crosses the room and begins to touch her hair.*] I want from you honesty. There should be nothing false between us. No false pride. [*Pause.*]

SONG: Yes, I am. I am your Butterfly.

GALLIMARD: Then let me be honest with you. It is because of you that I was promoted tonight. You have changed my life forever. My little Butterfly, there should be no more secrets: I love you. [*He starts to kiss her roughly. She resists slightly.*]

SONG: No . . . no . . . gently . . . please, I've never . . .

GALLIMARD: No?

SONG: I've tried to appear experienced, but . . . the truth is . . . no.

GALLIMARD: Are you cold?

SONG: Yes. Cold.

GALLIMARD: Then we will go very, very slowly. [*He starts to caress her; her gown begins to open.*]

SONG: No . . . let me . . . keep my clothes . . .

GALLIMARD: But . . .

SONG: Please . . . it all frightens me. I'm a modest Chinese girl.

GALLIMARD: My poor little treasure.

SONG: I am your treasure. Though inexperienced, I am not . . . ignorant. They teach us things, our mothers, about pleasing a man.

GALLIMARD: Yes?

SONG: I'll do my best to make you happy. Turn off the lights.

[GALLIMARD *gets up and heads for a lamp.* SONG, *propped up on one elbow, tosses her hair back and smiles.*]

SONG: Monsieur Gallimard?

GALLIMARD: Yes, Butterfly?

SONG: "Vieni, vieni!"

GALLIMARD: "Come, darling."

SONG: "Ah! Dolce notte!"

GALLIMARD: "Beautiful night."

SONG: "Tutto estatico d'amor ride il ciel!"

GALLIMARD: "All ecstatic with love, the heavens are filled with laughter." [*He turns off the lamp. Blackout.*]

ACT TWO
SCENE 1

M. GALLIMARD'*s cell. Paris. Present.*
Lights up on GALLIMARD. *He sits in his cell, reading from a leaflet.*

GALLIMARD: This, from a contemporary critic's commentary on *Madame Butterfly*: "Pinkerton suffers from . . . being an obnoxious bounder whom every man in the audience itches to kick." Bully for us men in the audience! Then, in the same note: "Butterfly is the most irresistibly appealing of Puccini's 'Little Women.' Watching the succession of her humiliations is like watching a child under torture." [*He tosses the pamphlet over his shoulder.*] I suggest that, while we men may all want to kick Pinkerton, very few of us would pass up the opportunity to be Pinkerton. [GALLIMARD *moves out of his cell.*]

Scene 2

GALLIMARD *and Butterfly's* [SONG*'s*] *flat. Beijing. 1960.*

We are in a simple but well-decorated parlor. GALLIMARD *moves to sit on a sofa, while* SONG, *dressed in a chong sam,*[1] *enters and curls up at his feet.*

GALLIMARD: [*To us.*] We secured a flat on the outskirts of Peking. Butterfly, as I was calling her now, decorated our "home" with Western furniture and Chinese antiques. And there, on a few stolen afternoons or evenings each week, Butterfly commenced her education.

SONG: The Chinese men—they keep us down.

GALLIMARD: Even in the "New Society"?[2]

SONG: In the "New Society," we are all kept ignorant equally. That's one of the exciting things about loving a Western man. I know you are not threatened by a woman's education.

GALLIMARD: I'm no saint, Butterfly.

SONG: But you come from a progressive society.

GALLIMARD: We're not always reminding each other how "old" we are, if that's what you mean.

SONG: Exactly. We Chinese—once, I suppose, it is true, we ruled the world. But so what? How much more exciting to be part of the society ruling the world today. Tell me—what's happening in Vietnam?

GALLIMARD: Oh, Butterfly—you want me to bring my work home?

SONG: I want to know what you know. To be impressed by my man. It's not the particulars so much as the fact that you're making decisions which change the shape of the world.

GALLIMARD: Not the world. At best, a small corner.

[TOULON *enters, and sits at a desk upstage.*]

Scene 3

French embassy. Beijing. 1961.

GALLIMARD *moves downstage, to* TOULON*'s desk.* SONG *remains upstage, watching.*

---

1. A dress usually with a high collar and split skirt.

2 The Communist society based on, among other things, the principle of equality.

TOULON: And a more troublesome corner is hard to imagine.

GALLIMARD: So, the Americans plan to begin bombing?

TOULON: This is very secret, Gallimard: yes. The Americans don't have an embassy here. They're asking us to be their eyes and ears. Say Jack Kennedy signed an order to bomb North Vietnam, Laos. How would the Chinese react?

GALLIMARD: I think the Chinese will squawk—

TOULON: Uh-huh.

GALLIMARD: —but, in their hearts, they don't even like Ho Chi Minh.[1] [*Pause.*]

TOULON: What a bunch of jerks. Vietnam was *our* colony. Not only didn't the Americans help us fight to keep them, but now, seven years later, they've come back to grab the territory for themselves. It's very irritating.

GALLIMARD: With all due respect, sir, why should the Americans have won our war for us back in '54 if we didn't have the will to win it ourselves?

TOULON: You're kidding, aren't you? [*Pause.*]

GALLIMARD: The Orientals simply want to be associated with whoever shows the most strength and power. You live with the Chinese, sir. Do you think they like Communism?

TOULON: I live in China. Not with the Chinese.

GALLIMARD: Well, I—

TOULON: *You* live with the Chinese.

GALLIMARD: Excuse me?

TOULON: I can't keep a secret.

GALLIMARD: What are you saying?

TOULON: Only that I'm not immune to gossip. So, you're keeping a native mistress. Don't answer. It's none of my business. [*Pause.*] I'm sure she must be gorgeous.

GALLIMARD: Well . . .

TOULON: I'm impressed. You have the stamina to go out into the streets and hunt one down. Some of us have to be content with the wives of the expatriate community.

GALLIMARD: I do feel . . . fortunate.

TOULON: So, Gallimard, you've got the inside knowledge—what *do* the Chinese think?

1. See headnote (p. 1103) for a discussion of Ho Chi Minh.

GALLIMARD: Deep down, they miss the old days. You know, cappuccinos, men in tuxedos—

TOULON: So what do we tell the Americans about Vietnam?

GALLIMARD: Tell them there's a natural affinity between the West
and the Orient.

TOULON: And that you speak from experience?

GALLIMARD: The Orientals are people too. They want the good
things we can give them. If the Americans demonstrate the will
to win, the Vietnamese will welcome them into a mutually bene-
ficial union.

TOULON: I don't see how the Vietnamese can stand up to American
firepower.

GALLIMARD: Orientals will always submit to a greater force.

TOULON: I'll note your opinions in my report. The Americans always love to hear how "welcome" they'll be. [*He starts to exit.*]

GALLIMARD: Sir?

TOULON: Mmmm?

GALLIMARD: This . . . rumor you've heard.

TOULON: Uh-huh?

GALLIMARD: How . . . widespread do you think it is?

TOULON: It's only widespread within this embassy. Where nobody
talks because everybody is guilty. We were worried about you,
Gallimard. We thought you were the only one here without a secret. Now you go and find a lotus blossom . . . and top us all. [*He
exits.*]

GALLIMARD: [*To us.*] Toulon knows! And he approves! I was learning
the benefits of being a man. We form our own clubs, sit behind
thick doors, smoke—and celebrate the fact that we're still boys.
[*He starts to move downstage, towards* SONG.] So, over the—
[*Suddenly* COMRADE CHIN *enters.* GALLIMARD *backs away.*]

GALLIMARD: [*To* SONG.] No! Why does she have to come in?

SONG: Rene, be sensible. How can they understand the story without her? Now, don't embarrass yourself.
[GALLIMARD *moves down center.*]

GALLIMARD: [*To us.*] Now, you will see why my story is so amusing
to so many people. Why they snicker at parties in disbelief.
Please—try to understand it from my point of view. We are all
prisoners of our time and place. [*He exits.*]

SCENE 4
[GALLIMARD *and Butterfly's* (SONG'*s) flat. Beijing. 1961.*]

SONG: [*To us.*] 1961. The flat Monsieur Gallimard rented for us. An evening after he has gone.

CHIN: Okay, see if you can find out when the Americans plan to start bombing Vietnam. If you can find out what cities, even better.

SONG: I'll do my best, but I don't want to arouse his suspicions.

CHIN: Yeah, sure, of course. So, what else?

SONG: The Americans will increase troops in Vietnam to 170,000 soldiers with 120,000 militia and 11,000 American advisors.

CHIN: [*Writing.*] Wait, wait. 120,000 militia and—

SONG: —11,000 American—

CHIN: —American advisors. [*Beat.*] How do you remember so much?

SONG: I'm an actor.

CHIN: Yeah. [*Beat.*] Is that how come you dress like that?

SONG: Like what, Miss Chin?

CHIN: Like that dress! You're wearing a dress. And every time I come here, you're wearing a dress. Is that because you're an actor? Or what?

SONG: It's a . . . disguise, Miss Chin.

CHIN: Actors, I think they're all weirdos. My mother tells me actors are like gamblers or prostitutes or—

SONG: It helps me in my assignment. [*Pause.*]

CHIN: You're not gathering information in any way that violates Communist Party principles, are you?

SONG: Why would I do that?

CHIN: Just checking. Remember: when working for the Great Proletarian State, you represent our Chairman Mao[1] in every position you take.

SONG: I'll try to imagine the Chairman taking my positions.

CHIN: We all think of him this way. Good-bye, comrade. [*She starts to exit.*] Comrade?

SONG: Yes?

---

1. Mao Tse-tung (1893–1976), Communist leader of China.

CHIN: Don't forget: there is no homosexuality in China!

SONG: Yes, I've heard.

CHIN: Just checking. [*She exits.*]

SONG: [*To us.*] What passes for a woman in modern China.

[GALLIMARD *sticks his head out from the wings.*]

GALLIMARD: Is she gone?

SONG: Yes, Rene. Please continue in your own fashion.

SCENE 5

Beijing. 1961–63.

GALLIMARD *moves to the couch where* SONG *still sits. He lies down in her lap, and she strokes his forehead.*

GALLIMARD: [*To us.*] And so, over the years 1961, '62, '63, we settled into our routine, Butterfly and I. She would always have prepared a light snack and then, ever so delicately, and only if I agreed, she would start to pleasure me. With her hands, her mouth . . . too many ways to explain, and too sad, given my present situation. But mostly we would talk. About my life. Perhaps there is nothing more rare than to find a woman who passionately listens.

[SONG *remains upstage, listening, as* HELGA *enters and plays a scene downstage with* GALLIMARD.]

HELGA: Rene, I visited Dr. Bolleart this morning.

GALLIMARD: Why? Are you ill?

HELGA: No, no. You see, I wanted to ask him . . . that question we've been discussing.

GALLIMARD: And I told you, it's only a matter of time. Why did you bring a doctor into this? We just have to keep trying—like a crapshoot, actually.

HELGA: I went, I'm sorry. But listen: he says there's nothing wrong with me.

GALLIMARD: You see? Now, will you stop—?

HELGA: Rene, he says he'd like you to go in and take some tests.

GALLIMARD: Why? So he can find there's nothing wrong with both of us?

HELGA: Rene, I don't ask for much. One trip! One visit! And then, whatever you want to do about it—you decide.

GALLIMARD: You're assuming he'll find something defective!

HELGA: No! Of course not! Whatever he finds—if he finds nothing, we decide what to do about nothing! But go!

GALLIMARD: If he finds nothing, we keep trying. Just like we do now.

HELGA: But at least we'll know! [*Pause.*] I'm sorry. [*She starts to exit.*]

GALLIMARD: Do you really want me to see Dr. Bolleart?

HELGA: Only if you want a child, Rene. We have to face the fact that time is running out. Only if you want a child. [*She exits.*]

GALLIMARD: [*To* SONG.] I'm a modern man, Butterfly. And yet, I don't want to go. It's the same old voodoo. I feel like God himself is laughing at me if I can't produce a child.

SONG: You men of the West—you're obsessed by your odd desire for equality. Your wife can't give you a child, and *you're* going to the doctor?

GALLIMARD: Well, you see, she's already gone.

SONG: And because this incompetent can't find the defect, you now have to subject yourself to him? It's unnatural.

GALLIMARD: Well, what is the "natural" solution?

SONG: In Imperial China, when a man found that one wife was inadequate, he turned to another—to give him his son.

GALLIMARD: What do you—? I can't . . . marry you, yet.

SONG: Please. I'm not asking you to be my husband. But I am already your wife.

GALLIMARD: Do you want to . . . have my child?

SONG: I thought you'd never ask.

GALLIMARD: But, your career . . . your—

SONG: Phooey on my career! That's your Western mind, twisting itself into strange shapes again. Of course I love my career. But what would I love most of all? To feel something inside me—day and night—something I know is yours. [*Pause.*] Promise me . . . you won't go to this doctor. Who is this Western quack to set himself as judge over the man I love? I know who is a man, and who is not. [*She exits.*]

GALLIMARD: [*To us.*] Dr. Bolleart? Of course I didn't go. What man would?

SCENE 6

Beijing. 1963.

Party noises over the house speakers. RENEE *enters, wearing a revealing gown.*

GALLIMARD: 1963. A party at the Austrian embassy. None of us could remember the Austrian ambassador's name, which seemed somehow appropriate. [*To* RENEE.] So, I tell the Americans, Diem[1] must go. The U.S. wants to be respected by the Vietnamese, and yet they're propping up this nobody seminarian as her president. A man whose claim to fame is his sister-in-law imposing fanatic "moral order" campaigns? Oriental women—when they're good, they're very good, but when they're bad, they're Christians.

RENEE: Yeah.

GALLIMARD: And what do you do?

RENEE: I'm a student. My father exports a lot of useless stuff to the Third World.

GALLIMARD: How useless?

RENEE: You know. Squirt guns, confectioner's sugar, hula hoops . . .

GALLIMARD: I'm sure they appreciate the sugar.

RENEE: I'm here for two years to study Chinese.

GALLIMARD: Two years?

RENEE: That's what everybody says.

GALLIMARD: When did you arrive?

RENEE: Three weeks ago.

GALLIMARD: And?

RENEE: I like it. It's primitive, but . . . well, this is the place to learn Chinese, so here I am.

GALLIMARD: Why Chinese?

RENEE: I think it'll be important someday.

GALLIMARD: You do?

RENEE: Don't ask me when, but . . . that's what I think.

GALLIMARD: Well, I agree with you. One hundred percent. That's very farsighted.

RENEE: Yeah. Well, of course, my father thinks I'm a complete weirdo.

---

1. See headnote (p. 1103) for a discussion of Ngo Dinh Diem.

GALLIMARD: He'll thank you someday.

RENEE: Like when the Chinese start buying hula hoops?

GALLIMARD: There're a billion bellies out there.

RENEE: And if they end up taking over the world—well, then I'll be lucky to know Chinese too, right? [*Pause.*]

GALLIMARD: At this point, I don't see how the Chinese can possibly take—

RENEE: You know what I *don't* like about China?

GALLIMARD: Excuse me? No—what?

RENEE: Nothing to do at night.

GALLIMARD: You come to parties at embassies like everyone else.

RENEE: Yeah, but they get out at ten. And then what?

GALLIMARD: I'm afraid the Chinese idea of a dance hall is a dirt floor and a man with a flute.

RENEE: Are you married?

GALLIMARD: Yes. Why?

RENEE: You wanna . . . fool around? [*Pause.*]

GALLIMARD: Sure.

RENEE: I'll wait for you outside. What's your name?

GALLIMARD: Gallimard. Rene.

RENEE: Weird. I'm Renee too. [*She exits.*]

GALLIMARD: [*To us.*] And so, I embarked on my first extra-extramarital affair. Renee was picture perfect. With a body like those girls in the magazines. If I put a tissue paper over my eyes, I wouldn't have been able to tell the difference. And it was exciting to be with someone who wasn't afraid to be seen completely naked. But is it possible for a woman to be *too* uninhibited, *too* willing, so as to seem almost too . . . masculine?

[*Chuck Berry blares from the house speakers, then comes down in volume as* RENEE *enters, toweling her hair.*]

RENEE: You have a nice weenie.

GALLIMARD: What?

RENEE: Penis. You have a nice penis.

GALLIMARD: Oh. Well, thank you. That's very . . .

RENEE: What—can't take a compliment?

GALLIMARD: No, it's very . . . reassuring.

RENEE: But most girls don't come out and say it, huh?

GALLIMARD: And also . . . what did you call it?

RENEE: Oh. Most girls don't call it a "weenie," huh?

GALLIMARD: It sounds very—

RENEE: Small, I know.

GALLIMARD: I was going to say, "young."

RENEE: Yeah. Young, small, same thing. Most guys are pretty, uh, sensitive about that. Like, you know, I had a boyfriend back home in Denmark. I got mad at him once and called him a little weeniehead. He got so mad! He said at least I should call him a great big weeniehead.

GALLIMARD: I suppose I just say "penis."

RENEE: Yeah. That's pretty clinical. There's "cock," but that sounds like a chicken. And "prick" is painful, and "dick" is like you're talking about someone who's not in the room.

GALLIMARD: Yes. It's a . . . bigger problem than I imagined.

RENEE: I—I think maybe it's because I really don't know what to do with them—that's why I call them "weenies."

GALLIMARD: Well, you did quite well with . . . mine.

RENEE: Thanks, but I mean, really *do* with them. Like, okay, have you ever looked at one? I mean, really?

GALLIMARD: No, I suppose when it's part of you, you sort of take it for granted.

RENEE: I guess. But, like, it just hangs there. This little . . . flap of flesh. And there's so much fuss that we make about it. Like, I think the reason we fight wars is because we wear clothes. Because no one knows—between the men, I mean—who has the bigger . . . weenie. So, if I'm a guy with a small one, I'm going to build a really big building or take over a really big piece of land or write a really long book so the other men don't know, right? But, see, it never really works, that's the problem. I mean, you conquer the country, or whatever, but you're still wearing clothes, so there's no way to prove absolutely whose is bigger or smaller. And that's what we call a civilized society. The whole world run by a bunch of men with pricks the size of pins. [*She exits.*]

GALLIMARD: [*To us.*] This was simply not acceptable.

[*A high-pitched chime rings through the air. SONG, dressed as Butterfly, appears in the upstage special. She is obviously distressed. Her body swoons as she attempts to clip the stems of flowers she's arranging in a vase.*]

GALLIMARD: But I kept up our affair, wildly, for several months. Why? I believe because of Butterfly. She knew the secret I was trying to hide. But, unlike a Western woman, she didn't confront me, threaten, even pout. I remembered the words of Puccini's *Butterfly*:

SONG: "Noi siamo gente avvezza/ alle piccole cose/ umili e silenziose."

GALLIMARD: "I come from a people/ Who are accustomed to little/ Humble and silent." I saw Pinkerton and Butterfly, and what she would say if he were unfaithful . . . nothing. She would cry, alone, into those wildly soft sleeves, once full of possessions, now empty to collect her tears. It was her tears and her silence that excited me, every time I visited Renee.

TOULON: [*Offstage.*] Gallimard!

[TOULON *enters.* GALLIMARD *turns towards him. During the next section,* SONG, *up center, begins to dance with the flowers. It is a drunken dance, where she breaks small pieces off the stems.*]

TOULON: They're killing him.

GALLIMARD: Who? I'm sorry? What?

TOULON: Bother you to come over at this late hour?

GALLIMARD: No . . . of course not.

TOULON: Not after you hear my secret. Champagne?

GALLIMARD: Um . . . thank you.

TOULON: You're surprised. There's something that you've wanted, Gallimard. No, not a promotion. Next time. Something in the world. You're not aware of this, but there's an informal gossip circle among intelligence agents. And some of ours heard from some of the Americans—

GALLIMARD: Yes?

TOULON: That the U.S. will allow the Vietnamese generals to stage a coup . . . and assassinate President Diem.

[*The chime rings again.* TOULON *freezes.* GALLIMARD *turns up stage and looks at Butterfly, who slowly and deliberately clips a flower off its stem.* GALLIMARD *turns back towards* TOULON.]

GALLIMARD: I think . . . that's a very wise move!

[TOULON *unfreezes.*]

TOULON: It's what you've been advocating. A toast?

GALLIMARD: Sure. I consider this a vindication.

TOULON: Not exactly. "To the test. Let's hope you pass."

[*They drink. The chime rings again.* TOULON *freezes.* GALLIMARD *turns upstage, and* SONG *clips another flower.*]

GALLIMARD: [*To* TOULON.] The test?

TOULON: [*Unfreezing.*] It's a test of everything you've been saying. I personally think the generals probably will stop the Communists. And you'll be a hero. But if anything goes wrong, then your opinions won't be worth a pig's ear. I'm sure that won't happen. But sometimes it's easier when they don't listen to you.

GALLIMARD: They're your opinions too, aren't they?

TOULON: Personally, yes.

GALLIMARD: So we agree.

TOULON: But my opinions aren't on that report. Yours are. Cheers.

[TOULON *turns away from* GALLIMARD *and raises his glass. At that instant* SONG *picks up the vase and hurls it to the ground. It shatters.* SONG *sinks down amidst the shards of the vase, in a calm, childlike trance. She sings softly, as if reciting a child's nursery rhyme.*]

SONG: [*Repeat as necessary.*] "The whole world over, the white man travels, setting anchor, wherever he likes. Life's not worth living, unless he finds, the finest maidens, of every land . . ."

[GALLIMARD *turns downstage towards us.* SONG *continues singing.*]

GALLIMARD: I shook as I left his house. That coward! That worm! To put the burden for his decisions on my shoulders!

I started for Renee's. But no, that was all I needed. A schoolgirl who would question the role of the penis in modern society. What I wanted was revenge. A vessel to contain my humiliation. Though I hadn't seen her in several weeks, I headed for Butterfly's. [GALLIMARD *enters* SONG's *apartment.*]

SONG: Oh! Rene . . . I was dreaming!

GALLIMARD: You've been drinking?

SONG: If I can't sleep, then yes, I drink. But then, it gives me these dreams which—Rene, it's been almost three weeks since you visited me last.

GALLIMARD: I know. There's been a lot going on in the world.

SONG: Fortunately I am drunk. So I can speak freely. It's not the world, it's you and me. And an old problem. Even the softest

skin becomes like leather to a man who's touched it too often. I
confess I don't know how to stop it. I don't know how to become
another woman.

GALLIMARD: I have a request.

SONG: Is this a solution? Or are you ready to give up the flat?

GALLIMARD: It may be a solution. But I'm sure you won't like it.

SONG: Oh, well, that's very important. "Like it?" Do you think I
    "like" lying here alone, waiting, always waiting for your return?
    Please—don't worry about what I may not "like."

GALLIMARD: I want to see you . . . naked. [*Silence.*]

SONG: I thought you understood my modesty. So you want me to—
    what—strip? Like a big cowboy girl? Shiny pasties on my breasts?
    Shall I fling my kimono over my head and yell "ya-hoo" in the
    process? I thought you respected my shame!

GALLIMARD: I believe you gave me your shame many years ago.

SONG: Yes—and it is just like a white devil to use it against me. I
    can't believe it. I thought myself so repulsed by the passive Ori-
    ental and the cruel white man. Now I see—we are always most
    revolted by the things hidden within us.

GALLIMARD: I just mean—

SONG: Yes?

GALLIMARD: —that it will remove the only barrier left between us.

SONG: No, Rene. Don't couch your request in sweet words. Be your-
    self—a cad—and know that my love is enough, that I submit—
    submit to the worst you can give me. [*Pause.*] Well, come. Strip
    me. Whatever happens, know that you have willed it. Our love,
    in your hands. I'm helpless before my man.

    [GALLIMARD *starts to cross the room.*]

GALLIMARD: Did I not undress her because I knew, somewhere deep
    down, what I would find? Perhaps. Happiness is so rare that our
    mind can turn somersaults to protect it.

    At the time, I only knew that I was seeing Pinkerton stalking
    towards his Butterfly, ready to reward her love with his lecherous
    hands. The image sickened me, pulled me to my knees, so I was
    crawling towards her like a worm. By the time I reached her,
    Pinkerton . . . had vanished from my heart. To be replaced by
    something new, something unnatural, that flew in the face of all
    I'd learned in the world—something very close to love.

[*He grabs her around the waist; she strokes his hair.*]

GALLIMARD: Butterfly, forgive me.

SONG: Rene . . .

GALLIMARD: For everything. From the start.

SONG: I'm . . .

GALLIMARD: I want to—

SONG: I'm pregnant. [*Beat.*] I'm pregnant. [*Beat.*] I'm pregnant. [*Beat.*]

GALLIMARD: I want to marry you!

SCENE 7

GALLIMARD *and Butterfly's flat. Beijing. 1963.*

Downstage, SONG *paces as* COMRADE CHIN *reads from her notepad.* *Upstage,* GALLIMARD *is still kneeling. He remains on his knees throughout the scene, watching it.*

SONG: I need a baby.

CHIN: [*From pad*]: He's been spotted going to a dorm.

SONG: I need a baby.

CHIN: At the Foreign Language Institute.

SONG: I need a baby.

CHIN: The room of a Danish girl . . . What do you mean, you need a baby?!

SONG: Tell Comrade Kang—last night, the entire mission, it could've ended.

CHIN: What do you mean?

SONG: Tell Kang—he told me to strip.

CHIN: *Strip?!*

SONG: Write!

CHIN: I tell you, I don't understand nothing about this case anymore. Nothing.

SONG: He told me to strip, and I took a chance. Oh, we Chinese, we know how to gamble.

CHIN: [*Writing.*] ". . . told him to strip."

SONG: My palms were wet, I had to make a split-second decision.

CHIN: Hey! Can you slow down?! [*Pause.*]

SONG: You write faster, I'm the artist here. Suddenly, it hit me—"All he wants is for her to submit. Once a woman submits, a man is always ready to become 'generous.' "

CHIN: You're just gonna end up with rough notes.

SONG: And it worked! He gave in! Now, if I can just present him with a baby. A Chinese baby with blond hair—he'll be mine for life!

CHIN: Kang will never agree! The trading of babies has to be a counterrevolutionary act!

SONG: Sometimes, a counterrevolutionary act is necessary to counter a counterrevolutionary act. [*Pause.*]

CHIN: Wait.

SONG: I need one . . . in seven months. Make sure it's a boy.

CHIN: This doesn't sound like something the Chairman would do. Maybe you'd better talk to Comrade Kang yourself.

SONG: Good. I will.

    [CHIN *gets up to leave.*]

SONG: Miss Chin? Why, in the Peking Opera, are women's roles played by men?

CHIN: I don't know. Maybe, a reactionary remnant of male—

SONG: No. [*Beat.*] Because only a man knows how a woman is supposed to act.

    [CHIN *exits.* SONG *turns upstage, towards* GALLIMARD.]

GALLIMARD: [*Calling after* CHIN.] Good riddance! [*To* SONG.] I could forget all that betrayal in an instant, you know. If you'd just come back and become Butterfly again.

SONG: Fat chance. You're here in prison, rotting in a cell. And I'm on a plane, winging my way back to China. Your President pardoned me of our treason, you know.

GALLIMARD: Yes, I read about that.

SONG: Must make you feel . . . lower than shit.

GALLIMARD: But don't you, even a little bit, wish you were here with me?

SONG: I'm an artist, Rene. You were my greatest . . . acting challenge. [*She laughs.*] It doesn't matter how rotten I answer, does it? You still adore me. That's why I love you, Rene. [*She points to us.*] So—you were telling your audience about the night I announced I was pregnant.

    [GALLIMARD *puts his arms around* SONG*'s waist. He and* SONG *are in the positions they were in at the end of Scene 6.*]

SCENE 8
Same.

GALLIMARD: I'll divorce my wife. We'll live together here, and then later in France.
SONG: I feel so . . . ashamed.
GALLIMARD: Why?
SONG: I had begun to lose faith. And now, you shame me with your generosity.
GALLIMARD: Generosity? No, I'm proposing for very selfish reasons.
SONG: Your apologies only make me feel more ashamed. My outburst a moment ago!
GALLIMARD: Your outburst? What about my request?!
SONG: You've been very patient dealing with my . . . eccentricities. A Western man, used to women freer with their bodies—
GALLIMARD: It was sick! Don't make excuses for me.
SONG: I have to. You don't seem willing to make them for yourself. [*Pause.*]
GALLIMARD: You're crazy.
SONG: I'm happy. Which often looks like crazy.
GALLIMARD: Then make me crazy. Marry me. [*Pause.*]
SONG: No.
GALLIMARD: What?
SONG: Do I sound silly, a slave, if I say I'm not worthy?
GALLIMARD: Yes. In fact you do. No one has loved me like you.
SONG: Thank you. And no one ever will. I'll see to that.
GALLIMARD: So what is the problem?
SONG: Rene, we Chinese are realists. We understand rice, gold, and guns. You are a diplomat. Your career is skyrocketing. Now, what would happen if you divorced your wife to marry a Communist Chinese actress?
GALLIMARD: That's not being realistic. That's defeating yourself before you begin.
SONG: We must conserve our strength for the battles we can win.
GALLIMARD: That sounds like a fortune cookie!
SONG: Where do you think fortune cookies come from?
GALLIMARD: I don't care.
SONG: You do. So do I. And we should. That is why I say I'm not

worthy. I'm worthy to love and even to be loved by you. But I am not worthy to end the career of one of the West's most promising diplomats.

GALLIMARD: It's not that great a career! I made it sound like more than it is!

SONG: Modesty will get you nowhere. Flatter yourself, and you flatter me. I'm flattered to decline your offer. [*She exits.*]

GALLIMARD: [*To us.*] Butterfly and I argued all night. And, in the end, I left, knowing I would never be her husband. She went away for several months—to the countryside, like a small animal. Until the night I received her call.

[*A baby's cry from offstage.* SONG *enters, carrying a child.*]

SONG: He looks like you.

GALLIMARD: Oh! [*Beat; he approaches the baby.*] Well, babies are never very attractive at birth.

SONG: Stop!

GALLIMARD: I'm sure he'll grow more beautiful with age. More like his mother.

SONG: "Chi vide mai/ a bimbo del Giappon . . ."

GALLIMARD: "What baby, I wonder, was ever born in Japan"—or China, for that matter—

SONG: ". . . occhi azzurrini?"

GALLIMARD: "With azure eyes"—they're actually sort of brown, wouldn't you say?

SONG: "E il labbro."

GALLIMARD: "And such lips!" [*He kisses* SONG.] *And such lips.*

SONG: "E i ricciolini d'oro schietto?"

GALLIMARD: "And such a head of golden"—if slightly patchy— "curls?"

SONG: I'm going to call him "Peepee."

GALLIMARD: Darling, could you repeat that because I'm sure a rickshaw just flew by overhead.

SONG: You heard me.

GALLIMARD: "Song Peepee"? May I suggest Michael, or Stephan, or Adolph?

SONG: You may, but I won't listen.

GALLIMARD: You can't be serious. Can you imagine the time this child will have in school?

SONG: In the West, yes.

GALLIMARD: It's worse than naming him Ping Pong or Long Dong or—

SONG: But he's never going to live in the West, is he? [*Pause.*]

GALLIMARD: That wasn't my choice.

SONG: It is mine. And this is my promise to you: I will raise him, he will be our child, but he will never burden you outside of China.

GALLIMARD: Why do you make these promises? I want to be burdened! I want a scandal to cover the papers!

SONG: [*To us.*] Prophetic.

GALLIMARD: I'm serious.

SONG: So am I. His name is as I registered it. And he will never live in the West. [SONG *exits with the child.*]

GALLIMARD: [*To us.*] It is possible that her stubbornness only made me want her more. That drawing back at the moment of my capitulation was the most brilliant strategy she could have chosen. It is possible. But it is also possible that by this point she could have said, could have done . . . anything, and I would have adored her still.

SCENE 9

Beijing. 1966.

A driving rhythm of Chinese percussion fills the stage.

GALLIMARD: And then, China began to change. Mao became very old, and his cult became very strong. And, like many old men, he entered his second childhood. So he handed over the reins of state to those with minds like his own. And children ruled the Middle Kingdom with complete caprice. The doctrine of the Cultural Revolution[1] implied continuous anarchy. Contact between Chinese and foreigners became impossible. Our flat was confiscated. Her fame and my money now counted against us.

[*Two dancers in Mao suits and red-starred caps[2] enter, and begin*

---

1. See headnote (p. 1101) for a discussion of Mao Tse-tung and the Cultural Revolution. *Middle Kingdom:* China.

2. That is, official dress of the Cultural Revolution. "Mao suits," popularized by Mao Tse-tung, were drab, masculine suits incorporating military elements and were meant to help level China's hierarchical society.

crudely mimicking revolutionary violence, in an agitprop fashion.]

GALLIMARD: And somehow the American war went wrong too. Four hundred thousand dollars were being spent for every Viet Cong killed; so General Westmoreland's remark that the Oriental does not value life the way Americans do was oddly accurate.[3] Why weren't the Vietnamese people giving in? Why were they content instead to die and die and die again?

[TOULON *enters.*]

TOULON: Congratulations, Gallimard.

GALLIMARD: Excuse me, sir?

TOULON: Not a promotion. That was last time. You're going home.

GALLIMARD: What?

TOULON: Don't say I didn't warn you.

GALLIMARD: I'm being transferred . . . because I was wrong about the American war?

TOULON: Of course not. We don't care about the Americans. We care about your mind. The quality of your analysis. In general, everything you've predicted here in the Orient . . . just hasn't happened.

GALLIMARD: I think that's premature.

TOULON: Don't force me to be blunt. Okay, you said China was ready to open to Western trade. The only thing they're trading out there are Western heads. And, yes, you said the Americans would succeed in Indochina. You were kidding, right?

GALLIMARD: I think the end is in sight.

TOULON: Don't be pathetic. And don't take this personally. You were wrong. It's not your fault.

GALLIMARD: But I'm going home.

TOULON: Right. Could I have the number of your mistress? [*Beat.*] Joke! Joke! Eat a croissant for me.

[TOULON *exits.* SONG, *wearing a Mao suit, is dragged in from the wings as part of the upstage dance. They "beat" her, then lampoon the acrobatics of the Chinese opera, as she is made to kneel onstage.*]

3. This notorious claim, made by General William Westmoreland (1914–   ), commander of the U.S. forces in Vietnam, came to symbolize American misunderstanding of the Vietnamese.

GALLIMARD: [*Simultaneously.*] I don't care to recall how Butterfly and I said our hurried farewell. Perhaps it was better to end our affair before it killed her.

[GALLIMARD *exits.* COMRADE CHIN *walks across the stage with a banner reading: "The Actor Renounces His Decadent Profession!" She reaches the kneeling* SONG. *Percussion stops with a thud. Dancers strike poses.*]

CHIN: Actor-oppressor, for years you have lived above the common people and looked down on their labor. While the farmer ate millet—

SONG: I ate pastries from France and sweetmeats from silver trays.

CHIN: And how did you come to live in such an exalted position?

SONG: I was a plaything for the imperialists!

CHIN: What did you do?

SONG: I shamed China by allowing myself to be corrupted by a foreigner . . .

CHIN: What does this mean? The People demand a full confession!

SONG: I engaged in the lowest perversions with China's enemies!

CHIN: What perversions? Be more clear!

SONG: I let him put it up my ass!

[*Dancers look over, disgusted.*]

CHIN: Aaaa-ya! How can you use such sickening language?!

SONG: My language . . . is only as foul as the crimes I committed . . .

CHIN: Yeah. That's better. So—what do you want to do now?

SONG: I want to serve the people.

[*Percussion starts up, with Chinese strings.*]

CHIN: What?

SONG: I want to serve the people!

[*Dancers regain their revolutionary smiles, and begin a dance of victory.*]

CHIN: What?!

SONG: I want to serve the people!!

[*Dancers unveil a banner: "The Actor Is Rehabilitated!"* SONG *remains kneeling before* CHIN, *as the dancers bounce around them, then exit. Music out.*]

SCENE 10
A commune. Hunan Province. 1970.

CHIN: How you planning to do that?

SONG: I've already worked four years in the fields of Hunan, Comrade Chin.

CHIN: So? Farmers work all their lives. Let me see your hands.
[SONG *holds them out for her inspection.*]

CHIN: Goddamn! Still so smooth! How long does it take to turn you actors into good anythings? Hunh. You've just spent too many years in luxury to be any good to the Revolution.

SONG: I served the Revolution.

CHIN: Serve the Revolution? Bullshit! You wore dresses! Don't tell me—I was there. I saw you! You and your white vice-consul! Stuck up there in your flat, living off the People's Treasury! Yeah, I knew what was going on! You two . . . homos! Homos! Homos! [*Pause; she composes herself.*] Ah! Well . . . you will serve the people, all right. But not with the Revolution's money. This time, you use your own money.

SONG: I have no money.

CHIN: Shut up! And you won't stink up China anymore with your pervert stuff. You'll pollute the place where pollution begins— the West.

SONG: What do you mean?

CHIN: Shut up! You're going to France. Without a cent in your pocket. You find your consul's house, you make him pay your expenses—

SONG: No.

CHIN: And you give us weekly reports! Useful information!

SONG: That's crazy. It's been four years.

CHIN: Either that, or back to rehabilitation center!

SONG: Comrade Chin, he's not going to support me! Not in France! He's a white man! I was just his plaything—

CHIN: Oh, yuck! Again with the sickening language? Where's my stick?

SONG: You don't understand the mind of a man. [*Pause.*]

CHIN: Oh, no? No, I don't? Then how come I'm married, huh? How come I got a man? Five, six years ago, you always tell me those kind of things, I felt very bad. But not now! Because what does the Chairman say? He tells us *I'm* now the smart one, you're now the nincompoop! *You're* the blackhead, the harebrain, the nitwit! You think you're so smart? You understand "The Mind of a Man"? Good! Then *you* go to France and be a pervert for Chairman Mao!

[CHIN *and* SONG *exit in opposite directions.*]

SCENE 11
[*Paris. 1968–70.*
GALLIMARD *enters.*]

GALLIMARD: And what was waiting for me back in Paris? Well, better Chinese food than I'd eaten in China. Friends and relatives. A little accounting, regular schedule, keeping track of traffic violations in the suburbs. . . . And the indignity of students shouting the slogans of Chairman Mao at me—in French.

HELGA: Rene? Rene? [*She enters, soaking wet.*] I've had a . . . a problem. [*She sneezes.*]

GALLIMARD: You're wet.

HELGA: Yes, I . . . coming back from the grocer's. A group of students, waving red flags, they—

[GALLIMARD *fetches a towel.*]

HELGA: —they ran by, I was caught up along with them. Before I knew what was happening—

[GALLIMARD *gives her the towel.*]

HELGA: Thank you. The police started firing water cannons at us. I tried to shout, to tell them I was the wife of a diplomat, but—you know how it is. . . . [*Pause.*] Needless to say, I lost the groceries. Rene, what's happening to France?

GALLIMARD: What's—? Well, nothing, really.

HELGA: Nothing?! The storefronts are in flames, there's glass in the streets, buildings are toppling[1]—and I'm wet!

GALLIMARD: Nothing! . . . that I care to think about.

HELGA: And is that why you stay in this room?

---

1. In May 1968, university students and workers throughout France staged a spontaneous revolution against the conservative Fifth Republic government.

GALLIMARD: Yes, in fact.

HELGA: With the incense burning? You know something? I hate incense. It smells so sickly sweet.

GALLIMARD: Well, I hate the French. Who just smell—period!

HELGA: And the Chinese were better?

GALLIMARD: Please—don't start.

HELGA: When we left, this exact same thing, the riots—

GALLIMARD: No, no . . .

HELGA: Students screaming slogans, smashing down doors—

GALLIMARD: Helga—

HELGA: It was all going on in China, too. Don't you remember?!

GALLIMARD: Helga! Please! [*Pause.*] You have never understood China, have you? You walk in here with these ridiculous ideas, that the West is falling apart, that China was spitting in our faces. You come in, dripping of the streets, and you leave water all over my floor. [*He grabs* HELGA's *towel, begins mopping up the floor.*]

HELGA: But it's the truth!

GALLIMARD: Helga, I want a divorce. [*Pause;* GALLIMARD *continues mopping the floor.*]

HELGA: I take it back. China is . . . beautiful. Incense, I like incense.

GALLIMARD: I've had a mistress.

HELGA: So?

GALLIMARD: For eight years.

HELGA: I knew you would. I knew you would the day I married you. And now what? You want to marry her?

GALLIMARD: I can't. She's in China.

HELGA: I see. You want to leave. For someone who's not here, is that right?

GALLIMARD: That's right.

HELGA: You can't live with her, but still you don't want to live with me.

GALLIMARD: That's right. [*Pause.*]

HELGA: Shit. How terrible that I can figure that out. [*Pause.*] I never thought I'd say it. But, in China, I was happy. I knew, in my own way, I knew that you were not everything you pretended to be. But the pretense—going on your arm to the embassy ball, visiting your office and the guards saying, "Good morning, good morning, Madame Gallimard"—the pretense . . . was very good indeed. [*Pause.*] I hope everyone is mean to you for the rest of your life. [*She exits.*]

GALLIMARD: [*To us.*] Prophetic.

[MARC *enters with two drinks.*]

GALLIMARD: [*To* MARC.] In China, I was different from all other men.

MARC: Sure. You were white. Here's your drink.

GALLIMARD: I felt . . . touched.

MARC: In the head? Rene, I don't want to hear about the Oriental love goddess. Okay? One night—can we just drink and throw up without a lot of conversation?

GALLIMARD: You still don't believe me, do you?

MARC: Sure I do. She was the most beautiful, et cetera, et cetera, blasé blasé. [*Pause.*]

GALLIMARD: My life in the West has been such a disappointment.

MARC: Life in the West is like that. You'll get used to it. Look, you're driving me away. I'm leaving. Happy, now? [*He exits, then returns.*] Look, I have a date tomorrow night. You wanna come? I can fix you up with—

GALLIMARD: Of course. I would love to come. [*Pause.*]

MARC: Uh—on second thought, no. You'd better get ahold of yourself first. [*He exits;* GALLIMARD *nurses his drink.*]

GALLIMARD: [*To us.*] This is the ultimate cruelty, isn't it? That I can talk and talk and to anyone listening, it's only air—too rich a diet to be swallowed by a mundane world. Why can't anyone understand? That in China, I once loved, and was loved by, very simply, the Perfect Woman.

[SONG *enters, dressed as Butterfly in wedding dress.*]

GALLIMARD: [*To* SONG.] Not again. My imagination is hell. Am I asleep this time? Or did I drink too much?

SONG: Rene?

GALLIMARD: God, it's too painful! That you speak?

SONG: What are you talking about? Rene—touch me.

GALLIMARD: Why?

SONG: I'm real. Take my hand.

GALLIMARD: Why? So you can disappear again and leave me clutching at the air? For the entertainment of my neighbors who—?

[SONG *touches* GALLIMARD.]

SONG: Rene?

[GALLIMARD *takes* SONG's *hand. Silence.*]

GALLIMARD: Butterfly? I never doubted you'd return.

SONG: You hadn't . . . forgotten—?

GALLIMARD: Yes, actually, I've forgotten everything. My mind, you see—there wasn't enough room in this hard head—not for the world *and* for you. No, there was only room for one. [*Beat.*] Come, look. See? Your bed has been waiting, with the Klimt[2] poster you like, and—see? The xiang lu [incense burner] you gave me?

SONG: I . . . I don't know what to say.

GALLIMARD: There's nothing to say. Not at the end of a long trip. Can I make you some tea?

SONG: But where's your wife?

GALLIMARD: She's by my side. She's by my side at last.

[GALLIMARD *reaches to embrace* SONG. SONG *sidesteps, dodging him.*]

GALLIMARD: Why?!

SONG: [*To us.*] So I did return to Rene in Paris. Where I found—

GALLIMARD: Why do you run away? Can't we show them how we embraced that evening?

SONG: Please. I'm talking.

GALLIMARD: You have to do what I say! I'm conjuring you up in *my* mind!

SONG: Rene, I've never done what you've said. Why should it be any different in your mind? Now split—the story moves on, and I must change.

GALLIMARD: I welcomed you into my home! I didn't have to, you know! I could've left you penniless on the streets of Paris! But I took you in!

SONG: Thank you.

GALLIMARD: So . . . please . . . don't change.

SONG: You know I have to. You know I will. And anyway, what difference does it make? No matter what your eyes tell you, you can't ignore the truth. You already know too much.

---

2. Gustav Klimt (1862–1928), Austrian artist known for highly stylized, often sexually charged paintings.

[GALLIMARD *exits.* SONG *turns to us.*]

SONG: The change I'm going to make requires about five minutes. So I thought you might want to take this opportunity to stretch your legs, enjoy a drink, or listen to the musicians. I'll be here, when you return, right where you left me. [SONG *goes to a mirror in front of which is a wash basin of water. She starts to remove her makeup as stagelights go to half and houselights come up.*]

ACT THREE
SCENE 1

A courthouse in Paris. 1986.

As he promised, SONG *has completed the bulk of his transformation, onstage by the time the houselights go down and the stagelights come up full. He removes his wig and kimono, leaving them on the floor. Underneath, he wears a well-cut suit.*

SONG: So I'd done my job better than I had a right to expect. Well, give him some credit, too. He's right—I was in a fix when I arrived in Paris. I walked from the airport into town, then I located, by blind groping, the Chinatown district. Let me make one thing clear: whatever else may be said about the Chinese, they are stingy! I slept in doorways three days until I could find a tailor who would make me this kimono on credit. As it turns out, maybe I didn't even need it. Maybe he would've been happy to see me in a simple shift and mascara. But . . . better safe than sorry.

That was 1970, when I arrived in Paris. For the next fifteen years, yes, I lived a very comfy life. Some relief, believe me, after four years on a fucking commune in Nowheresville, China. Rene supported the boy and me, and I did some demonstrations around the country as part of my "cultural exchange" cover. And then there was the spying.

[SONG *moves upstage, to a chair.* TOULON *enters as a judge, wearing the appropriate wig and robes. He sits near* SONG. *It's 1986, and* SONG *is testifying in a courtroom.*]

SONG: Not much at first. Rene had lost all his high-level contacts. Comrade Chin wasn't very interested in parking-ticket statistics. But finally, at my urging, Rene got a job as a courier, handling sensitive documents. He'd photograph them for me, and I'd pass them on to the Chinese embassy.

JUDGE: Did he understand the extent of his activity?

SONG: He didn't ask. He knew that I needed those documents, and that was enough.

JUDGE: But he must've known he was passing classified information.

SONG: I can't say.

JUDGE: He never asked what you were going to do with them?

SONG: Nope. [*Pause.*]

JUDGE: There is one thing that the court—indeed, that all of France—would like to know.

SONG: Fire away.

JUDGE: Did Monsieur Gallimard know you were a man?

SONG: Well, he never saw me completely naked. Ever.

JUDGE: But surely, he must've . . . how can I put this?

SONG: Put it however you like. I'm not shy. He must've felt around?

JUDGE: Mmmmm.

SONG: Not really. I did all the work. He just laid back. Of course we did enjoy more . . . complete union, and I suppose he *might* have wondered why I was always on my stomach, but. . . . But what you're thinking is, "Of course a wrist must've brushed . . . a hand hit . . . over twenty years!" Yeah. Well, Your Honor, it was my job to make him think I was a woman. And chew on this: it wasn't all that hard. See, my mother was a prostitute along the Bundt[1] before the Revolution. And, uh, I think it's fair to say she learned a few things about Western men. So I borrowed her knowledge. In service to my country.

JUDGE: Would you care to enlighten the court with this secret knowledge? I'm sure we're all very curious.

SONG: I'm sure you are. [*Pause.*] Okay, Rule One is: Men always believe what they want to hear. So a girl can tell the most obnoxious lies and the guys will believe them every time—"This is my first time"—"That's the biggest I've ever seen"—or *both*, which, if you really think about it, is not possible in a single lifetime. You've maybe heard those phrases a few times in your own life, yes, Your Honor?

---

1. Financial district in Shanghai.

JUDGE: It's not my life, Monsieur Song, which is on trial today.

SONG: Okay, okay, just trying to lighten up the proceedings. Tough room.

JUDGE: Go on.

SONG: Rule Two: As soon as a Western man comes into contact with the East—he's already confused. The West has sort of an international rape mentality towards the East. Do you know rape mentality?

JUDGE: Give us your definition, please.

SONG: Basically, "Her mouth says no, but her eyes say yes."

The West thinks of itself as masculine—big guns, big industry, big money—so the East is feminine—weak, delicate, poor . . . but good at art, and full of inscrutable wisdom—the feminine mystique.

Her mouth says no, but her eyes say yes. The West believes the East, deep down, *wants* to be dominated—because a woman can't think for herself.

JUDGE: What does this have to do with my question?

SONG: You expect Oriental countries to submit to your guns, and you expect Oriental women to be submissive to your men. That's why you say they make the best wives.

JUDGE: But why would that make it possible for you to fool Monsieur Gallimard? Please—get to the point.

SONG: One, because when he finally met his fantasy woman, he wanted more than anything to believe that she was, in fact, a woman. And second, I am an Oriental. And being an Oriental, I could never be completely a man. [*Pause.*]

JUDGE: Your armchair political theory is tenuous, Monsieur Song.

SONG: You think so? That's why you'll lose in all your dealings with the East.

JUDGE: Just answer my question: did he know you were a man? [*Pause.*]

SONG: You know, Your Honor, I never asked.

SCENE 2

Same.

Music from the "Death Scene" from Butterfly *blares over the house speakers. It is the loudest thing we've heard in this play.*

GALLIMARD *enters, crawling towards* SONG's *wig and kimono.*

GALLIMARD: Butterfly? Butterfly?

[SONG *remains a man, in the witness box, delivering a testimony we do not hear.*]

GALLIMARD: [*To us.*] In my moment of greatest shame, here, in this courtroom—with that . . . person up there, telling the world . . . What strikes me especially is how shallow he is, how glib and obsequious . . . completely . . . without substance! The type that prowls around discos with a gold medallion stinking of garlic. So little like my Butterfly.

Yet even in this moment my mind remains agile, flip-flopping like a man on a trampoline. Even now, my picture dissolves, and I see that . . . witness . . . talking to me.

[SONG *suddenly stands straight up in his witness box, and looks at* GALLIMARD.]

SONG: Yes. You. White man. [SONG *steps out of the witness box, and moves downstage towards* GALLIMARD. *Light change.*]

GALLIMARD: [*To* SONG.] Who? Me?

SONG: Do you see any other white men?

GALLIMARD: Yes. There're white men all around. This is a French courtroom.

SONG: So you are an adventurous imperialist. Tell me, why did it take you so long? To come back to this place?

GALLIMARD: What place?

SONG: This theater in China. Where we met many years ago.

GALLIMARD: [*To us.*] And once again, against my will, I am transported.

[*Chinese opera music comes up on the speakers.* SONG *begins to do opera moves, as he did the night they met.*]

SONG: Do you remember? The night you gave your heart?

GALLIMARD: It was a long time ago.

SONG: Not long enough. A night that turned your world upside down.

GALLIMARD: Perhaps.

SONG: Oh, be honest with me. What's another bit of flattery when you've already given me twenty years' worth? It's a wonder my head hasn't swollen to the size of China.

GALLIMARD: Who's to say it hasn't?

SONG: Who's to say? And what's the shame? In pride? You think I could've pulled this off if I wasn't already full of pride when we met? No, not just pride. Arrogance. It takes arrogance, really—to believe you can will, with your eyes and your lips, the destiny of another. [*He dances.*] C'mon. Admit it. You still want me. Even in slacks and a button-down collar.

GALLIMARD: I don't see what the point of—

SONG: You don't? Well maybe, Rene, just maybe—I want you.

GALLIMARD: You do?

SONG: Then again, maybe I'm just playing with you. How can you tell? [*Reprising his feminine character, he sidles up to* GALLIMARD.] "How I wish there were even a small cafe to sit in. With men in tuxedos, and cappuccinos, and bad expatriate jazz." Now you want to kiss me, don't you?

GALLIMARD: [*Pulling away.*] What makes you—?

SONG: —so sure? See? I take the words from your mouth. Then I wait for you to come and retrieve them. [*He reclines on the floor.*]

GALLIMARD: Why?! Why do you treat me so cruelly?

SONG: Perhaps I *was* treating you cruelly. But now—I'm being nice. Come here, my little one.

GALLIMARD: I'm not your little one!

SONG: My mistake. It's I who am *your* little one, right?

GALLIMARD: Yes, I—

SONG: So come get your little one. If you like. I may even let you strip me.

GALLIMARD: I mean, you were! Before . . . but not like this!

SONG: I was? Then perhaps I still am. If you look hard enough. [*He starts to remove his clothes.*]

GALLIMARD: What—what are you doing?

SONG: Helping you to see through my act.

GALLIMARD: Stop that! I don't want to! I don't—

SONG: Oh, but you asked me to strip, remember?

GALLIMARD: What? That was years ago! And I took it back!

SONG: No. You postponed it. Postponed the inevitable. Today the inevitable has come calling.

[*From the speakers, cacophony:* Butterfly *mixed in with Chinese gongs.*]

GALLIMARD: No! Stop! I don't want to see!

SONG: Then look away.

GALLIMARD: You're only in my mind! All this is in my mind! I order you! To stop!

SONG: To what? To strip? That's just what I'm—

GALLIMARD: No! Stop! I want you—!

SONG: You want me?

GALLIMARD: To stop!

SONG: You know something, Rene? Your mouth says no, but your eyes say yes. Turn them away. I dare you.

GALLIMARD: I don't have to! Every night, you say you're going to strip, but then I beg you and you stop!

SONG: I guess tonight is different.

GALLIMARD: Why? Why should that be?

SONG: Maybe I've become frustrated. Maybe I'm saying "Look at me, you fool!" Or maybe I'm just feeling . . . sexy. [*He is down to his briefs.*]

GALLIMARD: Please. This is unnecessary. I know what you are.

SONG: Do you? What am I?

GALLIMARD: A—a man.

SONG: You don't really believe that.

GALLIMARD: Yes, I do! I knew all the time somewhere that my happiness was temporary, my love a deception. But my mind kept the knowledge at bay. To make the wait bearable.

SONG: Monsieur Gallimard—the wait is over. [SONG *drops his briefs. He is naked. Sound cue out. Slowly, we and* SONG *come to the realization that what we had thought to be* GALLIMARD's *sobbing is actually his laughter.*]

GALLIMARD: Oh, God! What an idiot! Of course!

SONG: Rene—what?

GALLIMARD: Look at you! You're a man! [*He bursts into laughter again.*]

SONG: I fail to see what's so funny!

GALLIMARD: "You fail to see—!" I mean, you never did have much of a sense of humor, did you? I just think it's ridiculously funny that I've wasted so much time on just a man!

SONG: Wait. I'm not "just a man."

GALLIMARD: No? Isn't that what you've been trying to convince me of?

SONG: Yes, but what I mean—

GALLIMARD: And now, I finally believe you, and you tell me it's not true? I think you must have some kind of identity problem.

SONG: Will you listen to me?

GALLIMARD: Why?! I've been listening to you for twenty years. Don't I deserve a vacation?

SONG: I'm not just any man!

GALLIMARD: Then, what exactly are you?

SONG: Rene, how can you ask—? Okay, what about this? [*He picks up Butterfly's robes, starts to dance around. No music.*]

GALLIMARD: Yes, that's very nice. I have to admit.

[SONG *holds out his arm to* GALLIMARD.]

SONG: It's the same skin you've worshiped for years. Touch it.

GALLIMARD: Yes, it does feel the same.

SONG: Now—close your eyes. [SONG *covers* GALLIMARD*'s eyes with one hand. With the other,* SONG *draws* GALLIMARD*'s hand up to his face.* GALLIMARD, *like a blind man, lets his hands run over* SONG*'s face.*]

GALLIMARD: This skin, I remember. The curve of her face, the softness of her cheek, her hair against the back of my hand . . .

SONG: I'm your Butterfly. Under the robes, beneath everything, it was always me. Now, open your eyes and admit it—you adore me. [*He removes his hand from* GALLIMARD*'s eyes.*]

GALLIMARD: You, who knew every inch of my desires—how could you, of all people, have made such a mistake?

SONG: What?

GALLIMARD: You showed me your true self. When all I loved was the lie. A perfect lie, which you let fall to the ground—and now, it's old and soiled.

SONG: So—you never really loved me? Only when I was playing a part?

GALLIMARD: I'm a man who loved a woman created by a man. Everything else—simply falls short. [*Pause.*]

SONG: What am I supposed to do now?

GALLIMARD: You were a fine spy, Monsieur Song, with an even finer accomplice. But now I believe you should go. Get out of my life!

SONG: Go where? Rene, you can't live without me. Not after twenty years.

GALLIMARD: I certainly can't live with you—not after twenty years of betrayal.

SONG: Don't be so stubborn! Where will you go?

GALLIMARD: I have a date . . . with my Butterfly.

SONG: So, throw away your pride. And come . . .

GALLIMARD: Get away from me! Tonight, I've finally learned to tell fantasy from reality. And, knowing the difference, I choose fantasy.

SONG: *I'm* your fantasy!

GALLIMARD: You? You're as real as hamburger. Now get out! I have a date with my Butterfly and I don't want your body polluting the room! [*He tosses* SONG'*s suit at him.*] Look at these—you dress like a pimp.

SONG: Hey! These are Armani slacks and—! [*He puts on his briefs and slacks.*] Let's just say . . . I'm disappointed in you, Rene. In the crush of your adoration, I thought you'd become something more. More like . . . a woman.

But no. Men. You're like the rest of them. It's all in the way we dress, and make up our faces, and bat our eyelashes. You really have so little imagination!

GALLIMARD: You, Monsieur Song? Accuse me of too little imagination? You, if anyone, should know—I am pure imagination. And in imagination I will remain. Now get out! [GALLIMARD *bodily removes* SONG *from the stage, taking his kimono.*]

SONG: Rene! I'll never put on those robes again! You'll be sorry!

GALLIMARD: [*To* SONG.] I'm already sorry! [*Looking at the kimono in his hands*] Exactly as sorry . . . as a Butterfly.

SCENE 3

M. GALLIMARD'*s prison cell. Paris. Present.*

GALLIMARD: I've played out the events of my life night after night, always searching for a new ending to my story, one where I leave this cell and return forever to my Butterfly's arms.

Tonight I realize my search is over. That I've looked all along in the wrong place. And now, to you, I will prove that my love was not in vain—by returning to the world of fantasy where I first met her.

[*He picks up the kimono; dancers enter.*]

GALLIMARD: There is a vision of the Orient that I have. Of slender women in chong sams and kimonos who die for the love of unworthy foreign devils. Who are born and raised to be the perfect women. Who take whatever punishment we give them, and bounce back, strengthened by love, unconditionally. It is a vision that has become my life.

[*Dancers bring the wash basin to him and help him make up his face.*]

GALLIMARD: In public, I have continued to deny that Song Liling is a man. This brings me headlines, and is a source of great embarrassment to my French colleagues, who can now be sent into a coughing fit by the mere mention of Chinese food. But alone, in my cell, I have long since faced the truth.

And the truth demands a sacrifice. For mistakes made over the course of a lifetime. My mistakes were simple and absolute—the man I loved was a cad, a bounder. He deserved nothing but a kick in the behind, and instead I gave him . . . all my love.

Yes—love. Why not admit it all? That was my undoing, wasn't it? Love warped my judgment, blinded my eyes, rearranged the very lines on my face . . . until I could look in the mirror and see nothing but . . . a woman.

[*Dancers help him put on the Butterfly wig.*]

GALLIMARD: I have a vision. Of the Orient. That, deep within its almond eyes, there are still women. Women willing to sacrifice themselves for the love of a man. Even a man whose love is completely without worth.

[*Dancers assist* GALLIMARD *in donning the kimono. They hand him a knife.*]

GALLIMARD: Death with honor is better than life . . . life with dishonor. [*He sets himself center stage, in a seppuku*[1] *position.*] The love of a Butterfly can withstand many things—unfaithfulness, loss, even abandonment. But how can it face the one sin that implies all others? The devastating knowledge that, underneath it all, the object of her love was nothing more, nothing less than . . . a man. [*He sets the tip of the knife against his body.*] It is 19__. And

---

1. Better known in the West as hara-kiri; a ritual suicide accomplished by stabbing oneself in the stomach. By tradition, one may repair dishonor by having the courage to perform seppuku.

I have found her at last. In a prison on the outskirts of Paris. My name is Rene Gallimard—also known as Madame Butterfly. [GALLIMARD *turns upstage and plunges the knife into his body, as music from the "Love Duet" blares over the speakers. He collapses into the arms of the dancers, who lay him reverently on the floor. The image holds for several beats. Then a tight special up on* SONG, *who stands as a man, staring at the dead* GALLIMARD. *He smokes a cigarette; the smoke filters up through the lights. Two words leave his lips.*]

SONG: Butterfly? Butterfly?
   [*Smoke rises as lights fade slowly to black.*]
   [*END OF PLAY.*]

1988

*

Biographical Sketches

Chinua Achebe (*b. 1930*)   Achebe was born in Ogidi, an Igbo-speaking town in eastern Nigeria. His father was a Christian churchman. He was educated in English at church schools, at Government College in Umuahia, and at University College in Ibadan. In 1953, he received his B.A. from London University and then studied broadcasting at the BBC. He worked for a time at the Nigerian Broadcasting Corporation in Lagos. After the Nigerian civil war, he moved to the United States. Since 1990, he has been Charles P. Stevenson, Jr., Professor of Languages and Literature at Bard College. Achebe is known mainly for his essays, short stories, and novels. A volume of his poetry was joint winner of the Commonwealth Poetry Prize in 1972.

John Agard (*b. 1949*)   Born and raised in Guyana, Agard moved to England in 1977. The rhythm of the West Indies—a special mixture of African and European styles—pervades Agard's poetry. Many of his poems were written to be performed, and he considers himself part of a movement that has rediscovered the oral roots of poetry. Agard calls himself a poetsonian, playing on the term *calypsonian*, which refers to a performer of calypso song and dance. He writes poems for adults and children alike and works as a playwright, performer, and anthologist. Together with the BBC and other organizations, Agard has sought to increase the place of poetry in everyday British life. His books include *Man to Pan, Mangoes and Bullets, We Animals Would Like a Word with You*, and *From the Devil's Pulpit*.

Paul Allen (*b. 1945*) Allen teaches courses in writing poetry and writing song lyrics at the College of Charleston in Charleston, South Carolina, where he is Associate Professor of English. His first book of poems, *American Crawl*, received the Vassar Miller Poetry Prize and was nominated for a Pulitzer and a National Book Award. In 2000, Glebe Street Records released Allen's *The Man with the Hardest Belly: Poems & Songs*. Forthcoming is another poetry collection, *The Clean Plate Club*.

Matthew Arnold (*1822–1888*) Arnold was a sort of jack-of-all-trades: a preeminent poet of the Victorian era, a pioneer in the field of literary criticism, an educator, a government official, and an influential public figure. Arnold's father was the headmaster of Rugby, a prestigious English prep school, and Arnold grew up knowing many of the leading intellectual and literary men of his day. He was educated at Winchester, Rugby, and Balliol College, Oxford, later serving as fellow of Oriel College, Oxford. In 1851, he married Frances Lucy Wightman, and when the newlyweds visited Dover on their honeymoon, Arnold wrote the earliest drafts of "Dover Beach." Arnold was well-known in his own day as an arbiter of culture, and his theories of literary criticism are still highly influential today.

Margaret Atwood (*b. 1939*) Atwood spent the first eleven years of her life in sparsely populated areas of northern Ontario and Quebec, where her father, an entomologist, spent eight months of each year doing research in the forest. The Atwood family stayed in a cabin heated by a wood stove and lit by kerosene lanterns. One of Atwood's few sources of entertainment was reading, and she soon began to write too, beginning with poems, plays, comic books, and an unfinished novel about an ant. By sixteen, she had decided that all she wanted to do was write. Atwood received her bachelor's degree from Victoria College at the University of Toronto and her master's degree from Radcliffe College. She also studied at Harvard University. Together with a friend, Atwood published her first book of poems on a small flatbed press and sold copies for fifty cents each. She has received numerous prizes for her poetry as well as for her fiction.

W. H. (Wystan Hugh) Auden (*1907–1973*) Born to a medical officer and a nurse, Auden attended Christ Church College, Oxford, where he distinguished himself more as a poet than as a student. While at Oxford, Auden formed friendships with such writers as Stephen Spender, C. Day

Lewis, and Christopher Isherwood. Not only was Auden the principal poet of his generation, but he was also a playwright, librettist, editor, and essayist. He is widely admired for his technical virtuosity, his success with diverse poetic forms and themes, and his encyclopedic intellectual range. Auden moved to New York City's Greenwich Village in 1939 and became a U.S. citizen in 1946. For many years, he was actively involved in politics, vigorously opposing fascism. But he shocked audiences on both sides of the Atlantic when he repudiated the political scene by publishing "In Memory of W. B. Yeats" in the *New Republic*. Auden received the Pulitzer Prize for his body of work and served as Chancellor of the Academy of American Poets.

Elizabeth Bishop (*1911–1979*)   Bishop lost both of her parents early in her life. She was shuttled between her father's wealthy Massachusetts family and her mother's rural Nova Scotia family throughout her childhood. She was educated at Vassar College, where she fell in with a group of young, talented writers. In 1935, she met Marianne Moore, whose work deeply impressed her and whose friendship was to become a stabilizing force in her life. The *Partisan Review*'s March 1940 publication of "The Fish" launched Bishop's career, and from then on her work frequently appeared in such magazines as the *New Yorker*. Bishop went on to win virtually every poetry prize in the country. She served as Chancellor of the Academy of American Poets, a member of the American Academy of Arts and Letters, and a consultant in poetry to the Library of Congress in 1949–50. She taught at the University of Washington, Harvard University, New York University, and, just prior to her death, the Massachusetts Institute of Technology.

William Blake (*1757–1827*)   Though Blake is today considered one of the earliest and greatest figures of English Romanticism, at the time of his death he was a little-known artist and an entirely unknown poet. Having been apprenticed at the age of fourteen, Blake's only formal education was in art, and he was an accomplished painter and engraver. For most of his life, he made his living illustrating books and magazines, giving drawing lessons, and engraving designs made by other artists. From childhood, though, he spent most of his spare time reading and often tried his hand at poetry. By adulthood, he was dissatisfied with the reigning poetic tradition and was testing new forms and techniques. In 1789, the year that the French Revolution began, he published *Songs of Innocence*, a series of poems accompanied by his own illustrations. In 1794, he published a parallel series, *Songs of Experience*. Together, Blake wrote, these two series portray "the two Contrary States of the Human Soul." He was a devout Christian who saw a close relationship between his religion and his art, declaring that "all he knew was in the Bible" and that the "Old and New Testaments are the Great Code of Art."

Anne Bradstreet (*1612/13–1672*) Bradstreet's father, Thomas Dudley, steward of the earl of Lincoln's estate, took care to see that his daughter received a better education than most other young women of her day. At sixteen, she married Simon Bradstreet, a recent graduate of Cambridge University and assistant to her father. Simon Bradstreet was soon appointed to assist in preparations of the Massachusetts Bay Company, and so the Bradstreets and Dudleys sailed with John Winthrop to Massachusetts. In leaving Old England for New England, Anne Bradstreet gave up a life of relative comfort and culture for the wilderness of the New World. When visiting England in 1650, Bradstreet's brother-in-law published a volume of her poetry without her consent. This volume, *The Tenth Muse,* was the first book of poetry written by a resident of the New World and was widely read throughout England. The verses for which she is remembered today were not published until 1678, in a posthumous edition. Bradstreet was an ambitious poet whose work is firmly grounded in English religious, political, and cultural history.

Gwendolyn Brooks (*1917–2000*) Born in Topeka, Kansas, and raised in Chicago, Brooks began writing poetry at the age of seven. After graduating from high school, she attended art school at the South Side Community Art Center. Her main interest, however, was poetry, and she soon demonstrated her talent by winning contests sponsored by *Poetry* magazine and various other organizations. She published her first book of poetry in 1945. Her second book of poems, *Annie Allen*, won Brooks the distinction of being the first African American to be awarded the Pulitzer Prize, which she received in 1950. Brooks's early works concentrate on what Langston Hughes called the "ordinary aspects of black life," but her later poetry deals more with issues of African American consciousness and activism.

Elizabeth Barrett Browning (*1806–1861*) The eldest of twelve children, Barrett Browning was the first in her family to be born in England in over two hundred years, as the Barretts had lived in Jamaica for centuries. Living at home under her father's strict rule, Barrett Browning began writing poetry at an early age, publishing her first volume when she was only thirteen and gaining a considerable following by the time she was in her thirties. Her 1844 collection, *Poems*, caught the eye of Robert Browning, and the two exchanged 574 letters over a period of twenty months. Her father did not want any of his children to marry, and so she was forced to elope. The two settled in Italy, where Elizabeth bore a son, saw her chronic lung condition improve, and published *Sonnets from the Portuguese*, a sequence of forty-four sonnets that record the stages of her love for Robert Browning. Critics have compared the imagery of the sonnet sequence with that of Shakespeare and the skillful use of form with that of Petrarch.

Robert Browning (*1812–1889*) Born in a suburb of London, Browning spent much of his childhood in his father's extensive library. From early on, his aim was to become a poet; he abandoned his schooling in order to dedicate his energies to the realization of that goal. His parents supported him until he was in his thirties. Browning admired the poetry of Elizabeth Barrett and began to correspond with her in 1844. Two years later, they were married. In 1849, they moved to Italy because the climate there helped Elizabeth's lung condition. After Elizabeth died, in 1861, Browning returned to London and began to establish his literary reputation. Today he is recognized as one of England's most prolific poets.

Lynne Bryer (*1946–1994*) Bryer, a white South African, received her master's in English from Rhodes University in Grahamstown in 1969. She worked in the publishing industry in London and Cape Town before opening her own publishing house, Chameleon Press. As a publisher, Bryer provided a venue for new and progressive writing in South Africa. She received the prestigious AA Life Vita Arthur Nortje Poety Award in 1991. She died from cancer at the age of forty-eight.

Lewis Carroll (*1832–1898*) Charles Lutwidge Dodgson was the man behind the pen name of Lewis Carroll. Dodgson was born in Daresbury, Cheshire, England, to an Anglican clergyman who eventually had eleven children. He was educated at Richmond School, Rugby, and Christ Church, Oxford. A man of diverse interests, Dodgson was actively engaged in many fields: mathematics, logic, photography, art, theater, religion, medicine, and science. In 1855, he finally attained a college mastership at Oxford, a position that he was to hold until 1881. For some time, he aspired to the priesthood, and he went so far as to be ordained a deacon in 1861. Dodgson was happiest in the company of children, for whom he created puzzles, clever games, and charming letters. He was particularly close to the children of Henry Liddell, dean of Christ Church, and wrote most of his stories for their amusement. Alice Liddell was his favorite, and it is she who stars in *Alice in Wonderland* and *Through the Looking-Glass*.

Raymond Carver (*1938–1988*)   Carver was born in Clatskanie, Oregon, and grew up in Yakima, Washington. His father worked on the railroad and in the lumber mills and, like Carver, was an alcoholic. His mother worked as a waitress and a retail clerk. The marriage was tumultuous. Carver himself married at nineteen and had two children by the time he was twenty. His marriage, like that of his parents, was notable for its turmoil, and he suffered from acute alcoholism and was frequently hospitalized. While supporting his family by working menial jobs, Carver took classes at Chico State in California with the novelist John Gardner and eventually transferred to and graduated from Humboldt State College and the Iowa Writer's Workshop. He was a Guggenheim Fellow in 1979 and was twice awarded grants from the National Endowment for the Arts. He also won *Poetry* magazine's Levinson Prize and was elected to the American Academy and Institute of Arts and Letters. Though he spent most of his life in California, he lived in Port Angeles, Washington, during the ten years before his death from cancer.

John Cheever (*1912–1982*)   Cheever's formal education ended when he was expelled from Thayer Academy at the age of seventeen for smoking, and soon after his father, who had left the family a few years before, lost all his money in the stock market crash of 1929. Cheever wrote his first short story about his expulsion, titling it "Expelled," and Malcolm Cowley, who was to become a lifelong friend, published it in the *New Republic*. After travel in Europe, Cheever returned to America, settling in New York City and becoming friends with such writers as John Dos Passos, E. E. Cummings, James Agee, and James Farrell. He lived in poverty in New York as he established himself as a writer. After serving in the Pacific in World War II, he married and had three children. He wrote about the manners and morals of middle-class urban and suburban America and was known primarily as a prolific short story writer until his first novel won the National Book Award in 1958. *The Stories of John Cheever* won the Pulitzer Prize in 1978.

Anton Chekhov (*1860–1904*)   Born in the small town of Taganrog in Russia, Chekhov began writing short stories while attending medical school at the University of Moscow. He began practicing medicine in 1884 while at the same time writing short stories, comic sketches, and plays to support his family. Chekhov's first big success was the Moscow Art Theater's production of his play *The Seagull* in 1897. Chekhov eventually left medicine to write full-time. In early 1897, he suffered a lung hemorrhage and was forced to spend most of his time in the Crimea for the sake of his health, though he still occasionally traveled to Moscow to participate in the productions of his plays. He died of tuberculosis in a German health resort at the age of forty-four.

Kate Chopin (*1851–1904*) Chopin was born Katherine O'Flaherty in St. Louis to an Irish immigrant father and a Catholic mother of French heritage. Her father, a successful businessman, died in a train wreck when she was four. She grew up in the company of strong, loving women: her mother, grandmother, and great-grandmother. When she entered the St. Louis Academy of the Sacred Heart, she had already read a great deal of English and French literature. Chopin moved to Louisiana after her marriage to Oscar Chopin in 1870. After her husband's death, in 1884, Chopin returned to St. Louis with her six children and lived there with her mother and then, after her mother's death, on her own. She began writing and soon earned a national reputation as a writer of local-color fiction. She is best known for her short stories and her novel *The Awakening*.

Samuel Taylor Coleridge (*1772–1834*) Coleridge was born in the small town of Ottery St. Mary in Devonshire, England, the youngest of ten children. When his father died, in 1781, Coleridge was sent to a London charity school for children of the clergy, Christ's Hospital, where he read widely and finished first in his class. He went on to attend Jesus College, Cambridge, though he was forced to leave without a degree after he fell into debt. After a brief stint in the army and an attempt at lecturing, he married Sara Fricker and tried to settle down. He became friends with William Wordsworth, and the two men collaborated on a number of literary projects, notably *Lyrical Ballads*. Coleridge spent two years in Malta trying unsuccessfully to recover from painful rheumatism. Upon his return, he dissolved his unhappy marriage, which had been strained by his love for another woman. As the years passed, he became more estranged from his family and more addicted to opium to ease his pain. Coleridge was also a literary critic.

Billy Collins (*b. 1941*) Collins lives in New York and is a professor of English at Lehman College of the City University of New York. In addition to serving as the U.S. Poet Laureate in 2001, he has received fellowships from the National Endowment for the Arts and the Guggenheim Foundation, and his work has been published in such venues as *Poetry*, *American Poetry Review*, *American Scholar*, *Harper's*, the *Paris Review*, the *Atlantic Monthly*, and the *New Yorker*. Collins's collections include *Picnic, Lightning*; *The Art of Drowning*; *Questions about Angels*; *Nine Horse*; *Sailing Alone Around the Room*; and the CD *The Best Cigarette*. He has won numerous awards, among them the Pushcart Prize and the National Poetry Series publication prize.

Stephen Crane (*1871–1900*)   The son of a Methodist minister and a social reformer mother, Crane rebelled against his parents by rejecting all religious and social traditions. At Syracuse University, he distinguished himself more as a baseball player than as a scholar, and he was unsure of what to do with his life when he graduated. But by 1891, he had found an occupation: he wanted to write. He wrote for several newspapers but never lasted long at any of them. Until the syndicated publication of *The Red Badge of Courage*, which he regarded as a potboiler, he lived a life of extreme privation. The same newspaper that syndicated the novel hired him to work as a roving reporter in the West and Mexico, where he gathered material for his writing. His first volume of poetry, *The Black Riders and Other Lines*, earned praise from critics but not from the general public. In 1897, he moved to England, where he befriended some of the age's finest writers, including Henry James and Joseph Conrad. He died of tuberculosis at the age of twenty-eight.

E. E. (Edward Estlin) Cummings (*1894–1962*)   Cummings was born in Cambridge, Massachusetts, to particularly supportive parents who encouraged him to develop his creative gifts. His father was a former Harvard professor who had become a Unitarian minister, and Cummings received both his B.A. and his M.A. from Harvard University. While there, he wrote poetry in the pre-Raphaelite and Metaphysical traditions and published it in the *Harvard Advocate*. Cummings joined the Ambulance Corps the day after the United States entered World War I. During the war, he spent three months in a French prison because his outspoken antiwar convictions led the French to accuse him of treason. He transmuted this experience into his first literary success, *The Enormous Room*. After the war, he shuttled among New York City's Greenwich Village, Paris, and New Hampshire. He showed little interest in wealth or his growing celebrity.

Emily Dickinson (*1830–1886*)   Dickinson's grandfather founded Amherst College, and her father was a state senator and U.S. congressman. Dickinson attended Amherst Academy and spent a year at the Mount Holyoke Female Seminary (now Mount Holyoke College). She spent the rest of her life in her father's Amherst mansion. Visitors were scarce, and Dickinson herself rarely ventured out. Though she was a prolific poet, her talents were not recognized in her day: only ten of her poems were published in her lifetime. After her death, over seventeen hundred poems were discovered bound neatly in booklets. Four years later, Thomas Wentworth Higginson, an editor for the *Atlantic Monthly* with whom Dickinson had corresponded, smoothed and regularized some of her poems and published them in a book. Editors did not restore her idiosyncratic expressions and punctuation until the twentieth century.

John Donne (*1572–1631*)   The first and greatest of a group that came to be known as the Metaphysical poets, Donne wrote in a revolutionary style that combined highly intellectual conceits, or metaphors, with complex, compressed phrasing. Born into a Catholic family at a time when Catholics were a persecuted minority, Donne felt his religion was central to his identity and to much of his poetry. He studied at both Oxford and Cambridge Universities but took a degree from neither school because to do so he would have had to subscribe to the Thirty-nine Articles, the tenets of Anglicanism. From Oxford and Cambridge, Donne went to Lincoln's Inn, where he studied law. Two years later, he relented and joined the Anglican Church, motivated in no small part by the recent death of his brother, who had been imprisoned for his Catholicism. After he secretly married the daughter of an aristocrat, Donne was briefly imprisoned himself. This politically disastrous marriage dashed his worldly hopes and forced him to struggle for years to support a large and growing family. During this time, he wrote on the lawfulness of suicide (*Bianthanatos*). He eventually managed to reestablish himself and by 1615 was sufficiently well-known that King James I appointed him dean of St. Paul's Cathedral in London. Most of his published works were sermons; Donne circulated his poetry among learned people, but it was not published until after his death.

Rita Dove (*b. 1952*)   Growing up in Akron, Dove wrote stories and plays for her classmates to perform. After being named a President's Scholar, Dove went on to attend Miami University in Ohio, study for a year at Tübingen University in Germany as a Fulbright scholar, and receive an M.F.A. in creative writing from the University of Iowa. She was also awarded fellowships from the Guggenheim Foundation and the National Endowment for the Arts. She served as Poet Laureate of the United States between 1993 and 1995, the youngest person ever to do so. In 1987, Dove was awarded the Pulitzer Prize for Poetry. She has taught creative writing at Arizona State University and is currently the Commonwealth Professor of English at the University of Virginia and an associate editor of *Callaloo*, the journal of African American and African arts and letters.

T. S. (Thomas Stearns) Eliot (*1888–1965*)   T. S. Eliot was born into a New England family in St. Louis. His grandfather founded Washington University and the first Unitarian Church in St. Louis. Eliot traveled to New England for college, received his B.A. and M.A. from Harvard University, and eventually abandoned his doctoral studies in philosophy. He went to England in 1914, read Greek philosophy at Oxford, and published "The Love Song of J. Alfred Prufrock" the next year, with Ezra Pound's help. Eliot became a British citizen in 1927, and in that same year he shocked many of his fellow modernists by declaring that he had become a "classicist in literature, royalist in politics, and Anglo-Catholic in religion." Accordingly, his later works explore religious questions in a quieter idiom. Working for the publishing house of Faber & Faber in London, Eliot helped publish a number of young poets and eventually became the director of the firm. His unhappy marriage to Vivienne Haigh-Wood ended in 1933, and he married Valerie Fletcher in 1956. Eliot was awarded the Nobel Prize for Literature in 1948.

Louise Erdrich (*b. 1954*)   Erdrich is the daughter of a French Ojibwa mother and a German American father; the eldest of their seven children, she grew up in North Dakota near the Turtle Mountain Reservation. Both of her parents taught at a Bureau of Indian Affairs school in an era when the primary aim of these schools was to acculturate their Native American pupils. Erdrich recalls that while she was growing up, her mother read stories out loud and her father regularly recited poetry. She attended public schools until she enrolled at Dartmouth College in 1972 as part of the school's first coeducational class. During her junior year, she published a poem in *Ms.* magazine and won the American Academy of Poets Prize. After graduating from Dartmouth, Erdrich taught poetry and writing to young people through a position at the State Arts Council of North Dakota. Later on, she devoted herself full-time to her own writing, working to support herself until she was able to live on what she earned from her poems and novels. Erdrich is best known for her award-winning first novel, *Love Medicine*.

William Faulkner (*1897–1962*)   Faulkner was born to an old Mississippi family: his great-grandfather was a local legend, having been a colonel in the Civil War, a lawyer, a railroad builder, a financier, a politician, and a writer who was shot and killed by a rival in 1889. After dropping out of high school in 1915, Faulkner drifted about the country working in various capacities. Though he never saw active service during his stint in the British Royal Flying Corps, he returned to Mississippi with what he claimed was a war wound. After beginning to write, he went to New Orleans and met Sherwood Anderson, who helped him develop his writing style and get his work published. His early novels and short stories were not very popular. His reputation as a writer was established only after the 1946 publication of *The Portable Faulkner*, edited by Malcolm Cowley. He was awarded the Nobel Prize in 1950 and died of a heart attack at the age of sixty-five.

Carolyn Forché (*b. 1950*)   Born in Detroit, Forché attended the Justin Morrill College at Michigan State University, where she studied five languages, creative writing, English literature, and international relations. Her first poetry collection, *Gathering the Tribes*, won the Yale Series of Younger Poets Award. In 1977, she traveled to Spain to translate the work of the Salvadoran-exiled poet Claribel Alegría and, upon her return, received a John Simon Guggenheim Foundation Fellowship, which enabled her to work as a human rights activist in El Salvador for two years. Her experiences there informed her second book, *The Country between Us*, which received the Poetry Society of America's Alice Fay di Castagnola Award and was the Lamont Selection of the Academy of American Poets. In March 1994, Forché's third book of poetry, *The Angel of History*, received the Los Angeles Times Book Award. Forché has worked as a correspondent in Beirut for National Public Radio's *All Things Considered* and as a human rights liaison in South Africa. She has held three fellowships from the National Endowment for the Arts. Forché teaches in the M.F.A. program in poetry at George Mason University in Virginia.

Robert Frost (*1874–1963*)   When Frost was eleven, his father died of tuberculosis and his mother moved the family from San Francisco to New England, where she raised him and his sister on her salary as a schoolteacher. Frost studied classics in high school, and he and his future wife, Elinor Miriam White, were the co-valedictorians of their class. Frost entered and dropped out of both Dartmouth and Harvard. He married White, and while he tried to make his name known in literary circles, the young couple taught in a private school Frost's mother had opened. After the death of Frost's first child, his grandfather bought a farm in Derry, New Hampshire, for Frost and his wife, and the growing family lived there for a decade. Still struggling to get his work into print, he journeyed across the Atlantic to meet Ezra Pound, T. S. Eliot, W. B. Yeats, and other literary figures in London. Under Pound's patronage, Frost's work soon appeared in *Poetry* magazine, and his first book followed. In 1961, well over eighty years old, Frost read a poem at John F. Kennedy's inauguration.

Gabriel García Márquez (*b. 1928*) Born in Aracataca, Colombia, García Márquez lived with his maternal grandparents until he was eight, when his parents took him in after his grandfather died and his grandmother's eyesight deteriorated. He studied law halfheartedly at the Universidad Nacional and the Universidad de Cartagena, spending more of his time on literature than law. He finally abandoned the law in 1950 and supported himself by working as a journalist in Latin America, Europe, and the United States. His first published work was *Leaf Storm* (1955). In 1967, he published what is still his most famous novel, *One Hundred Years of Solitude*, which chronicles six generations of a Colombian family and uses their town as a microcosm of Latin America. Within a week of its publication, all eight thousand copies had been sold, and the book was gaining García Márquez international acclaim. He won the Nobel Prize for Literature in 1982. Garciá Márquez currently lives in Mexico City.

Charlotte Perkins Gilman (*1860–1935*) Gilman was born in Hartford, to a father who was a minor literary figure and a mother whose family had lived in Rhode Island since the middle of the seventeenth century. After Gilman's father deserted the family, her mother moved back to Rhode Island, where she raised her two children on her own. Gilman's childhood was lonely. Later, she supported herself for some time as a governess, an art teacher, and a designer of greeting cards. After marrying the artist Charles Stetson, Gilman became severely depressed. Convinced that her marriage was threatening her sanity, she moved with her daughter to California and in 1892 divorced her husband. Her husband then married her best friend, the writer Grace Ellery Channing, and Gilman sent her daughter to live with them, for which she was widely criticized in the press. She pursued a double career as a writer and a lecturer on women, labor, and social organization.

Allen Ginsberg (*1926–1998*) Ginsberg's childhood in Paterson, New Jersey, was overshadowed by his mother's severe mental illness. Intent on following his father's advice to become a labor lawyer, Ginsberg enrolled at Columbia University in New York. He soon became friends with fellow students Lucien Carr and Jack Kerouac, as well as locals William S. Burroughs and Neal Cassady. He and his friends experimented with drugs, took cross-country treks, and worked to develop a new poetic vision. Ginsberg eventually graduated from Columbia in 1948 and went to San Francisco, where he did some graduate work, performed odd jobs, and spent eight months in a psychiatric hospital. In 1956, his first book of poems, *Howl and Other Poems*, was published with an introduction by his mentor William Carlos Williams. With the publication of *Howl*, Ginsberg was catapulted to fame as a member of the Beat Generation and as a significant poet in his own right.

Susan Glaspell (*1882–1948*)   Glaspell was born in Davenport, Iowa, earned a bachelor's degree in philosophy from Drake University, and started her writing career as a reporter in Des Moines. After a few years, including a period in graduate school at the University of Chicago, she returned to Davenport and wrote short stories for magazines. In 1913, she and George Cook, a writer from a prominent Davenport family, relocated to New York City's Greenwich Village, where they married and became vital figures in the literary, bohemian scene. Each summer they vacationed in Provincetown, Massachusetts, and there, in 1915, they founded the Provincetown Players. A semiprofessional group distinguished by its association with such radicals as the journalist and communist John Reed and the sonneteer Edna St. Vincent Millay, this company launched not only Glaspell's career as a playwright but also Eugene O'Neill's, and it enjoyed success in Greenwich Village. Glaspell and Cook had been living in Greece for two years when Cook died, in 1924. Glaspell returned to America, where she wrote mostly fiction and a memoir of Cook's life. She died of cancer in Provincetown.

Thomas Gray (*1716–1771*)   Perhaps the most important years of Gray's life were those in which he attended Eton College. There he met two boys, Horace Walpole and Richard West, who would be his lifelong friends. Gray's feelings for them were homosexual, but there is no evidence that the feelings were mutual. Gray went on to Cambridge, where he studied Greek and history and led a fairly secluded life. At Cambridge, Gray shone academically, emerging as one of England's best scholars. When West died of tuberculosis, in 1742, Gray began writing poetry, most of which was inspired by his grief for his beloved friend.

Thomas Hardy (*1840–1928*)   Hardy was the son of a master mason in Upper Bockhampton and was apprenticed to a local architect at the age of fifteen. He wrote novels in his spare time and managed to publish one in

1871 but continued to make his living as an architect until his thirty-third year, after which he devoted himself entirely to literature. He spent the next quarter century writing novels. After his *Jude the Obscure* was harshly criticized, he abandoned fiction for poetry. Much of his writing is situated in or is about Wessex, the fictional area of England centered in Dorset. In Hardy's later years, he wrote his autobiography, which he arranged to have published after his death under the name of a friend. Hardy took a pessimistic view of the human condition and held that indifferent forces—not any divine plan—circumscribe human lives. This perspective is evident in both his novels and his poetry. Hardy is buried in Westminster Abbey, though his heart was removed and lies at Stinsford Church near his former residence.

Nathaniel Hawthorne (*1804–1864*) Hawthorne was born in Salem, Massachusetts, and descended from Puritan immigrants, one of whom had been a judge in the Salem witch trials. His father, a sea captain, died in 1808, and his mother's family took responsibility for his education. He attended Bowdoin College, after which he returned to Salem and dedicated himself to writing. He had difficulty getting his early works published, and only a few of his novels and short stories found their way into print. Soon after the publication of his *Twice-Told Tales* in 1837, he became engaged and went to work at the Boston Custom House to save enough money for his marriage. He abandoned his writing for years, convinced that it was the product of his loneliness, but after losing his post as surveyor of the Port of Salem in 1846, he returned to his old craft, writing *The Scarlet Letter* and *The House of Seven Gables*, among other works.

Robert Hayden (*1913–1980*) Hayden was born Asa Bundy Sheffey in Detroit. His childhood was tumultuous, as he was shuttled between the home of his parents and that of a foster family next door. His impaired vision kept him from participating in sports, so he spent most of his free time reading. With the help of a scholarship, he studied at Detroit City College (now Wayne State University) and at the University of Michigan with W. H. Auden. He taught at Fisk University for over twenty years and at the University of Michigan for more than ten. Hayden produced ten volumes of poetry during his lifetime, though he did not receive acclaim for his work until late in his life. In the 1960s, he resisted pressure to express the activist sentiments that were growing stronger in the African American community and thereby alienated himself from a growing African American literary movement. In 1976, he became the first black American to be appointed Consultant in Poetry to the Library of Congress (later called the Poet Laureate).

Seamus Heaney (*b. 1939*) Heaney was born on a farm in Mossbawn, County Derry, Northern Ireland. He was among the first to take advantage of reforms that allowed Catholics access to a top-notch education in that province of Great Britain, which traditionally discriminated against Catholics in favor of Protestants. Educated, and subsequently appointed as a lecturer in English, at Queen's University, Belfast, Heaney began to publish work in university magazines under the pseudonym Incertus. He produced his first volume, *Eleven Poems*, in 1965. After experiencing six years of civil strife in Northern Ireland, Heaney published *North*, his most political book of poems by far. He has held teaching positions at the University of California at Berkeley, Carysfort College in Dublin, and Oxford University and has served as the Boylston Professor of Rhetoric and Oratory at Harvard University. He won the Nobel Prize for Literature in 1995.

Ernest Hemingway (*1899–1961*) Hemingway was born and raised in Oak Park, Illinois, one of six children. Most of his summers were spent in the family's cottage in northern Michigan, where many of his stories are set. After graduating from high school, Hemingway went to work on the *Kansas City Star*. When the United States entered World War I, Hemingway, unable to join the army because of an eye problem, joined the Ambulance Corps. He returned from the war a decorated hero. In 1920, he married and went to Paris, where he met Gertrude Stein, Sherwood Anderson, Ezra Pound, and F. Scott Fitzgerald and worked at becoming a writer. After the 1926 publication of his first novel, *The Sun Also Rises*, he became an international celebrity. His first marriage broke up not long afterward, and over the course of his life he remarried three times. He was awarded a Pulitzer Prize in 1953 and a Nobel Prize in 1954. After being hospitalized several times for depression and paranoia, he killed himself at the age of sixty-one.

O. Henry (*1862–1910*) Born William Sidney Porter in Greensboro, North Carolina, Henry grew up in the South during the post–Civil War depression. He left school at the age of fifteen and eventually moved to Texas, where he was married. He joined the *Houston Post* as a reporter and columnist when his humorous weekly, the *Rolling Stone*, failed. In 1895, he fled to Honduras to escape prosecution for embezzlement, but he was convicted when he returned to Texas in 1897 to be with his dying wife. In 1898, he entered a penitentiary at Columbus, Ohio. During his three years in prison, he wrote short stories to support his daughter. His first work, "Whistling Dick's Christmas Stocking," which appeared in *McClure's*

Magazine in 1899, was a huge success. After being released from prison, he moved to New York City and began writing full-time. Ten collections of his works have been published, three posthumously, and over six hundred of his short stories were published during his lifetime. In 1918, the O. Henry Memorial Award, which gives awards annually for the best magazine stories, was established in his honor.

Robert Herrick (*1591–1674*)   Herrick was the seventh child of a Cheapside, London, goldsmith who committed suicide only fifteen months after the poet's birth. He was apprenticed to his goldsmith uncle, Sir William Herrick. Herrick eventually decided to leave business and pursue his education, attending St. John's College, Cambridge. There, he earned a bachelor of arts in 1617 and a master's in 1620 and, perhaps more important, became the eldest of the Sons of Ben, poets who idolized Ben Jonson. He would have liked nothing better than to live a life of leisured study, discussing literature and socializing with Jonson. For a number of reasons, though, he took religious orders and reluctantly moved to Dean Priory, Devonshire. In 1647, the Protectorate government expelled Herrick from his post for his support of Charles I. He fled to London, where in 1648 he published a volume of over fourteen hundred poems with two different titles: *Hesperides* for those on secular subjects and *Noble Numbers* for those on sacred subjects. These poems did not fare well in the harsh Puritan climate and went unnoticed until the nineteenth century. Herrick was eventually restored to his Devonshire post, and he lived out his last years there quietly.

Gerard Manley Hopkins (*1844–1889*)   Hopkins was the eldest of eight children of a marine-insurance adjustor (shipwrecks later figured in his poetry, particularly the wreck of the *Deutschland*). While studying at Balliol College, Oxford, Hopkins was drawn to the religious revival that John Henry Newman was leading there. He followed in Newman's footsteps and, despite his family's opposition, converted from the Anglican to the Roman Catholic Church. He was twenty-two years old at the time. A few years later, he joined the Jesuit order, burning all of his early poetry, which he considered "too worldly." From then on, he asked the rector to approve the subjects of his poems, most of which were either devotional or occasional. Hopkins kept most of his later poetry to himself, only occasionally including poems in letters to his friends. Consequently, it was not until after his death that his work was published. Near the end of his life, he was appointed professor of Greek at University College, Dublin. He died there of typhoid at age forty-four.

A. E. (Alfred Edward) Housman (*1859–1936*)   Housman was born in Fockbury, Worcestershire. His father was a solicitor from Lancashire; his mother was Cornish. He was raised in the High Church wing of the Church of England but converted to paganism at eight, became a deist at thirteen, and switched to outright atheism at twenty-one. Housman did well at school and won a scholarship to St. John's College, Oxford, where he studied classics, ancient history, and philosophy. "Oxford had not much effect on me," he said, "except that there I met my greatest friend." The friend in question was Moses Jackson, who was willing to be Housman's friend although Housman wanted a more intimate relationship. Housman shocked his friends and teachers at Oxford by failing his final examinations. His biographers often attribute this failure to the psychological turmoil that resulted from his suppressed love for Jackson. Housman next obtained a job in the civil service and pursued his classical studies. In 1908, he was appointed the Chair of Latin at University College, London, and he served as professor of Latin at Cambridge from 1911 until his death. Most of his poetry came in a creative burst that lasted about a year in the mid-1890s. He published his first book, *A Shropshire Lad*, in 1896. Housman aimed to write poetry that was both compact and moving. His work was influenced by Greek and Latin lyric poetry, by the traditional ballad, and by the German poet Heinrich Heine.

Langston Hughes (*1902–1967*)   Hughes, born in Joplin, Mississippi, was a major figure of the intellectual and literary movement known as the Harlem Renaissance. His parents separated when he was young, and he grew up with his maternal grandmother, residing only intermittently with his mother in Detroit and Cleveland and with his father in Mexico. Hughes was elected Class Poet in high school and went on to attend Columbia University. After a year of college, he dropped out and began to travel and write and publish poetry. His work was included in important African American periodicals like *Opportunity* and *Crisis* and anthologies like *The New Negro* and *Caroling Dusk*. Hughes graduated from Lincoln University in 1929 and began to travel again, working as a correspondent and columnist. When the Great Depression brought the Harlem Renaissance to an abrupt end, he became involved in activist politics, including the American Communist Party. In addition to writing poetry and novels, Hughes also founded theaters and produced plays.

David Henry Hwang (*b. 1957*)   Hwang (pronounced "Wong") was born to first-generation Chinese immigrants (his father a banker, his mother a professor of piano) in Los Angeles. In 1978, he wrote his first play, *F.O.B.*, which tells the story of a newly arrived Chinese immigrant ("fresh off the boat") who exemplifies both the impulse to hasten assimilation into American culture by repudiating one's heritage and the counterimpulse to nourish and sustain one's heritage. After graduating from Stanford University in 1979, Hwang attended the Yale School of Drama for two years. During that time, F.O.B. was picked up by the influential National Playwrights Conference at the Eugene O'Neill Theater Center in Waterford, Connecticut. Subsequently produced off-Broadway, the play won an Obie Award as best new play. In his works that followed, including *The Dance and the Railroad* and *Family Devotions*, Hwang continued to explore the Asian experience in America while widening his focus to general issues of race, gender, and culture. In 1988, the immensely successful Broadway production of *M. Butterfly* garnered a Pulitzer Prize nomination and a Tony Award. *Golden Child* won an Obie for its 1996 off-Broadway production and a Tony nomination for its 1998 Broadway production.

Henrik Ibsen (*1828–1906*)　Ibsen was born to a well-to-do family in a lumber town south of Christiana (later called Oslo), Norway. His father's business crashed when Ibsen was six, and the family experienced the humiliations that follow a financial reversal. At fifteen, Ibsen was apprenticed to a druggist; he went to Christiana six years later and, failing to enter the university there, eventually found work in the theater, as an assistant stage manager in Bergen. Here he wrote the plays of his first period, romantic, mythological works celebrating Norway's national independence. Frustrated and poor, Ibsen left Norway at thirty-six, partly subsidized by government grants, for the warmer climates of Italy and Germany, where he lived for the next three decades. The production of *The League of Youth* in 1869 began the second of Ibsen's periods, this one of realistic drama exemplified by *A Doll House*, which he wrote in 1879. His plays during these twelve or so years revolutionized the European stage, and on the strength of this achievement Ibsen is often called the father of modern theater. During his third period, Ibsen's work remained realistic but made increasing use of symbol and metaphor, and it was preoccupied with the place of the artist in the world. He died after a series of strokes that left him an invalid in his final years, which he spent in Norway.

Randall Jarrell (*1914–1965*)　Jarrell was born in Nashville but spent most of his childhood in California. At Vanderbilt University, he met the Fugitives, a group of poets, professors, and students who launched a conservative, modern, distinctly southern movement in American letters. He studied psychology as an undergraduate student and English as a graduate student. John Crowe Ransom, one of Jarrell's professors, became his mentor, and Jarrell followed him to Kenyon College in 1937, where Jarrell began his career as an academic. From then on, he was always linked with a university: after Kenyon, the University of Texas, Sarah Lawrence College, and from 1947 until his death the Women's College of the University of North Carolina, Greensboro. Jarrell spent World War II in the army, and during these years he published the critically acclaimed *Little Friend, Little Friend*. Jarrell sought to infuse his poetry with what he called the "dailiness of life" and wished to keep its tone familiar, even colloquial.

Ben Jonson (*1572–1637*) Poet, playwright, actor, scholar, critic, translator, and leader of a literary school, Jonson was born the son of an already deceased clergyman and the stepson of a master bricklayer of Westminster. He won a scholarship to a prestigious London grammar school, where he learned from the great scholar William Camden. He had an eventful early career, serving in the army at Flanders, killing an associate in a duel and narrowly escaping the death penalty, and converting to Catholicism. In the middle of all this, Jonson managed to write a number of plays, including *Every Man in His Humor* (in which Shakespeare played the lead role), *Volpone*, *The Alchemist*, and *Bartholomew Fair*. Jonson was a favorite of King James I, who made him England's Poet Laureate and granted him a substantial pension in 1616. In the same year, Jonson published *The Works of Benjamin Jonson* and by doing so made it clear that he considered writing his profession. This gesture broke with the Elizabethan tradition of circulating poems only among the aristocracy until a poet's death, at which point the author's poems were made available to the general public.

James Joyce (*1882–1941*) Joyce was born in Dublin to a feckless father who drifted steadily down the financial and social scale over the course of his life. He was educated at a series of Jesuit institutions, including Clongowes Wood College, Belvedere College, and University College, in Dublin. He was very religious in his youth, but during his last year at Belvedere College he began turning away from Catholicism. He refused to become involved in any of the nationalist activities of his fellow students, choosing instead to live a life of exile. After graduation, he moved to the Continent, where he lived in Paris, Trieste, and Zurich and was supported by a series of patrons. His works include a series of stories entitled *Dubliners*; *A Portrait of the Artist as a Young Man*; *Ulysses*, which was banned for a dozen years in the United States; and *Finnegans Wake*.

Franz Kafka (*1883–1924*)   Born in Prague to a middle-class Jewish family, Kafka attended a prestigious German high school and went on to earn a degree in law in 1906. He held a position in the civil service for many years, working for the Workers' Accident Insurance Organization. Though he never married, he was engaged twice to the same woman and lived with an actress in Berlin for some time before dying of tuberculosis in Vienna. Before his death, he directed his friend Max Brod to destroy his three novels and his numerous unfinished manuscripts. Brod disobeyed Kafka's instructions, and Kafka's work subsequently became known all over the world. His three novels are *The Trial, The Castle*, and *America*. His stories have been collected in English translation in three volumes: *The Great Wall of China, The Penal Colony*, and *The Complete Stories*.

John Keats (*1795–1821*)   Keats's father was head ostler at a London livery stable and inherited the business after marrying his employer's daughter. Keats was sent to the Reverend John Clarke's private school at Enfield, where he was a noisy, high-spirited boy. His teacher, Charles Cowden Clarke, took Keats under his wing, encouraging his passion for reading, poetry, music, and theater. After both his parents died, his uncle took him out of school and apprenticed him to an apothecary and surgeon. He subsequently studied at Guy's Hospital, London. After qualifying to practice as an apothecary, he abandoned medicine for poetry, over his guardian's vehement protests. The decision was influenced by Keats's friendship with Leigh Hunt, then editor of the *Examiner* and a leading political radical, minor poet, and prolific critic and essayist. Keats was one of Hunt's protégés, and Hunt introduced him to such great writers as William Hazlitt, Charles Lamb, and Percy Bysshe Shelley. In February 1820, Keats coughed up blood and realized that he had tuberculosis, which had already claimed the lives of his mother and brother. He died at the age of twenty-five, with his third book barely off the press.

Galway Kinnell (*b. 1927*)   Kinnell was born in Providence. He earned his B.A. from Princeton, where he and classmate W. S. Merwin read each other their poems, and his master's at Rochester. But the process of writing poetry has for Kinnell been largely a process of de-education. He views all poetry as an attempt at self-transcendence, and he consequently dramatizes the process by which he steps out of himself and into other things and creatures. Kinnell has fused a life of poetry with one of politics: he has run an adult education program in Chicago, lived as a journalist in Iran, and worked in the field registering voters for the Congress of Racial Equality in Louisiana. He served in the navy in 1945 and 1946 and has taught at over twenty colleges and universities. He has earned various awards, including the 1983 Pulitzer Prize, and grants, including those from the Rockefeller Foundation and the National Endowment for the Arts.

Yusef Komunyakaa (*b. 1947*) Yusef Komunyakaa was born in Bogalusa, Louisiana, in 1947, the eldest of five children. He graduated from Bogalusa's Central High School in 1965 and later joined the army to serve in Vietnam. While in Vietnam, he began to write, serving as a correspondent and later as managing editor of the *Southern Cross*. For his work with the paper, Komunyakaa received the Bronze Star. Upon leaving the army in the early 1970s, he enrolled at the University of Colorado. Before graduating with his B.A. in 1975, he took a creative writing course and discovered that he had a talent for poetry. He went on to take his M.A. in creative writing at Colorado State University in 1978, eventually leaving Colorado for the University of California, Irvine, where he received his M.F.A. He has published thirteen books of poems, among them *Neon Vernacular*, a Pulitzer Prize winner, and *Thieves of Paradise*, a National Book Award finalist. Komunyakaa is interested in the influence that jazz music has had on poetry and was, along with Sascha Feinstein, the co-editor of *The Jazz Poetry Anthology*. Komunyakaa is a professor in the Creative Writing Program at Princeton.

Maxine Kumin (*b. 1925*) Born in Philadelphia and educated at Radcliffe College, Kumin settled in the suburbs of Boston to raise a family and write poetry. There, Kumin "workshopped" many of her poems with her close friends Anne Sexton, John Holmes, and George Starbuck. Over the years, she has published twelve books of poetry, including *Up Country: Poems of New England*, which was awarded the Pulitzer Prize in 1973. She is also the author of five novels, a collection of short stories, more than twenty children's books, several books of essays, and a memoir. Kumin has served as a Consultant in Poetry to the Library of Congress as well as Poet Laureate of New Hampshire. She has received grants from such prestigious foundations as the National Endowment for the Arts, the National Council on the Arts, and the American Academy of Poets. She has taught at many colleges and universities, among them Princeton, Columbia, Tufts, Washington University, Randolph-Macon, and the University of Massachusetts.

Philip Larkin (*1922–1985*) Larkin was born in Coventry, England, and after being deemed unfit for military service, he attended Oxford University during World War II. The misery of his undergraduate years is depicted in *Jill*, the first of his two novels. At Oxford, Larkin belonged to the group of writers that came to be known as the Movement. Members of this group refused to employ rhetorical excess in their poetry, opting instead to use more even-tempered, conversational idioms. Though his first book of poetry was strongly influenced by W. B. Yeats, his later works were more like those of Thomas Hardy, Wilfred Owen, and W. H. Auden. Larkin believed that to these people, technique mattered less than content; the same might be said of Larkin himself. After taking his Oxford degree, Larkin went to work as a university librarian for a number of universities, though mainly at the University of Hull. When Sir John Betjeman died, in 1984, it was widely assumed that Larkin would succeed him as Poet Laureate. Larkin died before a successor to Betjeman could be appointed, however, and so the author of such colorful poems as "This Be the Verse" and "High Windows" never penned a royal birthday ode.

D. H. Lawrence (*1885–1930*)   Lawrence was born in the mining village of Eastwood, Nottinghamshire, in England. His mother was better educated and more genteel than her husband, who was a miner, and she struggled to have her children grow up to be like her. Lawrence was aware of the struggle between his parents and sided with his mother during his youth and his father later in his life. After the death of an elder brother, though, he became the center of his mother's emotional life, a place he found suffocating. After graduating from a Nottingham high school he had attended on scholarship, he worked as a clerk and a teacher. He earned a teacher's certificate at Nottingham University College. The publication of a group of his poems in the *English Review* in 1909 helped earn him a reputation as a promising young writer. He taught school in the suburb of Croyburg, England, until 1912, when he moved to Germany with Frieda von Richthofen, who was eventually divorced by her husband. In 1914, she and Lawrence married. He lived in Italy, Australia, Mexico, and the south of France, where he died of tuberculosis. His three greatest novels are *Sons and Lovers*, *The Rainbow*, and *Women in Love*.

Li-Young Lee (*b. 1957*)   Lee's great-grandfather was president of China from 1912 to 1916, and his family was wealthy and well connected even after the Communist revolution. His father was once Mao Tse-tung's doctor. In the midst of political upheaval, the family fled to Indonesia, and Lee was born in Jakarta in 1957. Oppression of the Chinese minority in that city set the family on an odyssey that ended in the mid-1960s in a small Pennsylvania town, where Lee's father became pastor of the Presbyterian church. Lee studied at the University of Pittsburgh, the University of Arizona, and the State University of New York at Brockport. He has published *The Rose* and *The City in Which I Love You*, both books of poetry, and *The Winged Seed*, a critically acclaimed memoir.

Robert Lowell (*1917–1977*)   Lowell came from a well-established New England family. He took a dim view of his family, though, and published an unattractive portrait of it in one of his later books, *Life Studies*. Lowell's life was turbulent, in great part because he suffered from manic depression. He attended St. Mark's School, then enrolled in Harvard, where he studied English literature for two years before abruptly transferring to Kenyon College so that he could study the classics, logic, and philosophy under John Crowe Ransom. He then attended Louisiana State University to work with Robert Penn Warren and Cleanth Brooks. He converted to Catholicism and became an active pacifist, opposing both World War II and the Vietnam War.

Susan Ludvigson (*b. 1942*)   Ludvigson was born in Rice Lake, Wisconsin, and is the author of seven books of poetry and two chapbooks. Her work appears regularly in such magazines and journals as the *Atlantic Monthly*, the *Nation*, the *Ohio Review*, and *Antioch Review*. She has received a writer's Fulbright Fellowship as well as grants and fellowships from the Guggenheim Foundation, the Rockefeller Foundation, the National Endowment for the Arts, and the North and South Carolina arts commissions, as well as other institutions. Ludvigson represented the United States at the First International Women Writers Congress in Paris. She is professor of English and Poet-in-Residence at Winthrop University.

Archibald MacLeish (*1892–1982*)   MacLeish grew up in Glencoe, Illinois. He described his father as a "devout, cold, rigorous man of very beautiful speech" and his mother, who had taught at Vassar College before becoming his father's third wife, as having come of a "very passionate people with many mad among them." He attended Hotchkiss School in Connecticut and then earned his B.A. from Yale and his J.D. from Harvard. He went to France to serve in World War I. In the years following the war, MacLeish worked as a lawyer in Boston. In 1923, having found that his work distracted him from poetry, he moved to France to participate in the modernist movement and published four books of poetry. He returned to America in 1928 and retraced by foot and muleback the route that Cortez's conquering army took through Mexico. The literary product of this journey, *Conquistador*, won a Pulitzer Prize in 1932. As World War II approached, he served as Librarian of Congress, Director of the Office of Facts and Figures, and Assistant Secretary of State. In 1949, he returned to Harvard, where he served as Boylston Professor of English Rhetoric until 1962.

Christopher Marlowe (*1564–1593*)   Marlowe was born to a shoemaker in Canterbury only two months before the birth of William Shakespeare. He attended Corpus Christi College in Cambridge, holding a six-year scholarship ordinarily awarded to students preparing for the ministry. At the end of his studies, he did not take holy orders but began to write plays. He won fame at age twenty-three with his tragedy *Tamburlaine* but lived only six more years. During this time, he wrote five more plays: a sequel to *Tamburlaine*; *The Massacre at Paris*; two major tragedies, *The Jew of Malta* and *Dr. Faustus*; and a chronicle history play, *Edward II*. Marlowe's productivity was remarkable considering his tumultuous and short life. He was killed by a dagger during an argument over a bill in a tavern when he was only twenty-nine.

Andrew Marvell (*1621–1678*)   Marvell was born in Yorkshire, England, and was educated at Cambridge University. He completed his bachelor of arts in 1638, just a few years before the start of the English Civil War. What he did after his years at Cambridge is uncertain, though it is well-known that he supported the Puritan cause during the war. In 1650, he served as the private tutor of the daughter of the Lord General of the Puritan troops, and in 1657 he was appointed to assist Oliver Cromwell's blind Latin secretary, the poet John Milton. Beginning in 1659, Marvell represented his hometown of Hull in Parliament. He survived the Restoration and managed to save Milton from imprisonment and possible execution.

James Alan McPherson (*b. 1943*)   Born in Savannah, McPherson received his B.A. from Morris Brown College, his L.L.B. from Harvard, and his M.F.A. from the University of Iowa. His literary career began when he received first prize in the *Atlantic Monthly* short story contest in 1965, and in 1969 his first collection of short stories, *Hue and Cry*, was published. Since then, he has received numerous fellowships and awards for his fiction. He has taught English at the University of California at Santa Cruz, Harvard University, Morgan State University, and the University of Virginia, and he has been a professor of English at the University of Iowa since 1981.

Edna St. Vincent Millay (*1892–1950*) Millay was born in the small coastal town of Rockland, Maine. Her parents divorced when she was a child, and her mother supported herself and her family of four by working as a nurse. Millay wrote her first poem at age five and as a child submitted her poetry regularly to various magazines. She attended Vassar College through the generosity of a benefactor who was impressed by her writing. She graduated when she was twenty-five years old, and her first book of poetry was published that same year. Millay then moved to Greenwich Village in New York City, where she fell in with the literary and political rebels who lived there. She seemed to embody all the qualities of the modern woman of the 1920s: she was talented, energetic, independent, and liberated. Of course, she was not completely typical: she was openly bisexual, and even when she did marry, hers was a "sexually open" marriage. In the same year that she married and moved to the Berkshires, Millay was awarded the Pulitzer Prize.

John Milton (*1608–1674*) Milton was the eldest son of a self-made London businessman. As a child, he exhibited unusual scholastic gifts: he had already learned Latin and Greek and was well on his way to mastering Hebrew and most of the European languages before he entered Cambridge University. After graduation, Milton retired to his father's house, where he read for six years. His father then sent him abroad for a year of travel and study. After returning to England, Milton became embroiled in political controversy. He wrote pamphlets defending everything from free speech to the execution of Charles I. When the monarchy was restored, Milton found himself impoverished and imprisoned, and he had lost his sight. Still, he spent his later years writing the masterpieces for which he is known today: *Paradise Lost, Paradise Regained*, and *Samson Agonistes*.

Marianne Moore (*1887–1972*) Moore was born in Kirkwood, Missouri, a suburb of St. Louis. When she was young, her father abandoned her family. Moore was raised in the home of her grandfather, a Presbyterian pastor, until his death, after which Moore's family lived at first with other relatives in Missouri and then on their own in Carlisle, Pennsylvania. She graduated from Bryn Mawr College in 1906 and went on to work as a schoolteacher at the U.S. Indian School in Carlisle. She and her mother moved to New York City in 1918, and Moore began to work at the New York Public Library. In New York, she met such influential poets as William Carlos Williams and Wallace Stevens and began to contribute her poetry to *Egoist, Poetry, Others*, and *Dial*, the prestigious literary magazine Moore eventually came to edit. In 1921, Hilda Doolittle published Moore's first book of poetry without her knowledge. Moore was widely recognized for her work: her *Collected Poems* won the Bollingen Prize, the National Book Award, and the Pulitzer Prize. Moore lived with her mother and brother in Brooklyn for most of her adult life.

Joyce Carol Oates (*b. 1938*)   Oates describes her childhood in Lockport, New York, as having been "a daily scramble for existence." After receiving a typewriter as a gift at age fourteen, she began to write "novel after novel," continuing to do so throughout high school and college. While at Syracuse University on scholarship, she won the prestigious *Mademoiselle* fiction contest. After graduating as valedictorian of her class, she earned an M.A. in English at the University of Wisconsin. Between 1968 and 1978, Oates taught at the University of Windsor in Canada. At the same time, she published two or three new books each year. Oates has taught at Princeton University since 1978, where she is Roger S. Berlind Distinguished Professor of the Humanities. She and her husband operate a small press and publish a literary magazine, the *Ontario Review*. She has received the National Book Award and has been nominated twice for the Nobel Prize in Literature.

Tim O'Brien (*b. 1946*)   O'Brien is from Worthington, Minnesota. He graduated from Macalester College in 1968 with a B.A. in political science. He had intended to join the State Department, but he was drafted, so he instead served in Vietnam as an infantry foot soldier—even though he opposed the war. He returned from the war—where his division was involved in the My Lai massacre of 1968—with a Purple Heart. After Vietnam, he did graduate work at Harvard but left to work as an intern at the *Washington Post*. Just as he was accepting a job as a national affairs reporter at the *Post*, his memoir, *If I Die in a Combat Zone, Box Me Up and Send Me Home*, was published. After a year as a reporter, O'Brien left the newspaper and dedicated himself full-time to writing fiction. His novels have won the National Book Award and have been nominated for both the National Book Critics Circle Award and the Pulitzer Prize.

Flannery O'Connor (*1925–1964*)   O'Connor lived with her mother in Milledgeville, Georgia, for most of her life. She began to suffer from disseminated lupus in 1950 but halted the progress of the rare disease with injections of a cortisone derivative. The cortisone weakened her bones so much that from 1955 on, she was forced to rely on crutches, but she refused to indulge in self-pity or to restrict her activities. O'Connor wrote, trav-

*

Permissions Acknowledgments

Stories

Chinua Achebe: "Uncle Ben's Choice" from *Girls at War and Other Stories.* © Chinua Achebe. Reprinted by permission of the author.

Raymond Carver: "Cathedral" from *Cathedral* by Raymond Carver. Copyright © 1981 by Raymond Carver. Reprinted by permission of Alfred A. Knopf, a Division of Random House, Inc.

John Cheever: "The Swimmer" from *The Stories of John Cheever* by John Cheever. Copyright © 1964 by John Cheever. Reprinted by permission of Alfred A. Knopf, a Division of Random House, Inc.

Anton Chekhov: "In Exile" from *Anton Chekhov: Selected Stories* by Anton Chekhov, translated by Ann Dunnigan, copyright © 1960 by Ann Dunnigan. Used by permission of Dutton Signet, a division of Penguin Putnam, Inc.

William Faulkner: "A Rose for Emily" from *Collected Stories of William Faulkner* (New York: Random House, 1950). Reprinted by permission.

Gabriel García Márquez: "A Very Old Man with Enormous Wings" from *Leaf Storm and Other Stories* by Gabriel García Márquez. Copyright © 1971 by Gabriel García Márquez. Reprinted by permission of HarperCollins Publishers, Inc.

Ernest Hemingway: "Hills Like White Elephants" from *Men without Women* by Ernest Hemingway. Copyright 1927 by Charles Scribner's Sons. Copyright renewed 1955 by Ernest Hemingway. Reprinted with permission of Scribner, a Division of Simon & Schuster.

James Joyce: "Araby" from *Dubliners* by James Joyce, copyright 1916 by B. W. Heubsch. Definitive text copyright © 1967 by the Estate of James Joyce.

Used by permission of Viking Penguin, a division of Penguin Putnam, Inc.

Franz Kafka: "A Hunger Artist" from *Franz Kafka: The Complete Stories* by Nahum N. Glatzer, editor, Willa and Edwin Muir, translators. Copyright © 1971 by Schocken Books. Reprinted by permission of Schocken Books, a division of Random House, Inc.

James Alan McPherson: "A Loaf of Bread" from *Elbow Room*. Reprinted with permission of the author.

Joyce Carol Oates: "Where Are You Going, Where Have You Been?" from *The Wheel of Love and Other Stories,* published by Vanguard. Copyright © 1970 by Joyce Carol Oates. Reprinted by permission of John Hawkins & Associates, Inc.

Tim O'Brien: "The Things They Carried" from *The Things They Carried*. Copyright © 1990 by Tim O'Brien. Reprinted by permission of Houghton Mifflin Company. All rights reserved.

Flannery O'Connor: "A Good Man Is Hard to Find" from *A Good Man Is Hard to Find and Other Stories,* copyright 1953 by Flannery O'Connor and renewed 1981 by Regina O'Connor, reprinted by permission of Harcourt, Inc.

Frank O'Connor: "Guests of the Nation" from *Collected Stories of Frank O'Connor*. Copyright © 1981 by Harriet O'Donovan, Executrix of the Estate of Frank O'Connor. Reprinted by permission of Alfred A. Knopf, a division of Random House, Inc., and by Joan Daves Agency/Writers House, Inc., on behalf of the Proprietors.

Tillie Olsen: "I Stand Here Ironing," copyright © 1956, 1957, 1960, 1961 by Tillie Olsen, from *Tell Me a Riddle* by Tillie Olsen, introduction by John Leonard. Used by permission of Dell Publishing, a division of Random House, Inc.

Katherine Anne Porter: "The Jilting of Granny Weatherall" from *Flowering Judas and Other Stories,* copyright 1930 and renewed 1958 by Katherine Anne Porter, reprinted by permission of Harcourt, Inc.

Leslie Marmon Silko: "Yellow Woman" copyright © 1981 by Leslie Marmon Silko. Reprinted from *Storyteller* by permission of Seaver Books, New York.

John Steinbeck: "The Chrysanthemums," copyright 1937, renewed © 1965 by John Steinbeck from *The Long Valley*. Used by permission of Viking Penguin, a division of Penguin Putnam, Inc.

John Updike: "A & P" from *Pigeon Feathers and Other Stories*. Copyright © 1962 by John Updike. Reprinted by permission of Alfred A. Knopf, a division of Random House, Inc.

Alice Walker: "Everyday Use" from *In Love and Trouble: Stories of Black Women,* copyright © 1973 by Alice Walker, reprinted by permission of Harcourt, Inc.

Eudora Welty: "A Worn Path" from *A Curtain of Green and Other Stories,* copyright 1941 and renewed 1969 by Eudora Welty, reprinted by permission of Harcourt, Inc.

Edith Wharton: "Roman Fever" from *Roman Fever and Other Stories*. Copyright 1934 by *Liberty Magazine;* copyright renewed © 1962 by William R. Tyler. Reprinted with the permission of Scribner, a division of Simon & Schuster.

Poems

John Agard: "Palm Tree King" from *Mangoes and Bullets,* published by Pluto Press 1985. Reprinted by kind permission of the author and Caroline Sheldon Literary Agency.

Paul Allen: "The Man with the Hardest Belly" from *American Crawl,* University of North Texas Press, 1997. Reprinted by permission of the author.

Margaret Atwood: "You Fit into Me" from *Power Politics.* Copyright © 1971 by Margaret Atwood. Reprinted by permission of House of Anansi Press Limited.

W. H. Auden: "In Memory of W. B. Yeats" and "Musée des Beaux Arts" from *W. H. Auden: Collected Poems,* edited by Edward Mendelson. Copyright © 1940 and renewed 1968 by W. H. Auden. Reprinted by permission of Random House, Inc., and Faber and Faber Ltd.

Elizabeth Bishop: "One Art," "Sestina," and "The Fish" from *The Complete Poems 1927–1979.* Copyright © 1979, 1983 by Alice Helen Methfessel. Reprinted by permission of Farrar, Straus and Giroux, LLC.

Gwendolyn Brooks: "The Bean Eaters," "the mother," and "We Real Cool" from *Blacks.* Reprinted by permission of the author.

Lynne Bryer: "The Way" from *Illuminations.* Reprinted by permission.

Billy Collins: "On Turning Ten" from *The Art of Drowning* by Billy Collins, © 1995. "Picnic, Lightning" from *Picnic, Lightning* by Billy Collins, © 1998. Reprinted by permission of the University of Pittsburgh Press. "Sonnet" from *Poetry,* Vol. CLXXIII, No. 4 (February 1999), copyright © 1999 by The Modern Poetry Association. Reprinted by permission of the Editor of *Poetry* and by the author.

E. E. Cummings: "in Just-" and "Buffalo Bill 's" from *Complete Poems: 1904–1962* by E. E. Cummings, edited by George J. Firmage. Copyright 1923, 1951, © 1991 by the Trustees for the E. E. Cummings Trust. Copyright © 1976 by George James Firmage. Used by permission of Liveright Publishing Corporation.

Emily Dickinson: "After great pain, a formal feeling comes—" from *The Poems of Emily Dickinson,* Thomas H. Johnson, ed., Cambridge, Mass.: The Belknap Press of Harvard University Press, Copyright © 1951, 1955, 1979, 1983 by the President and Fellows of Harvard College. Reprinted by permission of the publishers and Trustees of Amherst College.

Rita Dove: "Daystar" from *Thomas and Beulah,* Carnegie Mellon University Press, © 1986 by Rita Dove. "The House Slave" from *The Yellow House on the Corner,* Carnegie Mellon University Press, © 1980 by Rita Dove. Reprinted by permission of the author.

T. S. Eliot: "The Love Song of J. Alfred Prufrock" from *Collected Poems 1909–1962.* Reprinted by permission of Faber and Faber Ltd.

Louise Erdrich: "Captivity" and "Indian Boarding School: The Runaways" from *Jacklight* by Louise Erdrich, © 1984 by Louise Erdrich. Reprinted by permission of The Wylie Agency, Inc.

Carolyn Forché: "The Colonel" from *The Country between Us.* Copyright © 1981 by Carolyn Forché. Originally appeared in *Women's International Resource Exchange.* Reprinted by permission of HarperCollins Publishers, Inc.

Robert Frost: "Design" and "Stopping by Woods on a Snowy Evening" from *The Poetry of Robert Frost,* edited by Edward Connery Lathem. Copyright 1936, 1951, by Robert Frost, © 1964 by Lesley Frost Ballantine, copyright 1923, 1969 by Henry Holt and Company. Reprinted by permission of Henry Holt and Company, LLC.

Allen Ginsberg: "A Supermarket in California" from *Collected Poems 1947–1980* by Allen Ginsberg. Copyright © 1955 by Allen Ginsberg. Copyright renewed. Reprinted by permission of HarperCollins Publishers, Inc.

Robert Hayden: "Those Winter Sundays" from *Collected Poems of Robert Hayden,* edited by Frederick Glaysher. Copyright © 1966 by Robert Hayden. Used by permission of Liveright Publishing Corporation.

Seamus Heaney: "Digging" and "Punishment" from *Open Ground: Selected Poems 1966–1996* by Seamus Heaney. Copyright © 1998 by Seamus Heaney. Reprinted by Permission of Farrar, Straus and Giroux, LLC, and by permission of Faber and Faber Ltd.

Langston Hughes: "Harlem," "The Negro Speaks of Rivers," and "Theme for English B" from *Collected Poems* by Langston Hughes. Copyright © 1994 by the Estate of Langston Hughes. Reprinted by permission of Alfred A. Knopf, Inc., a division of Random House, Inc.

Randall Jarrell: "The Death of the Ball Turret Gunner" from *The Complete Poems* by Randall Jarrell. Copyright © 1969, renewed 1997 by Mary von S. Jarrell. Reprinted by permission of Farrar, Straus and Giroux, LLC.

Galway Kinnell: "Blackberry Eating" from *Three Books* by Galway Kinnell. Copyright © 1993 by Galway Kinnell. Previously published in *Moral Acts, Mortal Words* (1980). Reprinted by permission of Houghton Mifflin Company. All rights reserved.

Yusef Komunyakaa: "Facing It" and "We Never Know" from *Dien Cai Dau,* © 1988 by Yusef Komunyakaa and reprinted by permission of Wesleyan University Press.

Maxine Kumin: "Woodchucks" from *Selected Poems 1960–1990* by Maxine Kumin. Copyright © 1972 by Maxine Kumin. Used by permission of W. W. Norton & Company, Inc.

Philip Larkin: "Aubade" from *Collected Poems* by Philip Larkin. Copyright © 1988, 1989 by the Estate of Philip Larkin. Reprinted by permission of Farrar, Straus and Giroux, LLC, and by Faber and Faber Ltd.

Li-Young Lee: "The Gift" and "Visions and Interpretations" from *Rose: Poems* by Li-Young Lee, copyright © 1986 by Li Young Lee. Reprinted with the permission of BOA Editions Ltd.

Robert Lowell: "Skunk Hour" from *Selected Poems* by Robert Lowell. Copyright © 1976 by Robert Lowell. Reprinted by permission of Farrar, Straus and Giroux, LLC.

Susan Ludvigson: "After Love" from *Everything Winged Must Be Dreaming*. Reprinted by permission of the author.

Archibald MacLeish: "Ars Poetica" from *Collected Poems 1917–1982*. Copyright © 1985 by The Estate of Archibald MacLeish. Reprinted by permission of Houghton Mifflin Company. All rights reserved.

Edna St. Vincent Millay: Sonnet XXX of *Fatal Interview* and "What lips my lips have kissed" from *Collected Poems*. Copyright © 1923, 1931, 1951, 1958 by Edna St. Vincent Millay and Norma Millay Ellis. All rights reserved. Reprinted by permission of Elizabeth Barnett, literary executor.

Marianne Moore: "Poetry" from *The Complete Poems of Marianne Moore*. Copyright 1935 by Marianne Moore; copyright renewed © 1963 by Marianne Moore and T. S. Eliot. Reprinted with the permission of Simon & Schuster.

Sharon Olds: "Sex Without Love" and "The One Girl at the Boys' Party" from *The Dead and the Living* by Sharon Olds. Copyright © 1983 by Sharon Olds. Reprinted by permission of Alfred A. Knopf, a division of Random House, Inc.

Marge Piercy: "Barbie doll" from *Circles on the Water* by Marge Piercy. Copyright © 1982 by Marge Piercy. Reprinted by permission of Alfred A. Knopf, a division of Random House, Inc.

Sylvia Plath: "Daddy" from *Ariel* by Sylvia Plath. Copyright © 1963 by Ted Hughes. "Metaphors" from *The Collected Poems of Sylvia Plath*. Copyright © 1960 by Ted Hughes. Copyright renewed. Reprinted by permission of HarperCollins Publishers, Inc., and Faber and Faber Ltd.

Ezra Pound: "In a Station of the Metro" and "The River-Merchant's Wife: A Letter" from *Personae,* copyright © 1926 by Ezra Pound. Reprinted by permission of New Directions Publishing Corp.

John Crowe Ransom: "Bells for John Whiteside's Daughter" from *Selected Poems*. Copyright 1924 by Alfred A. Knopf and renewed 1952 by John Crowe Ransom. Reprinted by permission of the publisher.

Theodore Roethke: "I Knew a Woman" from *The Collected Poems of Theodore Roethke,* copyright 1954 by Theodore Roethke. "My Papa's Waltz," copyright 1942 by Hearst Magazines from *The Collected Poems of Theodore Roethke*. "Root Cellar," copyright 1943 by Modern Poetry Association, Inc., from *The Collected Poems of Theodore Roethke*. Used by permission of Doubleday, a division of Random House, Inc.

Bruce Springsteen: "The River" by Bruce Springsteen. Copyright © 1980 by Bruce Springsteen (ASCAP). Reprinted by permission.

William Stafford: "Traveling through the Dark" from *The Way It Is: New and Selected Poems*. Copyright 1962, 1998 by the Estate of William Stafford. Reprinted with the permission of Graywolf Press, St. Paul, Minnesota.

Wallace Stevens: "Anecdote of the Jar," "Sunday Morning," and "The Emperor of Ice-Cream" from *Collected Poems*. Copyright 1923 and renewed 1951 by Wallace Stevens. Reprinted by permission of Alfred A. Knopf, a division of Random House, Inc.

Plays

son. Used by permission of Dutton Signet, a division of Penguin Group (USA), Inc.

Every effort has been made to contact the copyright holders of each of these selections. Rights holders of any selections not credited should contact W. W. Norton & Company, Inc., 500 Fifth Avenue, New York, NY 10110, in order for a correction to be made in the next reprinting of our work.

*

Index of Authors, Titles, and First Lines of Poems